HALSBURY'S
Laws of England

FIFTH EDITION
2015

Volume 8

This is volume 8 of the Fifth Edition of Halsbury's Laws of England, containing the title CHARITIES.

The title CHARITIES replaces the title CHARITIES contained in volume 8 (2010). Upon receipt of volume 8 (2015), volume 8 (2010) may be archived.

For a full list of volumes comprised in a current set of Halsbury's Laws of England please see overleaf.

Fifth Edition volumes:

1 (2008), 2 (2008), 3 (2011), 4 (2011), 5 (2013), 6 (2011), 7 (2008), 8 (2015), 9 (2012), 10 (2012), 11 (2009), 12 (2009), 13 (2009), 14 (2009), 15 (2009), 16 (2011), 17 (2011), 18 (2009), 19 (2011), 20 (2014), 21 (2011), 22 (2012), 23 (2013), 24 (2010), 25 (2010), 26 (2010), 27 (2010), 28 (2010), 29 (2014), 30 (2012), 31 (2012), 32 (2012), 33 (2013), 34 (2011), 35 (2011), 36 (2011), 37 (2013), 38 (2013), 38A (2013), 39 (2014), 40 (2014), 41 (2014), 41A (2014), 42 (2011), 43 (2011), 44 (2011), 45 (2010), 46 (2010), 47 (2014), 47A (2014), 48 (2008), 49 (2008), 50 (2008), 51 (2013), 52 (2014), 53 (2014), 54 (2008), 55 (2012), 56 (2011), 57 (2012), 58 (2014), 58A (2014), 59 (2014), 59A (2014), 60 (2011), 61 (2010), 62 (2012), 63 (2012), 64 (2012), 65 (2015), 66 (2015), 67 (2008), 68 (2008), 69 (2009), 70 (2012), 71 (2013), 72 (2009), 73 (2009), 74 (2011), 75 (2013), 76 (2013), 77 (2010), 78 (2010), 79 (2014), 80 (2013), 81 (2010), 82 (2010), 83 (2010), 84 (2013), 84A (2013), 85 (2012), 86 (2013), 87 (2012), 88 (2012), 88A (2013), 89 (2011), 90 (2011), 91 (2012), 92 (2010), 93 (2008), 94 (2008), 95 (2013), 96 (2012), 97 (2010), 97A (2014), 98 (2013), 99 (2012), 100 (2009), 101 (2009), 102 (2010), 103 (2010), 104 (2014)

Additional Materials:

Sentencing and Disposition of Offenders (*Release and Recall of Prisoners*) containing vol **92** (2010) paras 761–820; *Tort* (*Conversion and Wrongful Interference with Goods*) containing vol **45**(**2**) (Reissue) paras 542–686

Consolidated Index and Tables:

2014 Consolidated Index (A–E), 2014 Consolidated Index (F–O), 2014 Consolidated Index (P–Z), 2015 Consolidated Table of Statutes, 2015 Consolidated Table of Statutory Instruments, etc, 2015 Consolidated Table of Cases (A–G), 2015 Consolidated Table of Cases (H–Q), 2015 Consolidated Table of Cases (R–Z, ECJ Cases)

Updating and ancillary materials:

2014 Annual Cumulative Supplement; Monthly Current Service; Annual Abridgments 1974–2013

March 2015

HALSBURY'S
Laws of England

Volume 8

2015

Members of the LexisNexis Group worldwide

United Kingdom	LexisNexis, a Division of Reed Elsevier (UK) Ltd, Lexis House, 30 Farringdon Street, LONDON, EC4A 4HH, and 9–10, St Andrew Square, EDINBURGH, EH2 2AF
Australia	Reed International Books Australia Pty Ltd trading as LexisNexis, Chatswood, New South Wales
Austria	LexisNexis Verlag ARD Orac GmbH & Co KG, Vienna
Benelux	LexisNexis Benelux, Amsterdam
Canada	LexisNexis Canada, Markham, Ontario
China	LexisNexis China, Beijing and Shanghai
France	LexisNexis SA, Paris
Germany	LexisNexis GmbH, Dusseldorf
Hong Kong	LexisNexis Hong Kong, Hong Kong
India	LexisNexis India, New Delhi
Italy	Giuffrè Editore, Milan
Japan	LexisNexis Japan, Tokyo
Malaysia	Malayan Law Journal Sdn Bhd, Kuala Lumpur
New Zealand	LexisNexis New Zealand Ltd, Wellington
Singapore	LexisNexis Singapore, Singapore
South Africa	LexisNexis, Durban
USA	LexisNexis, Dayton, Ohio

FIRST EDITION	*Published in 31 volumes between 1907 and 1917*
SECOND EDITION	*Published in 37 volumes between 1931 and 1942*
THIRD EDITION	*Published in 43 volumes between 1952 and 1964*
FOURTH EDITION	*Published in 56 volumes between 1973 and 1987, with reissues between 1988 and 2008*
FIFTH EDITION	*Published between 2008 and 2014, with reissues from 2014*

A CIP Catalogue record for this book is available from the British Library.

ISBN 13 (complete set, standard binding): 9781405734394

ISBN 13: 9781405780582

ISBN 978-1-4057-8058-2

9 781405 780582

Typeset by Letterpart Limited, Caterham on the Hill, Surrey CR3 5XL
Printed and bound by CPI Group (UK) Ltd, Croydon, CR0 4YY
Visit LexisNexis at www.lexisnexis.co.uk

HALSBURY ADVISORY BOARD

Editors of this Volume

SIMON HETHERINGTON, LLB

and

AMANDA WRIGHT, LLB

Commissioning Editor

CLAIRE TURPIN, LLB, MSc

Indexer

JAMES A. WARD, BA, LLB,
a Solicitor of the Senior Courts of England and Wales

Managing Editor

HELEN HALVEY, LLB

CHARITIES

Consultant Editor
THEA LONGLEY
a Solicitor of the Senior Courts of England and Wales;
Partner, Bates Wells Braithwaite

The law stated in this volume is in general that in force on 1 February 2015, although subsequent changes have been included wherever possible.

Any future updating material will be found in the Current Service and annual Cumulative Supplement to Halsbury's Laws of England.

TABLE OF CONTENTS

HOW TO USE HALSBURY'S LAWS OF ENGLAND

Volumes

Each text volume of Halsbury's Laws of England contains the law on the titles contained in it as at a date stated at the front of the volume (the operative date).

Information contained in Halsbury's Laws of England may be accessed in several ways.

First, by using the tables of contents.

Each volume contains both a general Table of Contents, and a specific Table of Contents for each title contained in it. From these tables you will be directed to the relevant part of the work.

Readers should note that the current arrangement of titles can be found in the Current Service.

Secondly, by using tables of statutes, statutory instruments, cases or other materials.

If you know the name of the Act, statutory instrument or case with which your research is concerned, you should consult the Consolidated Tables of statutes, cases and so on (published as separate volumes) which will direct you to the relevant volume and paragraph.

(Each individual text volume also includes tables of those materials used as authority in that volume.)

Thirdly, by using the indexes.

If you are uncertain of the general subject area of your research, you should go to the Consolidated Index (published as separate volumes) for reference to the relevant volume(s) and paragraph(s).

(Each individual text volume also includes an index to the material contained therein.)

Updating publications

The text volumes of Halsbury's Laws should be used in conjunction with the annual Cumulative Supplement and the monthly Noter-Up.

The annual Cumulative Supplement

The Supplement gives details of all changes between the operative date of the text volume and the operative date of the Supplement. It is arranged in the same volume, title and paragraph order as the text volumes. Developments affecting particular points of law are noted to the relevant paragraph(s) of the text volumes.

For narrative treatment of material noted in the Cumulative Supplement, go to the Annual Abridgment volume for the relevant year.

Destination Tables

In certain titles in the annual *Cumulative Supplement*, reference is made to Destination Tables showing the destination of consolidated legislation. Those Destination Tables are to be found either at the end of the titles within the annual *Cumulative Supplement*, or in a separate *Destination Tables* booklet provided from time to time with the *Cumulative Supplement*.

The Noter-Up

The Noter-Up is contained in the Current Service Noter-Up booklet, issued monthly and noting changes since the publication of the annual Cumulative Supplement. Also arranged in the same volume, title and paragraph order as the text volumes, the Noter-Up follows the style of the Cumulative Supplement.

For narrative treatment of material noted in the Noter-Up, go to the relevant Monthly Review.

REFERENCES AND ABBREVIATIONS

ACT	Australian Capital Territory
A-G	Attorney General
Admin	Administrative Court
Admlty	Admiralty Court
Adv-Gen	Advocate General
affd	affirmed
affg	affirming
Alta	Alberta
App	Appendix
art	article
Aust	Australia
B	Baron
BC	British Columbia
C	Command Paper (of a series published before 1900)
c	chapter number of an Act
CA	Court of Appeal
CAC	Central Arbitration Committee
CA in Ch	Court of Appeal in Chancery
CB	Chief Baron
CCA	Court of Criminal Appeal
CCR	County Court Rules 1981 (as subsequently amended)
CCR	Court for Crown Cases Reserved
CJEU	Court of Justice of the European Union
C-MAC	Courts-Martial Appeal Court
CO	Crown Office
COD	Crown Office Digest
CPR	Civil Procedure Rules
Can	Canada
Cd	Command Paper (of the series published 1900–18)
Cf	compare
Ch	Chancery Division
ch	chapter
cl	clause
Cm	Command Paper (of the series published 1986 to date)

Cmd	Command Paper (of the series published 1919–56)
Cmnd	Command Paper (of the series published 1956–86)
Comm	Commercial Court
Comr	Commissioner
Court Forms (2nd Edn)	Atkin's Encyclopaedia of Court Forms in Civil Proceedings, 2nd Edn. See note 2 post.
CrimPR	Criminal Procedure Rules
DC	Divisional Court
DPP	Director of Public Prosecutions
EAT	Employment Appeal Tribunal
EC	European Community
ECJ	Court of Justice of the European Community (before the Treaty of Lisbon (OJ C306, 17.12.2007, p 1) came into force on 1 December 2009); European Court of Justice (after the Treaty of Lisbon (OJ C306, 17.12.2007, p 1) came into force on 1 December 2009)
EComHR	European Commission of Human Rights
ECSC	European Coal and Steel Community
ECtHR Rules of Court	Rules of Court of the European Court of Human Rights
EEC	European Economic Community
EFTA	European Free Trade Association
EGC	European General Court
EWCA Civ	Official neutral citation for judgments of the Court of Appeal (Civil Division)
EWCA Crim	Official neutral citation for judgments of the Court of Appeal (Criminal Division)
EWHC	Official neutral citation for judgments of the High Court
Edn	Edition
Euratom	European Atomic Energy Community
EU	European Union
Ex Ch	Court of Exchequer Chamber
ex p	ex parte
Fam	Family Division
Fed	Federal
Forms & Precedents (5th Edn)	Encyclopaedia of Forms and Precedents other than Court Forms, 5th Edn. See note 2 post.
GLC	Greater London Council
HC	High Court
HC	House of Commons

TABLE OF STATUTES

TABLE OF STATUTORY INSTRUMENTS

TABLE OF CHARITY COMMISSION DECISIONS ETC

PARA

C

PARA

Construction Industry Training Board v A-G [1971] 3 All ER 449, [1971] 1 WLR 1303, [1971] RA 343, 115 Sol Jo 505; affd [1973] Ch 173, [1972] 2 All ER 1339, [1972] 3 WLR 187, [1972] RA 241, 116 Sol Jo 466, CA 1, 6, 21–23, 32, 249, 254, 317, 534, 539, 550, 592, 624
Cook v Duckenfield (1743) 2 Atk 562 .... 74, 201, 535, 606
Cookstown Roman Catholic Church Trustees v IRC (1953) 34 TC 350, 46 R & IT 788, L(TC) 1651 .... 29, 31, 65
Cooper v Coles [1987] QB 230, [1987] 1 All ER 91, [1986] 3 WLR 888, 150 JP 523, 130 Sol Jo 839, [1986] LS Gaz R 3672 465
Cooper v Gordon (1869) LR 8 Eq 249, 33 JP 761, 38 LJ Ch 489, 17 WR 908, 20 LT 732 602
Cooper's Conveyance Trusts, Re, Crewdson v Bagot [1956] 3 All ER 28, [1956] 1 WLR 1096, 100 Sol Jo 620 .... 5, 140, 142–144, 171, 174
Cooper's Settlement, Re, Cooper v Cooper [1962] Ch 826, [1961] 3 All ER 636, [1961] 3 WLR 1029, 105 Sol Jo 887 423
Corbett, Re, Corbett v Lord Cobham [1903] 2 Ch 326, 72 LJ Ch 775, 52 WR 74, 88 LT 591 77
Corbyn, Re, Midland Bank Executor and Trustee Co Ltd v A-G [1941] Ch 400, [1941] 2 All ER 160, 110 LJ Ch 200, 85 Sol Jo 256, 165 LT 372, 57 TLR 483 45
Corbyn v French (1799) 4 Ves 418, 31 ER 213, [1775–1802] All ER Rep 444 .... 163, 171
Corcoran, Re, Corcoran v O'Kane [1913] 1 IR 1 31
Corelli, Re, Watt v Bridges [1943] Ch 332, [1943] 2 All ER 519, 112 LJ Ch 348, 87 Sol Jo 327, 169 LT 265, 59 TLR 437 .... 60, 65
Costabadie v Costabadie (1847) 6 Hare 410, 16 LJ Ch 259, 11 Jur 345, 9 LTOS 20 529
Cottam's Will Trusts, Re, Midland Bank Executor and Trustee Co Ltd v Huddersfield Corpn [1955] 3 All ER 704, [1955] 1 WLR 1299, 99 Sol Jo 889 .... 11, 14
Coulthurst, Re, Coutts & Co v Coulthurst [1951] Ch 661, [1951] 1 All ER 774, 95 Sol Jo 188, [1951] 1 TLR 651, CA 13, 18–19
Courtauld-Thomson Trusts, Re (1954) Times, 18 December 60
Coventry Corpn v A-G (1720) 2 Eq Cas Abr 192, 7 Bro Parl Cas 235, HL 295, 534, 635
Cowan v Milbourn (1867) LR 2 Exch 230, 31 JP 423, 36 LJ Ex 124, 15 WR 750, 16 LT 290 66
Cowan v Scargill [1985] Ch 270, [1984] 2 All ER 750, [1984] 3 WLR 501, [1984] IRLR 260, [1984] ICR 646, 128 Sol Jo 550 .... 418, 423
Cox, Re, Baker v National Trust Co Ltd and connected appeal [1955] AC 627, [1955] 2 All ER 550, [1955] 3 WLR 42, 99 Sol Jo 383, [1955] 3 DLR 497, 16 WWR 49, PC 2, 6, 18, 22, 60
Cox, Re, Cox v Davie (1877) 7 Ch D 204, 47 LJ Ch 72, 26 WR 74, 37 LT 457 19
Coxe v Basset (1796) 3 Ves 155 .... 86, 104
Coxen, Re, McCallum v Coxen [1948] Ch 747, [1948] 2 All ER 492, [1948] LJR 1590, 92 Sol Jo 442 .... 3, 60, 87, 97
Crafton v Frith (1851) 4 De G & Sm 237, 20 LJ Ch 198, 15 Jur 737, 17 LTOS 137 .... 19, 95
Craigdallie v Aikman (1813) 1 Dow 1 331
Craigdallie v Aikman (1820) 2 Bligh 529, HL 114
Cramp v Playfoot (1858) 4 K & J 479 87
Cranston, Re, Webb v Oldfield [1898] 1 IR 431 44
Cranstoun, Re, National Provincial Bank v Royal Society for the Encouragement of Arts, Manufactures and Commerce [1932] 1 Ch 537, 101 LJ Ch 152, 76 Sol Jo 111, 146 LT 568, 48 TLR 226 24
Crawford v Forshaw [1891] 2 Ch 261, 60 LJ Ch 683, 39 WR 484, 65 LT 32, [1891–4] All ER Rep Ext 1895, CA 385
Cross v Lloyd-Greame (1909) 74 Sol Jo 152, 102 LT 163, 26 TLR 171 .... 6, 15, 146, 212
Crowe, Re, National Westminster Bank Ltd v Balfour (1979) unreported 168
Cunnack v Edwards [1896] 2 Ch 679, 61 JP 36, 65 LJ Ch 801, 45 WR 99, 75 LT 122, 12 TLR 614, CA 18, 62
Cunningham, Re, Dulcken v Cunningham [1914] 1 Ch 427, 83 LJ Ch 342, 110 LT 371 172
Cunningham v Foot (1878) 3 App Cas 974, 26 WR 858, 38 LT 889, HL 76
Cunningham and Bradley and Wilson, Re [1877] WN 258, 12 LJNC 214 290
Currie, Re, McClelland v Gamble [1985] NI 299 169
Currie v Pye (1811) 17 Ves 462 643

PARA

PARA

H

PARA

K

L

M

PARA

O

PARA

Ofrex (George Drexler) Foundation (Trustees) v IRC [1966] Ch 675, [1965] 3 All ER 529, [1965] 3 WLR 1168, 42 TC 524, 44 ATC 295, [1965] TR 307, 109 Sol Jo 775, L(TC) 2160 .... 96, 137, 142
Ogden, Re, Taylor v Sharp (1909) 25 TLR 382, CA 23
Oldham Borough Council v A-G (1992) Times, 13 April; revsd [1993] Ch 210, [1993] 2 All ER 432, [1993] 2 WLR 224, 91 LGR 71, [1992] 39 LS Gaz R 30, 136 Sol Jo LB 252, CA 146, 214–215
Oliphant v Hendrie (1784) 1 Bro CC 571 57
Ommanney v Butcher (1823) Turn & R 260, 37 ER 1098, [1814–23] All ER Rep 154 ... 4, 59, 80, 90, 273, 513, 534–535, 537
Oppenheim v Tobacco Securities Trust Co Ltd [1951] AC 297, [1951] 1 All ER 31, [1951] 1 TLR 118, HL 4, 6, 17, 22, 34, 60
Orchard Street Schools (Trustees), Re [1878] WN 211 .... 139, 183, 449
O'Reilly v Mackman [1983] 2 AC 237, [1982] 3 All ER 1124, [1982] 3 WLR 1096, 126 Sol Jo 820, HL 530
Osmund, Re, Midland Bank Executor and Trustee Co Ltd v A-G [1944] Ch 206, [1944] 1 All ER 262, 113 LJ Ch 141, 88 Sol Jo 111, 170 LT 156, 60 TLR 222, CA 23
O'sullivan v English Folk Dance and Song Society [1955] 2 All ER 845, [1955] 1 WLR 907, 53 LGR 549, 48 R & IT 471, 119 JP 484, 99 Sol Jo 526, CA 437
O'sullivan v Management Agency and Music Ltd [1985] QB 428, [1985] 3 All ER 351, [1984] 3 WLR 448, 128 Sol Jo 548, CA 454
Over Seventies Housing Association v Westminster City Council [1974] RA 247, 230 Estates Gazette 1593 .... 1, 14, 314, 432, 434
Ovey, Re, Broadbent v Barrow (1885) 29 Ch D 560, 54 LJ Ch 752, 33 WR 821, 52 LT 849, 1 TLR 401 .... 149, 171
Oxfam v City of Birmingham District Council [1976] AC 126, [1975] 2 All ER 289, [1975] 2 WLR 874, 73 LGR 442, [1975] RA 169, 139 JP 450, 119 Sol Jo 340, HL 432, 435
Oxford Group v IRC [1949] 2 All ER 537, 31 TC 221, 28 ATC 204, 42 R & IT 438, [1949] TR 281, 93 Sol Jo 525, L(TC) 1495, CA 28, 65, 94
Oxford Union Society v City of Oxford (1957) 2 RRC 54 437

P

P (A Barrister) v General Council of the Bar [2005] 1 WLR 3019, [2005] PNLR 32 526
Packe, Re, Sanders v A-G [1918] 1 Ch 437, 87 LJ Ch 300, 62 Sol Jo 488, 118 LT 693; on appeal sub nom Packe, Re, Campion v A-G (1918) 145 LT Jo 111, CA 163
Page v Hull University Visitor. See R v Lord President of the Privy Council, ex p Page
Paice v Archbishop of Canterbury (1807) 14 Ves 364 .... 61, 180, 513, 535, 619
Palatine Estate Charity, Re (1888) 39 Ch D 54, 57 LJ Ch 751, 36 WR 732, 58 LT 925, 4 TLR 499 .... 33, 119
Pardoe, Re, McLaughlin v A-G [1906] 2 Ch 184, 75 LJ Ch 455, 54 WR 561, 94 LT 567, 22 TLR 4512 .... 33, 49, 608
Pare v Clegg (1861) 26 JP 53, 29 Beav 589, 30 LJ Ch 742, 7 Jur NS 1136, 9 WR 795, 4 LT 669 .... 50, 66
Park v Cho [2014] EWHC 55 (Ch), [2014] PTSR 769, [2014] All ER (D) 151 (Jan) 594
Parke v Daily News Ltd [1962] Ch 927, [1962] 2 All ER 929, [1962] 3 WLR 566, 106 Sol Jo 704 68
Parker, Re (1859) 4 H & N 666, 29 LJ Ex 66, 5 Jur NS 1058, 7 WR 660 33
Parker's Trusts, Re (1863) 27 JP 644, 9 Jur NS 884, 11 WR 937, 9 LT 72, sub nom Parker's Charity, Re 32 Beav 654, 2 New Rep 434 .... 31, 113, 119, 137
Parkes, Re, Cottrell v Parkes (1909) 25 TLR 523 157
Parkinson's Case (1689) Comb 143, 3 Mod Rep 265, 1 Show 74, Carth 92, Holt KB 143 .... 244, 532
Parr v A-G (1842) 8 Cl & Fin 409, 6 Jur 245, HL 247
Patel v University of Bradford Senate [1978] 3 All ER 841, [1978] 1 WLR 1488, 122 Sol Jo 791; affd [1979] 2 All ER 582, [1979] 1 WLR 1066, 123 Sol Jo 436, CA 244, 514, 517, 524–525
Patten, Re, Westminster Bank v Carlyon [1929] 2 Ch 276, 98 LJ Ch 419, [1929] All ER Rep 416, 141 LT 295, 45 TLR 504 49
Pauling's Settlement Trusts, Re, Younghusband v Coutts & Co [1964] Ch 303, [1963] 3 All ER 1, [1963] 3 WLR 742, 107 Sol Jo 492, CA 451

PARA

Rees, Re, Jones v Evans [1920] 2 Ch 59, 89 LJ Ch 382, [1920] All ER Rep 138, 123 LT 567 .... 30, 108, 181
Reeve v A-G (1843) 3 Hare 191, 7 Jur 1168, 1 LTOS 432 .... 15, 49, 164, 180, 207, 273, 535
Regentford v Charity Commission for England and Wales [2014] UKUT 0364 (TCC) 559, 580
Reinshaw Park Golf Club v Chesterfield RDC (1957} 1 RRC 291, 50 R & IT 267 437
Rendall v Blair (1890) 45 Ch D 139, 59 LJ Ch 641, 38 WR 689, 63 LT 265, 6 TLR 386, [1886–90] All ER Rep Ext 1214, CA 592, 594, 609
Reresby v Farrer (1700) 2 Vern 414, 1 Eq Cas Abr 100 pl 7 442
Resch's Will Trusts, Re, Le Cras v Perpetual Trustee Co Ltd [1969] 1 AC 514, [1968] 3 WLR 1153, [1968] ALR 161, [1967] 2 NSWR 706, sub nom Le Cras v Perpetual Trustee Co Ltd [1967] 3 All ER 915, PC 8, 11, 19, 245
Restell, Re, Royal Hospital for Incurables v Restell (1901) 17 TLR 395 137–138
Richardson, Re, Shuldham v Royal National Lifeboat Institution (1887) 56 LJ Ch 784, 35 WR 710, 57 LT 17, [1886–90] All ER Rep Ext 1850 .... 45, 75, 138, 180–181
Richardson's Will, Re (1887) 58 LT 45, 4 TLR 153 .... 163, 619
Richmond Corpn v A-G [1965] RA 117, 11 RRC 89, [1965] RVR 224, 193 Estates Gazette 733; revsd sub nom Richmond Parish Charity Lands, Re [1965] RA 343, 11 RRC 283, 109 Sol Jo 755, [1965] RVR 590, CA 48, 121, 163, 214
Richmond upon Thames London Borough Council v Rogers. See Hampton Fuel Allotment Charity, Re
Richmond-upon-Thames London Borough Council v A-G (1982) 81 LGR 156 48
Rickard, Re, Rickard v Robson (1862) 26 JP 709, 31 Beav 244, 31 LJ Ch 897, 8 Jur NS 665, 135 RR 422, 10 WR 657, 7 LT 87 .... 61, 141
Rickards v A-G. See A-G v Rickards
Rickerby v Nicolson [1912] 1 IR 343 93
Rider's Will Trusts, Re, Nelson v Rider [1958] 3 All ER 135, [1958] 1 WLR 974, 102 Sol Jo 636 418
Rigall v Foster (1853) 18 Jur 39 602
Rigley's Trusts, Re (1866) 36 LJ Ch 147, 15 WR 190, 15 LT 499 .... 33, 61, 95
Riland's Estate, Re, Phillips v Robinson [1881] WN 173 93
Roach v Hammond (1715) Gilb Ch 92, Prec Ch 401, sub nom Anon 2 Eq Cas Abr 438 17
Roadley, Re, Iveson v Wakefield [1930] 1 Ch 524, 99 LJ Ch 232, 144 LT 64, 46 TLR 215 .... 15, 19, 43
Roberts, Re, Repington v Roberts-Gawen (1881) 19 Ch D 520, 45 LT 450, CA 140, 142
Roberts, Re, Stenton v Hardy [1963] 1 All ER 674, [1963] 1 WLR 406, 107 Sol Jo 175 .... 151, 171
Roberts' Settlement Trusts, Re (1961) 40 ATC 428, [1961] TR 401 146
Robertson, Re, Colin v Chamberlin [1930] 2 Ch 71, 99 LJ Ch 284, 143 LT 36, 46 TLR 276 .... 33, 172
Robinson, Re, Besant v German Reich [1931] 2 Ch 122, 100 LJ Ch 321, 145 LT 254, 47 TLR 264 .... 58, 180, 182, 206, 213
Robinson, Re, Davis v Robinson [1951] Ch 198, [1950] 2 All ER 1148, 94 Sol Jo 839, [1951] 1 TLR 132 43
Robinson, Re, Wright v Tugwell [1892] 1 Ch 95, 40 WR 137, 66 LT 81; on appeal [1897] 1 Ch 85, 61 JP 132, 66 LJ Ch 97, 45 WR 181, 41 Sol Jo 96, 76 LT 95, 13 TLR 72, CA 31, 75, 119, 137–138
Robinson, Re, Wright v Tugwell [1923] 2 Ch 332, 92 LJ Ch 340, 67 Sol Jo 619, 129 LT 527, 39 TLR 509 .... 31, 75, 137, 163, 169, 180
Robinson v Smith (1908) 24 TLR 573 113
Robinson v Wood (1858) 27 LJ Ch 726, 4 Jur NS 625, 6 WR 728, [1843–60] All ER Rep 318, 31 LTOS 311 137
Roche, Re (1842) 1 Con & Law 306, 2 Dr & War 287 296
Rodwell v Minister of Health [1947] KB 404, [1947] 1 All ER 80, 45 LGR 60, 111 JP 72, [1947] LJR 568, 91 Sol Jo 43, 176 LT 193, 63 TLR 45 15
Rogers v Thomas (1837) 2 Keen 8 60
Rogerson, Re, Bird v Lee [1901] 1 Ch 715, 70 LJ Ch 444, 84 LT 200, [1900–3] All ER Rep Ext 1552 .... 61, 87
Rolls v Miller (1884) 27 Ch D 71, 53 LJ Ch 682, 32 WR 806, [1881–5] All ER Rep 915, 50 LT 597, CA 19, 82
Rooke v Dawson [1895] 1 Ch 480, 59 JP 231, 64 LJ Ch 301, 13 R 270, 43 WR 313, 39 Sol Jo 232, 72 LT 248, 11 TLR 189 592

PARA

T

Tacon, Re, Public Trustee v Tacon [1958] Ch 447, [1958] 1 All ER 163, [1958] 2 WLR 66, 102 Sol Jo 53, CA 163, 167
Talbot, Re, Jubb v Sheard [1933] Ch 895, 102 LJ Ch 362, [1933] All ER Rep 126, 77 Sol Jo 388, 149 LT 401, 49 TLR 462 .... 137, 143, 174
Tatham v Drummond (1864) 4 De GJ & Sm 484, 34 LJ Ch 1, 10 Jur NS 1087, 5 New Rep 24, 13 WR 61, 11 LT 324 44
Taylor, Re, Martin v Freeman (1888) 58 LT 538, 4 TLR 302 .... 61, 87, 168, 171, 606, 619
Taylor, Re, Midland Bank Executor and Trustee Co Ltd v Smith [1940] Ch 481, [1940] 2 All ER 637, 109 LJ Ch 188, 84 Sol Jo 289, 163 LT 51, 56 TLR 588; affd [1940] Ch 834, CA 60, 62
Taylor v Linley. See Linley v Taylor
Taylor v Mogg (1858) 27 LJ Ch 816, 5 Jur NS 137, 32 LTOS 220 643
Taylor v Roe [1894] 1 Ch 413, 63 LJ Ch 282, 3 R 306, 42 WR 426, 38 Sol Jo 142, 70 LT 232 650
Taylor's Charity, Re, ex p Blackburne (1820) 1 Jac & W 297 .... 295, 385
Tempest, Re (1866) 1 Ch App 485, 35 LJ Ch 632, 12 Jur NS 539, 14 WR 850, 14 LT 688 289
Templemoyle Agricultural School, Re (1869) IR 4 Eq 295 168–169
Tennant Plays Ltd (or Tennent Plays Ltd) v IRC [1948] 1 All ER 506, 30 TC 107, 41 R & IT 297, [1948] TR 49, 92 Sol Jo 308, CA 94
Tetley, Re, A-G v National Provincial and Union Bank of England. See A-G v National Provincial and Union Bank of England
Thackrah, Re, Thackrah v Wilson [1939] 2 All ER 4, 83 Sol Jo 216 28
Tharp, Re, Longrigg v People's Dispensary for Sick Animals of the Poor Inc [1942] 2 All ER 358; revsd [1943] 1 All ER 257, 87 Sol Jo 102, CA 160, 171
Thellusson v Woodford (1799) 4 Ves 227; affd sub nom Thellusson v Woodford; Woodford v Thellusson (1805) 1 Bos & PNR 357, 8 RR 104, 11 Ves 112, 32 ER 1030, [1803–13] All ER Rep 30, HL 48
Thetford School Case (1609) 8 Co Rep 130b 134–135, 254
Thomas v Charity Commission for England and Wales (2012) First-tier Tribunal, General Regulatory Chamber (Charity), 19 October 189
Thomas v Howell (1874) LR 18 Eq 198, 43 LJ Ch 511 .... 6, 25, 60, 136
Thomas v Pritchard [1903] 1 KB 209, 67 JP 71, 72 LJKB 23, 20 Cox CC 376, 51 WR 58, 47 Sol Jo 32, 87 LT 688, 19 TLR 10, DC 623
Thomas v University of Bradford [1987] AC 795, [1987] 1 All ER 834, [1987] 2 WLR 677, [1987] ICR 245, 131 Sol Jo 296, [1987] LS Gaz R 980, [1987] NLJ Rep 220, HL 514, 517–518, 523–525, 530
Thomas v University of Bradford (No 2) [1992] 1 All ER 964 .... 518, 528
Thompson, Re, Public Trustee v Lloyd [1934] Ch 342, 103 LJ Ch 162, [1933] All ER Rep 805, 150 LT 451 60
Thompson v Corby (1860) 24 JP 581, 27 Beav 649, 8 WR 267, 3 LT 73 19
Thompson v Federal Taxation Comr (1959) 102 CLR 315, [1960] ALR 184, 33 ALJR 384 (Aust HC), Aust HC 6
Thompson v Thompson (1844) 13 LJ Ch 455, 1 Coll 381, 8 Jur 839, 3 LTOS 452 ..... 15, 19, 25, 50, 57, 66, 86, 93, 182
Thompson's Settlement Trusts, Re, Thompson v Alexander [1905] 1 Ch 229, 74 LJ Ch 133, 91 LT 835, 21 TLR 86 256
Thomson v Honourable Society of the Inner Temple Trustees (30 May 1967, unreported) 447
Thomson v London University (1864) 33 LJ Ch 625, 10 Jur NS 669, 12 WR 733, 10 LT 403 .... 514, 525, 529
Thomson v Shakespear (1860) John 612, 29 LJ Ch 140, 6 Jur NS 118, 8 WR 124, 1 LT 398; affd (1860) 24 JP 309, 1 De GF & J 399, 29 LJ Ch 276, 6 Jur NS 281, 8 WR 265, 2 LT 479 .... 36, 62, 141, 209
Thornber v Wilson (1855) 19 JP 675, 3 Drew 245, 24 LJ Ch 667, 3 WR 388, 25 LTOS 309 32
Thorne v Heard and Marsh [1895] AC 495, 64 LJ Ch 652, 11 R 254, 44 WR 155, 73 LT 291, 11 TLR 464, HL 447
Thorne v University of London [1966] 2 QB 237, [1966] 2 All ER 338, [1966] 2 WLR 1080, 110 Sol Jo 231, CA 525, 529

PARA

Y

CHARITIES

1. CHARITABLE PURPOSES

(1) ESSENTIALS OF CHARITABLE PURPOSES

1. Meaning of 'charity'. For the purposes of the law of England and Wales, 'charity' means an institution which is established for charitable purposes[1] only and is subject to the control of the High Court in the exercise of its jurisdiction with respect to charities[2]. Unless the context otherwise requires, 'institution' means an institution whether incorporated or not, and includes a trust or undertaking[3].

References to 'charity' in any Act of Parliament should be construed in their technical legal sense, unless a different definition of that term applies by virtue of that Act or any other enactment[4]. A reference in any enactment or document to a charity within the meaning of the Charitable Uses Act 1601[5], or of the preamble to it, is to be construed as a reference to a charity as defined above[6].

The Charities Act 1960 established a register of charities[7], which is continued by the Charities Act 2011[8], and it is the duty of the charity trustees[9] of any charity which is required to be registered[10] to apply for registration[11]. The effect of registration is that an institution is for all purposes other than rectification of the register conclusively presumed to be or to have been a charity at any time when it is or was on the register of charities[12]. The legislation does not provide, however, that an institution which, if it were a charity, would be required to be registered, but which is not registered, is for that reason not a charity[13].

1 As to the meaning of 'charitable purposes' see PARA 2.

2 Charities Act 2011 ss 1(1), 10(1). This definition does not apply for the purposes of an enactment if a different definition of that term applies for those purposes by virtue of that or any other enactment, or, in the Charities Act 2006, where the context otherwise requires: Charities Act 2011 s 1(2); Charities Act 2006 s 78(7). As to the limitation of the meaning of 'charity' in relation to ecclesiastical property see PARA 196.

'Enactment', in the Charities Act 2011, except where the context otherwise requires, generally includes any provision of subordinate legislation within the meaning of the Interpretation Act 1978 (see **STATUTES AND LEGISLATIVE PROCESS**), and a provision of a Measure of the Church Assembly or of the General Synod of the Church of England: see the Charities Act 2011 ss 9(1), 23(4), 27(2), 58(7), 245(4), 246(5), 331(1). In the Charities Act 2006 s 75(5) it includes any provision made by or under an Act of the Scottish Parliament or Northern Ireland legislation: s 78(4), (7) (s 78(4) amended by the Charities Act 2011 Schs 7, 10).

The requirement that an institution be subject to the control of the High Court in the exercise of the court's jurisdiction with respect to charities is satisfied if the institution is subject to that jurisdiction in any significant respect: see *Construction Industry Training Board v A-G* [1971] 3 All ER 449, [1971] 1 WLR 1303; affd [1973] Ch 173, [1972] 2 All ER 1339, CA. As to what is meant by 'the court's jurisdiction with respect to charities' cf the Charities Act 2011 s 62(5) (see PARA 217), s 68 (see PARAS 184–185), s 115(8) (see PARA 592); and see *Construction Industry Training Board v A-G*. See also the *Report of the Charity Commissioners for England and Wales for 1990* (HC Paper (1990–91) no 362) App A (a). It does not have to be subject to that jurisdiction which the court exercises only over charities and not over other trusts or other corporate bodies, and it is sufficient if the court is competent to restrain the institution from applying its property ultra vires or in breach of trust: *Construction Industry Training Board v A-G* [1973] Ch 173, [1972] 2 All ER 1339, CA.

For territorial limits on the operation of the Charities Act 2006 see s 80(2)–(9) (amended by the Charities Act 2011 Sch 7 Pt 2 para 125, Sch 10). For territorial limits on the operation of the Charities Act 2011 see s 356. With limited exceptions, neither Act extends to Scotland or Northern Ireland.

3 Charities Act 2006 s 78(5), (7); Charities Act 2011 s 9(3), (4). The four principal institutional structures for charities – that is to say, the four kinds of institution which might be referred to as

charities – are trusts (see PARA 68 et seq), charitable incorporated organisations (CIOs) (see PARA 226 et seq), unincorporated associations (see PARA 218 et seq) and other charitable companies (see PARA 240 et seq).

It is possible for a charity to change its structure: see *Change your charity structure* (Charity Commission, December 2014) (available, at the date at which this volume states the law, on the government website). As to the Charity Commission see PARAS 543–578. As to the Charity Commission's publications see PARA 547.

4 See the Charities Act 2011 s 1(2); and *Income Tax Special Purposes Comrs v Pemsel* [1891] AC 531 at 580, HL, per Lord Macnaghten; *Chesterman v Federal Taxation Comr* [1926] AC 128, PC; *Adamson v Melbourne and Metropolitan Board of Works* [1929] AC 142, PC. See also *Ashfield Municipal Council v Joyce* [1978] AC 122, [1976] 3 WLR 617, PC.

As to the meaning of 'charity' for tax purposes see INCOME TAXATION vol 58A (2014) PARA 1622.

5 Ie 43 Eliz 1 c 4 (1601).

6 Charities Act 2011 Sch 7 para 1.

7 See the Charities Act 1960 s 4(1) (repealed).

8 See the Charities Act 2011 s 29(1); and PARA 307.

9 As to the meaning of 'charity trustees' see PARA 255.

10 As to charities which are not required to be registered see the Charities Act 2011 s 30(2); and PARA 308.

11 See the Charities Act 2011 s 35(1); and PARA 309.

12 Charities Act 2011 s 37(1); and PARA 314. See also *Wynn v Skegness UDC* [1966] 3 All ER 336, [1967] 1 WLR 52; *Re Murawski's Will Trusts, Lloyds Bank Ltd v Royal Society for the Prevention of Cruelty to Animals* [1971] 2 All ER 328, [1971] 1 WLR 707.

13 See *Over Seventies Housing Association v Westminster City Council* [1974] RA 247; and PARA 314.

2. Charitable purposes. Charitable uses or trusts form a distinct head of equity[1], and it is the court's duty to determine whether particular purposes are charitable[2]. The popular use of the expressions 'charity', 'charitable', 'charitable objects' and 'charitable purposes' does not coincide with their technical legal meaning according to the law of England[3]. The word 'charitable', when used in its legal sense, covers many objects which a layman might not consider to be included under that word, but it excludes some benevolent or philanthropic activities which a layman might consider charitable[4]. Not every object which is beneficial to the community is charitable[5].

For the purposes of the law of England and Wales, 'charitable purposes' means purposes which are for the public benefit[6], and fall within any of the following descriptions of purposes[7]:

(1) the prevention or relief of poverty[8];
(2) the advancement of education[9];
(3) the advancement of religion[10];
(4) the advancement of health or the saving of lives[11];
(5) the advancement of citizenship or community development[12];
(6) the advancement of the arts, culture, heritage or science[13];
(7) the advancement of amateur sport[14];
(8) the advancement of human rights, conflict resolution or reconciliation or the promotion of religious or racial harmony or equality and diversity[15];
(9) the advancement of environmental protection or improvement[16];
(10) the relief of those in need by reason of youth, age, ill-health, disability, financial hardship or other disadvantage[17];
(11) the advancement of animal welfare[18];
(12) the promotion of the efficiency of the armed forces of the Crown, or of the efficiency of the police, fire and rescue services or ambulance services[19];

(13) any other purposes recognised as charitable under the old law[20], including facilities for recreation or other leisure-time occupation, if the facilities are provided in the interests of social welfare[21];

(14) any purposes that may reasonably be regarded as analogous to, or within the spirit of, a purpose falling within heads (1)–(13) above[22]; and

(15) any purposes that may reasonably be regarded as analogous to, or within the spirit of, a purpose which has been recognised under head (14) above[23].

Where any of the terms used in heads (1) to (13) above has a particular meaning under charity law, the term is to be taken as having the same meaning where it appears above[24]. Accordingly, the cases previously decided on the subject remain relevant except in so far as they are contradicted by any provision in the Charities Act 2011[25].

All charitable purposes must fall within one or more of these categories of purposes, though not every institution or trust whose purpose might be brought within one of them is necessarily a charity[26], for it must, further, be publicly beneficial and of a public nature[27]. Many charitable purposes do not fit neatly within a single category[28]. Where a trust is described merely as being for charitable purposes, and a class of objects to be benefited is defined, the purposes of the trust cannot be taken to be confined to that particular charitable purpose which would render a trust for that class valid as a charity, but rather the purposes must be construed as being all the categories of charitable objects, and the trust must be interpreted in the light of the application of all categories to the class of objects to be benefited[29].

Where a purpose is clearly charitable the court will not generally inquire into the efficacy of the activities carried on in pursuance of that purpose[30], but such activities may be relevant in so far as they demonstrate whether there is any charitable tendency in a given purpose[31].

An activity which is charitable in the legal sense is not any the less charitable because it is being carried on without any regular organisation by a person who may discontinue it at any time[32]. Such an activity would come within the statutory definition of charity as a trust or undertaking[33].

The Value Added Tax Act 1994 contains various references to 'relevant charitable purposes', but 'charitable purpose' there bears a limited meaning and is not to be taken as the same as that which underpins the law relating to charities[34].

1 *Income Tax Special Purposes Comrs v Pemsel* [1891] AC 531 at 580, HL, per Lord Macnaghten; cited in *Royal College of Surgeons of England v National Provincial Bank Ltd* [1952] AC 631 at 650, [1952] 1 All ER 984 at 992, HL.

2 *National Anti-Vivisection Society v IRC* [1948] AC 31 at 63, [1947] 2 All ER 217 at 232, HL, per Lord Simonds.

3 *Income Tax Special Purposes Comrs v Pemsel* [1891] AC 531 at 580, 583, HL, per Lord Macnaghten. As to the popular meaning see *Income Tax Special Purposes Comrs v Pemsel* at 552 per Lord Halsbury LC, at 564 per Lord Bramwell, and at 572 per Lord Herschell; and *Baird's Trustees v Lord Advocate* (1888) 15 R 682, Ct of Sess; *Verge v Somerville* [1924] AC 496 at 502, PC. As to the meaning of 'charity' see PARA 1.

4 *Re Shaw, Public Trustee v Day* [1957] 1 All ER 745 at 752, [1957] 1 WLR 729 at 736, per Harman J.

5 *National Anti-Vivisection Society v IRC* [1948] AC 31 at 41, [1947] 2 All ER 217 at 220, HL, per Lord Wright. See *Helena Partnerships Ltd (formerly Helena Housing Ltd) v Revenue and Customs Comrs (Attorney General intervening)* [2012] EWCA Civ 569, [2012] 4 All ER 111, [2012] PTSR 1409 (provision of housing).

6 Charities Act 2011 s 2(1)(b); Charities Act 2006 s 78(2)(b) (amended by Charities Act 2011 Sch 7 Pt 2 para 123(1)(b)). This definition does not apply in the Charities Act 2006 where the context otherwise requires: s 78(7). As to the public benefit test see PARA 4.

This requirement is known as the 'public benefit requirement': Charities Act 2011 s 4(1).

7 Charities Act 2011 s 2(1)(a); Charities Act 2006 s 78(2)(b). This definition does not apply where the context otherwise requires: Charities Act 2011 s 2(3); Charities Act 2006 s 78(7). Any reference in any enactment or document (in whatever terms) to charitable purposes, or institutions having purposes that are charitable under charity law is to be construed in accordance with the definition above: Charities Act 2011 s 2(2).

For the most part, references to 'charitable purposes' in the Charities Act 2011 are, unless the context otherwise requires, to purposes which are exclusively charitable as defined in s 2(1): s 11 (which applies to s 11 and from that section onwards).

8 Charities Act 2011 s 3(1)(a). See PARA 12 et seq.

9 Charities Act 2011 s 3(1)(b). 'Religion' includes: (1) a religion which involves belief in more than one god; and (2) a religion which does not involve belief in a god: s 3(2)(a). See PARA 27 et seq.

10 Charities Act 2011 s 3(1)(c). See PARA 22 et seq.

11 Charities Act 2011 s 3(1)(d). The 'advancement of health' includes the prevention or relief of sickness, disease or human suffering: s 3(2)(b). See PARA 34.

12 Charities Act 2011 s 3(1)(e). This includes: (1) rural or urban regeneration; and (2) the promotion of civic responsibility, volunteering, the voluntary sector or the effectiveness or efficiency of charities: s 3(2)(c). See PARA 35.

13 Charities Act 2011 s 3(1)(f). See PARA 36.

14 Charities Act 2011 s 3(1)(g). 'Sport' means sports or games which promote health by involving physical or mental skill or exertion: s 3(2)(d). See PARAS 6, 38.

15 Charities Act 2011 s 3(1)(h). See PARA 39 et seq.

16 Charities Act 2011 s 3(1)(i). See PARA 42.

17 Charities Act 2011 s 3(1)(j). This includes relief given by the provision of accommodation or care to the persons mentioned: s 3(2)(e). See PARA 43.

18 Charities Act 2011 s 3(1)(k). See PARA 44.

19 Charities Act 2011 s 3(1)(l). 'Fire and rescue services' means services provided by fire and rescue authorities under Part 2 of the Fire and Rescue Services Act 2004 (see **FIRE AND RESCUE SERVICES**): Charities Act 2011 s 3(2)(f). See PARA 45.

20 'The old law' means the law relating to charities as in force immediately before 1 April 2008 (ie the day on which the Charities Act 2006 s 2 (now repealed) came into force): Charities Act 2011 s 3(4). See PARA 46 et seq.

21 Charities Act 2011 s 3(1)(m)(i). The facilities referred to in the text are charitable purposes by virtue of s 5: see PARA 52 et seq.

22 Charities Act 2011 s 3(1)(m)(ii). See PARA 56.

23 Charities Act 2011 s 3(1)(m)(iii). See PARA 56.

24 Charities Act 2011 s 3(3).

25 Previously, charitable purposes derived from the Charitable Uses Act 1601 (43 Eliz 1 c 4 (1601)) (repealed) and were classified into four principal divisions: the relief of poverty; the advancement of education; the advancement of religion; and other purposes beneficial to the community not falling under any of the preceding heads: see *Income Tax Special Purposes Comrs v Pemsel* [1891] AC 531 at 583, HL, per Lord Macnaghten. The classification was taken from the argument of Sir Samuel Romilly in *Morice v Bishop of Durham* (1805) 10 Ves 522 at 532 per Lord Eldon LC. See also *Re Macduff, Macduff v Macduff* [1896] 2 Ch 451 at 466, CA, per Lindley LJ.

26 *Re Macduff, Macduff v Macduff* [1896] 2 Ch 451 at 474, CA, per Rigby LJ.

27 See PARAS 4–6.

28 *Re Hopkins' Will Trusts, Naish v Francis Bacon Society Inc* [1965] Ch 669 at 678, [1964] 3 All ER 46 at 51 per Wilberforce J; cf *Trustees of City of Belfast YMCA v Northern Ireland Valuation Comr* [1969] NI 3, CA.

29 *Re Cox, Baker v National Trust Co Ltd* [1955] AC 627, [1955] 2 All ER 550, PC.

30 *Re Shaw's Will Trusts, National Provincial Bank Ltd v National City Bank Ltd* [1952] Ch 163, [1952] 1 All ER 49.

31 See eg *Southwood v A-G* [2000] WTLR 1199, CA.

32 *Re Marchant, Weaver v Royal Society for the Prevention of Cruelty to Animals* (1910) 54 Sol Jo 425; *Re Mann, Hardy v A-G* [1903] 1 Ch 232; *Re Webster, Pearson v Webster* [1912] 1 Ch 106; and see *Re Kerin* (1966) Times, 24 May. Cf the position of unincorporated associations established for charitable purposes, as to which see PARAS 28, 62.

33 See the Charities Act 2011 s 9(3); the Charities Act 2006 s 78(5); and PARA 1.

34 See Value Added Tax Act 1994 Sch 8 Pt II Group 5 note (6); and VALUE ADDED TAX vol 99 (2012) PARA 228. In that provision the phrase is used to determine whether certain activities may be zero-rated for the purposes of VAT. See eg *Capernwray Missionary Fellowship of Torchbearers v Revenue and Customs Comrs* [2014] UKFTT 626 (TC), [2014] SFTD 1051.

3. Purposes must be exclusively charitable. To be a charity in law, a trust or institution must be established for purposes which are exclusively charitable[1]; a charitable trust can be enforced by the court at the suit of the Attorney General, for the court knows what are charitable purposes and can apply the trust property accordingly, but a trust for benevolent purposes cannot be so enforced and is therefore void for uncertainty[2]. However, a distinction must be drawn between: (1) the designated purposes of the trust; (2) the designated means of carrying out those purposes; and (3) the consequences of carrying them out. Trust purposes of an otherwise charitable nature do not lose that nature merely because the trustees, by way of furtherance of those purposes, have incidental powers to carry on activities which are not themselves charitable. The distinction is between: (a) those non-charitable activities which are merely subsidiary or incidental to a charitable purpose; and (b) those non-charitable activities so authorised which in themselves form part of the trust purpose. In the latter but not the former case, the reference to non-charitable activities will deprive the trust of its charitable status[3].

Where there is a benefit to individuals which cannot be regarded as subordinate to the general benefit of the community, the requirements of charity will not be satisfied[4].

1 See the Charities Act 2011 s 1(1)(a); and PARA 1. As to the meaning of 'charitable purposes' see PARA 2. If it is established partly for charitable and partly for non-charitable purposes, it may in some circumstances be validated by the Charitable Trusts (Validation) Act 1954: see PARAS 98–103. In determining whether purposes are charitable it may be necessary to refer not only to the body's constitution but also, in cases of doubt and ambiguity, to extrinsic evidence, including its activities: *Southwood v A-G* [1998] 40 LS Gaz R 37, Times, 26 October; affd [2000] WTLR 1199, CA; *Incorporated Council of Law Reporting for England and Wales v A-G* [1972] Ch 73 at 91 per Sachs LJ and at 99 per Buckley LJ; *IRC v Oldham Training and Enterprise Council* [1996] STC 1218 at 1234–1235 per Lightman J. See also *Application for the Registration of the Ethnic-English Trust and the Ironside Community Trust*, Decision of the Charity Commission, 28 June 2007. As to decisions of the Charity Commission see PARA 547.

2 *Chichester Diocesan Fund and Board of Finance Inc v Simpson* [1944] AC 341 at 371, [1944] 2 All ER 60 at 74, HL, per Lord Simonds; the same case in the Court of Appeal, sub nom *Re Diplock, Wintle v Diplock* [1941] Ch 253 at 259, [1941] 1 All ER 193 at 199, per Sir Wilfrid Greene MR; *Morice v Bishop of Durham* (1804) 9 Ves 399 at 404 per Sir William Gaunt MR (on appeal (1805) 10 Ves 522 at 539 per Lord Eldon LC); *IRC v Broadway Cottages Trust Ltd* [1955] Ch 20 at 29, [1954] 3 All ER 120 at 124, CA, per Jenkins LJ; and see PARA 65. As to the Attorney General see PARAS 589, 596, 605 et seq; and CONSTITUTIONAL AND ADMINISTRATIVE LAW vol 20 (2014) PARA 273 et seq.

3 *McGovern v A-G* [1982] Ch 321, [1981] 3 All ER 493. See also *Re Coxen, McCallum v Coxen* [1948] Ch 747, [1948] 2 All ER 492; *Royal College of Surgeons of England v National Provincial Bank Ltd* [1952] AC 631, [1952] 1 All ER 984, HL; *Neville Estates Ltd v Madden* [1962] Ch 832, [1961] 3 All ER 769; *Incorporated Council of Law Reporting for England and Wales v A-G* [1972] Ch 73 at 84, [1971] 3 All ER 1029 at 1033, CA, per Russell LJ; *A-G v Ross* [1985] 3 All ER 334, [1986] 1 WLR 252.

4 See *Helena Partnerships Ltd (formerly Helena Housing Ltd) v Revenue and Customs Comrs (Attorney General intervening)* [2012] EWCA Civ 569 at [107], [2012] 4 All ER 111, [2012] PTSR 1409. See also *Wirral Independent Recycling Enterprise ('WIRE') Ltd v Revenue and Customs Comrs* [2012] UKFTT 267 (TC), [2012] SWTI 2101.

4. Public benefit requirement. The Charities Act 2011 provides that a purpose is not charitable unless it is for the 'public benefit' and the element of public benefit is thus a necessary condition of legal charity[1]. This principle was previously established at common law[2] and for the purposes of the Charities Act 2011 any reference to public benefit is a reference to that term as it is understood at common law[3]. There are two distinct elements in this requirement: (1) the purpose must have an identifiable benefit[4]; and (2) the benefit of the purpose must be available to a sufficient section of the public[5]. The line of distinction between purposes of a public and a private nature is fine and practically incapable of definition[6].

The Charity Commission has a statutory objective to promote awareness and understanding of the operation of the public benefit requirement[7] and must issue guidance in pursuance of that objective[8]. Charity trustees must have regard to it when exercising any powers or duties to which the guidance is relevant[9].

1 See the Charities Act 2011 s 2(1)(b); and PARA 2.

2 See *Oppenheim v Tobacco Securities Trust Co Ltd* [1951] AC 297 at 305, [1951] 1 All ER 31 at 33, HL, per Lord Simonds; *Jones v Williams* (1767) Amb 651 (where 'charity' is defined as a gift to a general public use which extends to the poor as well as to the rich); *Ommanney v Butcher* (1823) Turn & R 260 at 273 per Plumer MR; *Goodman v Saltash Corpn* (1882) 7 App Cas 633 at 650, HL, per Earl Cairns; *Re Christchurch Inclosure Act* (1888) 38 ChD 520 at 532, CA, per Lindley LJ; affd sub nom *A-G v Meyrick* [1893] AC 1, HL. As to the meaning of 'private charity' see PARA 59.

3 See the Charities Act 2011 s 4(3). This is subject to s 4(2) (see PARA 5 text and note 3): Charities Act 2011 s 4(4).

4 See PARA 5.

5 See PARA 6.

6 *Re Drummond, Ashworth v Drummond* [1914] 2 Ch 90 at 96 per Eve J; *A-G v Pearce* (1740) 2 Atk 87; *Hall v Derby Borough Urban Sanitary Authority* (1885) 16 QBD 163, DC; *Shaw v Halifax Corpn* [1915] 2 KB 170 at 182, CA, per Kennedy LJ. See also *Helena Partnerships Ltd (formerly Helena Housing Ltd) v Revenue and Customs Comrs (Attorney General intervening)* [2012] EWCA Civ 569, [2012] 4 All ER 111, [2012] PTSR 1409, and PARA 3 text and note 4.

7 See the Charities Act 2011 s 14; and PARA 544. As to the meaning of 'public benefit requirement' see PARA 2 note 6.

8 See the Charities Act 2011 s 17(1). The Commission may from time to time revise any such guidance (s 17(2)) and must carry out such public and other consultation as it considers appropriate before issuing any such guidance or, unless it considers that it is unnecessary to do so, before revising any such guidance (s 17(3)). Any consultation initiated by the Charity Commission for England and Wales before 1 April 2008 (ie the day on which the Charities Act 2006 s 4 (now repealed) came into force) is effective for these purposes as if it had been initiated by the Commission on or after that day: Charities Act 2006 s 75(3), Sch 10 para 1 (repealed), Charities Act 2011 Sch 8 Pt 1 para 6. The Commission must publish any guidance issued or revised under these provisions in such manner as it considers appropriate: s 17(4). As to the Charity Commission see PARAS 543–578. As to such guidance see *PB1: Public benefit: the public benefit requirement* (Charity Commission, September 2013); *PB2: Public benefit: running a charity* (Charity Commission, September 2013); *PB3: Public benefit: reporting* (Charity Commission, September 2013) (all available, at the date at which this volume states the law, on the government website). As to the Charity Commission's publications see PARA 547.

9 Charities Act 2011 s 17(5). Certain charities have a duty to include in their annual report a statement as to the manner in which they have fulfilled the public benefit requirement: see PARA 374 text and notes 10–15.

5. Proof of public benefit. The question whether a purpose will or may be operative for the public benefit is a question to be answered by the court by forming an opinion on the evidence before it[1], having strict regard to the conditions of the gift[2].

It is not to be presumed that a purpose of a particular description is for the public benefit[3]. The purpose must be one capable of being of benefit to the community[4].

Despite this it is likely that the old common law position still stands, namely that a purpose may be so obviously beneficial to the community that to call evidence on the question would be absurd[5]; in some cases the purpose is so clearly beneficial there is little need to provide evidence to prove it[6]. If the purpose of the gift is held to be beneficial to the public, it is not relevant for the court to inquire whether one means or another of achieving that purpose is most effective[7]. However, if the element of public benefit is incapable of proof one way or the other, the court will not recognise the trust as being of a charitable nature[8].

A donor's opinion with regard to whether the gift will be beneficial to the public[9], even when based on religious belief[10], and his motive[11], are both immaterial. The fact that a donor expressly refers to his 'general charitable intention' cannot impose on a gift a general charitable intention or make it charitable if, on the face of it, it has only a particular intention which is not charitable[12]. It is for the court to consider each case upon its own special circumstances[13].

As circumstances differ from age to age, a purpose regarded in one age as for the public benefit and charitable may in another be regarded differently, so that a gift in the will of a testator dying in 1700 might be held valid upon the evidence then before the court but, upon different evidence, held invalid if he died in 1900[14]. The converse may also be possible[15]. This is not to say that a charitable trust, when it has once been established, can ever fail: a charity once established in perpetuity does not die, though its nature may be changed[16].

Indirect benefits received by persons whose needs it is the charity's purpose to relieve, and which are received otherwise than as recipients of the main service, and wider benefits (received by the community at large), can be taken into consideration as part of the public benefit requirement[17].

1 *National Anti-Vivisection Society v IRC* [1948] AC 31 at 44, [1947] 2 All ER 217 at 219, HL, per Lord Wright (approving *Re Hummeltenberg, Beatty v London Spiritualistic Alliance Ltd* [1923] 1 Ch 237, and overruling *Re Foveaux, Cross v London Anti-Vivisection Society* [1895] 2 Ch 501 at 507 per Chitty J); applied in *Re Moss, Hobrough v Harvey* [1949] 1 All ER 495. See also *Re Grove-Grady, Plowden v Lawrence* [1929] 1 Ch 557 at 572, CA, per Lord Hanworth MR, and at 583, 588, per Russell LJ; compromised on appeal sub nom *A-G v Plowden* [1931] WN 89, HL; *Application for Registration of Living in Radiance*, Decision of the Charity Commissioners, 25 August 2005, at 6.2. As to decisions of the Charity Commission see PARA 547.

2 *Re Pinion, Westminster Bank Ltd v Pinion* [1965] Ch 85, [1964] 1 All ER 890, CA; revsg on this point Wilberforce J [1965] Ch 85, [1963] 2 All ER 1049.

3 Charities Act 2011 s 4(2). The full significance of this provision is unclear. It is taken to be a reference to the presumption under the old law that the relief of poverty, the advancement of education and the advancement of religion (see PARAS 12–33) satisfied the requirement of benefit to a sufficient section of the community unless the contrary appeared: see PARA 6 note 8. See, however, *A-G v Charity Commission for England and Wales* [2012] UKUT 420 (TCC), [2012] WTLR 977, 15 ITELR 521, where the Tribunal asserted that there is no presumption that a trust for the relief of poverty is for the public benefit.

4 *A-G v Charity Commission for England and Wales* [2012] UKUT 420 (TCC) at [83], [2012] WTLR 977, 15 ITELR 521.

5 *Re Shaw's Will Trusts, National Provincial Bank Ltd v National City Bank Ltd* [1952] Ch 163, [1952] 1 All ER 49; and see PARA 21. The court may have a predisposition as to whether a purpose is to the public benefit, but will look at the terms of the trust critically and that predisposition may be displaced: *R (on the application of Independent Schools Council) v Charity Commission for England and Wales; A-G v Charity Commission for England and Wales* [2011] UKUT 421 (TCC), [2012] Ch 214, [2012] 1 All ER 127.

6 *PB1: Public benefit: the public benefit requirement* (Charity Commission, September 2013) Pt 3 (available, at the date at which this volume states the law, on the government website). As to the Charity Commission's publications see PARA 547. As to the meaning of 'public benefit requirement' see PARA 2 note 6. See also *R (on the application of Independent Schools Council) v Charity Commission for England and Wales; A-G v Charity Commission for England and Wales* [2011] UKUT 421 (TCC), [2012] Ch 214, [2012] 1 All ER 127.

7 *Re Shaw's Will Trusts, National Provincial Bank Ltd v National City Bank Ltd* [1952] Ch 163, [1952] 1 All ER 49.
8 *Gilmour v Coats* [1949] AC 426, [1949] 1 All ER 848, HL; *McGovern v A-G* [1982] Ch 321, [1981] 3 All ER 493. See also *PB1: Public benefit: the public benefit requirement* (Charity Commission, September 2013) Pt 3, where the Charity Commission indicates that it will not consider a purpose to be charitable if it cannot be shown to be beneficial.
9 See the cases cited in note 1.
10 *Gilmour v Coats* [1949] AC 426 at 456–457, [1949] 1 All ER 848 at 861, HL, per Lord Reid; *Keren Kayemeth Le Jisroel Ltd v IRC* [1932] AC 650, HL.
11 *Hoare v Osborne* (1866) LR 1 Eq 585 at 588 per Kindersley V-C; *Re Delany, Conoley v Quick* [1902] 2 Ch 642 at 649 per Farwell J; *Re King, Kerr v Bradley* [1923] 1 Ch 243 at 245 per Romer J.
12 *Re Sanders' Will Trusts, Public Trustee v McLaren* [1954] Ch 265, [1954] 1 All ER 667 (appeal settled (1954) Times, 22 July, CA); and see PARA 91.
13 *Re Foveaux, Cross v London Anti-Vivisection Society* [1895] 2 Ch 501 at 504 per Chitty J, cited with approval by Lord Simonds in *National Anti-Vivisection Society v IRC* [1948] AC 31 at 67, [1947] 2 All ER 217 at 234, HL.
14 *National Anti-Vivisection Society v IRC* [1948] AC 31 at 74, [1947] 2 All ER 217 at 238, HL, per Lord Simonds.
15 *Gilmour v Coats* [1949] AC 426 at 443, [1949] 1 All ER 848 at 853, HL, per Lord Simonds.
16 *National Anti-Vivisection Society v IRC* [1948] AC 31 at 74, [1947] 2 All ER 217 at 238, HL, per Lord Simonds. However, a charitable trust may be established for a specific, strictly limited purpose (see *Gibson v South American Stores (Gath and Chaves) Ltd* [1950] Ch 177, [1949] 2 All ER 985, CA) or subject to a gift over on the happening of a certain event, e g the failure of the original charitable purpose (see *Re Cooper's Conveyance Trusts, Crewdson v Bagot* [1956] 3 All ER 28, [1956] 1 WLR 1096); such trusts are not necessarily established in perpetuity and could be said to die, or at least to be potentially mortal; see also PARA 140. The failure of a charitable trust's original purpose in the absence of a gift over will trigger the court's cy-près jurisdiction: see PARA 179 et seq.
17 *R (on the application of Independent Schools Council) v Charity Commission for England and Wales; A-G v Charity Commission for England and Wales* [2011] UKUT 421 (TCC), [2012] Ch 214, [2012] 1 All ER 127.

6. Benefit to sufficient section of community. To satisfy the public benefit requirement[1], a purpose must benefit the community, or an appreciably important class of the community[2], which must be sufficiently defined[3] and identifiable by some quality of a public nature[4], but may be restricted within narrow limits[5]. It may be a community abroad[6].

The question what is a sufficient section of the public must be considered in the light of the particular purpose, for they are interdependent; the argument that what is a sufficient section to support a valid trust in one category must be sufficient to support a valid trust in any other category cannot be accepted[7]. It is not to be presumed that a purpose of a particular description is for the public benefit[8]. In ascertaining whether a purpose is public or private, the salient point to be considered is whether the class to be benefited, or from which the beneficiaries are to be selected, constitutes a substantial body of the public[9].

The beneficiaries must not be numerically negligible[10], and must not be ascertained or determined by their connection with a private individual or private individuals or with a company or other employer[11]; nor may they be merely particular private individuals pointed out by the donor or a fluctuating class of private individuals[12]. A class of trusts for the relief of poverty, known as the 'poor relations cases', forms an exception to this principle[13]. The fact that funds have been publicly subscribed for a purpose is not a test of whether the purpose is of a public nature, though it may afford some indication[14].

An orphanage for the children of deceased railway employees has been held to be a public charity[15]; a 'seamen's mission' for the benefit of seamen in port in the Port of London and the London dock areas is charitable[16], and a statutory body established to promote and improve the standard of training within the whole of one industry in England, Scotland and Wales has been held to be established for exclusively charitable purposes[17]. But a trust for all members of a trade union which was open to all members of the printing industry, but to which not all members of the industry in fact belonged, was held not to be charitable[18], nor was a society for the relief of the sickness of its own members, who numbered over 400,000, charitable[19].

A trust to provide for the education of children of employees or former employees of a group of companies is private[20]; a contributory fund for the relief of air raid victims among the contributors who were employees of a particular company is private[21]; similarly a trust to contribute to the holiday expenses of the workpeople employed in a certain department of a company's business has been held to be a trust for private individuals, and so not charitable[22]. A gift on trust for the children and remoter issue of Presbyterians living at a certain date and descended from Presbyterian settlers in the colony of New South Wales hailing from or born in the north of Ireland was held not to be for the benefit of a section of the community, in the sense in which these words have been interpreted in the authorities[23]. A gift for the education of descendants of named persons, irrespective of their means, is private[24]. Pupils at a particular school may be a sufficient section of the public[25]. A gift to a named community house, construed as a gift for its purposes, was held charitable, the necessary element of public benefit consisting in the assistance rendered by the community house to members of the public in need[26]. A gift to a class which would be held to be private on this principle may nevertheless be a valid charitable gift if the purposes of the gift are restricted to the relief of poverty[27], and a bequest for the relief of such poor persons as the testator's trustees may choose is charitable[28].

On the other hand, where the choice is to be made from a number of named individuals[29], or where the class of beneficiaries is so restricted that the gift is, in effect, one to particular individuals[30], the gift may be held to be not in the nature of a charitable gift at all, but rather a direct beneficial gift to the individuals in question or some of them[31]. Similarly, where although there is a benefit to the section of the community, there is at the same time a benefit to individuals which cannot be regarded as subordinate, the elements of charity will not be made out[32].

1 See PARAS 4–5.

2 *Verge v Somerville* [1924] AC 496 at 499, PC; *Oppenheim v Tobacco Securities Trust Co Ltd* [1951] AC 297 at 305, [1951] 1 All ER 31 at 33, HL, per Lord Simonds. See also *R (on the application of Independent Schools Council) v Charity Commission for England and Wales; A-G v Charity Commission for England and Wales* [2011] UKUT 421 (TCC), [2012] Ch 214, [2012] 1 All ER 127; *A-G v Charity Commission for England and Wales* [2012] UKUT 420 (TCC), [2012] WTLR 977, 15 ITELR 521.

3 *Keren Kayemeth Le Jisroel Ltd v IRC* [1932] AC 650, HL; *Williams' Trustees v IRC* [1947] AC 447 at 457, [1947] 1 All ER 513 at 519, HL, per Lord Simonds; *Northern Ireland Valuation Comr v Lurgan Borough Council* [1968] NI 104 at 153–156, CA, per McVeigh LJ.

4 *Keren Kayemeth Le Jisroel Ltd v IRC* [1932] AC 650, HL; *Williams' Trustees v IRC* [1947] AC 447, [1947] 1 All ER 513, HL; *Re Compton, Powell v Compton* [1945] Ch 123, [1945] 1 All ER 198, CA; *Re Hobourn Aero Components Ltd's Air Raid Distress Fund, Ryan v Forrest* [1946] Ch 194, [1946] 1 All ER 501, CA; see also *Dingle v Turner* [1972] AC 601 at 623, [1972] 1 All ER 878 at 889, HL, per Lord Cross of Chelsea; *Charter v Race Relations Board* [1973] AC 868 at 907, [1973] 1 All ER 512 at 533, HL, per Lord Cross of Chelsea.

5 See the cases cited in notes 15–25; and PARA 59.

6 As to foreign charitable purposes see PARAS 57–58.

7 *IRC v Baddeley* [1955] AC 572 at 615, [1955] 1 All ER 525 at 549, HL, per Lord Somervell of Harrow; *Re Dunlop, Northern Bank Executor and Trustee Co Ltd v A-G for Northern Ireland* [1984] NI 408; cf *Dingle v Turner* [1972] AC 601 at 624, [1972] 1 All ER 878 at 889, HL, per Lord Cross of Chelsea.

8 See the Charities Act 2011 s 4(2); and PARA 5. Previously there was a presumption that the relief of poverty, the advancement of education and the advancement of religion (see PARAS 12–33) satisfied the requirement unless the contrary appeared: *National Anti-Vivisection Society v IRC* [1948] AC 31 at 42, [1947] 2 All ER 217 at 220, HL, per Lord Wright. In the same case Lord Simonds, at 65, 233, put it rather more widely, saying that the assumption should be made when a purpose appears broadly to fall within one of the familiar categories of charity, adding that the court will not be astute in such a case to defeat upon doubtful evidence the avowed benevolent intention of a donor. See also *Re Watson, Hobbs v Smith* [1973] 3 All ER 678, [1973] 1 WLR 1472; *Re Hetherington* [1990] Ch 1, sub nom *Re Hetherington, Gibbs v McDonnell* [1989] 2 All ER 129. However, the gift failed for this reason in *Gilmour v Coats* [1949] AC 426, [1949] 1 All ER 848, HL. In the absence of further judicial consideration decisions taken on this matter before the Charities Act 2006 s 3(2) (now repealed) came into force must tentatively remain good law.

9 *Shaw v Halifax Corpn* [1915] 2 KB 170 at 181, CA, per Buckley LJ; *Verge v Somerville* [1924] AC 496 at 499, PC; *A-G v Pearce* (1740) 2 Atk 87; *Hall v Derby Borough Urban Sanitary Authority* (1885) 16 QBD 163, DC.

10 *Oppenheim v Tobacco Securities Trust Co Ltd* [1951] AC 297 at 306, [1951] 1 All ER 31 at 34, HL, per Lord Simonds; *A-G v Charity Commission for England and Wales* [2012] UKUT 420 (TCC), [2012] UKUT 420 (TCC), [2012] WTLR 977, 15 ITELR 521. But see *Cross v Lloyd-Greame* (1909) 102 LT 163.

11 *Oppenheim v Tobacco Securities Trust Co Ltd* [1951] AC 297, [1951] 1 All ER 31, HL; *Re Compton, Powell v Compton* [1945] Ch 123, [1945] 1 All ER 198, CA; *Caffoor v Income Tax Comr, Colombo* [1961] AC 584, [1961] 2 All ER 436, PC; *Davies v Perpetual Trustee Co Ltd* [1959] AC 439, [1959] 2 All ER 128, PC; and see *IRC v Educational Grants Association Ltd* [1967] Ch 993 at 1009, [1967] 2 All ER 893 at 896, CA, per Lord Denning MR.

12 *A-G v Pearce* (1740) 2 Atk 87; *A-G v Comber* (1824) 2 Sim & St 93; *Goodman v Saltash Corpn* (1882) 7 App Cas 633 at 650, HL, per Earl Cairns; *Re Drummond, Ashworth v Drummond* [1914] 2 Ch 90. See also *Charter v Race Relations Board* [1973] AC 868, [1973] 1 All ER 512, HL; and the cases cited in notes 29–30. As to the difficulty of distinguishing a section of the public from a fluctuating class of individuals cf *Dingle v Turner* [1972] AC 601 at 624, [1972] 1 All ER 878 at 889, HL, per Lord Cross of Chelsea.

13 *Oppenheim v Tobacco Securities Trust Co Ltd* [1951] AC 297 at 305, 308, [1951] 1 All ER 31 at 33, 35, HL, per Lord Simonds. These cases 'stick out like a sore thumb from the general rule': *IRC v Educational Grants Association Ltd* [1967] Ch 993 at 1011, [1967] 2 All ER 893 at 898, CA, per Harman LJ; 'a hallowed, if illogical, exception': *Re Scarisbrick, Cockshott v Public Trustee* [1951] Ch 622 at 639, [1951] 1 All ER 822 at 830, CA, per Sir Raymond Evershed MR. See also *Dingle v Turner* [1972] AC 601, [1972] 1 All ER 878, HL; and see PARA 17.

The Charity Commission's position appears to be that the 'poor relations' cases continue to be good law: *PB1: Public benefit: the public benefit requirement* (Charity Commission, September 2013) Annex A (available, at the date at which this volume states the law, on the government website) continues to envisage an exception of this nature. This is supported by the Upper Tribunal's analysis in *A-G v Charity Commission for England and Wales* [2012] UKUT 420 (TCC), [2012] WTLR 977, 15 ITELR 521.

As to the Charity Commission's publications see PARA 547.

14 *Shaw v Halifax Corpn* [1915] 2 KB 170, CA; *Hall v Derby Borough Urban Sanitary Authority* (1885) 16 QBD 163, DC (these were decisions on whether a particular foundation was a 'public charity' within the meaning of local Acts); see also *Re Hobourn Aero Components Ltd's Air Raid Distress Fund, Ryan v Forrest* [1946] Ch 194, [1946] 1 All ER 501, CA; *Re Forster, Gellatly v Palmer* [1939] Ch 22, [1938] 3 All ER 767. The funds may be levied by taxation (*A-G v Brown* (1818) 1 Swan 265; *A-G v Dublin Corpn* (1827) 1 Bli NS 312 at 334, 336, HL; *A-G v Eastlake* (1853) 11 Hare 205; *Re St Bride's, Fleet Street, Church or Parish Estate* (1877) 35 ChD 147n; *Re St Botolph Without Bishopsgate Parish Estates* (1887) 35 ChD 142 at 150–151, per North J; see also *A-G v Shrewsbury Corpn* (1843) 6 Beav 220), or given by the Crown (*A-G v Blizard* (1855) 21 Beav 233; contra, *A-G v Galway Corpn* (1829) 1 Mol 95). The trust property may be purchased under statutory authority for public purposes: *Re St Pancras Burial Ground* (1866) LR 3 Eq 173.

15 *Hall v Derby Borough Urban Sanitary Authority* (1885) 16 QBD 163: see note 14.

16 *Finch v Poplar Borough Council* (1967) 66 LGR 324.

17 *Construction Industry Training Board v A-G* [1971] 3 All ER 449, [1971] 1 WLR 1303; affd without dealing with this point [1973] Ch 173, [1972] 2 All ER 1339, CA.
18 *Re Mead's Trust Deed, Briginshaw v National Society of Operative Printers and Assistants* [1961] 2 All ER 836, [1961] 1 WLR 1244.
19 *Waterson v Hendon Borough Council* [1959] 2 All ER 760, [1959] 1 WLR 985; but see *Re Forster, Gellatly v Palmer* [1939] Ch 22, [1938] 3 All ER 767.
20 *Oppenheim v Tobacco Securities Trust Co Ltd* [1951] AC 297, [1951] 1 All ER 31, HL (where the number of employees exceeded 110,000); disapproving *Re Rayner, Cloutman v Regnart* (1920) 89 LJCh 369; and approving *Re Compton, Powell v Compton* [1945] Ch 123, [1945] 1 All ER 198, CA; and *Re Hobourn Aero Components Ltd's Air Raid Distress Fund, Ryan v Forrest* [1946] Ch 194, [1946] 1 All ER 501, CA; *Re Cox, Baker v National Trust Co Ltd* [1955] AC 627, [1955] 2 All ER 550, PC; and *IRC v Educational Grants Association Ltd* [1967] Ch 993, [1967] 2 All ER 893, CA.
21 *Re Hobourn Aero Components Ltd's Air Raid Distress Fund, Ryan v Forrest* [1946] Ch 194, [1946] 1 All ER 501, CA.
22 *Re Drummond, Ashworth v Drummond* [1914] 2 Ch 90 (where the employees concerned numbered between 400 and 500); approved in *Re Compton, Powell v Compton* [1945] Ch 123, [1945] 1 All ER 198, CA.
23 *Davies v Perpetual Trustee Co Ltd* [1959] AC 439, [1959] 2 All ER 128, PC; cf *Re Tree, Idle v Tree* [1945] Ch 325, [1945] 2 All ER 65.
24 *Re Compton, Powell v Compton* [1945] Ch 123, [1945] 1 All ER 198, CA.
25 *Oppenheim v Tobacco Securities Trust Co Ltd* [1951] AC 297 at 306, [1951] 1 All ER 31 at 34, HL, per Lord Simonds, and at 309, 36 per Lord Normand; *Perpetual Trustees Co Ltd v Ferguson* (1951) 51 SRNSW 256, NSW SC, though see, as to the particular schools in question in that case, *Thompson v Federal Taxation Comr* (1959) 102 CLR 315, Aust HC.
26 *Re Banfield, Lloyds Bank Ltd v Smith* [1968] 2 All ER 276, [1968] 1 WLR 846. However, in *Re Duffy* [2013] EWHC 2395 (Ch) a gift to the amenity fund of a residential care home for the general benefit of the staff and residents was not charitable.
27 See PARA 17.
28 *A-G v Pearce* (1740) 2 Atk 87; and see PARA 124.
29 *Liley v Hey* (1842) 1 Hare 580. As to gifts for the benefit of individuals see PARA 60.
30 *A-G v Hughes* (1689) 2 Vern 105, revsg sub nom *A-G v Baxter* (1684) 1 Vern 248, explained in *Moggridge v Thackwell* (1803) 7 Ves 36 at 76 per Lord Eldon LC; affd (1807) 13 Ves 416, HL; *Thomas v Howell* (1874) LR 18 Eq 198.
31 See the cases cited in note 30. If the gifts had been charitable, they would have failed under the law of mortmain (now repealed: see PARA 84).
32 See *Helena Partnerships Ltd (formerly Helena Housing Ltd) v Revenue and Customs Comrs (Attorney General intervening)* [2012] EWCA Civ 569 at [107], [2012] 4 All ER 111, [2012] PTSR 1409 (provision of housing).

7. **Preference given to limited class.** Where a trust is held to be primarily for the benefit of a sufficient section of the community, there is authority to the effect that it is not invalidated by a direction to give preference, in applying part of the available income, to a smaller class which would not in itself be a sufficient section of the community[1], such as the employees of a particular company[2] or the descendants of the founder of the charity[3]. The authorities upon which these propositions are based are weakened by the abolition of the presumption of public benefit for purposes which advance education under which they were decided[4] and the Charity Commission's position is that a fund that gives preference to the children from a particular family, however large a group, would not benefit a section of the public[5].

In any case, where the preferential direction is mandatory, extends to the whole of the income and is in favour of a class which will almost certainly always exhaust the whole income, the absolute priority of the preferential class prevents the trust from being for the benefit of a sufficient section of the community[6].

1 *Re Koettgen's Will Trusts, Westminster Bank Ltd v Family Welfare Association Trustees Ltd* [1954] Ch 252, [1954] 1 All ER 581.

2 *Re Koettgen's Will Trusts, Westminster Bank Ltd v Family Welfare Association Trustees Ltd* [1954] Ch 252, [1954] 1 All ER 581.

3 The 'Founder's Kin' cases, explained in *Caffoor v Income Tax Comr, Colombo* [1961] AC 584 at 602, [1961] 2 All ER 436 at 444, PC: they should probably be regarded as belonging more to history than to doctrine.

4 See PARA 6 note 8.

5 See *The Advancement of Education for the Public Benefit* (Charity Commission, December 2008) para E3 (available, at the date at which this volume states the law, on the government website). At the date at which this volume states the law, this guidance was under review; it should be read together with the public benefit guidance (see PARA 4 note 8). As to the Charity Commission's publications see PARA 547. As to the Charity Commission see PARAS 543–578.

6 *Caffoor v Income Tax Comr, Colombo* [1961] AC 584, [1961] 2 All ER 436, PC (doubting *Re Koettgen's Will Trusts, Westminster Bank Ltd v Family Welfare Association Trustees Ltd* [1954] Ch 252, [1954] 1 All ER 581). See *Re Martin* (1977) 121 Sol Jo 828 (right of residence to testator's daughters in old people's home).

8. Benefit to rich as well as poor. An object may be charitable in the legal sense notwithstanding that it will benefit the rich as well as the poor[1], but it is difficult to believe that a trust would be held charitable if the poor were excluded from its benefit[2]. The Charity Commission's position has been that, whatever restrictions there are on public benefit, charities must in all cases ensure that people in poverty are not excluded from the opportunity to benefit from each of their aims[3].

1 *Jones v Williams* (1767) Amb 651; *Income Tax Special Purposes Comrs v Pemsel* [1891] AC 531 at 583, HL, per Lord Macnaghten; *Verge v Somerville* [1924] AC 496 at 499, PC; see also *Re Hillier, Dauncey v Finch and A-G* [1944] 1 All ER 480; *R (on the application of Independent Schools Council) v Charity Commission for England and Wales; A-G v Charity Commission for England and Wales* [2011] UKUT 421 (TCC) at [196] et seq, [2012] Ch 214, [2012] 1 All ER 127.

2 *Re Macduff, Macduff v Macduff* [1896] 2 Ch 451 at 464, CA, per Lindley LJ; *A-G v Duke of Northumberland* (1877) 7 ChD 745 at 752 per Jessel MR; and see *Re Resch's Will Trusts, Le Cras v Perpetual Trustee Co Ltd* [1969] 1 AC 514 at 542, sub nom *Le Cras v Perpetual Trustee Co Ltd* [1967] 3 All ER 915 at 923, PC. See *Joseph Rowntree Memorial Trust Housing Association Ltd v A-G* [1983] Ch 159, [1983] 1 All ER 288, where it was said that it is not necessarily fatal to charitable status that the benefit cannot be withdrawn if a beneficiary ceases to qualify.

3 *Charities and Public Benefit* (Charity Commission, January 2008) para F11. However, elements of this guidance were held to be erroneous: see *R (on the application of Independent Schools Council) v Charity Commission for England and Wales; A-G v Charity Commission for England and Wales* [2011] UKUT 421 (TCC) at [226] et seq, [2012] Ch 214, [2012] 1 All ER 127. See now *PB1: Public benefit: the public benefit requirement* (Charity Commission, September 2013) Pt 5 (available, at the date at which this volume states the law, on the government website). See also *Review Decision made on the Application for Registration of Odstock Private Care Ltd*, Charity Commission Review Decision, 25 September 2007 (relief of sickness not charitable where service charges prevented those in poverty from benefiting either directly or indirectly). As to decisions of the Charity Commission see PARA 547; and as to the Charity Commission's publications see PARA 547.

9. Discrimination. A person does not contravene the provisions which make it unlawful to discriminate against a person on the ground of a protected characteristic[1] only by restricting the provision of benefits to persons who share a protected characteristic, if he is acting in pursuance of a charitable instrument[2], and the provision of the benefits is a proportionate means of achieving a legitimate aim, or is to prevent or compensate for a disadvantage linked to the protected characteristic[3].

Moreover, the Equality Act 2010 is not contravened by a charity requiring its members to assert or imply membership of a religion or acceptance of a belief;

nor for a person to restrict participation in an activity for the purpose of promoting or supporting a charity, to persons of one sex[4].

If a charitable instrument enables the provision of benefits to persons of a class defined by reference to colour it has effect for all purposes as if it enabled the provision of those benefits to persons of the class which results if colour is ignored; or where the original class is defined by reference to colour only, to persons generally[5].

A Minister has power in certain circumstances to modify a trust deed or instruments relating to educational charities, if the deed or instrument restricts the benefits to persons of one sex, if the Minister is satisfied that the modification or removal of the restriction would be conducive to the advancement of education without sex discrimination[6].

1 Ie the Equality Act 2010: see generally DISCRIMINATION. The protected characteristics are age, disability, gender reassignment, marriage and civil partnership, pregnancy and maternity, race, religion or belief, sex, and sexual orientation: Equality Act 2010 s 4. As to the effect of the Marriage (Same Sex Couples) Act 2013 see s 1(1), 11(1); and MATRIMONIAL AND CIVIL PARTNERSHIP LAW vol 72 (2009) PARA 1 et seq.

2 As to the meaning of 'charitable instrument' see the Equality Act 2010 s 194(4); and DISCRIMINATION vol 33 (2013) PARA 312.

A charity must show weighty and convincing reasons for seeking to change its governing instrument in order to avail itself of the charities exception: see *Catholic Care (Diocese of Leeds) v Charity Commission for England and Wales* [2012] UKUT 395 (TCC), [2013] 2 All ER 1114, [2013] 1 WLR 2105, where an adoption charity which screened only heterosexual couples sought to amend its memorandum of association to make explicit that it would only provide adoption services to heterosexual couples.

3 Equality Act 2010 s 193(1), (2). See DISCRIMINATION vol 33 (2013) PARA 312. There is also protection for the Charity Commission in the exercise of its functions, where the regulator thinks that the Commission's action is expedient, having regard to the charitable instrument: see ss 193(8), 194(5); and DISCRIMINATION vol 33 (2013) PARA 312. The Commission has published guidance on the operation of the Equality Act 2010 in the charities sector: see *Equality Act guidance for charities* (Charity Commission, February 2013) (available, at the date at which this volume states the law, on the government website). As to the Charity Commission's publications see PARA 547.

4 See Equality Act 2010 s 193(5)–(7). See DISCRIMINATION vol 33 (2013) PARA 312.

5 Equality Act 2010 s 193(4); and see DISCRIMINATION vol 33 (2013) PARA 61. See eg *Re Harding, Gibbs v Harding* [2007] EWHC 3 (Ch), [2008] Ch 235, [2007] 1 All ER 747 (where the deceased's intended gift to the black community of Hackney, Haringey, Islington and Tower Hamlets was held to be a valid charitable gift but without the reference to colour).

6 See Equality Act 2010 Sch 14; and DISCRIMINATION vol 33 (2013) PARA 170.

10. Trading by or on behalf of charities. A charity may carry on trade provided it falls into one of the following categories: (1) primary purpose trading; (2) ancillary trading; and (3) non-primary purpose trading that does not involve significant risk to the resources of the charity[1].

Primary purpose trading is trading which contributes directly to one or more of the objects of a charity as set out in its governing document[2], for example the provision of educational services by a charitable school or college in return for course fees or the sale of goods manufactured by disabled people who are beneficiaries of a charity for the disabled[3]. Ancillary trading is trading which contributes indirectly to the successful furtherance of the purposes of the charity[4], such as the sale of food and drink in a restaurant or bar by a theatre charity to members of an audience[5]. Non-primary purpose trading is trading intended to raise funds for the charity[6]. The significant risk to be avoided as regards non-primary purpose trading is where the turnover is insufficient to meet the costs of carrying on the trade and the difference has to be financed out of the assets of the charity[7].

A charity may establish a non-charitable trading subsidiary company, but must ensure that any investment in the trading subsidiary is within the investment powers of the charity and can be justified as an appropriate investment of the charity's resources[8]. Such a subsidiary must be used in respect of any trading where there would be a significant risk to the assets of the charity if it were to carry on non-primary purpose trading itself[9].

1 See *CC35: Trustees, trading and tax: how charities may lawfully trade* (Charity Commission, April 2007) para C2 (available, at the date at which this volume states the law, on the government website). As to the Charity Commission's publications see PARA 547.

2 See *CC35: Trustees, trading and tax* (Charity Commission, April 2007) para C6.

3 See *CC35: Trustees, trading and tax* (Charity Commission, April 2007) para C6.

4 See *CC35: Trustees, trading and tax* (Charity Commission, April 2007) para C7.

5 See *CC35: Trustees, trading and tax* (Charity Commission, April 2007) para C7.

6 See *CC35: Trustees, trading and tax* (Charity Commission, April 2007) para C8.

7 See *CC35: Trustees, trading and tax* (Charity Commission, April 2007) para C8.

8 See *CC35: Trustees, trading and tax* (Charity Commission, April 2007) para D8.

9 See *CC35: Trustees, trading and tax* (Charity Commission, April 2007) para D1.

11. Charity trading or charging for services. The provision of benefits to the public may be charitable notwithstanding that a charge is made[1], or a contribution required from beneficiaries[2]. An institution may carry on a trade or business in order to achieve its purposes and still be charitable, so long as no part of any profit made can be distributed to members or applied otherwise than for charitable purposes[3]. It is not necessary, for it to be charitable, that a gift for the provision of homes for the aged should provide for all the needs of the beneficiaries[4], and the provision of such accommodation may be charitable even if it is to be let to the beneficiaries at economic rents[5].

1 *Scottish Burial Reform and Cremation Society Ltd v Glasgow Corpn* [1968] AC 138, [1967] 3 All ER 215, HL; *Brighton College v Marriott* [1926] AC 192, HL; *IRC v Falkirk Temperance Cafe Trust* 1927 SC 261, Ct of Sess; *The Abbey, Malvern Wells, Ltd v Minister of Local Government and Planning* [1951] Ch 728, [1951] 2 All ER 154; *Re Resch's Will Trusts, Le Cras v Perpetual Trustee Co Ltd* [1969] 1 AC 514, sub nom *Le Cras v Perpetual Trustee Co Ltd* [1967] 3 All ER 915, PC; *Incorporated Council of Law Reporting for England and Wales v A-G* [1972] Ch 73, [1971] 3 All ER 1029, CA; *Joseph Rowntree Memorial Trust Housing Association Ltd v A-G* [1983] Ch 159, [1983] 1 All ER 288. See also *R (on the application of Independent Schools Council) v Charity Commission for England and Wales; A-G v Charity Commission for England and Wales* [2011] UKUT 421 (TCC), [2012] Ch 214, [2012] 1 All ER 127.

2 *Re Estlin, Prichard v Thomas* (1903) 72 LJCh 687; *Re Clarke, Bracey v Royal National Lifeboat Institution* [1923] 2 Ch 407; *Re Chaplin, Neame v A-G* [1933] Ch 115; *IRC v Peeblesshire Nursing Association* 1927 SC 215, Ct of Sess; *Re Cottam's Will Trusts, Midland Bank Executor and Trustee Co Ltd v Huddersfield Corpn* [1955] 3 All ER 704, [1955] 1 WLR 1299.

3 *Brighton College v Marriott* [1926] AC 192, HL; *Incorporated Council of Law Reporting for England and Wales v A-G* [1972] Ch 73 at 86, 90, [1971] 3 All ER 1029 at 1034, CA per Russell LJ, and at 1038 per Sachs LJ. See PARA 10.

4 *Re Payling's Will Trusts, Armstrong v Payling* [1969] 3 All ER 698, [1969] 1 WLR 1595; cf *Re Monk, Giffen v Wedd* [1927] 2 Ch 197, CA.

5 *Re Cottam's Will Trusts, Midland Bank Executor and Trustee Co Ltd v Huddersfield Corpn* [1955] 3 All ER 704, [1955] 1 WLR 1299; *Scottish Burial Reform and Cremation Society Ltd v Glasgow Corpn* [1968] AC 138 at 156, [1967] 3 All ER 215 at 224, HL, per Lord Wilberforce; though see also *IRC v Peeblesshire Nursing Association* 1927 SC 215 at 222, Ct of Sess, per Lord Sands (provision charitable if at less than cost price).

(2) PARTICULAR CHARITABLE PURPOSES

(i) Prevention or Relief of Poverty

12. Prevention or relief of poverty. A purpose is charitable under the first statutory description of charitable purposes if it is for the prevention or relief of poverty[1].

The view of the Charity Commission has been that 'prevention' refers to that which addresses the causes of poverty[2], including, for example, providing money management and debt counselling advice[3]. 'Relief' refers to that which addresses the consequences of poverty[4] and implies that the persons in question have a need attributable to their condition as poor persons which requires alleviating, and which those persons could not alleviate, or would find difficulty in alleviating, themselves from their own resources[5]. The word 'relief' is not synonymous with 'benefit'[6].

1 Charities Act 2011 s 3(1)(a); and PARA 2. See also *A-G v Charity Commission for England and Wales* [2012] UKUT 420 (TCC), [2012] WTLR 977, 15 ITELR 521.

2 See *Charitable purposes* (Charity Commission, September 2013) para 3 (available, at the date at which this volume states the law, on the government website). As to the Charity Commission's publications see PARA 547.

3 See *Charitable purposes* (Charity Commission, September 2013) para 3.

4 See *Charitable purposes* (Charity Commission, September 2013) para 3.

5 *Joseph Rowntree Memorial Trust Housing Association Ltd v A-G* [1983] Ch 159, [1983] 1 All ER 288.

6 *Joseph Rowntree Memorial Trust Housing Association Ltd v A-G* [1983] Ch 159, [1983] 1 All ER 288; *Re Dunlop, Northern Bank Executor and Trustee Co Ltd v A-G for Northern Ireland* [1984] NI 408.

13. Meaning of 'poverty'. 'Poverty' is a relative term, not confined to destitution[1]. It may be taken as being where persons have to 'go short' in the ordinary understanding of that term, due regard being had to their status in life and so forth[2]. It is the Charity Commission's view that in current social and economic circumstances, poverty includes many disadvantages and difficulties arising from, or which cause, the lack of financial or material resources[3].

1 *Trustees of Mary Clark Home v Anderson* [1904] 2 KB 645; *Re Estlin, Prichard v Thomas* (1903) 72 LJCh 687; *Re Gardom, Le Page v A-G* [1914] 1 Ch 662, CA (revsd without affecting this point sub nom *Le Page v Gardom* (1915) 84 LJCh 749, HL); *Shaw v Halifax Corpn* [1915] 2 KB 170, CA; *Re Clarke, Bracey v Royal National Lifeboat Institution* [1923] 2 Ch 407; *Re De Carteret, Forster v De Carteret* [1933] Ch 103. Cf *Re Drummond, Ashworth v Drummond* [1914] 2 Ch 90 (persons employed at a weekly wage of 15 shillings held not poor within the meaning of the preamble to the ancient statute of the Charitable Uses Act 1601 (43 Eliz 1 c 4 (1601)) (now wholly repealed: see PARA 2 note 25; and PARA 46); and see *Re Central Employment Bureau for Women and Students' Careers Association Inc* [1942] 1 All ER 232; *Spiller v Maude* (1881) 32 ChD 158n (not more than £50 per annum in 1850); *Re Lacy, Royal General Theatrical Fund Association v Kydd* [1899] 2 Ch 149.

2 *Re Coulthurst, Coutts & Co v Coulthurst* [1951] Ch 661 at 666, [1951] 1 All ER 774 at 776, CA, per Sir Raymond Evershed MR; *Re Niyazi's Will Trusts* [1978] 3 All ER 785, [1978] 1 WLR 910. As to the review of the guidance see PARA 12 note 2.

3 See *Charitable purposes* (Charity Commission, September 2013) para 3 (available, at the date at which this volume states the law, on the government website). As to the Charity Commission see PARAS 543–578. As to the Charity Commission's publications see PARA 547.

14. Contribution by beneficiaries. Relief is charitable where it is given by way of bounty and not by way of bargain[1], but this does not mean that it cannot be charitable if the beneficiaries contribute to the cost of the benefits they receive[2].

1 *IRC v Society for Relief of Widows and Orphans of Medical Men* (1926) 136 LT 60 at 65 per Rowlatt J (relief of distressed widows of the medical profession who paid subscriptions; the chief income was derived from investments, donations and legacies; *Spiller v Maude* (1881) 32 ChD 158n applied); see also *Blair v Duncan* [1902] AC 37, HL; and *Verge v Somerville* [1924] AC 496, PC.

2 *Re Estlin, Prichard v Thomas* (1903) 72 LJCh 687; *Re Clarke, Bracey v Royal National Lifeboat Institution* [1923] 2 Ch 407; *Re Chaplin, Neame v A-G* [1933] Ch 115; *Re Cottam's Will Trusts, Midland Bank Executor and Trustee Co Ltd v Huddersfield Corpn* [1955] 3 All ER 704, [1955] 1 WLR 1299. Cf *IRC v Peeblesshire Nursing Association* 1927 SC 215, Ct of Sess per Lord Sands; *Over Seventies Housing Association v Westminster City Council* [1974] RA 247; *Joseph Rowntree Memorial Trust Housing Association Ltd v A-G* [1983] Ch 159, [1983] 1 All ER 288. See generally PARA 11.

15. General and particular relief. Gifts have satisfied the requirement of charity where they are general and indefinite[1] or for the poor of a particular parish, town or other place[2] or even on a particular estate[3], or for persons of a particular religious denomination attending a certain chapel[4], or for members of a particular regiment[5], or for a particular class of poor or the poor of a particular class, as poor gentlewomen[6], distressed gentlefolk[7], persons of moderate means[8] or widows of limited means with small dependent children[9], or persons who are not self-supporting[10], housekeepers[11], tradesmen of a particular kind[12], unsuccessful literary men[13], servants[14], old and worn-out clerks of a particular firm[15], poor and incapacitated employees of a company[16], or by reference to employment in the public sector[17], or necessitous employees of a limited company and their dependants[18], members of a particular club who fall on evil days[19], 'poor struggling youths of merit'[20], poor pious persons[21], poor emigrants[22] or persons descended from residents of a particular borough in a particular year needing assistance to improve their condition in life by emigrating[23], inmates of a workhouse[24] or hospital[25], debtors[26], 50 old men and 50 old women of a particular place, being 'needy and deserving'[27], the widows and orphans of poor clergymen[28] or of seamen of a particular port[29] or of the victims of a particular disaster[30], or widows and orphans living in a particular parish[31], or indigent bachelors and widowers 'who have shown sympathy with science'[32]. A gift for the working classes, including those still working, is not, by implication or otherwise, for the relief of poor people[33], but a gift for the construction of a working men's hostel has been held to be charitable[34]. A gift for the relief of domestic distress is charitable[35]. A fund to pay for the education at a particular school of sons of old boys who fell or were disabled in the war was for the relief of poverty[36].

1 *A-G v Peacock* (1676) Cas *temp* Finch 245 (for the good of poor people for ever); *A-G v Syderfen* (1683) 1 Vern 224; *A-G v Rance* (1728) cited in Amb 422; *Nash v Morley* (1842) 5 Beav 177; *Re Darling, Farquhar v Darling* [1896] 1 Ch 50 (to the poor and the service of God).

2 *Woodford Inhabitants v Parkhurst* (1639) Duke 70; *A-G v Pearce* (1740) 2 Atk 87; *A-G v Clarke* (1762) Amb 422; *A-G v Exeter Corpn* (1826) 2 Russ 45; subsequent proceedings (1827) 3 Russ 395; *A-G v Bovill* (1840) 1 Ph 762; *A-G v Blizard* (1855) 21 Beav 233; *Re Roadley, Iveson v Wakefield* [1930] 1 Ch 524 (poor of a parish); *A-G v Wilkinson* (1839) 1 Beav 370; *Russell v Kellett* (1855) 3 Sm & G 264; *Re Lucas, Rhys v A-G* [1922] 2 Ch 52 (poor of a township); *Re Lousada, Bacon v Bacon* (1887) 82 LT Jo 358 ('London poor'); *Salter v Farey* (1843) 7 Jur 831; *Re Lambeth Charities* (1853) 22 LJCh 959; *Re St Alphage, London Wall* (1888) 59 LT 614.

3 *Bristow v Bristow* (1842) 5 Beav 289; see also *A-G v Persse* (1842) 2 Dr & War 67.

4 *Re Wall, Pomeroy v Willway* (1889) 42 ChD 510.

5 *Re Donald, Moore v Somerset* [1909] 2 Ch 410.

6 *A-G v Power* (1809) 1 Ball & B 145; *Re Estlin, Prichard v Thomas* (1903) 72 LJCh 687; *Trustees of Mary Clark Home v Anderson* [1904] 2 KB 645; *Re Gardom, Le Page v A-G* [1914]

1 Ch 662, CA (on appeal sub nom *Le Page v Gardom* (1915) 84 LJCh 749, HL); *Shaw v Halifax Corpn* [1915] 2 KB 170, CA. See, however, PARA 9.

7 *Re Young, Young v Young* [1951] Ch 344, [1950] 2 All ER 1245.

8 *Re Clarke, Bracey v Royal National Lifeboat Institution* [1923] 2 Ch 407.

9 *Re De Carteret, Forster v De Carteret* [1933] Ch 103.

10 *Re Central Employment Bureau for Women and Students' Careers Association Inc* [1942] 1 All ER 232.

11 *A-G v Pearce* (1740) 2 Atk 87.

12 *Re White's Trusts* (1886) 33 ChD 449.

13 *Thompson v Thompson* (1844) 1 Coll 381 at 395 per Knight Bruce V-C.

14 *Reeve v A-G* (1843) 3 Hare 191; *Loscombe v Wintringham* (1850) 13 Beav 87.

15 *Re Gosling, Gosling v Smith* (1900) 48 WR 300.

16 *Re Rayner, Cloutman v Regnart* (1920) 89 LJCh 369.

17 *A-G v Charity Commission for England and Wales* [2012] UKUT 420 (TCC) at [83], [2012] WTLR 977, 15 ITELR 521.

18 *Dingle v Turner* [1972] AC 601, [1972] 1 All ER 878, HL (poor employees); *Gibson v South American Stores (Gath and Chaves) Ltd* [1950] Ch 177, [1949] 2 All ER 985, CA.

19 *Re Young's Will Trusts, Westminster Bank Ltd v Sterling* [1955] 3 All ER 689, [1955] 1 WLR 1269.

20 *Milne's Executors v Aberdeen University Court* (1905) 7 F 642, Ct of Sess.

21 *Nash v Morley* (1842) 5 Beav 177.

22 *Barclay v Maskelyne* (1858) 32 LTOS 205. See *Re Sidney, Hingeston v Sidney* [1908] 1 Ch 488, CA ('emigration uses' not charitable).

23 *Re Tree, Idle v Tree* [1945] Ch 325, [1945] 2 All ER 65.

24 *A-G v Vint* (1850) 3 De G & Sm 704.

25 *Reading Corpn v Lane* (1601) Duke 81.

26 *A-G v Painter Stainers' Co* (1788) 2 Cox Eq Cas 51; *A-G v Ironmongers' Co* (1834) 2 My & K 576.

27 *Re Reed* (1893) 10 TLR 87; and see *Re Wall, Pomeroy v Willway* (1889) 42 ChD 510.

28 *Waldo v Caley* (1809) 16 Ves 206; see also *Re Friend of the Clergy's Charters, Friend of the Clergy v A-G* [1921] 1 Ch 409.

29 *Powell v A-G* (1817) 3 Mer 48.

30 *Pease v Pattinson* (1886) 32 ChD 154; *Re Hartley Colliery Accident Relief Fund, Plummer v Jordan* (1908) 102 LT 165n; *Cross v Lloyd-Greame* (1909) 102 LT 163 (where the victims were only six in number).

31 *A-G v Comber* (1824) 2 Sim & St 93; *Russell v Kellett* (1855) 3 Sm & G 264.

32 *Weir v Crum-Brown* [1908] AC 162, HL.

33 *Re Sanders' Will Trusts, Public Trustee v McLaren* [1954] Ch 265, [1954] 1 All ER 667; distinguishing *Re Glyn's Will Trusts, Public Trustee v A-G* [1950] 2 All ER 1150n. As to the phrase 'working classes' see *Rodwell v Minister of Health* [1947] KB 404 at 411, [1947] 1 All ER 80 at 82 per Morris J; *HE Green & Sons v Minister of Health (No 2)* [1948] 1 KB 34 at 38, [1947] 2 All ER 469 at 471 per Denning J; *Belcher v Reading Corpn* [1950] Ch 380 at 392, [1949] 2 All ER 969 at 984 per Romer J; *Guinness Trust (London Fund) v Green* [1955] 2 All ER 871 at 873, [1955] 1 WLR 872 at 875, CA, per Denning LJ; *Re Niyazi's Will Trusts* [1978] 3 All ER 785 at 788, [1978] 1 WLR 910 at 915 per Megarry V-C.

34 *Re Niyazi's Will Trusts* [1978] 3 All ER 785, [1978] 1 WLR 910.

35 *Kendall v Granger* (1842) 5 Beav 300 at 303 per Lord Langdale MR.

36 *Cawdron v Merchant Taylors' School* [2009] EWHC 1722 (Ch) at [39], [2010] PTSR 507.

16. Poor of a particular religion. The relief of the poor of a particular church or religious denomination, such as Jews[1], Presbyterians[2], Moravians[3], Unitarians[4], Irvingites[5] or Methodists[6], is charitable, and has always been so, notwithstanding the law of superstitious uses[7]; so also is a gift for ministers 'persecuted or in poverty' on account of preaching certain doctrines[8].

1 *De Costa v De Paz* (1754) 2 Swan 487n; *Re Haendler, A-G v Revel* (1931) Times, 4 July; and see *A-G v Mathieson, Re Wilkinson and Fell's Contract* [1907] 2 Ch 383 at 392, CA, per Cozens-Hardy MR (Mildmay Mission to the Jews).

2 *A-G v Wansay* (1808) 15 Ves 231.

3 *Income Tax Special Purposes Comrs v Pemsel* [1891] AC 531, HL.

4 *A-G v Shore* (1843) 11 Sim 592; *Shore v Wilson* (1842) 9 Cl & Fin 355 at 507–508, HL, per Maule J.

5 *A-G v Lawes* (1849) 8 Hare 32.
6 *Dawson v Small* (1874) LR 18 Eq 114.
7 See PARA 63.
8 *A-G v Lawes* (1849) 8 Hare 32.

17. Gifts to poor relations. Perpetual trusts for the benefit of poor relations or descendants are charitable[1], though the charitable nature of these trusts is, perhaps, anomalous as lacking the necessary public element[2].

Gifts for poor relations intended for immediate distribution are also charitable[3], but some gifts to relations are construed as being intended to be confined to statutory next of kin and these are not charitable, the object then being not to relieve poverty among a class but to benefit specific individuals[4]. Such gifts are confined to the statutory next of kin if all members of the class are entitled to participate[5], but not if the beneficiaries are poor relations to be selected[6], nor if a contrary intention appears from the will[7]. Poor relations who become rich must not participate[8], and a gift for the poorest of the testator's kindred can only be charitable when intended for persons who are actually poor[9].

A gift for the poor, giving a preference to poor relations, is charitable[10]. An inquiry may be directed as to who are poor relations[11].

1 *White v White* (1802) 7 Ves 423 (trust for apprenticing poor relations); *A-G v Price* (1810) 17 Ves 371 (poor kinsmen in a particular place); *Isaac v Defriez* (1754) Amb 595 (poorest relations); *Browne v Whalley* [1866] WN 386; *Gillam v Taylor* (1873) LR 16 Eq 581 (lineal descendants); *Re Drake's Will Trusts, Drake v Drake* [1971] Ch 179, [1970] 3 All ER 32, CA ('male descendants' construed as not limited to males descended solely through males, overruling *Bernal v Bernal* (1838) 3 My & Cr 559); *A-G v Duke of Northumberland* (1877) 7 ChD 745; contra, *Liley v Hey* (1842) 1 Hare 580; *Peek v Peek* (1869) 17 WR 1059.

2 *Re Compton, Powell v Compton* [1945] Ch 123, [1945] 1 All ER 198, CA; approved in *Oppenheim v Tobacco Securities Trust Co Ltd* [1951] AC 297, [1951] 1 All ER 31, HL. The Charity Commission's position is that the poor relations cases continue to be good law under the Charities Act 2011: see *PB1: Public benefit: the public benefit requirement* (Charity Commission, September 2013) Annex A (available, at the date at which this volume states the law, on the government website), which continues to envisage an exception of this nature. This is supported by the Upper Tribunal's analysis in *A-G v Charity Commission for England and Wales* [2012] UKUT 420 (TCC) at [48]–[65], [2012] WTLR 977, 15 ITELR 521. The reasoning in the 'poor relations' cases is not conclusive as to whether they satisfy both limbs of the public benefit test, or whether they are a well-established and anomalous exception which require to satisfy the first limb only; however, the Upper Tribunal declined to decide the point, absent which the authorities continue to confirm that such trusts are charitable if they satisfy the first limb: see *A-G v Charity Commission for England and Wales* at [65]. As to the Charity Commission see PARAS 543–578. As to the Charity Commission's publications see PARA 547.

3 *A-G v Buckland (or Bucknall)* (1742) cited in Amb 71n; *Mahon v Savage* (1803) 1 Sch & Lef 111; and see *Re Shepherd, Smithem v Shepherd* (1921) 152 LT Jo 18. In no charitable disposition which is valid because of its public character is there any warrant for distinguishing between trusts maintained for a period and trusts for immediate distribution: *Re Scarisbrick, Cockshott v Public Trustee* [1951] Ch 622 at 639, [1951] 1 All ER 822 at 830, CA, per Sir Raymond Evershed MR.

4 *Re Scarisbrick, Cockshott v Public Trustee* [1951] Ch 622 at 638, [1951] 1 All ER 822 at 828, CA, per Sir Raymond Evershed MR.

5 *Re Scarisbrick, Cockshott v Public Trustee* [1951] Ch 622 at 640, [1951] 1 All ER 822 at 831, CA, per Sir Raymond Evershed MR.

6 *Re Scarisbrick, Cockshott v Public Trustee* [1951] Ch 622, [1951] 1 All ER 822, CA ('such relations of my son and daughters as in the opinion of the survivor of my said son and daughters shall be in needy circumstances'); cf *Re Cohen, Cowan v Cohen* [1973] 1 All ER 889, [1973] 1 WLR 415 (relatives in special need).

7 *Carr v Bedford* (1678) 2 Rep Ch 146; *Griffith v Jones* (1686) 2 Rep Ch 394; *Edge v Salisbury* (1749) Amb 70 ('nearest relations'); *Brunsden v Woolredge* (1765) Amb 507 ('mother's poor relations'); *Widmore v Woodroffe* (1766) Amb 636 ('most necessitous of my relations'); *Gower*

v Mainwaring (1750) 2 Ves Sen 87 at 110 per Lord Hardwicke LC ('friends and relations' means 'relations'); see also *Roach v Hammond* (1715) Prec Ch 401; *Anon* (1716) 1 P Wms 327 ('poor relations'); *Green v Howard* (1779) 1 Bro CC 31 ('testator's relations'). As to such a bequest's being void for uncertainty when not confined to statutory next of kin see *Widmore v Woodroffe* (1766) Amb 636 at 640 per Lord Hardwicke LC; *Mahon v Savage* (1803) 1 Sch & Lef 111; *Brandon v Brandon* (1819) 3 Swan 312 ('nearest and next of kin').

8 *Mahon v Savage* (1803) 1 Sch & Lef 111.

9 *A-G v Duke of Northumberland* (1877) 7 ChD 745; and see *A-G v Price* (1810) 17 Ves 371.

10 *Waldo v Caley* (1809) 16 Ves 206.

11 *A-G v Price* (1810) 17 Ves 371; *A-G v Sidney Sussex College, Cambridge* (1865) 34 Beav 654; revsd without affecting this point (1866) 21 ChD 514n.

18. Gifts to other limited classes of the poor. By analogy with the poor relations cases[1], it has been held that trusts for the relief of necessitous employees of a limited company and their dependants[2], for the benefit of widows and orphaned children of deceased officers and ex-officers of a bank (the terms of the gift indicating that it was intended for the relief of privation)[3], for fellow members of a club who may fall on evil days[4], for the sons of old boys who were disabled or killed in war[5], and trusts for the relief of poverty by reference to employment within the public sector[6], are charitable, despite the lack of a sufficient section of the public as objects of the charity. These trusts would not be valid charitable trusts if not restricted to the relief of poverty[7].

On the same principle, gifts to friendly societies for the relief of poverty among members are charitable[8], though such gifts are not charitable where the purpose is the relief of sickness or distress generally[9]. It may be that the validity of a trust to assist emigration by persons residing in a particular area before a certain date and their descendants depends on the presence of the element of relief of poverty[10].

1 See PARA 17.

2 *Dingle v Turner* [1972] AC 601, [1972] 1 All ER 878, HL (poor employees); *Gibson v South American Stores (Gath and Chaves) Ltd* [1950] Ch 177, [1949] 2 All ER 985, CA; see also *Re Gosling, Gosling v Smith* (1900) 48 WR 300 (old and worn-out clerks of a banking firm), doubted in *Gibson v South American Stores (Gath and Chaves) Ltd*; *Re Rayner, Cloutman v Regnart* (1920) 89 LJCh 369 (poor and incapacitated employees of a company), distinguishing *Re Drummond, Ashworth v Drummond* [1914] 2 Ch 90.

3 *Re Coulthurst, Coutts & Co v Coulthurst* [1951] Ch 661, [1951] 1 All ER 774, CA.

4 *Re Young's Will Trusts, Westminster Bank Ltd v Sterling* [1955] 3 All ER 689, [1955] 1 WLR 1269.

5 See *Cawdron v Merchant Taylors' School* [2009] EWHC 1722 (Ch), [2010] PTSR 507.

6 *A-G v Charity Commission for England and Wales* [2012] UKUT 420 (TCC) at [83], [2012] WTLR 977, 15 ITELR 521.

7 See *Re Cox, Baker v National Trust Co Ltd* [1955] AC 627, [1955] 2 All ER 550, PC. As to the relief of poverty see PARA 12 et seq.

8 *Spiller v Maude* (1881) 32 ChD 158n; *Pease v Pattinson* (1886) 32 ChD 154; *Re Buck, Bruty v Mackey* [1896] 2 Ch 727; *Re Lacy, Royal General Theatrical Fund Association v Kydd* [1899] 2 Ch 149; *IRC v Society for Relief of Widows and Orphans of Medical Men* (1926) 136 LT 60; cf *Dingle v Turner* [1972] AC 601 at 617, [1972] 1 All ER 878 at 883, HL, per Lord Cross.

9 *Re Hobourn Aero Components Ltd's Air Raid Distress Fund, Ryan v Forrest* [1946] Ch 194, [1946] 1 All ER 501, CA; *Waterson v Hendon Borough Council* [1959] 2 All ER 760, [1959] 1 WLR 985; *Re Clark's Trust* (1875) 1 ChD 497; *Cunnack v Edwards* [1896] 2 Ch 679, CA; but cf *Re Forster, Gellatly v Palmer* [1939] Ch 22, [1938] 3 All ER 767.

10 *Re Tree, Idle v Tree* [1945] Ch 325, [1945] 2 All ER 65, as explained in *Davies v Perpetual Trustee Co Ltd* [1959] AC 439, [1959] 2 All ER 128, PC.

19. Relief of poverty inferred or indirect. In some cases an unexpressed intention to relieve poverty may be inferred from the nature of the gift[1]. The relief of poverty may also be effected indirectly. Thus, bequests in aid of the granting of allotments[2], the apprenticing of poor children[3], and the distribution of doles[4], are charitable.

Similarly, the following are charitable: the establishment, maintenance and support of institutions or funds for the relief of various forms of poverty or distress, such as soup kitchens[5], hospitals and dispensaries[6] and, as conducive to the work of hospitals, funds for providing accommodation for relatives who come from a distance to visit patients critically ill in hospital[7], funds for homes of rest for nurses[8] and funds to provide extra comforts for nurses at Christmas[9], funds to provide extra amenities for patients in paying beds in hospitals[10], nursing homes or societies for persons of moderate means[11], convalescent homes[12], homes of rest[13], a house to be maintained by the local authority as a children's home[14], asylums[15], almshouses[16], homes for lady teachers[17] or ladies in reduced circumstances[18] or working girls[19], orphanages[20], institutions for the benefit of impoverished actors[21], and the sick and poor funds of a parish church[22]. Neighbourhood law centres formed for the purpose of giving legal aid and advice to poor persons have been registered as charities[23], as have trusts to provide low interest or interest-free loans to assist poor persons to purchase freehold or leasehold housing accommodation[24]. Gifts to religious communities having for their object the relief of the poor are charitable[25].

1 See eg *A-G v Comber* (1824) 2 Sim & St 93 (widows and orphans); *Thompson v Corby* (1860) 27 Beav 649 (aged widows and spinsters); *Re Dudgeon, Truman v Pope* (1896) 74 LT 613 (respectable single women over 60 years of age); *Re Wall, Pomeroy v Willway* (1889) 42 ChD 510 (Unitarians of over 50 years of age attending a particular chapel); *Re Gosling, Gosling v Smith* (1900) 48 WR 300 (pensioning old and worn-out clerks); *Re Lucas, Rhys v A-G* [1922] 2 Ch 52 (small weekly payments to oldest respectable inhabitants of named place); *Verge v Somerville* [1924] AC 496, PC (Australian Repatriation Fund); *Re Roadley, Iveson v Wakefield* [1930] 1 Ch 524 (maintenance of patients from named parishes at named hospitals); *Re Coulthurst, Coutts & Co v Coulthurst* [1951] Ch 661, [1951] 1 All ER 774, CA (widows and orphaned children of deceased officers and deceased ex-officers of bank considered by reason of financial circumstances most deserving); *Re Niyazi's Will Trusts* [1978] 3 All ER 785, [1978] 1 WLR 910 (gift for construction of working men's hostel); *Cawdron v Merchant Taylors' School* [2009] EWHC 1722 (Ch), [2010] PTSR 507 (education of sons of old boys injured or killed in war). Cf *Re Sidney, Hingeston v Sidney* [1908] 1 Ch 488, CA (emigration uses: not charitable); *Re Drummond, Ashworth v Drummond* [1914] 2 Ch 90 (holiday fund for employees of a company: not charitable); *A-G for Northern Ireland v Forde* [1932] NI 1, CA (gift to widows of persons resident on estate: not charitable).

2 *Crafton v Frith* (1851) 4 De G & Sm 237. See also the Charities Act 2011 s 298; and PARA 226.

3 *A-G v Minshull* (1798) 4 Ves 11; *A-G v Earl Winchelsea* (1791) 3 Bro CC 373; *A-G v Wansay* (1808) 15 Ves 231.

4 *A-G v Minshull* (1798) 4 Ves 11; *A-G v Bovill* (1840) 1 Ph 762; *Thompson v Thompson* (1844) 1 Coll 381 at 392 per Knight Bruce V-C.

5 *Biscoe v Jackson* (1887) 35 ChD 460, CA.

6 *Pelham v Anderson* (1764) 2 Eden 296; *A-G v Gascoigne* (1833) 2 My & K 647; *A-G v Kell* (1840) 2 Beav 575; *Wharton v Masterman* [1895] AC 186, HL; *Re Cox, Cox v Davie* (1877) 7 ChD 204; *Re Garrard, Gordon v Craigie* [1907] 1 Ch 382; *Re Weir Hospital* [1910] 2 Ch 124, CA; *Re Welsh Hospital (Netley) Fund, Thomas v A-G* [1921] 1 Ch 655; *Re Roadley, Iveson v Wakefield* [1930] 1 Ch 524; *Re Resch's Will Trusts, Le Cras v Perpetual Trustee Co Ltd* [1969] 1 AC 514, sub nom *Le Cras v Perpetual Trustee Co Ltd* [1967] 3 All ER 915, PC. Hospitals give in-patients continuous treatment; dispensaries give out-patients occasional medical and surgical aid: *Re Ford* [1945] 1 All ER 288. Not all hospitals are charitable, but a gift in a will may be construed as a gift only to hospitals not run for profit, which are charitable: *Re Smith's Will Trusts, Barclays Bank Ltd v Mercantile Bank Ltd* [1962] 2 All ER 563, [1962] 1 WLR 763, CA.

7 *Re Dean's Will Trusts, Cowan v Board of Governors of St Mary's Hospital, Paddington* [1950] 1 All ER 882.

8 *Re White's Will Trusts, Tindall v Board of Governors of United Sheffield Hospitals* [1951] 1 All ER 528.

9 *Re Bernstein's Will Trusts, National Westminster Bank Ltd v Board of Governors of United Liverpool Hospitals* (1971) 115 Sol Jo 808.
10 *Re Adams, Gee v Barnet Group Hospital Management Committee* [1968] Ch 80, [1967] 3 All ER 285, CA.
11 *Re Clarke, Bracey v Royal National Lifeboat Institution* [1923] 2 Ch 407. Cf *IRC v Peeblesshire Nursing Association* 1927 SC 215, Ct of Sess.
12 *IRC v Trustees of Roberts Marine Mansions* (1927) 43 TLR 270, CA (seaside home at reduced charges for members of drapery and allied trades requiring rest and change of air for the benefit of their health).
13 *Re Estlin, Prichard v Thomas* (1903) 72 LJCh 687 (home of rest for lady teachers); *Re James, Grenfell v Hamilton* [1932] 2 Ch 25 (home of rest for certain religious sisters and clergy and persons chosen by mother superior); *Re Chaplin, Neame v A-G* [1933] Ch 115 (home of rest to afford means of recuperation from strain).
14 *Re Sahal's Will Trusts, Alliance Assurance Co Ltd v A-G* [1958] 3 All ER 428, [1958] 1 WLR 1243; though see also *Re Cole, Westminster Bank Ltd v Moore* [1958] Ch 877, [1958] 3 All ER 102, CA.
15 *Harbin v Masterman* (1871) LR 12 Eq 559; *Harbin v Masterman* [1894] 2 Ch 184, CA; affd sub nom *Wharton v Masterman* [1895] AC 186, HL (asylum for destitute orphans); *Henshaw v Atkinson* (1818) 3 Madd 306 (blind asylum).
16 *Mayor of London's Case* (1639) Duke 83; *Re Whiteley, Bishop of London v Whiteley* [1910] 1 Ch 600; and see *Chamberlayne v Brockett* (1872) 8 Ch App 206. Cf *Re Brown, Brown v Brown* (1900) 32 OR 323 (luxuries for inmates of poorhouse).
17 *Re Estlin, Prichard v Thomas* (1903) 72 LJCh 687 (the ladies in question paid part of the expenses of board and lodging). See, however, PARA 9.
18 *Trustees of Mary Clark Home v Anderson* [1904] 2 KB 645; *Re Gardom, Le Page v A-G* [1914] 1 Ch 662, CA; *Shaw v Halifax Corpn* [1915] 2 KB 170, CA; *Re Armitage, Ellam v Norwich Corpn* [1972] Ch 438, sub nom *Re Armitage's Will Trusts, Ellam v City and County of Norwich* [1972] 1 All ER 708. See, however, PARA 9.
19 *Rolls v Miller* (1884) 27 ChD 71, CA. See, however, PARA 9.
20 *Hall v Derby Borough Urban Sanitary Authority* (1885) 16 QBD 163, DC; *Harbin v Masterman* [1894] 2 Ch 184, CA (affd sub nom *Wharton v Masterman* [1895] AC 186, HL); *Re Clergy Society* (1856) 2 K & J 615; *Re Douglas, Obert v Barrow* (1887) 35 ChD 472.
21 *Spiller v Maude* (1881) 32 ChD 158n; *Re Lacy, Royal General Theatrical Fund Association v Kydd* [1899] 2 Ch 149.
22 *Re Garrard, Gordon v Craigie* [1907] 1 Ch 382 (conceded in argument).
23 *Report of the Charity Commissioners for England and Wales for 1974* (HC Paper (1974–75) no 381) paras 67–72.
24 *Report of the Charity Commissioners for England and Wales for 1990* (HC Paper (1990–91) no 362) App A (e).
25 *Cocks v Manners* (1871) LR 12 Eq 574; *Re Delany, Conoley v Quick* [1902] 2 Ch 642, and cases there cited.

(ii) The Advancement of Education

20. Advancement of education. A purpose is charitable under the second statutory description of charitable purposes if it is for the advancement of education[1].

It is a necessary element that education must be capable of being 'advanced', which the Charity Commission has explained as promoting, sustaining and increasing individual and collective knowledge and understanding of specific areas of study, skills and expertise[2].

Education may be described as formal education, community education, physical education and development of young people, training (including vocational training) and life-long learning, research and adding to collective knowledge and understanding of specific areas of study and expertise, and the development of individual capabilities, competences, skills and understanding[3].

Accordingly, many different types of charity are capable of advancing education as so described. The Charity Commission lists a number, though not exhaustively, including: schools, colleges and universities and organisations supporting the work of education establishments, or associated with them[4]; pre-schools and out-of-school education; youth sporting facilities; organisations providing life skills training[5] such as the Duke of Edinburgh award schemes, Scouts and Guides; research foundations and think tanks; learned societies[6]; museums, galleries, libraries and scientific institutes; organisations which fund education; organisations that educate the public in a particular subject[7]; and information media[8].

1 See the Charities Act 2011 s 3(1)(b); and PARA 2.

2 *Charitable purposes* (Charity Commission, September 2013) para 4 (available, at the date at which this volume states the law, on the government website). As to the Charity Commission's publications see PARA 547.

3 *Charitable purposes* (Charity Commission, September 2013) para 4.

4 Eg parent-teacher organisations, prize funds, standard-setting organisations, teacher training organisations, student unions and examinations boards: *Charitable purposes* (Charity Commission, September 2013) para 4.

5 Eg the Duke of Edinburgh award schemes, Scouts and Guides: *Charitable purposes* (Charity Commission, September 2013) para 4.

6 Eg the Royal Geographical Society: *Charitable purposes* (Charity Commission, September 2013) para 4.

7 Eg in human rights, climate change, physics, personal financial management: *Charitable purposes* (Charity Commission, September 2013) para 4. See the Commission's observations regarding the boundaries between education about climate change and the adoption and promotion of a political position: *Operational Compliance Report: The Global Warming Policy Foundation* (Charity Commission, September 2014) (available, at the date at which this volume states the law, on the government website).

The promulgation of humanism has been accepted by the Charity Commission as a charitable purpose falling within this category: see PARA 50 text and note 13.

8 'Information media' is taken by the Charity Commission to include the internet, radio, television, libraries, information centres, university presses, seminars, conferences and lectures: *Charitable purposes* (Charity Commission, September 2013) para 4.

21. Advancement of education for the public benefit. In addition to the guidance of the Charity Commission as to the purposes which fall in the second statutory description[1], it is well established that the advancement and propagation of education and learning generally are charitable purposes[2], even in the absence of any element of poverty in the class of beneficiaries[3], but a gift being clearly educational is not sufficient to stop the court from requiring evidence of public benefit[4].

If the sole object of a school is to provide for the education of people whose families can afford to pay, it will lack the purposes necessary to qualify as a charity; but if its constitution allows for the education of poorer children, even if it does not in practice do so, it may still be established for charitable purposes[5]. The granting of bursaries and scholarships, or making classes, teachers, and educational facilities available to students outside the school itself, would be evidence of public benefit; but making playing fields available to the community would not[6].

It need not be confined to education by a teacher in a classroom[7], and it need not be connected with teaching or education in the conventional sense[8]. Thus the purposes of a students' union attached to a medical college[9], or a polytechnic[10], have been held to be charitable.

This category of charitable purposes extends to the improvement of a useful branch of human knowledge and its public dissemination[11], though a gift which merely tends to the increase of knowledge may not be charitable[12], and research of a private character, for example for the benefit of the members of a particular society, would not normally be charitable[13]. The promotion of academic research may be a charitable purpose if the research is of educational value to the researcher, or if it is so directed as to lead to something which will pass into the store of educational material or to improve the sum of communicable knowledge in an area which education may cover[14]. The principles in relation to research are as follows[15].

(1) A trust for research will ordinarily qualify as a charitable trust if, but only if: (a) the subject matter of the proposed research is a useful subject of study; and (b) it is contemplated that knowledge acquired as a result of the research will be disseminated to others; and (c) the trust is for the benefit of the public, or a sufficiently important section of the public[16].

(2) In the absence of a contrary context, however, the court will be readily inclined to construe a trust for research as importing subsequent dissemination of the results thereof[17].

(3) Furthermore, if a trust for research is to constitute a valid trust for the advancement of education, it is not necessary either: (a) that a teacher/pupil relationship should be in contemplation; or (b) that the persons to benefit from the knowledge to be acquired should be persons who are already in the course of receiving 'education' in the conventional sense[18].

(4) In any case where the court has to determine whether a bequest for the purposes of research is or is not of a charitable nature, it must pay due regard to any admissible extrinsic evidence which is available to explain the wording of the will in question or the circumstances in which it was made[19].

Where a gift is clearly educational the court will not inquire into the efficacy of the method of education advocated[20].

The furtherance of 'religious and mental improvement' has been deemed charitable[21], as has the Scout movement[22].

Education in political matters in the interests of one party only is not charitable[23]; nor is adult education with particular reference to the memorandum of one political party[24]. If the essential or dominant purpose is not education but a political object it is not charitable[25].

Many purposes which fall to be considered under this division of charitable purposes may also be considered charitable as being for the advancement of the arts, culture, heritable or science[26], and may be accepted as falling under either or both of these categories[27].

1 See PARA 20.

2 *Whicker v Hume* (1858) 7 HL Cas 124; *President of United States of America v Drummond* (1838) cited in 7 HL Cas 155; *R (on the application of Independent Schools Council) v Charity Commission for England and Wales; A-G v Charity Commission for England and Wales* [2011] UKUT 421 (TCC), [2012] Ch 214, [2012] 1 All ER 127.

3 *R v Income Tax Special Comrs, ex p University College of North Wales* (1909) 78 LJKB 576 at 578, CA, per Cozens-Hardy MR.

4 See the Charities Act 2011 s 4(2); and PARA 5. Previously where a gift was clearly educational the court did not require evidence of public benefit, although this did not prevent evidence being admissible to enable the court to decide whether there was any educational tendency in the gift: *Re Pinion, Westminster Bank Ltd v Pinion* [1965] Ch 85, [1964] 1 All ER 890, CA; affg on this point [1965] Ch 85, [1963] 2 All ER 1049.

5 *R (on the application of Independent Schools Council) v Charity Commission for England and Wales; A-G v Charity Commission for England and Wales* [2011] UKUT 421 (TCC) at [177] et seq, [2012] Ch 214, [2012] 1 All ER 127.

6 *R (on the application of Independent Schools Council) v Charity Commission for England and Wales; A-G v Charity Commission for England and Wales* [2011] UKUT 421 (TCC) at [196] et seq, [2012] Ch 214, [2012] 1 All ER 127.

7 *Royal Choral Society v IRC* [1943] 2 All ER 101, CA; *Re Koeppler Will Trusts, Barclays Bank Trust Co Ltd v Slack* [1986] Ch 423, [1985] 2 All ER 869, CA. And see *Charitable purposes* (Charity Commission, September 2013) para 4 (available, at the date at which this volume states the law, on the government website). As to the Charity Commission's publications see PARA 547.

8 See *Re Compton, Powell v Compton* [1945] Ch 123 at 127, [1945] 1 All ER 198 at 200, CA, per Lord Greene MR; *Re Hopkins' Will Trusts, Naish v Francis Bacon Society Inc* [1965] Ch 669 at 680, [1964] 3 All ER 46 at 52 per Wilberforce J; *Re Koeppler Will Trusts, Barclays Bank Trust Co Ltd v Slack* [1986] Ch 423, [1985] 2 All ER 869, CA (conferences for highly qualified participants on recognised academic subjects held to be for the advancement of education). But see also *Re Shaw, Public Trustee v Day* [1957] 1 All ER 745, [1957] 1 WLR 729; on appeal [1958] 1 All ER 245n, CA.

9 *London Hospital Medical College v IRC* [1976] 2 All ER 113, [1976] 1 WLR 613 (union existed solely to further educational purposes of college: benefits received by students incidental to implementation of those purposes).

10 *A-G v Ross* [1985] 3 All ER 334, [1986] 1 WLR 252. Note the *Attorney General's Guidance on Expenditure by Student Unions: Report of Charity Commissioners for England and Wales for 1983* (HC Paper (1983–84) no 447) App A. See also the Further and Higher Education Act 1992 s 77 (see EDUCATION vol 36 (2011) PARA 812), which permits the transformation of polytechnics into universities with the consent of the Privy Council.

11 *Incorporated Council of Law Reporting for England and Wales v A-G* [1972] Ch 73 at 102, [1971] 3 All ER 1029 at 1046, CA, per Buckley LJ. See also *Vancouver Society of Immigrant and Visible Minority Women v Minister of National Revenue* (1999) 169 DLR (4th) 34, Can SC (structured transmission of useful information and training).

12 *Re Shaw, Public Trustee v Day* [1957] 1 All ER 745, [1957] 1 WLR 729, following *Whicker v Hume* (1858) 7 HL Cas 124; and *Re Macduff, Macduff v Macduff* [1896] 2 Ch 451, CA.

13 See *Re British School of Egyptian Archaeology, Murray v Public Trustee* [1954] 1 All ER 887 at 890, [1954] 1 WLR 546 at 551 per Harman J; *Re Hopkins' Will Trusts, Naish v Francis Bacon Society Inc* [1965] Ch 669 at 681, [1964] 3 All ER 46 at 53 per Wilberforce J.

14 See *Re Hopkins' Will Trusts, Naish v Francis Bacon Society Inc* [1965] Ch 669 at 680, [1964] 3 All ER 46 at 52 per Wilberforce J. See also *Incorporated Council of Law Reporting for England and Wales v A-G* [1972] Ch 73, [1971] 3 All ER 1029, CA.

15 *Re Besterman's Will Trusts* (21 January 1980, unreported) per Slade J, cited by the same judge in *McGovern v A-G* [1982] Ch 321 at 352–353, [1981] 3 All ER 493 at 518. See also *Re Koeppler Will Trusts, Barclays Bank Trust Co Ltd v Slack* [1986] Ch 423, [1985] 2 All ER 869, CA.

16 *Re Besterman's Will Trusts* (21 January 1980, unreported) per Slade J, cited by the same judge in *McGovern v A-G* [1982] Ch 321 at 352–353, [1981] 3 All ER 493 at 518.

17 *Re Besterman's Will Trusts* (21 January 1980, unreported) per Slade J, cited by the same judge in *McGovern v A-G* [1982] Ch 321 at 352–353, [1981] 3 All ER 493 at 518.

18 *Re Besterman's Will Trusts* (21 January 1980, unreported) per Slade J, cited by the same judge in *McGovern v A-G* [1982] Ch 321 at 352–353, [1981] 3 All ER 493 at 518.

19 *Re Besterman's Will Trusts* (21 January 1980, unreported) per Slade J, cited by the same judge in *McGovern v A-G* [1982] Ch 321 at 352–353, [1981] 3 All ER 493 at 518.

20 *Re Shaw's Will Trusts, National Provincial Bank Ltd v National City Bank Ltd* [1952] Ch 163, [1952] 1 All ER 49.

21 *Re Scowcroft, Ormrod v Wilkinson* [1898] 2 Ch 638; *Barralet v A-G* [1980] 3 All ER 918, sub nom *Re South Place Ethical Society, Barralet v A-G* [1980] 1 WLR 1565 (study and dissemination of ethical principles and the cultivation of a rational religious sentiment).

22 *Re Webber, Barclays Bank Ltd v Webber* [1954] 3 All ER 712, [1954] 1 WLR 1500, following *Re Alexander* (1932) Times, 30 June (instruction of boys of all classes in the principles of loyalty, discipline and good citizenship). Though not within the contemplation of that decision, the Guide movement must be presumed to fall within its reach, and is explicitly mentioned in the Charity Commission's guidance: see *Charitable purposes* (Charity Commission, September 2013) para 7; and PARA 35.

23 *Bonar Law Memorial Trust v IRC* (1933) 49 TLR 220.

24 *Re Hopkinson, Lloyds Bank Ltd v Baker* [1949] 1 All ER 346; see also PARA 60.

25 *Re Bushnell, Lloyds Bank Ltd v Murray* [1975] 1 All ER 721, [1975] 1 WLR 1596. See also *Webb v O'Doherty* (1991) 3 Admin LR 731, (1991) Times, 11 February (the funds of a students' union, an educational charity, could not be used to campaign for an end to the First Gulf War, a political purpose). Education of the public in the subject of militarism and disarmament was political and not a charitable object: *Southwood v A-G* [2000] WTLR 1199, CA.

26 Ie under the Charities Act 2011 s 3(1)(f); see PARAS 2, and 36.

27 See eg *Re Shakespeare Memorial Trust, Earl of Lytton v A-G* [1923] 2 Ch 398; *Re Hopkins' Will Trusts, Naish v Francis Bacon Society Inc* [1965] Ch 669, [1964] 3 All ER 46; *Construction Industry Training Board v A-G* [1971] 3 All ER 449, [1971] 1 WLR 1303 (affd without dealing with this point [1973] Ch 173, [1972] 2 All ER 1339, CA); *Incorporated Council of Law Reporting for England and Wales v A-G* [1972] Ch 73, [1971] 3 All ER 1029, CA.

22. Education of limited class. Gifts for the education of special classes of persons forming a section of the community[1], such as women and girls who are not self-supporting[2], or the daughters of missionaries[3], or persons professing particular religious doctrines[4], or the employees in the whole of a particular industry[5], and gifts for educational purposes with a provision for the participation of the founder's kin, are charitable[6].

However, gifts for the education of descendants of named persons[7], or for the education of employees or of children of employees or former employees of a limited company[8], are not charitable, and an institute maintained for the promotion of efficiency, progress and general development among persons engaged or employed in insurance was held to be for the benefit, not of the public, but of the insurance profession[9].

1 See *Oppenheim v Tobacco Securities Trust Co Ltd* [1951] AC 297 at 305, [1951] 1 All ER 31 at 33, HL, per Lord Simonds. As to whether purposes satisfy the requirement of benefiting a sufficient section of the community see PARA 6. For provision as to discrimination see PARA 9.
2 *Re Central Employment Bureau for Women and Students' Careers Association Inc* [1942] 1 All ER 232. See, however, PARA 9.
3 *German v Chapman* (1877) 7 ChD 271, CA.
4 *Income Tax Special Purposes Comrs v Pemsel* [1891] AC 531, HL; *Walsh v Gladstone* (1843) 1 Ph 290; *Carbery v Cox* (1852) 3 I Ch R 231n (Roman Catholics); *Re Michel's Trust* (1860) 28 Beav 39 (Jews).
5 *Construction Industry Training Board v A-G* [1971] 3 All ER 449, [1971] 1 WLR 1303; affd without dealing with this point [1973] Ch 173, [1972] 2 All ER 1339, CA.
6 *Spencer v All Souls' College* (1762) Wilm 163; *A-G v Sidney Sussex College, Cambridge* (1866) 21 ChD 514n; *Re Lavelle, Concannon v A-G* [1914] 1 IR 194 (explained in *Re Compton, Powell v Compton* [1945] Ch 123, [1945] 1 All ER 198, CA); and see *Re Koettgen's Will Trusts, Westminster Bank Ltd v Family Welfare Association Trustees Ltd* [1954] Ch 252, [1954] 1 All ER 581; and PARA 7. See also *Cawdron v Merchant Taylors' School* [2009] EWHC 1722 (Ch), [2010] PTSR 507, where the education of sons or relatives of former old boys of the school who had fallen in the war was held to be charitable, though this was considered under the general head of relief of poverty.
7 *Re Compton, Powell v Compton* [1945] Ch 123, [1945] 1 All ER 198, CA. Cf *Laverty v Laverty* [1907] 1 IR 9 (education of 'any boy or man' of a particular surname: not charitable); and see *Davies v Perpetual Trustee Co Ltd* [1959] AC 439, [1959] 2 All ER 128, PC.
8 *Oppenheim v Tobacco Securities Trust Co Ltd* [1951] AC 297, [1951] 1 All ER 31, HL, doubting *Re Rayner, Cloutman v Regnart* (1920) 89 LJCh 369; *Re Leverhulme, Cooper v Leverhulme* [1943] 2 All ER 143. See also *Re Cox, Baker v National Trust Co Ltd* [1955] AC 627, [1955] 2 All ER 550, PC; *IRC v Educational Grants Association Ltd* [1967] Ch 993, [1967] 2 All ER 893, CA.
9 *Chartered Insurance Institute v London Corpn* [1957] 2 All ER 638, [1957] 1 WLR 867, DC (where the question at issue was whether the institute was an organisation whose main objects were concerned with the advancement of education, so as to entitle it to rating relief); but see *Royal College of Nursing v St Marylebone Corpn* [1959] 3 All ER 663, [1959] 1 WLR 1077, CA.

23. Education in particular subjects. The promotion of education in particular subjects, such as art[1], artistic taste[2], the appreciation of the fine arts[3], music[4] or the music of one particular composer[5], choral singing[6], playing the organ[7], drama[8], the arts of social intercourse[9], the Irish language[10], archaeology[11], commercial education[12], training for industrial employment[13], craftsmanship[14], the art and science of government[15], economic and sanitary science[16], psychological healing[17], or Christian knowledge[18], is charitable. But education in the cause of a particular political party is not charitable[19]; nor is the presentation of 'classical, artistic, cultural and educational dramatic works'[20]. A trust whose purpose is the mere increase of knowledge is not charitable in the legal sense[21], and gifts to the Simplified Spelling Society[22] and for investigations into the efficacy of a new alphabet[23] have been held not to be charitable.

1 *Re Allsop, Gell v Carver* (1884) 1 TLR 4 (school of art). A gift to 'encourage artistic pursuits' is not charitable: *Re Ogden, Taylor v Sharp* (1909) 25 TLR 382, CA; and see *Gwynn v Cardon* (c 1800) cited in 10 Ves 533; *Re Bootham Ward Strays, York, IRC v Scott* [1892] 2 QB 152 at 165, CA, per Lord Herschell. The promotion of art is charitable: *Re Town and Country Planning Act 1947, Crystal Palace Trustees v Minister of Town and Country Planning* [1951] Ch 132, [1950] 2 All ER 857n, doubting *Re Ogden, Taylor v Sharp*.

2 *Royal Choral Society v IRC* [1943] 2 All ER 101 at 105, CA, per Lord Greene MR; and see *Re Hopkins' Will Trusts, Naish v Francis Bacon Society Inc* [1965] Ch 669, [1964] 3 All ER 46.

3 *Re Shaw's Will Trusts, National Provincial Bank Ltd v National City Bank Ltd* [1952] Ch 163, [1952] 1 All ER 49.

4 *IRC v Glasgow Musical Festival Association* 1926 SC 920, Ct of Sess (society engaged in stimulating public interest in music and encouraging those members of the public who have musical gifts to cultivate them); *Shillington v Portadown Urban Council* [1911] 1 IR 247; *Re Henry Wood National Memorial Trust, Armstrong v Moiseiwitsch* (1965) 109 Sol Jo 876 (gift to build a concert hall). A gift to any musical or literary society in a district is not charitable: *Re King, Henderson v Cranmer* [1931] WN 232.

5 *Re Delius, Emanuel v Rosen* [1957] Ch 299, sub nom *Re Delius' Will Trusts, Emanuel v Rosen* [1957] 1 All ER 854.

6 *Royal Choral Society v IRC* [1943] 2 All ER 101, CA; and see *Re Levien, Lloyds Bank Ltd v Worshipful Co of Musicians* [1955] 3 All ER 35, [1955] 1 WLR 964 (individual singer).

7 *Re Levien, Lloyds Bank Ltd v Worshipful Co of Musicians* [1955] 3 All ER 35, [1955] 1 WLR 964.

8 *Re Shakespeare Memorial Trust, Earl of Lytton v A-G* [1923] 2 Ch 398.

9 *Re Shaw's Will Trusts, National Provincial Bank Ltd v National City Bank Ltd* [1952] Ch 163, [1952] 1 All ER 49.

10 *A-G v Flood* (1816) Hayes & Jo App xxi at xxxviii; and see *Brownjohn v Gale* [1869] WN 133.

11 *Yates v University College, London* (1873) 8 Ch App 454 (affd (1875) LR 7 HL 438); *Re British School of Egyptian Archaeology, Murray v Public Trustee* [1954] 1 All ER 887, [1954] 1 WLR 546 (Egyptology).

12 *Re Koettgen's Will Trusts, Westminster Bank Ltd v Family Welfare Association Trustees Ltd* [1954] Ch 252, [1954] 1 All ER 581 (conceded).

13 *Construction Industry Training Board v A-G* [1971] 3 All ER 449, [1971] 1 WLR 1303; affd without dealing with this point [1973] Ch 173, [1972] 2 All ER 1339, CA.

14 *IRC v White and A-G* (1980) 55 TC 651.

15 *Re Arthur McDougall Fund Trusts, Thompson v Fitzgerald* [1956] 3 All ER 867, [1957] 1 WLR 81.

16 *Re Berridge, Berridge v Turner* (1890) 63 LT 470, CA.

17 *Re Osmund, Midland Bank Executor and Trustee Co Ltd v A-G* [1944] Ch 206, [1944] 1 All ER 262, CA.

18 *A-G v Stepney* (1804) 10 Ves 22.

19 *Re Hopkinson, Lloyds Bank Ltd v Baker* [1949] 1 All ER 346; *Bonar Law Memorial Trust v IRC* (1933) 49 TLR 220. Education of the public in the subject of militarism and disarmament was political and not a charitable object: *Southwood v A-G* [1998] 40 LS Gaz R 37, Times, 26 October; affd [2000] WTLR 1199, CA.

20 *Associated Artists Ltd v IRC* [1956] 2 All ER 583, [1956] 1 WLR 752.

21 See the cases cited in PARA 21.

22 *Trustees of Sir GB Hunter (1922) C Trust v IRC* (1929) 45 TLR 344.

23 *Re Shaw, Public Trustee v Day* [1957] 1 All ER 745, [1957] 1 WLR 729; appeal dismissed by consent on terms [1958] 1 All ER 245n, CA.

24. Preservation of objects of educational value. The preservation of objects of historic interest for public inspection is a charitable purpose[1], whether they be specimen buildings[2] or a collection of armour, antiques and articles of vertu[3]. However, the preservation intact of a collection of paintings, furniture and other objects as a museum to be open to the public may not be charitable if the gift, carried out in accordance with the donor's intentions, is shown to have no possible educational value[4].

1 These may also fall under the sixth statutory description of charitable purposes as being for the advancement of culture or heritage: See the Charities Act 2011 s 3(1)(f); and PARAS 2, 36.
2 *Re Cranstoun, National Provincial Bank Ltd v Royal Society for the Encouragement of Arts, Manufactures and Commerce* [1932] 1 Ch 537. See the *Report of the Charity Commissioners for England and Wales for 1990* (HC Paper (1990–91) no 362) App A (b) (Settle and Carlisle Railway Trust registered as a charity).
3 *Re Spence, Barclays Bank Ltd v Stockton-on-Tees Corpn* [1938] Ch 96, [1937] 3 All ER 684.
4 *Re Pinion, Westminster Bank Ltd v Pinion* [1965] Ch 85, [1964] 1 All ER 890, CA.

25. Educational institutions. The establishment and support of colleges[1], schools[2], professorships[3], fellowships[4], lectureships[5], scholarships[6] and prizes[7], and the providing of schoolteachers[8], are charitable purposes. Gifts to learned societies and institutions for the advancement of science[9], such as the Royal Society or the Royal Geographical Society[10], the Royal Literary Society[11], the Royal College of Surgeons[12] and the Zoological Society[13], are charitable[14]. However, institutions which, on the true construction of their constitutions, are for the benefit of a particular profession are not charitable[15]. A trust to buy books for Trinity College, Oxford, was treated as charitable on the ground that a large, well-assorted library tends to the promotion of education[16]. An institution established for the purpose of publishing material essential for the study of a learned science may be charitable, notwithstanding that the material is directly of use primarily to the members of a profession as a professional tool[17].

1 *Porter's Case* (1592) 1 Co Rep 24 b; *Plate v St John's College* (1638) Duke 77; *A-G v Comber* (1824) 2 Sim & St 93; *Christ's College, Cambridge, Case* (1757) 1 Wm Bl 90; *A-G v Whorwood* (1750) 1 Ves Sen 534 at 536 per Lord Hardwicke LC; *Walsh v Gladstone* (1843) 1 Ph 290 (Roman Catholic college); *R v Income Tax Special Comrs, ex p University College of North Wales* (1909) 78 LJKB 576, CA (college founded to give instruction in all the branches of a liberal education, except theology, and drawing revenue from a government grant, fees from pupils, donations, etc, as well as from investments); *Royal College of Surgeons of England v National Provincial Bank Ltd* [1952] AC 631, [1952] 1 All ER 984, HL (college incorporated for promotion and encouragement of the study and practice of the art and science of surgery); and see *Aberdeen University v Irvine* (1868) LR 1 Sc & Div 289, HL; *Wallis v Solicitor-General for New Zealand* [1903] AC 173, PC. On the other hand, the support of a staff training college for employees of a limited company who attend compulsorily is not charitable: *Re Leverhulme, Cooper v Leverhulme* [1943] 2 All ER 143.
2 *Gibbons v Maltyard* (1592) Poph 6; *Rugby School Case* (1626) Duke 80; *A-G v Nash* (1792) 3 Bro CC 588; *Kirkbank v Hudson* (1819) 7 Price 212; *A-G v Earl of Lonsdale* (1827) 1 Sim 105 at 109 per Leath V-C (school for gentlemen's sons); *Hartshorne v Nicholson* (1858) 26 Beav 58; *Re Sir Robert Peel's School at Tamworth, ex p Charity Comrs* (1868) 3 Ch App 543; *Re Allsop, Gell v Carver* (1884) 1 TLR 4 (school of art); *Re Gilchrist Educational Trust* [1895] 1 Ch 367; *Smith v Kerr* [1902] 1 Ch 774 at 778, CA, per Collins MR (ancient Inns of Chancery); *Re Hawkins, Walrond v Newton* (1906) 22 TLR 521 (school for religious teaching and elementary education); *Brighton College v Marriott* [1926] AC 192 at 204, HL, per Lord Blanesburgh (school for sons of noblemen and gentlemen); *The Abbey, Malvern Wells, Ltd v Ministry of Local Government and Planning* [1951] Ch 728, [1951] 2 All ER 154 (school for girls carried on by private company but dividends bound to be applied under trust deed in promoting work of school), distinguishing *Re Girls' Public Day School Trust Ltd, Girls' Public Day School Trust Ltd v Minister of Town and Country Planning* [1951] Ch 400 (school for girls carried on by private company, but certain shareholders not obliged to apply benefits for purposes of school: not charitable).
3 *Yates v University College, London* (1873) 8 Ch App 454 (affd (1875) LR 7 HL 438 (professorship of archaeology)); *Re Buckland, Buckland v Bennett* (1887) 22 LJNC 7 (professorship of economic fish culture).
4 *Jesus College Case* (1615) Duke 78.
5 *A-G v Cambridge Margaret and Regius Professors* (1682) 1 Vern 55.

6 *R v Newman* (1670) 1 Lev 284; *Re Levitt* (1885) 1 TLR 578; *University College of North Wales v Taylor* [1908] P 140, CA; *Re Williams, Taylor v Wales University* (1908) 24 TLR 716.
7 *Thompson v Thompson* (1844) 1 Coll 381 at 398 per Knight Bruce V-C; *Farrer v St Catharine's College, Cambridge* (1873) LR 16 Eq 19; *Re Mariette, Mariette v Aldenham School Governing Body* [1915] 2 Ch 284; *Chesterman v Federal Taxation Comr* [1926] AC 128, PC.
8 *Hynshaw v Morpeth Corpn* (1629) Duke 69; *A-G v Earl of Winchelsea* (1791) 3 Bro CC 373.
9 As to the meaning of 'science' see PARA 36 note 1.
10 *Beaumont v Oliveira* (1869) 4 Ch App 309; *Royal Society of London and Thompson* (1881) 17 ChD 407.
11 *Thomas v Howell* (1874) LR 18 Eq 198.
12 *Royal College of Surgeons of England v National Provincial Bank Ltd* [1952] AC 631, [1952] 1 All ER 984, HL (college incorporated to promote study and practice of surgery charitable, although members obtained incidental professional advantages), explaining *Re Royal College of Surgeons of England* [1899] 1 QB 871, CA. See also *Royal College of Nursing v St Marylebone Corpn* [1959] 3 All ER 663, [1959] 1 WLR 1077, CA.
13 *Re Lopes, Bence-Jones v Zoological Society of London* [1931] 2 Ch 130; followed in *North of England Zoological Society v Chester RDC* [1959] 3 All ER 116, [1959] 1 WLR 773, CA.
14 In addition to advancing education, these purposes may also fall under the sixth statutory description of charitable purposes as being for the advancement of science: see the Charities Act 2011 s 3(1)(f); and PARAS 2, 36.
15 Eg *Chartered Insurance Institute v London Corpn* [1957] 2 All ER 638, [1957] 1 WLR 867.
16 *A-G v Marchant* (1866) LR 3 Eq 424 at 430 per Kindersley V-C; and cf *Re Good, Harington v Watts* [1905] 2 Ch 60.
17 *Incorporated Council of Law Reporting for England and Wales v A-G* [1972] Ch 73, [1971] 3 All ER 1029, CA; though see also, as to law reporting, *Incorporated Council of Law Reporting for State of Queensland v Taxation Comr* (1971) 45 ALJR 552, Aust HC (charitable but not educational), following *Incorporated Council of Law Reporting for the State of Queensland v Federal Taxation Comr* (1924) 34 CLR 580, Aust HC.

26. Games and tournaments. The promotion of organised games at a boarding school and the provision of prizes for events in school sports are charitable purposes as being for the advancement of that part of the educational work of the school which has to do with the physical development of the students[1]. This has been extended to a trust to promote the physical education and development of pupils at schools and universities, as an addition to such part of their education as relates to their mental education, by providing facilities and assistance for association football and other games or sports[2]. The promotion of annual chess tournaments with prizes, open to young men resident in a particular city, is charitable, for the game possesses educational value[3].

A trust to provide an annual school treat has been held charitable as tending to the advancement of education[4]; and a trust to provide an annual outing for children of members of an ex-serviceman's club has been held charitable as serving an educational purpose[5]; but a gift to provide a pennyworth of sweets each for all children resident in a parish, unconfined to children who had attended school, has been held not charitable[6].

Where the promotion of a game or tournament has no educational value, it may nevertheless be charitable under the seventh statutory description of charitable purposes if it advances amateur sport[7].

1 *Re Mariette, Mariette v Aldenham School Governing Body* [1915] 2 Ch 284; and see *Re Gray, Todd v Taylor* [1925] Ch 362 (regimental sporting fund: charitable as promoting efficiency of army). Cf *Re Nottage, Jones v Palmer* [1895] 2 Ch 649, CA (see PARA 65); *Re Harrow School Governors and Murray's Contract* [1927] 1 Ch 556 (provision of school sanatorium an educational purpose within the Education Act 1921 s 117 (repealed)); *Trustees of City of Belfast YMCA v Northern Ireland Valuation Comr* [1969] NI 3, CA.
2 *IRC v McMullen* [1981] AC 1, [1980] 1 All ER 884, HL.
3 *Re Dupree's Deed Trusts, Daley v Lloyds Bank* [1945] Ch 16, [1944] 2 All ER 443.
4 *Re Mellody, Brandwood v Haden* [1918] 1 Ch 228.
5 *Re Ward's Estate, Ward v Ward* (1937) 81 Sol Jo 397.

6 *Re Pleasants, Pleasants v A-G* (1923) 39 TLR 675.
7 See the Charities Act 2011 s 3(1)(g); and PARAS 2, 37.

(iii) The Advancement of Religion

27. Advancement of religion. A purpose is charitable under the third statutory description of charitable purposes if it is for the advancement of religion[1]. The words 'advancement of religion', as used to denote one class of legally charitable objects, mean the promotion of spiritual teaching in a wide sense, and the maintenance of the doctrines on which it rests and of the observances that serve to promote and manifest it[2]. To advance religion means to promote it, to spread its message ever wider among mankind, and to take some positive steps to sustain and increase religious belief; and these things are done in a variety of ways which may be comprehensively described as pastoral and missionary[3].

Religion is concerned with man's relations with the supernatural and, whilst there is no statutory or common law definition of religion, two essential attributes are (1) faith in a supreme being[4]; and (2) worship of that supreme being[5].

Taking part in acts or practices expressing belief or showing reverence is not necessary to the concept of 'worship'; what is necessary is that the relationship with the supreme being is characterised by some or all of deep respect, homage, adoration, devotion, obeisance, submission, prayer and meditation[6].

The court will not adjudicate upon the truth of religious rites, but can address questions of religious belief and practice where its jurisdiction is invoked to enforce the contractual rights of members of a community against other members or its governing body or to ensure that property held on trust is used for the purposes of the trust[7].

1 See the Charities Act 2011 s 3(1)(c); and PARA 2.
2 *Keren Kayemeth Le Jisroel Ltd v IRC* [1931] 2 KB 465 at 477, CA, per Lord Hanworth MR; affd without defining 'advancement of religion' [1932] AC 650, HL (acquisition of land in Asia Minor for settling Jews: not a religious purpose). The promotion of a particular doctrine is not necessarily taken by the Charity Commission as being for the advancement of religion in a charitable sense: see *Application for Registration of Good News for Israel,* Decision of the Charity Commissioners, 5 February 2004. As to decisions of the Charity Commission see PARA 547.
3 *United Grand Lodge of Ancient Free and Accepted Masons of England v Holborn Borough Council* [1957] 3 All ER 281 at 285, [1957] 1 WLR 1080 at 1090 per Donovan J. See *Charitable purposes* (Charity Commission, September 2013) para 5 (available, at the date at which this volume states the law, on the government website). As to the Charity Commission's publications see PARA 547.
4 Or in more than one supreme being: see the Charities Act 2011 s 3(2)(a)(i); and PARA 2. Previously there was some doubt on this point (see *Bowman v Secular Society Ltd* [1917] AC 406 at 448–450, HL, per Lord Parker; and *Yeap Cheah Neo v Ong Cheng Neo* (1875) LR 6 PC 381), but the Charity Commission has long recognised polytheistic religions as capable of being the subject of a trust to advance religion.

A supreme being need not be a god: see the Charities Act 2011 s 3(2)(a)(ii); and PARA 2. Although 'god' is not defined, the Charity Commission's position is that 'god' and 'supreme being' are not synonymous and so, in the case of a belief system without a god, faith in a supreme being other than a personified deity is still required: *Charitable purposes* (Charity Commission, September 2013) para 5.

In the same place the Charity Commission's guidance refers to a 'supreme being or entity' which is taken to include a 'spiritual principle' other than a supreme being. It is submitted that this is incorrect: if faith in any supreme being is no longer a prerequisite of religion then charity law is arguably stripped of any meaningful way of determining what constitutes religion. For the discussion of this issue in the House of Lords, see 673 HL Official Report (5th series) col 138 et seq, 28 June 2005; and 674 HL Official Report (5th series) col 292 et seq, 12 October 2005.

The promulgation of humanism has been accepted by the Charity Commission as a charitable purpose; however, it is not registered under this category, but in relation to the advancement of education (see PARA 20 et seq), the promotion of religious and racial harmony (see PARA 41), and 'other charitable purposes' (see PARA 50 text and note 13).

As to the Charity Commission see PARAS 543–578.

5 *Barralet v A-G* [1980] 3 All ER 918 at 924, sub nom *Re South Place Ethical Society, Barralet v A-G* [1980] 1 WLR 1565 at 1571–1572 per Dillon J. See however PARA 29.

6 See *The advancement of religion for the public benefit* (Charity Commission, December 2008) Annex A.

In the context of identifying premises as a 'place of religious worship' for the purposes of Places of Worship Registration Act 1855, the Supreme Court has held that the Church of Scientology fulfils the criteria for registration: see *R (on the application of Hodkin) v Registrar General of Births, Deaths and Marriages* [2013] UKSC 77, [2014] AC 610, [2014] 1 All ER 737, overruling *R v Registrar General, ex p Segerdal* [1970] 2 QB 697, [1970] 3 All ER 886, CA (Church of Scientology). As to registration of places of worship see **ECCLESIASTICAL LAW** vol 34 (2011) PARA 47. This raises questions about the refusal of the Charity Commission to register the Church of Scientology as a charity: *Church of Scientology's Application for Registration as a Charity* [2005] WTLR 1151.

7 *Shergill v Khaira* [2014] UKSC 33, [2014] 3 All ER 243.

28. Religious purposes. Gifts to 'religious societies' or for 'religious purposes' are prima facie charitable[1], but particular religious societies or purposes are not necessarily charitable[2]. A religious society can exist only as an organised body, with a written or oral constitution[3], devoted to promoting the spiritual teaching of that body[4], and is charitable only in so far as its objects serve charitable religious purposes and its powers are limited to ancillary ends, as distinct from subsidiary activities not in themselves religious or charitable[5].

Charitable religious purposes are those which tend directly or indirectly to the instruction or edification of the public[6]. The presence of the necessary element of public benefit is a question of fact to be determined by the court upon proof by means of evidence cognisable by it, and does not depend on doctrinal belief[7]. The celebration of a religious rite, such as the saying of masses, in public has been held to confer a sufficient public benefit because of the edifying and improving effect of such celebration on the members of the public who attend[8]. Moreover, where there is a gift for a religious purpose which could be carried out in a way which is beneficial to the public, but could also be carried out in a way which would not have a sufficient element of public benefit, the gift is to be construed as a gift to be carried out only by the methods that are charitable, all non-charitable methods being excluded[9].

Religious orders and communities are usually unincorporated associations, and unless property held by them is impressed with charitable trusts it is subject to the law relating to unincorporated associations[10]. The general principle that unincorporated associations supported by their members to provide benefits for themselves are not charitable does not apply with full force to associations for religious purposes[11]. A purely contemplative or secluded order or community is not charitable, there being no element of benefit to the public from their activity of which the court will take cognisance[12]; but a gift to a community which is in contact with the general public may satisfy the requirement of public benefit[13].

Gifts which contain a public religious element and are charitable in this way are gifts for 'promoting religion'[14], for the 'worship of God'[15], for the 'spread of the Gospel'[16] or of Christianity[17], or to be used 'in the service of my Lord and Master'[18], or 'for God's work'[19], for purposes 'having regard to the glory of God in the spiritual welfare of His creatures'[20], or for the distribution of Bibles[21] or of other religious books[22], or for organised religious pilgrimages[23], or for the maintenance of institutions formed for the promotion of religion, such as the

United Society for the Propagation of the Gospel[24], the Protestant Alliance[25], the Irish Church Mission[26], the Church Missionary Society[27], the Society for Promoting Christian Knowledge[28], the Sunday School Association[29], the Young Men's Christian Association[30], the Church Army[31], the Salvation Army[32], or to 'the following religious societies namely ...'[33]. Religion may be promoted by the provision of organised recreational facilities[34].

1 *Re White, White v White* [1893] 2 Ch 41 at 53, CA, per Lindley LJ; *Arnott v Arnott* [1906] 1 IR 127; *Dunne v Byrne* [1912] AC 407 at 411, PC; *Re Ward, Public Trustee v Ward* [1941] Ch 308, sub nom *Re Ward, Public Trustee v Berry* [1941] 2 All ER 125, CA (educational or charitable or religious purposes for Roman Catholics in the British Empire: charitable).
2 *Re White, White v White* [1893] 2 Ch 41 at 51–52, CA, per Lindley LJ; *MacLaughlin v Campbell* [1906] 1 IR 588; *Gilmour v Coats* [1949] AC 426 at 449, [1949] 1 All ER 848 at 856, HL, per Lord Simonds and at 454, 859 per Lord Reid (purposes of convent of strictly cloistered nuns not charitable).
3 *Re Thackrah, Thackrah v Wilson* [1939] 2 All ER 4 (the Oxford Group; a company called The Oxford Group was afterwards incorporated: see *Oxford Group v IRC* [1949] 2 All ER 537, CA; and note 5).
4 *Keren Kayemeth Le Jisroel Ltd v IRC* [1931] 2 KB 465 at 469, CA, per Rowlatt J; approved on appeal [1932] AC 650, HL.
5 *Oxford Group v IRC* [1949] 2 All ER 537, CA (the advancement of the Christian religion in accordance with the principles of the Oxford Group Movement; the maintenance, support and assistance of the Oxford Group Movement in every way: not charitable); *Neville Estates Ltd v Madden* [1962] Ch 832, [1961] 3 All ER 769.
6 *Cocks v Manners* (1871) LR 12 Eq 574 at 585 per Wickens V-C; *Re Delany, Conoley v Quick* [1902] 2 Ch 642 at 648 per Farwell J; *Chesterman v Federal Taxation Comr* [1926] AC 128 at 131, PC; *Re Williams, Public Trustee v Williams* [1927] 2 Ch 283 at 287 per Clauson J; cf *Re Banfield, Lloyds Bank Ltd v Smith* [1968] 2 All ER 276, [1968] 1 WLR 846; *Re Warre's Will Trusts, Wort v Salisbury Diocesan Board of Finance* [1953] 2 All ER 99, [1953] 1 WLR 725. The study and dissemination of ethical principles and the cultivation of a rational religious sentiment is not a charitable religious purpose: *Barralet v A-G* [1980] 3 All ER 918, sub nom *Re South Place Ethical Society, Barralet v A-G* [1980] 1 WLR 1565.
7 *Re Coats' Trusts, Coats v Gilmour* [1948] Ch 340 at 347, [1948] 1 All ER 521 at 526, CA, per Lord Greene MR; on appeal sub nom *Gilmour v Coats* [1949] AC 426 at 446, [1949] 1 All ER 848 at 854, HL, per Lord Simonds. See also PARA 5.
8 *Re Hetherington* [1990] Ch 1, sub nom *Re Hetherington, Gibbs v McDonnell* [1989] 2 All ER 129 (such is not the case in relation to the celebration of a religious rite in private); *Re Caus, Lindeboom v Camille* [1934] Ch 162; and see *Gilmour v Coats* [1949] AC 426, [1949] 1 All ER 848, HL. The Charity Commission accepted that the practices of a spiritualist church fell within the scope of religious practices for charitable purposes: see *Sacred Hands Spiritual Centre's Application for Registration as a Charity* [2006] WTLR 873.
9 *Re Hetherington* [1990] Ch 1, sub nom *Re Hetherington, Gibbs v McDonnell* [1989] 2 All ER 129.
10 See the extensive discussion in *Leahy v A-G for New South Wales* [1959] AC 457, [1959] 2 All ER 300, PC.
11 *Neville Estates Ltd v Madden* [1962] Ch 832, [1961] 3 All ER 769.
12 *Cocks v Manners* (1871) LR 12 Eq 574; *Gilmour v Coats* [1949] AC 426, [1949] 1 All ER 848, HL.
13 *Cocks v Manners* (1871) LR 12 Eq 574; *Re Braham, Daw v Samuel* (1892) 36 Sol Jo 712; *Re Charlesworth, Robinson v Archdeacon of Cleveland* (1910) 101 LT 908; *Neville Estates Ltd v Madden* [1962] Ch 832, [1961] 3 All ER 769; *Re Banfield, Lloyds Bank Ltd v Smith* [1968] 2 All ER 276, [1968] 1 WLR 846; though see *Re Warre's Will Trusts, Wort v Salisbury Diocesan Board of Finance* [1953] 2 All ER 99, [1953] 1 WLR 725 (sed quaere). See also *Northern Ireland Valuation Comr v Trustees of the Redemptorist Order* [1971] NI 114, CA.
14 *A-G v Stepney* (1804) 10 Ves 22; *Baker v Sutton* (1836) 1 Keen 224; *Wilkinson v Lindgren* (1870) 5 Ch App 570; contra, *Browne v Yeall* (1791) 7 Ves 50n, doubted in *Morice v Bishop of Durham* (1805) 10 Ves 522 at 539 per Lord Eldon LC and in *Re Macduff, Macduff v Macduff* [1896] 2 Ch 451 at 471–472, CA, per Rigby LJ. Cf *Dunne v Byrne* [1912] AC 407, PC, explained in *Re Bain, Public Trustee v Ross* [1930] 1 Ch 224 at 230, CA, per Lord Hanworth MR.
15 *A-G v Pearson* (1817) 3 Mer 353 at 409 per Lord Eldon LC.
16 *Re Lea, Lea v Cooke* (1887) 34 ChD 528.

17 *A-G v Stepney* (1804) 10 Ves 22; *A-G v London Corpn* (1790) 1 Ves 243; *Re Hood, Public Trustee v Hood* [1931] 1 Ch 240, CA (spreading Christian principles and minimising drink traffic).
18 *Powerscourt v Powerscourt* (1824) 1 Mol 616; *Felan v Russell* (1842) 4 I Eq R 701; *Re Darling, Farquhar v Darling* [1896] 1 Ch 50.
19 *Re Barker's Will Trusts, Barker v Crouch* (1948) 64 TLR 273.
20 *Townsend v Carus* (1844) 3 Hare 257.
21 *A-G v Stepney* (1804) 10 Ves 22.
22 *Thornton v Howe* (1862) 31 Beav 14; *Re Watson, Hobbs v Smith* [1973] 3 All ER 678, [1973] 1 WLR 1472.
23 *Re McCarthy* [1958] IR 311. It does not appear that this decision depended on any characteristic peculiar to Irish law.
24 *Re Maguire* (1870) LR 9 Eq 632.
25 *Re Delmar Charitable Trust* [1897] 2 Ch 163 (defence of doctrines of the Reformation).
26 *A-G v Becher* [1910] 2 IR 251 (conversion of Roman Catholics to Protestantism).
27 *Re Clergy Society* (1856) 2 K & J 615.
28 *Re Clergy Society* (1856) 2 K & J 615.
29 *R v Income Tax Special Comrs, ex p Essex Hall* [1911] 2 KB 434, CA.
30 *Trustees of City of Belfast YMCA v Northern Ireland Valuation Comr* [1969] NI 3, CA.
31 *Re Smith, Walker v Battersea General Hospital* (1938) 54 TLR 851; cf *Re Church Army* (1906) 75 LJCh 467, CA.
32 *Re Smith, Walker v Battersea General Hospital* (1938) 54 TLR 851; and see *Re Fowler, Fowler v Booth* (1914) 31 TLR 102, CA.
33 *Re White, White v White* [1893] 2 Ch 41 at 53, CA. See *Re Macduff, Macduff v Macduff* [1896] 2 Ch 451 at 466, CA, per Lindley LJ, and at 474, per Rigby LJ. See also the consideration of *Re White, White v White*, in *Re Smith's Will Trusts, Barclays Bank Ltd v Mercantile Bank Ltd* [1961] 3 All ER 824, [1961] 1 WLR 1387; on appeal [1962] 2 All ER 563, [1962] 1 WLR 763, CA.
34 *Trustees of City of Belfast YMCA v Northern Ireland Valuation Comr* [1969] NI 3, CA.

29. Religious denominations. There is no distinction in the matter of charity between one sort of religion and another, whether monotheistic, polytheistic or non-theistic[1], or between one sect and another[2], or between the established church and other churches[3]. Gifts to 'the Church of England'[4] or 'the Church of Rome'[5] for its use are charitable. The advancement of the Roman Catholic and Jewish religions and of all dissenting denominations, and the maintenance and benefit of their schools and chapels are also charitable purposes[6]; the promotion of faith-healing is charitable, perhaps as being for the advancement of religion[7], and the Charity Commission has accepted the registration of a spiritualist church[8]. However, gifts for denominational institutions or purposes are not necessarily for religious purposes, and are therefore not charitable[9].

1 In addition to many Christian sects, the Charity Commission has registered trusts for the advancement of the Hindu, Sikh, Islamic and Buddhist religions; and see PARA 27. As to the Charity Commission see PARAS 543–578.
2 *Thornton v Howe* (1862) 31 Beav 14 at 19–20 per Romilly MR; *Re Watson, Hobbs v Smith* [1973] 3 All ER 678, [1973] 1 WLR 1472. As to the Unification Church see *Report of the Charity Commissioners for England and Wales for 1982* (HC Paper (1982–83) no 370) App C. The Attorney General appealed against the refusal of the Charity Commissioners to accede to his request to remove the trusts from the register, but the appeal was eventually discontinued: see the statement of the Attorney General in 126 HC Official Report (6th Series), 3 February 1988 cols 977–978, and the debate in the House of Lords, 493 HL Official Report (5th Series), 10 February 1988, col 247 et seq. As to the Attorney General see PARAS 589, 596, 605 et seq; and CONSTITUTIONAL AND ADMINISTRATIVE LAW vol 20 (2014) PARA 273 et seq.
3 *Gilmour v Coats* [1949] AC 426 at 458, [1949] 1 All ER 848 at 862, HL, per Lord Reid.
4 *Re Barnes, Simpson v Barnes* (1922) [1930] 2 Ch 80n.
5 *Re Schoales, Schoales v Schoales* [1930] 2 Ch 75.
6 See *Neville Estates Ltd v Madden* [1962] Ch 832, [1961] 3 All ER 769. See also *Application for Registration of Good News for Israel*, Decision of the Charity Commissioners, 5 February 2004. As to decisions of the Charity Commission see PARA 547.

7 *Re Kerin* (1966) Times, 24 May, although on appeal the order in this case was wholly set aside by consent. However faith healing even without a religious element has been recognised as charitable: *Re Le Cren Clarke, Funnell v Stewart* [1996] 1 All ER 715, [1996] 1 WLR 288.

8 It was formerly doubtful whether the promotion of spiritualism is charitable (cf *Re Hummeltenberg, Beatty v London Spiritualistic Alliance Ltd* [1923] 1 Ch 237), but more recently the Charity Commission has registered a spiritualist church: *Sacred Hands Spiritual Centre's Application for Registration as a Charity* [2006] WTLR 873.

9 *MacLaughlin v Campbell* [1906] 1 IR 588 (Roman Catholic purposes: not charitable); *Re Stratton, Knapman v A-G* [1931] 1 Ch 197, CA (bequest to vicar for time being of parish for parochial institutions or purposes: not charitable); *Re Jackson, Midland Bank Executor and Trustee Co Ltd v Archbishop of Wales* [1930] 2 Ch 389 (bequest to archbishop to be applied in any manner he might think best for helping to carry on the work of the Church in Wales: not charitable); *Trustees of Cookstown Roman Catholic Church v IRC* (1953) 34 TC 350 (religious, educational and other parochial requirements: not charitable). See also *Application for Registration of Good News for Israel*, Decision of the Charity Commissioners, 5 February 2004.

30. Missionary purposes. The expression 'missionary purposes' is ambiguous and may comprise objects which are not charitable[1]; but the context[2] or surrounding circumstances[3] may show that the testator used the expression in the more restricted, popular sense of Christian missionary work, in which sense a gift for missionary purposes is charitable[4].

Carrying out missionary and outreach work are expressly envisaged by the Charity Commission as ways of advancing religion[5].

1 *Re Rees, Jones v Evans* [1920] 2 Ch 59; *Scott v Brownrigg* (1881) 9 LR Ir 246.

2 *Dunne v Duignan* [1908] 1 IR 228 (where, also, the words 'foreign missions' were distinguished from 'missionary purposes'); *Re Hall, Hall v Hall* (1915) 31 TLR 396 (the City Mission in London); *Jackson v A-G* [1917] 1 IR 332 (Presbyterian missions and orphans); *Re Moon's Will Trusts, Foale v Gillians* [1948] 1 All ER 300 (bequest to trustees of named church for mission work in district served by it).

3 *Re Rees, Jones v Evans* [1920] 2 Ch 59; *Re Kenny, Clode v Andrews* (1907) 97 LT 130; *Re Redish, Armfield-Marrow v Bennet* (1909) 26 TLR 42; *Re Moon's Will Trusts, Foale v Gillians* [1948] 1 All ER 300.

4 See the cases cited in notes 2–3; and *A-G v Becher* [1910] 2 IR 251; *Income Tax Special Purposes Comrs v Pemsel* [1891] AC 531, HL.

5 See *Charitable purposes* (Charity Commission, September 2013) para 5 (available, at the date at which this volume states the law, on the government website). As to the Charity Commission's publications see PARA 547.

31. Support of clergy and church purposes. The following purposes are charitable: the establishment of a bishopric[1], the provision of clergy[2] or preachers[3], or the increase of their stipends[4], even though conditional upon their preaching certain doctrines[5] or a sermon in commemoration of the testator[6], or permitting free sittings[7], or wearing a black gown in the pulpit[8], or preaching to a particular class of persons such as prisoners[9], or making certain payments[10], or upon condition that the benefice is never held in plurality[11].

A society of clergymen holding meetings to discuss pastoral matters and education is charitable, so that a gift to pay the expenses of the members' dinners, in order to encourage attendance at meetings, was held charitable[12]; as were gifts for the augmentation of livings or for the purchase of advowsons for the spread of particular religious views[13], and trusts for the benefit of parishioners to nominate the parson[14].

A gift for the assistance of the education of candidates for holy orders[15], or of a rentcharge to a vicar so long as he forgoes tithes[16], or for pensioning a perpetual curate, is charitable[17]. A gift to a society for the relief of infirm, sick and aged Roman Catholic secular priests in a particular diocese[18], and a gift for active or retired evangelistic workers, including missionaries, required to be

Protestants and to hold certain beliefs, tend to the advancement of religion and are charitable[19]. A gift of cottages to be used as rest homes for retired aged missionaries is charitable[20].

A gift to a parish church is charitable, having been regarded formerly as for the benefit of the parson and parishioners and their successors for ever[21], and latterly as for church purposes, that is, purposes connected with the services of the church[22]. Gifts, also, for such objects connected with a church as the minister shall think fit[23], for church expenses generally[24], or to provide a clerk[25], a sexton[26], an organist[27] or choristers[28], are charitable; but gifts for parish work or purposes[29] are not, and gifts for diocesan purposes[30] may not be, charitable, not being restricted to the advancement of religion. A gift for the benefit of the choir of a parish church serves to maintain and improve the religious services of the church, and so is for the advancement of religion and charitable[31]. In the context of a particular will, a church may be entitled under a gift to charitable institutions[32].

1 *A-G v Bishop of Chester* (1785) 1 Bro CC 444.

2 *Dundee Magistrates v Dundee Presbytery* (1861) 4 Macq 228, HL; *Pennington v Buckley* (1848) 6 Hare 451 at 453 per Wigram V-C (gift for benefit of unbeneficed curates).

3 *Pember v Knighton* (1639) Duke 381; *Penstred v Payer* (1639) Duke 381; *Grieves v Case* (1792) 4 Bro CC 67; cf *Re Braham, Daw v Samuel* (1892) 36 Sol Jo 712 (reader and lecturer for Hebrew congregation).

4 *A-G v Brereton* (1752) 2 Ves Sen 425; *A-G v Sparks* (1753) Amb 201; *Middleton v Clitherow* (1798) 3 Ves 734; *Widmore v Woodroffe* (1766) Amb 636 (Queen Anne's Bounty); *Gibson v Representative Church Body* (1881) 9 LR Ir 1; *Re Maguire* (1870) LR 9 Eq 632 (gift to Additional Curates' Aid Society); *Re Macnamara, Hewitt v Jeans* (1911) 104 LT 771.

5 *A-G v Molland* (1832) 1 You 562.

6 *Durour v Motteux* (1749) 1 Ves Sen 320; *Re Parker's Charity* (1863) 32 Beav 654; cf *Re Arber, Taylor v Shelton* (1919) Times, 13 December (annual payment to church bellringers in consideration of their ringing the bells on the anniversary of testator's death: not charitable).

7 *Re Randell, Randell v Dixon* (1888) 38 ChD 213.

8 *Re Robinson, Wright v Tugwell* [1897] 1 Ch 85, CA. As to subsequent removal of condition see *Re Robinson, Wright v Tugwell* [1923] 2 Ch 332; and PARA 180.

9 *Re Hussey's Charities, Cheyne v Apreece, Symons v Delaval* (1861) 30 LJCh 491.

10 *Re Corcoran, Corcoran v O'Kane* [1913] 1 IR 1.

11 *Re Macnamara, Hewitt v Jeans* (1911) 104 LT 771.

12 *Re Charlesworth, Robinson v Archdeacon of Cleveland* (1910) 101 LT 908.

13 *Re Hunter, Hood v A-G* [1897] 2 Ch 105, CA. However, such gifts are not charitable if no trust of the advowson is declared, on which ground the House of Lords reversed this decision: *Hunter v A-G* [1899] AC 309, HL. The sale of advowsons is now prohibited: see the Patronage (Benefices) Measure 1986 s 3(1); and ECCLESIASTICAL LAW vol 34 (2011) PARA 583.

14 *Re St Stephen, Coleman Street, Re St Mary the Virgin, Aldermanbury* (1888) 39 ChD 492; *Hunter v A-G* [1899] AC 309 at 322, HL, per Lord Davey; *Foley v A-G* (1721) 7 Bro Parl Cas 249, HL; *A-G v Scott* (1750) 1 Ves Sen 413; *A-G v Webster* (1875) LR 20 Eq 483 at 491 per Jessel MR. Cf on the other hand *A-G v Parker* (1747) 1 Ves Sen 43; *A-G v Forster* (1804) 10 Ves 335 at 340 per Lord Eldon LC; *A-G v Newcombe* (1807) 14 Ves 1 at 10 per Lord Eldon LC, where such a trust was considered valid but not charitable. See also *Edenborough v Archbishop of Canterbury* (1826) 2 Russ 93. However, a trust of an advowson merely to appoint a fit and proper person to fill the vacant living, without any beneficiary, is not charitable: *Re Church Patronage Trust, Laurie v A-G* [1904] 2 Ch 643, CA.

15 *Re Williams, Public Trustee v Williams* [1927] 2 Ch 283.

16 *Milbank v Lambert* (1860) 28 Beav 206. As to tithes see ECCLESIASTICAL LAW vol 34 (2011) PARA 975 et seq.

17 *A-G v Parker* (1747) 1 Ves Sen 43. See also *A-G v Brereton* (1752) 2 Ves Sen 425 at 426–427 per Lord Hardwicke LC.

18 *Re Forster, Gellatly v Palmer* [1939] Ch 22, [1938] 3 All ER 767. This gift could not, however, be upheld as being for the relief of poverty.

19 *Re Mylne, Potter v Dow* [1941] Ch 204, [1941] 1 All ER 405. Cf *Baptist Union of Ireland (Northern) Corpn Ltd v IRC* [1945] NI 99 (fund for Baptist ministers who paid subscriptions and their widows and orphans: charitable).

20 *Re White's Will Trusts, Barrow v Gillard* [1955] Ch 188, [1954] 2 All ER 620.
21 *Re St Andrew, Holborn* (undated) cited in *Cheeseman v Partridge* (1739) 1 Atk 436 at 437.
22 *Re Gare, Filmer v Carter* [1952] Ch 80, [1951] 2 All ER 863. See further PARA 119.
23 *Re Bain, Public Trustee v Ross* [1930] 1 Ch 224, CA (gift to vicar for such objects connected with the church as he should think fit; church objects and parochial activities distinguished); *Re Martley, Simpson v Cardinal Bourne* (1931) 47 TLR 392 (for the benefit of the work of the cathedral); *Re Eastes, Pain v Paxon* [1948] Ch 257, [1948] 1 All ER 536 (gift to vicar and churchwardens of a particular church for any purposes in connection with the church). However, see also *Re Stratton, Knapman v A-G* [1931] 1 Ch 197, CA (gift to vicar of parish 'for parochial institutions or purposes': not charitable); *Re Davies, Lloyds Bank Ltd v Mostyn* (1932) 49 TLR 5, CA (gift to archbishop for work connected with the Roman Catholic church in the archdiocese: not charitable); *Farley v Westminster Bank Ltd* [1939] AC 430, [1939] 3 All ER 491, HL (gift to vicars and churchwardens of named churches for parish work: not charitable).
24 *Re Scowcroft, Ormrod v Wilkinson* [1898] 2 Ch 638 at 642 per Stirling J.
25 *Durour v Motteux* (1749) 1 Ves Sen 320.
26 *Durour v Motteux* (1749) 1 Ves Sen 320.
27 *A-G v Oakaver* (1736) cited in 1 Ves Sen 536; *Re Scowcroft, Ormrod v Wilkinson* [1898] 2 Ch 638. Cf *Re Arber, Taylor v Shelton* (1919) Times, 13 December (see note 6).
28 *Turner v Ogden* (1787) 1 Cox Eq Cas 316. The contrary decision in *A-G v Oakaver* (1736) cited in 1 Ves Sen 536 was discussed and not followed in *Re Royce, Turner v Wormald* [1940] Ch 514, [1940] 2 All ER 291.
29 *Farley v Westminster Bank Ltd* [1939] AC 430, [1939] 3 All ER 491, HL (work); *Trustees of Cookstown Roman Catholic Church v IRC* (1953) 34 TC 350; *Re Stratton, Knapman v A-G* [1931] 1 Ch 197, CA.
30 *Re Rumball, Sherlock v Allan* [1956] Ch 105, [1955] 3 All ER 71, CA; *Re Van Wart, Ramsay v Bourne* (1911) Times, 17 February (this report is misleading: see the order made in the case, set out in *Re Rumball, Sherlock v Allan* [1956] Ch 105 at 119, [1955] 3 All ER 71 at 78, CA); *Re Beddy* (1953) unreported, discussed in *Re Rumball, Sherlock v Allan*; *Re Davies, Lloyds Bank Ltd v Mostyn* (1932) 49 TLR 5, CA; contra, *Re Macgregor, Thompson v Ashton* (1932) 32 SRNSW 483, NSW SC (gift for diocesan purposes charitable).
31 *Re Royce, Turner v Wormald* [1940] Ch 514, [1940] 2 All ER 291; and see *Re Hendry, Watson v Blakeney* (1887) 56 LT 908 (choir fund apparently charitable).
32 *Re Nesbitt's Will Trusts, Dr Barnardo's Homes National Incorporated Association v United Newcastle-upon-Tyne Hospitals Board of Governors* [1953] 1 All ER 936, [1953] 1 WLR 595.

32. Gifts to holders of religious offices. If a gift is expressed to be made to the holder of a particular religious office for the time being, it must be determined whether it is intended as a beneficial gift to the person holding that office when the gift takes effect[1], or whether it is to be held by that person and his successors in office as trustees[2].

If the latter is found to be the case, and if the duties and functions of the office are charitable in nature, the gift will be interpreted as a gift on trust for the charitable purposes inherent in the office[3]. Thus the following gifts were charitable: gifts to a minister and his successors[4], to a dissenting minister for the time being[5], to a vicar and churchwardens for the time being to be applied as they think fit, without any specified object[6], to a vicar[7], and to women holding certain offices in a religious order or their successors[8].

Where the gift is not merely expressed to be to the holder of a religious office and other words are added which might themselves indicate the nature of the trusts imposed by the gift, the court has to decide whether the words following the gift are intended merely to indicate that, within the scope of the trusts properly appropriate to the nature of the office by which the donee is described, the discretion is entirely the donee's, or whether by the added words the donor is himself intending to state, or at least to indicate, the trusts on which the donee is to hold the property[9].

In the former case the added words do not render inapplicable the prima facie presumption that the gift is charitable; in the latter case the question is whether the trusts indicated by the added words are themselves exclusively charitable. Thus the following gifts are charitable: gifts to a named vicar for his work[10], to the vicar of a named church to be used for his work in the parish[11], to a Roman Catholic archbishop to be used for such purposes as he should think fit[12], one to be applied as directed by a bishop for the general purposes of his diocese[13], and a gift to the editors of a missionary periodical for such objects as they might think fit, being construed as intended for the benefit of associated missionary activities for which they distributed gifts[14]. On the other hand, a gift to a Roman Catholic archbishop and his successors to be used and expended wholly or in part as he might judge most conducive to religion in the diocese is not charitable[15], for where the trusts of a gift are clearly set out they cannot be modified or limited in scope by reference to the position or character of the trustee[16]. Where the holder of the charitable office in question is not given sole control over the application of the property, the presumption that the purposes of the gift are the charitable purposes of the office does not apply[17].

1 See eg *Re Meehan, Tobin and Tobin v Cohalan and Meehan* [1960] IR 82 (gift to a bishop for the time being absolutely: an 'O'Hagan clause', ie designed to catch any charitable legacies which might fail under the law of mortmain or otherwise, so that the purpose of the clause would be frustrated if it had been held to be a gift on charitable trusts); see also *Re Van Wart, Ramsay v Bourne* (1911) Times, 17 February, as explained in *Re Rumball, Sherlock v Allan* [1956] Ch 105, [1955] 3 All ER 71, CA. As to the repeal of the law of mortmain see PARA 84.

2 In the absence of special considerations such as those indicated in note 1, a gift in virtue of office must be a gift on trust: see *Re Flinn, Public Trustee v Flinn* [1948] Ch 241 at 244, [1948] 1 All ER 541 at 542 per Jenkins J.

3 *Re Flinn, Public Trustee v Flinn* [1948] Ch 241, [1948] 1 All ER 541. The principle is not confined to the holders of religious offices, but most of the cases are in this field. See, however, *Re Spensley's Will Trusts, Barclays Bank Ltd v Staughton* [1954] Ch 233, [1954] 1 All ER 178, CA (National Trust); *Re Endacott, Corpe v Endacott* [1960] Ch 232, [1959] 3 All ER 562, CA (parish council).

4 *A-G v Molland* (1832) 1 You 562; *Thornber v Wilson* (1855) 3 Drew 245 (gift to the Roman Catholic minister of a particular chapel for a period of years); *Re Davies, Lloyd v Cardigan County Council* [1915] 1 Ch 543.

5 *A-G v Cock* (1751) 2 Ves Sen 273; *A-G v Sparks* (1753) Amb 201. The same does not apply to a gift for the particular minister in office: *Doe d Phillips v Aldridge* (1791) 4 Term Rep 264.

6 *Re Garrard, Gordon v Craigie* [1907] 1 Ch 382; see also *Thornber v Wilson* (1855) 3 Drew 245; *Re Delany, Conoley v Quick* [1902] 2 Ch 642 at 646 per Farwell J; and distinguish cases where the gift fails for uncertainty: *Fowler v Fowler* (1864) 33 Beav 616.

7 *Re Simson, Fowler v Tinley* [1946] Ch 299, [1946] 2 All ER 220.

8 *Re Delany, Conoley v Quick* [1902] 2 Ch 642. See, however, PARA 9.

9 See *Re Rumball, Sherlock v Allan* [1956] Ch 105 at 115, [1955] 3 All ER 71 at 75, CA, per Lord Evershed MR. See also *Re Spensley's Will Trusts, Barclays Bank Ltd v Staughton* [1954] Ch 233, [1954] 1 All ER 178, CA.

10 See *Re Simson, Fowler v Tinley* [1946] Ch 299, [1946] 2 All ER 220.

11 *Re Simson, Fowler v Tinley* [1946] Ch 299, [1946] 2 All ER 220, distinguishing *Farley v Westminster Bank Ltd* [1939] AC 430, [1939] 3 All ER 491, HL.

12 *Re Flinn, Public Trustee v Flinn* [1948] Ch 241, [1948] 1 All ER 541, distinguishing *Re Davidson, Minty v Bourne* [1909] 1 Ch 567, CA (gift to Roman Catholic archbishop for the time being to be distributed between charitable, religious or other societies, institutions, persons or objects in connection with the Roman Catholic faith in England); *Re Rumball, Sherlock v Allan* [1956] Ch 105, [1955] 3 All ER 71, CA (gift to bishop for the time being to be used as he thinks fit in his diocese: charitable).

13 *Re Money's Will Trusts, Mawdesley v Jerusalem and East Mission* (1965) 109 Sol Jo 68 (where the principle was applied even though the bishop was not the trustee of the fund, since his power to direct the purposes for which the property should be applied was clearly a fiduciary one). See also the comments of Jenkins LJ in *Re Rumball, Sherlock v Allan* [1956] Ch 105 at 124, [1955] 3 All ER 71 at 81, CA, on *Re Beddy* (1953, unreported).

14 *Re Norman, Andrew v Vine* [1947] Ch 349, [1947] 1 All ER 400.

15 *Dunne v Byrne* [1912] AC 407, PC; and see *Re Davidson, Minty v Bourne* [1909] 1 Ch 567, CA; *Re Stratton, Knapman v A-G* [1931] 1 Ch 197, CA; *Re Davies, Lloyds Bank Ltd v Mostyn* (1932) 49 TLR 5, CA; *Farley v Westminster Bank Ltd* [1939] AC 430, [1939] 3 All ER 491, HL.

16 *Dunne v Byrne* [1912] AC 407 at 410, PC, per Lord Macnaghten. Conversely, where the expressed trusts are charitable they cannot be rendered non-charitable by the character of the trustees: *Re Arthur McDougall Fund Trusts, Thompson v Fitzgerald* [1956] 3 All ER 867, [1957] 1 WLR 81; *Construction Industry Training Board v A-G* [1971] 3 All ER 449, [1971] 1 WLR 1303; affd without dealing with this point [1973] Ch 173, [1972] 2 All ER 1339, CA.

17 *Re Spensley's Will Trusts, Barclays Bank Ltd v Staughton* [1954] Ch 233, [1954] 1 All ER 178, CA, disapproving on this point Vaisey J at [1952] Ch 886, [1952] 2 All ER 49.

33. **Religious buildings and burial grounds.** The following have been held to be charitable purposes: the provision, maintenance, repair and ornamentation of a parish church[1] or of a church, chapel or meeting house of any particular Christian denomination[2], the upkeep of a chapel and Sunday school, which may include maintaining both the fabric and the services[3], the provision or repair of a chancel[4], spire[5], organ[6], bells[7], gallery[8], clock[9], stained-glass window[10], or monument in a church[11] and the continuation of the seating in a parish church[12].

Gifts for maintaining or providing a churchyard[13] or cemetery[14], or a burial ground for a particular sect[15], or for headstones to the graves of certain almshouse pensioners[16], are also charitable, as is the repair of a parsonage[17].

A company established to promote cheap and sanitary methods of disposing of the dead, in particular cremation, has been held to be established for charitable purposes by analogy with the cases on burial[18].

1 *Re Robertson, Colin v Chamberlin* [1930] 2 Ch 71; *Re Parker* (1859) 4 H & N 666; *Clephane v Edinburgh Magistrates* (1864) 4 Macq 603, HL; *A-G v Ruper* (1722) 2 P Wms 125; *A-G v Brown* (1818) 1 Swan 265 at 297 per Lord Eldon LC; *A-G v Vivian* (1826) 1 Russ 226; *A-G v Love* (1857) 23 Beav 499; *Re Donington Church Estate, Re Charitable Trusts Act 1853* (1860) 2 LT 10; *Re Church Estate Charity, Wandsworth* (1871) 6 Ch App 296; *A-G v Dartmouth Corpn* (1883) 48 LT 933; *Re St Alphage, London Wall* (1888) 59 LT 614; *Re Eighmie, Colbourne v Wilks* [1935] Ch 524 (maintenance of parish church and its decorations).

2 *Re Manser, A-G v Lucas* [1905] 1 Ch 68 at 73 per Warrington J; *Re Williams, James v Williams* (1910) 26 TLR 307 (liquidation of debts on Congregational chapels); *Holmes v A-G* (1981) Times, 12 February (meeting room of the Exclusive Brethren, formerly the Plymouth Brethren); *Broxtowe Borough Council v Birch* [1981] RA 215.

3 *Re Strickland's Will Trusts, National Guarantee and Suretyship Association Ltd v Maidment* [1936] 3 All ER 1027.

4 *Hoare v Osborne* (1866) LR 1 Eq 585.

5 *Re Palatine Estate Charity* (1888) 39 ChD 54.

6 *A-G v Oakaver* (1736) cited in 1 Ves Sen 536.

7 *Turner v Ogden* (1787) 1 Cox Eq Cas 316; and see *Re Palatine Estate Charity* (1888) 39 ChD 54 at 59 per Stirling J.

8 *A-G v Day* [1900] 1 Ch 31.

9 *Re Church Estate Charity, Wandsworth* (1871) 6 Ch App 296; *Re Hendry, Watson v Blakeney* (1887) 56 LT 908.

10 *Re King, Kerr v Bradley* [1923] 1 Ch 243.

11 *Hoare v Osborne* (1866) LR 1 Eq 585; *Re Rigley's Trusts* (1866) 36 LJCh 147; *Re Barker, Sherrington v Dean and Chapter of St Paul's Cathedral* (1909) 25 TLR 753. As to tombs and monuments not forming part of a church see PARA 61.

12 *Re Raine, Walton v A-G* [1956] Ch 417, [1956] 1 All ER 355.

13 *Re Vaughan, Vaughan v Thomas* (1886) 33 ChD 187; *Re Douglas, Douglas v Simpson* [1905] 1 Ch 279; *Re Eighmie, Colbourne v Wilks* [1935] Ch 524 (bequest to rector and churchwardens for keeping burial ground and private monument in it in repair; grave and monument in cemetery adjoining churchyard which had been closed for burials).

14 *A-G v Blizard* (1855) 21 Beav 233.

15 *Re Manser, A-G v Lucas* [1905] 1 Ch 68 (bequest for maintenance of Quaker burial ground).

16 *Re Pardoe, McLaughlin v A-G* [1906] 2 Ch 184. As to private tombs see PARA 61.

17 *A-G v Bishop of Chester* (1785) 1 Bro CC 444.

18 *Scottish Burial Reform and Cremation Society Ltd v Glasgow Corpn* [1968] AC 138, [1967] 3 All ER 215, HL. However, this probably now falls under the thirteenth category of charitable purpose, as a purpose recognised as charitable under existing law but not listed in the Charities Act 2011 s 3(1)(a)–(l) (see PARA 2), rather than the advancement of religion: see s 3(1)(m); and PARAS 2, 56.

(iv) The Advancement of Health or the Saving of Lives

34. Advancement of health and the saving of lives. A purpose is charitable under the fourth statutory description of charitable purposes if it is for the advancement of health or the saving of lives[1], which purposes include the prevention or relief of sickness, disease or human suffering[2], as well as the promotion of health[3]. Accordingly there is considerable overlap with the relief of those in need by reason of age, ill-health and disability[4].

The relief of sickness extends beyond the treatment or provision of care, such as a hospital, to the provision of items, services and facilities to ease the suffering or assist the recovery of people who are sick, convalescent, disabled or infirm or to provide comforts for patients[5]. The relief of illness may be through complementary and alternative medicine[6]. Institutions that provide rescue services, such as lifeboats, mountain rescue, fire, ambulance, air ambulance and first aid services, or which assist the work of the police and rescue services may be charitable under this category[7] in addition to being charitable for the promotion of the efficiency of the police, fire and rescue services or ambulance services[8].

As a purpose previously falling under the fourth head of charity[9], there must be a benefit to a definite community or section of the community[10]; it must be identifiable as such[11]; it must be of appreciable importance[12]; and it must not depend on any personal relationship to a particular individual or individuals[13]. Where the benefit does not extend to the whole community, the section of the community must be substantial enough to give the trust a public character[14]. What is a sufficiently substantial class may vary according to the nature of the benefit to be provided[15], and it is particularly important to keep in mind the necessary element of general public utility[16].

1 See the Charities Act 2011 s 3(1)(d); and PARA 2. The saving of lives includes a range of charitable activity directed towards saving people whose lives are in danger and protecting life and property: Charitable purposes (Charity Commission, September 2013) para 6 (available, at the date at which this volume states the law, on the government website). As to the Charity Commission's publications see PARA 547.

2 See the Charities Act 2011 s 3(2)(b); and PARA 2.

3 See *Charitable purposes* (Charity Commission, September 2013) para 6.

4 Ie under the Charities Act 2011 s 3(1)(j); and see PARA 43.

5 See *Charitable purposes* (Charity Commission, September 2013) para 6.

That guidance provides many examples of charities falling within this description including: hospitals and healing centres, and charities supporting their work or associated with them, eg hospital leagues of friends; hospital radio; medical research charities; charities providing services and facilities for medical practitioners, such as homes for nurses; charities that ensure the proper standards of medical practice, eg the General Medical Council; charities that promote activities that have a proven beneficial effect on health; charities set up to assist the victims of natural disasters or war; the provision of life saving or self-defence classes; the provision of blood transfusion services.

6 This is now encompassed within *Charitable purposes* (Charity Commission, September 2013) para 6. See *Application for Registration of NFSH Charitable Trust Ltd*, Decision of the Charity Commissioners, 15 August 2002, at para 7.7 in which it was held that promotion of spiritual healing was charitable as being for the relief of stress and the promotion of health, provided that the healer did not claim to diagnose illness, make unfounded claims to cure any illness and the

purpose of the healing was to promote relief of illness rather than to promote the well-being of healthy people. As to decisions of the Charity Commission see PARA 547.

7 See *Charitable purposes* (Charity Commission, September 2013) para 6.

8 Ie under the Charities Act 2011 s 3(1)(l); see PARAS 2, 45.

9 Ie the fourth division mentioned by Lord Macnaghten in *Income Tax Special Purposes Comrs v Pemsel* [1891] AC 531 at 583, HL, per Lord Macnaghten: see PARA 46.

10 *Verge v Somerville* [1924] AC 496 at 499, PC.

11 *Keren Kayemeth Le Jisroel Ltd v IRC* [1932] AC 650, HL; *Williams' Trustees v IRC* [1947] AC 447, [1947] 1 All ER 513, HL.

12 *National Anti-Vivisection Society v IRC* [1948] AC 31 at 65, [1947] 2 All ER 217 at 233, HL, per Lord Simonds; *Verge v Somerville* [1924] AC 496 at 499, PC.

13 *Oppenheim v Tobacco Securities Trust Co Ltd* [1951] AC 297 at 306, [1951] 1 All ER 31 at 34, HL, per Lord Simonds; *Re Compton, Powell v Compton* [1945] Ch 123, [1945] 1 All ER 198, CA.

14 See PARA 6.

15 *IRC v Baddeley* [1955] AC 572 at 615, [1955] 1 All ER 525 at 549, HL, per Lord Somervell of Harrow.

16 *IRC v Baddeley* [1955] AC 572 at 590, [1955] 1 All ER 525 at 532, HL, per Viscount Simonds.

(v) The Advancement of Citizenship or Community Development

35. Advancement of citizenship or community development. A purpose is charitable under the fifth statutory description of charitable purposes if it is for the advancement of citizenship or community development[1], which includes urban and rural regeneration[2] and the promotion of civic responsibility, volunteering, the voluntary sector or the effectiveness or efficiency of charities[3]. Activities which are charitable under this category include good citizenship award schemes[4], Scout and Guide groups[5] and social investment[6]. The promotion of 'community capacity building'[7], which the Charity Commission defines as developing the capacity and skills of the members of a community in such a way that they are better able to identify, and help meet, their needs and to participate more fully in society[8], for example by providing training or instruction or developing transferable skills such as team-working and problem solving[9], is also charitable.

For a purpose to be charitable it must also conform to the established requirements with regard to public benefit[10].

1 See the Charities Act 2011 s 3(1)(e); and PARA 2.

2 See the Charities Act 2011 s 3(2)(c)(i); and PARA 2. See also *RR2: The Promotion of Urban and Rural Regeneration* (Charity Commission, March 1999) (available, at the date at which this volume states the law, on the government website). As to the Charity Commission's publications see PARA 547.

3 See the Charities Act 2011 s 3(2)(c)(ii); and PARA 2. See also the *Report of the Charity Commissioners for England and Wales for 1990* (HC Paper (1990–91) no 362) App A(f) (to improve the efficiency of charities by the provision to charitable organisations of advice and assistance in the field of information technology is charitable); and the *Report for 1969* (HC Paper (1969–70) no 276) para 20.

4 See *Charitable purposes* (Charity Commission, September 2013) para 7 (available, at the date at which this volume states the law, on the government website).

5 See *Charitable purposes* (Charity Commission, September 2013) para 7. These purposes are also charitable as being for the advancement of education: see *Re Webber, Barclays Bank Ltd v Webber* [1954] 3 All ER 712, [1954] 1 WLR 1500, following *Re Alexander* (1932) Times, 30 June; and PARA 21 note 23.

6 See *Charitable purposes* (Charity Commission, September 2013) para 7. See also the *Decision of the Charity Commissioners to Register the Charity Bank Ltd as a Charity*, Decision of the Charity Commissioners, 17 April 2002. As to decisions of the Charity Commission see PARA 547.

7 See the *Charitable purposes* (Charity Commission, September 2013) para 7. See also *RR5: The Promotion of Community Capacity Building* (Charity Commission, November 2000).

8 See *RR5: The Promotion of Community Capacity Building* (Charity Commission, November 2000) para 7.
9 See *RR5: The Promotion of Community Capacity Building* (Charity Commission, November 2000) Annex A15.
10 See PARA 34 notes 9–16. As to public benefit generally see PARA 4 et seq.

(vi) The Advancement of the Arts, Culture, Heritage or Science

36. Advancement of the arts, culture, heritage or science. A purpose is charitable under the sixth statutory description of charitable purposes if it is for the advancement of the arts, culture, heritage or science[1]. Facilities the provision of which is charitable include a library[2], museum[3], public hall[4], reading room[5], botanical garden[6], observatory[7], or a war memorial of a useful character[8], where the facilities are open to the public[9]. A gift to the National Trust is charitable[10], as is a gift to promote the finding of the original manuscripts of plays attributed to Shakespeare[11]. There is clearly considerable scope for overlap between the advancement of the arts, culture, heritage or science and the advancement of education, and purposes may fall under both descriptions[12].

For a purpose to be charitable it must also conform to the established requirements with regard to public benefit[13].

1 See the Charities Act 2011 s 3(1)(f); and PARA 2. The concepts of 'arts', 'culture', 'heritage' and 'science' are undefined, but 'science' has been held to embrace a wide and ascertainable range of subjects: see *Weir v Crum-Brown* [1908] AC 162 at 168–169, HL, per Lord Macnaghten. See, however *Charitable purposes* (Charity Commission, September 2013) para 8 (available, at the date at which this volume states the law, on the government website), where the Commission sets out the meanings it gives to the terms. As to the Charity Commission's publications see PARA 547.
2 *Abbott v Fraser* (1874) LR 6 PC 96; *Re Scowcroft, Ormrod v Wilkinson* [1898] 2 Ch 638 at 642 per Stirling J.
3 *British Museum Trustees v White* (1826) 2 Sim & St 594; *Re Allsop, Gell v Carver* (1884) 1 TLR 4; *Re Holburne, Coates v Mackillop* (1885) 53 LT 212; and see *Re Scowcroft, Ormrod v Wilkinson* [1898] 2 Ch 638.

For guidance on the Charity Commission's approach to whether museums and art galleries are charitable, in particular by reference to whether the collections and exhibits satisfy the criterion a merit, see *RR10: Museums and art galleries* (Charity Commission, August 2002) (available, at the date at which this volume states the law, on the government website).
4 *Re Spence, Barclays Bank Ltd v Stockton-on-Tees Corpn* [1938] Ch 96, [1937] 3 All ER 684.
5 *Re Scowcroft, Ormrod v Wilkinson* [1898] 2 Ch 638.
6 *Townley v Bedwell* (1801) 6 Ves 194; *Harrison v Southampton Corpn* (1854) 2 Sm & G 387.
7 *Harrison v Southampton Corpn* (1854) 2 Sm & G 387.
8 *Murray v Thomas* [1937] 4 All ER 545; cf *Re Lord Mayor of Belfast's Air Raid Distress Fund* [1962] NI 161.
9 This does not, therefore, apply where the intention is to benefit the founder and subscribers only: *Thomson v Shakespear* (1860) John 612 at 616 per Page Wood V-C (affd 1 De GF & J 399 (museum)); *Carne v Long* (1860) 2 De GF & J 75 (library); *Re Prevost, Lloyds Bank Ltd v Barclays Bank Ltd* [1930] 2 Ch 383 (London Library); and see *Re Russell Institution, Figgins v Baghino* [1898] 2 Ch 72 (literary and scientific institution); *Re Jones, Clegg v Ellison* [1898] 2 Ch 83 (horticultural society); *Re Pitt Rivers, Scott v Pitt Rivers* [1902] 1 Ch 403, CA (museum and pleasure ground).
10 *Re Verrall, National Trust for Places of Historic Interest or Natural Beauty v A-G* [1916] 1 Ch 100; and see *Re Spensley's Will Trusts, Barclays Bank Ltd v Staughton* [1952] Ch 886, [1952] 2 All ER 49; revsd [1954] Ch 233, [1954] 1 All ER 178, CA. As to the National Trust see NATIONAL CULTURAL HERITAGE vol 77 (2010) PARA 979 et seq.
11 *Re Hopkins' Will Trusts, Naish v Francis Bacon Society Inc* [1965] Ch 669, [1964] 3 All ER 46. See also PARA 23.
12 For example, gifts to learned societies and institutions which advance the arts or science can be charitable under the second statutory description of charitable purposes: see PARA 25. See generally *Charitable purposes* (Charity Commission, September 2013) para 8.
13 See PARA 34 notes 9–16. As to public benefit generally see PARA 4 et seq.

(vii) The Advancement of Amateur Sport

37. Advancement of amateur sport. A purpose is charitable under the seventh statutory description of charitable purposes if it is for the advancement of amateur sport[1]. Dangerous sports which involve risks which go far beyond the usual risks of injury associated with energetic physical exercise, such as boxing or so-called 'extreme' sports, may not be conducive to physical health and institutions seeking charitable status will need to show medical evidence of the risks involved in the sport and details of the steps taken to minimise the dangers to personal safety if they are to be considered charitable under this purpose[2].

For a purpose to be charitable it must also conform to the established requirements with regard to public benefit[3].

For an amateur sports club to be charitable, open membership is essential if it is to meet the requirement of public benefit[4], save where reasonable restrictions are necessary to enable the club to operate effectively[5]. A club may operate a waiting list for membership on a first come, first served basis where it is oversubscribed[6], and is not required to provide facilities for the elderly or disabled[7]. For membership to be open, membership subscriptions must be affordable for the majority of the community the club serves[8], there must be no test of skill for admission[9], any clothing and equipment needed must be affordable[10], and the extent to which facilities and resources are devoted to competitive play must not damage the principle of genuinely open membership[11]. If the true purpose of a club is competitive success, and not community participation, it is not charitable[12].

1 See the Charities Act 2011 s 3(1)(g); and PARA 2. 'Sport' is defined as meaning sport or games which promote health by involving physical or mental skill or exertion: see s 3(2)(d); and PARA 2.

The Charity Commission's position was formerly that sport must be capable of improving physical health and fitness (see *RR11: Charitable Status and Sport* (Charity Commission, April 2003) para 7(ii) (available, at the date at which this volume states the law, on the government website)) but at the date at which this volume states the law this guidance is under review in light of the modern statutory definition of 'sport' set out in the Charities Act 2011 s 3(2)(d); in other respects, however, that guidance may be taken to represent the Charity Commission's approach with regard to this head of statutory purpose. Accordingly, the following activities may be sports notwithstanding the Charity Commission's assertion to the contrary: angling; ballooning; billiards, pool and snooker; crossbow, rifle and pistol shooting; flying; gliding; motor sports; parachuting. For an example see *Application for Registration of Hitchin Bridge Club*, Decision of the Charity Commission, 28 February 2011. As to decisions of the Charity Commission see PARA 547; and as to the Charity Commission's publications see PARA 547.

2 See *RR11: Charitable Status and Sport* (Charity Commission, April 2003) paras 22–24. If an organisation uses a dangerous sport as a means of achieving a different charitable purpose, the benefit to the public of the organisation's object may outweigh the dangers inherent in the sport: see *RR11: Charitable Status and Sport* (Charity Commission, April 2003) para 25.

3 See PARA 34 notes 9–16. As to public benefit generally see PARA 4 et seq.

4 See *RR11: Charitable Status and Sport* (Charity Commission, April 2003) para 14; and note 2. Although these guidelines are directed towards community amateur sports clubs, which, if registered with HMRC, are no longer charitable (see PARA 38), they remain (pending revision) relevant to other amateur sports clubs: *Charitable purposes* (Charity Commission, September 2013) para 9 (available, at the date at which this volume states the law, on the government website).

5 See *RR11: Charitable Status and Sport* (Charity Commission, April 2003) paras 14–17.

6 See *RR11: Charitable Status and Sport* (Charity Commission, April 2003) para 16. See also notes 2, 5.

7 See *RR11: Charitable Status and Sport* (Charity Commission, April 2003) para 21. There should, however, be no bar to participation by the elderly or disabled where the sport is suitable and the club's facilities can reasonably be used by these groups: para 21. See also notes 2, 5.

8 See *RR11: Charitable Status and Sport* (Charity Commission, April 2003) para 18. See also notes 2, 5.
9 See *RR11: Charitable Status and Sport* (Charity Commission, April 2003) para 19. See also notes 2, 5.
10 See *RR11: Charitable Status and Sport* (Charity Commission, April 2003) para 26. See also notes 2, 5.
11 See *RR11: Charitable Status and Sport* (Charity Commission, April 2003) para 27. See also notes 2, 5.
12 See *RR11: Charitable Status and Sport* (Charity Commission, April 2003) para 28. See also notes 2, 5.

38. Community amateur sports clubs. A registered sports club[1], that is, a sports club registered with Her Majesty's Revenue and Customs as a community amateur sports club (CASC), which is established for charitable purposes[2], is to be treated as not being so established, and accordingly cannot be a charity[3].

1 A 'registered sports club' means a registered club within the meaning of the Corporation Tax Act 2010 Pt 13, Ch 9 (community amateur sports clubs: see CAPITAL GAINS TAXATION vol 6 (2011) PARA 892): Charities Act 2011 s 6(2).
2 As to the meaning of 'charitable purpose' see PARA 2. As to the advancement of amateur sport as a charitable purpose see PARA 37.
3 Charities Act 2011 s 6(1). Thus a sports club can be registered as a charity or a CASC, but not both: *Charitable purposes* (Charity Commission, September 2013) para 9 (available, at the date at which this volume states the law, on the government website). It should be noted, therefore, that *RR11: Charitable Status and Sport* (Charity Commission, April 2003) (available, at the date at which this volume states the law, on the government website) (see PARA 37) must be read in light of that. As to the Charity Commission's publications see PARA 547.

(viii) The Advancement of Human Rights, Conflict Resolution or Reconciliation, or the Promotion of Religious or Racial Harmony or Equality and Diversity

39. Advancement of human rights. A purpose is charitable under the eighth statutory description of charitable purposes if it is for the advancement of human rights[1]. The advancement of human rights includes the following: monitoring abuses of human rights[2]; obtaining redress for victims of human rights abuse[3]; relieving need among the victims of human rights abuse or their dependants[4]; research into human rights issues[5]; educating the public about human rights[6]; technical advice to governments and others on human rights matters[7]; contributing to the sound administration of human rights law[8]; commenting on proposed human rights legislation[9]; raising awareness of human rights issues[10]; promoting popular support for human rights[11]; advocating the adoption of, and compliance with, international and regional codes of human rights, and the incorporation of human rights into domestic law[12]; and promoting respect for human rights by individuals and corporations[13].

It is charitable to pursue the elimination of infringements of human rights[14], and to encourage a government to respect its own human rights legislation[15]. Where a country's domestic law is inconsistent with international standards, a charity may campaign for legislation or changes in government policy provided that political means are not the dominant method by which the organisation will pursue its charitable objects[16].

For a purpose to be charitable it must also conform to the established requirements with regard to public benefit[17].

1 See the Charities Act 2011 s 3(1)(h); and PARA 2. See also *Charitable purposes* (Charity Commission, September 2013) para 10 (available, at the date at which this volume states the law, on the government website). As to the Charity Commission's publications see PARA 547.

2 See *RR12: The Promotion of Human Rights* (Charity Commission, January 2005) para 17.
3 See *RR12: The Promotion of Human Rights* (Charity Commission, January 2005) para 18.
4 See *RR12: The Promotion of Human Rights* (Charity Commission, January 2005) para 19. This purpose may also be charitable under the tenth statutory description of purposes as being for the relief of those in need by reason of disadvantage: see the Charities Act 2011 s 3(1)(j); and PARAS 2, 43.
5 See *RR12: The Promotion of Human Rights* (Charity Commission, January 2005) para 20. This purpose may also be charitable under the second statutory description of purposes as being for the advancement of education: see the Charities Act 2011 s 3(1)(b); see PARAS 2, 21 et seq.
6 See *RR12: The Promotion of Human Rights* (Charity Commission, January 2005) para 21. This purpose may also be charitable under the second statutory description of purposes as being for the advancement of education: see the Charities Act 2006 s 2(2)(b); see PARAS 2, 21 et seq.
7 See *RR12: The Promotion of Human Rights* (Charity Commission, January 2005) para 22.
8 See *RR12: The Promotion of Human Rights* (Charity Commission, January 2005) para 23.
9 See *RR12: The Promotion of Human Rights* (Charity Commission, January 2005) para 24.
10 See *RR12: The Promotion of Human Rights* (Charity Commission, January 2005) para 25.
11 See *RR12: The Promotion of Human Rights* (Charity Commission, January 2005) paras 26–28.
12 See *RR12: The Promotion of Human Rights* (Charity Commission, January 2005) paras 29–30.
13 See *RR12: The Promotion of Human Rights* (Charity Commission, January 2005) para 31.
14 See *RR12: The Promotion of Human Rights* (Charity Commission, January 2005) para 32. See also *Human Dignity Trust v Charity Commission for England and Wales* (2014) First-tier Tribunal, General Regulatory Chamber (Charity), 9 July.

Means of pursuing the elimination of infringement of human rights include: the procurement of the abolition of torture by all lawful means; the procurement of the abolition of torture, extra-judicial killing and disappearance; and the elimination of slavery, the slave trade and other forms of unlawful forced labour, where this does not involve trying to change the domestic law of any country: *RR12: The Promotion of Human Rights* (Charity Commission, January 2005) para 32.

15 See *RR12: The Promotion of Human Rights* (Charity Commission, January 2005) para 18. See also *Human Dignity Trust v Charity Commission for England and Wales* (2014) First-tier Tribunal, General Regulatory Chamber (Charity), 9 July.
16 See *RR12: The Promotion of Human Rights* (Charity Commission, January 2005) paras 31, 33–36. Where political means are the dominant method by which the purpose is pursued, the purpose is not charitable as being for a political purpose: paras 31, 33–36. As to political purposes see PARA 67.
17 See PARA 34 notes 9–16. As to public benefit generally see PARA 4 et seq.

40. Advancement of conflict resolution or reconciliation. A purpose is charitable under the eighth statutory description of charitable purposes if it is for the advancement of conflict resolution or reconciliation[1]. The advancement of conflict resolution and reconciliation includes: the resolution of international conflicts and relieving the suffering, poverty and distress arising through conflict on a national or international scale by identifying the causes of the conflict and seeking to resolve such conflict[2]; the promotion of restorative justice[3]; and purposes directed towards mediation, conciliation or reconciliation as between persons, organisations, authorities or groups involved or likely to become involved in dispute or inter-personal conflict[4].

For a purpose to be charitable it must also conform to the established requirements with regard to public benefit[5].

1 See the Charities Act 2011 s 3(1)(h); and PARA 2.
2 See also *Charitable purposes* (Charity Commission, September 2013) para 10 (available, at the date at which this volume states the law, on the government website). See also *Application for Registration of Charity of Concordis International Trust*, Decision of the Charity Commissioners, 23 July 2004. As to decisions of the Charity Commission see PARA 547; and as to the Charity Commission's publications see PARA 547.
3 See *Charitable purposes* (Charity Commission, September 2013) para 10. See also *Application for Registration of Restorative Justice Consortium Ltd*, Decision of the Charity Commissioners, 15 January 2003.

4 See *Charitable purposes* (Charity Commission, September 2013) para 10. See also *Report of the Charity Commissioners for England and Wales for 1983* (HC Paper (1983–84) no 447) paras 28–34 (family conciliation services charitable); and *Application for Registration of Charity of Concordis International Trust*, Decision of the Charity Commissioners, 23 July 2004 (mediating with parties to national or international conflict charitable).

5 See PARA 34 notes 9–16. As to public benefit generally see PARA 4 et seq.

41. Promotion of religious or racial harmony or equality and diversity. A purpose is charitable under the eighth statutory description of charitable purposes if it is for the promotion of religious or racial harmony or equality and diversity[1]. This includes a range of charitable activity directed towards actively promoting harmony and the lessening of conflict between people from differing races or religions or belief systems and eliminating discrimination and promoting diversity in society[2].

For a purpose to be charitable it must also conform to the established requirements with regard to public benefit[3].

1 See the Charities Act 2011 s 3(1)(h); and PARA 2.

2 See *Charitable purposes* (Charity Commission, September 2013) para 10 (available, at the date at which this volume states the law, on the government website). As to the Charity Commission's publications see PARA 547.

The Charity Commission had for some time prior to the reform of the law by the Charities Act 2006 accepted that promoting good race relations, endeavouring to eliminate discrimination on grounds of race and encouraging equality of opportunity between persons of different racial groups are prima facie charitable purposes: *Report of the Charity Commissioners for England and Wales for 1983* (HC Paper (1983–84) no 447) paras 15–20. This report, prepared before the decision in *Re Koeppler Will Trusts, Barclays Bank Trust Co Ltd v Slack* [1984] Ch 243, [1984] 2 All ER 111; revsd [1986] Ch 423, [1985] 2 All ER 869, CA, took the view that the authority of *Re Strakosch, Temperley v A-G* [1949] Ch 529, [1949] 2 All ER 6, CA (and by implication *Anglo-Swedish Society v IRC* (1931) 47 TLR 295) was undermined by the race relations legislation. The Inland Revenue did not challenge the view of the Charity Commissioners.

The promulgation of humanism has been accepted by the Charity Commission as a charitable purpose falling within this category: see PARA 50 text and note 13.

3 See PARA 34 notes 9–16. As to public benefit generally see PARA 4 et seq.

(ix) The Advancement of Environmental Protection or Improvement

42. Advancement of environmental protection or improvement. A purpose is charitable under the ninth statutory description of charitable purposes if it is for the advancement of environmental protection or improvement[1]. The advancement of environmental protection or improvement includes the conservation of a particular animal, bird, or other species or wildlife in general; a specific plant species, habitat or area of land, including areas of natural beauty and scientific interest; flora, fauna and the environment generally[2]. It is charitable to preserve vegetables valuable to man[3]. Independent expert evidence that is authoritative and objective may be required to show that a particular species, land or habitat to be conserved is worthy of conservation[4]. The promotion of sustainable development and biodiversity is charitable, as is the promotion of recycling and sustainable waste management and research projects into the use of renewable energy sources[5].

There is old authority to the effect that a trust to establish a refuge for animals and birds of all kinds is not charitable where that refuge is closed to the public as not affording any advantage to animals useful to mankind, or any protection from cruelty to animals generally[6]. However, the Charity Commission regards this as out of date, and has indicated that if an organisation can make out a case for the limiting or excluding of physical access to a site or property, it can still satisfy the public benefit requirement by putting in place alternative means of informing the public about the charity and its activities[7], for example through: (1) access to part of the site if access to the whole is harmful; (2) facilities to view the site from the outside; (3) viewing through video cameras, telescopes or other equipment, (4) computer simulations and internet sites; (5) TV and radio coverage; or (6) videos, books, discussions and lectures[8].

For a purpose to be charitable it must also conform to the established requirements with regard to public benefit[9].

1 See the Charities Act 2011 s 3(1)(i); and PARA 2.
2 See *Charitable purposes* (Charity Commission, September 2013) para 11 (available, at the date at which this volume states the law, on the government website). Cf *A-G v Whorwood* (1750) 1 Ves Sen 534 at 536 per Lord Hardwicke LC (not charitable to feed sparrows). Conservation purposes relating to fauna may also be charitable under the eleventh statutory description of purposes as being for the advancement of animal welfare: see the Charities Act 2011 s 3(1)(k); and PARA 44. As to the Charity Commission's publications see PARA 547.
3 *London University v Yarrow* (1857) 1 De G & J 72, 26 LJ Ch 430.
4 See *Charitable purposes* (Charity Commission, September 2013) para 11.
5 See *Charitable purposes* (Charity Commission, September 2013) para 11.
6 *Re Grove-Grady, Plowden v Lawrence* [1929] 1 Ch 557, [1929] All ER Rep 158, CA; compromised on appeal sub nom *A-G v Plowden* [1931] WN 89, 171 LT Jo 308, HL. See also *Re Glyn's Will Trusts* (1953) Times, 28 March (sanctuary for birds and wild flowers open to such members of the public as the trustees deem fit: not charitable).
7 See *RR9: Preservation and Conservation* (Charity Commission, February 2001) Annex paras A19–A21 (available, at the date at which this volume states the law, on the government website). See also *Re Sawtell* [1978] 2 NSWLR 200 at 211, NSW SC, per Holland J.
8 See *RR9: Preservation and Conservation* (Charity Commission, February 2001) Annex para A20.
9 See PARA 34 notes 9–16. As to public benefit generally see PARA 4 et seq.

(x) The Relief of Those in Need

43. Relief of those in need. A purpose is charitable under the tenth statutory description of charitable purposes if it is for the relief of those in need by reason of youth, age, ill-health, disability, financial hardship or other disadvantage[1], including relief given by the provision of accommodation or care to such persons[2].

Purposes for the relief of those in need by reason of youth include the prevention of cruelty to children[3] and the gift of a house to be maintained by a local authority as a children's home[4]. However, a gift for the general benefit and general welfare of children has been held not to be exclusively charitable[5].

Purposes for the relief of those in need by reason of age include: the provision of free cottages for old women of the working classes of the age of 60 or upwards[6]; and the maintenance of aged persons in a nursing home[7]. Gifts to the old people over 65 years of a named locality as trustees think best have been upheld as charitable[8]. Previously, aged persons have been held proper objects of charity under a gift not containing any express direction or indication of relief[9]; but it does not appear that the element of relief is necessarily implied in any gift to the aged. Persons not under 50 years of age were previously held to be aged[10].

The relief of those in need by reason of ill-health or disability includes a home of rest for those needing it[11], and gifts for patients in named hospitals[12], for the benefit of the blind[13], for the sick and for the wounded[14]. Faith-healing may be charitable as being for the relief of ill-health[15]. A gift to pay money to the eventual discoverers of the cause of and a cure for cancer was held to be exclusively charitable[16], as have gifts to religious communities having for their object the relief of the sick[17].

There is a clear overlap between the relief of those in need by reason of financial hardship and the relief of poverty[18]. Given the low threshold for what constitutes 'poverty', it is difficult to conceive of a purpose which would fall under the tenth statutory description of purposes but not under the first[19].

Other examples of the relief of those in need include the relief of refugees[20], a community providing a temporary home of rest and the comfort of friendship to those who need it[21], funds for the relief of victims of air raids[22] or floods[23], and the provision of housing such as almshouses, housing associations and Registered Social Landlords[24].

The social relief, resettlement and rehabilitation of persons under a disability or deprivation (including disaster funds) are charitable, though the Charity Commission's position is that these purposes fall under the thirteenth statutory description[25].

It seems that the Charity Commission regards the relief of unemployment as a charitable purpose, though it is not clear under which statutory description it falls[26].

For a purpose to be charitable it must also conform to the established requirements with regard to public benefit[27].

1 See the Charities Act 2011 s 3(1)(j); *Charitable purposes* (Charity Commission, September 2013) para 11 (available, at the date at which this volume states the law, on the government website); and PARA 2. As to the Charity Commission's publications see PARA 547.

2 See the Charities Act 2006 s 3(2)(e); and PARA 2.

3 *Income Tax Special Purposes Comrs v Pemsel* [1891] AC 531 at 572, HL, where, however, Lord Herschell discusses 'charity' in its popular sense.

4 *Re Sahal's Will Trusts, Alliance Assurance Co Ltd v A-G* [1958] 3 All ER 428, [1958] 1 WLR 1243.

5 *Re Cole, Westminster Bank Ltd v Moore* [1958] Ch 877, [1958] 3 All ER 102, CA.

6 *Re Glyn's Will Trusts, Public Trustee v A-G* [1950] 2 All ER 1150n. See, however, PARA 9.

7 *Re Bradbury, Needham v Reekie* [1950] 2 All ER 1150n, 94 Sol Jo 839. However, in *Re Duffy* [2013] EWHC 2395 (Ch) a gift to the amenity fund of a residential care home for the general benefit of the staff and residents was not charitable.

8 *Re Robinson, Davis v Robinson* [1951] Ch 198, [1950] 2 All ER 1148.

9 *Re Shepherd, Firman v Shepherd* (1952) unreported (trust to divide income equally among the 21 oldest inhabitants of a locality without a means test).

10 *Re Wall, Pomeroy v Willway* (1889) 42 ChD 510. However, the average expectation of life has increased since 1889, and a more advanced age might now be held to be the minimum.

11 Cf the preamble to the Charitable Uses Act 1601 (43 Eliz 1 c 4 (1601)) (now wholly repealed: see PARA 2 note 25; and PARA 46) and see *Re Estlin, Prichard v Thomas* (1903) 72 LJCh 687; *Re James, Grenfell v Hamilton* [1932] 2 Ch 25; *Re Chaplin, Neame v A-G* [1933] Ch 115; but see *Re Morris' Will Trusts* (1962) Times, 25 January, where a gift to provide a home of rest was held not to be intended to relieve the impotent.

12 *Re Roadley, Iveson v Wakefield* [1930] 1 Ch 524.

13 *Re Elliott, Raven v Nicholson* (1910) 102 LT 528; and *Re Fraser, Yeates v Fraser* (1883) 22 ChD 827.

14 *Re Hillier, Dauncey v Finch and A-G* [1944] 1 All ER 480.

15 *Re Kerin* (1966) Times, 24 May. However, on appeal the order in this case was wholly set aside by consent.

16 *Re Watson's Settlement Trusts, Dawson v Reid* [1959] 2 All ER 676, [1959] 1 WLR 732.

17 *Cocks v Manners* (1871) LR 12 Eq 574; *Re Delany, Conoley v Quick* [1902] 2 Ch 642, and cases there cited; *Re Banfield, Lloyds Bank Ltd v Smith* [1968] 2 All ER 276, [1968] 1 WLR 846.

18 Ie under the Charities Act 2011 s 3(1)(a): see PARAS 2, 12.

19 See PARA 13.

20 *Re Morrison, Wakefield v Falmouth* (1967) 111 Sol Jo 758.

21 *Re Banfield, Lloyds Bank Ltd v Smith* [1968] 2 All ER 276, [1968] 1 WLR 846.
22 *Re Lord Mayor of Belfast's Air Raid Distress Fund* [1962] NI 161; and see *Re Hobourn Aero Components Ltd's Air Raid Distress Fund, Ryan v Forrest* [1946] Ch 194 at 200, 202, [1946] 1 All ER 501 at 506, 507, CA, obiter per Lord Greene MR.
23 *Re North Devon and West Somerset Relief Fund Trusts, Baron Hylton v Wright* [1953] 2 All ER 1032, [1953] 1 WLR 1260.
24 See *Charitable purposes* (Charity Commission, September 2013) para 12. As to housing associations see **HOUSING** vol 56 (2011) PARA 11. As to Registered Social Landlords see **HOUSING** vol 56 (2011) PARA 123 et seq.
25 See *Charitable purposes* (Charity Commission, September 2013) para 15. As to the thirteenth statutory description see the Charities Act 2011 s 3(1)(m); and PARAS 2, 46.
26 See *RR3: Charities for the relief of unemployment* (Charity Commission, March 1999) (available, at the date at which this volume states the law, on the government website). However, in *Charitable purposes* (Charity Commission, September 2013), the Commission does not list this as an example purpose under either the tenth or the thirteenth statutory description.
27 See PARA 34 notes 9–16. As to public benefit generally see PARA 4 et seq.

(xi) The Advancement of Animal Welfare

44. Advancement of animal welfare. A purpose is charitable under the eleventh statutory description of charitable purposes if it is for the advancement of animal welfare[1]. Trusts for the protection or benefit of animals, whether useful to man or not, are charitable, as being calculated to promote human morality by encouraging kindness, discouraging cruelty and stimulating humane sentiments to the benefit of mankind[2], unless outweighed by consequences detrimental to the public benefit[3]. Accordingly the following gifts are charitable: gifts to such institutions as the RSPCA[4], a home for lost dogs[5] or for starving and forsaken cats[6], a veterinary college[7] and vegetarian societies[8], or to a periodical devoted to propaganda against cruelty to animals[9], or for the welfare of cats and kittens needing care and attention[10], or for the establishment of an animals' hospital[11], humane slaughterhouses[12], a fund to provide rewards for policemen for helping to bring to justice cases of cruelty to animals[13], and to preserve animals valuable to man[14]. Animal sanctuaries may be charitable under this category as well as under the ninth statutory description of charitable purposes as being for the advancement of environmental protection or improvement[15].

For a purpose to be charitable it must also conform to the established requirements with regard to public benefit[16].

1 See the Charities Act 2011 s 3(1)(k); and PARA 2. See also the *Charitable purposes* (Charity Commission, September 2013) para 13 (available, at the date at which this volume states the law, on the government website), which reflects many of the principles established by the cases set out in notes 2–15. As to the Charity Commission's publications see PARA 547.
2 *Re Wedgwood, Allen v Wedgwood* [1915] 1 Ch 113, CA; *Re Moss, Hobrough v Harvey* [1949] 1 All ER 495; *Re Green's Will Trusts, Fitzgerald-Hart v A-G* [1985] 3 All ER 455. Cf *Re Joy, Purday v Johnson* (1888) 60 LT 175; and see *A-G v Whorwood* (1750) 1 Ves Sen 534 at 536 per Lord Hardwicke LC (trust to feed sparrows: not charitable). Trusts for the prevention of cruelty to animals abroad are charitable: *Armstrong v Reeves* (1890) 25 LR Ir 325; *Re Jackson, Bell v Adlam* (1910) Times, 11 June. Gifts for the benefit of specific animals are not charitable: *Re Dean, Cooper-Dean v Stevens* (1889) 41 ChD 552; *Re Howard, Oakley v Aldridge* (1908) Times, 30 October. As to the enforceability of such gifts see PARA 60 note 25; and **TRUSTS AND POWERS** vol 98 (2013) PARA 8.

In appropriate circumstances, such protection or benefit may be extended to animals which are dangerous or harmful to man, despite Kennedy LJ's dicta otherwise in *Re Wedgwood, Allen v Wedgwood*: *Application for Registration of the Wolf Trust (formerly known as Wild Bite)*, Decision of the Charity Commissioners, 30 January 2003, para 4.2. As to decisions of the Charity Commission see PARA 547.

3 *National Anti-Vivisection Society v IRC* [1948] AC 31 at 41, 49, [1947] 2 All ER 217 at 219, 224, HL, per Lord Wright, and at 72–73 and 237 per Lord Simonds (anti-vivisection society not charitable, overruling *Re Foveaux, Cross v London Anti-Vivisection Society* [1895] 2 Ch 501); applied in *Animal Defence and Anti-Vivisection Society v IRC* (1950) 66 (pt 2) TLR 1091. See also *Hanchett-Stamford v A-G* [2008] EWHC 330 (Ch), [2009] Ch 173, [2008] 4 All ER 323, (prevention of cruelty to performing animals where this necessitates a change in the law is not charitable).

4 *Tatham v Drummond* (1864) 4 De GJ & Sm 484; *Armstrong v Reeves* (1890) 25 LR Ir 325 (Society of Carlsruhe for the Protection of Animals).

5 *Re Douglas, Obert v Barrow* (1887) 35 ChD 472, CA; *Adamson v Melbourne and Metropolitan Board of Works* [1929] AC 142 at 148, PC.

6 *Swifte v A-G for Ireland (No 2)* [1912] 1 IR 133.

7 *London University v Yarrow* (1857) 1 De G & J 72 at 80 per Lord Cranworth LC.

8 *Re Cranston, Webb v Oldfield* [1898] 1 IR 431, CA; *Re Slatter, Howard v Lewis* (1905) 21 TLR 295.

9 *Marsh v Means* (1857) 3 Jur NS 790; and see *Re Cranston, Webb v Oldfield* [1898] 1 IR 431 at 443, CA, per Lord Ashbourne LC (lectures).

10 *Re Moss, Hobrough v Harvey* [1949] 1 All ER 495.

11 *London University v Yarrow* (1857) 1 De G & J 72.

12 *Tatham v Drummond* (1864) 4 De GJ & Sm 484; and see *Re Wedgwood, Allen v Wedgwood* [1915] 1 Ch 113 at 116, CA, per Lord Cozens-Hardy MR; *Re Winton* (1953) Times, 31 January.

13 *Re Herrick, Colohan v A-G* (1918) 52 ILT 213. Cf *Re Hollywood, Smyth v A-G* (1917) 52 ILT 51.

14 *London University v Yarrow* (1857) 1 De G & J 72.

15 See the Charities Act 2011 s 3(1)(i); and PARAS 2, 42.

16 See PARA 34 notes 9–16. As to public benefit generally see PARA 4 et seq.

(xii) The Promotion of the Efficiency of the Armed Forces of the Crown, or of the Efficiency of the Police, Fire and Rescue Services or Ambulance Services

45. Efficiency of armed forces and of the police, fire, rescue or ambulance services. A purpose is charitable under the twelfth statutory description of charitable purposes if it is for the promotion of the efficiency of the armed forces of the Crown, or of the efficiency of the police, fire and rescue services or ambulance services[1].

This includes ensuring that those forces are properly trained and equipped during times of conflict; and providing facilities and benefits for the armed forces[2]. Similarly it is also charitable to promote the efficiency of the police, fire, rescue or ambulance services as they exist for the prevention and detection of crime, the preservation of public order and to protect the public[3].

Gifts tending to this end include a gift for the benefit of a volunteer corps[4], for teaching shooting[5], for the maintenance of a library for a regimental officers' mess[6] or for the mess generally[7], to form a regimental fund for the promotion of sport[8], to provide a prize to be competed for by cadets[9], for the upkeep of bedrooms and attendance for the men of a regiment[10], for the training of boys to become officers in the navy or mercantile marine[11], for promoting the defence of the United Kingdom from attack by hostile aircraft[12], to provide a lifeboat[13], to the Royal National Lifeboat Institution[14]. The principle does not extend to a gift that can be applied solely for the benefit of former members of the navy, army or air force[15], however, a gift to two institutions, one for sailors, the other for soldiers, has been held to be a charitable gift[16].

For a purpose to be charitable it must also conform to the established requirements with regard to public benefit[17].

1 See the Charities Act 2011 s 3(1)(l); and PARA 2. See also *Re Good, Harington v Watts* [1905] 2 Ch 60 at 66 per Farwell J; *IRC v City of Glasgow Police Athletic Association* [1953] AC 380

at 391, [1953] 1 All ER 747 at 749, HL, per Lord Normand: the association was held not to be established exclusively for that purpose, and not to be charitable because the recreation of members of the association was one of its main purposes. As to the meaning of 'fire and rescue services' see PARA 2 note 19.

2 The Charity Commission gives an extensive list, covering a broad range, of purposes which would be encompassed within this statutory description, in addition to the examples established by the cases in notes 4–16: see *Charitable purposes* (Charity Commission, September 2013) para 14 (available, at the date at which this volume states the law, on the government website). As to the Charity Commission's publications see PARA 547.

3 See *Charitable purposes* (Charity Commission, September 2013) para 14.

4 *Re Lord Stratheden and Campbell, Alt v Lord Stratheden and Campbell* [1894] 3 Ch 265. Property given for the use of a volunteer corps may, however, be regulated by statutory provisions, in which case it is not held on charitable trusts: *Re Edis's Trust, Campbell-Smith v Davies* [1972] 2 All ER 769, [1972] 1 WLR 1135.

5 *Re Stephens, Giles v Stephens* (1892) 8 TLR 792. See also *Charitable Status: Rifle and Pistol Clubs for Instruction and Practice in Shooting (The City of London Rifle and Pistol Club and the Burnley Rifle Club)* Decisions of the Charity Commissioners (1993) vol 1 p 4. As to decisions of the Charity Commission see PARA 547.

6 *Re Good, Harington v Watts* [1905] 2 Ch 60. The decision on the facts, though not the ratio, in this case and in *Re Gray, Todd v Taylor* [1925] Ch 362, was doubted by Lord Normand in *IRC v City of Glasgow Police Athletic Association* [1953] AC 380 at 391, [1953] 1 All ER 747 at 749, HL.

7 *Re Donald, Moore v Somerset* [1909] 2 Ch 410 at 422 per Warrington J.

8 *Re Gray, Todd v Taylor* [1925] Ch 362. See note 6.

9 *Re Barker, Sherrington v Dean and Chapter of St Paul's Cathedral* (1909) 25 TLR 753.

10 *Re Barker, Sherrington v Dean and Chapter of St Paul's Cathedral* (1909) 25 TLR 753.

11 *Re Corbyn, Midland Bank Executor and Trustee Co Ltd v A-G* [1941] Ch 400, [1941] 2 All ER 160.

12 *Re Driffill, Harvey v Chamberlain* [1950] Ch 92, [1949] 2 All ER 933.

13 *Johnston v Swann* (1818) 3 Madd 457.

14 *Thomas v Howell* (1874) LR 18 Eq 198; *Re Richardson, Shuldham v Royal National Lifeboat Institution* (1887) 56 LJCh 784; *Re David, Buckley v Royal National Lifeboat Institution* (1889) 41 ChD 168 (affd (1890) 43 ChD 27, CA).

15 *Re Good, Harington v Watts* [1905] 2 Ch 60 (gift for old officers of regiment); *Re Meyers, London Life Association v St George's Hospital* [1951] Ch 534, [1951] 1 All ER 538 (gift for welfare, benefit or assistance of members of navy, army or air force, whether past, present or future, or their wives or children).

16 *Re Smith, Blyth v A-G* (1920) 36 TLR 416, CA.

17 See PARA 34 notes 9–16. As to public benefit generally see PARA 4 et seq.

(xiii) Other Charitable Purposes Prior to the Charities Act 2006

46. Charitable purposes prior to the Charities Act 2006 remain charitable. A purpose is charitable under the thirteenth statutory description of purposes if it does not fall under any of the twelve statutory descriptions of charitable purposes[1] but was recognised as charitable under charity law[2] as in force immediately before 1 April 2008[3].

Prior to that date, charitable purposes were decided by reference to the preamble to the Charitable Uses Act 1601[4], which contained a varied list of purposes[5], and made it clear that at least those purposes were charitable[6]. The objects enumerated in the preamble were as follows: the relief of aged, impotent and poor people; the maintenance of sick and maimed soldiers and mariners, schools of learning and free schools and scholars of universities; the repair of bridges, ports, havens, causeways, churches, sea banks and highways; the education and preferment of orphans; the relief, stock or maintenance for houses of correction; marriages of poor maids; supportation, aid and help of young tradesmen, handicraftsmen and persons decayed; the relief or redemption of prisoners or captives; the aid or ease of any poor inhabitants concerning payment of fifteens[7], setting out of soldiers[8] and other taxes.

The list was not exhaustive[9]; but to decide whether a beneficial purpose was beneficial in a way which the law regarded as charitable, it was the practice of the courts to refer to the list in the preamble. The objects there enumerated and all others 'which by analogies are deemed within its spirit and intendment' were charitable in the legal sense[10]. No other objects were in law charitable[11]; however, when a purpose had been proved to be of general public utility or beneficial to the community, it was held to be charitable unless there was some reason for holding that it was not within the spirit and intendment of the preamble[12]. The purposes named in the preamble, which received a very wide construction[13], were regarded only as instances of charities[14].

Notwithstanding that neither the ancient statute nor the preamble were on the statute book immediately before 1 April 2008[15], it was still the general law that a purpose was not charitable unless it was within the spirit and intendment of the preamble[16]. The preamble never had any statutory operation, and the vast body of case law derived from it was unaffected by its repeal[17]. Charitable purposes were classified into four principal 'heads' of charity[18]: (1) the relief of poverty; (2) the advancement of education; (3) the advancement of religion; and (4) other purposes beneficial to the community not falling under any of the preceding heads, including certain additional purposes declared to be charitable by the Recreational Charities Act 1958[19]. All claims to bring a purpose under the head of charity had to assert that it came within one or more of these four divisions[20].

1 Ie under the Charities Act 2011 s 3(1)(a)–(l): see PARAS 2, 12–45.

2 As to the meaning of 'charity law' see PARA 2 note 20.

3 See the Charities Act 2006 ss 2(2), 3(1)(m)(i), (3), (4); and PARA 2. The date mentioned in the text is the day on which the Charities Act 2006 s 2 (repealed) came into force.

4 43 Eliz 1 c 4 (1601) (now wholly repealed: see PARA 2 note 25).

5 *Income Tax Special Purposes Comrs v Pemsel* [1891] AC 531 at 581, HL, per Lord Macnaghten; *Re Macduff, Macduff v Macduff* [1896] 2 Ch 451 at 467, CA, per Lindley LJ; *Re Foveaux, Cross v London Anti-Vivisection Society* [1895] 2 Ch 501 at 504, per Chitty J; *Re Nottage, Jones v Palmer* [1895] 2 Ch 649 at 656, CA, per Rigby LJ.

6 *National Anti-Vivisection Society v IRC* [1948] AC 31 at 64–65, [1947] 2 All ER 217 at 233, HL, per Lord Simonds.

7 'Fifteens' or 'fifteenths' were taxes on personalty.

8 See PARA 48.

9 *National Anti-Vivisection Society v IRC* [1948] AC 31 at 64, [1947] 2 All ER 217 at 233, HL, per Lord Simonds.

10 *Morice v Bishop of Durham* (1804) 9 Ves 399 at 405, per Grant MR (on appeal (1805) 10 Ves 522); *Income Tax Special Purposes Comrs v Pemsel* [1891] AC 531 at 581, HL, per Lord Macnaghten; *Re Macduff, Macduff v Macduff* [1896] 2 Ch 451 at 467, CA, per Lindley LJ; *Verge v Somerville* [1924] AC 496 at 502, PC.

11 *Gilmour v Coats* [1949] AC 426 at 442, [1949] 1 All ER 848 at 852, HL, per Lord Simonds (unless they are declared to be so by statute; see eg the Charities Act 2011 s 5 (recreational and similar trusts); and PARAS 47–49).

12 *Incorporated Council of Law Reporting for England and Wales v A-G* [1972] Ch 73, [1971] 3 All ER 1029, CA. But see *Barralet v A-G* [1980] 3 All ER 918, sub nom *Re South Place Ethical Society, Barralet v A-G* [1980] 1 WLR 1565, where Dillon J cast some doubt on this proposition.

13 *Cocks v Manners* (1871) LR 12 Eq 574 at 585, per Wickens V-C.

14 *London University v Yarrow* (1857) 1 De G & J 72 at 79 per Lord Cranworth LC; *Re Foveaux, Cross v London Anti-Vivisection Society* [1895] 2 Ch 501 at 504 per Chitty J.

15 Ie the day on which the Charities Act 2006 s 2 came into force: see note 3.

16 See *Scottish Burial Reform and Cremation Society Ltd v Glasgow Corpn* [1968] AC 138, [1967] 3 All ER 215, HL.

17 *Incorporated Council of Law Reporting for England and Wales v A-G* [1971] Ch 626 at 644, [1971] 1 All ER 436 at 445 per Foster J; affd [1972] Ch 73, [1971] 3 All ER 1029, CA.

18 This is the so-called *Pemsel* classification: see *Income Tax Special Purposes Comrs v Pemsel* [1891] AC 531 at 583, HL, per Lord Macnaghten. The classification was taken from the argument of Sir Samuel Romilly in *Morice v Bishop of Durham* (1805) 10 Ves 522 at 532 per Lord Eldon LC. See also *Re Macduff, Macduff v Macduff* [1896] 2 Ch 451 at 466, CA, per Lindley LJ.

19 The Recreational Charities Act 1958 was repealed by the Charities Act 2011 s 354(4), Sch 10. See now Charities Act 2011 s 5; and PARAS 52–55.

20 *National Anti-Vivisection Society v IRC* [1948] AC 31 at 52, [1947] 2 All ER 217 at 226, HL, per Lord Porter. Many charitable purposes do not fit neatly within a single category: *Re Hopkins' Will Trusts, Naish v Francis Bacon Society Inc* [1965] Ch 669 at 678, [1964] 3 All ER 46 at 51 per Wilberforce J; cf *Trustees of City of Belfast YMCA v Northern Ireland Valuation Comr* [1969] NI 3, CA.

47. General benefit of community. A gift in general terms for the benefit of a country or district, not indicating a specific purpose, is charitable, apparently on the principle that it is impliedly for purposes recognised by the law as charitable[1]. Examples are gifts 'to my country England'[2]; and gifts, whether general or for specific purposes, for the benefit of the inhabitants of a county[3], town[4], ward[5] or parish[6], and gifts in general terms for the benefit of the inhabitants, or a class of the inhabitants[7], of particular localities[8], for example a borough[9], city[10], town[11], village[12], or parish[13], or the occupiers of certain cottages on a manor[14], or the free inhabitants of ancient tenements in a particular place[15]. However, a trust for defined purposes which are not charitable is not rendered charitable by the fact that the area of benefit is a particular locality[16]. The provision of housing stock is not a charitable purpose within this category[17].

1 *Williams' Trustees v IRC* [1947] AC 447 at 459, [1947] 1 All ER 513 at 521, HL, per Lord Simonds; and see *Re Strakosch, Temperley v A-G* [1949] Ch 529, [1949] 2 All ER 6, CA. The leading case is *Goodman v Saltash Corpn* (1882) 7 App Cas 633, HL (applied in *Peggs v Lamb* [1994] Ch 172, [1994] 2 All ER 15), the decision in which was later described by Lord Ashbourne in *Harris v Earl of Chesterfield* [1911] AC 623 at 633, HL, as a splendid effort of equitable imagination. See also *Alfred F Beckett Ltd v Lyons* [1967] Ch 449, [1967] 1 All ER 833, CA.

2 *Re Smith, Public Trustee v Smith* [1932] 1 Ch 153, CA, explaining dicta in *A-G v National Provincial and Union Bank of England* [1924] AC 262, HL.

3 *A-G v Earl of Lonsdale* (1827) 1 Sim 105.

4 *Wrexham Corpn v Tamplin* (1873) 21 WR 768; *A-G v Dartmouth Corpn* (1883) 48 LT 933; *Re Baynes, Public Trustee v Leven Corpn* [1944] 2 All ER 597 (gift to Common Good Fund of town council in Scotland).

5 *Baylis v A-G* (1741) 2 Atk 239.

6 *West v Knight* (1669) 1 Cas in Ch 134; *Dolan v Macdermot* (1868) 3 Ch App 676; *A-G v Lord Hotham* (1823) Turn & R 209; *A-G v Earl of Lonsdale* (1827) 1 Sim 105; *A-G v Webster* (1875) LR 20 Eq 483; *Re St Bride's, Fleet Street, Church or Parish Estate* (1877) 35 ChD 147n; *Re St Botolph Without Bishopsgate Parish Estates* (1887) 35 ChD 142; *Re St Alphage, London Wall* (1888) 59 LT 614; *Re St Stephen, Coleman Street, Re St Mary the Virgin, Aldermanbury* (1888) 39 ChD 492; *Re Parish of St Nicholas Acons* (1889) 60 LT 532; *Re Norton's Will Trusts, Lightfoot v Goldson* [1948] 2 All ER 842 (any use trustees think best for benefit of church and parish, but preferably for certain purposes that might, however, prove impracticable).

7 Eg the native inhabitants of Dacca (*Mitford v Reynolds* (1842) 1 Ph 185), the freemen of a borough (*Re Norwich Town Close Estate Charity* (1888) 40 ChD 298, CA), or the schoolchildren of a town (*Re Mellody, Brandwood v Haden* [1918] 1 Ch 228), or, possibly, the 21 oldest inhabitants of a locality without a means test (*Re Shepherd, Firman v Shepherd* (1952) unreported; see PARA 43).

8 See *Goodman v Saltash Corpn* (1882) 7 App Cas 633 at 642, HL, per Lord Selborne LC; *Peggs v Lamb* [1994] Ch 172, [1994] 2 All ER 15.

9 *Re Norwich Town Close Estate Charity* (1888) 40 ChD 298, CA; and see *Stanley v Norwich Corpn* (1887) 3 TLR 506; but cf *Prestney v Colchester Corpn and A-G* (1882) 21 ChD 111 at 119 per Hall V-C. See also *Re Harding, Gibbs v Harding* [2007] EWHC 3 (Ch), [2008] Ch 235, [2007] 1 All ER 747.
10 *A-G v Carlisle Corpn* (1828) 2 Sim 437; *Mitford v Reynolds* (1842) 1 Ph 185.
11 *A-G v Cashel Corpn* (1842) 3 Dr & War 294; *A-G v Galway Corpn* (1829) 1 Mol 95; *Shillington v Portadown Urban Council* [1911] 1 IR 247.
12 *Wright v Hobert* (1723) 9 Mod Rep 64.
13 *Re Mann, Hardy v A-G* [1903] 1 Ch 232.
14 *A-G v Meyrick* [1893] AC 1, HL. In *Wilson v Barnes* (1886) 38 ChD 507, CA, a gift for the benefit of the copyhold tenants of a manor was held charitable; but copyhold tenure has been abolished (see CUSTOM AND USAGE vol 32 (2012) PARA 43).
15 *Goodman v Saltash Corpn* (1882) 7 App Cas 633, HL.
16 *Re Sanders' Will Trusts, Public Trustee v McLaren* [1954] Ch 265, [1954] 1 All ER 667; and see *Re Gwyon, Public Trustee v A-G* [1930] 1 Ch 255 at 261 per Eve J, applying Lord Shaw's dictum in the Scottish case of *Houston v Burns* [1918] AC 337 at 349, HL; *Re King, Henderson v Cranmer* [1931] WN 232; *D'Aguiar v Guyana IRC* (1970) 49 ATC 33, PC. However, a gift for public purposes in a town may be charitable even though, in general, public purposes are not exclusively charitable: see *Re Spence, Barclays Bank Ltd v Stockton-on-Tees Corpn* [1938] Ch 96, [1937] 3 All ER 684; *Re Allen, Hargreaves v Taylor* [1905] 2 Ch 400. See also *A-G of the Cayman Islands v Wahr Hansen* [2001] 1 AC 75, [2000] 3 All ER 642, PC.
17 See *Helena Partnerships Ltd (formerly Helena Housing Ltd) v Revenue and Customs Comrs (Attorney General intervening)* [2012] EWCA Civ 569, [2012] 4 All ER 111, [2012] PTSR 1409, referring specifically to the spirit and intendment of the preamble to the Charitable Uses Act 1601 (repealed).

48. Objects of practical utility. Objects of general public utility or benefit of a practical kind mentioned in the preamble to the Charitable Uses Act 1601[1] include the repair of bridges, ports, highways and similar instances[2]. These, together with many purposes which have been held charitable by analogy, would normally be provided now by some public authority as public works[3], services or facilities[4], and some benefits which would be charitable have been to some extent superseded in other ways[5], but gifts for such purposes do not thereby cease to be charitable. The provision of the means for public recreation is charitable[6], as is a gift to the Royal Humane Society[7]. The preamble includes the aid or ease of poor inhabitants concerning payment of taxes. Analogous cases beneficial to the community, all of which are charitable[8], are gifts for the benefit of the country to be applied by the Chancellor of the Exchequer[9], or for relief of taxes[10], or in reduction of the National Debt[11], or in reduction of rates[12].

The preservation of public order[13], the defence of the country (such as trusts for national or local defence) and the rehabilitation of ex-offenders and the prevention of crime[14] are also charitable. The provision of housing stock is not a charitable purpose within this category[15].

1 43 Eliz 1 c 4 (1601) (now wholly repealed: see PARA 2 note 25).
2 See PARA 46.
3 As to 'public works' see the view taken earlier in *Dolan v Macdermot* (1867) LR 5 Eq 60 at 62 per Lord Romilly MR; affd (1868) 3 Ch App 676.
4 Eg repairing highways (*A-G v Governors of Harrow School* (1754) 2 Ves Sen 551; *A-G v Day* [1900] 1 Ch 31); building bridges (*Forbes v Forbes* (1854) 18 Beav 552); protecting the sea coast against encroachment (*A-G v Brown* (1818) 1 Swan 265; *Wilson v Barnes* (1886) 38 ChD 507, CA); providing a fire brigade for the benefit of a locality in 1876 (*Re Wokingham Fire Brigade Trusts, Martin v Hawkins* [1951] Ch 373, [1951] 1 All ER 454); providing a town with water (*Jones v Williams* (1767) Amb 651), light (*A-G v Heelis* (1824) 2 Sim & St 67 at 76–77 per Leach V-C; *A-G v Eastlake* (1853) 11 Hare 205), or other improvements (*Howse v Chapman* (1799) 4 Ves 542; *A-G v Heelis*; *A-G v Brown*), or with fortifications (*A-G v Carlisle Corpn* (1828) 2 Sim 437; *A-G v Dartmouth Corpn* (1883) 48 LT 933); or building a courthouse (Duke on Charitable Uses 109, 136), or workhouse (*A-G v Blizard* (1855) 21 Beav 233; *Re St Botolph Without Bishopsgate Parish Estates* (1887) 35 ChD 142; *Webster v Southey*

(1887) 36 ChD 9; but cf *Burnaby v Barsby* (1859) 4 H & N 690); or providing a cemetery (*A-G v Blizard*), or cheap and sanitary methods of disposing of the dead (*Scottish Burial Reform and Cremation Society Ltd v Glasgow Corpn* [1968] AC 138, [1967] 3 All ER 215, HL); but see *Auckland Harbour Board v IRC* [1959] NZLR 204. In *Richmond-upon-Thames London Borough Council v A-G* (1982) 81 LGR 156 Warner J declined to decide the question whether the provision of municipal offices or of a town hall could be a valid charitable purpose.

5 The relief of poverty has been a national responsibility since the National Assistance Act 1948 came into force (see SOCIAL SERVICES AND COMMUNITY CARE vol 95 (2013) PARAS 5, 25 et seq, 63 et seq). See also *Richmond Corpn v A-G* [1965] RA 117; revsd sub nom *Re Richmond Parish Charity Lands* [1965] RA 343, CA.

6 *Re Hadden, Public Trustee v More* [1932] 1 Ch 133; *Shillington v Portadown Urban Council* [1911] 1 IR 247 (providing the means of obtaining healthy recreation, including, inter alia, music and instruments for the town band); *Re Morgan, Cecil-Williams v A-G* [1955] 2 All ER 632, [1955] 1 WLR 738; and see *IRC v Baddeley* [1955] AC 572 at 589, [1955] 1 All ER 525 at 532, HL, per Viscount Simonds, at 615 and 549 per Lord Somervell of Harrow, and at 594 and 535 per Lord Reid; *Alexandra Park Trustees v Haringey London Borough* (1967) 66 LGR 306; *Brisbane City Council v A-G for Queensland* [1979] AC 411, [1978] 3 All ER 30, PC; *Liverpool City Council v A-G* (1992) Times, 1 May. This may possibly not apply if the facilities are not open air facilities: see *Northern Ireland Valuation Comr v Lurgan Borough Council* [1968] NI 104 at 125, CA, per Lord Macdermott CJ, and see also at 134 per Curran LJ (there cannot be a valid charity for recreation or other leisure-time occupation which does not comply with the Recreational Charities Act 1958 (repealed: see now the Charities Act 2011 s 5) (see PARAS 52–55)). The Charity Commissioners (now the Charity Commission) have not accepted the 'open air' point, and held that the provision of a public ice skating rink is charitable apart from the Recreational Charities Act 1958 (now the Charities Act 2011 s 5), and also under it: *Report of the Charity Commissioners for England and Wales for 1984* (HC Paper (1984–85) no 394) paras 19–25.

7 *Beaumont v Oliveira* (1869) 4 Ch App 309.

8 A similar analogy (to the 'setting out of soldiers' in the preamble to the statute of Elizabeth I: see PARA 46) was applied in *Re Good, Harington v Watts* [1905] 2 Ch 60 (gift to maintain library and purchase plate for officers' mess).

9 *Nightingale v Goulbourn* (1848) 2 Ph 594.

10 *A-G v Bushby* (1857) 24 Beav 299.

11 *Thellusson v Woodford* (1799) 4 Ves 227 (affd (1805) 11 Ves 112, HL); *Newland v A-G* (1809) 3 Mer 684; *Ashton v Lord Langdale* (1851) 4 De G & Sm 402 at 403 per Shadwell V-C; *Income Tax Special Purposes Comrs v Pemsel* [1891] AC 531 at 544, HL, per Lord Halsbury LC.

12 *Doe d Preece v Howells* (1831) 2 B & Ad 744; and see *A-G v Limerick Corpn* (1817) 6 Dowl 136.

13 *IRC v City of Glasgow Police Athletic Association* [1953] AC 380 at 391, [1953] 1 All ER 747 at 749, HL, per Lord Normand. Note also the promotion of the efficiency of the police, fire and rescue services or ambulance services, with which there may be overlap in individual cases: see the Charities Act 2011 s 3(1)(l): and PARAS 2, 45.

14 See *Charitable purposes* (Charity Commission, September 2013) para 15 (available, at the date at which this volume states the law, on the government website). As to the Charity Commission's publications see PARA 547.

15 See *Helena Partnerships Ltd (formerly Helena Housing Ltd) v Revenue and Customs Comrs (Attorney General intervening)* [2012] EWCA Civ 569, [2012] 4 All ER 111, [2012] PTSR 1409, referring specifically to the spirit and intendment of the preamble to the Charitable Uses Act 1601 (repealed).

49. Other public purposes. It is charitable to promote industry and commerce for the public benefit[1]; to further the sound development and administration of the law by the dissemination of accurate reports of judicial decisions[2]; to encourage good domestic servants[3], good housewifery and horticulture[4]; and to promote agriculture[5]. Among funds which have been held to be charitable are funds to promote marriage among the Jews[6], for the repatriation of men from New South Wales who had served in the First World War[7], for reclaiming fallen women[8], for the assistance or support of unmarried mothers[9], and for promoting the spiritual and moral welfare of seamen in port[10]. A gift for a peal of bells to be rung to commemorate the restoration of the monarchy has been held charitable[11]; and the erection of a monument[12], not of the donor[13], or memorial[14] may perhaps be charitable, as may the promotion of certain patriotic purposes[15].

1 *Re Town and Country Planning Act 1947, Crystal Palace Trustees v Minister of Town and Country Planning* [1951] Ch 132, [1950] 2 All ER 857n.
2 *Incorporated Council of Law Reporting for England and Wales v A-G* [1972] Ch 73, [1971] 3 All ER 1029, CA; *Incorporated Council of Law Reporting for the State of Queensland v Comr of Taxation* (1971) 45 ALJR 552, Aust HC.
3 *Reeve v A-G* (1843) 3 Hare 191; *Loscombe v Wintringham* (1850) 13 Beav 87. Cf *Re Patten, Westminster Bank v Carlyon* [1929] 2 Ch 276 (staff Christmas fund at a club: not charitable).
4 *Re Pleasants, Pleasants v A-G* (1923) 39 TLR 675.
5 *IRC v Yorkshire Agricultural Society* [1928] 1 KB 611, CA; *Re Pleasants, Pleasants v A-G* (1923) 39 TLR 675; *Brisbane City Council v A-G for Queensland* [1979] AC 411, [1978] 3 All ER 30, PC; and see *Re Clifford* as reported in (1912) 81 LJCh 220 at 222 per Swinfen Eady J (restocking of a river with fish might be for the benefit of the community). But a fund to provide cheap loans to assist planters and agriculturalists is not charitable unless the purposes of the loans themselves are restricted to the promotion of agriculture: *Hadaway v Hadaway* [1955] 1 WLR 16, PC. See also PARA 42.
6 *Re Cohen, National Provincial and Union Bank of England Ltd v Cohen* (1919) 36 TLR 16.
7 *Verge v Somerville* [1924] AC 496, PC.
8 *Mahony v Duggan* (1880) 11 LR Ir 260. See, however, PARA 9.
9 *Re Andrae Estate, Sims v Public Trustee* (1967) 61 WWR 182 (Alta). See, however, PARA 9.
10 *Finch v Poplar Borough Council* (1967) 66 LGR 324; and see *Wynn v Skegness UDC* [1966] 3 All ER 336, [1967] 1 WLR 52 (holiday centre for miners, their wives and families in need of a change of air).
11 *Re Pardoe, McLaughlin v A-G* [1906] 2 Ch 184. Cf *Re Arber, Taylor v Shelton* (1919) Times, 13 December (in commemoration of testator's death: not charitable).
12 The Charity Commissioners (now the Charity Commission) have treated some such cases as charitable, eg the Wellington Monument in Somerset and the Cobden Obelisk at Midhurst. See the comments on the statement on the text made by the Charity Commissioners in their *Report for 1981* (HC Paper (1981–82) no 363) paras 68–70, in relation to registration of the Mountbatten Statue Appeal trust. As to the Charity Commission see PARA 543.
13 *Re Endacott, Corpe v Endacott* [1960] Ch 232, [1959] 3 All ER 562, CA. The fact that the memorial was to be useful did not save it. See also PARA 54.
14 The cases were considered in *Re Lord Mayor of Belfast's Air Raid Distress Fund* [1962] NI 161, and the question was also discussed in *Murray v Thomas* [1937] 4 All ER 545. In each of those cases the memorial was to be of a useful character, such as a building or hall, but Clauson J in *Murray v Thomas* was inclined to the view that a war memorial might be charitable even though it was not of a useful character; this is borne out by the express inclusion of war memorials in the Charity Commission's guidance: see note 15.
15 *Charitable purposes* (Charity Commission, September 2013) para 15 (available, at the date at which this volume states the law, on the government website). As to the Charity Commission's publications see PARA 547.

50. Spread of particular doctrines. The promulgation of particular doctrines or principles not subversive of morality or otherwise pernicious[1], and not in furtherance of the principles of a particular political party[2], nor involving pressure on the legislature to achieve a political object in changing the law of the land[3], may be charitable, as, for instance: Conservative principles combined with mental and moral improvement[4], Socialism[5], kindness to animals[6], temperance[7], 'extending the knowledge of those doctrines in the various branches of literature to which I have turned my attention and pen, in order to ascertain what appeared to be truth, and to teach it to those who would listen'[8], or carrying on the teachings of Rudolf Steiner, which are 'directed to the mental or moral improvement of man'[9]. The promotion of ethical standards of conduct of work and compliance with the law may be a valid charitable purpose[10].

The question whether the promulgation of a particular doctrine or principle will or may benefit the public must be answered by the court by forming an opinion upon the evidence before it[11]. The same consideration applies to the dissemination of information useful to the community[12].

The promulgation of humanism has been recognised as a charitable purpose by the Charity Commission[13].

1 See PARA 65. An inquiry may be ordered into the nature of the doctrines: *Russell v Jackson* (1852) 10 Hare 204.

2 *Bonar Law Memorial Trust v IRC* (1933) 49 TLR 220 (gift to commemorate a Conservative leader by an educational centre for subjects deemed desirable to governing body composed of leader and chairman ex officio and other members of Conservative party: not charitable), distinguishing *Re Scowcroft, Ormrod v Wilkinson* [1898] 2 Ch 638. See also PARA 67.

3 See PARA 67. See *Re Bushnell, Lloyds Bank Ltd v Murray* [1975] 1 All ER 721, [1975] 1 WLR 1596.

4 *Re Scowcroft, Ormrod v Wilkinson* [1898] 2 Ch 638 at 642 per Stirling J. Cf *Re Jones, Public Trustee v Earl of Clarendon* (1929) 45 TLR 259 (Primrose League: not a charity).

5 *Russell v Jackson* (1852) 10 Hare 204 (subject to its being found on inquiry not to be illegal; the Socialist party was not formed until 1904). See *Pare v Clegg* (1861) 29 Beav 589.

6 *Marsh v Means* (1857) 3 Jur NS 790.

7 *Re Hood, Public Trustee v Hood* [1931] 1 Ch 240 at 250, CA, per Lord Hanworth MR, and at 252–253, CA, per Romer LJ; *IRC v Falkirk Temperance Café Trust* 1927 SC 261, Ct of Sess. Distinguish *IRC v Temperance Council of Christian Churches of England and Wales* (1926) 136 LT 27 (promotion of temperance mainly by political means: not charitable).

8 *Thompson v Thompson* (1844) 1 Coll 381 at 395 per Shadwell V-C (where it was admitted that the testator's writings contained nothing irreligious, illegal or immoral).

9 *Re Price, Midland Bank Executor and Trustee Co Ltd v Harwood* [1943] Ch 422, [1943] 2 All ER 505.

10 See *Charitable Status: Public Concern at Work (1993)* Decisions of the Charity Commissioners (1994) vol 2 p 5; and the *Charitable purposes* (Charity Commission, September 2013) para 15 (available, at the date at which this volume states the law, on the government website). As to decisions of the Charity Commission see PARA 547; and as to the Charity Commission's publications see PARA 547.

11 *National Anti-Vivisection Society v IRC* [1948] AC 31, [1947] 2 All ER 217, HL; approving observations in *Re Hummeltenberg, Beatty v London Spiritualistic Alliance Ltd* [1923] 1 Ch 237 at 242 per Russell J, which were adopted in *Re Grove-Grady, Plowden v Lawrence* [1929] 1 Ch 557, CA, and overruling the dictum of Chitty J in *Re Foveaux, Cross v London Anti-Vivisection Society* [1895] 2 Ch 501, that where the merits of a particular object are controversial the court stands neutral.

12 See *Re Besterman's Will Trusts* (21 January 1980, unreported); *McGovern v A-G* [1982] Ch 321, [1981] 3 All ER 493.

13 Revised objects of the British Humanist Association were approved by the Commission in November 2011, under the general headings of the advancement of education (see PARA 20 et seq), promoting religious and racial harmony (see PARA 41), and 'other charitable purposes'.

51. Miners' welfare trusts. Until 1 April 2010[1], certain trusts known as miners' welfare trusts were to be treated as charitable[2].

As from that date, such a trust is no longer charitable unless it constitutes a charity in accordance with the Charities Act 2011[3].

1 Ie the date on which the repeal of the Recreational Charities Act 1958 s 2 by the Charities Act 2006 came into force.

2 See the Miners' Welfare Act 1952 s 16(1) (prospectively repealed); and **MINES, MINERALS AND QUARRIES** vol 76 (2013) PARA 89. They were to be so treated by virtue of the Recreational Charities Act 1958 s 2(1) (now repealed). See also *Wynn v Skegness UDC* [1966] 3 All ER 336, [1967] 1 WLR 52.

3 Ie under the Charities Act 2011 s 1(1) (see PARA 1): see the Charities Act 2006 Sch 8 para 10.

(xiv) Recreational Charities

52. Recreation and other leisure-time occupation. It is deemed by statute to be[1], and always to have been, charitable to provide, or assist in the provision of, facilities for recreation or other leisure-time occupation, if the facilities are provided in the interests of social welfare[2]. This applies in particular to the provision of facilities at village halls, community centres and women's institutes, and to the provision and maintenance of grounds and buildings to be used for the purpose of recreation or leisure-time occupation, and extends to the provision of facilities for those purposes by the organising of any activity[3]. The activities do not have to have an educational element[4].

1 Ie by the Charities Act 2011 s 5 (consolidating the provisions of the Recreational Charities Act 1958). As to whether trusts for the type of purpose mentioned in this paragraph are or can be charitable if they do not comply with the provisions of the Act see PARA 48 note 6; and *Northern Ireland Valuation Comr v Lurgan Borough Council* [1968] NI 104 at 125, 134, 166, CA.

Nothing in the Charities Act 2011 s 5 derogates from the public benefit requirement: see PARA 54.

Further guidance on the Charity Commission's approach to charitable status under s 5 can be gleaned from *RR4: The Recreational Charities Act 1958* (Charity Commission, August 2000) (available, at the date at which this volume states the law, on the government website), considering the provisions of the 1958 Act which have now been so consolidated. As to the Charity Commission's publications see PARA 547.

2 Charities Act 2011 s 5(1). See also s 3(1)(m)(i); and PARA 2. As to the interests of social welfare see s 5(2), (3); and PARA 53.

3 Charities Act 2011 s 5(4). There seems to be no reason and little scope for applying the ejusdem generis rule of construction to s 5(1) by reference to this provision, even though it is not expressed to be without prejudice to the generality of s 5(1).

4 See *Charitable Status: Fairfield (Croydon) Ltd—The Recreation Charities Act 1958 (1995)* Decisions of the Charity Commissioners (1997) vol 5 p 7. As to decisions of the Charity Commission see PARA 547.

53. The interests of social welfare. The statutory requirement that the facilities be provided in the interests of social welfare[1] cannot be satisfied if the 'basic conditions' are not met[2]. The basic conditions are: (1) that the facilities are provided with the object of improving the conditions of life for the persons for whom the facilities are primarily intended[3]; and (2) that either those persons have need of the facilities by reason of their youth, age, infirmity or disability, poverty, or social and economic circumstances[4], or the facilities are to be available to members of the public at large or to male, or to female, members of the public at large[5].

1 Ie the requirement under the Charities Act 2011 s 5(1): see PARA 52. The Charities Act 2011 contains no definition of 'social welfare'. There are decisions on the words 'social welfare' under the Rating and Valuation (Miscellaneous Provisions) Act 1955 s 8 (repealed; replaced by the General Rate Act 1967 s 40, (itself repealed and replaced by the Local Government Finance Act 1988 s 47): see PARA 437), but these may be misleading: see *Northern Ireland Valuation Comr v Lurgan Borough Council* [1968] NI 104 at 126, 151, CA.

2 Charities Act 2011 s 5(2).

3 Charities Act 2011 s 5(3)(a). This appears to contemplate that there may be a primary and a secondary class of beneficiaries: see (discussing an early iteration of the Recreational Charities Act 1958 s 1(2) (repealed), but still of interest) *Wynn v Skegness UDC* [1966] 3 All ER 336, [1967] 1 WLR 52. The provision was discussed in *IRC v McMullen* [1978] 1 All ER 230, [1978] 1 WLR 664; affd [1979] 1 All ER 588, [1979] 1 WLR 130, CA, but revsd on other grounds [1981] AC 1, [1980] 1 All ER 884, HL. At first instance Walton J said that the persons for whom the facilities are primarily intended must be to some extent and in some way deprived persons, and this view was shared by the majority in the Court of Appeal. The dissenting judgment of Bridge LJ was, however, said to be clearly correct in the Scottish case of *Guild v IRC* [1992] 2 AC 310, [1992] 2 All ER 10, HL (a tax case where the English law of charities was applicable as part of the law of Scotland). It suffices that the facilities are provided with the object of improving the conditions of life for members of the community generally.

Provision of bar facilities at a rugby club does not improve conditions of life for those for whom the facilities were primarily intended: *Charitable Status: North Tawton Rugby Union*

Football Club (1995) Decisions of the Charity Commissioners (1997) vol 5 p 7. Provision of an internet café for the use of the local community living or working in an area of social and economic deprivation can be charitable under the 1958 Act: *Application for Registration of Community Server*, Decision of the Charity Commissioners, 15 September 2003. As to decisions of the Charity Commission see PARA 547.

4 Charities Act 2011 s 5(3)(b)(i).

5 Charities Act 2011 s 5(3)(b)(ii).

54. Public benefit and recreational charities. Nothing in the general provision as to recreational and similar trusts[1] is to be taken to derogate from the principle that, to be charitable, a trust or institution must be for the public benefit[2]. Although the Charities Act 2011 lays down certain requirements of its own as to the section of the public which is to benefit[3], these do not seem to exclude the application of the test of benefit for a sufficient section of the public, and they operate subject to this overriding principle[4].

1 Ie nothing in the Charities Act 2011 s 5: see PARAS 52–53.

2 Charities Act 2011 s 5(5). As to the meaning of 'for the public benefit' in this context see *Wynn v Skegness UDC* [1966] 3 All ER 336 at 345, [1967] 1 WLR 52 at 63 per Ungoed-Thomas J.

3 See PARA 53.

4 See *Charitable Status: North Tawton Rugby Union Football Club (1995)* Decisions of the Charity Commissioners (1997) vol 5 p 7. See also PARA 6. As to decisions of the Charity Commission see PARA 547.

55. Past transactions. Although the Recreational Charities Act 1958, which came into force on 13 March 1958 when it received the royal assent, was declaratory and therefore retrospective in effect, it did not apply to make charitable any trust, or to validate any disposition, of property if, before 17 December 1957, that property, or any property representing or forming part of it, or any income arising from any such property, had been paid or conveyed to, or applied for the benefit of, the persons entitled by reason of the invalidity of the trust or disposition[1].

The Act did not affect any order made or judgment given, whether before or after 13 March 1958, in legal proceedings begun before 17 December 1957[2]; and nothing in the Act required anything properly done before 17 December 1957, or anything done or to be done in pursuance of a contract entered into before that day, to be treated for any purpose as wrongful or ineffectual[3].

Nothing in the Act required anything to be treated, for the purposes of any enactment, as having been charitable at a time before 13 March 1958, so as to invalidate anything done or any determination given before that date[4].

The repeal of the Recreational Charities Act 1958 by the Charities Act 2011 did not affect any saving described above capable of having continuing effect[5].

1 Recreational Charities Act 1958 s 3(2)(a) (repealed).

2 Recreational Charities Act 1958 s 3(2)(b).

3 Recreational Charities Act 1958 s 3(2)(c).

4 Recreational Charities Act 1958 s 3(3) (repealed).

5 Charities Act 2011 Sch 8 para 11.

(xv) Purposes Analogous to, or within the Spirit of, another Charitable Purpose

56. Recognising new charitable purposes. The Charities Act 2011 establishes as charitable: (1) any purposes that may reasonably be regarded as analogous to, or within the spirit of, any purposes falling within the Charities Act 2011 or the existing law[1]; and (2) any purposes that may reasonably be regarded as analogous to, or within the spirit of, any purposes which have been recognised under charity law as falling within head (1)[2].

Historically, in order to find whether a novel purpose was charitable the courts considered that it must fall within the 'spirit and intendment' of the preamble to the Charitable Uses Act 1601[3] and sought to find an analogy with purposes mentioned in the preamble itself[4], or with purposes previously held to be within its spirit and intendment[5]. Even in the absence of such analogy, objects beneficial to the public, or of public utility, were prima facie within the spirit and intendment of the preamble and, in the absence of any ground for holding that they are outside its spirit and intendment, were therefore charitable in law[6]. The effect of the Charities Act 2011 is to preserve this general approach whilst removing the need to find that a novel purpose falls within the spirit and intendment of the 1601 Act[7].

The Charity Commission has published guidance on the approach it takes in recognising new charitable purposes, which reflects the principles described above[8].

For a novel purpose to be recognised as charitable, it must satisfy the public benefit requirement[9].

1 See the Charities Act 2011 s 3(1)(m)(ii); and PARA 2. As to purposes falling within the Charities Act 2011 and the existing law see PARA 2 et seq.
2 See the Charities Act 2011 s 3(1)(m)(iii); and PARA 2. For a modern example of registration being refused, notwithstanding that the purposes might be for the public benefit, because they had not been recognised as charitable under the law, see *Independent Press Regulation Trust*, Decision of the Charity Commission, October 2014. As to decisions of the Charity Commission see PARA 547.
3 Ie 43 Eliz 1 c 4 (1601). Now wholly repealed: see PARA 2 note 25; and PARA 46. See *Re Macduff, Macduff v Macduff* [1896] 2 Ch 451 at 466–467, CA, per Lindley LJ, and at 473–475 per Rigby LJ; *Langham v Peterson* (1903) 87 LT 744; *Re Good, Harington v Watts* [1905] 2 Ch 60 at 66 per Farwell J; *A-G v National Provincial and Union Bank of England* [1924] AC 262, HL; *General Medical Council v IRC* (1928) 97 LJKB 578, CA.
4 See PARA 46.
5 See the cases cited in note 3; and *Williams' Trustees v IRC* [1947] AC 447, [1947] 1 All ER 513, HL; *Re Strakosch, Temperley v A-G* [1949] Ch 529, [1949] 2 All ER 6, CA; *Incorporated Council of Law Reporting for England and Wales v A-G* [1971] Ch 626, [1971] 1 All ER 436.
6 *Incorporated Council of Law Reporting for England and Wales v A-G* [1972] Ch 73 at 88, 95, 104, [1971] 3 All ER 1029 at 1036, CA, per Russell LJ, at 1042 per Sachs LJ, and at 1048 per Buckley LJ; *Scottish Burial Reform and Cremation Society Ltd v Glasgow Corpn* [1968] AC 138, [1967] 3 All ER 215, HL; *IRC v McMullen* [1979] 1 All ER 588, [1979] 1 WLR 130, CA (revsd, without discussing this point [1981] AC 1, [1980] 1 All ER 884, HL). In *Barralet v A-G* [1980] 3 All ER 918, sub nom *Re South Place Ethical Society, Barralet v A-G* [1980] 1 WLR 1565, however, Dillon J doubted whether this more generous approach is permissible in the light of earlier House of Lords decisions such as *Williams' Trustees v IRC* [1947] AC 447, [1947] 1 All ER 513, HL. See also *A-G v Heelis* (1824) 2 Sim & St 67; *Brisbane City Council v A-G for Queensland* [1979] AC 411 at 422, [1978] 3 All ER 30 at 33, PC.
7 See the Charities Act 2011 s 3(1)(m)(ii), (iii); and PARA 2.
8 See *RR1a: Recognising new charitable purposes* (Charity Commission, October 2001) (available, at the date at which this volume states the law, on the government website). As to the Charity Commission's publications see PARA 547.
9 See PARA 4 et seq. As to the meaning of 'public benefit requirement' see PARA 2 note 6.

(xvi) Charitable Purposes Abroad

57. Choice of law. If in an English court the question arises of the validity of a gift by will for purposes which may be charitable but which are to be carried out entirely abroad, the question is determined, in the case of a gift of immovable property, by the law of the country in which the property is situated[1] and, in the case of movable property, by the law of the country in which the testator was domiciled at the date of his death[2]. Formerly the English law as to gifts for superstitious uses[3] was applied to gifts to be applied abroad[4] even though the gifts were valid according to the foreign law[5], but English rules as to mortmain and perpetuities were not so applied[6].

1 *Re Hoyles, Row v Jagg* [1911] 1 Ch 179, CA (mortgages on land in Ontario); *Philipson-Stow v IRC* [1961] AC 727, [1960] 3 All ER 814, HL (land in South Africa). As to the distinction between immovables and movables see CONFLICT OF LAWS vol 19 (2011) PARA 676 et seq.
2 *Re Levick's Will Trusts, Ffennell v IRC* [1963] 1 All ER 95, [1963] 1 WLR 311. In some old charity cases the gift has apparently been tested both by English and by foreign law: *Thompson v Thompson* (1844) 1 Coll 381. As to domicile see CONFLICT OF LAWS vol 19 (2011) PARA 336 et seq.
3 See PARA 63.
4 *De Garcin v Lawson* (1798) 4 Ves 433n.
5 *Re Elliott, Elliott v Elliott* [1891] WN 9.
6 *Fordyce v Bridges* (1848) 2 Ph 497 at 515 per Lord Cottenham LC (perpetuity); *Oliphant v Hendrie* (1784) 1 Bro CC 571; *Mackintosh v Townsend* (1809) 16 Ves 330 (mortmain); though see also *A-G v Mill* (1827) 3 Russ 328; affd (1831) 2 Dow & Cl 393, HL; and cf *Jewish National Fund Inc v Royal Trust Co and Richter* [1965] SCR 784, 53 DLR (2d) 577, Can SC. As to the repeal of the law of mortmain see PARA 83; as to perpetuities see PARA 142.

58. Test for validity under English law. If the validity of a gift falls to be determined under English domestic law, the test is not necessarily the same in all cases as for a gift to be applied in England. It is well established that trusts for charitable purposes generally[1], for the relief of the poverty or those in need[2] or for the advancement of education[3], religion[4] or animal welfare[5] abroad are valid under English law. The fact that the activities of a charity are to be exercised abroad does not make it non-charitable if it otherwise satisfies the tests[6].

However, not all purposes which are charitable in England would be charitable if they were to be carried out abroad[7]. Gifts for some purposes previously falling under the fourth head of charity[8] have been upheld[9], but public policy might prevent the recognition, as being charitable under English domestic law, of a gift for the improvement of the army of a foreign state[10]. There is also authority that the reduction of the national debt of a foreign state is not charitable[11].

The test which should be applied in these cases has never been formulated by an English court, but in Australia the test is whether the purpose is beneficial to the foreign community and not inimical to the general concept of legal charity as understood by the local law[12].

1 *Re Vagliano, Vagliano v Vagliano* (1905) 75 LJCh 119.
2 Eg *Ironmongers' Co v A-G* (1844) 10 Cl & Fin 908, HL; *Re Robinson, Besant v German Reich* [1931] 2 Ch 122; *Re Geck, Freund v Steward* (1893) 69 LT 819, CA; *Re Niyazi's Will Trusts* [1978] 3 All ER 785, [1978] 1 WLR 910. This applies even if inhabitants of a country of alien ideology are to benefit: *Re Burnham* (1958) 17 DLR (2d) 298 (BC); and cf *Re Robinson, Besant v German Reich* at 128 per Maugham J. As to charitable trusts for the relief of poverty or the relief of those in need see PARAS 12–19.
3 *Re Davis' Trusts* (1889) 61 LT 430; *Re Shaw's Will Trusts, National Provincial Bank Ltd v National City Bank Ltd* [1952] Ch 163, [1952] 1 All ER 49. As to charitable trusts for the advancement of education see PARAS 21–26.
4 *Income Tax Special Purposes Comrs v Pemsel* [1891] AC 531, HL. As to charitable trusts for the advancement of religion see PARAS 27–33.
5 *Armstrong v Reeves* (1890) 25 LR Ir 325. As to charitable trusts for the advancement of animal welfare see PARA 44.
6 *Keren Kayemeth Le Jisroel Ltd v IRC* [1931] 2 KB 465 at 477, CA, per Lord Hanworth MR (affd without considering this point [1932] AC 650, HL); *Re Robinson, Besant v German Reich* [1931] 2 Ch 122.

7 *Camille and Henry Dreyfus Foundation Inc v IRC* [1954] Ch 672 at 684, [1954] 2 All ER 466 at 471, CA, per Evershed MR, and at 704 and 485 per Jenkins LJ; affd without considering this point [1956] AC 39, [1955] 3 All ER 97, HL.

8 Ie the fourth division mentioned by Lord Macnaghten in *Income Tax Special Purposes Comrs v Pemsel* [1891] AC 531 at 583, HL, per Lord Macnaghten: see PARA 46.

9 *Re Lowin* [1967] 2 NSWR 140, NSW CA (revsg [1965] NSWR 1624) (musical competitions in Vienna); *Re Stone, Perpetual Trustee Co Ltd v Stone* (1970) 91 WN NSW 704 (reclamation and afforestation of land in Israel); *Re Jacobs, Westminster Bank Ltd v Chinn* (1970) 114 Sol Jo 515 (see note 9; and *Report of the Charity Commissioners for England and Wales for 1970* (HC Paper (1970–71) no 409) p 28) (improvement and reclamation of land in Israel); although cf *Jewish National Fund Inc v Royal Trust Co and Richter* [1965] SCR 784, 53 DLR (2d) 577, Can SC.

10 *Camille and Henry Dreyfus Foundation Inc v IRC* [1954] Ch 672 at 684, [1954] 2 All ER 466 at 471, CA, per Evershed MR, and at 704 and 485 per Jenkins LJ; affd without considering this point [1956] AC 39, [1955] 3 All ER 97, HL. Cf *Habershon v Vardon* (1851) 4 De G & Sm 467 (gift held non-charitable as contrary to public policy).

11 *Camille and Henry Dreyfus Foundation Inc v IRC* [1954] Ch 672 at 704, [1954] 2 All ER 466 at 485 per Jenkins LJ; affd without discussing this point [1956] AC 39, [1955] 3 All ER 97, HL. However, the Jubilee Debt Campaign (registered charity 1055675) which pursues the object of the relief of poverty in the third world through debt cancellation has been registered by the Charity Commission. As to the register of charities see PARA 307 et seq.

12 *Re Stone, Perpetual Trustee Co Ltd v Stone* (1970) 91 WN NSW 704 at 717, applying *Re Lowin* [1967] 2 NSWR 140, NSW CA; and *Camille and Henry Dreyfus Foundation Inc v IRC* [1954] Ch 672, [1954] 2 All ER 466, CA, affd without considering this point [1956] AC 39, [1955] 3 All ER 97, HL. In the absence of binding decisions, the principles on which the Charity Commission proceeds are set out in the *Report of the Charity Commissioners for England and Wales for 1992* (HC Paper (1992–93) no 651) para 76. See *Re Jacobs, Westminster Bank Ltd v Chinn* (1970) 114 Sol Jo 515, where the point was not discussed in the judgment.

(3) NON-CHARITABLE PURPOSES

(i) Gifts for Private Charities or Individuals

59. 'Private charities'. Bequests for private charitable purposes[1] are not recognised by the courts as charitable in the legal sense[2], except where, by the use of the word 'private', a testator may be said to have drawn a distinction between charities available for all and charities which are restricted to a special class or administered by individuals without the intervention of any corporate organisation[3].

1 As to the ambiguity of the expression 'private charity' see *A-G v Pearce* (1740) 2 Atk 87 ('each particular object may be private, but it is the extensiveness which will constitute it a public charity'); *Nash v Morley* (1842) 5 Beav 177; *Hall v Derby Sanitary Authority* (1885) 16 QBD 163 at 171 per Manisty J, and at 173 per Smith J; *Re Slevin, Slevin v Hepburn* [1891] 2 Ch 236, CA.

2 *Ommanney v Butcher* (1823) Turn & R 260; *Ellis v Selby* (1836) 1 My & Cr 286 at 292–293 per Lord Cottenham LC; *Nash v Morley* (1842) 5 Beav 177 at 183 per Lord Langdale MR. See also, for a modern reassertion of this position, *Attorney General v Charity Commission for England and Wales* [2012] UKUT 420 (TCC) at [42], [2012] WTLR 977, 15 ITELR 521.

3 *Re Sinclair's Trust* (1884) 13 LR Ir 150 at 154 per Porter MR. With this interpretation of the word 'private', it may be possible to reconcile *Waldo v Caley* (1809) 16 Ves 206, where a gift for 'charitable purposes as well of a public as a private nature' was held good; *Johnston v Swann* (1818) 3 Madd 457, where a trust for public and private charities was held good; and *Horde v Earl of Suffolk* (1833) 2 My & K 59, where a trust 'to distribute in charity to private individuals or public institutions' was held good.

60. Gifts for benefit of individuals. Gifts for the benefit of particular individuals or a fluctuating body of particular individuals[1], whether named by the testator or to be selected by his trustees[2] or by any other person[3], are never charitable, although they may be upheld as gifts to individuals if the recipients can deal with the capital and income of the gifts as they please[4]. Examples are gifts for persons residing in a particular street[5], for the children of the testator's tenants on a particular estate[6], for a city company whose property was impressed with no charitable trust[7], for the members of a religious community associated only for the purpose of working out their own salvation[8], even though involving intercessory prayer and other spiritual exercises affording edification by example[9], for poor relations limited to statutory next of kin[10], for descendants of named persons[11], for the workpeople employed in a certain department of a company's business[12], for employees of a particular company who give financial subscriptions[13], for all the employees of a public company[14], or for children of past and present employees of a group of companies[15], unless the gifts are to relieve poor employees or past employees of the company or group[16].

The following have also been held not to be charitable: bequests for the benefit of an orphan school kept by an individual substantially at his own expense[17], for the support of any boy or man of a particular surname[18], for keeping a portrait in repair[19], for providing a particular estate with labourers' cottages[20], to a livery company for giving a dinner on the testator's birthday to which certain churchwardens should be invited[21], for a private chapel with chaplain and choristers[22], for a Church of England retreat house[23], for the suppression of cruelty to animals by the private prayers of members of a society[24], for the maintenance of particular animals[25], a gift of a house to provide a commodious residence for the High Commissioner of Australia for the time being[26], a devise of a house to a college as a residence for a fellow who should 'sometimes give entertainment to the poor'[27], a conveyance of land to be used as a recreation ground for the benefit of the employees of a named company[28], for establishing a hotel for distinguished overseas visitors to Stratford-upon-Avon[29], and a fund to maintain a building of national architectural interest which was used largely for the private purposes of the body to which it belonged[30].

1 *Goodman v Saltash Corpn* (1882) 7 App Cas 633 at 650, HL, per Earl Cairns.

2 *Liley v Hey* (1842) 1 Hare 580; *Thomas v Howell* (1874) LR 18 Eq 198; *Edge v Salisbury* (1749) Amb 70.

3 *A-G v Hughes* (1689) 2 Vern 105.

4 *Cocks v Manners* (1871) LR 12 Eq 574; *Re Clarke, Clarke v Clarke* [1901] 2 Ch 110; *Re Smith, Johnson v Bright-Smith* [1914] 1 Ch 937; *Re Drummond, Ashworth v Drummond* [1914] 2 Ch 90 at 97 per Eve J. See also *Re Taylor, Midland Bank Executor and Trustee Co Ltd v Smith* [1940] Ch 481, [1940] 2 All ER 637; appeal dismissed by consent [1940] Ch 834, CA (gift to bank staff fund having purposes charitable and non-charitable: not charitable, but valid; *Cocks v Manners* and *Re Clarke, Clarke v Clarke* applied).

5 *Rogers v Thomas* (1837) 2 Keen 8.

6 *Browne v King* (1885) 17 LR Ir 488; and cf *Bristow v Bristow* (1842) 5 Beav 289.

7 *A-G v Haberdashers' Co* (1834) 1 My & K 420; *Re Meech's Will, Butchers' Co v Rutland* [1910] 1 Ch 426.

8 *Cocks v Manners* (1871) LR 12 Eq 574; *Stewart v Green* (1870) IR 5 Eq 470; *Re Delany* (1881) 9 LR Ir 226. See also *Re Delany, Conoley v Quick* [1902] 2 Ch 642, where the objects of the convent were charitable; *Neville Estates Ltd v Madden* [1962] Ch 832, [1961] 3 All ER 769; *Re Banfield, Lloyds Bank Ltd v Smith* [1968] 2 All ER 276, [1968] 1 WLR 846.

9 *Gilmour v Coats* [1949] AC 426, [1949] 1 All ER 848, HL. See also *Neville Estates Ltd v Madden* [1962] Ch 832, [1961] 3 All ER 769; *Re Banfield, Lloyds Bank Ltd v Smith* [1968] 2 All ER 276, [1968] 1 WLR 846.

10 *Edge v Salisbury* (1749) Amb 70, where 'nearest relations' was construed to mean statutory next of kin; *Brunsden v Woolredge* (1765) Amb 507; *Widmore v Woodroffe* (1766) Amb 636; *Goodinge v Goodinge* (1749) 1 Ves Sen 231; *Doyley v A-G* (1735) 4 Vin Abr 485, pl 16; *Salusbury v Denton* (1857) 3 K & J 529. See also *Gower v Mainwaring* (1750) 2 Ves Sen 87; and PARA 15.

11 *Re Compton, Powell v Compton* [1945] Ch 123, [1945] 1 All ER 198, CA. See also *Davies v Perpetual Trustee Co Ltd* [1959] AC 439, [1959] 2 All ER 128, PC.
12 *Re Drummond, Ashworth v Drummond* [1914] 2 Ch 90.
13 *Re Hobourn Aero Components Ltd's Air-Raid Distress Fund, Ryan v Forrest* [1946] Ch 194, [1946] 1 All ER 501, CA.
14 *Wernher's Charitable Trust v IRC* [1937] 2 All ER 488. See also *Re Cox, Baker v National Trust Co Ltd* [1955] AC 627, [1955] 2 All ER 550, PC; *Re Koettgen's Will Trusts, Westminster Bank Ltd v Family Welfare Association Trustees Ltd* [1954] Ch 252, [1954] 1 All ER 581; *Caffoor (Trustees of Abdul Gaffoor Trust) v Income Tax Comr, Colombo* [1961] AC 584, [1961] 2 All ER 436, PC.
15 *Oppenheim v Tobacco Securities Trust Co Ltd* [1951] AC 297, [1951] 1 All ER 31, HL.
16 *Gibson v South American Stores (Gath and Chaves) Ltd* [1950] Ch 177, [1949] 2 All ER 985, CA; following *Re Gosling, Gosling v Smith* (1900) 48 WR 300, and *Re Sir Robert Laidlaw's Will Trusts* (1935, unreported). See further PARA 18.
17 *Clark v Taylor* (1853) 1 Drew 642; cf *Re Marchant, Weaver v Royal Society for the Prevention of Cruelty to Animals* (1910) 54 Sol Jo 425.
18 *Laverty v Laverty* [1907] 1 IR 9.
19 *Re Gassiot, Fladgate v Vintners' Co* (1901) 70 LJCh 242.
20 *Re Tunno, Raikes v Raikes* [1886] WN 154, where the object was the benefit of the owner of the estate.
21 *Re Barnett, Waring v Painter Stainers Co* (1908) 24 TLR 788; but see *Re Coxen, McCallum v Coxen* [1948] Ch 747, [1948] 2 All ER 492 (bequest to provide dinner to charity trustees meeting for trust business: charitable as promoting efficient management of charity).
22 *Hoare v Hoare* (1886) 56 LT 147 at 150 per Chitty J.
23 *Re Warre's Will Trusts, Wort v Salisbury Diocesan Board of Finance* [1953] 2 All ER 99, [1953] 1 WLR 725.
24 *Re Joy, Purday v Johnson* (1888) 60 LT 175 at 178 per Chitty J, where the real object contemplated by the testator was the improvement of the members of the society, not the suppression of cruelty to animals, which is a valid charitable purpose. As to trusts for the advancement of animal welfare see PARA 44.
25 *Re Dean, Cooper-Dean v Stevens* (1889) 41 ChD 552; *Re Howard, Oakley v Aldridge* (1908) Times, 30 October. If a trust or condition for maintaining specified animals does not violate any rule against remoteness, it is not in itself unlawful. There may be no beneficiary directly interested in seeing to its enforcement; but when a trustee accepts a trust, the execution of which includes a lawful direction, or where an annuitant accepts an annuity subject to a lawful condition, the courts have not abstained from recognising such obligations. In *Pettingall v Pettingall* (1842) 11 LJCh 176 (applied in *Re Thompson, Public Trustee v Lloyd* [1934] Ch 342) the executor was held, upon the construction of the will, to be a beneficial legatee of the surplus of an annual sum which he was directed to apply to the keeping of a mare; the court enforced the obligation by requiring full information to be given when required respecting the animal, by giving liberty to apply, and by an undertaking to maintain the animal comfortably. In *Mitford v Reynolds* (1848) 16 Sim 105 at 116, 120 per Shadwell V-C, there was a charitable bequest, after deducting the annual amount required for the keep of specified horses; the court's order included provision for the horses. In *Re Dean, Cooper-Dean v Stevens*, a trust annuity for the maintenance of certain horses and dogs was held valid. A proper way of providing for specified animals has been said to be by giving an annuity to a custodian payable so long as any of them are living: *Re Howard, Oakley v Aldridge*. See also *Re Endacott, Corpe v Endacott* [1960] Ch 232, [1959] 3 All ER 562, CA.
26 *Re Spensley's Will Trusts, Barclays Bank Ltd v Staughton* [1954] Ch 233, [1954] 1 All ER 178, CA. But see *Re Courtauld-Thomson Trusts* (1954) Times, 18 December, where a gift to apply income, and, if necessary, capital, in defraying the expenses of residence of a Minister of the Crown in certain property, the subject matter of another disposition, was held to be a valid charitable trust.
27 *A-G v Whorwood* (1750) 1 Ves Sen 534.
28 *Wernher's Charitable Trust v IRC* [1937] 2 All ER 488.
29 *Re Corelli, Watt v Bridges* [1943] Ch 332, [1943] 2 All ER 519.
30 *Trades House of Glasgow v IRC* 1970 SLT 294, Ct of Sess.

61. Monuments and tombs. Gifts for building, maintaining or repairing a monument or tomb which does not form part of the fabric or ornament of a church[1], whether as a memorial or burying place of the donor alone[2] or of himself and his family[3], cannot be supported as charities, though they may be valid as private trusts if they do not offend the law against perpetuities[4]. However, these cases are anomalous and should not be followed except where the one is exactly like another[5].

Gifts for monuments and tombs may not be construed as charitable even when expressed through a charitable gift to be applied preferably in a particular way 'and a small provision for keeping in repair the graves of my wife's parents'[6]. So, too, a bequest to an infirmary for the purpose of maintaining the testator's grave and headstone is void; and a further bequest of personalty for the general purposes of the infirmary subject to its accepting the prior bequest takes effect free from the condition[7]. However, a bequest for maintaining a burial ground, and in particular the grave of the testator's wife, is good[8], and the direction with regard to the particular grave is merely a special obligation ancillary to the repair of the burial ground and not a separate trust[9].

Where a fund is bequeathed to trustees upon trust out of the income to keep a tomb not forming part of a church[10] in repair, and as to the residue[11], surplus[12], balance[13] or remainder[14], upon trust for charitable objects, the gift is construed as a bequest of the whole fund charged with a gift that fails, and not as a gift of the residue after a void gift[15], and accordingly the whole fund, including the amount necessary to satisfy the invalid object, is applicable to the valid charitable object[16].

As in the case of gifts for the repair of tombs, a condition attaching to a gift, that a tomb which is not part of the fabric of a church be kept in repair, is not charitable but is not of itself illegal. If such a condition is limited within the perpetuity period, so that no remote interest will arise on its determination, it may be a valid condition[17]; and a perpetual condition of this sort attaching to a valid charitable gift, with a gift over on breach of the condition to another charity, has been held valid[18]. However, where the gift over is not to a charity, the condition is void and the original bequest takes effect free from the condition[19], and if the condition attaches to a non-charitable gift, that gift fails and with it the gift over[20].

By contrast, a bequest to trustees of a sum of money upon trust to invest it and pay the income to a cemetery company during such period as the company should keep specified graves in order, and if the graves should not be kept in order to pay the income to charitable organisations entitled to the balance of the testator's residuary income not required for another charitable purpose, has been held not to infringe the rule against perpetuities or the rule against inalienability and to be a valid gift[21].

Local authorities and burial authorities have power to agree with any person to maintain private monuments and memorials in certain circumstances in consideration of the payment of a sum by him, provided that no such agreement imposes on the authority an obligation of maintenance with respect to a period exceeding 99 years from the date of the agreement[22]. A burial authority also has power to agree with any person, on such terms and conditions as it thinks proper, to maintain any grave, vault, tombstone or other memorial in a cemetery for a period not exceeding 100 years from the date of the agreement[23].

1 *Trimmer v Danby* (1856) 25 LJCh 424; *Hoare v Osborne* (1866) LR 1 Eq 585; *Re Rigley's Trusts* (1866) 36 LJCh 147; *Re Barker, Sherrington v Dean and Chapter of St Paul's Cathedral* (1909) 25 TLR 753.

2 *Mellick v Asylum President and Guardians* (1821) Jac 180; *Adnam v Cole* (1843) 6 Beav 353; *Lloyd v Lloyd* (1852) 2 Sim NS 255; *Willis v Brown* (1838) 2 Jur 987.

3 *Gravenor v Hallum* (1767) Amb 643; *Durour v Motteux* (1749) 1 Ves Sen 320; *Doe d Thompson v Pitcher* (1815) 3 M & S 407; *Re Rickard, Rickard v Robson* (1862) 31 Beav 244;

Fowler v Fowler (1864) 33 Beav 616; *Hoare v Osborne* (1866) LR 1 Eq 585; *Re Rigley's Trusts* (1866) 36 LJCh 147; *Fisk v A-G* (1867) LR 4 Eq 521; *Hunter v Bullock* (1872) LR 14 Eq 45; *Dawson v Small* (1874) LR 18 Eq 114; *Re Williams* (1877) 5 ChD 735; *Re Birkett* (1878) 9 ChD 576; *Yeap Cheah Neo v Ong Cheng Neo* (1875) LR 6 PC 381; *Re Vaughan, Vaughan v Thomas* (1886) 33 ChD 187; *Re Rogerson, Bird v Lee* [1901] 1 Ch 715; *Toole v Hamilton* [1901] 1 IR 383. As to the maintenance of graveyards see PARA 33.

4 *Mellick v Asylum President and Guardians* (1821) Jac 180; *Trimmer v Danby* (1856) 25 LJCh 424; *Roche v M'Dermott* [1901] 1 IR 394 at 399. A trust in a will to keep up a tomb for as long as the law for the time being permits is valid for 21 years from the time of the testator's death: *Pirbright v Salwey* [1896] WN 86, followed in *Re Hooper, Parker v Ward* [1932] 1 Ch 38. Cf *Re Moore, Prior v Moore* [1901] 1 Ch 936, where the addition of words 'that is to say until the period of twenty-one years from the death of the last survivor of all persons who shall be living at my death' rendered the trust void for uncertainty. As to the rule against perpetuities see further PARA 142. But see now the Perpetuities and Accumulations Act 1964, the Perpetuities and Accumulations Act 2009; and **PERPETUITIES AND ACCUMULATIONS**.

5 *Re Endacott, Corpe v Endacott* [1960] Ch 232 at 251, [1959] 3 All ER 562 at 571, CA, per Harman LJ, and at 246 and 568 per Lord Evershed MR.

6 *Re Norton's Will Trusts, Lightfoot v Goldson* [1948] 2 All ER 842.

7 *Re Elliott, Lloyds Bank Ltd v Burton-on-Trent Hospital Management Committee* [1952] Ch 217, [1952] 1 All ER 145, where the prior bequest was admitted to be void as creating a perpetuity and, the condition precedent being therefore illegal, its effect on the further bequest as *malum prohibitum* was decided by reference to the civil law. See also **WILLS AND INTESTACY** vol 102 (2010) PARA 130.

8 See *Re Hooper, Parker v Ward* [1932] 1 Ch 38.

9 *Re Manser, A-G v Lucas* [1905] 1 Ch 68.

10 The repair of a tomb forming part of a church is charitable: see PARA 33.

11 *Fisk v A-G* (1867) LR 4 Eq 521; *Re Vaughan, Vaughan v Thomas* (1886) 33 ChD 187.

12 *Hoare v Osborne* (1866) LR 1 Eq 585; *Dawson v Small* (1874) LR 18 Eq 114; *Re Williams* (1877) 5 ChD 735.

13 *Hunter v Bullock* (1872) LR 14 Eq 45; and cf *Re Taylor, Martin v Freeman* (1888) 58 LT 538, where in a special case a bequest of 'the balance' was not construed as residuary. As to what constitutes a residuary gift to charity see generally *Paice v Archbishop of Canterbury* (1807) 14 Ves 364; *A-G v Goulding* (1788) 2 Bro CC 428; *Harbin v Masterman* (1871) LR 12 Eq 559; *Harbin v Masterman* [1894] 2 Ch 184, CA (affd sub nom *Wharton v Masterman* [1895] AC 186, HL).

14 *Re Birkett* (1878) 9 ChD 576.

15 The principle on which this class of cases is to be distinguished from the class (of which *Mitford v Reynolds* (1842) 1 Ph 185, forms one: see PARA 87), in which the charity took only the surplus after the amount necessary for the invalid object had been ascertained, and not the entire fund, is that the direction for the upkeep of the tomb created only a moral obligation: *Re Rogerson, Bird v Lee* [1901] 1 Ch 715 at 719 per Joyce J; *Re Dalziel, Midland Bank Executor and Trustee Co Ltd v St Bartholomew's Hospital* [1943] Ch 277, [1943] 2 All ER 656, where a gift over showed that no mere moral obligation was intended.

16 *Re Rogerson, Bird v Lee* [1901] 1 Ch 715; and see the cases cited in notes 11–14. Cf *Fowler v Fowler* (1864) 33 Beav 616 (where the gift of the surplus, after a trust to repair a tomb, was held void for uncertainty on the ground that the amount required for repairing a tomb could not be ascertained); *Re Rigley's Trusts* (1866) 36 LJCh 147 (where the court directed an inquiry to ascertain in what proportions a gift valid as to part and invalid as to the other part, namely the repair of a private tomb, should be divided). An affidavit of a competent person as to the cost of such repairs has been accepted: *Re Vaughan, Vaughan v Thomas* (1886) 33 ChD 187; *Re Birkett* (1878) 9 ChD 576 at 579 per Jessel MR. The principle of these 'tomb cases' has been held inapplicable to a somewhat analogous gift for maintaining a memorial masonic temple: *Re Porter, Porter v Porter* [1925] Ch 746.

17 *Lloyd v Lloyd* (1852) 2 Sim NS 255 at 264 per Lord Cranworth V-C; *Re Dean, Cooper-Dean v Stevens* (1889) 41 ChD 552 at 557 per North J; *Pirbright v Salwey* [1896] WN 86. The ratio decidendi of the two last cited cases is 'anomalous and not easy to explain' (Jarman on Wills (8th Edn, 1951) p 286 note (s)); but *Pirbright v Salwey* was followed in *Re Hooper, Parker v Ward* [1932] 1 Ch 38 (Maugham J). In *Lloyd v Lloyd* there were two trusts for the repair of tombs: one of the inheritance on a trust to repair a tomb, which the court held void as a perpetuity (*Lloyd v Lloyd* at 266 per Lord Cranworth V-C); the other a condition that two annuitants should out of their life estates keep a tomb in repair, which was held binding on the annuitants. In that case, at 264, Kindersley V-C said that he was satisfied that a condition simply for keeping a tomb in repair was not a charitable one, and was not of itself illegal; it might be

illegal to vest property in trustees in perpetuity for such a purpose; but the direction that the annuitants should out of their life interests keep the tomb in repair was quite lawful and they were obliged, out of their annuities, to do so according to the direction of the will.

18 *Re Tyler, Tyler v Tyler* [1891] 3 Ch 252, CA. The principle of the decision was that the rule against perpetuities does not apply to a transfer, in certain events, of property from one charity to another. As to the validity of gifts over see PARA 143.

19 *Re Davies, Lloyd v Cardigan County Council* [1915] 1 Ch 543.

20 *Re Dalziel, Midland Bank Executor and Trustee Co Ltd v St Bartholomew's Hospital* [1943] Ch 277, [1943] 2 All ER 656.

21 *Re Chardon, Johnston v Davies* [1928] Ch 464; *Re Chambers' Will Trusts, Official Trustees of Charitable Funds v British Union for Abolition of Vivisection* [1950] Ch 267. Tudor on Charities (5th Edn, 1929) p 701 sets out clauses of the will and the court order omitted from the report of *Re Chardon, Johnston v Davies*, and notes that the decision in that case was not affected by the presence of charitable interests. See also the article 'The Upkeep of a Tomb' (1950) 100 L Jo 524, explaining the decision on the basis that the legatees were free to dispose of the income as they pleased so long as the graves were kept in repair. Such a gift would now be affected by the Perpetuities and Accumulations Act 1964 s 12: see PARA 144; and **PERPETUITIES AND ACCUMULATIONS** vol 80 (2013) PARA 48. See also the Perpetuities and Accumulations Act 2009.

On the other hand, a gift of income for an indefinite period to a society for the furtherance of non-charitable purposes is void: *Re Wightwick's Will Trusts, Official Trustees of Charitable Funds v Fielding-Ould* [1950] Ch 260, [1950] 1 All ER 689, citing *Re Dutton, ex p Peake* (1878) 4 ExD 54; *Re Clark's Trust* (1875) 1 ChD 497; *Re Swain, Phillips v Poole* (1908) 99 LT 604; *Cocks v Manners* (1871) LR 12 Eq 574 at 586 per Wickens V-C; *Re Clarke, Clarke v Clarke* [1901] 2 Ch 110; *Re Drummond, Ashworth v Drummond* [1914] 2 Ch 90. See also *Re Elliott, Lloyds Bank Ltd v Burton-on-Trent Hospital Management Committee* [1952] Ch 217, [1952] 1 All ER 145 (see the text and note 7); *Re Conner, Provincial Bank of Ireland Ltd v General Cemetery Co of Dublin and Lucas* [1960] IR 67.

22 See the Parish Councils and Burial Authorities (Miscellaneous Provisions) Act 1970 s 1(1); and **CREMATION AND BURIAL** vol 24 (2010) PARA 1227. As to burial authorities see **CREMATION AND BURIAL** vol 24 (2010) PARA 1116 et seq.

23 See the Local Authorities' Cemeteries Order 1977, SI 1977/204, art 10(7); and see **CREMATION AND BURIAL** vol 24 (2010) PARA 1227.

62. Gifts for associations and perpetual institutions. An association or institution may benefit its members in the course of carrying out its main charitable purpose, and this alone will not prevent its being a charity[1]. It is a question of fact whether there is so much personal benefit, intellectual or professional, to the members of a society or body as to be incapable of being disregarded[2].

Gifts for associations or institutions whose objects are solely or substantially for the private advantage of their members are not charitable[3], as, for example, gifts to societies for promoting the interests of the members of a profession[4], and gifts for friendly and other mutual benefit societies[5] not requiring poverty as an essential element to entitle a member to the benefits of the society[6], the Corps of Commissionaires[7], a trade union or its benevolent fund[8], a sacred harmonic society[9], a mechanics' institute[10], a library[11], chess club[12], or museum[13], established for subscribers only. However, this principle does not apply with full force to associations established for religious purposes, although it would if they were wholly secluded and contemplative[14].

On the winding up of associations of this kind the funds may be divisible among the members for the time being[15], but, where there is no resulting trust for subscribers and the members are only entitled by their contract of membership to a limited interest in the funds of the association, any surplus after satisfying the contractual rights of members passes to the Crown as bona vacantia[16].

A gift to a perpetual unincorporated non-charitable institution may be construed as a gift to the individual members of the institution for the time being; and may be valid, if it is not, and when paid will not become, subject to any trust which prevents the existing members from spending the money as they please[17]. If, however, the gift is one which, by reason of its own terms or of the constitution of the institution in whose favour it is made, tends to a perpetuity, it is bad[18], except in the case of a gift authorised by the Literary and Scientific Institutions Act 1854[19], notwithstanding that such an institution is perpetual and non-charitable and that the members pay subscriptions[20].

1 See *IRC v Yorkshire Agricultural Society* [1928] 1 KB 611 at 630, CA, per Atkin LJ; and PARA 25 note 12.

2 *Midland Counties Institution of Engineers v IRC* (1928) 14 TC 285 at 293, CA, per Rowlatt J; *London Hospital Medical College v IRC* [1976] 2 All ER 113 at 122, [1976] 1 WLR 613 at 623 per Brightman J ('a matter of degree').

3 A society engaged in joint operation for the sake of gain may be a partnership, but a society for charitable purposes is not: see PARTNERSHIP vol 79 (2014) PARA 6.

4 *R v Income Tax Special Comrs, ex p Headmasters' Conference, R v Income Tax Special Comrs, ex p Incorporated Association of Preparatory Schools* (1925) 41 TLR 651; *Geologists' Association v IRC* (1928) 14 TC 271, CA (combination of members for scientific purposes and mutual improvement, all the benefits being enjoyed primarily by the members); followed in *Midland Counties Institution of Engineers v IRC* (1928) 14 TC 285, CA (association of persons for mutual improvement in technical and professional knowledge); *Honourable Co of Master Mariners v IRC* (1932) 17 TC 298 (association to foster professional interests); *Chartered Insurance Institute v London Corpn* [1957] 2 All ER 638, [1957] 1 WLR 867, DC.

So, too, the General Medical Council, a body formed to register and regulate the members of a profession was held on the above principles not to be charitable: *General Medical Council v IRC* (1928) 97 LJKB 578, CA; and see *General Nursing Council for Scotland v IRC* 1929 SC 664, Ct of Sess (council not a body established for charitable purposes only; funds partly benefited professional interest); *General Nursing Council for England and Wales v St Marylebone Borough Council* [1959] AC 540, [1959] 1 All ER 325, HL). However, more recently the Charity Commission has taken the view that because its purpose is primarily for the benefit of the public and not for the benefit of the profession, it can be registered as a charity: see *Application for Registration as a Charity by the General Medical Council*, Decision of the Charity Commissioners, 2 April 2001, at para 10.3. And see further PARA 34, especially note 6. As to decisions of the Charity Commission see PARA 547.

5 *Re Clark's Trust* (1875) 1 ChD 497; *Cunnack v Edwards* [1896] 2 Ch 679, CA; *Re Topham, Public Trustee v Topham* [1938] 1 All ER 181 (club having for object the religious, intellectual, physical and social improvement of its members and associated with a church); *Lord Nuffield v IRC* (1946) 175 LT 465 (trust to organise mutual insurance associations to meet expenditure necessitated by illness, not charitable); and see the cases cited in note 15. The receipt of donations and subscriptions is not sufficient to make a friendly society charitable: *Re Clark's Trust* at 500 per Hall V-C; *Re Buck, Bruty v Mackey* [1896] 2 Ch 727 at 733 per Kekewich J; *Braithwaite v A-G* [1909] 1 Ch 510. See, however, *Re Forster, Gellatly v Palmer* [1939] Ch 22, [1938] 3 All ER 767.

6 See the cases cited in PARA 18 notes 7–8.

7 *Re Clarke, Clarke v Clarke* [1901] 2 Ch 110.

8 *Re Amos, Carrier v Price* [1891] 3 Ch 159. See also *Re Estlin, Prichard v Thomas* (1903) 72 LJCh 687.

9 *Re Allsop, Gell v Carver* (1884) 1 TLR 4; but see *Royal Choral Society v IRC* [1943] 2 All ER 101, CA.

10 *Re Dutton, ex p Peake* (1878) 4 ExD 54; *Re Sheraton's Trusts* [1884] WN 174.

11 *Carne v Long* (1860) 2 De GF & J 75; *Re Swain, Phillips v Poole* (1908) 99 LT 604; *Re Prevost, Lloyds Bank Ltd v Barclays Bank Ltd* [1930] 2 Ch 383.

12 *Re Swain, Phillips v Poole* (1908) 99 LT 604.

13 *Thomson v Shakespear* (1860) 1 De GF & J 399; *Laverty v Laverty* [1907] 1 IR 9; *Re Joy, Purday v Johnson* (1888) 60 LT 175.

14 *Neville Estates Ltd v Madden* [1962] Ch 832, [1961] 3 All ER 769; and see PARA 28.

15 *Brown v Dale* (1878) 9 ChD 78; *Re Russell Institution, Figgins v Baghino* [1898] 2 Ch 72; *Re Jones, Clegg v Ellison* [1898] 2 Ch 83; *Re Printers and Transferrers Amalgamated Trades Protection Society* [1899] 2 Ch 184; *Re Lead Co's Workmen's Fund Society, Lowes v Governor*

and Co for Smelting Down Lead with Pit and Sea Coal [1904] 2 Ch 196; *Re Customs and Excise Officers' Mutual Guarantee Fund, Robson v A-G* [1917] 2 Ch 18; *Re St Andrew's Allotment Association's Trusts, Sargeant v Probert* [1969] 1 All ER 147, [1969] 1 WLR 229; *Re Sick and Funeral Society of St John's Sunday School, Golcar* [1973] Ch 51, [1972] 2 All ER 439; *Re GKN Bolts and Nuts Ltd Sports and Social Club, Leek v Donkersley* [1982] 2 All ER 855, [1982] 1 WLR 774. Contra, *Re West Sussex Constabulary's Widows, Children and Benevolent (1930) Fund Trusts, Barnett v Ketteringham* [1971] Ch 1, [1970] 1 All ER 544. See also *Re Grant's Will Trusts, Harris v Anderson* [1979] 3 All ER 359, [1980] 1 WLR 360; *Conservative and Unionist Central Office v Burrell (Inspector of Taxes)* [1980] 3 All ER 42 (affd without discussion of this point [1982] 2 All ER 1, [1982] 1 WLR 522, CA).

16 *Cunnack v Edwards* [1896] 2 Ch 679, CA. As to the court's jurisdiction to dissolve such societies on sufficient cause being shown see *Blake v Smither* (1906) 22 TLR 698; and on the question of dissolution generally see *Re William Denby & Son Ltd Sick and Benevolent Fund, Rowling v Wilks* [1971] 2 All ER 1196, [1971] 1 WLR 973. As to bona vacantia see CROWN AND CROWN PROCEEDINGS vol 29 (2014) PARA 145 et seq.

17 *Cocks v Manners* (1871) LR 12 Eq 574; *Re Clarke, Clarke v Clarke* [1901] 2 Ch 110 at 114 per Byrne J; *Re Smith, Johnson v Bright-Smith* [1914] 1 Ch 937; *Re Drummond, Ashworth v Drummond* [1914] 2 Ch 90 at 97 per Eve J; *Bourne v Keane* [1919] AC 815 at 874, HL, per Lord Buckmaster, and at 916, per Lord Parmoor; *Re Delany, Conoley v Quick* [1902] 2 Ch 642; *Re Turkington, Owen v Benson* [1937] 4 All ER 501 (gift to local masonic lodge as a fund to build local temple: held that members could not be trustees for themselves); *Re Taylor, Midland Bank Executor and Trustee Co Ltd v Smith* [1940] Ch 481, [1940] 2 All ER 637 (on appeal [1940] Ch 834, CA) (gift for bank staff association fund, formed for purposes only partly charitable, to be administered according to rules of fund under which committee could deal with it as it pleased; on appeal, parties agreed); *Re Price, Midland Bank Executor and Trustee Co Ltd v Harwood* [1943] Ch 422, [1943] 2 All ER 505 (gift to Anthroposophical Society to be used at the discretion of the chairman and executive council for carrying on the teachings of the founder: capital and income being held to be available); *Re Lipinski's Will Trusts, Gosschalk v Levy* [1976] Ch 235, [1977] 1 All ER 33 (a non-charitable purpose trust which is directly or indirectly for the benefit of ascertained individuals is valid). Contrast *Re Grant's Will Trusts, Harris v Anderson* [1979] 3 All ER 359, [1980] 1 WLR 360. See also generally *Leahy v A-G for New South Wales* [1959] AC 457, [1959] 2 All ER 300, PC; *Neville Estates Ltd v Madden* [1962] Ch 832, [1961] 3 All ER 769; *Re Recher's Will Trusts, National Westminster Bank Ltd v National Anti-Vivisection Society* [1972] Ch 526, [1971] 3 All ER 401.

18 *Re Clarke, Clarke v Clarke* [1901] 2 Ch 110 at 114 per Byrne J; *Thomson v Shakespear* (1860) 1 De GF & J 399; *Carne v Long* (1860) 2 De GF & J 75; *Re Dutton, ex p Peake* (1878) 4 ExD 54; *Re Amos, Carrier v Price* [1891] 3 Ch 159; *Re Swain, Phillips v Poole* (1908) 99 LT 604; *Re Clifford, Mallam v McFie* [1912] 1 Ch 29, 81 LJCh 220; *Re Macaulay's Estate, Macaulay v O'Donnell* [1943] Ch 435n, HL (gift to local lodge of Theosophical Society for the maintenance and improvement of the local Theosophical Lodge denotes permanency and endowment). The invalidity of such gifts is not saved by the Perpetuities and Accumulations Act 1964: see s 15(4); and PERPETUITIES AND ACCUMULATIONS vol 80 (2013) PARA 5.

19 See NATIONAL CULTURAL HERITAGE vol 77 (2010) PARA 945.

20 See the Literary and Scientific Institutions Act 1854 s 30; and NATIONAL CULTURAL HERITAGE vol 77 (2010) PARA 959. See also *Re Badger, Mansell v Viscount Cobham* [1905] 1 Ch 568 at 573 per Buckley J.

(ii) Superstitious Uses

63. Superstitious uses. Certain kinds of gift have in the past been held void as being for superstitious uses, whether or not their validity would otherwise depend on whether they were valid charitable gifts. A superstitious use may be defined as one which has for its object the propagation or the rites of a religion not tolerated by the law[1].

The Act of Uniformity 1558 made all forms of religion other than that of the Church of England illegal, and consequently gifts for the clergy or the buildings of Roman Catholics or Protestant dissenters, or for the propagation of the doctrines and principles of Roman Catholicism or the Jewish religion[2], were held void for superstition upon the common law principle that no disposition of property for purposes which are illegal can effect the intended purposes[3].

The effect of the Act of Uniformity 1558 was, however, alleviated by a succession of relieving Acts[4], and the Act of Uniformity itself has now been almost wholly repealed. The result is that there are now no religions proscribed by law[5]. It has been said that dispositions connected with relics, the veneration of saints or the sustenance of miracle producers might be held invalid despite the relieving Acts[6], but even if these practices were regarded as superstitious, such dispositions would not in themselves fall within the definition of superstitious uses[7]. If they were to be held invalid it might be on the ground that they were not charitable, there being no evidence of public benefit of which the court could take cognisance[8].

1 This is not exhaustive but will serve as a working definition: *Bourne v Keane* [1919] AC 815 at 845, 874, 916, HL, per Lord Birkenhead LC. See also *R v Lady Portington* (1692) 1 Salk 162.
2 See eg *Jones' Case* (1690) [1893] 2 Ch 49n, HL; *A-G v Todd* (1837) 1 Keen 803; *Smart v Prujean* (1801) 6 Ves 560; *De Garcin v Lawson* (1798) 4 Ves 433n; *Doe d Wellard v Hawthorn* (1818) 2 B & Ald 96; *Cary v Abbot* (1802) 7 Ves 490; *A-G v Power* (1809) 1 Ball & B 145; *De Themmines v De Bonneval* (1828) 5 Russ 288; *De Costa v De Paz* (1754) 2 Swan 487n.
3 *Bourne v Keane* [1919] AC 815 at 847, HL, per Lord Birkenhead LC.
4 See the Toleration Act 1688 (repealed); the Nonconformist Relief Act 1779 (repealed); the Places of Religious Worship Act 1812 (repealed); the Roman Catholic Relief Act 1829 (see ECCLESIASTICAL LAW vol 34 (2011) PARAS 65, 558); the Roman Catholic Charities Act 1832 (repealed); the Liberty of Religious Worship Act 1855 (repealed); the Roman Catholic Relief Act 1926 (repealed); the Religious Disabilities Act 1846 (repealed) (Jews). As to the effect of the Toleration Act 1688 see *Evans' Case* (1767) cited in 3 Mer 375n.
5 Cf *Thornton v Howe* (1862) 31 Beav 14; and see PARA 29.
6 *Bourne v Keane* [1919] AC 815 at 855, HL, per Lord Birkenhead LC.
7 See the text to note 1.
8 Cf *Gilmour v Coats* [1949] AC 426, [1949] 1 All ER 848, HL; and PARAS 27, 28. As to the public benefit see PARA 4 et seq.

64. Gifts for masses for the dead. Gifts for masses were among the gifts void as being for superstitious uses; even after the relieving Acts[1] it was believed that gifts for masses for the dead were void for superstition[2], but this was based on a misunderstanding[3]. It seems that no gifts can now be rendered void on this ground[4]. Such a gift may well be charitable, for it is clearly for the advancement of religion, and the element of public benefit required is satisfied at least where the masses are to be celebrated in public[5].

1 As to the relieving Acts see PARA 63 text and note 4.
2 See *West v Shuttleworth* (1835) 2 My & K 684.
3 See *Bourne v Keane* [1919] AC 815, HL, overruling *West v Shuttleworth* (1835) 2 My & K 684 and the cases following it.
4 The Roman Catholic Charities Act 1860 (repealed) seems to have assumed that there could still be trusts void for superstition, but it was a remedial Act and, if there could be no such trusts, the remedy is merely superfluous: see *Bourne v Keane* [1919] AC 815 at 856, HL, per Lord Birkenhead LC, and at 896, per Lord Atkinson. Lord Birkenhead LC said in that case, at 860, that the decision did not mean that there are now no superstitious uses, but he did not suggest any, nor have any come to light since 1919.
5 *Re Hetherington* [1990] Ch 1, sub nom *Re Hetherington, Gibbs v McDonnell* [1989] 2 All ER 129, following *Re Caus, Lindeboom v Camille* [1934] Ch 162, notwithstanding doubts expressed in *Gilmour v Coats* [1949] AC 426, [1949] 1 All ER 848, HL. As to the requirement for public benefit see PARA 4 et seq. As to religious purposes see PARA 28.

(iii) Non-charitable Public Purposes

65. Non-charitable public objects. Although purposes beneficial to the public or of public utility are prima facie charitable[1], certain public purposes have been held not to be charitable because they do not fall within the spirit and intendment of the preamble to the Charitable Uses Act 1601[2]. Such a purpose may possibly in the future be upheld as charitable[3] under the Charities Act 2011 as reasonably being either regarded as (1) analogous to, or within the spirit of, any purposes falling within the Act or the existing law[4]; or (2) analogous to, or within the spirit of, any purposes which have been recognised under charity law as falling within (1)[5]. However, until such time the following have been held not to be charitable: bequests for purposes of benevolence[6] or benevolence and liberality[7], for patriotic[8], civil or religious[9], philanthropic[10], parochial[11], missionary[12], pious[13], or Roman Catholic[14] purposes, or worthy causes[15], or for parish work[16], or for social or recreational purposes in connection with certain churches[17], or for purposes most conducive to the good of religion in a diocese[18], or for purposes conducive to the attainment of the objects of an association not limited to the advancement of religion[19], or for helping to carry on the work of the Church in Wales[20], or for executing the Papal office[21], or for purposes of hospitality[22] or general utility[23] or for emigration uses[24], or for simplifying spelling[25], or for increasing the sum of available knowledge[26], or for the storage of books[27]. Although the provision of the means of public recreation may be charitable[28], trusts for the promotion of religious, social and physical well-being[29], and for religious, moral, social and recreative purposes[30] and for giving aid and advice to the community generally[31] have been held not to be charitable. A gift to provide 'some useful memorial to myself' is not charitable[32]; nor is a gift for the general benefit and welfare of children for the time being in a local authority home[33]. The protection of the interests of holders in the United Kingdom of foreign bonds[34] is not charitable; nor is a pig marketing board[35] or a statutory body set up to administer a harbour[36], and a body established to help the government resist strikes threatening essential public services is also not charitable[37].

1 *Incorporated Council of Law Reporting for England and Wales v A-G* [1972] Ch 73, [1971] 3 All ER 1029, CA; and see PARA 46.

2 Ie 43 Eliz 1 c 4 (1601) (now wholly repealed: see PARA 2 note 25; and PARA 46). A trust to distribute income among organisation or institution operating for the public good was held not exclusively charitable: see *A-G of the Cayman Islands v Wahr Hansen* [2001] 1 AC 75, [2000] 3 All ER 642, PC.

3 Although note that the question of what falls within the spirit and intendment of the Charitable Uses Act 1601 tended not to be answered restrictively: *Vancouver Regional FreeNet Association v Minister of National Revenue* (1996) 137 DLR (4th) 206, Can CA (provision of public internet access within the spirit and intendment of the repair of bridges, ports, causeways and highways).

4 See the Charities Act 2011 s 3(1)(m)(ii); and PARA 2.

5 See the Charities Act 2011 3(1)(m)(iii); and PARA 2.

6 *James v Allen* (1817) 3 Mer 17; *Re Jarman's Estate, Leavers v Clayton* (1878) 8 ChD 584; *A-G for New Zealand v Brown* [1917] AC 393, PC; *A-G for New Zealand v New Zealand Insurance Co Ltd* [1936] 3 All ER 888, PC.

7 *Morice v Bishop of Durham* (1805) 10 Ves 522.

8 *A-G v National Provincial and Union Bank of England* [1924] AC 262, HL.

9 *Re Friends' Free School, Clibborn v O'Brien* [1909] 2 Ch 675.

10 *Re Macduff, Macduff v Macduff* [1896] 2 Ch 451, CA.

11 *Re Stratton, Knapman v A-G* [1931] 1 Ch 197, CA; *Cookstown Roman Catholic Church Trustees v IRC* (1953) 34 TC 350 (parochial requirements).

12 As to missionary purposes see PARA 30.

13 *Heath v Chapman* (1854) 2 Drew 417 at 425–426 per Page Wood V-C.

14 *MacLaughlin v Campbell* [1906] 1 IR 588; and see *Re Davidson, Minty v Bourne* [1909] 1 Ch 567, CA. Cf *Re Schoales, Schoales v Schoales* [1930] 2 Ch 75 (gift to the Roman Catholic Church for its use: charitable).

15 *Re Gillingham Bus Disaster Fund, Bowman v Official Solicitor* [1958] Ch 300 at 305, [1958] 1 All ER 37 at 39 per Harman J; affd [1959] Ch 62, [1958] 2 All ER 749, CA, where there are

dicta arguably supporting the opposite proposition. See *Re Atkinson's Will Trusts, Atkinson v Hall* [1978] 1 All ER 1275, [1978] 1 WLR 586 where the inclusion of 'worthy causes' in the list in the text was approved.

16 *Farley v Westminster Bank Ltd* [1939] AC 430, [1939] 3 All ER 491, HL.

17 *Londonderry Presbyterian Church House Trustees v IRC* [1946] NI 178, CA.

18 *Dunne v Byrne* [1912] AC 407, PC.

19 *Oxford Group v IRC* [1949] 2 All ER 537, CA; followed in *Associated Artists Ltd v IRC* [1956] 2 All ER 583, [1956] 1 WLR 752. See also PARA 28 note 5.

20 *Re Jackson, Midland Bank Executor and Trustee Co Ltd v Archbishop of Wales* [1930] 2 Ch 389.

21 *Re Moore, Moore v Pope Benedict XV* [1919] 1 IR 316.

22 *Re Hewitt's Estate, Gateshead Corpn v Hudspeth* (1883) 53 LJCh 132; and see *A-G v Whorwood* (1750) 1 Ves Sen 534; and *Re Corelli, Watt v Bridges* [1943] Ch 332, [1943] 2 All ER 519 (hostel for distinguished visitors from far countries).

23 *Kendall v Granger* (1842) 5 Beav 300; *Re Woodgate* (1886) 2 TLR 674.

24 *Re Sidney, Hingeston v Sidney* [1908] 1 Ch 488, CA; *Keren Kayemeth Le Jisroel Ltd v IRC* [1932] AC 650, HL (trust for settlement of Jews in Palestine and elsewhere); but cf *Verge v Somerville* [1924] AC 496, PC (cited in PARA 49 note 7) and *Re Tree, Idle v Tree* [1945] Ch 325, [1945] 2 All ER 65 (cited in PARA 18 note 9).

25 *Sir GB Hunter (1922) C Trust (Trustees) v IRC* (1929) 45 TLR 344; *Re Shaw, Public Trustee v Day* [1957] 1 All ER 745, [1957] 1 WLR 729.

26 *Whicker v Hume* (1858) 7 HL Cas 124 at 155 per Lord Chelmsford LC; *Re Macduff, Macduff v Macduff* [1896] 2 Ch 451 at 472–473, CA, per Rigby LJ; *Re Shaw, Public Trustee v Day* [1957] 1 All ER 745, [1957] 1 WLR 729.

27 *Re Hawkins, Walrond v Newton* (1906) 22 TLR 521.

28 See the Charities Act 2011 s 5; and PARAS 52–55.

29 *IRC v Baddeley* [1955] AC 572, [1955] 1 All ER 525, HL.

30 *Londonderry Presbyterian Church House Trustees v IRC* [1946] NI 178, CA.

31 *D'Aguiar v Guyana IRC* (1970) 49 ATC 33, PC.

32 *Re Endacott, Corpe v Endacott* [1960] Ch 232, [1959] 3 All ER 562, CA.

33 *Re Cole, Westminster Bank Ltd v Moore* [1958] Ch 877, [1958] 3 All ER 102, CA; but see *Re Sahal's Will Trusts, Alliance Assurance Co Ltd v A-G* [1958] 3 All ER 428, [1958] 1 WLR 1243.

34 *Foreign Bondholders Corpn v IRC* [1944] 1 KB 403, [1944] 1 All ER 420, CA.

35 *Pig Marketing Board (Northern Ireland) Ltd v IRC* [1945] NI 155.

36 *Auckland Harbour Board v IRC* [1959] NZLR 204.

37 *Trustees for the Roll of Voluntary Workers v IRC* 1942 SC 47, Ct of Sess.

66. Purposes contrary to public policy. A gift for a purpose not permitted by the law is void and cannot be charitable[1]. Similarly, if the gift is for a purpose contrary to public policy it is not a good charitable gift. Thus, gifts to pay the fines of imprisoned criminals[2], or which tend to promote revolution in a friendly foreign state[3], or for propagating doctrines subversive of morality[4] or disseminating pernicious knowledge[5], may be held void. A gift for a purpose contrary to ecclesiastical law, but not otherwise illegal, is not invalid on that ground[6], and the propagation of doctrines subversive of Christianity is not necessarily contrary to public policy[7].

1 Cf the cases on superstitious uses: see PARA 63. As to gifts for illegal purposes, or which tend towards the promotion of illegality, see **GIFTS** vol 52 (2014) PARAS 263–265.

2 *Thrupp v Collett* (1858) 26 Beav 125. The reference in the preamble to the Charitable Uses Act 1601 (43 Eliz 1 c 4 (1601)) (now wholly repealed: see PARA 2 note 25; and PARA 46) to the relief and redemption of prisoners or captives may be taken to refer to prisoners of war or Christian captives in Barbary (cf *Ironmongers' Co v A-G* (1844) 10 Cl & Fin 908, HL), or debtors other than those in contempt of court (cf *Re Prison Charities* (1873) LR 16 Eq 129).

3 *Habershon v Vardon* (1851) 4 De G & Sm 467 (political restoration of the Jews to Jerusalem, then under Turkish sovereignty).

4 *Thornton v Howe* (1862) 31 Beav 14; *Thompson v Thompson* (1844) 1 Coll 381 at 397 per Shadwell V-C; and see *Russell v Jackson* (1852) 10 Hare 204 (socialism); *Pare v Clegg* (1861) 29 Beav 589. It is to be presumed that what amounts to a doctrine subversive of morality is an

evolving concept, and that gifts for the propagation of socialist doctrine would no longer fall within this description, even if it were not for other reasons to be considered charitable. As to political purposes see PARA 67.

5 *Re Macduff, Macduff v Macduff* [1896] 2 Ch 451 at 474, CA, per Rigby LJ.

6 *Re Bowman, Secular Society Ltd v Bowman* [1915] 2 Ch 447 at 470, CA, per Warrington LJ; on appeal sub nom *Bowman v Secular Society Ltd* [1917] AC 406, HL.

7 *Bowman v Secular Society Ltd* [1917] AC 406, HL, overruling *Briggs v Hartley* (1850) 19 LJCh 416, and *Cowan v Milbourn* (1867) LR 2 Exch 230. It seems that this authority extends to doctrines subversive of all religion (see *Bowman v Secular Society Ltd* at 420 per Lord Finlay LC), although the House of Lords only treated the society as anti-Christian. See also *Thompson v Thompson* (1844) 1 Coll 381.

67. Political purposes. A trust for the attainment of political objects is not charitable, not because it is illegal (for everyone is at liberty to advocate or promote by any lawful means a change in the law), but because the court has no means of judging whether a proposed change in the law will or will not be for the public benefit, and therefore cannot say that a gift to secure the change is a charitable gift[1]. Political purposes include[2]: (1) furthering the interests of a political party; (2) procuring, or opposing[3], changes in the law of England and Wales, or another country; (3) procuring a reversal of government policy or a particular decision of government authority in England and Wales, or another country; (4) attempting to sway public opinion on controversial social issues[4]. Any purpose with the object of influencing the legislature is a political purpose[5], even where this is consistent with the way the law is heading[6]; and a trust for furthering the views of a particular political party, whether under the guise of an educational centre[7] or a fund for adult education on party lines[8], is not charitable; but a trust for a purpose which is charitable is not rendered non-charitable even if the trust instrument envisages the use of political means to achieve the charitable object[9].

Although charities may not have political objects, political activity may be carried out by charities, but only as a means of supporting their charitable purposes[10]. Political activity cannot be the continuing and sole activity of a charity[11]. The Charity Commission has published guidance on the political activity that is compatible with charitable status generally[12], and in particular on the activity that a charity can appropriately undertake during elections or referendums[13].

1 *Bowman v Secular Society Ltd* [1917] AC 406 at 442, HL, per Lord Parker, dealing with a society advocating the disestablishment of the Church; *National Anti-Vivisection Society v IRC* [1948] AC 31, [1947] 2 All ER 217, HL (society having as its main purpose the compulsory abolition of vivisection by Act of Parliament: not charitable); *Re Jones, Public Trustee v Earl of Clarendon* (1929) 45 TLR 259 (Primrose League: not a charity); *English-Speaking Union v Westminster City Council* (1959) 4 RRC 97, DC; *Re Bushnell, Lloyds Bank Ltd v Murray* [1975] 1 All ER 721, [1975] 1 WLR 1596 (trust for propagation of doctrines of socialist medicine not charitable); *McGovern v A-G* [1982] Ch 321, [1981] 3 All ER 493. See also *IRC v Temperance Council of Christian Churches of England and Wales* (1926) 136 LT 27; *Re Hood, Public Trustee v Hood* [1931] 1 Ch 240 at 250, CA, per Lord Hanworth MR, and at 252 per Lawrence LJ (trust to promote temperance mainly by political means: not charitable, though the advancement of temperance otherwise is charitable). See also *Human Dignity Trust v Charity Commission for England and Wales* (2014) First-tier Tribunal, General Regulatory Chamber (Charity), 9 July.

2 *McGovern v A-G* [1982] Ch 321, [1981] 3 All ER 493. As to where other public purposes are charitable see PARA 49. As to non-charitable public objects see PARA 65.

3 *Re Koeppler Will Trusts, Barclays Bank Trust Co Ltd v Slack* [1984] Ch 243, [1984] 2 All ER 111; revsd [1986] Ch 423, [1985] 2 All ER 869, CA, without affecting relevant dictum.

4 See eg *Southwood v A-G* [2000] WTLR 1199, CA, where a trust to advance education of the public in militarism and disarmament, which defined policies of certain government and challenged them, was political, not charitable.

5 *IRC v Temperance Council of Christian Churches of England and Wales* (1926) 136 LT 27; cf *Re Shaw, Public Trustee v Day* [1957] 1 All ER 745, [1957] 1 WLR 729, where the achievement of the purpose (the promotion of a new alphabet) would have involved legislation (an appeal was dismissed by consent on terms [1958] 1 All ER 245n, CA). See also *Baldry v Feintuck* [1972] 2 All ER 81 at 85, [1972] 1 WLR 552 at 558 per Brightman J; *Webb v O'Doherty* (1991) 3 Admin LR 731, (1991) Times, 11 February (campaigning in the sense of seeking to influence public opinion on political matters not a charitable activity).

6 *Hanchett-Stamford v A-G* [2008] EWHC 330 (Ch) at [22], [2009] Ch 173, [2008] 4 All ER 323 per Lewison J (prevention of cruelty to performing animals necessitating a change in the law to ban such performances not charitable despite the passing of the Animal Welfare Act 2006, which creates offences of causing distress to animals but does not go so far as to prohibit performing animals).

7 *Bonar Law Memorial Trust v IRC* (1933) 49 TLR 220; and see PARA 50 note 2.

8 *Re Hopkinson, Lloyds Bank Ltd v Baker* [1949] 1 All ER 346.

9 *National Anti-Vivisection Society v IRC* [1948] AC 31 at 51, 61, 76, [1947] 2 All ER 217 at 225, HL, per Lord Wright, at 231 per Lord Simonds, and at 239 per Lord Normand; *Re Hood, Public Trustee v Hood* [1931] 1 Ch 240, CA.

10 See *CC9: Speaking Out: Guidance on Campaigning and Political Activity by Charities* (Charity Commission, March 2008) para D5 (available, at the date at which this volume states the law, on the government website). As to the Charity Commission's publications see PARA 547. See also *Human Dignity Trust v Charity Commission for England and Wales* (2014) First-tier Tribunal, General Regulatory Chamber (Charity), 9 July.

11 See *CC9: Speaking Out: Guidance on Campaigning and Political Activity by Charities* (Charity Commission, March 2008) para D5.

12 See *CC9: Speaking Out: Guidance on Campaigning and Political Activity by Charities* (Charity Commission, March 2008).

13 See *Charities, Elections and Referendums* (Charity Commission, July 2014) (available, at the date at which this volume states the law, on the government website).

2. CREATION OF CHARITABLE TRUSTS

(1) FORMAL REQUIREMENTS AND RESTRICTIONS

(i) Creation by Assurance

68. Realty and personalty. As a general rule, realty and personalty of all descriptions, including advowsons[1] and easements[2], may be given to a charity by deed or by will.

Since the repeal of the mortmain laws[3], restrictions on the assurance of land in favour of charity exist only in the form of personal and corporate incapacity. Limited owners and persons under disability may make charitable gifts only in accordance with their particular powers or in the manner and form prescribed by enabling statutes. A corporation may only make charitable gifts within the framework of its constitution and for objects contemplated by it[4], if it is created by statute[5], or registered under the Companies Acts[6], or the Charities Act 2011[7] or is a municipal corporation[8]. A corporation created by royal charter, however, has prima facie the same power of disposition as a natural person[9].

1 *A-G v Ward* (1829) 7 LJOS Ch 114; *A-G v Archbishop of York* (1853) 17 Beav 495; *A-G v St John's Hospital, Bedford* (1864) 10 Jur NS 897; *Re St Stephen, Coleman Street, Re St Mary the Virgin, Aldermanbury* (1888) 39 ChD 492; *Hunter v A-G* [1899] AC 309 at 322, HL, per Lord Davey; *Re Church Patronage Trust, Laurie v A-G* [1904] 2 Ch 643, CA. But see the Patronage (Benefices) Measure 1986 s 3, prohibiting the sale of advowsons; and **ECCLESIASTICAL LAW** vol 34 (2011) PARA 583.

2 The contrary was stated in Duke on Charitable Uses, ed Bridgman (1805) 137–138, but there seems to be no reason why such a grant should not be made, and in many cases charities must be entitled to easements (see **REAL PROPERTY AND REGISTRATION** vol 87 (2012) PARA 802 et seq).

3 See PARAS 83–84.

4 It may not be ultra vires for a company to give away its property to charity, if it is done bona fide in the interests of the company: see *Hutton v West Cork Rly Co* (1883) 23 ChD 654 at 673, CA, per Bowen LJ; *Evans v Brunner, Mond & Co* [1921] 1 Ch 359; *Re Lee, Behrens & Co Ltd* [1932] 2 Ch 46; but see also *Parke v Daily News Ltd* [1962] Ch 927, [1962] 2 All ER 929.

5 *Baroness Wenlock v River Dee Co* (1883) 36 ChD 675n, CA; on appeal (1885) 10 App Cas 354, HL.

6 As to the registration of companies see **COMPANIES** vol 14 (2009) PARA 111 et seq.

7 Ie as a charitable incorporated organisation: see PARA 230.

8 See **LOCAL GOVERNMENT** vol 69 (2009) PARA 3; **LONDON GOVERNMENT**. See generally **GIFTS**.

9 See *Sutton's Hospital Case* (1612) 10 Co Rep 1a, 23a at 30b, Ex Ch. As to the limitation of powers of chartered corporations see **CORPORATIONS** vol 24 (2010) PARA 431; **GIFTS** vol 52 (2014) PARA 208.

69. Facilities for giving land, etc to charity. The Universities of Oxford, Cambridge and Durham and certain colleges[1], and the Crown Estates Commissioners with the consent of Her Majesty under the royal sign manual[2] may give limited areas of land for certain charitable purpose.

Particular classes of donor have also been given facilities for giving limited areas of land for special charitable purposes. These include any life tenant, a lord of a manor in respect of common land, a beneficiary under a trust, the guardian of a minor, and various corporate or public bodies and trustees holding land in a corporate, public or charitable capacity, who may grant land as a site for a school and certain allied purposes[3], or for enlarging a churchyard or burial ground[4]. Similar provisions apply to assist gifts for the promotion of science, literature and the fine arts, including libraries and reading rooms[5]; or for a place of worship, a minister's residence or a burial place[6].

Former powers for endowing or augmenting a minister's income or providing a church or chapel for a new parish[7] and of corporations, trustees of charitable institutions and persons absolutely entitled for giving to the Church Commissioners[8] land for providing a church, chapel, churchyard or parsonage[9] have been replaced by more extensive powers conferred on any corporation, any trustees for charitable purposes, the Crown Estates Commissioners, the Chancellor of the Duchy of Lancaster, the Duke of Cornwall and government departments to give or convey land to the Church Commissioners for churches, churchyards or burial grounds, residences for incumbents or other ecclesiastical persons, or for providing access to or improving the amenities of any of the foregoing[10].

In some cases the court has allowed subscriptions and donations in favour of charity to be made out of the estate of a person who lacks capacity[11], but it can only authorise a gift or settlement where this is in the best interests of the patient[12]. A capital sum may in some circumstances be paid to charity under a power of advancement in discharge of the moral obligation of a wealthy beneficiary under a settlement[13].

1 See the Universities and College Estates Act 1925 ss 15, 16; and EDUCATION vol 36 (2011) PARA 1575.

2 See the Crown Estate Act 1961 s 4; and CROWN AND CROWN PROCEEDINGS vol 29 (2014) PARA 208. As to the Crown Estate Commissioners see CROWN AND CROWN PROCEEDINGS vol 29 (2014) PARA 194.

3 See the School Sites Act 1841 ss 2, 6, 10; and EDUCATION vol 36 (2011) PARA 1541.

4 See the Consecration of Churchyards Act 1867 s 4, applying certain provisions of the School Sites Act 1841; and CREMATION AND BURIAL; ECCLESIASTICAL LAW vol 34 (2011) PARA 834 et seq.

5 See the Literary and Scientific Institutions Act 1854; and NATIONAL CULTURAL HERITAGE vol 77 (2010) PARA 939 et seq.

6 See the Places of Worship Sites Act 1873; the Places of Worship Sites Amendment Act 1882; and ECCLESIASTICAL LAW vol 34 (2011) PARA 831. See also the Reverter of Sites Act 1987 ss 1, 6, 7; and PARAS 70–71.

7 New Parishes Act 1843 s 22 (repealed); New Parishes Act 1844 s 11 (repealed); New Parishes Act 1856 s 4 (repealed). See the New Parishes Measure 1943; and ECCLESIASTICAL LAW.

8 These Commissioners have replaced the Ecclesiastical Commissioners: see the Church Commissioners Measure 1947; and ECCLESIASTICAL LAW vol 34 (2011) PARA 67 et seq.

9 Church Building Act 1818 s 33 (repealed); Church Building Act 1819 (repealed); Church Building Act 1822 ss 2, 3 (both repealed); Church Building Act 1831 ss 2, 7 (both repealed); Church Building Act 1838 ss 6–9 (all repealed). See the New Parishes Measure 1943; and ECCLESIASTICAL LAW.

10 See the New Parishes Measure 1943 ss 13, 14 (note that the amendments made to s 14 by the Charities Act 1960 Sch 6 are not affected by the repeal of that Act by the Charities Act 2006, and the consolidation effected by the Charities Act 2011: see Charities Act 2011 Sch 8 para 19(2)); and ECCLESIASTICAL LAW vol 34 (2011) PARAS 827–828.

11 *Re Frost* (1870) 5 Ch App 699; *Re Strickland* (1871) 6 Ch App 226. As to mental capacity see the Mental Capacity Act 2005 ss 1(2), 2; and MENTAL HEALTH AND CAPACITY vol 75 (2013) PARAS 601, 603.

12 See the Mental Capacity Act 2005 ss 4, 16, 18(b), (h); and MENTAL HEALTH AND CAPACITY vol 75 (2013) PARAS 606, 724.

13 *Re Clore's Settlement Trusts, Sainer v Clore* [1966] 2 All ER 272, [1966] 1 WLR 955. See also *X v A* [2005] EWHC 2706 (Ch), [2006] 1 All ER 952, [2006] 1 WLR 741.

70. Rights of reverter. Land granted under the School Sites Act 1841 and the other similar nineteenth century enactments for the establishment of schools and churches and other charitable purposes may now be put to alternative use if, the land being no longer used for the purpose of the grant[1], the person entitled to the land cannot be traced[2].

Where any relevant enactment provides for land to revert to the ownership of any person at any time, being a time when the land ceases, or has ceased for a specified period, to be used for particular purposes, the enactment has effect, and is deemed always to have had effect[3], as if it provided (instead of for the reverter) for the land to be vested after that time, on the trust arising under this provision, in the persons in whom it was vested immediately before that time[4]. The trust so arising in relation to any land is a trust for the persons who, but for these provisions, would from time to time be entitled to the ownership of the land by virtue of its reverter with a power, without consulting them, to sell the land and to stand possessed of the net proceeds of sale (after payment of costs and expenses) and of the net rents and profits until sale (after payment of rates, taxes, costs of insurance, repairs and other outgoings) in trust for those persons; but they are not to be entitled by reason of their interest to occupy the land[5]. Where a trust in relation to any land has arisen or is treated as having arisen[6] and immediately before that time the land was vested in any persons in their capacity as the minister and churchwardens of any parish[7], those persons are treated as having become trustees[8] in that capacity and, accordingly, their interest in the land passes and, if the case so requires, is treated as having passed to their successors from time to time[9].

These provisions do not confer any right on any person as a beneficiary in relation to any property in respect of which that person's claim was statute-barred[10] before 17 August 1987[11] or in relation to any property derived from any such property or in relation to any rents or profits received, or breach of trust committed, before that date[12].

Where any property is held by any persons as trustees of a trust which has arisen[13] and there are no beneficiaries of that trust[14], the trustees have no power to act in relation to that property except[15]: (1) for the purposes for which they could have acted if these provisions[16] had not been passed[17]; or (2) for the purpose of securing the establishment of a scheme of the Charity Commission[18] or the making of an order under the special powers[19] as to trusts for religious education[20].

1 Ie the relevant statutory purpose under which the grant was made, rather than the purposes specified in the grant itself if narrower: see *Fraser v Canterbury Diocesan Board of Finance (No 2)* [2005] UKHL 65 at [14]–[20], [2006] 1 AC 377, [2006] 1 All ER 315 per Lord Hoffmann, and at [57]–[59] per Lord Walker of Gestingthorpe. See also *St Mary and St Michael Parish Advisory Co Ltd v Westminster Roman Catholic Diocese Trustee* [2006] EWHC 762 (Ch), [2006] All ER (D) 82 (Apr).

2 See the Reverter of Sites Act 1987; the text and notes 3–20; and PARA 71. The need for reform in this area was identified by the Law Commission in its report *Rights of Reverter* (Cmnd 8410) (1981). Nothing in the Reverter of Sites Act 1987 requires any land which is or has been the subject of any grant, conveyance or other assurance under any relevant enactment to be treated as or as having been settled land: Reverter of Sites Act 1987 s 6(1). The power conferred by the School Sites Act 1841 s 14 (power of sale etc) is exercisable at any time in relation to land which, but for the exercise of the power, a trust might subsequently arise under the Reverter of Sites Act 1987 s 1; and the exercise of that power in respect of any land prevents any trust from arising under s 1 in relation to that land or any land representing the proceeds of sale of that land: s 6(2); and see **EDUCATION** vol 36 (2011) PARA 1541. 'Relevant enactment' means any enactment contained in the School Sites Acts (see **EDUCATION** vol 36 (2011) PARA 1541), the Literary and Scientific Institutions Act 1854 (see **NATIONAL CULTURAL HERITAGE** vol 77 (2010) PARA 939 et seq) or the Places of Worship Sites Act 1873 (see **ECCLESIASTICAL LAW** vol 34 (2011) PARA 831): Reverter of Sites Act 1987 s 7(1). References to land include references to: (1) any part of any land which has been the subject of a grant, conveyance or other assurance under any

relevant enactment; and (2) any land an interest in which (including any future or contingent interest arising under any such enactment) belongs to the Crown, the Duchy of Lancaster or the Duchy of Cornwall: s 7(2).

3 Ie subject to the Reverter of Sites Act 1987 s 4: see PARA 71.

4 Reverter of Sites Act 1987 s 1(1).

5 Reverter of Sites Act 1987 s 1(2) (amended by the Trusts of Land and Appointment of Trustees Act 1996 Sch 2 para 6). The amendments made by the Trusts of Land and Appointment of Trustees Act 1996 do not affect any entailed interest created before its commencement (1 January 1997): s 25(4). The amendments made by the Trusts of Land and Appointment of Trustees Act 1996 in consequence of the abolition of the doctrine of conversion do not affect a trust created by a will if the testator died before 1 January 1997, and do not affect personal representatives of a person who died before that date: see s 25(5).

6 Ie under the Reverter of Sites Act 1987 s 1(1) at such a time as is mentioned in that provision: see the text and notes 3–4.

7 For these purposes, 'churchwardens' include chapel wardens, 'minister' includes a rector, vicar or perpetual curate, and 'parish' includes a parish of the Church in Wales: Reverter of Sites Act 1987 s 1(6).

8 Ie under the Reverter of Sites Act 1987 s 1.

9 Reverter of Sites Act 1987 s 1(3) (as amended: see note 5).

10 The reference to a person's claim being statute-barred is a reference to the Limitation Act 1980 providing that no proceedings are brought by that person to recover the property in respect of which the claim subsists: Reverter of Sites Act 1987 s 1(6). As to limitation see further **LIMITATION PERIODS**.

11 Ie the commencement of the Reverter of Sites Act 1987.

12 Reverter of Sites Act 1987 s 1(4) (as amended: see note 5). Anything validly done before 17 August 1987 in relation to any land which by virtue of s 1 is deemed to have been held at the time in trust is, if done by the beneficiaries, deemed, so far as necessary for preserving its validity, to have been done by the trustees: s 1(4).

13 See note 8.

14 Ie in consequence the Reverter of Sites Act 1987 s 1(4): see the text and notes 10–12.

15 Reverter of Sites Act 1987 s 1(5).

16 Ie the Reverter of Sites Act 1987.

17 Reverter of Sites Act 1987 s 1(5)(a).

18 Ie a scheme under the Reverter of Sites Act 1987 s 2: see PARA 71. As to the Charity Commission see PARAS 543–578.

19 Ie under the Education Act 1996 s 554: see **EDUCATION** vol 36 (2011) PARA 1628.

20 Reverter of Sites Act 1987 s 1(5)(b) (amended by the Education Act 1996 Sch 37 para 67). An order made under the Education Act 1996 s 554 (see PARA 185) with respect to so much of any endowment as consists of land in relation to which a trust under the Reverter of Sites Act 1987 s 1 has arisen or will arise after the land ceased or ceases to be used for particular purposes, or any other property subject to a trust under that provision may extinguish any rights to which a person is or may become entitled as a beneficiary under the trust: s 5(1) (s 5 amended by the Education Act 1996 Sch 37 para 67). The Secretary of State or the Welsh Ministers may not by an order under the Education Act 1996 s 554 extinguish any such rights unless he or they are satisfied that all reasonably practicable steps to trace the persons who are or may become entitled to any of those rights have been taken and that either: (1) there is no claim by any person to be a person who is or may become entitled which is outstanding, or which has at any time been accepted as valid by the trustees or by persons whose acceptance binds or will bind the trustees, or which has been upheld in proceedings that have been concluded; or (2) consent to the making of an order under s 554 has been given by every person whose claim to be such a person is outstanding or has been so accepted or upheld: Reverter of Sites Act 1987 s 5(2) (as so amended). A claim by any person to be a beneficiary under a trust is outstanding if it has been notified to the trustees, it has not been withdrawn and proceedings for determining whether it ought to have been upheld have not been commenced or (if commenced) have not been concluded: s 7(3). Proceedings in relation to any person's claim are not treated as concluded where the time for appealing is unexpired or an appeal is pending unless that person has indicated his intention not to appeal or to continue with his appeal: s 7(4).

Where applications for the extinguishment of the rights of any beneficiaries are made with respect to the same trust property to the Secretary of State, or the Welsh Ministers, under the Education Act 1996 s 554 and to the Charity Commission under the Reverter of Sites Act 1987 s 2 (see PARA 71) the Commission must not consider or further consider the application made to it unless the Secretary of State, or the Welsh Ministers, either consent to the consideration of the application made to the Charity Commission before the application made to him or them or disposes of the application made to him or them without extinguishing the rights of one or more of the beneficiaries: s 5(3) (amended by the Education Act 1996 Sch 37 para 67; and the Charities Act 2006 Sch 8 para 84).

Trustees of a trust arising under the Reverter of Sites Act 1987 s 1 may pay or apply capital money for the purposes of any provision of s 5 or the Education Act 1996 s 554: Reverter of Sites Act 1987 s 5(4) (amended by the Education Act 1996 Sch 37 para 67).

As to the Secretary of State and the Welsh Ministers see PARA 585.

71. Charity Commission's schemes under the Reverter of Sites Act 1987. Where any persons hold any property as trustees of a trust which has arisen under the provisions of the Reverter of Sites Act 1987[1], the Charity Commission[2], on the application of the trustees[3], may by order[4] establish a scheme which extinguishes the rights of the beneficiaries under the trust and requires the trustees to hold the property on trust for such charitable purposes as may be specified in the order[5]. The charitable purposes must be such as the Charity Commission considers appropriate[6], having regard to: (1) the desirability of securing that the property is held for charitable purposes (the 'new purposes') which are close to the purposes, whether charitable or not, for which the trustees held the relevant land[7] before the cesser of use in consequence of which the trust arose (the 'former purposes')[8]; and (2) the need for the new purposes to be capable of having a significant social or economic effect[9]. In determining the character of the former purposes, the Commission may, if it thinks it appropriate to do so, give greater weight to the persons or locality benefited by those purposes than to the nature of the benefit[10].

1 Ie under the Reverter of Sites Act 1987 s 1: see PARA 70.
2 As to the Charity Commission see PARAS 543–578.
3 As to the application by trustees see PARA 72.
4 As to orders to establish schemes of the Charity Commission see PARA 73.
5 Reverter of Sites Act 1987 s 2(1) (amended by the Charities Act 2006 Sch 8 para 82(1), (2)). The Reverter of Sites Act 1987 s 2(1) is expressed to be subject to the provisions of ss 2(2)–(8), 3, 4 (see the text and notes 6–10; and PARAS 72–73): see s 2(1). An order may contain any such provision as may be contained in an order made by the High Court for establishing a scheme for the administration of a charity and has the same effect as an order so made: s 2(2). As to the general jurisdiction and powers of the court in relation to the settlement of schemes see PARA 183 et seq.
6 Reverter of Sites Act 1987 s 2(3) (substituted by the Charities Act 2006 Sch 8 para 82(3)).
7 'Relevant land', in relation to a trust which has arisen under Reverter of Sites Act 1987 s 1 (see PARA 70), means the land which but for the Reverter of Sites Act 1987 would have reverted to the persons who are the first beneficiaries under the trust: s 7(1).
8 Reverter of Sites Act 1987 s 2(3A)(a) (s 2(3A), (3B) added by the Charities Act 2006 Sch 8 para 82(3)).
9 Reverter of Sites Act 1987 s 2(3A)(b) (as added: see note 8).
10 Reverter of Sites Act 1987 s 2(3B) (as added: see note 8).

72. Applications for Charity Commission schemes under the Reverter of Sites Act 1987. The Charity Commission may not make any order[1] establishing a scheme under the Reverter of Sites Act 1987[2] unless the trustees have satisfied the requirements for the making of an application for a scheme. These requirements are satisfied if, before the application is made[3]:

(1) notices[4] have been published in two national newspapers and in a local newspaper circulating in the locality where the relevant land[5] is situated[6];

(2) each of the notices specified a period for the notification to the trustees of claims by beneficiaries, being a period ending not less than three months after the date of publication of the last of those notices to be published[7];

(3) that period has ended[8];

(4) for a period of not less than 21 days during the first month of that period, a copy of one of the notices was affixed to an object on the relevant land in such a position and manner as, so far as practicable, to make the notice easy for members of the public to see and read it without going on to the land[9]; and

(5) the trustees have considered what other steps could be taken to trace the persons who are or may be beneficiaries and to inform those persons of the application for the scheme and have taken such of the steps considered by them as it was reasonably practicable for them to take[10].

The above requirements do not apply in the case of an application made in respect of any trust if the time when the trust is treated as having arisen was before 17 August 1987[11].

The Commission must refuse to consider an application by the trustees under these provisions unless it is accompanied by a statutory declaration by the applicants that the requirements for the making of an application[12] are satisfied with respect to the making of the application or, if the declaration so declares, do not apply, and that one of two specified conditions[13] is identified in the declaration and fulfilled[14]. The declaration is conclusive for these purposes of the matters declared in it[15].

1 As to orders to establish Charity Commission schemes see PARA 73. As to the Charity Commission see PARAS 543–578.
2 Ie under the Reverter of Sites Act 1987 s 2: see PARAS 71, 73.
3 Reverter of Sites Act 1987 s 3(1).
4 A notice must: (1) set out the circumstances that have resulted in a trust having arisen under the Reverter of Sites Act 1987 s 1 (see PARA 70); (2) state that an application is to be made for the establishment of a scheme with respect to the property subject to the trust; and (3) contain a warning to every beneficiary that, if he wishes to oppose the extinguishment of his rights, he ought to notify his claim to the trustees in the manner, and within the period, specified in the notice: s 3(2).
5 As to the meaning of 'relevant land' see PARA 71 note 7. As to references to land see PARA 70 note 1.
6 Reverter of Sites Act 1987 s 3(1)(a).
7 Reverter of Sites Act 1987 s 3(1)(b).
8 Reverter of Sites Act 1987 s 3(1)(c).
9 Reverter of Sites Act 1987 s 3(1)(d). Where at the time when the trustees publish a notice for the purposes of s 3(2) (see note 4) the relevant land is not under their control and it is not reasonably practicable for them to arrange for a copy to be affixed as so required, s 3(1)(d) is to be disregarded: s 3(3).
10 Reverter of Sites Act 1987 s 3(1)(e).
11 Reverter of Sites Act 1987 s 3(4). The section goes on to say 'and more than 12 years have elapsed since then', which by the date at which this volume states the law has become otiose.
12 Ie the requirements under the Reverter of Sites Act 1987 s 3: see the text and notes 1–12.
13 Ie one of the conditions in the Reverter of Sites Act 1987 s 2(6): see PARA 73 head (2) in the text.
14 Reverter of Sites Act 1987 s 2(7) (amended by the Charities Act 2006 Sch 8 para 82(1), (5)).
15 Reverter of Sites Act 1987 s 2(7) (see note 14).

73. Orders of the Charity Commission establishing schemes under the Reverter of Sites Act 1987. The Charity Commission[1] may not make any order establishing a scheme under the Reverter of Sites Act 1987[2] unless:

(1) the requirements[3] for making an application for the order are satisfied or do not apply[4];

(2) one of the following conditions is fulfilled[5]:

 (a) there is no claim by any person to be a beneficiary in respect of rights proposed to be extinguished which is outstanding[6] or which has at any time been accepted as valid by the trustees or by persons whose acceptance binds them or which has been upheld in proceedings that have been concluded[7]; or

(b) consent to the establishment of such a scheme has been given by every person whose claim to be a beneficiary in respect of those rights is outstanding or has been so accepted or upheld[8];

(3) public notice of the Commission's proposals has been given inviting representations to be made to it within a period specified in the notice, being a period ending not less than a month after the date of the giving of the notice[9]; and

(4) that period has ended and the Commission has taken into consideration any representations which have been made within that period and not withdrawn[10].

An order made on an application[11] with respect to any trust must be so framed as to secure that if a person who, but for the making of the order, would have been a beneficiary under the trust and has not consented to the establishment of a scheme under these provisions, notifies a claim to the trustees within the period of five years after the date of the making of the order, that person may be paid an amount equal to the value of his rights at the time of their extinguishment[12].

Where an order[13] is made by the Commission: (i) public notice of it must be given in such manner as it thinks sufficient and appropriate[14]; and (ii) a copy of the order must, for not less than one month after the date of giving the notice, be available for public inspection at all reasonable times at the Commission's office and at some convenient place in the locality where the land is situated[15]. The notice must contain such particulars of the order, or such directions for obtaining information about it, as the Commission thinks sufficient and appropriate[16].

An appeal against an order[17] may be brought to the Tribunal[18] by any of the following: (A) the Attorney General[19]; (B) the trustees of the trust established under the order[20]; (C) a beneficiary of, or the trustees of, the trust in respect of which the application for the order had been made[21]; (D) any person interested in the purposes for which the last mentioned trustees or any of their predecessors held the relevant land[22] before the cesser of use in consequence of which the trust arose[23]; (E) any two or more inhabitants of the locality where that land is situated[24]; or (F) any other person who is or may be affected by the order[25].

Trustees of a trust which has arisen[26] may pay or apply capital money for certain purposes[27] under the Reverter of Sites Act 1987[28].

1 As to the Charity Commission see PARAS 543–578.
2 Ie a scheme under the Reverter of Sites Act 1987 s 2: see PARA 71.
3 Ie the requirements of the Reverter of Sites Act 1987 s 3: see PARA 72.
4 Reverter of Sites Act 1987 s 2(5)(a) (amended by the Charities Act 2006 Sch 8 para 82(1), (4)). The reference in the text to when the requirements for making an application for the order do not apply is a reference to where they do not apply by virtue of the Reverter of Sites Act 1987 s 3(4) (see PARA 72): see s 2(5)(a) (as so amended).
5 Reverter of Sites Act 1987 s 2(5)(b) (amended by the Charities Act 2006 Sch 8 para 82(1), (4)).
6 As to where a claim is outstanding see PARA 70 note 20.
7 Reverter of Sites Act 1987 s 2(6)(a).
8 Reverter of Sites Act 1987 s 2(6)(b).
9 Reverter of Sites Act 1987 s 2(5)(c) (amended by the Charities Act 2006 Sch 8 para 82(1), (4)). The notice must contain such particulars of the Commission's proposals or such directions for obtaining information about them and must be given in such manner as it thinks sufficient and appropriate; a further such notice is not required where the Commission decides, before proceeding with any proposals of which notice has been given, to modify them: Reverter of Sites Act 1987 s 2(8) (amended by the Charities Act 2006 Sch 8 para 82(1), (6)).

10 Reverter of Sites Act 1987 s 2(5)(d) (amended by the Charities Act 2006 Sch 8 para 82(1), (4)).
11 As to the application by trustees see PARA 72.
12 Reverter of Sites Act 1987 s 2(4).
13 Ie under the Reverter of Sites Act 1987 s 2: see the text and notes 1–12; and PARA 71.
14 Reverter of Sites Act 1987 s 4(1)(a) (amended by the Charities Act 2006 Sch 8 para 83(1), (2)).
15 Reverter of Sites Act 1987 s 4(1)(b) (amended by the Charities Act 2006 Sch 8 para 83(1), (2)).
16 Reverter of Sites Act 1987 s 4(1) (amended by the Charities Act 2006 Sch 8 para 83(1), (2)).
17 See note 13.
18 As to the Tribunal see PARA 579 et seq. The Charities Act 2011 Pt 17 Ch 2, and Sch 6, apply to orders under the Reverter of Sites Act 1987 s 2: s 4(2) (substituted by the Charities Act 2011 Sch 7 para 48).
19 Reverter of Sites Act 1987 s 4(2)(a) (as substituted: see note 18). As to the Attorney General see PARAS 589, 596, 605 et seq; and CONSTITUTIONAL AND ADMINISTRATIVE LAW vol 20 (2014) PARA 273 et seq.
20 Reverter of Sites Act 1987 s 4(2))(b) (as substituted: see note 18).
21 Reverter of Sites Act 1987 s 4(2)(c) (as substituted: see note 18).
22 As to the meaning of 'relevant land' see PARA 71 note 7.
23 Reverter of Sites Act 1987 s 4(2)(d) (as substituted: see note 18). The reference to the trust arising in the text is a reference to a trust arising under the Reverter of Sites Act 1987 s 1 (see PARA 70).
24 Reverter of Sites Act 1987 s 4(2)(e) (as substituted: see note 18). The substitution made by the Charities Act 2006 Sch 8 para 83(3) does not affect the operation of the Reverter of Sites Act 1987 in relation to any appeal brought in the High Court before 18 March 2008 (ie the day on which the substitution came into force): Charities Act 2006 Sch 10 para 18 (repealed, though the continuity of the law is unaffected: Charities Act 2011 Sch 8 para 1).
25 Reverter of Sites Act 1987 s 4(2)(f) (as substituted: see note 18).
26 Ie under the Reverter of Sites Act 1987 s 1: see PARA 70.
27 Ie for the purposes of the Reverter of Sites Act 1987 s 2 (see the text and notes 1–12), s 3 (see PARA 72) or s 4 (see note 16) (see the text and notes 13–24).
28 Reverter of Sites Act 1987 s 4(5). The Charities Act 2011 ss 337, 339, (see PARAS 554, 555) (supplemental provisions with respect to orders and appeals) apply in relation to, and to appeals against, orders under the Reverter of Sites Act 1987 s 2 as they apply in relation to, and to appeals against, orders under the Charities Act 2011: Reverter of Sites Act 1987 s 4(4) (substituted by the Charities Act 2011 Sch 7 para 48).

74. Writing generally necessary. Assurances in favour of a charity generally take the form of a conveyance on trust or a declaration of trust; but an express trust is not necessary, since the Crown as parens patriae is the trustee of funds given to charity without trustees or objects selected or without any express trust[1].

Charitable trusts declared in respect of land[2] since 1925 must be manifested and proved by some writing signed by some person who is able to declare the trust or by his will[3], but trusts of personalty are valid without evidence in writing[4].

A charitable trust[5], like a private trust[6], may be created by informal as well as by technical language, provided that the donor's intention to devote the property to charity is clear. Precatory or recommendatory words have frequently been held to create trusts where the testator's intention has been held to be imperative[7]. Similarly, provisions in which the word 'condition' occurs may create trusts[8].

In the case of a charitable gift, the court pays more regard to the intention than to the form of conveyance; for this reason an estate in fee simple might pass to a charity even though the conveyance contained no words of limitation, if it was clear that a gift to charity in perpetuity was intended[9]. A gift which is exclusively charitable made by will may be widened, and so invalidated, by codicil if that is the necessary implication from the words used[10].

A gift may be made to charity by means of a power of appointment[11]. An exercise of a power defective as not complying with the terms of the power will be good if not otherwise invalid[12].

A voluntary conveyance of lands to charity is not avoided by a subsequent conveyance for value unless it was made with the intention of defrauding the purchaser under the subsequent conveyance[13].

1 *Moggridge v Thackwell* (1803) 7 Ves 36 at 69, 83 per Lord Eldon LC (affd (1807) 13 Ves 416, HL); *Morice v Bishop of Durham* (1805) 10 Ves 522 at 541 per Lord Eldon LC; *Ommanney v Butcher* (1823) Turn & R 260 at 271 per Plumer MR: provided there is certainty of intention (see PARA 85). See also PARA 513. As to the law of trusts generally see **TRUSTS AND POWERS.**

2 As to the meaning of 'land' see the Law of Property Act 1925 s 205(1)(ix); and **REAL PROPERTY AND REGISTRATION** vol 87 (2012) PARA 7.

3 See the Law of Property Act 1925 s 53(1)(b). In the absence of such writing there would be a resulting trust for the settlor (cf *Hodgson v Marks* [1971] Ch 892, [1971] 2 All ER 684, CA, a non-charity trust case). The requirement of evidence in writing does not apply to resulting, implied or constructive trusts (see the Law of Property Act 1925 s 53(2)) but a charitable trust is hardly likely to arise in these forms. However, see *Re Tyler's Fund Trusts, Graves v King* [1967] 3 All ER 389, [1967] 1 WLR 1269.

4 *Lyell v Kennedy* (1889) 14 App Cas 437 at 457, HL, per Lord Selborne. See further **DEEDS AND OTHER INSTRUMENTS** vol 32 (2012) PARA 224; **TRUSTS AND POWERS** vol 98 (2013) PARA 59.

5 *Salusbury v Denton* (1857) 3 K & J 529; *Goodman v Saltash Corpn* (1882) 7 App Cas 633 at 642, HL, where Lord Selborne LC said it was immaterial whether the words used were 'trust', 'intent', 'purpose', 'proviso' or 'condition'.

6 *Brown v Higgs* (1803) 8 Ves 561; *Re Williams, Williams v Williams* [1897] 2 Ch 12 at 21–22, CA, per Lindley LJ. A private trust is for the benefit of ascertained or ascertainable individuals. As to private trusts see **TRUSTS AND POWERS** vol 98 (2013) PARA 38.

7 *Re Burley, Alexander v Burley* [1910] 1 Ch 215; and see **TRUSTS AND POWERS** vol 98 (2013) PARA 66. See also *A-G v Davies* (1802) 9 Ves 535 at 546 per Lord Eldon LC; *Kirkbank v Hudson* (1819) 7 Price 212; and *Pilkington v Boughey* (1841) 12 Sim 114. In those cases the trust was established, but held void as infringing the mortmain law then in force. The mortmain statutes have been repealed: see PARAS 83–84.

8 See PARA 75.

9 *A-G v Berwick-upon-Tweed Corpn* (1829) Taml 239 at 246 per Leach MR. If there was no indication that a gift to charity in perpetuity was intended, a grant to a person for the benefit of a charity containing no words of limitation would, it is conceived, have given the charity the benefit of the grant merely during the life of the grantee.

10 *Wheeler v Sheer* (1730) Mos 288, where a gift for such charitable uses as the testator should appoint by codicil was followed by a codicil giving the property to such uses and purposes (omitting the word 'charitable') as he should direct; explained in *Moggridge v Thackwell* (1803) 7 Ves 36 at 79 per Lord Eldon LC; *Mills v Farmer* (1815) 1 Mer 55 at 72 per Lord Eldon LC. See also *Charitable Donations Comrs v Sullivan* (1841) 1 Dr & War 501 at 507.

11 *Cook v Duckenfield* (1743) 2 Atk 562 at 567 per Lord Hardwicke LC. As to powers of appointment see **TRUSTS AND POWERS** vol 98 (2013) PARA 42 et seq.

12 *Sayer v Sayer, Innes v Sayer* (1849) 7 Hare 377; affd sub nom *Innes v Sayer* (1851) 3 Mac & G 606, where a number of authorities are cited. See **TRUSTS AND POWERS** vol 98 (2013) PARA 629.

13 *Ramsay v Gilchrist* [1892] AC 412, PC. See also the Law of Property Act 1925 s 173; and **MISREPRESENTATION** vol 76 (2013) PARA 864 et seq. See also *A-G v Newcastle Corpn* (1842) 5 Beav 307 at 312 per Lord Langdale MR (affd sub nom *Newcastle-upon-Tyne Corpn v A-G* (1845) 12 Cl & Fin 402, HL); *Trye v Gloucester Corpn* (1851) 14 Beav 173.

75. Condition creating a trust. A trust is created where the whole of the property is devoted to purposes which exclude all the donee's beneficial interest, even though the words used are primarily words of condition[1]; or where property is given upon condition that a fixed and definite sum, which does not exhaust the entire revenue, shall be applied in a specified charitable way[2]. On the other hand, where property is given on condition that an indefinite sum shall be expended for a certain purpose, it is a gift upon condition, and not a trust; and the donee is entitled to the beneficial interest in the property[3]. It is a gift upon condition and not a trust where the gift is on condition that, for example, the donees perform certain duties[4], or a minister preach in a black gown[5].

1 *A-G v Master, Wardens etc of the Wax Chandlers' Co* (1873) LR 6 HL 1 ('for this intent and purpose and upon this condition'); *Merchant Taylors' Co v A-G* (1871) 6 Ch App 512 ('to this intent and upon this condition'); *Wright v Wilkin* (1862) 2 B & S 259, Ex Ch. See also *Goodman v Saltash Corpn* (1882) 7 App Cas 633 at 642, HL, per Lord Selborne LC; *Re Christchurch Inclosure Act* (1888) 38 ChD 520 at 531, CA, per Lindley LJ; Duke on Charitable Uses, ed Bridgman (1805) 123–124, 137.

2 *A-G v Grocers' Co* (1843) 6 Beav 526. See also *Re Richardson, Shuldham v Royal National Lifeboat Institution* (1887) 56 LJCh 784 (condition to construct and maintain lifeboats attached to a legacy to a charitable society construed as a trust).

3 *Jack v Burnett* (1846) 12 Cl & Fin 812, HL (gift to a college on condition that three bursars should be maintained); *Re Tyler, Tyler v Tyler* [1891] 3 Ch 252, CA (condition that a tomb should be kept in repair); *Re Rosenblum, Rosenblum v Rosenblum* (1924) 131 LT 21.

4 *A-G v Christ's Hospital* (1830) 1 Russ & M 626; *A-G v Cordwainers' Co* (1833) 3 My & K 534 at 543 per Leach MR: the imposition of a penalty for non-performance of the condition implies a benefit, if the condition be performed, and is inconsistent with any other intention than that the testator meant to give a beneficial interest to the company upon the terms of complying with the directions contained in his will.

5 *Re Robinson, Wright v Tugwell* [1897] 1 Ch 85, CA; but see *Robinson, Wright v Tugwell* [1923] 2 Ch 332, where this condition was dispensed with.

76. Charge or trust for charity is binding. According to the ancient equitable doctrine that no person can acquire an estate with notice of a charitable use without being bound by it, the grantee or devisee of an estate subject to a charge in favour of a charity is a trustee, at any rate until separate trustees of the charge are appointed[1]. If, however, the conveyance or will appoints trustees of the charge, it seems that no fiduciary obligation is imposed on the grantee or devisee[2].

There is a distinction between a charge and a trust in favour of charity[3]. If a devise is made subject to the payment of an annuity to a charitable institution, it is a question of construction[4] whether the devisee is a trustee of the annuity for the charity, or the charity merely has a right to recover the annuity as a charge[5]. A charitable trust may be so limited as to affect part only of the property granted or devised, as where property is given subject to[6], or in trust to make[7], specified charitable payments which do not exhaust the whole estate[8]. In those cases where the donor has not expressed a general intention to devote the whole property to charity, the donee takes beneficially subject only to the specific appropriation[9], unless it appears that he was intended to take only as a trustee, in which case a resulting trust arises in favour of the donor and his successors in title[10].

Where property is impressed with trusts which serve more one charitable purpose, it is appropriate to consider the property as a composite whole, even if the result may be that one purpose becomes thereby subordinate to the other[11].

1 *Charitable Donations and Bequests Comrs v Wybrants* (1845) 2 Jo & Lat 182 at 198 per Lord Sugden LC. See also the non-charity cases of *Hodge v Churchward* (1847) 16 Sim 71, and *Cunningham v Foot* (1878) 3 App Cas 974, HL.

2 *Cunningham v Foot* (1878) 3 App Cas 974 at 987, HL, per Lord Cairns LC.

3 See *Charitable Donations and Bequests Comrs v Wybrants* (1845) 2 Jo & Lat 182 at 198 per Lord Sugden LC.

4 See *Cunningham v Foot* (1878) 3 App Cas 974, HL.

5 The question is of importance in relation to the operation of the Limitation Acts; cf the cases cited in note 1.

6 *Southmolton Corpn v A-G* (1854) 5 HL Cas 1; *A-G v Dean and Canons of Windsor* (1860) 8 HL Cas 369. Cf gifts on condition: see PARAS 136–137.

7 *Beverley Corpn v A-G* (1857) 6 HL Cas 310.

8 *Merchant Taylors' Co v A-G* (1871) 6 Ch App 512 at 520 per James LJ; *A-G v Cordwainers' Co* (1833) 3 My & K 534; *A-G v Trinity College, Cambridge* (1856) 24 Beav 383.
9 *A-G v Bristol Corpn* (1820) 2 Jac & W 294; *A-G v Master, Wardens etc of the Wax Chandlers' Co* (1873) LR 6 HL 1 at 9 per Lord Chelmsford; *A-G v Grocers' Co* (1843) 6 Beav 526; *A-G v Skinners' Co* (1827) 2 Russ 407.
10 *Re Stanford, Cambridge University v A-G* [1924] 1 Ch 73. See also PARA 172.
11 *Dore v Leicestershire County Council* [2010] EWHC 1387 (Ch), [2010] All ER (D) 78 (Jun) (property was historically used principally for the purposes of a school and partially for the benefit of the community, but although the management of the property was chiefly for the former, it was possible to carry out both purposes and neither was extinguished).

77. Equitable doctrines. The ordinary law as to ademption applies to legacies given to charities[1], as, presumably, do the doctrines of performance, satisfaction and election[2]. Where a legacy is given to the trustees of an endowment fund, it may be adeemed by a gift to the same trustees by the testator during his life[3].

1 *Twining v Powell* (1845) 2 Coll 262; *Makeown v Ardagh* (1876) IR 10 Eq 445. See **EQUITABLE JURISDICTION** vol 47 (2014) PARA 176 et seq; **WILLS AND INTESTACY** vol 102 (2010) PARA 155 et seq.
2 As to election, satisfaction and ademption, and performance see **REAL PROPERTY AND REGISTRATION** vol 87 (2012) PARA 191.
3 *Re Corbett, Corbett v Lord Cobham* [1903] 2 Ch 326.

78. Merger of charities. A merger of charities means two or more separate charities coming together to form one organisation, either by a single new charity being formed to continue the work of both, or one of the charities assuming control of the other or others[1].

A charity may merge with another if its governing instrument so allows, or, absent that, if the Charity Commission[2] grants the power to merge[3].

The objects of the two (or more charities) must be compatible, or a strong case must be made to the Commission why a merger should proceed so that the Commission can grant the necessary powers to alter the charity's objects. The trustees will need to show, for example, that the charity's trusts have ceased to be an effective use of the charity's funds either because they can no longer be furthered or because they do not allow the funds to be put to best use[4].

Mergers of charities may be notified to the Commission for inclusion in the register of charity mergers[5].

1 See *Making mergers work: helping you succeed* (Charity Commission, September 2009) para 1.1 (available, at the date at which this volume states the law, on the government website). As to publications of the Charity Commission see PARA 547.
2 See *Making mergers work: helping you succeed* (Charity Commission, September 2009) para 1.1.
3 As to the Charity Commission see PARAS 543–578.
4 See *Making mergers work: helping you succeed* (Charity Commission, September 2009) para 3.1.
5 As to the register of charity mergers see PARAS 322, 323. As to pre-merger vesting declarations see PARA 417.

(ii) Creation without an Assurance

79. Charity established by voluntary subscriptions. A charity created or established by voluntary subscriptions does not differ from charities established in other ways, provided that a fund exists which is subject to a charitable trust[1].

1 *A-G v Kell* (1840) 2 Beav 575; *Re Welsh Hospital (Netley) Fund, Thomas v A-G* [1921] 1 Ch 655; *Re British Red Cross Balkan Fund, British Red Cross Society v Johnson* [1914] 2 Ch 419; *Re North Devon and West Somerset Relief Fund Trusts, Baron Hylton v Wright*

[1953] 2 All ER 1032, [1953] 1 WLR 1260; *Re Lord Mayor of Belfast's Air Raid Distress Fund* [1962] NI 161; cf *Re Gillingham Bus Disaster Fund, Bowman v Official Solicitor* [1959] Ch 62, [1958] 2 All ER 749, CA. As to funds raised by contributions see PARA 106.

80. Secret trusts. A donor may make an effective disposition in favour of charity by means of a non-charitable gift affected by a secret trust for charity, whether or not mentioned in the instrument of gift, as by a direction to a donee to use a gift for the charitable purposes agreed between donor and donee[1]. A testator also may make a testamentary disposition to charity subject to a secret trust for non-charitable purposes[2].

The requisites for establishing the existence of a secret trust in favour of charity do not differ from those for other secret trusts[3]. They include the necessity of the testator's intention being communicated to the donee and accepted by him[4], and the admissibility of evidence to prove the terms of a secret charitable trust when its existence is admitted[5]; but where there is no communication in a testator's lifetime of his intention to create a secret trust for charity[6], or where no secret trust is proved[7], the donee takes absolutely, unless it appears that he is a trustee and takes upon a resulting trust[8]. A secret trust is a personal obligation binding the individual donee: if he renounces or disclaims, or dies in the lifetime of the donor, the trust cannot operate[9].

1 *Re Huxtable, Huxtable v Crawfurd* [1902] 2 Ch 793, CA; cf *Re Tyler's Fund Trust, Graves v King* [1967] 3 All ER 389, [1967] 1 WLR 1269.
2 *Re Young, Young v Young* [1951] Ch 344, [1950] 2 All ER 1245.
3 As to secret trusts see further **TRUSTS AND POWERS** vol 98 (2013) PARA 87 et seq. As to evidence of secret trusts see **WILLS AND INTESTACY** vol 102 (2010) PARAS 220–222.
4 *Re Huxtable, Huxtable v Crawfurd* [1902] 2 Ch 793, CA; *Moss v Cooper* (1861) 1 John & H 352.
5 *Edwards v Pike* (1759) 1 Eden 267.
6 *Juniper v Batchellor* (1868) 19 LT 200; *Carter v Green* (1857) 3 K & J 591; *Littledale v Bickersteth* (1876) 24 WR 507.
7 *Re Downing's Residuary Estate* (1888) 60 LT 140; *Baldwin v Baldwin* (1856) 22 Beav 413.
8 *Ommanney v Butcher* (1823) Turn & R 260.
9 *Re Maddock, Llewelyn v Washington* [1902] 2 Ch 220 at 231, CA, per Cozens-Hardy LJ. However, it is at least arguable, based on the remarks in *Blackwell v Blackwell* [1929] AC 318 at 328, HL, per Lord Buckmaster, and at 341 per Lord Warrington of Clyffe, that the intended beneficiaries of a secret charitable trust ought not to be deprived of the benefit by the disclaimer of the donee after the death of the donor, and that therefore the trust ought to stand in such a case. See further **TRUSTS AND POWERS** vol 98 (2013) PARA 87.

(iii) Establishment not to Contravene General Law

81. Charity constituting nuisance. Except under statutory authority, a charity or charitable institution may not be established in such manner or place as to constitute a nuisance[1], and an injunction[2] will be granted to restrain the establishment of a charity which, though charitable, will constitute a nuisance[3].

1 As to nuisance see **NUISANCE** vol 78 (2010) PARA 101 et seq.
2 As to injunctions see **CIVIL PROCEDURE** vol 11 (2009) PARA 331 et seq.
3 *Baines v Baker* (1752) Amb 158; *Metropolitan Asylum District Managers v Hill* (1881) 6 App Cas 193, HL; *Fleet v Metropolitan Asylums Board* (1886) 2 TLR 361, CA; *Matthews v Sheffield Corpn* (1887) 31 Sol Jo 773; *Bendelow v Wortley Union Guardians* (1887) 57 LJCh 762; *A-G v Manchester Corpn* [1893] 2 Ch 87; *A-G v Nottingham Corpn* [1904] 1 Ch 673. For the class of hospital which has been held to constitute a nuisance see *Tod-Heatly v Benham* (1888) 40 ChD 80, CA.

82. Charity in breach of restrictive covenant. Charitable institutions such as hospitals and institutions for educating and lodging girls, may not be established in premises subject to a restrictive covenant for use as a private dwelling house only, and not for the purposes of trade or business; and an injunction will be granted to restrain the establishment of an institution which, though charitable, will constitute a breach of covenant[1].

1 *German v Chapman* (1877) 7 ChD 271, CA (institution for education and lodging of girls); *Bramwell v Lacy* (1879) 10 ChD 691; *Portman v Home Hospitals Association* (1879) 27 ChD 81n; *Frost v King Edward VII Welsh etc Association* [1918] 2 Ch 180 (compromised on appeal 35 TLR 138, CA) (hospitals); *Rolls v Miller* (1884) 27 ChD 71, CA (institution for working girls); and see *Barnard Castle UDC v Wilson* [1901] 2 Ch 813 at 817 per Buckley LJ (carrying on a school is carrying on a business), affd on this point but revsd on other grounds [1902] 2 Ch 746 at 755, CA, per Vaughan Williams LJ, and at 758 per Stirling LJ. Cf *C & G Homes Ltd v Secretary of State for Health* [1991] Ch 365, [1991] 2 All ER 841, CA. As to restrictive covenants generally see REAL PROPERTY AND REGISTRATION vol 87 (2012) PARA 1076 et seq.

(iv) Repeal of Law of Mortmain

83. Mortmain restrictions. Before 29 July 1960[1], assurances inter vivos of land, or of personal estate to be laid out in the purchase of land, in favour of charity were, with various exceptions, subject to certain restrictions: they had to take effect in possession; they might be made subject to certain reservations only; if not for valuable consideration, they had to be made not less than a certain period before the death of the donor; and they had to comply with certain provisions as to form and recording. If these restrictions were not complied with, the assurance was void.

Land might be assured by will to charity, but unless the recipient charity was authorised to retain the land by an order of the court or the Charity Commissioners (now the Charity Commission)[2], the land had to be sold within one year after the testator's death or such extended period as might be duly determined.

The law of mortmain also prohibited the assurance of land to charitable and other corporations otherwise than under royal licence or statutory authority. Any land assured contrary to this prohibition was forfeit to the Crown.

1 Ie the date of the passing of the Charities Act 1960 (repealed). The various restrictions mentioned in the text were contained principally in the Mortmain and Charitable Uses Act 1888, the Mortmain and Charitable Uses Act 1891 and the Mortmain and Charitable Uses Act Amendment Act 1892, which were all, together with any enactments amending them, repealed by the Charities Act 1960: see s 38(1) (repealed). The full list of mortmain repeals is contained in Sch 7 Pt II (repealed).

2 As to the Charity Commission see PARA 543.

84. Repeal and consequential provisions. The law of mortmain was repealed by the Charities Act 1960[1]. Various provisions consequential on the repeal were made as follows.

No right or title to any property may be defeated or impugned, and no assurance or disposition of property may be treated as void or voidable, by virtue of any of the enactments relating to mortmain which have been repealed[2], or any other enactment relating to mortmain, if on 29 July 1960 the possession was in accordance with that right or title or with that assurance or disposition, and no step has been taken to assert a claim by virtue of any such enactment[3]. However, this provision does not validate any assurance or disposition so as to defeat a right or title acquired by adverse possession before 29 July 1960[4].

In relation to the wills of persons dying before 29 July 1960, the repeal of the Mortmain and Charitable Uses Act 1891 abrogates any requirement to sell land then unsold, but it does not enable effect to be given to a direction to lay out personal estate in land without an order under that Act, nor does it affect the power to make such an order[5].

1 See the Charities Act 1960 ss 38(1), 48(2), Sch 7 Pt II (all repealed); and PARA 83 note 1.
2 See PARA 83 note 1.
3 Charities Act 1960 s 38(2) (repealed).
4 Charities Act 1960 s 38(2) proviso (repealed).
5 Charities Act 1960 s 38(3) (repealed).

(2) ESSENTIAL REQUIREMENTS

(i) Imperative Words creating a Trust

85. Words of trust. As in the case of an ordinary trust, there must be certainty of intention on the donor's part to make a gift[1]. The words used must be such that on the whole they ought to be construed as imperative[2]; a mere expression of desire or hope will not create a trust of any kind[3]. The word 'trust' itself need not be used[4].

In the absence of a binding contract an expression of intention in a deceased's lifetime to give money to charity is not effective after death[5].

1 As to certainty of intention see **TRUSTS AND POWERS** vol 98 (2013) PARAS 64–67.
2 *Knight v Knight* (1840) 3 Beav 148 at 173 per Lord Langdale MR. See *Liverpool City Council v A-G* (1992) Times, 1 May.
3 See eg *Re Adams and Kensington Vestry* (1884) 27 ChD 394, CA. See also eg *Re Wedgwood Museum Trust Ltd, Young v A-G* [2011] EWHC 3782 (Ch), [2011] All ER (D) 204 (Dec) (nothing to suggest that there was a special charitable trust; assets were held as part of the corporate assets and not on separate trust, and were therefore available to the pension scheme creditor).
4 As to where writing is generally necessary see PARA 74. See also **TRUSTS AND POWERS** vol 98 (2013) PARA 65. As to whether contractual rights and obligations are created by subscribing to a charity see *Brooks v Richardson* [1986] 1 All ER 952, [1986] 1 WLR 385.
5 *Re Hudson, Creed v Henderson* (1885) 54 LJCh 811; *Sinnett v Herbert* (1871) LR 12 Eq 201; *Re Smith, Champ v Marshallsay* (1890) 64 LT 13.

(ii) Certainty as to Subject Matter

86. Certainty as to trust fund. The general rule of equity that a gift will fail if the trust property cannot clearly be identified applies to charitable trusts[1]. Thus, if the amount of a gift purporting to be made in favour of a charity cannot be ascertained, the gift fails[2], although a gift of a sum 'not exceeding' a named figure is construed as a gift of the named sum[3].

1 As to certainty of subject matter in relation to trusts generally see **TRUSTS AND POWERS** vol 98 (2013) PARAS 68–69.
2 *Hartshorne v Nicholson* (1858) 26 Beav 58 (where the amount of the gift was left blank). See also *Ewen v Bannerman* (1830) 2 Dow & Cl 74, HL; *Cherry v Mott* (1836) 1 My & Cr 123 (where an amount could only be ascertained by entering into an impossible contract); and the non-charity case of *Asten v Asten* [1894] 3 Ch 260. In *Dundee Magistrates v Morris* (1858) 3 Macq 134, HL (considered in *Fisk v A-G* (1867) LR 4 Eq 521, and *Re Birkett* (1878) 9 ChD 576), a will, in which the testator directed that a hospital for 100 boys should be established in Dundee without stating what amount should be applied to this object, was held to furnish a sufficient means of ascertaining the amount of the legacy. See also *Macduff v Spence's Trustees* 1909 SC 178, Ct of Sess (a trust to apply the interest of a fund or so much thereof as the trustees might deem expedient to charitable objects held valid; but this case is probably not good law in England).
3 *Thompson v Thompson* (1844) 1 Coll 381 at 395 per Knight Bruce V-C; *Gough v Bult* (1848) 16 Sim 45. However, see *Coxe v Basset* (1796) 3 Ves 155; and cf *Re Mills, Midland Bank*

Executor and Trustee Co Ltd v Board of Governors of United Birmingham Hospitals [1953] 1 All ER 835, [1953] 1 WLR 554; *Re Vernon* (1957) Times, 27 June.

87. Gift of uncertain surplus. Where there is a gift of a fund to be applied in the first place to a particular purpose with a gift over of the surplus, then if the first purpose cannot be carried out because it is unlawful, but the amount which would have been required can be reasonably ascertained, the gift to charity of the surplus over that amount is valid[1]. But where the first purpose is so indefinite that the amount required for it cannot be reasonably ascertained, so that there is no ascertainable surplus, the gift fails entirely[2]. The result is the same where the testator, although estimating the cost of effecting the first purpose, gives his executors a discretion to exceed that amount[3]. An inquiry may be directed to ascertain the amount needed to fulfil the primary invalid purpose[4].

However, where a fund is given primarily for a charitable purpose, but is subject to an invalid charge, as, for example, for the perpetual repair of a tomb not forming part of a church, there is no apportionment, for the whole fund goes to charity[5].

1 *Dundee Magistrates v Morris* (1858) 3 Macq 134, HL; *Mitford v Reynolds* (1842) 1 Ph 185. See also *A-G v Parsons* (1803) 8 Ves 186 at 192 per Lord Eldon LC; and *Re Coxen, McCallum v Coxen* [1948] Ch 747 at 752, [1948] 2 All ER 492 at 498 per Jenkins J.

2 *Chapman v Brown* (1801) 6 Ves 404, explained in *Re Birkett* (1878) 9 ChD 576 at 579 per Jessel MR; *Cherry v Mott* (1836) 1 My & Cr 123 at 134 per Lord Langdale MR; *Cramp v Playfoot* (1858) 4 K & J 479; *Peek v Peek* (1869) 17 WR 1059; *Kirkmann v Lewis* (1869) 38 LJCh 570; *Re Taylor, Martin v Freeman* (1888) 58 LT 538; *Re Porter, Porter v Porter* [1925] Ch 746; *Re Dalziel, Midland Bank Executor and Trustee Co Ltd v St Bartholomew's Hospital* [1943] Ch 277, [1943] 2 All ER 656. The principle underlying this rule is that if the entire fund might have been properly applied to the first purpose, if it had been lawful, there would be no ascertainable residue for the second.

3 *Limbrey v Gurr* (1819) 6 Madd 151.

4 *Chapman v Brown* (1801) 6 Ves 404 at 410 per Grant MR; *Mitford v Reynolds* (1842) 1 Ph 185 at 199 per Lord Lyndhurst LC. See also *Dundee Magistrates v Morris* (1858) 3 Macq 134, HL. Where the invalid purpose was the repair of a tomb it was held that the gift failed to the extent of the capital representing the annual amount necessary to keep that tomb in repair, treating the capital as invested in consols: *Re Vaughan, Vaughan v Thomas* (1886) 33 ChD 187 at 194 per North J.

5 *Kelly v A-G* [1917] 1 IR 183; *Re Rogerson, Bird v Lee* [1901] 1 Ch 715, following *Fisk v A-G* (1867) LR 4 Eq 521, *Re Birkett* (1878) 9 ChD 576, and *Re Vaughan, Vaughan v Thomas* (1886) 33 ChD 187. In cases of this kind the obligation to repair the tomb is a moral one and is not legally binding: *Hunter v Bullock* (1872) LR 14 Eq 45; *Dawson v Small* (1874) LR 18 Eq 114 at 118 per Bacon V-C; *Re Williams* (1877) 5 ChD 735; *Re Taylor, Martin v Freeman* (1888) 58 LT 538; *Re Rogerson, Bird v Lee* [1901] 1 Ch 715 at 719 per Joyce J; *Re Manser, A-G v Lucas* [1905] 1 Ch 68 at 75 per Warrington J; *Re Dalziel, Midland Bank Executor and Trustee Co Ltd v St Bartholomew's Hospital* [1943] Ch 277, [1943] 2 All ER 656. As to monuments and tombs see PARA 61.

88. Perpetual gift of income. A gift of income in perpetuity to a charity does not necessarily carry with it the right to capital, as it would in the case of a gift to an individual, unless there is an intention discoverable from the terms of the gift that the capital should go with the income[1].

1 *Re Levy, Barclays Bank Ltd v Board of Guardians and Trustees for Relief of Jewish Poor* [1960] Ch 346, [1960] 1 All ER 42, CA.

89. Additions to trust property. When trustees hold an interest in land on charitable trusts and subsequently acquire a further interest in the same land, whether by gift or prescription, the whole is held subject to the original charitable trusts[1]. Similarly, where a right of presentation in connection with a charitable corporation had been exercised for centuries by a municipal corporation, it was held that the municipal corporation held the right on trust for the charitable purposes for which it was originally created[2]. Where trustees of land for charitable purposes acquire neighbouring land and there is no evidence as to the source of the purchase money, it will not necessarily be presumed that the money used came out of the rents and profits of the original land, so that the whole is subject to the original trusts[3].

If land is purchased partly with money belonging to a charity, the charity is entitled to such proportion of the land as the money contributed by the charity bears to the whole price[4]. Where a fund is given to specified charitable objects in fixed proportions, and the fund has increased, the rule is to apportion the accretions pro rata between the different objects[5]. Where the funds of one charity are inextricably mixed with the funds of another charity, both charities are entitled to participate pro rata in the increased value of the aggregate funds[6].

1 *A-G v Cashel Corpn* (1842) 3 Dr & War 294.
2 *A-G v St John's Hospital, Bedford* (1864) 10 Jur NS 897.
3 *A-G v Master, Wardens etc of the Wax Chandlers' Co* (1873) LR 6 HL 1; but see *Re Ambleside Charity* (1870) 18 WR 663. These cases may be reconciled by contrasting the different nature and circumstances of the trustees in question.
4 *A-G v Newcastle Corpn* (1842) 5 Beav 307 (appeal compromised sub nom *Newcastle-upon-Tyne Corpn v A-G* (1845) 12 Cl & Fin 402, HL).
5 *A-G v Marchant* (1866) LR 3 Eq 424 (accretions arising from increased income). As to surplus income see PARAS 131–135.
6 *Edinburgh Corpn v Lord Advocate* (1879) 4 App Cas 823, HL.

(iii) Trusts Exclusively Charitable

A. APART FROM STATUTE

90. Court must be able to execute trust. The validity of a charitable trust does not depend on the application of the test of certainty of objects which is applicable to private trusts[1], but as with all trusts its validity does depend on whether it can be executed by the court[2]. Provided a trust is restricted in its objects or purposes to that which the law regards as charitable, it does not fail because the particular objects are not defined[3], for the court can execute a charitable trust by means of a scheme, notwithstanding that the particular objects are not stated[4]. The application of the trust property to charity must be obligatory[5]; and a gift cannot be treated as valid merely because the trustees have always applied the property to charity if they have a discretion under the trust instrument to apply it to non-charitable purposes[6], although some such dispositions were validated by the Charitable Trusts (Validation) Act 1954[7].

1 See *IRC v Broadway Cottages Trust* [1955] Ch 20, [1954] 3 All ER 120, CA; and TRUSTS AND POWERS vol 98 (2013) PARA 70.
2 See *Morice v Bishop of Durham* (1805) 10 Ves 522. A trust of residue for charitable purposes is not rendered void for uncertainty by the fact that the trustees have power to retain investments indefinitely, for that alone cannot prevent the court from having jurisdiction to execute the trust in case of maladministration: *Dick v Audsley* [1908] AC 347, HL.
3 *Morice v Bishop of Durham* (1805) 10 Ves 522 at 527–528 per Lord Eldon LC: if the bequest is in trust for charity, it is no objection that the charity is not particularly defined, neither is it necessary that the testator should use the word 'charity'. See also *Ommanney v Butcher* (1823) Turn & R 260; *Re Douglas, Obert v Barrow* (1887) 35 ChD 472 at 485, CA, per Cotton LJ; *Re Macduff, Macduff v Macduff* [1896] 2 Ch 451 at 463, CA, per Lindley LJ, and at 469–470 per Rigby LJ; *Re Garrard, Gordon v Craigie* [1907] 1 Ch 382; *Chichester Diocesan Fund and Board of Finance Inc v Simpson* [1944] AC 341 at 348, [1944] 2 All ER 60 at 62, HL, per Viscount Simon LC.

4 In *Application for Registration of Environment Foundation*, Decision of the Charity Commissioners, 24 January 2003, at para 3, there is dicta to the effect that the use of the qualifying phrase 'by such means as are charitable' to limit the scope of a purpose that is otherwise not exclusively charitable does not save a trust from failure where this leads to lack of certainty and clarity in the charitable objects; however, this appears to be at least partly based on the erroneous belief that the rule of certainty of objects applies equally to charitable objects as it does to the objects of a private trust. As to schemes see PARA 179 et seq. As to decisions of the Charity Commission see PARA 547.

5 *Re Macduff, Macduff v Macduff* [1896] 2 Ch 451 at 465, CA, per Lindley LJ, and at 470 per Rigby LJ; and see *A-G v Lawes* (1849) 8 Hare 32 at 42 per Knight Bruce V-C; *Morice v Bishop of Durham* (1805) 10 Ves 522 at 541 per Lord Eldon LC; *James v Allen* (1817) 3 Mer 17 at 19 per Grant MR; *Nash v Morley* (1842) 5 Beav 177 at 183 per Lord Langdale MR; *Re Douglas, Obert v Barrow* (1887) 35 ChD 472 at 482, CA, per Cotton LJ; *Re Davidson, Minty v Bourne* [1909] 1 Ch 567, CA; *Re Warre's Will Trusts, Wort v Salisbury Diocesan Board of Finance* [1953] 2 All ER 99, [1953] 1 WLR 725 (residence for missioners and for a retreat house); *Re Harpur's Will Trusts, Haller v A-G* [1962] Ch 78, [1961] 3 All ER 588, CA. Cases when part is clearly given to charity should be distinguished: see PARA 95.

6 *Re Jarman's Estate, Leavers v Clayton* (1878) 8 ChD 584 at 587 per Hall V-C.

7 As to the Charitable Trusts (Validation) Act 1954 see PARAS 98–103.

91. Clear charitable intention necessary. The question whether any particular gift is or is not charitable is not one for speculative reasoning as to what was the donor's intention, even though his general wishes may be discoverable. No gift is to be deemed charitable unless, in express terms or by necessary implication, the donor has signified a clear intention to devote the property to charitable purposes[1]. To ascertain the intention of a testator, a fair interpretation must be put upon the provisions of a will taken together[2].

Purposes or objects which are not defined or indicated are not presumed to be charitable[3], except where a general intention to give to charity is to be gathered from the instrument[4], or where the nature of the gift permits such a presumption[5].

A recital of a charitable intention cannot render charitable a trust whose expressed objects are not charitable[6]; but, if the objects of the trust are ambiguous, the recital may be referred to for the purpose of explaining and ascertaining what was the donor's meaning[7].

Where executors had transferred land to a local authority, which had covenanted to use it as a recreation ground[8] and for no other purpose, it was held that the land was not held on charitable trusts[9]. It was further held that the Attorney General was not entitled to sue the local authority on its personal covenants[10].

1 *Hunter v A-G* [1899] AC 309 at 315, HL, per Earl of Halsbury LC, and at 319 per Lord Shand. Where no charitable intention is manifest, the court will not execute a trust to distribute a fund among such persons or such purposes as may appear just to the trustees: *Harris v Du Pasquier* (1872) 26 LT 689; *Gibbs v Rumsey* (1813) 2 Ves & B 294; *Fowler v Garlike* (1830) 1 Russ & M 232; and see *Buckle v Bristow* (1864) 13 WR 68.

2 *Hunter v A-G* [1899] AC 309 at 320, HL, per Lord Davey.

3 *Buckle v Bristow* (1864) 13 WR 68.

4 *Mills v Farmer* (1815) 1 Mer 55 at 95 per Lord Eldon LC; *Re Willis, Shaw v Willis* [1921] 1 Ch 44, CA.

5 As to the inference of charitable intention see PARA 92. The cases on gifts for the benefit of a particular locality may be regarded as a special example of such a presumption or implication: see PARA 47.

6 Cf *Re Sanders' Will Trusts, Public Trustee v McLaren* [1954] Ch 265, [1954] 1 All ER 667.

7 *A-G v Jesus College, Oxford* (1861) 29 Beav 163 at 168 per Romilly MR.

8 It was common ground that the provision of a recreation ground was a charitable purpose: see PARA 48.

9 *Liverpool City Council v A-G* (1992) Times, 1 May. See however, *University of London v Prag* [2014] EWHC 3564 (Ch) at [66], [2014] All ER (D) 79 (Nov), where *Liverpool City Council v A-G* was distinguished as being based on a purely contractual arrangement, and possibly inapplicable where all the relevant matters were set out in a deed.

10 *Liverpool City Council v A-G* (1992) Times, 1 May. As to the Attorney General see PARAS 589, 596, 605 et seq; and CONSTITUTIONAL AND ADMINISTRATIVE LAW vol 20 (2014) PARA 273 et seq.

92. Inference of charitable intention. A gift to or for the benefit of a charitable society, without further explanation, is construed as a gift for its general purposes[1]. A gift to a charitable corporation is an absolute gift to it and makes the property given applicable for the objects stated in the corporation's memorandum or charter as part of its general corporate property[2].

A gift on trust to the holder of an office whose functions are charitable in nature[3] is not for that reason a charitable gift if express trusts are attached to the gift by the donor; but where no express trusts are declared, it may sometimes be inferred that the trusts of the gift are the charitable trusts of the trustee's office[4].

1 See *Re White, White v White* [1893] 2 Ch 41 at 52, CA, per Lindley LJ; *Green v Rutherforth* (1750) 1 Ves Sen 462 at 472 per Lord Hardwicke LC; *Re Vernon's Will Trusts, Lloyds Bank Ltd v Group 20 Hospital Management Committee (Coventry)* [1972] Ch 300n, [1971] 3 All ER 1061n; *Re Finger's Will Trusts, Turner v Ministry of Health* [1972] Ch 286, [1971] 3 All ER 1050. If the association is established for charitable purposes, no objection on the ground of perpetuity can arise. As to gifts to unincorporated associations see PARA 62.

2 As to the property of charitable corporations see PARA 254.

3 The same applies to a gift on trust to a charitable society: *A-G v Sibthorp* (1830) 2 Russ & M 107; *A-G v Dean and Canons of Windsor* (1858) 24 Beav 679 at 701–702 per Romilly MR (gifts to dean and canons); *Gloucester Corpn v Wood* (1843) 3 Hare 131 (on appeal sub nom *Gloucester Corpn v Osborn* (1847) 1 HL Cas 272) (gift to municipal corporation); and see *Doe d Toone v Copestake* (1805) 6 East 328; *Aston v Wood* (1868) LR 6 Eq 419 (gift to trustees of nonconformist chapel); *Re Freeman, Shilton v Freeman* [1908] 1 Ch 720, CA; *Re Friends' Free School, Clibborn v O'Brien* [1909] 2 Ch 675.

4 Most of the cases on this point arise out of gifts to holders of religious offices. As to gifts to the holders of religious offices see PARA 32.

93. Alternative, subsidiary or cumulative purposes. Gifts expressed in the alternative, such as for 'charitable or other purposes'[1], 'charitable or public purposes'[2], 'charitable or benevolent purposes'[3], or in other alternative terms admitting non-charitable objects[4], are not charitable. Where the word 'or' is used, it must be determined whether it is used exegetically[5] (meaning 'that is to say'; 'in other words') or disjunctively (that is, separating two alternatives)[6].

The word 'and' is similarly ambiguous: gifts for 'charitable and benevolent' purposes[7] and similar gifts[8] have been held charitable on the ground that the objects indicated must possess both characteristics; but where, upon the true construction of a gift, those words create not cumulative characteristics which each object must possess, but cumulative classes of objects, the trust is not charitable[9]. It may sometimes be the case, however, that the context shows that a word which would normally admit non-charitable objects bears in the particular will a restricted meaning admitting only such objects of the kind which it indicates as are also charitable[10].

1 *Ellis v Selby* (1836) 1 My & Cr 286; *Re Chapman, Hales v A-G* [1922] 2 Ch 479, CA.

2 *Vezey v Jamson* (1822) 1 Sim & St 69; *Re Davis, Thomas v Davis* [1923] 1 Ch 225; *Blair v Duncan* [1902] AC 37, HL; *Langham v Peterson* (1903) 87 LT 744.

Where a gift is 'for the benefit of the schools, and charitable institutions, and poor, and other objects of charity, and any other public objects', the words 'or any other public objects' must be ejusdem generis with the specified ones, and therefore for charitable objects: *Re Bennett, Gibson v A-G* [1920] 1 Ch 305. Cf *A-G of the Cayman Islands v Wahr Hansen* [2001] 1 AC 75, [2000]

3 All ER 642, PC where general statements of benevolent or philanthropic objects were not to be artificially construed so as to be impliedly limited to charitable purposes only when there were clear indications that no such implied limitation had been intended.

3 *Houston v Burns* [1918] AC 337, HL; *Re Jarman's Estate, Leavers v Clayton* (1878) 8 ChD 584; *Re Riland's Estate, Phillips v Robinson* [1881] WN 173; *Chichester Diocesan Fund and Board of Finance Inc v Simpson* [1944] AC 341, [1944] 2 All ER 60, HL; *A-G for New Zealand v Brown* [1917] AC 393, PC.

4 *Shaw's Trustees v Esson's Trustees* (1905) 8 F 52, Ct of Sess (charitable, benevolent or religious objects at discretion of trustees); *Re Davidson, Minty v Bourne* [1909] 1 Ch 567, CA (charitable, religious or other objects in connection with the Roman Catholic faith); *Ellis v IRC* (1949) 31 TC 178, CA; *Re Macduff, Macduff v Macduff* [1896] 2 Ch 451, CA (purposes 'charitable, philanthropic or ...'); *Down v Worrall* (1833) 1 My & K 561 (pious and charitable purposes or otherwise); *Thompson v Thompson* (1844) 1 Coll 381 at 399 per Knight Bruce V-C; *Re Sidney, Hingeston v Sidney* [1908] 1 Ch 488, CA (charitable or emigration uses).

5 See *Rickerby v Nicholson* [1912] 1 IR 343 (religious or charitable purposes); *Re Salter, Rea v Crozier* [1911] 1 IR 289 (charitable or religious purposes); *Re Sinclair's Trusts* (1884) 13 LR Ir 150 (any charitable or religious purpose); *McPhee's Trustees v McPhee* 1912 SC 75, Ct of Sess; *Re Tomkinson, M'Crea and Bell v A-G of Duchy of Lancaster* (1929) 74 Sol Jo 77 (to such charities or to such religious bodies) in which the gifts were held to be valid.

6 See *Chichester Diocesan Fund and Board of Finance Inc v Simpson* [1944] AC 341, [1944] 2 All ER 60, HL, where the possible interpretations are discussed. In view of the technical meaning of the word 'charitable' in English law, there are obvious difficulties in the way of the exegetical construction, for it might tend to widen 'charitable' rather than to restrict 'benevolent'.

7 *Re Best, Jarvis v Birmingham Corpn* [1904] 2 Ch 354; *Caldwell v Caldwell* (1921) 91 LJPC 95, HL; *Jemmit v Verril* (1826) Amb 585n.

8 *A-G v Herrick* (1772) Amb 712 ('charitable and pious uses'); *Re Lloyd, Greame v A-G* (1893) 10 TLR 66 ('religious and benevolent' purposes); *Re Sutton, Stone v A-G* (1885) 28 ChD 464 ('charitable and deserving objects'). See also *Blair v Duncan* [1902] AC 37 at 44, HL, per Lord Davey ('charitable and public purposes'), *Baker v Sutton* (1836) 1 Keen 224 ('religious and charitable institutions and purposes'); *Re Scowcroft, Ormrod v Wilkinson* [1898] 2 Ch 638 ('furtherance of Conservative principles and religious and mental improvement').

9 *Re Eades, Eades v Eades* [1920] 2 Ch 353 ('religious, charitable and philanthropic objects'); *Williams v Williams, Williams v Kershaw* (1835) 5 Cl & Fin 111n ('benevolent, charitable and religious purposes'); *A-G v Dartmouth Corpn* (1883) 48 LT 933 ('charitable, needful and necessary' purposes); and see *A-G v National Provincial and Union Bank of England* [1924] AC 262, HL ('such patriotic purposes or objects and such charitable institution or institutions or charitable object or objects in the British Empire' as trustees should select, though note that in such an instance it is at least possible that the later widening of the scope of purposes which the Charity Commission envisages as appropriate for registration might now lead to a different decision; see PARA 49 text and note 15); *A-G of the Bahamas v Royal Trust Co* [1986] 3 All ER 423, [1986] 1 WLR 1001, PC (education and welfare); and the Scottish case, *Edgar etc v Cassells* 1922 SC 395, Ct of Sess ('benevolent, charitable and religious institutions in G' construed distributively, though such construction did not render the gift void by Scottish law). The question is whether the gift is for purposes which are both charitable and benevolent or for charitable purposes and for benevolent purposes. The more numerous the qualifications enumerated, the more likely is the latter conclusion: *Re Eades, Eades v Eades*.

10 *Dolan v Macdermot* (1868) 3 Ch App 676; *Re Bennett, Gibson v A-G* [1920] 1 Ch 305; *Re Ludlow, Bence-Jones v A-G* (1923) 93 LJCh 30, CA.

94. Construction of objects of companies and other bodies. Similar considerations apply to the objects of companies and other corporate or unincorporated bodies. If a company is formed for a number of objects, some of which, being main objects, permit expenditure on non-charitable activities, or some of which, though subsidiary, are not merely ancillary to the main objects and are not charitable, the company is not formed for charitable purposes only[1]. However, if the non-charitable activities do not represent a collateral or independent purpose, but are incidental to, and consequent upon, the way in which the charitable purpose for which alone the body was formed is carried on, the body is charitable[2]. Where such a body has a written constitution, it is not permissible to look at its activities rather than its specified objects to decide what its objects are[3]. It is, however, permissible to refer to outside evidence in order to decide whether the ascertained objects can be carried out only in a way which is exclusively charitable[4].

1 *Oxford Group Ltd v IRC* [1949] 2 All ER 537, 31 TC 221, CA; *Ellis v IRC* (1949) 31 TC 178 (on appeal 31 TC 178, CA); *Associated Artists Ltd v IRC* [1956] 2 All ER 583, [1956] 1 WLR 752; *IRC v City of Glasgow Police Athletic Association* [1953] AC 380, [1953] 1 All ER 747, HL. See also *Helena Partnerships Ltd (formerly Helena Housing Ltd) v Revenue and Customs Comrs (Attorney General intervening)* [2012] EWCA Civ 569, [2012] 4 All ER 111, [2012] PTSR 1409 (registered social landlord was not formed exclusively for charitable purposes; the provision of housing stock was not in itself a charitable purpose).

2 *Institution of Civil Engineers v IRC* [1932] 1 KB 149, CA; *Royal College of Surgeons of England v National Provincial Bank Ltd* [1952] AC 631, [1952] 1 All ER 984, HL; *Royal College of Nursing v St Marylebone Corpn* [1959] 3 All ER 663, [1959] 1 WLR 1077, CA; *Neville Estates Ltd v Madden* [1962] Ch 832, [1961] 3 All ER 769.

3 *Bowman v Secular Society Ltd* [1917] AC 406, HL; *Keren Kayemeth Le Jisroel Ltd v IRC* [1931] 2 KB 465, CA; *Tennant Plays Ltd v IRC* [1948] 1 All ER 506, CA; *Berry v St Marylebone Borough Council* [1958] Ch 406, [1957] 3 All ER 677, CA; *Incorporated Council of Law Reporting for England and Wales v A-G* [1972] Ch 73, [1971] 3 All ER 1029, CA; affg [1971] Ch 626, [1971] 1 All ER 436.

4 See *Incorporated Council of Law Reporting for England and Wales v A-G* [1972] Ch 73, [1971] 3 All ER 1029, CA.

95. Intention to devote part to charity. Even if some of the objects of a trust are prima facie non-charitable[1], or illegal[2], the gift may be good if there is an overriding intention that some part of the property be applied to charity. If it can be ascertained what are the proper proportions to be attributed to the several objects, the court will direct an inquiry[3], but if from the nature of the gift it appears impracticable to do so the court will divide the fund equally between the different objects[4], and the gift will only fail as to the proportion appropriated to the non-charitable objects. In simple cases the amount sufficient for the non-charitable purpose may be ascertained by affidavit[5].

Apportionment between a void part and a valid part is not, however, possible where on its true construction the gift is one entire gift to an entire class with uncertainty in the criteria specified for the selection of beneficiaries from that class[6].

1 *Hunter v A-G* [1899] AC 309 at 323–324, HL, per Lord Davey; *Wilkinson v Lindgren* (1870) 5 Ch App 570; *Pocock v A-G* (1876) 3 ChD 342, CA; *Re Douglas, Obert v Barrow* (1887) 35 ChD 472, CA; *Re Hurley, Nichols v Pargiter* (1900) 17 TLR 115; *Re Allen, Hargreaves v Taylor* [1905] 2 Ch 400; *Re Hood, Public Trustee v Hood* [1931] 1 Ch 240, CA. See also *A-G v Fletcher* (1835) 5 LJCh 75; *Dolan v Macdermot* (1868) 3 Ch App 676; *Wrexham Corpn v Tamplin* (1873) 21 WR 768; *Adnam v Cole* (1843) 6 Beav 353; *Hoare v Osborne* (1866) LR 1 Eq 585; *Re Rigley's Trusts* (1866) 36 LJCh 147; *Re Vaughan, Vaughan v Thomas* (1886) 33 ChD 187. It is immaterial whether the non-charitable objects are definite or indefinite: *Re Clarke, Bracey v Royal National Lifeboat Institution* [1923] 2 Ch 407.

2 *A-G v Hartley* (1793) 4 Bro CC 412; *Carter v Green* (1857) 3 K & J 591; *Salusbury v Denton* (1857) 3 K & J 529, following *Doyley v A-G* (1735) 4 Vin Abr 485, pl 16, at 486 per Lord Cowper; but distinguish *Down v Worrall* (1833) 1 My & K 561, where the trustees had a discretion to apply a fund either for charitable purposes or for an individual. Illegal purposes, being contrary to public policy, cannot be charitable: see PARA 66.

3 *Adnam v Cole* (1843) 6 Beav 353; *Hoare v Osborne* (1866) LR 1 Eq 585 at 588 per Kindersley V-C; *Re Rigley's Trusts* (1866) 36 LJCh 147; and see *Re Gardom, Le Page v A-G* [1914] 1 Ch 662; revsd on another point [1914] 1 Ch 662 at 674, CA, per Cozens-Hardy MR; and affd sub nom *Le Page v Gardom* (1915) 84 LJCh 749, HL.

4 *Doyley v A-G* (1735) 4 Vin Abr 485, pl 16, at 486 per Lord Cowper; *Crafton v Frith* (1851) 4 De G & Sm 237; *Re Hall's Charity* (1851) 14 Beav 115; *Salusbury v Denton* (1857) 3 K & J 529; *Hoare v Osborne* (1866) LR 1 Eq 585 at 588–589 per Kindersley V-C; *A-G v Marchant*

(1866) LR 3 Eq 424; *Hunter v A-G* [1899] AC 309 at 323–324, HL, per Lord Davey; *Re Clarke, Bracey v Royal National Lifeboat Institution* [1923] 2 Ch 407; *Re Gavacan, O'Meara v A-G* [1913] 1 IR 276; *Re King, Henderson v Cranmer* [1931] WN 232.

5 *Re Vaughan, Vaughan v Thomas* (1886) 33 ChD 187 at 194 per North J.

6 *Re Wright's Will Trusts* (1982) (1999) 13 TLI 48, CA.

96. Power to revoke charitable trusts. If trusts are declared which are charitable, but there is a power to revoke the trusts and declare new ones which need not necessarily be charitable, the existence of the unexercised power does not make the original trusts non-charitable while they last[1].

1 *Gibson v South American Stores (Gath and Chaves) Ltd* [1950] Ch 177, [1949] 2 All ER 985, CA; cf *George Drexler Ofrex Foundation Trustees v IRC* [1966] Ch 675, [1965] 3 All ER 529; *Re Sir Robert Peel's School, Tamworth, ex p Charity Comrs* (1868) 3 Ch App 543. See also *IRC v Yorkshire Agricultural Society* [1928] 1 KB 611 at 633, CA, per Atkin LJ. See also PARA 137 note 17.

97. Incidental non-charitable benefits. A gift may be charitable notwithstanding that the attainment of its purposes incidentally produces benefits of a non-charitable character[1] or that non-charitable benefits are conferred for the purpose of promoting the principal charitable purpose[2].

It is acceptable in certain circumstances for charity trustees to be paid out of the charity for their services[3]. However, if it proposed that trustees should be paid simply for acting as trustees, the Charity Commission[4] needs to be satisfied that this does not have the effect of extending the purposes of the institution so that it is incapable of being a charity since it would exist at least in part to benefit the trustee or trustees[5].

1 See the cases cited in PARA 94 note 2.

2 Cf *Re Coxen, MacCallum v Coxen* [1948] Ch 747, [1948] 2 All ER 492 (provision for an annual dinner and for payment of fees to trustees for their attendance at meetings, held ancillary to management of large fund for the benefit of orthopaedic hospitals). See also *Re Charlesworth, Robinson v Archdeacon of Cleveland* (1910) 101 LT 908 (cited in PARA 31 note 12); *Queen's University of Belfast v A-G for Northern Ireland* [1966] NI 115 (provision for payment of annual sum to each of four outside electors, ancillary to promotion of research by award of elective studentships).

3 See the Charities Act 2011 ss 185, 186; and PARA 336. In *Li Quan v Bray* [2014] EWHC 3340 (Fam), [2014] All ER (D) 339 (Oct) a charitable trust established to promote the conservation of Chinese tigers could not be regarded as a post-nuptial settlement formed partly for the support of the husband and wife who were directors of the charity.

4 As to the Charity Commission see PARAS 543–578.

5 As to the policy of the Charity Commission towards remuneration of trustees under what is now the Charities Act 2011 see *CC11: Trustee expenses and payments* (Charity Commission, March 2012) Pt F (available, at the date at which this volume states the law, on the government website). As to the Charity Commission's publications see PARA 547.

B. CHARITABLE TRUSTS (VALIDATION) ACT 1954

98. Dispositions affected by the Charitable Trusts (Validation) Act 1954. Certain dispositions which would have been invalid under the general law as not being for charitable purposes only were validated retrospectively by the Charitable Trusts (Validation) Act 1954[1].

The Act applies to any disposition of property to be held or applied for objects declared by an imperfect trust provision[2], and to any covenant[3] to make such a disposition, where apart from the Act the disposition or covenant is invalid under the law of England and Wales, but would be valid if the objects were exclusively charitable[4].

A covenant entered into before 30 July 1954[5] is not, however, enforceable by virtue of the Act unless confirmed by the covenantor after that date, but a disposition made in accordance with such a covenant is to be treated for the purposes of the Act as confirming the covenant and any previous disposition in accordance with it[6]. A disposition in settlement or other disposition creating more than one interest in the same property is treated for the purposes of the Act as a separate disposition in relation to each of the interests created[7].

1 The Charitable Trusts (Validation) Act 1954 does not affect trust instruments coming into operation on or after 16 December 1952: see s 1(2); and PARA 100. The Act binds the Crown: s 6. The ordinary principles as to certainty of object (see PARA 93) apply to such instruments.

2 As to the meaning of 'imperfect trust provision' see PARA 99.

3 'Covenant' includes any agreement, whether under seal or not; and 'covenantor' is to be construed accordingly: Charitable Trusts (Validation) Act 1954 s 1(4).

4 Charitable Trusts (Validation) Act 1954 s 2(1). Cf *Vernon (William Vernon & Sons Ltd Employees Fund Trustees) v IRC* [1956] 3 All ER 14, [1956] 1 WLR 1169, where the trusts, though not exclusively charitable, were apparently not invalid, so that the Charitable Trusts (Validation) Act 1954 did not affect them. The Act does not apply if the invalidity has already been acted upon: see s 2(2); and PARA 101.

5 Ie the commencement of the Charitable Trusts (Validation) Act 1954.

6 Charitable Trusts (Validation) Act 1954 s 3(6).

7 Charitable Trusts (Validation) Act 1954 s 2(3). It was held by a majority of the Court of Appeal that contributions to an appeal fund, whose purposes were defraying funeral expenses of victims of an accident, caring for disabled victims and then to apply the rest of the funds to such worthy cause or causes in memory of the victims, were dispositions to which the Charitable Trusts (Validation) Act 1954 could apply but were not dispositions creating three separate interests in the money given: *Re Gillingham Bus Disaster Fund, Bowman v Official Solicitor* [1959] Ch 62, [1958] 2 All ER 749, CA.

99. Imperfect trust provisions. For the purposes of the Charitable Trusts (Validation) Act 1954, 'imperfect trust provision' means any provision declaring objects for which property is to be held or applied, and so describing those objects that, consistently with the terms of the provision, the property could be used exclusively for charitable purposes, but could nevertheless be used for purposes which are not charitable[1]. The trust declared need not be so imperfect as to be invalid[2].

It has been held[3] that a gift for such worthy causes as trustees may think fit is not a disposition to which the Act applies[4], and that the Act was intended to cure dispositions such that the whole of the money could be devoted to charity by excluding words which are too wide or too vague[5]. In a later case, however, it was held that imperfect trust provisions are not solely those which declare the objects of the trust in such a form as to include by express reference some legally charitable purpose as well as some non-charitable purpose[6]. Thus the Act has been held to validate trusts for welfare purposes amongst employees of companies[7] and members of a trade union[8] which would otherwise have failed as being partly for non-charitable purposes, and also because the beneficiaries were not a sufficient section of the public, by limiting the purposes to the relief of poverty among the specified class[9].

The Act does not apply to a trust which is purely a private discretionary trust with no flavour of charity, but which might be validated if the beneficiaries were required to be poor[10]. Similarly it does not apply to a trust with only one expressed object, where that object is not charitable[11]. A trust for 'such purposes as my trustees may think fit' might not be validated by the Act, notwithstanding that the trustees could properly choose charitable objects[12].

The Act does not apply to a gift to be divided between institutions and associations of a particular type, because such a gift does not declare the objects for which property is to be held or applied[13].

1 Charitable Trusts (Validation) Act 1954 s 1(1). Where some of the trust property is required to be held for a non-charitable purpose the Act cannot, therefore, apply: *Vernon (William Vernon & Sons Ltd Employees Fund Trustees) v IRC* [1956] 3 All ER 14, [1956] 1 WLR 1169. If no one could object to an exclusively charitable application, the provision in question satisfies the condition: *Ulrich v Treasury Solicitor* [2005] EWHC 67 (Ch), [2005] 1 All ER 1059, [2006] 1 WLR 33, applied in *Cawdron v Merchant Taylors' School* [2009] EWHC 1722 (Ch), [2010] PTSR 507.

2 See *Re Harpur's Will Trusts, Haller v A-G* [1962] Ch 78, [1961] 3 All ER 588, CA.

3 Although Buckley J, in *Re Wykes, Riddington v Spencer* [1961] Ch 229 at 239, sub nom *Re Wykes' Will Trusts, Riddington v Spencer* [1961] 1 All ER 470 at 474, treated this as obiter dictum, it appears that it was an alternative ground for decision: see *Re Harpur's Will Trusts, Haller v A-G* [1962] Ch 78 at 95, [1961] 3 All ER 588 at 594, CA, per Harman LJ; *Re Saxone Shoe Co Ltd's Trust Deed, Re Abbott's Will Trusts, Abbott v Pearson* [1962] 2 All ER 904 at 915, [1962] 1 WLR 943 at 957 per Cross J.

4 *Re Gillingham Bus Disaster Fund, Bowman v Official Solicitor* [1958] Ch 300, [1958] 1 All ER 37; affd [1959] Ch 62, [1958] 2 All ER 749, CA.

5 *Re Gillingham Bus Disaster Fund, Bowman v Official Solicitor* [1958] Ch 300 at 306, [1958] 1 All ER 37 at 40 per Harman J.

6 *Re Wykes, Riddington v Spencer* [1961] Ch 229 at 238, sub nom *Re Wykes' Will Trusts, Riddington v Spencer* [1961] 1 All ER 470 at 477 per Buckley J. In *Re Gillingham Bus Disaster Fund, Bowman v Official Solicitor* [1959] Ch 62 at 80, [1958] 1 All ER 749 at 758, CA, Ormerod LJ was of the same view, and cf Lord Evershed MR at 75, 755; see also *Ulrich v Treasury Solicitor* [2005] EWHC 67 (Ch) at [28]–[32], [2005] 1 All ER 1059, [2006] 1 WLR 33 per Hart J. Some persuasive support for this view may be given by *Re McCullough* [1966] NI 73; *Re Ashton, Siddall v Gordon* [1955] NZLR 192, NZ CA; *Leahy v A-G for New South Wales* [1959] AC 457, [1959] 2 All ER 300, PC (all decided on similar statutory provisions).

7 *Re Wykes, Riddington v Spencer* [1961] Ch 229, sub nom *Re Wykes' Will Trusts, Riddington v Spencer* [1961] 1 All ER 470; *Ulrich v Treasury Solicitor* [2005] EWHC 67 (Ch), [2005] 1 All ER 1059, [2006] 1 WLR 33.

8 *Re Mead's Trust Deed, Briginshaw v National Society of Operative Printers and Assistants* [1961] 2 All ER 836, [1961] 1 WLR 1244.

9 As to the relief of poverty among limited classes such as these see PARA 18.

10 *Re Saxone Shoe Co Ltd's Trust Deed, Re Abbott's Will Trusts, Abbott v Pearson* [1962] 2 All ER 904, [1962] 1 WLR 943. In *Re Wykes, Riddington v Spencer* [1961] Ch 229, sub nom *Re Wykes' Will Trusts, Riddington v Spencer* [1961] 1 All ER 470, the reference to welfare purposes permitted a flavour of charity to be discerned, but Buckley J did not base his decision on that. In *Re McCullough* [1966] NI 73, Lowry J said that no specific indication of a charitable intention was required; but see *Re Ashton, Siddall v Gordon* [1955] NZLR 192, NZ CA.

11 *Buxton v Public Trustee* (1962) 41 TC 235. The object was 'to promote and aid the improvement of international relations and intercourse'.

12 See *Leahy v A-G for New South Wales* [1959] AC 457, [1959] 2 All ER 300, PC, approving *Re Hollole* [1945] VLR 295 (a gift to a trustee to be disposed by him as he may deem best). See also *Re Wykes, Riddington v Spencer* [1961] Ch 229 at 243, sub nom *Re Wykes' Will Trusts, Riddington v Spencer* [1961] 1 All ER 470 at 476 per Buckley J.

13 *Re Harpur's Will Trusts, Haller v A-G* [1961] Ch 38, [1960] 3 All ER 237; affd [1962] Ch 78, [1961] 3 All ER 588, CA.

100. Effect of the Charitable Trusts (Validation) Act 1954. The effect of the Charitable Trusts (Validation) Act 1954 is that any imperfect trust provision[1] contained in an instrument taking effect before 16 December 1952[2] has, and is deemed to have had, effect, in relation to any disposition or covenant[3] to which the Act applies[4]: (1) as respects the period before 30 July 1954[5], as if the whole of the declared objects were charitable[6]; and (2) as respects the period thereafter, as if the provision had required the property to be held or applied for the declared objects in so far only as they authorise use for charitable purposes[7]. A document inviting gifts of property to be held or applied for objects declared by the document is treated for these purposes as an instrument taking effect when it is first issued[8].

Thus the imperfect trust provision itself is not validated, unless it is also the disposition; and there may well be provisions for purposes which would fall within the definition of imperfect trust provision but which would not be invalid as dispositions, and would therefore not be affected[9], because they do not have effect in relation to any disposition to which the Act applies[10].

1 As to the meaning of 'imperfect trust provision' see PARA 99.
2 Ie the date of publication of the *Report of the Committee on the Law and Practice relating to Charitable Trusts* Cmd 8710 (1952) (the Nathan Report) and it was made known that the government would introduce legislation enacted by the Charitable Trusts (Validation) Act 1954: see 179 HL Official Report (5th series), 16 December 1952, col 998; and 509 HC Official Report (5th series), 8 December 1952, written answers col *154*.
3 As to the meaning of 'covenant' see PARA 98 note 3.
4 Charitable Trusts (Validation) Act 1954 s 1(2). As to dispositions and covenants to which the Charitable Trusts (Validation) Act 1954 applies see PARAS 98, 101.
5 Ie the date of the commencement of the Charitable Trusts (Validation) Act 1954.
6 Charitable Trusts (Validation) Act 1954 s 1(2)(a).
7 Charitable Trusts (Validation) Act 1954 s 1(2)(b).
8 Charitable Trusts (Validation) Act 1954 s 1(3). In *Re Gillingham Bus Disaster Fund, Bowman v Official Solicitor* [1958] Ch 300, [1958] 1 All ER 37; affd [1959] Ch 62, [1958] 2 All ER 749, CA, a letter published in a newspaper, announcing the establishment of the fund, was held to be a document within this provision.
9 Ie by the Charitable Trusts (Validation) Act 1954 s 2(1): see PARA 98.
10 See *Harpur's Will Trusts, Haller v A-G* [1962] Ch 78 at 91, [1961] 3 All ER 588 at 592, CA, per Lord Evershed MR.

101. Savings: dispositions already treated as invalid. The Charitable Trusts (Validation) Act 1954 does not apply to any disposition if, before 16 December 1952[1], property comprised in, or representing that comprised in, the disposition in question or another disposition made for the objects declared by the same imperfect trust provision, or income arising from any such property, has been paid or conveyed to, or applied for the benefit of, the persons entitled by reason of the invalidity of the disposition in question or the other disposition, as the case may be[2].

The purpose of this provision is to prevent the Act being applied where an imperfect trust provision has been recognised to be invalid and the invalidity acted on[3].

1 See PARA 100.
2 Charitable Trusts (Validation) Act 1954 s 2(2).
3 *Re St Andrew's (Cheam) Lawn Tennis Club Trust; Philippe v Cameron* [2012] EWHC 1040 (Ch), [2012] 3 All ER 746.

102. Transitional provisions in relation to legal proceedings and tax payments. The Charitable Trusts (Validation) Act 1954 contained transitional provisions enabling effect to be given to its provisions in legal proceedings begun before the commencement of the Act on 30 July 1954, as well as those begun afterwards[1], and even enabling certain judgments and orders[2] to be varied in accordance with the provisions of the Act[3].

The operation of the Act did not affect retrospectively any liability to tax, nor did it invalidate anything done or any determination given before the commencement of the Act[4].

1 Charitable Trusts (Validation) Act 1954 s 4(1) (repealed).

2 This did not, however, include orders or judgments made or given before the commencement of the Charitable Trusts (Validation) Act 1954 in proceedings begun before 16 December 1952 (as to which date see PARA 100): see the Charitable Trusts (Validation) Act 1954 s 4(2) (repealed).
3 See the Charitable Trusts (Validation) Act 1954 s 4(3) (repealed).
4 See the Charitable Trusts (Validation) Act 1954 s 4(4).

103. Savings: adverse claims. No proceedings may be begun by any person to enforce his right to any property[1] comprised in, or representing that comprised in a disposition to which the Charitable Trusts (Validation) Act 1954 applies[2] after 30 July 1955[3] or after the expiration of one year beginning with the date on which the right first accrues to him or to some person through whom he claims, whichever is the later, unless before or after its accrual, the right either[4]: (1) has been concealed by the fraud of some person administering the imperfect trust provision[5] or his agent[6]; or (2) or has been acknowledged by some such person or his agent by means of a written acknowledgment given to the person having the right or his agent and signed by the person making it, or by means of a payment or transfer of property in respect of the right[7]. If the period prescribed for any person to bring proceedings to recover any property expires without his having recovered the property or begun proceedings to do so, his title to the property is extinguished[8].

Subject to the limitation period set out above, where a disposition to which the Charitable Trusts (Validation) Act 1954 applies was made before, and is not confirmed[9] after, 30 July 1954, the Act does not prejudice a person's right, by reason of the invalidity of the disposition, to property comprised in, or representing that comprised in, the disposition as against the persons administering the imperfect trust provision or the persons on whose behalf they do so, unless the right accrued to him or some person through whom he claims before 16 December 1946[10]. However, the persons administering the imperfect trust provision, and any trustee for them or for the persons on whose behalf they do so, are entitled, as against a person whose right to the property is saved by this last provision, to deal with the property as if his right to the property had not been so saved, unless they have express notice of a claim by him to enforce his right to the property[11].

For the purposes of these provisions, a right by reason of the invalidity of a disposition to property comprised in, or representing that comprised in, the disposition is deemed not to accrue to anyone so long as he is under a disability or has a future interest only, or so long as the disposition is subject to another disposition made by the same person, and the whole of the property or the income arising from it is held or applied for the purposes of that disposition[12]. The other disposition may be a disposition deemed to be separate by virtue of the Act itself[13].

1 Ie the right by virtue of the Charitable Trusts (Validation) Act 1954 s 3(1): see the text and notes 9–11.
2 As to dispositions to which the Charitable Trusts (Validation) Act 1954 applies see PARAS 98, 101.
3 Ie after the expiration of one year beginning with 30 July 1954 i e the commencement of the Charitable Trusts (Validation) Act 1954.
4 Charitable Trusts (Validation) Act 1954 s 3(2).
5 As to the meaning of 'imperfect trust provision' see PARA 99.
6 Charitable Trusts (Validation) Act 1954 s 3(2)(a).
7 Charitable Trusts (Validation) Act 1954 s 3(2)(b).
8 Charitable Trusts (Validation) Act 1954 s 3(2). This provision is not to be taken as extending the time for bringing any proceedings beyond the period of limitation prescribed by any other statute: s 3(2). The Limitation Act 1980 s 38(2), (5), (6) (see LIMITATION PERIODS vol 68 (2008)

PARAS 1025, 1170) applies for the purposes of the Charitable Trusts (Validation) Act 1954 as it does for the purposes of the Limitation Act 1980 to define the circumstances in which a person is deemed to be under a disability or to claim through another person: Charitable Trusts (Validation) Act 1954 s 3(4) (amended by the Limitation Act 1980 Sch 3 para 4). Rights may accrue to a person for the purposes of this provision notwithstanding that the person or persons to whom they accrue are not ascertained: *Re Harpur's Will Trusts, Haller v A-G* [1961] Ch 38 at 49, [1960] 3 All ER 237 at 243 per Cross J.

9 See PARA 98 text to note 5.

10 Charitable Trusts (Validation) Act 1954 s 3(1). As to claiming through another person see note 8.

11 Charitable Trusts (Validation) Act 1954 s 3(1). There is also provision for the preservation of the right of a person, whose rights are saved by s 3(1), by virtue of his interest in the property to damages or other relief in respect of any dealing with the property, if the person dealing with the property had at the time express notice of a claim by him to enforce his right to the property: see s 3(5).

12 Charitable Trusts (Validation) Act 1954 s 3(3).

13 *Re Chitty's Will Trust, Thomas's Will Trusts, Ransford v Lloyds Bank Ltd* [1970] Ch 254, sub nom *Re Thomas's Will Trust* [1969] 3 All ER 1492. As to what are deemed to be separate dispositions see PARA 98.

C. POWERS OF APPOINTMENT IN FAVOUR OF CHARITY

104. Test for validity of power of appointment. Powers of appointment, whether mere powers or trust powers, are subject to a different test as to certainty of objects from that applicable to trusts as such[1]. The test for powers is whether it can be said of any person or institution whether he or it is or is not an object of the power as defined in the instrument creating the power[2]. Therefore, although the court will not establish a charitable trust where the testator has merely given power to trustees to distribute an indefinite sum in charity[3], a power in a will to distribute income to charitable institutions or 'such other organisation or body not registered as a charity but in the opinion of my trustees having charitable objects' is not invalid, though a trust in those terms would be[4].

A power to appoint to charitable and non-charitable indefinite objects is as invalid as a gift to such objects, and consequently, if a testator makes a gift to charitable and non-charitable objects in such shares and proportions as another person may nominate, the power of appointment is invalid and the subject matter of the gift is divided equally between the objects, the gift failing as to the proportions attributable to the non-charitable objects[5]. However, the inclusion of definite non-charitable institutions together with charity generally as discretionary objects under a trust which does not involve a perpetuity does not render the trust uncertain as to its objects[6].

1 As to powers of appointment see generally **TRUSTS AND POWERS; WILLS AND INTESTACY.**

2 See *Whishaw v Stephens* [1970] AC 508, sub nom *Re Gulbenkian's Settlement Trusts, Whishaw v Stephens* [1968] 3 All ER 785, HL; *McPhail v Doulton* [1971] AC 424, [1970] 2 All ER 228, HL.

3 *Coxe v Basset* (1796) 3 Ves 155 (power given to trustees to continue charities and benefactions or to bestow any other).

4 *Re Wootton's Will Trusts, Trotter v Duffin* [1968] 2 All ER 618, [1968] 1 WLR 681.

5 *Re Clarke, Bracey v Royal National Lifeboat Institution* [1923] 2 Ch 407.

6 *Re Douglas, Obert v Barrow* (1887) 35 ChD 472, CA.

(3) ASCERTAINMENT OF OBJECTS OF THE TRUST

(i) Construction in general

105. Benignant construction of charitable bequests. A benignant construction is placed on charitable bequests[1]. If a testator declares his intention to give the whole of his estate to charity, but specifically appropriates part only, the general intention in favour of charity prevails, and the proportion not appropriated by him will be appropriated by the court to charity[2]. Similarly, precatory recommendations in favour of particular charities do not prevent partial application in other ways[3].

The court infers from very slight circumstances that a testator means to give the whole of an estate to charitable purposes[4]; but no such inference is made if the testator is aware that the specific charitable payments which he directs do not exhaust the property given to the trustee[5]; nor can a charitable intention be inferred from the mere fact that the trustees are a charitable society and are given a wide discretion[6]. The court's leniency towards charitable gifts is also exemplified by the cases in which gifts apparently to charitable institutions have been construed as gifts for charitable purposes carried on by the institutions[7].

A gift to a legatee 'for the charitable purposes agreed upon between us' does not imply a general charitable intention, but only a limited charitable intention for the purposes agreed[8], and evidence is admissible to show what these purposes are, but not to limit the amount of the gift[9].

1 *Weir v Crum-Brown* [1908] AC 162 at 167, HL, per Lord Loreburn LC; *IRC v McMullen* [1981] AC 1 at 11, [1980] 1 All ER 884 at 890, HL, per Lord Hailsham of St Marylebone LC, with whom three other Law Lords expressly agreed; *Guild v IRC* [1992] 2 AC 310, [1992] 2 All ER 10, HL; but note *Scottish Burial Reform and Cremation Society Ltd v Glasgow City Corpn* [1968] AC 138 at 153, [1967] 3 All ER 215 at 222, HL, per Lord Upjohn. Thus, where a gift is capable of two constructions, one which would make it void and the other which would render it effectual, the latter must be adopted: *Bruce v Deer Presbytery* (1867) LR 1 Sc & Div 96 at 97, HL, per Lord Chelmsford LC; *Houston v Burns* [1918] AC 337 at 341–342, HL, per Lord Finlay LC; and see *Re Bain, Public Trustee v Ross* [1930] 1 Ch 224 at 230, CA, per Lord Hanworth MR. Compare the similar maxim of civil law that where there is an ambiguity, a benignant construction should be given if possible (*semper in dubiis benigniora praeferenda sunt*): Dig, lib 1 tit xvii s 56. See also *Dundee Magistrates v Morris* (1858) 3 Macq 134 at 155, HL, per Lord Chelmsford LC, and at 166 per Lord Cranworth. Cf *A-G of the Cayman Islands v Wahr Hansen* [2001] 1 AC 75, [2000] 3 All ER 642, PC (benignant construction of inter vivos settlement negatived by contrary indications).

2 *Beverley Corpn v A-G* (1857) 6 HL Cas 310 at 318 per Lord Cranworth LC, approving the doctrine laid down in *Arnold v A-G* (1698) Show Parl Cas 22, HL, and in *A-G v Johnson* (1753) Amb 190.

3 *Moggridge v Thackwell* (1803) 7 Ves 36; affd (1807) 13 Ves 416, HL.

4 *A-G v Skinners' Co* (1827) 2 Russ 407.

5 *Beverley Corpn v A-G* (1857) 6 HL Cas 310 at 320 per Lord Cranworth LC. See *A-G v Bristol Corpn* (1820) 2 Jac & W 294; *A-G v Drapers' Co* (1840) 2 Beav 508; *A-G v Dean and Canons of Windsor* (1860) 8 HL Cas 369. See also PARA 131.

6 *Re Freeman, Shilton v Freeman* [1908] 1 Ch 720, CA; but see also PARA 90.

7 This is important when there is a question as to whether the stated objects of the gift have failed: see generally PARA 147 et seq.

8 *Re Huxtable, Huxtable v Crawfurd* [1902] 2 Ch 793 at 796, CA, per Vaughan Williams LJ. See also the cases relating to secret charitable trusts: PARA 80.

9 *Re Huxtable, Huxtable v Crawfurd* [1902] 2 Ch 793 at 796, CA, per Vaughan Williams LJ; *Re Blackwell, Blackwell v Blackwell* [1929] AC 318, HL. As to secret trusts see PARA 80; and TRUSTS AND POWERS vol 98 (2013) PARAS 87–92.

106. Fund raised by contributions. When a fund raised from numerous contributories for somewhat indefinite purposes is vested in trustees, the trustees have prima facie implied authority to declare the trusts; and trusts so declared will be binding until set aside at the instance of the Attorney General or of one or more of the donors[1].

The precise ambit of this rule is unclear; it cannot be used to widen the purposes of a gift for a specific charitable purpose so as to defeat the claim of a donor by way of resulting trust on initial failure of the purpose[2].

Donations given via a website to be held for distribution to various charitable purposes give rise to a trust[3].

1 *A-G v Mathieson, Re Wilkinson and Fell's Contract* [1907] 2 Ch 383 at 394, CA, per Cozens-Hardy MR; *A-G v Clapham* (1855) 4 De GM & G 591 at 626 per Lord Cranworth LC; *Re Lord Mayor of Belfast's Air Raid Distress Fund* [1962] NI 161; *Re Henry Wood National Memorial Trust, Armstrong v Moiseiwitsch* [1967] 1 All ER 238n, [1966] 1 WLR 1601. As to the Attorney General see PARAS 589, 596, 605 et seq; and CONSTITUTIONAL AND ADMINISTRATIVE LAW vol 20 (2014) PARA 273 et seq.

2 Cf *Re Henry Wood National Memorial Trust, Armstrong v Moiseiwitsch* [1967] 1 All ER 238n, [1966] 1 WLR 1601.

3 *Charity Commission for England and Wales v Framjee* [2014] EWHC 2507 (Ch), [2015] 1 WLR 16, (2014) 17 ITELR 271 (the Dove Trust).

(ii) Extrinsic Evidence

107. Contemporaneous evidence. Evidence is admissible of contemporaneous documents and usage[1], of the circumstances attending the execution of the trust document[2], of the donor's contemporaneous acts[3], of the early application or distribution of the fund[4], and of the construction placed on doubtful questions which arose in the early administration of the trust[5]. The donee's contemporaneous acts are of little value for the purpose of placing a construction upon any instrument of gift executed by a donor; they only show the intention and the view with which the donee accepted the gift[6].

1 *Shore v Wilson* (1842) 9 Cl & Fin 355, HL; *Drummond v A-G for Ireland* (1849) 2 HL Cas 837 at 857 per Lord Brougham; *Aberdeen University v Irvine* (1868) LR 1 Sc & Div 289, HL; *A-G v Anderson* (1888) 57 LJCh 543. As to the presumption of a charitable trust from usage see PARA 112.

2 *A-G v Anderson* (1888) 57 LJCh 543.

3 *A-G v Trinity College, Cambridge* (1856) 24 Beav 383 at 399 per Romilly MR; *A-G v Dean and Canons of Windsor* (1860) 8 HL Cas 369 at 402 per Lord Campbell LC; *A-G v Dartmouth Corpn* (1883) 48 LT 933.

4 *Shore v Wilson* (1842) 9 Cl & Fin 355 at 569, HL, per Tindal LJ; *A-G v Brazen Nose College* (1834) 2 Cl & Fin 295, HL.

5 *A-G v Caius College* (1837) 2 Keen 150.

6 *A-G v Trinity College, Cambridge* (1856) 24 Beav 383. It is not so where the trusts are accepted conditionally or subject to certain qualifications, which the court may collect from contemporaneous transactions as evidenced by documents or usage: *A-G v Drapers' Co, Howell's Charity* (1843) 6 Beav 382 at 386 per Lord Langdale MR and cases there cited.

108. Inadmissible evidence. Parol evidence is not admissible for the purpose of interpreting a patent ambiguity, as where a blank is left in a trust deed or will[1], though it may be admitted to cure a latent ambiguity, that is to say, to ascertain the meaning the testator affixed to the expressions he used[2].

Evidence of intention is not admissible to cure an error in description[3]. Nor is evidence of counsel's opinion given at or prior to the execution of a trust deed admissible on its construction, because it merely amounts to evidence of the intention of the party executing it and to admit it would be a breach of the parol evidence rule[4].

Where the document of trust is lost, the court will take into consideration existing copies[5].

1 *Baylis v A-G* (1741) 2 Atk 239. As to ambiguities see DEEDS AND OTHER INSTRUMENTS vol 32 (2012) PARA 408; WILLS AND INTESTACY vol 102 (2010) PARA 219.

2 *Shore v Wilson* (1842) 9 Cl & Fin 355 at 390, HL, per Lord Lyndhurst ('godly preachers of Christ's holy Gospel'); *Drummond v A-G for Ireland* (1849) 2 HL Cas 837 at 862 per Lord Brougham ('Protestant dissenters'); *A-G v Clapham* (1855) 4 De GM & G 591 at 627 per Lord Cranworth LC; *A-G v Beverley Corpn* (1855) 6 De GM & G 256 at 268 per Turner LJ; *A-G v Dartmouth Corpn* (1883) 48 LT 933 ('charitable, needful, and necessary uses'); *Edge v Salisbury* (1749) Amb 70 ('relations'); *Re Kenny, Clode v Andrews* (1907) 97 LT 130; *Re Rees, Jones v Evans* [1920] 2 Ch 59 ('missionary'). See also *Re Kilvert's Trusts* (1871) 7 Ch App 170 at 173 per James LJ; *Re How, How v How* [1930] 1 Ch 66; *Re Moon's Will Trusts, Foale v Gillians* [1948] 1 All ER 300; and see PARA 109.

3 *National Society for the Prevention of Cruelty to Children v Scottish National Society for the Prevention of Cruelty to Children* [1915] AC 207 at 214, HL, per Lord Dunedin; *British Home and Hospital for Incurables v Royal Hospital for Incurables* (1903) 89 LT 495; revsd on other grounds (1904) 90 LT 601, CA.

4 *Rabin v Gerson Berger Association Ltd* [1986] 1 All ER 374, [1986] 1 WLR 526, CA. As to the admission of extrinsic evidence see DEEDS AND OTHER INSTRUMENTS vol 32 (2012) PARA 385 et seq.

5 *A-G v Cashel Corpn* (1842) 3 Dr & War 294; *A-G v Archbishop of York* (1853) 17 Beav 495; and see *A-G v Boultbee* (1794) 2 Ves 380; affd (1796) 3 Ves 220.

109. Extrinsic evidence to explain latent ambiguity. Extrinsic evidence is admissible in the case of latent ambiguity, as where a description in a will applies equally to more than one institution[1], to determine which institution the testator had in his mind[2]. Examples of admissible extrinsic evidence are to show that one of the institutions which claimed the legacy did not exist when the testator was resident in the locality[3], or that the testator was interested in[4], or had declared he would leave a legacy to[5], or had subscribed to[6] and referred in his books in a particular way to[7], a particular charity.

The fact that a dissolved charity satisfied the description given by the testator better than an existing society does not prevent an existing society, which satisfies the description sufficiently, from taking the legacy[8].

1 The fact that an existing institution is accurately described does not preclude all possibility of there being ambiguity: *National Society for the Prevention of Cruelty to Children v Scottish National Society for the Prevention of Cruelty to Children* [1915] AC 207 at 212, HL, per Lord Loreburn, and at 214 per Lord Dunedin. There is no absolute rule that a person, whether juridical or natural, answering the description in the will must have the gift whatever other considerations arise: *Re Meyers, London Life Association v St George's Hospital* [1951] Ch 534, [1951] 1 All ER 538. As to ambiguities see DEEDS AND OTHER INSTRUMENTS vol 32 (2012) PARA 408; WILLS AND INTESTACY vol 102 (2010) PARA 219.

2 *Middleton v Clitherow* (1798) 3 Ves 734; *Wilson v Squire* (1842) 1 Y & C Ch Cas 654 at 656 per Wigram V-C; *Re Briscoe's Trusts* (1872) 26 LT 149; *Re Fearn's Will* (1879) 27 WR 392; *Re Raven, Spencer v National Association for the Prevention of Consumption and other Forms of Tuberculosis* [1915] 1 Ch 673 at 681 per Warrington J; *Re King, King v Long* (1918) 53 ILT 60; *Re Satterthwaite's Will Trusts, Midland Bank Executor and Trustee Co Ltd v Royal Veterinary College* [1966] 1 All ER 919, [1966] 1 WLR 277, CA; *Re Nesbitt's Will Trusts, Dr Barnardo's Homes National Incorporated Association v United Newcastle-upon-Tyne Hospitals Board of Governors* [1953] 1 All ER 936, [1953] 1 WLR 595. An inquiry may be directed to decide which the testator intended to benefit: *Middleton v Clitherow*; *Re Dymond, Dymond v A-G* (1906) Times, 2 April. See also the non-charity cases *Charter v Charter* (1874) LR 7 HL 364 at 370–371 per Lord Chelmsford, and at 376 per Lord Hatherley; *Re Beale, Beale v Royal Hospital for Incurables* (1890) 6 TLR 308, CA; and PARA 108.

3 *King's College Hospital v Wheildon* (1854) 18 Beav 30.

4 *Gibson v Coleman* (1868) 18 LT 236.

5 *A-G v Hudson* (1720) 1 P Wms 674.

6 *Bunting v Marriott* (1854) 19 Beav 163; *Re Kilvert's Trusts* (1871) 7 Ch App 170 at 173 per James LJ; *Makeown v Ardagh* (1876) IR 10 Eq 445; *Re Fearn's Will* (1879) 27 WR 392; *Re Bradley, Oldershaw v Governesses' Benevolent Institution* (1887) 3 TLR 668; *Re Howard, Crofton v Lord's Day Observance Society* (1899) 43 Sol Jo 380.

7 *British Home and Hospital for Incurables v Royal Hospital for Incurables* (1904) 90 LT 601, CA.

8 *Coldwell v Holme* (1854) 2 Sm & G 31; *Re Magrath, Histed v Queen's University of Belfast* [1913] 2 Ch 331 (where the existing institution was in effect the defunct institution reconstituted).

110. Trivial error in description. A trivial error in describing the legatee does not invalidate the gift if the testator's intention is clear[1]; and where an institution is accurately described, a direction as to the use to be made of the money not applicable to the circumstances is immaterial[2].

The context of the will is also important, and may show that the description of a charity is exact, and not loose[3] or that the testator did not intend to benefit institutions of a particular character[4].

In short, the course to be adopted to find what legatee answers the description given in a will is the same in the case of a legacy to a charity as in the case of a legacy to an ordinary legatee[5].

1 *Makeown v Ardagh* (1876) IR 10 Eq 445. Examples are a vicar who is described as a rector (*Hopkinson v Ellis* (1842) 5 Beav 34), or a society which had changed its name but not its objects (*Re Kilvert's Trusts* (1871) 7 Ch App 170). As to the misdescription of property or persons see WILLS AND INTESTACY vol 102 (2010) PARA 270 et seq.

2 *Smith v Ruger* (1859) 5 Jur NS 905.

3 *Bradshaw v Thompson* (1843) 2 Y & C Ch Cas 295, where the description was ambiguous, and a general hospital was held entitled to take a legacy in preference to an ophthalmic hospital, because in other gifts in the same will, where the testator intended to benefit institutions for particular complaints, he had said so in express terms; *Re Alchin's Trusts, ex p Furley, ex p Earl Romney* (1872) LR 14 Eq 230; and see *Wallace v A-G* (1864) 33 Beav 384 at 392 per Romilly MR; *British Home and Hospital for Incurables v Royal Hospital for Incurables* (1904) 90 LT 601, CA.

4 Eg rate-supported institutions: *Lechmere v Curtler* (1855) 24 LJCh 647; *Re Davies' Trusts* (1872) 21 WR 154.

5 *Re Kilvert's Trusts* (1871) 7 Ch App 170 at 174 per Mellish LJ. See WILLS AND INTESTACY vol 102 (2010) PARAS 213, 217.

111. Usage in construction of trust instrument. The true construction of ancient instruments of trust may be aided by evidence of long usage and acquiescence[1], and where such instruments may be construed in two ways the court inclines, if possible, to the one supported by long usage[2] rather than assumes that a breach of trust has been committed[3]. But usage cannot be held to sanction a clear breach of trust[4], nor as a rule can evidence of long usage be admitted to vary a trust the terms of which are unambiguous[5].

1 *A-G v Bristol Corpn* (1820) 2 Jac & W 294 at 321 per Lord Eldon LC; *A-G v Smythies* (1833) 2 Russ & M 717 at 749 per Lord Brougham LC. As to the interpretation of deeds and the principles of construction see DEEDS AND OTHER INSTRUMENTS vol 32 (2012) PARA 364 et seq.

2 See the cases cited in note 1; and *A-G v Rochester Corpn* (1854) 5 De GM & G 797 at 822 per Turmer LJ.

3 *A-G v Sidney Sussex College* (1869) 4 Ch App 722 at 732 per Lord Hatherley LC. See also *Bruce v Deer Presbytery* (1867) LR 1 Sc & Div 96, HL.

4 *A-G v Bristol Corpn* (1820) 2 Jac & W 294 at 321 per Lord Eldon LC; *Drummond v A-G for Ireland* (1849) 2 HL Cas 837 at 861 per Lord Brougham; *A-G v Rochester Corpn* (1854) 5 De GM & G 797 at 822 per Turner LJ: *A-G v St John's Hospital, Bedford* (1865) 2 De GJ & Sm 621; and see *Re Swansea Free Grammar School* [1894] AC 252, PC. In some cases, however, a legal origin for long usage inconsistent with the instrument of trust has been presumed: *Queen's*

College, Cambridge, Case (1821) Jac 1; *A-G v Middleton* (1751) 2 Ves Sen 327 at 330 per Lord Hardwicke LC; *Re Parish of St Nicholas Acons* (1889) 60 LT 532; *A-G v Dalton* (1851) 13 Beav 141.

5 *A-G v Calvert* (1857) 23 Beav 248 at 263 per Romilly MR; *A-G v St Cross Hospital* (1853) 17 Beav 435; *A-G v Gould* (1860) 28 Beav 485 at 501 per Romilly MR; *A-G v West* (1858) 27 LJCh 789; *A-G v Ewelme Hospital* (1853) 17 Beav 366.

(iii) Presumption of Charitable Trust from Usage

112. Presumption from usage. In the absence of any document declaring the trusts of a fund, their nature may be determined by usage[1]. Where property has been held from time immemorial for the use and repair of what originally was the only church in a parish, the money is not applicable for the purposes of a new church in the same parish[2]. The trustees' accounts showing the application of the income of a fund for a long period may determine the charitable purposes on which the fund is held[3]. However, where trustees remain in adverse possession of the trust property after the legal title has reverted to the grantors, they do so on the trusts of the original grant, and cannot themselves declare fresh trusts of the property[4].

The court will presume whatever may be necessary, even an Act of Parliament[5], to give long standing usage a legal origin and render it valid[6]; it will be guided by the earliest evidence of usage, and will if possible presume that what was then done and long afterwards continued was rightly done[7]; but when the deed of foundation is produced, and is clear, nothing can be presumed to the contrary of what it established[8].

1 *A-G v St Cross Hospital* (1853) 17 Beav 435 at 464–465 per Romilly MR; *A-G v Bishop of Worcester* (1851) 9 Hare 328 at 359 per Turner V-C; and see *A-G v Boultbee* (1794) 2 Ves 380 (where regard was had to the terms of an entry in an ancient book kept by the trustees for entering their proceedings); *Goodman v Saltash Corpn* (1882) 7 App Cas 633, HL.

2 *Re Church Estate Charity, Wandsworth* (1871) 6 Ch App 296; but see PARA 89.

3 *Re St Bride's, Fleet Street, Church or Parish Estate* (1877) 35 ChD 147n.

4 *Re Ingleton Charity, Croft v A-G* [1956] Ch 585, [1956] 2 All ER 881 (the reverter in that case was automatic, under the School Sites Act 1841).

5 *A-G v Ewelme Hospital* (1853) 17 Beav 366; *A-G v Mercers' Co, Re St Paul's School* (1870) 18 WR 448 at 449 per James V-C.

6 *A-G v Mercers' Co, Re St Paul's School* (1870) 18 WR 448; *Cocksedge v Fanshaw* (1779) 1 Doug KB 119; *Goodman v Saltash Corpn* (1882) 7 App Cas 633 at 640, 644, HL, per Lord Selborne LC (where from long enjoyment by free inhabitants of a borough of a right of fishery a charitable trust in their favour under a lost grant to the corporation was presumed); *Haigh v West* [1893] 2 QB 19 at 26, CA, per Charles J (where enrolment of a lost grant was presumed); and see *Lord Fitzhardinge v Purcell* [1908] 2 Ch 139 at 165 per Parker J; *Harris v Earl of Chesterfield* [1911] AC 623, HL.

7 *A-G v Dalton* (1851) 13 Beav 141 at 142 per Lord Langdale MR.

8 *A-G v St Cross Hospital* (1853) 17 Beav 435; *A-G v Ewelme Hospital* (1853) 17 Beav 366; *A-G v Gould* (1860) 28 Beav 485; and see *Edinburgh Corpn v Lord Advocate* (1879) 4 App Cas 823, HL.

113. Instances of usage. A charitable trust may be presumed from such circumstances as the receipt for a long period of a rentcharge by a charity[1], or the letting of certain rights of pasturage by a parish vestry[2], or the exercise by the free inhabitants of a borough of a right of oyster fishery[3].

Various periods of uninterrupted usage have been held sufficient to establish charitable trusts[4]. Statutes now repealed prescribed various periods of usage for the establishment of the trusts of Roman Catholic and dissenting charities, in the absence of written instruments[5].

1 *A-G v West* (1858) 27 LJCh 789; and see *Stanley v Norwich Corpn* (1887) 3 TLR 506 (where certain rents had been paid to freemen of a city for a long period).

2 *Haigh v West* [1893] 2 QB 19 at 26, CA, per Charles J; and see *A-G v Cashel Corpn* (1842) 3 Dr & War 294.

3 *Goodman v Saltash Corpn* (1882) 7 App Cas 633, HL; and cf *Lord Fitzhardinge v Purcell* [1908] 2 Ch 139 at 165 per Parker J.

4 *A-G v West* (1858) 27 LJCh 789 (30 years); *A-G v Moor* (1855) 20 Beav 119 (100 years); *Re Parker's Charity* (1863) 32 Beav 654 (100 years); *Bunting v Sargent* (1879) 13 ChD 330 at 336 (105 years) per Jessel MR; *Robinson v Smith* (1908) 24 TLR 573 (over 100 years); *Re Parish of St Nicholas Acons* (1889) 60 LT 532 (200 years); *Queen's College, Cambridge, Case* (1821) Jac 1 (250 years); *Re St Alphage, London Wall* (1888) 59 LT 614 (300 years); *A-G v Mercers' Co, Re St Paul's School* (1870) 18 WR 448 (350 years).

5 See the Roman Catholic Charities Act 1860 s 5 and the Nonconformists' Chapels Act 1844 s 2. Both were repealed by the Charities Act 1960 s 39(1), Sch 5 (repealed), but not so as to affect the operation of charities which took effect before the passing of the two Acts: see the Charities Act 1960 s 39(2) (repealed by the Charities Act 2006 Sch 9, but without prejudice to such charities: see the Charities Act 2006 Sch 10 para 22). As to the beneficiaries of religious trusts and the form of worship intended see PARA 118.

(iv) Beneficiaries of Religious Trusts

114. Denomination intended by founder to be followed. One principle applicable to all charities without exception is that the founder's intentions are to be carried into effect so far as they are capable of being so, and so far as they are not contrary to law or morality. If, therefore, the founder has directed that only persons conforming to particular religious doctrines shall be recipients of his bounty, his will must be followed[1].

1 *A-G v Calvert* (1857) 23 Beav 248 at 255 per Romilly MR; *Re Malling Abbey Trusts, Beaumont v Dale* (1915) 31 TLR 397, CA (Church of England); *Craigdallie v Aikman* (1820) 2 Bli 529, HL (Scottish seceders); *A-G v Pearson* (1817) 3 Mer 353 at 410 per Lord Eldon LC; *Milligan v Mitchell* (1837) 3 My & Cr 72 (Scottish dissenters).

115. Presumptions as to particular denominations. A trust for the purpose of building a church or otherwise for maintaining and propagating the worship of God, containing no more precise expression of intention, is construed as a trust for the advancement of the established religion of the country[1]. Where the instrument of foundation was made before the Reformation, it was construed as though made after that event[2]. The expression 'Presbyterian' does not denote any particular doctrine or mode of worship[3]. In the absence of express direction, there is a presumption, in the case of eleemosynary[4] and educational charities[5], against the founder's intention being that the recipients must be persons holding a particular form of religious belief. Thus, in eleemosynary charities the founder's religious opinions and tenets are wholly to be disregarded. The presumption is that he intended to include persons of all persuasions, and the burden of proof lies on those who seek to exclude any[6].

In gifts to educational charities the founder's opinions are only of value where some directions may have been given by him relative to the religious instruction to be given to the pupils to be taught, and then only for the purpose of explaining and elucidating any obscurity or ambiguity which may be found in such direction[7].

1 *A-G v Pearson* (1817) 3 Mer 353 at 409 per Lord Eldon LC; *A-G v Calvert* (1857) 23 Beav 248 at 258 per Romilly MR.

2 *A-G v Calvert* (1857) 23 Beav 248 at 260 per Romilly MR; and see *Glasgow College v A-G* (1848) 1 HL Cas 800.

3 *A-G v Bunce* (1868) LR 6 Eq 563 at 574 per Malins V-C. With regard to Presbyterian trusts see *Westwood v McKie* (1869) 21 LT 165; *General Assembly of the Free Church of Scotland v Lord Overtoun, Macalister v Young* [1904] AC 515, HL.
4 As to the meaning of 'eleemosynary corporation' see PARA 225.
5 As to educational charities see **EDUCATION** vol 36 (2011) PARA 860.
6 *A-G v Calvert* (1857) 23 Beav 248 at 259 per Romilly MR; *A-G v St John's Hospital, Bath* (1876) 2 ChD 554.
7 *A-G v Calvert* (1857) 23 Beav 248 at 258–259 per Romilly MR; *A-G v Clifton* (1863) 32 Beav 596; and see *Re St Leonard, Shoreditch, Parochial Schools* (1884) 10 App Cas 304, PC.

116. Presumptions in case of gift expressly for religious purpose. In the case of a charity for the support of a religious establishment generally, or the purpose of religious instruction, two presumptions arise: first, that the founder intended to support an establishment belonging to some particular form of religion, and that he intended some particular doctrine of religion to be taught; and secondly, that this establishment and doctrine were those which he himself supported and professed; the court will look carefully at his course of life and conduct and spell out expressions, not merely in the instrument of foundation, but in his will and works, to ascertain what were the doctrines and opinions entertained and professed by him[1].

1 *A-G v Calvert* (1857) 23 Beav 248 at 256 per Romilly MR; *Shore v Wilson* (1842) 9 Cl & Fin 355, HL; *General Assembly of the Free Church of Scotland v Lord Overtoun, Macalister v Young* [1904] AC 515 at 613, HL, per Earl of Halsbury LC.

117. Ascertainment of founder's intention. The founder's intention is a question of fact[1], not always easily ascertained[2]. Where there is no expressed intention[3], or where the language is ambiguous[4], and in those cases only, the objects and mode of executing the trust may be ascertained from a consideration of extrinsic circumstances. Thus, where vague expressions, such as 'Protestant dissenters', are used, extrinsic evidence is admissible to show what denominations are intended to be included[5].

Nevertheless, evidence is not admissible to contradict an express trust[6], or to sanction a breach of trust[7], or to show the sense in which words were used by particular individuals[8], other than the authors of the trusts in question[9].

Reference also may be made to contemporaneous statutes to see in what sense the words were used in the age in which the deeds were executed[10], to contemporaneous deeds relating to the same chapel[11], or to a contemporaneous declaration of trust[12], or to the ecclesiastical history of the period[13]; and where the trust is for the benefit of an existing congregation of dissenters, the character of the congregation may be made the subject of inquiry[14].

The founder's meaning may be explained by evidence as to the character of the congregation for whose benefit the gift was made[15].

1 *Shore v Wilson* (1842) 9 Cl & Fin 355, HL.
2 *Foley v Wontner* (1820) 2 Jac & W 245.
3 *A-G v Murdoch* (1849) 7 Hare 445; affd (1852) 1 De GM & G 86.
4 *A-G v Calvert* (1857) 23 Beav 248 at 263 per Romilly MR; *A-G v Gould* (1860) 28 Beav 485.
5 *Shore v Wilson* (1842) 9 Cl & Fin 355 at 390, HL, per Lord Lyndhurst. In some cases Unitarians were held not entitled to participate; but it has been said that upon most occasions they would now be considered to be Protestant dissenters (*Drummond v A-G for Ireland* (1849) 2 HL Cas 837 at 863 per Lord Campbell); and see *Re Hutchinson's Trusts* [1914] 1 IR 271. As to presumption arising from usage see also PARAS 112–113.
6 *A-G v Clapham* (1855) 4 De GM & G 591.
7 *Drummond v A-G for Ireland* (1849) 2 HL Cas 837.
8 *Drummond v A-G for Ireland* (1849) 2 HL Cas 837 at 863 per Lord Campbell; *Re How, How v How* [1930] 1 Ch 66.

9 *Drummond v A-G for Ireland* (1849) 2 HL Cas 837 at 858 per Lord Brougham; and see PARA 108.
10 *Drummond v A-G for Ireland* (1849) 2 HL Cas 837 at 863 per Lord Campbell; *Shore v Wilson* (1842) 9 Cl & Fin 355 at 413, HL, per Campbell A-G. See also PARA 108.
11 *A-G v Anderson* (1888) 57 LJCh 543.
12 *A-G v Clapham* (1855) 4 De GM & G 591 at 626 per Lord Cranworth LC.
13 *A-G v Bunce* (1868) LR 6 Eq 563 at 571–572 per Malins V-C.
14 *A-G v Murdoch* (1849) 7 Hare 445; affd (1852) 1 De GM & G 86; and see *Dill v Watson* (1836) 2 Jo Ex Ir 48. Many denominations of dissenters, in order to secure uniformity in the trusts of their chapels, schools and other property, have used model deeds which were in fact carefully prepared deeds relating to particular chapels, schools, etc, by reference to which the trusts of other chapels, etc could be declared. Denominations which used such model deeds include the Methodist Church, the Baptists, the United Reformed Church, the Fellowship of Independent Evangelical Churches, Unitarians, the Calvinistic Methodist or Presbyterian Church of Wales.
15 *A-G v Molland* (1832) 1 You 562, where teaching 'the Gospel of Christ under the name of orthodoxy' was so explained.

118. Form of worship intended. It is not essential for the trusts of religious charities to be in writing in order that they may be enforced by the court[1]. The court may ascertain what form of religious worship was intended from the established usage of the congregation[2].

It was provided by statute that, in the case of Nonconformist chapels where there was no written instrument specifying particular forms of worship or opinions, 25 years' usage was to be taken as conclusive evidence of what might be taught or observed there[3]; and that in the case of Roman Catholic charities, if the trusts of the charity were not ascertained by means of any written document, 20 years' consistent usage was deemed conclusive evidence of the trusts on which the property was settled[4]. These provisions have now been repealed, but without prejudice to their operation as applied to charities taking effect before the repeals[5].

1 See also PARA 74.
2 *A-G v Pearson* (1817) 3 Mer 353 at 400 per Lord Eldon LC; *A-G v Murdoch* (1849) 7 Hare 445; affd (1852) 1 De GM & G 86; *Drummond v A-G for Ireland* (1849) 2 HL Cas 837. For a form of order directing an inquiry as to usage see *A-G v Pearson* at 420 per Lord Eldon LC. As to usage being presumptive evidence of trusts see PARA 112.
3 Nonconformists' Chapels Act 1844 s 2 (repealed).
4 Roman Catholic Charities Act 1860 s 5 (repealed).
5 Charities Act 1960 s 39(1), (2), Sch 5 (repealed).

119. Gifts for benefit of a church. A fund given for the 'reparation' of a church may in a proper case be applied in the erection of new buildings[1] and paying the salaries of persons who look after the fabric or ornaments of the building[2].

The income of a fund directed to be employed by the churchwardens of a parish 'about the parish church' is applicable to general expenditure about the church as a whole, including repairs to the chancel, although the churchwardens are not concerned with chancel repairs, which formerly fell on the rector as owner of the great tithes[3].

The endowment of a church means that the income only of the fund is to be applied for the benefit of the incumbent[4].

A gift to a parish church may be construed to be a gift to the parson and parishioners and their successors for ever[5], for their benefit, intended to be devoted to purposes in the parish connected with the services of the church, such purposes now being activities properly directed by the parochial church council[6].

Gifts to a vicar[7] and to a dissenting minister[8] may also be gifts for the benefit of the office, and not merely personal legacies to the holder of the office at the date of the gift.

A charitable bequest to a bishop 'to be applied by him for such general or special purposes in connection with' a named cathedral church 'as he in his absolute and uncontrolled discretion may think fit' may be applied in paying the stipend of an honorary canon having a stall in the cathedral, even though his main work lies outside the parish in which the cathedral is situated, or of a canon missioner with duties inside the cathedral, even though he is liable to be employed in the diocese outside the parish, but not of a canon missioner with general diocesan duties and having only an honorary stall in the cathedral[9].

1 *Re Palatine Estate Charity* (1888) 39 ChD 54. See *A-G v Master, Wardens etc of the Wax Chandlers' Co* (1873) LR 6 HL 1; *Re Booth's Charities* (1866) 14 WR 761.

2 *Re Palatine Estate Charity* (1888) 39 ChD 54 (this includes the verger or organ tuner, but not the organist).

3 *A-G v Parr* [1920] 1 Ch 339. Tithes have been abolished: see the Tithe Act 1936; and ECCLESIASTICAL LAW vol 34 (2011) PARA 975 et seq. As to chancel repairs see ECCLESIASTICAL LAW vol 34 (2011) PARA 868 et seq.

4 *Re Robinson, Wright v Tugwell* [1892] 1 Ch 95 at 100 per North J; on appeal [1897] 1 Ch 85, CA.

5 *Cheeseman v Partridge* (1739) 1 Atk 436. As to gifts to holders of religious offices see PARA 32.

6 *Re Gare, Filmer v Carter* [1952] Ch 80, [1951] 2 All ER 863.

7 *Re Parker's Charity* (1863) 32 Beav 654. See also *Re Garrard, Gordon v Craigie* [1907] 1 Ch 382.

8 *A-G v Cock* (1751) 2 Ves Sen 273; and see *Cheeseman v Partridge* (1739) 1 Atk 436 (schoolmaster).

9 *Re Whitehead* (1908) Times, 14 October.

(v) Gifts for Institutions, Parishioners or Parishes

120. Gifts for institutions. Where gifts are made to an existing charitable institution or to its governors or treasurer, generally[1] or for promoting certain definite objects which are in fact the objects of that institution[2], the gifts are applicable by the trustees, governors, or other officials for the general purposes of the institution.

A gift to an existing institution for a purpose which is in fact within the objects of the institution is prima facie a gift for the performance of that purpose by the institution in the course of its own activities. Thus, a gift of a fund to a city company to be employed in apprenticing young men should prima facie be applicable for apprenticing them in the craft in which the corporate body was engaged[3]; and where there is a gift to a college for the purpose of educating the descendants of a testator[4], education at that particular college, and not elsewhere, is presumed to be intended[5].

1 *Green v Rutherforth* (1750) 1 Ves Sen 462 at 472 per Lord Hardwicke LC (a gift to a college); *Re White, White v White* [1893] 2 Ch 41 at 52, CA, per Lindley LJ.

2 *Incorporated Society in Dublin v Richards* (1841) 1 Dr & War 258 at 294, 332 per Lord Sugden LC.

3 *A-G v Sidney Sussex College* (1869) 4 Ch App 722 at 730 per Lord Hatherley LC.

4 A gift for the education of descendants of named persons would now be regarded as a family trust and not charitable: *Re Compton, Powell v Compton* [1945] Ch 123 at 136, [1945] 1 All ER 198 at 205, CA, per Lord Greene MR.

5 *A-G v Sidney Sussex College* (1869) 4 Ch App 722 at 731 per Lord Hatherley LC.

121. Gifts for parishioners or for the poor. Where children of parishioners of a certain parish are alone eligible as objects of a charity, the word 'parishioner' has hitherto been taken in its ordinary sense of a person occupying premises liable to be rated in the parish[1].

A charity for the poor of a parish was not to be applied in such a way as to relieve those who had otherwise to support the poor by means of the poor rate[2]; but this principle did not apply to a gift which was intended in aid of poor rate[3].

1 *Etherington v Wilson* (1875) 1 ChD 160, CA. See also *A-G v Parker* (1747) 3 Atk 576; *Edenborough v Archbishop of Canterbury* (1826) 2 Russ 93; *A-G v Rutter, Sellon v Nicholls* (1768) 2 Russ 101n ('inhabitants and parishioners'); *Carter v Cropley* (1857) 8 De GM & G 680 at 687 per Bruce LJ; *Kensit v Rector of St Ethelburga, Bishopsgate Within* [1900] P 80. For a detailed analysis of the cases relating to 'parishioners' or 'inhabitants' see Tudor on Charities (7th Edn, 1984) p 210 et seq.

The effect of the Local Government Finance Act 1988 has not been considered in this regard. That Act abolished domestic rates and replaced them with the community charge, which was subsequently replaced by the council tax in 1993 (see the Local Government Finance Act 1992; and LOCAL GOVERNMENT FINANCE vol 70 (2012) PARA 51).

2 This principle was established in cases deciding that persons receiving poor law relief were not proper objects of such a charity: see *A-G v Leage* [1881] WN 167; *A-G v Bovill* (1840) 1 Ph 762; *Deptford Churchwardens v Sketchley* (1847) 8 QB 394 at 405 per Lord Denman CJ; *A-G v Wilkinson* (1839) 1 Beav 370; *A-G v Exeter Corpn* (1827) 3 Russ 395. See also *A-G v Price* (1744) 3 Atk 108; *A-G v Gutch* (1830) cited in Shelford on Mortmain (1836) 628; *A-G v Clarke* (1762) Amb 422; *Bishop of Hereford v Adams* (1802) 7 Ves 324; *A-G v Rochester Corpn* (1854) 5 De GM & G 797; *Re Sekforde's Charity* (1861) 4 LT 321. The poor law has been replaced by the modern social security system: see WELFARE BENEFITS AND STATE PENSIONS vol 104 (2014) PARA 1 et seq.

3 *A-G v Blizard* (1855) 21 Beav 233; *Re Richmond Parish Charity Lands, Richmond Corpn v Morell* (1965) 11 RRC 89; revsd on appeal on some points (1965) 11 RRC 283, CA (the same charity as in *A-G v Blizard*, after the abolition of the poor rate). See also PARA 48.

(vi) Uncertainty of Objects

122. Uncertainty of objects in general. Where a clear charitable intention is expressed, a gift which is otherwise valid is never allowed to fail on account of the uncertainty of the object, but the particular mode of application will be directed by the Crown in some cases, and by the court in others[1].

Effect will therefore be given to bequests for charitable purposes generally[2], or for a particular charitable purpose generally, such as the relief of poverty[3], or for the advancement of education[4] or religion[5], and to charitable gifts where the testator has indicated the class of objects to be benefited, such as the poor of a particular place[6] or the clergy of a particular sect[7], without prescribing the particular way in which his intention is to be carried into effect. In all of these cases the law supplies the mode of effectuating the intention[8].

1 *Moggridge v Thackwell* (1803) 7 Ves 36, where Lord Eldon considered the earlier cases; *Morice v Bishop of Durham* (1804) 9 Ves 399 at 404 per Grant MR (on appeal (1805) 10 Ves 522); *Mills v Farmer* (1815) 1 Mer 55; *Re White, White v White* [1893] 2 Ch 41 at 53, CA, per Lindley LJ; *Re Forester, Jervis v Forester* (1897) 13 TLR 555; *Re Pyne, Lilley v A-G* [1903] 1 Ch 83; *Re Bennett, Sucker v A-G* [1960] Ch 18, [1959] 3 All ER 295. Where the court has jurisdiction, schemes may also be directed by the Charity Commission (see the Charities Act 2011 s 69(1)(a); and PARA 189) or the Tribunal (see the Charities Act 2011 s 315, Sch 6, Table; and PARA 199). As to the Charity Commission see PARAS 543–578; as to the Tribunal see PARA 579 et seq.

2 *A-G v Herrick* (1772) Amb 712; *Morice v Bishop of Durham* (1805) 10 Ves 522 at 54 Lord Eldon LC; *Miller v Rowan* (1837) 5 Cl & Fin 99 at 109, HL, per Lord Brougham. As to where no trust is created and property is given to charity generally see PARA 513.

3 *A-G v Rance* (1728) cited in Amb 422. As to the relief of poverty see PARA 12 et seq.

4 *Whicker v Hume* (1858) 7 HL Cas 124. As to the advancement of education see PARA 21 et seq.

5 *Re White, White v White* [1893] 2 Ch 41 at 52, CA, per Lindley LJ. As to the advancement of religion see PARA 27 et seq.
6 *A-G v Wilkinson* (1839) 1 Beav 370.
7 *A-G v Hickman* (1732) 2 Eq Cas Abr 193 pl 14; *A-G v Gladstone* (1842) 13 Sim 7.
8 *Mills v Farmer* (1815) 1 Mer 55 at 95 per Lord Eldon LC. See also PARAS 513, 535.

123. Description by locality. In case of ambiguity, where the testator describes the institution he intends to benefit as being in a particular locality, prima facie[1] the legacy will go to an institution situated in the locality named, though the name used is more like that of an institution in another locality[2]. On the other hand, a legacy to the hospitals of London was not limited to hospitals within the City of London[3]; while a gift to 'all and every the hospitals', without further description, was confined to hospitals in the locality where the testatrix resided[4].

1 For cases in which other indications in the will contradictory to the description by locality have been followed see *Re Morgan, Marriott v Society for Abolition of Vivisection* (1909) 25 TLR 303; *British Home and Hospital for Incurables v Royal Hospital for Incurables* (1904) 90 LT 601, CA.
2 *Wilson v Squire* (1842) 1 Y & C Ch Cas 654; *Re Lycett, Riley v King's College Hospital* (1897) 13 TLR 373 (where the 'King's Cross Hospital' was construed to mean the Great Northern Hospital, King's Cross, in preference to the King's Cross Hospital at Dundee); *Bradshaw v Thompson* (1843) 2 Y & C Ch Cas 295 (where the 'Westminster Hospital, Charing Cross' was construed to mean the Charing Cross Hospital rather than the Westminster Hospital or the Royal Westminster Ophthalmic Hospital). See also *General Lying-in Hospital v Knight* (1851) 21 LJCh 537; *Re Kilvert's Trusts* (1871) 7 Ch App 170 at 173 per James LJ; *Re Clergy Society* (1856) 2 K & J 615; *Buxton v Blakiston* (1886) 2 TLR 293; *Re Glubb, Barnfield v Rogers* (1897) 14 TLR 66.
3 *Wallace v A-G* (1864) 33 Beav 384; and see *Ditcham v Chivis* (1828) 4 Bing 706; *Beckford v Crutwell* (1832) 5 C & P 242.
4 *Masters v Masters* (1718) 1 P Wms 421 at 425.

(vii) Delegation of Ascertainment of Objects

124. Power to determine object. Power to determine the particular object to be benefited may be delegated[1], so long as charitable and no other objects may benefit[2]. Thus, a direction to trustees to divide a fund at their discretion among such charitable institutions or objects as they think expedient is valid[3]; so, too, a bequest to such charitable objects of a definite class as the trustees select is valid and not void for uncertainty[4]. Whether the discretion extends to the whole gift or only to part of it is a question of construction[5], as is the question whether the trustees may appoint capital or only income to the selected objects[6].

The court will modify an apportionment which is not in accordance with the testator's wishes[7]. Where, however, trustees are given the widest possible discretion within certain limits in the choice of objects, they need not exercise their discretion in accordance with the known views of the testator[8].

Where the power to determine the particular object is delegated to a person who fails to exercise the power, the gift to charity does not fail on that account. Thus, a gift is not invalidated by a trustee neglecting to appoint[9] or an executor renouncing[10], or by the appointment of an executor being revoked[11], or by the death in the testator's lifetime of any person entrusted with the nomination of the particular object[12], or by the name of the intended nominator being left blank[13], or by the trustees declining to act[14] or dying without exercising the discretion[15]. In such cases the court will distribute the money after an inquiry[16].

A direction to trustees to apply residue for such charitable institutions or such other charitable objects as they might in their absolute discretion select does not enable them to set up and distribute the residue to a charitable foundation having a permanent existence[17].

1 *A-G v National Provincial and Union Bank of England* [1924] AC 262 at 264, HL, per Lord Cave LC. As to who may exercise discretionary power see PARA 385.
2 *Chichester Diocesan Fund and Board of Finance Inc v Simpson* [1944] AC 341 at 371, [1944] 2 All ER 60 at 74, HL, per Lord Simonds; see also at 348, 62 per Viscount Simon LC, at 350, 63 per Lord Macmillan, and at 356, 66 per Lord Wright.
3 *Waldo v Caley* (1809) 16 Ves 206; *Horde v Earl of Suffolk* (1833) 2 My & K 59; *Re Lea, Lea v Cooke* (1887) 34 ChD 528; *Cleland's Trustees v Cleland* 1907 SC 591, Ct of Sess; *Dick's Trustees v Dick* 1907 SC 953, Ct of Sess; affd sub nom *Dick v Audsley* [1908] AC 347, HL. See also the cases on cumulative purposes cited in PARA 93, and cf the cases on alternative purposes there cited, where the bequests were held void for uncertainty.
4 See *Re Garrard, Gordon v Craigie* [1907] 1 Ch 382; *Re Bennett, Gibson v A-G* [1920] 1 Ch 305; *Re Bain, Public Trustee v Ross* [1930] 1 Ch 224, CA; *Re Norman, Andrew v Vine* [1947] Ch 349, [1947] 1 All ER 400; *Re Flinn, Public Trustee v Flinn* [1948] Ch 241, [1948] 1 All ER 541; *Re Eastes, Pain v Paxon* [1948] Ch 257, [1948] 1 All ER 536.
5 See eg *Re Hall's Charity* (1851) 14 Beav 115.
6 *Re Beesty's Will Trusts, Farrar v Royal Alfred Merchant Seamen's Society* [1966] Ch 223, [1964] 3 All ER 82.
7 *A-G v Buller* (1822) Jac 407. See also *A-G v Rochester Corpn* (1676) Cas *temp* Finch 193; *A-G v Rochester Corpn* (1833) 6 Sim 273.
8 *Re Squire's Trusts, Chester and Flower v Oxford and Cambridge Universities and A-G* (1901) 17 TLR 724.
9 *A-G v Boultbee* (1796) 3 Ves 220; *Re Douglas, Obert v Barrow* (1887) 35 ChD 472 at 485, CA, per Cotton LJ.
10 *A-G v Fletcher* (1835) 5 LJCh 75. A power for executors to nominate is not exercisable by trustees subsequently appointed: *Hibbard v Lamb* (1756) Amb 309.
11 *White v White* (1778) 1 Bro CC 12; *Moggridge v Thackwell* (1803) 7 Ves 36 at 78 per Lord Eldon LC.
12 *Moggridge v Thackwell* (1803) 7 Ves 36 (affd (1807) 13 Ves 416, HL); *Re Willis, Shaw v Willis* [1921] 1 Ch 44, CA.
13 *Baylis v A-G* (1741) 2 Atk 239.
14 *Doyley v A-G* (1735) 2 Eq Cas Abr 194.
15 *A-G v Bucknall* (1742) 2 Atk 328.
16 *Doyley v A-G* (1735) 2 Eq Cas Abr 194.
17 *Re Muller's Estate* (22 June 1990, unreported): *Report of the Charity Commissioners for England and Wales for 1990* (HC Paper (1990–91) no 362) App D(a).

125. Founder's right to nominate beneficiaries. The right of nominating the beneficiaries of a charity belongs naturally to the founder and his heirs or nominees[1], until forfeited by neglect or improper use[2].

This right of nomination, while capable of alienation[3], does not necessarily pass upon the alienation of land to which it is attached. Thus, the owner of a manor to which a right of patronage is attached can alienate the manor without parting with the right of patronage[4].

1 *A-G v Leigh* (1721) 3 P Wms 145n (inmates of almshouses); *Green v Rutherforth* (1750) 1 Ves Sen 462; *Philips v Bury* (1694) 2 Term Rep 346 at 352–353, HL, per Holt CJ. It is not clear what effect the abolition of descent to the heir has upon rights of patronage. As to the old rules of descent see WILLS AND INTESTACY vol 102 (2010) PARA 480.
2 *A-G v Leigh* (1721) 3 P Wms 145n; Tudor on Charities (7th Edn, 1984) p 405.
3 *A-G v Brentwood School* (1832) 3 B & Ad 59; *A-G v Boucherett* (1858) 25 Beav 116 (cases of school patronage); *Re Church Patronage Trust, Laurie v A-G* [1904] 2 Ch 643, CA (advowson). The sale of advowsons is now prohibited: see the Patronage (Benefices) Measure 1986 s 3(1); and ECCLESIASTICAL LAW vol 34 (2011) PARA 583.
4 *A-G v Ewelme Hospital* (1853) 17 Beav 366. Where the owner of lands granted out of them a perpetual rentcharge in support of a charity, and subsequently conveyed away the fee simple, it

was held that his heir was not thereby deprived of the right of nominating the objects of the charity: *A-G v Rigby* (1732) 3 P Wms 145. Descent to the heir has been abolished: see note 1.

126. Right vested in trustees or others. Trustees to whom a testator gives the direction and management of a school provided by him are entitled to nominate and appoint the scholars[1]. The transfer to local authorities of the powers of vestries[2] has not affected any right of electing almsmen vested by deed in the minister, churchwardens, overseers and ratepayers of a parish[3] or any right vested in trustees of electing the minister of a parish[4].

1 *A-G v Dean and Canons of Christ Church* (1822) Jac 474 at 486 per Plumer MR (revsd on another point (1826) 2 Russ 321); and see *A-G v Scott* (1750) 1 Ves Sen 413.

2 See LOCAL GOVERNMENT vol 69 (2009) PARA 4.

3 *A-G v Drapers' Co* (1858) 4 Drew 299. Overseers were abolished by the Rating and Valuation Act 1925 s 62 (repealed) and their powers transferred to the rating authorities, or to such other local authorities or persons as were mentioned in the Overseers Order 1927, SR & O 1927/55 (lapsed). Domestic rates were abolished by the Local Government Finance Act 1988 and replaced by the community charge, itself replaced by the council tax in 1993: see the Local Government Finance Act 1992; LOCAL GOVERNMENT FINANCE vol 70 (2012) PARA 51.

4 *Carter v Cropley* (1857) 8 De GM & G 680. See also *Shaw v Thompson* (1876) 3 ChD 233; and cf *Re Hayle's Estate* (1862) 31 LJCh 612. As to transfer to the parochial church council see ECCLESIASTICAL LAW vol 34 (2011) PARA 308.

127. Church Commissioners' powers. In orders made by it under the Bishops Trusts Substitution Act 1858[1], the Charity Commission[2] is not entitled to make any order in relation to any advowson or right of patronage or presentation, part of the possessions of a see, which might be exchanged or otherwise disposed of by scheme of the Church Commissioners; nor may any orders relating to any ecclesiastical patronage be made under that Act without the consent of the Church Commissioners[3].

1 See PARA 270.

2 As to the Charity Commission see PARAS 543–578.

3 See the Bishops Trusts Substitution Act 1858 s 2 (amended by the Church Commissioners Measure 1947 ss 1, 2, 18(2)); and PARA 270. As to the Church Commissioners see ECCLESIASTICAL LAW vol 34 (2011) PARA 66 et seq.

128. Beneficiaries' qualifications. Where by the instrument establishing a charity the beneficiaries are required to possess certain qualifications, as, for example, to be parishioners of a certain parish[1], or to have been pupils for a number of years at a certain school[2], or where, other things being equal, preference is to be given to freemen of a certain town[3], the conditions imposed by the instrument must be complied with. However, the parties exercising the right of nomination need not take into consideration the motives with which the proposed beneficiaries secured the necessary qualifications[4]; and where compliance with certain religious forms is annexed as a condition to a charitable gift no further religious test can properly be required[5].

1 *Etherington v Wilson* (1875) 1 ChD 160, CA. As to the effect of a union of benefices upon charitable trusts relating to the united parishes see the Mission and Pastoral Measure 2011 Sch 3 para 9; and PARA 269.

2 *Re Storie's University Gift* (1860) 2 De GF & J 529.

3 *Re Nettle's Charity* (1872) LR 14 Eq 434 (election to scholarship).

4 *Etherington v Wilson* (1875) 1 ChD 160, CA, where the proposed beneficiary had become a parishioner temporarily to obtain the required qualification.

5 *A-G v Calvert* (1857) 23 Beav 248.

129. Nomination by subscribers' votes. Subscribers to a charity who are entitled to votes in proportion to the amount of their subscriptions may vote for any candidate they please. There is nothing illegal in a bargain between two subscribers by which the candidate of one is to be given the votes of both at an election in consideration of the candidate of the other having similar treatment at another election, and such a contract is enforceable at law[1].

1 *Bolton v Madden* (1873) LR 9 QB 55.

130. Improper nomination. A nomination which fails to comply with the directions of the instrument establishing the charity may be set aside[1], unless it is made in good faith under a mistaken construction of a scheme[2]. On setting aside an improper nomination the court has no jurisdiction to nominate proper beneficiaries, where by the charity's constitution the nomination rests with the trustees[3].

No application to the court to set aside the election of any person may be made by any other person who claims to be the proper object of a charity unless the making of the application is authorised by the Charity Commission[4].

Where the objects of a charity have been nominated for many years by the wrong persons, the court will not compel them to account for the payments made[5].

1 *Re Nettle's Charity* (1872) LR 14 Eq 434.
2 *Re Storie's University Gift* (1860) 30 LJCh 193 at 199 per Turner LJ.
3 *Re Storie's University Gift* (1860) 30 LJCh 193 at 198 per Turner LJ.
4 See the Charities Act 2011 s 115(2); and PARA 594. As to the Charity Commission see PARAS 543–578.
5 *A-G v Rigby* (1732) 3 P Wms 145.

(4) SURPLUS INCOME

131. Whole property given: surplus and later accretion. Where, at the date of the bequest, the property given is more than sufficient to satisfy the purposes specified in the will, and it also appears that the testator intended to give the whole property to charity, but was mistaken only as to the quantum, the whole is applicable to increase the charities specified or cy-près[1].

Where, however, it appears on the face of a will that the testator knew that the value of his estate was or might be more than the amount of the specific appropriation, and he has expressed no intention of devoting the whole to charity, the surplus does not go to charity, but either goes beneficially to the donees to whom the property is given in trust for the charitable purposes[2] or results to the testator and those claiming under him[3].

Where there is a direction to make specific charitable payments out of the income, it is a question of construction in each case whether the intention is to devote the whole property to charity[4]. Where the surplus income is directed to be applied in repairing the premises given to the charity, the whole property is held to have been devoted to charity[5].

If property, or the whole of the income arising from it[6], as, for example, a rentcharge equal to the annual value of the land charged[7], is given to charity any subsequent increase in the value of the property accrues to the charity[8].

A gift of income to a charity in perpetuity does not necessarily carry with it a right to the capital; it depends on the terms of the gift[9].

1 *Re Monk, Giffen v Wedd* [1927] 2 Ch 197, CA; *A-G v Earl of Winchelsea* (1791) 3 Bro CC 373; *A-G v Minshull* (1798) 4 Ves 11; *Arnold v A-G* (1698) Show Parl Cas 22, HL. For cases on

surplus capital see PARA 172. Surplus income may in these circumstances be applied by a scheme under the Charities Act 2011 s 62(1)(b) (see PARA 214). As to cy-près applications by scheme see PARA 209 et seq.

2 *A-G v Skinners' Co* (1827) 2 Russ 407 at 443 per Lord Eldon LC; *A-G v Skinners' Co* (1833) 5 Sim 596. See also *Re Jordeyn's Charity* (1833) 1 My & K 416; *A-G v Trinity College, Cambridge* (1856) 24 Beav 383; and the cases cited in PARA 133 note 4.

3 *Re Stanford, Cambridge University v A-G* [1924] 1 Ch 73.

4 *A-G v Bristol Corpn* (1820) 2 Jac & W 294 at 315, 318 per Lord Eldon LC; *Beverley Corpn v A-G* (1857) 6 HL Cas 310 at 333 per Lord Wensleydale; *A-G v Dean and Canons of Windsor* (1860) 8 HL Cas 369 at 393–394 per Lord Campbell LC, and at 406 per Lord Cranworth.

5 *Beverley Corpn v A-G* (1857) 6 HL Cas 310 at 324 per Lord Chelmsford LC; *Merchant Taylors' Co v A-G* (1871) 6 Ch App 512; *A-G v Master, Wardens etc of the Wax Chandlers' Co* (1873) LR 6 HL 1.

6 *A-G v Skinners' Co* (1827) 2 Russ 407 at 411 per Lord Eldon LC (gift of rents and profits equivalent to gift of the lands themselves); *Southmolton Corpn v A-G* (1854) 5 HL Cas 1 at 31–32 per Lord St Leonards; *Beverley Corpn v A-G* (1857) 6 HL Cas 310.

7 *Kennington Hastings Case* (1612) Duke 71; *Hynshaw v Morpeth Corpn* (1629) Duke 69; *Eltham Inhabitants v Warreyn* (1634) Duke 67; *Sutton Colefield Case* (1635) Duke 68.

8 *Ex p Jortin* (1802) 7 Ves 340; *A-G v Bristol Corpn* (1820) 2 Jac & W 294; *A-G v Wilson* (1834) 3 My & K 362.

9 *Re Levy, Barclays Bank Ltd v Board of Guardians and Trustees for the Relief of the Jewish Poor* [1960] Ch 346, [1960] 1 All ER 42, CA.

132. Gift of surplus: surplus and later accretion. If a testator gives particular sums, not exhausting the entire income, for specified charitable purposes, and gives the remainder of the income for other charitable purposes, a question of construction arises whether any increase in the income is divisible pro rata among the specified objects and the objects entitled to the residue[1], or whether the whole residue of the augmented income passes to the objects entitled to the residue[2].

If there is an express gift of surplus income of the donee who is charged with the payments, this may be interpreted in two ways: either (1) as a gift of the residue, whatever it may amount to, in which case the residuary donee is entitled to any increased income[3]; or (2) as a gift of an aliquot proportion of the whole, in which case the donee shares rateably with the other donees in any increase[4]. The question into which of these two classes a gift falls is a matter of construction, to be solved in each particular case by considering the instrument of foundation as a whole[5]. The court is not entitled to take a broad view of the parties' rights based on the donor's supposed intention[6]. Such words as 'overplus', 'surplus', or 'residue' do not necessarily indicate that the gift is residuary[7]. An express gift of surplus will be disregarded where, if effect were given to it, the donor's intention would be defeated[8].

1 *A-G v Caius College* (1837) 2 Keen 150. See *A-G v Coopers' Co* (1812) 19 Ves 187; *A-G v Solly* (1835) 5 LJCh 5.

2 *Re Avenon's Charity, A-G v Pelly* (1912) 56 Sol Jo 241, reported on further consideration [1913] 2 Ch 261 (where the surplus, having exceeded what was necessary for the residuary purpose, was all applied cy-près to the residuary purpose); *Re Lepton's Charity, Ambler v Thomas* [1972] Ch 276, [1971] 1 All ER 799.

3 *Southmolton Corpn v A-G* (1854) 5 HL Cas 1; *Beverley Corpn v A-G* (1857) 6 HL Cas 310 at 326 per Lord Chelmsford LC; *Re Rowe, Merchant Taylors' Co v London Corpn* (1914) 30 TLR 528.

4 *A-G v Drapers' Co, Kendrick's Charity* (1841) 4 Beav 67; *A-G v Jesus College, Oxford* (1861) 29 Beav 163; and see the cases cited in note 3.

5 *A-G v Dean and Canons of Windsor* (1860) 8 HL Cas 369 at 405–406 per Lord Cranworth.

6 *Re Lepton's Charity, Ambler v Thomas* [1972] Ch 276, [1971] 1 All ER 799, where the disparity resulting from the increase of income was alleviated by the application of the Charities Act 1960 s 13(1)(a)(ii), (e)(iii) (repealed) (see now the Charities Act 2011 s 62; and PARA 214).

7 *Beverley Corpn v A-G* (1857) 6 HL Cas 310; *Southmolton Corpn v A-G* (1854) 5 HL Cas 1 at 25–26 per Lord Cranworth LC. As to the expression 'or thereabouts' see also *A-G v Trinity College, Cambridge* (1856) 24 Beav 383 at 392–393 per Romilly MR. No difficulty arises where the instrument expressly directs the surplus income (*Re Jordeyn's Charity* (1833) 1 My & K 416; *Southmolton Corpn v A-G* at 5 per Lord Cranworth LC), or any subsequent increase (*Charitable Donations and Bequests Comrs v Baroness De Clifford* (1841) 1 Dr & War 245), to be applied for charitable or other purposes or for the benefit of the donees (*A-G v Gascoigne* (1833) 2 My & K 647, where the executors took beneficially; *A-G v Skinners' Co* (1827) 2 Russ 407; *A-G v Drapers' Co, Kendrick's Charity* (1841) 4 Beav 67).

8 *Re Ashton's Charity* (1859) 27 Beav 115 (gift of surplus to six 'almswomen', who would have ceased to be almswomen if they received the whole of the largely increased surplus income, treated as a gift to charity generally).

133. No gift of surplus: surplus and later accretion. If, at the time of the gift, the specific payments do not exhaust the whole income, and there is no express gift of the surplus, but there is a clear intention, whether express or implied, to attach a charitable trust to the whole property, the surplus will be devoted to charity, however deficient may be the appropriation of the whole income, for the general charitable intention will prevail[1].

In such a case the donees will not be entitled to the surplus or increase unless they are themselves a charity[2], or there are other circumstances from which a contrary intention can be inferred[3]. If, however, there is no general intention to devote the whole to charity, the surplus income belongs to the parties charged with making the payments, and not to the charities[4], notwithstanding that such specific payments, by lapse of time or change of circumstances, have become insufficient to satisfy the purposes for which they were originally made[5]; for the absence of any disposition of the surplus is prima facie an indication of an intention to benefit the donee[6].

This rule has been frequently applied in the case of gifts to corporations such as colleges[7], city companies[8], or local authorities[9], or a dean and canons[10], subject to or charged with specific charitable payments which do not exhaust the income; but the principle is not confined to gifts to such bodies[11].

1 *Arnold v A-G* (1698) Show Parl Cas 22, HL; *A-G v Sparks* (1753) Amb 201; *A-G v Painter Stainers' Co* (1788) 2 Cox Eq Cas 51; *A-G v Haberdashers' Co* (1792) 4 Bro CC 103; *A-G v Bristol Corpn* (1820) 2 Jac & W 294 at 318 per Lord Eldon LC; *A-G v Skinners' Co* (1827) 2 Russ 407 at 442 per Lord Eldon LC; *Mystery of Mercers v A-G* (1828) 2 Bli NS 165, HL; *A-G v Drapers' Co* (1840) 2 Beav 508; *A-G v Coopers' Co* (1840) 3 Beav 29; *A-G v Grocers' Co* (1843) 6 Beav 526 at 546 per Lord Langdale MR; *Southmolton Corpn v A-G* (1854) 5 HL Cas 1 at 32 per Lord St Leonards; *Beverley Corpn v A-G* (1857) 6 HL Cas 310 at 318 per Lord Chelmsford LC; *A-G v Dean and Canons of Windsor* (1860) 8 HL Cas 369; *Shepherd v Bristol Corpn* (1818) 3 Madd 319 at 352 per Leach V-C; affd on this point but revsd on other grounds sub nom *A-G v Bristol Corpn* at 318 per Lord Eldon LC.

2 *A-G v Trinity College, Cambridge* (1856) 24 Beav 383 at 399 per Romilly MR; and see *A-G v Bristol Corpn* (1820) 2 Jac & W 294.

3 *A-G v Drapers' Co* (1840) 2 Beav 508.

4 *A-G v Bristol Corpn* (1820) 2 Jac & W 294 at 307 per Lord Eldon LC; *A-G v Skinners' Co* (1827) 2 Russ 407 at 443 per Lord Eldon LC; *A-G v Cordwainers' Co* (1833) 3 My & K 534; *A-G v Brazen Nose College* (1834) 2 Cl & Fin 295, HL; *A-G v Fishmongers' Co, Kneseworth's Will* (1841) 5 My & Cr 11; *A-G v Grocers' Co* (1843) 6 Beav 526; *Jack v Burnett* (1846) 12 Cl & Fin 812, HL; *Southmolton Corpn v A-G* (1854) 5 HL Cas 1 at 34 per Lord St Leonards; *A-G v Trinity College, Cambridge* (1856) 24 Beav 383; *A-G v Dean and Canons of Windsor* (1860) 8 HL Cas 369; *Merchant Taylors' Co v A-G* (1871) 6 Ch App 512 at 519 per James LJ.

5 *A-G v Gascoigne* (1833) 2 My & K 647; *Charitable Donations and Bequests Comrs v Baroness De Clifford* (1841) 1 Dr & War 245.

6 *A-G v Trinity College, Cambridge* (1856) 24 Beav 383 at 392 per Romilly MR. See also *A-G v Master, Wardens etc of the Wax Chandlers' Co* (1873) LR 6 HL 1 at 19 et seq.

7 *A-G v Catherine Hall, Cambridge* (1820) Jac 381; *A-G v Brazen Nose College* (1834) 2 Cl & Fin 295, HL; *Jack v Burnett* (1846) 12 Cl & Fin 812, HL; *A-G v Trinity College, Cambridge* (1856) 24 Beav 383; *A-G v Sidney Sussex College* (1869) 4 Ch App 722; *Re Lavelle, Concannon v A-G* [1914] 1 IR 194.
8 *A-G v Cordwainers' Co* (1833) 3 My & K 534; *A-G v Fishmongers' Co, Kneseworth's Will* (1841) 5 My & Cr 11; *A-G v Grocers' Co* (1843) 6 Beav 526; *A-G v Master, Wardens etc of the Wax Chandlers' Co* (1873) LR 6 HL 1 at 9 per Lord Chelmsford, and at 19 per Lord Cairns.
9 *A-G v Bristol Corpn* (1820) 2 Jac & W 294; *Southmolton Corpn v A-G* (1854) 5 HL Cas 1 at 34 per Lord St Leonards; *Beverley Corpn v A-G* (1857) 6 HL Cas 310.
10 *A-G v Dean and Canons of Windsor* (1860) 8 HL Cas 369.
11 *Merchant Taylors' Co v A-G* (1871) 6 Ch App 512 at 519 per James LJ. See *A-G v Smythies* (1833) 2 Russ & M 717 at 741 per Lord Brougham LC (master of an almshouse); and cf *A-G v Master of Brentwood School* (1833) 1 My & K 376; *A-G v Governors of Atherstone Free School* (1834) 3 My & K 544.

134. No gift of surplus: no surplus but later accretion. If there is no express gift of surplus income, but the specific payments exhaust the entire income at the time of the gift, any subsequent increase[1] in the income is applicable to similar purposes and prima facie in similar proportions[2]. The deficiency in case of a decrease in the income is apportionable in the same way[3]. However, the court may, within certain limits, vary the proportions[4].

This rule is equally applicable whether the donor thought at the time that he was disposing of the entire income[5], or there are words that might have been interpreted as limiting the extent of the benevolent purpose had they stood alone, but such words are coupled with other words which show that the benevolent purpose operates to the extent of the whole fund[6].

1 *Southmolton Corpn v A-G* (1854) 5 HL Cas 1 at 32 per Lord St Leonards.
2 *Thetford School Case* (1609) 8 Co Rep 130b.
3 *Thetford School Case* (1609) 8 Co Rep 130b; *Sutton Colefield Case* (1635) Duke 68; *A-G v Townsend* (1670) Duke 34; *Arnold v A-G* (1698) Show Parl Cas 22, HL; *A-G v Coventry Corpn* (1702) Colles 280, HL; *A-G v Johnson* (1753) Amb 190; *A-G Haberdashers' Co* (1792) 4 Bro CC 103; *A-G v Coopers' Co* (1812) 19 Ves 187; *A-G v Bristol Corpn* (1820) 2 Jac & W 294 at 315, 317–318, 322 per Lord Eldon LC; *Mystery of Mercers v A-G* (1828) 2 Bli NS 165, HL; *A-G v Wilson* (1834) 3 My & K 362; *A-G v Brazen Nose College* (1834) 2 Cl & Fin 295 at 328, HL, per Lord Brougham LC; *A-G v Barham* (1835) 4 LJCh 128; *A-G v Coopers' Co* (1840) 3 Beav 29; *A-G v Christ's Hospital* (1841) 4 Beav 73; *A-G v Gilbert* (1847) 10 Beav 517; *Southmolton Corpn v A-G* (1854) 5 HL Cas 1; *Beverley Corpn v A-G* (1857) 6 HL Cas 310 at 320 per Lord Chelmsford LC; *A-G v Master, Wardens etc of the Wax Chandlers' Co* (1873) LR 6 HL 1.
4 *A-G v Dean and Canons of Windsor* (1860) 8 HL Cas 369 at 452 per Lord Kingsdown; *A-G v Marchant* (1866) LR 3 Eq 424 at 430 per Kindersley V-C.
5 *A-G v Marchant* (1866) LR 3 Eq 424 at 430 per Kindersley V-C; and see *A-G v Bristol Corpn* (1820) 2 Jac & W 294 at 332 per Lord Eldon.
6 *A-G v Painter Stainers' Co* (1788) 2 Cox Eq Cas 51 at 55.

135. Whether donees take surplus and increase. The donees are entitled to the surplus where it has been charged with the expense of repairs[1], or where they have bound themselves by penalties or covenanted to pay fixed sums to charity whether the income of the property is sufficient or not[2].

Donees will not take beneficially where there has been long usage to the contrary, or where by the instrument of foundation they are given power to regulate the charity[3].

Speaking generally, the increase will belong to the donee, first, if the gift be to the donee subject to certain payments to others; secondly, if the gift be upon condition of making certain payments subject to a forfeiture upon non-performance of the condition; or, thirdly, if the donee might be a loser by the insufficiency of the fund[4].

In the case of a gift to a particular body for the benefit of the body with a provision that certain members or officials are to receive specific annual sums, the body is entitled to the bulk of the property with the full increase, and the particular members or officers are entitled only to the sums specifically given them[5]. Thus, where property is given not for purposes of individual benefit, but for the performance of duties, any increase of income exceeding reasonable remuneration for the performance of those duties will be applied to other charitable purposes[6].

A gift of the income of property to maintain poor scholars, each having so much a day, is a gift to them of the whole, and entitles them to the surplus[7].

1 *A-G v Skinners' Co* (1827) 2 Russ 407; *A-G v Coopers' Co* (1840) 3 Beav 29.
2 *Jack v Burnett* (1846) 12 Cl & Fin 812 at 828, HL, per Lord Cottenham LC. See also *A-G v Bristol Corpn* (1820) 2 Jac & W 294 at 303 per Lord Eldon LC; and cf *A-G v Merchant Venturers' Co, Bristol* (1848) 17 LJCh 137.
3 *A-G v Mercers' Co, Re St Paul's School* (1870) 18 WR 448.
4 *Jack v Burnett* (1846) 12 Cl & Fin 812 at 828, HL, per Lord Cottenham.
5 *Southmolton Corpn v A-G* (1854) 5 HL Cas 1 at 32–33 per Lord St Leonards; and see *A-G v Bristol Corpn* (1820) 2 Jac & W 294 at 317 per Lord Eldon LC. In the case of a gift to a corporation consisting of a master and almsmen, with a direction that the almsmen should receive fixed stipends, the almsmen were not allowed to share rateably with the master in the increased income: *A-G v Smythies* (1833) 2 Russ & M 717 at 747–748 per Lord Brougham LC; *Re Ashton's Charity* (1859) 27 Beav 115, where the increased income was applied to charity generally.
6 *Thetford School Case* (1609) 8 Co Rep 130b; *A-G v Bristol Corpn* (1820) 2 Jac & W 294; *A-G v Smythies* (1833) 2 Russ & M 717 at 747 per Lord Brougham LC. Distinguish the case of a gift to a college for its maintenance with a provision that each scholar should have a certain sum, in which case the scholars are not entitled to share in any increased income: *A-G v Smythies* at 747 per Lord Brougham LC.
7 *A-G v Master of Brentwood School* (1833) 1 My & K 376 at 394 per Leach MR; and see *A-G v Governors of Atherstone Free School* (1834) 3 My & K 544 at 555 per Lord Brougham LC.

(5) CONDITIONAL AND LIMITED INTERESTS

136. Conditions precedent. A charitable gift may be made subject to conditions precedent, for example, that the gift shall take effect only if the testator's estate is sufficient for the intended object[1] or amounts to a certain sum[2]. Gifts to hospitals were frequently made subject to conditions precedent relating to nationalisation[3].

A legacy to a fund raised for the purpose of effecting a particular charitable object may be construed as a gift on condition that the particular object proves to be practicable[4]; and a gift may be made for a particular charitable purpose on condition that other property is given for the same object[5].

Such gifts of realty fail if the condition is not[6], or cannot be[7], fulfilled or offends against the rule against perpetuities[8], unless the fulfilment of the condition is not essential to the gift[9]. In the case of gifts of personalty subject to conditions precedent which are illegal, a distinction is drawn between illegality involving that which is inherently wrong[10] and that which is wrong only because it is prohibited by law[11]; in the latter case the invalidity of the condition does not avoid the gift and the donee takes free from the condition[12].

Cases of gifts subject to conditions precedent are to be distinguished from cases in which there is an immediate outright gift to charity but the particular application directed is postponed and may depend on the occurrence of events contingent and uncertain[13].

1 *Cherry v Mott* (1836) 1 My & Cr 123.

2 *Thomas v Howell* (1874) LR 18 Eq 198; and see *Re Swain, Monckton v Hands* [1905] 1 Ch 669, CA.
3 *Re Frere, Kidd v Farnham Group Hospital Management Committee* [1951] Ch 27, [1950] 2 All ER 513; *Re Buzzacott, Munday v King's College Hospital* [1953] Ch 28, [1952] 2 All ER 1011; *Connell's Trustees v Milngavie District Nursing Association* 1953 SC 230, Ct of Sess; *Re Lowry's Will Trusts, Barclays Bank Ltd v United Newcastle-upon-Tyne Hospitals Board of Governors of* [1967] Ch 638, [1966] 3 All ER 955.
4 *Re London University Medical Sciences Institute Fund, Fowler v A-G* [1909] 2 Ch 1, CA.
5 *McCormick v Queen's University of Belfast* [1958] NI 1.
6 *Cherry v Mott* (1836) 1 My & Cr 123.
7 *Re Emson, Grain v Grain* (1905) 74 LJCh 565.
8 See PARA 142.
9 *Re Selinger's Will Trusts, Midland Bank Executor and Trustee Co Ltd v Levy* [1959] 1 All ER 407, [1959] 1 WLR 217 (a suitable charity to be found within one year of testator's death; if none found legacy to be revoked; held only to be intended to prevent delay in administration, so that where administration was delayed for other reasons, the gift took effect, even though a recipient was not found until two years after the death).
10 Ie *malum in se*.
11 Ie *malum prohibitum*. See *Re Piper, Dodd v Piper* [1946] 2 All ER 503 at 505, where Romer J observed: 'the difference between *malum prohibitum* and *malum in se* has never been very precisely defined or considered'.
12 *Re Elliott, Lloyds Bank Ltd v Burton-on-Trent Hospital Management Committee* [1952] Ch 217, [1952] 1 All ER 145 (condition relating to upkeep of a grave, involving only *malum prohibitum*); *Re Hepplewhite's Will Trusts* (1977) Times, 21 January (gift subject to several conditions, some valid, some invalid: gift good subject only to valid conditions). As to distinctions between various types of impossibility see *Re Moore, Trafford v Maconochie* (1888) 39 ChD 116, CA.
13 *Chamberlayne v Brockett* (1872) 8 Ch App 206; *Re Swain, Monckton v Hands* [1905] 1 Ch 669, CA.

137. Conditions subsequent. Charitable gifts may be made subject to conditions subsequent which come into effect if, after the gift has taken effect, some act is omitted to be done[1] or some act is done[2]. However, a mere intention to make the enjoyment of the gift conditional is inoperative unless it is actually carried out[3]. There have been many examples of conditions subsequent relating to the nationalisation of charitable institutions[4].

Conditions subsequent include: (1) common law conditions[5], a breach of which involves forfeiture to the grantor or his representatives[6]; (2) conditions enforceable in equity[7]; and (3) conditions followed by executory limitations or gifts over[8].

If the condition infringes the rule against perpetuities[9], or is illegal[10], or involves a breach of trust[11], or is repugnant to the gift[12], or is void for uncertainty[13], the charity takes the gift discharged from the condition and, if there is a gift over, that also fails[14]. Where trustees are given a discretionary power to exclude certain institutions from benefit under a charitable gift, the validity of that power is governed by the same principles as a gift over[15]; thus if the power involves perpetuity and is not restricted to charity it is bad and the initial gift to charity is unfettered[16].

Charitable trusts have sometimes been declared subject to express powers of revocation, but there has apparently been no decision on the validity of such a power except as regards the rule against perpetuities[17].

However, if the condition itself is not bad but the gift over cannot take effect because it is to a person who is not an object of the power which is exercised by the gift, the prior estate is defeated on the fulfilment of the condition and the property is held upon a resulting trust or falls into residue[18].

1 *A-G v Christ's Hospital* (1790) 3 Bro CC 165 (children from particular parish to be maintained); *Re Tyler, Tyler v Tyler* [1891] 3 Ch 252, CA (keeping a tomb in repair); *Re*

Conington's Will (1860) 6 Jur NS 992 (incumbent of particular church to be maintained and special services to be held); *Re Robinson, Wright v Tugwell* [1892] 1 Ch 95 (approved [1897] 1 Ch 85, CA) (black gown to be worn in pulpit; but see *Re Robinson, Wright v Tugwell* [1923] 2 Ch 332, where this condition was dispensed with); *Re Parker's Charity* (1863) 32 Beav 654 (anniversary sermon).

2 *Milbank v Lambert* (1860) 28 Beav 206 (vicar not to collect tithes); *Re Barrett's Trusts, Dyson v Sheffield Corpn* (1910) 26 TLR 330.

3 *Yates v University College, London* (1875) LR 7 HL 438 (where the testator omitted to make rules compliance with which was required by the gift); *University College of North Wales v Taylor* [1908] P 140, CA (where the condition intended to be attached to the gift was contained in a memorandum excluded from probate as not being sufficiently referred to in the will for identification).

4 Eg *Royal College of Surgeons of England v National Provincial Bank Ltd* [1952] AC 631, [1952] 1 All ER 984, HL; *Re Bawden's Settlement, Besant v London Hospital Board of Governors* [1953] 2 All ER 1235, [1954] 1 WLR 33n; *Mollison's Trustees v Aberdeen General Hospitals Board of Management* 1953 SC 264, Ct of Sess.

5 *Re Hollis' Hospital Trustees and Hague's Contract* [1899] 2 Ch 540; *Re Da Costa, Clarke v Church of England Collegiate School of St Peter* [1912] 1 Ch 337.

6 Shep Touch 117, 119, 120; Co Litt 201a.

7 See the cases cited in PARA 75 (where words of condition created a trust). See also the cases where charities accepting property subject to conditions were held bound to perform them, eg *A-G v Caius College* (1837) 2 Keen 150 at 163 per Lord Langdale MR; and PARA 138.

8 See *Christ's Hospital v Grainger* (1849) 1 Mac & G 460; *Re Conington's Will* (1860) 6 Jur NS 992; *Re Tyler, Tyler v Tyler* [1891] 3 Ch 252, CA; *Royal College of Surgeons of England v National Provincial Bank Ltd* [1952] AC 631, [1952] 1 All ER 984, HL.

9 *Re Talbot, Jubb v Sheard* [1933] Ch 895; *Re Bawden's Settlement, Besant v London Hospital Board of Governors* [1953] 2 All ER 1235, [1954] 1 WLR 33n.

10 *Re Amos, Carrier v Price* [1891] 3 Ch 159 at 167 per North J (contrary to the Mortmain Acts).

11 *Re Tyler, Tyler v Tyler* [1891] 3 Ch 252, CA.

12 *Lydiatt v Foach* (1700) 2 Vern 410; *Watson v Hinsworth Hospital* (1707) 2 Vern 596 (condition that rent of property given to charity should never be raised); *A-G v Catherine Hall, Cambridge* (1820) Jac 381 at 395 per Lord Eldon LC; *A-G v Greenhill* (1863) 33 Beav 193 (conditions restricting alienation); *Re Restell, Royal Hospital for Incurables v Restell* (1901) 17 TLR 395; *Hope v Gloucester Corpn* (1855) 7 De GM & G 647. See also the cases cited in PARA 163 note 11.

13 See *Re Hayes' Will Trusts, Dobie v National Hospital Board of Governors* [1953] 2 All ER 1242, [1954] 1 WLR 22 (gift to 29 institutions with power to trustees to exclude any if impracticable or inequitable that they should share). The requirement of certainty is stricter for a condition subsequent than for a condition precedent: *Blathwayt v Baron Cawley* [1976] AC 397, [1975] 3 All ER 625, HL; *Re Barlow's Will Trusts* [1979] 1 All ER 296, [1979] 1 WLR 278.

14 See *Yates v University College, London* (1875) LR 7 HL 438, followed in *Re Barnett, Waring v Painter-Stainers' Co* (1908) 24 TLR 788; *Re Barker, Sherrington v Dean and Chapter of St Paul's Cathedral* (1909) 25 TLR 753; *Re Dalziel, Midland Bank Executor and Trustee Co Ltd v St Bartholomew's Hospital* [1943] Ch 277, [1943] 2 All ER 656. Conversely, gifts to individuals subject to conditions which infringed the mortmain laws were taken by the legatee free from the condition: *Doe d Burdett v Wrighte* (1819) 2 B & Ald 710; *Poor v Mial* (1821) 6 Madd 32; *Henchman v A-G* (1834) 3 My & K 485. As to the repeal of the law of mortmain see PARA 83.

15 *Re Hayes' Will Trusts, Dobie v National Hospital Board of Governors* [1953] 2 All ER 1242, [1954] 1 WLR 22; *George Drexler Ofrex Foundation Trustees v IRC* [1966] Ch 675, [1965] 3 All ER 529.

16 *Re Bawden's Settlement, Besant v London Hospital Board of Governors* [1953] 2 All ER 1235, [1954] 1 WLR 33n. The condition upon which a gift over effected under such a power would take effect would be the trustees' decision to exercise the power; since they cannot effect it if the power is bad, the condition can never occur.

17 In *Re Sir Robert Peel's School at Tamworth, ex p Charity Comrs* (1868) 3 Ch App 543, the validity of the power was assumed but the decision turned on a quite different point; in *Gibson v South American Stores (Gath and Chaves) Ltd* [1950] Ch 177, [1949] 2 All ER 985, CA, the validity of the power was not in issue. In *Re Watson's Settlement Trusts, Dawson v Reid* [1959] 2 All ER 676, [1959] 1 WLR 732 the power of revocation was not limited to the perpetuity period and permitted new non-charitable trusts to be declared; accordingly it was held to be invalid. Under the mortmain laws such a power, if attached to a gift of realty, would have

rendered the gift void. Apparently the perpetuity period in the case of a revocable settlement by deed runs from the moment when it is no longer revocable: Morris and Leach *Rule against Perpetuities* (2nd Edn, 1962) p 57. As to the rule against perpetuities see PARA 142. As to the repeal of the law of mortmain see PARAS 83–84.

18 *Robinson v Wood* (1858) 27 LJCh 726. This also applied in relation to gifts over which could not take effect because of the laws of mortmain (now repealed): see *Doe d Blomfield v Eyre* (1848) 5 CB 713.

138. Acceptance of conditional gift. Where a gift subject to a condition is accepted, the condition must be fulfilled, whether or not the subject matter of the gift is adequate for the purpose[1]. The subsequent abandonment of the benefit of a gift to which a condition is attached does not relieve the party who accepted it from the burden of fulfilling the condition[2]. Trustees are not bound to accept property subject to a special trust or condition[3].

As a rule, donees who accept conditional gifts are entitled to have the property vested in them[4]. Where the condition is a continuing one and there are no special trustees to hold the fund, it may be retained in court and the income paid out so long as the conditions are performed[5].

1 *A-G v Christ's Hospital* (1790) 3 Bro CC 165; *A-G v Andrew* (1798) 3 Ves 633 at 646 per Lord Eldon LC; *A-G v Caius College* (1837) 2 Keen 150; *Jack v Burnett* (1846) 12 Cl & Fin 812 at 828, HL, per Lord Cottenham LC; *A-G v Master, Wardens etc of the Wax Chandlers' Co* (1873) LR 6 HL 1 at 19 per Lord Cairns; *Re Richardson, Shuldham v Royal National Lifeboat Institution* (1887) 56 LJCh 784; and see *A-G v Merchant Venturers' Co, Bristol* (1848) 17 LJCh 137. In some cases where inadequate funds were given the gift has been construed as conditional upon sufficient funds becoming available: see eg *Re London University Medical Sciences Institute Fund, Fowler v A-G* [1909] 2 Ch 1, CA; and PARA 175.

2 *A-G v Christ's Hospital* (1830) 1 Russ & M 626.

3 *A-G v Andrew* (1798) 3 Ves 633 (affd sub nom *Andrew v Master and Wardens of Merchant Taylors' Co* (1800) 7 Ves 223, HL); *A-G v Caius College* (1837) 2 Keen 150.

4 *A-G v Christ's Hospital* (1790) 3 Bro CC 165; *Re Richardson, Shuldham v Royal National Lifeboat Institution* (1887) 56 LJCh 784. See also *Re Lopes, Bence-Jones v Zoological Society of London* [1931] 2 Ch 130; *Re Restell, Royal Hospital for Incurables v Restell* (1901) 17 TLR 395.

5 *Re Robinson, Wright v Tugwell* [1892] 1 Ch 95; approved [1897] 1 Ch 85, CA.

139. Condition with gift over strictly enforced. The rule of equity under which relief is given against a forfeiture on breach of condition[1] does not apply where there is a gift over on breach[2]. Thus, where property is given upon certain charitable trusts, with a proviso that in certain events it is to be transferred and held upon other charitable trusts, the property will pass upon the happening of the particular event[3]. If the event be the trustees' neglect of the terms of their trust, the gift over will take effect notwithstanding the general rule that a charitable purpose is not defeated by the trustee's failure or neglect or the failure of trust machinery[4], and that the position of one beneficiary under a trust ought not to be prejudiced as against other beneficiaries by any neglect on the trustee's part[5]. However, even in such a case, the court has power to make a scheme which will defeat the gift over and preserve the substance of the prior gift[6].

On the other hand, where the gift over is to be considered as a collateral remedy to secure the testator's charitable intention expressed in the prior gift, the trustee's neglect to observe a condition[7] or perform a trust in strict accordance with the directions in the will[8] may not occasion a forfeiture. The dividing line between the two classes of case is very difficult to find.

The onus of proof on the question whether a forfeiture has taken place lies on the party alleging it[9]. The court construes forfeiture clauses strictly[10].

If the right of a beneficiary entitled under a gift over or forfeiture becomes barred by limitation[11], the trustees or the beneficiaries under the prior gift hold the property free from the gift over, but on the trusts of the original gift[12]. They cannot themselves declare new trusts of the property[13].

1 *Cage v Russel* (1681) 2 Vent 352; *Hollinrake v Lister* (1826) 1 Russ 500 at 508 per Lord Gifford MR. See WILLS AND INTESTACY vol 102 (2010) PARA 149.

2 *Simpson v Vickers* (1807) 14 Ves 341.

3 *Re Malling Abbey Trusts, Beaumont v Dale* (1915) 31 TLR 397, CA; *Royal College of Surgeons of England v National Provincial Bank Ltd* [1952] AC 631, [1952] 1 All ER 984, HL.

4 *Brown v Higgs* (1803) 8 Ves 561 at 574 per Lord Eldon LC.

5 *Re Jones, Williams v Rowlands* [1948] Ch 67, [1947] 2 All ER 716.

6 *Re Hanbey's Will Trusts, Cutlers' Co v President and Governors of Christ's Hospital, London* [1956] Ch 264, [1955] 3 All ER 874, where no scheme was ordered, however, owing to the prolonged though honest breaches of trust and the difficulty of settling any useful scheme which would apply the trust properly cy-près with the objects the testator had in mind in his will.

7 *A-G v Christ's Hospital* (1830) 1 Russ & M 626. See also *Re Selinger's Will Trusts, Midland Bank Executor and Trustee Co Ltd v Levy* [1959] 1 All ER 407, [1959] 1 WLR 217 (condition as to time, held not to be of the essence of the gift and non-fulfilment of the condition not to cause a forfeiture).

8 *Re Hanbey's Will Trusts, Cutlers' Co v President and Governors of Christ's Hospital, London* [1956] Ch 264, [1955] 3 All ER 874; *Re Parish of Upton Warren* (1833) 1 My & K 410; *Re Richardson's Will* (1887) 58 LT 45.

9 *Re Hartshill Endowment* (1861) 30 Beav 130; and see *Re Conington's Will* (1860) 6 Jur NS 992. In both these cases the question was whether a condition requiring the performance of the Church of England service had been satisfied.

10 *Re Jones, Williams v Rowlands* [1948] Ch 67, [1947] 2 All ER 716 (where a condition relating to the time within which certain buildings were to be erected was held not to have come into operation either because the trustees could not be said to have failed to complete what they had not been allowed to begin or because the condition was subject to an overriding condition which had not been fulfilled). See also *Re Beard's Trusts, Butlin v Harris* [1904] 1 Ch 270 (where a gift over on a school's becoming subject to a school board was held not to take effect on the school's coming under the control of a county council, and no forfeiture took place); *Re Gregory, How v Charrington* (1935) 52 TLR 130 (where a gift over if an orphanage was taken over for or subsidised by the state or by any public or local authority was held not to take effect although the school belonging to the orphanage was recognised as a public elementary school and received grants from a local authority in aid of teachers' salaries); and *Re Blunt's Trusts, Wigan v Clinch* [1904] 2 Ch 767 (where a forfeiture was held to have taken place, inasmuch as there was a bequest of an annuity for the support of national schools with a gift over if funds necessary for carrying on the schools should be raised under any statutory powers).

11 See *Re Trustees of Orchard Street Schools* [1878] WN 211. See also the Limitation Act 1980; and generally LIMITATION PERIODS. As to the time limit for actions in respect of trust property see s 21; and LIMITATION PERIODS vol 68 (2008) PARA 1140 et seq.

12 *Re Ingleton Charity, Croft v A-G* [1956] Ch 585, [1956] 2 All ER 881 (a case of automatic reverter under the School Sites Act 1841: see PARA 70). See also *Re Trustees of Orchard Street Schools* [1878] WN 211.

13 *Re Ingleton Charity, Croft v A-G* [1956] Ch 585, [1956] 2 All ER 881.

140. Gifts of limited interests. There may be a gift to charity of less than an absolute interest in property and, subject to the application of the rule against perpetuities[1], the interest given may be an interest determinable upon the happening of some event which is contingent and may never occur[2]. Thus, income may be given for the support of a school so long as it should continue to be carried on according to the trusts of its original deed[3], or to an incumbent so long as sittings in the parish church were free of pew-rents[4], or there may be a gift to a society during such time as it maintains two graves[5]. Similarly, there may be a gift to charity limited not to take effect until the occurrence of a particular event[6].

In such cases, the interest which is not disposed of belongs to the donor, and devolves as part of his estate[7].

If property is held for more than one charitable purpose, for example where contributions towards have it have come from more than one source, it should be viewed as a whole[8].

1 There is doubt as to whether the rule applies to these interests at common law; it does apply in relation to dispositions taking effect after 15 July 1964: see PARA 144.
2 *Lyons Corpn v Advocate-General of Bengal* (1876) 1 App Cas 91, PC; *Re Randell, Randell v Dixon* (1888) 38 ChD 213; *Re Hartshill Endowment* (1861) 30 Beav 130; *A-G v Molland* (1832) 1 You 562; *A-G v Pyle* (1738) 1 Atk 435. As to gifts of limited duration see PARA 174.
3 *Re Blunt's Trusts, Wigan v Clinch* [1904] 2 Ch 767.
4 *Re Randell, Randell v Dixon* (1888) 38 ChD 213. See also *Re Cooper's Conveyance Trusts, Crewdson v Bagot* [1956] 3 All ER 28, [1956] 1 WLR 1096.
5 *Re Chardon, Johnston v Davies* [1928] Ch 464 (a fuller account of the will, and the court's order, in this case are set out in Tudor on Charities (5th Edn, 1929) p 701); *Re Chambers' Will Trusts, Official Trustees of Charitable Funds v British Union for the Abolition of Vivisection* [1950] Ch 267 (distinguished in *Re Wightwick's Will Trusts, Official Trustees of Charitable Funds v Fielding-Ould* [1950] Ch 260, [1950] 1 All ER 689, where the limited gift was a gift on trust for non-charitable purposes and involved a perpetuity, and so failed).
6 *A-G v Earl of Craven* (1856) 21 Beav 392 at 400 per Romilly MR; *Yates v University College, London* (1875) LR 7 HL 438; *Re Roberts, Repington v Roberts-Gawen* (1881) 19 ChD 520, CA.
7 *A-G v Pyle* (1738) 1 Atk 435; *Re Randell, Randell v Dixon* (1888) 38 ChD 213; *Re Blunt's Trusts, Wigan v Clinch* [1904] 2 Ch 767.
8 See *Dore v Leicestershire County Council* [2010] EWHC 1387 (Ch), [2010] All ER (D) 78 (Jun); and PARA 76 note 11.

(6) RULES AGAINST REMOTENESS

141. Rule against perpetual trusts. Charitable trusts are exempt from the rule that a gift is void if its terms preclude the alienation of the capital of the fund for a period which may last longer than the perpetuity period[1], whereas a perpetual trust for a non-charitable purpose is void[2] and not less so because the trustee is a charitable society[3].

A charitable trust may, therefore, be made to last for any period, whether perpetual, indefinite or limited[4], and for the same reason a gift of income to a charity in perpetuity does not necessarily carry with it the capital, as it would in the case of a gift to an individual[5].

1 This is the rule referred to as the rule against perpetuities in eg *Chamberlayne v Brockett* (1872) 8 Ch App 206 at 211 per Lord Selborne LC; *A-G v Webster* (1875) LR 20 Eq 483 at 491 per Jessel MR; *Income Tax Special Purposes Comrs v Pemsel* [1891] AC 531 at 581–582, HL, per Lord Macnaghten. It has also been referred to as the rule against inalienability: *Re Chardon, Johnston v Davies* [1928] Ch 464; *Re Wightwick's Will Trusts, Official Trustees of Charitable Funds v Fielding-Ould* [1950] Ch 260, [1950] 1 All ER 689. It is to be distinguished from the rule against remoteness of vesting, commonly known as the rule against perpetuities (see PARA 142). It has not been affected by the Perpetuities and Accumulations Act 1964: see s 15(4). See also the Perpetuities and Accumulations Act 2009 s 2(1)–(3); and PARA 143. As to the perpetuity period see PARA 142 note 4; and **PERPETUITIES AND ACCUMULATIONS** vol 80 (2013) PARA 48. As to the general application of the rule against perpetuities see the Perpetuities and Accumulations Act 2009 s 1.
2 *Thomson v Shakespear* (1860) 1 De GF & J 399; *Carne v Long* (1860) 2 De GF & J 75; *Re Rickard, Rickard v Robson* (1862) 31 Beav 244; *Re Dutton, ex p Peake* (1878) 4 Ex D 54; *Re St Stephen, Coleman Street, Re St Mary the Virgin, Aldermanbury* (1888) 39 ChD 492 at 503 per Jay J; *Re Norwich Town Close Estate Charity* (1888) 40 ChD 298 at 307, CA, per Cotton LJ; *Income Tax Special Purposes Comrs v Pemsel* [1891] AC 531 at 581, HL, per Lord Macnaghten; and see PARA 62, especially the cases there cited on gifts to unincorporated associations. See also *A-G of the Cayman Islands v Wahr-Hansen* [2001] 1 AC 75, [2000] 3 All ER 642, PC.

3 *Re Tyler, Tyler v Tyler* [1891] 3 Ch 252 at 258, CA, per Lindley LJ; and see *Re Freeman, Shilton v Freeman* [1908] 1 Ch 720, CA. As to trusts for repairing tombs see PARA 61.

4 *Re Randell, Randell v Dixon* (1888) 38 ChD 213; *Re Bowen, Lloyd Phillips v Davis* [1893] 2 Ch 491.

5 *Re Levy, Barclays Bank Ltd v Board of Guardians and Trustees for the Relief of the Jewish Poor* [1960] Ch 346, [1960] 1 All ER 42, CA; *Re Beesty's Will Trusts, Farrar v Royal Alfred Merchant Seamen's Society* [1966] Ch 223, [1964] 3 All ER 82.

142. Rule against perpetuities. Charitable trusts are subject to the rule against perpetuities, which prevents the creation of interests in property which are to vest at too remote a time, in the same way as any other trust[1] except in one respect, that being the case of a gift over from one charity to another[2].

In the case of a disposition under an instrument taking effect before 16 July 1964[3], a charitable trust which need not take effect within the perpetuity period is void[4]. Thus, trusts for the benefit of charity limited to take effect after an indefinite failure of issue[5], or upon alienation[6], or upon the election of the next lieutenant-colonel of a regiment[7], or upon some other condition precedent which might not be fulfilled within the perpetuity period[8], failed[9].

In its application to dispositions under instruments taking effect after 15 July 1964[10], the rule was modified by the Perpetuities and Accumulations Act 1964[11]. The changes most relevant to charitable gifts are that, instead of a period of lives in being plus 21 years, the perpetuity period in relation to a disposition may be a period specified as such of up to 80 years[12], and that a disposition which is void at common law is to be treated as valid until it becomes established that the vesting of the disposition must occur, if at all, after the end of the perpetuity period[13]. Changes were also made in relation to possibilities of reverter and of resulting trusts[14]. Many of the decisions under the old law would have been different under the statute.

As from 6 April 2010[15] the rule against perpetuities is further modified by the Perpetuities and Accumulations Act 2009 and the following provisions apply to instruments taking effect[16] (or wills being executed) on or after that date[17]. The perpetuity period is 125 years from the date on which the trust is created irrespective of whether a perpetuity period is specified[18].

1 *Chamberlayne v Brockett* (1872) 8 Ch App 206. Thus an option to purchase land given to a charity is subject to the ordinary law as to perpetuities: *Worthing Corpn v Heather* [1906] 2 Ch 532. But distinguish this from the rule set out in PARA 141, from which gifts to charitable trusts are exempt.

2 This exception is discussed in PARA 143.

3 Ie the commencement date of the Perpetuities and Accumulations Act 1964. This Act affects instruments taking effect after 15 July 1964: see s 15(5); and PERPETUITIES AND ACCUMULATIONS vol 80 (2013) PARA 10. Dispositions made after that date but pursuant to an instrument taking effect before 16 July 1964 are not affected: see s 8(2); and PERPETUITIES AND ACCUMULATIONS vol 80 (2013) PARA 42. Where a disposition is made otherwise than by instrument, the Act applies as if it had been contained in an instrument taking effect when the disposition was made: s 15(6).

The Perpetuities and Accumulations Act 1964 does not apply in relation to an instrument taking effect on or after 6 April 2010, but this does not prevent it from applying in relation to an instrument so taking effect if it is a will executed before that day or it is an instrument made in the exercise of a special power of appointment and the instrument creating the power took effect before that day: s 15(5A) (added by the Perpetuities and Accumulations Act 2009 s 16).

4 Ie unless the prior limitation is in favour of charity: see PARA 143. The perpetuity period is defined as lives in being, plus 21 years: see PERPETUITIES AND ACCUMULATIONS vol 80 (2013) PARA 10 et seq. See, however, the text and notes 15–18.

5 *Charitable Donations and Bequests Comrs v Baroness De Clifford* (1841) 1 Dr & War 245; *Re Johnson's Trusts* (1866) LR 2 Eq 716 at 720 per Page Wood V-C; and see *Re Roberts, Repington v Roberts-Gawen* (1881) 19 ChD 520, CA.

6 *Pewterers' Co v Governors of Christ's Hospital* (1683) 1 Vern 161.
7 *Re Lord Stratheden and Campbell, Alt v Lord Stratheden and Campbell* [1894] 3 Ch 265.
8 *Chamberlayne v Brockett* (1872) 8 Ch App 206; *Re White's Trusts* (1886) 33 ChD 449; *Re Wightwick's Will Trusts, Official Trustees of Charitable Funds v Fielding-Ould* [1950] Ch 260, [1950] 1 All ER 689; *Re Mander, Westminster Bank Ltd v Mander* [1950] Ch 547, [1950] 2 All ER 191; *Re Cooper's Conveyance Trusts, Crewdson v Bagot* [1956] 3 All ER 28, [1956] 1 WLR 1096; *Re Watson's Settlement Trusts, Dawson v Reid* [1959] 2 All ER 676, [1959] 1 WLR 732; *George Drexler Ofrex Foundation Trustees v IRC* [1966] Ch 675, [1965] 3 All ER 529.
9 These cases are to be distinguished from those in which there is an immediate effective gift to charity, but the particular application directed may not be possible until some time in the future: see eg *Chamberlayne v Brockett* (1872) 8 Ch App 206; *Re Swain, Monckton v Hands* [1905] 1 Ch 669, CA.
10 See note 3.
11 As to the Perpetuities and Accumulations Act 1964 generally see **PERPETUITIES AND ACCUMULATIONS**.
12 See the Perpetuities and Accumulations Act 1964 s 1; and **PERPETUITIES AND ACCUMULATIONS** vol 80 (2013) PARA 20.
13 See the Perpetuities and Accumulations Act 1964 s 3(1); and **PERPETUITIES AND ACCUMULATIONS** vol 80 (2013) PARA 10. How the perpetuity period is to be determined under this wait-and-see provision is governed by s 3(4), (5): see **PERPETUITIES AND ACCUMULATIONS** vol 80 (2013) PARA 12. Under s 3(5), the only permissible lives in being in relation to a charitable gift are likely to be those of the settlor (see s 3(5)(a)) and of any person entitled to a prior interest (see s 3(5)(d)).
14 See the Perpetuities and Accumulations Act 1964 s 12; PARA 144; and **PERPETUITIES AND ACCUMULATIONS** vol 80 (2013) PARA 48.
15 Ie the date on which the relevant provisions of the Perpetuities and Accumulations Act 2009 came into force: see the Perpetuities and Accumulations Act 2009 (Commencement) Order 2010, SI 2010/37.
16 The provisions also apply in relation to an instrument made in the exercise of a special power of appointment only if the instrument creating the power takes effect on or after that date: Perpetuities and Accumulations Act 2009 s 15(1)(b).
17 See the Perpetuities and Accumulations Act 2009 s 15(1)(a).
18 See the Perpetuities and Accumulations Act 2009 s 5.

143. Validity of gifts over. An interest which is contingent upon the occurrence of an event which will cause a gift over to take effect is subject to the rule against perpetuities, so that, under the common law, if the event need not necessarily, or, under the Perpetuities and Accumulations Act 1964 or 2009[1], if it does not, happen within the perpetuity period, the gift over is void.

As from 6 April 2010[2] the Perpetuities and Accumulations Act 2009 provides the following relevant statutory exceptions to the rule against perpetuities in relation to charities[3]. The rule does not apply to an estate or interest created so as to vest in a charity on the occurrence of an event if immediately before the occurrence an estate or interest in the property concerned is vested in another charity[4]. Nor does the rule apply to a right exercisable by a charity on the occurrence of an event if immediately before the occurrence an estate or interest in the property concerned is vested in another charity[5].

It would appear[6] that there need be no connection between the event in question and the charitable purposes of the gift[7]. Additionally, the exception would not appear to extend to a non-charitable gift followed by a gift over in favour of charity, nor to a charitable gift with a gift over to private individuals[8] or in favour of purposes which need not necessarily be charitable[9].

Express gifts over to residue have generally been held not to be subject to the rule against perpetuities on the ground that they do no more than state the result which the law would imply in the absence of an express provision[10].

1 As to the Perpetuities and Accumulations Act 1964 and the Perpetuities and Accumulations Act 2009 generally see PARA 142; and **PERPETUITIES AND ACCUMULATIONS**.

2 Ie the date on which the relevant provisions of the Perpetuities and Accumulations Act 2009 came into force: see the Perpetuities and Accumulations Act 2009 (Commencement) Order 2010, SI 2010/37.

3 See the Perpetuities and Accumulations Act 2009 s 2(1). The exceptions created by s 2(2), (3) essentially give statutory force to a line of judicial authority begun in *Christ's Hospital v Grainger* (1849) 1 Mac & G 460; *Re Tyler, Tyler v Tyler* [1891] 3 Ch 252, CA; *Royal College of Surgeons of England v National Provincial Bank Ltd* [1952] AC 631, [1952] 1 All ER 984, HL.

4 Perpetuities and Accumulations Act 2009 s 2(2).

5 Perpetuities and Accumulations Act 2009 s 2(3).

6 The authorities mentioned in the text and notes 7–10 have not been explicitly expressed to apply under the Perpetuities and Accumulations Act 2009, but it is submitted that they are compatible with the provisions of s 2 and should be read so as to amplify that section.

7 In *Re Tyler, Tyler v Tyler* [1891] 3 Ch 252, CA, the event was failure to keep a family vault in good repair. Although a trust to apply part of the money to the repair of the vault would have been void, the court held that a condition creating a perpetual inducement to do a lawful act was not void. In *Re Martin, Barclays Bank Ltd v Board of Governors of St Bartholomew's Hospital* [1952] WN 339, there was a gift of income upon a similar condition, and if ever the gravestones were not in good repair, a gift over to another charity; the condition attached to the gift of income was void but the condition which gave rise to the gift over was held nevertheless to be valid. See also *Re Lopes, Bence-Jones v Zoological Society of London* [1931] 2 Ch 130 and, for cases in which the condition did relate to the purposes of the gift, see *Re Parish of Upton Warren* (1833) 1 My & K 410; *Christ's Hospital v Grainger* (1849) 1 Mac & G 460; *Re Hanbey's Will Trusts, Cutlers' Co v President and Governors of Christ's Hospital, London* [1956] Ch 264, [1955] 3 All ER 874. In *Royal College of Surgeons of England v National Provincial Bank Ltd* [1952] AC 631, [1952] 1 All ER 984, HL, the condition related to nationalisation of the hospital to which the prior gift was made.

8 *Re Bowen, Lloyd Phillips v Davis* [1893] 2 Ch 491 at 494 per Stirling J; *Re Barnett, Waring v Painter Stainers' Co* (1908) 24 TLR 788; *Re Peel's Release* [1921] 2 Ch 218; *Re Talbot, Jubb v Sheard* [1933] Ch 895; *Gibson v South American Stores (Gath and Chaves) Ltd* [1950] Ch 177, [1949] 2 All ER 985, CA; *Re Cooper's Conveyance Trusts, Crewdson v Bagot* [1956] 3 All ER 28, [1956] 1 WLR 1096; and see *Chamberlayne v Brockett* (1872) 8 Ch App 206 at 211 per Lord Selborne LC; *Worthing Corpn v Heather* [1906] 2 Ch 532; *Re Davies, Lloyd v Cardigan County Council* [1915] 1 Ch 543; *Re Wightwick's Will Trusts, Official Trustees of Charitable Funds v Fielding-Ould* [1950] Ch 260, [1950] 1 All ER 689.

9 *Re Friends' Free School, Clibborn v O'Brien* [1909] 2 Ch 675; *Re Da Costa, Clarke v Church of England Collegiate School of St Peter* [1912] 1 Ch 337; and see *Re Beard's Trusts, Butlin v Harris* [1904] 1 Ch 270 (where on construction it was held that there had been no forfeiture under the gift over). It has been held that where a gift to a charity is conditional on the performance of acts (not relating to the subject matter of the gift) extending to a possibly remote period, the charity is not bound by the condition, and is entitled to a clean conveyance, free from the condition, unless there is a gift over to another charity: *Re Da Costa, Clarke v Church of England Collegiate School of St Peter*; *Re Tyler, Tyler v Tyler* [1891] 3 Ch 252, CA. As to the ordinary rule that gifts subject to a condition must be accepted with whatever disadvantage that condition may carry see *A-G v Christ's Hospital* (1790) 3 Bro CC 165; *A-G v Christ's Hospital* (1830) 1 Russ & M 626 at 628 per Leach MR. For an example of an alternative ultimate trust for charity see *Re Davey, Prisk v Mitchell* [1915] 1 Ch 837, CA.

10 *Re Randell, Randell v Dixon* (1888) 38 ChD 213. But see *Re Engels, National Provincial Bank Ltd v Mayer* [1943] 1 All ER 506. This accordingly depends on the application of the rule against perpetuities to possibilities of reverter and of resulting trusts: see PARA 142.

144. Limited gifts and undisposed interests. The rule against perpetuities[1] is concerned only with the commencement of interests, not with their duration[2]. Thus, where a sum of money was given to a school so long as it should continue endowed, it was held to be given only for that period, so that when the school ceased to be endowed the gift fell into residue[3]. Where property would fall into residue by operation of law, the interest disposed of having come to an end, an express direction that it should do so will not bring the case within the rule against perpetuities[4]. However, the interest which may arise by forfeiture on breach of a common law condition is subject to the rule[5].

In relation to dispositions taking effect after 15 July 1964[6], possibilities of reverter on the determinable estate in fee simple and possibilities of a resulting trust on the determination of any other determinable interest in property are subject to the rule against perpetuities as if they were rights of re-entry or similar rights arising on breach of a condition subsequent[7]. If the provision in that form would be void at common law, it is necessary to wait until it is established that the condition cannot be satisfied within the relevant perpetuity period[8]. If the provision falls to be treated as void for remoteness, the determinable interest becomes an absolute interest[9]. These statutory provisions apply not only to gifts expressed to last so long as some state of affairs persists[10], but also to limited gifts for charitable purposes which subsequently fail[11].

1 See PARA 142.
2 *Re Chardon, Johnston v Davies* [1928] Ch 464.
3 *A-G v Pyle* (1738) 1 Atk 435, where, however, the rule against perpetuities was not mentioned.
4 *Re Randell, Randell v Dixon* (1888) 38 ChD 213; *Re Blunt's Trusts, Wigan v Clinch* [1904] 2 Ch 767; and see *Lyons Corpn v Advocate-General of Bengal* (1876) 1 App Cas 91, PC; *Walsh v Secretary of State for India* (1863) 10 HL Cas 367. But see, contra, *Re Engels, National Provincial Bank Ltd v Mayer* [1943] 1 All ER 506.
5 *Re Trustees of Hollis' Hospital and Hague's Contract* [1899] 2 Ch 540; *Re Da Costa, Clarke v Church of England Collegiate School of St Peter* [1912] 1 Ch 337. See also *Hopper v Liverpool Corpn* (1943) 88 Sol Jo 213.
6 See PARA 142 note 3.
7 See the Perpetuities and Accumulations Act 1964 s 12(1); and **PERPETUITIES AND ACCUMULATIONS** vol 80 (2013) PARA 48.
8 See the Perpetuities and Accumulations Act 1964 s 3; PARA 142; and **PERPETUITIES AND ACCUMULATIONS** vol 80 (2013) PARAS 10, 12.
9 See the Perpetuities and Accumulations Act 1964 s 12(1).
10 Eg *Re Chardon, Johnston v Davies* [1928] Ch 464.
11 Eg *Re Cooper's Conveyance Trusts, Crewdson v Bagot* [1956] 3 All ER 28, [1956] 1 WLR 1096. This type of gift is almost invariably accompanied by some express direction or condition relating to failure of the purpose. As to gifts of limited duration see PARA 174.

145. Accumulations. As from 6 April 2010[1] the following provisions apply to an instrument to the extent that it provides for property to be held on trust for charitable purposes[2]. If the instrument imposes or confers on the trustees a duty or power to accumulate income[3] and, apart from these provisions the duty or power would last beyond the end of the statutory period[4], it ceases to have effect at the end of that period unless the instrument provides for the duty or power to cease to have effect on the death of the settlor, or on the death of one of the settlors, determined by name or by the order of their deaths[5]. If a duty or power ceases to have effect under these provisions the income to which the duty or power would have applied apart from these provisions must go to the person who would have been entitled to it if there had been no duty or power to accumulate or be applied for the purposes for which it would have had to be applied if there had been no such duty or power[6].

There was judicial authority[7] to the effect that earlier statutory restrictions on accumulations[8] applied to charitable funds directed to be accumulated beyond the time permitted by the statute[9]; and that if an accumulation is directed of a fund the capital and income of which are given absolutely to a charity, the charity is entitled to stop the accumulation and demand immediate payment of the fund[10].

1 Ie the date on which the relevant provisions of the Perpetuities and Accumulations Act 2009 came into force: see the Perpetuities and Accumulations Act 2009 (Commencement) Order 2010, SI 2010/37.

2 Perpetuities and Accumulations Act 2009 s 14(1). However this does not apply where the provision is made by a court or the Charity Commission for England and Wales: s 14(2).
3 These provisions apply whether or not the duty or power to accumulate extends to income produced by the investment of income previously accumulated: Perpetuities and Accumulations Act 2009 s 14(7). See generally **PERPETUITIES AND ACCUMULATIONS** vol 80 (2013) PARA 129 et seq.
4 The statutory period is a period of 21 years starting with the first day when the income must or may be accumulated (as the case may be): Perpetuities and Accumulations Act 2009 s 14(4).
5 Perpetuities and Accumulations Act 2009 s 14(3), (5).
6 Perpetuities and Accumulations Act 2009 s 14(6).
7 It seems probable that this would continue to be the case, though there has been no judicial decision expressly adopting the authorities in light of the provisions of the Perpetuities and Accumulations Act 2009 (see text and notes 1–6).
8 Ie the Law of Property Act 1925 s 164; the Perpetuities and Accumulations Act 1964 s 13.
9 *Martin v Maugham* (1844) 14 Sim 230; *Re Bradwell, Goode v Board of Trustees for Methodist Church Purposes* [1952] Ch 575, [1952] 2 All ER 286.
10 *Wharton v Masterman* [1895] AC 186, HL; *Re Travis, Frost v Greatorex* [1900] 2 Ch 541, CA. The trust amounts to a directory provision of a kind which the trustees ought prima facie to bear in mind and carry out: *Re Knapp, Spreckley v A-G* [1929] 1 Ch 341 at 344 per Maugham J.

(7) FINALITY

146. Alteration of trusts. When a charitable trust has once been declared and established, the trusts cannot be varied or added to by the founder, whether an individual[1] or a body of subscribers[2], or by the trustees[3], unless a valid power of appointment or revocation[4] was reserved at the time the trusts were declared. In general, only the court or the Charity Commission[5] or the Tribunal[6] in the exercise of the jurisdiction to make cy-près schemes[7] can alter charitable trusts once they are declared[8]. Exceptionally, in respect of certain small unincorporated charities, the charity trustees themselves have power, with the concurrence of the Charity Commission, to modify the trusts of the charity[9].

1 *Re Hartshill Endowment* (1861) 30 Beav 130.
2 *A-G v Kell* (1840) 2 Beav 575; *A-G v Bovill* (1840) 1 Ph 762.
3 See *Cross v Lloyd-Greame* (1909) 102 LT 163; *Baldry v Feintuck* [1972] 2 All ER 81, [1972] 1 WLR 552. Note, however, the principle of *A-G v Mathieson, Re Wilkinson and Fell's Contract* [1907] 2 Ch 383, CA, that where funds are subscribed by the public for some charitable purpose and later the trustees declare the trusts on which the funds are held, that declaration of trust is binding unless and until rectified at the suit of the Attorney General: see PARA 106. See also *Li Quan v Bray* [2014] EWHC 3340 (Fam), [2015] Fam Law 29, [2014] All ER (D) 339 (Oct), where a charitable trust could not be regarded as a post-nuptial settlement and could not be invaded by court order. As to post-nuptial settlements see **SETTLEMENTS** vol 91 (2012) PARA 504. As to the Attorney General see PARAS 589, 596, 605 et seq; and **CONSTITUTIONAL AND ADMINISTRATIVE LAW** vol 20 (2014) PARA 273 et seq.
4 As to the validity of powers of revocation see PARAS 96, 137 note 17. See also *Re Holloway's Trusts, Greenwell v Ryan* (1909) 26 TLR 62 (express power to vary the trusts); *Re Harrison, Harrison v A-G* (1915) 85 LJCh 77; *Re Jewish Orphanage Endowment Trusts, Sebag-Montefiore v Rothschild Executor and Trustee Co* [1960] 1 All ER 764, [1960] 1 WLR 344 (power to modify contained in a scheme). Even if there is power to alter the trusts, it may be expressly or impliedly limited: *Baldry v Feintuck* [1972] 2 All ER 81, [1972] 1 WLR 552 (attempt to alter purposes of students' union of a university to permit application of funds partly for charitable purposes not connected with education and partly for non-charitable purposes).
5 See the Charities Act 2011 ss 69, 70; and PARA 189. As to the Charity Commission see PARAS 543–578.
6 See the Charities Act 2011 s 315; and PARA 579. As to the Tribunal see PARA 579 et seq.
7 Alternatively, jurisdiction may be exercised under the Variation of Trusts Act 1958. Such cases can rarely arise, but in *Re Roberts' Settlement Trusts* [1961] TR 401, the court approved, on behalf of the settlor's future wives, an arrangement excluding the settlor and any wife of his

from benefit under a charitable trust. As to the Variation of Trusts Act 1958 generally see **TRUSTS AND POWERS** vol 98 (2013) PARA 647 et seq.

8 See PARA 212. As to cy-près schemes generally see PARA 209 et seq. The duty of the court is to construe the trust instrument and carry out its charitable directions. If the conditions for cy-près application are not satisfied the court has no jurisdiction (apart from the Variation of Trusts Act 1958 (see note 7); and the Charities Act 2011 ss 267–280 (see the text and note 9) to alter the terms of the trust, no matter how beneficial such alterations may be: *Re Weir Hospital* [1910] 2 Ch 124, CA; *Oldham Borough Council v A-G* [1993] Ch 210, [1993] 2 All ER 432, CA.

9 See the Charities Act 2011 ss 267–280; and PARAS 218–221.

3. FAILURE OF STATED CHARITABLE OBJECTS

(1) FAILURE OF STATED OBJECTS

(i) Failure of Objects generally

147. In general. In many cases it is impossible to carry out the charitable objects specified by the donor. This impossibility may extend to only some of the provisions of the gift, or to the whole gift: for example, there may be gifts to a charitable institution which has either ceased to exist[1] or changed its nature[2], or gifts which are insufficient[3] or more than sufficient[4] to carry out the stated purposes.

In considering these cases the first problem is to ascertain what the objects of the gift are. Owing to the leniency with which the court treats charitable gifts, it does not follow that, because the actual objects stated in the instrument cannot strictly be carried out, the stated object has failed. For example, gifts to an unincorporated charitable association are normally construed as gifts for the purposes of that institution, and therefore the object of the gift does not necessarily fail if the institution itself ceases to exist: the object of the gift is the purpose, not the institution[5].

Having ascertained the object of the gift, the next problem is to decide whether it has failed[6]. Again the court adopts a lenient view in deciding whether there has been a failure. Thus, a gift to a perpetually endowed charitable institution does not fail if the institution is dissolved, provided that some of its funds remain held on charitable trusts, which may not necessarily be the same trusts[7].

Even when the object of the gift has been ascertained and it has been shown that the object has failed, the gift itself will not necessarily fail. In certain cases the gift can be applied cy-près for charitable purposes similar to those which have failed[8]. However, in cases of initial failure, a cy-près application can normally only be made where the donor has shown a general charitable intention[9], since the justification for a cy-près application is that the court is giving effect to the presumed intention of the donor.

1 See PARA 151. As to the position where a charity has been entered on the register of charity mergers see PARAS 322–323.
2 See PARAS 152–156.
3 See PARA 163.
4 See PARA 165.
5 See PARA 149.
6 See PARA 151. For a view of the law which equates this question with the question of the existence of a general charitable intention see PARA 168.
7 See PARA 151 et seq.
8 As to cy-près applications see generally PARA 209 et seq.
9 As to general charitable intention see PARA 168.

(ii) Gifts to Charitable Institutions

A. IN GENERAL

148. Lapse of charitable gifts by will. Problems on gifts to non-existent institutions have always arisen in relation to gifts by will. In such cases, under the general law, the gift will lapse if the legatee 'predeceases' the testator[1].

Therefore two problems have to be considered: (1) was the object of the testator's bounty the institution itself, or rather the purposes it carried on; and (2) has either the institution itself ceased to exist[2] or, if it is a gift for a purpose, has the purpose ceased to be practicable[3] before the date of death?

1 As to the doctrine of lapse see WILLS AND INTESTACY vol 102 (2010) PARA 160 et seq.
2 As to the position where a charity has been entered on the register of charity mergers see PARAS 322–323.
3 As to whether purposes are still practicable see PARA 150.

B. WHERE THE INSTITUTION CEASED TO EXIST BEFORE THE GIFT TOOK EFFECT

(A) Gifts for Purposes or for the Institution

149. Construction. In principle, gifts to named charitable institutions must be construed in exactly the same way as gifts to non-charitable institutions or to individuals. However, because charitable institutions are established for some charitable purpose or purposes, it may be possible for the court to decide that on its true construction a particular gift is for the work carried on by the institution, and not simply for the institution itself. However, this will not save the gift if the purpose itself has ceased to exist[1].

The authorities establish that there is a distinction between incorporated and unincorporated bodies in this context[2]. A gift to an incorporated body is not a gift upon trust for its purposes unless there is something in the context which shows that it is[3]; but a gift to an unincorporated association established for charitable purposes is a gift upon trust for those purposes unless there is something in the gift to show that the continued existence of the association is of the essence of the gift[4].

Where the gift is not to the institution itself by its proper name but to, say, a 'home' or 'hospital', the conclusion that a purpose gift is intended is almost, if not absolutely, inescapable[5]. It has been held that the gift is a gift for purposes in some cases where the named institution has once existed but has ceased to exist before the gift takes effect[6], or where the named institution was in fact merely an informal establishment carried on by the testatrix herself for charitable work[7]. In other cases, however, even where the gift was clearly intended for the benefit of the work carried on by the named institution, it has been held not to be a gift for purposes but solely a gift to the institution[8]. Again, a gift may be construed as one not to augment generally the endowment of a charity running, inter alia, a specified home, but exclusively for the benefit of patients at that home[9]. Where the existence of the institution itself is essential to the gift, the gift cannot be treated as a gift simply for its purposes[10].

Where the institution has ceased to exist, but has been replaced by another carrying on the identical work and functions, the gift may be construed as a misdescription of the latter institution[11].

1 *Re Spence, Ogden v Shackleton* [1979] Ch 483, sub nom *Re Spence's Will Trusts, Ogden v Shackleton* [1978] 3 All ER 92; *Re Prescott* [1990] 2 IR 342.
2 *Re Finger's Will Trusts, Turner v Ministry of Health* [1972] Ch 286, [1971] 3 All ER 1050; *Re Vernon's Will Trusts, Lloyds Bank Ltd v Group 20 Hospital Management Committee (Coventry)* [1972] Ch 300n, [1971] 3 All ER 1061n.
3 *Re Finger's Will Trusts, Turner v Ministry of Health* [1972] Ch 286, [1971] 3 All ER 1050; *Bowman v Secular Society Ltd* [1917] AC 406 at 442, HL, per Lord Finlay LC; *Re Cain, National Trustees Executors and Agency Co of Australasia Ltd v Jeffrey* [1950] VLR 382 at 389 per Dean J. For a case in which there was such an indication in the context see *Re Meyers, London Life Association v St George's Hospital* [1951] Ch 534, [1951] 1 All ER 538.

4 *Re Vernon's Will Trusts, Lloyds Bank Ltd v Group 20 Hospital Management Committee (Coventry)* [1972] Ch 300n, [1971] 3 All ER 1061n; *Re Finger's Will Trusts, Turner v Ministry of Health* [1972] Ch 286, [1971] 3 All ER 1050. Some unincorporated associations are enabled by statute to hold property for purposes without the interposition of any trust, charitable or otherwise: see *Re Edis's Trusts, Campbell-Smith v Davies* [1972] 2 All ER 769, [1972] 1 WLR 1135.

5 *Re Finger's Will Trusts, Turner v Ministry of Health* [1972] Ch 286 at 296, [1971] 3 All ER 1050 at 1058 per Goff J.

6 *Re Souter, Brook v Talbot* (1907) Times, 24 January; *Re Withall, Withall v Cobb* [1932] 2 Ch 236; *Re Watt, Hicks v Hill* [1932] 2 Ch 243n, CA; *Re Morgan's Will Trusts, Lewarne v Minister of Health* [1950] Ch 637, [1950] 1 All ER 1097; *Re Glass, Public Trustee v South-West Middlesex Hospital Management Committee* [1950] Ch 643n, [1950] 2 All ER 953n; *Re Meyers, London Life Association v St George's Hospital* [1951] Ch 534, [1951] 1 All ER 538; *Re Hutchinson's Will Trusts, Gibbons v Nottingham Area No 1 Hospital Management Committee* [1953] Ch 387, [1953] 1 All ER 996; *Re Griffiths, Powell v Griffiths* (23 July 1958, unreported), cited in [1963] 1 All ER 680n; *Re Morrison, Wakefield v Falmouth* (1967) 111 Sol Jo 758; *Re Finger's Will Trusts, Turner v Ministry of Health* [1972] Ch 286, [1971] 3 All ER 1050; *Phillips v Royal Society for the Protection of Birds* [2012] EWHC 618 (Ch), [2012] All ER (D) (Apr).

7 *Re Webster, Pearson v Webster* [1912] 1 Ch 106.

8 *Re Goldney, Goldney v Queen Elizabeth Hospital for Children* (1946) 115 LJCh 337; *Re Pochin, Midland Bank Executor and Trustee Co v Godkin* [1948] Ch 182n. Cf *Phillips v Royal Society for the Protection of Birds* [2012] EWHC 618 (Ch), [2012] All ER (D) (Apr).

9 *Re Spence, Ogden v Shackleton* [1979] Ch 483, sub nom *Re Spence's Will Trusts, Ogden v Shackleton* [1978] 3 All ER 92, distinguishing *Re Lucas, Sheard v Mellor* [1948] Ch 424, [1948] 2 All ER 22, CA.

10 See *Clark v Taylor* (1853) 1 Drew 642 (as explained in *Re Slevin, Slevin v Hepburn* [1891] 2 Ch 236, CA); *Langford v Gowland* (1862) 3 Giff 617; *Fisk v A-G* (1867) LR 4 Eq 521; *Makeown v Ardagh* (1876) IR 10 Eq 445; *Re Ovey, Broadbent v Barrow* (1885) 29 ChD 560; *Re Rymer, Rymer v Stanfield* [1895] 1 Ch 19, CA; *Re Brightwen, Shelly v Shelly* (1907) Times, 7 February; *Re Harwood, Coleman v Innes* [1936] Ch 285; *Re Stemson's Will Trusts, Carpenter v Treasury Solicitor* [1970] Ch 16, [1969] 2 All ER 517; and see the cases cited in note 8.

11 *Re Magrath, Histed v Queen's University of Belfast* [1913] 2 Ch 331; following *Coldwell v Holme* (1854) 2 Sm & G 31.

150. Purposes still practicable. If the gift is construed as a gift for purposes, it appears that the gift will not lapse, notwithstanding the disappearance of the institution itself, if the purposes of the former institution are still being carried on by some other body; the gift is applicable by way of a scheme for those purposes[1]. It has been held that if the institution has ceased to exist and there is no longer any need to carry on its purposes, the purposes have ceased to exist and the object has failed[2].

1 See the cases cited in PARA 149 note 6.

2 *Re Slatter's Will Trusts, Turner v Turner* [1964] Ch 512, [1964] 2 All ER 469; *Re Spence, Ogden v Shackleton* [1979] Ch 483, sub nom *Re Spence's Will Trusts, Ogden v Shackleton* [1978] 3 All ER 92. The case of an institution becoming redundant because its purposes have been fulfilled is one of failure through impracticability: see PARA 163 text to note 1.

(B) Tests for Non-existence of the Institution

151. In general. If the gift is construed as being to the institution itself, the question is whether that institution, as a charity, has ceased to exist[1]. It may be still in existence even though its operations are diminished[2], and even if its continued existence is precarious[3], but not if it is merely nugatory[4]. The closure of one branch of a large charity does not affect the validity of a gift to the charity[5] unless the gift can only be construed as a gift to that particular branch[6]. The non-existence of an institution which was intended to be a trustee for charitable purposes which can still be effected does not affect the validity of the gift[7].

Apart from factual problems, there is a general rule that a perpetual charity endowed with funds can never cease to exist so long as it has endowments, however much its constitution may have been altered[8]. Particular instances are dealt with in the following paragraphs.

1 As to the position where a charity has been entered on the register of charity mergers see PARAS 322–323.

2 *Re Buck, Bruty v Mackey* [1896] 2 Ch 727; *Re Waring, Hayward v A-G* [1907] 1 Ch 166.

3 *Re Roberts, Stenton v Hardy* [1963] 1 All ER 674, [1963] 1 WLR 406.

4 *Re Meyers, London Life Association v St George's Hospital* [1951] Ch 534, [1951] 1 All ER 538; *Connell's Trustees v Milngavie District Nursing Association* 1953 SC 230, Ct of Sess.

5 *Re Bradfield, Bradfield v Hancock* (1892) 36 Sol Jo 646.

6 *Re Slatter's Will Trusts, Turner v Turner* [1964] Ch 512, [1964] 2 All ER 469.

7 *Marsh v A-G* (1860) 2 John & H 61. As to failure of or disclaimer by trustees see PARA 164.

8 *Re Faraker, Faraker v Durell* [1912] 2 Ch 488, CA; *Re Lucas, Sheard v Mellor* [1948] Ch 424, [1948] 2 All ER 22, CA; *Re Vernon's Will Trusts, Lloyds Bank Ltd v Group 20 Hospital Management Committee (Coventry)* [1972] Ch 300n, [1971] 3 All ER 1061n.

152. Alteration by scheme. If, before the gift takes effect, a named charity has been consolidated with others under a scheme made by the Charity Commission[1], it is nevertheless still in existence and the gift is payable to the trustees of the consolidated funds[2]. Similarly if, under a scheme for the administration of the assets of the named charity, a new charity is established elsewhere for similar purposes, the gift may be payable to the trustees of the new charity[3].

1 As to the Charity Commission see PARAS 543–578. As to schemes see PARA 179 et seq.

2 *Re Faraker, Faraker v Durell* [1912] 2 Ch 488, CA.

3 *Re Lucas, Sheard v Mellor* [1948] Ch 424, [1948] 2 All ER 22, CA; and see *Re Vernon's Will Trusts, Lloyds Bank Ltd v Group 20 Hospital Management Committee (Coventry)* [1972] Ch 300n, [1971] 3 All ER 1061n.

153. Alteration of objects by the institution itself. If a named charity, having power to do so, alters its name and objects so as to include further charitable objects before a gift to it takes effect, the gift is nevertheless payable to it under its new name[1].

1 *Re Bagshaw, Westminster Bank Ltd v Taylor* [1954] 1 All ER 227, [1954] 1 WLR 238.

154. Dissolution of institution under power in its constitution. Where a company established for charitable purposes is wound up[1], or an unincorporated association is dissolved under powers contained in its own constitution[2], it is no longer in existence, notwithstanding that its assets cannot be devoted to any purposes that are not charitable[3]. But where the assets and functions of a company had been transferred under the National Health Service Act 1946, a gift in augmentation of those assets was held to be payable to the body to which the assets had been transferred, despite the subsequent dissolution of the company before the death of the testator[4].

Where some part of the operation of a charity is taken over by another prior to the former ceasing to exist, this does not of itself amount to an amalgamation[5].

1 *Re Stemson's Will Trusts, Carpenter v Treasury Solicitor* [1970] Ch 16, [1969] 2 All ER 517; followed in *Re Finger's Will Trusts, Turner v Ministry of Health* [1972] Ch 286, [1971] 3 All ER 1050.

2 *Re Finger's Will Trusts, Turner v Ministry of Health* [1972] Ch 286, [1971] 3 All ER 1050.

3 Such a company will not be restored to the register of companies under the Companies Act 2006 s 1029 (see COMPANIES vol 15 (2009) PARA 1535) in order to take a legacy on a death after the dissolution: *Re Servers of the Blind League* [1960] 2 All ER 298, [1960] 1 WLR 564 (decided under earlier legislation).

4 *Re Vernon's Will Trusts, Lloyds Bank Ltd v Group 20 Hospital Management Committee (Coventry)* [1972] Ch 300n, [1971] 3 All ER 1061n.

5 *Phillips v Royal Society for the Protection of Birds* [2012] EWHC 618 (Ch), [2012] All ER (D) (Apr), where the transfer of some birds from one registered charity to another prior to the former ceasing to exist, did not include assets.

155. Alteration of objects and amalgamation under statute. If an amalgamation or change of constitution is effected by or under a statute, the consequences may depend upon the construction of the statute[1]. The fact that hospitals became nationalised under the National Health Service Act 1946 did not mean that they ceased to be charitable[2], nor did they cease to be eligible as objects of a gift divisible among hospitals which, in the trustees' opinion, were most in need of it[3]. Gifts to or for the benefit of voluntary hospitals which, before the testator's death, had become vested in the Minister of Health or in a specially constituted board of governors, were upheld as being for the purposes of the charitable work of the voluntary hospitals still being carried on by the nationalised hospitals[4].

1 Cf *Re Donald, Moore v Somerset* [1909] 2 Ch 410.

2 *Re Dean's Will Trusts, Cowan v Board of Governors of St Mary's Hospital, Paddington* [1950] 1 All ER 882, 94 Sol Jo 239.

3 *Re Perreyman, National Provincial Bank Ltd v Perreyman* [1953] 1 All ER 223, 96 Sol Jo 851.

4 *Re Morgan's Will Trusts, Lewarne v Minister of Health* [1950] Ch 637, [1950] 1 All ER 1097; *Re Glass, Public Trustee v South-West Middlesex Hospital Management Committee* [1950] Ch 643n, [1950] 2 All ER 953n; *Re Frere, Kidd v Farnham Group Hospital Management Committee* [1951] Ch 27, [1950] 2 All ER 513; *Re Meyers, London Life Association v St George's Hospital* [1951] Ch 534, [1951] 1 All ER 538. See also PARA 149. And, as to gifts to hospitals being subject to conditions precedent or subsequent connected with nationalisation, see PARAS 136, 137.

156. Informal amalgamation. Gifts to two named societies which, before the gifts took effect, merged with one another were held both to be payable to the united society[1]. A gift to a society which amalgamated with another to which the testatrix later subscribed was held to be payable to the new society[2]. Where a legacy is construed as being for the benefit of a particular charitable activity which, at the date of the will, is carried on by one organisation but, at the date of the testator's death, is carried on by another, the change of machinery does not affect the validity of the gift[3]. Similarly, a change in the constitution of a named institution does not affect the validity of a gift to it on trust for some special charitable purpose[4].

1 *Re Joy, Purday v Johnson* (1888) 60 LT 175; cf *Re Wilson, Wardle v Lemon* (1909) 25 TLR 465 (legacy to fund formerly used for benefit of two villages, but before testator's death restricted to one of them, the other starting its own separate fund: legacy divided between the two funds in proportion to the population of the two villages).

2 *Re Pritt, Morton v National Church League* (1915) 85 LJCh 166.

3 *Re Wedgwood, Sweet v Cotton* [1914] 2 Ch 245. See also *Re Adams, Harle v Adams* (1888) 4 TLR 757; *Re Dawson's Will Trusts, National Provincial Bank Ltd v National Council of the YMCA Inc* [1957] 1 All ER 177, [1957] 1 WLR 391. Cf *Phillips v Royal Society for the Protection of Birds* [2012] EWHC 618 (Ch), [2012] All ER (D) (Apr).

4 *Re Dean's Will Trusts, Cowan v Board of Governors of St Mary's Hospital, Paddington* [1950] 1 All ER 882, 94 Sol Jo 239; *Re White's Will Trusts, Tindall v Board of Governors of United Sheffield Hospitals* [1951] 1 All ER 528, 95 Sol Jo 205.

C. OTHER CASES

157. Gift where institution never existed. Where the named institution has never existed, the stated object has normally failed. The gift will, therefore, lapse unless there is a general charitable intention which enables it to be applied cy-près[1].

1 *Re Davis, Hannen v Hillyer* [1902] 1 Ch 876; and see PARA 170. In *Re Parkes, Cottrell v Parkes* (1909) 25 TLR 523, it was held in such a case that the donor's intention was to benefit certain purposes, rather than a particular institution: cf PARA 149. As to cy-près schemes see PARA 209 et seq.

158. Gift where institution ceased to exist after gift took effect. A legacy to an orphanage which was in existence at the date of the testator's death but which closed before the estate was distributed was held to have vested in the orphanage absolutely on the testator's death, and not to have been divested on the closure of the orphanage[1]. The same principle was applied in the case of a reversionary legacy for a school which closed during the prior life interest[2].

A gift to a company established for charitable purposes from a person who dies after the company goes into liquidation but before it is formally dissolved need not fail according to its terms[3].

1 *Re Slevin, Slevin v Hepburn* [1891] 2 Ch 236, CA; following *Hayter v Trego* (1830) 5 Russ 113. See also *Re Buck, Bruty v Mackey* [1896] 2 Ch 727; *Re Hunter, Lloyds Bank Ltd v Mistress and Governors of Girton College, Cambridge* [1951] Ch 190, [1951] 1 All ER 58. See also *Phillips v Royal Society for the Protection of Birds* [2012] EWHC 618 (Ch), [2012] All ER (D) (Apr), applying *Re Slevin, Slevin v Hepburn.*

2 *Re Soley, Grover v Drapers' Co* (1900) 17 TLR 118.

3 *Re ARMS (Multiple Sclerosis Research) Ltd, Alleyne v A-G* [1997] 2 All ER 679, [1997] 1 WLR 877 (where the property was in the event distributable among the creditors).

159. Gift where institution ceases on death of donor. If the institution to whom a charitable gift is to be made ceases to exist on the death of the donor, there is an initial failure[1] of the gift[2]. If the purposes of the institution, though not the institution itself, continue after the donor's death the gift will not be allowed to fail merely because the particular institution used to attain a charitable end has ceased to exist[3].

If the purposes or the institution can be seen to have continued after the death, but subsequently cease, there may be a subsequent failure of charitable objects[4], but the gift will not fail. However, if the donor is essential to the functioning of the institution then the gift will be deemed to fail at the moment of death[5]. If a general or paramount charitable intention can be found in the gift, it may still be saved and applied cy-près[6].

1 As to initial failure of purposes see PARA 167 et seq.

2 *Kings v Bultitude* [2010] EWHC 1795 (Ch), (2010) 13 ITELR 391.

3 See *Re Broadbent, Imperial Cancer Research Fund v Bradley* [2001] EWCA Civ 714, (2001) 3 ITELR 787; *Kings v Bultitude* [2010] EWHC 1795 (Ch), (2010) 13 ITELR 391.

4 See *Re Slevin, Slevin v Hepburn* [1891] 2 Ch 236, CA; and as to subsequent failure of objects generally see PARA 173 et seq.

5 *Kings v Bultitude* [2010] EWHC 1795 (Ch), (2010) 13 ITELR 391.

6 See *Kings v Bultitude* [2010] EWHC 1795 (Ch), (2010) 13 ITELR 391, where, however, no such general or paramount intention was found: the testatrix made a gift of residue to the 'trustee' of a church which was 'dogged in pursuing its separate path', and ceased to function at her death; held that on the facts, the gift did not demonstrate a general charitable intention.

160. Gift where institution unascertainable. If a gift is made to a named institution whose identity cannot be ascertained, then, depending on the testator's apparent intention, the court may hold that a particular institution was intended to take but that it has not been shown to exist or to have existed[1], or that no particular institution was intended[2]. In the latter case the gift is treated as a gift for the indicated charitable purposes. On the other hand, a particular institution may have been intended, but it may be impossible to decide which of various possible claimants is the one intended by the testator[3]. In such a case the principle applicable is that uncertainty of objects does not invalidate a gift that is clearly charitable[4].

1 *Re Goldschmidt, Commercial Union Assurance Co Ltd v Central British Fund for Jewish Relief and Rehabilitation* [1957] 1 All ER 513, [1957] 1 WLR 524; cf *Re Tharp, Longrigg v People's Dispensary for Sick Animals of the Poor Inc* [1942] 2 All ER 358; revsd [1943] 1 All ER 257, CA, on the construction of the gift. As to gifts where the institution never existed see PARA 157.
2 *Simon v Barber* (1829) 3 Hare 195n.
3 See *Bennett v Hayter* (1839) 2 Beav 81; *Gibson v Coleman* (1868) 18 LT 236; *Re Alchin's Trust, ex p Furley, ex p Earl Romney* (1872) LR 14 Eq 230; *Re Songest, Mayger v Forces' Help Society and Lord Roberts' Workshops* [1956] 2 All ER 765, [1956] 1 WLR 897, CA (for the eventual outcome of this case see [1956] 3 All ER 489n, [1956] 1 WLR 1311, CA); *Re Satterthwaite's Will Trusts, Midland Bank Executor and Trustee Co Ltd v Royal Veterinary College* [1966] 1 All ER 919, [1966] 1 WLR 277, CA.
4 See PARA 90. The property will be applied by scheme, usually by division between some or all of the claimants likely to have been intended: see PARA 206.

161. Disclaimer of gift. A gift on trust cannot be invalidated by the trustee's refusal to accept the trusts[1] unless it is of the essence of the gift that the named trustee should act[2]. Where a gift is to a charitable institution absolutely, however, and the institution disclaims, the gift may fail in the same way as would an absolute gift to an individual[3].

1 See PARA 164.
2 See *Re Lysaght, Hill v Royal College of Surgeons* [1966] Ch 191, [1965] 2 All ER 888.
3 See *Re Slevin, Slevin v Hepburn* [1891] 2 Ch 236 at 242, CA, per Kay LJ. In one case such a gift has been held not to fail: *Denyer v Druce* (1829) Taml 32; and see dicta in *Simon v Barber* (1829) 3 Hare 195n.

(iii) Other Cases where Object Fails

162. Gift to be applied in illegal manner. If the purpose of a gift is illegal or contrary to public policy, the gift cannot be charitable and will not be allowed to take effect[1]. But if the purpose is charitable, and only the particular manner of effecting it is illegal, then the court will give effect to the gift despite the failure of the intended manner of application[2].

The same is true where income is directed to be accumulated for an excessive period and then to be applied for charitable purposes[3]: the direction to accumulate is treated as mere machinery, the failure of which cannot prevent the property from being devoted to charity[4]. Similarly, if a gift is initially valid, the fact that a subsequent statute makes it illegal to carry it out exactly as directed does not cause any part of the gift to lapse[5].

If property is given for charitable purposes and the trustees have discretion to apply it in various ways, they may not apply it in an illegal manner, and the fact that the donor has purported to permit an illegal as well as a legal mode of application does not cause any kind of failure[6].

1 *Thrupp v Collett* (1858) 26 Beav 125; *Sims v Quinlan* (1865) 17 I Ch R 43. As to purposes contrary to public policy see PARA 66.

2 *A-G v Vint* (1850) 3 De G & Sm 704. See also cases of gifts void as being for superstitious uses but nevertheless charitable, eg *De Costa v De Paz* (1754) 2 Swan 487n; *Cary v Abbot* (1802) 7 Ves 490. As to superstitious uses see PARA 63.

3 *Martin v Maugham* (1844) 14 Sim 230; followed reluctantly in *Re Bradwell, Goode v Board of Trustees for Methodist Church Purposes* [1952] Ch 575, [1952] 2 All ER 286; distinguished in *Re Lushington, Wynyard v A-G* [1963] NZLR 313; on appeal sub nom *Re Lushington, Manukau County v Wynyard* [1964] NZLR 161, NZ CA, where there was held to be no general charitable intention.

4 *Re Bradwell, Goode v Board of Trustees for Methodist Church Purposes* [1952] Ch 575, [1952] 2 All ER 286. As to accumulations generally, and their effect on charitable trusts, see PARA 145.

5 *A-G v Green* (1789) 2 Bro CC 492.

6 See eg *Sorresby v Hollins* (1740) 9 Mod Rep 221; *Faversham Corpn v Ryder* (1854) 5 De GM & G 350; *Salusbury v Denton* (1857) 3 K & J 529; *Sinnett v Herbert* (1871) LR 12 Eq 201 (on appeal (1872) 7 Ch App 232).

163. Impracticable gifts. The purpose for which a charitable gift is made may fail because it has already been fulfilled[1], or because it is impossible to carry it out at all[2], as where the gift postulates the existence of an institution[3] or a state of affairs[4] or class of objects[5] which does not exist or ceases to exist[6]. The purpose of a gift may also be impracticable because insufficient money has been given[7], or because the property given and intended to be used is unsuitable[8], or because no suitable site can be found[9]. The donor may have attached conditions to the gift which render it unlikely or impossible that the purposes can ever be achieved[10], or conditions which are repugnant to the fulfilment of the primary charitable purpose so that, as it stands, the gift is self-defeating[11].

When the fund given is inadequate for the intended purpose at the date when it ought to be applied to that purpose according to the terms of the gift, it should not be retained and accumulated until it is sufficient, but should be dealt with there and then[12]. In some cases where inadequate funds were given the gift has been construed as conditional upon sufficient funds becoming available, so that if they do not become available the gift never takes effect at all[13].

The intended purpose need not be immediately practicable[14]; the question is whether at the relevant date[15] it is practicable to carry the donor's intentions into effect, or whether at that date there is any reasonable prospect that it will be practicable to do so at some future time[16].

The burden of proof in relation to impracticability lies on the party who alleges that the gift has failed through impracticability[17].

1 *Corbyn v French* (1799) 4 Ves 418; *Bunting v Marriott* (1854) 19 Beav 163.

2 See *A-G v Bishop of Oxford* (1785) 1 Bro CC 444n, discussed in *Corbyn v French* (1799) 4 Ves 418; *Re Welstead* (1858) 25 Beav 612; *A-G v Combe* (1679) 2 Cas in Ch 18; *Brantham v East Burgold* (circa 1790) cited 2 Ves 388; and cf *New v Bonaker* (1867) LR 4 Eq 655.

3 Eg a particular school: *Incorporated Society v Price* (1844) 1 Jo & Lat 498; *Re Templemoyle Agricultural School* (1869) IR 4 Eq 295; cf *Marsh v Means* (1857) 3 Jur NS 790 (for continuing publication of a certain periodical which was not published after the date of the will).

4 Eg that property given as a burial ground will continue to be available for the purpose (*Campbell v Liverpool Corpn* (1870) LR 9 Eq 579; and cf *Re St Pancras Burial Ground* (1866) LR 3 Eq 173; *A-G v Glyn* (1841) 12 Sim 84); or that certain public services will continue to be available on a voluntary basis only (*Re Mackenzie, Moir v Angus County Council* [1962] 2 All ER 890, [1962] 1 WLR 880 (education); though see also *Re Leitch* [1965] VR 204, decided on a similar bequest; *Re Hillier, Hillier v A-G* [1954] 2 All ER 59, [1954] 1 WLR 700, CA (hospital buildings); *Re Wokingham Fire Brigade Trusts, Martin v Hawkins* [1951] Ch 373, [1951] 1 All ER 454 (local fire brigade); and see also *Richmond Corpn v A-G* [1965] RA 117, revsd sub nom *Re Richmond Parish Charity Lands* [1965] RA 343, CA (gift in aid of the poor rate)).

5 *A-G v London Corpn* (1790) 1 Ves 243 (infidels in Virginia); *A-G v Hicks* (1810) 3 Bro CC 166n as noted in 29 ER 468 (leprous patients); *A-G v Ironmongers' Co* (1834) 2 My & K 576 (British slaves in Barbary); *A-G v Lawes* (1849) 8 Hare 32 (persecuted ministers of a particular

sect); *A-G v Bunce* (1868) LR 6 Eq 563 (Presbyterians at Devizes); *Re Prison Charities* (1873) LR 16 Eq 129 (poor persons imprisoned for debt); *Re Geikie, Robson v Paterson* (1911) 27 TLR 484 (members of a particular church); *Re Welsh Hospital (Netley) Fund, Thomas v A-G* [1921] 1 Ch 655 (sick and wounded Welsh soldiers); *Re Colonial Bishoprics Fund 1841* [1935] Ch 148 (bishops in South Africa in connection with the Church of England). But see also *A-G v Earl of Craven* (1856) 21 Beav 392 (poor infected by plague).

6 However, a temporary absence of objects will not cause a failure, or even a temporary failure: *Aylet v Dodd* (1741) 2 Atk 238.

7 Eg *Cherry v Mott* (1836) 1 My & Cr 123; *Re Queen's School, Chester* [1910] 1 Ch 796; *Re Good's Will Trusts, Oliver v Batten* [1950] 2 All ER 653; *Re Whittaker, Nobel v A-G* [1951] 2 TLR 955; *Re Winton* (1953) Times, 31 January; *Re Dover's Battle of Britain Memorial Hospital Fund* (1955) Times, 29 June; *Re Ulverston and District New Hospital Building Trusts, Birkett v Barrow and Furness Hospital Management Committee* [1956] Ch 622, [1956] 3 All ER 164, CA. Note, however, that if trustees have accepted a conditional gift they may be under a duty to fulfil the condition even if the gift is insufficient to do so: see PARA 138.

8 *Re Packe, Sanders v A-G* [1918] 1 Ch 437 (appeal settled sub nom *Re Packe, Campion v A-G* (1918) 145 LT Jo 111, CA); *A-G for New South Wales v Perpetual Trustee Co Ltd* (1940) 63 CLR 209, Aust HC; *Hay v Murdoch* [1952] WN 145, HL. See also *A-G v Earl of Lonsdale* (1827) 1 Sim 105 (land given inter vivos to charitable trustees by tenant for life; trusts impracticable after his death); and *McCormick v Queen's University of Belfast* [1958] NI 1.

9 *Chamberlayne v Brockett* (1872) 8 Ch App 206; *Re White's Trusts* (1886) 33 ChD 449; *Biscoe v Jackson* (1887) 35 ChD 460, CA.

10 *Re Wilson, Twentyman v Simpson* [1913] 1 Ch 314; *Re Mitchell's Will Trusts, Jago v A-G* (1966) 110 Sol Jo 291. Cf *A-G v Minshull* (1798) 4 Ves 11 (gift to apprentice poor children, with a maximum of £10 for each child which became impracticably small); *Re Stewart's Will Trusts* [1983] NI 283. See further, as to conditional gifts, PARA 136 et seq.

11 *Re Richardson's Will* (1887) 58 LT 45; *Re Robinson, Wright v Tugwell* [1923] 2 Ch 332 (condition that preacher wear black gown in pulpit, which would alienate congregation); *Re Dominion Students' Hall Trust, Dominion Students' Hall Trust v A-G* [1947] Ch 183 (colour bar condition incompatible with primary object of promoting community among all members of Commonwealth); *Re Lysaght, Hill v Royal College of Surgeons* [1966] Ch 191, [1965] 2 All ER 888 (condition excluding Catholics and Jews; the trustee, essential to the gift, would not accept the gift subject to the condition); cf *Re Meres' Will Trusts* (1957) Times, 4 May (condition that only males of pure English, Irish or Scottish parentage be eligible to benefit: void for uncertainty, but the main gift held valid); *Harris v Sharp* (7 December 1987, unreported), ChD, discussed [1988] Conv (NS) 288 (D Partington). Trustees are not bound to accept property subject to a special trust or condition: see PARA 138.

12 *Re Whittaker, Nobel v A-G* [1951] 2 TLR 955.

13 Eg see *Re London University Medical Sciences Institute Fund, Fowler v A-G* [1909] 2 Ch 1, CA; and PARA 175.

14 See *A-G v Bishop of Chester* (1785) 1 Bro CC 444; *Re Villers-Wilkes, Bower v Goodman* (1895) 11 TLR 250; *Chamberlayne v Brockett* (1872) 8 Ch App 206; *Biscoe v Jackson* (1887) 35 ChD 460, CA; *Sinnett v Herbert* (1872) 7 Ch App 232; *A-G v Lady Downing* (1767) Wilm 1; *A-G v Bowyer* (1798) 3 Ves 714 at 728 per Lord Hardwicke LC; *Re Swain, Monckton v Hands* [1905] 1 Ch 669, CA.

15 Ie in the case of a will, the date of the testator's death; and in the case of an inter vivos gift, the date of the gift: *Re Moon's Will Trusts, Foale v Gillians* [1948] 1 All ER 300; *Re Wright, Blizard v Lockhart* [1954] Ch 347, [1954] 2 All ER 98, CA; and see PARA 167.

16 See the inquiry directed in *Re White's Will Trusts, Barrow v Gillard* [1955] Ch 188, [1954] 2 All ER 620.

17 *Re Tacon, Public Trustee v Tacon* [1958] Ch 447 at 454, [1958] 1 All ER 163 at 164, CA, per Lord Evershed MR.

164. Failure of or disclaimer by trustee. Following the general rule that equity does not want for a trustee, the fact that the intended trustee of a gift for charitable purposes[1], or a person to whom a power of selection is given[2], dies before the testator does not generally cause a failure of the gift, for the identity of the trustee is normally regarded as mere machinery[3], and in the exercise of its general jurisdiction over the administration of trusts the court can always remedy failures of machinery[4].

The same is true if an executor is given a power of selection but the appointment is later revoked[5]. If substantially the whole of a small estate is given on trust for a charitable institution and there is no executor who proves, letters of administration with the will annexed may properly be granted to an officer of the institution[6].

Similarly, the refusal of the intended trustee to accept the gift[7] does not constitute a failure of the gift unless it is of the essence of the gift that the intended trustee should act[8], or unless the gift is impracticable if the intended trustee does not act[9]. Again, the gift will not fail if the intended trustee is incapable in law of accepting the trust[10], or if there is no person able to give a good receipt for the gift[11].

A gift upon trust will not normally fail by reason of the default or neglect of the trustees[12], but this principle cannot be applied when that default or neglect is the condition upon which a gift over is expressed to operate[13].

1 *Moggridge v Thackwell* (1792) 1 Ves 464 per Lord Thurlow; reheard by Lord Eldon (1803) 7 Ves 36; affd (1807) 13 Ves 416, HL; *A-G v Hickman* (1732) 2 Eq Cas Abr 193 pl 14; *A-G v Lady Downing* (1767) Wilm 1; *A-G v Gladstone* (1842) 13 Sim 7; *A-G v Sturge* (1854) 19 Beav 597.

2 *Re Willis, Shaw v Willis* [1921] 1 Ch 44, CA; *A-G v Hickman* (1732) 2 Eq Cas Abr 193 pl 14.

3 See eg *Re Morrison, Wakefield v Falmouth* (1967) 111 Sol Jo 758; but for an exceptional case see *Re Lysaght, Hill v Royal College of Surgeons* [1966] Ch 191, [1965] 2 All ER 888.

4 If necessary a scheme will be directed for the administration of the trusts. As to administrative schemes see PARA 180.

5 *White v White* (1778) 1 Bro CC 12.

6 *Re M'Auliffe's Goods* [1895] P 290; followed in *Re Lalor's Goods* (1901) 85 LT 643. See also *Walsh v Gladstone* (1843) 1 Ph 290 (legacy to person who predeceased testator 'to be applied to the use of' a named college: held, on the evidence, that it would be proper to pay the legacy over to the president of the college).

7 *Doyley v A-G* (1735) 4 Vin Abr 485 pl 16; *A-G v Andrew* (1798) 3 Ves 633 (affd sub nom *Andrew v Master and Wardens of the Merchant Taylors' Co* (1800) 7 Ves 223, HL); *Denyer v Druce* (1829) Taml 32; *A-G v Fletcher* (1835) 5 LJCh 75; *Reeve v A-G* (1843) 3 Hare 191; *Barclay v Maskelyne* (1858) 32 LTOS 205; *Re Burley, Alexander v Burley* [1910] 1 Ch 215; *Re Wilson-Barkworth, Burstall v Deck* (1933) 50 TLR 82; *Re Lawton, Gartside v A-G* [1936] 3 All ER 378.

8 *Re Lysaght, Hill v Royal College of Surgeons* [1966] Ch 191, [1965] 2 All ER 888; and cf *Marquess of Bute's Trustees v Marquess of Bute* (1905) 7 F 49, Ct of Sess.

9 *New v Bonaker* (1867) LR 4 Eq 655 (gift to the President and Vice-President of the United States and the Governor of Pennsylvania). As to impracticability see PARA 163.

10 *Re Hampton, Public Trustee v Hampton* (1918) 88 LJCh 103 (the Public Trustee cannot act as trustee of any charitable trust); *Tufnell v Constable* (1838) 7 Ad & El 798 (churchwardens); *Re Woolnough's Will Trusts* (1959) Times, 22 October; *Re Armitage, Ellam v Norwich Corpn* [1972] Ch 438, [1972] 1 All ER 708 (local authorities). Formerly gifts to corporations were sometimes void under the mortmain laws (repealed: see PARAS 83–84); but gifts to corporations on trust were sometimes upheld as to the trust, though the corporation could not act as a trustee: see *Sonley v Clock-makers' Co* (1780) 1 Bro CC 81 (private trust); *Incorporated Society in Dublin v Richards* (1841) 1 Dr & War 258. But there were conflicting decisions: see eg *A-G v Flood* (1816) Hayes & Jo App xxi; affd (1817) Hayes 611.

11 *Re Meyers, London Life Association v St George's Hospital* [1951] Ch 534, [1951] 1 All ER 538.

12 *A-G v Boultbee* (1794) 2 Ves 380; affd (1796) 3 Ves 220. This applies even if there is a gift over: *Re Parish of Upton Warren* (1833) 1 My & K 410; and see *A-G v Leigh* (1721) 3 P Wms 145n. As to surplus income and gifts over see PARA 131 et seq.

13 *Christ's Hospital v Grainger* (1849) 1 Mac & G 460; *Re Hanbey's Will Trusts, Cutlers' Co v President and Governors of Christ's Hospital, London* [1956] Ch 264, [1955] 3 All ER 874.

165. Gift of more than is needed for purpose. If a gift for a specific purpose is of an amount of capital more than is required or appropriate for the purpose, then, as to the surplus, the donor has failed to devote his gift to a specified charitable purpose which can be carried out, and in that sense there is a failure of objects[1]. The same applies to gifts in response to public appeals, where the total sum subscribed is more than can be used for the specified purpose[2]. The question may also arise where the income of a fund subject to a continuing trust for charity is, from the start, greater than is necessary for the specified purpose[3], or becomes so in the course of time by reason of an increase in the income[4] or the decay of the particular charity named[5].

1 *Re Connolly, Walton v Connolly* (1914) 110 LT 688, CA; *Re King, Kerr v Bradley* [1923] 1 Ch 243; *Re Stanford, Cambridge University v A-G* [1924] 1 Ch 73; *Re Monk, Giffen v Wedd* [1927] 2 Ch 197, CA; *Re Royce, Turner v Wormald* [1940] Ch 514, [1940] 2 All ER 291; *Re Raine, Walton v A-G* [1956] Ch 417, [1956] 1 All ER 355. As to whether the surplus is held on resulting trust or is applicable cy-près see PARA 172.

2 Eg *Re North Devon and West Somerset Relief Fund Trusts, Hylton v Wright* [1953] 2 All ER 1032, [1953] 1 WLR 1260. For cases where the sum raised is too small to be used for the specified purpose see PARA 163 text and note 7.

3 Eg *Arnold v A-G* (1698) Show Parl Cas 22, HL.

4 *A-G v Coopers' Co* (1812) 19 Ves 187.

5 *A-G v Ironmongers' Co* (1834) 2 My & K 576; *Re Slevin, Slevin v Hepburn* [1891] 2 Ch 236 at 240, CA, per Kay LJ. As to surplus income see PARAS 131–135.

(2) CONSEQUENCES OF FAILURE OF STATED OBJECTS

(i) Consequences of Failure of Objects

166. Failure of gift or application cy-près. If it is established that the stated objects of a charitable gift fail, there are two possible consequences: either the property can be applied cy-près[1] for such charitable purposes as the court or the Charity Commission considers appropriate having regard to the statutory considerations[2], or the whole gift fails. In general, no cy-près application is possible unless the donor has shown a general charitable intention[3], but there are three exceptions to this requirement: (1) where the gift has taken effect but has failed subsequently[4]; (2) where the amount of the gift is, from the outset, surplus to what is required to achieve the stated object, but the donor has shown an intention to devote the property wholly to charity[5]; and (3) in the case of public subscriptions[6]. In all such cases of cy-près application, the application is made by way of scheme[7]. If no cy-près application is possible, the gift fails and will result to the donor.

1 As to the cy-près doctrine see PARA 209 et seq.

2 See the Charities Act 2011 s 67(1)–(3); and PARA 211. As to the statutory considerations see PARA 214; as to the Charity Commission see PARAS 543–578.

3 See PARA 168.

4 As to subsequent failure see PARAS 173–174.

5 See PARA 172.

6 Ie by virtue, in part, of the Charities Act 2011 ss 63–66: see PARAS 176–177. As to the failure of public appeals for charitable purposes see PARA 175 et seq.

7 As to the making of cy-près schemes see PARA 209 et seq.

(ii) Initial Failure

167. When ascertained. For the purpose of deciding whether a charitable gift can take effect in the first place, the situation must be considered as at the date when the gift first vests in interest in charity, whether in possession[1] or in reversion[2], and whether the gift is to an institution or for a purpose[3]. If the reversionary gift is defeasible, the possibility that it will be divested is to be ignored[4]; the question must be decided by reference to the value of the whole fund at the relevant date, not the value at that date of the reversionary interest[5].

If the institution to whom the gift is to be made ceases to exist on the death of the donor, there is an initial failure of the gift[6].

1 *Re Slevin, Slevin v Hepburn* [1891] 2 Ch 236, CA.

2 *Re Moon's Will Trusts, Foale v Gillians* [1948] 1 All ER 300; *Re Wright, Blizard v Lockhart* [1954] Ch 347, [1954] 2 All ER 98, CA; *Re Woodhams, Lloyds Bank Ltd v London College of Music* [1981] 1 All ER 202, [1981] 1 WLR 493.

3 *Re Wright, Blizard v Lockhart* [1954] Ch 347, [1954] 2 All ER 98, CA. See *Harris v Sharp* (7 December 1987, unreported), ChD, discussed [1988] Conv (NS) 288 (D Partington). See also *Kings v Bultitude* [2010] EWHC 1795 (Ch), (2010) 13 ITELR 391; *Phillips v Royal Society for the Protection of Birds* [2012] EWHC 618 (Ch), [2012] All ER (D) (Apr).

4 *Re Tacon, Public Trustee v Tacon* [1958] Ch 447, [1958] 1 All ER 163, CA: the position in relation to a true contingent gift is undecided.

5 *Re Tacon, Public Trustee v Tacon* [1958] Ch 447, [1958] 1 All ER 163, CA. See *Re Martin* (1977) 121 Sol Jo 828 (inflation taken into account, applying *Re Tacon*). See also the form of inquiry directed in *Re White's Will Trusts, Barrow v Gillard* [1955] Ch 188, [1954] 2 All ER 620.

6 *Kings v Bultitude* [2010] EWHC 1795 (Ch), (2010) 13 ITELR 391, where the gift might have been saved if a general or paramount charitable intention had been found. See also PARA 159.

168. General charitable intention. A gift will not lapse if, although the indicated purpose of the gift has failed at the moment when the gift should take effect, the court can find an intention on the donor's part more general than a bare intention that the impracticable direction be carried into execution as an indispensable part of the trust declared[1]. 'General charitable intention' means a paramount intention to give the property in the first instance for a general charitable purpose rather than a particular charitable purpose and to graft on to the general gift a direction as to the donor's intentions as to the manner in which the general gift is to be carried into effect[2]. The general charitable purpose may be directed to a particular form of charity rather than to charity generally[3].

The process of ascertaining whether there is a general charitable intention may involve considering whether one or more of the directions given by the donor were essential to his intended purpose[4], and this may be decided by construing the gift[5]. Often, however, the words used give little assistance, and more is to be gained from an examination of the nature of the charitable trust itself and what is involved in the project[6]. The fact that a donor refers expressly to his general charitable intention cannot give to the gift a general charitable character when, on the face of it, it is particular and non-charitable[7]. It has been held that the court cannot find a general charitable intention in relation to a gift which is for a non-charitable purpose[8]; and it cannot construct a general charitable intention from mere guesswork[9].

The meaning of 'general charitable intention' has more recently been restated in terms of paramount charitable intention[10]. Under this restatement, the question whether the specified objects have failed and the question of the presence of a general charitable intention are merged into one question, namely whether the impossibility of performing part of the expressed trusts defeats the essential charitable purpose of the donor, or whether this essential purpose can be carried out in a modified way. If the essential purpose of the gift can still be carried out in a modified way, the general or paramount charitable intention takes effect and the court can give effect to it by means of a cy-près scheme[11].

1 For this formulation of the meaning of a general charitable intention see *A-G for New South Wales v Perpetual Trustee Co Ltd* (1940) 63 CLR 209 at 225, Aust HC, per Dixon and Evatt JJ.

2 *Re Wilson, Twentyman v Simpson* [1913] 1 Ch 314 at 320–321 per Parker J (the locus classicus on the point). See also *Re Templemoyle Agricultural School* (1869) IR 4 Eq 295 at 301 per Chatterton V-C.

3 See *Re Taylor, Martin v Freeman* (1888) 58 LT 538 at 542 per Kay J.

4 See *Re Lysaght, Hill v Royal College of Surgeons* [1966] Ch 191, [1965] 2 All ER 888, where the gift contained two incompatible directions: the Royal College of Surgeons was to act as trustee but refused to do so if the gift remained subject to a condition relating to religious discrimination. It was held that the trusteeship of the college was essential to the gift, and that the condition as to religious discrimination was not.

5 *A-G for New South Wales v Perpetual Trustee Co Ltd* (1940) 63 CLR 209 at 227, Aust HC (and see at 225–228 generally).

6 *A-G for New South Wales v Perpetual Trustee Co Ltd* (1940) 63 CLR 209 at 227, Aust HC. See also *Re Broadbent, Imperial Cancer Research Fund v Bradley* [2001] EWCA Civ 714, (2001) 3 ITELR 787. For a case in which no general charitable intention could be found see *Kings v Bultitude* [2010] EWHC 1795 (Ch), (2010) 13 ITELR 391; and PARA 159.

7 *Re Sanders' Will Trusts, Public Trustee v McLaren* [1954] Ch 265, [1954] 1 All ER 667 (appeal settled (1954) Times, 22 July, CA).

8 *Re Jenkins' Will Trusts, Public Trustee v British Union for the Abolition of Vivisection* [1966] Ch 249, [1966] 1 All ER 926. Cf *Re Satterthwaite's Will Trusts, Midland Bank Executor and Trustee Co Ltd v Royal Veterinary College* [1966] 1 All ER 919, [1966] 1 WLR 277, CA.

9 *Re Crowe, National Westminster Bank Ltd v Balfour* (1979, unreported); noted in *Report of the Charity Commissioners for England and Wales for 1979* (HC Paper (1979–80) no 608) paras 40–45.

10 *Re Lysaght, Hill v Royal College of Surgeons* [1966] Ch 191, [1965] 2 All ER 888. However, this restatement seems to be used in tandem with, rather than in place of, 'general charitable intention': see *Kings v Bultitude* [2010] EWHC 1795 (Ch), (2010) 13 ITELR 391; and PARA 159.

11 As to cy-près schemes see PARA 209 et seq.

169. Examples of general charitable intention. A general charitable intention has been found where a deed contained alternative gifts, all related to one general purpose[1], and where a legacy was one of nine to institutions concerned with animal welfare[2], and where the bulk of an estate after a life interest was specifically dedicated to charity and the particular institution which had ceased to exist was mainly only a co-ordinating body[3]. Where residue is divided between charitable purposes or institutions and the gift of one share fails as to its stated objects, it may be relatively easy to find a general charitable intention[4]. There is no rule that, where a legacy to charity fails and residue is also given to charity, there can be no general charitable intention in relation to the legacy[5]. In most cases the question of whether there is or is not a general charitable intention depends upon the construction of the particular will, and no general principle can be derived from them[6].

Sometimes where the failure is caused by the donor's attaching some impracticable condition to his gift, the condition is held to be an inessential part of the gift and the donor's general charitable intention to be directed towards only the essential elements in the gift[7]. Similarly, when the precise direction, as distinct from the general purpose, is illegal, it may be regarded as inessential[8].

A general charitable intention may be manifested not only in a gift by deed or will, but also in a gift in response to a public appeal[9], but these cases are more often approached on the basis of an intention to make an outright, or only a limited, gift of property to charity, whether or not the purpose of the appeal can be effected[10].

Very slight indications of a general charitable intention will suffice where there is a gift to an institution, apparently charitable[11], which has never existed[12]. It is difficult[13], though not impossible[14], to find a general charitable intention where there is a gift to a particular institution which ceased to exist before the gift took effect[15], and a parallel principle applies where a particular purpose has become impracticable or impossible of accomplishment before the gift took effect[16].

1 *Re Templemoyle Agricultural School* (1869) IR 4 Eq 295. See also *Re Tyler's Fund Trusts, Graves v King* [1967] 3 All ER 389, [1967] 1 WLR 1269 (gift by deed for charitable institutions to be named in a later document).

2 *Re Satterthwaite's Will Trusts, Midland Bank Executor and Trustee Co Ltd v Royal Veterinary College* [1966] 1 All ER 919, [1966] 1 WLR 277, CA. Cf *Re Jenkins' Will Trusts, Public Trustee v British Union for the Abolition of Vivisection* [1966] Ch 249, [1966] 1 All ER 926.

3 *Re Finger's Will Trusts, Turner v Ministry of Health* [1972] Ch 286, [1971] 3 All ER 1050.

4 *Re Whittaker, Nobel v A-G* [1951] 2 TLR 955; *Re Griffiths, Powell v Griffiths* (23 July 1958, unreported) cited in [1963] 1 All ER 680n. Cf *Kings v Bultitude* [2010] EWHC 1795 (Ch), (2010) 13 ITELR 391, where no charitable intention was found.

5 *Lyons Corpn v Advocate-General of Bengal* (1876) 1 App Cas 91, PC; and see PARA 171 text and note 8.

6 See eg *Biscoe v Jackson* (1887) 35 ChD 460, CA (gift to establish cottage hospital and soup kitchen: general charitable intention of benefiting poor of parish); *Re Winton* (1953) Times, 31 January (gift for building humane slaughterhouse for horses: held not limited to that specific purpose); *Re Currie* [1985] NI 299. In *Kings v Bultitude* [2010] EWHC 1795 (Ch), (2010) 13 ITELR 391, the question was determined partly by reference to the will, and partly by reference to general evidence of the importance of the testatrix to the legatee institution.

7 *Re Lysaght, Hill v Royal College of Surgeons* [1966] Ch 191, [1965] 2 All ER 888, cited in PARA 166 note 4; *A-G for New South Wales v Perpetual Trustee Co Ltd* (1940) 63 CLR 209, Aust HC; *Re Bloomfield's Bequest* (1920) 54 ILT 213; *Re Robinson, Wright v Tugwell* [1923] 2 Ch 332; *Brantham v East Burgold* (circa 1790) cited 2 Ves 388; *Re Woodhams, Lloyds Bank Ltd v London College of Music* [1981] 1 All ER 202, [1981] 1 WLR 493 (music college refused to accept gift for scholarships restricted to orphans; restriction inessential part of gift and general charitable intention prevailed).

8 *A-G v Vint* (1850) 3 De G & Sm 704. As to where gifts are to be applied in an illegal manner see PARA 162.

9 Eg *Re North Devon and West Somerset Relief Fund Trusts, Hylton v Wright* [1953] 2 All ER 1032, [1953] 1 WLR 1260. As to donations via websites see PARA 106.

10 As to the failure of gifts in relation to general or limited charitable purposes see PARA 176. Since the Charities Act 1960 s 14 (repealed; see now the Charities Act 2011 ss 63–66) the question has become less important: see PARAS 175–178.

11 Its description or the context may show that it would have been charitable: *Re Maguire* (1870) LR 9 Eq 632; *Re Clergy Society* (1856) 2 K & J 615; *Re Knox, Fleming v Carmichael* [1937] Ch 109, [1936] 3 All ER 623.

12 *Re Davis, Hannen v Hillyer* [1902] 1 Ch 876. See also *Re Bailey, Bailey v Working Ladies' Guild* (1931) 75 Sol Jo 415 (no indication of more general intention from context, but gift applied cy-près); *Re Barnard, Majendie v Duke of Northumberland* (1890) 7 TLR 73.

13 *Re Harwood, Coleman v Innes* [1936] Ch 285. See also *Re Hunter, Genn v A-G of British Columbia* [1973] 3 WWR 197 (BC SC).

14 *Re Finger's Will Trusts, Turner v Ministry of Health* [1972] Ch 286, [1971] 3 All ER 1050.

15 As to the position when the gift in a will fails at the moment of death of the donor see PARA 159.

16 *Re Spence, Ogden v Shackleton* [1979] Ch 483, sub nom *Re Spence's Will Trusts, Ogden v Shackleton* [1978] 3 All ER 92.

170. Effect of general charitable intention. If a general charitable intention[1] is found, failure of the particular directions in the gift will not cause the gift itself to fail, for the donor's true intention may still be carried out, and where necessary a scheme will be directed[2] or the property applied by the Attorney General, to whom the power of the Crown to dispose of charitable gifts under the sign manual has been delegated[3].

If a gift to a non-existent institution is saved by the presence of a general charitable intention, the person or authority administering the purposes of the gift under a scheme may be entitled to a share of residue divisible between institutions which are beneficiaries under the instrument[4].

1 As to general charitable intention see PARAS 168–169.
2 As to cy-près schemes see PARA 209 et seq.
3 As to the jurisdiction of the Crown over charities see PARAS 512–513. As to the Attorney General see PARAS 589, 596, 605 et seq; and **CONSTITUTIONAL AND ADMINISTRATIVE LAW** vol 20 (2014) PARA 273 et seq.
4 *Re Davis, Hannen v Hillyer* [1902] 1 Ch 876.

171. Intention to benefit particular charity only. In some cases it has been held that every element in the gift was essential to the donor's intention and that, if the particular directions fail, an application of the property in any other way would be contrary to the donor's intention[1]. Frequently an intention to benefit charity only in a particular form appears from the fact that the donor has laid down detailed directions or conditions[2], or has expressly made the conditions of the essence of the gift[3].

In the case of a legacy to a correctly named, known institution which ceased to exist before the date of the testator's death, it may be difficult to find a general charitable intention[4], the more so if the gift is expressed to be 'for the benefit of that institution'[5], or if the testator placed particular reliance on the institution named carrying out his wishes[6]. A gift to an institution which has never existed may be held to be limited in intention to the supposed institution, and to lapse in consequence[7].

It has been said that, where residue is given to charity, it is difficult to find a general charitable intention in relation to a legacy whose objects fail[8]. If a legacy which is only for a particular charitable purpose fails at the moment of the testator's death, it falls into residue or passes as on an intestacy.

When gifts of realty for charitable purposes were void under the mortmain laws[9], ancillary gifts of personalty were held to fail also, as being dependent on the validity of the gift of realty[10], unless they could be construed as being for an independent purpose, whether private[11] or charitable[12].

1 *A-G v Bishop of Oxford* (1786) 1 Bro CC 444n, as explained in *Corbyn v French* (1799) 4 Ves 418.
2 *Re Wilson, Twentyman v Simpson* [1913] 1 Ch 314; *Russell v Kellett* (1855) 3 Sm & G 264; *Re Good's Will Trusts, Oliver v Batten* [1950] 2 All ER 653; *Hay v Murdoch* [1952] WN 145, HL.
3 Eg by a direction that if they are not fulfilled the gift is to fall into residue: *Re Randell, Randell v Dixon* (1888) 38 ChD 213. See also *Re Cooper's Conveyance Trusts, Crewdson v Bagot* [1956] 3 All ER 28, [1956] 1 WLR 1096; *Re Peel's Release* [1921] 2 Ch 218; and PARA 172.
4 *Re Harwood, Coleman v Innes* [1936] Ch 285; *Re Rymer, Rymer v Stanfield* [1895] 1 Ch 19, CA; but see *Re Finger's Will Trusts, Turner v Ministry of Health* [1972] Ch 286, [1971] 3 All ER 1050, citing *Re Roberts, Stenton v Hardy* [1963] 1 All ER 674 at 681, [1963] 1 WLR 406 at 416 per Wilberforce J. See *Kings v Bultitude* [2010] EWHC 1795 (Ch), (2010) 13 ITELR 391, where no general charitable intention could be found, and the institution was held to cease to exist at the moment of the death of the testatrix.
5 *Langford v Gowland* (1862) 3 Giff 617. See also *Re Spence, Ogden v Shackleton* [1979] Ch 483, sub nom *Re Spence's Will Trusts, Ogden v Shackleton* [1978] 3 All ER 92 (gift to defunct old people's home expressed with particularity showed no general charitable intention).
6 *Re Stemson's Will Trusts, Carpenter v Treasury Solicitor* [1970] Ch 16, [1969] 2 All ER 517. For other cases in which gifts to charitable institutions which had ceased to exist were held not to show a general charitable intention see *Clark v Taylor* (1853) 1 Drew 642; *Re Ovey, Broadbent v Barrow* (1885) 29 ChD 560; *Kings v Bultitude* [2010] EWHC 1795 (Ch), (2010) 13 ITELR 391.
7 See *Re Tharp, Longrigg v People's Dispensary for Sick Animals of the Poor Inc* [1942] 2 All ER 358; revsd [1943] 1 All ER 257, CA, on the ground that the named institution was a misdescription of an existing body.
8 *Re Goldschmidt, Commercial Union Assurance Co Ltd v Central British Fund for Jewish Relief and Rehabilitation* [1957] 1 All ER 513, [1957] 1 WLR 524; but see *Lyons Corpn v Advocate-General of Bengal* (1876) 1 App Cas 91, PC; and PARA 169 note 5.
9 As to the repeal of the mortmain laws see PARAS 83–84.

10 See eg *A-G v Whitchurch* (1796) 3 Ves 141; *A-G v Hinxman* (1820) 2 Jac & W 270; *Re Taylor, Martin v Freeman* (1888) 58 LT 538.
11 *Blandford v Thackerell* (1793) 2 Ves 238.
12 *A-G v Stepney* (1804) 10 Ves 22.

172. Surplus: intention to devote whole to charity. In a number of cases where the property given is more than is needed for the specified charitable purpose, it has been held that the gift is a valid charitable gift as to the whole, and that the surplus should be applied cy-près[1], sometimes on the basis that there was a general charitable intention[2]. In other cases this result has been achieved on the basis that the donor intended to devote to charity the whole of the property given[3]. However, if the donor's intention was to limit his gift to the amount necessary for the particular purpose named, any surplus is held on a resulting trust, or falls into residue, or passes as on an intestacy, as the case may be[4].

1 As to cy-près schemes see PARA 209 et seq.
2 *Re Royce, Turner v Wormald* [1940] Ch 514, [1940] 2 All ER 291. As to general charitable intention see PARA 169 et seq.
3 *Re Douglas, Douglas v Simpson* [1905] 1 Ch 279; *Re King, Kerr v Bradley* [1923] 1 Ch 243; *Re Monk, Giffen v Wedd* [1927] 2 Ch 197, CA (where the principle applied was explained by Sargant LJ at 211 as an application of the rule in *Lassence v Tierney* (1849) 1 Mac & G 551, on the basis of an absolute gift of the whole to trustees for charity, followed by a specific direction as to the application of part only of the property); *Re Robertson, Colin v Chamberlin* [1930] 2 Ch 71; *Re Raine, Walton v A-G* [1956] Ch 417, [1956] 1 All ER 355 (where there was held to be no general charitable intention but nevertheless an intention to give the property outright to charity, and the property did not pass as on an intestacy). Each of these cases concerned a gift of residue. See also cases on surplus income (see PARAS 131–135); and cases on outright gifts in relation to subsequent failure (see PARA 173).
4 *Re Stanford, Cambridge University v A-G* [1924] 1 Ch 73.

(iii) Subsequent Failure

173. Outright gift. A donor may give the whole interest in the property to charity or only an interest of limited duration[1]. Whether or not the gift is outright is a matter of construction[2]. If it is shown that the donor intended to part with his whole interest in the property, and therefore to make an outright gift, the question of general charitable intention is irrelevant[3]. A charity once established does not die and its property, being irrevocably devoted to charity, is applied for other charitable purposes[4]. Thus property given outright by will or inter vivos[5] to a charitable institution[6] or for charitable purposes[7] which vests effectively in charity does not fall into residue if, later, the institution closes[8] or the purposes become impracticable[9].

1 As to gifts of limited duration see PARA 174.
2 See also PARA 174 note 2.
3 *Re Wokingham Fire Brigade Trusts, Martin v Hawkins* [1951] Ch 373, [1951] 1 All ER 454 (approved in *Re Ulverston and District New Hospital Building Trusts, Birkett v Barrow and Furness Hospital Management Committee* [1956] Ch 622, [1956] 3 All ER 164, CA); *Re British School of Egyptian Archaeology, Murray v Public Trustee* [1954] 1 All ER 887, [1954] 1 WLR 546. See also *Campbell v Liverpool Corpn* (1870) LR 9 Eq 579; *Re St Pancras Burial Ground* (1866) LR 3 Eq 173; *Wallis v Solicitor-General for New Zealand* [1903] AC 173, PC. The same is true in Scots law: *Anderson's Trustees v Scott* 1914 SC 942, Ct of Sess; *Davidson's Trustees v Arnott* 1951 SC 42, Ct of Sess. In some cases of subsequent failure, the court has considered the question of general charitable intention (*Re Welsh Hospital (Netley) Fund, Thomas v A-G* [1921] 1 Ch 655; *Re North Devon and West Somerset Relief Fund Trusts, Hylton v Wright* [1953] 2 All ER 1032, [1953] 1 WLR 1260; *Re British School of Egyptian Archaeology, Murray v Public Trustee* above, although as to this, see *Re Ulverston and District New Hospital*

Building Trusts above), but there seem to be no cases of gifts by will in which this has been considered relevant, apart from the special category of cases on capital surplus (see *Re Monk, Giffen v Wedd* [1927] 2 Ch 197, CA; and PARA 172). There are possibly ambiguous observations in *Re Cunningham, Dulcken v Cunningham* [1914] 1 Ch 427; *Incorporated Society v Price* (1844) 1 Jo & Lat 498; *Lyons Corpn v Advocate-General of Bengal* (1876) 1 App Cas 91, PC, although see the same case at 111 per Sir Montague E Smith ('an absolute charitable gift, capable of being applied cy-près').

4 Cf *National Anti-Vivisection Society v IRC* [1948] AC 31 at 74, [1947] 2 All ER 217 at 238, HL, per Lord Simonds.

5 In theory there is no difference between gifts inter vivos and gifts by will, but the principle established by *Re Slevin, Slevin v Hepburn* [1891] 2 Ch 236, CA, is not easy to apply to gifts inter vivos: see *Re British School of Egyptian Archaeology, Murray v Public Trustee* [1954] 1 All ER 887 at 891, [1954] 1 WLR 546 at 552 per Harman J.

6 *Re Slevin, Slevin v Hepburn* [1891] 2 Ch 236, CA; *Re Soley, Grover v Drapers' Co* (1900) 17 TLR 118.

7 *Re Geikie, Robson v Paterson* (1911) 27 TLR 484; *Re Moon's Will Trusts, Foale v Gillians* [1948] 1 All ER 300; *Re Wright, Blizard v Lockhart* [1954] Ch 347, [1954] 2 All ER 98, CA.

8 See the cases mentioned in note 6.

9 See the cases mentioned in note 7.

174. Gift of limited duration. If a gift is only for a specific charitable purpose and is limited to that purpose, and the donor parts with his interest in the property only to the extent necessary for the achievement of that purpose, a subsequent failure of that purpose brings to an end the charity's interest in the property given, so that what remains of it is held upon resulting trust for the donor or falls into residue[1]. The question is one of the construction of the gift and may, therefore, turn only on the drafting[2]. In the cases in which a limited gift has been found, there has generally been an express condition or direction relating to failure of the purpose[3], and the efficacy of that direction has depended also on its validity as regards the rule against perpetuities[4]. However, the limited intention may perhaps be inferred from the circumstances of the gift[5].

1 The possibility of such cases was recognised in *Re Slevin, Slevin v Hepburn* [1891] 2 Ch 236 at 239, CA, per Kay LJ.

2 Cf *Re Peel's Release* [1921] 2 Ch 218 (gift to be used 'for ever thereafter' for a charitable purpose with a reverter condition if it should cease to be so used: held to be an initial outright gift to charity, subject to gift over which was void for remoteness) with *Re Cooper's Conveyance Trusts, Crewdson v Bagot* [1956] 3 All ER 28, [1956] 1 WLR 1096 (conveyance on trust for a charitable purpose 'and for no other purpose whatsoever' with provision as to the event of a failure of the purpose: held to be only a limited gift to charity, which reverted, on failure of the purpose, to the grantor's heirs). See also *Bath and Wells Diocesan Board of Finance v Jenkinson* (2000) Times, 6 September, [2000] All ER (D) 1142.

3 *Re Randell, Randell v Dixon* (1888) 38 ChD 213 (gift to endure so long as sittings in a particular church were free from pew-rents); *Re Blunt's Trusts, Wigan v Clinch* [1904] 2 Ch 767 (annuity for support of a school so long as it was carried on the trusts of its original trust deed); *Re Cooper's Conveyance Trusts, Crewdson v Bagot* [1956] 3 All ER 28, [1956] 1 WLR 1096. See also *Christ's Hospital v Grainger* (1849) 1 Mac & G 460; *Re Hanbey's Will Trusts, Cutlers' Co v President and Governors of Christ's Hospital, London* [1956] Ch 264, [1955] 3 All ER 874. Cf gifts of land as sites for schools subject to reverter under the School Sites Acts, eg *Bankes v Salisbury Diocesan Council of Education Inc* [1960] Ch 631, [1960] 2 All ER 372; and see EDUCATION vol 36 (2011) PARA 1541.

4 See *Re Bowen, Lloyd Phillips v Davis* [1893] 2 Ch 491; *Re Peel's Release* [1921] 2 Ch 218; *Re Talbot, Jubb v Sheard* [1933] Ch 895. As to the rule against perpetuities see PARA 142. As to the application of the rule against perpetuities to gifts of this kind see PARA 144.

5 *Gibson v South American Stores (Gath and Chaves) Ltd* [1950] Ch 177, [1949] 2 All ER 985, CA (revsg on this point [1949] Ch 572, [1949] 2 All ER 18). Although it was there said that there was no general charitable intention, the court appears to have held also that there was only a limited gift in the sense indicated above: see *Gibson v South American Stores (Gath and Chaves) Ltd*, CA, above at 201 and at 998–999 per Lord Evershed MR. The presence of a power of revocation may have had the same effect as the express gift over in the cases cited in

note 3. *Burgess' Trustees v Crawford* 1912 SC 387, Ct of Sess, cannot now be regarded as good authority in England, in the light of *Re Wright, Blizard v Lockhart* [1954] Ch 347, [1954] 2 All ER 98, CA.

(iv) Failure of Public Appeals for Charitable Purposes

175. Types of failure. The question of the failure of a charitable purpose frequently has to be considered in relation to property given by the public in different ways in response to an appeal; the appeal may be for a temporary purpose which requires less money than is given for it[1], or it may be for a purpose which cannot be achieved at all because of the lack of money subscribed[2].

Strictly speaking, it may be that where money is subscribed over a period of time and only at the end of the period does it become clear that the purpose is impracticable, the case is one of subsequent failure, for it could not have been said at the moment of each gift that there was no reasonable prospect that the purpose would at some future time be practicable[3]; but in practice such cases are treated as cases of initial failure[4], or of gifts upon a condition that the purpose be found practicable[5].

Furthermore, the courts do not always make a distinction between cases of initial failure in this sense and context and cases where a surplus is left after satisfying the objects of the appeal[6]. The cases establish that different considerations apply to property received from different sources, and this has been partly recognised and partly modified by statute[7].

Donations given via a website to be held for distribution to various charitable purposes give rise to a trust, and if the funds held by the administering body are frozen following intervention by the Charity Commission, there will be a distribution between the various purposes for which the fund was established[8].

1 *Re Hartley Colliery Accident Relief Fund, Plummer v Jordan* (1908) 102 LT 165n; *Re Welsh Hospital (Netley) Fund, Thomas v A-G* [1921] 1 Ch 655; *Re North Devon and West Somerset Relief Fund Trusts, Hylton v Wright* [1953] 2 All ER 1032, [1953] 1 WLR 1260 (the Lynmouth flood disaster).

2 *Re Ulverston and District New Hospital Building Trusts, Birkett v Barrow and Furness Hospital Management Committee* [1956] Ch 622, [1956] 3 All ER 164, CA; *Re Hillier, Hillier v A-G* [1954] 2 All ER 59, [1954] 1 WLR 700, CA.

3 See the form of inquiry ordered in *Re White's Will Trusts, Barrow v Gillard* [1955] Ch 188, [1954] 2 All ER 620; and PARA 167.

4 Eg in the cases cited in note 2. The distinction which is sometimes made is between the case in which the purpose is never capable of achievement at all, and that in which the question arises after the purpose has to some extent been achieved: see *Re Ulverston and District New Hospital Building Trusts, Birkett v Barrow and Furness Hospital Management Committee* [1956] Ch 622 at 635–636, [1956] 3 All ER 164 at 171, CA, per Jenkins LJ. As to initial failure see PARAS 167–172.

5 *Re London University Medical Sciences Institute Fund, Fowler v A-G* [1909] 2 Ch 1, CA; see also PARA 136.

6 Eg in *Re North Devon and West Somerset Relief Fund Trusts, Hylton v Wright* [1953] 2 All ER 1032, [1953] 1 WLR 1260.

7 See the Charities Act 2011 ss 63–66; and PARAS 176–178.

8 See *Charity Commission for England and Wales v Framjee* [2014] EWHC 2507 (Ch), (2014) 17 ITELR 271, [2014] All ER (D) 287 (Jul) (the Dove Trust). As to the power of the Charity Commission to protect charities from mismanagement see PARA 567.

176. General or limited purpose: anonymous gifts. If the circumstances of the gift are such that a general charitable intention[1] may be found, the failure of the purpose will not cause a failure of the gift, whether it is initially impracticable[2] or, a fortiori, an unapplied surplus is left[3].

However, if the purpose of the appeal was only a limited charitable purpose and that purpose failed, it had been established that anonymous gifts and money collected by way of whist drives, raffles and similar activities were devoted irrevocably to charity[4], and this was confirmed by statute[5].

Property given for specific charitable purposes[6] which fail is applicable cy-près[7] as if given for charitable purposes generally, where it belongs to a donor[8] who cannot be identified[9]. Property is conclusively presumed, without any advertisement or inquiry, to belong to donors who cannot be identified, in so far as it consists[10]: of (1) the proceeds of cash collections made by means of collecting boxes or by other means not adapted for distinguishing one gift from another[11]; or (2) the proceeds of any lottery, competition, entertainment, sale or similar money-raising activity, after allowing for property given to provide prizes or articles for sale or otherwise to enable the activity to be undertaken[12].

1 As to general charitable intention see PARA 168 et seq.
2 *Re Hillier, Hillier v A-G* [1954] 2 All ER 59, [1954] 1 WLR 700, CA.
3 *Re North Devon and West Somerset Relief Fund Trusts, Hylton v Wright* [1953] 2 All ER 1032, [1953] 1 WLR 1260.
4 See *Re Hillier, Hillier v A-G* [1953] 2 All ER 1547, [1954] 1 WLR 9; and compare the non-charity case *Re West Sussex Constabulary's Widows, Children and Benevolent (1930) Fund Trusts, Barnett v Ketteringham* [1971] Ch 1, [1970] 1 All ER 544 (contributions by way of raffles etc are made outright, for the relationship is one of contract not of trust; anonymous gifts are presumed to be given outright, for it would be absurd to impute any other intention to the donors; both therefore became bona vacantia).
5 See the Charities Act 2011 s 64(1); and the text to notes 6–12.
6 As to the meaning of 'charitable purposes' see PARA 2.
7 As to cy-près schemes see PARA 209 et seq.
8 For these purposes, unless the context otherwise requires, references to 'donor' include persons claiming through or under the original donor: Charities Act 2011 s 66(2)(a), (3).
9 See the Charities Act 2011 s 63(1)(a); and PARA 177.
10 Charities Act 2011 s 64(1). See PARA 177.
11 Charities Act 2011 s 64(1)(a).
12 Charities Act 2011 s 64(1)(b).

177. Limited purpose: gifts irrevocable or resulting trust. It was sometimes held that, where identifiable donors could be presumed to have made outright gifts, the gift might not fail even though the particular purpose of the gift had failed[1]. This principle has been given some statutory recognition. Where property given[2] for specific charitable purposes[3] which fail[4] belongs to a donor[5] who has executed in the prescribed form[6] a disclaimer of his right to have the property returned[7], it is applicable cy-près as if given for charitable purposes generally[8].

Property given for specific charitable purposes which fail is applicable cy-près as if given for charitable purposes generally where it belongs to a donor who after the prescribed advertisements[9] and inquiries have been published and made, and the prescribed period beginning with the publication of those advertisements has expired, cannot be identified or cannot be found[10]. Where the prescribed advertisements and inquiries have been published and made by or on behalf of trustees with respect to any such property, the trustees are not liable to any person in respect of the property if no claim by him to be interested in it is received by them before the expiry of the prescribed period[11]. The court[12] or the Charity Commission may by order direct certain property[13] be treated, without any advertisement or inquiry, as belonging to donors who cannot be identified where it appears to the court or the Commission either[14]: (1) that it would be unreasonable, having regard to the amounts likely to be returned to the donors, to incur expense with a view to returning the property[15]; or (2) that it would be unreasonable, having regard to the nature, circumstances and amounts of the gifts, and to the lapse of time since the gifts were made, for the donors to expect the property to be returned[16].

The following applies where a person has given property[17] for specific charitable purposes[18] which fail[19] and the property is given in response to a solicitation[20] which is:

(a) made for specific charitable purposes[21]; and
(b) accompanied by a statement to the effect that property given in response to it will, in the event of those purposes failing, be applicable cy-près as if given for charitable purposes generally, unless the donor makes a relevant declaration[22] at the time of making the gift[23].

Where the donor has not made a relevant declaration the property is applicable cy-près as if given for charitable purposes generally[24] by a donor[25] who has executed a disclaimer in the prescribed form of his right to have the property returned[26].

However where the donor has made a relevant declaration[27], the trustees holding the property must take the prescribed[28] steps for the purpose of informing the donor of the failure of the purposes[29], inquiring whether he wishes to request the return of the property (or a sum equal to its value)[30], and if within the prescribed period he makes such a request, returning the property (or such a sum) to him[31]. If those trustees have taken all appropriate prescribed steps but they have failed to find the donor[32] or the donor does not within the prescribed period request the return of the property (or a sum equal to its value)[33], the property is applicable cy-près as if given for charitable purposes generally[34] by a donor[35] who has executed a disclaimer in the prescribed form of his right to have the property returned[36].

Subject to the above statutory provisions, property given for specific charitable purposes which fail from the first with no general charitable intention, so far as it was given by identifiable donors, is held upon resulting trust for them[37] rateably in the proportion that each donor's gift bore to the whole sum given[38].

1 *Re Dover's Battle of Britain Memorial Hospital Fund* (1955) Times, 29 June. But in so far as this case depended on assuming that all donors gave on the same terms, it must be read in the light of *Re Ulverston and District New Hospital Building Trusts, Birkett v Barrow and Furness Hospital Management Committee* [1956] Ch 622, [1956] 3 All ER 164, CA. See also *Re British School of Egyptian Archaeology, Murray v Public Trustee* [1954] 1 All ER 887, [1954] 1 WLR 546; *Munster and Leinster Bank v A-G* (1954) 91 ILT 34.

2 For these purposes, unless the context otherwise requires, references to 'property given' include property for the time being representing property originally given or property derived from it: Charities Act 2011 s 66(2)(b), (3).

3 As to the meaning of 'charitable purpose' see PARA 2.

4 For these purposes, a charitable purpose is deemed to 'fail' where any difficulty in applying property to those purposes makes that property or the part not applicable cy-près available to be returned to the donors: Charities Act 2011 s 66(1). As to cy-près schemes see PARA 209 et seq.

5 As to the meaning of 'donor' see PARA 176 note 8.

6 For these purposes, 'prescribed' means prescribed by regulations made by the Charity Commission, which it must publish in such manner as it thinks fit: Charities Act 2011 s 66(4), (5). As to the Charity Commission see PARAS 543–578. Regulations of the Charity Commission are not made by statutory instrument, but are published by the Commission. For the regulations applicable under s 66(4) see the Charities (Failed Appeals) Regulations 2008 (available, at the date at which this volume states the law, on the government website).

7 A donor who disclaims is deemed to have parted with all his interest at the time the gift was made: see the Charities Act 2011 s 63(1)(b), (3); and note 19.

8 Charities Act 2011 s 63(1)(b). Section 63 applies to property notwithstanding that it was so given before the commencement of the relevant statutory provision: see Sch 8 para 17.

9 As respects the advertisements which are to be published, regulations may make provision as to the form and content of such advertisements as well as the manner in which they are to be published: Charities Act 2011 s 66(6).
10 Charities Act 2011 s 63(1)(a). See PARA 176. See also note 8.
11 Charities Act 2011 s 63(2). The prescribed period referred to in the text is the period mentioned in s 63(1)(a) (see the text and note 11): see s 63(2).
12 'Court' means the High Court and, within the limits of its jurisdiction, any other court in England and Wales having a jurisdiction in respect of charities concurrent (within any limit of area or amount) with that of the High Court, and includes any judge or officer of the court exercising the jurisdiction of the court: Charities Act 2011 s 353(1).
13 Ie property not falling within the Charities Act 2011 s 64(1) (which is so treated without any order or any advertisement or inquiry): see PARA 176 text and notes 10–12. The significance of s 64 is that property falling within that section is applicable cy-près without the expense of advertisements and inquiries.
14 Charities Act 2011 s 64(2).
15 Charities Act 2011 s 64(2)(a).
16 Charities Act 2011 s 64(2)(b).
17 For these purposes, it is irrelevant whether any consideration is or is to be given in return for the property in question: Charities Act 2011 s 65(8)(b).
18 Charities Act 2011 s 65(1)(a), (4)(a), (7)(a).
19 Charities Act 2011 s 65(4)(b), (7)(b).
20 Charities Act 2011 s 65(1)(b), (4)(a). For these purposes 'solicitation' means a solicitation made in any manner and however communicated to the persons to whom it is addressed: s 65(8)(a).
21 Charities Act 2011 s 65(2)(a).
22 A 'relevant declaration' is a declaration in writing by the donor to the effect that, in the event of the specific charitable purposes failing, he wishes the trustees holding the property to give him the opportunity to request the return of the property in question (or a sum equal to its value at the time of the making of the gift): Charities Act 2011 s 65(3).
23 Charities Act 2011 s 65(2)(b). Where any appeal consists of both solicitations that are accompanied by statements within s 65(2)(b) and solicitations that are not so accompanied, a person giving property as a result of the appeal is to be taken to have responded to the former solicitations and not the latter, unless he proves otherwise: s 65(8)(c).
24 Ie the Charities Act 2011 s 14(1) applies.
25 Ie a donor within the Charities Act 2011 s 63(1)(b).
26 See the Charities Act 2011 s 65(7).
27 See the Charities Act 2011 s 65(4)(c).
28 See note 6.
29 Charities Act 2011 s 65(5)(a).
30 Charities Act 2011 s 65(5)(b).
31 Charities Act 2011 s 65(5)(c).
32 Charities Act 2011 s 65(6)(a).
33 Charities Act 2011 s 65(6)(b).
34 Ie the Charities Act 2011 s 63(1) applies.
35 Ie a donor within the Charities Act 2011 s 63(1)(b).
36 Charities Act 2011 s 65(6).
37 *Re Henry Wood National Memorial Trust, Armstrong v Moiseiwitsch* (1965) 109 Sol Jo 876.
38 *Re British Red Cross Balkan Fund, British Red Cross Society v Johnson* [1914] 2 Ch 419. The rule in *Clayton's Case* (1816) 1 Mer 572 (see **EQUITABLE JURISDICTION** vol 47 (2014) PARA 241) does not apply to the fund that is left for distribution. Where property is applied cy-près by the Charities Act 2011 s 63, the donor is deemed to have parted with all his interest at the time when the gift was made; but where property is so applied as belonging to donors who cannot be identified or cannot be found, and is not so applied by virtue s 64 (see PARA 176): (1) the scheme must specify the total amount of that property; and (2) the donor of any part of that amount is entitled, if he makes a claim not later than six months after the date on which the scheme is made, to recover from the charity for which the property is applied a sum equal to that part, less any expenses properly incurred by the charity trustees after that date in connection with claims relating to his gift; and (3) the scheme may include directions as to the provision to be made for meeting any such claim: s 63(4). Where:
    (a) any sum is, in accordance with any such directions, set aside for meeting any such claims (s 63(6)(a)); but
    (b) the aggregate amount of any such claims actually made exceeds the relevant amount (s 63(6)(b)),

then, if the Charity Commission so directs, each of the donors in question is entitled only to such proportion of the relevant amount as the amount of his claim bears to the aggregate amount referred to in head (b) above: s 63(7). For these purposes 'relevant amount' means the amount of the sum so set aside after deduction of any expenses properly incurred by the charity trustees in connection with claims relating to the donors' gifts: s 63(6). As to the meaning of 'charity' see PARA 1. As to the meaning of 'charity trustees' see PARA 255. As to the Charity Commission see PARAS 543–578. As to directions given by the Commission see PARA 554. As to schemes see PARA 179 et seq.

178. Cy-près application on subsequent failure. Independently of the statutory provisions[1], where property has been given in response to a public appeal and a surplus was left after the purposes had been carried out so far as possible, the property has generally been held to be applicable cy-près[2], even without regard to the question of general charitable intention[3]. In any case of subsequent failure in which, under the general law, the surplus assets are not applicable cy-près[4], the statutory provisions would now operate to make the surplus applicable cy-près so far as it belongs to unidentifiable donors or donors who have disclaimed[5].

1 Ie the Charities Act 2011 ss 63–66: see PARAS 176–177.

2 *Re Hartley Colliery Accident Relief Fund, Plummer v Jordan* (1908) 102 LT 165n; *Re Welsh Hospital (Netley) Fund, Thomas v A-G* [1921] 1 Ch 655; *Re North Devon and West Somerset Relief Fund Trusts, Hylton v Wright* [1953] 2 All ER 1032, [1953] 1 WLR 1260.

3 *Re Wokingham Fire Brigade Trusts, Martin v Hawkins* [1951] Ch 373, [1951] 1 All ER 454, approved in *Re Ulverston and District New Hospital Building Trusts, Birkett v Barrow and Furness Hospital Management Committee* [1956] Ch 622, [1956] 3 All ER 164, CA, where Jenkins LJ said that the question of general charitable intention could also have been ignored in *Re North Devon and West Somerset Relief Fund Trusts, Hylton v Wright* [1953] 2 All ER 1032, [1953] 1 WLR 1260. See also *Re British School of Egyptian Archaeology, Murray v Public Trustee* [1954] 1 All ER 887 at 892, [1954] 1 WLR 546 at 553, where Harman J compared the questions of general charitable intention and out and out gift to charity. The only case in which such a surplus after subsequent failure has been held on resulting trust appears to be *Re British Red Cross Balkan Fund, British Red Cross Society v Johnson* [1914] 2 Ch 419; it is there stated to have been admitted, but the Attorney General was not a party and the concession may not have been correctly made or binding on him. As to cy-près schemes see PARA 209 et seq. As to general charitable intention see PARA 168 et seq. As to the Attorney General see PARAS 589, 596, 605 et seq; and **CONSTITUTIONAL AND ADMINISTRATIVE LAW** vol 20 (2014) PARA 273 et seq.

4 Alternatively, where they do not pass as bona vacantia; the distinction is academic, but is adverted to in *Re Hillier, Hillier v A-G* [1953] 2 All ER 1547, [1954] 1 WLR 9, and in *Re Ulverston and District New Hospital Building Trusts, Birkett v Barrow and Furness Hospital Management Committee* [1956] Ch 622, [1956] 3 All ER 164, CA. For the cases in which property reverts to the donor on a subsequent failure of the charitable purposes see PARA 174.

5 The provisions of the Charities Act 2011 s 64(2), 66(1) (see PARA 177) indicate that the provision applies to subsequent as well as to initial failure.

4. SCHEMES AND THE CY-PRÈS DOCTRINE

(1) SCHEMES

(i) Direction of Schemes

179. Jurisdiction. When it is necessary to define the objects or regulate the mode of administration of a charity, a scheme is usually directed either by the court[1], the Charity Commission[2] or the Tribunal[3]. Where, however, there is a gift to charity generally, without the interposition of any trust, and it is necessary to apply the gift to some specific charitable purposes, the application is directed by the Attorney General, to whom the power of the Crown to dispose of charitable gifts under the sign manual has been delegated[4].

1 See PARA 183 et seq.
2 See PARA 189 et seq. As to the Charity Commission see PARAS 543–578.
3 As to the Tribunal see PARA 579 et seq.
4 See PARA 513. As to the Attorney General see PARAS 589, 596, 605 et seq; and CONSTITUTIONAL AND ADMINISTRATIVE LAW vol 20 (2014) PARA 273 et seq.

180. General principles for direction of schemes. A scheme is the method generally employed by the court in administering a charitable trust and is not necessarily, or generally, a scheme for the application of the fund cy-près[1]. It may be used to give effect to the donor's intention, for example by dealing not only with the method of administration but also with the substance of the trust, and by defining it[2]. A scheme will be directed where the trusts of the instrument of foundation are ambiguous or insufficient, or where no particular objects are defined[3], or where there are no trustees, or the trustees are dead[4] or refuse to act[5], or where there has been an increase in the revenue of the charity[6], or the persons managing the charity have misapplied its property[7], or where the charity's investment powers have become inadequate in changed economic circumstances[8], or where a legacy to a charity is to be confined to a particular part of its activities[9], or where for any other reason it is thought expedient to regulate the administration of the charity[10], or to remove or modify conditions or directions imposed in the trust[11].

Schemes may be directed even where there is an unlimited discretion as to distribution left to trustees[12], but in such a case the scheme is framed as far as possible to meet the trustees' wishes[13].

Where legacies[14] or annual sums[15] are given to be distributed in charity at the discretion of private individuals or public institutions, and no permanent trust is intended, schemes for the application of the money are not essential, though in many cases they have been directed by the court[16].

A scheme is generally necessary on any application of a charitable fund cy-près[17], unless the trust is altered only in detail[18].

Under a scheme sanctioned by the court containing general terms without any reference to any foreign country, a charity must be administered and the trusts of the scheme carried into effect within the jurisdiction[19].

A scheme may confer upon the trustees or governors of the charity power to alter some of its provisions[20].

1 *Re Robinson, Besant v German Reich* [1931] 2 Ch 122 at 128 per Maugham J. As to the cy-près doctrine see PARA 209 et seq.

2 *Re Gott, Glazebrook v Leeds University* [1944] Ch 193, [1944] 1 All ER 293.

3 *A-G v Clarke* (1762) Amb 422; *Re White, White v White* [1893] 2 Ch 41, CA. See *Re Mason's Orphanage and London and North-Western Rly Co* (1895) 65 LJCh 32 at 34 per Stirling J (on appeal [1896] 1 Ch 596, CA); and PARA 209.

4 *Moggridge v Thackwell* (1803) 7 Ves 36 (affd (1807) 13 Ves 416, HL); *A-G v Gladstone* (1842) 13 Sim 7; *Re Stanes' Will, Re Trustee Relief Act* (1853) 21 LTOS 261. As to the failure of trustees see PARA 207.

5 *Reeve v A-G* (1843) 3 Hare 191; and see PARA 207.

6 Eg *A-G v Caius College* (1837) 2 Keen 150; *A-G v Warden etc of Louth Free School* (1851) 14 Beav 201; *Re Campden Charities* (1881) 18 ChD 310, CA.

7 *A-G v Coopers' Co* (1812) 19 Ves 187.

8 *Re Royal Society's Charitable Trusts* [1956] Ch 87, [1955] 3 All ER 14, where the court's functions in relation to administrative schemes are considered; *Steel v Wellcome Custodian Trustees Ltd* [1988] 1 WLR 167 (exceptional case where foundation of scheme was a perfectly general power to apply the fund in the acquisition of any property whatsoever as if the trustees were absolutely and beneficially entitled). See also *Re Shipwrecked Fishermen and Mariners' Royal Benevolent Society Charity* [1959] Ch 220, [1958] 3 All ER 465; *Re Royal Naval and Royal Marine Children's Homes, Portsmouth, Lloyds Bank Ltd v A-G* [1959] 2 All ER 716n, [1959] 1 WLR 755; *Re University of London Charitable Trusts* [1964] Ch 282, [1963] 3 All ER 859. As to the investment powers of charities generally and the power to make common investment schemes see PARAS 423, 426.

9 *Re Spence, Ogden v Shackleton* [1979] Ch 483, sub nom *Re Spence's Will Trusts, Ogden v Shackleton* [1978] 3 All ER 92.

10 See *A-G v St Olave's Grammar School, Southwark* (1837) Coop Pr Cas 267; *A-G v Dedham School* (1857) 23 Beav 350; *Re Forbes, Forbes v Forbes* (1910) 27 TLR 27.

11 *Re Robinson, Wright v Tugwell* [1923] 2 Ch 332 (removing 'abiding' condition that a black gown should be worn in the pulpit); *Re Dominion Students' Hall Trust* [1947] Ch 183 (removing colour bar from trust for Dominion students); *Re Lysaght, Hill v Royal College of Surgeons* [1966] Ch 191, [1965] 2 All ER 888 (removing provision for religious discrimination); *Re Woodhams, Lloyds Bank Ltd v London College of Music* [1981] 1 All ER 202, [1981] 1 WLR 493 (modifying restrictions on beneficiaries); *Re JW Laing Trust, Steward's Co Ltd v A-G* [1984] Ch 143, [1984] 1 All ER 50 (obligation to distribute whole of capital and income within ten years of settlor's death removed where trust fund set up in 1922 with £15,000 and worth £24m at time of application); *Re Stewart's Will Trusts* [1983] NI 283.

12 *A-G v Stepney* (1804) 10 Ves 22; *Waldo v Caley* (1809) 16 Ves 206 at 211 per Grant MR; *Jemmit v Verril* (1826) Amb 585n; *Barclay v Maskelyne* (1858) 32 LTOS 205; *Re Hurley, Nichols v Pargiter* (1900) 17 TLR 115; and cf *Re Barnett* (1860) 29 LJCh 871; *Dick v Audsley* [1908] AC 347 at 351, HL, per Lord Loreburn LC.

13 *Bennett v Honywood* (1772) Amb 708 at 710 per Lord Apsley LC; *A-G v Gaskell* (1831) 9 LJOS Ch 188; *Re Delmar Charitable Trust* [1897] 2 Ch 163 at 168 per Stirling J.

14 *A-G v Glegg* (1738) Amb 584; *Johnston v Swann* (1818) 3 Madd 457; *Re Barnett* (1860) 29 LJCh 871; *Re Lea, Lea v Cooke* (1887) 34 ChD 528; and see *Re Garrard, Gordon v Craigie* [1907] 1 Ch 382.

15 *Horde v Earl of Suffolk* (1833) 2 My & K 59. See also *Waldo v Caley* (1809) 16 Ves 206; *Powerscourt v Powerscourt* (1824) 1 Mol 616; *Shrewsbury v Hornby* (1846) 5 Hare 406; *Mahon v Savage* (1803) 1 Sch & Lef 111; *Re Lea, Lea v Cooke* (1887) 34 ChD 528.

16 *A-G v Doyley* (1735) 7 Ves 58n; *A-G v Stepney* (1804) 10 Ves 22; *Paice v Archbishop of Canterbury* (1807) 14 Ves 364; *Baker v Sutton* (1836) 1 Keen 224; *Pocock v A-G* (1876) 3 ChD 342, CA; *Re Hurley, Nichols v Pargiter* (1900) 17 TLR 115.

17 *Martin v Maugham* (1844) 14 Sim 230; *Biscoe v Jackson* (1887) 35 ChD 460, CA; *Re Bradwell, Goode v Board of Trustees for Methodist Church Purposes* [1952] Ch 575, [1952] 2 All ER 286.

18 *Re Richardson, Shuldham v Royal National Lifeboat Institution* (1887) 56 LJCh 784.

19 *Re Mirrlees' Charity, Mitchell v A-G* [1910] 1 Ch 163.

20 *Re Jewish Orphanage Endowment Trusts, Sebag-Montefiore v Rothschild Executor and Trustee Co* [1960] 1 All ER 764, [1960] 1 WLR 344.

181. Where a scheme is not required. Legacies to or for the benefit of established institutions, whether incorporated[1] or not[2], or to their presidents[3], trustees, treasurers or officers[4], as part of their general funds or upon similar trusts to those upon which the general funds are held, may be paid without a scheme being directed[5]. A gift to an individual engaged in a charitable activity for the purposes of that activity may also be paid to that individual without a scheme[6]. Similarly, unless the Attorney General objects, a gift for the purposes of an institution which has ceased to exist may be paid, without a formal scheme, to another institution carrying on the same work[7]; and a legacy may be paid to a trustee without a scheme upon an undertaking to apply the legacy to the charitable purposes of the bequest and render accounts to the Attorney General[8].

On the same principle, legacies for the benefit of a parish church[9], or a Roman Catholic[10] or dissenters'[11] chapel, may be paid to the churchwardens and trustees respectively.

A scheme is not necessary in the case of a gift to an institution for its general purposes but subject to special conditions, as, for example, that certain lifeboats should be maintained[12], or that a particular person should have rights of nomination to a hospital[13].

1 *Emery v Hill* (1826) 1 Russ 112; *Society for the Propagation of the Gospel v A-G* (1826) 3 Russ 142; *A-G v Christ's Hospital* (1830) 1 Russ & M 626; *Re Richardson, Shuldham v Royal National Lifeboat Institution* (1887) 56 LJCh 784.

2 *Re M'Auliffe's Goods* [1895] P 290. See also *Re Lalor's Goods* (1901) 85 LT 643.

3 *Walsh v Gladstone* (1843) 1 Ph 290 (president of a college).

4 *Wellbeloved v Jones* (1822) 1 Sim & St 40 at 43 per Leach V-C; *Emery v Hill* (1826) 1 Russ 112.

5 See also *Minet v Vulliamy* (1819) cited in 1 Russ 113n; *Carter v Green* (1857) 3 K & J 591; and *Re Surfleet's Estate, Rawlings v Smith* (1911) 105 LT 582 (where the gifts were to institutions whose objects included the purchase of land); *Makeown v Ardagh* (1876) IR 10 Eq 445. Cf *Wellbeloved v Jones* (1822) 1 Sim & St 40; *Sons of the Clergy Corpn v Mose* (1839) 9 Sim 610 (where the gifts were on trusts not identical with the purposes of the institutions).

6 *Re Rees, Jones v Evans* [1920] 2 Ch 59.

7 See eg *Re Finger's Will Trusts, Turner v Ministry of Health* [1972] Ch 286, [1971] 3 All ER 1050. As to the Attorney General see PARAS 589, 596, 605 et seq; and CONSTITUTIONAL AND ADMINISTRATIVE LAW vol 20 (2014) PARA 273 et seq.

8 *Re Reddish, Penton v Waters* [1934] WN 198. See *Re Wedgwood, Sweet v Cotton* [1914] 2 Ch 245.

9 *A-G v Ruper* (1722) 2 P Wms 125.

10 *De Windt v De Windt* (1854) 23 LJCh 776.

11 *Bunting v Marriott* (1854) 19 Beav 163.

12 *Re Richardson, Shuldham v Royal National Lifeboat Institution* (1887) 56 LJCh 784.

13 *A-G v Christ's Hospital* (1830) 1 Russ & M 626. Cf *Re Lopes, Bence-Jones v Zoological Society of London* [1931] 2 Ch 130, where there was a scheme.

182. Property situated or payable abroad. The court will not direct a scheme to be settled where the charity's property is out of the jurisdiction, or is a fund payable to trustees out of the jurisdiction[1]. In such a case the court may direct an inquiry whether the trust can be carried into effect according to the law of the particular country[2], and may pay the money to the persons selected by the testator as the instruments of his benevolence, if they are proper persons to act as trustees[3], but not otherwise[4], or may appoint new trustees for the purpose[5], or may retain the fund in court and direct payment of the dividends to the persons entrusted by the testator with the application of them[6], or may retain the fund in court to await the result of an application to the foreign court[7], or may give liberty to carry into effect a scheme to be settled by the foreign court[8].

The court may direct a scheme to be settled where trusts, which have been established within the jurisdiction for the endowment of a charitable object out of the jurisdiction, become impracticable but the fund and the trustees are within the jurisdiction[9].

Where a scheme became necessary, for lack of objects, in relation to funds administered by an institution which had become subject to a foreign state, the court refused to allow the institution to continue to administer the trusts[10].

1 Eg in Scotland (*Edinburgh Corpn v Aubery* (1753) Amb 236; *A-G v Lepine* (1818) 2 Swan 181; *Emery v Hill* (1826) 1 Russ 112; *Re Marr's Will Trusts, Walker v A-G* [1936] Ch 671); Switzerland (*Minet v Vulliamy* (1819) cited in 1 Russ 113n); France (*Martin v Paxton* (1824) cited in 1 Russ 116); United States of America (*Society for the Propagation of the Gospel v A-G* (1826) 3 Russ 142; *New v Bonaker* (1867) LR 4 Eq 655); Germany (*Re Robinson, Besant v German Reich* [1931] 2 Ch 122 at 129 per Maugham J). As to foreign charitable purposes see PARAS 57–58.

2 *Thompson v Thompson* (1844) 1 Coll 381 at 394 per Shadwell V-C (Scotland). See *New v Bonaker* (1867) LR 4 Eq 655 (United States of America).

3 *Edinburgh Corpn v Aubery* (1753) Amb 236; *A-G v Lepine* (1818) 2 Swan 181; *Minet v Vulliamy* (1819) cited in 1 Russ 113n; *Martin v Paxton* (1824) cited in 1 Russ 116; *Emery v Hill* (1826) 1 Russ 112; *Collyer v Burnett* (1829) Taml 79; *Mitford v Reynolds* (1842) 1 Ph 185 at 197 per Lord Lyndhurst LC. See also *New v Bonaker* (1867) LR 4 Eq 655; *Lyons Corpn v Advocate-General of Bengal* (1876) 1 App Cas 91, PC.

4 *Lyons Corpn v East India Co* (1836) 1 Moo PCC 175.

5 *A-G v Stephens* (1834) 3 My & K 347. See also *A-G v Fraunces* [1866] WN 280, where a fund given to a school in a parish in the United States of America was directed to be paid to the governors of another school in the same parish, the original school having disappeared.

6 *A-G v Lepine* (1818) 2 Swan 181. See also *A-G v Sturge* (1854) 19 Beav 597, where the official charged by the testator with the distribution of a fund had died, and the court directed payment to be made to the holder of the office for the time being.

7 *Forbes v Forbes* (1854) 18 Beav 552; *Re Fraser, Yeates v Fraser* (1883) 22 ChD 827.

8 *Re Marr's Will Trusts, Walker v A-G* [1936] Ch 671. Cf *Re Lipton's Trustees* 1943 SC 521, Ct of Sess; *Re Neech's Executors* 1947 SC 119, Ct of Sess.

9 *Re Colonial Bishoprics Fund 1841* [1935] Ch 148.

10 *A-G v London Corpn* (1790) 3 Bro CC 171. The charity had been administered in the United States of America, but the founder's will did not confine its scope to America.

(ii) Settlement of Schemes by the Court

183. General jurisdiction and powers. In general the court has jurisdiction in every case to make schemes to regulate the administration of a charity, and, subject to certain restrictions, the Charity Commission has equal concurrent jurisdiction with the court[1].

However, only the court now makes schemes in contentious cases or cases which involve special complexities or difficult question of law or fact[2]. Formerly it was the rule that the court would make a scheme if it became necessary in the course of an administration action or any charitable proceedings[3].

Where the court undertakes the execution of charitable trusts it will not retain the funds under its direct control but will direct a scheme in accordance with which the trustees will administer the funds[4].

The court may make a scheme supplemental to the original trusts and temporary in effect[5] or a scheme effective only until the happening of a certain event[6].

If the original trusts are altered by a scheme, a gift over on alteration or non-compliance with the trusts will not take effect[7].

1 See the Charities Act 2011 ss 69(1), 70(1); and PARA 189. As to the jurisdiction of the court and the Commission in relation to ecclesiastical charities see PARA 196. In most cases an application to the court for a scheme may only be made with the leave of the Commission: see PARA 594. As to the Charity Commission see PARAS 543–578.

2 See the Charities Act 2011 s 70(8); and PARA 189 note 2.

3 See eg *Re Huxtable, Huxtable v Crawfurd* [1902] 2 Ch 793, CA; *Wellbeloved v Jones* (1822) 1 Sim & St 40; *A-G v Haberdashers' Co* (1852) 15 Beav 397. Now it is usual to refer the matter to the Commission under the Charities Act 2011 s 69(3) for it to settle a scheme: see PARA 191.

4 *A-G v Solly* (1835) 5 LJCh 5; *A-G v Haberdashers' Co* (1791) 1 Ves 295; *A-G v Haberdashers' Co* (1852) 15 Beav 397 at 406 per Romilly MR. See *A-G v Governors of Harrow School* (1754) 2 Ves Sen 551; *A-G v Townley* (1829) Shelford's Law of Mortmain 442.

5 See *A-G v Price* (1908) 24 TLR 761; revsd [1912] 1 Ch 667, CA; on appeal sub nom *Price v A-G* [1914] AC 20, HL. Cf *A-G v Edalji* (1907) 97 LT 292.

6 *Re Royal Naval and Royal Marine Children's Homes, Portsmouth, Lloyds Bank Ltd v A-G* [1959] 2 All ER 716n, [1959] 1 WLR 755.

7 *Re Bacon's Charity* (7 December 1878, unreported) per Jessel MR; a report of the case is on the files of the Charity Commission and it is noted at Tudor on Charities (4th Edn, 1906) 187 note (q). See also *Re Parish of Upton Warren* (1833) 1 My & K 410; *Christ's Hospital v Grainger* (1849) 1 Mac & G 460 at 464 per Lord Cottenham LC; *Re Trustees of the Orchard Street Schools* [1878] WN 211; *Re Hanbey's Will Trusts, Cutlers' Co v President and Governors of Christ's Hospital, London* [1956] Ch 264, [1955] 3 All ER 874. Quaere whether the court would make a scheme having the effect of defeating a resulting trust (as distinct from a gift over to another charity) on non-compliance with the trusts and whether, if the event on which the resulting trust was to arise had already happened, there would be jurisdiction to make such a scheme.

184. Schemes in relation to chartered charities. Before 1961 the court and the Charity Commissioners (now the Charity Commission)[1] had only very limited jurisdiction over charities established by royal charter[2], and the appropriate procedure for any substantial alteration was the grant and acceptance of a new charter, although it was doubtful whether this could alter the purposes for which funds already held could be applied, at least in the case of an eleemosynary corporation[3].

Now, however, where a royal charter establishing or regulating a body corporate is amendable by the grant and acceptance of a further charter, a scheme relating to the body corporate or to the administration of property held by the body (including a scheme for the cy-près application[4] of any such property) may be made by the court[5] under the court's jurisdiction with respect to charities notwithstanding that the scheme cannot take effect without the alteration of the charter[6]. The scheme must be so framed that it, or such part of it as cannot take effect without the alteration of the charter, does not purport to come into operation unless or until Her Majesty thinks fit to amend the charter in such manner as will permit the scheme or that part of it to have effect[7].

Where under the court's jurisdiction with respect to charities, or under powers conferred by the Charities Act 2011, a scheme is made with respect to a body corporate, and it appears to Her Majesty expedient, having regard to the scheme, to amend any royal charter relating to that body, Her Majesty may, on the application of that body, amend the charter accordingly by Order in Council in any way in which the charter could be amended by the grant and acceptance of a further charter[8]. Any such Order in Council may be revoked or varied in like manner as the charter it amends[9].

1 As to the Charity Commission see PARAS 543–578.

2 See *Re Whitworth Art Gallery Trusts, Manchester Whitworth Institute v Victoria University of Manchester* [1958] Ch 461, [1958] 1 All ER 176.

3 As to the meaning of 'eleemosynary corporation' see PARA 225.

4 As to cy-près applications see PARA 209 et seq.

5 As to the meaning of 'court' see PARA 177 note 12.

6 Charities Act 2011 s 68(1), (2)(a). The powers conferred by s 68 (which replaces the Charities Act 1993 s 15) have been extensively used: see the *Report of the Charity Commissioners for England and Wales for 1965* (HC Paper (1966–67) no 108) pp 8–9; *Report of the Charity Commissioners for England and Wales for 1967* (HC Paper (1967–68) no 261) pp 15–18.

7 Charities Act 2011 s 68(2)(b).

8 See the Charities Act 2011 s 68(3), (4). See eg the Royal College of Ophthalmologists (Charter Amendment) Order 1998, SI 1998/2552; the Royal College of Physicians (Charter Amendment)

Order 1999, SI 1999/667; the Licensed Victuallers' National Homes (Charter Amendment) Order 2000, SI 2000/1348; the Institution of Chemical Engineers (Charter Amendment) Order 2004, SI 2004/1986.

9 Charities Act 2011 s 68(4).

185. Schemes in relation to certain statutory charities. The court has no inherent jurisdiction to alter such of the trusts of a charity as are established by or by virtue of a statute[1]. However, the Charities Act 2011 provides that the jurisdiction of the court[2] with respect to charities[3] is not to be restricted or excluded in relation to certain classes of charities by the statutes by or under which they are established[4]. The specified classes are as follows:

(1) charities established or regulated by any provision of the Seamen's Fund Winding-up Act 1851[5];
(2) charities established or regulated by schemes under statutory provisions relating to endowed schools and elementary education[6];
(3) fuel allotments[7];
(4) charities established or regulated under any provision of the Municipal Corporations Act 1883 or by any scheme under any such provision[8];
(5) charities regulated by schemes under the London Government Act 1899[9];
(6) charities established or regulated by orders or regulations under certain provisions[10] of the Regimental Charitable Funds Act 1935[11];
(7) parochial charities regulated by the Charities Act 2011[12].

A scheme established for any such charity may modify or supersede in relation to it the provision made by any such enactment or instrument as if made by a scheme of the court, and may also make any such authorised[13] provision[14].

1 *Re Shrewsbury Grammar School* (1849) 1 Mac & G 324 at 333 per Lord Cottenham LC; *A-G v Governors of Christ's Hospital* [1896] 1 Ch 879; *Trustees of the London Parochial Charities v A-G* [1955] 1 All ER 1, [1955] 1 WLR 42. See also *Warren v Clancy* [1898] 1 IR 127, CA; *Re Imprisoned Debtors Discharge Society's Act 1856* (1912) 28 TLR 477, CA. As to the amendment of statutes establishing or regulating charities see also PARA 193.

2 As to the meaning of 'court' see PARA 177 note 12.

3 As to the meaning of 'charity' see PARA 1.

4 See the Charities Act 2011 s 68(5).

5 Charities Act 2011 Sch 5 para 1(a). The Seamen's Fund Winding-up Act 1851 was repealed by the Charities Act 1960 Sch 5 (repealed).

6 Charities Act 2011 Sch 5 para 1(b). The statutory provisions referred to in the text are the Endowed Schools Act 1869 to 1948, the Elementary Education Act 1870 s 75, the Education Act 1973 s 2 (all repealed) and the Education Act 1996 s 554: Charities Act 2011 Sch 5 para 1(b). As to schemes under the Endowed Schools Acts and power to make new provision as to the use of endowments see the Education Act 1996 ss 553–556; and EDUCATION vol 36 (2011) PARAS 1627–1628. As to rights of reverter see PARA 70.

7 Charities Act 2011 Sch 5 para 1(c), which defines 'fuel allotments' as land which under any enactment relating to inclosure or any instrument having an effect under any such enactment, is vested in trustees upon trust that the land or the rents and profits of the land be used for the purpose of providing poor persons with fuel. Notwithstanding anything in the Commons Act 1876 s 19, a scheme for the administration of a fuel allotment may contain certain provisions for the disposal or exchange of the allotment or for its use for any purposes specified in the scheme: see the Charities Act 2011 Sch 5 para 2; and AGRICULTURAL LAND vol 1 (2008) PARA 513. As to other types of allotment under the Inclosure Acts see PARA 195.

8 Charities Act 2011 Sch 5 para 1(d). The relevant provisions of the Municipal Corporations Act 1883 were repealed by the Charities Act 1960 s 39(1), Sch 5 (repealed).

9 Charities Act 2011 Sch 5 para 1(e). The relevant provisions of the London Government Act 1899 have been repealed.

10 Ie the Regimental Charitable Funds Act 1935 s 2: see ARMED FORCES.

11 Charities Act 2011 Sch 5 para 1(f).

12 Charities Act 2011 Sch 5 para 1(g). As to the regulation of parochial charities see ss 298–302 and orders made thereunder: see PARAS 267–269.

13 Ie authorised by the Charities Act 2011 Sch 5: see the text and notes 2–12.

14 Charities Act 2011 s 68(6).

186. Attorney General's consent. The application or consent of the Attorney General is probably necessary to an alteration of a scheme by the court[1]. In a proper case it is his duty to make the necessary application[2].

The court will not, upon the motion of one of the interested parties[3], alter a scheme which it has settled with the approval of the Attorney General.

1 *A-G v Stewart* (1872) LR 14 Eq 17; and see *A-G v Hall* (1875) 3 Seton's Form of Decrees, Judgments and Orders (7th Edn, 1912) 1259. See also *Re Royal Society's Charitable Trusts* [1956] Ch 87, [1955] 3 All ER 14. As to the Attorney General see PARAS 589, 596, 605 et seq; and CONSTITUTIONAL AND ADMINISTRATIVE LAW vol 20 (2014) PARA 273 et seq.

2 *A-G v Bishop of Worcester* (1851) 9 Hare 328 at 360 per Turner V-C.

3 *Re Sekeford's Charity* (1861) 5 LT 488.

187. Alteration of schemes settled by court. A scheme settled by the court for the administration of a charity can be altered by the court if the lapse of time and change of circumstances render it in the interest of the charity that the alteration should be made[1]. Schemes so settled are not altered except upon substantial grounds, and upon clear evidence, not only that the existing scheme does not operate beneficially, but that it can be made to do so consistently with the object of the foundation[2]. A scheme for applying the income of a charity remains in force only until further order or the establishment of a new scheme[3].

If the trusts of a scheme settled by the court are later shown not to be charitable in law, the scheme must be corrected by a further scheme[4]. A scheme making an unfair distribution among the objects of a charity may be altered[5].

1 *A-G v St John's Hospital, Bath* (1865) 1 Ch App 92 at 106 per Turner LJ; *Glasgow College v A-G* (1848) 1 HL Cas 800; and see *A-G v London Corpn* (1790) 3 Bro CC 171; *A-G v Bovill* (1840) 1 Ph 762; *A-G v Rochester Corpn* (1854) 5 De GM & G 797; *Re Hussey's Charities, Cheyne v Apreece, Symons v Delaval* (1861) 7 Jur NS 325 (where a gift to a clergyman for prisoners was divided on the formation of a second prison); *A-G v Hankey* (1867) LR 16 Eq 140n. As to the alteration of a scheme of a charity abroad see *A-G v London Corpn* (1790) 3 Bro CC 171; *Lyons Corpn v Advocate-General of Bengal* (1876) 1 App Cas 91 at 110, PC. As to the procedure for settling schemes see PARAS 619–620.

For special statutory provisions for the alteration of schemes affecting schools see eg the Education Act 1973 ss 1(2), 2 (repealed). Previously the Endowed Schools Acts 1869 to 1948 (repealed) (see PARA 185 note 6) had contained special provisions for the alteration of schemes. As to schemes under the Endowed Schools Acts and power to make new provision as to the use of endowments see the Education Act 1996 ss 553–556; and EDUCATION vol 36 (2011) PARAS 1627–1628. As to rights of reverter see PARA 70.

2 *A-G v Bishop of Worcester* (1851) 9 Hare 328; and see *Re Sekeford's Charity* (1861) 5 LT 488; *A-G v Stewart* (1872) LR 14 Eq 17.

3 *Re Betton's Charity* [1908] 1 Ch 205.

4 See *Vernon v IRC* [1956] 3 All ER 14, [1956] 1 WLR 1169.

5 *A-G v Buller* (1822) Jac 407. Other types of provision which have been altered include those relating to religious instruction (*A-G v St John's Hospital, Bath* (1876) 2 ChD 554), the number of governors (*Re Browne's Hospital v Stamford* (1889) 60 LT 288), and the granting of building leases (*Re Henry Smith's Charity, Hartlepool* (1882) 20 ChD 516, CA).

188. Court's powers where scheme not directed. Where the matter is before the court, and it is not thought necessary to direct a scheme, the court may, as the case requires, refer the apportionment of funds to the master[1], or retain a measure of control by giving any of the parties leave to apply if necessary[2], or order the person applying the fund to account for its distribution[3], or direct payment of the capital into court and payment of the dividends to the person entrusted with their distribution[4].

1 *White v White* (1778) 1 Bro CC 12; *Re Hyde's Trusts* (1873) 22 WR 69.
2 *Waldo v Caley* (1809) 16 Ves 206 at 211 per Grant MR; *Horde v Earl of Suffolk* (1833) 2 My & K 59; *Re Lea, Lea v Cooke* (1887) 34 ChD 528 at 535 per North J.
3 *A-G v Glegg* (1738) Amb 584; *A-G v Governors etc of Sherborne Grammar School* (1854) 18 Beav 256.
4 *M'Coll v Atherton* (1848) 12 Jur 1042. As to where a scheme is not required see PARA 181.

(iii) Settlement of Schemes by the Charity Commission

189. General jurisdiction. The Charity Commission[1] may by order exercise the same jurisdiction and powers as are exercisable by the High Court in charity proceedings for the following purposes[2]: (1) establishing a scheme for the administration of a charity[3]; (2) appointing, discharging or removing a charity trustee[4] or trustee for a charity, or removing an officer or employee[5]; (3) vesting or transferring property, or requiring or entitling any person to call for or make any transfer of property or any payment[6].

In relation to a charity[7] whose gross income does not in the aggregate exceed £500 a year[8], the Commission may exercise its jurisdiction to make schemes on the application of any one or more of the charity trustees or of any person interested in the charity[9] or, if it is a local charity[10], of any two or more inhabitants of the area of the charity[11]. In relation to any other charity, the Commission must not exercise its jurisdiction[12] to make schemes except on the application of the charity[13] or on a reference to it by the court[14] for the purpose[15] or on the application of the Attorney General[16].

Unless the scheme is made under a court order, the Commission must give notice of its intention to act to each of the charity trustees, except any that cannot be found or has no known address in the United Kingdom[17] or who is party or privy to the application for the exercise of the jurisdiction[18].

The Commission does not have jurisdiction to try or determine the title in law or in equity to any property as between a charity or trustee for a charity and a person holding or claiming the property or an interest in it adversely to the charity, or to try or determine any question as to the existence or extent of any charge or trust[19].

1 As to the Charity Commission see PARAS 543–578.
2 Charities Act 2011 s 69(1). The Commission must not exercise its jurisdiction under the Charities Act 2011 s 16 in any case (not referred to it by order of the court) which, by reason of its contentious character, or of any special question of law or of fact which it may involve, or for other reasons, the Commission may consider more fit to be adjudicated on by the court: s 70(8). Mere opposition to a scheme is insufficient to oust the Commission's jurisdiction: *Bartley v Charity Commission for England and Wales* (2014) First-tier Tribunal, General Regulatory Chamber (Charity), 21 July, para 35.

Some of the guidance given to Charity Commission staff is set out in the *Report of the Charity Commissioners for England and Wales for 1989* (HC Paper (1989–90) no 343) paras 73–75. As to the jurisdiction of the courts in relation to charities see PARA 534 et seq.
3 Charities Act 2011 s 69(1)(a). As to the meaning of 'charity' see PARA 1. An appeal against an order by the Commission under s 69(1) lies to the Tribunal at the instance of the Attorney General (in the case of s 69(1)(a)), the charity trustees of the charity to which the order relates or (if a body corporate) the charity itself (in the case of s 69(1)(b)), any person discharged or removed by the order, or any other person who is or may be affected by the order: Charities Act 2011 ss 315(2), 319(1), (2), Sch 6 Table Cols 1, 2. The Tribunal has the power to quash, substitute or amend the order: see Table Col 3. For an example of such a scheme which was quashed in its entirety by the Tribunal see *Thomas v Charity Commission for England and*

Wales (2012) First-tier Tribunal, General Regulatory Chamber (Charity), 19 October. As to the Attorney General see PARAS 589, 596, 605 et seq; and **CONSTITUTIONAL AND ADMINISTRATIVE LAW** vol 20 (2014) PARA 273 et seq.

As to the meaning of 'person who is or may be affected' within the meaning of Sch 6 see PARA 317 note 8.

4 As to the meaning of 'charity trustees' see PARA 255.

5 Charities Act 2011 s 69(1)(b).

6 Charities Act 2011 s 69(1)(c). A person guilty of disobedience to an order of the Commission under s 69 requiring a transfer of property or payment to be called for or made, may on the application of the Commission to the High Court be dealt with as for disobedience to an order of the High Court: see s 336; and PARA 556.

No vesting or transfer of any property in pursuance of any provision of Pt 6 (ss 61–116) operates as a breach of covenant or condition against alienation or gives rise to a forfeiture: s 116.

7 Exempt charities, other than those for whom provisions for increased regulation under the Charities Act 2006 Sch 5 (repealed) were not brought into force prior to the commencement of the Charities Act 2011, are excluded from this provision: see the Charities Act 2011 Sch 9 para 16. As to exempt charities see PARAS 318–324.

8 If the Minister thinks it expedient to do so in consequence of changes in the value of money or with a view to increasing the number of charities in respect of which the Commission may exercise its jurisdiction under the Charities Act 2011 s 69 in accordance with s 70(3), he may by order amend that provision by substituting a different sum for the sum for the time being specified there: s 72. At the date at which this volume states the law no such orders had been made. As to the Minister see PARA 586.

9 As the meaning of 'interested in the charity' see PARA 593 note 4.

10 'Local charity' means, in relation to any area, a charity established for purposes which are by their nature or by the trusts of the charity directed wholly or mainly to the benefit of that area or of part of it: Charities Act 2011 s 293.

11 Charities Act 2011 s 70(3).

12 Charities Act 2011 s 70(2). See, however, PARAS 192, 195.

13 Charities Act 2011 s 70(2)(a). The application must be made by all or a majority of the charity trustees. Once an application has been made, it cannot effectively be withdrawn: *Re Poor's Lands Charity, Bethnal Green* [1891] 3 Ch 400 (decided under previous legislation).

14 Ie on an order of the court under the Charities Act 2011 s 69(3): see PARA 191. As to ecclesiastical charities see also PARA 196.

15 See the Charities Act 2011 s 70(2)(b).

16 Charities Act 2011 s 70(2)(c). Exempt charities are excluded from this provision: see Sch 9 para 16; and note 7.

17 'United Kingdom' means Great Britain and Northern Ireland: Interpretation Act 1978 s 5, Sch 1. 'Great Britain' means England, Scotland and Wales: Union with Scotland Act 1706, preamble art I; Interpretation Act 1978 s 22(1), Sch 2 para 5(a). Neither the Isle of Man nor the Channel Islands are within the United Kingdom. See further **CONSTITUTIONAL AND ADMINISTRATIVE LAW** vol 20 (2014) PARA 3.

18 Charities Act 2011 s 71(1). Notice may be given by post, addressed to the recipient's last known address in the United Kingdom: s 71(2).

19 Charities Act 2011 s 70(1). A transfer of property by virtue of an order under s 69 does not amount to the Commission trying or determining title to property: *Bartlett v Charity Commission for England and Wales* (2014) First-tier Tribunal, General Regulatory Chamber (Charity), 21 July, para 35.

190. Public notice. The Charity Commission[1] may not make any order to establish a scheme for the administration of a charity, or submit such a scheme to the court[2] or the Minister[3] for an order giving it effect, unless before doing so the Commission has complied with the statutory publicity requirements[4].

The statutory publicity requirements are: (1) that the Commission must give public notice[5] of its proposals inviting representations to be made to it within a period specified in the notice[6]; and (2) that in the case of a scheme relating to a local charity (other than an ecclesiastical charity) in a parish or in a community in Wales, the Commission must communicate a draft of the scheme to the parish or community council[7]. The time when any such notice is given or any such communication takes place is to be decided by the Commission[8].

The Commission may determine that either or both of the statutory publicity requirements is or are not to apply in relation to a particular scheme if it is satisfied that by reason of the nature of the scheme, or for any other reason, compliance with the requirement or requirements is unnecessary[9].

Where the Commission gives public notice of any proposals under these provisions, it must take into account any representations made to it within the period specified in the notice[10] and may without further notice proceed with the proposals either without modifications or with such modifications as it thinks desirable[11].

Where the Commission makes an order[12] to establish a scheme for the administration of a charity, a copy of the order must be available, for at least a month after the order is published, for public inspection at all reasonable times[13] at the Commission's office[14] and, if the charity is a local charity, at some convenient place in the area of the charity[15], save where the Commission is satisfied that for any reason it is unnecessary for a copy of the scheme to be available locally[16].

1 As to the Charity Commission see PARAS 543–578.
2 As to the meaning of 'court' see PARA 177 note 12.
3 As to the Minister see PARA 586.
4 Charities Act 2011 s 88(1).
5 'Public notice' is not defined but must contain such particulars of the proposals, or such directions for obtaining information about them, as the Commission thinks sufficient and appropriate, and given in such manner as the Commission thinks sufficient and appropriate: Charities Act 2011 s 88(8).
6 Charities Act 2011 s 88(2)(a).
7 Charities Act 2011 s 88(2)(b). Where a parish has no council, a draft of the scheme must be communicated to the chairman of the parish meeting: s 88(2)(b)(i). In the case of a community that has no council, communication is to the county council or county borough council: s 88(2)(b)(ii). As to the meaning of 'local charity' see PARA 189 note 10. As to the meaning of 'ecclesiastical charity' see PARA 267 note 4.
8 Charities Act 2011 s 88(3).
9 Charities Act 2011 s 88(4).
10 Charities Act 2011 s 88(5)(a).
11 Charities Act 2011 s 88(5)(b).
12 Ie an order under the Charities Act 2011.
13 Charities Act 2011 s 88(6). As to the supply of copies see PARA 307 note 16.
14 Charities Act 2011 s 88(6)(a).
15 Charities Act 2011 s 88(6)(b).
16 Charities Act 2011 s 88(7).

191. Schemes on reference by the court. Where the court[1] directs a scheme for the administration of a charity[2] to be established, it may by order refer the matter to the Charity Commission[3] for it to prepare or settle a scheme in accordance with such directions, if any, as the court sees fit to give[4]. Any such order may provide for the scheme to be put into effect by order of the Commission[5] without any further court order[6].

1 As to the meaning of 'court' see PARA 177 note 12.
2 As to the meaning of 'charity' see PARA 1.
3 As to the Charity Commission see PARAS 543–578.
4 Charities Act 2011 s 69(3)(a).
5 Ie as if prepared under the Charities Act 2011 s 69(1): see PARA 189.
6 Charities Act 2011 s 69(3)(b).

192. Powers on trustees' refusal or inability to apply for scheme. Where the Charity Commission[1] is satisfied with regard to any charity[2], other than an exempt charity[3], that the charity trustees[4] ought in the interests of the charity to apply for a scheme, but have unreasonably refused or neglected to do so, and the Commission has given the charity trustees an opportunity to make representations to them, the Commission may proceed as if an application for a scheme had been made by the charity[5].

The purposes of a charity may not be altered under this provision unless 40 years have elapsed since the date of its foundation[6].

Where a charity cannot apply to the Commission for a scheme by reason of any vacancy among the charity trustees or the absence or incapacity of any of them, but such an application is made by such number of the charity trustees as the Commission considers appropriate in the circumstances of the case, the Commission may nevertheless proceed as if the application were an application made by the charity[7].

1 As to the Charity Commission see PARAS 543–578.
2 As to the meaning of 'charity' see PARA 1.
3 As to exempt charities see PARAS 318–324.
4 As to the meaning of 'charity trustees' see PARA 255.
5 Charities Act 2011 s 70(4), (5)(a).
6 Charities Act 2011 s 70(5)(b).
7 Charities Act 2011 s 70(6).

193. Schemes amending statutory provisions. Where it appears to the Charity Commission[1] that a scheme for the administration of a charity[2] should be established, but also that it is necessary or desirable for the scheme to alter some statutory provision establishing or regulating the charity or to make some other provision which is beyond the Commission's normal powers, or where it appears to the Commission that it is for any reason proper for the scheme to be subject to parliamentary review, it may settle a scheme[3], and effect may be given to it by an order of the Minister[4]. Where the scheme goes beyond the powers otherwise exercisable in altering the provisions of a public general Act, the order may not be made unless the draft is approved by resolution of each House of Parliament[5]. Any provision of a scheme brought into effect under this procedure may be modified or superseded by the court[6] or the Commission as if it were a scheme brought into effect by order of the Commission[7] in the exercise of its ordinary powers[8].

The Commission must not proceed under these provisions without the like application, and the like notice to the charity trustees[9], as would be required if it was proceeding (without an order of the court) under its ordinary jurisdiction[10]; but on any application for a scheme, or in a case where it acts because the charity trustees have unreasonably refused or neglected to act[11], or are unable to do so[12], it may proceed under these provisions or under its ordinary powers[13], as appears to it to be appropriate[14].

1 As to the Charity Commission see PARAS 543–578.
2 As to the meaning of 'charity' see PARA 1.
3 Charities Act 2011 s 73(1).
4 See the Charities Act 2011 s 73(2), (3). As to the Minister see PARA 586. Such orders of the Minister must be made by statutory instrument: see the Charities Act 2011 s 347(1), (2). For examples of orders that have been made see the Charities (The Hundred Acres Charity, Enfield) Order 1974, SI 1974/1839; the Charities (National Trust for Places of Historic Interest or Natural Beauty) Order 1975, SI 1975/1155; the Charities (The Marine Society) Order 1976, SI 1976/147; the Charities (Cheltenham College) Order 1976, SI 1976/1809; the Charities (The

New College of Cobham) Order 1978, SI 1978/1155; the Charities (Booth Charities) Order 1985, SI 1985/1935; the Charities (William Lambe (London) Trust) Order 1986, SI 1986/2003; the Charities (University of Liverpool) Order 1988, SI 1988/1068; the Charities (Borough Lands Charity, Chippenham) Order 1990, SI 1990/843; the Charities (Royal Russell School) Order 1998, SI 1998/2883; the Charities (Seamen's Hospital Society) Order 1999, SI 1999/73; the Charities (The Royal Philanthropic Society) Order 1994, SI 1994/1235; the Charities (The Bridge House Estates) Order 1995, SI 1995/1047; the Charities (The Royal School for the Blind) Order 1996, SI 1996/1667; the Charities (The Shrubbery) Order 2003, SI 2003/1688; the Charities (Alexandra Park and Palace) Order 2004, SI 2004/160; the Charities (National Trust) Order 2005, SI 2005/712; the Charities (Bridge House Estates) Order 2007, SI 2007/550; the Charities (Incorporated Church Building Society) (England and Wales) Order 2013, SI 2013/641; and the Charities (People's Dispensary for Sick Animals) Order 2015, SI 2015/198. Formerly a special Act was necessary; now expenditure of charity money on promoting legislation is restricted by the Charities Act 2011 s 74(1) (see PARA 331).

Exempt charities, other than those for whom provisions for increased regulation under the Charities Act 2006 Sch 5 (repealed) were not brought into force prior to the commencement of the Charities Act 2011, are excluded from this provision. As to exempt charities see PARAS 318–325. And as to the increased regulation of exempt charities see PARA 319.

5 Charities Act 2011 s 73(4).
6 As to the meaning of 'court' see PARA 177 note 12.
7 Ie under the Charities Act 2011 s 69: see PARAS 189, 191–192, 298.
8 Charities Act 2011 s 73(5). However, where a scheme requires the positive approval of Parliament (see the text to note 6), the order giving effect to it may direct that the scheme must not be modified or superseded by a scheme brought into effect otherwise than under s 73, and may also direct that any modifying or superseding scheme is subject to the same limitation: see s 73(6).
9 As to the meaning of 'charity trustees' see PARA 255.
10 See note 8.
11 See the Charities Act 2011 s 70(5); and PARA 192.
12 See the Charities Act 2011 s 70(6); and PARA 192.
13 See note 8.
14 Charities Act 2011 s 73(7).

194. Interim order in lieu of scheme. If the Charity Commission[1] is satisfied: (1) that in existing circumstances the whole of the income of a charity cannot be effectively applied for the purposes of the charity[2]; and (2) that if those circumstances continue a scheme might be made for applying the surplus cy-près[3]; and (3) that for any reason it is not yet desirable to make such a scheme[4], it may by order authorise the charity trustees[5] at their discretion, though subject to any conditions imposed by the order, to apply accrued or accruing income[6] for any purposes for which it might be made applicable by such a scheme[7]. Any application authorised by the order is deemed to be within the purposes of the charity[8].

1 As to the Charity Commission see PARAS 543–578.
2 Charities Act 2011 s 75(1)(a). As to the meaning of 'charity' see PARA 1.
3 Charities Act 2011 s 75(1)(b).
4 Charities Act 2011 s 75(1)(c).
5 As to the meaning of 'charity trustees' see PARA 255.
6 The order may not, however, extend to more than £300 out of income accrued before the date of the order, nor to income accruing more than three years after that date, nor to more than £100 out of the income accruing in any of those three years: Charities Act 2011 s 75(4).
7 Charities Act 2011 s 75(2).
8 Charities Act 2011 s 75(3).

195. Special jurisdiction. There may be special cases in which, by virtue of some statutory provision, the Charity Commission[1] has jurisdiction to modify schemes that the court cannot modify[2].

Provisions with respect to allotments for recreation grounds, field gardens or other public or parochial purposes contained in any Inclosure Act, award or order made thereunder, and any provisions with respect to the management of any such allotments contained in any such Act, order, or award, may, on the application of any district or parish council interested in the allotment, be dealt with by a scheme of the Charity Commission in the exercise of its ordinary jurisdiction as if the provisions had been established by the founder in the case of a charity having a founder[3].

Any employee organisation[4] in the coal industry where members or members and their dependants constitute a substantial proportion of the beneficiaries under a relevant trust[5] and where neither the organisation nor its members are entitled to appoint any of the trustees of that trust, may apply to the Charity Commission for a scheme making such amendments to the provisions regulating the trust as the Commission considers appropriate for the purpose of securing fair representation amongst the trustees of those persons employed in the coal industry who may benefit under the trust[6]. These provisions apply to any trust for purposes which are exclusively charitable: (1) which is a trust of property wholly or partly representing an application of money from the miners' welfare fund constituted under the Mining Industry Act 1920[7] or the body known as the Coal Industry Social Welfare Organisation[8]; (2) which is a trust expressed to be for the benefit of (a) persons currently or formerly employed in the coal industry or any class of such persons or their dependants[9]; or (b) members of the mining community in general or of the mining community of a particular area, whether or not any other persons are also beneficiaries[10]; or (3) under the terms of which all or a majority of the trustees are appointed by the body mentioned in head (1) above or are appointed by the Coal Authority and an employee organisation[11].

1 As to the Charity Commission see PARAS 543–578.

2 See eg *Trustees of the London Parochial Charities v A-G* [1955] 1 All ER 1, [1955] 1 WLR 42. The Charities Act 2011 ss 73–75 (see PARAS 193–194) provides for a similar situation.

3 Commons Act 1899 s 18 (amended by the Charities Act 2006 Sch 8 para 10). For the purposes of the Commons Act 1899 s 18 the Broads Authority is treated as a district council: s 18 (amended by the Norfolk and Suffolk Broads Act 1988 Sch 6 para 1). As to the Broads Authority see **WATER AND WATERWAYS** vol 101 (2009) PARA 734. As to field gardens see **AGRICULTURAL LAND** vol 1 (2008) PARA 512.

A national park authority has the same power to make an application under the Commons Act 1899 s 18 as a local authority: Environment Act 1995 s 70, Sch 9 para 1(4). As to national park authorities see **OPEN SPACES AND COUNTRYSIDE** vol 78 (2010) PARA 526 et seq.

4 For these purposes, 'employee organisation' means any organisation appearing to the Charity Commission to represent in respect of their employment a substantial number of persons whose employers are licensed operators within the meaning of the Coal Industry Act 1994, or who are all employed by the same licensed operator: Coal Industry Act 1987 s 5(4) (as substituted and amended: see note 5).

5 Ie a trust to which the Coal Industry Act 1987 s 5 (amended by the Coal Industry Act 1994 s 67, Sch 9 para 36(b); and the Charities Act 2006 Sch 8 para 80, Sch 10 para 18) applies: see the text and notes 8–11.

6 Coal Industry Act 1987 s 5(1) (amended by the Charities Act 2006 Sch 8 para 80(2)). See also **MINES, MINERALS AND QUARRIES** vol 76 (2013) PARA 90.

7 Ie the Mining Industry Act 1920 s 20 (repealed).

8 Coal Industry Act 1987 s 5(3)(a). As to provisions relating to the Coal Industry Social Welfare Organisation see the Miners' Welfare Act 1952 s 12 (prospectively repealed); and **MINES, MINERALS AND QUARRIES** vol 76 (2013) PARA 89.

9 Coal Industry Act 1987 s 5(3)(b)(i).

10 Coal Industry Act 1987 s 5(3)(b)(ii).

11 Coal Industry Act 1987 s 5(3)(c). The statutory wording refers to the British Coal Corporation, however this has been replaced by the Coal Authority: see **MINES, MINERALS AND QUARRIES** vol 76 (2013) PARA 51 et seq.

196. Schemes in relation to ecclesiastical charities. The definition of 'charity' in the Charities Act 2011[1] does not apply to any ecclesiastical corporation[2] in respect of the corporate property of the corporation[3] or to any trust of property for purposes for which the property has been consecrated[4]. Nor is it applicable to any diocesan board of finance (or any subsidiary thereof) within the meaning of the Endowments and Glebe Measure 1976 for any diocese in respect of the diocesan glebe land of that diocese within the meaning of that Measure[5]. This notwithstanding, the power of the court[6] to make schemes in its charity jurisdiction, and the Charity Commission's jurisdiction to make schemes[7], extend to the making of schemes with respect to consecrated chapels belonging to charities[8] which are no longer needed for the purposes of the charity[9]. Such schemes may provide for the demolition of the chapel or disposal of the material arising from the demolition, for the sale or other disposal of the chapel or site of it and the application of the proceeds, for its appropriation to such uses as may be specified or generally described in the scheme, and for supplementary and incidental matters[10].

In relation to a charity established for ecclesiastical purposes of the Church of England, being a charity whose administration or purposes are affected by a pastoral scheme or order[11], the Charity Commission's powers to make schemes[12] may be exercised on the application of the diocesan board of finance for the relevant diocese[13]. This power also extends to charities affected by a pastoral (church buildings disposal) scheme under the Mission and Pastoral Measure 2011[14].

Nothing in the New Parishes Measure 1943 enables the Church Commissioners[15] to deal with the endowment of a charity within the meaning of the Charities Act 2011 without the consent of the Charity Commission[16].

1 See the Charities Act 2011 s 1(1); and PARA 1.

2 Ie any corporation in the Church of England, whether sole or aggregate, which is established for spiritual purposes: Charities Act 2011 s 10(3). As to ecclesiastical matters see further ECCLESIASTICAL LAW.

3 Charities Act 2011 s 10(2)(a). However, in respect of a corporation aggregate having some non-ecclesiastical purposes, the definition of 'charity' does extend to its corporate property held for those purposes: see s 10(2)(a).

4 See the Charities Act 2011 s 10(2)(c).

5 Charities Act 2011 s 10(2)(b), (4). As to diocesan boards of finance see ECCLESIASTICAL LAW vol 34 (2011) PARAS 241–242.

6 Ie under the Charities Act 2011: see PARA 183 et seq.

7 Ie under the Charities Act 2011 s 69: see PARA 189. As to the Charity Commission see PARAS 543–578.

8 For these purposes, a consecrated chapel held on charitable trusts for the purpose of religious worship by the beneficiaries and staff of a charity and not by the general public is deemed to belong to that charity, notwithstanding that the trusts on which the chapel is held are separate from those of the charity, but this does not apply to a chapel held on separate trusts relating to the use thereof for religious worship: Mission and Pastoral Measure 2011 s 67(4). As to the meaning of 'charity' see PARA 1; definition applied by s 106(1) (amended by the Charities Act 2011 Sch 7 Pt 2 para 148).

9 Mission and Pastoral Measure 2011 s 67(1) (substituted by the Charities Act 2011 Sch 7 Pt 2 para 146). Where a scheme is made under the Mission and Pastoral Measure 2011, the bishop may, if he thinks it proper to do so, by order under his seal direct that s 74(1) and s 78, if applicable, apply to the chapel as they apply to the buildings mentioned in those provisions, and those provisions then apply accordingly: s 67(2). The scheme, so far as it relates to the chapel, does not have effect unless and until such an order is made, or the bishop directs that the scheme may have effect without such an order: s 67(2). 'Bishop' means the bishop of the diocese concerned: s 106(1).

10 Mission and Pastoral Measure 2011 s 67(3).

11 As to such schemes and orders see the Mission and Pastoral Measure 1983; and ECCLESIASTICAL LAW vol 34 (2011) PARA 641 et seq.
12 Ie under the Charities Act 2011 s 69: see PARA 189.
13 Mission and Pastoral Measure 2011 Sch 3 para 9(6) (amended by the Charities Act 2011 Sch 7 Pt 2 para 149). They may also be exercised in accordance with the Charities Act 2011 ss 69–71 (see PARA 189): Mission and Pastoral Measure 2011 Sch 3 para 9(6) (as so amended). Any schemes or orders made by the Charity Commission for purposes arising in connection with a pastoral scheme or order may be made before the date on which the pastoral scheme or order comes into operation, but not so as to take effect before that date: Sch 3 para 9(7).
14 See Mission and Pastoral Measure 2011 s 77(3) (amended by the Charities Act 2011 Sch 7 Pt 2 para 147); and ECCLESIASTICAL LAW vol 34 (2011) PARAS 641, 895.
15 As to the Church Commissioners see ECCLESIASTICAL LAW vol 34 (2011) PARA 66 et seq.
16 New Parishes Measure 1943 s 31 (amended by the Charities Act 1960 s 48, Sch 6; the Education Act 1973 s 1(4), (5), Sch 2 Pt III; the Charities Act 1993 Sch 6 para 3(4); the Charities Act 2006 Sch 8 para 31; the Church of England (Miscellaneous Provisions Measure 2010 Sch 1 para 10; and the Charities Act 2011 Sch 7 Pt 2 para 10). The repeal of the Charities Act 1960 by the Charities Act 2006 Sch 8 para 83(3) does not affect the amendments made by that Act: Charities Act 2006 Sch 10 para 23.

197. Schemes in relation to redundant places of worship. Statutory provision is made with respect to the transfer of certain redundant places of worship[1]. These provisions apply in relation to any premises[2] if the premises are held by or in trust for a charity (the 'relevant charity'), and the whole or part of the premises has been used as a place of public worship, but the premises are not a church subject to the provisions of the Pastoral Measure 1983 or the Mission and Pastoral Measure 2011[3]. The essence of the provisions is to enable the court to make a scheme for the acquisition of a redundant place of worship by the Secretary of State, the Historic Building and Monuments Commission or a prescribed charity[4].

1 See the Redundant Churches and Other Religious Buildings Act 1969 ss 4, 5; and ECCLESIASTICAL LAW vol 34 (2011) PARA 907.
2 'Premises' includes a part of a building: Redundant Churches and Other Religious Buildings Act 1969 s 4(13) (s 4 substituted by the Charities Act 1992 Sch 5 para 1).
3 Redundant Churches and Other Religious Buildings Act 1969 s 4(1) (as substituted: see note 2): see ECCLESIASTICAL LAW vol 34 (2011) PARA 907. The Pastoral Measure 1983 is replaced by the Mission and Pastoral Measure 2011: see further ECCLESIASTICAL LAW. As to the Historic Buildings and Monuments Commission for England see NATIONAL CULTURAL HERITAGE vol 77 (2010) PARA 803 et seq.
4 See ECCLESIASTICAL LAW vol 34 (2011) PARA 907.

198. Schemes in relation to reserve forces charities. Statutory provision is made for the treatment of charitable property held for the purposes of any body of a reserve force which has been, or is to be, disbanded or amalgamated with another body[1].

A warrant of Her Majesty may designate[2] any unit of a reserve force[3] as the successor to any unit or other body of the same or any other reserve force which has been or is to be disbanded[4]. The Secretary of State[5] must send a copy of any such warrant to the Charity Commission[6], the Department of Health and Social Services for Northern Ireland, and a trustee of each charity[7] in England and Wales or Northern Ireland, or a person concerned in the management or control of each recognised body[8], affected by the warrant[9].

The effect of designating the successor to a disbanded unit is that on and after the day on which a warrant comes into force, any charitable property[10] which is held for the purposes of the disbanded unit in question is to be held for the corresponding purposes, or most nearly corresponding purposes, of the successor unit designated by the warrant[11]. If the Charity Commission considers that this effect[12] should not apply to all or any of the charitable property held for the purposes of a disbanded unit, it may make an order[13] providing that it does not apply or ceases to apply to that property or part[14]. If a charity affected by a warrant or any trustee of, or person interested in, such a charity considers that this effect[15] should not apply to all or any of the property held by the charity for the purposes of the disbanded unit in question, then the charity, trustee or person interested, as the case may be, may apply to the court[16] for an order providing that it will cease to apply to that property or part[17].

In any case where: (1) the Secretary of State requests the Charity Commission to make provision with respect to any charitable property which is held for the purposes of a unit of a reserve force that has been or is to be disbanded[18]; or (2) an order is made as to the exclusion of charitable property from the effect of designation of a successor to the disbanded unit[19] the Commission may, notwithstanding the limit on jurisdiction to make schemes for the protection of charities[20], exercise such jurisdiction with respect to the property to which the request or order relates[21].

These provisions[22] do not apply to any property held by a charity for the purposes of a unit that has been or is to be disbanded if, under the terms on which the property is so held[23]: (a) any interest of the charity in the property is determined on the disbanding of that unit[24]; and (b) any other person or charity has an interest in the property contingent upon the determination of the interest of the charity[25].

1 See the Reserve Forces Act 1996 s 120. As to the succession to charitable property in relation to Scotland see Sch 5 Pt III paras 9–14 (amended by virtue of SI 1999/678). As to the succession to charitable property in relation to Northern Ireland see the Reserve Forces Act 1996 Sch 5 Pt IV paras 15–20. See also ARMED FORCES.

2 'Warrant' means a warrant making such a designation: Reserve Forces Act 1996 Sch 5 para 2.

3 As to the meaning of 'reserve forces' see the Reserve Forces Act 1996 s 1(2); and ARMED FORCES vol 3 (2011) PARA 470.

4 Reserve Forces Act 1996 Sch 5 para 1(1). 'Disbanded unit' means a unit for which a successor is designated under Sch 5 para 1: Sch 5 para 2. References to disbandment of a body of a reserve force (however expressed) include references to its amalgamation with another unit or body: Sch 5 para 2.

5 As to the Secretary of State see PARA 585.

6 As to the Charity Commission see PARAS 543–578.

7 As to the meaning of 'charity' see PARA 1; definition applied by the Reserve Forces Act 1996 Sch 5 para 2 (amended by the Charities Act 2011 Sch 7 Pt 2 para 69).

8 'Recognised body' has the same meaning as in the Law Reform (Miscellaneous Provisions) (Scotland) Act 1990 Pt I: Reserve Forces Act 1996 Sch 5 para 2.

9 Reserve Forces Act 1996 Sch 5 para 1(2) (amended by SI 1999/678; and the Charities Act 2006 Sch 8 para 181(2)). A copy of such a warrant may be sent by post; and any such copy must be sent so as to arrive on or before the day on which the warrant comes into force and, in any event, not more than 14 days from the day on which the warrant is made: Reserve Forces Act 1996 Sch 5 para 1(3).

10 For these purposes, 'charitable property' means any property belonging to a charity: Reserve Forces Act 1996 Sch 5 para 3(2).

11 Reserve Forces Act 1996 Sch 5 para 3(1). The same jurisdiction and powers are exercisable in relation to any charity owning property to which Sch 5 para 3(1) applies as would be exercisable if that were not a provision of an Act of Parliament regulating that charity: Sch 5 para 3(3).

12 Ie the effect of the Reserve Forces Act 1996 Sch 5 para 3(1): see the text and notes 10–11.

13 Any such order may be made at any time within the period of six months beginning with the day on which the warrant is made: Reserve Forces Act 1996 Sch 5 para 4(2).

14 Reserve Forces Act 1996 Sch 5 para 4(1) (amended by the Charities Act 2006 Sch 8 para 181(3)). Neither a warrant nor any order under the Reserve Forces Act 1996 Sch 5 para 4 or Sch 5 para 5 (see the text and notes 15–17) affects the validity of anything done or omitted

with respect to any property affected by the warrant or order before a copy of the warrant or order is received by a trustee of the charity in question: Sch 5 para 7.

15 See note 12.

16 For meaning of 'court' for these purposes see PARA 177 note 12; definition applied by the Reserve Forces Act 1996 Sch 5 para 5(3) (amended by the Charities Act 2011 Sch 7 Pt 2 para 69).

17 Reserve Forces Act 1996 Sch 5 para 5(1). Such an application (1) may be made at any time within the period of six months beginning with the day on which the warrant comes into force; and (2) is subject to the Charities Act 2011 s 115(2)–(5) (proceedings not to be begun without the consent of the Charity Commission or leave of a judge of the High Court) (see PARA 594), and for the purposes of s 115(5) an application for an order of the Commission authorising proceedings under the Reserve Forces Act 1996 Sch 5 para 5 is deemed to be refused if it is not granted during the period of one month beginning with the day on which the application is received by the Commission: Sch 5 para 5(2) (amended by the Charities Act 2011 Sch 7 Pt 2 para 69). See also note 14.

18 Reserve Forces Act 1996 Sch 5 para 6(a) (Sch 5 para 6 substituted by the Charities Act 2011 Sch 7 para 69).

19 Reserve Forces Act 1996 Sch 5 para 6(b) (as substituted: see note 18). The reference in the text to an order is a reference to an order made under Sch 5 para 4 or Sch 5 para 5 (see the text and notes 12–17) excluding any charitable property from the operation of Sch 5 para 3(1) (see the text and notes 10–11): see Sch 5 para 6(b) (as so substituted).

20 Ie under the Charities Act 2011 s 70(2): see PARA 189.

21 Reserve Forces Act 1996 Sch 5 para 6 (as substituted see note 18).

22 Ie the Reserve Forces Act 1996 Sch 5 paras 3–7: see the text and notes 10–21.

23 Reserve Forces Act 1996 Sch 5 para 8.

24 Reserve Forces Act 1996 Sch 5 para 8(a).

25 Reserve Forces Act 1996 Sch 5 para 8(b).

(iv) Appeals

199. Right of appeal to the Tribunal from orders of Charity Commission. Where the Charity Commission[1] exercises the same jurisdiction and powers as are exercisable by the High Court in charity proceedings[2], an appeal against any such order may be brought to the Tribunal[3] by the Attorney General[4]. Such an appeal may also be brought to the Tribunal by the charity trustees or (if a body corporate) the charity itself in the case of a scheme for the administration of the charity[5], or by any person discharged or removed by the order, or by any other person who is or may be affected by the order[6].

The Tribunal has the power to do any of the following: (1) quash the order in whole or in part and, if appropriate, remit the matter to the Commission; (2) substitute for all or part of the order any other order which could have been made by the Commission; (3) add to the order anything which could have been contained in an order made by the Commission[7].

Apart from cases in which, by reason of lapse of time and changed circumstances, the provisions of a scheme are no longer practicable[8], the court will only interfere with a scheme settled by the Charity Commission where it has acted ultra vires or the scheme contains something wrong in principle[9].

1 As to the Charity Commission see PARAS 543–578.

2 Ie under the Charities Act 2011 s 69(1): see PARA 189.

3 As to the Tribunal see PARA 579 et seq.

4 Charities Act 2011 s 319(1), Sch 6 Table Col 1. As to the Attorney General see PARAS 589, 596, 605 et seq; and CONSTITUTIONAL AND ADMINISTRATIVE LAW vol 20 (2014) PARA 273 et seq.

5 Charities Act 2011 s 319(2)(a), Sch 6 Table Col 2.

6 Charities Act 2011 s 319(2)(b), Sch 6 Table Col 2. As to the meaning of 'person who is or may be affected' within the meaning of Sch 6 see PARA 317 note 8.

7 Charities Act 2011 Sch 6 Table Col 3.

8 As to the alteration of schemes settled by court in these circumstances see PARA 187.

9 *Re Campden Charities* (1881) 18 ChD 310, CA; *Re Campden Charities (No 2)* (1883) 24 ChD 213; *Re Weir Hospital* [1910] 2 Ch 124 at 134, CA, per Cozens-Hardy MR. See also *Re Shaftoe's Charity* (1878) 3 App Cas 872, PC; *Re Sutton Coldfield Grammar School* (1881) 7 App Cas 91, PC; *Re Faraker, Faraker v Durell* [1912] 2 Ch 488, CA.

(2) SCHEMES WHERE DONOR'S DIRECTIONS ARE INADEQUATE

200. Particular purpose not defined. Where the mode of executing a charitable gift is originally undefined, it is impossible, of course, to select an object cy-près to that which has failed[1]. However, the donor's intention will be carried out as far as possible by the application of the gift to charitable objects to be nominated by the Crown, the court[2] or the Charity Commission[3], as the case may be.

1 *Barclay v Maskelyne* (1858) 4 Jur NS 1294 at 1297 per Wood V-C.

2 *White v White* (1778) 1 Bro CC 12; *Mills v Farmer* (1815) 1 Mer 55 at 96, 102 per Lord Eldon LC. As to the nomination of charitable objects by the Crown or the court see PARAS 513, 534. Whether the selection of objects is by the Crown or the court, the same principles apply: *Moggridge v Thackwell* (1803) 7 Ves 36 at 87 per Lord Eldon LC; *A-G v Wansay* (1808) 15 Ves 231 at 233 per Lord Eldon LC; *Re Slevin, Slevin v Hepburn* [1891] 2 Ch 236 at 243, CA, per Kay LJ.

3 See the Charities Act 2011 ss 69–71; and PARAS 189, 191–192, 298. As to the Charity Commission see PARAS 543–578.

201. Indications of donor's intention. In cases where no particular purpose is named by the donor any indications throwing light on the donor's intentions will be considered[1], for example his religious opinions[2], his interest in a particular locality[3], the nature of other charitable bequests in the same will[4], precatory directions in favour of a certain class[5], or even wishes expressed in an unattested codicil[6].

If no indication can be gathered as to his particular intention, the donor's general intention must be considered. Thus, a gift for the poor generally could not properly be applied for a purpose unconnected with the relief of poverty, such as the rebuilding of a church[7].

1 *Cook v Duckenfield* (1743) 2 Atk 562; *Ironmongers' Co v A-G* (1844) 10 Cl & Fin 908 at 922, 924–929, HL.

2 *Re Ashton's Charity* (1859) 27 Beav 115 at 120 per Romilly MR. See also *Ironmongers' Co v A-G* (1844) 10 Cl & Fin 908 at 922, 924–929, HL.

3 *Re Mann, Hardy v A-G* [1903] 1 Ch 232. A gift to 'the ward of Bread Street' was directed to be disposed of as the aldermen of the ward thought fit: *Baylis v A-G* (1741) 2 Atk 239.

4 *Mills v Farmer* (1815) 1 Mer 55 at 103, 722 per Lord Eldon LC; *Ironmongers' Co v A-G* (1844) 10 Cl & Fin 908, HL; *Lyons Corpn v Advocate-General of Bengal* (1876) 1 App Cas 91 at 114, PC.

5 Eg 'clergymen who have large families and good characters': *Moggridge v Thackwell* (1803) 7 Ves 36. See also *A-G v London Corpn* (1790) 3 Bro CC 171.

6 *A-G v Madden* (1843) 2 Con & Law 519.

7 *A-G v Peacock* (1676) Cas *temp* Finch 245. As to the relief of poverty see PARA 12 et seq.

202. Court's discretion. If no particular charitable purpose is indicated, and if the general charitable intention is subject to no restrictions, express or implied, the court's discretion in the application of the fund in what seems the most expedient manner is unlimited[1]. Thus, gifts for charity generally may be applied for the benefit of hospitals[2], schools[3] or other charitable institutions[4]; while bequests for the poor may be used for educational purposes[5], for the benefit of scholars at a particular school[6], for the testator's poor relations[7], or for poor foreign refugees of whom the testator himself had been one[8].

Similarly, where the name of the charity legatee is left blank, the gift is applied under a scheme[9].

1 *Philpott v St George's Hospital* (1859) 27 Beav 107; *Re Ashton's Charity* (1859) 27 Beav 115. See also *Mills v Farmer* (1815) 1 Mer 55. As to the meaning of 'general charitable intention' see PARA 168.
2 *Legge v Asgill* (1818) 3 Hare 194n; affd Turn & R 265n.
3 *A-G v Syderfen* (1683) 1 Vern 224. See also *Pieschel v Paris* (1825) 2 Sim & St 384; *Re Campden Charities* (1881) 18 ChD 310, CA.
4 *Re Dickason* (1837) 3 Hare 195n.
5 *Bishop of Hereford v Adams* (1802) 7 Ves 324; *Wilkinson v Malin* (1832) 2 Cr & J 636; *A-G v Bovill* (1840) 1 Ph 762; *London School Board v Faulconer* (1878) 8 ChD 571. See, however, *Re Lambeth Charities* (1853) 22 LJCh 959; *A-G v Duke of Northumberland* (1889) 5 TLR 719, CA.
6 *A-G v Peacock* (1676) Cas *temp* Finch 245 (Christ's Hospital).
7 *Ware v A-G* (1824) 3 Hare 194n; contra *Sanford v Gibbons* (1829) 3 Hare 195n. As to the class of cases known as the 'poor relations' cases see PARA 17.
8 *A-G v Rance* (1728) cited in Amb 422.
9 *Pieschel v Paris* (1825) 2 Sim & St 384; *Re White, White v White* [1893] 2 Ch 41, CA; and see *Re Macduff, Macduff v Macduff* [1896] 2 Ch 451, CA.

203. Failure of machinery for ascertaining objects. A scheme will also be directed where the machinery for ascertaining the intended objects of a charitable trust breaks down, as where the bequest is for charitable and non-charitable purposes in shares to be determined by persons who fail to make the necessary apportionment[1], or where objects are intended to be, but are not, named by the donor[2] or others[3], or where a fund is to be divided among a particular class at the discretion of persons who fail to make the division[4].

1 *Doyley v A-G* (1735) 4 Vin Abr 485 pl 16; *Salusbury v Denton* (1857) 3 K & J 529.
2 *A-G v Syderfen* (1683) 1 Vern 224; *Mills v Farmer* (1815) 1 Mer 55; and see *Charitable Donations Comrs v Sullivan* (1841) 1 Dr & War 501.
3 *White v White* (1778) 1 Bro CC 12; *A-G v Boultbee* (1796) 3 Ves 220; *Moggridge v Thackwell* (1803) 7 Ves 36; *A-G v Fletcher* (1835) 5 LJCh 75; *Pocock v A-G* (1876) 3 ChD 342, CA; *Re Willis, Shaw v Willis* [1921] 1 Ch 44, CA.
4 *A-G v Gladstone* (1842) 13 Sim 7; and see *A-G v Wansay* (1808) 15 Ves 231; *Pease v Pattinson* (1886) 32 ChD 154.

204. Continuing charitable trust. Where a donor's intention was to establish a continuing charitable trust[1], the execution of which he committed to trustees other than an existing charitable institution engaged in that particular charitable purpose, or an officer or officers of such an institution, a scheme will generally be directed[2] if the donor has not prescribed all the details of administration, even though such details are expressly confined to the trustees' discretion[3]. In a simple case a scheme may not be necessary[4]. The principle is that, wherever a permanent charitable trust was intended, the court will not part with a fund of which it has once obtained control without seeing that a proper trust is established[5].

1 A scheme is not usually directed where immediate distribution is authorised: see PARA 208.
2 See PARAS 180–181.
3 *Wellbeloved v Jones* (1822) 1 Sim & St 40; *Sons of the Clergy Corpn v Mose* (1839) 9 Sim 610; *A-G v Stepney* (1804) 10 Ves 22; *Re Mann, Hardy v A-G* [1903] 1 Ch 232; *Re Webster, Pearson v Webster* [1912] 1 Ch 106; and see PARA 181.
4 *Nash v Morley* (1842) 5 Beav 177 at 185 per Lord Langdale MR.
5 *Wellbeloved v Jones* (1822) 1 Sim & St 40.

205. Institutions which cannot be identified. If a gift is made to a named institution and the testator appears to have intended a particular institution to take, but it cannot be decided which of two or more existing institutions was intended, the gift will be applied by way of scheme[1], usually by being divided between the possible claimants[2].

1 As to schemes generally see PARA 179 et seq.

2 *Re Songest, Mayger v Forces Help Society and Lord Roberts' Workshops* [1956] 2 All ER 765, [1956] 1 WLR 897, CA; *Simon v Barber* (1829) 3 Hare 195n; *Bunting v Marriott* (1854) 19 Beav 163; *Re Hussey's Charities, Cheyne v Apreece, Symons v Delaval* (1861) 30 LJCh 491; and see the cases cited in the notes to PARA 160. As to gifts to institutions which have never existed see PARA 157.

206. Institutions which do not exist. If a gift is made to an institution which has never existed or which has ceased to exist before the gift takes effect, but is made in such circumstances that the non-existence of the institution does not cause the gift to fail[1], a scheme[2] is necessary to apply the gift for the same purposes as those of the named institution[3].

1 For the considerations which govern the efficacy of a gift to such an institution see PARAS 149–150, 157, 159, 170.

2 As to schemes generally see PARA 179 et seq.

3 *Re Clergy Society* (1856) 2 K & J 615; *Re Davis, Hannen v Hillyer* [1902] 1 Ch 876; *Re Finger's Will Trusts, Turner v Ministry of Health* [1972] Ch 286, [1971] 3 All ER 1050, and the cases cited in the notes to PARA 148. As to whether this is properly called a cy-près application see *Re Robinson, Besant v German Reich* [1931] 2 Ch 122 at 128–129 per Maugham J.

207. Failure of trustees. A scheme[1] has been directed if the trustees died or, being an institution, ceased to exist, or refused to act, whether or not the trust authorised an immediate distribution[2]. Where the trustee appointed was appointed in the capacity of holder of an office which ceased to exist before the testator's death, the matter was referred to the master to approve a proper person to be trustee in place of that officer[3].

1 As to schemes generally see PARA 179 et seq.

2 *Moggridge v Thackwell* (1803) 7 Ves 36; *A-G v Gladstone* (1842) 13 Sim 7; *Reeve v A-G* (1843) 3 Hare 191; *A-G v Lawes* (1849) 8 Hare 32; *Re Stanes' Will, Re Trustee Relief Act* (1853) 21 LTOS 261; *Re Fraser, Yeates v Fraser* (1883) 22 ChD 827; *Re Wilson-Barkworth, Burstall v Deck* (1933) 50 TLR 82; and see the cases cited in PARA 203 note 3.

3 *A-G v Stephens* (1834) 3 My & K 347.

208. Immediate distribution not requiring scheme. A scheme[1] will not usually be directed where the donor has authorised an immediate distribution[2] or a distribution at intervals for a limited period[3] and the trustees are in existence and accept the trust[4].

1 As to schemes generally see PARA 179 et seq.

2 *Re Barnett* (1860) 29 LJCh 871.

3 *Waldo v Caley* (1809) 16 Ves 206; *Powerscourt v Powerscourt* (1824) 1 Mol 616; *Horde v Earl of Suffolk* (1833) 2 My & K 59.

4 For such cases in which a scheme has been directed see PARA 180.

(3) CY-PRÈS SCHEMES

(i) Cy-près Schemes in general

209. The cy-près doctrine. Where a clear charitable intention is expressed, it will not be permitted to fail because the mode, if specified, cannot be executed, but the law will substitute another mode cy-près[1], that is, as near as possible to the mode specified by the donor[2].

An application cy-près results from the exercise of the court's ordinary jurisdiction to administer a charitable trust of which the particular mode of application has not been defined by the donor[3]. Where he has in fact prescribed a particular mode of application and that mode is incapable of being performed, but he had a charitable intention which transcended the particular mode of application prescribed, the court, in the exercise of this jurisdiction, can carry out the charitable intention as though the particular direction had not been expressed at all[4].

However, where the particular mode of application prescribed by the donor was the essence of his intention, which may be shown by a condition[5] or by particularity of language[6], and that mode is incapable of being performed, there is nothing left upon which the court can found its jurisdiction, so that in such circumstances the court has no power to direct any other charitable application in place of that which has failed[7].

Where the particular mode of application does not exhaust a gift, these principles apply to the surplus[8].

There can be no question under English law of a cy-près application of property subject to trusts which are not charitable in law[9].

1 See *Moggridge v Thackwell* (1803) 7 Ves 36 at 69 per Lord Eldon LC (affd (1807) 13 Ves 416, HL); *Mills v Farmer* (1815) 1 Mer 55; *A-G v Bristol Corpn* (1820) 2 Jac & W 294 at 308 per Lord Eldon LC; *Chamberlayne v Brockett* (1872) 8 Ch App 206. As to the statutory conditions for cy-près application see PARA 214.

2 See the cases cited in note 1. See also *A-G v Whitchurch* (1796) 3 Ves 141 at 144 per Arden MR; *Cary v Abbot* (1802) 7 Ves 490; *Clephane v Edinburgh Corpn* (1869) LR 1 Sc & Div 417 at 421, HL, per Lord Westbury; *Ironmongers' Co v A-G* (1844) 10 Cl & Fin 908 at 922, HL, per Lord Campbell; *Re Avenon's Charity, A-G v Pelly* (1912) 106 LT 295, reported on further consideration [1913] 2 Ch 261.

3 See PARAS 180, 200.

4 *Re Wilson, Twentyman v Simpson* [1913] 1 Ch 314 at 321 per Parker J; and see *Re Monk, Giffen v Wedd* [1927] 2 Ch 197, CA. See also *Re JW Laing Trust, Steward's Co Ltd v A-G* [1984] Ch 143, [1984] 1 All ER 50 (obligation to distribute capital assets of trust fund within a certain time became inexpedient: scheme approved to remove obligation).

5 *Re Wilson, Twentyman v Simpson* [1913] 1 Ch 314.

6 *Re Good's Will Trusts, Oliver v Batten* [1950] 2 All ER 653.

7 *Re Good's Will Trusts, Oliver v Batten* [1950] 2 All ER 653.

8 See PARAS 131, 172.

9 *A-G v Haberdashers' Co* (1834) 1 My & K 420; *Thomson v Shakespear* (1860) 1 De GF & J 399; *Carne v Long* (1860) 2 De GF & J 75; *Re Clark's Trust* (1875) 1 ChD 497; and see *Pease v Pattinson* (1886) 32 ChD 154.

210. Cy-près and gifts to institutions. In the case of a gift to a non-existent institution which does not lapse by reason of the non-existence of the institution[1], the court, having held that the donor's benevolence is not restricted to the named institution, gives effect to that benevolence by applying the gift for the purposes carried on by a defunct institution or, in the case of one which has never existed, for the purposes indicated by the donor so far as ascertainable. This may not necessarily be a cy-près application[2], but it sometimes appears to fall within the cy-près doctrine[3].

1 As to when such a gift does or does not lapse see PARAS 149–150, 169.
2 See PARA 206 note 3.
3 As to the cy-près doctrine see PARA 209.

211. What objects are cy-près. The power of the court or the Charity Commission[1] to make schemes for the application of property cy-près must be exercised in accordance with the following provisions[2] of the Charities Act 2011[3]. Where any property given for charitable purposes[4] is applicable cy-près, the court or the Commission may make a scheme providing for the property to be applied for such charitable purposes[5], and (if the scheme provides for the property to be transferred to another charity)[6] by or on trust for such other charity[7], as it considers appropriate, having regard to the following matters[8]:

(1) the spirit of the original gift[9];
(2) the desirability of securing that the property is applied for charitable purposes which are close to the original purpose[10]; and
(3) the need for the relevant charity[11] to have purposes which are suitable and effective in the light of current social and economic circumstances[12].

If a scheme provides for the property to be transferred to another charity, the scheme may impose on the trustees of that charity a duty to secure that the property is applied for purposes which are, so far as is reasonably practicable, similar in character to the original purposes[13].

A charity may be cy-près to the original object even though it seems to have no trace of resemblance to it[14], if no other can be found which has a nearer connection[15].

Objects already adequately provided for should not be chosen for the purpose of an application cy-près[16], nor should the application be made in such a way as merely to relieve the rates[17], taxes or other public funds.

1 As to the Charity Commission see PARAS 543–578.
2 Ie the Charities Act 2011 s 67.
3 Charities Act 2011 s 67(1).
4 This applies to property given for charitable purposes whether before, on or after the commencement of the Charities Act 2011: see Sch 8 para 17. As to the meaning of 'charitable purposes' see PARA 2. 'Property given' includes property for the time being representing the property originally given or property derived from it: s 67(5).
5 Charities Act 2011 s 67(2)(a).
6 References in the statutory provisions to the transfer of property to a charity are references to its transfer to the charity, or to the charity trustees, or to any trustee for the charity, or to any person nominated by the charity trustees to hold it in trust for the charity, as the scheme may provide: Charities Act 2011 s 67(6).
7 Charities Act 2011 s 67(2)(b).
8 Charities Act 2011 s 67(2).
9 Charities Act 2011 s 67(3)(a). See eg *Ground, Pople, Lemieux and Lawrence v Charity Commission for England and Wales* (2011) First-tier Tribunal, General Regulatory Chamber (Charity), 6 December.
10 Charities Act 2011 s 67(3)(b).
11 'Relevant charity' means the charity by or on behalf of which the property is to be applied under the scheme: Charities Act 2011 s 67(3).
12 Charities Act 2011 s 67(3)(c).
13 Charities Act 2011 s 67(4). References to the original purposes of a gift must be read, where the application of the property given has been altered or regulated by a scheme or otherwise, as referring to the purposes for which the property is for the time being applicable: s 67(7).

14 *A-G v Boultbee* (1794) 2 Ves 380 (affd (1796) 3 Ves 220); *Clephane v Edinburgh Corpn* (1869) LR 1 Sc & Div 417 at 421, HL, per Lord Westbury.
15 *A-G v Ironmongers' Co* (1841) Cr & Ph 208 at 227 per Lord Brougham; affd sub nom *Ironmongers' Co v A-G* (1844) 10 Cl & Fin 908, HL (but the will in that case was so phrased that the only proper application of the fund whose objects had failed was to one of the other purposes benefited under the same will).
16 *Re Prison Charities* (1873) LR 16 Eq 129.
17 *Re Prison Charities* (1873) LR 16 Eq 129; *Re Poplar and Blackwall Free School* (1878) 8 ChD 543; *A-G v Duke of Northumberland* (1889) 5 TLR 237; varied on appeal 5 TLR 719, CA.

212. No application cy-près without a scheme. However desirable it may be, in no circumstances can trustees of a charity apply the trust funds cy-près on their own initiative, without the direction of the court or of the Charity Commission[1]. The Commission may make interim orders in lieu of a cy-près scheme for a limited period[2]. Where the case permits and requires the property or some part of it to be applied cy-près, a trust for charitable purposes[3] places a trustee under a duty to secure its effective use for charity[4] by taking steps to enable it to be so applied[5].

1 *A-G v Coopers' Co* (1812) 19 Ves 187; *A-G v Vivian* (1826) 1 Russ 226; *A-G v Kell* (1840) 2 Beav 575; *A-G v Bushby* (1857) 24 Beav 299; *Ward v Hipwell* (1862) 3 Giff 547; *Re Campden Charities* (1881) 18 ChD 310 at 328–329, CA, per Jessel MR; *Cross v Lloyd-Greame* (1909) 102 LT 163; and see *Re Weir Hospital* [1910] 2 Ch 124 at 133, CA, per Cozens-Hardy MR. See also PARAS 146, 335. As to the Charity Commission see PARAS 543–578.
2 See the Charities Act 2011 s 75; and PARA 194.
3 As to the meaning of 'charitable purposes' see PARA 2.
4 As to the meaning of 'charity' see PARA 1.
5 Charities Act 2011 s 61. This provision is declaratory.

(ii) When Property may be applied Cy-près

213. Failure of stated charitable objects. Before the Charities Act 1960 came into force no property could be applied cy-près unless it was clearly established that the donor's directions could not be carried into effect at all[1]. The specified purpose might be impracticable or impossible[2] for a number of reasons, such as that it had already been fulfilled[3], or that its objects had ceased to exist[4], or that insufficient money was available[5]. The purpose might be an illegal mode of achieving a lawful purpose[6], or the gift might be dependent on named trustees accepting the trust[7], or might be connected with another gift which was void[8]. Alternatively the property available might be more than could be used for the specified purpose[9].

The question of a cy-près application may also arise in connection with gifts to charitable institutions, as where the named institution has never existed[10], or has ceased to exist before the gift takes effect[11].

1 *A-G v Boultbee* (1794) 2 Ves 380 at 387 per Arden MR (affd (1796) 3 Ves 220); *Re Weir Hospital* [1910] 2 Ch 124, CA.
2 As to impracticable gifts see PARA 163.
3 *Bunting v Marriott* (1854) 19 Beav 163; and see PARA 163 note 1.
4 *A-G v London Corpn* (1790) 3 Bro CC 171; and see PARA 163 note 5.
5 *Cherry v Mott* (1836) 1 My & Cr 123; and see PARA 163 note 7.
6 *A-G v Vint* (1850) 3 De G & Sm 704. As to where gifts are to be applied in an illegal manner see PARA 162.
7 *Re Lysaght, Hill v Royal College of Surgeons* [1966] Ch 191, [1965] 2 All ER 888; and see PARA 164. See also PARA 214 note 3.
8 *A-G v Whitchurch* (1796) 3 Ves 141; and see PARA 171.
9 *Re King, Kerr v Bradley* [1923] 1 Ch 243; and see PARA 165.
10 *Re Davis, Hannen v Hillyer* [1902] 1 Ch 876; and see PARA 157.

11 *Re Finger's Will Trusts, Turner v Ministry of Health* [1972] Ch 286, [1971] 3 All ER 1050; and see PARAS 149, 159. As to whether in the case of gifts to institutions the application is always correctly described as a cy-près application see *Re Robinson, Besant v German Reich* [1931] 2 Ch 122 at 128–129 per Maugham J.

214. Statutory conditions for cy-près application. The Charities Act 2011 specifies the circumstances in which the original purposes[1] of a charitable gift can be altered to allow the property given or part of it to be applied cy-près[2]. They are as follows:

(1) where the original purposes, in whole or in part: (a) have been, as far as may be, fulfilled[3]; or (b) cannot be carried out, or cannot be carried out according to the directions given and to the spirit of the gift[4];

(2) where the original purposes provide a use for part only of the property available by virtue of the gift[5];

(3) where the property available by virtue of the gift and other property applicable for similar purposes can be more effectively used in conjunction, and to that end can suitably be made applicable to common purposes, regard being had to the appropriate considerations[6];

(4) where the original purposes were laid down by reference to an area which then was, but has since ceased to be, a unit for some other purpose, or by reference to a class of persons or to an area which has for any reason ceased to be suitable, regard being had to the appropriate considerations, or to be practical in administering the gift[7];

(5) where the original purposes, in whole or in part, have, since they were laid down: (a) been adequately provided for by other means[8]; or (b) ceased, as being useless or harmful to the community or for other reasons, to be in law charitable[9]; or (c) ceased in any other way to provide a suitable and effective method of using the property available by virtue of the gift, regard being had to the appropriate considerations[10].

These statutory conditions appear to supersede completely the old law on failure of stated objects as an occasion for a cy-près application[11].

If the above requirements are not satisfied the court has no jurisdiction to alter the terms of a charitable gift[12].

1 Where the application of the property given has been altered or regulated by a scheme or otherwise, references to the original purposes of a gift are to be construed as referring to the purposes for which the property is for the time being applicable: Charities Act 2011 s 62(4). See also *Re JW Laing Trust, Steward's Co Ltd v A-G* [1984] Ch 143, [1984] 1 All ER 50 (clause relating to distribution of capital assets within a certain time not an original purpose under what is now the Charities Act 2011 s 62). Note that cases mentioned in this paragraph were decided under earlier legislation.

2 Charities Act 2011 s 62(1). This provision only affects the conditions which must be satisfied in so far as they require a failure of the original purposes: see s 62(3); and PARA 215.

3 Charities Act 2011 s 62(1)(a)(i). The cases on impossibility and impracticability (see PARA 163) are included within these categories.

4 Charities Act 2011 s 62(1)(a)(ii). 'The spirit of the gift' means the basic intention underlying the gift, that intention being ascertainable from the terms of the relevant instrument read in the light of admissible evidence: see *Re Lepton's Charity, Ambler v Thomas* [1972] Ch 276 at 285, sub nom *Re Lepton's Will Trusts, Re Lepton's Charity, Ambler v Thomas* [1971] 1 All ER 799 at 803 per Pennycuick V-C. Under the old law (see PARA 213) it was only the letter of the gift that could be considered.

Re Lysaght, Hill v Royal College of Surgeons [1966] Ch 191, [1965] 2 All ER 888, appears to fall within the Charities Act 2011 s 62(1)(a)(ii), although the statutory provision from which it is derived is not mentioned in the report, the argument having centred on whether there was any form of general charitable intention.

For an example of a scheme directed where the spirit of the original gift was taken into consideration see *White v Williams* [2010] EWHC 940 (Ch), [2010] PTSR 1575, [2010] All ER (D) 40 (May).

5 Charities Act 2011 s 62(1)(b). This comprises the cases on surplus capital and income: see PARAS 131 et seq, 165.

6 Charities Act 2011 s 62(1)(c). The 'appropriate considerations' are, on the one hand, the spirit of the gift concerned and, on the other, the social and economic circumstances prevailing at the time of the proposed alteration of the original purposes: s 62(2).

7 Charities Act 2011 s 62(1)(d). The precursor provision to this was applied in *Peggs v Lamb* [1994] Ch 172, [1994] 2 All ER 15. Cf the power to make schemes enlarging the area of local charities under the Charities Act 2011 s 62(5), (6) (see PARA 217), and the provisions as to dissolution and alteration of parishes (see PARA 269). See also *Richmond Corpn v A-G* [1965] RA 117; on appeal sub nom *Re Richmond Parish Charity Lands* [1965] RA 343, CA.

8 Charities Act 2011 s 62(1)(e)(i).

9 Charities Act 2011 s 62(1)(e)(ii). Cf *National Anti-Vivisection Society v IRC* [1948] AC 31, [1947] 2 All ER 217, HL.

10 Charities Act 2011 s 62(1)(e)(iii). In *Re Lepton's Charity, Ambler v Thomas* [1972] Ch 276, sub nom *Re Lepton's Will Trusts, Re Lepton's Charity, Ambler v Thomas* [1971] 1 All ER 799, a testator gave £3 a year out of a fund to a minister and the residue (originally £2 a year) to the poor; since his death the income had risen so that the poor received almost £800. The 'original purposes' of the gift were held to refer to the gift as a whole, and not to the two parts of the gift separately. See also *Re Royal Kilmainham Hospital* [1966] IR 451 (decided under similar Republic of Ireland legislation); *Varsani v Jesani* [1999] Ch 219, [1998] 3 All ER 273, CA (charity established to promote interests of religious sect which later split into two factions), considered in *White v Williams* [2010] EWHC 940 (Ch), [2010] PTSR 1575, [2010] All ER (D) 40 (May) (scheme directed largely because of a schism in the church in question); see also *Ground, Pople, Lemieux and Lawrence v Charity Commission for England and Wales* (2011) First-tier Tribunal, General Regulatory Chamber (Charity), 6 December.

11 See the Charities Act 2011 s 62(3); and note 2. See also and PARA 213.

12 See *Re Weir Hospital* [1910] 2 Ch 124, CA; *Oldham Borough Council v A-G* [1993] Ch 210, [1993] 2 All ER 432, CA. As to alteration of trusts see PARA 146.

215. Necessity for general charitable intention. On an initial failure[1] of the stated objects of a charitable gift, the property may only be applied cy-près if the donor had a general charitable intention[2] or, in the case of a surplus, if the donor intended to devote to charity the whole of the property given[3]. Where the failure occurs after the gift has once taken effect, the property will be applied cy-près unless the gift was expressly limited to the particular purpose which has failed[4]. The statutory conditions for cy-près applications[5] do not dispense with the necessity for considering these factors[6].

1 As to what constitutes initial failure see PARA 167 et seq. As to the failure of stated charitable objects generally see PARA 213.

2 As to general charitable intention see PARAS 168–172.

3 See PARA 172.

4 As to what constitutes subsequent failure see PARAS 173–174.

5 See PARA 214.

6 See the Charities Act 2011 s 62(3); and *Re JW Laing Trust, Steward's Co Ltd v A-G* [1984] Ch 143, [1984] 1 All ER 50; *Oldham Borough Council v A-G* (1992) Times, 13 April (revsd [1993] Ch 210, [1993] 2 All ER 432, CA); cf *Re Lysaght, Hill v Royal College of Surgeons* [1966] Ch 191, [1965] 2 All ER 888. Note that cases mentioned in this paragraph were decided under earlier legislation.

216. Property of unidentifiable or disclaiming donors. Under the law as it stood before the Charities Act 1960, property given for a specific charitable purpose was not necessarily applicable cy-près if that purpose was or became impracticable, unless a general charitable intention could be shown[1]. Now, however, such property may be applied cy-près as if given for charitable purposes generally, where it belongs to a donor who cannot be found or identified after the prescribed advertisements and inquiries have been published and made and the prescribed period beginning with the publication of those advertisements has expired; or where it belongs to a donor who has executed a disclaimer in the prescribed form of his right to have the property returned[2].

1 See eg *Re Hillier, Hillier v A-G* [1954] 2 All ER 59, [1954] 1 WLR 700, CA; and PARAS 175–178.

2 See the Charities Act 2011 ss 63–66; and PARAS 176–177. In certain cases, advertisements and inquiries are unnecessary or may be dispensed with by the court or the Charity Commission: see s 64(1), (2); and PARA 177. As to the Charity Commission see PARAS 543–578.

The scheme must specify the amount of any property applied as belonging to donors who cannot be identified or found otherwise than under s 64(1) or (2), and may make provision for meeting any claim by any such donor: see s 63(3)–(5); and PARA 177. Schemes have been made by virtue of these provisions in a number of cases: see the *Report of the Charity Commissioners for England and Wales for 1965* (HC Paper (1966–67) no 108) p 8; *Report of the Charity Commissioners for England and Wales for 1969* (HC Paper (1969–70) no 276) p 20.

(4) SCHEMES EXTENDING AREA OF LOCAL CHARITIES

217. Schemes extending area of local charities. Where property is held for charitable purposes which are laid down by reference to one of certain types of area, the court[1] may by scheme made under the court's jurisdiction with respect to charities[2], provide for enlarging the area to another specified area[3].

This does not affect the court's general powers to make cy-près schemes[4].

1 As to the meaning of 'court' see PARA 177 note 12.

2 As to the court's jurisdiction with respect to charities see PARA 534 et seq.

3 See the Charities Act 2011 s 62(5).

Where the existing area is Greater London, the permissible enlargement is any area comprising Greater London: Sch 4 para 1. As to Greater London see **LONDON GOVERNMENT** vol 71 (2013) PARA 14.

Where the existing area is any area in Greater London and not in, or partly in, the City of London the permissible enlargements are: (1) any area in Greater London and not in, or partly in the City of London; (2) the area of Greater London, exclusive of the City of London; (3) any area comprising the area of Greater London, exclusive of the City of London; (4) any area partly in Greater London and partly in any adjacent parish or parishes (civil or ecclesiastical) and not partly in the City of London: Sch 4 para 2.

Where the existing area is a district, the permissible enlargement is any area comprising the district: Sch 4 para 3. As to the City of London see **LONDON GOVERNMENT** vol 71 (2013) PARA 16.

Where the existing area is a Welsh county or county borough the permissible enlargement is any area comprising that county or county borough: Sch 4 para 4.

Where the existing area is any area in a district, the permissible enlargement is: (a) any area in the district; (b) the district; (c) any area comprising the district; (d) any area partly in the district and partly in any adjacent district or in any adjacent Welsh county or county borough: Sch 4 para 5.

Where the existing area is any area in a Welsh county or county borough, the permissible enlargements are: (i) any area in the county or county borough; (ii) the county or county borough; (iii) any area comprising the county or county borough; (iv) any area partly in the county or county borough and partly in any adjacent Welsh county or county borough or in any adjacent district: Sch 4 para 6.

Where the existing area is a parish (civil or ecclesiastical), or two or more parishes, or an area in a parish, or partly in each of two or more parishes, the permissible enlargement is any area not extending beyond the parish or parishes comprising or adjacent to the existing area: see Sch 4 para 7.

In Wales, where the existing area is a community, or two or more communities, or an area in a community, or partly in each of two or more communities, the permissible enlargement is any area not extending beyond the community or communities comprising or adjacent to the existing area: see Sch 4 para 8.

As to local government areas and authorities in England and Wales see LOCAL GOVERNMENT vol 69 (2009) PARA 22 et seq. As to parishes see also ECCLESIASTICAL LAW vol 34 (2011) PARA 262 et seq.

4 Charities Act 2011 s 62(6). For the conditions in which cy-près schemes may be made see s 62(1); and PARA 214. Note also the provisions as to alteration or dissolution of parishes (as to which see PARA 269).

(5) SPECIAL PROVISIONS FOR UNINCORPORATED CHARITIES AND SPECIAL TRUSTS

218. Small unincorporated charities: power to transfer property. The Charities Act 2011 makes provision for a small unincorporated charity to transfer its property[1]. For a charity to fall within this provision, its gross income[2] in its last financial year[3] must not have exceeded £10,000[4] and the charity must not hold any land on trusts[5] which stipulate that the land is to be used for the purposes, or any particular purposes, of the charity[6]. The provisions do not apply to a charitable company or other body corporate[7].

The charity trustees[8] of a charity which comes within these provisions may resolve[9] that all the property of the charity should be transferred to such other charity[10] or be divided between two or more other charities[11], as is or are specified in the resolution[12]. Each charity specified may be either a registered charity or one not required to be registered[13]. Such a resolution can be passed only if the trustees are satisfied that it is expedient in the interests of furthering the purposes for which the property is held by the transferor charity for the property to be transferred in accordance with the resolution[14], and that the purposes, or any of the purposes, of any charity to which property is to be transferred under the resolution are substantially similar to the purposes, or any of the purposes, of the transferor[15].

Where any one of the resolutions mentioned above has been passed by the charity trustees, they must send a copy to the Charity Commission[16] together with a statement of their reasons for passing it[17]. Having received the copy of the resolution the Commission may direct the charity trustees to give public notice of the resolution in such manner as is specified in the direction[18], and, if it gives such a direction, the Commission must take into account any representations[19] made to it by persons appearing to it to be interested in the charity[20]. When considering the resolution, the Commission may direct the charity trustees to provide additional information or explanations relating to the circumstances in and by reference to which they passed the resolution[21], or relating to their compliance with the statutory[22] requirements[23].

Such a resolution takes effect at the end of the period of 60 days beginning with the date on which the copy of it was received by the Charity Commission[24], unless the Commission before the end of that period[25] notifies the charity trustees in writing that it objects to the resolution[26], or if the running of the 60 day period is suspended under the statutory provisions[27]. The Commission may object to the resolution either on procedural grounds (that is, that any statutory obligation imposed on the charity trustees has not been complied with in connection with the resolution), or on the merits of the proposals contained in the resolution[28].

Where such a resolution has taken effect, the charity trustees must arrange for all the property of the transferor charity to be transferred in accordance with the resolution, and on terms that any property so transferred: (1) is to be held by the charity to which it is transferred in accordance with the requirement set out below[29]; but (2) when so held is nevertheless to be subject to any restrictions on expenditure to which it was subject as property of the transferor charity[30]. The charity trustees must arrange for the property to be so transferred by such date after the resolution takes effect as they agree with the charity trustees of the transferee charity or charities concerned[31]. The charity trustees of any charity to which property is transferred under this provision must secure, so far as is reasonably practicable, that the property is applied for such of its purposes as are substantially similar to those of the transferor charity; but this requirement does not apply if those charity trustees consider that complying with it would not result in a suitable and effective method of applying the property[32].

For the purpose of enabling any property to be transferred to a charity under these statutory provisions, the Charity Commission may, at the request of the charity trustees of that charity, make orders vesting any property of the transferor charity in the transferee charity, in its charity trustees or in any trustee for that charity, or in any other person nominated by those charity trustees to hold property in trust for that charity[33].

1 See the Charities Act 2011 ss 267–272: and the text and notes 2–23. Modified rules are applicable to small charities with a permanent endowment (see ss 273, 274; and PARA 219): s 267(3).

A charity is deemed for the purposes of the Charities Act 2011 to have a permanent endowment unless all property held for the purposes of the charity may be expended for those purposes without distinction between capital and income, and 'permanent endowment' means, in relation to any charity, property held subject to a restriction on its being expended for the purposes of the charity: s 353(3).

2 'Gross income', in relation to a charity, means its gross recorded income from all sources, including special trusts: Charities Act 2011 s 353(1). 'Special trust' means property which is held and administered by or on behalf of a charity for any special purposes of the charity, and is so held and administered on separate trusts relating only to that property but a special trust does not, by itself, constitute a charity for the purposes of Pt 8 (ss 130–176): s 287. As to the meaning of 'charity' see PARA 1.

3 'Financial year' is to be construed, in relation to a charitable company, in accordance with the Companies Act 2006 s 390 (see COMPANIES vol 15 (2009) PARA 711), and, in relation to any other charity, in accordance with regulations made under the Charities Act 2011 s 132(3) (see PARA 344): s 353(1). Accordingly the financial year of a charity which is not a company ('relevant charity') is, for the purposes of the Charities Act 2011 and regulations made under that Act, to be determined in accordance with the following: Charities (Accounts and Reports) Regulations 2008, SI 2008/629, reg 3(1). The first financial year of a relevant charity is the period beginning with the day on which the charity is established and ending with its accounting reference date or such other date, not more than seven days before or after the accounting reference date, as the charity trustees may determine: reg 3(2). Subsequent financial years of a relevant charity begin with the day immediately following the last day of the charity's previous financial year and end with its accounting reference date or such other date, not more than seven days before or after the accounting reference date, as the charity trustees may determine: reg 3(3). For this purpose, the 'accounting reference date' of a relevant charity is:

(1) in relation to the first financial year of the charity, such date, not less than six months and not more than 18 months after the date on which the charity was established as the charity trustees may determine (reg 3(4)(a));

(2) in relation to a subsequent financial year of the charity:

 (a) the date 12 months after the previous accounting reference date of the charity (reg 3(4)(b)(i)); or

 (b) subject to reg 3(5) and reg 3(7), such other date, not less than six months and not more than 18 months after the previous accounting reference date of the charity as the charity trustees may determine (reg 3(4)(b)(ii)).

The charity trustees may only exercise the power in head (2) in respect of a restricted financial year with the consent of the Commission: reg 3(5). For this purpose 'restricted financial year' means a financial year beginning immediately after:

(i) a financial year in respect of which the charity trustees had exercised the power in head

(b) above or in the Charities (Accounts and Reports) Regulations 2005, SI 2005/572, reg 6(4)(b) (revoked) (Charities (Accounts and Reports) Regulations 2008, SI 2008/629, reg 3(6)(a));

(ii) a financial year ('A') where A began immediately after a financial year in respect of which the charity trustees had exercised the power in head (b) above or in the Charities (Accounts and Reports) Regulations 2005, SI 2005/572, reg 6(4)(b) (revoked) (Charities (Accounts and Reports) Regulations 2008, SI 2008/629, reg 3(6)(b)).

The charity trustees may exercise their power under head (b) above so as to determine an accounting reference date less, or more, than 12 months from the beginning of the financial year only where they satisfied that there are exceptional reasons to do so: reg 3(7).

4 The Minister may by order amend the Charities Act 2011 s 267(1) by substituting a different sum for the sum for the time being specified there: s 285(2). At the date at which this volume states the law no such order had been made. As to the Minister see PARA 586. As to the making of orders generally see ss 347, 348; and PARA 590.

5 'Trusts', in relation to a charity, means the provisions establishing it as a charity and regulating its purposes and administration, whether those provisions take effect by way of trust or not, and in relation to other institutions has a corresponding meaning: Charities Act 2011 s 353(1).

6 Charities Act 2011 s 267(1). The requirement that a charity must satisfy the gross income limit in order to fall within this provision does not apply in the case of a resolution by the charity trustees of a charity to transfer all its property to a charitable incorporated organisation or to divide its property between two or more charitable incorporated organisations: s 267(2). As to the Minister see PARA 586.

7 Charities Act 2011 s 267(1)(c). As to the meaning of 'company' see PARA 246.

8 As to the meaning of 'charity trustees' see PARA 255.

9 Any resolution must be passed by a majority of not less than two-thirds of the charity trustees voting on the resolution: Charities Act 2011 s 268(4).

10 For these purposes, references to the transfer of property to a charity are references to its transfer to the charity, or to the charity trustees, or to any trustee for the charity, or to a person nominated by the charity trustees to hold it in trust for the charity, as the charity trustees may determine: Charities Act 2011 s 267(4).

11 Ie in such manner as is specified in the resolution: Charities Act 2011 s 268(1)(b).

12 Charities Act 2011 s 268(1). No transfer or vesting of any property under Pt 13 (ss 267–286) operates as a breach of any covenant or condition against alienation or gives rise to forfeiture: s 286.

13 Charities Act 2011 s 268(2). As to the register see PARA 307 et seq.

14 Charities Act 2011 s 268(3)(a).

15 Charities Act 2011 s 268(3)(b).

16 As to the Charity Commission see PARAS 543–578.

17 Charities Act 2011 s 268(5).

18 Charities Act 2011 s 269(1)(a).

19 To be taken into account, such representations must have been made within the period of 28 days beginning with the date when public notice of the resolution was given by the charity trustees: Charities Act 2011 s 269(1)(b)(ii).

20 Charities Act 2011 s 269(1)(b).

21 Charities Act 2011 s 269(2)(a).

22 Ie those under the Charities Act 2011 s 268.

23 Charities Act 2011 s 269(2)(b).

24 Charities Act 2011 s 270.

25 Or that period as modified by the statutory provisions, if applicable: see note 28.

26 See the Charities Act 2011 s 271(3).

Appeal against the decision of the Commission to notify charity trustees that it objects to a resolution under s 271 (or s 275: see PARA 220) lies to the Tribunal at the instance of the Attorney General, the charity trustees or any other person who is or may be affected by the decision: s 319(2), Sch 6 Table cols 1, 2. The Tribunal has power to quash the decision: Sch 6 Table col 3. As to the meaning of 'person who is or may be affected' within the meaning of Sch 6 see PARA 317 note 8. As to the Tribunal see PARA 579 et seq. As to the Attorney General see PARAS 589, 596, 605 et seq; and **CONSTITUTIONAL AND ADMINISTRATIVE LAW** vol 20 (2014) PARA 273 et seq.

27 See the Charities Act 2011 s 271(4), (5).

If the Commission directs the charity trustees to give public notice of a resolution (ie under the Charities Act 2011 s 269(1)) then the running of the 60 day period is suspended as from the date on which the direction is given to the charity trustees, until the end of the period of 42 days beginning with the date on which public notice of the resolution is given by the charity trustees: s 271(4).

If the Commission directs the charity trustees to provide any information or explanations (ie under s 269(2)) then the running of the 60 day period is suspended as from the date on which the direction is given to the charity trustees, until the date on which the information or explanations is or are provided to the Commission: s 271(5).

Once the period of time, or the total period of time, during which the 60 day period is suspended exceeds 120 days, the resolution (if not previously objected to by the Commission) is to be treated as if it had never been passed: s 271(6), (7).

28 Charities Act 2011 s 271(1)–(3).

29 Charities Act 2011 s 272(2)(a). The requirement referred to is that set out in s 272(3): see text and note 32.

30 Charities Act 2011 s 272(2)(b).

31 Charities Act 2011 s 272(2).

32 Charities Act 2011 s 272(3).

33 Charities Act 2011 s 272(4).

219. Transfer where charity has permanent endowment. Special rules apply to resolutions to transfer the property of a charity to such other charity or charities under the statutory provisions for small unincorporated charities[1] where the charity in question has a permanent endowment[2], whether or not the charity's trusts contain provision for the termination of the charity[3].

In the case of charity all the property of which is comprised in its permanent endowment, the statutory provisions apply to any or all of such property[4] subject to the following modifications[5]:

(1) if the property comprised in its permanent endowment is to be transferred to a single charity, the charity trustees must be satisfied[6] that the proposed transferee charity has purposes which are substantially similar to all of the purposes of the transferor charity[7];

(2) if the property comprised in its permanent endowment is to be transferred to two or more charities, the charity trustees must be satisfied[8] that the proposed transferee charities, taken together, have purposes which are substantially similar to all of the purposes of the transferor charity, and that each of the proposed transferee charities has purposes which are substantially similar to one or more of the purposes of the transferor charity[9];

(3) in the case of a transfer to two or more charities the resolution must provide for the property comprised in the permanent endowment of the charity to be divided between the transferee charities in such a way as to take account of such guidance as may be given by the Charity Commission[10] for these purposes[11];

(4) the requirement that the charity trustees of any charity to which property is transferred must secure, so far as is reasonably practicable, that the property is applied for such of its purposes as are substantially similar to those of the transferor charity[12], must apply in the case of every such transfer and in complying with that requirement the charity trustees of a transferee charity must secure that the application of property transferred to the charity takes account of any such Commission guidance[13].

In the case of a charity with both a permanent endowment and unrestricted property[14], such a resolution must relate to both its permanent endowment and its unrestricted property[15]. The statutory provisions apply in relation to the unrestricted property of the charity as if references in those provisions were references to any or all of its unrestricted property[16]. The statutory provisions apply in relation to the permanent endowment subject to the modifications above[17].

1 Ie the provisions contained within the Charities Act 2011 ss 268–272 (see PARA 218).
2 See the Charities Act 2011 s 267(3); and PARA 218.
3 Charities Act 2011 s 273(1).
4 Charities Act 2011 s 273(3). References for these purposes to all or any of the property of a charity are references to all or any of the property comprised in its permanent endowment: s 274(2).
5 See the Charities Act 2011 s 273(3), 274(1). References in the following modifications to the transfer of property to a charity are references to its transfer to the charity, or to the charity trustees, or to any trustee for the charity, or to a person nominated by the charity trustees to hold it in trust for the charity, as the charity trustees may determine: ss 267(4).
6 Ie rather than being satisfied as mentioned in the Charities Act 2011 s 268(3)(b). As to s 268(3)(b) see PARA 218 text and note 15. For the purposes of the statutory provisions contained in ss 268–272, any reference to any obligation imposed on the charity trustees by or under s 268 or s 269 (see PARA 218) includes a reference to any obligation imposed on them by virtue of s 274(3)–(5): s 274(6).
7 See the Charities Act 2011 s 274(3).
8 Ie rather than being satisfied as mentioned in the Charities Act 2011 s 268(3)(b). See note 6.
9 See the Charities Act 2011 s 274(4).
10 As to the Charity Commission see PARAS 543–578. Any guidance given by the Commission for these purposes may take such form and be given in such manner as the Commission considers appropriate: Charities Act 2011 s 274(8).
11 Charities Act 2011 s 274(5). See note 6.
12 Ie the requirement in the Charities Act 2011 s 272(3); on which see PARA 218.
13 Charities Act 2011 s 274(7).
14 Ie property other than permanent endowment: Charities Act 2011 s 273(2).
15 Charities Act 2011 s 273(2)(a).
16 Charities Act 2011 s 273(2)(b)(i).
17 Ie the modifications detailed in text and notes 4–11: Charities Act 2011 s 273(2)(b)(ii), (4)–(11).

220. Small unincorporated charities: power to modify purposes. The Charities Act 2011 makes provision for a small unincorporated charity to modify its purposes[1]. For a charity to fall within this provision, its gross income[2] in its last financial year[3] must not have exceeded £10,000[4] and the charity must not hold any land on trusts[5] which stipulate that the land is to be used for the purposes, or any particular purposes, of the charity[6]. The provisions do not apply to a charitable company or other body corporate[7]. The charity trustees[8] may resolve[9] that the trusts of the charity should be modified by replacing all or any of the purposes of the charity with other charitable purposes[10] specified in the resolution[11]. Such a resolution can be passed only where the charity trustees are satisfied that it is expedient in the interests of the charity for the purposes in question to be replaced and that, in so far as is reasonably practicable, the new purposes consist of or include purposes that are similar in character to those that are to be replaced[12].

The procedure, if a resolution is passed, is exactly the same as in the case of a resolution to transfer the charity property[13].

The trusts of the charity concerned are to be taken to be have been modified in accordance with the terms of the resolution as from the time when it takes effect under this procedure[14].

1 See the Charities Act 2011 s 275; and notes 2–13.
2 As to the meaning of 'gross income' see PARA 218 note 2. As to the meaning of 'charity' see PARA 1. As to the meaning of 'special trust' see PARA 218 note 2.
3 As to the meaning of 'financial year' see PARA 218 note 3.

4 The Minister may by order amend the Charities Act 2011 s 275(1) by substituting a different sum for the sum for the time being specified there: s 285(1), (2). At the date at which this volume states the law no such order had been made. As to the Minister see PARA 586. As to the making of orders generally see ss 347, 348; and PARA 590.
5 As to the meaning of 'trusts' see PARA 218 note 5.
6 Charities Act 2011 s 275(1).
7 Charities Act 2011 s 275(1)(c). As to the meaning of 'company' see PARA 246.
8 As to the meaning of 'charity trustees' see PARA 255.
9 Any resolution must be passed by a majority of not less than two-thirds of the charity trustees voting on the resolution: Charities Act 2011 s 275(5).
10 Charities Act 2011 s 275(3). As to the meaning of 'charitable purposes' see PARA 2.
11 Charities Act 2011 s 275(2).
12 Charities Act 2011 s 275(4).
13 See the Charities Act 2011 ss 275(6), 276–278. The procedure is identical to that described in ss 268(5), 269–271: see PARA 218.
14 Charities Act 2011 s 279.

221. Small unincorporated charities: power to modify powers or procedures. The Charities Act 2011 makes provision for any charity which is not a company or other body corporate[1] to modify its powers or procedures[2]. The charity trustees[3] may resolve that any provision of the trusts of the charity relating to any of the powers exercisable by the charity trustees in the administration of the charity, or regulating the procedure to be followed in any respect in connection with its administration, should be modified in such manner as is specified in the resolution[4]. Where the charity is an unincorporated association with a body of members distinct from the charity trustees, any such resolution must be approved by a further resolution which is passed at a general meeting of the body[5]. The trusts are to be taken to have been so modified as from such date as specified in the resolution or, in the case of an unincorporated association with a body of members distinct from the charity trustees, the date when any such further resolution was passed[6], if later[7].

1 See the Charities Act 2011 s 280(1). As to the meaning of 'company' see PARA 246.
2 See the Charities Act 2011 s 280.
3 As to the meaning of 'charity trustees' see PARA 255.
4 Charities Act 2011 s 280(2). Where the trustees have passed a resolution under s 280(2) and (if s 280(4) applies) a further resolution has been passed under s 280(4) the trusts of the charity are to be taken to have been modified in accordance with the terms of the resolution: s 280(5).
5 Charities Act 2011 s 280(3), (4). This must either be by a majority of not less than two-thirds of the members entitled to attend and vote at the meeting who vote on the resolution, or by a decision taken without a vote and without any expression of dissent in response to the question put to the meeting: s 280(4)(a), (b).
6 Ie under the Charities Act 2011 s 280(4).
7 See the Charities Act 2011 s 280(6).

222. Small unincorporated charities: general power to spend capital. The Charities Act 2011 makes provision for a small unincorporated charity to spend its capital[1]. The provision applies to any available endowment fund[2] of a charity which is not a company or a body corporate[3], save where the fund falls under the statutory provision for larger unincorporated associations to spend capital given for a particular purpose[4]. Where the charity trustees[5] are satisfied that the purposes set out in the trusts to which the fund is subject could be carried out more effectively if the capital of the fund, or the relevant portion of the capital, could be expended as well as income accruing to it, rather than just such income[6], then the charity trustees may resolve that the fund, or a portion of it, ought to be freed from the restrictions with respect to expenditure of capital that apply to it[7]. Once the charity trustees have passed such a resolution, the fund or portion may be expended in carrying out the purposes set out in the trusts to which the fund is subject without regard to the restrictions with respect to capital expenditure[8]. The fund or portion may be so expended as from such date as is specified for the purpose in the resolution[9].

1 See the Charities Act 2011 s 281; and notes 2–9.
2 For these purposes 'available endowment fund' means the whole of the charity's permanent endowment if it is all subject to the same trusts, or any part of its permanent endowment which is subject to any particular trusts that are different from those to which any other part is subject: Charities Act 2011 s 281(7).
3 Charities Act 2011 s 281(1).
4 Charities Act 2011 s 281(2). As to the statutory provision for larger unincorporated associations to spend capital given for a particular purpose see ss 282–284 and PARA 223.
5 As to the meaning of 'charity trustees' see PARA 255.
6 Charities Act 2011 s 281(4).
7 Charities Act 2011 s 281(3).
8 Charities Act 2011 s 281(5).
9 Charities Act 2011 s 281(6).

223. Larger unincorporated charities: power to spend capital given for particular purpose. The Charities Act 2011 makes provision for a larger unincorporated charity to spend its capital[1]. The provision applies to any available endowment fund[2] of a charity which is not a company or a body corporate[3], where: (1) the capital of the fund consists entirely of property given[4] by a particular individual, by a particular institution by way of grant or otherwise, or by two or more individuals or institutions in pursuit of a common purpose[5]; (2) the relevant charity's gross income[6] in its last financial year exceeded £1,000 and the market value[7] of the endowment fund exceeds £10,000[8]. Where the charity trustees[9] are satisfied that the purposes set out in the trusts to which the fund is subject could be carried out more effectively if the capital of the fund, or the relevant portion of the capital, could be expended as well as income accruing to it, rather than just such income[10], then the charity trustees may resolve that the fund, or a portion of it, ought to be freed from the restrictions with respect to expenditure of capital that apply to it[11].

Once the charity trustees have passed such a resolution, a copy must be passed to the Charity Commission[12], together with a statement of their reasons for passing it[13]. The Commission may direct the charity trustees to give public notice of the resolution in such manner as is specified in the direction[14], and if it gives such a direction, the Commission must take into account any representations made to it by persons appearing to it to be interested in the charity[15]. The Commission may also direct the charity trustees to provide the Commission with additional information or explanations relating to the circumstances in and by reference to which they have decided to act under the statutory provision, or their compliance with any obligation imposed on them by or under the statutory provision[16].

When considering whether to concur with the resolution the Commission must take into account any evidence available to it as to the wishes of the donor or donors of the endowment fund, and any changes in the circumstances relating to the charity since the making of the gift or gifts, including, in particular, its financial position, the needs of its beneficiaries, and the social, economic and legal environment in which it operates[17]. The Commission must not concur with the resolution unless it is satisfied that: (a) its implementation would accord with the spirit of the gift or gifts, even though it would be inconsistent with the restrictions with respect to expenditure of capital that apply; and (b) the charity trustees have complied with their obligations imposed on them by or under the statutory provision[18].

The Commission must notify the charity trustees in writing, before the end of a period of three months beginning with the 'relevant date', either that it concurs with the resolution, or that it does not concur with it[19]. The 'relevant date' means the date on which the Commission receives a copy of the resolution, save where the Commission directs the charity trustees to give public notice of the resolution when it means the date when that notice is given[20]. Where the charity trustees are notified by the Commission that it concurs with the resolution, or the period of three months has elapsed without the Commission notifying them that it does not concur with the resolution, the fund or portion may be expended in carrying out the purposes set out in the trusts to which the fund is subject without regard to the restrictions with respect to expenditure of capital that apply[21]. The charity trustees may not otherwise implement such a resolution[22].

1 See the Charities Act 2011 ss 282–284; and notes 2–22.
2 As to the meaning of 'available endowment fund' see the Charities Act 2011 s 281(7); and PARA 222 note 2 (definition applied by s 282(5)).
3 See the Charities Act 2011 s 282(1). As to the meaning of 'company' see PARA 246.
4 This includes the giving under a will: Charities Act 2011 s 282(6). As to wills generally see **WILLS AND INTESTACY**.
5 Charities Act 2011 s 282(1)(a).
6 As to the meaning of 'gross income' see PARA 218 note 2.
7 'Market value', in relation to an endowment fund, means the market value of the fund as recorded in the accounts for the last financial year of the relevant charity, or if no such value was so recorded, the current market value of the fund as determined on a valuation carried out for the purpose: Charities Act 2011 s 282(5).
8 Charities Act 2011 s 282(1)(b). The Minister may by order amend s 282(1)(b) by substituting a different sum for either of the sums for the time being specified there: s 285(1), (2). At the date at which this volume states the law no such order had been made. As to the Minister see PARA 586.
9 As to the meaning of 'charity trustees' see PARA 255.
10 Charities Act 2011 s 282(3).
11 Charities Act 2011 s 282(2).
12 As to the Charity Commission see PARAS 543–578.
13 Charities Act 2011 s 282(4)(a).
14 Charities Act 2011 s 283(1)(a).
15 Where those representations are made to it within the period of 28 days beginning with the date when public notice of the resolution is given by the charity trustees: Charities Act 2011 s 283(1)(b).
16 Charities Act 2011 s 283(2).
17 Charities Act 2011 s 284(1).
18 Charities Act 2011 s 284(2). The provisions referred to are ss 282, 283.
19 Charities Act 2011 s 284(3).

Appeal against the decision of the Commission not to concur with the resolution of charity trustees lies to the Tribunal at the instance of the Attorney General, the charity trustees or any other person who is or may be affected by the decision: s 319(2), Sch 6 Table cols 1, 2. The Tribunal has power to quash the decision and (if appropriate) remit the matter to the Commission: Sch 6 Table col 3. As to the meaning of 'person who is or may be affected' within the meaning of Sch 6 see PARA 317 note 8. As to the Tribunal see PARA 579 et seq. As to the Attorney General see PARAS 589, 596, 605 et seq; and **CONSTITUTIONAL AND ADMINISTRATIVE LAW** vol 20 (2014) PARA 273 et seq.
20 Charities Act 2011 s 284(4).
21 Charities Act 2011 s 284(5).
22 Charities Act 2011 s 282(4)(b).

224. Power to spend capital subject to special trusts. The Charities Act 2011 makes provision for a charity to spend capital subject to a special trust[1] which, as the result of a direction by the Charity Commission[2], is to be treated as a separate charity for the purposes of the Act[3]. The provision applies to any available endowment fund[4] of such a special trust[5]. Where the charity trustees[6] are satisfied that the purposes set out in the trusts to which the fund is subject could be carried out more effectively if the capital of the fund, or the relevant portion of the capital, could be expended as well as income accruing to it, rather than just such income[7], then they may resolve that the fund, or a portion of it, ought to be freed from the restrictions with respect to expenditure of capital that apply to it[8].

In relation to a larger fund, namely where:

(1) the market value[9] of the fund exceeds £10,000[10]; and
(2) the capital of the fund consists entirely of property given[11] by a particular individual, by a particular institution (by way of grant or otherwise) or by two or more individuals or institutions in pursuit of a common purpose,

then, if such a resolution is passed, the same procedure as applies in the case of a resolution in respect of a larger unincorporated charity to spend its capital must be followed[12]. The charity trustees must send a copy of the resolution to the Commission together with a statement of their reasons for passing it[13]. Where the charity trustees are notified by the Charity Commission that it concurs with the resolution, or the period of three months has elapsed without the Commission notifying them that it does not concur with the resolution[14], then the fund may be expended in carrying out the purposes set out in the trusts to which the fund is subject without regard to these restrictions[15], from such date as is specified for this purpose in the resolution[16].

Where the fund does not fall within the description of a larger fund[17], then if such a resolution is passed the fund may be expended in carrying out the purposes set out in the trusts to which the fund is subject without regard to these restrictions[18], from such date as is specified for this purpose in the resolution[19].

1 As to the meaning of 'special trust' see PARA 218 note 2.
2 Ie a direction under the Charities Act 2011 s 12(1) (see PARA 550): s 288(1). As to the Charity Commission see PARAS 543–578.
3 Charities Act 2011 s 288(1).
4 As to the meaning of 'available endowment fund' see the Charities Act 2011 s 281; and PARA 222 (definition applied by s 288(7)).
5 Charities Act 2011 s 288(1).
6 As to the meaning of 'charity trustees' see PARA 255.
7 Charities Act 2011 ss 288(4), 289(3).
8 Charities Act 2011 ss 288(3), 289(2).
9 As to the meaning of 'market value' see the Charities Act 2011 s 282; and PARA 223 note 7 (definition applied by s 289(5).
10 Charities Act 2011 s 289(1)(b). The Minister may by order amend s 289(1)(b) by substituting a different sum for the sum for the time being specified there: s 292. At the date at which this volume states the law no such order had been made. As to the Minister see PARA 586.
11 Including under a will: Charities Act 2011 s 289(6). As to wills generally see **WILLS AND INTESTACY**.
12 Charities Act 2011 ss 289(4)(b), 290, 291. The procedure is identical to that described in ss 282–284: see PARA 223.
13 Charities Act 2011 ss 289(4)(a).
14 Charities Act 2011 s 291(5).
15 Charities Act 2011 s 291(5).
16 Charities Act 2011 s 291(6).
17 The Charities Act 2011 s 288 does not apply to a fund if ss 289–291 (see text and notes 15–19) apply: s 288(2).
18 Charities Act 2011 s 288(5).
19 Charities Act 2011 s 288(6).

5. CORPORATE STRUCTURES FOR CHARITIES

(1) TYPES OF CORPORATE STRUCTURES

225. The various types of charitable corporate structures. There are various types of corporate structures for charities. Most recently, the Charities Act 2011 introduced charitable incorporated organisations ('CIOs')[1]. Then there are charitable companies registered under the Companies Acts[2]. Finally there are charitable corporations whose corporate purpose is charitable[3]; and this includes eleemosynary corporations, established for the perpetual distribution of the free alms or bounty of the founder[4].

In the case of a charitable company or corporation much of the general law relating to companies and corporations will apply[5]; however, there are exceptions[6].

1 See PARA 226 et seq.
2 See PARA 240 et seq.
3 See PARA 244 et seq. As to the different classes of corporation, and as to the powers of corporations generally, see **CORPORATIONS**. As to the incorporation of charity trustees see PARA 263. As to charitable purposes see PARA 2 et seq.
4 1 Bl Com 459; 1 Kyd on Corporations 25; Shelford's Law of Mortmain 23; and see PARA 256. Corporations which are wholly ecclesiastical are taken out of the definition of a 'charity' by the Charities Act 2011 s 10 (see PARA 196). As to what are eleemosynary charities see *Re Armitage, Ellam v Norwich Corpn* [1972] Ch 438, sub nom *Re Armitage's Will Trusts* [1972] 1 All ER 708.
5 See eg PARA 255 note 5. As to companies and corporations generally see **COMPANIES; CORPORATIONS**.
6 See eg PARA 240.

(2) CHARITABLE INCORPORATED ORGANISATIONS

226. Charitable incorporated organisations. The Charities Act 2011 makes provision for the creation and regulation of charitable[1] incorporated organisations[2] or 'CIO's[3]. A CIO is a body corporate[4] constituted, registered and regulated by the Charity Commission[5].

1 As to the meaning of 'charitable' see PARA 1.
2 Charities Act 2011 Pt 11 (ss 204–250).
3 Charities Act 2011 s 204.
4 Charities Act 2011 s 205(1).
5 See the Charities Act 2011 ss 206–244; and PARA 227 et seq. As to the Charity Commission see PARAS 543–578.

227. Constitution and name. A charitable incorporated organisation ('CIO')[1] must have a constitution[2], a principal office in England or Wales[3], and one or more members[4]. The constitution must state the name of the CIO[5], its purposes[6], whether its principal office is in England or Wales[7] and whether or not its members are liable to contribute to its assets if it is wound up, and if they are so liable up to what amount[8]. The constitution must also make provision (1) about who is eligible for membership and how a person becomes a member[9]; (2) about the appointment of one or more persons who are to be charity trustees of the CIO and about any condition of eligibility for appointment[10]; and (3) containing directions about the application of property of the CIO on its dissolution[11]. The constitution must provide for such other matters, and comply with such requirements, as are specified in regulations made by the Minister[12] and must be in the form specified in regulations by the Charity Commission[13] or as near to that form as the circumstances admit[14].

Subject to anything in its constitution, a CIO has power to do anything which is calculated to further its purposes or is conducive or incidental to doing so[15] and a CIO must use and apply its property in furtherance of its purposes and in accordance with its constitution[16].

The name of a CIO must appear in legible characters in every location, and in every description of document or communication, in which a charitable company would be required[17] to state its registered name, and in all conveyances[18] purporting to be executed by the CIO[19]. Where the name of the CIO does not include 'charitable incorporated organisation' or 'CIO'[20], then its status as a CIO must be stated in legible characters in all the locations, documents communications and conveyances in which its name must appear by virtue of the statutory provisions[21]. Any legal proceedings brought by a CIO to enforce a right arising out of a contract or conveyance in connection with which there was a failure to comply with the requirement to disclose its name and status[22] must be dismissed if the defendant to the proceedings shows[23]:

(a) that he has a claim against the claimant arising out of the contract or conveyance that he has been unable to pursue by reason of the failure to comply[24]; or
(b) that he has suffered some financial loss in connection with the contract or conveyance by reason of the failure to comply[25],

unless the court before which the proceedings are brought is satisfied that it is just and equitable to permit the proceedings to continue[26].

1 As to the creation of a charitable incorporated organisation see PARA 226.
2 Charities Act 2011 s 205(2)(a). The constitution must be in English if its principal office is in England and may be in either English or Welsh if its principal office is in Wales: s 206(4).
3 Charities Act 2011 s 205(2)(b).
4 Charities Act 2011 s 205(2)(c). The members may be either not liable to contribute to the assets of the CIO if it is wound up or liable to do so up to a maximum amount each: s 205(3).
5 Charities Act 2011 s 206(1)(a).
6 Charities Act 2011 s 206(1)(b).
7 Charities Act 2011 s 206(1)(c).
8 Charities Act 2011 s 206(1)(d).
9 Charities Act 2011 s 206(2)(a).
10 Charities Act 2011 s 206(2)(b).
11 Charities Act 2011 s 206(2)(c).
12 Charities Act 2011 s 206(3). See the Charitable Incorporated Organisations (General) Regulations 2012, SI 2012/3012, Pt III (regs 13–18).
13 As to the Charity Commission see PARAS 543–578. Regulations of the Charity Commission are not made by statutory instrument, but are published by the Commission. For the form of constitution set out by the Commission see the Charities Act 2011 (Charitable Incorporated Organisations) (Constitutions) Regulations 2012 (available, at the date at which this volume states the law, on the government website), which sets out different constitutions for CIOs, depending on whether (1) its voting members are its charity trustees, (2) it has a voting membership in addition to the charity trustees, and (3) it has voting members other than its charity trustees.
14 Charities Act 2011 s 206(5). As to regulations made under this provision see notes 12, 13.
15 Charities Act 2011 s 216(1).
16 Charities Act 2011 s 217(1).
17 Ie required by regulations under the Companies Act 2006 s 82: see **COMPANIES** vol 14 (2009) PARA 220.
18 Conveyance means any instrument creating, transferring, varying or extinguishing an interest in land: Charities Act 2011 s 211(2).
19 Charities Act 2011 s 211(1).

20 Or the Welsh equivalent, 'sefydliad elusennol corfforedig' or 'SEC': Charities Act 2011 s 212(1), (2). It is irrelevant whether or not there are full stops after each letter and whether or not capital letters are used in either the English or Welsh abbreviation: s 212(1), (2).
21 Charities Act 2011 s 212(3). This statement must be in English, except that in the case of a document which is otherwise wholly in Welsh the statement may be in Welsh: s 211(4).
22 Charities Act 2011 s 213(1); and see the text and notes 17–21.
23 See the Charities Act 2011 s 213(2). Section 213 does not affect the right of any person to enforce such rights as he may have against another person in any proceedings brought by that person: s 213(3).
24 Charities Act 2011 s 213(2)(a).
25 Charities Act 2011 s 213(2)(b).
26 Charities Act 2011 s 213(2).

228. Amendment of constitution. A charitable incorporated organisation ('CIO')[1] may by resolution of its members[2] amend its constitution[3]. Such a resolution must be passed by a 75 per cent majority[4] of those voting at a general meeting of the CIO or unanimously by the CIO's members otherwise than at a general meeting[5]. However, the power of a CIO to amend its constitution is not exercisable in any way which would result in the CIO's ceasing to be a charity[6]. A resolution containing an amendment which would make any regulated alteration[7] is to that extent ineffective unless the prior written consent of the Charity Commission[8] has been obtained to the making of the amendment[9].

A CIO must send to the Commission a copy of a resolution containing an amendment to its constitution[10], together with a copy of the constitution as amended[11], and such other documents[12] and information as the Commission may require[13], by the end of the period of 15 days beginning with the date of passing of the resolution[14]. An amendment does not take effect until it has been registered[15].

The Commission must refuse to register an amendment if in the opinion of the Commission the CIO had no power to make it[16], or the amendment would change the name of the CIO, and the Commission could have refused an application for the constitution and registration of a CIO with the name specified in the amendment under the provisions on unsuitable names[17]. The Commission may refuse to register an amendment if the amendment would make a regulated alteration and the prior written consent of the Commission had not been obtained[18].

An appeal against a decision of the Commission to refuse to register such an amendment lies to the Tribunal[19] at the instance of the Attorney General, the CIO, the charity trustees of the CIO or any other person who is or may be affected by the decision[20]. The Tribunal has the power to quash the decision and, if appropriate, remit the matter to the Commission or direct the Commission to register the amendment[21].

1 As to the creation of a charitable incorporated organisation see PARA 226.
2 'Members', in relation to a charity with a body of members distinct from the charity trustees, means any of those members: Charities Act 2011 s 353(1).
3 Charities Act 2011 s 224(1). A single resolution may provide for more than one amendment: s 224(1). The date of passing of such a resolution is the date of the general meeting at which it was passed, or if it was passed otherwise than at a general meeting, the date on which provision in the CIO's constitution or in regulations about the procedure of CIOs deems it to have been passed, but that date may not be earlier than that on which the last member agreed to it: s 224(3). As to a CIO's constitution see PARA 227.
4 This percentage includes those voting by proxy or by post, if voting that way is permitted: Charities Act 2011 s 224(2)(a).
5 Charities Act 2011 s 224(2)(a), (b).
6 Charities Act 2011 s 225. As to the meaning of 'charity' see PARA 1.

7 The following are 'regulated alterations': (1) any alteration of the CIO's purposes; (2) any alteration of any provision of the CIO's constitution directing the application of property of the CIO on its dissolution; (3) any alteration of any provision of the CIO's constitution where the alteration would provide authorisation for any benefit to be obtained by charity trustees or members of the CIO or persons connected with them: Charities Act 2011 s 226(2). For these purposes 'benefit' means a direct or indirect benefit of any nature, except that it does not include any remuneration within the meaning of s 185 (see PARA 336) whose receipt may be authorised under s 185: ss 226(3), 248.

For the purposes of these provisions, the following persons are 'connected' with a charity trustee or member of a CIO: (a) a child, parent, grandchild, grandparent, brother or sister of the trustee or member; (b) the spouse or civil partner of the trustee or member or of any person falling within head (a) above; (c) a person carrying on business in partnership with the trustee or member with any person falling within head (a) or head (b); (d) an institution which is controlled by the trustee member or by any person falling within head (a), (b) or (c), or by two or more such persons, when taken together; and (e) a body corporate in which the trustee member or any connected person falling within heads (a)–(c) has a substantial interest, or two or more such persons falling, when taken together, have a substantial interest: Charities Act 2011 ss 226(3), 249(1), (2). As to the effect of the Marriage (Same Sex Couples) Act 2013 see s 1(1), 11(1); and **MATRIMONIAL AND CIVIL PARTNERSHIP LAW** vol 72 (2009) PARA 1 et seq. The provisions in the Charities Act 2011 ss 350–352 (see PARA 401) apply for the purposes of s 249: s 249(3).

As to the meaning of 'charity trustees' see PARA 255.

8 As to the Charity Commission see PARAS 543–578.

9 Charities Act 2011 s 226(1). Where the Commission does register such an amendment s 226(1) does not apply: s 227(5).

10 Charities Act 2011 s 227(1).

11 Charities Act 2011 s 227(1)(a).

12 As to the meaning of 'document' see PARA 263 note 2.

13 Charities Act 2011 s 227(1)(b).

14 Charities Act 2011 s 227(1). As to the date of the passing of the resolution see note 3.

15 Charities Act 2011 s 227(2).

16 Eg because the effect of making it would be that the CIO ceased to be a charity, or that the CIO or its constitution did not comply with any requirement imposed by or by virtue of the Charities Act 2011 or any other enactment: see s 227(3)(a).

17 Charities Act 2011 s 227(3). As to the provisions on names unsuitable for a CIO see s 208; and PARA 230.

18 Charities Act 2011 s 227(4). See also note 9.

19 As to the Tribunal see PARA 579 et seq.

20 Charities Act 2011 s 319(2), Sch 6 Table Cols 1, 2. As to the meaning of 'person who is or may be affected' within the meaning of Sch 6 see PARA 317 note 8. As to the Attorney General see PARAS 589, 596, 605 et seq; and **CONSTITUTIONAL AND ADMINISTRATIVE LAW** vol 20 (2014) PARA 273 et seq.

21 Charities Act 2011 Sch 6 Table Col 3.

229. Offences connected with CIO name and status. In the case of failure, without reasonable excuse, to comply with the requirements regarding name and status[1] an offence is committed by every charity trustee[2] of the charitable incorporated organisation ('CIO')[3] who is in default[4], and any other person who on the CIO's behalf signs or authorises the signing of the offending document, communication or conveyance, or otherwise commits or authorises the offending act or omission[5].

A person who, in whatever way, holds any body out as being a CIO when it is not, is guilty of an offence[6], but it is a defence for a person charged with such an offence to prove that he believed on reasonable grounds that the body was a CIO[7].

1 Ie the requirements under the Charities Act 2011 s 212: see PARA 227.

2 As to the meaning of 'charity trustees' see PARA 255.

3 As to the creation of a charitable incorporated organisation see PARA 226.

4 As to the meaning of 'in default' for these purposes see the Companies Act 2006 ss 1121–1123 (COMPANIES vol 14 (2009) PARA 315); applied by the Charities Act 2011 s 214(3).

5 Charities Act 2011 s 214(1). A person guilty of an offence under s 214(1) is liable on summary conviction to a fine not exceeding level 3 on the standard scale and, for continued contravention, a daily default fine not exceeding one-tenth of level 3 on the standard scale: s 214(2). As to the meaning of 'daily default fine' for these purposes see the Companies Act 2006 s 1125 (COMPANIES vol 15 (2009) PARA 1622); applied by the Charities Act 2011 s 214(3). As to the standard scale see SENTENCING AND DISPOSITION OF OFFENDERS vol 92 (2010) PARA 142.

6 Charities Act 2011 s 215(1). A person guilty of such an offence is liable on summary conviction to fine not exceeding level 3 on the standard scale: s 215(3).

7 Charities Act 2011 s 215(2).

230. Registration. Any one or more persons (the 'applicants') may apply to the Charity Commission[1] for a charitable incorporated organisation ('CIO')[2] to be constituted and for its registration as a charity[3]. The applicants must supply the Commission with: (1) a copy of the proposed constitution[4]; (2) such other documents or information as may be prescribed by CIO regulations[5]; and (3) such other documents or information as the Commission may require for the purposes of the application[6].

The Commission must refuse an application for registration if it is not satisfied that the CIO would be a charity at the time it would be registered[7], or if the CIO's proposed constitution does not comply with one or more of the statutory requirements and any regulations made thereunder[8]. The Commission may refuse such an application if the proposed name of the CIO is the same as, or is in the opinion of the Commission too like, the name of any other charity whether registered or not[9], or if the Commission is of the opinion that the proposed name falls foul of the general statutory provisions on unsuitable charity names[10].

If the Commission grants an application for registration it must register the CIO to which the application relates as a charity under the register of charities[11]. Upon registration, the CIO becomes by virtue of such registration a body corporate whose constitution is that proposed in the application, whose name is that specified in the constitution, and whose first member or members are the applicants[12]. All property for the time being vested in any or all of the applicants on trust for the charitable purposes of the CIO, when incorporated, becomes vested in the CIO upon its registration[13].

The entry relating to a CIO's registration in the register of charities must include the date of registration[14] and a note saying that it is constituted as a CIO[15]. A copy of the entry must be sent to the CIO at its principal office[16].

An appeal against a decision of the Commission to grant or not to grant an application for the constitution of a CIO and its registration as a charity lies to the Tribunal[17] at the instance of the Attorney General, or any other person who is or may be affected by the decision[18]. The Tribunal has the power to quash the decision, if appropriate, remit the matter to the Commission, and direct the Commission to rectify the register of charities or grant the application, as appropriate[19].

1 As to the Charity Commission see PARAS 543–578.

2 As to the creation of a charitable incorporated organisation see PARA 226.

3 Charities Act 2011 s 207(1). As to the meaning of 'charity' see PARA 1. No application may be made for a CIO to be constituted and registered where the resulting charity would be an exempt charity: Charitable Incorporated Organisations (General) Regulations 2012, SI 2012/3012, reg 5.

Provisions of the Charities Act 2011 regarding the registration of charities generally are modified in their application to CIOs: see the Charitable Incorporated Organisations (General) Regulations 2012, SI 2012/3012, reg 6. The provisions in question are the Charities Act 2011 s 29 (the register) (modified); ss 30–34 (charities required to be registered; removal from the register) (disapplied); s 35 (duties of trustees in connection with registration) (modified); s 36 (claims and objections to registration) (modified); s 38 (right to inspect register) (modified). As to the registration of charities see PARA 307 et seq.

As to exempt charities see PARAS 318–320.

4 Charities Act 2011 s 207(2)(a). As to the constitution see PARA 227.

5 Charities Act 2011 s 207(2)(b). 'CIO regulations' are regulations made by the Minister under Pt 11 (ss 204–250): s 247. For the purposes of s 207, see the Charitable Incorporated Organisations (General) Regulations 2012, SI 2012/3012, regs 7–9. As to the Minister see PARA 586. As to the meaning of 'document' see PARA 263 note 2.

6 Charities Act 2011 s 207(2)(c).

7 Charities Act 2011 s 208(1)(a).

8 Charities Act 2011 s 208(1)(b). The statutory requirements are those set out in s 206: see PARA 227.

9 Charities Act 2011 s 208(2)(a).

10 See the Charities Act 2011 s 208(2)(b). The statutory requirements are those set out in s 42(2)(b)–(e) (see PARA 312), reading s 42(2)(b) as referring to the proposed purposes of the CIO and to the activities which it is proposed it should carry on: s 208(2)(b).

11 Charities Act 2011 s 209(1). As to the register see PARA 307.

12 Charities Act 2011 s 210(1).

13 See the Charities Act 2011 s 210(2).

14 Charities Act 2011 s 209(2)(a).

15 Charities Act 2011 s 209(2)(b).

16 Charities Act 2011 s 209(3).

17 As to the Tribunal see PARA 579 et seq.

18 Charities Act 2011 s 319(2), Sch 6 Table Cols 1, 2. As to the meaning of 'person who is or may be affected' within the meaning of Sch 6 see PARA 317 note 8. As to the Attorney General see PARAS 589, 596, 605 et seq; and CONSTITUTIONAL AND ADMINISTRATIVE LAW vol 20 (2014) PARA 273 et seq.

19 Charities Act 2011 Sch 6 Table Col 3. In the case of a decision to grant an application, the persons who made the application are not entitled to bring an appeal, but in the case of a decision not to grant an application, the persons who made the application are so entitled: Sch 6, Table.

231. Application for conversion into CIO by charitable company or registered society. The Charities Act 2011 provides for the conversion of a charitable company[1] or a charity[2] which is a registered society[3] into a charitable incorporated organisation ('CIO')[4]. Such a conversion may not be made by a company or registered society having a share capital if any of the shares are not fully paid up[5], or by an exempt charity[6].

In order to apply for conversion[7], the company or registered society must supply the Charity Commission[8] with:

(1) a copy of a resolution[9] of the company or registered society that it be converted into a CIO[10];

(2) a copy of the proposed constitution of the CIO[11];

(3) a copy of a resolution of the company or registered society adopting the proposed constitution[12];

(4) such other documents or information as may be prescribed by CIO regulations[13]; and

(5) such other documents[14] or information as the Commission may require for the purposes of the application[15].

In the case of a company limited by guarantee which makes an application for conversion, whether or not it also has a share capital, the proposed constitution of the CIO must provide for the members to be liable to contribute to its assets if it is wound up, and for the amount up to which they are so liable[16].

Upon any application for conversion the Charity Commission must notify the appropriate registrar[17], along with such other persons, if any, as the Commission thinks appropriate in the particular case[18]. The Commission must consult those to whom it has given such notice about whether the application should be granted[19]. CIO regulations may make provision about circumstances in which it would not be appropriate to grant an application for conversion[20]. The Commission must refuse an application for conversion if it is not satisfied that the CIO would be a charity at the time it would be registered[21], or if the CIO's proposed constitution does not comply with one or more of the statutory requirements and any regulations made thereunder[22], or in the case of an application made by a company limited by guarantee, if the CIO's proposed constitution does not comply with the statutory requirements for winding up[23]. The Commission may refuse an application if the proposed name of the CIO is the same as, or is in the opinion of the Commission too like, the name of any other charity whether registered or not[24], or if the Commission is of the opinion that the proposed name falls foul of the general statutory provisions on unsuitable charity names[25], or where, having considered any representations received from those whom it has consulted[26], the Commission considers, having regard to any relevant regulations[27], that it would not be appropriate to grant the application[28].

An appeal against a decision of the Commission not to grant an application for the conversion of a charitable company or a registered society into a CIO and the CIO's registration as a charity lies to the Tribunal[29] at the instance of the Attorney General, the charity which made the application, the charity trustees of the charity or any other person who is or may be affected by the decision[30]. The Tribunal has the power to: (1) quash the decision and, if appropriate, remit the matter to the Commission; and (2) direct the Commission to grant the application[31].

1 As to the meaning of 'charitable company' see PARA 241 note 1. As to the meaning of 'charitable' see PARA 1; and as to the meaning of 'company' see PARA 246.

2 As to the meaning of 'charity' see PARA 1.

3 Ie a registered society within the meaning of the Co-operative and Community Benefit Societies Act 2014: see the Charities Act 2011 s 229(1) (amended by the Co-operative and Community Benefit Societies Act 2014 Sch 4, Pt 2 para 182); and FINANCIAL SERVICES AND INSTITUTIONS vol 50 (2008) PARA 2395. As to community benefit societies as charities see further PARA 245.

4 Charities Act 2011 ss 228(1), 229(1). As to the creation of a charitable incorporated organisation see PARA 226. See also *Change your charity structure* (Charity Commission, December 2014) (available, at the date at which this volume states the law, on the government website). As to the Charity Commission see PARAS 543–578. As to the Charity Commission's publications see PARA 547.

5 Charities Act 2011 ss 228(2)(a), 229(2)(a).

6 Charities Act 2011 ss 228(2)(b), 229(2)(b). As to exempt charities see PARAS 318–320.

7 Such an application is referred to as an 'application for conversion': Charities Act 2011 s 230(3).

8 As to the Charity Commission see PARAS 543–578.

9 The resolution must be a special resolution or a unanimous written resolution signed by or on behalf of all the members of the company or registered society who would be entitled to vote on a special resolution: Charities Act 2011 ss 228(4), 229(4). In the case of a company the Companies Act 2006 Pt 3 Ch 3 (ss 29–30) (see COMPANIES) does not apply to such a resolution: Charities Act 2011 s 228(5). In the case of a registered society, 'special resolution' has the meaning given in the Co-operative and Community Benefit Societies Act 2014 s 113 (see FINANCIAL SERVICES AND INSTITUTIONS): Charities Act 2011 s 229(5) (as amended: see note 3).

10 Charities Act 2011 ss 228(3)(a), 229(3)(a).

11 Charities Act 2011 ss 228(3)(b), 229(3)(b).

12 Charities Act 2011 ss 228(3)(c), 229(3)(c).

13 Charities Act 2011 ss 228(3)(d), 229(3)(d). As to the meaning of 'CIO regulations' see PARA 230 note 5. At the date at which this volume states the law no CIO regulations have effect for the purposes of these provisions.
14 As to the meaning of 'document' see PARA 260 note 2.
15 Charities Act 2011 ss 228(3)(e), 229(3)(e).
16 Charities Act 2011 s 228(6). That amount must not be less than the amount up to which they were liable to contribute to the assets of the company if it was wound up: s 228(7). If the amount each member of the company is liable to contribute to its assets on its winding up is £10 or less the guarantee is extinguished on the conversion of the company into a CIO and the requirements of s 228(6), (7) do not apply: s 228(8).
17 Charities Act 2011 s 230(1)(a). The 'appropriate registrar' means the registrar of companies in the case of a charitable company; or in the case of a registered society, the Financial Conduct Authority and, if the society is a PRA-authorised person within the meaning of the Financial Services and Markets Act 2000 s 2B (see FINANCIAL SERVICES AND INSTITUTIONS vol 48 (2008) PARA 5B), the Prudential Regulation Authority: s 230(2) (amended by SI 2013/496). As to the registrar of companies see COMPANIES vol 14 (2009) PARA 131 et seq. As to the Financial Conduct Authority and the Prudential Regulation Authority see FINANCIAL SERVICES AND INSTITUTIONS vol 48 (2008) PARAS 5A, 5B.
18 Charities Act 2011 s 230(1)(b).
19 Charities Act 2011 s 230(1).
20 Charities Act 2011 s 231(3). At the date at which this volume states the law no such regulations had been made.
21 Charities Act 2011 s 231(1)(a).
22 Charities Act 2011 s 231(1)(b). The statutory requirements are those set out in s 206: see PARA 227.
23 Charities Act 2011 s 231(1)(c). As to the statutory requirements for winding up see the Charities Act 2011 s 228(6), (7) (see the text and note 16).
24 See the Charities Act 2011 s 231(2)(a).
25 See the Charities Act 2011 s 231(2)(b). The statutory requirements are those set out in s 42(2)(b)–(e) (see PARA 312), reading s 42(2)(b) as referring to the proposed purposes of the CIO and to the activities which it is proposed it should carry on: s 231(2)(b).
26 Ie under the Charities Act 2011 s 230(1): see the text and note 19.
27 Ie under the Charities Act 2011 s 231(3): see the text and note 20.
28 Charities Act 2011 s 231(2)(c).
29 As to the Tribunal see PARA 579 et seq.
30 Charities Act 2011 s 319(2), Sch 6 Table Cols 1, 2. As to the meaning of 'person who is or may be affected' within the meaning of Sch 6 see PARA 317 note 8. As to the Attorney General see PARAS 589, 596, 605 et seq; and CONSTITUTIONAL AND ADMINISTRATIVE LAW vol 20 (2014) PARA 273 et seq.
31 Charities Act 2011 Sch 6 Table Col 3.

232. Consequence of conversion by charitable company or registered society to a CIO. If the Charity Commission[1] refuses an application for conversion, it must so notify the appropriate registrar[2]. If the Commission grants an application for conversion, it must register the charitable incorporated organisation ('CIO')[3] to which the application related in the register of charities[4], and send to the appropriate registrar a copy of each of the resolutions made by the converting company[5] or registered society[6] as part of the application[7] and a copy of the entry in the register relating to the CIO[8]. The registration of the CIO in the register of charities is provisional only until the appropriate registrar cancels the registration of the company or registered society[9]. The appropriate registrar must register the documents[10] sent to him by the Commission[11], cancel the registration of the company in the register of companies or of the society in the mutual societies register[12], and notify the Commission that he has done so[13]. When the appropriate registrar cancels the registration of the company or of the registered society, the company or registered society is thereupon converted into a CIO being a body corporate[14] whose constitution is that proposed in the application for conversion[15], whose name is that specified in the constitution[16], and whose first members are the members of the converting company or society immediately before the moment of conversion[17].

If the converting company or registered society had a share capital, upon the conversion of the company or registered society all the shares must be cancelled and no former holder of any cancelled share has any right in respect of it after its cancellation[18], but this does not affect any right which accrued in respect of a share before its cancellation[19].

The entry relating to a CIO's registration in the register of charities must include: (1) a note saying that it is constituted as a CIO[20]; (2) the date of registration[21]; and (3) a note of the name of the company or society which was converted into the CIO[22]. A copy of the entry must be sent to the CIO at its principal office[23].

The conversion of a charitable company or of a registered society into a CIO does not affect, in particular, any liability to which the company or registered society was subject by virtue of its being a charitable company or registered society[24].

1 As to the Charity Commission see PARAS 543–578.
2 Charities Act 2011 s 231(4). As to the meaning of 'appropriate registrar' see PARA 231 note 17.
3 As to the creation of a charitable incorporated organisation see PARA 226.
4 Charities Act 2011 s 232(1)(a). As to the meaning of 'charity' see PARA 1; and as to the register of charities see PARA 307.
5 As to the meaning of 'company' see PARA 246.
6 Ie a registered society within the meaning of the Co-operative and Community Benefit Societies Act 2014: see PARA 231; and **FINANCIAL SERVICES AND INSTITUTIONS**.
7 Ie the resolutions referred to under the Charities Act 2011 s 228(3)(a), (c) or s 229(3)(a), (c): see PARA 231.
8 Charities Act 2011 s 232(1)(b), (2).
9 Charities Act 2011 s 232(3).
10 As to the meaning of 'document' see PARA 263 note 2.
11 Charities Act 2011 s 232(4)(a). The documents referred to in the text are those sent under s 232(1)(b): see the text and note 8.
12 Charities Act 2011 s 232(4)(b).
13 Charities Act 2011 s 232(4).
14 Charities Act 2011 s 233(1).
15 Charities Act 2011 s 233(1)(a).
16 Charities Act 2011 s 233(1)(b).
17 Charities Act 2011 s 233(1)(c).
18 Charities Act 2011 s 233(2).
19 Charities Act 2011 s 233(3).
20 Charities Act 2011 s 232(5)(a). This information is to be included only when the appropriate registrar has notified the Commission as required by s 232(4) (see the text to notes 4–8): s 232(6).
21 Charities Act 2011 s 232(5)(b). This information is to be included only when the appropriate registrar has notified the Commission as required by s 232(4) (see the text to notes 4–8): s 232(6).
22 Charities Act 2011 s 232(5)(c).
23 Charities Act 2011 s 232(7).
24 Charities Act 2011 s 233(4).

233. Application for conversion into CIO by community interest company. CIO regulations[1] may make provision for the conversion of a community interest company[2] into a charitable incorporated organisation ('CIO')[3] and for the CIO's registration as a charity[4]. The regulations may, in particular, apply, apply with modifications specified in the regulations, or disapply, any of the relevant statutory provisions[5].

1 As to the meaning of 'CIO regulations' see PARA 230 note 5. At the date at which this volume states the law no CIO regulations have effect for the purposes of these provisions.
2 As to community interest companies see COMPANIES vol 14 (2009) PARA 82. As to the meaning of 'company' see PARA 246.
3 As to the creation of a charitable incorporated organisation see PARA 226.
4 Charities Act 2011 s 234(1).
5 Charities Act 2011 s 234(2). The relevant statutory provisions are ss 228–233 (see PARAS 231–232); and the Companies (Audit, Investigations and Community Enterprise) Act 2004 ss 53–55 (see COMPANIES).

234. Amalgamation of CIOs. Any two or more charitable incorporated organisations[1] (the 'old CIOs') may apply to the Charity Commission[2] to be amalgamated, and for the incorporation and registration as a charity[3] of a new CIO (the 'new CIO') as their successor[4].

To make an application for amalgamation, the old CIOs must supply the Commission with (1) a copy of the proposed constitution[5]; (2) such other documents or information as may be prescribed by CIO regulations[6]; and (3) such other documents or information as the Commission may require for the purposes of the application[7]; (4) a copy of a resolution of each of the old CIOs approving the proposed amalgamation[8]; and (5) a copy of a resolution of each of the old CIOs adopting the proposed constitution of the new CIO[9]. The resolutions must have been passed by a 75 per cent majority of those voting at a general meeting of the CIO[10], or unanimously by the CIO's members otherwise than at a general meeting[11].

Each old CIO must give notice of the proposed amalgamation in the way or ways that in the opinion of its charity trustees[12] will make it most likely to come to the attention of those who would be affected by the amalgamation[13], and send a copy of the notice to the Commission[14]. The notice must invite any person who considers that he would be affected by the proposed amalgamation to make written representations to the Commission no later than a date determined by the Commission and specified in the notice[15].

The Commission must refuse an application for registration if it is not satisfied that the CIO would be a charity at the time it would be registered[16], or if the CIO's proposed constitution does not comply with one or more of the statutory requirements and any regulations made thereunder[17], or if it considers that there is a serious risk that the new CIO would be unable properly to pursue its purposes[18].

The Commission may refuse such an application if the proposed name of the CIO is the same as, or is in the opinion of the Commission too like, the name of any other charity whether registered or not[19], or if the Commission is of the opinion that the proposed name falls foul of the general statutory provisions on unsuitable charity names[20]. The Commission may also refuse an application if it is not satisfied that the provision in the constitution of the new CIO is the same, or substantially the same, as the provision in the constitutions of each of the old CIOs about the following matters[21]:

(a) the purposes of the CIO[22];
(b) the application of property of the CIO on its dissolution[23]; and
(c) authorisation for any benefit[24] to be obtained by charity trustees or members of the CIO or persons connected with them[25].

If the Commission grants an application for amalgamation, it must register the new CIO in the register of charities[26] and by virtue of registration the new CIO thereupon becomes a body corporate[27] whose constitution is that proposed in the application for amalgamation[28], whose name is that specified in the constitution[29], and whose first members are the members of the old CIOs immediately before the new CIO was registered[30]. Upon the registration of the new CIO all the property, rights and liabilities of each of the old CIOs become the property, rights and liabilities of the new CIO[31] and each of the old CIOs must be dissolved[32]. Any gift which is expressed as a gift to one of the old CIOs and takes effect on or after the date of registration of the new CIO takes effect as a gift to the new CIO[33].

The entry relating to the registration in the register of the charity constituted as the new CIO must include:

(i) a note that it is constituted as a CIO[34];
(ii) the date of the charity's registration[35];
(iii) a note that the CIO was formed following amalgamation, and of the name of each of the old CIOs[36].

A copy of the entry must be sent to the charity at the principal office of the new CIO[37].

An appeal against a decision of the Commission not to grant such an application for amalgamation lies to the Tribunal[38] at the instance of the Attorney General, the charity which made the application, the charity trustees of the CIOs or any other person who is or may be affected by the decision[39]. The Tribunal has the power to: (A) quash the decision and, if appropriate, remit the matter to the Commission; and (B) direct the Commission to grant the application[40].

An appeal to the Tribunal also lies against a decision of the Commission to grant such an application for amalgamation, at the instance of the Attorney General or any creditor of any of the CIOs being amalgamated[41]. The Tribunal has the power to quash the decision and, if appropriate, remit the matter to the Commission[42].

1 As to the creation of a new charitable incorporated organisation see PARA 226.
2 As to the Charity Commission see PARAS 543–578.
3 As to the meaning of 'charity' see PARA 1.
4 Charities Act 2011 s 235(1). Such an application is referred to as an 'application for amalgamation': s 237(7).
5 Charities Act 2011 s 235(2)(a).
6 Charities Act 2011 s 235(2)(b). As to the meaning of 'CIO regulations' see PARA 230 note 5. See the Charitable Incorporated Organisations (General) Regulations 2012, SI 2012/3012, regs 9–11.
7 Charities Act 2011 s 235(2)(c).
8 Charities Act 2011 s 235(3)(a).
9 Charities Act 2011 s 235(3)(b).
10 Charities Act 2011 s 235(4)(a). This percentage includes those voting by proxy or by post, if voting that way is permitted: s 235(4)(a). The date of passing of such a resolution is the date of the general meeting at which it was passed: s 235(5)(a).
11 Charities Act 2011 s 235(4)(b). The date of the passing of such a resolution is the date on which provision in the CIO's constitution or in CIO regulations made under s 223 (see PARA 239 note 2) deems it to have been passed, but that date may not be earlier than that on which the last member agreed to it: s 235(5)(b).
12 As to the meaning of 'charity trustees' see PARA 255.
13 Charities Act 2011 s 236(1)(a).
14 Charities Act 2011 s 236(1)(b).
15 Charities Act 2011 s 236(2).
16 Charities Act 2011 s 237(1)(a).
17 Charities Act 2011 s 237(1)(b).
18 Charities Act 2011 s 237(2).
19 Charities Act 2011 s 237(3)(a).
20 Charities Act 2011 s 237(3)(b).
21 Charities Act 2011 s 237(4).

22 Charities Act 2011 s 237(5)(a).
23 Charities Act 2011 s 237(5)(b).
24 As to the meaning of 'benefit' see PARA 228 note 7; definition applied by the Charities Act 2011 s 237(6).
25 Charities Act 2011 s 237(5)(c). As to determining whether a person is connected with a charity trustee or member of the CIO see PARA 228 note 7.
26 Charities Act 2011 s 238(1).
27 Charities Act 2011 s 239(1).
28 Charities Act 2011 s 239(1)(a).
29 Charities Act 2011 s 239(1)(b).
30 Charities Act 2011 s 239(1)(c).
31 Charities Act 2011 s 239(2)(a). No such vesting or transfer operates as a breach of a covenant or condition against alienation or gives rise to a forfeiture: s 250.
32 Charities Act 2011 s 239(2)(b).
33 Charities Act 2011 s 239(3).
34 Charities Act 2011 s 238(2)(a).
35 Charities Act 2011 s 238(2)(b).
36 Charities Act 2011 s 238(2)(c).
37 Charities Act 2011 s 238(3).
38 As to the Tribunal see PARA 579 et seq.
39 Charities Act 2011 s 319(2), Sch 6 Table Cols 1, 2. As to the meaning of 'person who is or may be affected' within the meaning of Sch 6 see PARA 317 note 8. As to the Attorney General see PARAS 589, 596, 605 et seq; and CONSTITUTIONAL AND ADMINISTRATIVE LAW vol 20 (2014) PARA 273 et seq.
40 Charities Act 2011 Sch 6 Table Col 3.
41 Charities Act 2011 s 319(2), Sch 6 Table Cols 1, 2.
42 Charities Act 2011 Sch 6 Table Col 3.

235. Transfer of undertaking of CIO. A charitable incorporated organisation ('CIO')[1] may resolve that all its property, rights and liabilities should be transferred to another CIO specified in the resolution[2]. Such a resolution must be passed by a 75 per cent majority of those voting at a general meeting of the CIO[3], or unanimously by the CIO's members otherwise than at a general meeting[4]. Where a CIO has passed such a resolution, it must send to the Charity Commission[5] a copy of the resolution[6], and a copy of a resolution of the transferee CIO agreeing to the transfer to it[7]. Upon receipt of the copy resolutions, the Commission may direct the transferor CIO to give public notice of its resolution in such manner as is specified in the direction[8] and, if it gives such a direction, must take into account any representations made to it by persons appearing to it to be interested in the transferor CIO, where those representations are made to it within the period of 28 days beginning with the date when public notice of the resolution is given by the transferor CIO[9].

The resolution does not take effect until confirmed by the Commission[10]. The Commission must refuse to confirm the resolution if it considers that there is a serious risk that the transferee CIO would be unable properly to pursue the purposes of the transferor CIO[11]. The Commission may refuse to confirm the resolution if it is not satisfied that the provision in the constitution of the transferee CIO is the same, or substantially the same, as the provision in the constitution of the transferor CIO about the following matters[12]:

(1) the purposes of the CIO[13];
(2) the application of property of the CIO on its dissolution[14]; and
(3) authorisation for any benefit[15] to be obtained by charity trustees[16] or members of the CIO or persons connected with them[17].

If the Commission does not notify the transferor CIO within the relevant period[18] that it is either confirming or refusing to confirm the resolution, the resolution is to be treated as confirmed by the Commission on the day after the end of that period[19].

If the resolution is confirmed, or treated as confirmed, by the Commission then all the property, rights and liabilities of the transferor CIO become the property, rights and liabilities of the transferee CIO in accordance with the resolution[20] and the transferor CIO must be dissolved[21]. Any gift which is expressed as a gift to the transferor CIO and takes effect on or after the date on which the resolution is confirmed or treated as confirmed, takes effect as a gift to the transferee CIO[22].

An appeal against a decision of the Commission not to confirm such a resolution lies to the Tribunal[23] at the instance of the Attorney General, the CIO, the charity trustees of the CIO, or any other person who is or may be affected by the decision[24]. The Tribunal has power to: (a) quash the decision and, if appropriate, remit the matter to the Commission; and (b) direct the Commission to confirm the resolution[25].

An appeal to the Tribunal also lies against a decision of the Commission to confirm such a resolution at the instance of the Attorney General or any creditor of the CIO[26]. The Tribunal has the power to quash the decision and, if appropriate, remit the matter to the Commission[27].

1 As to the creation of a charitable incorporated organisation see PARA 226.
2 Charities Act 2011 s 240(1). No such vesting or transfer operates as a breach of a covenant or condition against alienation or gives rise to a forfeiture: s 250.
3 Charities Act 2011 s 240(3)(a). This percentage includes those voting by proxy or by post, if voting that way is permitted: s 240(3)(a). The date of passing of such a resolution is the date of the general meeting at which it was passed: s 240(4)(a).
4 Charities Act 2011 s 240(3)(b). The date of the passing of such a resolution is the date on which provision in the CIO's constitution or in regulations made under s 223 (see PARA 239 note 2) deems it to have been passed, but that date may not be earlier than that on which the last member agreed to it: s 240(4)(b).
5 As to the Charity Commission see PARAS 543–578.
6 Charities Act 2011 s 240(2)(a).
7 Charities Act 2011 s 240(2)(b).
8 Charities Act 2011 s 241(a).
9 Charities Act 2011 s 241(b).
10 Charities Act 2011 s 240(5).
11 Charities Act 2011 s 242(1).
12 Charities Act 2011 s 242(2).
13 Charities Act 2011 s 242(3)(a).
14 Charities Act 2011 s 242(3)(b).
15 As to the meaning of 'benefit' for these purposes see PARA 228 note 7.
16 As to the meaning of 'charity trustees' see PARA 255.
17 Charities Act 2011 s 242(3)(c). As to the rules which apply for determining whether a person is connected with a charity trustee or member of the CIO see PARA 228 note 7.
18 'Relevant period' means, in a case where the Commission directs the transferor CIO under the Charities Act 2011 s 241 to give public notice of its resolution (see the text and notes 9–10), the period of six months beginning with the date when that notice is given: s 243(2)(a). In any other case, 'relevant period' means a period of six months beginning with the date when both of the copy resolutions referred to in s 240(2) (see the text and notes 6–7) have been received by the Commission: s 243(2)(b). The Commission may at any time within the relevant period give the transferor CIO a notice extending the relevant period by such period not exceeding six months as is specified in the notice: s 243(3). Such a notice must set out the Commission's reasons for the extension: s 243(4).
19 Charities Act 2011 s 243(1).
20 Charities Act 2011 s 244(1)(a).
21 Charities Act 2011 s 244(1)(b).

22 Charities Act 2011 s 244(2).
23 As to the Tribunal see PARA 579 et seq.
24 Charities Act 2011 s 319(2), Sch 6 Table Cols 1, 2. As to the meaning of 'person who is or may be affected' within the meaning of Sch 6 see PARA 317 note 8. As to the Attorney General see PARAS 589, 596, 605 et seq; and CONSTITUTIONAL AND ADMINISTRATIVE LAW vol 20 (2014) PARA 273 et seq.
25 Charities Act 2011 Sch 6 Table Col 3.
26 Charities Act 2011 s 319(2), Sch 6 Table Cols 1, 2.
27 Charities Act 2011 Sch 6 Table Col 3.

236. Winding up, insolvency and dissolution of CIO. CIO regulations[1] may make provision about the winding up of charitable incorporated organisations ('CIOs')[2], their insolvency[3], their dissolution[4] and their revival and restoration to the register following dissolution[5]. Such regulations may, in particular, make provision:

(1) about the transfer on the dissolution of a CIO of its property and rights, including property and rights held on trust for the CIO, to the official custodian or another person or body[6];
(2) requiring any person in whose name any stocks, funds or securities are standing in trust for a CIO to transfer them into the name of the official custodian or another person or body[7];
(3) about the disclaiming, by the official custodian or other transferee of a CIO's property, of title to any of that property[8];
(4) about the application of a CIO's property cy-près[9];
(5) about circumstances in which charity trustees[10] may be personally liable for contributions to the assets of a CIO or for its debts[11]; and
(6) about the reversal on a CIO's revival of anything done on its dissolution[12].

A CIO is subject to the same insolvency and dissolution procedures as a registered company, and accordingly provisions of the Insolvency Act 1986 and subordinate legislation are applied subject to modifications[13]. In particular, provision is made for the voluntary winding up of a CIO by its members[14], or the winding up of a CIO by the court[15], and the application of the surplus in accordance with the CIO's constitution[16].

In circumstances where the Insolvency Act 1986 does not apply, a CIO may apply for dissolution[17], or be dissolved by the Charity Commission[18].

Appeal against decisions in relation to the winding up or dissolution of a CIO under the provisions mentioned above lies to the Tribunal[19].

1 As to the meaning of 'CIO regulations' see PARA 230 note 5. Such regulations may apply any enactment (including subordinate legislation) which would not otherwise apply, either without modification or with modifications specified in the regulations, and disapply, or modify (in ways specified in the regulations) the application of, any enactment which would otherwise apply: Charities Act 2011 s 245(3), (4).

See the Charitable Incorporated Organisations (Insolvency and Dissolution) Regulations 2012, SI 2012/3013, made for the purposes of these provisions.

2 Charities Act 2011 s 245(1)(a); Charitable Incorporated Organisations (Insolvency and Dissolution) Regulations 2012, SI 2012/3013. As to the creation of a charitable incorporated organisation see PARA 226.
3 Charities Act 2011 s 245(1)(b). See the Charitable Incorporated Organisations (Insolvency and Dissolution) Regulations 2012, SI 2012/3013, reg 3; and text and notes 13–16.
4 Charities Act 2011 s 245(1)(c). See the Charitable Incorporated Organisations (Insolvency and Dissolution) Regulations 2012, SI 2012/3013, regs 4–22; and text and notes 17–18.
5 Charities Act 2011 s 245(1)(d). See the Charitable Incorporated Organisations (Insolvency and Dissolution) Regulations 2012, SI 2012/3013, regs 33–41.
6 Charities Act 2011 s 245(2)(a). See the Charitable Incorporated Organisations (Insolvency and Dissolution) Regulations 2012, SI 2012/3013, regs 23–26. No such vesting or transfer operates

as a breach of a covenant or condition against alienation or gives rise to a forfeiture: Charities Act 2011 s 250. As to the official custodian see PARA 300 et seq.

7 Charities Act 2011 s 245(2)(b).

8 Charities Act 2011 s 245(2)(c). See the Charitable Incorporated Organisations (Insolvency and Dissolution) Regulations 2012, SI 2012/3013, regs 27–29.

9 Charities Act 2011 s 245(2)(d). As to the doctrine of cy-près see PARA 179 et seq.

10 As to the meaning of 'charity trustees' see PARA 255.

11 Charities Act 2011 s 245(2)(e). See the Insolvency Act 1986 s 74 (applied with modifications by the Charitable Incorporated Organisations (Insolvency and Dissolution) Regulations 2012, SI 2012/3013, Schedule.

12 Charities Act 2011 s 245(2)(f). See the Charitable Incorporated Organisations (Insolvency and Dissolution) Regulations 2012, SI 2012/3013, regs 33–41.

13 As to the provisions of the Insolvency Act 1986 applied for the purposes of CIOs see the Charitable Incorporated Organisations (Insolvency and Dissolution) Regulations 2012, SI 2012/3013, reg 3, Schedule; and generally see **COMPANY AND PARTNERSHIP INSOLVENCY**.

14 Insolvency Act 1986 s 84 (substituted for this purpose by SI 2012/3013, Schedule para 1(4)).

15 Insolvency Act 1986 s 122 (substituted for this purpose by SI 2012/3013, Schedule para 1(4)). Note that, inter alia, a CIO may be wound up by the court if it does not commence business within a year of registration, or suspends business for a whole year: Insolvency Act 1986 s 122(1)(b) (as so substituted).

16 Insolvency Act 1986 s 84 (substituted for this purpose by SI 2012/3013, Schedule para 1(4).

17 Charitable Incorporated Organisations (Insolvency and Dissolution) Regulations 2012, SI 2012/3013, regs 4–15.

18 Charitable Incorporated Organisations (Insolvency and Dissolution) Regulations 2012, SI 2012/3013, regs 16–20. The Charity Commission must dissolve a CIO where the CIO is not operating, is no longer a charity, or is being wound up; dissolution is effected by the removal of the CIO from the register of charities.

19 See the Charities Act 2011 Sch 6 Table cols 1–3 (amended by SI 2012/3014). As to the Tribunal see PARA 579 et seq.

237. Charitable incorporated organisations and third parties. The validity of an act done, or purportedly done, by a charitable incorporated organisation ('CIO')[1] must not be called into question on the ground that it lacked constitutional capacity[2]. Nor may the power of the charity trustees[3] of a CIO to act so as to bind the CIO, or authorise others to do so, be called into question on the ground of any constitutional limitations on their powers[4].

A party to an arrangement or transaction with a CIO is not bound to inquire whether it is within the CIO's constitutional capacity[5], or as to any constitutional limitations on the powers of its charity trustees to bind the CIO or authorise others to do so[6]. If a CIO purports to transfer or grant an interest in property, the fact that the act was beyond its constitutional capacity, or that its charity trustees in connection with the act exceeded their constitutional powers, does not affect the title of a person who subsequently acquires the property or any interest in it for full consideration without actual notice of any such circumstances affecting the validity of the CIO's act[7].

Nothing in the provisions described above absolves the CIO's charity trustees from their duty to act within the CIO's constitution and in accordance with any constitutional limitations on their powers[8], or prevents a person from bringing proceedings to restrain the doing of an act which would be beyond the CIO's constitutional capacity, or beyond the constitutional powers of the CIO's charity trustees[9]. However, no such proceedings may be brought in respect of an act to be done in fulfillment of a legal obligation arising from a previous act of the CIO[10].

1 As to the creation of a charitable incorporated organisation see PARA 226.

2 Charities Act 2011 s 218(1). This applies only in favour of a person who gives full consideration in money or money's worth in relation to the act in question, and does not know that the act is beyond the CIO's constitutional capacity: s 218(3). The burden of proving that a person knew

that an act was beyond the CIO's constitutional capacity lies on the person making that allegation: see s 218(6). References to a CIO's lack of 'constitutional capacity' are to lack of capacity because of anything in its constitution: s 218(7)(a).

3 As to the meaning of 'charity trustees' see PARA 255.

4 Charities Act 2011 s 218(2). This applies only in favour of a person who gives full consideration in money or money's worth in relation to the act in question, does not know that the act is beyond the constitutional powers of its charity trustees and who dealt with the CIO in good faith (which he is presumed to have done unless the contrary is proved): s 218(3). The burden of proving that a person knew that an act was beyond the constitutional powers of its charity trustees lies on the person making that allegation: s 218(6). Nothing in s 218(2) affects any liability incurred by the CIO's charity trustees (or any one of them) for acting beyond his or their constitutional powers: s 219(4). References to 'constitutional limitations' on the powers of a CIO's charity trustees are to limitations on their powers under its constitution, including limitations deriving from a resolution of the CIO in general meeting, or from an agreement between the CIO's members, and 'constitutional powers' is to be construed accordingly: s 218(7)(b).

5 Charities Act 2011 s 218(4)(a).

6 Charities Act 2011 s 218(4)(b).

7 Charities Act 2011 s 218(5). No such vesting or transfer operates as a breach of a covenant or condition against alienation or gives rise to a forfeiture: s 250.

8 Charities Act 2011 s 219(5).

9 Charities Act 2011 s 219(1).

10 Charities Act 2011 s 219(2). This does not prevent the Charity Commission from exercising any of its powers: s 219(3). As to the Charity Commission see PARAS 543–578.

238. Members and trustees of charitable incorporated organisations. It is the duty of each member of a charitable incorporated organisation ('CIO')[1], and each charity trustee[2] of a CIO, to exercise his powers, and in the case of a charity trustee to perform his functions, in his capacity as such, in the way he decides, in good faith, would be most likely to further the purposes of the CIO[3].

The CIO's charity trustees must manage the affairs of the CIO and may for that purpose exercise all the powers of the CIO[4]. Each charity trustee of a CIO must in the performance of his functions in that capacity exercise such care and skill as is reasonable in the circumstances, having regard in particular to any special knowledge or experience that he has or holds himself out as having and, if he acts as a charity trustee in the course of a business or profession, to any special knowledge or experience that it is reasonable to expect of a person acting in the course of that kind of business or profession[5].

A charity trustee of a CIO may not benefit personally from any arrangement or transaction entered into by the CIO if, before the arrangement or transaction was entered into, he did not disclose to all the charity trustees of the CIO any material interest of his in it or in any other person or body party to it, whether that interest is direct or indirect[6].

A charity trustee of a CIO is entitled to be reimbursed by the CIO, or may pay out of the CIO's funds, expenses properly incurred by him in the performance of his functions as such[7].

If the CIO is one whose members are liable to contribute to its assets if it is wound up, then its constitution binds the CIO and its members for the time being to the same extent as if its provisions were contained in a contract to which the CIO and each of its members was a party, and which contained obligations on the part of the CIO and each member to observe all the provisions of the constitution[8]. Money payable by a member to the CIO under the constitution is a debt due from him to the CIO, and is of the nature of an ordinary contract debt[9].

Subject to anything in a CIO's constitution, a trustee of the CIO may be a member but need not be; a member may be a trustee but need not be; and the membership and trustees may, but need not be, identical[10].

1 As to the creation of a charitable incorporated organisation see PARA 226.
2 As to the meaning of 'charity trustees' see PARA 255.
3 Charities Act 2011 ss 220, 221(1).
4 Charities Act 2011 s 216(2). Subject to anything in its constitution, a CIO has power to do anything which is calculated to further its purposes or is conducive or incidental to doing so: s 216(1). As to the constitution of a CIO and its amendment see PARAS 227, 228.
5 Charities Act 2011 s 221(2). CIO regulations may permit a CIO's constitution to provide that this duty does not apply, or does not apply in so far as is specified in the constitution: s 221(3), (4). As to the meaning of 'CIO regulations' see PARA 230 note 5. See the Charitable Incorporated Organisations (General) Regulations 2012, SI 2012/3012, reg 33(3)(l), applying the duty of care imposed on trustees by the Trustee Act 2000 Sch 1 para 3 to charity trustees of a CIO.
6 Charities Act 2011 s 222(1). Nothing in s 222(1) confers authority for a charity trustee of a CIO to benefit personally from any arrangement or transaction entered into by the CIO: s 222(2).
7 Charities Act 2011 s 222(3).
8 Charities Act 2011 s 217(2).
9 Charities Act 2011 s 217(3).
10 See Charities Act 2011 s 206(6).

239. Further regulations. CIO regulations[1] make provision about the procedure of charitable incorporated organisations ('CIOs')[2]. Subject to any such regulations, to any other requirement imposed by or by virtue of the Charities Act 2011 or any other enactment, and anything in the CIO's constitution, a CIO may regulate its own procedure[3], but this must include provision for the holding of a general meeting of its members[4].

CIO regulations may make further provision about applications for registration of CIOs, the administration of CIOs, the conversion of charitable companies, registered societies and community interest companies into CIOs, the amalgamation of CIOs and in relation to CIOs generally[5]. The regulations may, in particular, make provision about[6]:

(1) the execution of deeds and documents[7];
(2) the electronic communication of messages or documents relevant to a CIO or to any dealing with the Charity Commission in relation to one[8];
(3) the maintenance of registers of members and of charity trustees[9]; and
(4) the maintenance of other registers, for example, a register of charges over the CIO's assets[10].

The regulations may, in relation to charities constituted as CIOs, disapply or modify the application of any of the provisions of the Charities Act 2011 relating to the registration of charities[11].

1 As to the meaning of 'CIO regulations' see PARA 230 note 5.
2 Charities Act 2011 s 223(1). As to the creation of a charitable incorporated organisation see PARA 226. See the Charitable Incorporated Organisations (General) Regulations 2012, SI 2012/3012, regs 35–46.
3 Charities Act 2011 s 223(2). As to the constitution of a CIO see PARA 227.
4 Charities Act 2011 s 223(3). The regulations may in particular make provision about such meetings: s 223(3).
5 Charities Act 2011 s 246(1); Charitable Incorporated Organisations (General) Regulations 2012, SI 2012/3012. The regulations, in addition to the specific provisions mentioned in PARA 227 et seq and text and notes 2, 6–11, make general provision relating to the service of documents and communications; fraudulent trading (applying specified provisions of the Companies Act 2006); pre-merger vesting declarations (modifying the Charities Act 2011

ss 310, 312: see PARA 417); and accounts and statements (in relation to the Charities Act 2011 s 133: see PARA 342): Charitable Incorporated Organisations (General) Regulations 2012, SI 2012/3012, regs 47, 48, 49–59, 60, 61, 62.

The regulations may apply any enactment (including subordinate legislation) which would not otherwise apply, either without modification or with modifications specified in the regulations, disapply, or modify (in ways specified in the regulations) the application of any enactment which would otherwise apply: Charities Act 2011 s 246(3), (5).

6 Charities Act 2011 s 246(2).

7 Charities Act 2011 s 246(2)(2)(a); Charitable Incorporated Organisations (General) Regulations 2012, SI 2012/3012, regs 20–22. As to the meaning of 'document' see PARA 263 note 2.

8 Charities Act 2011 s 246(2)(b); and see the Charitable Incorporated Organisations (General) Regulations 2012, SI 2012/3012, reg 50, Sch 2. As to the Charity Commission see PARAS 543–578.

9 Charities Act 2011 s 246(2)(c); Charitable Incorporated Organisations (General) Regulations 2012, SI 2012/3012, regs 26–30. As to the meaning of 'charity trustees' see PARA 255.

10 Charities Act 2011 s 246(2)(d).

11 See the Charities Act 2011 s 246(4). The general statutory provisions relating to the registration of charities are ss 29–38: see PARA 307 et seq.

(3) CHARITABLE COMPANIES REGISTERED UNDER THE COMPANIES ACTS

240. Exemption from requirement of 'limited' as part of name. A private company[1] is exempt from the statutory requirements[2] relating to the use of 'limited'[3] as part of the company name if it is a charity[4].

1 As to the meaning of 'company' see PARA 246.

2 See the Companies Act 2006 s 59; and COMPANIES vol 14 (2009) PARA 200.

3 For companies registered in Wales the equivalent in Welsh ('cyfyngedig') is permitted: see the Companies Act 2006 s 59(2); and COMPANIES vol 14 (2009) PARA 200. The abbreviations 'ltd.' and 'cyf.' are also allowed: see s 59(1), (2); and COMPANIES vol 14 (2009) PARA 200.

4 See the Companies Act 2006 s 60(1)(a); and COMPANIES vol 14 (2009) PARA 201.

241. Status of charitable company to appear on correspondence. Where a charitable company's name does not include the word 'charity' or the word 'charitable'[1], the fact that the company is a charity must be stated in legible characters[2] in (1) every location, and in every description of document or communication, in which it is required[3] to state its registered name[4]; and (2) all conveyances[5] purporting to be executed by the company[6].

Failure to comply with these requirements without reasonable excuse is an offence by the company and every officer of the company who is in default[7].

Any legal proceedings brought by such a company[8] to enforce a right arising out of a contract or conveyance in connection with which there was a failure to comply with these requirements must be dismissed if the defendant to the proceedings shows[9]:

(a) that he has a claim against the company arising out of the contract or conveyance that he has been unable to pursue by reason of the company's failure to comply with the requirements[10]; or

(b) that he has suffered some financial loss in connection with the contract or conveyance by reason of the company's failure to comply with the requirements[11],

unless the court before which the proceedings are brought is satisfied that it is just and equitable to permit the proceedings to continue[12].

1 As to the meaning of 'charity' and 'charitable' generally see PARA 1. 'Charitable company' means a charity which is a company: Charities Act 2011 s 193.

2 Charities Act 2011 s 194(1). Where a company's name includes the word 'elusen' or the word 'elusennol' (the Welsh equivalents of the words 'charity' and 'charitable'), s 194(1) does not apply in relation to any document which is wholly in Welsh: s 194(2). The statement required by s 194(1) must be in English, except that, in the case of a document which is otherwise wholly in Welsh, the statement may be in Welsh if it consists of or includes the word 'elusen' or the word 'elusennol': s 194(3). See also s 5; and PARA 311.

3 Ie required by regulations under the Companies Act 2006 s 82: see **COMPANIES** vol 14 (2009) PARA 220.

4 Charities Act 2011 s 194(1)(a).

5 'Conveyance' means any instrument creating, transferring, varying or extinguishing an interest in land: Charities Act 2011 s 194(4).

6 Charities Act 2011 s 194(1)(b).

7 See the Charities Act 2011 s 196(1). For this purpose a shadow director of the company is treated as an officer of the company if the failure to comply is in relation to s 194(1)(a) (see the text and note 4) and that person would be treated as an officer of the company for the purposes of the corresponding requirement of regulations under the Companies Act 2006 s 82 (see **COMPANIES** vol 14 (2009) PARA 220): Charities Act 2011 s 196(2). As to the meaning of 'shadow director' for these purposes see the Companies Act 2006 ss 84, 251 (**COMPANIES** vol 14 (2009) PARAS 220, 479); and the Charities Act 2011 s 196(4). 'Officer' in relation to a body corporate includes a director, manager or secretary: Companies Act 2006 s 1173; Charities Act 2006 s 196(4).

A person guilty of such an offence is liable on summary conviction to a fine not exceeding level 3 on the standard scale and, for continued contravention, a daily default fine not exceeding one-tenth of level 3 on the standard scale: Charities Act 2011 s 196(3). As to the standard scale see **SENTENCING AND DISPOSITION OF OFFENDERS** vol 92 (2010) PARA 142. As to the meaning of 'daily default fine' for these purposes see the Companies Act 2006 ss 84, 1125 (**COMPANIES** vol 14 (2009) PARA 220; **COMPANIES** vol 15 (2009) PARA 1622); and the Charities Act 2011 s 196(4).

8 Ie a company to which the Charities Act 2011 s 194 (see the text and notes 1–6) applies.

9 See the Charities Act 2011 s 195(1), (2).

10 Charities Act 2011 s 195(2)(a). The requirements referred to in the text are the requirements under s 194.

11 Charities Act 2011 s 195(2)(b). The requirements referred to in the text are the requirements under s 194.

12 Charities Act 2011 s 195(2). This does not affect the right of any person to enforce such rights as he may have against another person in any proceedings brought by that person: s 195(3).

242. Trusts not affected by alteration of objects. A charitable company or other corporation which has power to alter its constitution cannot, by altering its objects so that it ceases to be charitable, affect the application of: (1) any property acquired under any disposition or agreement previously made otherwise than for full consideration in money or money's worth, or any property representing property so acquired; (2) any property representing income which has accrued before the alteration is made; or (3) the income from any such property[1].

Where a charity is a company, any 'regulated alteration' is ineffective without the prior written consent of the Charity Commission[2]. The following are regulated alterations: (a) any alteration of the company's articles of association adding, removing or altering a statement of the company's objects[3]; (b) any alteration of any provision of its articles of association directing the application of property of the company on its dissolution[4]; and (c) any alteration of any provision of its articles of association where the alteration would provide authorisation for any benefit[5] to be obtained by directors or members of the company or persons connected with them[6].

Where a company that has made a regulated alteration[7] is required to send to the registrar of companies a copy of its articles as amended[8], to forward to the registrar a copy of the special resolution effecting alteration[9] or to give notice to the registrar of the amendment[10], the copy or notice must be accompanied by a copy of the Commission's consent[11]. If more than one of these provisions applies and they are complied with at different times, the company need not send a further copy of the Commission's consent if a copy was sent on an earlier occasion[12].

1 See the Charities Act 2011 s 197(1), (2). See also *IRC v Yorkshire Agricultural Society* [1928] 1 KB 611 at 633, CA; and *Baldry v Feintuck* [1972] 2 All ER 81, [1972] 1 WLR 552, as to unincorporated associations.
2 See the Charities Act 2011 s 198(1). As to the Charity Commission see PARAS 543–578. An appeal against a decision of the Commission to give or withhold consent under s 198(1) lies to the Tribunal at the instance of the Attorney General, the charity trustees of the charity, the body corporate itself and any other person who is or may be affected by the decision: see the Charities Act 2011 s 319(2), Sch 6 Table Cols 1, 2. The Tribunal has the power to quash the decision and (if appropriate) remit the matter to the Commission: see Sch 6 Table col 3. As to the meaning of 'person who is or may be affected' within the meaning of Sch 6 see PARA 317 note 8. As to the Attorney General see PARAS 589, 596, 605 et seq; and **CONSTITUTIONAL AND ADMINISTRATIVE LAW** vol 20 (2014) PARA 273 et seq.
3 Charities Act 2011 s 198(2)(a).
4 Charities Act 2011 s 198(2)(b).
5 For these purposes benefit means a direct or indirect benefit of any nature, except that it does not include any remuneration within the meaning of the Charities Act 2011 s 185 (see PARA 336) whose receipt may be authorised under that section: s 199.
6 Charities Act 2011 s 198(2)(c). For these purposes the following persons are connected with a director or member of a charitable company: (1) a child, parent, grandchild, grandparent, brother or sister of the director or member; (2) the spouse or civil partner of the director or member or of any person falling within (1); (3) a person carrying on business in partnership with the director or member or with any person falling within (1) or (2); (4) an institution which is controlled (a) by the director or member or by any person falling within (1), (2) or (3), or (b) by two or more persons falling within (a), when taken together; (5) a body corporate in which (a) the director or member or any connected person falling within any of (1) to (3) has a substantial interest, or (b) two or more persons falling within sub-paragraph (i), when taken together, have a substantial interest: s 200(1). As to the meaning of 'child' see PARA 401 note 9; as to the meaning of 'spouse' see PARA 401 note 12; and as to the meaning of 'civil partner' see PARA 401 note 13. As to the effect of the Marriage (Same Sex Couples) Act 2013 see s 1(1), 11(1); and **MATRIMONIAL AND CIVIL PARTNERSHIP LAW** vol 72 (2009) PARA 1 et seq.
7 Ie in accordance with the Charities Act 2011 s 198(2).
8 Ie as required by the Companies Act 2006 s 26 (see **COMPANIES** vol 14 (2009) PARA 236).
9 Ie as required by the Companies Act 2006 s 30 (see **COMPANIES** vol 14 (2009) PARA 231).
10 Ie as required by the Companies Act 2006 s 31 (see **COMPANIES** vol 14 (2009) PARA 240).
11 Charities Act 2011 s 198(3). The provisions of the Companies Act 2006 s 30(2)–(4) (offence of failing to comply with s 30) apply in relation to a failure to comply with the Charities Act 2011 s 198(3) as in relation to a failure to comply with the Companies Act 2006 s 30: Charities Act 2011 s 198(5).
12 Charities Act 2011 s 198(4).

243. Requirement of consent of Charity Commission to certain acts. In the case of a charitable company[1]:

(1) any approval given by its members for certain specified purposes[2]; and
(2) any affirmation given by its members of unapproved property transactions and loans[3],

is ineffective without the prior written consent of the Charity Commission[4].

An appeal against a decision to give or withhold such consent lies to the Tribunal at the instance of the Attorney General[5], the charity trustees of the Charity concerned, the body corporate itself and any other person who may be affected by the decision[6]. The Tribunal has the power to quash the decision and (if appropriate) remit the matter to the Commission[7].

Nor may a company that is a charity do, without the prior written consent of the Commission, any act that does not require approval by its members under a listed provision of the Companies Act 2006[8], but would require such approval but for an exemption in the provision in question that disapplies the need for approval on the part of the members of a body corporate which is a wholly-owned subsidiary of another body corporate[9].

1 As to the meaning of 'charitable company' see PARA 241 note 1.

2 Charities Act 2011 s 201(1)(a). The specified purposes are those of the following provisions of the Companies Act 2006: (1) s 188 (directors' long-term service contracts) (see COMPANIES vol 14 (2009) PARA 563); (2) s 190 (substantial property transactions with directors etc) (see COMPANIES vol 14 (2009) PARA 564); (3) ss 197, 198, 200 (loans and quasi-loans to directions etc) (see COMPANIES vol 14 (2009) PARAS 568–570); (4) s 201 (credit transactions for the benefit of directors etc) (see COMPANIES vol 14 (2009) PARA 571); (5) s 203 (related arrangements) (see COMPANIES vol 14 (2009) PARA 572); (6) s 217 (payments to directors for loss of office) (see COMPANIES vol 14 (2009) PARA 579); and (7) s 218 (payments to directors for loss of office: transfer of undertaking etc) (see COMPANIES vol 14 (2009) PARA 580): Charities Act 2011 s 201(2).

3 Charities Act 2011 s 201(1)(b). As to the affirmation of unapproved property transactions and loans see the Companies Act 2006 ss 196 and 214; and COMPANIES vol 14 (2009) PARAS 567, 577.

4 Charities Act 2011 s 201(1). As to the Charity Commission see PARAS 543–578.

5 As to the Tribunal see PARA 579. As to the Attorney General see PARAS 589, 596, 605 et seq; and CONSTITUTIONAL AND ADMINISTRATIVE LAW vol 20 (2014) PARA 273 et seq.

6 See the Charities Act 2011 s 319(2), Sch 6 Table Cols 1, 2. As to the meaning of 'person who is or may be affected' within the meaning of Sch 6 see PARA 317 note 8.

7 Charities Act 2011 Sch 6 Table Col 3.

8 Ie a provision listed in the Charities Act 2011 s 201(2) (see note 2): s 202(3).

9 Charities Act 2011 s 202(1), (2). If a company acts in contravention of s 202, the exemption referred to must be treated as of no effect in relation to the act: s 202(4).

(4) CHARITABLE CORPORATIONS GENERALLY

(i) Establishment of other Types of Charitable Corporation

244. Colleges and hospitals. The two principal kinds of charitable corporations used to be hospitals and colleges, the former being created for the maintenance and relief of the poor and impotent, and the latter for the promotion of learning and the support of persons engaged in literary pursuits[1].

Colleges and hospitals, in the strict legal sense of the latter term, are both institutions where the persons benefited by the charity are themselves incorporated[2]. The colleges of Oxford and Cambridge are eleemosynary corporations[3], but the halls are not[4]. The universities of Oxford and Cambridge are civil and not eleemosynary corporations[5]. More modern universities have been founded by royal charter and are eleemosynary corporations[6].

In other than the strict legal sense[7], however, the expression 'hospital' has been used to denote various kinds of corporate institutions[8] for the relief of the poor or infirm, such as corporations where the estate of inheritance only is vested in the master or warden[9], or hospitals managed by an incorporated body of governors or trustees[10].

Hospitals for the sick did not cease to be charities merely because of the coming into effect of the National Health Service Act 1946[11]; and the chartered corporation of a hospital was not automatically dissolved thereby[12], but the Minister of Health was given power to dissolve the original corporation of a hospital which had been nationalised[13].

Not all hospitals are charitable institutions[14]. Some are managed commercially[15], with a view to the profit of private individuals, and there are hospitals the services of which are not available to a sufficient section of the public[16]. However, the mere fact that a hospital is supported by the payment of fees does not prevent its being a charitable corporation[17], and the same is true of schools[18]. Furthermore, the Charity Commission has power to authorise the committee of management of a voluntary hospital to provide facilities for paying patients in certain circumstances[19].

1 1 Kyd on Corporations 25; *Philips v Bury* (1694) Skin 447 at 484, HL.

2 Shelford's Law of Mortmain (1836) 24; *Philips v Bury* (1694) Skin 447 at 484, HL ('if in an hospital the master and poor are incorporated, it is a college, having a common seal to act by, although it hath not the name of a college'). See also *A-G v Wyggeston's Hospital* (1853) 16 Beav 313; *A-G v St Cross Hospital* (1853) 17 Beav 435; *A-G v St John's Hospital, Bedford* (1865) 2 De GJ & Sm 621; *Sutton's Hospital Case* (1612) 10 Co Rep 1a at 23a, 31a, Ex Ch; *Lord Colchester v Kewney* (1866) 35 LJ Ex 204 at 206 per Channell B (affd (1867) LR 2 Exch 253).

3 *R v Vice-Chancellor of Cambridge* (1765) 3 Burr 1647 at 1652, 1656 per Lord Aston CJ; and see *Parkinson's Case* (1689) Carth 92 at 93 per Lord King LC; *Anon* (1698) 12 Mod Rep 232; *Philips v Bury* (1694) Skin 447 at 494, HL; *Patel v University of Bradford Senate* [1978] 3 All ER 841, [1978] 1 WLR 1488 (affd [1979] 2 All ER 582, [1979] 1 WLR 1066, CA). As to the meaning of 'eleemosynary corporation' see PARA 225.

4 *R v Hertford College* (1878) 3 QBD 693 at 694, CA, per Lord Coleridge CJ.

5 *R v Vice-Chancellor of Cambridge* (1765) 3 Burr 1647; *Patel v University of Bradford Senate* [1978] 3 All ER 841, [1978] 1 WLR 1488 (affd [1979] 2 All ER 582, [1979] 1 WLR 1066, CA); Shelford's Law of Mortmain 25.

6 The charters normally, probably always, provide that inter alios, the members of the academic staff and all the undergraduates are members of the university: see *Patel v University of Bradford Senate* [1978] 3 All ER 841, [1978] 1 WLR 1488 (affd [1979] 2 All ER 582, [1979] 1 WLR 1066, CA).

7 See *Sutton's Hospital Case* (1612) 10 Co Rep 1a at 31a; Shelford's Law of Mortmain 24.

8 *Moses v Marsland* [1901] 1 KB 668, DC; and see *Dean and Chapter of York v Middleborough* (1828) 2 Y & J 196 at 216 per Alexander LCB.

9 Co Litt 342a; Shelford's Law of Mortmain 24.

10 There were formerly many hospitals of this kind. The Charterhouse and Sutton's Hospital are ancient examples of this class (see *Sutton's Hospital Case* (1612) 10 Co Rep 1a). The word 'hospital' is, of course, used also in reference to unincorporated institutions or hospitals managed by unincorporated bodies of governors or trustees. Some modern hospitals are of this latter kind, especially those which have no endowment and are supported by voluntary subscriptions. For a discussion of the various meanings of the word 'hospital' see *Trustees of the Mary Clark Home v Anderson* [1904] 2 KB 645 at 653 per Channell J. As to hospitals see further **HEALTH SERVICES**.

11 *Re Frere, Kidd v Farnham Group Hospital Management Committee* [1951] Ch 27, [1950] 2 All ER 513. As to the history of the national health legislation see **HEALTH SERVICES** vol 54 (2008) PARA 3 et seq. As to the effect of nationalisation on gifts to hospitals see PARA 155.

12 *Re Kellner's Will Trusts, Blundell v Royal Cancer Hospital* [1950] Ch 46, [1949] 2 All ER 774, CA.

13 See the National Health Service Act 1977 s 129, Sch 14 para 6 (repealed); and **HEALTH SERVICES** vol 54 (2008) PARA 4.

14 See *Re Smith's Will Trusts, Barclays Bank Ltd v Mercantile Bank Ltd* [1962] 2 All ER 563, [1962] 1 WLR 763, CA (revsg [1961] 3 All ER 824, [1961] 1 WLR 1387); *Re Resch's Will Trusts, Le Cras v Perpetual Trustee Co Ltd* [1969] 1 AC 514, sub nom *Le Cras v Perpetual Trustees Co Ltd* [1967] 3 All ER 915, PC.

15 *Re Resch's Will Trusts, Le Cras v Perpetual Trustee Co Ltd* [1969] 1 AC 514 at 540, sub nom *Le Cras v Perpetual Trustees Co Ltd* [1967] 3 All ER 915 at 921, PC.

16 As to the requirement of benefit to a sufficient section of the community see PARA 6.

17 *Re Resch's Will Trusts, Le Cras v Perpetual Trustee Co Ltd* [1969] 1 AC 514, sub nom *Le Cras v Perpetual Trustees Co Ltd* [1967] 3 All ER 915, PC. As to the meaning of 'charitable corporation' see PARA 225. As to contributions by beneficiaries of charity see PARA 11.

18 *The Abbey, Malvern Wells, Ltd v Ministry of Local Government and Planning* [1951] Ch 728, [1951] 2 All ER 154.

19 See the Voluntary Hospitals (Paying Patients) Act 1936; and PARA 578. As to the Charity Commission see PARAS 543–578.

245. Community benefit societies and friendly societies. Community benefit societies[1] and registered friendly societies[2] which have exclusively charitable purposes are exempt charities[3].

Community benefit societies must observe requirements as to their name and status which are comparable to certain of those applicable in relation to charitable companies[4].

1 Community benefit societies (formerly industrial and provident societies) are established under the Co-operative and Community Benefit Societies Act 2014: see **FINANCIAL SERVICES AND INSTITUTIONS**.
2 Friendly societies are established under Friendly Societies Act 1992: see **FINANCIAL SERVICES AND INSTITUTIONS**.
3 As to exempt charities see PARA 318 et seq. See also *CC23: Exempt Charities* (Charity Commission, September 2013) Annexes 1–3 (available, at the date at which this volume states the law, on the government website). As to the Charity Commission see PARAS 543–578. As to the Charity Commission's publications see PARA 547.
4 See the Co-operative and Community Benefit Societies Act 2014 s 12.

246. Other charitable corporations. Besides colleges and hospitals, there are other corporations created solely for the fulfilment of charitable purposes, as where charity trustees[1], governors[2], or the schoolmaster[3], or the schoolmaster and usher[4], have been respectively incorporated for charitable or educational objects. Charitable corporations have also in many cases been created by Act of Parliament[5], or by registration under the Companies Acts, and by charter, to carry into effect various charitable purposes.

For the purposes of the Charities Act 2011, 'company' means a company registered under the Companies Act 2006 in England and Wales or Scotland[6].

1 See PARA 263.
2 *Eden v Foster* (1726) 2 P Wms 325 (grammar school).
3 *Whiston v Dean and Chapter of Rochester* (1849) 7 Hare 532 (cathedral school).
4 *A-G v Price* (1744) 3 Atk 108 at 109 per Lord Hardwicke LC (free school); *Re Chelmsford Grammar School* (1855) 1 K & J 543 at 561 per Page-Wood V-C.
5 Eg the RPFC (ie the Royal Patriotic Fund Corporation) which was established under the Patriotic Fund Reorganisation Act 1903 (repealed), which Act was superseded by the Armed Forces (Pensions and Compensation) Act 2004 s 6; Royal Patriotic Fund Corporation (Transfer of Property, Rights and Liabilities) Order 2005, SI 2005/3308: see **ARMED FORCES** vol 3 (2011) PARA 757.
6 Charities Act 2011 s 353(1).

247. Local authorities. Local authorities are trustees of their corporate property for public purposes for the benefit of the ratepayers[1], and as such they are subject to the court's trust jurisdiction[2] and are charity trustees[3]; but they do not come within the definition of charitable corporations because they are not established exclusively for charitable purposes[4].

1 *A-G v Aspinall* (1837) 2 My & Cr 613, approved in *Parr v A-G* (1842) 8 Cl & Fin 409, HL; and see *Re Brown's Mortgage, Wallasey Corpn v A-G* [1945] Ch 166, [1945] 1 All ER 397.
2 *A-G v Wilson* (1840) Cr & Ph 1; *A-G v Lichfield Corpn* (1848) 11 Beav 120; *A-G v De Winton* [1906] 2 Ch 106. See also *A-G v Newcastle-upon-Tyne Corpn and North-Eastern Rly Co* (1889) 23 QBD 492, CA. In *A-G v Aspinall* (1837) 2 My & Cr 613, the argument that the statutory remedies under the Municipal Corporations Act 1835 (repealed) ousted the court's equitable jurisdiction over breaches of trust was rejected.
3 *A-G v Dublin Corpn* (1827) 1 Bli NS 312, HL; *A-G v Liverpool Corpn* (1835) 1 My & Cr 171 at 201 per Pepys MR; *A-G v Stafford Corpn* [1878] WN 74.

4 See PARA 225. As to the transfer of powers on local government reorganisation see PARAS 271–272. As to local government reorganisation generally see further **LOCAL GOVERNMENT** vol 69 (2009) PARA 5 et seq.

(ii) Foundation and Dissolution

248. Meaning of 'foundation'. Historically, the expression 'foundation' as applied to the establishment of charitable corporations[1] is used in two distinct senses. It denotes: (1) the incorporation of a body of persons; and (2) the original endowment of the incorporated body[2].

1 As to the meaning of 'charitable corporation' see PARA 225. It is not clear to what extent early case law concerning foundations and endowments has any application to a charitable incorporated organisation ('CIO') or to a company formed under the Companies Act 2006. As to CIOs see PARA 226 et seq; and as to companies formed under the Companies Act 2006 see **COMPANIES**.

2 Shelford's Law of Mortmain 323–324; *Sutton's Hospital Case* (1612) 10 Co Rep 1a at 23a, 33a.

249. Modes of creation. A charitable corporation may be created: (1) by royal charter[1]; (2) by royal charter giving authority to the holder of an office to create corporations indefinitely[2]; (3) by persons acting under royal licence[3]; (4) by special Act of Parliament[4]; (5) under the Companies Act 2006[5]; and (6) by the Charity Commission[6].

There is now a power to create charitable incorporated organisations ('CIOs') under the Charities Act 2011[7].

No particular form of words need be used for the creation of a corporation by charter or Act of Parliament, provided the intention to incorporate is clear[8].

The Crown can establish or found a corporation which has had no previous embryonic existence as an unincorporated body of persons, but as a matter of history and of practice this never occurs[9].

1 This used to be the most usual form of incorporation. For examples see *Re Clergy Society* (1856) 2 K & J 615, and modern universities. However, charitable companies are thought to be now more common than charitable corporations founded by royal charter.

2 'In this manner the Chancellor of the University of Oxford has power by charter to erect corporations and has actually often exerted it' (1 Bl Com 474).

3 For examples see *Sutton's Hospital Case* (1612) 10 Co Rep 1a at 23a, 31a; *Ex p Kirkby Ravensworth Hospital* (1808) 15 Ves 305; *A-G v Dulwich College* (1841) 4 Beav 255.

4 Eg the Church Building Society, the Construction Industry Training Board and the other Industrial Training Boards: see *Construction Industry Training Board v A-G* [1973] Ch 173, [1972] 2 All ER 1339, CA.

5 See generally **COMPANIES**. For examples see *Re St Hilda's Incorporated College, Cheltenham* [1901] 1 Ch 556; *Incorporated Council of Law Reporting for England and Wales v A-G* [1972] Ch 73, [1971] 3 All ER 1029, CA. See PARA 248 note 1.

6 See the Charities Act 2011 Pt 12 (ss 251–266). The powers conferred by that Act replace those under the Charitable Trustees Incorporation Act 1872 (repealed). It was formerly often found more convenient to make use of the corporate capacity of the official custodian, but this use was restricted by the Charities Act 1992 (repealed): see PARAS 300–306. As to corporations formed in this way see PARA 263. As to the Charity Commission see PARAS 543–578. As to the official custodian see PARA 300 et seq.

7 See the Charities Act 2011 Pt 11 (ss 204–250); and PARA 226 et seq. See PARA 248 note 1.

8 *Sutton's Hospital Case* (1612) 10 Co Rep 1a at 23a, 28a; Shelford's Law of Mortmain 27.

9 *A-G v National Hospital for the Relief and Cure of the Paralysed and Epileptic* [1904] 2 Ch 252 at 256 per Kekewich J.

250. The founder. The person providing the original endowment is usually regarded as the founder, rather than the person performing the act of incorporation[1].

If the Monarch joins with an individual in endowing a corporation, the Monarch alone is founder[2], but if two or more private individuals contribute to the original endowment, they together constitute the founder[3]. A private individual who has founded a charitable corporation does not cease to be founder by reason of the corporation being subsequently endowed by the Monarch[4].

Where a charity is established by subscriptions the original subscribers alone are the founders. Additional contributions do not constitute a new foundation[5].

1 *Sutton's Hospital Case* (1612) 10 Co Rep 1a at 23a, 33a; *Anon* (1698) 12 Mod Rep 232. See also *St John's College, Cambridge v Todington* (1757) 1 Burr 158 at 200 per Lord Mansfield. See PARA 248 note 1.

2 2 Co Inst 68.

3 *Re St Leonard, Shoreditch, Parochial Schools* (1884) 10 App Cas 304 at 308, PC.

4 2 Co Inst 68.

5 *Re St Leonard, Shoreditch, Parochial Schools* (1884) 10 App Cas 304, PC.

251. Founder's right to provide for government and administration. A charitable corporation, in so far as it is charitable, is the 'creature of the founder'[1]. The founder may accordingly provide for the government and administration of his 'creature' and the application in perpetuity of the revenues[2]. Moreover, he and his appointees have the perpetual right of patronage and visitation[3].

However, he may not alter the corporation's constitution by increasing the number of corporators, or vary the trusts or application of the endowment or revenues[4], unless special powers for this purpose are reserved by the charter of incorporation[5].

It appears that if the number of members of the corporation is not originally fixed, the corporation itself may add to the number[6].

1 *St John's College, Cambridge v Todington* (1757) 1 Burr 158. See PARA 248 note 1. As to the meaning of 'charitable corporation' see PARA 225. As to who is the founder see PARA 250.

2 *Green v Rutherforth* (1750) 1 Ves Sen 462 at 472 per Lord Hardwicke LC; *Philips v Bury* (1694) Skin 447 at 482–483, HL.

3 As to patronage see PARA 125; and ECCLESIASTICAL LAW vol 34 (2011) PARA 550 et seq. As to visitation see PARA 514 et seq.

4 *A-G v Dulwich College* (1841) 4 Beav 255; and see *Ex p Bolton* (1789) 2 Bro CC 662.

5 *R v Vice-Chancellor of Cambridge* (1765) 3 Burr 1647 at 1656 per Lord Mansfield; *St John's College, Cambridge v Todington* (1757) 1 Burr 158. A power to alter the corporation's statutes or byelaws does not imply a power to alter its objects or constitution: *Ex p Bolton* (1789) 2 Bro CC 662; *A-G v Dulwich College* (1841) 4 Beav 255 at 266 per Lord Langdale MR.

6 *A-G v Talbot* (1748) 3 Atk 662 at 675 per Lord Hardwicke LC.

252. Control over chartered corporations. Although charitable corporations created by royal charter are the 'creatures of the Crown', yet so long as they exist and are capable of discharging their functions, they are not subject to control by the Crown except such control as is reserved by the charter[1]. However, when a corporation is dissolved, or an integral part of it is gone, the Crown may grant a new charter[2], or on failure of objects the court may dispose of the funds cy-près[3]; the court also has jurisdiction to regulate and control by scheme a charity founded by royal charter[4].

1 *R v Pasmore* (1789) 3 Term Rep 199. See, however, *Queen's College, Cambridge, Case* (1821) Jac 1 at 20–21 per Lord Eldon LC, where it was held that, in the case of a royal foundation, the Crown had an implied power to dispense with the statutes. As to the meaning of 'charitable corporation' see PARA 225. As to creation by royal charter see PARA 249.

2 *R v Pasmore* (1789) 3 Term Rep 199.

3 *A-G v Hicks* (1810) 3 Bro CC 166n as noted in 29 ER 468. See also the Charities Act 2011 s 68(1), (2); and PARA 184. As to the cy-près doctrine see PARA 209.

4 *Re Whitworth Art Gallery Trusts, Manchester Whitworth Institute v Victoria University of Manchester* [1958] Ch 461, [1958] 1 All ER 176. As to the settlement of schemes by the court see PARA 183.

253. Dissolution of charitable corporation. A charitable corporation may be dissolved in the same way as any other corporation[1]. When a charitable corporation has been dissolved, it is no longer in existence, notwithstanding that all its assets are still traceable and may not be applied for any other than charitable purposes[2].

A charitable company[3] may be wound up both on the petition of any creditor or contributory or itself[4], and also on the petition of the Attorney General[5]. Further, a petition may be presented by the Charity Commission if, after it has instituted an inquiry[6], it is satisfied that there is or has been misconduct or mismanagement in the administration of the charity, or that it is necessary or desirable to act for the purpose of protecting the property of the charity or securing a proper application for the purposes of the charity of that property or of property coming to the charity[7]. The Commission may make an application[8] to restore a charitable company to the register of companies[9].

The powers exercisable by the Commission under these provisions are exercisable by it of its own motion, but only with the agreement of the Attorney General on each occasion[10].

A charitable company which has been dissolved and struck off the register will not be restored to the register in order to take a legacy on a death after the date of dissolution[11]. On the other hand bequests received after a charitable company has gone into liquidation but before it is formally dissolved are, unless the terms of the bequest otherwise provide, available for distribution amongst the creditors[12].

Charitable incorporated organisations ('CIOs') may be wound up or dissolved under the relevant provisions of the Charities Act 2011[13].

1 See **COMPANY AND PARTNERSHIP INSOLVENCY** vol 16 (2011) PARA 380 et seq. As to the meaning of 'charitable corporation' see PARA 225.

2 *Re Stemson's Will Trusts, Carpenter v Treasury Solicitor* [1970] Ch 16, [1969] 2 All ER 517; but see *Re Vernon's Will Trusts, Lloyds Bank Ltd v Group 20 Hospital Management Committee (Coventry)* [1972] Ch 300n, [1971] 3 All ER 1061n. See also PARA 154.

3 As to the meaning of 'charitable company' see PARA 241 note 1.

4 See the Insolvency Act 1986 s 124; and **COMPANY AND PARTNERSHIP INSOLVENCY** vol 17 (2011) PARA 1319.

5 Charities Act 2011 s 113(1), (2). As to the Attorney General see PARAS 589, 596, 605 et seq; and **CONSTITUTIONAL AND ADMINISTRATIVE LAW** vol 20 (2014) PARA 273 et seq. The powers given to the Charity Commission by s 114 (see PARA 558) to take legal proceedings do not extend to presenting a petition for the winding up of a charitable company: s 114(2). The affairs of the first company to be wound up under s 113(1) (as originally enacted in the Charities Act 1960 s 30(1) (repealed)) came before the court in *Liverpool and District Hospital for Diseases of the Heart v A-G* [1981] Ch 193, [1981] 1 All ER 994. As to the Charity Commission see PARAS 543–578.

6 Ie under the Charities Act 2011 s 46: see PARA 559.

7 Charities Act 2011 ss 76(1)(a), (b), 113(3).

8 Ie under the Companies Act 2006 s 1029 (see **COMPANIES** vol 15 (2009) PARA 1535).

9 Charities Act 2011 s 203(1).

10 Charities Act 2011 ss 113(4), 203(2).

11 *Re Servers of the Blind League* [1960] 2 All ER 298, [1960] 1 WLR 564.

12 *Re ARMS (Multiple Sclerosis Research) Ltd, Alleyne v A-G* [1997] 2 All ER 679, [1997] 1 WLR 877.

13 See PARA 236.

(iii) Corporate Property

254. Property is held on trust. As charitable corporations exist solely for the accomplishment of charitable purposes, they are sometimes said to be but trustees for charity[1], whether the beneficiaries are members of the corporation, as in the case of hospitals[2] and colleges[3], or not[4]. It has accordingly been held that, in the absence of special powers, corporate property may only be invested in the manner permitted by law in respect of trust funds[5], and the governors or directors of the corporation, though not strictly trustees themselves, are in a fiduciary position and may not receive remuneration for work done[6].

In other cases the courts have refused to interfere with the property or affairs of a charitable corporation in the absence of a special trust[7], but the court has jurisdiction to restrain such a corporation from applying its property in unauthorised ways, and may have other jurisdiction over its internal affairs[8]. Perhaps the true meaning of the so-called rule that the court's jurisdiction to intervene in the affairs of a charity depends on the existence of a trust, is that the court has no jurisdiction to intervene unless there has been placed on the holder of the assets in question a legally binding restriction, arising either by way of trust in the strict traditional sense or, in the case of a corporate body, under the terms of its constitution, which obliges him or it to apply the assets in question for exclusively charitable purposes; for the jurisdiction of the court necessarily depends on the existence of a person or body who is subject to such obligation and against whom the court can act in personam so far as necessary for the purposes of enforcement[9].

1 *Lydiatt v Foach* (1700) 2 Vern 410; and see *Construction Industry Training Board v A-G* [1973] Ch 173 at 187, [1972] 2 All ER 1339 at 1348, CA, per Buckley LJ. The property of non-charitable corporations is not held on trust: *Bowman v Secular Society Ltd* [1917] AC 406 at 440, HL, per Lord Parker. As to the meaning of 'charitable corporation' see PARA 225.

2 *Lydiatt v Foach* (1700) 2 Vern 410; *A-G v Wyggeston's Hospital* (1853) 16 Beav 313; *A-G v St Cross Hospital* (1853) 17 Beav 435.

3 *Thetford School Case* (1609) 8 Co Rep 130b; but see *A-G v Whorwood* (1750) 1 Ves Sen 534 at 536 obiter per Lord Hardwicke LC.

4 *Re Manchester Royal Infirmary, Manchester Royal Infirmary v A-G* (1889) 43 ChD 420; *Re Dominion Students' Hall Trust, Dominion Students' Hall Trust v A-G* [1947] Ch 183; *Soldiers', Sailors' and Airmen's Families Association v A-G* [1968] 1 All ER 448n, [1968] 1 WLR 313. See also *Re Church Army* (1906) 75 LJCh 467, CA; *The Abbey, Malvern Wells, Ltd v Ministry of Local Government and Planning* [1951] Ch 728, [1951] 2 All ER 154; and the cases cited in PARA 246.

5 *Re Manchester Royal Infirmary, Manchester Royal Infirmary v A-G* (1889) 43 ChD 420; *Soldiers', Sailors' and Airmen's Families Association v A-G* [1968] 1 All ER 448n, [1968] 1 WLR 313. In the former case, but not in the latter, the decision was based partly on the fact that the funds had been held on trust before becoming vested in the corporation.

6 *Re French Protestant Hospital* [1951] Ch 567, [1951] 1 All ER 938.

7 *A-G v Magdalen College, Oxford* (1847) 10 Beav 402, decided on the principle that matters of internal regulation were entrusted by the founder to the jurisdiction of the visitor.

8 Cf *Construction Industry Training Board v A-G* [1973] Ch 173, [1972] 2 All ER 1339, CA; affg [1971] 3 All ER 449, [1971] 1 WLR 1303. The court's jurisdiction has always been said to depend on the existence of a trust, but a limited company or other corporation is capable of being subject to the court's charity jurisdiction and therefore of being a charity for the purpose of the Charities Act 2011: see ss 113, 353(1); and PARA 1 note 2.

9 *Liverpool and District Hospital for Diseases of the Heart v A-G* [1981] Ch 193 at 214, [1981] 1 All ER 994 at 1009–1010 per Slade J. Even when these conditions are fulfilled, the particular terms of the trust or constitution in question may operate substantially or partially to oust the jurisdiction of the court: see the Charities Act 2011 s 1(1); *Construction Industry Training Board v A-G* [1973] Ch 173 at 181–182, [1972] 2 All ER 1339 at 1343–1344, CA, per Russell LJ; *A-G v Magdalen College, Oxford* (1847) 10 Beav 402.

6. TRUSTEES

(1) CHARITY TRUSTEES

255. Charity trustees. 'Charity trustees' means the persons having the general control and management of the administration of a charity[1].

Regardless of the type of legal entity, or the name they are given[2], those falling within the statutory definition[3] will be regarded as the trustees. In the case of charitable companies, the trustees should be the directors.

Many of the general provisions of the Trustee Act 1925 apply to charity trustees[4], and in the case of a charitable company much of the general law relating to companies will apply[5].

1 Charities Act 2011 s 177. As to trustees generally see **TRUSTS AND POWERS** vol 98 (2013) PARA 194 et seq.

2 Eg 'committee', 'board' or 'governors'.

3 Ie the definition as set out in the Charities Act 2011 s 177: see the text to note 1.

4 See eg PARA 285. As to the Trustee Act 1925 see **TRUSTS AND POWERS**.

5 Eg in the case of a charitable company limited by guarantee, the trustees/directors will be appointed in line with the constitution of the company, and members of the company will have a statutory right to remove them. As to companies generally see **COMPANIES**; and see also **CORPORATIONS**. As to charitable incorporated organisations ('CIOs') see PARA 226 et seq.

(2) CORPORATIONS AND QUASI-CORPORATIONS AS TRUSTEES

256. Eleemosynary and civil corporations. Corporations, no less than individuals, may as a rule be trustees for charitable purposes[1].

Eleemosynary corporations are trustees of their corporate property, whether their members participate in the charity or not[2]. They may also undertake the execution of special trusts connected with the objects of their foundation[3].

Civil corporations, as, for example, livery companies of the City of London[4] and municipal corporations[5], are in many cases also trustees of charities. Local authorities are also trustees of the municipal property[6], and may hold property on special trusts, for example for the benefit of the borough freemen[7].

1 *Flood's Case* (1616) Hob 136; *A-G v Tancred* (1757) 1 Eden 10 at 14 per Henley, Lord Keeper; *A-G v Master of Brentwood School* (1833) 1 My & K 376 at 390 per Leach MR; *A-G v Liverpool Corpn* (1835) 1 My & Cr 171 at 201 per Pepys MR; *Incorporated Society in Dublin v Richards* (1841) 1 Dr & War 258 at 302–303, 307, 331 per Lord Sugden LC. For other instances of corporations acting as trustees for charities see also *Bene't (or Corpus Christi) College, Cambridge v Bishop of London* (1778) 2 Wm Bl 1182 (devise to college for charitable use); *A-G v Landerfield* (1743) 9 Mod Rep 286 (devise to hospital); *Society for Propagation of the Gospel v A-G* (1826) 3 Russ 142; *Re Manchester Royal Infirmary, Manchester Royal Infirmary v A-G* (1889) 43 ChD 420. As to the incorporation of charity trustees see PARA 263.

As to the need for a corporate trustee to be a trust corporation see PARA 257. As to the capacity of a corporation to be a trustee jointly with an individual or individuals see the Bodies Corporate (Joint Tenancy) Act 1899; *Re Thompson's Settlement Trusts, Thompson v Alexander* [1905] 1 Ch 229; and **CORPORATIONS** vol 24 (2010) PARA 448; **TRUSTS AND POWERS** vol 98 (2013) PARAS 10, 304.

2 *Lydiatt v Foach* (1700) 2 Vern 410 at 412 per North, Lord Keeper. As to the meaning of 'eleemosynary corporation' see PARA 225. As to where the property of charitable corporations is held on trust see PARA 254.

3 Eg in the case of educational foundations, trusts for additional fellowships (*A-G v Talbot* (1748) 3 Atk 662; *A-G v Whorwood* (1750) 1 Ves Sen 534 at 537 per Lord Hardwicke LC; *A-G v Flood* (1816) Hayes & Jo App xxi at p xxxv per Lord Brougham LC; *Re Catharine Hall, ex p Inge* (1831) 2 Russ & M 590 at 596 per Lord Eldon LC; and as to the necessity for the

visitor's consent see *A-G v Master and Fellows of Catharine Hall, Cambridge* (1820) Jac 381 at 400 per Lord Eldon LC); for scholarships or prizes (*A-G v Talbot* above); for maintenance of schools connected with the foundation (*A-G v Caius College* (1837) 2 Keen 150); for presentation to livings connected with the foundation (*Green v Rutherforth* (1750) 1 Ves Sen 462 at 473 per Lord Hardwicke LC).

4 *A-G v Grocers' Co* (1843) 6 Beav 526.

5 See the Municipal Corporations Act 1882 s 133 (amended by the Charities Act 2006 Sch 8 para 7); and *Colchester Corpn v Lowten* (1813) 1 Ves & B 226; *A-G v Shrewsbury Corpn* (1843) 6 Beav 220; *Viscount Gort v A-G* (1817) 6 Dow 136, HL; *Christ's Hospital v Grainger* (1848) 16 Sim 83 (on appeal (1849) 1 Mac & G 460); *Re Ludlow Charities* (1837) 3 My & Cr 262. For the position under the Municipal Corporations Act 1835 (repealed) see *A-G v Exeter Corpn* (1852) 2 De GM & G 507 at 515 per Lord St Leonards LC; and Tudor on Charities (7th Edn, 1984) pp 313, 362. See also the Charitable Trusts Act 1853 s 65 (repealed by the Municipal Corporations Act 1882 s 5, Sch 1: and see s 133); and *Re Huntingdon Municipal Charities* (1859) 27 Beav 214.

6 See PARA 247.

7 *Goodman v Saltash Corpn* (1882) 7 App Cas 633, HL; *Prestney v Colchester Corpn and A-G* (1882) 21 ChD 111.

257. Trust corporations. Certain powers which may be required to be exercised by trustees can be exercised by corporate trustees only if they are trust corporations[1]. Of particular relevance to charities is the power to give good receipt for property transactions[2].

If a corporate trustee is appointed by the Charity Commission under a scheme, it will be deemed a trust corporation automatically[3], otherwise it must seek certification as a trust corporation[4] in order to be able to give good receipt.

A corporation may be so designated if it is constituted under the laws of the United Kingdom or any part of it and satisfies the Lord Chancellor that it undertakes the administration of trusts without remuneration, or that by its constitution it is required to apply the whole of its net income after payment of outgoings for charitable, ecclesiastical or public purposes, and is prohibited from distributing, directly or indirectly, any part of that income by way of profits among any of its members, and is authorised by him to act in relation to such trusts as a trust corporation[5].

A corporate body established by royal charter may be a trust corporation[6], and in certain circumstances a charitable incorporated organisation ('CIO')[7] is treated as a trust corporation[8].

1 As to trust corporations see **TRUSTS AND POWERS** vol 98 (2013) PARAS 238, 239.

2 See the Law of Property Act 1925 s 27(1); the Settled Land Act 1925 ss 94, 95; and **TRUSTS AND POWERS** vol 98 (2013) PARA 239.

3 See the Charities Act 2011 Sch 7 para 3.

4 See the Law of Property Act 1925 s 27(1); the Settled Land Act 1925 ss 94, 95; and **TRUSTS AND POWERS** vol 98 (2013) PARA 239. Application for such a certificate is made to the Ministry of Justice.

5 See the Law of Property (Amendment) Act 1926 s 3(1); and **TRUSTS AND POWERS** vol 98 (2013) PARAS 238, 239. As to the meaning of United Kingdom see PARA 189.

6 See the Public Trustee Rules 1912, SI 1912/348, r 30; the Trustee Act 1925 s 68(1)(18); and **TRUSTS AND POWERS** vol 98 (2013) PARA 234. The body must have an appropriate power in its constitution,, and the powers of the body must be considered in each case.

7 As to CIOs see PARAS 226–239.

8 Where a CIO holds specified trust property as trustee by virtue of the Charities Act 2011 s 310 (as modified) (see PARA 417), the CIO is to be treated for the purposes of the provisions identified in the Charities Act 2011 Sch 7 para 3 (application of certain enactments to trust corporations) as if it were a corporation appointed by the court to be trustee: Charitable Incorporated Organisations (General) Regulations 2012, SI 2012/3012, reg 61(4).

258. Corporations with limited capacity. Corporations may have only a limited capacity for holding property on trust[1]. A corporation created by or under statute[2] or otherwise[3] for a particular purpose has no capacity beyond the object for which it was established. Local authorities may not act as trustees for an ecclesiastical charity or a charity for the relief of poverty[4].

Real or personal property vested in a corporation[5] passes automatically to the corporation's successors, and statutory provision has been made to deal with the problem of vacancies[6].

1 Tudor on Charities (7th Edn, 1984) pp 362–363. It is sometimes said that colleges in universities cannot undertake trusts inconsistent with their foundation, but the cases cited as authority (*A-G v Whorwood* (1750) 1 Ves Sen 534; *A-G v Tancred* (1757) 1 Eden 10 at 15 per Henley, Lord Keeper) do not appear to justify the proposition.

2 See *National Guaranteed Manure Co v Donald* (1859) 28 LJEx 185 at 188; *Putney Overseers v London and South Western Rly Co* (1891) 60 LJQB 438 at 439 per Lord Esher MR, CA, per Lord Esher MR.

3 See *Incorporated Society v Price* (1844) 1 Jo & Lat 498. The Chamberlain of the City of London is a corporation sole for the purpose of taking recognisances, obligations, etc, in trust for the portions of orphans: *Fulwood's Case* (1591) 4 Co Rep 64b, 65a; *Byrd v Wilford* (1596) Cro Eliz 464, Ex Ch.

4 Local Government Act 1972 s 139(3). It would seem that this includes all charities directed to the relief of individual distress: *Re Armitage, Ellam v Norwich Corpn* [1972] Ch 438, [1972] 1 All ER 708 ('eleemosynary charity' as referred to in the Local Government Act 1933 s 268 (repealed)). Gifts to local authorities on trust for such a charity do not fail owing to the trustee's incapacity: see *Re Woolnough's Will Trusts* (1959) Times, 22 October; *Re Armitage, Ellam v Norwich Corpn* above. Some local authorities have special statutory powers enabling them to act as trustees of such trusts.

5 For a corporate trustee to give good receipt for property transactions it must be a trust corporation: see PARA 257.

6 See the Law of Property Act 1925 s 180; and CORPORATIONS vol 24 (2010) PARAS 355–356, 448. Formerly personalty could not be vested in a corporation sole as such; there is a possible doubt, on the strict construction of s 180(1), as to whether it is effective as apparently intended: see CORPORATIONS vol 24 (2010) PARA 450. A parson, seised of property in right of his church, may be in a different position: see *Duke of Marlborough v St John* (1852) 5 De G & Sm 174; *Ecclesiastical Comrs v Wodehouse* [1895] 1 Ch 552; Littleton s 644; 1 Co Inst 300b, 341b; and cf *Power v Banks* [1901] 2 Ch 487.

259. Churchwardens and incumbents. Churchwardens possess a quasi-corporate capacity to hold personalty[1], but not realty[2], for church purposes[3].

Under the School Sites Acts grants of land might formerly be made to the minister, churchwardens and overseers of the poor[4], and may still, in certain circumstances, be made to the minister and churchwardens alone[5], and their successors, as a corporation, for the charitable purposes mentioned in the Acts. Otherwise a minister and churchwardens do not, as a rule, form a corporation[6].

Certain property[7], that is to say certain real property held on charitable trusts for ecclesiastical purposes of the Church of England, and personal property held on permanent trusts[8], if it is vested in an incumbent or churchwardens[9] or in an ecclesiastical corporation sole acting as joint trustee with an incumbent or churchwardens[10] or if the presently acting trustee is the parochial church council but not validly appointed[11], must be brought to the attention of the diocesan authority[12], with a view to being vested in the board as custodian trustee[13]. Subject to objections and representations received, the board must make a vesting declaration[14] vesting the property in itself as custodian trustee[15], and also a scheme for the charity's management, limited to the establishment or continuance of managing trustees[16]. The exercise of these powers is without prejudice to the jurisdiction of the court and the Charity Commission to make administrative schemes[17].

Incumbents and churchwardens no longer[18] have the capacity to acquire interests in land or personalty to which the Incumbents and Churchwardens (Trusts) Measure 1964 applies[19], except an interest in personalty by gift or under a will, without the consent of the diocesan authority[20].

1 Shelford's Law of Mortmain 28; *A-G v Ruper* (1722) 2 P Wms 125; and see *Tufnell v Constable* (1838) 7 Ad & El 798.

2 Shelford's Law of Mortmain 29; *A-G v Ruper* (1722) 2 P Wms 125; *Gravenor v Hallum* (1767) Amb 643 at 644 per Lord Camden LC; *Withnell v Gartham* (1795) 6 Term Rep 388 at 396 per Lord Kenyon CJ. It is otherwise in the City of London: *Fell v Official Trustee of Charity Lands* [1898] 2 Ch 44 at 51, CA, per Lindley MR. In some early cases it appears that churchwardens were created corporations by letters patent with power to hold land: Shelford's Law of Mortmain 29; 1 Kyd on Corporations 31. As to actions by and against the churchwardens see ECCLESIASTICAL LAW vol 34 (2011) PARA 278.

3 Property vested in churchwardens alone was not affected by the Local Government Act 1894 (repealed) or by the Overseers Order 1927, SR & O 1927/55 (lapsed); nor did those enactments interfere with their powers, duties and liabilities, so far as they related to the affairs of the church or to charities generally. The Parochial Church Councils (Powers) Measure 1956 s 4 (see ECCLESIASTICAL LAW vol 34 (2011) PARA 308 et seq) gives to parochial church councils certain of the powers, duties and liabilities which the churchwardens formerly had. As to churchwardens generally see ECCLESIASTICAL LAW vol 34 (2011) PARA 270 et seq.

4 See the School Sites Act 1841 s 7. Overseers were abolished by the Rating and Valuation Act 1925 s 62, and their functions transferred to rating or other local authorities by s 1(2); and the Overseers Order 1927, SR & O 1927/55 (lapsed).

5 See the School Sites Act 1844 ss 4, 5.

6 In the City of London the minister and churchwardens may by custom be a corporation for the execution of charitable trusts (see Tudor on Charities (4th Edn, 1906) p 264 note (f); *A-G v Leage* [1881] WN 167, set out in Tudor on Charities (4th Edn, 1906) p 1041), or may be incorporated for such purposes by a private Act, as in the case of the vicar and churchwardens of St Martin's-in-the-Fields (1 Anne, sess 2, c xxi (1702)).

7 There are various exceptions: glebe and similar property, church movables and ornaments etc, property vested in the official custodian for charities, church educational endowments (defined in the Diocesan Education Committees Measure 1955 s 3 (repealed); see now the Diocesan Boards of Education Measure 1991 s 10), land acquired as sites of proposed churches, parsonage houses etc under the New Parishes Measure 1943 ss 16(1), (2), s 17 (see ECCLESIASTICAL LAW vol 34 (2011) PARAS 849, 877–878), land held on a yearly tenancy or term certain of a year or less: see the Incumbents and Churchwardens (Trusts) Measure 1964 s 2(2) (amended by the Endowments and Glebe Measure 1976 s 47(4), Sch 8). As to the official custodian see PARA 300 et seq.

8 'Permanent trusts' means any trust of property which is a permanent endowment within the meaning of the Charities Act 2011 s 353(3) (see PARA 218 note 1): Incumbents and Churchwardens (Trusts) Measure 1964 s 1 (definition amended by the Charities Act 2011 Sch 7 Pt 2 para 13).

9 'Incumbent' includes any minister with a separate cure of souls but does not include a curate in charge of a conventional district: Incumbents and Churchwardens (Trusts) Measure 1964 s 1. 'Incumbent or churchwardens' means any incumbent and the churchwardens of the parish comprising the benefice of that incumbent or of any parish comprised in any united benefice of that incumbent and is deemed to refer to them or any of them jointly or severally: s 1.

10 Ie either where no present or past trustee, other than the personal representatives of a sole surviving trustee, is or has been any person other than those specified (Incumbents and Churchwardens (Trusts) Measure 1964 s 2(1)(a)) or where the presently acting trustees, whether or not validly appointed, are the persons specified, unless they are so acting in contravention of the terms of the trust (s 2(1)(b)).

11 Ie if immediately previously the trusts have been administered by an incumbent or churchwardens with or without an ecclesiastical corporation sole as joint trustee, unless they were acting in contravention of the terms of the trust: Incumbents and Churchwardens (Trusts) Measure 1964 s 2(1)(c).

12 'Diocesan authority' means the diocesan board of finance, or any existing or future body appointed by the diocesan synod to act as trustees of diocesan trust property: Incumbents and Churchwardens (Trusts) Measure 1964 s 1 (definition amended by the Synodical Government Measure 1969 s 4(7)). As to diocesan boards of finance see ECCLESIASTICAL LAW vol 34 (2011) PARAS 241–242.

13 See the Incumbents and Churchwardens (Trusts) Measure 1964 ss 2(1), (2) (as amended: see note 7), 3(1), (2); and ECCLESIASTICAL LAW vol 34 (2011) PARA 995. 'Custodian trustee' has the same meaning as in the Public Trustee Act 1906 (see TRUSTS AND POWERS vol 98 (2013) PARA 232 et seq): Incumbents and Churchwardens (Trusts) Measure 1964 s 1. The duties of the board of finance on its becoming aware of the existence of property falling within those provisions are laid down in the Incumbents and Churchwardens (Trusts) Measure 1964 s 3(2), Schedule. The board must give notice to persons interested, including the Charity Commission, of the proposal as to vesting: see Schedule para 2 (amended by the Charities Act 2006 Sch 8 para 45). As to the Charity Commission see PARAS 543–578.

14 This has the effect specified in the Trustee Act 1925 s 40(1)(b) (see TRUSTS AND POWERS vol 98 (2013) PARA 306): see the Incumbents and Churchwardens (Trusts) Measure 1964 s 3(3). Any person in whom is vested an interest to which the Measure applies but which cannot be vested in the board by a vesting declaration alone is under a duty to transfer it to the board: see s 3(4).

15 See the Incumbents and Churchwardens (Trusts) Measure 1964 s 3(2). The vesting declaration will vest subject to all trusts, charges etc affecting it: see s 3(5).

16 Incumbents and Churchwardens (Trusts) Measure 1964 Schedule para 6. The trustees should be the incumbent or churchwardens jointly with, where appropriate, an ecclesiastical corporation sole: Schedule para 6.

17 See the Incumbents and Churchwardens (Trusts) Measure 1964 s 3(6) (amended by the Charities Act 2006 Sch 8 para 43). For the jurisdiction to make administrative schemes see PARAS 179, 189.

18 Ie since 1 January 1965 (the commencement of the Incumbents and Churchwardens (Trusts) Measure 1964).

19 See text and note 7.

20 Incumbents and Churchwardens (Trusts) Measure 1964 s 4.

260. Local authorities as trustees of charities connected with education. A local authority may be constituted trustee of property for purposes connected with education[1]. An intention that a school vest in the authority as trustee is deemed to be an intention to establish a new community school, community special school or maintained nursery school[2].

1 See the Education Act 1996 s 529; and EDUCATION vol 36 (2011) PARA 1625. Although these provisions do not specifically mention the appointment of local authority as trustee of property held on charitable trusts, it would seem clear that such will fall within the scope of the provision.

It appears that education authorities' statutory functions do not give them ipso facto an interest in the establishment of independent educational charities in their areas: *Re Belling, London Borough of Enfield v Public Trustee* [1967] Ch 425, [1967] 1 All ER 105. As to the transfer of the property of registered educational charities following the coming into force of the Local Government Act 1972 see PARAS 271–272.

2 See the Education Act 1996 s 529(1A)–(3); and EDUCATION vol 36 (2011) PARA 1625. As to community schools, community special schools and maintained nursery schools see EDUCATION vol 35 (2011) PARA 98 et seq.

261. Public Trustee and custodian trustees. The Public Trustee may not accept any trust exclusively for religious or charitable purposes[1] or involving the selection of charitable objects of a settlor's bounty[2], but this does not extend to bodies corporate entitled to act as custodian trustees under the Public Trustee Act 1906[3].

1 Public Trustee Act 1906 s 2(5). As to the Public Trustee see TRUSTS AND POWERS vol 98 (2013) PARA 206 et seq.

2 *Re Hampton, Public Trustee v Hampton* (1918) 88 LJCh 103.

3 See the Public Trustee Act 1906 s 4(3); and TRUSTS AND POWERS vol 98 (2013) PARA 233. See also *Re Cherry's Trusts, Robinson v Wesleyan Methodist Chapel Purposes Trustees* [1914]

1 Ch 83. As to corporations entitled to act as custodian trustees see the Public Trustee Rules 1912, SR & O 1912/348, r 30; and TRUSTS AND POWERS vol 98 (2013) PARA 234.

262. Non-corporate bodies. A Roman Catholic bishop[1], a dissenting minister[2], a principal of a college, a mayor or bailiff of a city[3], or the officers of a corporate body[4], and their respective successors, are not recognised by the law as corporations, and consequently cannot be trustees for charitable purposes in a corporate capacity, though the particular individuals named may act as trustees[5].

1 *A-G v Power* (1809) 1 Ball & B 145 at 149 per Lord Manners LC; and see *Re Lalor's goods* (1901) 85 LT 643.
2 *A-G for Ireland v Lee* (1869) IR 4 Eq 84.
3 *A-G v Gilbert* (1847) 10 Beav 517.
4 *A-G v Tancred* (1757) 1 Eden 10 at 14 per Henley, Lord Keeper. See also PARA 257.
5 See the cases cited in notes 2–4. As to examples of corporations sole see CORPORATIONS vol 24 (2010) PARA 315.

263. Certificates of incorporation of charity trustees as a body corporate. Where the charity trustees[1] of a charity apply[2] to the Charity Commission for a certificate of incorporation of the trustees as a body corporate, and the Commission considers that the incorporation of the trustees would be in the interests of the charity, the Commission may grant such a certificate, subject to such conditions or directions[3] as it thinks fit to insert in it[4]. The Commission must not, however, grant such a certificate in a case where the charity appears to it to be required to be registered[5] but is not so registered[6]. On the grant of such a certificate the trustees of the charity become a body corporate by such name as is specified in the certificate and any relevant rights or liabilities[7] of those trustees become rights or liabilities of that body[8]. A certificate of incorporation is conclusive evidence that all the preliminary requirements for incorporation[9] have been complied with, and the date of incorporation mentioned in the certificate is deemed to be the date at which incorporation has taken place[10].

The certificate of incorporation vests in the body corporate all real and personal estate, of whatever nature or tenure, belonging to or held by any person or persons in trust for the charity, and thereupon any person or persons in whose name or names any stocks, funds or securities are standing in trust for the charity, must transfer them into the name of the body corporate, but this does not apply to property vested in the official custodian[11].

After their incorporation the trustees may sue and be sued in their corporate name, and have the same powers, and are subject to the same restrictions and limitations, as respects the holding, acquisition and disposal of property for or in connection with the purposes of the charity as they had or were subject to while unincorporated[12]. Any relevant legal proceedings[13] that might have been continued or commenced by or against the trustees may be continued or commenced by or against them in their corporate name[14]. After a certificate of incorporation has been granted all trustees of the charity, notwithstanding their incorporation, are chargeable for such property as comes into their hands, and are answerable and accountable for their own acts, receipts, neglects, and defaults, and for the due administration of the charity and its property, in the same manner and to the same extent as if no such incorporation had been effected[15]. After the incorporation of the trustees of any charity, every relevant donation, gift and disposition of property[16], made to or in favour of the charity, or the charity trustees, or otherwise for the purposes of the charity, takes effect as if made to or in favour of the incorporated body[17] or otherwise for the same purposes[18].

The Commission may amend a certificate of incorporation either on the application of the incorporated body to which it relates or of its own motion[19]. Before making any such amendment of its own motion, the Commission must by notice in writing inform the charity trustees of the relevant charity[20] of its proposals, and invite those trustees to make representations to it within a time specified in the notice, being not less than one month from the date of the notice[21]. The Commission must take into consideration any representations made by those trustees within the time so specified, and may then (without further notice) proceed with its proposals either without modification or with such modifications as appear to it to be desirable[22]. The Commission may amend a certificate of incorporation either by making an order specifying the amendment or by issuing a new certificate of incorporation taking account of the amendment[23].

The Commission must keep a record of all applications for, and certificates of, incorporation and must keep all documents sent to it for such period as it thinks fit[24].

An appeal against a decision of the Commission to grant or not to grant a certificate of incorporation[25], to amend a certificate of incorporation, or not to amend a certificate of incorporation[26] lies to the Tribunal at the instance of the Attorney General[27], the charity trustees of the charity, or any other person who is affected or may be affected by the decision or, as the case may be, the amended certificate or incorporation[28]. In the case of a decision to grant or not to grant a certificate of incorporation, the Tribunal has the power to quash the decision, or any conditions or directions inserted in the certificate, and, if appropriate, remit the matter to the Commission; in the case of a decision to amend a certificate of incorporation, the Tribunal has the power to quash the decision and, if appropriate, remit the matter to the Commission; in the case of a decision not to amend a certificate of incorporation, the Tribunal has the power to do any of the following: (1) quash the decision and, if appropriate, remit the matter to the Commission; (2) make any order the Commission could itself have made under the provisions above[29].

1 As to the meaning of 'charity trustees' see PARA 255.

2 Every application to the Charity Commission for a certificate of incorporation must be in writing and signed by the charity trustees of the charity concerned and be accompanied by such documents or information as the Commission may require for the purpose of the application: Charities Act 2011 s 256(1). The Commission may require any statement contained in any such application, or any document or information so supplied to be verified in such manner as it may specify: s 256(2). 'Document' includes information recorded in any form, and, in relation to information recorded otherwise than in legible form, any reference to its production is to be construed as a reference to the furnishing of a copy of it in legible form, and any reference to the furnishing of a copy of, or extract from, it is accordingly to be construed as a reference to the furnishing of a copy of, or extract from, it in legible form: s 353(2). As to the Charity Commission see PARAS 543–578. As to the meaning of 'charity' see PARA 1.

Before a certificate of incorporation is granted, trustees of the charity must have been effectually appointed to the satisfaction of the Commission: Charities Act 2011 s 257.

3 All conditions and directions inserted in any certificate of incorporation are binding upon and must be performed or observed by the trustees as trusts of the charity, and the Charities Act 2011 s 336 (see PARA 556) (enforcement of orders of the Commission) applies to any trustee who fails to perform or observe any such condition or direction as it applies to a person guilty of disobedience to any such order of the Commission as is mentioned in that provision: s 255(1), (2).

4 Charities Act 2011 s 251(1), (2).

5 Ie under the Charities Act 2011 s 30: see PARA 307 et seq.

6 Charities Act 2011 s 251(3).

7 Ie rights or liabilities in connection with any property vesting in the body corporate under the Charities Act 2011 s 252 (see the text and note 11).
8 Charities Act 2011 s 251(4). The transfer of rights and liabilities does not affect the operation of s 254 (see the text and note 15): s 251(4). A body incorporated under s 50 need not have a common seal: s 251(7).

Where a certificate of incorporation is granted, vacancies in the number of the trustees of the charity must from time to time be filled up so far as required by the constitution or settlement of the charity, or by any conditions or directions in the certificate, by such legal means as would have been available for the appointment of new trustees of the charity if no certificate of incorporation had been granted, or otherwise as required by such conditions or directions: s 259(1), (2).

No vesting or transfer of any property in pursuance of any provision of Part 12 operates as a breach of a covenant or condition against alienation or gives rise to a forfeiture: s 266.
9 Ie under the Charities Act 2011 Pt 12 (ss 251–266).
10 Charities Act 2011 s 258(1), (2).
11 Charities Act 2011 s 252(1)–(3). As to the official custodian see PARA 300 et seq.
12 Charities Act 2011 s 251(5)(a), (b).
13 For these purposes, 'relevant legal proceedings' means legal proceedings in connection with any property vesting in the body corporate under the Charities Act 2011 s 252 (see the text and note 11): s 251(6).
14 Charities Act 2011 s 251(5).
15 Charities Act 2011 s 254.
16 For these purposes a donation, gift or disposition of property is a relevant one, whether of real or personal property, and whether made by deed, will or otherwise, if it was lawfully made before the incorporation but has not actually taken effect, or is lawfully made thereafter: Charities Act 2011 s 253(2).
17 For these purposes, 'incorporated body' means a body incorporated under the Charities Act 2011 s 251 (see the text and notes 1–8, 12–14): s 265.
18 Charities Act 2011 s 253(1).
19 Charities Act 2011 s 262(1).
20 For these purposes, 'relevant charity', in relation to an incorporated body, means the charity the charity trustees of which have been incorporated as that body: Charities Act 2011 s 265.
21 Charities Act 2011 s 262(2), (3).
22 Charities Act 2011 s 262(4).
23 Charities Act 2011 s 262(5).
24 Charities Act 2011 s 264(1), (2). Documents must be open to inspection at all reasonable times: s 264(3). Any person provided with a copy or extract of any such document may require it to be certified by a certificate signed by a member of staff of the Commission: s 264(4).
25 Ie a decision of the Commission to grant or not to grant a certificate of incorporation under the Charities Act 2011 s 251(1).
26 Ie a decision of the Commission to amend or not to amend a certificate of incorporation of a charity under the Charities Act 2011 s 262(1).
27 As to the Tribunal see PARA 579 et seq. As to the Attorney General see PARAS 589, 596, 605 et seq; and **CONSTITUTIONAL AND ADMINISTRATIVE LAW** vol 20 (2014) PARA 273 et seq.
28 See the Charities Act 2011 s 319(2), Sch 6 Table Cols 1, 2. As to the meaning of 'person who is or may be affected' within the meaning of Sch 6 see PARA 317 note 8.
29 See the Charities Act 2011 Sch 6 Table Col 3.

264. Execution of documents by incorporated body. There are provisions which have effect as respects the execution of documents by an incorporated body[1].

If an incorporated body has a common seal, a document[2] may be executed by the body by the affixing of its common seal[3].

Whether or not it has a common seal, a document may be executed by an incorporated body either: (1) by being signed by a majority of the charity trustees of the relevant charity and expressed, in whatever form of words, to be executed by the body[4]; or (2) by being executed in pursuance of an authority conferred[5] by the trustees of the relevant charity[6]. Such an authority (a) suffices for any document if it is given in writing or by resolution of a meeting of the trustees of the relevant charity, notwithstanding the want of any formality that would otherwise[7] be required in giving an authority[8]; (b) may be given so as to make the powers conferred exercisable by any of the trustees, or may be restricted to named persons or in any other way[9]; (c) subject to any such restriction, and until it is revoked, has effect, notwithstanding any change in the trustees of the relevant charity, as a continuing authority given by the trustees from time to time of the charity and exercisable by such charity trustees[10].

A document duly executed by an incorporated body which makes it clear on its face that it is intended by the person or persons making it to be a deed has effect, upon delivery, as a deed; and it is to be presumed, unless a contrary intention is proved, to be delivered upon its being so executed[11].

In favour of a purchaser[12] a document is deemed to have been duly executed by such a body if it purports to be signed by a majority of the trustees of the relevant charity, or by such of the trustees of the relevant charity as are authorised by the trustees of that charity to execute it in the name and on behalf of the body[13]. Where the document makes it clear on its face that it is intended by the person or persons making it to be a deed, it is deemed to have been delivered upon its being executed[14].

1 Charities Act 2011 s 260(1). As to the meaning of 'incorporated body' see PARA 263 note 17.
2 As to the meaning of 'document' see PARA 263 note 2.
3 Charities Act 2011 s 260(2).
4 Charities Act 2011 s 260(3)(a).
5 The trustees of the relevant charity in the case of an incorporated body may, subject to the trusts of the charity, confer on any two or more of their number a general authority, or an authority limited in such manner as the trustees think fit, to execute in the name and on behalf of the body documents for giving effect to transactions to which the body is a party: Charities Act 2011 s 261(1). In any such authority to execute a document in the name and on behalf of an incorporated body there is, unless the contrary intention appears, implied authority also to execute it for the body in the name and on behalf of the official custodian or of any other person, in any case in which the trustees could do so: s 261(3). As to the meaning of 'trusts' see PARA 218 note 5. As to the meaning of 'charity trustees' see PARA 255. As to the meaning of 'relevant charity' see PARA 263 note 20. As to the official custodian see PARA 300 et seq.
6 Charities Act 2011 s 260(3)(b).
7 Ie apart from the Charities Act 2011 s 261(1): see note 5.
8 Charities Act 2011 s 261(2)(a).
9 Charities Act 2011 s 261(2)(b).
10 Charities Act 2011 s 261(2)(c).
11 Charities Act 2011 s 260(4).
12 For these purposes, 'purchaser' means a purchaser in good faith for valuable consideration and includes a lessee, mortgagee or other person who for valuable consideration acquires an interest in property: Charities Act 2011 s 260(6).
13 Charities Act 2011 s 260(5)(a), (b).
14 Charities Act 2011 s 260(5).

265. Power of Charity Commission to dissolve incorporated body. Where the Charity Commission[1] is satisfied: (1) that an incorporated body[2] has no assets or does not operate[3]; or (2) that the relevant charity[4] in the case of an incorporated body has ceased to exist[5]; or (3) that the institution[6] previously constituting, or treated by the Commission as constituting, any such charity has ceased to be, or, as the case may be, was not at the time of the body's incorporation, a charity[7]; or (4) that the purposes of the relevant charity in the case of an incorporated body have been achieved so far as is possible or are in practice incapable of being achieved[8], the Commission may of its own motion make an order dissolving the body as from such date as is specified in the order[9].

Where the Commission is satisfied, on the application of the charity trustees[10] of the relevant charity in the case of an incorporated body, that it would be in the interests of the charity for that body to be dissolved, the Commission may make an order dissolving the body as from such date as is specified in the order[11].

An order made under these provisions with respect to an incorporated body has the effect of vesting in the trustees of the relevant charity, in trust for that charity, all property for the time being vested in the body, or in any other person, apart from the official custodian[12], in trust for that charity[13]. If the Commission so directs in the order (a) all or any specified[14] part of that property vests, instead of vesting in the trustees of the relevant charity, in a specified person as trustee for, or nominee of, that charity, or in such persons (other than the trustees of the relevant charity) as may be specified[15]; (b) any specified investments, or any specified class or description of investments, held by any person in trust for the relevant charity must be transferred to the trustees of that charity, or to any such person or persons as is or are mentioned in head (a) above[16].

In relation to certain orders[17] which are made with respect to an incorporated body, any rights or liabilities of the body become rights or liabilities of the trustees of the relevant charity, and any legal proceedings that might have been continued or commenced by or against the body may be continued or commenced by or against those trustees[18].

Any order made by the Commission under these provisions may be varied or revoked by a subsequent order so made[19].

An appeal against such an order lies to the Tribunal at the instance of the Attorney General[20], the charity trustees of the charity or any other person who is or may be affected by the order[21]. The Tribunal has the power to do any of the following: (i) quash the order and, if appropriate, remit the matter to the Commission; (ii) substitute for the order any other order which could have been made by the Commission; (iii) add to the order anything which could have been contained in an order made by the Commission[22].

1 As to the Charity Commission see PARAS 543–578.
2 As to the meaning of 'incorporated body' see PARA 263 note 17.
3 Charities Act 2011 s 263(1)(a).
4 As to the meaning of 'relevant charity' see PARA 263 note 20.
5 Charities Act 2011 s 263(1)(b).
6 As to the meaning of 'institution' see PARA 1.
7 Charities Act 2011 s 263(1)(c).
8 Charities Act 2011 s 263(1)(d).
9 Charities Act 2011 s 263(1). A person guilty of disobedience to an order of the Commission under the Charities Act 2011 s 263 may on the application of the Commission to the High Court be dealt with as for disobedience to an order of the High Court: s 336(1), (2). The power of the Commission to discharge an order at any time within 12 months after it has been made does not apply to orders under s 263: see s 337(4)(a); and PARA 554. As to orders of the Commission generally see s 337; and PARA 554.
10 As to the meaning of 'charity trustees' see PARA 255.
11 Charities Act 2011 s 263(2).
12 As to the official custodian see PARA 300 et seq.
13 Charities Act 2011 s 263(3).
14 For these purposes, 'specified' means specified by the Commission in the order: Charities Act 2011 s 263(4).
15 Charities Act 2011 s 263(4)(a).
16 Charities Act 2011 s 263(1)(b).
17 Ie any order under the Charities Act 2011 s 263 by virtue of which: (1) any property vested as mentioned in s 263(3) (see the text and notes 12–13) is vested in the charity trustees of the relevant charity, or in any person as trustee for, or nominee of, that charity; or (2) any investments held by any person in trust for the relevant charity are required to be transferred to the charity trustees of that charity, or to any person as trustee for, or nominee of, that charity: s 263(6).
18 Charities Act 2011 s 263(5). See also s 266; and PARA 263 note 8.

19 Charities Act 2011 s 337(6).
20 As to the Tribunal see PARA 579 et seq. As to the Attorney General see PARAS 589, 596, 605 et seq; and **CONSTITUTIONAL AND ADMINISTRATIVE LAW** vol 20 (2014) PARA 273 et seq.
21 See the Charities Act 2011 s 319(2), Sch 6 Table Cols 1, 2. As to the meaning of 'person who is or may be affected' within the meaning of Sch 6 see PARA 317 note 8.
22 See the Charities Act 2011 Sch 6 Table Col 3.

(3) TRUSTEES OF PAROCHIAL AND DIOCESAN CHARITIES

266. Parochial recreation grounds and allotments. Trustees who hold property for the purposes of a public recreation ground or of allotments for the benefit of the inhabitants of a parish or community[1] having a parish or community council[2] or for other charitable purposes (except those of an ecclesiastical charity[3]) connected with such a parish may transfer the property to the parish or community council or to persons appointed by the council, provided that the Charity Commission[4] approves and the council consents[5]. The council or its appointees take the property on the same trusts and subject to the same conditions as the trustees did[6].

An appeal against a decision of the Commission to withhold approval for such a transfer lies to the Tribunal at the instance of the Attorney General[7], the trustees, the parish or community council or any other person who is or may be affected by the decision[8]. The Tribunal has the power to quash the decision and, if appropriate, remit the matter to the Commission[9].

1 As to local government areas and authorities in England and Wales see **LOCAL GOVERNMENT** vol 69 (2009) PARA 22 et seq.
2 Charities Act 2011 s 298(1)(a), (b).
3 As to the meaning of 'ecclesiastical charity' see PARA 267 note 4.
4 As to the Charity Commission see PARAS 543–578.
5 See the Charities Act 2011 s 298(1), (2). This provision applies to property held for any public purposes as it applies to property held for charitable purposes: s 298(1).

No vesting or transfer of any property in pursuance of any provision of Pt 15 (ss 293–304) operates as a breach of covenant or condition against alienation or gives rise to a forfeiture: s 304.

Sections 298–302 do not affect the trusteeship, control or management of any foundation or voluntary school within the meaning of the School Standards and Framework Act 1998 (see **EDUCATION** vol 35 (2011) PARA 108); nor do they apply to the Isles of Scilly, and they have effect subject to orders made under any enactment relating to local government with respect to local government areas or to the powers of local authorities: Charities Act 2011 s 303(2), (3).
6 Charities Act 2011 s 298(2).
7 As to the Tribunal see PARA 579 et seq. As to the Attorney General see PARAS 589, 596, 605 et seq; and **CONSTITUTIONAL AND ADMINISTRATIVE LAW** vol 20 (2014) PARA 273 et seq.
8 See the Charities Act 2011 s 319(2), Sch 6 Table Cols 1, 2. As to the meaning of 'person who is or may be affected' within the meaning of Sch 6 see PARA 317 note 8.
9 See the Charities Act 2011 Sch 6 Table Col 3.

267. Local representatives as trustees of rural parochial charities. If the charity trustees[1] of a parochial charity[2] in a parish[3], other than an ecclesiastical charity[4] or one founded less than 40 years previously, do not include persons elected by the local government electors, ratepayers[5] or parish inhabitants or appointed by the parish council[6] or meeting, the council or meeting may appoint additional charity trustees to such number as the Charity Commission may allow[7]. If there is only a sole charity trustee of such a charity and he is not so elected or appointed, the Commission may approve the increase of the number of charity trustees to three, of whom one may be nominated by the person holding the office of the sole trustee and one by the council or meeting[8].

Trustees appointed under this provision hold office for four years and are eligible for re-appointment on retiring[9].

1 As to the meaning of 'charity trustees' see PARA 255.

2 'Parochial charity' means, in relation to any parish or, in Wales, community, a charity the benefits of which are, or the separate distribution of the benefits of which is, confined to the inhabitants of the parish or community, or of a single ancient ecclesiastical parish which included that parish or community or part of it, or of an area consisting of that parish or community with not more than four neighbouring parishes or communities: Charities Act 2011 s 303(1).

3 Or, in Wales, a community: Charities Act 2011 s 299(1). As to local government areas and authorities in England and Wales see LOCAL GOVERNMENT vol 69 (2009) PARA 22 et seq.

4 'Ecclesiastical charity' includes a charity the endowment of which is held for one or more of the following purposes: (1) for any spiritual purpose which is a legal purpose; or (2) for the benefit of any spiritual person or ecclesiastical officer as such; or (3) for use (if a building) as a church, chapel, mission room or Sunday school or otherwise by any particular church or denomination, and any building which in the Charity Commission's opinion has been erected or provided within 40 years before 5 March 1894 mainly by or at the cost of members of any particular church or denomination; or (4) for the maintenance, repair or improvement of any such building or for the maintenance of divine service in it; (5) otherwise for the benefit of any particular church or denomination or any of its members as such: Local Government Act 1894 s 75(2) (amended by the Charities Act 2006 Sch 8 para 9); applied by the Charities Act 2011 s 353(1). Where any endowment of a charity, other than a building held for any of the above purposes, is held in part only for some of the above purposes, the charity is an ecclesiastical charity so far as that endowment is concerned: Local Government Act 1894 s 75(2) proviso (as so applied).

5 Domestic rates were abolished by the Local Government Finance Act 1988 and replaced by the community charge, itself replaced by the council tax in 1993: see the Local Government Finance Act 1992; and LOCAL GOVERNMENT FINANCE vol 70 (2012) PARA 51.

6 Or, in Wales, the community council: Charities Act 2011 s 298(2).

7 Charities Act 2011 s 299(1), (2). This does not affect the trusteeship, control or management of any foundation or voluntary school: see PARA 266 note 5. As to limitations on the provisions of the Charities Act 2011 s 299 see s 303(3); and PARA 266 note 5.

8 Charities Act 2011 s 299(3).

9 Charities Act 2011 s 302(1). If no previous appointment has been made under s 299 or the corresponding provision of the Local Government Act 1894 or the Charities Act 1960, and more than one trustee is appointed, half of those appointed must be appointed for a term of two years: Charities Act 2011 s 302(2). Appointments to fill casual vacancies are for the remainder of the term of the previous appointment: s 302(3).

268. Appointment of trustees of parochial charities. Before the passing of the Local Government Act 1894, the inhabitants of a rural parish, in vestry or not, or a select vestry were sometimes entitled to appoint charity trustees[1] for, or trustees or beneficiaries of, a charity[2]. In such a case (other than as regards ecclesiastical charities[3]) where the parish or community has its own council[4], the appointment is now to be made by the parish or community council or, in the case of beneficiaries, by persons appointed by the parish or community council, and where the parish or community does not have a council, the appointment is to be made by the parish meeting (or in the case of a community, the county council or county borough council)[5].

In some cases, before the passing of the Local Government Act 1894, overseers as such or churchwardens as such were charity trustees of or trustees for parochial charities in rural parishes, alone or jointly with others[6]. In such a case (other than as regards ecclesiastical charities) the former overseer or churchwarden trustees are replaced by trustees appointed by the parish or community council or, if there is no such council, by the parish meeting (or in the case of a community, the county council or county borough council)[7], to a number not greater than that of the former overseer or churchwarden trustees[8].

If, before 1 April 1927[9], outside Greater London (other than the outer London boroughs) overseers of a parish as such were charity trustees of or trustees for any charity, alone or jointly, they are replaced by trustees appointed by the parish or community council or, if there is none, by the parish meeting (or in the case of a community, the county council or county borough council)[10], to a number not greater than that of the former overseer trustees[11]. Where after 1 April 1974 an existing urban parish is not comprised in a parish, the power of appointing trustees rests with the district council[12].

Charity trustees and trustees for a charity appointed under these provisions must be appointed for four years, but are eligible for re-appointment on retiring[13].

1 As to the meaning of 'charity trustees' see PARA 255.
2 See the Charities Act 2011 s 300(1). As to the meaning of 'charity' see PARA 1.
This does not affect the trusteeship, control or management of any foundation or voluntary school: see PARA 266 note 5. As to limitations on the provisions of the Charities Act 2011 s 300 see s 303(2), (3); and PARA 266 note 5.
3 As to the meaning of 'ecclesiastical charity' see PARA 267 note 4.
4 As to local government areas and authorities in England and Wales see **LOCAL GOVERNMENT** vol 69 (2009) PARA 22 et seq.
5 Charities Act 2011 s 300(1), (2). In other cases persons such as the rector and the lord of the manor were trustees, together with overseers or churchwardens; in such cases they seem to continue as trustees, together with persons appointed by the parish council in place of the churchwardens or overseers.
6 See the Charities Act 2011 s 300(3).
7 Charities Act 2011 s 300(3), (4).
8 Charities Act 2011 s 300(4). As to overseers see PARA 259 note 4.
9 Ie the date on which overseers were abolished by the Rating and Valuation Act 1925 s 62, and their functions transferred to rating or other local authorities by s 1(2); and the Overseers Order 1927, SR & O 1927/55 (lapsed). See **LOCAL GOVERNMENT** vol 69 (2009) PARA 1 et seq; **LOCAL GOVERNMENT FINANCE**.
10 Charities Act 2011 s 301(1), (2). As to the London boroughs see **LONDON GOVERNMENT** vol 71 (2013) PARA 15.
11 Charities Act 2011 s 301(2).
12 Charities Act 2011 s 301(3).
13 Charities Act 2011 s 302(1). However, an appointment to fill a casual vacancy must be for the remainder of the term of the previous appointment: s 302(3).

269. Dissolution of parishes: ecclesiastical charities. If a benefice is dissolved by a pastoral scheme[1], and any property of a charity established for ecclesiastical purposes of the Church of England is vested in or under the management or control of the incumbent of that benefice or a corporation of which he or she is a member, the trusts of the charity or the constitution of the corporation have effect with the substitution of the incumbent of the new benefice created by the union or, as the case may be, of a benefice, incorporating part of the area of the dissolved benefice, specified by order of the Charity Commission[2]. Corresponding provision is made in the case of the churchwardens and parochial church council of a dissolved benefice[3] and where a team ministry is established by a pastoral scheme for an area comprising the whole or a major part of the area of a benefice[4]. Changes in the vesting of property under these provisions take effect without any conveyance or other assurance[5].

If a pastoral scheme unites one parish with another or alters the area of a parish, the purposes of a charity defined by reference to the area of one of the parishes are altered by the substitution of a reference to the united or altered parish, and the trusts of the charity have effect accordingly[6].

If there is a condition of any benefaction as to attendance at or the performance of divine service or any other act at a church, and the church ceases to be used for divine service by virtue of a declaration of closure for regular public worship made by a pastoral church buildings scheme, the condition is to be taken as referring to the parish church of the parish in which the church originally specified or its site is situated[7].

Where any property of a charity established for ecclesiastical purposes of the Church of England is vested in or under the management or control of the incumbent of a benefice or a corporation of which the incumbent is a member, and the benefice becomes vacant or the bishop declares a suspension period in respect of the benefice, then, during the period of the vacancy or suspension, as the case may be, the trusts of the charity or the constitution of the corporation have effect, without any conveyance or other assurance, with the substitution for the incumbent of that benefice of the priest in charge of that benefice[8].

Schemes or orders made by the Charity Commission for purposes arising in connection with a pastoral scheme or order may be made before the date on which the pastoral scheme or order comes into operation, but not so as to take effect before that date[9].

1 Ie under the Mission and Pastoral Measure 2011: see ECCLESIASTICAL LAW vol 34 (2011) PARA 640 et seq.
2 Mission and Pastoral Measure 2011 Sch 3 para 9(1). As to the Charity Commission see PARAS 543–578. These provisions do not apply to any fund or property for which provision is made (under s 77, though the Measure appears to refer to s 76, and the amendment mentioned in note 9 is, it is submitted, to be read into this provision as well in order to make sense of the provision) (see ECCLESIASTICAL LAW vol 34 (2011) PARAS 892, 913): Sch 3 para 9(10).
3 See the Mission and Pastoral Measure 2011 Sch 3 para 9(2). Unless otherwise dealt with by the Sch 3 para 9, property held by or on behalf of the parochial church council of a dissolved parish vests in or is held on behalf of the parochial church council of the parish in which the parish church of the dissolved parish is situated: see Sch 3 para 9(8).
4 See the Mission and Pastoral Measure 2011 Sch 3 para 9(3).
5 Mission and Pastoral Measure 2011 Sch 3 para 9(4), (8).
6 See the Mission and Pastoral Measure 2011 Sch 3 para 9(5).
7 Mission and Pastoral Measure 2011 Sch 3 para 9(9). See also s 77(4) where similar provisions apply in relation to giving sermons in church affected by a declaration of closure for regular public worship, with the proviso that the sermons may be given in such other church as the bishop may, with the Charity Commission's approval, direct.
8 Mission and Pastoral Measure 2011 s 90(1), (2).
9 Mission and Pastoral Measure 2011 Sch 3 para 9(7). This does not apply to any fund or property for which provision is made under s 77 (trusts for the repair etc, of buildings closed for regular public worship and contents) (see ECCLESIASTICAL LAW vol 34 (2011) PARAS 892, 913): s 90(3) (amended by the Church of England (Miscellaneous Provisions) Measure 2014 Sch 2 para 19(1), (8)).

270. Alteration of diocesan boundaries: bishops as trustees. Upon the application of the bishops concerned, or one of them, the Charity Commission[1] may make orders vesting charity property held upon trust by the bishop of one diocese in the bishop of another diocese, and substituting one bishop for another as trustee, in cases where the limits of dioceses have been altered[2].

1 As to the Charity Commission see PARAS 543–578.
2 See the Bishops Trusts Substitution Act 1858 ss 1, 2; and ECCLESIASTICAL LAW vol 34 (2011) PARA 582. The order may not deal with advowsons or similar rights which could be dealt with by a scheme of the Church Commissioners, nor may it deal with any ecclesiastical patronage or similar right without the consent of the Church Commissioners: see s 2 (amended by virtue of the Church Commissioners Measure 1947 ss 1, 2, 18(2)). The order may not affect trusts of a visitatorial or any other nature or character relating to the halls or colleges of Oxford or Cambridge Universities or to the colleges of Winchester, Eton or Westminster: see the Bishops

Trusts Substitution Act 1858 s 4; and PARA 522. The Act does not extend to endowments of an eleemosynary or any other character governed by a specific Act of Parliament: s 5. Any costs necessarily incident to effecting the transfers are to be defrayed by order of the Charity Commission out of the property, real or personal, as it may direct, which are to be transferred: see s 3 (amended by the Charities Act 2006 Sch 8 paras 3–5). As to the Church Commissioners see ECCLESIASTICAL LAW vol 34 (2011) PARA 66 et seq.

(4) TRUSTEES OF LOCAL AUTHORITY CHARITIES

271. Transfer of local authority charities outside London. In consequence of the reorganisation of local government outside Greater London effected by the Local Government Act 1972[1], property held on charitable trusts by existing local authorities was transferred to the new authorities established by that Act.

On 1 April 1974, where any property was held, as sole trustee, exclusively for charitable purposes[2] by an existing[3] local authority[4] for an area outside Greater London[5], other than the parish council, parish meeting or representative body of an existing rural parish in England[6], but including the corporation of a borough included in a rural district, that property vested[7], on the same trusts[8], in a new[9] local authority[10].

Where property was held by one of the existing authorities in heads (1) to (4) below, and so held for the benefit of, or of the inhabitants of, or of any particular class or body of persons in, a specified area, the property vested in the new authority specified in heads (1) to (4) below, the area of which comprises the whole or the greater part of that specified area[11]. Where the property was so held but was not held for such a benefit, it vested in the new authority specified in heads (1) to (4) below, the area of which comprises the whole or the greater part of the area of the existing authority, that is to say[12]:

(1) where the existing authority was a county[13] council, the new authority is the council of the new county[14];

(2) where the existing authority was the council of a borough or urban district in England, the new authority is the council of the parish constituted by reference to existing urban district and borough boundaries[15] or, where there was no such parish, the council of the district[16];

(3) where the existing authority was the council of a borough or urban district in Wales, the new authority is the council of the community or, where there is no such council, the council of the district[17]; and

(4) where the existing authority was a rural district council, then, if the rural district is co-extensive with a parish, the new authority is the parish council, and in any other case the new authority is the council of the district[18].

Where the property was held by an existing county council or county borough council for the purposes of a registered educational charity[19] then: (a) if the property was so held for the benefit of, or of the inhabitants of, or of any particular class or body of persons in, a specified area, the property vested in the new authority which is the local education authority for the whole or the greater part of that specified area[20]; and (b) in any other case, the property vested in the new authority which is the local education authority for the whole or the greater part of the area of the existing county council or county borough council by which the property is held[21].

Further, where the property was held by the corporation of a borough included in a rural district, it vested in the parish council for the parish consisting of the area of the existing borough[22].

Where the property was held by the parish council, parish meeting or representative body of an existing rural parish in Wales, then: (i) in the case of property held by an existing parish council, the property vested in the community council for the community or group of communities, the area or areas of which are co-extensive with the area of the parish or parishes for which the existing parish council act[23]; (ii) in the case of property held by the parish meeting or representative body of an existing parish the area of which is comprised in a community for which there is a community council, the property vested in that community council[24]; and (iii) in any other case, the property vested in the council of the district which comprises the area of the existing rural parish[25].

Where, on 1 April 1974, any power with respect to a charity[26] (not being a charity incorporated under the Companies Acts or by charter[27]) was under the trusts of the charity or by virtue of any enactment vested in, or in the holder of an office connected with, certain existing local authorities[28], that power vested in, or in the holder of the corresponding office connected with, or (if there is no such office) the proper officer[29] of, the corresponding[30] new authority[31].

Nothing in these provisions affects any power of Her Majesty, the court[32] or any other person to alter the trusts of any charity, nor do they apply in a case to which the provisions relating to Welsh Church funds apply[33].

1 See further LOCAL GOVERNMENT vol 69 (2009) PARA 22 et seq.

2 As to the meaning of 'charitable purposes' see PARA 1; definition applied by the Local Government Act 1972 s 210(11); Interpretation Act 1978 s 17(2)(a).

3 'Existing', in relation to a local government or other area or a local authority or other body means that area or body as it existed immediately before 26 October 1972 (the passing of the Local Government Act 1972): s 270(1).

4 'Local authority' means a county council, a district council, a London borough council or a parish council but, in relation to Wales, means a county council, county borough council or community council: Local Government Act 1972 s 270(1) (definition amended by the Local Government Act 1985 s 102, Sch 16 para 8, Sch 17; and the Local Government (Wales) Act 1994 s 1(5)). For these purposes, 'local authority', in relation to a parish, includes a parish meeting and the representative body of a parish: Local Government Act 1972 s 210(11).

5 As to the transfer of powers on local government reorganisation in Greater London see PARA 272.

6 'Wales' means the combined area of the preserved counties, and 'England' does not include any area which is included in any of the preserved counties: Local Government Act 1972 s 269 (substituted by the Local Government (Wales) Act 1994 s 1(3), Sch 2 para 8).

7 Ie in accordance with the Local Government Act 1972 s 210(2)–(5): see the text and notes 11–25.

8 As to the meaning of 'trusts' see PARA 218 note 5; definition applied by the Local Government Act 1972 s 210(11); Interpretation Act 1978 s 17(2)(a).

9 'New', in relation to any area or authority, means an area or authority established by or under the Local Government Act 1972, including one established by virtue of any provision of the Local Government (Wales) Act 1994: Local Government Act 1972 s 270(1) (amended by the Local Government (Wales) Act 1994 s 66(5), Sch 15 para 57).

10 Local Government Act 1972 s 210(1). As to local government areas and authorities in England and Wales see LOCAL GOVERNMENT vol 69 (2009) PARA 22 et seq.

11 Local Government Act 1972 s 210(2).

12 Local Government Act 1972 s 210(2).

13 'County', without more, means, in relation to England, a metropolitan county or a non-metropolitan county, but in the expression 'county council' means, in relation to England, a non-metropolitan county only: Local Government Act 1972 s 270(1) (amended by the Local Government Act 1985 s 102, Sch 16 para 8).

14 Local Government Act 1972 s 210(2)(a).

15 Ie the council of the parish constituted under the Local Government Act 1972 s 1, Sch 1 Pt V: see LOCAL GOVERNMENT vol 69 (2009) PARA 27 et seq.
16 Local Government Act 1972 s 210(2)(b). 'District', without more, means, in relation to England, a metropolitan district or a non-metropolitan district: s 270(1).
17 Local Government Act 1972 s 210(2)(c).
18 Local Government Act 1972 s 210(2)(d).
19 Ie established under the Charities Act 1960 s 4 (repealed: now re-enacted in the Charities Act 2011 s 29 (see PARA 307 et seq)) in any part of that register maintained by the Secretary of State by virtue of the Charities Act 1960 s 2 (repealed) (educational charities): Local Government Act 1972 s 210(3). As to the meaning of 'charity' see PARA 1; definition applied by the Local Government Act 1972 s 210(11); Interpretation Act 1978 s 17(2)(a).
20 Local Government Act 1972 s 210(3)(a).
21 Local Government Act 1972 s 210(3)(b).
22 Local Government Act 1972 s 210(4).
23 Local Government Act 1972 s 210(5)(a). As to property held by a Welsh borough or urban district council see the text to note 16.
24 Local Government Act 1972 s 210(5)(b).
25 Local Government Act 1972 s 210(5)(c).
26 References in the Local Government Act 1972 s 210(6) to a power with respect to a charity do not include references to a power of any person by virtue of being a charity trustee of it; but where under the trusts of any charity, not being a charity incorporated under the Companies Acts or by charter, the charity trustees on 1 April 1974 included either an existing local authority to which s 210(1) (see the text and notes 1–10) applies or the holder of an office connected with such an existing local authority, those trustees instead included the corresponding new authority as defined in s 210(6) or, as the case may require, the holder of the corresponding office connected with, or (if there is no such office) the proper officer of, that authority: s 210(7). As to the meaning of 'charity trustees' see PARA 255; definition applied by s 210(11); Interpretation Act 1978 s 17(2)(a).
27 As to modes of creation of charitable corporations see PARA 249.
28 Ie existing authorities to which the Local Government Act 1972 s 210(1) applies: see the text and notes 1–10.
29 Any reference in the Local Government Act 1972 to a proper officer is, in relation to any purpose and any local authority or other body or any area, to be construed as a reference to an officer appointed for that purpose by that body or for that area, as the case may be: s 270(3).
30 Ie the new authority in which, had the property of the charity been vested in the existing local authority, that property would have been vested under the Local Government Act 1972 s 210(2)–(5) (see the text and notes 11–25): see s 210(6).
31 Local Government Act 1972 s 210(6).
32 As to the meaning of 'court' see PARA 177 note 12; definition applied by the Local Government Act 1972 s 210(11); Interpretation Act 1978 s 17(2)(a).
33 Local Government Act 1972 s 210(10). The reference in the text to the provisions relating to Welsh Church funds is a reference to s 211 (see LOCAL GOVERNMENT vol 69 (2009) PARA 579): see s 210(10).

272. Transfer of local authority charities in London. In consequence of the reorganisation of local government administration in and around London under the London Government Act 1963, it became necessary to transfer property held on charitable trusts by the London and Middlesex County Councils and the councils of metropolitan and county boroughs within Greater London, and to transfer powers in respect of a charity vested in those councils or certain others or in the holders of offices connected with such a council. Such property and powers were accordingly vested in either the Greater London Council or the Inner London Education Authority, or in one of the London borough councils, or in the holder of the appropriate office connected with the appropriate council[1]. Apart from those provisions, the Secretary of State for the Environment[2] had power by order to make such incidental, consequential, transitional or supplementary provision as appeared necessary or proper[3].

Under further reorganisation by the Local Government Act 1985 the Greater London Council was abolished[4] and a new Inner London Education Authority was established[5]. It was provided that where, immediately before the abolition date, any property was held exclusively for charitable purposes by the Greater London Council, and the Inner London Education Authority was the charity trustee of the charity to which the property related, that property should on that date vest in the new Inner London Education Authority[6]. Subject to this it was further provided that the Home Secretary could by order make such provision in relation to any charity as appeared to him necessary or expedient in consequence of the abolition of the Greater London Council[7].

Subsequently the new Inner London Education Authority was abolished by the Education Reform Act 1988[8]. Where, immediately before the abolition date, any property was held exclusively for charitable purposes by the Inner London Education Authority as sole trustee and the charity was primarily for the benefit of the area of a single inner London council[9], that property became vested on that date for the like purposes in that council[10]. In other areas where property was held exclusively for charitable purposes by the Inner London Education Authority as sole trustee, that property became vested on that date for the like purposes in the London Residuary Body[11] or in such other person appointed before that date[12].

1 For details of the provisions transferring property and powers in respect of charities see the London Government Act 1963 s 81(1) (repealed) (property held by the London or Middlesex County Council), s 81(2) (repealed) (property held by borough councils), s 81(3) (repealed) (powers with respect to a charity vested in such a council or in the holder of an office connected with it), s 81(4) (repealed) (powers with respect to a charity established wholly or mainly for the benefit of an area within Greater London, vested in various county councils), s 81(6) (repealed) (powers with respect to other charities). See also s 81(7) (repealed) (charity trustees, including the holder of an office connected with a borough council within the Greater London area), and s 81(5) (repealed) (power for the Inner London Education Authority to nominate an inner London borough council, or the holder of an office connected with it, in whom powers with respect to a charity were to vest).

2 See the Secretary of State for the Environment Order 1970, SI 1970/1681 (lapsed).

3 See the London Government Act 1963 s 84(1); and LONDON GOVERNMENT vol 71 (2013) PARA 9. For an example of the exercise of this power and its interaction with transitional provisions of s 81 (repealed) see *Re Alexandra Park and Palace Acts, Alexandra Park Trustees v Haringey London Borough Council* (1967) 66 LGR 306.

4 See the Local Government Act 1985 s 1(1). The abolition date was 1 April 1986: s 1(2).

5 Ie as from the abolition date (see note 4): Local Government Act 1985 s 18 (repealed).

6 Local Government Act 1985 s 90(1) (repealed).

7 See the Local Government Act 1985 s 90(2) (amended by the Education Reform Act 1988 Sch 13 Pt 1). Nothing in the Local Government Act 1985 s 90 affects any power of Her Majesty, the court or any other person to alter the trusts of any charity: s 90(3).

8 Education Reform Act 1988 s 162(1) (repealed). The abolition date was 1 April 1990: s 162(1), (2).

9 For these purposes, a charity is a charity primarily for the benefit of the area of a single inner London council if the charity is established for purposes which are by their nature or by the trusts of the charity directed wholly or mainly to the benefit of an area which falls wholly or mainly within that council's area: Education Reform Act 1988 s 192(9). 'Inner London council' means the council of an inner London borough or (in its capacity as a local authority) the Common Council of the City of London: s 163(2). As to the meaning of 'charity' see PARA 1; and as to the meaning of 'trusts' see PARA 218 note 5; definitions applied by s 192(11) (amended by the Charities Act 1993 s 98(1), Sch 6 para 30). As to the London borough councils and the Common Council of the City of London see LONDON GOVERNMENT vol 71 (2013) PARAS 20 et seq, 34 et seq.

10 Education Reform Act 1988 s 192(1). See further EDUCATION vol 35 (2011) PARA 24. Powers vested in officers of the Inner London Education Authority vested in the corresponding inner London council officer, if any, and otherwise in an officer appointed, with his consent and that of the council, by the Charity Commissioners (now the Charity Commission): see s 192(2), (3). The appointment was to be made within two years of the abolition date, and in the meantime the London Residuary Body was to be treated as having been appointed: see s 192(7).

11 As to the London Residuary Body see EDUCATION vol 36 (2011) PARA 900.
12 See the Education Reform Act 1988 s 192(4). Powers with respect to such charities vested in, or in the holder of any office connected with, the Inner London Education Authority, became vested in the London Residuary Body or in such other person as the Charity Commissioners might appoint: see s 192(5). The appointment was to be made within two years of the abolition date, and in the meantime the London Residuary Body was to be treated as having been appointed: see s 192(7). References in s 192(1)–(5) to a power with respect to a charity do not include references to any power of any person by virtue of being a charity trustee of that charity: see s 192(6). There is provision for the replacement of charity trustees where they included the Inner London Education Authority or the holder of an office connected with the Inner London Education Authority: see s 192(6). As to the meaning of 'charity trustees' see PARA 255; definition applied by s 192(11) (see note 9).

(5) APPOINTMENT OF TRUSTEES

(i) Initial Appointment

273. Donor's failure to appoint trustee. The appointment of the first trustees of a charity rests with the donor, but a charitable gift is not defeated by his failure to provide machinery for carrying his charitable purpose into effect[1]. Where money is given to charity generally and indefinitely without trustees or objects selected, the Crown, as parens patriae, is the constitutional trustee, and disposes of the fund under the sign manual[2]. Where there is a devise for such charity as the testator has by writing appointed, and no writing is to be found, the Crown will appoint[3]. Where the donor intends to create a trust, but appoints no trustee, the court disposes of the fund by means of a scheme[4].

1 As to the failure of or disclaimer by trustee see PARA 164.
2 *Moggridge v Thackwell* (1803) 7 Ves 36 at 83, 86 per Lord Eldon LC; *Cary v Abbot* (1802) 7 Ves 490; *Morice v Bishop of Durham* (1805) 10 Ves 522 at 541 per Lord Eldon LC; *Ommanney v Butcher* (1823) Turn & R 260 at 271 per Plumer MR. As to the Crown's jurisdiction over charities see PARAS 512–513.
3 *A-G v Syderfen* (1683) 1 Vern 224.
4 *Mills v Farmer* (1815) 1 Mer 55 at 94–95 per Lord Eldon LC; *Reeve v A-G* (1843) 3 Hare 191 at 196–197 per Shadwell V-C. As to general principles for the direction of schemes see PARA 180.

274. Who is the initial trustee. In general, no problem arises in determining who has been appointed trustee and who should act, and if any question does arise it is determined by a process of construction[1]. However, where the gift is to a local branch of a large charitable institution, the byelaws of the institution may require the gift to be transferred to the main institution, although its application may be restricted to the area of the branch[2]. Such byelaws do not extend to gifts which the local branch is to hold on special trusts, not for the general purposes of the institution[3].

1 See eg *Re Lavers* (1908) Times, 7 November, where property was to be vested in trustees 'commonly called the X Trustees (the same who have the right of presentation of the vicarage of Y)'. The right of presentation was not vested in the X Trustees, and it was held that the testator intended to appoint those in whom it was vested.
2 *Royal National Lifeboat Institution v Turver* (1915) 31 TLR 340.
3 *Royal National Lifeboat Institution v Turver* (1915) 31 TLR 340.

(ii) Who may or should be appointed New Trustees

275. General principles. Vacancies among trustees should be filled by persons who are likely best to discharge the duties imposed upon them by the trust[1].

The fact that three new trustees are appointed, of whom two hold opposite views on an important matter affecting the charity, is not sufficient reason for upsetting an appointment[2]; but a suspicion that former trustees have used their powers for political ends is sufficient to prevent their re-appointment[3]. There is no objection to trustees being related to one another[4].

In order to qualify for tax relief[5], a charity must satisfy Her Majesty's Revenue and Customs as to various aspects of its management[6]. The managers of a body of persons or trust must be fit and proper persons in order to satisfy the condition, and in so far as charity trustees are managers they will fall within the scope of this provision[7].

1 *Baker v Lee* (1860) 8 HL Cas 495 at 513 per Lord Cranworth.

2 *Re Burnham National Schools* (1873) LR 17 Eq 241 at 250 per Jessel MR.

3 *Re Norwich Charities* (1837) 2 My & Cr 275.

4 *Re Lancaster Charities, Re Charitable Trusts Act 1853* (1860) 3 LT 582. However, the Charity Commission sometimes takes objection in cases of charities in small parishes, with small bodies of trustees, to a preponderance of members of one family if the trustees co-opt one another. As to the Charity Commission see PARAS 543–578.

5 See CAPITAL GAINS TAXATION vol 6 (2011) PARA 878 et seq; INCOME TAXATION vol 58A (2014) PARA 1618 et seq.

6 See the Finance Act 2010 s 30, Sch 6 paras 1, 4; and INCOME TAXATION vol 58A (2014) PARA 1622.

7 See further PARA 438.

276. Disqualification for acting as charity trustee. A person is disqualified for being a charity trustee[1] or trustee for a charity[2] in one of the following cases:

(1) Case A: he has been convicted of any offence involving dishonesty or deception[3];

(2) Case B: he has been adjudged bankrupt or sequestration of his estate has been awarded and (in either case) he has not been discharged or he is the subject of a bankruptcy restrictions order or an interim order[4], unless leave has been granted under the Company Directors Disqualification Act 1986[5] for him to act as director of the charity or charity trustee of the CIO[6];

(3) Case C: he has made a composition or arrangement with, or granted a trust deed for, his creditors and has not been discharged in respect of it[7];

(4) Case D: he has been removed from the office of charity trustee or trustee for a charity by an order made by the Charity Commission[8] or, before the transfer of their functions to Commission, the Charity Commissioners[9], or by the High Court, on the grounds of any misconduct or mismanagement in the administration of the charity for which he was responsible or to which he was privy, or which he by his conduct contributed to or facilitated[10];

(5) Case E: he has been removed under certain Scottish legislation[11] from being concerned in the management or control of any body[12];

(6) Case F: he is subject to a disqualification order or disqualification undertaking under the Company Directors Disqualification Act 1986, to a disqualification order under Part II of the Companies (Northern Ireland) Order 1989[13] or to an order made under the Insolvency Act 1986 regarding disabilities on revocation of a county court administration order[14];

(7) Case G: he is subject to (a) a moratorium period under a debt relief order[15], or (b) a debt relief restrictions order or interim order[16], unless

leave has been granted under the Company Directors Disqualification Act 1986 for him to act as director of the charity or charity trustee of the CIO[17].

On the application of a disqualified person, with certain exceptions[18], the Commission may waive his disqualification either generally or in relation to a particular charity or a particular class of charities[19]. Any such waiver must be notified in writing to the person concerned[20]. If a person disqualified under Case D or E makes such an application five years or more after the date on which his disqualification took effect then, subject to the same exceptions[21], the Commission must grant the application unless satisfied that, by reason of any special circumstances, it should be refused[22].

An appeal against such a decision of the Commission to waive or not to waive a person's disqualification lies to the Tribunal at the instance of the Attorney General[23], the person who applied for the waiver or any other person who is or may be affected by the decision[24]. The Tribunal has the power to do any of the following: (i) quash the decision and, if appropriate, remit the matter to the Commission; (ii) substitute for the decision any other decision of a kind which could have been made by the Commission[25].

1 As to the meaning of 'charity trustees' see PARA 255.
2 As to the meaning of 'charity' see PARA 1.
3 Charities Act 2011 s 178(1) Case A. This applies whether the conviction occurred before or after 14 March 2012 (the commencement of s 178(1)), but does not apply to any conviction which is a spent conviction under the Rehabilitation of Offenders Act 1974: Charities Act 2011 s 179(1). As to spent convictions and the Rehabilitation of Offenders Act 1974 see **SENTENCING AND DISPOSITION OF OFFENDERS** vol 92 (2010) PARA 660 et seq.
4 Charities Act 2011 s 178(1) Case B. This applies whether the adjudication of bankruptcy or the sequestration occurred before or after 14 March 2012: s 179(2). See **BANKRUPTCY AND INDIVIDUAL INSOLVENCY**.
5 Ie under the Company Directors Disqualification Act 1986 s 11: see **BANKRUPTCY AND INDIVIDUAL INSOLVENCY** vol 5 (2013) PARA 729 et seq.
6 See the Charities Act 2011 s 180(1) (amended by SI 2012/3014). As to charitable incorporated organisations (CIOs) see PARA 226 et seq.
7 Charities Act 2011 s 178(1) Case C. This applies whether the composition or arrangement was made, or the trust deed was granted, before or after 14 March 2012: s 179(3). See **BANKRUPTCY AND INDIVIDUAL INSOLVENCY**.
8 As to the Charity Commission see PARAS 543–578.
9 Ie under the Charities Act 2011 s 79(2)(a) (see PARA 567) or under an earlier corresponding enactment: s 178(1) Case D. The enactments referred to are the Charities Act 1993 s 18(2)(i) (repealed), the Charities Act 1960 s 20(1A)(i) (repealed); or s 20(1)(i) (repealed) as it stood before 1 November 1992 (ie the commencement of the Charities Act 1992 s 8): see the Charities Act 2011 s 179(5)(b). The 'Charity Commissioners' means the Charity Commissioners for England and Wales: Charities Act 2011 s 179(5)(a).
10 Charities Act 2011 s 178(1) Case D. This applies in relation to orders made and removals effected before or after 14 March 2012: s 179(4). The Commission must keep, in such manner as it thinks fit, a register of all persons who have been removed from office as mentioned in Case D either by an order of the Commission made before or after 14 March 2012 or by an order of the High Court made after 1 January 1993 (the commencement of the Charities Act 1992 s 45(1)): Charities Act 2011 s 182(1)). Where any person is removed by the High Court, the court must notify the Commission of his removal: s 182(1). Entries in the register must be available for public inspection in legible form at all reasonable times: s 182(2).
11 Ie the Law Reform (Miscellaneous Provisions) (Scotland) Act 1990 s 7 (repealed) (powers of Court of Session to deal with management of charities); and the Charities and Trustee Investment (Scotland) Act 2005 s 34(5)(e) (powers of the Court of Session).
12 See the Charities Act 2011 ss 178(1) Case E, 179(6). This applies in relation to orders made and removals effected before or after 14 March 2012: s 179(4).
13 Ie the Companies (Northern Ireland) Order 1989, SI 1989/2404, Pt II.
14 Charities Act 2011 s 178(1) Case F. This applies in relation to orders made and removals effected before or after 14 March 2012: s 179(4). A person is not, however, disqualified under

Case F from being a charity trustee or a trustee for a charitable company or CIO in the following circumstances (Charities Act 2011 s 180(2) (amended by SI 2012/2024, SI 2012/3014)):

(1) in the case of a person subject to a disqualification order or disqualification undertaking under the Company Directors Disqualification Act 1986, if leave for the purposes of s 1(1)(a) or s 1A(1)(a) (see **COMPANIES** vol 15 (2009) PARA 1575 et seq) has been granted for him to act as director of the charity (Charities Act 2011 s 180(2));

(2) in the case of a person subject to a disqualification order under the Company Directors Disqualification (Northern Ireland) Order 2002, SI 2002/3150, if leave has been granted by the High Court in Northern Ireland for him to act as director of the charity (Charities Act 2011 s 180(2)); or

(3) in the case of a person subject to an order under the Insolvency Act 1986 s 429(2) (see **BANKRUPTCY AND INDIVIDUAL INSOLVENCY** vol 5 (2013) PARA 914), if leave has been granted by the court which made the order for him so to act (Charities Act 2011 s 180(2)).

15 Ie under the Insolvency Act 1986 Pt VIIA (ss 251A–251X) (see **BANKRUPTCY AND INDIVIDUAL INSOLVENCY** vol 5 (2013) PARA 91).

16 Ie under the Insolvency Act 1986 Sch 4ZB (see **BANKRUPTCY AND INDIVIDUAL INSOLVENCY** vol 5 (2013) PARA 91.

17 Charities Act 2011 ss 178(1) Case G, 180(1) (added and amended respectively by SI 2012/2404).

18 No waiver can be granted in relation to any charitable company or CIO if the person concerned is for the time being prohibited by virtue of a disqualification order or disqualification undertaking under the Company Directors Disqualification Act 1986, or of s 11(1), 12(2), 12A or 12B of that Act (**COMPANIES** vol 15 (2009) PARAS 1590–1591), from acting as director of the company or charity trustee of the CIO, and leave has not been granted for him to act as director of any company or trustee of any CIO: Charities Act 2011 s 181(5) (amended by SI 2012/3014). As to the meaning of 'company' see PARA 246.

19 Charities Act 2011 s 181(1), (2).

20 Charities Act 2011 s 181(4).

21 Ie those detailed in the Charities Act 2011 s 181(5) (see note 18).

22 Charities Act 2011 s 181(3). This provision applies whether the disqualification took effect before, on or after 27 February 2007: Charities Act 2006 Sch 10 para 11 (repealed, though the continuity of the law is unaffected: Charities Act 2011 Sch 8 para 1).

23 As to the Tribunal see PARA 579 et seq. As to the Attorney General see PARAS 589, 596, 605 et seq; and **CONSTITUTIONAL AND ADMINISTRATIVE LAW** vol 20 (2014) PARA 273 et seq.

24 See the Charities Act 2011 s 319(2), Sch 6 Table Cols 1, 2. As to the meaning of 'person who is or may be affected' within the meaning of Sch 6 see PARA 317 note 8.

25 See the Charities Act 2011 Sch 6 Table Col 3.

277. Person acting as a charity trustee while disqualified. Any person who acts as a charity trustee[1] or trustee for a charity[2] while he is disqualified for being such a trustee by virtue of the relevant provisions of the Charities Act 2011[3] is guilty of an offence[4], except where the charity concerned is a company or a CIO[5] and the disqualified person is disqualified by virtue only of certain specified matters[6] relating to insolvency[7]. However, no proceedings may be instituted except by or with the consent of the Director of Public Prosecutions[8]. However, acts done as charity trustee or trustee for a charity by a person disqualified by virtue of the relevant provisions of the Charities Act 2011[9] are not invalid by reason only of that disqualification[10].

Where the Charity Commission[11] is satisfied that any person has acted as charity trustee or trustee for a charity (excluding, until a day to be appointed, an exempt charity[12]) while disqualified for being such a trustee[13], and that, while so acting he has received from the charity any sums by way of remuneration or expenses, or any benefit in kind, in connection with his acting as charity trustee or trustee for the charity, it may by order direct him to repay to the charity the whole or part of any such sums, or (as the case may be) to pay to the charity the whole or part of the monetary value, as determined by it, of any such benefit[14].

This does not apply to any sums received by way of remuneration or expenses in respect of any time when the person concerned was not disqualified for being a charity trustee or trustee for the charity[15].

An appeal against such an order of the Commission lies to the Tribunal at the instance of the Attorney General[16], the person subject to the order or any other person who is or may be affected by the order[17]. The Tribunal has the power to do any of the following: (1) quash the order and, if appropriate, remit the matter to the Commission; (2) substitute for the order any other order which could have been made by the Commission[18].

1 As to the meaning of 'charity trustees' see PARA 255.
2 As to the meaning of 'charity' see PARA 1.
3 Ie under the Charities Act 2011 s 178: see PARA 276.
4 Charities Act 2011 s 183(1). A person guilty of such an offence is liable on summary conviction to imprisonment for a term not exceeding 12 months or a fine not exceeding the statutory maximum, or both; and on conviction on indictment to imprisonment for a term not exceeding two years or a fine, or both: s 183(2). As to the statutory maximum see **SENTENCING AND DISPOSITION OF OFFENDERS** vol 92 (2010) PARA 140.
5 As to the meaning of 'company' see PARA 246. As to charitable incorporated organisations (CIOs) see PARA 226 et seq.
6 Ie where he is disqualified by virtue only of the Charities Act 2011 s 178(1) Cases B, F or G: see PARA 276.
7 Charities Act 2011 s 183(2) (amended by SI 2012/3014).
8 Charities Act 2011 s 345(1), (2)(e). As to the Director of Public Prosecutions see **CRIMINAL PROCEDURE** vol 27 (2010) PARAS 23, 33 et seq.
9 See note 3.
10 Charities Act 2011 s 184(1).
11 As to the Charity Commission see PARAS 543–578.
12 A transitional modification to the Charities Act 2011 s 184 is made by virtue of Sch 9 para 25, so as to exclude exempt charities other than those for whom the equivalent previous statutory provisions had not been brought into force. As to exempt charities see further PARA 318.
13 See note 3.
14 Charities Act 2011 s 184(2), (3). A person guilty of disobedience to any order made by the Commission under s 184 may on the application of the Commission to the High Court be dealt with as for disobedience to an order of the High Court: s 336(1), (2); and see PARA 556.
15 Charities Act 2011 s 184(4).
16 As to the Tribunal see PARA 579 et seq. As to the Attorney General see PARAS 589, 596, 605 et seq; and **CONSTITUTIONAL AND ADMINISTRATIVE LAW** vol 20 (2014) PARA 273 et seq.
17 See the Charities Act 2011 s 319(2), Sch 6 Table Cols 1, 2. As to the meaning of 'person who is or may be affected' within the meaning of Sch 6 see PARA 317 note 8.
18 See the Charities Act 2011 Sch 6 Table Col 3.

278. Qualification under trust instrument necessary. In selecting trustees, regard must be had to any directions contained in the scheme[1] or other instrument[2] regulating the charity. Thus, where trustees are required to be residents in a certain locality, persons not possessing the necessary qualification should not be appointed[3], although in special circumstances the residential area may be extended[4]. In the absence of express direction in the instrument regulating the charity, new trustees who reside at a distance from the charitable institution may be appointed[5], but as a rule it is expedient to appoint trustees from the neighbourhood[6].

1 *Foord v Baker* (1859) 27 Beav 193, where the scheme provided that no person who had a beneficial interest in the charity estate should act as a trustee. As to schemes see PARA 179 et seq.
2 *A-G v Earl of Stamford* (1843) 1 Ph 737 at 748, 755 per Lord Cottenham LC, where a residential qualification was required by the trust deed. See also *A-G v Pearson* (1817) 3 Mer 353 at 403 per Lord Eldon LC, where, however, the trust deed was silent on this point.
3 *A-G v Cowper* (1785) 1 Bro CC 439; *A-G v France* (1780) cited in *A-G v Cowper* (1785) 1 Bro CC 439; *A-G v Earl of Stamford* (1843) 1 Ph 737. See also *A-G v Earl of Devon* (1846) 16

LJCh 34 at 45 per Shadwell V-C, where the trustees were to be 'near inhabiting'. In *A-G v Earl of Stamford* (1849) 16 Sim 453, the requirement that trustees be supplied from within a parish was held to be satisfied by persons whose daily work was within the parish, but who resided a short distance outside.

4 *Re Sekforde's Charity* (1861) 4 LT 321 (radius of six miles from charitable institution).

5 *Re Lancaster Charities, Re Charitable Trusts Act 1853* (1860) 7 Jur NS 96: 'it is not always desirable to entrust the management of charities to a purely local interest'.

6 *A-G v Moises* (1879) reported in Tudor on Charities (4th Edn, 1906) pp 1036, 1038.

279. Religious opinions of trustees. Where a charity is established exclusively for the benefit of members of the Church of England or for the instruction of children on Church of England lines, then, independently of any express provision[1] in the instrument regulating the charity, only members of that church should be appointed trustees[2]. The same principle applies in the case of charities for the exclusive benefit of dissenting sects[3].

Where a charity is established for purposes connected with a parish church, it is proper, though of course not necessary, to appoint the parson and the churchwardens as trustees[4].

It is the practice of the Charity Commission to insert in any scheme relating to a parochial ecclesiastical charity a provision giving the parochial church council of the parish some direct representation on the governing body of the charity[5].

Where a charity is substantially eleemosynary in character, the religious opinions of proposed trustees or governors must not be taken into consideration[6].

1 For an example of express provision see *Re Church Patronage Trust, Laurie v A-G* [1904] 2 Ch 643, CA.

2 *Re Norwich Charities* (1837) 2 My & Cr 275 at 305 per Lord Cottenham LC; *Re Scarborough Corpn* (1837) 1 Jur 36; *Re Stafford Charities* (1857) 25 Beav 28; *Baker v Lee* (1860) 8 HL Cas 495 at 513 per Lord Cranworth; *A-G v Clifton* (1863) 32 Beav 596; *Re Burnham National Schools* (1873) LR 17 Eq 241 at 247; *A-G v Bishop of Limerick* (1870) 18 WR 1192; and see *Re Hodgson's School* (1878) 3 App Cas 857 at 866, PC.

3 *A-G v Pearson* (1817) 3 Mer 353; *Shore v Wilson* (1842) 9 Cl & Fin 355 at 389, HL, per Alderson B; *Re Drogheda Charitable and Trust Estates* (1846) 2 Jo & Lat 422; *A-G v Calvert* (1857) 23 Beav 248; *Baker v Lee* (1860) 8 HL Cas 495; *A-G v St John's Hospital, Bath* (1876) 2 ChD 554 at 565–566 per Malins V-C.

4 *Re Donington Church Estate, Re Charitable Trusts Act 1853* (1860) 2 LT 10 (in this case the court declined to appoint the overseers of the poor and the surveyor of highways as trustees, apparently on the ground that they would probably be dissenters, and because the rector and churchwardens objected to their appointment). In one case in Ireland the Ecclesiastical Commissioners for Ireland were made trustees: see *Re Bishop Gore's Charity* (1844) Drury *temp* Sug 536.

5 As to non-ecclesiastical charities see also the Charities Act 2011 s 299; and PARA 267. As to the Charity Commission see PARAS 543–578.

6 *Re Norwich Charities* (1837) 2 My & Cr 275; *A-G v Calvert* (1857) 23 Beav 248; *Baker v Lee* (1860) 8 HL Cas 495 at 513 per Lord Cranworth; *A-G v Tottenham* (1870) IR 5 Eq 241; *A-G v St John's Hospital, Bath* (1876) 2 ChD 554.

280. No restriction on number. The statutory limitation on the number of trustees of settlements of land does not apply in the case of land vested in trustees for charitable, ecclesiastical or public purposes, or where the net proceeds of the sale of the land are held for those purposes[1].

1 See the Trustee Act 1925 s 34(3)(a), (b); and TRUSTS AND POWERS vol 98 (2013) PARAS 244, 262.

(iii) Appointment under Express Powers

281. Strict and directory powers. Express powers for the appointment of new trustees contained in the instrument or scheme founding or regulating a charity may be construed by the court as being in character either strict powers or directory powers. Strict powers can only be exercised in accordance with the exact circumstances prescribed by the settlement[1]; but non-fulfilment of the prescribed conditions does not prevent the execution of a directory power[2]. The same principle of construction applies also to directions contained in decrees of the court[3] and Acts of Parliament[4]. Appointments under express powers are now rare, since in almost all cases a statutory power is available[5].

1 For a case where a power was apparently construed as strict see *Foley v Wontner* (1820) 2 Jac & W 245.

2 *A-G v Floyer* (1716) 2 Vern 748 (where there was a direction in a will that, when six trustees were reduced to three, others should be appointed, and the sole surviving trustee was allowed to appoint others); and see TRUSTS AND POWERS vol 98 (2013) PARA 258 et seq. See also *A-G v Bishop of Litchfield* (1801) 5 Ves 825; *A-G v Cuming* (1843) 2 Y & C Ch Cas 139; *Doe d Dupleix v Roe* (1794) 1 Anst 86 at 91 per Eyre CB (new trustees validly appointed before number reduced to figure named in trust deed); *A-G v Cowper* (1785) 1 Bro CC 439 (residential qualification construed as directory).

3 *A-G v Scott* (1750) 1 Ves Sen 413 at 415 per Lord Hardwicke LC.

4 *Doe d Read v Godwin* (1822) 1 Dow & Ry KB 259.

5 As to the statutory power of appointment see PARA 285. As to powers generally see TRUSTS AND POWERS.

282. Court's powers. The court may sanction the appointment of an association registered under the Companies Acts as sole trustee in place of retiring trustees, notwithstanding that the trust deed does not authorise the appointment of a sole trustee[1].

Where the court is administering a charitable trust, trustees ought not to exercise any power they may have of appointing new trustees without the sanction of the court[2]. However, if proper persons are selected, the appointment is valid[3].

Where the trust instrument is lost, but there have been many appointments in the past, the court presumes that the earliest usage was in accordance with the terms of the lost instrument[4]. Where the instrument is not explicit the court may direct an inquiry as to who are entitled to appoint new trustees[5].

1 *Re Barnardo* (1907) Times, 14 June. As to the Companies Acts see COMPANIES vol 14 (2009) PARA 16.

2 *A-G v Clack* (1839) 1 Beav 467.

3 *A-G v Lawson* (1866) 36 LJCh 130 at 135 per Kindersley V-C.

4 *A-G v Dalton* (1851) 20 LJCh 569 at 573–574 per Romilly MR. As to usage see *A-G v Pearson* (1817) 3 Mer 353 at 403 per Lord Eldon LC; *A-G v St Cross Hospital* (1853) 17 Beav 435.

5 *Davis v Jenkins* (1814) 3 Ves & B 151 at 155, 159 per Lord Eldon LC.

283. Vesting of property in new trustees. Where, under the trusts of a charity[1], trustees of property held for the purposes of the charity may be appointed or discharged by resolution of a meeting of the charity trustees[2] or other persons, a memorandum declaring a trustee to have been so appointed or discharged, is sufficient evidence of the fact if the memorandum is signed by the person presiding at the meeting or in some other manner directed by the meeting, and attested by two persons present at the meeting[3]. Such a memorandum, if executed as a deed, has the same effect as the statutory provisions which relate to vesting declarations as respects trust property in deeds appointing or discharging trustees[4], as if the appointment or discharge were effected by the deed[5].

The court has power under the Trustee Act 1925 to vest any interest in land, stock or thing in action in any trustee of a charity over which the court would have jurisdiction upon action duly instituted, whether the trustee was appointed under an express power or by the court[6].

1 As to the meaning of 'trusts' in this context see PARA 218 note 5.
2 As to the meaning of 'charity trustees' see PARA 255.
3 Charities Act 2011 s 334(1), (2). This provision applies to a memorandum made at any time: s 334(5). Section 83 applies in relation to any institution to which the Literary and Scientific Institutions Act 1854 applies (see **NATIONAL CULTURAL HERITAGE** vol 77 (2010) PARA 939) as it applies in relation to a charity: Charities Act 2011 s 334(6).
No vesting or transfer of any property in pursuance of s 334 operates as a breach of a covenant or condition against alienation or gives rise to a forfeiture: s 334(7).
4 Ie the Trustee Act 1925 s 40: see **TRUSTS AND POWERS** vol 98 (2013) PARA 306.
5 Charities Act 2011 s 334(3). This only applies to memoranda made after 1 January 1961 (ie the commencement of the Charities Act 1960): Charities Act 2011 s 334(5). The similar provisions of the Trustee Appointment Act 1850, the Trustee Appointment Act 1869, the Trustees Appointment Act 1890 (and, so far as it applied those Acts, the School Sites Act 1852) were repealed by the Charities Act 1960, but where at 1 January 1961 the provisions of those Acts as to the appointment of trustees applied in relation to any land, they continue to have effect as if they were declared as part of the trusts on which the land is held: Charities Act 1960 s 35(6); Charities Act 2006 Sch 10 para 21. As to the continuity of the law see PARA 73 note 4.
6 See the Trustee Act 1925 s 52; and **TRUSTS AND POWERS** vol 98 (2013) PARA 310. An application for a vesting order is made using the Part 8 procedure: see **CIVIL PROCEDURE** vol 11 (2009) PARA 127 et seq.

284. Evidence of vesting. A duly signed and attested[1] memorandum declaring a trustee to be appointed or discharged by resolution of a meeting of charity trustees, is sufficient evidence of the fact of the appointment or discharge[2]. On proof of the signature, whether by evidence or presumption, the document is presumed to have been duly signed and attested unless the contrary is shown[3].

1 For the requirements as to signature and attestation, and the cases in which these provisions are applicable to appointments and discharges see PARA 283.
2 Charities Act 2011 s 334(2). This applies to a memorandum made at any time: s 334(5). See also s 334(6), (7); PARA 283 note 3. As to the meaning of 'charity trustees' see PARA 255.
3 See the Charities Act 2011 s 334(4). This provision applies to a memorandum made at any time: s 334(5).

(iv) Appointment under Statutory Powers

285. Appointment of trustees under the Trustee Act 1925. The general provisions of the Trustee Act 1925 as to the appointment of new trustees[1] and the vesting of trust property in new or continuing trustees[2] apply to charitable trusts as much as to any others[3].

1 See the Trustee Act 1925 s 36; and **TRUSTS AND POWERS** vol 98 (2013) PARA 27 et seq. As to the appointment of new trustees generally see **TRUSTS AND POWERS** vol 98 (2013) PARA 258 et seq.
2 Trustee Act 1925 s 40: see **TRUSTS AND POWERS** vol 98 (2013) PARA 305 et seq.
3 Cf *Re Coates to Parsons* (1886) 34 ChD 370.

286. Trustees of religious or educational societies and church trusts. Various statutes[1] gave powers of appointment of new trustees to congregations, societies and bodies in relation to trusts of land for various religious or educational purposes. These provisions have been repealed[2], but their operation is preserved in the cases where they applied in relation to any land at the commencement of the Charities Act 1960[3].

1 See the Trustee Appointment Act 1850, the Trustee Appointment Act 1869, the Trustees Appointment Act 1890, and, so far as it applied to any of those Acts, the School Sites Act 1852.
2 Ie by the Charities Act 1960 48(2), Sch 7 Pt I.
3 See the Charities Act 2006 Sch 10 para 21; and PARA 283. The Charities Act 1960 (repealed) commenced on 1 January 1961.

287. Parochial charities: reorganisation of parishes, etc. Special statutory provision is made in relation to the appointment of trustees of non-ecclesiastical parochial charities[1], and to cope with the consequences of changes of local secular[2] and ecclesiastical[3] organisation[4].

1 See the Charities Act 2011 s 299(2); and PARA 267.
2 See the Charities Act 2011 s 299; and PARA 267.
3 See in particular the Mission and Pastoral Measure 2011 Sch 3 para 9; and PARA 269. See also the City of London (Guild Churches) Act 1952 s 28; and ECCLESIASTICAL LAW vol 34 (2011) PARA 330 et seq.
4 See generally PARAS 269–270.

(v) Appointment by the Court

288. Court's general jurisdiction. Apart from any statutory jurisdiction, the High Court has an inherent jurisdiction to appoint new trustees of charities[1], even where there is in existence a power of appointment capable of being executed[2], and under this jurisdiction can appoint additional trustees[3].

The court has no power to appoint judicial trustees for any charity[4].

1 *A-G v London Corpn* (1790) 3 Bro CC 171; *A-G v Stephens* (1834) 3 My & K 347.
2 *A-G v Clack* (1839) 1 Beav 467. It is not proper to apply to the court in ordinary cases where a power of appointment is capable of being exercised: *Re Gibbon's Trusts* (1882) 45 LT 756; *Re Higginbottom* [1892] 3 Ch 132.
3 *Re Burnham National Schools* (1873) LR 17 Eq 241 at 246; *Re Browne's Hospital v Stamford* (1889) 60 LT 288.
4 See the Judicial Trustees Act 1896 s 6(2); and TRUSTS AND POWERS vol 98 (2013) PARA 200.

289. Jurisdiction under the Trustee Act 1925. Whenever it is expedient to appoint a new trustee or new trustees of any trust, whether charitable or otherwise, and it is found inexpedient, difficult or impracticable to do so without the court's assistance, the court may make an order for the appointment of a new trustee either in substitution for or in addition to any existing trustee or trustees, although there is no existing trustee[1], and for vesting the property in the new trustee or trustees without any conveyance[2].

Thus, the court may appoint new trustees of charities where the old trustees have died[3], where a trustee corporation is in liquidation or has been dissolved[4], where an official person nominated as trustee no longer exists in his official character[5], and where the trustees disclaim or decline to act[6], or are abroad[7], are removed for misconduct[8], lack capacity to exercise functions as trustee[9], or are bankrupt[10].

1 See the Trustee Act 1925 s 41(1); and TRUSTS AND POWERS vol 98 (2013) PARA 289. The Trustee Act 1925 applies to charities: see *Re Coates to Parsons* (1886) 34 ChD 370, a case decided on the corresponding provision of the Conveyancing Act 1881 s 31 (repealed). An application for a vesting order is made using the Part 8 procedure: see CIVIL PROCEDURE vol 11 (2009) PARA 127 et seq. The consent of the Charity Commission may be necessary before proceedings are begun: see the Charities Act 2011 s 115; and PARA 594. As to the Charity Commission see PARAS 543–578.
2 See the Trustee Act 1925 ss 44–52, 58; and TRUSTS AND POWERS vol 98 (2013) PARA 315 et seq. See also *A-G v Langham* (1887) 82 LT Jo 246 (where the court vested charity lands in the Attorney General, the trustee being a person mentally disordered).

3 *Re Nightingale's Charity* (1844) 3 Hare 336. As to the principles upon which the court proceeds in appointing trustees see generally *Re Tempest* (1866) 1 Ch App 485.
4 See the Trustee Act 1925 s 41(1); and **TRUSTS AND POWERS** vol 98 (2013) PARAS 289, 296. See also *Re Yarm Free Grammar School* (1853) 10 Hare, App I, V; *Re No 9 Bomore Road* [1906] 1 Ch 359; *Re Nos 56, 58, Albert Road, Norwood* [1916] 1 Ch 289. Cf the Law of Property Act 1925 s 181 (see **CORPORATIONS** vol 24 (2010) PARA 506) and the Companies Act 2006 s 1012 (see **COMPANIES** vol 15 (2009) PARA 1531).
5 *A-G v Stephens* (1834) 3 My & K 347.
6 *Re Beverley Grammar School* (1839) 9 LJCh 91; and see *Re Lincoln Primitive Methodist Chapel, Re Charitable Trusts Act 1853 and Trustee Act 1850* (1855) 1 Jur NS 1011, where the court confirmed the appointment of the new trustees. As to disclaimer by trustees see PARA 164.
7 See *Re Lincoln Primitive Methodist Chapel, Re Charitable Trusts Act 1853 and Trustee Act 1850* (1855) 1 Jur NS 1011.
8 *Ex p Greenhouse* (1815) 1 Madd 92.
9 See the Trustee Act 1925 s 41(1); and **TRUSTS AND POWERS** vol 98 (2013) PARA 296. See also the Trustee Act 1925 ss 36(9), 54; the Court of Protection Rules 2007, SI 2007/1744, r 52(1)–(3); and **MENTAL HEALTH AND CAPACITY** vol 75 (2013) PARA 740; **TRUSTS AND POWERS** vol 98 (2013) PARAS 278, 291.
10 See the Trustee Act 1925 s 41(1); and **TRUSTS AND POWERS** vol 98 (2013) PARA 296.

290. Filling of vacancies. Where it was not intended that the whole number of trustees originally appointed should always be kept up, the court, before filling vacancies, requires to be satisfied that the number of the existing trustees is insufficient[1]. Thus the court has refused to appoint new trustees at the expense of the charity where ten trustees out of 15[2], and 11 out of 13[3], remained to execute the trusts. In other cases where two-thirds or three-quarters of the trustees remained[4], or where the intention was that the full number should be kept up[5], the court has filled up the vacancies.

1 *Re Worcester Charities* (1847) 2 Ph 284; *Re Shrewsbury Charities* (1849) 1 Mac & G 84; and see *Re Hereford Charities, Re Gloucester Charities* (1842) 6 Jur 289. Jessel MR apparently considered that, where the appointment was by donees of a power, it was the rule in charity cases to keep up the full number of trustees: *Re Cunningham and Bradley and Wilson* [1877] WN 258.
2 *Re Worcester Charities* (1847) 2 Ph 284. See also *Re Hereford Charities, Re Gloucester Charities* (1842) 6 Jur 289; *Re Coates to Parsons* (1886) 34 ChD 370 at 377–378 per North J.
3 *Re Marlborough School* (1843) 13 LJCh 2.
4 *Re Hereford Charities, Re Gloucester Charities* (1842) 6 Jur 289; *Re Bedford Charity* (undated) cited in 10 Hare App I, IVn.
5 *Davis v Jenkins* (1814) 3 Ves & B 151 at 158–159 per Lord Eldon LC. As to the number of new trustees appointed by the court see **TRUSTS AND POWERS** vol 98 (2013) PARA 290.

291. Provision for future appointments. In making an order appointing new trustees[1], or on the settlement of a scheme, the court may give directions or provide for future appointments, and may allow the trustees to appoint others as occasion requires[2].

1 *Re East Bergholt Town Lands* (1853) 2 Eq Rep 90.
2 *Re Puckering's Charity* (1854) Seton's Judgments and Orders (7th Edn) 1264.

(vi) Appointment by the Charity Commission

292. Jurisdiction. The Charity Commission[1] has the same jurisdiction and powers as the court in relation to the appointment of a charity trustee[2] or trustee for a charity[3], and as to vesting or transferring property and requiring or entitling persons to call for or make transfers of property or payments[4]. It may only exercise its jurisdiction in certain circumstances[5], and may not make any order under this jurisdiction, other than an order relating to the official custodian or an order appointing such number of additional charity trustees as it considers necessary for the proper administration of the charity[6], without first complying with the statutory publicity requirement[7], save where the Commission is satisfied that for any reason such compliance is unnecessary[8]. The statutory publicity requirement is that the Commission must give public notice of its proposals, inviting representations to be made to it within a period specified in the notice[9]. Such notice is to contain such particulars of the proposals, or such directions for obtaining information about them, as the Commission thinks sufficient and appropriate, and is to be given in such manner as the Commission thinks sufficient and appropriate[10]. Where the Commission gives notice of any proposals under these provisions, it must take into account any representations made to it within the period specified in the notice, and may (without further notice) proceed with the proposals either without modifications or with such modifications as it thinks desirable[11].

If a corporate trustee is appointed by the Charity Commission under a scheme, it will be deemed a trust corporation[12].

1 As to the Charity Commission see PARAS 543–578.
2 As to the meaning of 'charity trustees' see PARA 255.
3 As to the meaning of 'charity' see PARA 1.
4 See the Charities Act 2011 s 69(1)(b), (c); and PARA 189.
5 See the Charities Act 2011 s 70(2); and PARA 189.
6 Ie an order under the Charities Act 2011 s 76(3)(b): see PARA 253. As to the official custodian see PARA 300 et seq.
7 See the Charities Act 2011 s 89(1).
8 See the Charities Act 2011 s 89(4). In which case the publicity requirement does not apply in relation to the particular order.
9 Charities Act 2011 s 89(2). The time when any such notice is given is to be decided by the Commission: s 89(3).
10 Charities Act 2011 s 89(7).
11 Charities Act 2011 s 89(6).
12 See the Charities Act 2011 Sch 7 para 3; and PARA 257.

293. Practice. When appointing trustees on the settlement of a scheme[1], the Charity Commission[2] may introduce a representative element, and may arrange in suitable cases that the representative element shall constitute a majority of the trustees. In framing new schemes, the number of the trustees is sometimes increased, and sometimes reduced. Provision is also frequently made for ex officio and co-optative trustees.

1 As to schemes see PARA 179 et seq.
2 As to the Charity Commission see PARAS 543–578.

(6) REMOVAL AND DISCHARGE OF TRUSTEES

(i) Removal by the Court

294. Court's general jurisdiction. In all cases which may require such a remedy the court has jurisdiction to remove existing trustees and substitute new ones. This jurisdiction is merely ancillary to the court's principal duty, which is the protection of trusts[1], and does not depend upon the existence in the instrument of foundation of an express power of removal[2].

1 *Letterstedt v Broers* (1884) 9 App Cas 371 at 386, PC. For a form of decree removing a trustee see *A-G v Drummond* (1842) 3 Dr & War 162.
2 As to the exercise of express powers of removal see *A-G v Pearson* (1817) 3 Mer 353 at 412–415 per Lord Eldon LC.

295. Removal of trustee for breach of trust. The court has removed trustees who have wilfully committed breaches of trust, as by converting a dissenting chapel to the use of a sect contrary to the founder's wishes[1], transferring the property of one charity to another[2], misapplying increased revenues[3], or allowing Unitarians to participate in a charity founded for Protestant dissenters[4]. A trustee who was lessee of part of a charity estate in defiance of the provisions of the scheme was ordered to resign his office or give up his lease[5]. Corporations who are trustees of charities may similarly be removed for breaches of trust[6]. However, charity trustees are not necessarily removed where they have innocently committed a breach of trust[7].

Trustees who, having committed breaches of trust, refuse to retire voluntarily, may be made to pay the costs of proceedings necessary for the appointment of other trustees[8].

Where inconvenience as regards the receipt of dividends arose from the trustees' being holders of annual offices, the court appointed others to hold the funds, but allowed the office-holders to retain certain rights of nomination[9].

1 *A-G v Pearson* (1835) 7 Sim 290 at 309 per Shadwell V-C; *A-G v Aust* (1865) 13 LT 235. See also *A-G v Munro* (1848) 2 De G & Sm 122 (where a minister of the Established Church of Scotland seceded from that body to the Free Church, and was removed from his charge); *A-G v Anderson* (1888) 57 LJCh 543.
2 *Newsome v Flowers* (1861) 30 Beav 461.
3 *Coventry Corpn v A-G* (1720) 7 Bro Parl Cas 235, HL.
4 *Shore v Wilson* (1842) 9 Cl & Fin 355, HL; *Drummond v A-G for Ireland* (1849) 2 HL Cas 837 at 861 per Lord Brougham.
5 *Foord v Baker* (1859) 27 Beav 193.
6 *A-G v Earl of Clarendon* (1810) 17 Ves 491 at 499 per Grant MR. See also *A-G v Governors of Foundling Hospital* (1793) 2 Ves 42 at 46 per Lord Commissioner Eyre; *A-G v Dixie, ex p Bosworth School* (1805) 13 Ves 519; *Ex p Kirkby Ravensworth Hospital* (1808) 15 Ves 305 at 314 per Lord Eldon LC; *Ex p Greenhouse* (1815) 1 Madd 92.
7 *A-G v Stafford Corpn* (1740) Barn Ch 33; *A-G v Caius College* (1837) 2 Keen 150.
8 *A-G v Murdoch* (1856) 2 K & J 571.
9 *Re Taylor's Charity, ex p Blackburne* (1820) 1 Jac & W 297.

296. Removal of trustees on other grounds. A reason sufficient to prevent the appointment of a trustee is not necessarily a sufficient ground for removing an existing trustee[1]. Where no breach of trust has been committed, trustees, if otherwise unexceptionable, are not removed merely on the ground of not possessing the required religious[2] or residential[3] qualification, or on the ground of temporary absence from the United Kingdom[4], or because they were appointed irregularly[5]. Bankruptcy is not necessarily[6], though it is usually[7], a ground for removal.

1 *A-G v Clapham* (1853) 10 Hare 540 at 613 per Page Wood V-C (trustees of a chapel); revsd on appeal without affecting this point (1855) 4 De GM & G 591; and see (1855) 4 De GM & G at 632 per Lord Cranworth LC. As to disqualification for acting as a charity trustee see PARA 276.
2 *Baker v Lee* (1860) 8 HL Cas 495 at 513 per Lord Cranworth; *A-G v Clifton* (1863) 32 Beav 596 at 601 per Romilly MR; *A-G v Bishop of Limerick* (1870) 18 WR 1192.
3 *A-G v Earl of Clarendon* (1810) 17 Ves 491; *A-G v Earl of Stamford* (1843) 1 Ph 737 at 747–748 per Lord Cottenham LC; and see *A-G v Clifton* (1863) 32 Beav 596 at 601 per Romilly MR.
4 *Re Moravian Society* (1858) 4 Jur NS 703.
5 *A-G v Cuming* (1843) 2 Y & C Ch Cas 139 at 150–151 per Shadwell V-C; *A-G v Daugars* (1864) 33 Beav 621.
6 *Archbold v Ireland Charitable Bequests Comrs* (1849) 2 HL Cas 440. As to disqualification on the ground of bankruptcy see PARA 276.
7 *Bainbrigge v Blair* (1839) 1 Beav 495; *Re Roche* (1842) 1 Con & Law 306; *Re Barker's Trusts* (1875) 1 ChD 43.

(ii) Removal by the Charity Commission

297. Jurisdiction. The Charity Commission[1] has the same jurisdiction and powers as the High Court to discharge or remove a charity trustee[2] or trustee for a charity[3], or to remove an officer or employee[4]. The jurisdiction is exercisable upon and subject to the same conditions as the jurisdiction to appoint new trustees[5]. It also has jurisdiction to remove charity trustees and other persons where it is necessary for the protection of the charity[6].

1 As to the Charity Commission see PARAS 543–578.
2 As to the meaning of 'charity trustees' see PARA 255.
3 As to the meaning of 'charity' see PARA 1.
4 See the Charities Act 2011 s 69(1)(b); and PARA 189.
5 Ie the Charities Act 2011 s 89; see PARA 292. Before making an order removing a charity trustee, or trustee for a charity, or an officer, agent or employee of a charity, the Commission must give him one month's notice of its proposals, inviting representations to be made to it within a period specified in the notice, save where the person cannot be found or has no known address in the United Kingdom: s 89(5). As to the meaning of United Kingdom see PARA 189.
6 See the Charities Act 2011 ss 76–83; and PARA 558 et seq.

(iii) Discharge and Retirement

298. Discharge by order of Charity Commission. The Charity Commission[1] may exercise its jurisdiction to discharge a charity trustee[2] or trustee for a charity[3] on his own application[4].

1 As to the Charity Commission see PARAS 543–578.
2 As to the meaning of 'charity trustees' see PARA 255.
3 As to the meaning of 'charity' see PARA 1.
4 Charities Act 2011 s 70(7). Notice must be given to the other trustees: see s 71(1), (2); and PARA 189.

299. Retirement without a new appointment. Under the Trustee Act 1925, a trustee may retire from the trust by deed, provided that after his discharge there will be a trust corporation[1] or at least two individuals to act as trustees, and provided that his co-trustees and any person entitled to appoint new trustees consent by deed to his retirement[2]. There may also be express provision in the trust instrument for the possibility of retirement without a new appointment.

1 As to trust corporations see PARA 257.
2 See the Trustee Act 1925 s 39; and TRUSTS AND POWERS vol 98 (2013) PARA 331 et seq.

(7) THE OFFICIAL CUSTODIAN FOR CHARITIES

300. Status and capacity. The official custodian for charities is the successor for all purposes both of the Official Trustee of Charity Lands and of the Official Trustees of Charitable Funds[1]. He is a corporation sole having perpetual succession and using an official seal, which is officially and judicially noticed[2]. His function is to act as trustee for charities in the cases provided for by the Charities Act 2011[3]. In relation to property vested in him in trust for a charity, he may not exercise any powers of management, and is in the position of a corporate custodian trustee[4] save that he may not charge fees[5].

1 Previously provided for by the Charities Act 1960 s 48(6) (repealed), which also vested in the official custodian property previously vested in the official trustee or official trustees, and provided that any Act, scheme, deed or other document referring to or relating to the official trustee or official trustees is, so far as the context permits, to have effect as if the official

custodian had been mentioned instead: s 48(6)(a), (b) (repealed). Despite the repeal of the Charities Act 1960 s 48(6), the official custodian continues to be treated as the successor of both offices for all purposes as if the functions of the official trustee or trustees had been functions of the official custodian and as if the official trustee or trustees had been, and had discharged their functions as, holder of the office of official custodian; subsequent repeals of legislation have preserved that position: Charities Act 2006 Sch 10 para 26(1) (repealed); Charities Act 2011 Sch 8 para 18. See the Charities Act 2011 s 90; PARA 302.

Any scheme, order, certificate or other document issued under or for the purposes of the Charitable Trusts Acts 1853 to 1939 and having effect in accordance with the Charities Act 1960 s 48(4) (repealed) immediately before the commencement of that repeal continues to have the same effect, and to be enforceable or liable to be discharged in the same way, as would have been the case if that repeal had not come into force; any such document, and any document under the seal of the official trustees of charitable funds may be proved as if the Charities Act 1960 had not been passed: Charities Act 2006 Sch 10 para 25.

2 See the Charities Act 2011 s 21(1), Sch 2 para 1. The office is held by such individual as the Charity Commission may from time to time designate: s 21(3). As to the Charity Commission see PARAS 543–578.

3 Charities Act 2011 s 21(2). These cases are discussed in the ensuing paragraphs. He may also act as trustee for shared church buildings under the Sharing of Church Buildings Act 1969 s 2, and the ownership of an existing or proposed church building which is subject to a sharing agreement and which is, or will be, owned by all or some of the sharing churches may be vested in him: see s 2(2); and **ECCLESIASTICAL LAW** vol 34 (2011) PARA 955. The vesting of ownership in the official custodian is by order under the Charities Act 2011: see the Sharing of Church Buildings Act 1969 s 2(4) (amended by the Charities Act 2011 Sch 7 para 19). As to vesting property in the official custodian see PARA 302. The purposes of a sharing agreement must be limited to purposes which are exclusively charitable according to the law of England and Wales: Sharing of Church Buildings Act 1969 s 2(5). See generally **ECCLESIASTICAL LAW** vol 34 (2011) PARA 953 et seq.

4 Ie a corporation appointed under the Public Trustee Act 1906 s 4: see **TRUSTS AND POWERS** vol 98 (2013) PARA 232.

5 See the Charities Act 2011 s 91(1), (2); and PARA 304.

301. Performance of functions; accounts. The official custodian for charities[1] must perform his duties in accordance with directions, general or special, given by the Charity Commission[2]; his expenses, so far as they are not reimbursed to or recovered by him as trustee for any charity[3], must be defrayed by the Commission[4]. Anything which is required to or may be done by, to or before the official custodian may be done by, to or before any member of the staff of the Commission generally or specially authorised by it to act for him during a vacancy in his office or otherwise[5]. He must keep accounts and records relating to them as directed by the Treasury in such form, in such manner and at such times as may be so directed[6]. The accounts so prepared must be examined and certified by the Comptroller and Auditor General[7], who must send to the Commission a copy of the accounts as certified by him together with his report on them[8].

1 As to the official custodian for charities see PARA 300.

2 Charities Act 2011 s 21(4). As to the Charity Commission see PARAS 543–578.

3 As to the meaning of 'charity' see PARA 1.

4 Charities Act 2011 Sch 2 para 2. As to service of directions see the Charities Act 2011 s 339; and PARA 555.

5 Charities Act 2011 Sch 2 para 3.

6 Charities Act 2011 Sch 2 para 5.

7 As to the Comptroller and Auditor General see **CONSTITUTIONAL AND ADMINISTRATIVE LAW** vol 20 (2014) PARAS 494–496.

8 Charities Act 2011 Sch 2 para 6. The Commission must publish and lay before Parliament a copy of the documents so received: Sch 2 para 7.

302. Vesting property in official custodian. Prior to 1 September 1992[1], the court could by order vest any property held by or in trust for a charity in the official custodian for charities[2], or authorise or require persons in whom such property was vested to transfer it to him, or appoint any person to transfer such property to him[3]. The Charity Commissioners (now the Charity Commission) had the same powers in this respect[4]. Personal property[5] held by or in trust for a charity or comprised in a testamentary gift to a charity could be transferred to the official custodian with his agreement[6].

Under the Charities Act 1992 the provision relating to personal property[7] was repealed[8], and the official custodian was required to divest himself of all the property he holds in that capacity, except any land[9] and any property other than land vested in him by virtue of an order of the Charity Commissioners acting under their power to act for the protection of charities[10]. Further, the power of the court is now limited to land or an interest in land[11].

Any funds vested in the Accountant General[12] and held by him in trust for any charity or ecclesiastical corporation[13] in the Church of England may be transferred to the official custodian or the appropriate authority[14] if, on an application made to him by the Charity Commission[15] or the Church Commissioners, the Accountant General thinks fit so to direct[16]. Any funds so transferred vest in and are held by the official custodian or the appropriate authority respectively in trust for the charity or ecclesiastical corporation upon the trusts on which the funds were held before the transfer[17].

1 Ie date on which the Charities Act 1992 s 29 (repealed) came into force.

2 As to the official custodian for charities see PARA 300.

3 Charities Act 1960 s 16(1) (repealed: see now the Charities Act 2011 s 90(1); and the text and note 11).

4 See the Charities Act 1960 s 18(1)(c) (repealed). This was subject to the conditions contained in s 18(4), (5) (repealed) as to exercise of the jurisdiction. These provisions are re-enacted in the Charities Act 2011 ss 69, 70: see PARA 189. As to the Charity Commission see PARA 543.

5 In this provision 'personal property' extended to any real security but did not include any interest in land other than by way of security: Charities Act 1960 s 16(2) (repealed) (see the text and note 7).

6 Charities Act 1960 s 16(2) (repealed) (see the text and note 7). In the case of a testamentary gift to a charity, the official custodian's receipt was a complete discharge of the personal representative: s 16(2) (repealed).

7 Ie the Charities Act 1960 s 16(2) (repealed).

8 See the Charities Act 1992 ss 47, 78(2), Sch 3 para 4, Sch 7 (s 47, Sch 3 repealed). Any provision of the trusts of a charity, or of any directions given by an order of the Commissioners (now the Charity Commission) made in connection with a transaction requiring the sanction of an order under the Charities Act 1960 s 29(1) (repealed), ceased to have effect if and to the extent that it required or authorised personal property (including any mortgage or other real security, but excluding any interest in land other than such an interest by way of mortgage or other security) of the charity to be transferred to or held by the official custodian: Charities Act 1992 s 30(2) (repealed). See also s 30(3) (repealed).

9 For these purposes, 'land' did not include any interest in land by way of mortgage or other security: Charities Act 1992 s 29(13) (repealed).

10 See Charities Act 1992 s 29(1), (2) (repealed). The disposal of any property by the official custodian in accordance with the Charities Act 1992 s 29 operated to discharge him from his trusteeship of that property: s 30(4) (repealed). As to the Charity Commission's power to act for the protection of charities see PARA 558 et seq.

11 See the Charities Act 2011 s 90(2). The court may by order vest in the official custodian any land held by or in trust for a charity, authorise or require the persons in whom any such land is vested to transfer it to him or appoint any person to transfer any such land to him, but this does not apply to any interest in land by way of mortgage or other security: s 90(1), (2). As to the concurrent jurisdiction of the Commission see PARA 189.

12 As to the Accountant General see COURTS AND TRIBUNALS vol 24 (2010) PARA 751.

13 'Ecclesiastical corporation' means a capitular body within the meaning of the Cathedrals Measure 1963 (see ECCLESIASTICAL LAW vol 34 (2011) PARAS 343–344, 369) or the incumbent of a benefice (see ECCLESIASTICAL LAW vol 34 (2011) PARA 269): Administration of Justice Act 1982 s 41(3) (s 41(1)–(3) amended by the Church of England (Miscellaneous Provisions) Measure 2006 Sch 5 para 25(b)). As from the relevant date, any reference in the Administration of Justice Act 1982 s 41(3) to a capitular body is to be construed as a reference to the corporate body of the cathedral: see the Cathedrals Measure 1999 ss 36(2), 38(2), (3); and ECCLESIASTICAL LAW. 'Relevant date', in relation to any cathedral existing at the passing of the Cathedrals Measure 1999, means the date appointed by the Archbishops of Canterbury and York under s 38(2): see s 35(1). See further ECCLESIASTICAL LAW vol 34 (2011) PARA 344 et seq.

14 The 'appropriate authority' is, in the case of funds held in trust for a cathedral, the corporate body of that cathedral established under the Cathedrals Measure 1999 s 9(1)(a) and, in the case of funds held in trust for a benefice, the Diocesan Board of Finance for the diocese in which that benefice is situated: s 41(3) (as amended: see note 13).

15 As to the Charity Commission see PARAS 543–578.

16 Administration of Justice Act 1982 s 41(1) (as amended: see note 13).

17 Administration of Justice Act 1982 s 41(2) (as amended: see note 13).

303. Divestment of land subject to the Reverter of Sites Act 1987. Where any land is vested in the official custodian for charities[1] in trust for a charity and it appears to the Charity Commission[2] that the provisions of the Reverter of Sites Act 1987[3] which replace a right of reverter by trust will, or are likely to, operate in relation to the land at a particular time or in particular circumstances, the concurrent jurisdiction[4] of the Commission in relation to the discharge of a trustee for a charity[5] may, at any time before those provisions of that Act operate, be exercised by it of its own motion for the purpose of making an order discharging the official custodian from his trusteeship of the land, and making consequential vesting orders and giving consequential directions[6]. Where: (1) the provisions of the Reverter of Sites Act 1987[7] have already operated in relation to any land which, immediately before the time when that provision operated, was vested in the official custodian in trust for a charity[8]; and (2) it remains vested in him but on the trust arising under that Act[9], the court[10] or the Commission (of its own motion) may make an order discharging the official custodian from his trusteeship of the land, and make such vesting orders and give such directions as appear to it to be necessary or expedient in consequence[11]. Where, in certain circumstances[12], an order is made discharging the official custodian from his trusteeship of any land, the persons in whom the land is to be vested on the discharge of the official custodian are the relevant charity trustees[13] unless the court (or as the case may be) the Commission is satisfied that it would be appropriate for it to be vested in some other persons[14].

An appeal against such an order made by the Commission to lies to the Tribunal at the instance of the Attorney General[15], the charity trustees of the charity, the charity itself (if a body corporate) or any other person who is or may be affected by the order[16]. The Tribunal has the power to do any of the following: (a) quash the order and, if appropriate, remit the matter to the Commission; (b) substitute for the order any other order which could have been made by the Commission; (c) add to the order anything which could have been contained in an order made by the Commission[17].

1 As to the official custodian for charities see PARA 300.

2 As to the Charity Commission see PARAS 543–578.

3 Ie the Reverter of Sites Act 1987 s 1: see PARA 70.

4 Under the Charities Act 2011 s 69: see PARAS 189, 191–192, 298.

5 As to the meaning of 'charity' see PARA 1.

6 Charities Act 2011 s 92(1), (2). The vesting or transfer of any property in accordance with such an order does not operate as a breach of any covenant or condition against alienation or give rise to a forfeiture: see PARA 189 note 6.
7 See note 3. Any reference to the Reverter of Sites Act 1987 s 1 (see PARA 70) operating in relation to any land is a reference to a trust arising in relation to the land under that provision: Charities Act 2011 s 92(3).
8 Charities Act 2011 s 93(1)(a).
9 Charities Act 2011 s 93(1)(b).
10 As to the meaning of 'court' see PARA 177 note 12.
11 Charities Act 2011 s 93(2). Where the Reverter of Sites Act 1987 s 1 (see PARA 70) has operated in relation to any such land as is mentioned in the Charities Act 2011 s 93(1)(a) and the land remains vested in the official custodian as mentioned in s 93(1)(b) (see the text to notes 8, 9), then, all the powers, duties and liabilities that, apart from s 93, would be those of the official custodian as trustee of the land are instead those of the charity trustees of the charity concerned; and those trustees have power in his name and on his behalf to execute and do all assurances and things which they could properly execute or do in their own name and on their own behalf if the land were vested in them: s 95(1), (2). This is not to be taken to require or authorise those trustees to sell the land at a time when it remains vested in the official custodian: s 95(3).
12 Ie where an order: (1) is made by the court under the Charities Act 2011 s 90(3) (see PARA 305) or by the Commission under s 69 (see PARAS 189, 191–192, 298), on the grounds that the Reverter of Sites Act 1987 s 1 (see PARA 70) will, or is likely to, operate in relation to the land; or (2) is made by the court or the Commission under the Charities Act 2011 s 93 (see the text and notes 7–11): s 94(1).
13 For these purposes, the 'relevant charity trustees' means: (1) in relation to an order mentioned in note 12 head (1), the charity trustees of the charity in trust for which the land is vested in the official custodian immediately before the time when the order takes effect; or (2) in relation to an order mentioned in note 12 head (2), the charity trustees of the charity in trust for which the land was vested in the official custodian immediately before the time when the Reverter of Sites Act 1987 s 1 operated in relation to the land: Charities Act 2011 s 94(3). As to the meaning of 'charity trustees' generally see PARA 255.
14 Charities Act 2011 s 94(2). Where the official custodian has been discharged from his trusteeship of any land by an order under s 93 (see the text and notes 7–11), and the land has been vested in the charity trustees or other persons in accordance with s 94 (see the text and notes 12–13), the land is to be held by those trustees, or as the case may be by those persons, as trustees on the terms of the trust arising under the Reverter of Sites Act 1987 s 1 (see PARA 70): Charities Act 2011 s 95(4). The official custodian is not liable to any person in respect of any loss or misapplication of any land vested in him in accordance with that provision (semble, the Reverter of Sites Act 1987 s 1) unless it is occasioned by or through any wilful neglect or default of his or of any person acting for him: Charities Act 2011 s 95(5). But the Consolidated Fund is liable to make good to any person any sums for which the official custodian may be liable by reason of any such neglect or default: s 95(6). As to the Consolidated Fund see **CONSTITUTIONAL AND ADMINISTRATIVE LAW** vol 20 (2014) PARA 480 et seq; **PARLIAMENT** vol 78 (2010) PARAS 1028–1031.
15 As to the Tribunal see PARA 579 et seq. As to the Attorney General see PARAS 589, 596, 605 et seq; and **CONSTITUTIONAL AND ADMINISTRATIVE LAW** vol 20 (2014) PARA 273 et seq.
16 See the Charities Act 2011 s 319(2), Sch 6 Table Cols 1, 2. As to the meaning of 'person who is or may be affected' within the meaning of Sch 6 see PARA 317 note 8.
17 See the Charities Act 2011 Sch 6 Table Col 3.

304. Management of property vested in official custodian. As regards land vested in the official custodian for charities[1] in trust for a charity, the charity trustees[2] have the power in his name and on his behalf to execute and do all assurances and things which they could properly execute or do in their own name and on their own behalf if the land were vested in them[3]. However, if any land is so vested in the official custodian by virtue of an order under the Charity Commission's powers to act for the protection of charities[4], the power conferred on the charity trustees[5] is not exercisable by them in relation to any transaction affecting that land, unless the transaction is authorised by order of the court[6] or the Charity Commission[7]. Where any land is vested in the official custodian in trust for a charity[8], the charity trustees have the same power to make obligations entered into by them binding on the land as if it were vested in them, and any covenant, agreement or condition which is enforceable by or against the official custodian by reason of the land being vested in him is enforceable by or against the charity trustees as if the land were vested in them[9]. These provisions do not authorise any charity trustees or charity to impose any personal liability on the official custodian[10].

Where property is vested in the official custodian in trust for a charity, he must not exercise any powers of management, but, as trustee of any property, he has all the same powers, duties and liabilities, and is entitled to the same rights and immunities, and is subject to the control and orders of the court, as a corporation appointed custodian trustee[11], except that he has no power to charge fees[12]. However, where the official custodian is entitled as trustee for a charity to the custody of securities or documents of title relating to the trust property, he may permit them to be in the possession or under the control of the charity trustees without thereby incurring any liability[13].

1 As to the official custodian for charities see PARA 300.
2 As to the meaning of 'charity trustees' see PARA 255. In the case of a corporate charity, references in the Charities Act 2011 s 91(3)–(5) to 'charity trustees' should be read as references to 'the charity': s 91(6).
3 Charities Act 2011 s 91(3). Charity trustees are not required to obtain the official custodian's permission or to join him in proceedings claiming possession of charitable property: *Muman v Nagasena* [1999] 4 All ER 178, [2000] 1 WLR 299, CA.
4 Ie an order under the Charities Act 2011 s 76(3)(c): see PARA 567. As to the Charity Commission see PARAS 543–578.
5 Ie by the Charities Act 2011 s 91(3): see the text and notes 1–3.
6 As to the meaning of 'court' see PARA 177 note 12.
7 Charities Act 2011 s 91(4).
8 As to the meaning of 'charity' see PARA 1.
9 Charities Act 2011 s 91(5).
10 Charities Act 2011 s 91(7).
11 Ie under the Public Trustee Act 1906 s 4: see **TRUSTS AND POWERS** vol 98 (2013) PARA 232. As to the liability of the official custodian see PARA 306.
12 Charities Act 2011 s 91(1), (2).
13 Charities Act 2011 s 91(8).

305. Discharge and termination of trusts; effect of orders. The court[1] may by order discharge the official custodian for charities[2] from his trusteeship as regards all or any property vested in him in trust for a charity[3]. Where the official custodian is discharged from his trusteeship of any property, or the trusts on which he holds any property come to an end, the court may make such vesting orders and give such directions as may seem to the court to be necessary or expedient in consequence[4]. No person is liable for any loss occasioned by his acting in conformity with such an order or any order vesting property in the official custodian[5], or by his giving effect to anything done in pursuance of such orders, and no person is excused from so doing by reason of the order having been in any respect improperly obtained[6].

1 As to the meaning of 'court' see PARA 177 note 12. This power may also be exercised by the Charity Commission: see the Charities Act 2011 s 69(1); and PARA 189. As to the Commission's powers see PARA 302. As to the Charity Commission see PARAS 543–578.
2 As to the official custodian for charities see PARA 300.
3 Charities Act 2011 s 90(3).
4 Charities Act 2011 s 90(4). The vesting or transfer of any property in accordance with such an order does not operate as a breach of any covenant or condition against alienation or give rise to a forfeiture: see PARA 189 note 6.

5 Ie under the Charities Act 2011 s 90 (see PARA 302; and text and notes 1–4).
6 Charities Act 2011 s 90(5), (6).

306. Liability of official custodian. The official custodian for charities[1] is not liable as trustee for any charity in respect of any loss or of the misapplication of any property, unless it is occasioned by or through his wilful neglect or default[2] or that of any person acting for him[3]. The Consolidated Fund is liable to make good to any charity any sums for which the official custodian is liable by reason of such neglect or default[4].

1 As to the official custodian for charities see PARA 300.
2 'Wilful default' has been considered judicially in other contexts (eg *Re Vickery, Vickery v Stephens* [1931] 1 Ch 572; *Re Lucking's Will Trusts, Renwick v Lucking* [1967] 3 All ER 726, [1968] 1 WLR 866; *Re City Equitable Fire Insurance Co Ltd* [1925] Ch 407, CA), but it is doubtful whether those decisions are useful in relation to the official custodian's liability. See also *Bartlett v Barclays Bank Trust Co Ltd (No 2)* [1980] Ch 515 at 546, [1980] 2 All ER 92 at 97, where Brightman LJ considers the meaning of the phrase in relation to the duties of a trustee: '... passive breach of trust, an omission by a trustee to do something which, as a prudent trustee, he ought to have done, as distinct from an active breach of trust, that is to say, doing something which the trustee ought not to have done. If an instance of such wilful default is pleaded and proved, as are a number of such instances in the present case, the court is entitled to order an account on the footing of wilful default.' It is conceived that this could be applied by analogy to the official custodian.
3 Charities Act 2011 Sch 2 para 4(1). As to the power to delegate his functions see Sch 2 para 3; and PARA 301.
4 Charities Act 2011 Sch 2 para 4(2). As to the Consolidated Fund see **CONSTITUTIONAL AND ADMINISTRATIVE LAW** vol 20 (2014) PARA 480 et seq; **PARLIAMENT** vol 78 (2010) PARAS 1028–1031.

7. CHARITY REGISTRATION; LOCAL AUTHORITY FUNCTIONS

(1) REGISTRATION OF CHARITIES

(i) Obligation to Register

307. The register. The Charities Act 2011 makes provision for a register of charities[1]. It is the duty of the Charity Commission to continue to keep the register[2], in which every charity must be entered[3] apart from the following[4]: (1) exempt charities[5]; (2) charities which are specifically excepted[6]; and (3) charities whose gross income does not exceed £5,000[7]. A qualifying excepted charity must be registered in the register if it so requests[8]; and a charity voluntarily so registered must be removed from the register if it so requests[9]. The register must contain the name of every registered charity and CIO[10] and such other particulars of, and such other information relating to, every such charity as the Commission thinks fit[11]. An institution which the Commission no longer considers is a charity must be removed from the register[12]; if the removal is due to any change in its trusts, the removal has effect from the date of the change[13]. A charity which ceases to exist or does not operate must also be removed[14]. The register, including entries cancelled on removal of an institution, must be kept open to public inspection at all reasonable times[15], and copies or particulars of the trusts of a registered charity or the constitution of a CIO, as supplied to the Commission, must be kept by them so long as it remains registered and must be open to public inspection at all reasonable times[16]. Where any information contained in the register is not in documentary form, it must be made available for public inspection in legible form at all reasonable times[17].

The Commission must, on request, furnish any person with copies of, or extracts from, any document in its possession which is for the time being open to inspection[18].

1 See the Charities Act 2011 s 29.
2 See the Charities Act 2011 s 29(1). The Commission must keep the register in such manner as its think fit: s 29(2). As to the Charity Commission see PARAS 543–578.
3 Charities Act 2011 s 30(1).
4 Charities Act 2011 s 30(2).
5 Charities Act 2011 s 30(2)(a). As to such charities see PARAS 308, 318–320.
6 See the Charities Act 2011 s 30(2)(b), (c); and PARA 308.
7 Charities Act 2011 s 30(2)(d). The Minister may by order substitute a different sum for the sum for the time being specified, but only if he considers it expedient to do so in consequence of changes in the value of money or with a view to extending the scope of the exception from registration: see s 32(1)(b), (2)(b). At the date at which this volume states the law, no such order had been made. Note that a charitable incorporated organisation (CIO) with an income of less than £5,000 can register. As to CIOs see PARA 226 et seq.
8 See the Charities Act 2011 s 30(3)(a), (b). Section 30(3)(a) ceases to have effect on a day to be appointed: see PARA 308 note 2.
9 Charities Act 2011 s 34(3).
10 The Charities Act 2011 s 29(2) is applied with modifications to CIOs by the Charitable Incorporated Organisations (General) Regulations 2012, SI 2012/3012, reg 5.
11 Charities Act 2011 s 29(2).
12 Charities Act 2011 s 34(1)(a).
13 Charities Act 2011 s 34(2).
14 Charities Act 2011 s 34(1)(b).
15 Charities Act 2011 s 38(1). If the Commission so determines, this will not apply to any particular information contained in the register and specified in the determination: s 38(3).

An appeal against a decision of the Commission not to make such a determination lies to the Tribunal at the instance of the Attorney General, the charity trustees of the charity to which the information relates, the charity itself (if a body corporate), or any other person who is or may be affected by the decision: s 319(2), Sch 6 Table Cols 1, 2. The Tribunal has the power to quash the decision and, if appropriate, remit the matter to the Commission: Sch 6 Table Col 3. As to the meaning of 'person who is or may be affected' within the meaning of Sch 6 see PARA 317 note 8. As to the Attorney General see PARAS 589, 596, 605 et seq; and **CONSTITUTIONAL AND ADMINISTRATIVE LAW** vol 20 (2014) PARA 273 et seq.

16 Charities Act 2011 s 38(4); applied with modifications to charitable incorporated organisations (CIOs) (see note 10). However, a person is not required to supply the Commission with copies of schemes for the administration of a charity made otherwise than by the court, or to notify the Commission of any change made with respect to a registered charity by such a scheme, or require a person, if he refers the Commission to a document or copy already in the possession of the Commission, to supply a further copy of the document: s 35(4). But where a copy of any such document relating to a registered charity is in the possession of the Commission, a copy of it must be open to inspection under s 38(4) as if supplied to the Commission: s 38(5).

17 Charities Act 2011 s 38(2).

18 Charities Act 2011 s 18. As to the meaning of 'document' see PARA 263 note 2. As to the fees payable see the Charities Act 2011 s 19; the Charity Commissioners' Fees (Copies and Extracts) Regulations 1992, SI 1992/2986; and PARA 557.

308. Charities not obliged to be registered. The categories of charities which are not required to be registered are:

(1) exempt charities[1];

(2) until a day to be appointed[2], any charity which for the time being is permanently or temporarily excepted by order of the Charity Commission[3], or by regulations[4] made by the Minister, which complies with any conditions of the exception and whose gross income[5] does not exceed £100,000[6]; and

(3) any charity whose gross income does not exceed £5,000[7].

1 Charities Act 2011 s 30(2)(a). As to exempt charities see PARAS 318–320.

2 The relevant provisions of the Charities Act 2011, namely ss 30(2)(b), (c), (3)(a), 31, 32(1)(a), (2)(a), (3), 33 cease to have effect on such day as the Minister may by order appoint: s 33. As to the Minister see PARA 586. At the date at which this volume states the law, no such order had been made.

3 As to the Charity Commission see PARAS 543–578.

4 Such regulations must be made under the Charities Act 2011 s 30(2)(c) as are necessary to secure that any institution ceasing to be an exempt charity by virtue of an order under s 23 is excepted under s 30(2)(c), subject to compliance with any conditions of the exception and the financial limit mentioned in that provision: s 31(3). No regulations may be made under s 30(2)(c) so as to except on or after 31 January 2009 any charity that was not excepted immediately before that day: s 31(2). But this does not prevent regulations made before that date, and taking effect as made under that provision, from being varied or revoked: s 31(5).

5 Gross income is construed, in relation to a particular time, as a reference to the charity's gross income in its financial year immediately preceding that time or, if the Charity Commission so determines, as a reference to the amount which the Commission estimates to be the likely amount of the charity's gross income in such financial year of the charity as is specified in the determination: Charities Act 2011 s 30(4).

In relation to the gross income limit, the Minister may by order substitute a different sum for the sum for the time being specified, but only if he considers it expedient to do so with a view to reducing the scope of the exception from registration: s 32(1)(b), (2)(b). At the date at which this volume states the law, no such order had been made.

6 See the Charities Act 2011 s 30(2)(b)–(c). This provision, with the following provisions described in this note, ceases to have effect on a day to be appointed: see note 2.

Such charities are referred to as 'excepted charities'. See also *Excepted Charities* (Charity Commission, June 2014) (available, at the date at which this volume states the law, on the government website). As to the Charity Commission's publications see PARA 547.

No order may be made under the Charities Act 2011 s 30(2)(b) so as to except on or after 31 January 2009 any charity that was not excepted immediately before that day: s 31(1). But this does not prevent an order which was made before that date, and took effect as made under that provision, from being varied or revoked: s 31(4).

Note that these charities are not necessarily excepted from other obligations under the Charities Act 2011.

Statutory instruments have been made excepting certain charities or types of charity from registration: see the Charities (Exception of Voluntary Schools from Registration) Regulations 1960, SI 1960/2366; the Charities (Exception of Certain Charities for Boy Scouts and Girl Guides from Registration) Regulations 1961, SI 1961/1044; the Charities (Exception from Registration and Accounts) Regulations 1965, SI 1965/1056; the Charities (Exception of Universities from Registration) Regulations 1966, SI 1966/965 (amended by SI 2012/3012); the Charities (Exception from Registration) Regulations 1996, SI 1996/180 (amended by SI 2001/260, SI 2002/1598, SI 2007/2655, SI 2012/1734, SI 2012/3012, SI 2014/242); the Charities Act 1993 (Exception from Registration) Regulations 2008, SI 2008/3268 (amended by SI 2011/1725, SI 2012/3012); and the Charities (Exception from Registration) Regulations 2010, SI 2010/502 (amended by SI 2012/3012). In other cases charities have been excepted individually by order: see eg the *Report of the Charity Commissioners for England and Wales for 1963* (HC Paper (1963–64) no 298) p 10 (Roman Catholic Church and Church of Wales charities).

7 Charities Act 2011 s 30(2)(d). The Charity Commission may still take regulatory action in regard to a charity which falls below the income threshold: see eg *Operational Compliance Report: House the Homeless* (Charity Commission, October 2014) (available, at the date at which this volume states the law, on the government website). As to the Charity Commission's publications see PARA 547.

309. Duty to apply for registration. Where a charity required to be registered[1] is not registered, it is the duty of the charity trustees[2] to apply for it to be registered and to supply the Charity Commission with the required documents and information[3]. The required documents and information are: (1) copies of the charity's trusts[4] or, if they are not set out in any extant document, particulars of them[5]; (2) such other documents or information as may be prescribed by regulations made by the Minister[6]; and (3) such other documents or information as the Commission may require for the purposes of the application[7].

Any person not fulfilling these duties may be required by order of the Commission to make good the default[8].

1 Ie by virtue of the Charities Act 2011 s 30(1); see PARA 307.
2 As to the meaning of 'charity trustees' see PARA 255.
3 Charities Act 2011 s 35(1). As to the Charity Commission see PARAS 543–578.
4 As to the meaning of 'trusts' see PARA 218 note 5.
5 Charities Act 2011 s 35(2)(a).
6 Charities Act 2011 s 35(2)(b). At the date at which this volume states the law, no regulations have been made or take effect under this provision.
7 Charities Act 2011 s 35(2)(c).
8 See the Charities Act 2011 s 335; and PARA 556. Disobedience to such an order attracts the same sanctions as a contempt of court: see s 336; and PARA 556.

310. Continuing duty to supply information. Where an institution is for the time being registered, it is the duty of the charity trustees[1], or the last charity trustees, to notify the Charity Commission[2] if the institution[3] ceases to exist, or if there is any change in its trusts[4] or in the particulars of it entered in the register, and, so far as appropriate, must supply particulars of any such change and copies of any new trusts or alterations to the trusts[5]. Any person failing to do so may be required by order to make good the default[6].

In the case of a charitable incorporated organisation ('CIO')[7], the charity trustees must within 28 days notify the Commission if there is any change in the particulars of the CIO entered in the register; and so far as appropriate, supply the Commission with particulars of any such change[8].

1 As to the meaning of 'charity trustees' see PARA 255.
2 As to the Charity Commission see PARAS 543–578.
3 As to the meaning of 'institution' see PARA 1.
4 As to the meaning of 'trusts' see PARA 218 note 5.
5 Charities Act 2011 s 35(3). They need not, however, supply copies of schemes made otherwise than by the court, or copies of documents already in the possession of the Commission, or notify the Commission of any change made with respect to a registered charity by such a scheme: see s 35(4); and PARA 307.

It is submitted that the duty is not applicable in a case where the trusts have been modified under ss 267–279, 282–284, or 288 (see PARAS 218–220, 223–224), for the Commission will then have all the relevant information. These provisions do not contain a provision specifically excluding s 35(3); if, however, a resolution of the trustees under these provisions can be construed as a 'scheme for the administration of a charity' the duty would be excluded by s 35(4)(a).
6 See the Charities Act 2011 s 335; and PARA 556.
7 As to charitable incorporated organisations see PARA 226 et seq.
8 Charities Act 2011 s 35(3) (substituted for this purpose by the Charitable Incorporated Organisations (General) Regulations 2012, SI 2012/3012, reg 6).

311. Publication of registered charity's status. Where a charity[1] is a registered charity whose gross income[2] in its last financial year[3] exceeded £10,000[4], the fact that it is a registered charity must be stated in legible characters[5]:

(1) in all notices, advertisements and other documents issued by or on behalf of the charity and soliciting money or other property for the benefit of the charity[6];
(2) in all bills of exchange, promissory notes, endorsements, cheques and orders for money or goods purporting to be signed on behalf of the charity[7]; and
(3) in all bills rendered by the charity and in all its invoices, receipts and letters of credit[8].

If any person[9] issues or authorises the issue of any document falling within head (1) or (3) above or signs any document falling within head (2) above, and in either case the fact that the charity is a registered charity is not stated[10], he is guilty of an offence[11]. However, no proceedings for such an offence may be instituted except by or with the consent of the Director of Public Prosecutions[12].

1 As to the meaning of 'charity' see PARA 1.
2 As to the meaning of 'gross income' see PARA 218 note 2.
3 As to the meaning of 'financial year' see PARA 218 note 3.
4 Charities Act 2011 s 39(1). The Minister may by order substitute a different sum for the sum for the time being specified: s 40. At the date at which this volume states the law, no such order had been made.
5 Charities Act 2011 s 39(2). The statement must be in English, except that, in the case of a document which is otherwise wholly in Welsh, the statement may be in Welsh if it consists of or includes the words 'elusen cofrestredig' (the Welsh equivalent of 'registered charity'): s 39(3).
6 Charities Act 2011 s 39(2)(a). This provision has effect whether the solicitation is express or implied, and whether the money or other property is to be given for any consideration or not: s 39(4).
7 Charities Act 2011 s 39(2)(b).
8 Charities Act 2011 s 39(2)(c). See also s 194(1); and PARA 241.
9 'Person' includes a body of persons corporate or unincorporate: Interpretation Act 1978 s 5, Sch 1. As to offences by corporate bodies see the Charities Act 2011 s 346; and PARA 588.
10 Ie the statement as required by the Charities Act 2011 s 39(2): see the text and notes 5–8.
11 Charities Act 2011 s 41(1), (2). A person guilty of such an offence is liable on summary conviction to a fine not exceeding level 3 on the standard scale: s 41(3). As to the standard scale see **SENTENCING AND DISPOSITION OF OFFENDERS** vol 92 (2010) PARA 142.
12 Charities Act 2011 s 345(1), (2)(a). As to the Director of Public Prosecutions see **CRIMINAL PROCEDURE** vol 27 (2010) PARA 23.

312. Direction for change of name of charity. In certain circumstances the Charity Commission[1] may give a direction to the charity trustees[2] requiring the name of the charity to be changed to such other name as the charity trustees may determine with the approval of the Commission[3]. The circumstances specified are if[4]:

(1) it is a registered charity and its name (the 'registered name') (a) is the same as, or (b) is in the opinion of the Commission too like, the name, at the time when the registered name was entered in the register in respect of the charity, of any other charity (whether registered or not)[5];

(2) the name[6] of the charity is in the opinion of the Commission likely to mislead the public as to the true nature of (a) the purposes of the charity as set out in its trusts, or (b) the activities which the charity carries on under its trusts in pursuit of those purposes[7];

(3) the name[8] of the charity includes any word or expression for the time being specified in regulations made by the Minister[9] and the inclusion in its name of that word or expression is in the opinion of the Commission likely to mislead the public in any respect as to the status of the charity[10];

(4) the name[11] of the charity is in the opinion of the Commission likely to give the impression that the charity is connected in some way with Her Majesty's government or any local authority, or with any other body of persons or any individual, when it is not so connected[12]; or

(5) the name of the charity is in the opinion of the Commission offensive[13].

A change of name by a charity under these provisions does not affect any rights or obligations of the charity; and any legal proceedings that might have been continued or commenced by or against it in its former name may be continued or commenced by or against it in its new name[14].

An appeal against a direction under these provisions requiring the name of a charity to be changed lies to the Tribunal at the instance of the Attorney General[15], the charity trustees of the charity to which the direction relates, the charity itself (if a body corporate) or any other person who is or may be affected by the direction[16]. The Tribunal has the power to quash the direction and, if appropriate, remit the matter to the Commission, as well as the power to substitute for the direction any other direction which could have been given by the Commission[17].

Until a day to be appointed, these provisions do not apply to an exempt charity[18].

1 As to the Charity Commission see PARAS 543–578.

2 Charities Act 2011 s 42(5). For these purposes, any reference to charity trustees in relation to a charity which is a company, is to be read as a reference to the directors of the company: s 45(1). As to a direction to change name of a charitable company see PARA 313. As to the meaning of 'charity trustees' generally see PARA 255.

3 Charities Act 2011 s 42(1). On receiving such a direction the charity trustees must give effect to it notwithstanding anything in the trusts of the charity, and, having done so, must without delay notify the Commission of the charity's new name and of the date on which the change occurred: s 43(1), (2). This is without prejudice to s 35(3) (see PARA 310): s 43(3).

4 Charities Act 2011 s 42(2).

5 Charities Act 2011 s 42(2)(a). Any direction on this ground must be given within 12 months of the time when the registered name was entered in the register in respect of the charity: s 42(3). For the purposes of this provision minor variations in names are to be disregarded.

6 Ie in relation to a registered charity the name by which it is registered: Charities Act 2011 s 42(4).

7 Charities Act 2011 s 42(2)(b).

8 See note 6.

9 As to the making of regulations see the Charities Act 2011 s 347; and PARA 590. As to the Minister see PARA 586.

The following are specified for this purpose: Assurance, Authority, Bank, Benevolent, British, Building Society, Charitable incorporated organisation, Church, Co-operative, England, English, Europe, European, Friendly Society, Grant-Maintained, Great Britain, Great British, Her Majesty, His Majesty, Industrial & Provident Society, International, Ireland, Irish, King, National, Nationwide, Northern Ireland, Northern Irish, Official, Polytechnic, Prince, Princess, Queen, Registered, Royal, Royale, Royalty, Sefydliad elusennol corfforedig, School, Scotland, Scottish, Trade Union, United Kingdom, University, Wales, Welsh, Windsor: Charities (Misleading Names) Regulations 1992, SI 1992/1901 (amended by SI 2012/3012).

10 Charities Act 2011 s 42(2)(c).

11 See note 6.

12 Charities Act 2011 s 42(2)(d).

13 Charities Act 2011 s 42(2)(e).

14 Charities Act 2011 s 44.

15 As to the Tribunal see PARA 579 et seq. As to the Attorney General see PARAS 589, 596, 605 et seq; and **CONSTITUTIONAL AND ADMINISTRATIVE LAW** vol 20 (2014) PARA 273 et seq.

16 See the Charities Act 2011 s 319(2), Sch 6 Table Cols 1, 2. As to the meaning of 'person who is or may be affected' within the meaning of Sch 6 see PARA 317 note 8.

17 See the Charities Act 2011 Sch 6 Table Col 3.

18 A transitional modification to the Charities Act 2011 s 42 is made by virtue of Sch 9 para 10, so as to exclude exempt charities other than those for whom the equivalent previous statutory provisions had not been brought into force. As to exempt charities see PARA 318 et seq.

313. Direction to change name of a charitable company. Where a direction[1] requiring the name of a charity[2] to be changed is given with respect to a charitable company, the direction must require the name of the charity to be changed by resolution of the directors of the company[3]. Where the name of such a charity is changed accordingly, the registrar of companies must[4] enter the new name on the register of companies in place of the former name[5] and issue a certificate of incorporation altered to meet the circumstances of the case[6].

1 Ie a direction under the Charities Act 2011 s 42: see PARA 312.

2 As to the meaning of 'charity' see PARA 1.

3 Charities Act 2011 s 45(2), (3). Where such a resolution of the directors is passed, the company must give notice of the change to the registrar of companies: s 45(4). As to the meaning of 'charitable company' see PARA 241 note 1.

4 Ie if satisfied that the new name complies with the requirements of the Companies Act 2006 Pt 5 (ss 53–85) (see **COMPANIES** vol 14 (2009) PARA 196 et seq): see the Charities Act 2011 s 45(5)(a).

5 Charities Act 2011 s 45(5)(a).

6 Charities Act 2011 s 45(5)(b). The change of name has effect from the date on which the altered certificate is issued: s 45(5).

(ii) Effect of, and Claims for and Objections to, Registration

314. Effect of registration. For all purposes other than rectification of the register of charities[1], any institution[2] must be conclusively presumed to have been a charity[3] at any time when it is or was on the register[4]. It has been held that the same presumption applies where a body which is not registered at a material date later becomes registered without any intervening alteration in its constitution or purposes[5].

Refusal of registration does not, however, conclusively establish that the body is not charitable[6].

However, if and for as long as an entry is in suspense, the institution is deemed not to be on the register for the purposes of this conclusive presumption[7].

1 As to the register see PARA 307 et seq.

2 As to the meaning of 'institution' see PARA 1.

3 As to the meaning of 'charity' see PARA 1.

4 Charities Act 2011 s 37(1). For examples of the application of this presumption see *Wynn v Skegness UDC* [1966] 3 All ER 336, [1967] 1 WLR 52; *Finch v Poplar Borough Council* (1967) 66 LGR 324.

5 *Re Murawski's Will Trusts, Lloyds Bank Ltd v Royal Society for the Prevention of Cruelty to Animals* [1971] 2 All ER 328, [1971] 1 WLR 707.

6 *Over Seventies Housing Association v Westminster City Council* [1974] RA 247, where refusal of registration did not prevent the body from arguing that it was a charity and therefore entitled to rating relief, though the argument in fact failed.

7 Charities Act 2011 s 37(2).

315. Objections to registration and claims for removal. Any person who is or may be affected by the registration of an institution[1] as a charity[2] or the registration of a charitable incorporated organisation ('CIO')[3] may object, on the ground that it is not a charity, to its being entered by the Charity Commission[4] in the register of charities, and if the institution is already registered any such person may apply to the Commission for it to be removed from the register on that ground[5]. Provision may be made by regulations made by the Minister[6] as to the manner in which any such objection or application is to be made, prosecuted or dealt with[7].

Questions affecting the registration of or the removal from the register of an institution may be considered afresh by the Commission, notwithstanding that they may have been determined on an appeal to the Tribunal[8], if it appears to the Commission that there has been a change of circumstances or that the decision is inconsistent with a later judicial decision[9].

1 As to the meaning of 'institution' see PARA 1.

2 As to the meaning of 'charity' see PARA 1.

3 As to charitable incorporated organisations see PARA 226 et seq.

4 As to the Charity Commission see PARAS 543–578.

5 Charities Act 2011 s 36(1); modified in relation to CIOs by the Charitable Incorporated Organisations (General) Regulations 2012, SI 2012/3012, reg 6. As to the meaning of 'person who is or may be affected' see also PARA 317 note 8.

6 As to the Minister see PARA 586.

7 Charities Act 2011 s 36(2). At the date at which this volume states the law, no such regulations had been made. The informal procedure adopted is described in the *Report of the Charity Commissioners for England and Wales for 1964* (HC Paper (1965–66) no 8) p 12. See also *R (on the application of International Peace Project 2000) v Charity Commission for England and Wales* [2009] EWHC (Admin) 3446 (application for judicial review of the Commission's failure to remove a charity from the register was refused because the alternative avenues of the informal procedures had not been explored).

8 See PARA 317. As to the Tribunal see PARA 579 et seq.

9 Charities Act 2011 s 36(5).

316. Disclosure of information to and by the Charity Commission. The Charities Act 2011 makes special provision for the disclosure of information to and by the Charity Commission[1].

Any relevant public authority may disclose information to the Commission if the disclosure is made for the purpose of enabling or assisting the Commission to discharge any of its functions[2], save that Revenue and Customs information[3] may be disclosed only if it relates to an institution, undertaking or body falling with one or more of the following categories[4]: (1) a charity[5]; (2) an institution which is established for charitable, benevolent or philanthropic purposes[6]; (3) an institution by or in respect of which a claim for tax exemption has at any time been made[7]; (4) a subsidiary undertaking of a charity[8]; and (5) a body entered in the Scottish Charity Register which is managed or controlled wholly or mainly in or from England or Wales[9].

The Charity Commission may disclose to any relevant public authority any information received by it in connection with any of its functions if the disclosure is made for the purpose of enabling or assisting the relevant public authority to discharge any of its functions or if the information so disclosed is otherwise relevant to the discharge of any of the functions of the relevant public authority[10], save that the Commission's power to disclose such information is exercisable subject to any express restriction subject to which the information was disclosed to the Commission[11].

Comparable provision to the above is made as to the disclosure of information by and to the principal regulators of exempt charities[12].

Nothing in the above provisions[13] authorises the making of a disclosure which contravenes the Data Protection Act 1998 or is prohibited by Part 1 of the Regulation of Investigatory Powers Act 2000[14].

1 See the Charities Act 2011 ss 54–59; and notes 2–14. As to the Charity Commission see PARAS 543–578. As to the disclosure of information in relation to inquiries see PARA 563.

2 Charities Act 2011 s 54(1). 'Relevant public authority' means any government department (including a Northern Ireland department), any local authority, any constable, and any other body or person discharging functions of a public nature (including a body or person discharging regulatory functions in relation to any description of activities): s 54(3).

3 'Revenue and Customs information' means information held as mentioned in the Commissioners for Revenue and Customs Act 2005 s 18(1): Charities Act 2011 s 55(4). As to Revenue and Customs see **INCOME TAXATION**.

4 Charities Act 2011 ss 54(2), 55(1).

5 Charities Act 2011 s 55(1)(a).

6 Charities Act 2011 s 55(1)(b).

7 Charities Act 2011 s 55(1)(c). 'Claim for tax exemption' means:

(1) a claim for exemption under the Income and Corporation Taxes Act 1988 s 505(1) (Charities Act 2011 s 55(5)(a));

(2) a claim under the Income Tax Act 2007 Pt 10 (Charities Act 2011 s 55(5)(b)); or

(3) a claim under the Corporation Tax Act 2010 Pt 11 if it is not (a) a claim for exemption under s 475, s 476 or s 477 (reliefs for eligible bodies and scientific research organisations), or (b) a claim made by virtue of s 490 or s 491 (application of exemptions to eligible bodies and scientific research organisations) (Charities Act 2011 s 55(5)(c)).

8 Charities Act 2011 s 55(1)(d). 'Subsidiary undertaking of a charity' means an undertaking (as defined by the Companies Act 2006 s 1161(1): see **COMPANIES** vol 14 (2009) PARA 26) in relation to which a charity is (or is to be treated as) a parent undertaking in accordance with the provisions of s 1162, Sch 7 or two or more charities would, if they were a single charity, be (or be treated as) a parent undertaking in accordance with those provisions: Charities Act 2011 s 55(2). For these purposes 'undertaking' includes a charity which is not an undertaking as defined by the Companies Act 2006 s 1161(1): Charities Act 2011 s 55(3).

9 Charities Act 2011 s 55(1)(e).

10 Charities Act 2011 s 56(1). For this purpose 'relevant public authority' has the same meaning as in note 2, but also includes any body or person discharging functions of a public nature (including a body or person discharging regulatory functions in relation to any description of activities) in a country or territory outside the United Kingdom: s 56(4). As to the meaning of the United Kingdom see PARA 189.

11 Charities Act 2011 s 56(2), (3). This restriction does not apply in relation to Revenue and Customs information disclosed to the Commission under s 54(1), but any such information may not be further disclosed (whether under s 56(1) or otherwise) except with the consent of the Commissioners for Her Majesty's Revenue and Customs: ss 56(2), 57(1), (2), (7). As to the Commissioners for Her Majesty's Revenue and Customs see **INCOME TAXATION** vol 58 (2014) PARA 33.

Any responsible person who discloses information in contravention of s 57(2) is guilty of an offence and liable, on summary conviction, to imprisonment for a term not exceeding 6 months or to a fine not exceeding the statutory maximum or both or, on conviction on indictment, to imprisonment for a term not exceeding two years or to a fine or both: s 57(4); modified by Sch 9 para 14, pending the commencement of the Criminal Justice Act 2003 s 154(1), which increases the sentencing powers of magistrates. However, it is a defence for a responsible person charged with such an offence to prove that he reasonably believed that the disclosure was lawful or that the information had already and lawfully been made available to the public: Charities Act 2011 s 57(5). 'Responsible person' means a person who is or was a member of the Charity Commission, a member of the staff of the Commission, a person acting on behalf of the Commission or a member of the staff of the Commission, or a member of a committee established by the Commission: s 57(8). As to the statutory maximum see SENTENCING AND DISPOSITION OF OFFENDERS vol 92 (2010) PARA 140.

12 See the Charities Act 2011 s 58; and PARA 321.

13 Or, as from the date on which the Charities Act 2011 s 58 takes effect, in those provisions as applied by s 58(1)–(3): see Sch 9 para 15; see PARA 321.

14 Charities Act 2011 s 59. As to the Data Protection Act 1998 see CONFIDENCE AND INFORMATIONAL PRIVACY. As to the Regulation of Investigatory Powers Act 2000 Pt 1 (ss 1–25) see POLICE AND INVESTIGATORY POWERS vol 84A (2013) PARA 657 et seq.

317. Appeals relating to registration. An appeal against any decision of the Charity Commission[1] to enter or not to enter an institution[2] in the register of charities[3], or to remove or not to remove an institution from the register, lies to the Tribunal[4] at the instance of the Attorney General[5], or the persons who are or claim to be the charity trustees[6] of the institution, the institution itself if a body corporate[7], or any other person who is or may be affected by the decision[8].

If the Commission decides to enter an institution in the register[9] or not to remove one from the register[10], or to restore a charitable incorporated organisation to the register[11], and there is an appeal to the Tribunal against that decision, then until it is known whether the decision is to stand or not, the entry in the register must be maintained, but must be in suspense and marked as such[12]. While the entry is in suspense, the institution is deemed not to be on the register for the purposes of the conclusive presumption as to charitable status[13] which arises from the fact of registration[14].

The Tribunal has the power to quash the order in whole or in part and (if appropriate) remit the matter to the Commission or direct the Commission to rectify the register[15].

1 As to the Charity Commission see PARAS 543–578.

2 As to the meaning of 'institution' see PARA 1.

3 Ie an appeal against a decision of the Commission under the Charities Act 2011 s 30, 34 (see PARA 307 et seq).

4 As to the Tribunal see PARA 579 et seq.

5 Charities Act 2011 s 319(2). As to the Attorney General see PARAS 589, 596, 605 et seq; and CONSTITUTIONAL AND ADMINISTRATIVE LAW vol 20 (2014) PARA 273 et seq.

6 As to the meaning of 'charity trustees' see PARA 255.

7 Previously, where the institution was a corporate body it could not itself appeal, but this point was not taken in the first two appeals to be heard: *Incorporated Council of Law Reporting for England and Wales v A-G* [1972] Ch 73, [1971] 3 All ER 1029, CA; *Construction Industry Training Board v A-G* [1973] Ch 173, [1972] 2 All ER 1339, CA (decided under earlier legislation).

8 Charities Act 2011 s 319(2), Sch 6 Table Cols 1, 2. A person to whom a decision not to remove the charity is addressed is a person affected by the decision: *Lasper v Charity Commission for England and Wales (Strike-out hearing)* (2010) First-tier Tribunal, General Regulatory Chamber (Charity), 1 November, para 3.10.

See also, in relation to the meaning of 'person who is or may be affected' in the Charities Act 2011 Sch 6 (though in relation to appeal under a different provision) *Colman v Charity Commission for England and Wales* (2014) First-tier Tribunal, General Regulatory Chamber (Charity), 17 April, para 18: 'in order for a person to be affected ... there must be an identifiable impact upon that person's legal rights at the time the order is made so as to merit a right of redress in the Tribunal. In order to be a person who "may" be affected ... there would have to be an identifiable impact on that person's legal rights which is sufficiently likely to occur to make it fair to allow them a right of appeal'; and *Nicholson v Charity Commission for England and Wales* (2014) First-tier Tribunal, General Regulatory Chamber (Charity), 2 September.

9 Charities Act 2011 s 36(3)(a).

10 Charities Act 2011 s 36(3)(b).
11 Charities Act 2011 s 36(3)(c) (added for this purpose by SI 2012/3012). As to charitable incorporated organisations (CIOs) see PARA 226 et seq.
12 See the Charities Act 2011 s 36(3), (4).
13 As to this presumption see the Charities Act 2011 s 37(1); and PARA 314.
14 Charities Act 2011 s 37(2). By analogy with *Re Murawski's Will Trusts, Lloyds Bank Ltd v Royal Society for the Prevention of Cruelty to Animals* [1971] 2 All ER 328, [1971] 1 WLR 707, the statutory presumption would probably be applied retrospectively if it was ultimately determined that the decision was to stand.
15 Charities Act 2011 Sch 6 Table Col 3.

(iii) Exempt Charities

318. Exempt charities. Certain charities[1] are largely exempt from the Charity Commission's jurisdiction[2]. They are known as 'exempt charities' for the purposes of the Charities Act 2011[3], and are not required to be entered in the register of charities[4].

The Act describes the categories of exempt charities[5], and further gives power to the Minister[6] to make by order such amendments to those categories as he considers appropriate for securing: (1) that (so far as they are charities) institutions of a particular description become or (as the case may be) cease to be exempt charities; (2) that (so far as it is a charity) a particular institution becomes or (as the case may be) ceases to be an exempt charity[7].

The Minister may also make orders for removing from the list of exempt charities an institution that has ceased to exist[8].

The provision for increased regulation of exempt charities introduced by the Charities Act 2006 and maintained by the Charities Act 2011[9] means that a number of charities previously exempt will lose their exemption and be subject to regulation by the Charity Commission[10].

1 The Charities Act 2011 creates categories of exempt charities (see note 5): s 22(1), Sch 3. Additionally, the Act recognises that other enactments may create exempt charities: s 22(2).
2 As to the Charity Commission see PARAS 543–578.
3 See the Charities Act 2011 s 22(1). Transitional modifications to the Charities Act 2011 ss 99, 103 (relating to common investment and common deposit schemes and funds) are made by Sch 9 para 2, so that such funds, where they allow investment only by exempt charities, are themselves exempt charities (see PARAS 426, 427). Specified provisions as to the preparation of accounts do not apply to an exempt charity: ss 143, 160(1), (3), 167 (see PARAS 343, 361, 367, 371).
4 See the Charities Act 2011 s 30(2)(a); and PARA 308.
5 See the Charities Act 2011 Sch 3. The exempt charities are:
   (1) Any institution which, if the Charities Act 1960 had not been passed, would be exempted from the powers and jurisdiction, under the Charitable Trusts Acts 1853 to 1939 (repealed), of the Charity Commissioners (now the Charity Commission) or Minister of Education (apart from any power of the Commissioners or Minister to apply those Acts in whole or in part to charities otherwise exempt) by the terms of any enactment not contained in those Acts other than the Places of Worship Registration Act 1855 s 9 (see ECCLESIASTICAL LAW): Charities Act 2011 Sch 3 para 1(1). This does not include (a) any Investment Fund or Deposit Fund within the meaning of the Church Funds Investment Measure 1958, (b) any investment fund or deposit fund within the meaning of the Methodist Church Funds Act 1960, or (c) the representative body of the Welsh Church or property administered by it: Charities Act 2011 Sch 3 para 1(2). Transitional modifications to Sch 3 para 1(2) have the effect of removing heads (a) and (b) until a day to be appointed: Sch 9 para 3. At the date at which this volume states the law, no such day had been appointed.
   (2) The universities of Oxford, Cambridge, London, Durham, Newcastle and Manchester; King's College London and Queen Mary and Westfield College in the University of London: Sch 3 paras 2, 3.
   (3) Any university (including the Open University), university college or institution in

England connected with it declared by Order in Council to be an exempt charity, except any college in the University of Oxford, any college or hall in the University of Cambridge or Durham, and any students' union: see Sch 3 para 4.

(4) An English higher education corporation (see EDUCATION vol 36 (2011) PARA 835): see Sch 3 para 5.

(5) A successor company to a higher education corporation: Sch 3 para 6.

(6) A further education corporation (see EDUCATION vol 36 (2011) PARA 729): Sch 3 para 7.

(7) A qualifying academy proprietor (see the Academies Act 2010 s 12(2); and EDUCATION vol 35 (2011) PARA 513): Charities Act 2011 Sch 3 para 8.

(8) The governing body of any foundation, voluntary or foundation special school (see EDUCATION vol 35 (2011) PARA 176 et seq): Charities Act 2011 Sch 3 para 9.

(9) Any foundation body established under the School Standards and Framework Act 1998 s 21 (see EDUCATION vol 35 (2011) PARA 108): Charities Act 2011 Sch 3 para 10.

(10) A sixth form college corporation within the meaning of the Further and Higher Education Act 1992 (see EDUCATION vol 36 (2011) PARA 758): Charities Act 2011 Sch 3 para 11.

(11) The Boards of Trustees of the Victoria and Albert Museum, the Science Museum, the Armouries, the Royal Botanic Gardens, Kew, the National Museums and Galleries on Merseyside, the trustees of the British Museum, the trustees of the Natural History Museum, the National Gallery, the Tate Gallery, the National Portrait Gallery and the Wallace Collection; the trustees of the Imperial War Museum, the trustees of the National Maritime Museum, and the British Library Board: Charities Act 2011 Sch 3 paras 12–25.

(12) Any institution administered by or on behalf of an institution included in heads (1)–(7), (10)–(11), except any college in the University of Oxford, or, any college or hall in the University of Cambridge or Durham, which is administered by or on behalf of the University; and any students' union: Sch 3 para 28(1), (2).

(13) Any institution which is administered by or on behalf of a body included in head (9) or (10) and established for the general purposes of, or for any special purpose of or in connection with, that body or any foundation, voluntary or foundation special school or schools: Sch 3 para 28(3).

(14) Any registered society within the meaning of the Co-operative and Community Benefit Societies and Credit Unions Act 2014) (see FINANCIAL SERVICES AND INSTITUTIONS vol 50 (2008) PARA 2395) which is also a non-profit registered provider of social housing: Charities Act 2011 Sch 3 para 26.

(15) Any registered society within the meaning of the Co-operative and Community Benefit Societies and Credit Unions Act 2014) (see FINANCIAL SERVICES AND INSTITUTIONS vol 50 (2008) PARA 2395) which is also registered in the register of social landlords under the Housing Act 1996 Pt 1: Charities Act 2011 Sch 3 para 27.

6 As to the Minister see PARA 586.

7 Charities Act 2011 s 23(1). Such an order may only be made if the Minister is satisfied that the order is desirable in the interests of ensuring appropriate or effective regulation of the charities or charity concerned in connection with compliance by the charity trustees of the charities or charity with their legal obligations in exercising control and management of the administration of the charities or charity: s 23(2). The Minister may by order make such amendments or other modifications of any enactment as he considers appropriate in connection with charities of a particular description becoming, or ceasing to be, exempt charities, or a particular charity becoming, or ceasing to be, an exempt charity, by virtue of these provisions: s 23(3).

The following Orders in Council were made under the Charities Act 1960 Sch 2 para (c) (repealed) or under the Charities Act 1993 Sch 2 para (c) (repealed) and now take effect under the Charities Act 2011 Sch 3 para 4. They designate numerous universities and institutions as exempt charities: see the Exempt Charities Order 1962, SI 1962/1343; the Exempt Charities Order 1965, SI 1965/1715; the Exempt Charities Order 1966, SI 1966/1460; the Exempt Charities Order 1967, SI 1967/821; the Exempt Charities Order 1969, SI 1969/1496; the Exempt Charities Order 1978, SI 1978/453; the Exempt Charities Order 1982, SI 1982/1661; the Exempt Charities Order 1983, SI 1983/1516; the Exempt Charities Order 1984, SI 1984/1976; the Exempt Charities Order 1987, SI 1987/1823; the Exempt Charities Order 1989, SI 1989/2394; the Exempt Charities Order 1993, SI 1993/2359; the Exempt Charities Order 1994, SI 1994/1905; the Exempt Charities (No 2) Order 1994, SI 1994/2956; the Exempt Charities Order 1995, SI 1995/2998; the Exempt Charities Order 1996, SI 1996/1637; the Exempt Charities (No 2) Order 1996, SI 1996/1932; the Exempt Charities (No 3) Order 1996, SI 1996/1933; the Exempt Charities Order 1999, SI 1999/3139; the Exempt

Charities Order 2000, SI 2000/1826; the Exempt Charities Order 2002, SI 2002/1626; the Exempt Charities Order 2003, SI 2003/1881; the Exempt Charities Order 2004, SI 2004/1995; the Exempt Charities Order 2006, SI 2006/1452; the Exempt Charities Order 2007, SI 2007/630; the Exempt Charities (No 2) Order 2007, SI 2007/1364; the Exempt Charities (No 3) Order 2007, SI 2007/2919; and the Exempt Charities Order 2011, SI 2011/1692. The Exempt Charities Order 2015, SI 2015/210, has been made under the Charities Act 2011 Sch 3 para 4(1)(a), declaring that with effect from 12 February 2015 the University of St Mark and St John is an exempt charity for the purposes of that Act.

8 Charities Act 2011 s 24. See note 7.

9 See PARA 319.

10 See *CC23: Exempt charities* (Charity Commission, September 2013) (available, at the date at which this volume states the law, on the government website). As to the Charity Commission's publications see PARA 547.

319. Increased regulation of exempt charities. The Charities Act 2006 contained provisions for the increased regulation of specified exempt charities[1] under the Act, and these provisions are maintained and developed by the Charities Act 2011[2]. These provide that such a charity is no longer exempt from: (1) the power of the Charity Commission to require a charity's name to be changed[3]; (2) the power of the Commission to institute inquiries with regard to charities, but only where this has been requested by the charity's principal regulator[4]; (3) the power of the Commission to call for documents and search records[5]; (4) the powers of the Commission under its concurrent jurisdiction with the High Court exercisable at the application of the Attorney General or applicants relating to a charity whose gross annual income does not exceed £500[6]; (5) the need to secure the consent of the court or Commission for a scheme providing for expenditure on promoting any Parliamentary Bill[7]; (6) the power of the Commission to act for the protection of charities[8]; (7) the power of the Commission to give directions about dormant bank accounts[9]; (8) charity proceedings[10]; and (9) the power of the Commission to order a person acting as charity trustee[11] while disqualified to repay sums received from a charity[12].

When the provisions are fully in force, all exempt charities must have a principal regulator[13]; those charities previously exempt which have no principal regulator will no longer be exempt and will be regulated by the Charity Commission[14].

1 The specified exempt charities were those specified in the Charities Act 2006 (Commencement No 7, Transitional and Transitory Provisions and Savings) Order 2010, SI 2010/503; and the Charities Act 2006 (Commencement No 8, Transitional Provisions and Savings) Order 2011, SI 2011/1728.

2 The Charities Act 2006 Sch 5 (repealed) modified various provisions of the Act so that the exemption from them which applied to exempt charities was removed for those charities or classes of charities which were so specified. With the consolidation of charities legislation into the Charities Act 2011, the exemptions which apply to exempt charities are now contained within or by reference to the specific provisions. This increased regulation takes effect in phases determined by the classes of charity for which they are brought into force, or were brought into force under the repealed provisions of the Charities Act 2006. See further *CC23: Exempt charities* (Charity Commission, September 2013) (available, at the date at which this volume states the law, on the government website). As to the Charity Commission see PARAS 543–578. As to the Charity Commission's publications see PARA 547.

3 Ie under the Charities Act 2011 s 42; see PARA 312.

4 Ie under the Charities Act 2011 ss 46, 47; see PARA 559.

5 Ie under the Charities Act 2011 ss 52, 53; see PARA 562.

6 Ie under the Charities Act 2011 ss 69, 70; see PARA 189. As to the Attorney General see PARAS 589, 596, 605 et seq; and CONSTITUTIONAL AND ADMINISTRATIVE LAW vol 20 (2014) PARA 273 et seq.

7 Ie under the Charities Act 2011 s 74(1), (2); see PARA 331.

8 Ie under the Charities Act 2011 ss 76, 77, 80–83; see PARAS 567, 572.

9 Ie under the Charities Act 2011 s 107; see PARA 575.
10 Ie under the Charities Act 2011 s 115; see PARAS 592–595.
11 As to the meaning of 'charity trustees' see PARA 255.
12 Ie under the Charities Act 2011 s 183; see PARA 277.
13 As to the principal regulators see PARA 320.
14 See further *CC23: Exempt charities* (Charity Commission, September 2013).

320. Exempt charities: principal regulators. The Minister[1] may make regulations prescribing any body or Minister of the Crown as the principal regulator of an exempt charity[2]. Where a principal regulator has been appointed in relation to an exempt charity[3], the following provisions apply. The principal regulator must do all that it or he reasonably can to meet the compliance objective: that is, to promote compliance by the charity trustees with their legal obligations in exercising control and management of the administration of the charity[4]. The Charity Commission[5] must consult the charity's principal regulator before exercising any specific power in relation to an exempt charity[6].

1 As to the Minister see PARA 586.
2 See the Charities Act 2011 s 25. As to the meaning of 'exempt charity see PARA 318. Such regulations may make such amendments or other modifications of any enactment as the Minister considers appropriate for the purpose of facilitating, or otherwise in connection with, the discharge by a principal regulator of its or his duty: s 27(1), (2).
3 The provisions for increased regulation of exempt charities take effect as they are brought into force in relation to specific charities or classes of charity: see PARAS 318, 319.
For persons prescribed as principal regulators of exempt charities see the Charities Act 2006 (Principal Regulators of Exempt Charities) Regulations 2010, SI 2010/501; the Charities Act 2006 (Principal Regulators of Exempt Charities) Regulations 2011, SI 2011/1726; the Charities Act 2006 (Principal Regulators of Exempt Charities) (No 2) Regulations 2011, SI 2011/1727; and the Charities Act 2011 (Principal Regulators of Exempt Charities) Regulations 2013, SI 2013/1764.
At the date at which this volumes states the law, few categories of exempt charity remain for which no principal regulator has been appointed. These are: community benefit societies (see PARAS 245, 318 note 5); any investment fund or deposit fund within the meaning of the Church Funds Investment Measure 1958 or the Methodist Church Funds Act 1960 (see PARA 318 note 5); common investment or deposit funds that are exempt charities (see PARA 318 note 3). See further *CC23: Exempt charities* (Charity Commission, September 2013) Annex 1 (available, at the date at which this volume states the law, on the government website). As to the Charity Commission's publications see PARA 547.
4 Charities Act 2011 s 26(1)–(3). As to the meaning of 'charity trustees' see PARA 255.
5 As to the Charity Commission see PARAS 543–578.
6 Charities Act 2011 s 28.

321. Disclosure of information to and by principal regulators of exempt charities. The Charities Act 2011 makes provision for the disclosure of information to and by the principal regulators of exempt charities[1].

Any relevant public authority may disclose information to the principal regulator of an exempt charity if the disclosure is made for the purpose of enabling or assisting the regulator to discharge any of its functions[2], save that Revenue and Customs information[3] may be disclosed only if it relates to the exempt charity in relation to which the principal regulator has functions as such or a subsidiary undertaking of the exempt charity[4].

The principal regulator of an exempt charity may disclose to any relevant public authority any information received by it in connection with any of its functions if the disclosure is made for the purpose of enabling or assisting the relevant public authority to discharge any of its functions or if the information so disclosed is otherwise relevant to the discharge of any of the functions of the relevant public authority[5], save that the power of the principal regulator to disclose such information is exercisable subject to any express restriction subject to which the information was disclosed to him or it[6].

Nothing in the above provisions authorises the making of a disclosure which contravenes the Data Protection Act 1998 or is prohibited by Part 1 of the Regulation of Investigatory Powers Act 2000[7].

1 The Charities Act 2011 ss 54–57 apply as modified by s 58: see s 58(1); and notes 2–7. As to the meaning of 'exempt charity' see PARA 318. 'Principal regulator', in relation to an exempt charity, means the Minister or body prescribed as principal regulator (see PARA 320): s 25.

2 Charities Act 2011 ss 54(1), 58(1), (2). As to the meaning of 'relevant public authority' see PARA 316 note 2.

3 As to the meaning of 'Revenue and Customs information' see PARA 316 note 3.

4 Charities Act 2011 s 55(1) (substituted in this regard by s 58(3)). For these purposes 'subsidiary undertaking of the exempt charity' means an undertaking PARA 25)) in relation to which: (1) the exempt charity is (or is to be treated as) a parent undertaking in accordance with the provisions of the Companies Act 2006 s 1162, Sch 7; or (2) the exempt charity and one or more other charities would, if they were a single charity, be (or be treated as) a parent undertaking in accordance with those provisions: Charities Act 2011 s 55(2) (as so substituted).

5 Charities Act 2011 ss 56(1), 58(2). As to the meaning of 'relevant public authority' see PARA 316 note 10.

6 Charities Act 2011 ss 56(2), (3), 58(2). This restriction does not apply in relation to Revenue and Customs information disclosed to the principal regulator of an exempt charity under s 54(1), but any such information may not be further disclosed (whether under s 54(1) or otherwise) except with the consent of the Commissioners for Her Majesty's Revenue and Customs: ss 56(2), 57(1), (2), 58(1). As to the Commissioners for Her Majesty's Revenue and Customs see INCOME TAXATION vol 58 (2014) PARA 33.

Any responsible person who discloses information in contravention of s 56(3) is guilty of an offence and liable, on summary conviction, to imprisonment for a term not exceeding six months (or, as from a day to be appointed, 12 months) in relation to an offence committed in England and Wales or to a fine not exceeding the statutory maximum or both or, on conviction on indictment, to imprisonment for a term not exceeding two years or to a fine or both: ss 57(4), 58(1). However, it is a defence for a responsible person charged with such an offence to prove that he reasonably believed that the disclosure was lawful or that the information had already and lawfully been made available to the public: ss 57(5), 58(1). As to the meaning of 'responsible person' means a person specified by regulations under s 25 (see PARA 318): s 57(8) (substituted in this regard by s 58(4)).

For persons specified as a 'responsible person' see the Charities Act 2006 (Principal Regulators of Exempt Charities) Regulations 2010, SI 2010/501; the Charities Act 2006 (Principal Regulators of Exempt Charities) Regulations 2011, SI 2011/1726; the Charities Act 2006 (Principal Regulators of Exempt Charities) (No 2) Regulations 2011, SI 2011/1727; and the Charities Act 2011 (Principal Regulators of Exempt Charities) Regulations 2013, SI 2013/1764.

Regulations under the Charities Act 2011 s 25 may also make such amendments or other modifications of any enactment as the Secretary of State considers appropriate for securing that any disclosure provisions that would otherwise apply in relation to the principal regulator of an exempt charity do not apply in relation to that body or person in its or his capacity as principal regulator: s 58(5), (7). For these purposes 'disclosure provisions' means provisions having effect for authorising, or otherwise in connection with, the disclosure of information by or to the principal regulator concerned: s 58(6).

7 Charities Act 2011 s 59. As to the Data Protection Act 1998 see CONFIDENCE AND INFORMATIONAL PRIVACY. As to the Regulation of Investigatory Powers Act 2000 Pt 1 (ss 1–25) see POLICE AND INVESTIGATORY POWERS vol 84A (2013) PARA 657 et seq.

(iv) Register of Charity Mergers

322. The register. The Charity Commission[1] must maintain a register of charity mergers, to be kept in such manner as it thinks fit[2]. The register must contain an entry in respect of every relevant charity merger which is notified to the Commission[3]. A 'relevant charity merger' is one which falls into one of the following categories: (1) a merger of two or more charities in connection with which the transferee has transferred[4] to it all the property of the transferor or transferors, each of which ceases to exist on after the transfer[5]; (2) a merger of two or more charities in connection with which both or all of them cease to exist, or will cease to exist, on or after the transfer of all their property to a new charity[6]; and (3) a merger as in head (1) or head (2) but which involves the transfer of all the unrestricted property of a charity which also has a permanent endowment, and whose trusts do not contain provision for the termination of the charity[7].

Notification of a relevant charity merger may be given to the Commission at any time after the transfer of property involved in the merger has taken place or, if more than one transfer of property is so involved, at any time after the last of those transfers has taken place[8]. The notification is to be given by the charity trustees[9] and must specify the transfer or transfers of property involved in the merger and the date or dates on which it or they took place and include a statement that appropriate arrangements have been made with respect to the discharge of any liabilities of the transferor charity or charities[10].

Where such notification is given, the Commission must enter on the register the date when the transfer or transfers of property involved took place and such other particulars of the merger as the Commission thinks fit[11].

Where a pre-merger vesting declaration[12] is made in connection with a relevant charity merger, then notification must be given to the Commission in respect of the merger once the transfer, or the last of the transfers, has taken place[13]. In addition to providing the information above, the notification must also contain the fact that the vesting declaration has been made, the date when it was made and the date on which the vesting of title under the declaration took place[14]. This additional information must be entered on the register by the Commission[15].

1 As to the Charity Commission see PARAS 543–578.

2 Charities Act 2011 s 305(1). The register must be open to public inspection at all reasonable times and where any information contained therein is not in documentary form it must be available for public inspection in legible form at all reasonable times: s 309(1), (2).

3 Charities Act 2011 s 305(2). Nothing in Pt 16 (ss 305–314) applies in a case where s 235 (amalgamation of CIOs) or s 240 (transfer of CIO's undertaking) applies: s 314. As to CIO amalgamations see PARA 234. As to CIO transfers of undertakings see PARA 235.

4 Any reference to a transfer of property under these provisions includes a transfer effected by a vesting declaration: Charities Act 2011 s 306(4)(a). A vesting declaration is one to which s 310(2) (see PARA 417) applies: s 306(4)(b).

No vesting or transfer of any property in pursuance of any provision of Pt 16 operates as a breach of covenant or condition against alienation or gives rise to a forfeiture: s 313.

5 Charities Act 2011 s 306(1)(a).

6 Charities Act 2011 s 306(1)(b).

7 See the Charities Act 2011 s 306(2), (3)(a). For these purposes any reference in head (1) or (2) to this charity ceasing to exist is omitted: s 306(3)(b).

8 Charities Act 2011 s 307(1).

9 As to the meaning of 'charity trustees' see PARA 255.

10 Charities Act 2011 s 307(3)(a), (b).

11 Charities Act 2011 s 308(1)(2)(a), (c).

12 Ie under the Charities Act 2011 s 310: see PARA 417.

13 Charities Act 2011 s 307(2).

14 Charities Act 2011 s 307(3)(c), (4).

15 Charities Act 2011 s 308(2)(b).

323. Effect of registration. Where a relevant charity merger[1] is registered in the register of charity mergers[2], any gift which is expressed as a gift to the transferor[3], and takes effect on or after the date of registration of the merger, takes effect as a gift to the transferee[4].

This provision does not apply in relation to an excluded gift, that is, if the transferor is a charity which prior to the merger had both a permanent endowment and other, unrestricted property and as such continues to exist after the merger[5], and the gift is intended to be held subject to the trusts on which the whole or part of the charity's permanent endowment is held[6].

Where a relevant charity merger takes place before the death of a testator whose will specifies a gift to the previous charity, so that the charity has ceased to exist before the gift comes into effect, the will cannot be taken to express a gift to the transferee[7].

1 As to the meaning of 'relevant charity merger' see the Charities Act 2011 s 306(1); and PARA 322).
2 Charities Act 2011 s 311(1). As to the register see PARA 322.
3 As to the meaning of 'transferor' see the Charities Act 2011 s 306; and PARA 322 (definition applied by s 312(1)).
4 See the Charities Act 2011 s 311(2). As to the meaning of 'transferee' see s 306; and PARA 417 (definition applied by s 312(1)). 'The obvious purpose of [s 311] is to ensure that money (or property) which the benefactor has specified should pass to a charity accompanies it into the entity into which the charity has been merged notwithstanding that the benefaction is not to take effect until a time which postdates the merger': *Berry v IBS-STL (UK) LTD (in liquidation)* [2012] EWHC 666 (Ch), [2012] All ER (D) 10 (Mar).
In practice merging charities may retain the transferor as a shell charity in order to preserve legacies, rather than winding up and registering the merger.
5 Ie the transferor is a charity within the Charities Act 2011 s 306(2) (see PARA 322).
6 See the Charities Act 2011 s 311(2), (3).
7 *Berry v IBS-STL (UK) LTD (in liquidation)* [2012] EWHC 666 (Ch), [2012] All ER (D) 10 (Mar) (trustees were entitled to distribute according to their discretion, and were not required to pay a portion of the residual estate to the successor charity, which had by that time gone into liquidation).

(v) Other Registration Requirements

324. Registration requirements generally. A charity may be liable to various registration requirements, depending on its activities. For instance, there will be registration requirements if it holds personal data[1], or if it is involved in certain educational activities or the provision of childcare[2], or if it is involved in the provision of certain types of social care[3]. There are also registration requirements where a lottery is promoted on behalf of a charity[4].

1 As to the requirement for data controllers to be registered by the Information Commissioner see CONFIDENCE AND INFORMATIONAL PRIVACY vol 19 (2011) PARA 130 et seq. As to the Information Commissioner see CONFIDENCE AND INFORMATIONAL PRIVACY vol 19 (2011) PARA 109 et seq.
2 See CHILDREN AND YOUNG PERSONS; EDUCATION. As to the Office for Standards in Education, Children's Services and Skills ('Ofsted') see EDUCATION vol 36 (2011) PARA 1350 et seq.
3 As to the requirement under the Health and Social Care Act 2008 for a service provider carrying out a regulated activity in England to register with the Care Quality Commission see SOCIAL SERVICES AND COMMUNITY CARE vol 95 (2013) PARA 97 et seq. As to the regulated activities see SOCIAL SERVICES AND COMMUNITY CARE vol 95 (2013) PARA 88 et seq; and as to the Care Quality Commission see SOCIAL SERVICES AND COMMUNITY CARE vol 95 (2013) PARA 217 et seq. As to registration of social workers etc in Wales see SOCIAL SERVICES AND COMMUNITY CARE vol 95 (2013) PARA 83.
4 See the Gambling Act 2005; and LICENSING AND GAMBLING.

(2) LOCAL AUTHORITIES' FUNCTIONS

(i) Local Indexes

325. Power to maintain a local index. A council[1] has power to maintain an index of local charities[2] or of any class of local charities in its area, and to publish information contained in the index or summaries or extracts from it[3]. Where any of a council's functions are carried out by a joint board, the board has the same powers as the council as respects local charities in the area which are established for purposes similar or complementary to those of the board[4]. A council may employ a voluntary organisation[5] as its agent for these purposes, on such terms and within such limits or in such cases as they may agree[6].

1 For these purposes 'council' means a county, or county borough, or district or London borough council, or the Common Council of the City of London: Charities Act 2011 s 296(1). As to the London borough councils and the Common Council of the City of London see LONDON GOVERNMENT vol 71 (2013) PARAS 20 et seq, 34 et seq. As to local government areas and authorities in England and Wales generally see LOCAL GOVERNMENT vol 69 (2009) PARA 22 et seq. The references to 'council' in the Charities Act 2011 ss 294–297 have effect as if the references to a council for any area included references to a national park authority and as if the relevant park were the authority's area: Environment Act 1995 s 70, Sch 9 para 15 (amended by the Charities Act 2011 Sch 7 para 68). As to national park authorities see OPEN SPACES AND COUNTRYSIDE vol 78 (2010) PARA 526 et seq.

2 As to the meaning of 'local charity' see PARA 189 note 10.

3 See the Charities Act 2011 s 294(1). Certain functions of a local authority in England and Wales carried out under these powers fall within the remit of the Secretary of State and the Welsh Ministers, following the dissolution of the Local Better Regulation Office: see the Regulatory Enforcement and Sanctions Act 2008 s 4, Sch 3 (amended by the Charities Act 2011 Sch 7 Pt 2 para 130); and the Local Better Regulation Office (Dissolution and Transfer of Functions, Etc) Order 2012, SI 2012/246.

4 Charities Act 2011 s 296(4).

5 'Voluntary organisation' means any body whose activities are carried on otherwise than for profit, not being a public or local authority: Charities Act 2011 s 296(3).

6 Charities Act 2011 s 296(2).

326. The index and its contents. The Charity Commission[1] must, on request, supply free of charge to a council[2] proposing to establish or maintaining an index of local charities, copies of any entries in the central register of charities relevant to the index, and particulars of any changes in entries of which copies have already been supplied; it may also arrange to supply particulars of such changes without further request[3].

An index maintained under these powers is required to be open to public inspection at all reasonable times[4].

1 As to the Charity Commission see PARAS 543–578.

2 As to the meaning of 'council' see PARA 325 note 1.

3 See the Charities Act 2011 s 294(2).

4 Charities Act 2011 s 294(3). See also PARA 325 note 2.

(ii) Review of Local Charities

327. Power to carry out reviews. A council[1] has power to initiate and carry out, in co-operation with the charity trustees[2], a review of the working of any group of local charities with the same or similar purposes in the council's area[3]. It may make to the Charity Commission[4] such report on the review and recommendations arising from it as the council, after consultation with the charity trustees, thinks fit[5]. It may also co-operate with other persons in a review of the working of local charities in its area, with or without other charities, or join with other persons in initiating and carrying out such a review[6]. The ancillary powers and provisions which exist in relation to the maintaining of local indexes[7] apply also to local reviews[8].

1 As to the meaning of 'council' see PARA 325 note 1.
2 As to the meaning of 'charity trustees' see PARA 255.
3 Charities Act 2011 s 295(1)(a). See also PARA 325 notes 2, 3.
4 As to the Charity Commission see PARAS 543–578.
5 Charities Act 2011 s 295(1)(b).
6 Charities Act 2011 s 295(2).
7 Ie as to the employment of voluntary organisations and the powers of joint boards: see PARA 325).
8 Charities Act 2011 s 296(2)–(4).

328. Scope of reviews. Reviews of local charities initiated under the Charities Act 2011[1] may not extend to any ecclesiastical charity[2], and may not extend to any charity without the consent of the charity trustees[3]. Reviews initiated by a district council may not extend to the working in any county of a local charity established for purposes similar or complementary to any services provided by county councils, unless the county council consents to the review's being so extended[4].

1 Ie under the Charities Act 2011 s 295: see PARA 327.
2 As to the meaning of 'ecclesiastical charity' see PARA 267 note 4.
3 See the Charities Act 2011 s 295(3). As to the meaning of 'charity trustees' see PARA 255.
4 See the Charities Act 2011 s 295(4). This does not apply to Wales: s 295(5). See also PARA 325 note 2.

(iii) Co-operation with and between Charities

329. Local authorities' powers. Any local council[1] or joint board discharging the functions of such a council may make arrangements with any charity established for purposes similar or complementary to services provided by the council or board for co-ordinating the activities of the council or board with those of the charity in the interests of persons who may benefit from those services or from the charity[2]. Whether or not such arrangements have been made with such a charity, it may also disclose to the charity, in the interests of those persons, information obtained in connection with the services provided by the council or board[3].

1 In this context, 'local council' means, in relation to England, the council of a district, county, London borough or parish, and includes also the Common Council of the City of London and the Council of the Isles of Scilly; and in relation to Wales it means the council of a county, county borough or community: Charities Act 2011 s 297(2). As to the London borough councils and the Common Council of the City of London see **LONDON GOVERNMENT** vol 71 (2013) PARAS 20 et seq, 34 et seq. As to local government areas and authorities in England and Wales generally see **LOCAL GOVERNMENT** vol 69 (2009) PARA 22 et seq. See also PARA 325 note 2.
2 Charities Act 2011 s 297(1)(a).
3 Charities Act 2011 s 297(1)(b).

330. Charity trustees' powers. Notwithstanding anything in the trusts[1] of a charity, where it appears to charity trustees[2] likely to promote or make more effective the work of the charity, they may co-operate in any review[3] of the working of charities or any class of charities[4], or make arrangements with a local authority[5] or with another charity for co-ordinating their activities with those of the authority or of the other charity[6], or publish information of other charities with a view to bringing them to the notice of those for whose benefit they are intended[7]. They may also defray the expense of doing any of those things out of any income or money applicable as income of the charity[8].

1 As to the meaning of 'trusts' see PARA 218 note 5.
2 As to the meaning of 'charity trustees' see PARA 255.
3 Ie whether or not initiated under the Charities Act 2011 s 295: see PARAS 327–328.
4 Charities Act 2011 s 297(3)(a).
5 Ie acting under the Charities Act 2011 s 297(1): see PARA 329. See also PARA 325 note 2.
6 Charities Act 2011 s 297(3)(b).
7 Charities Act 2011 s 297(3)(c).
8 Charities Act 2011 s 297(4).

8. CONDUCT AND ADMINISTRATION OF CHARITABLE TRUSTS

(1) DUTIES OF CHARITY TRUSTEES

(i) Duties in general

331. Observance of the trust. The duties of trustees of charitable trusts do not differ in principle from those of non-charitable trustees[1]. Their primary duty is to execute the trust in accordance with its terms, whether contained in a will, a deed, a scheme or any other instrument, and with the general law, in the interests of the intended beneficiaries[2].

It is a breach of trust for trustees to divert a charitable fund given for one object to another not contemplated by the donor[3], or for a trustee of more than one charity to mix the funds and apply them indiscriminately for the charities[4], or for trustees to vary the specific mode of application directed by the founder[5], or for the trustees of one charity to subscribe its funds to the funds of another charity unless the recipient charity is expressly or by implication a purpose or object of the donor charity[6]. If capital has been applied for income purposes, it should if possible be replaced out of future income[7].

It is a breach of trust to extend the benefits of a charity intended exclusively for members of one religion or sect to persons holding different religious beliefs[8]. If, but only if, an intention to that effect is expressed, this rule applies equally in the case of charities not established for purely religious purposes[9].

Chapels established for particular forms of worship or doctrinal teaching must not be converted by the trustees to other forms[10], even with the consent of the congregation[11]. However, congregations of the same sect may differ upon non-fundamental[12] doctrines, and yet remain proper objects of the same charity[13].

Although it is a breach of trust to alter or depart from the trusts of the foundation, it is competent for a congregation, or the majority if power is given to it, to make new regulations in matters not involving a contravention of the trusts, or to alter those in existence[14].

However, a charitable trust will be construed liberally, and an expenditure may be allowed which is not within a narrow reading of the words declaring the trust[15]. Thus, where a charity was established for the benefit of a guild and its poor brethren, the trustees committed no breach of trust by subscribing out of the trust fund towards the erection of a school in return for a right to have a number of boys educated there gratuitously[16].

Where a trustee of charity property inadvertently pays more than the income of the property to the charity, he has no claim against the charity for reimbursement[17].

Charities[18] are not permitted to spend money applicable for the purposes of the charity in promoting or preparing a Bill in Parliament, without the consent of the court or of the Charity Commission[19].

Charity trustees have statutory power to do various things to promote the work of the charity, notwithstanding the terms of the trusts of the charity[20], but a charity has no power to give a gratuitous guarantee in respect of the liability of a third party with whom it has no legal tie[21].

1 These include, eg, the duty not to deviate from the terms of the trust, not to profit from the trust, not to delegate the trust, to act impartially between the beneficiaries, to distribute the trust

property only to those properly entitled, and to invest prudently: see **TRUSTS AND POWERS** vol 98 (2013) PARA 387 et seq. As to the duty to act gratuitously and the position regarding the remuneration of charity trustees see PARA 336. See also PARA 332.

2 See *Andrews v M'Guffog* (1886) 11 App Cas 313 at 329, HL, per Lord Herschell LC. Trustees are also subject to a statutory duty of care: see the Trustee Act 2000 ss 1, 2, Sch 1; PARA 338; and **TRUSTS AND POWERS** vol 98 (2013) PARAS 389–390. See also PARA 332.

3 *A-G v Brandreth* (1842) 1 Y & C Ch Cas 200 (where a gift for the poor of one parish was wrongfully applied in aid of the poor of another parish); *Re St John the Evangelist, D'Aungre's Charity* (1888) 59 LT 617 (where funds given for the repair of one church were applied for another). See also *Wivelescom Case* (1629) Duke 94; *A-G v Vivian* (1826) 1 Russ 226; *A-G v Goldsmith's Co* (1833) Coop Pr Cas 292 at 309 per Leach MR; *Re Church Estate Charity, Wandsworth* (1871) 6 Ch App 296. As to the effect of a union of benefices upon charities connected with one of the united parishes or churches see PARA 269. A church in the City of London which becomes a guild church retains the benefit of a charity enjoyed by the church: see the City of London (Guild Churches) Act 1952 s 28.

4 *A-G v Newbury Corpn* (1838) Coop Pr Cas 72 at 77 per Lord Brougham LC; *Andrews v M'Guffog* (1886) 11 App Cas 313, HL. The rule is different where one fund is given for several charities: *A-G v Geary* (1817) 3 Mer 513.

5 Eg a gift for the benefit of decayed householders cannot be applied for the poor of the parish generally: *Ex p Fowlser* (1819) 1 Jac & W 70. Nor can a fund to provide a preacher be applied in aid of the poor (Duke on Charitable Uses 116), or property devised to discharge a tax be diverted to the use of certain poor persons (*A-G v Bushby* (1857) 24 Beav 299), or a grammar school, founded for classical teaching, be used for instruction in English, writing and arithmetic, or its surplus revenue be applied for enlarging the school chapel for the town use (*A-G v Earl of Mansfield* (1827) 2 Russ 501).

6 *Baldry v Feintuck* [1972] 2 All ER 81, [1972] 1 WLR 552. Cf the court's power to apply funds cy-près: see PARA 209 et seq.

7 *Andrews v M'Guffog* (1886) 11 App Cas 313 at 329, HL, per Lord Herschell LC.

8 *Shore v Wilson* (1842) 9 Cl & Fin 355, HL; *A-G v Calvert* (1857) 23 Beav 248 (charity restricted to members of Church of England). See also *Baker v Lee* (1860) 8 HL Cas 495 (non-eligibility of dissenters as trustees of Church of England charity); *A-G v Murdoch* (1852) 1 De GM & G 86; *A-G v Anderson* (1888) 57 LJCh 543 at 550 per Kekewich J (charities confined to Protestant dissenters and Presbyterians); *Drummond v A-G for Ireland* (1849) 2 HL Cas 837 (Unitarians excluded).

9 *A-G v Calvert* (1857) 26 LJCh 682 at 686 per Romilly MR; *Re Perry Almshouses, Re Ross' Charity* [1899] 1 Ch 21, CA.

10 *Craigdallie v Aikman* (1813) 1 Dow 1; *A-G v Pearson* (1817) 3 Mer 353 at 400, 418–419 per Lord Eldon LC; *Foley v Wontner* (1820) 2 Jac & W 245 at 247 per Lord Eldon LC; *Dill v Watson* (1836) 2 Jo Ex Ir 48; *Milligan v Mitchell* (1837) 3 My & Cr 72; *A-G v Munro* (1848) 2 De G & Sm 122; *A-G v Wilson* (1848) 16 Sim 210; *General Assembly of the Free Church of Scotland v Lord Overtoun, Macalister v Young* [1904] AC 515 at 613 et seq, HL, per Earl of Halsbury LC. But see *Westwood v McKie* (1869) 21 LT 165.

11 *Broom v Summers* (1840) 11 Sim 353; *A-G v Welsh* (1844) 4 Hare 572; *A-G v Murdoch* (1852) 1 De GM & G 86; *A-G v Rochester Corpn* (1854) 5 De GM & G 797; *Ward v Hipwell* (1862) 3 Giff 547; *A-G v Aust* (1865) 13 LT 235; and see *A-G v Anderson* (1888) 57 LJCh 543. As to the effect of acquiescence in a change of doctrine see *Cairncross v Lorimer* (1860) 3 Macq 827, HL.

12 It is for the court, not for the trustees, to decide what doctrines are fundamental and must be held by congregations to entitle them to participate in a charity: *Newsome v Flowers* (1861) 30 Beav 461.

13 *A-G v Gould* (1860) 28 Beav 485; *A-G v Etheridge* (1862) 32 LJCh 161 (cases relating to the doctrines of strict or free communion, both being admissible among the sect of Particular Baptists).

14 *Milligan v Mitchell* (1837) 3 My & Cr 72; *A-G v Murdoch* (1852) 1 De GM & G 86; *A-G v Gould* (1860) 28 Beav 485; *A-G v Anderson* (1888) 57 LJCh 543 at 549 per Kekewich J.

15 *A-G v Stamford Corpn* (1747) 2 Swan 591; *Wilkinson v Malin* (1832) 2 Tyr 544 at 570 per Lord Lyndhurst CB; *A-G v Foyster* (1794) 1 Anst 116 at 122 per Eyre CB.

16 *Anderson v Wrights of Glasgow* (1865) 12 LT 805, HL.

17 *A-G v Gibbs* (1847) 1 De G & Sm 156 at 160 per Knight Bruce V-C; affd 2 Ph 327.

18 This does not apply to those exempt charities for which the provision for increased regulation has not been brought into force: see the Charities Act 2011 Sch 9 para 17; and PARA 319.

19 See the Charities Act 2011 s 74(1). This applies regardless of anything in the trusts of the charity: s 74(2). For an example of the application of what is now s 74(1) see the *Report of the*

Charity Commissioners for England and Wales for 1986 (HC Paper (1986–87) no 306) App D. As to the Charity Commission see PARAS 543–578.

20 See the Charities Act 2011 s 297(3), (4); and PARA 330.

21 *Rosemary Simmons Memorial Housing Association Ltd v United Dominions Trust Ltd (Bates & Partners (a firm), third party)* [1987] 1 All ER 281, [1986] 1 WLR 1440.

332. Managing conflicts of interest. A trustee must not intentionally place himself in a position in which his interests may conflict with his duty; nor may he enter into engagements in which he has a personal interest which does or may conflict with the interests of the charity[1]. But the existence of an actual or potential conflict does not invalidate the appointment of a trustee, nor render it impossible for such trustees to take decisions in pursuance of their duty[2].

The Charity Commission has published guidance for charity trustees to identify, avoid or otherwise manage actual or potential conflicts of interest in the exercise of their functions[3]. That guidance summarises the Commission's view as to the legal duties and liabilities of trustees in relation to conflicts of interest, and indicates three overarching strands, namely, identifying, preventing and recording conflicts of interest. It provides examples of potential and actual conflicts, sets out steps that trustees ought to take to prevent conflicts arising or affecting the performance of their duties, and sets out the circumstances in which the Commission proposes to consider intervention in serious or high-risk cases[4].

1 See TRUSTS AND POWERS vol 98 (2013) PARA 367; and further, as to the position of charities in particular, *Mountstar (PTC) Ltd v Charity Commission for England and Wales* (2013) First-tier Tribunal, General Regulatory Chamber (Charity), 17 October.

2 See *Re Earl of Stamford, Payne v Stamford* [1896] 1 Ch 288; *Public Trustee v Paul Cooper & Co* [2001] WTLR 901, [1999] All ER (D) 1524; and TRUSTS AND POWERS vol 98 (2013) PARA 272.

3 See *Manage a conflict of interest in your charity* (Charity Commission, May 2013) (available, at the date at which this volume states the law, on the government website). As to the Charity Commission see PARA 543. As to the Charity Commission's publications see PARA 547.

4 The detailed guidance is set out in *CC29: Conflicts of interest: a guide for charity trustees* (Charity Commission, May 2014) (available, at the date at which this volume states the law, on the government website). A distinction is drawn between conflicts of interest which relate to possible benefits to the trustee, and those which arise from conflicts of loyalty (eg to other organisations of which the trustee may be a member).

333. Duty towards the trust property. It is the duty of charity trustees to protect the trust property[1]. It has been said that trustees are not bound to look with more prudence to the affairs of the charity than to their own[2], but more is expected from trustees acting for a permanent charity than can be expected from the ordinary prudence of a man in dealings between himself and other persons[3].

The deliberate destruction of charity property by trustees is a gross breach of trust[4].

1 See TRUSTS AND POWERS vol 98 (2013) PARAS 399–400. Thus, for example, it would be a breach of trust for trustees to alienate trust property improperly (*A-G v East Retford Corpn* (1833) 2 My & K 35; revsd (1838) 3 My & Cr 484), or negligently to permit others to appropriate it (*A-G v Leicester Corpn* (1844) 7 Beav 176). In particular they must reduce the property into possession and invest it properly in authorised investments: see PARA 423 et seq; and TRUSTS AND POWERS vol 98 (2013) PARAS 408–410.

2 *A-G v Dixie, ex p Bosworth School* (1805) 13 Ves 519 at 534 per Lord Eldon LC; *Learoyd v Whiteley* (1887) 12 App Cas 727 at 733, HL, per Lord Halsbury LC. But see *A-G v Kerr* (1840) 2 Beav 420 at 428 per Lord Langdale MR.

3 *White v Williams* [2011] EWHC 494 (Ch), [2011] PTSR 1151, [2011] All ER (D) 122 (Mar).

4 *Ex p Greenhouse* (1815) 1 Madd 92 at 108 per Plumer V-C, where the trustees of a chapel pulled it down.

334. Duty towards beneficiaries. It is improper for a trustee holding property subject to charitable trusts to retain the fund without taking any steps to apply the property for charity[1].

Where there is a temporary or permanent failure of the particular object of the charitable trust, the trustee may not merely retain the property for himself[2].

1 *A-G v Alford* (1855) 4 De GM & G 843 at 852 per Lord Cranworth LC.
2 *Aylet v Dodd* (1741) 2 Atk 238; *Incorporated Society v Price* (1844) 1 Jo & Lat 498 at 500 per Lord Sugden LC (trust to pay schoolmasters' salaries and maintain schools; schools discontinued): *A-G v Cambridge Corpn* (1836) 5 LJCh 357; *A-G v Bolton* (1796) 3 Anst 820; *A-G v West* (1858) 27 LJCh 789.

335. Duty to apply for scheme. If there is a failure of the objects of the trust, or if for any other reason the statutory conditions for a cy-près application are satisfied, the trustees are under a duty to secure the effective use of the charity property by taking steps to enable it to be applied cy-près[1]. Similarly, if there is some difficulty of administration, the trustees should apply to the Charity Commission[2] or to the court for directions.

1 See the Charities Act 2011 s 61; and PARA 212. The usual procedure is to apply to the Charity Commission for a scheme under s 69 or s 73: see PARA 189 et seq. As to cy-près schemes see PARA 209 et seq. In rare cases it may be proper to apply to the court, but the leave of the Commission is required: see PARA 594. Trustees may not apply the trust property cy-près on their own initiative: see PARA 212. As to the Charity Commission see PARAS 543–572.
2 As to the direction of schemes see PARA 179 et seq.

336. Remuneration. The equitable rule precluding private trustees from drawing remuneration for their services[1] may be overridden by express provision allowing remuneration[2]. Such an express provision will be strictly construed[3]. The same principle with regard to express provisions applies in the case of charitable trusts, but provision is made to deal with the remuneration of charity trustees in the absence of any express prohibition on remuneration in the trusts of the charity[4]. The provision applies to remuneration for services[5] provided by a person to or on behalf of a charity where he is a charity trustee, a trustee for the charity, or a person connected with the same[6] and the remuneration might result in that trustee obtaining any benefit[7].

The person is entitled to receive the remuneration out of the funds of the charity if the following conditions are met[8]. The conditions are:

(1) the amount or maximum amount[9] of the remuneration must be set out in an agreement in writing between the charity or its charity trustees, as the case may be, and the relevant person, under which the relevant person is to provide the services in question to or on behalf of the charity[10], and the amount or maximum amount of remuneration must not exceed what is reasonable in the circumstances for the provision by that person of the services in question[11];

(2) before entering into that agreement, the charity trustees must have decided that they were satisfied that it is in the best interests of the charity for the services to be provided by the relevant person to or on behalf of the charity for the amount or maximum amount of remuneration set out in the agreement[12];

(3) where, immediately after the agreement is entered into there is, in the case of the charity, more than one person who is a charity trustee and is: (a) a person in respect of whom such a remuneration agreement is in force, or (b) a person who is entitled to receive remuneration out of the funds of the charity otherwise than by virtue of such an agreement, or

(c) a person connected with a person falling within head (a) or (b), then the total number of them must constitute a minority of the persons for the time being holding office as charity trustees of the charity[13]; and

(4) the trusts of the charity must not contain any express provision that prohibits the relevant person from receiving the remuneration[14].

Before entering into such an agreement[15], the charity trustees must have regard to any guidance given by the Charity Commission concerning the making of such arrangements[16].

General provision is made to deal with the remuneration of professional trustees where there is an express provision in the trust instrument entitling him to receive payment out of the trust funds in respect of services provided by him to or on behalf of the trust[17] and where there is no such express provision[18]. The Secretary of State[19] may by regulations[20] make provision for the remuneration of trustees of charitable trusts[21] who are trust corporations[22] or act in a professional capacity[23]. This power includes power to make provision for the remuneration of a trustee who has been authorised[24] to exercise functions[25] as an agent of the trustees or to act as a nominee or custodian[26].

1 See *Brocksopp v Barnes* (1820) 5 Madd 90; *Barrett v Hartley* (1866) LR 2 Eq 789; and TRUSTS AND POWERS vol 98 (2013) PARA 370.

2 See *Willis v Kibble* (1839) 1 Beav 559; and TRUSTS AND POWERS vol 98 (2013) PARA 370.

3 *Re Gee (decd), Wood v Staples* [1948] Ch 284, [1948] 1 All ER 498.

4 See the Charities Act 2011 s 185. As to the meaning of 'charity trustees' see PARA 255. Note that the provisions allowing remuneration rarely apply, since it is usual for there to be an express prohibition on remuneration. As to the right of a trustee to be reimbursed for expenses etc see TRUSTS AND POWERS vol 98 (2013) PARA 342 et seq.

These provisions do not affect the payment of remuneration or provision of services provided by a person in his capacity as a charity trustee or trustee for a charity or under a contract of employment or any other remuneration which a person is entitled to receive out of the funds of a charity by virtue of any provision contained in the trusts of the charity, any order of the court or the Charity Commission or any statutory provision under another Act of Parliament: Charities Act 2011 s 185(3). 'Remuneration' for these purposes includes any benefit in kind: s 187. As to the Charity Commission see PARAS 543–578.

5 'Services' for these purposes includes goods that are supplied in connection with the provision of services: Charities Act 2011 s 187.

6 Charities Act 2011 s 185(1). For the purposes of these provisions, the following persons are 'connected' with a charity trustee or trustee for a charity: (1) a child, parent, grandchild, grandparent, brother or sister of the trustee; (2) the spouse or civil partner of the trustee or of any person falling within head (1) above; (3) a person carrying on business in partnership with the trustee or with any person falling within head (1) or head (2); (4) an institution which is controlled by the trustee or by any person falling within head (1), (2) or (3), or by two or more such persons, when taken together; and (5) a body corporate in which the trustee or any connected person falling within heads (1)–(3) has a substantial interest, or two or more such persons, when taken together, have a substantial interest: Charities Act 2011 s 188(1). The provisions in ss 350–352 (see PARA 401) apply for this purposes: s 188(2).

7 Charities Act 2011 s 185(1).'Benefit' means a direct or indirect benefit of any nature: s 187.

8 See the Charities Act 2011 s 185(2).

9 'Maximum amount' in relation to remuneration means the maximum amount of remuneration whether specified in or ascertainably under the terms of the agreement in question, and 'amount' includes monetary value: Charities Act 2011 s 187.

10 Charities Act 2011 s 185(2) Condition A(a).

11 Charities Act 2011 s 185(2) Condition A(b).

12 Charities Act 2011 s 185(2) Condition B. The statutory duty of care in the Trustee Act 2000 s 1(1) (see TRUSTS AND POWERS) applies to a charity trustee when making such a decision: Charities Act 2011 s 185(5). As to the statutory duty of care see PARA 338.

13 Charities Act 2011 s 185(2) Condition C. Such an agreement is in force so long as any obligations under the agreement have not been fully discharged by a party to it: s 185(6).

14 Charities Act 2011 s 185(2) Condition D.

15 Ie an agreement within the Charities Act 2011 s 185(2) Condition A.

16 Charities Act 2011 s 185(4). See *CC11: Trustee expenses and payments* (Charity Commission, March 2012) (available, at the date at which this volume states the law, on the government website). As to the Charity Commission see PARAS 543–578. As to the Charity Commission's publications see PARA 547.

17 See the Trustee Act 2000 s 28; and **TRUSTS AND POWERS** vol 98 (2013) PARA 371.

18 See the Trustee Act 2000 s 29; and **TRUSTS AND POWERS** vol 98 (2013) PARA 372.

19 As to the Secretary of State see PARA 585.

20 Regulations made under the Trustee Act 2000 s 30 may make different provision for different cases, and may contain such supplemental, incidental, consequential and transitional provisions as the Secretary of State considers appropriate: s 30(3). The power to make regulations under s 30 is exercisable by statutory instrument: s 30(4). At the date at which this volume states the law, no such regulations had been made.

21 'Charitable trust' means a trust under which property is held for charitable purposes: Trustee Act 2000 s 39(1). As to the meaning of 'charitable purposes' see PARA 2; definition applied by s 39(1) (amended by the Charities Act 2011 Sch 7 para 90).

22 'Trust corporation' has the same meaning as in the Trustee Act 1925 (see **TRUSTS AND POWERS** vol 98 (2013) PARA 238): Trustee Act 2000 s 39(1). See further, as to trust corporations, PARA 257.

23 Trustee Act 2000 s 30(1). For these purposes, a trustee acts in a professional capacity if he acts in the course of a profession or business which consists of or includes the provision of services in connection with: (1) the management or administration of trusts generally or a particular kind of trust; or (2) any particular aspect of the management or administration of trusts generally or a particular kind of trust, and the services he provides to or on behalf of the trust fall within that description: ss 28(5), 39(2).

24 Ie under a power conferred by Trustee Act 2000 Pt IV (ss 11–27) (see **TRUSTS AND POWERS** vol 98 (2013) PARA 429 et seq) or any other enactment or any provision of subordinate legislation, or by the trust instrument.

25 'Functions' includes powers and duties: Trustee Act 2000 s 39(2).

26 Trustee Act 2000 s 30(2). A person is a custodian in relation to assets if he undertakes the safe custody of the assets or of any documents or records concerning the assets: ss 17(2), 39(2). As to the remuneration of agents nominees and custodians see **TRUSTS AND POWERS** vol 98 (2013) PARA 343.

337. Disqualification of trustee receiving remuneration. Where any charity trustee[1] or trustee for a charity is or would be entitled to remuneration[2] under an agreement or proposed agreement within the relevant statutory provision[3], or is connected with a person who is or would be so entitled[4], then that trustee is disqualified from acting as such in relation to any decision or other matter connected with the agreement[5], though any act done by such a person which he is so disqualified is not invalid by reason only of that disqualification[6].

If the Charity Commission is satisfied that such a disqualified trustee has done any act which he was so disqualified from doing and he, or a person connected with him, has received or is to receive from the charity any remuneration under the agreement in question, it may make an order, as appropriate[7]: (1) requiring the disqualified trustee to reimburse to the charity the whole or part of the remuneration so received[8]; (2) to the extent that the remuneration consists of a benefit[9] in kind, requiring the disqualified trustee to reimburse to the charity the whole or part of the monetary value (as determined by the Commission) of the benefit in kind[10]; (3) directing that the disqualified trustee or, as the case may be, connected person is not to be paid the whole or part of the remuneration under the agreement in question[11].

If the Commission makes any such order, the disqualified trustee or, as the case may be, connected person accordingly ceases to have any entitlement under the agreement to so much of the remuneration, or its monetary value, as the order requires him to reimburse to the charity or, as the case may be, as it directs is not to be paid to him[12].

An appeal against such an order[13] of the Commission requiring a trustee or connected person to repay, or not to receive, remuneration lies to the Tribunal[14] at the instance of the Attorney General, the trustee or connected person, the other charity trustees of the charity concerned and any other person who is or may be affected by the order[15]. The Tribunal may do any of the following: (a) quash the order and, if appropriate remit the matter to the Commission; (b) substitute for the order any other order which could have been made by the Commission[16].

1 As to the meaning of 'charity trustee' see PARA 255.
2 As to the meaning of 'remuneration' see PARA 336 note 4.
3 Ie under an agreement or proposed agreement within the Charities Act 2011 s 185(2) Condition A (see PARA 336).
4 Charities Act 2011 s 186(1). As to the meaning of 'connected persons' see PARA 336 note 6.
5 Charities Act 2011 s 186(2).
6 Charities Act 2011 s 186(3).
7 Charities Act 2011 s 186(4). As to the Charity Commission see PARAS 543–578.
8 Charities Act 2011 s 186(5)(a).
9 As to the meaning of 'benefit' see PARA 336 note 7.
10 Charities Act 2011 s 186(5)(b).
11 Charities Act 2011 s 186(6).
12 Charities Act 2011 s 186(7).
13 Ie an order under the Charities Act 2011 s 186(5) or (6).
14 As to the Tribunal see PARA 579 et seq.
15 Charities Act 2011 s 319(2), Sch 6 Table Cols 1, 2. As to the meaning of 'person who is or may be affected' within the meaning of Sch 6 see PARA 317 note 8. As to the Attorney General see PARAS 589, 596, 605 et seq; and **CONSTITUTIONAL AND ADMINISTRATIVE LAW** vol 20 (2014) PARA 273 et seq.
16 Charities Act 2011 Sch 6 Table Col 3.

338. Statutory duty of care under the Trustee Act 2000. Trustees are subject to a statutory duty of care[1] in certain circumstances[2] in relation to: (1) investment[3]; (2) the acquisition of land[4]; (3) agents, nominees and custodians[5]; (4) the compounding of liabilities[6]; (5) insurance[7]; (6) reversionary interests, valuations and audit[8]. The duty of care does not apply if or in so far as it appears from the trust instrument that the duty is not meant to apply[9].

The duty of care required of a trustee is to exercise such care and skill as is reasonable in the circumstances having regard in particular to any special knowledge or experience that he has or holds himself out as having and, if he acts as trustee in the course of a business or profession, to any special knowledge or experience that it is reasonable to expect of a person acting in the course of that kind of business or profession[10].

1 See the Trustee Act 2000 ss 1(1), (2), 39(2); and **TRUSTS AND POWERS** vol 98 (2013) PARA 389. The new duty does not, however, alter the principles relating to the exercise of discretionary powers by trustees. As to the exercise of discretionary powers see **TRUSTS AND POWERS** vol 98 (2013) PARA 411. Note that the Trustee Act 2000 does not apply to an incorporated charity unless the incorporated charity is itself a trustee of an unincorporated charity.
2 See the Trustee Act 2000 s 2, Sch 1; and **TRUSTS AND POWERS** vol 98 (2013) PARA 390.
3 See the Trustee Act 2000 Sch 1 para 1. As to the power to invest see PARA 416 et seq; and **TRUSTS AND POWERS** vol 98 (2013) PARA 446 et seq.
4 See the Trustee Act 2000 Sch 1 para 2; and **TRUSTS AND POWERS** vol 98 (2013) PARAS 390, 475.
5 See the Trustee Act 2000 Sch 1 para 3. As to the power to delegate and employ agents see **TRUSTS AND POWERS** vol 98 (2013) PARA 425 et seq.
6 See the Trustee Act 2000 Sch 1 para 4.
7 See the Trustee Act 2000 Sch 1 para 5. As to the power to insure see **TRUSTS AND POWERS** vol 98 (2013) PARAS 513–514 et seq.
8 See the Trustee Act 2000 Sch 1 para 6.
9 See the Trustee Act 2000 Sch 1 para 7.

10 See the Trustee Act 2000 ss 1(1), (2), 39(2); and TRUSTS AND POWERS vol 98 (2013) PARA 389. See further, as to managing conflicts of interests by charity trustees, PARA 332.

339. Safeguarding children and vulnerable adults. The Charity Commission's guidance states that charity trustees are responsible for ensuring that those benefiting from, or working with, their charity, are not harmed in any way through contact with it. The trustees have a duty to act prudently and this means that they must take all reasonable steps within their power to ensure that this does not happen. It is particularly important where beneficiaries are vulnerable persons or children in the community[1].

1 See *Safeguarding Children and Young People* (Charity Commission, July 2014) (available, at the date at which this volume states the law, on the government website). This sets out the charity trustees' duties, including the essential contents of a child protection policy, in light of intergovernmental guidance, *Working Together to Safeguard Children* (Department of Education, March 2013) (available, at the date at which this volume states the law, on the government website). See further CHILDREN AND YOUNG PERSONS vol 9 (2012) PARA 172. As to the Charity Commission's publications see PARA 547.

340. Duty to report serious incidents. Charities with an income of more than £25,000 must include in their annual return[1] a statement that there have been no serious incidents that should have, but have not already, been brought to the attention of the Charity Commission[2]. This implies a duty to report such serious incidents to the Commission, by no later than the time the annual return is submitted[3]. Guidance has been published by the Charity Commission as to the nature and scope of this duty[4].

Trustees of a charity should report any serious incident that results in or risks loss of the charity's money or assets, damage to its property or harm to its work, beneficiaries or reputation[5]. Serious incidents are deemed by the Commission to include:

(1) fraud, theft or other significant loss;

(2) a large donation from an unknown or unverified source;

(3) links to terrorism or to any organisation that is proscribed due to terrorist activity;

(4) a disqualified person acting as a trustee[6];

(5) not having a policy to safeguard the charity's vulnerable beneficiaries[7];

(6) not having vetting procedures in place to check eligibility of prospective trustees[8], volunteers and staff;

(7) suspicions, allegations or incidents of abuse of vulnerable beneficiaries, and, more broadly, any actual or suspected criminal activity within or involving the charity[9].

1 As to the annual return see PARA 383.

2 Charities (Annual Return) Regulations 2013 (Charity Commission, December 2013) Schedule Pt C2 (available, at the date at which this volume states the law, on the government website). As to the Charities (Annual Return) Regulations see PARA 383 note 3.

3 See *Reporting Serious Incidents: guidance for trustees* (Charity Commission, December 2013) Pt B (available, at the date at which this volume states the law, on the government website). As to the Charity Commission's publications see PARA 547.

4 See *How to report a serious incident in your charity* (Charity Commission, June 2014) (available, at the date at which this volume states the law, on the government website).

5 See *How to report a serious incident in your charity* (Charity Commission, June 2014).

6 As to persons acting as trustee while disqualified see PARA 277.

7 As to the safeguarding of children and other vulnerable persons see PARA 339.

8 See further *CC30: Finding new trustees* (Charity Commission, September 2012) Pt 5 (available, at the date at which this volume states the law, on the government website).

9 See *How to report a serious incident in your charity* (Charity Commission, June 2014); and *Reporting Serious Incidents: guidance for trustees* (Charity Commission, December 2013) Pt D, where a detailed analysis of the various listed types of serious incident may be found.

(ii) Accounts, Reports and other Returns

A. ACCOUNTING RECORDS

341. Duty to keep accounting records. The charity trustees[1] of a charity[2], other than an exempt charity[3] and a charitable company[4], must ensure that accounting records are kept which are sufficient to show and explain all the charity's transactions, and which are such as to[5]: (1) disclose at any time, with reasonable accuracy, the financial position of the charity at that time[6]; and (2) enable the trustees to ensure that where any annual statements of account are prepared by them[7], those statements comply with the statutory requirements[8]. In particular they must contain entries showing from day to day all sums of money received and expended by the charity and the matters in respect of which the receipt and expenditure takes place, and a record of the assets and liabilities of the charity[9]. The charity trustees of a charity must preserve any accounting records made for these purposes for at least six years from the end of the financial year[10] of the charity in which they are made[11].

1 As to the meaning of 'charity trustees' see PARA 255.
2 As to the meaning of 'charity' see PARA 1.
3 See the Charities Act 2011 s 136(1); and PARA 381. As to exempt charities see PARA 318. As to the duty of charity trustees of an exempt charity see PARA 381.
4 Charities Act 2011 s 135. As to the meaning of 'charitable company' see PARA 241 note 1. Charitable companies prepare accounts under company law, but the applicable charity SORP applies to charitable companies as well as non-company charities: see generally *CC15b: Charity reporting and accounting: the essentials* (Charity Commission, January 2013) para 4.2 (available, at the date at which this volume states the law, on the government website). As to the SORP see PARA 345 note 12. As to the Charity Commission's publications see PARA 547.
5 Charities Act 2011 s 130(1).
6 Charities Act 2011 s 130(1)(a).
7 Ie under the Charities Act 2011 s 132(1): see PARA 342.
8 Charities Act 2011 s 130(1)(b). As to the statutory requirements see s 132(1) and the regulations made under it: see PARA 342.
9 Charities Act 2011 s 130(2).
10 As to the meaning of 'financial year' see PARA 218 note 3; and PARA 344.
11 Charities Act 2011 s 131(1). Where a charity ceases to exist within the six year period, the obligation to preserve the records continues to be discharged by the last charity trustees of the charity, unless the Charity Commission consents in writing to the records being destroyed or otherwise disposed of: s 131(2), (3). As to the Charity Commission see PARAS 543–578.

B. ANNUAL STATEMENTS OF ACCOUNTS

342. Annual statement of accounts. The charity trustees[1] of a charity[2], other than an exempt charity[3] and a charitable company[4], must prepare in respect of each financial year[5] of the charity a statement of accounts complying with such requirements as to its form and contents as may be prescribed by the regulations[6] made by the Minister[7]. However, where a charity's gross income[8] in any financial year does not exceed £250,000[9], the charity trustees may, in respect of that year, elect to prepare a receipts and payments account, and a statement of assets and liabilities instead of a statement of accounts[10]. The charity trustees of a charity must preserve any statement of accounts[11], or any account and statement[12], for at least six years from the end of the financial year to which any such statement relates or, as the case may be, to which any such account and statement relate[13].

1 As to the meaning of 'charity trustees' see PARA 255.
2 As to the meaning of 'charity' see PARA 1.
3 See the Charities Act 2011 s 136(1). As to exempt charities see PARA 318. As to the duty of charity trustees of an exempt charity see PARA 381.
4 Charities Act 2011 s 135. As to the meaning of 'charitable company' see PARA 241 note 1.
5 As to the meaning of 'financial year' see PARAS 218 note 3, 344 note 4.
6 Such regulations may not impose on the charity trustees of a charity that is a charitable trust created by any person (the 'settlor') any requirement to disclose, in any statement of accounts prepared by them under the identities of recipients of grants made out of the funds of the charity, or the amounts of any individual grants so made, if the disclosure would fall to be made at a time when the settlor or any spouse or civil partner of his was still alive: Charities Act 2011 s 132(4).

In the exercise of the previous statutory power the following regulations were made: the Charities (Accounts and Reports) Regulations 1995, SI 1995/2724 (revoked); the Charities (Accounts and Reports) Regulations 2000, SI 2000/2868 (revoked); the Charities (Accounts and Reports) Regulations 2005, SI 2005/572 (revoked); and the Charities (Accounts and Reports) Regulations 2008, SI 2008/629. At the date at which this volume states the law, the Charities (Accounts and Reports) Regulations 2008, SI 2008/629, continue to have effect. See PARA 344 et seq.

The Charities (Accounts and Reports) Regulations 2008, SI 2008/629, apply in respect of a financial year of a charity which begins on or after 1 April 2008, or, in the case of year which began before this date, a financial year in respect of which the charity trustees may make and make an accounts determination: reg 4(4), (6)(d). Such a determination may not be made if the charity is a special case charity, or if before 1 April 2008 they have approved the accounts of the charity prepared in respect of that financial year or authorised the signature of an annual report prepared in respect of that financial year in accordance with the Charities (Accounts and Reports) Regulations 2005, SI 2005/572 (revoked): Charities (Accounts and Reports) Regulations 2008, SI 2008/629, reg 4(7). As to the meaning of 'special case charity' see PARA 347 note 3.

Otherwise, the Charities (Accounts and Reports) Regulations 2005, SI 2005/572, continue to apply in respect of a financial year of a charity which began before 1 April 2008 (save that an auditor's duty under the Charities (Accounts and Reports) Regulations 2008, SI 2008/629, reg 7(5) applies only in respect of matters of which an auditor became aware of before 1 April 2008 and during a financial year ending on or before 31 March 2008): see reg 4(2)–(4).
7 Charities Act 2011 s 132(1). Before making any regulations under s 132 the Minister must consult such persons or bodies or persons as he considers appropriate: s 348(4). As to the making of regulations generally see s 347; and PARA 590. See also PARA 315 note 7. The regulations may make provision for the statement to be prepared in accordance with such methods and principles as are specified or referred to in the regulations, and as to any information to be provided by way of notes to the accounts: s 132(2). The regulations may also make provision for determining the financial years of a charity for the purposes of the Charities Act 2011 and any regulations made under it: s 132(3). As to the Minister see PARA 586. The duties of an auditor carrying out an audit of the accounts of a charity are, in the case of an audit carried out under s 144, specified where the auditor is carrying out an audit of a statement of accounts prepared under s 132(1), under the Charities (Accounts and Reports) Regulations 2008, SI 2008/629, reg 24 (see PARA 362): reg 20.
8 As to the meaning of 'gross income' see PARA 218 note 2.
9 The Minister may by order amend the specified sum: Charities Act 2011 s 174(1), (2). See also note 7. At the date at which this volume states the law, no such order had been made.
10 Charities Act 2011 s 133. As to the additional information to be supplied when a CIO (see PARA 226 et seq) elects to prepare these alternative documents see the Charitable Incorporated Organisations (General) Regulations 2012, SI 2012/3012, reg 62.

If the requirement to prepare group accounts applies to the charity trustees of a parent charity in relation to a financial year, the option of preparing these alternative documents is not available in relation to that year whatever the amount of the charity's gross income: Charities Act 2011 s 138(3)(b). As to group accounts see PARA 343. As to the meaning of 'parent charity' see PARA 343 note 2. The duties of an auditor carrying out an audit of the accounts of a charity are, in the case of an audit carried out under the Charities Act 2011 s 144, specified where the auditor is carrying out an audit of a receipts and payments account and a statement of assets and liabilities prepared under s 133, under the Charities (Accounts and Reports) Regulations 2008, SI 2008/629, reg 26 (see PARA 364): reg 20.

11 Ie prepared by them under the Charities Act 2011 s 132(1): see the text and notes 5–7.

12 Ie prepared by them under the Charities Act 2011 s 133: see the text and notes 8–10.

13 Charities Act 2011 s 134(1). The obligation to preserve the statement of accounts (or account and statement) continues to be discharged by the last charity trustees of the charity, unless the Charity Commission consents in writing to their being destroyed or otherwise disposed of; and this applies if a charity ceases to exist within the six year period mentioned in s 134(1) as it applies to any statement of accounts (or account and statement): s 134(2), (3).

343. Group accounts. The Charities Act 2011 makes special provision for group accounts[1]. These provisions apply to the preparation and auditing of accounts in respect of groups consisting of parent charities[2] and their subsidiary undertakings[3].

If a charity is a parent charity at the end of a particular financial year and, where it is a company, it is not required to prepare consolidated accounts for that year under the companies legislation[4] (whether or not such accounts are in fact prepared), then its charity trustees must prepare group accounts in respect of that year[5].

The charity trustees of a charity[6] which is a parent charity or a subsidiary undertaking must ensure that the accounting records kept in respect of the charity[7] not only comply with those statutory requirements but also are such as to enable the charity trustees of the parent charity to ensure that any group accounts prepared by them comply with the relevant requirements[8]. If a parent charity has a subsidiary undertaking in relation to which those statutory accounting requirements do not apply, the charity trustees of the parent charity must take reasonable steps to secure that the undertaking keeps such accounting records as to enable the trustees to ensure that, where any group accounts are prepared under the Charities Act 2011, those accounts comply with the relevant requirements[9].

If the requirement to prepare group accounts applies to the charity trustees of a parent charity (other than a parent charity which is a company) in relation to a financial year, then that requirement so applies in addition to the requirement to prepare a statement of account under the Charities Act 2011[10] and the option of preparing a receipts and payments account and a statement of assets and liabilities[11] is not available in relation to that year, whatever the amount of the charity's gross income for that year[12]. If the requirement to prepare group accounts applies to the charity trustees of a parent charity in relation to a financial year and the charity is a company, in addition to the duty to prepare individual accounts under the companies legislation[13], that requirement so applies[14].

However, the duty to prepare group accounts does not apply to the charity trustees of a parent charity in relation to a financial year if at the end of that year the charity is itself a subsidiary undertaking in relation to another charity[15] or if the aggregate gross income[16] of the group for that year does not exceed £1 million[17].

A subsidiary undertaking may be excluded from the group accounts in the following circumstances: (1) where the inclusion of the subsidiary undertaking is not material for the purposes of giving a true and fair view, save that two or more subsidiary undertakings may only be so excluded[18] if they are not material when taken together; (2) where severe long term restrictions substantially hinder the exercise of the rights of the parent charity over the assets or management of the undertaking; (3) where the information which is necessary for the preparation of the group accounts cannot be obtained without disproportionate expense or undue delay; (4) where the interest of the parent charity in the undertaking is held exclusively with a view to subsequent resale[19].

The charity trustees of a charity must preserve any group accounts prepared by them under the Charities Act 2011[20] for at least six years from the end of the financial year to which the accounts relate[21]. Where a charity ceases to exist within the six year period, the obligation to preserve the statement of accounts (or account and statement) continues to be discharged by the last charity trustees of the charity, unless the Charity Commission consents in writing to their being destroyed or otherwise disposed of[22].

The charity trustees of a parent charity must secure that, except where in their opinion there are good reasons against it, the financial year of each of its subsidiary undertakings coincides with its own financial year[23].

1 See the Charities Act 2011 ss 137–143; and notes 2–21. These provisions do not apply to exempt charities: see s 143; and PARA 381.

2 A charity is a 'parent charity' if it is, or is to be treated as, a parent undertaking in relation to one or more other undertakings in accordance with the Companies Act 2006 s 1162, Sch 7 (see **COMPANIES** vol 14 (2009) PARAS 26–27): Charities Act 2011 s 141(2). 'Group', in relation to a parent charity, means that charity and its subsidiary undertaking or undertakings, and any reference to the members of the group is to be construed accordingly: s 141(5).

3 Each undertaking in relation to which a parent charity is, or is to be treated as, a parent undertaking (see note 2) is a 'subsidiary undertaking' in relation to the parent charity: Charities Act 2011 s 141(3). However this does not have the result that any of the following is a 'subsidiary undertaking':

(1) any special trusts of a charity (s 141(4)(a));

(2) any institution which, by virtue of a direction under s 12(1) (see PARA 550) is to be treated as forming any part of a charity for the purposes of Pt 8 (ss 130–176) (s 141(4)(b)); and

(3) any charity to which a direction under s 12(2) (see PARA 550) applies for those purposes (s 141(4)(c)).

For these purposes 'undertaking' means an undertaking as defined by the Companies Act 2006 s 1161(1) or a charity which is not an undertaking as so defined: Charities Act 2011 s 141(6). As to the meaning of 'special trust' see PARA 218 note 2.

4 Ie under the Companies Act 2006 s 399 (see **COMPANIES** vol 15 (2009) PARA 775).

5 See the Charities Act 2011 s 138(1), (2). 'Group accounts' means consolidated accounts relating to the group and complying with such requirements as to their form and contents as may be prescribed by regulations made by the Minister: s 142(1). Such regulations may in particular provide for any such accounts to be prepared in accordance with such methods and principles as are specified or referred to in the regulations; for dealing with cases where the financial years of the members of the group do not all coincide; and as to any information to be provided by way of notes to the accounts: s 142(2). Such regulations may also make provision for determining the financial years of subsidiary undertakings for the purposes of these provisions and for imposing on the charity trustees of a parent charity requirements with respect to securing that such financial years coincide with that of the charity: s 142(3). As to the Minister see PARA 586. For the purposes of Pt 8 the financial years of subsidiary undertakings are to be determined in accordance with the Charities (Accounts and Reports) Regulations 2008, SI 2008/629, reg 10: reg 10(1). The financial year of a charitable subsidiary undertaking is to be determined in accordance with the Charities Act 2011 s 390 (see PARA 218): Charities (Accounts and Reports) Regulations 2008, SI 2008/629, reg 10(2). The financial year of a non-charitable subsidiary undertaking is a period in respect of which a profit and loss account of the undertaking is required to be made up (by its constitution or by the law under which it is established), whether that period is a year or not: reg 10(3).

6 As to the meaning of 'charity trustees' see PARA 255. As to the meaning of 'charity' see PARA 1.

7 Ie under the Charities Act 2011 s 130(1) (see PARA 341) or as the case may be the Companies Act 2006 s 386 (see **COMPANIES** vol 15 (2009) PARA 708).

8 Charities Act 2011 s 137(1). The 'relevant requirements' are the requirements of regulations under s 142 (see notes 5, and 12–17): s 137(1).

9 Charities Act 2011 s 137(3), (4).

10 Ie under the Charities Act 2011 s 132(1): see PARA 342.

11 Ie the documents mentioned in the Charities Act 2011 s 133: see PARA 342.
12 Charities Act 2011 s 138(3).
13 Ie the requirement in the Companies Act 2006 s 394 (see **COMPANIES** vol 15 (2009) PARA 716).
14 Charities Act 2011 s 138(4).
15 Charities Act 2011 s 139(1).
16 The Minister may by regulations make provision for determining the amount of the aggregate gross income for a financial year of a group consisting of a parent charity and its subsidiary undertaking or undertakings: Charities Act 2011 s 175. For these purposes, the Charities (Accounts and Reports) Regulations 2008, SI 2008/629, made under earlier legislation, continue to have effect. Accordingly the 'aggregate gross income' for a financial year of a group consisting of a parent charity and its subsidiary undertaking or undertakings is to be determined by eliminating all group transactions for that year from the group income for that year: Charities (Accounts and Reports) Regulations 2008, SI 2008/629, reg 9(1). 'Group income' means the aggregate of the gross income of the parent charity for the financial year, the gross income of each charitable subsidiary undertaking of that parent charity for the corresponding financial year, and the gross income of each non-charitable subsidiary undertaking of that parent charity for the corresponding financial year: reg 9(2)(c). 'Corresponding financial year' in relation to a subsidiary undertaking means: (1) in the case of a subsidiary undertaking whose financial year ends with that of the parent charity, that year; and (2) in any other case, the financial year of the subsidiary undertaking ending immediately before the end of the financial year of the parent charity: reg 9(2)(a), (3). If the figures for the corresponding financial year of a subsidiary undertaking cannot be obtained without disproportionate expense or undue delay, the latest available figures are to be taken: reg 9(4). 'Gross income' in relation to a non-charitable subsidiary undertaking means the amount of income of that undertaking that would be construed as its gross income were it a charity: reg 9(2)(b). 'Group transactions' means all income and expenditure relating to transactions between members of the group, and all gains and losses relating to transactions between members of the group: reg 9(2)(d). As to the meaning of 'member of a group' see the Charities Act 2011 s 141(5) (see note 5) (definition applied by the Charities (Accounts and Reports) Regulations 2008, SI 2008/629, reg 9(2)(e)).
17 Charities Act 2011 s 139(2) (amended with effect from 31 March 2015 by SI 2015/322).
18 Two or more subsidiary undertakings may only be excluded from the group accounts under head (1) if they are not material when taken together: Charities (Accounts and Reports) Regulations 2008, SI 2008/629, reg 19(2).
19 See the Charities Act 2011 s 139(2); and the Charities (Accounts and Reports) Regulations 2008, SI 2008/629, reg 19(1).

The Minister may prescribe circumstances in which a subsidiary undertaking may or, as the case may be, must be excluded from group accounts required to be prepared for a financial year: Charities Act 2011 s 139(3). Where, by virtue of such regulations, each of the subsidiary undertakings which are members of a group is either permitted or required to be excluded from any such group accounts for a financial year, the duty to prepare group accounts does not apply to the charity trustees of the parent charity in relation to that year: s 139(4).
20 Ie as prepared under the Charities Act 2011 s 138(2).
21 Charities Act 2011 s 140(1).
22 Charities Act 2011 s 140(2), (3).
23 Charities (Accounts and Reports) Regulations 2008, SI 2008/629, reg 11.

C. FORM AND CONTENT OF STATEMENTS GENERALLY

344. Application of requirements as to form and statements of accounts. There are statutory requirements[1] as to the form and content of a statement of accounts prepared by the charity trustees of a charity[2] in respect of a financial year[3]: (1) which begins before 1 April 2008[4]; or (2) which begins after that date, unless the charity is an exempt charity[5].

The charity trustees of a charity may not make an accounts determination[6] or a report determination[7] in respect of financial year beginning before 1 April 2008 if the charity is a special case or before that date they approved the accounts of the charity prepared in respect of that financial year or authorised the signature of an annual report[8] prepared in respect of that financial year[9].

1 The statutory requirements as to form and content of statements of account are set out in PARA 345 et seq.

2 As to the meaning of 'charity trustees' see PARA 255. As to the meaning of 'charity' see PARA 1.

3 See the Charities (Accounts and Reports) Regulations 2008, SI 2008/629, reg 4. As to the financial years to which these provisions apply see PARA 342 note 6.

The financial year of a charity which is not a company is, for the purposes of the Charities Act 2011 and regulations made under it, determined in accordance with the Charities (Accounts and Reports) Regulations 2008, SI 2008/629, reg 3: reg 3(1). The first financial year of a relevant charity is the period beginning with the day on which the charity is established and ending with its 'accounting reference date' or such other date, not more than seven days before or after the accounting reference date, as the charity trustees may determine: reg 3(2). The 'accounting reference date' in relation to the first financial year of the charity is such date, not less than six months and not more than 18 months, after the date on which the charity was established as the charity trustees may determine: reg 3(4)(a).

Subsequent financial years of a relevant charity begin with the day immediately following the last day of the charity's previous financial year and end with its 'accounting reference date' or such other date, not more than seven days before or after the accounting reference date, as the charity trustees may determine: reg 3(3). The 'accounting reference date' in relation to a subsequent financial year of the charity is the date 12 months after the previous accounting reference date of the charity or such date, not less than six months and not more than 18 months, after the previous accounting reference date as the charity trustees may determine, save that the charity trustees may only make such a determination with the consent of the Charity Commission in the case of: (1) a financial year beginning immediately after a financial year in respect of which the charity trustees made such a determination (or the equivalent determination in accordance with the Charities (Accounts and Reports) Regulations 2005, SI 2005/572, reg 6(4)(b)); or (2) a financial year where that year began immediately a financial year in respect of which the charity trustees had made such a determination (or the equivalent determination in accordance with the Charities (Accounts and Reports) Regulations 2005, SI 2005/572, reg 6(4)(b)): see the Charities (Accounts and Reports) Regulations 2008, SI 2008/629, reg 3(4)(b), (5)–(6). The charity trustees may exercise their power so as to determine an accounting reference date less, or more, than 12 months from the beginning of the financial year only where they are satisfied that there are exceptional reasons to do so: reg 3(7). As to the Charity Commission see PARAS 543–578.

4 See the Charities (Accounts and Reports) Regulations 2008, SI 2008/629, reg 4(2). In such a case the Charities (Accounts and Reports) Regulations 2005, SI 2005/572, generally continue to apply: see the Charities (Accounts and Reports) Regulations 2008, SI 2008/629, reg 4(2), (3).

5 See the Charities (Accounts and Reports) Regulations 2008, SI 2008/629, reg 4(4)(a), (5)(a). The relevant regulations (except the group provisions) also apply in respect of a transferred year: see reg 4(4)(b), (5)(b). 'Group accounts provisions' means Pt 3, Pt 4 Ch 3 and, Pt 4 Ch 3 in so far as it applies to audits carried out under the Charities Act 2011 s 151 (see PARA 359): Charities (Accounts and Reports) Regulations 2008, SI 2008/629, reg 4(6)(b). 'Transferred year' means a financial year of a charity which began before 1 April 2008 and in respect of which the charity trustees may make and make an accounts determination and a report determination: reg 4(6)(d). As to exempt charities see PARA 318 et seq.

6 'Accounts determination' means: (1) in relation to an investment fund, a determination that the Charities (Accounts and Reports) Regulations 2008, SI 2008/629, reg 6 rather than the Charities (Accounts and Reports) Regulations 2005, SI 2005/572, reg 4 is to apply to the statement of accounts prepared in respect of the financial year in question; (2) in relation to any other charity, a determination that the Charities (Accounts and Reports) Regulations 2008, SI 2008/629, reg 8 rather than the Charities (Accounts and Reports) Regulations 2005, SI 2005/572, reg 3 is to apply to the statement of accounts prepared in respect of the financial year in question: Charities (Accounts and Reports) Regulations 2008, SI 2008/629, reg 4(6)(a).

7 'Report determination' means: (1) in relation to an investment fund, a determination that the Charities (Accounts and Reports) Regulations 2008, SI 2008/629, reg 38 rather than the Charities (Accounts and Reports) Regulations 2005, SI 2005/572, reg 12, is to apply to the annual report prepared in respect of the financial year in question; (2) in relation to any other charity, a determination that the Charities (Accounts and Reports) Regulations 2008, SI 2008/62, reg 40 rather than the Charities (Accounts and Reports) Regulations 2005, SI 2005/572, reg 11 is to apply to the annual report prepared in respect of the financial year in question: Charities (Accounts and Reports) Regulations 2008, SI 2008/62, reg 4(6)(c).

8 Ie in accordance with the Charities (Accounts and Reports) Regulations 2005, SI 2005/572.

9 Charities (Accounts and Reports) Regulations 2008, SI 2008/629, reg 4(7).

345. Prescribed form and content of statements of accounts. The requirements as to form and content of statements of accounts[1] prepared by the charity trustees of a charity which is not an investment fund[2] or a special case charity[3] are as follows[4]. The statement must consist of a statement of financial activities which must show the total incoming resources and application of the resources, together with any other movements in the total resources, of the charity during the financial year[5]. The statement must also consist of a balance sheet which shows the state of affairs of the charity as at the end of the financial year[6].

The statement must be prepared in accordance with the following principles:

(1) the statement of financial activities must give a true and fair view of the incoming resources and application of the resources of the charity in the financial year in respect of which the statement is prepared[7];

(2) the balance sheet must give a true and fair view of the state of affairs of the charity at the end of that year[8];

(3) where compliance with certain requirements[9] would not be sufficient to give a true and fair view, the necessary additional information must be given in the statement of accounts or in notes to the accounts[10];

(4) if in special circumstances compliance with any of those requirements would be inconsistent with giving a true and fair view, the charity trustees must depart from the requirement to the extent necessary to give a true and fair view[11].

The statement must be prepared in accordance with the methods and principles set out in the *Statement of Recommended Practice for Accounting and Reporting by Charities* (the 'SORP')[12]. With respect to any amount required to be shown in the statement of financial activities or in the balance sheet, the statement must also show the corresponding amount[13] for the financial year immediately preceding that to which the statement or balance sheet relates[14]. Where a charity has more than one fund[15], only amounts corresponding to the entries in the statement of financial activities relating to the totals of both or all of the funds of the charity need be shown[16].

1 Ie the requirements as to the form and content of a statement of accounts to which the Charities (Accounts and Reports) Regulations 2008, SI 2008/629, apply: see PARA 344.
2 As to the requirements as to the form and content of a statement of accounts for investment funds see PARA 348.
3 As to the requirements as to the form and content of a statement of accounts for special case charities see PARA 347.
4 See the Charities (Accounts and Reports) Regulations 2008, SI 2008/629, reg 8(1), (2).
5 See the Charities (Accounts and Reports) Regulations 2008, SI 2008/629, reg 8(3)(a). As to the meaning of 'financial year' see PARA 344 note 4.
6 See the Charities (Accounts and Reports) Regulations 2008, SI 2008/629, reg 8(3)(b). The balance sheet must be signed by one or more of the charity trustees of the charity, each of whom has been authorised to do so, and must specify the date on which the statement of accounts of which the balance sheet forms part was approved by the charity trustees: reg 8(11).
7 Charities (Accounts and Reports) Regulations 2008, SI 2008/629, reg 8(4)(a).
8 Charities (Accounts and Reports) Regulations 2008, SI 2008/629, reg 8(4)(b).
9 Ie the requirements of the Charities (Accounts and Reports) Regulations 2008, SI 2008/629, reg 8(5)–(10): see the text and notes 12–16; and PARA 346.
10 Charities (Accounts and Reports) Regulations 2008, SI 2008/629, reg 8(4)(c).
11 Charities (Accounts and Reports) Regulations 2008, SI 2008/629, reg 8(4)(d).
12 Charities (Accounts and Reports) Regulations 2008, SI 2008/629, regs 2(1), 8(5).

The introduction of new accounting standards, namely the Financial Reporting Standard – FRS 102, has led to the development of two modular SORPS by the Charity Commission (and the Office of the Scottish Charity Regulator). These are the FRS 102 SORP, and the FRSSE SORP.

The applicable SORP depends on whether the charity prepares its accounts on the basis of the Financial Reporting Standard for Smaller Entities (FRSSE), or on the basis of the new FRS 102. Broadly speaking, a charity which meets any two of the following three criteria may use the FRSSE SORP. Those criteria are: (1) gross income not exceeding £6.5m; total assets not exceeding £3.26m: (3) employing no more than 50 staff. Larger charities must use FRS 102 SORP for accounting periods as from 1 January 2015. Smaller charities may choose to adopt FRS 102. See further *Charities SORP: Application guidance for charity accounting* (available, at the date at which this volume states the law, on the Charities SORP website).

Where in the financial year to which the statement of accounts relates the effect of the Charities (Accounts and Reports) Regulations 2008, SI 2008/629, reg 8(4), (5) (see the text and notes 7–11) is that there is nothing required to be shown in respect of a particular item, but an amount was required to be shown in respect of that item in the statement of accounts for the immediately preceding financial year, those provisions have effect as if such an amount were required to be shown in the statement of accounts in the financial year to which the statement relates, and that amount were nil: reg 8(9).

13 Where that corresponding amount is not comparable with the amount to be shown for the item in question in respect of the financial year to which the statement of financial activities or balance sheet relates, the former amount is to be adjusted: Charities (Accounts and Reports) Regulations 2008, SI 2008/629, reg 8(8).

14 Charities (Accounts and Reports) Regulations 2008, SI 2008/629, reg 8(6). This provision is expressed to be subject to reg 8(7)–(9) (see the text and notes 12–13, 15–16): see reg 8(6).

15 'Fund' means particular assets of a charity held on trusts which, as respects the purposes for which those assets are held, or as respects the powers of the charity trustees to use or apply those assets, are not identical with those on which other assets of the charity are held: Charities (Accounts and Reports) Regulations 2008, SI 2008/629, reg 2(1).

16 Charities (Accounts and Reports) Regulations 2008, SI 2008/629, reg 8(7).

346. Information provided in notes to the accounts. Specified information[1] must be provided by way of notes to the accounts[2]. Such information, in so far as not provided in the statement of financial activities or in the balance sheet, is as follows[3]:

(1) particulars of any material adjustment[4];

(2) a description of each of the accounting policies which have been adopted by the charity trustees[5] and are material in the context of the accounts of the charity, and the estimation techniques adopted by the charity trustees which are material to the presentation of the accounts; and a description of any material change to such policies and techniques, the reason for such change and its effect, if material, on the accounts, in accordance with the methods and principles set out in the *Statement of Recommended Practice for Accounting and Reporting by Charities* (the 'SORP')[6];

(3) a description of the nature and purpose of all material funds[7] of the charity in accordance with the methods and principles set out in the SORP[8];

(4) such particulars of the transactions of the charity, or of any subsidiary undertaking of the charity[9], entered into with a related party as are required to be disclosed by the SORP[10];

(5) such particulars of the cost to the charity of employing and providing pensions for staff as are required by the SORP to be disclosed[11];

(6) such particulars of the emoluments of staff employed by the charity as may be required by the SORP to be disclosed[12];

(7) a description of any incoming resources which represent capital, according to whether or not that capital is permanent endowment[13];

(8) an itemised analysis of any material movement between any of the restricted funds of the charity, or between a restricted and an

unrestricted fund[14] of the charity, together with an explanation of the nature and purpose of each of those funds[15];

(9) the name of any subsidiary undertaking of the charity, together with a description of the nature of the charity's relationship with that subsidiary undertaking and of its activities, including, where material, a statement of its turnover and net profit or loss for the corresponding financial year[16] of the institution or body corporate and any qualification expressed in an auditor's report on its accounts[17];

(10) particulars of any guarantee given by the charity, where any potential liability under the guarantee is outstanding at the date of the balance sheet[18];

(11) particulars of any loan outstanding at the date of the balance sheet (a) which was made to the charity, and which is secured by an express charge on any of the assets of the charity; or (b) which was made by the charity to any subsidiary undertaking of the charity[19];

(12) particulars of any fund of the charity which is in deficit at the date of the balance sheet[20];

(13) particulars of any remuneration paid to an auditor or independent examiner in respect of auditing or examining the accounts of the charity and particulars of any remuneration paid to him in respect of any other services rendered to the charity[21];

(14) such particulars of any grant made by the charity as may be required by the SORP to be disclosed[22];

(15) particulars of any ex gratia payment[23] made by the charity[24];

(16) an analysis of any entry in the statement of financial activities relating to resources expended on charitable activities as may be required by the SORP to be disclosed[25];

(17) such particulars of any support costs incurred by the charity as may be required by the SORP to be disclosed[26];

(18) an analysis of any entry in the balance sheet relating to fixed assets[27], debtors and creditors, according to the categories set out in the SORP[28];

(19) an analysis of all material changes during the financial year in question in the values of fixed assets, in accordance with the methods and principles set out in the SORP[29];

(20) in the case of any amount required by any of heads (1) to (19) above (other than heads (8), (14) or (19) to be disclosed)[30], the corresponding amount for the financial year immediately preceding that to which the accounts relate[31];

(21) a statement as to whether or not the accounts have been prepared in accordance with any applicable accounting standards and statements of recommended practice and particulars of any material departure from those standards and statements of practice and the reasons for such departure[32];

(22) where the charity trustees have exercised their powers[33] so as to determine an accounting reference date earlier or later than 12 months from the beginning of the financial year, a statement of their reasons for doing so[34];

(23) if the charity trustees have departed[35] from any requirements of the provisions relating to the form and content of statements of account[36], particulars of any such departure, the reasons for it, and its effect[37]; and

(24) any additional information: (a) which is required to ensure that the

statement of accounts complies with the requirements of the provisions relating to the form and content of statements of account[38]; or (b) which may reasonably assist the user to understand the statement of accounts[39].

1 Ie information specified in Charities (Accounts and Reports) Regulations 2008, SI 2008/629, Sch 2: see the text and notes 3–39.
2 Charities (Accounts and Reports) Regulations 2008, SI 2008/629, reg 8(10), Sch 2 para 1. As to when these provisions apply see PARA 342 note 6.
3 Charities (Accounts and Reports) Regulations 2008, SI 2008/629, Sch 2 para 1(1).
4 Charities (Accounts and Reports) Regulations 2008, SI 2008/629, Sch 2 para 1(1)(a). The material adjustment referred to in the text is the adjustment made pursuant to reg 8(8) (see PARA 345): Sch 2 para 1(1)(a).
5 As to the meaning of 'charity trustees' see PARA 255.
6 Charities (Accounts and Reports) Regulations 2008, SI 2008/629, Sch 2 para 1(1)(b), (c). As to the SORP see PARA 345 note 12.
7 As to the meaning of 'fund' see PARA 345 note 15.
8 Charities (Accounts and Reports) Regulations 2008, SI 2008/629, Sch 2 para 1(1)(d).
9 As to the meaning of 'subsidiary undertaking' see PARA 343 note 3 (definition applied by virtue of the Charities (Accounts and Reports) Regulations 2008, SI 2008/629, reg 2(1)).
10 Charities (Accounts and Reports) Regulations 2008, SI 2008/629, Sch 2 para 1(1)(e).
11 Charities (Accounts and Reports) Regulations 2008, SI 2008/629, Sch 2 para 1(1)(f).
12 Charities (Accounts and Reports) Regulations 2008, SI 2008/629, Sch 2 para 1(1)(g).
13 Charities (Accounts and Reports) Regulations 2008, SI 2008/629, Sch 2 para 1(1)(h).
14 'Unrestricted fund' means a fund which is to be used or applied in any way determined by the charity trustees for the furtherance of the objects of a charity, and 'restricted fund' means any other fund of a charity: Charities (Accounts and Reports) Regulations 2008, SI 2008/629, reg 2(1).
15 Charities (Accounts and Reports) Regulations 2008, SI 2008/629, Sch 2 para 1(1)(i).
16 As to the meaning of 'corresponding financial year' see the Charities (Accounts and Reports) Regulations 2008, SI 2008/629, reg 9(3); and PARA 343 note 16 (definition applied by Sch 2 para 1(3)(a)). As to the meaning of 'financial year' see PARA 344 note 4.
17 Charities (Accounts and Reports) Regulations 2008, SI 2008/629, Sch 2 para 1(1)(j).
18 Charities (Accounts and Reports) Regulations 2008, SI 2008/629, Sch 2 para 1(1)(k).
19 Charities (Accounts and Reports) Regulations 2008, SI 2008/629, Sch 2 para 1(1)(l).
20 Charities (Accounts and Reports) Regulations 2008, SI 2008/629, Sch 2 para 1(1)(m).
21 Charities (Accounts and Reports) Regulations 2008, SI 2008/629, Sch 2 para 1(1)(n).
22 Charities (Accounts and Reports) Regulations 2008, SI 2008/629, Sch 2 para 1(1)(o). However, this is subject to the proviso that the charity trustees of a charity that is a charitable trust created by any person are not required to disclose any information as to the identities of recipients of grants made out of the funds of the charity or the amounts of individual grants so made, if the disclosure of that information would fall to be made at a time when the settlor; or the spouse or civil partner of the settlor, is still alive: Sch 2 para 1(2), (3)(b).
23 'Ex gratia payment' means any such application of the property of a charity, or any such waiver by a charity of any entitlement to receive any property, as may be authorised under the Charities Act 2011 s 106(1), (2) (see PARA 430): Charities (Accounts and Reports) Regulations 2008, SI 2008/629, reg 2(1).
24 Charities (Accounts and Reports) Regulations 2008, SI 2008/629, Sch 2 para 1(1)(p).
25 Charities (Accounts and Reports) Regulations 2008, SI 2008/629, Sch 2 para 1(1)(q).
26 Charities (Accounts and Reports) Regulations 2008, SI 2008/629, Sch 2 para 1(1)(r).
27 'Fixed assets' means the assets of a charity which are intended for use or investment on a continuing basis: Charities (Accounts and Reports) Regulations 2008, SI 2008/629, reg 2(1).
28 Charities (Accounts and Reports) Regulations 2008, SI 2008/629, Sch 2 para 1(1)(s).
29 Charities (Accounts and Reports) Regulations 2008, SI 2008/629, Sch 2 para 1(1)(t).
30 Ie other than amounts required by the Charities (Accounts and Reports) Regulations 2008, SI 2008/629, Sch 2 para 1(i), (o), (t) to be disclosed: see heads (8), (14), (19) in the text.
31 Charities (Accounts and Reports) Regulations 2008, SI 2008/629, Sch 2 para 1(1)(u).
32 Charities (Accounts and Reports) Regulations 2008, SI 2008/629, Sch 2 para 1(1)(v).
33 Ie under the Charities (Accounts and Reports) Regulations 2008, SI 2008/629, reg 3(4)(b): see PARA 344.
34 Charities (Accounts and Reports) Regulations 2008, SI 2008/629, Sch 2 para 1(1)(w).

35 Ie under the Charities (Accounts and Reports) Regulations 2008, SI 2008/629, reg 8(4)(d): see PARA 345 text to note 11.
36 Ie the provisions of the Charities (Accounts and Reports) Regulations 2008, SI 2008/629, reg 8: see PARA 345.
37 Charities (Accounts and Reports) Regulations 2008, SI 2008/629, Sch 2 para 1(1)(x).
38 See note 37.
39 Charities (Accounts and Reports) Regulations 2008, SI 2008/629, Sch 2 para 1(1)(y).

D. FORM AND CONTENT OF STATEMENTS: SPECIAL CASES

347. Prescribed form and content of statements of accounts in special cases. There are statutory requirements[1] as to the form and content of a statement of accounts prepared by the charity trustees[2] of a special case charity[3].

The requirements as to form and content of such statement of accounts are as follows[4]. The statement must consist of an income and expenditure account and a balance sheet showing the state of affairs as at the end of the financial year in respect of which the statement of accounts is prepared[5]. It must also be prepared in accordance with the following principles:

(1) The income and expenditure account must give a true and fair view of the income and expenditure of the charity for the financial year in respect of which the statement of accounts is prepared[6].
(2) The balance sheet must give a true and fair view of the state of affairs of the charity at the end of that year[7].

1 Ie the requirements contained in the Charities (Accounts and Reports) Regulations 2008, SI 2008/629, reg 7: see the text and notes 4–7. As to the financial years to which these provisions apply see PARA 342 note 6.
2 Ie under the Charities Act 2011 s 132(1): see PARA 342.
3 See the Charities (Accounts and Reports) Regulations 2008, SI 2008/629, reg 7(1).

'Special case charity' is defined in reg 2(1) (amended by SI 2010/500; SI 2010/671), and means a charity which:

(1) is a registered social landlord within the meaning of the Housing Act 1996 and whose registration has been recorded under s 3(3)(a) (see HOUSING vol 56 (2011) PARA 123 et seq); or
(2) is a non-profit registered provider of social housing by virtue of the Housing and Regeneration Act 2008 s 278 (see HOUSING vol 56 (2011) PARA 41), and whose registration as a social landlord was the subject of a notice under the Housing Act 1996 s 3(3)(a); or
(3) is a non-profit registered provider of social housing whose registration as a provider of social housing has been the subject of a notice under the Housing and Regeneration Act 2008 s 120(1)(a); or
(4) has during the financial year in question (a) conducted an institution in relation to which a designation made, or having effect as if made, under the Education Reform Act 1988 s 129 has effect; (b) received financial support from funds administered by a higher education funding council or further education funding council within the meaning of the Further and Higher Education Act 1992 in respect of expenditure incurred or to be incurred by the charity in connection with that institution; and (c) incurred no expenditure for charitable purposes other than the purposes of that institution or any other such institution; or
(5) is a college or hall in the University of Cambridge; or
(6) was previously exempt under specific provisions which have since been revoked; or
(7) is a Welsh higher education corporation.

As to the meaning of 'charity trustees' see PARA 255.
4 Charities (Accounts and Reports) Regulations 2008, SI 2008/629, reg 7(2).
5 Charities (Accounts and Reports) Regulations 2008, SI 2008/629, reg 7(3). The balance sheet must be signed by at least one of the charity trustees of the charity, each of whom has been authorised to do so, and specify the date on which the statement of accounts of which the balance sheet forms part was approved by the charity trustees: reg 7(5).
6 Charities (Accounts and Reports) Regulations 2008, SI 2008/629, reg 7(4)(a).
7 Charities (Accounts and Reports) Regulations 2008, SI 2008/629, reg 7(4)(b).

E. FORM AND CONTENT OF STATEMENTS: INVESTMENT FUNDS

348. Prescribed form and content of statements of accounts: investment funds. There are statutory requirements[1] as to the form and content of a statement of accounts prepared by the charity trustees of an investment fund[2] in respect of a financial year[3].

The requirements as to form and content of such statement of accounts are as follows[4]. The statement of accounts must consist of: (1) a statement of total return which shows the net gain or loss on investments, gross income, total expenditure and total return of the investment fund, and the total amount distributed or due, including interest paid or payable, to participating charities out of the investment fund, during the financial year in respect of which the statement of accounts is prepared[5]; (2) a statement of changes in net assets providing a reconciliation between the net assets of the investment fund at the beginning of the relevant financial year and the net assets at the end of that year[6], save in the case of any financial year of a common deposit fund in which there are no gains or losses on disposal or revaluation of assets[7]; and (3) a balance sheet which shows the state of affairs of the investment fund as at the end of the relevant financial year[8].

In respect of every amount required to be shown in the statement of total return, statement of changes in net assets and the balance sheet, the corresponding amount for the financial year immediately preceding the relevant financial year must also be shown[9], save that, where the corresponding amount is not comparable with the amount to be shown for the item in question in respect of the relevant financial year, the former amount must be adjusted and particulars of any such material adjustment must be disclosed in a note to the accounts[10].

The statement must be prepared in accordance with the following principles[11]:

(a) the statement of total return must give a true and fair view of the incoming resources and application of the resources of the investment fund in the relevant financial year[12];

(b) the balance sheet must give a true and fair view of the state of affairs of the investment fund at the end of that year[13];

(c) the statement of changes in net assets must give a true and fair view of the movements in the net assets of the investment fund between their position at the beginning of the relevant financial year and their position at the end of that year[14];

(d) where compliance with certain requirements[15] would not be sufficient to give a true and fair view, the necessary additional information must be given in the accounts or in a note to the accounts[16];

(e) if in special circumstances compliance with any of those requirements would be inconsistent with giving a true and fair view, the charity trustees must depart from the requirement to the extent necessary to give a true and fair view, and particulars of the departure, the reasons for it and its effect must be given in a note to the accounts[17].

The values at which assets and liabilities of an investment fund are recorded in the balance sheet, and the recognition bases for gains and losses, must be determined in accordance with the methods and principles set out in the *Statement of Recommended Practice for Financial Statements of Authorised Funds* ('IMA SORP')[18].

1 Ie the requirements contained in the Charities (Accounts and Reports) Regulations 2008, SI 2008/629, reg 6: see the text and notes 3–11. As to the financial years to which these provisions apply see PARA 342 note 6.
2 Ie under the Charities Act 2001 s 132(1): see PARA 342. 'Investment fund' means a common deposit fund or a common investment fund: Charities (Accounts and Reports) Regulations 2008, SI 2008/629, reg 2(1). As to common investment funds see PARA 426. As to common deposit funds see PARA 427. As to the meaning of 'charity trustees' see PARA 1 note 10.
3 Charities (Accounts and Reports) Regulations 2008, SI 2008/629, reg 6(1). As to the meaning of 'financial year' see PARA 344 note 4.
4 Charities (Accounts and Reports) Regulations 2008, SI 2008/629, reg 6(2).
5 Charities (Accounts and Reports) Regulations 2008, SI 2008/629, reg 6(3)(a), Sch 1 para 1. This information must be analysed by reference to:
(1) net gains or losses on investments analysed as arising from non-derivative securities, derivative contracts and forward currency contracts (Sch 1 para 2(a));
(2) gains or losses on other assets (Sch 1 para 2(b));
(3) gross income, divided into dividends in respect of shares, scrip dividends, interest on securities, interest on deposits at banks and building societies, underwriting commission and other income (Sch 1 para 2(c));
(4) expenses incurred in the administration of the investment fund, divided into fees payable in respect of investment management services provided to the investment fund, fees payable in respect of the maintenance of the register of charities participating in the investment fund, fees payable in respect of any audit of the accounts of the investment fund, fees payable to the person carrying out such an audit in respect of other services for the investment fund provided by him, fees payable in respect of the safe custody of the assets of the investment fund, fees payable in respect of other administrative services provided to the investment fund and other expenditure divided into such categories as reasonably enable the user to gain an appreciation of the expenditure incurred (Sch 1 para 2(d));
(5) interest incurred in the administration of the investment fund (Sch 1 para 2(e));
(6) net income of the investment fund before taxation calculated as follows: A minus B where A is the total amount entered under head (3) above and B is the aggregate of the total amounts entered in that statement pursuance of heads (4) and (5) (Sch 1 para 2(f));
(7) tax borne by the investment fund in respect of income, profits or gains during the relevant financial year, divided into income tax or capital gains tax to which the investment fund is liable in the United Kingdom and overseas tax (Sch 1 para 2(g));
(8) net income of the investment fund after taxation calculated as follows: A minus B where A is the amount entered under head (6) above and B is the amount entered under head (7) above (Sch 1 para 2(h));
(9) total return of the investment fund before distributions which is calculated by aggregating the amounts entered under heads (1), (2) and (8) above (Sch 1 para 2(i));
(10) the amount distributed or due in respect of income and accumulation shares, and interest paid or payable to charities who have deposited sums during the relevant financial year (Sch 1 para 2(j));
(11) the change in value of the investment fund resulting from its activities calculated as follows: A minus B where A is the amount entered under head (8) and B is the amount entered under head (9) above (Sch 1 para 2(k)).

Where any of heads (1)–(11) require information to be divided into separate categories, the division of that information into such separate categories may, if the charity trustees so elect, be effected instead by means of a note to the accounts: see Sch 1 para 4. As to such a note see PARA 349.

In the case of a common investment fund established by a scheme which, in pursuance of the Charities Act 1960 s 22(5) (repealed) or the Charities Act 2011 s 98(1), (2), includes provision for enabling sums to be deposited by or on behalf of a charity on the basis that (subject to the provisions of the scheme) the charity is entitled to repayment of the sums deposited and to interest thereon at a rate determined by or under the scheme, the analysis in heads (1)–(11) above must distinguish between the amount of capital and income to be shared between charities participating otherwise than by way of deposit and the amount of capital and income that is required in respect of the liabilities of the investment fund for the repayment of deposits and for interest on deposits (including amounts required by way of reserve): Charities (Accounts and Reports) Regulations 2008, SI 2008/629, Sch 1 para 3.
6 Charities (Accounts and Reports) Regulations 2008, SI 2008/629, reg 6(3)(b), Sch 1 para 5. The reconciliation must show: (1) the value of the net assets at the beginning of the relevant financial

year; (2) the change in value of the investment fund calculated in accordance with head (11) of note 5; (3) the value of the net assets at the end of the relevant financial year; (4) particulars of any other items necessary to provide the reconciliation required by the statement of total return; and (5) in the case of a common investment fund, the amount or value of any property transferred to or withdrawn from the investment fund during the relevant financial year by participating charities and the amount of any distribution of income due in respect of accumulation shares: Sch 1 para 6.

In the case of a common investment fund to which Sch 1 para 3 applies (see note 5), this analysis must distinguish between the amount of capital and income to be shared between charities participating otherwise than by way of deposit and amount of capital and income that is required in respect of the liabilities of the investment fund for the repayment of deposits and for interest on deposits (including amounts required by way of reserve): Sch 1 para 7.

7 Charities (Accounts and Reports) Regulations 2008, SI 2008/629, reg 6(4).

8 Charities (Accounts and Reports) Regulations 2008, SI 2008/629, reg 6(3)(c), Sch 1 para 8. In the case of a common investment fund to which Sch 1 para 3 does not apply, this is shown by reference to:

(1) tangible fixed assets for use by the investment fund (Sch 1 para 9(a));
(2) investments (Sch 1 para 9(b));
(3) other assets, divided into debtors, deposits and loans, cash at bank and in hand, and others (Sch 1 para 9(c));
(4) total assets calculated by aggregating the amounts entered under heads (1)–(3) (Sch 1 para 9(d));
(5) derivative liabilities (Sch 1 para 9(e));
(6) other liabilities, divided into creditors, bank overdrafts, other loans and distributions payable to participating charities (Sch 1 para 9(f));
(7) total liabilities calculated by aggregating the amounts entered under heads (5) and (6) (Sch 1 para 9(g));
(8) net assets which is calculated as follows: A minus B where A is the amount entered under head (4) and B is the amount entered under head (7) (Sch 1 para 9(h)).

In the case of a common investment fund to which Sch 1 para 3 applies, this is shown by reference to heads (1)–(8) above in relation to the amount of capital and income to be shared between charities participating otherwise than by way of deposit, and by reference to heads (a)-(j) below (ie the provisions for common deposit funds) in relation to the amount of capital and income that is required in respect of the liabilities of the investment fund for the repayment of deposits and for interest on deposits (including amounts required by way of reserve): Sch 1 para 10.

In the case of a common deposit fund, the specified information is:

(a) cash at bank and in hand (Sch 1 para 11(a));
(b) debtors (Sch 1 para 11(b));
(c) deposits and investments, divided into deposits at the Bank of England, deposits with a person who has permission under the Financial Services and Markets Act 2000 Pt IV (see FINANCIAL SERVICES AND INSTITUTIONS) to accept deposits, other bank deposits, other deposits and other investments (Charities (Accounts and Reports) Regulations 2008, SI 2008/629, Sch 1 para 11(c));
(d) current assets not included in heads (a)–(c) (Sch 1 para 11(d));
(e) tangible fixed assets for use by the common deposit fund (Sch 1 para 11(e));
(f) gross assets which is calculated by aggregating the amounts entered under heads (a)–(e) (Sch 1 para 11(f));
(g) sums deposited by participating charities (Sch 1 para 11(g));
(h) other liabilities, divided into creditors, bank overdrafts, other loans and interest accrued or payable to participating charities (Sch 1 para 11(h));
(i) sums held as an income reserve on trust for existing depositors (Sch 1 para 11(i)); and
(j) total liabilities which is calculated by aggregating the amounts entered under heads (g), (h) and (i) (Sch 1 para 11(j)).

Despite the requirement in head (c) above to divide into separate categories the information to be provided by dividing the information into separate categories, the division of that information into those categories may, if the charity trustees so elect, be effected instead by means of a note to the accounts: Sch 1 para 12. As to such a note see PARA 349.

The balance sheet must, if the scheme or schemes regulating the investment fund allocates responsibility for preparing the accounts to a particular person, be signed and dated by that person, else by at least one of the charity trustees of the investment fund, each of whom has been authorised to do so: reg 6(7). Where the balance sheet is signed by the latter, it must specify the date on which the statement of accounts of which the balance sheet forms part was approved by the charity trustees: reg 6(8).

9 See the Charities (Accounts and Reports) Regulations 2008, SI 2008/629, reg 6(5), Sch 1 para 14(1). Where the effect of the principles according to which the statement must be prepared (ie Sch 1 para 13, on which see below text and notes 13–17) is that in the relevant financial year there was nothing required to be shown by one or more of the provisions specified in Sch 1 para 14(1) in respect of a particular item but an amount was required to be shown by that provision for that item in the statement of accounts prepared for the financial year immediately preceding the relevant financial year, Sch 1 para 14(1) has effect as if such an amount were required to be shown in the relevant financial year and that amount were nil: Sch 1 para 14(3).

10 See the Charities (Accounts and Reports) Regulations 2008, SI 2008/629, Sch 1 para 14(2).

11 See the Charities (Accounts and Reports) Regulations 2008, SI 2008/629, reg 6(5), Sch 1 para 13.

12 Charities (Accounts and Reports) Regulations 2008, SI 2008/629, Sch 1 para 13(1).

13 Charities (Accounts and Reports) Regulations 2008, SI 2008/629, Sch 1 para 13(2).

14 Charities (Accounts and Reports) Regulations 2008, SI 2008/629, Sch 1 para 13(3).

15 Ie the Charities (Accounts and Reports) Regulations 2008, SI 2008/629, Sch 1 paras 1–12 (see notes 7–8, 10), 16 (see PARA 349).

16 Charities (Accounts and Reports) Regulations 2008, SI 2008/629, Sch 1 para 13(4).

17 Charities (Accounts and Reports) Regulations 2008, SI 2008/629, Sch 1 para 13(5).

18 Charities (Accounts and Reports) Regulations 2008, SI 2008/629, reg 6(5), Sch 1 para 15. The Charities (Accounts and Reports) Regulations 2008, SI 2008/629, refer to the version of the SORP issued in 2005 (see Sch 1 para 17(1)), but this has been superseded by the current IMA SORP which was issued in 2014 on its website by the Investment Management Association.

349. Information provided in notes to the accounts: investment funds generally. Specified information[1] must be provided by way of notes to the accounts[2]. Such information, in so far as not provided in the statement of accounts, is as follows[3]:

(1) a description of the accounting policies adopted for the investment fund and, in particular, the basis of valuation of investments, the recognition of dividend income or interest and the conversion of any amounts expressed in currency other than pounds sterling[4];

(2) a description of the accounting assumptions made by the investment fund, including any material change in these assumptions, the reason for such change and its material effect on the accounts[5];

(3) where the charity trustees[6] have during the relevant financial year entered into any transaction, agreement or arrangement made for the purpose of minimising the risk of loss to the investment fund in consequence of fluctuations in interest rates or in the market value of securities or in the rates of foreign exchange, or entered into any other transaction in financial futures or options relating to shares, securities, foreign currency or into any other financial instrument the value of which is dependent on or derived from the price movements in one or more underlying assets, the nature of, and reason for, entering into that transaction, agreement or arrangement and the total value of, and the maximum extent of financial exposure as at the date of the balance sheet resulting from, that transaction, agreement or arrangement[7];

(4) a statement as to whether any remuneration or other benefits (together with the amount of such remuneration or, as the case may be, the monetary value of such benefits and the name of the person to whom the remuneration or benefit has been paid or is payable) has been paid or is payable to any person who is a charity trustee of the investment fund, or to whom functions in relation to management of the

investment fund have been delegated ('manager'), or connected with such a charity trustee or manager directly or indirectly from the property of the investment fund or from the property of any subsidiary undertaking of the investment fund[8];

(5) particulars of any transaction undertaken in the name of or on behalf of the investment fund in which any person referred to in head (4) has a material interest[9];

(6) an analysis of the amount and date of any distribution in respect of income and accumulation shares or payment of interest to participating charities[10];

(7) a note of any adjustments made in the statement of total return to reflect the amount of income included in the creation or cancellation price of a unit or share in the investment fund[11];

(8) the name of any subsidiary undertaking of the investment fund, together with a description of the nature of the investment fund's relationship with that subsidiary undertaking and of its activities, and, where material, a statement of the turnover and net profit or loss of the subsidiary undertaking for the corresponding financial year[12] and any qualification expressed in an auditor's report on the accounts of the subsidiary undertaking for that financial year[13];

(9) particulars of any loan or guarantee secured against any of the assets of the investment fund[14];

(10) an explanation of any amount entered in pursuance of income tax or capital gains tax to which the investment fund is liable in the United Kingdom[15] ('United Kingdom tax')[16];

(11) an analysis of any entry in the balance sheet relating to:

(a) tangible fixed assets for use by the investment fund, according to the following categories of: freehold interests in land and buildings; any other interest in land and buildings; payments on account and assets in course of construction; and plant, machinery, fixtures, fittings and equipment[17];

(b) debtors, according to the following categories of: amounts receivable in respect of securities sold; accrued income; other debtors; and, in the case of a common investment fund, amounts receivable in respect of property transferred to the investment fund[18];

(c) creditors, according to the following categories of: amounts payable in respect of securities purchased; accrued expenses; other creditors; and in the case of a common investment fund, amounts payable in respect of property withdrawn from the investment fund[19];

(12) the following particulars of any contingent liability: (a) its amount or estimated amount; (b) its legal nature; and (c) whether any valuable security has been provided by the investment fund in connection with that liability and, if so, what[20];

(13) particulars of any other financial commitments which have not been provided for and are relevant to assessment of the state of affairs of the investment fund[21];

(14) in the case of any amount required by any of the heads (1) to (13) to be disclosed, or the percentage of net assets represented by each category of certain investments required to be disclosed[22], or the percentage of

investment assets represented by each class of certain investments required to be disclosed[23], the corresponding amount or percentage for the financial year immediately preceding the relevant financial year[24];

(15) a statement as to whether or not the accounts have been prepared in accordance with any applicable accounting standards and statements of recommended practice and particulars of any material departure from those standards and practices and the reasons for such departure[25];

(16) where the charity trustees have exercised their powers for determining the accounting reference date[26] a statement of their reasons for doing so[27];

(17) any other information which is required[28] to be disclosed in a note to the accounts or which may reasonably assist the user to understand the statement of accounts[29];

(18) specified information in the case of a common investment fund and in the case of a common deposit fund[30].

1 Ie information specified in the Charities (Accounts and Reports) Regulations 2008, SI 2008/629, reg 6(6), Sch 1 para 16: see the text and notes 4–30.

2 Charities (Accounts and Reports) Regulations 2008, SI 2008/629, reg 6(6). These provisions apply to financial years beginning on or after 1 April 2008: see PARA 342 note 6.

3 Charities (Accounts and Reports) Regulations 2008, SI 2008/629, Sch 1 para 16(1). As to additional information to be provided in relation to a common investment fund see PARA 350 and as to additional information to be provided in relation to a common deposit fund see PARA 351.

4 Charities (Accounts and Reports) Regulations 2008, SI 2008/629, Sch 1 para 16(1)(a).

5 Charities (Accounts and Reports) Regulations 2008, SI 2008/629, Sch 1 para 16(1)(b).

6 As to the meaning of 'charity trustees' see PARA 255.

7 Charities (Accounts and Reports) Regulations 2008, SI 2008/629, Sch 1 para 16(1)(c).

8 Charities (Accounts and Reports) Regulations 2008, SI 2008/629, Sch 1 para 16(1)(d). A person 'A' is connected with a charity trustee or a person to whom functions in relation to the management of the investment fund have been delegated if: (1) A is the child, parent, grandchild, grandparent, brother or sister of the charity trustee or manager; (2) A is the spouse or the civil partner of the charity trustee or manager; or any person connected with a charity trustee or manager by virtue of head (1); (3) A is the trustee of any trust which is not a charity and the beneficiaries or potential beneficiaries of which include the charity trustee or manager or any person connected with that trustee or manager by virtue of head (1) or (2) and is acting in his capacity as trustee of that trust; (4) A is carrying on a business in partnership with the charity trustee or manager or any person connected with a trustee or manager by virtue of head (1), (2) or (3) and is acting in his capacity as such a business partner; or (5) A is a body corporate which is not a company which is connected with a charitable institution within the meaning of the Charities Act 1992 s 58(5) (see PARA 477 note 5) but in which the charity trustee or manager has (or the charity trustee or manager, any other trustee or manager of the investment fund or persons connected with him or them by virtue of head (1), (2), (3) or (4), taken together, have) a substantial interest: Charities (Accounts and Reports) Regulations 2008, SI 2008/629, Sch 1 para 17(2). As to the meaning of 'child' see the Charities Act 2011 s 350; and PARA 401 (definition applied by virtue of the Charities (Accounts and Reports) Regulations 2008, SI 2008/629, Sch 1 para 17(3)(a)). As to the effect of the Marriage (Same Sex Couples) Act 2013 see s 1(1), 11(1); and **MATRIMONIAL AND CIVIL PARTNERSHIP LAW** vol 72 (2009) PARA 1 et seq. Whether a person controls an institution is to be determined in accordance with the Charities Act 2011 s 351; and whether a person has a substantial interest in a body corporate is to be determined in accordance with s 352: Charities (Accounts and Reports) Regulations 2008, SI 2008/629, Sch 1 para 17(3)(b), (c).

9 Charities (Accounts and Reports) Regulations 2008, SI 2008/629, Sch 1 para 16(1)(e).

10 Charities (Accounts and Reports) Regulations 2008, SI 2008/629, Sch 1 para 16(1)(f).

11 Charities (Accounts and Reports) Regulations 2008, SI 2008/629, Sch 1 para 16(1)(g).

12 As to the meaning of 'corresponding financial year' see PARA 346 note 16: Charities (Accounts and Reports) Regulations 2008, SI 2008/629, Sch 1 para 16(4).

13 Charities (Accounts and Reports) Regulations 2008, SI 2008/629, Sch 1 para 16(1)(h).

14 Charities (Accounts and Reports) Regulations 2008, SI 2008/629, Sch 1 para 16(1)(i).

15 Ie any amount entered in pursuance of the Charities (Accounts and Reports) Regulations 2008, SI 2008/629, Sch 1 para 2(g)(i): see PARA 348 note 5 head (7).
16 Charities (Accounts and Reports) Regulations 2008, SI 2008/629, Sch 1 para 16(1)(j).
17 Charities (Accounts and Reports) Regulations 2008, SI 2008/629, Sch 1 para 16(1)(k)(i).
18 Charities (Accounts and Reports) Regulations 2008, SI 2008/629, Sch 1 para 16(1)(k)(ii).
19 Charities (Accounts and Reports) Regulations 2008, SI 2008/629, Sch 1 para 16(1)(k)(iii).
20 Charities (Accounts and Reports) Regulations 2008, SI 2008/629, Sch 1 para 16(1)(l).
21 Charities (Accounts and Reports) Regulations 2008, SI 2008/629, Sch 1 para 16(1)(m).
22 Ie the information required by the Charities (Accounts and Reports) Regulations 2008, SI 2008/629, Sch 1 para 1(2)(a)(iv) of the additional requirements for a common investment fund: see text and note 3.
23 Ie the information required by the Charities (Accounts and Reports) Regulations 2008, SI 2008/629, Sch 1 para 1(2)(a)(v) of the additional requirements for a common investment fund: see text and note 3.
24 Charities (Accounts and Reports) Regulations 2008, SI 2008/629, Sch 1 para 16(1)(n).
25 Charities (Accounts and Reports) Regulations 2008, SI 2008/629, Sch 1 para 16(1)(o).
26 Ie under the Charities (Accounts and Reports) Regulations 2008, SI 2008/629, reg 3(4)(b): see PARA 344 note 3.
27 Charities (Accounts and Reports) Regulations 2008, SI 2008/629, Sch 1 para 16(1)(p).
28 Ie required by the Charities (Accounts and Reports) Regulations 2008, SI 2008/629.
29 Charities (Accounts and Reports) Regulations 2008, SI 2008/629, Sch 1 para 16(1)(r).
30 See the Charities (Accounts and Reports) Regulations 2008, SI 2008/629, Sch 1 para 16(1)(q); and PARAS 350, 351.

350. Information provided in notes to the accounts: common investment funds. In addition to the information to be provided in relation to an investment fund[1], a common investment fund[2] must include in the notes to the accounts the following statements made up to the date of the balance sheet[3]:

(1) a portfolio statement, specifying details of each investment held by or on behalf of the investment fund, including: (a) its market value at that date and whether the investment in question is listed on a recognised stock exchange[4]; (b) the category of each such investment determined according to its geographical area or industrial sector[5]; (c) where the investment fund invests in more than one class of assets, the market value at that date of each class of investment[6]; (d) the percentage of net assets represented by each investment so held and by each category of investment specified under head (b)[7]; (e) the percentage of investment assets represented by each class of investments specified under head (c)[8]; and (f) an analysis of the credit rating of any interest-bearing securities held at that date, as may be required by the IMA SORP to be given[9];

(2) a statement of major changes in the portfolio, specifying: (a) where the relevant financial year is the first financial year of the investment fund and the aggregate value of purchases or sales of a particular investment during the financial year exceeds 2 per cent of net assets at the end of that year, or, where the relevant financial year is not the first financial year of the investment fund and the aggregate value of purchases or sales of a particular investment during the relevant financial year exceeds 2 per cent of net assets at the beginning of that year, that value[10]; (b) unless disclosed under head (a), the value of the 20 largest purchases and sales of a particular investment during the relevant financial year[11]; and (c) the total cost of purchase and net proceeds from sales of investments during the relevant financial year[12];

(3) a statement of the number of shares issued as at the beginning of the relevant financial year, the number of shares issued as at the date of the

balance sheet and the value of each income or accumulation share as at each of those dates, calculated by reference to the net asset value of the investment fund[13]; and

(4) a statement of the amount, if any, in the dividend equalisation reserve[14].

1 Ie the information specified under the Charities (Accounts and Reports) Regulations 2008, SI 2008/629, Sch 1 para 1(1) (see PARA 349).
2 'Common investment fund' means a common investment fund established by a scheme under the Charities Act 1960 s 22 (repealed) or the Charities Act 2011 s 96 (see PARA 426): Charities (Accounts and Reports) Regulations 2008, SI 2008/629, reg 2(2).
3 Charities (Accounts and Reports) Regulations 2008, SI 2008/629, Sch 1 para 16(1)(q)(i), (2).
4 Charities (Accounts and Reports) Regulations 2008, SI 2008/629, Sch 1 para 16(2)(a)(i). 'Recognised stock exchange' has the meaning given by the Income Tax Act 2007 s 1005: Charities (Accounts and Reports) Regulations 2008, SI 2008/629, Sch 1 para 17(1). See **INCOME TAXATION** vol 58 (2014) PARA 583.
5 Charities (Accounts and Reports) Regulations 2008, SI 2008/629, Sch 1 para 16(2)(a)(ii).
6 Charities (Accounts and Reports) Regulations 2008, SI 2008/629, Sch 1 para 16(2)(a)(iii).
7 Charities (Accounts and Reports) Regulations 2008, SI 2008/629, Sch 1 para 16(2)(a)(iv).
8 Charities (Accounts and Reports) Regulations 2008, SI 2008/629, Sch 1 para 16(2)(a)(v).
9 Charities (Accounts and Reports) Regulations 2008, SI 2008/629, Sch 1 para 16(2)(a)(vi). As to the IMA SORP see PARA 348 note 18.
10 Charities (Accounts and Reports) Regulations 2008, SI 2008/629, Sch 1 para 16(2)(b)(i).
11 Charities (Accounts and Reports) Regulations 2008, SI 2008/629, Sch 1 para 16(2)(b)(ii).
12 Charities (Accounts and Reports) Regulations 2008, SI 2008/629, Sch 1 para 16(2)(b)(iii).
13 Charities (Accounts and Reports) Regulations 2008, SI 2008/629, Sch 1 para 16(2)(c).
14 Charities (Accounts and Reports) Regulations 2008, SI 2008/629, Sch 1 para 16(2)(d). 'Dividend equalisation reserve' means income withheld from distribution with a view to avoiding fluctuations in the amounts distributed: Sch 1 para 17(1).

351. Information provided in notes to the accounts: common deposit funds. In addition to the information to be provided in relation to an investment fund[1], a common deposit fund[2] must include in the notes to the accounts the following information[3]:

(1) details of sums deposited by participating charities as at the date of the balance sheet, divided into: (a) sums repayable on demand; and (b) deposits with agreed maturity dates or periods of notice, divided into those repayable in not more than three months, those repayable in more than three months but not more than one year, those repayable in more than one year but not more than five years and those repayable in more than five years[4];

(2) details as at the date of the balance sheet of sums placed on deposit, divided into: (a) sums repayable on demand; and (b) other deposits, indicating whether they are repayable in not more than three months, more than three months but not more than one year, more than one year but not more than five years or more than five years[5];

(3) details as at the date of the balance sheet of investments other than deposits[6].

1 Ie the information specified under the Charities (Accounts and Reports) Regulations 2008, SI 2008/629, Sch 1 para 1(1) (see PARA 349).
2 A 'common deposit fund' means a common deposit fund established by a scheme under the Charities Act 1960 s 22A (repealed) or the Charities Act 2011 s 100: Charities (Accounts and Reports) Regulations 2008, SI 2008/629, reg 2(1). See PARA 427.
3 Charities (Accounts and Reports) Regulations 2008, SI 2008/629, Sch 1 para 16(1)(q)(ii), (3).
4 Charities (Accounts and Reports) Regulations 2008, SI 2008/629, Sch 1 para 16(3)(a).
5 Charities (Accounts and Reports) Regulations 2008, SI 2008/629, Sch 1 para 16(3)(b)(i).

6 Charities (Accounts and Reports) Regulations 2008, SI 2008/629, Sch 1 para 16(3)(b)(ii). These must be analysed in accordance with the requirements of head (1) in the text of the additional requirements for a common investment fund under Sch 1 para 16(2)(a) (see PARA 350): Sch 1 para 16(3)(b)(ii).

F. FORM AND CONTENT OF STATEMENTS: GROUP ACCOUNTS

352. Prescribed form and content of statements of group accounts: general requirements. The group accounts[1] prepared by the charity trustees[2] of any parent charity[3] must be prepared in accordance with applicable accounting principles[4] and, in particular, must make the following adjustments or include the following information[5]:

(1) the group accounts must incorporate in full the information contained in the individual accounts of the parent charity and its relevant subsidiary undertakings[6], subject to such consolidation adjustments, if any, as may be appropriate in accordance with applicable accounting principles[7];

(2) where the financial year of a relevant subsidiary undertaking differs from that of the parent charity, the group accounts must be made up from the accounts of the relevant subsidiary undertaking for its most recent financial year ending before the last day of the parent financial year, provided that financial year ended no more than three months before the parent financial year ended, or from interim accounts prepared by the relevant subsidiary undertaking as at the end of the parent financial year[8];

(3) where an undertaking becomes a subsidiary undertaking of a parent charity, that event must be accounted for in the group accounts by the acquisition method or merger method of accounting as appropriate in accordance with applicable accounting principles[9];

(4) where the parent charity or a relevant subsidiary undertaking has an interest in an associated undertaking or participates in the management of a joint venture and that associated undertaking or joint venture is not itself a subsidiary undertaking of the parent charity, or participates in a joint arrangement, the interest of the parent charity or subsidiary undertaking in that associated undertaking, joint venture or joint arrangement must appear in the group accounts as appropriate in accordance with applicable accounting principles[10];

(5) the consolidated balance sheet must identify as a separate item any minority interest in the net assets or liabilities of any relevant subsidiary undertaking as appropriate in accordance with applicable accounting principles[11]; and

(6) the consolidated statement of financial activities, consolidated income and expenditure account or consolidated statement of changes in net assets, as relevant, must identify as a separate item any minority interest in the net movement of the funds of a relevant subsidiary undertaking as appropriate in accordance with applicable accounting principles[12].

Where compliance with the group accounts requirements[13] is not sufficient to comply with any requirement to give a true and fair view[14], the necessary additional information must be given in the group accounts or a note to them[15]. If in special circumstances compliance with any of the group accounts requirements is inconsistent with a requirement to give a true and fair view, the charity trustees must depart from the relevant provision to the extent necessary to give a true and fair view, and the particulars of any such departure, the reasons for it and its effect must be given in a note to the group accounts[16].

1 As to group accounts see PARA 343.
2 As to the meaning of 'charity trustees' see PARA 255.
3 Ie any parent charity under the Charities Act 2011 s 138(2) (see PARA 343). As to the meaning of 'parent charity' see s 141(1); and PARA 343 note 2 (definition applied by virtue of the Charities (Accounts and Reports) Regulations 2008, SI 2008/629, reg 2(1)).
4 'Applicable accounting principles' means, in relation to a parent charity that is required to prepare group accounts: (1) the methods and principles set out in the financial reporting standards and statements of standard accounting practice issued by the Financial Reporting Council Ltd (the 'Council'); (2) any abstract issued by the Council which is relevant to the preparation of those accounts by that parent charity, and (3) any statement of recommended practice (including the SORP) issued by a body recognised by the Council for the purpose of issuing guidance on the standards in head (1) relevant to the preparation of those accounts by that parent charity: Charities (Accounts and Reports) Regulations 2008, SI 2008/629, reg 16(9)(a) (amended by SI 2012/1741). As to the bodies responsible for accounting standards see COMPANIES vol 15 (2009) PARA 699. As to the applicable SORP see PARA 345 note 12.
5 Charities (Accounts and Reports) Regulations 2008, SI 2008/629, reg 16(1), (2). This is in addition to complying with reg 13, 14 or 15 (see PARAS 347–349), as the case may be.
6 'Relevant subsidiary undertaking' means a subsidiary undertaking of the parent charity which is not excluded under the Charities (Accounts and Reports) Regulations 2008, SI 2008/629, reg 19 (see PARA 343) from the group accounts required to be prepared for the parent financial year: reg 16(9)(c). As to the meaning of 'subsidiary undertaking' see the Charities Act 2011 s 141; and PARA 343 note 3 (definition applied by virtue of the Charities (Accounts and Reports) Regulations 2008, SI 2008/629, reg 2(1)). 'Parent financial year' means the financial year of the parent charity in respect of which the group accounts are prepared: reg 16(9)(b).
7 Charities (Accounts and Reports) Regulations 2008, SI 2008/629, reg 16(3).
8 Charities (Accounts and Reports) Regulations 2008, SI 2008/629, reg 16(4).
9 Charities (Accounts and Reports) Regulations 2008, SI 2008/629, reg 16(5).
10 Charities (Accounts and Reports) Regulations 2008, SI 2008/629, reg 16(6).
11 Charities (Accounts and Reports) Regulations 2008, SI 2008/629, reg 16(7).
12 Charities (Accounts and Reports) Regulations 2008, SI 2008/629, reg 16(8).
13 'Group accounts requirements' means the general requirements under the Charities (Accounts and Reports) Regulations 2008, SI 2008/629, reg 16 (see notes 1–12), plus the additional requirements prescribed for parent charities that are special case charities, investment funds or other charities: see reg 17(4). As to these additional requirements see regs 13–15; and PARAS 353–355.
14 As to these requirements see PARAS 353 text and note 7, 354 text and note 7, 349 text and note 8.
15 Charities (Accounts and Reports) Regulations 2008, SI 2008/629, reg 17(1).
16 Charities (Accounts and Reports) Regulations 2008, SI 2008/629, reg 17(2), (3).

353. Prescribed form and content of statements of group accounts: parent charities that are not special case charities or investment funds. In addition to the general requirements as to the form and content of statements of group accounts[1], the group accounts prepared by the charity trustees[2] of a parent charity[3] other than a special case charity[4] or an investment fund[5] must consist of a consolidated statement of financial activities showing the total incoming resources and application of the resources, together with any other movements in the total resources, of the parent charity and its subsidiary undertakings in the relevant financial year, and a consolidated balance sheet showing the state of affairs of the parent charity and its subsidiary undertakings as at the end of the relevant financial year[6].

In addition, the group accounts must be prepared in accordance with the following principles: (1) the consolidated statement of financial activities must give a true and fair view of the total incoming resources of the parent charity and its subsidiary undertakings and the movements in the total resources of the group during the relevant financial year; and (2) the consolidated balance sheet must give a true and fair view of the state of affairs of the parent charity and its undertakings as at the end of the relevant financial year[7].

The group accounts prepared under the above provisions must, so far as practicable, comply with certain statutory requirements[8] as if a parent charity and its subsidiary undertakings were a single charity[9]; and in any case where the parent charity is a company, be prepared as if its charity trustees had been required to prepare a statement of accounts under the relevant provisions[10] of the Charities Act 2011[11].

1 As to the general requirements see PARA 352. As to group accounts see PARA 343.
2 As to the meaning of 'charity trustees' see PARA 255.
3 As to the meaning of 'parent charity' see the Charities Act 2011 s 141(1); and PARA 343 note 2 (definition applied by the Charities (Accounts and Reports) Regulations 2008, SI 2008/629, reg 2(1)).
4 Ie a charity to which the Charities (Accounts and Reports) Regulations 2008, SI 2008/629, reg 13 (see PARA 355) applies. As to the meaning of 'special case charity' see PARA 347 note 3.
5 Ie a charity to which the Charities (Accounts and Reports) Regulations 2008, SI 2008/629, reg 14 (see PARA 354) applies.
6 See the Charities (Accounts and Reports) Regulations 2008, SI 2008/629, reg 15(1)–(3).
7 See the Charities (Accounts and Reports) Regulations 2008, SI 2008/629, reg 15(1), (2), (4).
8 Ie the requirements of the Charities (Accounts and Reports) Regulations 2008, SI 2008/629, reg 8(6)–(10): see PARA 345.
9 Charities (Accounts and Reports) Regulations 2008, SI 2008/629, reg 15(1), (2), (5)(a).
10 Ie under the Charities Act 2011 s 132(1) (see PARAS 345–346).
11 Charities (Accounts and Reports) Regulations 2008, SI 2008/629, reg 15(1), (2), (5)(b).
Where reg 15(5)(b) applies, the provisions of Sch 2 para 1(1)(w) (see PARA 344 note 3) are substituted so as to require that where the company has exercised its power under the Companies Act 1985 s 225 (repealed: see now the Companies Act 2006 s 392; and **COMPANIES** vol 15 (2009) PARA 713) to determine an accounting reference date earlier or later than 12 months from the beginning of the financial year, it must provide a statement of the reasons for doing so: see the Charities (Accounts and Reports) Regulations 2008, SI 2008/629, reg 15(6).

354. Prescribed form and content of statements of group accounts: parent charities that are special case charities. In addition to the general requirements as to the form and content of statements of group accounts[1], the group accounts prepared by the charity trustees[2] of a parent charity[3] that is a special case charity[4] must consist of a consolidated income and expenditure account dealing with the income and expenditure of the parent charity and its subsidiary undertakings[5] for the relevant financial year, and a consolidated balance sheet dealing with the state of affairs of the parent charity and its subsidiary undertakings as at the end of the relevant financial year[6].

The group accounts must also be prepared in accordance with the following principles: (1) the consolidated income and expenditure account must give a true and fair view of the income and expenditure of the parent charity and its subsidiary undertakings as a whole in the relevant financial year; and (2) the consolidated balance sheet must give a true and fair view of the state of affairs of the parent charity and its subsidiary undertakings as at the end of the relevant financial year[7].

The group accounts must be signed by at least one of the charity trustees of the charity, each of whom has been authorised to do so, as if the parent charity and its subsidiary undertakings required to be included in the group accounts were a single charity[8].

1 As to the general requirements see PARA 352. As to group accounts see PARA 343.
2 As to the meaning of 'charity trustees' see PARA 255.

3 As to the meaning of 'parent charity' see the Charities Act 2011 s 141(1); and PARA 343 note 2 (definition applied by the Charities (Accounts and Reports) Regulations 2008, SI 2008/629, reg 2(1)).
4 As to the meaning of 'special case charity' see PARA 347 note 3.
5 As to the meaning of 'subsidiary undertaking' see the Charities Act 2011 s 141(1); and PARA 343 note 3 (definition applied by virtue of the Charities (Accounts and Reports) Regulations 2008, SI 2008/629, reg 2(1)).
6 See the Charities (Accounts and Reports) Regulations 2008, SI 2008/629, reg 14(1)–(3). As to the meaning of 'financial year' see PARA 344 note 4.
7 Charities (Accounts and Reports) Regulations 2008, SI 2008/629, reg 14(1), (2), (4).
8 See the Charities (Accounts and Reports) Regulations 2008, SI 2008/629, reg 14(1), (2), (5).

355. Prescribed form and content of statements of group accounts: parent charities that are investment funds. In addition to the general requirements as to the form and content of statements of group accounts[1], the group accounts prepared by the charity trustees[2] of a parent charity[3] that is an investment fund[4] must consist of a consolidated statement of total return dealing with the total return of the parent charity and its subsidiary undertakings[5] in the relevant financial year[6], a consolidated statement of changes in net assets dealing with the changes in the net assets of the parent and its subsidiary undertakings in the relevant financial year, and a consolidated balance sheet dealing with the state of affairs of the parent and its subsidiary undertakings as at the end of the relevant financial year[7].

The group accounts also must be prepared in accordance with the following principles: (1) the consolidated statement of total return must give a true and fair view of the total return of the parent charity and its subsidiary undertakings in the relevant financial year; (2) the consolidated statement of changes in net assets must give a true and fair view of the changes in the net assets of the parent charity and its subsidiary undertakings between their position at the beginning of the relevant financial year and their position at the end of that year; and (3) the consolidated balance sheet must give a true and fair view of the state of affairs of the parent charity and its subsidiary undertakings at the end of the relevant financial year[8].

The group accounts must so far as practicable, comply with the following accounting requirements for investment funds as if the parent charity and its subsidiary undertakings required to be included in the group accounts were a single charity: (a) the requirements for a statement of total return; (b) the requirements for a statement of changes in net assets; and (c) the requirements for information to be provided by way of notes to the accounts[9].

1 As to group accounts see PARA 343.
2 As to the meaning of 'charity trustees' see PARA 255.
3 As to the meaning of 'parent charity' see the Charities Act 2011 s 141; and PARA 343 note 2 (definition applied by the Charities (Accounts and Reports) Regulations 2008, SI 2008/629, reg 2(1)).
4 As to the meaning of 'investment fund' see PARA 348 note 2.
5 As to the meaning of 'subsidiary undertaking' see the Charities Act 2011 s 141; and PARA 343 note 3 (definition applied by virtue of the Charities (Accounts and Reports) Regulations 2008, SI 2008/629, reg 2(1)).
6 As to the meaning of 'financial year' see PARA 344 note 4.
7 Charities (Accounts and Reports) Regulations 2008, SI 2008/629, reg 13(1)–(3).
8 Charities (Accounts and Reports) Regulations 2008, SI 2008/629, reg 13(1), (2), (4).
9 See the Charities (Accounts and Reports) Regulations 2008, SI 2008/629, reg 13(1), (2), (5). As to the accounting requirements for investment funds see PARA 348.

G. ANNUAL AUDITS, EXAMINATIONS OR INDEPENDENT EXAMINATIONS

356. Annual audit or examination of charity accounts. If a charity's gross income[1] for a financial year[2] exceeds £1 million, or if it exceeds the accounts threshold[3] and at the end of the year the aggregate value of its assets before deduction of liabilities exceeds £3.26 million[4], the accounts of the charity for that year must be audited by a person who is: (1) eligible[5] for appointment as a statutory auditor[6]; or (2) a member of a body for the time being specified in regulations[7] and is under the rules of that body eligible for appointment as auditor of the charity[8].

If the gross income does not exceed £500,000, or the accounts threshold where the aggregate value of assets before deduction of liabilities exceeds £3.26 million, and its gross income or total expenditure in that year exceeds £25,000, the accounts of the charity for that year must, at the election of the charity trustees[9], either be examined by an independent examiner[10], or be audited by such person mentioned in head (1) or (2) above[11].

Where it appears to the Charity Commission that: (a) the requirement for an audit or, as the case may be, examination[12] has not been complied with in relation to a financial year of a charity within ten months from the end of that year[13]; or that (b) although it is not a case in which an audit is required[14], it would nevertheless be desirable for the accounts for that year to be audited by such a person mentioned in head (1) or (2) above[15], the Commission may by order require the accounts of the charity for that year to be audited by such a person[16]. Unless the circumstances are those set out in head (b) above, and the charity trustees themselves appoint an auditor in accordance with the order of the Commission, the auditor will be appointed by the Commission[17]. The expenses of any audit carried out by an auditor so appointed by the Commission, including the auditor's remuneration, are recoverable by it from the charity trustees of the charity concerned, who are personally liable, jointly and severally for those expenses[18]. To the extent that the expenses are not practically recoverable from the charity trustees they are recoverable from the charity funds[19].

An appeal against such an order of the Commission lies to the Tribunal[20] at the instance of the Attorney General, the charity trustees of the charity, the charity itself (if a body corporate), and any other person who is or may be affected by the order[21]. The Tribunal may: (i) quash the order; (ii) substitute for the order any other order which could have been made by the Commission; or (iii) add anything to the order which could have been contained in an order made by the Commission[22].

The above provisions do not apply to any exempt charity[23], certain charities which are not required to be registered[24], and are not registered[25], a charity which is audited in accordance with the companies legislation[26], or a charity which at any time in the relevant financial year is an English National Health Service charity or Welsh National Health Service charity[27].

1 As to the meaning of 'gross income' see PARA 218 note 2. As to the meaning of 'charity' see PARA 1.

2 As to the meaning of 'financial year' see PARAS 218 note 3, 344 note 4.

3 The accounts threshold is the sum specified in for the time being in the Charities Act 2011 s 133 (see PARA 342): s 144(1).

4 See the Charities Act 2011 s 144(1) (amended with effect from 31 March 2015 by SI 2015/321). As to the Minister's power to make an order substituting a different sum for the sum for the time being specified see the Charities Act 2011 s 174(1), (2). As to the Minister see PARA 586.

5 Ie in accordance with the Companies Act 2006 Pt 42: see COMPANIES.

6 Charities Act 2011 s 144(2)(a).
7 Ie under the Charities Act 2011 s 154: see PARA 361.
8 Charities Act 2011 s 144(2)(b).
9 As to the meaning of 'charity trustees' see PARA 255.
10 The independent examiner is an independent person who is reasonably believed by the trustees to have the requisite ability and practical experience to carry out a competent examination of the accounts: Charities Act 2011 s 145(1)(a). The Charity Commission may give guidance to charity trustees in connection with the selection of a person for appointment as an independent examiner, and give such directions as it thinks appropriate with respect to the carrying out of an examination under s 145(1)(a): s 145(5)(a), (b). Any such guidance or directions may either be of general application or apply to a particular charity only: s 145(5). However, this is subject to s 145(3), (4): s 145(2).

If the charity's gross income or total expenditure in a financial year exceeds £250,000, a person qualifies as an independent examiner for these purposes only if he is an independent person who is (1) a member of one of the following bodies: the Institute of Chartered Accountants in England and Wales; the Institute of Chartered Accountants of Scotland; the Institute of Chartered Accountants in Ireland; the Association of Chartered Certified Accountants; the Association of Authorised Public Accountants; the Association of Accounting Technicians; the Association of International Accountants; the Chartered Institute of Management Accountants; the Institute of Chartered Secretaries and Administrators; the Chartered Institute of Public Finance and Accountancy; the Institute of Financial Accountants; the Certified Public Accountants Association; or (2) a Fellow of the Association of Charity Independent Examiners: Charities Act 2011 s 145(3), (4) (s 145(4) amended with effect from 31 March 2015 by SI 2015/321).

As to the Charity Commission see PARAS 543–578. The Minister may by order amend the Charities Act 2011 s 145(3) or (4), and may substitute a new sum for that specified in s 145(3): see ss 145(6), 174(1), (2).
11 Charities Act 2011 s 145(1). The duties of an independent examiner with respect to the making of a report in respect of an examination carried out by him under s 145 are specified in the Charities (Accounts and Reports) Regulations 2008, SI 2008/629, reg 31 (see PARA 366): reg 20.
12 Ie under the Charities Act 2011 s 144(2) or s 145(1): see the text and notes 5–10.
13 Charities Act 2011 s 146(1)(a).
14 Ie under the Charities Act 2011 s 144(2): see the text and notes 5–7.
15 Charities Act 2011 s 146(1)(b).
16 Charities Act 2011 s 146(1).
17 Charities Act 2011 s 146(2).
18 Charities Act 2011 s 146(3)(a).
19 Charities Act 2011 s 146(3)(b).
20 As to the Tribunal see PARA 579 et seq.
21 Charities Act 2011 s 319(2), Sch 6 Table Cols 1, 2. As to the meaning of 'person who is or may be affected' within the meaning of Sch 6 see PARA 317 note 8. As to the Attorney General see PARAS 589, 596, 605 et seq; and **CONSTITUTIONAL AND ADMINISTRATIVE LAW** vol 20 (2014) PARA 273 et seq.
22 Charities Act 2011 Sch 6 Table Col 3.
23 See the Charities Act 2011 s 160(1). As to exempt charities see PARAS 318–320.
24 Ie under the Charities Act 2011 s 30(2)(d): see PARA 308.
25 See the Charities Act 2011 s 161(1); and PARA 381.
26 Ie the Companies Act 2006 Pt 16: see the Charities Act 2011 s 147(1); and PARA 566. As to the meaning of 'company' see PARA 246.
27 See the Charities Act 2011 s 148. As to English National Health Service charities see PARA 357. As to Welsh National Health Service charities see PARA 358.

357. Annual audit or examination of charity accounts: English NHS charities. In relation to the financial year[1] of a charity where, at any time in the year, the charity is an English NHS charity[2] and the charity meets the financial threshold so as to require an audit[3], the accounts of the charity for that financial year must be audited by a person appointed by the Audit Commission[4]. In any other case, the accounts of the charity for that financial year must, at the election of the Audit Commission, be audited by a person appointed by the Audit Commission or examined by a person so appointed[5]. The Comptroller and Auditor General may at any time examine and inspect the accounts of such a charity for the financial year, any records relating to those accounts and any report of a person so appointed to audit or examine those accounts[6].

As from a day to be appointed[7], in a case where the charity meets the financial threshold to require an audit, the audit must be conducted by a person who is eligible for appointment (1) as a statutory auditor[8]; or (2) as a local auditor[9]; or (3) who is a member of a specified body[10]. In any other case the accounts of the charity, must, at the election of the charity trustees, be audited by such a person or examined by a person qualified to be an independent examiner[11].

1 As to the meaning of 'financial year' see PARAS 218 note 3, 344 note 4.

2 Charities Act 2011 s 149(1). 'English NHS charity' means a charitable trust, the trustees of which are: (1) The National Health Service Commissioning Board; (2) a clinical commissioning group; (3) trustees for the NHS Commissioning board appointed in pursuance of the National Health Service Act 2006 Sch A1 para 11; (4) trustees for a clinical commissioning group appointed in pursuance of the National Health Service Act 2006 Sch 1A para 15: Charities Act 2011 s 149(7)(ba)–(bd) (added by the Health and Social Care Act 2012 Sch 5 para 184(c)). Until a day to be appointed, the following are also included: (a) a National Health Service trust all or most of whose hospitals, establishments and facilities are situated in England; (b) trustees appointed in pursuance of the National Health Service Act 2006 Sch 4 para 10 for a National Health Service trust falling within head (a); (c) special trustees appointed in pursuance of the National Health Services Reorganisation Act 1973 s 29(1), the National Health Service Act 1977 s 95(1) and the National Health Service Act 2006 s 212(1): Charities Act 2011 s 149(7)(c)–(e) (repealed as from a day to be appointed by the Health and Social Care Act 2012 Sch 14 Pt 2). At the date at which this volume states the law, no such day had been appointed. As to National Health Service bodies see **HEALTH SERVICES** vol 54 (2008) PARA 75 et seq.

As to the conversion of NHS charities into charities independent of the Department of Health see *Outline Guidance published by the Department of Health and the Association of NHS Charities* (November 2014).

3 Ie where the Charities Act 2011 s 144(1)(a) or (b) is satisfied; see PARA 356.

4 Charities Act 2011 s 149(2). 'Audit Commission means the Audit Commission for Local Authorities and the National Health Services in England: Charities Act 2011 s 144(8). These provisions are amended as from a day to be appointed by the Local Audit and Accountability Act 2014: see text and notes 7–10. At the date at which this volume states the law, no such day had been appointed.

The appointment of auditors by the Commission is governed by the Audit Commission Act 1998 s 3 (see **LOCAL GOVERNMENT** vol 69 (2009) PARA 758): see the Charities Act 2011 s 149(4). The duties of an auditor carrying out an audit of the accounts of a charity are, in the case of an audit carried out under s 149, specified by virtue of the Charities (Accounts and Reports) Regulations 2008, SI 2008/629, reg 27 (see PARA 362): reg 20. As to when an auditor appointed under the Charities Act 2011 s 149(2) or (3)(a) ceases to hold office see the Charities (Accounts and Reports) Regulations 2008, SI 2008/629, reg 35; and PARA 367. As to the examination of the accounts of England and Welsh National Health Service Charities see reg 32; and PARA 369.

5 Charities Act 2011 s 149(3). The Charity Commission may give such directions as it thinks appropriate with respect to the carrying out of an examination and any such directions may either be of general application or apply to a particular charity only: s 149(5). The duties of an examiner with respect to the making of a report in respect of an examination carried out by him under the Charities Act 2011 s 149 are specified in the Charities (Accounts and Reports) Regulations 2008, SI 2008/629, reg 32 (see PARA 369): reg 20.

These provisions are amended as from a day to be appointed by the Local Audit and Accountability Act 2014: see the text and notes 7–10. At the date at which this volume states the law, no such day had been appointed.

6 Charities Act 2011 s 149(6). As to the Comptroller and Auditor General see **CONSTITUTIONAL AND ADMINISTRATIVE LAW** vol 20 (2014) PARA 494 et seq.

7 Ie as from a day to be appointed under the Local Audit and Accountability Act 2014 s 49(1). At the date at which this volume states the law, no such day had been appointed.

8 Ie in accordance with the Companies Act 2006 Pt 42: see **COMPANIES.**

9 Ie in accordance with the Local Audit and Accountability Act 2014 Pt 4: see **LOCAL GOVERNMENT FINANCE.**

10 Charities Act 2011 s 149(2)(a)–(c) (added as from a day to be appointed by the Local Audit and Accountability Act 2014 Sch 12 para 119).

11 Charities Act 2011 s 149(3) (amended as from a day to be appointed by the Local Audit and Accountability Act 2014 Sch 12 para 119). The independent examiner is an independent person who is reasonably believed by the trustees to have the requisite ability and practical experience to carry out a competent examination of the accounts, and who falls within the descriptions set out in the Charities Act 2011 s 145(3) (see PARA 356 note 10) or is eligible for appointment as a local auditor (see note 8): s 149(3A) (added as from a day to be appointed by the Local Audit and Accountability Act 2014 Sch 12 para 119). The Charity Commission may give guidance to charity trustees of an English NHS charity in connection with the appointment of independent examiners, and such directions as it thinks appropriate with respect to the carrying out of an examination, and any such directions may either be of general application or apply to a particular charity only: Charities Act 2011 s 149(5) (substituted as from a day to be appointed by the Local Audit and Accountability Act 2014 Sch 12 para 119).

358. Annual audit or examination of charity accounts: Welsh NHS charities. In relation to the financial year[1] of a charity where, at any time in the year, the charity is a Welsh NHS charity[2], and the charity meets the financial threshold so as to require an audit[3], the accounts of the charity for that financial year must be audited by the Auditor General for Wales[4]. In any other case, the accounts of the charity for that financial year must, at the election of the Auditor General for Wales, be audited or examined by the Auditor General for Wales[5].

1 As to the meaning of 'financial year' see PARAS 218 note 3, 344 note 4.

2 Charities Act 2011 s 150(1). 'Welsh NHS charity' means a charitable trust, the trustees of which are: (1) a Local Health Board; (2) a National Health Service trust all or most of whose hospitals, establishments and facilities are situated in Wales; (3) trustees appointed in pursuance of the National Health Service (Wales) Act 2006 Sch 3 para 10 for a National Health Service trust falling within head (2); or (4) special trustees appointed in pursuance of the Health Services Reorganisation Act 1973 s 29(1), the National Health Service Act 1977 s 95(1) and the National Health Service (Wales) Act 2006 s 160(1) for such a National Health Service trust: Charities Act 2011 s 150(4).

As from a day to be appointed under the Health and Social Care Act 2012 s 306(4), heads (2) and (3) of the definition given above are amended so as to remove the requirement that all or most of the hospitals, etc, are situated in Wales: Charities Act 2011 s 150(4)(b), (c) (amended as from a day to be appointed by the Health and Social Care Act 2012 Sch 14 Pt 2). At the date at which this volume states the law, no such day had been appointed.

References in the Charities Act 2011 to an auditor or an examiner have effect in relation to s 150 as references to the Auditor General for Wales acting under s 150 as an auditor or examiner: s 152(5).

3 Ie under the Charities Act 2011 s 144(1); see PARA 356.

4 Charities Act 2011 s 150(2). The duties of an auditor carrying out an audit of the accounts of a charity are, in the case of an audit carried out under the Charities Act 2011 s 150, specified by virtue of the Charities (Accounts and Reports) Regulations 2008, SI 2008/629, reg 27 (see PARA 356): reg 20.

5 Charities Act 2011 s 150(3). The duties of an examiner with respect to the making of a report in respect of an examination carried out by him under s 43B are specified in the Charities (Accounts and Reports) Regulations 2008, SI 2008/629, reg 32 (see PARA 369): reg 20.

359. Annual audit of group accounts: larger groups. Where group accounts[1] are prepared for a financial year[2] of a parent charity[3] and either: (1) the aggregate gross income of the group in that year exceeds the relevant income threshold[4]; or (2) the aggregate gross income of the group in that year exceeds the relevant income threshold and at the end of the year the aggregate value of the assets of the group, before deduction of liabilities, exceeds the relevant assets threshold[5], then the group accounts for that year must be audited by a person who is eligible[6] to audit the charity[7].

This requirement also applies where group accounts are prepared for a financial year of a parent charity and the appropriate audit provision[8] applies in relation to the parent charity's own accounts for that year[9].

Where it appears to the Charity Commission that such auditing has not been complied with in relation to that year within ten months from the end of that year, the Commission may by order require the group accounts for that year to be audited[10] by a person who is either eligible for appointment as a statutory auditor or is a member of a body for the time being specified in regulations and is under the rules of that body eligible for appointment as auditor of the charity; and if it makes such an order, the auditor must be a person appointed by the Commission[11].

The expenses of such an audit are recoverable by the Commission from the charity trustees, who are jointly and severally liable for them, or where that appears impractical, from the funds of the parent charity[12].

If the audit requirement described above applies in relation to a financial year of a parent charity, the appropriate audit provision[13] applies in relation to the parent charity's own accounts for that year, whether or not it would otherwise so apply[14]; save where that parent charity is a company and its own accounts for that year are not required to be audited in accordance with the relevant provisions of the companies legislation[15] in which case the standard auditing provision under the Charities Act 2011[16] applies in relation to those accounts, whether or not it would otherwise so apply[17].

1 As to group accounts see PARA 343.
2 As to the meaning of 'financial year' see PARA 344 note 4.
3 Ie under the Charities Act 2011 s 138(2) (see PARA 343). As to the meaning of 'parent charity' see PARA 343 note 2 (definition applied by virtue of the Charities (Accounts and Reports) Regulations 2008, SI 2008/629, reg 2(1)).
4 The relevant income threshold is the sum prescribed as such for these purposes: see the Charities Act 2011 s 176(1), (3). With effect from 31 March 2015 the sum so prescribed is £1 million: Charities Act 2011 (Group Accounts) Regulations 2015, SI 2015/322, reg 4.
5 'Relevant assets threshold' is a reference to the sum prescribed by regulations made by the Minister: Charities Act 2011 s 176(2), (3). At the date at which this volume states the law, no such sum had been prescribed.
6 Ie under the Charities Act 2011 s 144(2)(a) or (b) (see PARA 356) or, in the case of an English NHS charity, by a person appointed by the Audit Commission (see PARA 357) (or, as from a day to be appointed, a person appointed by the charity trustees of the parent charity, who is a person falling within s 149(2)(a), (b) or (c): see PARA 357 text and note 9), or in the case of a Welsh NHS Charity, the Auditor General for Wales (see PARA 358): Charities Act 2011 s 151(4) (amended, as from a day to be appointed, by the Local Audit and Accountability Act 2014 Sch 12 para 120).

In the case of an English NHS charity, the Comptroller and Auditor General may at any time examine and inspect the accounts of the charity for the financial year, any records relating to those accounts, and any report of a person so appointed to audit or examine those accounts: see the Charities Act 2011 s 149(6) (applied by s 151(6) (amended, as from a day to be appointed, by the Local Audit and Accountability Act 2014 Sch 12 para 120)). As to the Comptroller and Auditor General see **CONSTITUTIONAL AND ADMINISTRATIVE LAW** vol 20 (2014) PARA 494 et seq.

At the date at which this volume states the law, no day had been appointed under the Local Audit and Accountability Act 2014 s 49(1) for the commencement of the amendments mentioned above.
7 See the Charities Act 2011 s 151(1), (4). The duties of an auditor carrying out an audit of the group accounts of a parent charity under s 151 are specified in the Charities (Accounts and Reports) Regulations 2008, SI 2008/629, reg 30 (see PARA 365): reg 21.
8 'Appropriate audit provision', in relation to a financial year of a parent charity, means the Charities Act 2011 s 144(2) (see PARA 356) or, in the case of an English NHS Charity s 149(2), or in the case of a Welsh NHS Charity s 150(2), or if the parent charity is a company, either s 144(2) or the Companies Act 2006 Pt 16 as the case may be: Charities Act 2011 s 151(3).
9 Charities Act 2011 s 151(2).
10 Ie by a person falling within the Charities Act 2011 s 144(2)(a) or (b): see PARA 356.
11 See the Charities Act 2011 s 153(1), (2).
12 Charities Act 2011 s 153(3). As to the meaning of 'charity trustees' see PARA 255.

13 As to the meaning of 'appropriate audit provision' see note 8.
14 Charities Act 2011 s 151(5)(a).
15 Ie under the Companies Act 2006 Pt 16 (see **COMPANIES**).
16 Ie the Charities Act 2011 s 144(2): see PARA 356.
17 Charities Act 2011 s 151(5)(b).

360. Annual audit or independent examination of group accounts: smaller groups. If group accounts[1] are prepared for a financial year[2] of a parent charity[3], and the provisions for auditing the accounts of larger groups[4] do not apply in relation to that year, then the following provisions apply[5].

Where they apply in relation to a financial year of a parent charity, the aggregate gross income[6] of the group in that year exceeds the relevant sum[7], and the provisions relating to English or Welsh NHS charities do not apply[8], the group accounts for that year must, at the election of the charity trustees[9] of the parent charity, be examined by an independent examiner[10] or audited by an appropriately qualified[11] person[12].

In respect of an English NHS charity[13] falling within these provisions, the group accounts must at the election of the Audit Commission be audited by a person appointed by the Audit Commission or examined by a person so appointed[14]. In the case of a Welsh NHS charity[15], the group accounts for that year must, at the election of the Auditor General for Wales, be audited or examined by the Auditor General for Wales[16].

1 As to group accounts see PARA 343.
2 As to the meaning of 'financial year' see PARA 344 note 4.
3 Ie under the Charities Act 2011 s 138(2) (see PARA 343). As to the meaning of 'parent charity' see PARA 343 note 2.
4 Ie the Charities Act 2011 s 151: see PARA 359.
5 Charities Act 2011 s 152(1).
6 As to the meaning of 'gross income' see PARA 218 note 2. As to the meaning of 'charity' see PARA 1.
7 Ie the sum specified in the Charities Act 2011 s 145(1): see PARA 356 note 11.
8 Ie the Charities Act 2011 s 152(6) or (7): see text and notes 13–16.
9 As to the meaning of 'charity trustees' see PARA 255.
10 Ie as defined in the Charities Act 2011 s 145(1)(a): see PARA 356 note 10.
11 Ie within the Charities Act 2011 s 144(2)(a) or (b): see PARA 356.
12 Charities Act 2011 s 152(2). If this applies to the group accounts for a year and the aggregate gross income of the group in that year exceeds the sum specified in s 145(3) (see PARA 356 note 10), a person qualifies as an independent examiner for the purposes of this provision only if he is independent and meets the requirements of s 145(3)(a) or (b): s 152(4). Section 152(2) is also subject to an order under s 153(1) (see PARA 359 text and note 11): s 152(3).

The Charity Commission may give guidance to charity trustees of a parent charity in connection with the selection of a person for appointment as an independent examiner, and give such directions as it thinks appropriate with respect to the carrying out of an examination under s 152(2): s 152(5)(a), (b). Any such guidance or directions may either be of general application or apply to a particular charity only: s 152(5).

If the group accounts for a financial year of a parent charity are to be examined or audited in accordance with s 152(2), s 145(1) (see PARA 356) applies in relation to the parent charity's own accounts for that year (whether or not it would otherwise so apply): s 152(8).
13 As to the meaning of 'English NHS charity' see PARA 357 note 2.
14 See the Charities Act 2011 s 152(6). As from a day to be appointed under the Local Audit and Accountability Act 2014 s 49(1), the election and appointment are the function of the trustees of the parent charity, and the independent examiner must fall within the Charities Act 2011 s 149(2)(a), (b) or (c) (see PARA 357): s 152(6) (prospectively amended by the Local Audit and Accountability Act 2014 Sch 12 para 121). At the date at which this volume states the law, no such day had been appointed.

Nothing in the Charities Act 2011 s 152(6) affects the operation of s 149(3)–(6) in relation to the parent charity's own accounts for the financial year in question: s 152(9).
15 As to the meaning of 'Welsh NHS charity' see PARA 358 note 2.

16 Charities Act 2011 s 152(7). Nothing in s 152(7) affects the operation of s 150(3) in relation to the parent charity's own accounts for the financial year in question: s 152(9).

361. Regulations and supplementary provisions relating to audits and examinations. The Minister[1] may by regulations make provision[2]:

(1) specifying bodies whose members may be eligible[3] for appointment as auditor of a charity[4];

(2) with respect to the duties of an auditor[5], including provision with respect to the making by him of a report on the statement of accounts[6], or the account and statement[7], or on company accounts prepared by the director of a company[8], or on group accounts[9], as the case may be[10];

(3) with respect to the making by an independent examiner[11] or an examiner of a report in respect of an examination[12] carried out by him[13];

(4) conferring on such an auditor or on an independent examiner or examiner a right of access with respect to books, documents[14] and other records, however kept, which relate to the charity concerned[15] or, for group accounts, to any member of the group[16];

(5) entitling such an auditor or an independent examiner or examiner to require information and explanations from past or present charity trustees or trustees for the charity, or from past or present officers or employees of the charity[17] or, for group accounts, of any member of the group[18];

(6) enabling the Charity Commission[19], in circumstances specified in the regulations, to dispense with the requirements for an audit or examination[20] in the case of a particular charity or in the case of any particular financial year of a charity[21].

If any person fails to afford to an auditor or an independent examiner any facility to which he is entitled in respect of head (4) or (5) above, the Commission may give him or the charity trustees[22] for the time being of the charity concerned, such directions as it thinks appropriate for securing that the default is made good[23].

An appeal against such an order of the Commission, or a decision not to make such an order, lies to the Tribunal at the instance of the Attorney General[24], the charity trustees of the charity, the charity itself (if a body corporate), the auditor, independent examiner or examiner (in the case of a decision not to make an order), and any other person who is or may be affected by the order[25]. The Tribunal has the power to do any of the following: (a) quash the order; (b) substitute for the order any other order which could have been made by the Commission; (c) make any order which the Commission could have made[26].

The above provisions do not apply to an exempt charity[27] or certain charities which are not required to be registered[28], and are not registered[29].

1 As to the Minister see PARA 586.

2 Charities Act 2011 s 154(1). Under this provision, the Charities (Accounts and Reports) Regulations 2008, SI 2008/629, take effect in respect of a financial year of a charity which begins on or after 1 April 2008, and the Charities (Accounts and Reports) Regulations 2005, SI 2005/572, continue to apply in respect of a financial year of a charity before this date: see PARA 342 note 6.

Before making any regulations under the Charities Act 2011 s 154 the Minister must consult such persons or bodies or persons as he considers appropriate: s 348(4).

3 Ie for the purposes of the Charities Act 2011 s 144(2)(b) or s 149(2)(c): see PARAS 356, 357.

4 Charities Act 2011 s 154(1)(a), (aa) (s 154(1)(aa) added as from a day to be appointed by the Local Audit and Accountability Act 2014 Sch 12 para 122). At the date at which this volume

states the law, no day had been appointed under the Local Audit and Accountability Act 2014 s 49(1) for the commencement of the amendment made by that Act.

5 Ie the duties of an auditor carrying out an audit of individual or group accounts under the Charities Act 2011 ss 144–146, 149, 150 (individual accounts: see PARAS 356–358), or ss 151–153 (group accounts: see PARAS 359, 360): s 154(3).

6 Ie under the Charities Act 2011 s 132(1): see PARA 342. As to the meaning of 'financial year' see PARAS 218 note 3, 344 note 4.

7 Ie for the financial year in question under the Charities Act 2011 s 132(3): see PARA 342.

8 Ie accounts prepared under the Companies Act 2006 s 394 (see **COMPANIES**).

9 Ie under the Charities Act 2011 s 138(2). As to group accounts see PARA 343.

10 Charities Act 2011 s 154(1)(b).

11 As to the meaning of 'independent examiner' see PARA 356 note 10.

12 Ie an examination under the Charities Act 2011 ss 145, 149, 150 (individual accounts: see PARAS 356–358) or s 152 (group accounts: see PARA 359, 360).

13 See the Charities Act 2011 s 154(1)(c).

14 As to the meaning of 'document' see PARA 263 note 2.

15 Charities Act 2011 s 154(1)(d)(i).

16 Charities Act 2011 s 154(1)(d)(ii).

17 Charities Act 2011 s 154(1)(e). In relation to group accounts, without prejudice to the generality of this provision, regulations made under head (5) in the text may make provision corresponding or similar to any provision made by the Companies Act 2006 ss 499, 500 (see **COMPANIES**) in connection with the rights exercisable by an auditor of a company in relation to a subsidiary undertaking of a company: Charities Act 2011 s 154(2).

18 Charities Act 2011 s 154(1)(e).

19 As to the Charity Commission see PARAS 543–578.

20 Ie under the Charities Act 2011 ss 144(2), 145(1), 151(4)(a), 152(2) (see PARAS 356–360).

21 Charities Act 2011 s 154(1)(f).

22 Or, where the audit or examination is of group accounts, to the charity trustees for the time being of such member of the group as the Commission thinks appropriate: Charities Act 2011 s 155(c).

23 Charities Act 2011 s 155. A person guilty of disobedience to an order of the Commission made under this provision may on the application of the Commission to the High Court be dealt with as for disobedience to an order of the High Court: s 336(1), (2)(a); and see PARA 556.

24 As to the Tribunal see PARA 579 et seq. As to the Attorney General see PARAS 589, 596, 605 et seq; and **CONSTITUTIONAL AND ADMINISTRATIVE LAW** vol 20 (2014) PARA 273 et seq.

25 Charities Act 2011 s 319(2), Sch 6 Table Cols 1, 2. As to the meaning of 'person who is or may be affected' within the meaning of Sch 6 see PARA 317 note 8.

26 Charities Act 2011 Sch 6 Table Col 3.

27 Charities Act 2011 s 160(1). As to exempt charities see PARAS 318–320.

28 Ie under the Charities Act 2011 s 30(2)(d): see PARA 308.

29 See the Charities Act 2011 s 161(1). See also PARA 381.

362. Auditor's report on statement of accounts. Where a statement of accounts has been prepared[1] for the financial year[2] in question, the auditor carrying out the audit of the accounts of a charity[3] must make a report on that statement to the charity trustees[4].

The report must (1) state the name and address of the auditor and the name of the charity concerned[5]; (2) be signed by him or, where the office of auditor is held by a body corporate or partnership, in its name by a person authorised to sign on its behalf[6]; (3) state that the auditor falls within certain statutory requirements[7]; (4) be dated and specify the financial year in respect of which the accounts to which it relates have been prepared[8]; and (5) specify that it is a report in respect of an audit carried out under the statutory provisions[9] relating to annual audits or examinations of charity accounts[10].

The report must also state whether in the auditor's opinion the statement of accounts complies with the relevant statutory requirements[11] and, in particular, whether the balance sheet gives a true and fair view of the state of affairs of the charity at the end of the relevant financial year and whether the statutory requirements[12] as to the true and fair view are satisfied[13].

Where the auditor has formed the opinion:

(a) that accounting records have not been kept in respect of the charity in accordance with the statutory duty[14]; or

(b) that the statement of accounts does not accord with those records[15]; or

(c) that any information contained in the statement of accounts is inconsistent in any material respect with any report of the charity trustees prepared in accordance with the statutory provisions[16] in respect of the financial year in question[17]; or

(d) that any information or explanation to which he is entitled[18] has not been afforded to him[19],

the auditor's report must contain a statement of the opinion he has formed and of his grounds for forming it[20].

The auditor must, in preparing his report, carry out such investigations as will enable him to form an opinion as to certain specified matters[21].

1 Ie under the Charities Act 2011 s 132(1) (see PARA 342).
2 As to the meaning of 'financial year' see PARA 344 note 4.
3 Ie under the Charities Act 2011 s 144 (see PARA 356). Under certain circumstances, the Charities (Accounts and Reports) Regulations 2008, SI 2008/629, reg 24 also applies (subject to the modifications mentioned in the relevant notes below) to the duties of an auditor carrying out an audit of the accounts of an English NHS Charity under the Charities Act 2011 s 149 (see PARA 357) or the Auditor General for Wales carrying out an audit of a Welsh NHS Charity under s 150 (see PARA 358): see the Charities (Accounts and Reports) Regulations 2008, SI 2008/629, regs 27(1), 28(1). Such circumstances are where: (1) the accounts of the charity in respect of the relevant financial year are required to be audited by the Charities Act 2011 s 149(2) or s 150(2), as appropriate; or (2) a statement of accounts has been prepared as required under s 132(1) for the relevant financial year: see the Charities (Accounts and Reports) Regulations 2008, SI 2008/629, regs 27(2), 28(2). As to the meaning of 'charity' see PARA 1. As to English NHS Charities see PARA 357. As to Welsh NHS Charities see PARA 358.
4 Charities (Accounts and Reports) Regulations 2008, SI 2008/629, reg 24(1). As to the meaning of 'charity trustees' see PARA 255. These provisions apply to financial years beginning on or after 1 April 2008: see PARA 342 note 6. In the case of an auditor appointed by the Charity Commission, any report required must instead be made to the Commission: reg 36(1). This does not apply in the case of an English or Welsh NHS Charity: reg 36(2). As to the Charity Commission see PARAS 543–578.
5 Charities (Accounts and Reports) Regulations 2008, SI 2008/629, reg 24(1)(a). This statement is not required of the Auditor General for Wales in the case of a Welsh NHS Charity: see reg 28(3)(a).
6 Charities (Accounts and Reports) Regulations 2008, SI 2008/629, reg 24(1)(b).
7 Charities (Accounts and Reports) Regulations 2008, SI 2008/629, reg 24(1)(c). The statutory requirements referred to in the text are the requirements of the Charities Act 2011 s 144(2)(a), or as the case may be, s 144(2)(b) (see PARA 356). However in the case of an English NHS Charity, the requirements are s 149(2) or as the case may be, s 145(1): Charities (Accounts and Reports) Regulations 2008, SI 2008/629, reg 27(3)(a). This statement is not required of the Auditor General of Wales in the case of a Welsh NHS Charity: reg 28(3)(b).
8 Charities (Accounts and Reports) Regulations 2008, SI 2008/629, reg 24(1)(d).
9 Ie under the Charities Act 2011 s 144 (see PARA 356) or, in the case of an English NHS Charity, s 149 (see PARA 357) or, in the case of a Welsh NHS Charity, s 150 (see PARA 358), and in accordance with regulations made under s 154 (see PARA 361): see the Charities (Accounts and Reports) Regulations 2008, SI 2008/629, regs 24(1)(e), 27(3)(b), 28(3)(b). Note that reg 27(3)(b) purports to amend reg 24(1)(d); however, it is submitted that this should instead refer to reg 24(1)(e).
10 Charities (Accounts and Reports) Regulations 2008, SI 2008/629, reg 24(1)(e).
11 Ie the Charities (Accounts and Reports) Regulations 2008, SI 2008/629, reg 6, 7 or 8 (see PARAS 339–342) as relevant: reg 24(1)(f)(i).
12 These requirements are as follows: (1) in the case of a statement of accounts prepared by the charity trustees of an investment fund (ie one to which the Charities (Accounts and Reports) Regulations 2008, SI 2008/629, reg 6 applies (see PARA 348)), that the statement of total return gives a true and fair view of the incoming resources and application of the resources of the investment fund in the relevant financial year, and the statement of changes in net assets gives a

true and fair view of the movements in the net assets of the investment fund between their position as at the beginning of the relevant financial year; (2) in the case of a special case charity (ie one to which reg 7 applies (see PARA 347)), that the income and expenditure account gives a true and fair view of the income and expenditure of the charity in the financial year in question; and (3) in the case of other charities (ie one to which reg 8 applies (see PARA 345)), that the statement of financial activities gives a true and fair view of the incoming resources and application of the resources of the charity in the relevant financial year: reg 24(2).

13 Charities (Accounts and Reports) Regulations 2008, SI 2008/629, reg 24(1)(f)(ii).

14 Charities (Accounts and Reports) Regulations 2008, SI 2008/629, reg 24(1)(g)(i). The statutory duty referred to in the text is the duty in accordance with the Charities Act 2011 s 130 (see PARA 341).

15 Charities (Accounts and Reports) Regulations 2008, SI 2008/629, reg 24(1)(g)(ii).

16 Ie under the Charities Act 2011 s 162: see PARA 371.

17 Charities (Accounts and Reports) Regulations 2008, SI 2008/629, reg 24(1)(g)(iii).

18 Ie under the Charities (Accounts and Reports) Regulations 2008, SI 2008/629, reg 33: see PARA 368.

19 Charities (Accounts and Reports) Regulations 2008, SI 2008/629, reg 24(1)(g)(iv).

20 Charities (Accounts and Reports) Regulations 2008, SI 2008/629, reg 24(1)(g).

21 Charities (Accounts and Reports) Regulations 2008, SI 2008/629, reg 24(3). The matters specified are those in reg 24(1)(f) (see the text and notes 13), and reg 24(1)(g) (see the text and notes 14).

363. Auditor's report on individual accounts under the Companies Act. Where individual accounts have been prepared by the charity trustees[1] of a charity which is a company under the relevant legislation[2], the duties of an auditor carrying out an audit of those accounts include the duty to make a report on those accounts to the charity trustees[3].

The report must (1) state the name and address of the auditor and the name of the charity concerned[4]; (2) be signed by him or, where the office of auditor is held by a body corporate or partnership, in its name by a person authorised to sign on its behalf[5]; (3) state that the auditor is a person who falls within certain statutory requirements[6]; (4) be dated and specify the financial year in respect of which the accounts to which it relates have been prepared[7]; (5) confirm that the accounts were not required to be audited in accordance with the relevant company provisions[8]; (6) specify that it is a report in respect of an audit carried out under the statutory provisions[9] relating to annual audits or examinations of charity accounts[10]; and (7) state whether, in the auditor's opinion: (a) the company's individual accounts comply with the statutory accounting requirements[11] and, in particular, whether the income and expenditure account gives a true and fair view of the income and expenditure of the charity for the relevant financial year and whether the balance sheet gives a true and fair view of the state of affairs of the charity as at the end of that year[12]; (b) in any case where the charity has prepared an additional statement of financial activities, that statement gives a true and fair view of the charity's incoming resources and application of resources in the relevant financial year[13]; and (c) in any case where the accounts state that they have been prepared in accordance with the methods and principles in the *Statement of Recommended Practice for Accounting and Reporting by Charities* (the 'SORP')[14], those methods and principles have been followed[15].

Where the auditor has formed the opinion:

(i) that accounting records have not been kept in respect of the charity in accordance with the statutory provisions[16];

(ii) that the charity's individual accounts do not accord with those records[17];

(iii) that any information contained in those accounts is inconsistent in any material respect with any report of the charity trustees prepared in accordance with the statutory provisions[18] in respect of the relevant financial year[19];

(iv) that any information or explanation to which he is entitled[20] has not been afforded to him[21],

the auditor's report must contain a statement of the opinion he has formed and of his grounds for forming it[22].

The auditor must, in preparing his report, carry out such investigations as will enable him to form an opinion as to certain specified matters[23].

1 As to the meaning of 'charity trustees' see PARA 255.
2 The Charities (Accounts and Reports) Regulations 2008, SI 2008/629, reg 25 refers to the Companies Act 1985 Pt VII Ch 1, however these provisions are repealed. See now the Companies Act 2006 Pt 15; and **COMPANIES**. The duties of an auditor carrying out an audit of the accounts of a charity are, in the case of an audit carried out under the Charities Act 2011 s 144 (see PARA 356), specified, where the auditor is carrying out an audit of individual accounts of a charity that is a charity prepared under the companies legislation, in the Charities (Accounts and Reports) Regulations 2008, SI 2008/629, reg 25: see reg 20.
3 Charities (Accounts and Reports) Regulations 2008, SI 2008/629, reg 25(1). These provisions apply to financial years beginning on or after 1 April 2008: see PARA 342 note 6. In the case of an auditor appointed by the Charity Commission, any report required must instead be made to the Commission: reg 36(1).
4 Charities (Accounts and Reports) Regulations 2008, SI 2008/629, reg 25(1)(a).
5 Charities (Accounts and Reports) Regulations 2008, SI 2008/629, reg 25(1)(b).
6 Charities (Accounts and Reports) Regulations 2008, SI 2008/629, reg 25(1)(c). The statutory requirements referred to in the text are the Charities Act 2011 s 144(2)(b) (see PARA 356).
7 Charities (Accounts and Reports) Regulations 2008, SI 2008/629, reg 25(1)(d).
8 Charities (Accounts and Reports) Regulations 2008, SI 2008/629, reg 25(1)(e). As to the relevant company provisions see note 2.
9 Ie under the Charities Act 2011 s 144 (see PARA 356) and in accordance with regulations made under s 154 (see PARA 361).
10 Charities (Accounts and Reports) Regulations 2008, SI 2008/629, reg 25(1)(f).
11 The Charities (Accounts and Reports) Regulations 2008, SI 2008/629, reg 25 refers to the Companies Act 1985 s 226A, however this provision has been repealed. See now the Companies Act 2006 s 396; and **COMPANIES**.
12 Charities (Accounts and Reports) Regulations 2008, SI 2008/629, reg 25(1)(g)(i).
13 Charities (Accounts and Reports) Regulations 2008, SI 2008/629, reg 25(1)(g)(ii).
14 As to the SORP see PARA 345 note 12.
15 Charities (Accounts and Reports) Regulations 2008, SI 2008/629, reg 25(1)(g)(iii).
16 Charities (Accounts and Reports) Regulations 2008, SI 2008/629, reg 25(1)(h)(i). The statutory provisions referred to in reg 25 are the Companies Act 1985 s 221. However s 221 is repealed. See now the Companies Act 2006 ss 386, 387; and **COMPANIES**.
17 Charities (Accounts and Reports) Regulations 2008, SI 2008/629, reg 25(1)(h)(ii).
18 Ie under the Charities Act 2011 s 162 (see PARA 371) or the Companies Act 1985 s 234. The Companies Act 1985 s 234 has been repealed; see now the Companies Act 2006; and **COMPANIES**.
19 Charities (Accounts and Reports) Regulations 2008, SI 2008/629, reg 25(1)(h)(iii).
20 Ie under the Charities (Accounts and Reports) Regulations 2008, SI 2008/629, reg 33: see PARA 368.
21 Charities (Accounts and Reports) Regulations 2008, SI 2008/629, reg 25(1)(h)(iv).
22 Charities (Accounts and Reports) Regulations 2008, SI 2008/629, reg 25(1)(h).
23 Charities (Accounts and Reports) Regulations 2008, SI 2008/629, reg 25(2). The matters specified are those in reg 25(1)(g) (see the text and notes 12–15), and reg 25(1)(h) (see the text and notes 16–22).

364. Auditor's report on annual accounts on the receipts and payments basis. Where a receipts and payments account and statement of assets and liabilities have been prepared[1] for the relevant financial year[2], the auditor must make a report on that account and statement to the charity trustees[3].

The report must: (1) state the name and address of the auditor and the name of the charity concerned[4]; (2) be signed by him or, where the office of auditor is held by a body corporate or partnership, in its name by a person authorised to sign on its behalf[5]; (3) state that the auditor falls within certain statutory requirements[6]; (4) be dated and specify the financial year in respect of which the accounts to which it relates have been prepared[7]; and (5) specify that it is a report in respect of an audit carried out under the statutory provisions[8] relating to annual audits or examinations of charity accounts[9].

The report must also state whether in the auditor's opinion the amount and statement properly present the receipts and payments of the charity for the financial year in question and its assets and liabilities as at the end of that year and whether in his opinion the account and statement adequately distinguish any material special trust or other restricted fund[10] of the charity[11].

Where the auditor has formed the opinion:

(a) that accounting records have not been kept in respect of the charity in accordance with the statutory[12] duty[13]; or
(b) that the account and statement do not accord with those records[14]; or
(c) that any information or explanation to which he is entitled[15] has not been afforded to him[16],

the report must contain a statement of that opinion and of his grounds for forming it[17].

The auditor must, in preparing his report, carry out such investigations as will enable him to form an opinion as to certain specified matters[18].

1 Ie under the Charities Act 2011 s 133: see PARA 342.
2 As to the meaning of 'financial year' see PARAS 218 note 3, 344 note 4. The provisions apply to financial years beginning on or after 1 April 2008: see PARA 342 note 6.
3 Charities (Accounts and Reports) Regulations 2008, SI 2008/629, reg 26(1). These regulations also apply in the case of an English NHS Charity in respect of an auditor appointed by the Audit Commission (ie under the Charities Act 2011 s 149(3)(a)) (Charities (Accounts and Reports) Regulations 2008, SI 2008/629, reg 27(1), (4)); and in the case of a Welsh NHS Charity in respect of the Auditor General for Wales where he has elected under the Charities Act 2011 s 150 that the accounts of the charity be audited (Charities (Accounts and Reports) Regulations 2008, SI 2008/629, reg 28(1), (4)). In the case of an auditor appointed by the Charity Commission, any report required must instead be made to the Commission, except in the case of an English or Welsh NHS Charity: Charities (Accounts and Reports) Regulations 2008, SI 2008/629, reg 36. As to the meaning of 'charity trustees' see PARA 255. As to English NHS Charities see PARA 357. As to Welsh NHS Charities see PARA 358.
4 Charities (Accounts and Reports) Regulations 2008, SI 2008/629, reg 26(1)(a). This statement is not required of the Auditor General for Wales in the case of a Welsh National Health Service Charity: see reg 28(5)(a).
5 Charities (Accounts and Reports) Regulations 2008, SI 2008/629, reg 26(1)(b).
6 Charities (Accounts and Reports) Regulations 2008, SI 2008/629, reg 26(1)(c). The statutory requirements referred to in the text are the requirements of the Charities Act 2011 s 144(2)(a), or as the case may be, s 144(2)(b) (see PARA 356) or, in the case of an English NHS Charity, s 149(3)(a): Charities (Accounts and Reports) Regulations 2008, SI 2008/629, reg 27(5). This statement is not required of the Auditor General of Wales in the case of a Welsh National Health Service Charity: see reg 28(5)(b).
7 Charities (Accounts and Reports) Regulations 2008, SI 2008/629, reg 26(1)(d).
8 Ie under the Charities Act 2011 s 144 (see PARA 356) or, in the case of an English NHS Charity, s 149 (see PARA 357) or, in the case of a Welsh NHS Charity, s 150 (see PARA 358), and in accordance with regulations made under s 154 (see PARA 361): see the Charities (Accounts and Reports) Regulations 2008, SI 2008/629, regs 26(1)(e), 27(5)(b), 28(5)(c). Note that in the Queen's Printer copy reg 27(5)(b) is labelled reg 27(6) and purports to amend reg 26(1)(d). It is submitted this is in error.
9 Charities (Accounts and Reports) Regulations 2008, SI 2008/629, reg 26(1)(e).
10 As to the meaning of 'restricted fund' see PARA 346 note 14.

11 Charities (Accounts and Reports) Regulations 2008, SI 2008/629, reg 26(1)(f). As to the meaning of 'special trust' see PARA 218 note 2.
12 Ie under Charities Act 2011 s 130: see PARA 341.
13 Charities (Accounts and Reports) Regulations 2008, SI 2008/629, reg 26(1)(g)(i).
14 Charities (Accounts and Reports) Regulations 2008, SI 2008/629, reg 26(1)(g)(ii).
15 Ie under the Charities (Accounts and Reports) Regulations 2008, SI 2008/629, reg 33: see PARA 368.
16 Charities (Accounts and Reports) Regulations 2008, SI 2008/629, reg 26(1)(g)(iii).
17 Charities (Accounts and Reports) Regulations 2008, SI 2008/629, reg 26(1)(g).
18 Charities (Accounts and Reports) Regulations 2008, SI 2008/629, reg 26(2). The matters specified are those in reg 26(1)(f) (see the text and notes 11), and reg 26(1)(g) (see the text and notes 13–17).

365. Auditor's report on group accounts. Where group accounts[1] are required to be audited[2] the auditor must make a report on those accounts to the charity trustees of the parent charity[3]. The report must: (1) state the name and address of the auditor and the name of the parent charity concerned[4]; (2) be signed by him or, where the office of auditor is held by a body corporate or partnership, in its name by a person authorised to sign on its behalf[5]; (3) state that the auditor falls within certain statutory requirements[6]; (4) be dated and specify the financial year in respect of which the accounts to which it relates have been prepared[7]; (5) where the parent charity is a company, confirm that the charity trustees were not required under certain company legislation[8] to prepare group accounts for that year[9]; and (6) specify that it is a report in respect of an audit carried out under the statutory provisions[10] relating to group accounts[11].

In the case of a parent charity that is an investment fund[12], the report must also state whether, in the auditor's opinion, the report complies with the appropriate requirements as to form and content[13], and in particular whether the consolidated statement of total return gives a true and fair view of the total return of the parent charity and its subsidiary undertakings during the relevant financial year, the consolidated statement of changes in net assets gives a true and fair view of the changes in the net assets of the parent charity and its subsidiary undertakings during the relevant financial year, and the consolidated balance sheet gives a true and fair view of the state of affairs of the parent charity and its subsidiary undertakings at the end of the relevant financial year[14].

In the case of a parent charity that is a special case charity[15], the report must also state whether, in the auditor's opinion, the report complies with the appropriate requirements as to form and content[16], and in particular whether the consolidated balance sheet gives a true and fair view of the state of affairs of the parent charity and its subsidiary undertakings at the end of the relevant financial year, and the consolidated income and expenditure account gives a true and fair view of the income and expenditure of the parent charity and its subsidiary undertakings as a whole in the relevant financial year[17].

In the case of any other parent charity[18], the report must also state whether, in the auditor's opinion, the report complies with the appropriate requirements as to form and content[19], and in particular whether the consolidated balance sheet gives a true and fair view of the state of affairs of the parent charity and its subsidiary undertakings as at the end of the relevant financial year, and the consolidated statement of financial activities gives a true and fair view of the total incoming resources of the parent charity and its subsidiary undertakings and the movements in the total resources of the group in the relevant financial year[20].

Where the auditor has formed the opinion that any information contained in the group accounts is inconsistent in any material respect with any report of the charity trustees prepared in accordance with the statutory provisions[21], or that any information or explanation to which he is entitled has not been afforded to him[22], the auditor's report must contain a statement of that opinion and of the grounds for forming it[23].

The auditor must, in preparing his report carry out such investigations as will enable him to form an opinion as to certain specified matters[24].

1 As to group accounts see PARA 343.
2 Ie under the Charities Act 2011 s 151 (see PARA 359).
3 Charities (Accounts and Reports) Regulations 2008, SI 2008/629, reg 30(1). As to the meaning of 'parent charity' see the Charities Act 2011 s 141; and PARA 343 and note 2 (definition applied by the Charities (Accounts and Reports) Regulations 2008, SI 2008/629, reg 2(1)).
4 Charities (Accounts and Reports) Regulations 2008, SI 2008/629, reg 30(1)(a).
5 Charities (Accounts and Reports) Regulations 2008, SI 2008/629, reg 30(1)(b).
6 Charities (Accounts and Reports) Regulations 2008, SI 2008/629, reg 30(1)(c)(i). The statutory requirements referred to in the text are the requirements of the Charities Act 2011 s 144(2)(a), or as the case may be, s 144(2)(b) (see PARA 356). These requirements do not apply where the audit is of an English NHS Charity, in which case the report must instead state that the auditor was appointed by the Audit Commission, or where the audit is of a Welsh NHS Charity, in which case the report must instead state that the auditor is the Auditor General for Wales: see the Charities (Accounts and Reports) Regulations 2008, SI 2008/629, reg 30(1)(c)(ii), (iii).
7 Charities (Accounts and Reports) Regulations 2008, SI 2008/629, reg 30(1)(d).
8 The legislation referred to in the text is the Companies Act 1985 s 227. However s 227 has been repealed. See now the Companies Act 2006 ss 399, 403; and COMPANIES.
9 Charities (Accounts and Reports) Regulations 2008, SI 2008/629, reg 30(1)(e).
10 See PARA 343.
11 Charities (Accounts and Reports) Regulations 2008, SI 2008/629, reg 30(1)(f).
12 As to the meaning of 'investment fund' see PARA 348 note 2.
13 Ie under the Charities (Accounts and Reports) Regulations 2008, SI 2008/629, reg 13 (see PARA 355).
14 Charities (Accounts and Reports) Regulations 2008, SI 2008/629, reg 30(1)(g)(i).
15 As to the meaning of 'special case charity' see PARA 347 note 3.
16 Ie under the Charities (Accounts and Reports) Regulations 2008, SI 2008/629, reg 14 (see PARA 354).
17 Charities (Accounts and Reports) Regulations 2008, SI 2008/629, reg 30(1)(g)(ii).
18 Ie a parent charity that is not an investment fund or a special case charity.
19 Ie under the Charities (Accounts and Reports) Regulations 2008, SI 2008/629, reg 15 (see PARA 353).
20 Charities (Accounts and Reports) Regulations 2008, SI 2008/629, reg 30(1)(g)(iii).
21 Ie under the Charities Act 2011 s 162 in respect of the relevant financial year (see PARA 371) or, where the parent charity is a company, with the report prepared in respect of that financial year under the Companies Act 1985 s 234. Section 234 has been repealed. See now the Companies Act 2006 s 415; and COMPANIES.
22 Ie under the Charities (Accounts and Reports) Regulations 2008, SI 2008/629, reg 33: see PARA 368.
23 Charities (Accounts and Reports) Regulations 2008, SI 2008/629, reg 30(1)(h).
24 Charities (Accounts and Reports) Regulations 2008, SI 2008/629, reg 30(2). The specified matters are those in reg 30(1)(g), (h): see notes 14–22.

366. Reports to charity trustees by an independent examiner. An independent examiner[1] who has carried out an examination of the accounts of a charity[2] under the statutory provisions providing for independent examination[3] must make a report to the charity trustees[4].

The report must: (1) state the independent examiner's name and address and the name of the charity concerned[5]; (2) be signed by him[6]; (3) be dated and specify the financial year[7] in respect of which the accounts to which it relates have been prepared[8]; (4) confirm, where the charity whose accounts are being examined is a company, that the accounts are not required to be audited under the companies legislation[9]; (5) specify, if the gross income exceeds the statutory sum[10], the basis on which he qualifies to act as independent examiner[11]; (6) state any, or any other, relevant professional qualifications or professional body of which he is a member[12]; (7) state, where the accounts are being examined under a dispensation from the Charity Commission[13], the date when the Commission dispensed with the audit requirement[14]; and (8) specify that it is a report in respect of an examination carried out under the statutory provisions[15] relating to annual audits or examinations of charity accounts and in accordance with any directions given by the Charity Commission[16] which are applicable[17].

The report must also state whether or not any matter has come to the examiner's attention in connection with the examination which gives him reasonable cause to believe that in any material respect[18]: (a) accounting records have not been kept in respect of the charity in accordance with the statutory duty[19]; (b) the accounts do not accord with those records[20]; and (c) in the case of an examination of accounts, the statement of accounts[21] does not comply with any of the relevant statutory requirements[22] other than any requirement to give a true and fair view[23].

The report must state whether or not any matter has come to the examiner's attention in connection with the examination to which, in his opinion, attention should be drawn in the report in order to enable a proper understanding of the accounts to be reached[24]. Further, where certain matters become apparent to the examiner during the course of an examination, the report must contain a statement to that effect[25]. The relevant matters are that: (i) there has been any material expenditure or action which appears not to be in accordance with the trusts of the charity[26]; or (ii) any information or explanation to which he is entitled[27] has not been afforded to him[28]; or (iii) in the case of an examination of accounts a statement of which has been prepared[29], any information contained in the statement of accounts is inconsistent in any material respect with any report of the charity trustees prepared under the statutory provisions relating to annual reports[30] in respect of the financial year in question[31].

1 As to the meaning of 'independent examiner' see PARA 356 note 10.
2 As to the meaning of 'charity' see PARA 1.
3 Ie under the Charities Act 2011 s 144: see PARA 356.
4 Charities (Accounts and Reports) Regulations 2008, SI 2008/629, reg 31. These provisions apply to financial years beginning on or after 1 April 2008: see PARA 342 note 6. As to the meaning of 'charity trustees' see PARA 255.
5 Charities (Accounts and Reports) Regulations 2008, SI 2008/629, reg 31(a).
6 Charities (Accounts and Reports) Regulations 2008, SI 2008/629, reg 31(b).
7 As to the meaning of 'financial year' see PARAS 218 note 3, 344 note 4.
8 Charities (Accounts and Reports) Regulations 2008, SI 2008/629, reg 31(c)(i).
9 Charities (Accounts and Reports) Regulations 2008, SI 2008/629, reg 31(c)(ii). The companies legislation referred to in the text is the Companies Act 1985 Pt 7. However Pt 7 has been repealed. See now the Companies Act 2006; and COMPANIES.
10 Ie the sum specified in the Charities Act 2011 s 145(3): see PARA 356 note 10.
11 Charities (Accounts and Reports) Regulations 2008, SI 2008/629, reg 31(d).
12 Charities (Accounts and Reports) Regulations 2008, SI 2008/629, reg 31(e).
13 Ie the Charities (Accounts and Reports) Regulations 2008, SI 2008/629, reg 34(3)(b) (see PARA 370). As to the Charity Commission see PARAS 543–578.
14 Charities (Accounts and Reports) Regulations 2008, SI 2008/629, reg 31(f). The audit requirement mentioned in the text is the Charities Act 2011 s 138(2) (see PARA 356).
15 See note 3.
16 Ie under Charities Act 2011 s 145(5)(b): see PARA 356. From time to time, the Charity Commission publishes guidance relating to independent examinations: see eg *CC32: The Independent Examination of Charity Accounts: Examiners' Guide* (Charity Commission, March

2012) (available, at the date at which this volume states the law, on the government website). As to the Charity Commission's publications see PARA 547.

17 Charities (Accounts and Reports) Regulations 2008, SI 2008/629, reg 31(g).

18 Charities (Accounts and Reports) Regulations 2008, SI 2008/629, reg 31(h).

19 Charities (Accounts and Reports) Regulations 2008, SI 2008/629, reg 31(h)(i). The statutory duty referred to in the text is a statutory duty under the Charities Act 2011 s 130 (see PARA 341) or, where the charity is a company, the Companies Act 1985 s 221: see the Charities (Accounts and Reports) Regulations 2008, SI 2008/629, reg 31(h)(i). The Companies Act 1985 s 221 has been repealed. See now the Companies Act 2006 s 386; and COMPANIES.

20 Charities (Accounts and Reports) Regulations 2008, SI 2008/629, reg 31(h)(ii).

21 Ie as prepared under the Charities Act 2011 s 132(1) (see PARA 342) or under the Companies Act 1985 Pt 7 (repealed: see now Companies Act 2006; and COMPANIES). In any case where the accounts under the Companies Act 1985 Pt 7 state they have been prepared in accordance with the *Statement of Recommended Practice for Accounting and Reporting by Charities* (the 'SORP'), the report must also state they have not in fact been prepared in accordance with the methods and principles set out in the SORP: see the Charities (Accounts and Reports) Regulations 2008, SI 2008/629, reg 31(h)(iv)(bb). As to the SORP see PARA 345 note 12.

22 As to the relevant statutory requirements see PARAS 345–348.

23 Charities (Accounts and Reports) Regulations 2008, SI 2008/629, reg 31(h)(iii), (iv).

24 Charities (Accounts and Reports) Regulations 2008, SI 2008/629, reg 31(i).

25 Charities (Accounts and Reports) Regulations 2008, SI 2008/629, reg 31(j).

26 Charities (Accounts and Reports) Regulations 2008, SI 2008/629, reg 31(j)(i).

27 Ie under the Charities (Accounts and Reports) Regulations 2008, SI 2008/629, reg 32: see PARA 369.

28 Charities (Accounts and Reports) Regulations 2008, SI 2008/629, reg 31(j)(ii).

29 Ie under the Charities Act 2011 s 132(1) (see PARA 342) or, in the case of a charitable company, the Companies Act 1985 Pt 7 (repealed: see now the Companies Act 2006; and COMPANIES).

30 Ie under the Charities Act 2011 s 162 (see PARA 371) and, in the case of a charitable company, the Companies Act 1985 s 234 (repealed: see now the Companies Act 2006 s 415; and COMPANIES vol 15 (2009) PARA 816).

31 See the Charities (Accounts and Reports) Regulations 2008, SI 2008/629, reg 31(j)(iii)–(iv).

367. Communications with Charity Commission and auditors etc. A person acting as an auditor, independent examiner or examiner appointed by or in relation to a charity[1], a person appointed to audit or report on any group accounts[2], or a person acting as an auditor of a charitable company[3], must immediately make a written report to the Charity Commission[4], detailing any matter of which he becomes aware in such capacity which relates to the activities or affairs of the charity or of an institution or body corporate connected with the charity[5] and which the person has reasonable cause to believe is, or is likely to be, of material significance for the exercise, in relation to the charity, of the Commission's functions in relation to the general power to institute inquiries[6] or the power[7] to act for the protection of charities[8]. If, in the course of acting as an auditor, independent examiner or examiner appointed by or in relation to a charity[9] a person becomes aware of any matter which does not appear to him to be one that he is required to report to the Commission[10], but which he has reasonable cause to believe is likely to be relevant for the purposes of the exercise by the Commission of any of its functions, he may make a report on the matter to the Commission[11].

Where the duty or power described above[12] has arisen in relation to a person acting in such capacity[13], it is not affected by the person subsequently ceasing to act in that capacity[14].

Where a person makes such a report, no duty to which he is subject is to be regarded as contravened merely because of any information or opinion contained in the report[15].

Where an auditor appointed by charity trustees[16] ceases for any reason to hold office he must send a statement to the charity trustees[17]. The statement must set out any circumstances connected with his ceasing to hold office which he considers should be brought to their attention or, if he considers that there are no circumstances, a statement that there are none[18]. Where the auditor sends a statement containing circumstances to be brought to the attention of the charity trustees, he must also send a copy to the Commission[19].

1 Ie a person appointed under the Charities Act 2011 ss 144–146, 149(2) or (3), or the Auditor General for Wales acting under s 150(2) or (3): s 156(1). See PARAS 356–364.
2 Ie under the Charities Act 2011 ss 151–153 (see PARAS 359–360): see s 158(1). Nothing in s 158 applies to exempt charities: s 160(3). As to exempt charities, and the increased regulation of them introduced by the Charities Act 2006 and maintained by the Charities Act 2011, see PARA 318 et seq.
3 Ie under the Companies Act 2006 Pt 16 Ch 2 (see **COMPANIES**): see the Charities Act 2011 s 159(1), (2). As to the meaning of 'charitable company' see PARA 241 note 1.
4 As to the Charity Commission see PARAS 543–578.
5 As to the meaning of 'charity' see PARA 1. A connected institution or body is an institution which is controlled by, or a body corporate in which a substantial interest is held by, the charity or any one or more of the charity trustees acting in his or their capacity as such: Charities Act 2011 s 157(1). For these purposes a person controls an institution if he is able to secure that the affairs of the institution are conducted in accordance with his wishes: ss 157(2), 351. A substantial interest in a body corporate is held if the person or institution in question (1) is interested in shares comprised in the equity share capital of that body of a nominal value of more than one-fifth of that share capital; or (2) is entitled to exercise, or control the exercise of, more than one-fifth of the voting power at any general meeting of that body: ss 157(2), 352(1). As to the meanings of 'equity share capital' and 'share' see the Companies Act 2006 ss 548, 540 respectively; and **COMPANIES** (definitions applied by the Charities Act 2011 s 352(3)). As to the meaning of 'charity trustees' see PARA 255.

In so far as this provision applies in relation to a person appointed to audit or report on any group accounts, the reference to the charity or any connected institution or body is to be construed as a reference to the parent charity or any of its subsidiary undertakings: s 158(2); and see note 2. As to the meaning of 'parent charity' see PARA 343 note 2. As to the meaning of 'subsidiary undertaking' see PARA 343 note 3.
6 Ie under the Charities Act 2011 ss 46, 47, 50: see PARAS 559–560.
7 Ie under the Charities Act 2011 ss 76, 79–82: see PARA 567 et seq.
8 Charities Act 2011 s 156(2), (3).
9 Ie acting in the capacity mentioned in the Charities Act 2011 s 156(1) (see text and note 1).
10 Ie one he is required to report under the Charities Act 2011 s 156(2).
11 Charities Act 2011 s 156(3).
12 Ie the duty or power under the Charities Act 2011 s 156(2) or (4).
13 Ie acting in the capacity mentioned in the Charities Act 2011 s 156(1) (see text and note 1).
14 Charities Act 2011 s 156(5).
15 Charities Act 2011 s 156(6).
16 Or a charity trustee of an English NHS charity under the Charities Act 2011 s 149(2) or (3)(a) (see PARA 357).
17 See the Charities (Accounts and Reports) Regulations 2008, SI 2008/629, reg 35(1)(a).
18 See the Charities (Accounts and Reports) Regulations 2008, SI 2008/629, reg 35(1)(a)(i), (ii).
19 See the Charities (Accounts and Reports) Regulations 2008, SI 2008/629, reg 35(1)(b).

368. Access to books, documents and records, and obtaining information and explanations. A person carrying out an audit or examination of the accounts of a charity[1] has a right of access to any books, documents[2] and other records (however kept) which relate to the charity[3] concerned and which the person concerned considers it necessary to inspect for the purposes of carrying out the audit or examination[4]. Such a person is entitled to require, in the case of the charity concerned, such information and explanations from past or present charity trustees[5] of, or trustees for, the charity, or from past or present officers[6] or employees of the charity, as he considers necessary to obtain for the purposes of carrying out the audit or, as the case may be, examination[7].

An auditor carrying out an audit of the group accounts of a parent charity[8] also has a right of access to any books, documents and other records (however kept) which relate to any of the subsidiary undertakings[9] included in group accounts and which the auditor considers it necessary to inspect for the purpose of carrying out the audit[10]. He also has the right to require, in the case of any such subsidiary undertaking, such information and explanations from, in the case of a subsidiary undertaking which is a charity, past or present charity trustees of, or trustees for, that charity, and, in the case of any subsidiary undertaking which is not a charity, from the subsidiary undertaking itself and from past or present officers or employees of that undertaking, as he considers it necessary to obtain for the purposes of carrying out the audit[11]. The auditor has the right to require the charity trustees of the parent charity to take all such steps as are reasonably open to them to obtain from any such subsidiary undertaking such information and explanations as he may reasonably require for the purposes of carrying out the audit[12].

1 Ie under the Charities Act 2011 ss 144, 149, 150 151: see PARAS 356–364.
2 As to the meaning of 'document' see PARA 263 note 2.
3 As to the meaning of 'charity' see PARA 1.
4 Charities (Accounts and Reports) Regulations 2008, SI 2008/629, reg 33(1). These provisions apply to financial years beginning on or after 1 April 2008: see PARA 342 note 6.
5 As to the meaning of 'charity trustees' see PARA 255.
6 For the purposes of this provision, 'officer' includes any auditor or other person appointed to scrutinise the accounts of any such undertaking: Charities (Accounts and Reports) Regulations 2008, SI 2008/629, reg 33(4).
7 Charities (Accounts and Reports) Regulations 2008, SI 2008/629, reg 33(2).
8 Ie under the Charities Act 2011 s 151: see PARA 359.
9 As to the meaning of subsidiary undertaking PARA 343.
10 Charities (Accounts and Reports) Regulations 2008, SI 2008/629, reg 33(3)(a).
11 Charities (Accounts and Reports) Regulations 2008, SI 2008/629, reg 33(3)(b).
12 Charities (Accounts and Reports) Regulations 2008, SI 2008/629, reg 33(3)(c).

369. Examination of the accounts of English and Welsh NHS charities. Where a person has carried out an examination of the accounts of an English NHS Charity[1], or the Auditor General for Wales has carried out an examination of the accounts of a Welsh NHS Charity[2], that person, or as the case may be the Auditor General for Wales, must make a report to the charity trustees[3] which:

(1) states the name of the charity concerned and, in the case of an examination in respect of an English NHS Charity[4], the name and address of the examiner[5];
(2) is signed by him[6];
(3) is dated and specified the financial year[7] in respect of which the accounts to which it relates have been prepared[8];
(4) in the case of an examination in respect of an English NHS Charity[9] states any relevant professional qualifications or professional body of which he is a member[10];
(5) specifies that it is a report in respect of an examination carried out in respect of an English or Welsh NHS Charity[11], and, in the case of an examination in respect of an English NHS Charity[12], in accordance with any directions given by the Commission[13] which are applicable[14];
(6) states whether or not any matter has come to the examiner's attention in connection with the examination which gives him reasonable cause to believe that in any material respect accounting records have not been kept in respect of the charity[15]; the accounts do not accord with those

records; in the case of an examination of a statement of accounts which has been prepared under certain provisions[16], the statement of accounts does not comply with certain requirements[17], as relevant, other than any requirement to give a true and fair view[18];

(7) states whether or not any matter has come to the examiner's or, as the case may be, the Auditor General for Wales', attention in connection with the examination to which, in his opinion, attention should be drawn in the report in order to enable a proper understanding of the accounts to be reached[19];

(8) contains a statement as to any of the following matters that has become apparent to the examiner or, as the case may be, the Auditor General for Wales, during the course of the examination, namely, that: (a) there has been any material expenditure or action which appears not to be in accordance with the trusts of the charity; or (b) any information or explanation to which he is entitled[20] has not been afforded to him; or (c) in the case of an examination of accounts a statement of which has been prepared[21], any information contained in the statement of accounts is inconsistent in any material respect with any report of the charity trustees prepared[22] in respect of the financial year in question[23].

1 Ie under the Charities Act 2011 s 149 (see PARA 357). As to the meaning of 'English NHS Charity' see PARA 357 note 2.
2 Ie under the Charities Act 2011 s 150 (see PARA 358). As to the meaning of 'Welsh NHS Charity' see PARA 358 note 2.
3 As to the meaning of 'charity trustees' see PARA 255.
4 Ie an examination under the Charities Act 2011 s 149 (see PARA 357).
5 Charities (Accounts and Reports) Regulations 2008, SI 2008/629, reg 32(a).
6 Charities (Accounts and Reports) Regulations 2008, SI 2008/629, reg 32(b).
7 As to the meaning of 'financial year' see PARAS 218 note 3, 344 note 4.
8 Charities (Accounts and Reports) Regulations 2008, SI 2008/629, reg 32(c).
9 Ie an examination under the Charities Act 2011 s 149 (see PARA 357).
10 Charities (Accounts and Reports) Regulations 2008, SI 2008/629, reg 32(d).
11 Ie an examination under the Charities Act 2011 s 149 (see PARA 357) or, as the case may be, s 150 (see PARA 358).
12 Ie an examination under the Charities Act 2011 s 149 (see PARA 357).
13 Ie given under the Charities Act 2011 s 149(5) (see PARA 357).
14 Charities (Accounts and Reports) Regulations 2008, SI 2008/629, reg 32(e).
15 Ie in accordance with the Charities Act 2011 s 130 (see PARA 341).
16 Ie in accordance with the Charities Act 2011 s 132(1) (see PARA 342).
17 Ie the requirements of the Charities (Accounts and Reports) Regulations 2008, SI 2008/629, reg 6, 7 or 8 (see PARAS 345–348).
18 Charities (Accounts and Reports) Regulations 2008, SI 2008/629, reg 32(f).
19 Charities (Accounts and Reports) Regulations 2008, SI 2008/629, reg 32(g).
20 Ie under the Charities (Accounts and Reports) Regulations 2008, SI 2008/629, reg 33 (see PARA 368).
21 Ie under the Charities Act 2011 s 132(1) (see PARA 342).
22 Ie prepared under the Charities Act 2011 s 162 (see PARA 371).
23 Charities (Accounts and Reports) Regulations 2008, SI 2008/629, reg 32(h).

370. Dispensation from audit or examination requirements. The Charity Commission[1] may, in certain circumstances[2], dispense with the statutory requirements for the audit or independent examination of charity accounts[3] in the case of a particular charity[4] or in respect of a particular financial year[5] of a charity[6].

Such circumstances are where the Commission:

(1) is satisfied that the accounts of the charity[7] concerned are required to be audited in accordance with any statutory provision contained in or

having effect under an Act of Parliament which, in the opinion of the Commission, imposes requirements which are sufficiently similar to the requirements for the audit of charity accounts under the Charities Act 2011[8] for those requirements to be dispensed with[9];

(2) is satisfied that the accounts of the charity[10] concerned have been audited by the Comptroller and Auditor General or by the Auditor General for Wales[11];

(3) is satisfied that the accounts of the charity concerned for the financial year in question have been or will be audited or, as the case may be, examined in accordance with requirements or arrangements which, in the opinion of the Commission, are sufficiently similar to the statutory requirements for the audit or independent examination of charity accounts[12] applicable to that financial year of that charity for those requirements to be dispensed with[13];

(4) considers that, although the financial year in question of the charity concerned is one to which the statutory requirements for the audit of charity accounts apply[14], there are exceptional circumstances which justify the examination of the accounts by an independent examiner instead of their audit in accordance with those requirements[15];

(5) in the case of group accounts[16], is satisfied that the group accounts of the parent charity concerned for the financial year in question have been, or will be, audited in accordance with requirements or arrangements which, in the opinion of the Commission, are sufficiently similar to the requirements for the audit of group accounts under the Charities Act 2011[17] for those requirements to be dispensed with[18].

The Commission must make it a condition of a dispensation that the charity trustees send to it any report made to the trustees with respect to the accounts of that charity for the relevant financial year of which it requests a copy[19]. The Commission may revoke a dispensation if the charity trustees fail to comply with a relevant condition[20].

1 As to the Charity Commission see PARAS 543–578.
2 Ie in the circumstances referred to in the Charities (Accounts and Reports) Regulations 2008, SI 2008/629, reg 34(2)–(5): see the text and notes 7–18.
3 Ie the requirements of the Charities Act 2011 ss 144(2), 151(4): see PARAS 356, 359.
4 As to the meaning of 'charity' see PARA 1.
5 As to the meaning of 'financial year' see PARA 218 note 3, 344 note 4.
6 See the Charities (Accounts and Reports) Regulations 2008, SI 2008/629, reg 34(1). These provisions apply to financial years beginning on or after 1 April 2008: see PARA 342 note 6.
7 Or, in the case of group accounts, the parent charity: see the Charities (Accounts and Reports) Regulations 2008, SI 2008/629, reg 34(4).
8 Ie under the Charities Act 2011 s 144(2) (see PARA 356) or, in the case of group accounts, s 151(4) (see PARA 359).
9 See the Charities (Accounts and Reports) Regulations 2008, SI 2008/629, reg 34(2)(a), (4)(a).
10 Or, in the case of group accounts, the parent charity: Charities (Accounts and Reports) Regulations 2008, SI 2008/629, reg 34(4).
11 Charities (Accounts and Reports) Regulations 2008, SI 2008/629, reg 34(2)(b), (4)(b). As to the Comptroller and Auditor General see **CONSTITUTIONAL AND ADMINISTRATIVE LAW** vol 20 (2014) PARA 494 et seq. As to the Auditor General for Wales see **CONSTITUTIONAL AND ADMINISTRATIVE LAW** vol 20 (2014) PARAS 400–402.
12 Ie the requirements of the Charities Act 2011 s 144: see PARA 356.
13 Charities (Accounts and Reports) Regulations 2008, SI 2008/629, reg 34(3)(a).
14 See note 8.
15 Charities (Accounts and Reports) Regulations 2008, SI 2008/629, reg 34(3)(b). The Commission must make it a condition of a dispensation granted under reg 34(3)(b) that the charity trustees comply with the requirements of the Charities Act 2011 s 145(1), (2) (see PARAS

356) as if they were able to make and had in fact made an election under that section that the accounts of the charity for the relevant financial year be examined by an independent examiner: Charities (Accounts and Reports) Regulations 2008, SI 2008/629, reg 34(7).

16 As to group accounts see PARA 343.

17 Ie the Charities Act 2011 ss 149(8), 151(4): see PARA 359.

18 Charities (Accounts and Reports) Regulations 2008, SI 2008/629, reg 34(5).

19 Charities (Accounts and Reports) Regulations 2008, SI 2008/629, reg 34(6).

20 See the Charities (Accounts and Reports) Regulations 2008, SI 2008/629, reg 34(8). The relevant conditions are those imposed under reg 34(6) and (7).

H. ANNUAL REPORTS, ANNUAL STATEMENTS AND ANNUAL RETURNS

371. Annual reports and annual statements. The charity trustees[1] of a charity[2] (other than an exempt charity[3], and certain charities which are not required to register and are not registered[4]) must prepare an annual report in respect of each financial year[5] of the charity[6]. The report must contain such a report by the trustees on the activities of the charity during that year[7], and such other information relating to the charity or to its trustees or officers[8], as is prescribed by regulations[9] made by the Minister[10].

Where in any financial year of a charity its gross income[11] exceeds £25,000[12], a copy of the annual report required to be so prepared in respect of that year must be transmitted to the Charity Commission by the charity trustees within ten months from the end of that year, or within such longer period as the Commission may for any special reason allow in the case of that report[13]. Where in any financial year of a charity its gross income does not exceed £25,000, a copy of the annual report required to be so prepared in respect of that year must, if the Commission so requests, be transmitted to it by the charity trustees: (1) in the case of a request made before the end of seven months from the end of the financial year to which the report relates, within ten months from the end of that year[14]; and (2) in the case of a request not so made, within three months from the date of the request[15]; or (3) in either case, within such longer period as the Commission may for any special reason allow in the case of that report[16].

Any copy of any annual report transmitted to the Commission under the above provisions must have attached to it a copy of the statement of accounts prepared for the financial year in question[17] or, as the case may be, a copy of the account and statement so prepared[18] together with[19]: (a) where the accounts of the charity for that year have been audited[20], a copy of the report made by the auditor on that statement of accounts or, as the case may be, on that account and statement[21]; (b) where the accounts of the charity for that year have been examined[22], a copy of the report made by the person carrying out the examination[23]. However, this requirement does not apply to a charitable company[24], and any copy of an annual report transmitted by the charity trustees of such a charity must instead have attached to it a copy of the charity's annual accounts prepared for the financial year in question under the provisions of the Companies Act 2006 which relate to accounts and reports[25], together with the following[26]: (i) where the accounts of the charity for that year have been audited under the provisions of the Companies Act 2006[27] a copy of the report made by the auditor on those accounts; or (ii) where the accounts of the charity for that year have been audited[28] a copy of the report made by the auditor on those accounts; or (iii) where the accounts of the charity for that year have been examined, a copy of the report made by the person carrying out the examination[29].

In addition to the statutory requirements[30] the Commission requires that an annual report includes a report of those activities undertaken by a charity to further its charitable purposes for the public benefit and a statement by the charity trustees as to whether they have complied with their statutory duty[31] to have regard to public benefit guidance[32].

1 As to the meaning of 'charity trustees' see PARA 255.
2 As to the meaning of 'charity' see PARA 1.
3 See the Charities Act 2011 s 167; and PARA 381. As to exempt charities see PARAS 318–320.
4 See the Charities Act 2011 s 30(2)(b), (c), (d) (see PARA 308): see s 168(1), (2); and PARA 381.
5 As to the meaning of 'financial year' see PARAS 218 note 3, 344 note 4.
6 Charities Act 2011 s 162(1). The charity trustees of a charity must preserve, for at least six years from the end of the financial year to which it relates, any annual report prepared by them under s 162(1) which they have not been required to transmit to the Charity Commission: s 165(2). Where a charity ceases to exist within the six year period, the obligation to preserve the records continues to be discharged by the last charity trustees of the charity, unless the Commission consents in writing to the records being destroyed or otherwise disposed of: s 165(3), (4). As to the Charity Commission see PARAS 543–578.
7 Charities Act 2011 s 162(1)(a).
8 Charities Act 2011 s 162(1)(b).
9 As to the regulations made under the power conferred by the Charities Act 2011 s 162, and the financial years to which they apply, see those noted in PARA 342 note 6.
10 Charities Act 2011 s 162(1). Before making such any regulations the Minister must consult such persons or bodies of persons as he considers appropriate: s 348(4). As to the making of regulations generally see s 348; and PARA 590. See also PARA 315 note 7. As to the contents, application of requirements as to annual reports see PARA 373 et seq. Such regulations may in particular make provision: (1) for any such report under s 162(1)(a) (see the text to note 6) to be prepared in accordance with such principles as are specified or referred to in the regulations; (2) enabling the Charity Commission to dispense with the requirement prescribed by virtue of s 162(1)(b) (see the text to note 8) in the case of a particular charity or a particular class of charities, or in the case of a particular financial year of a charity or of any class of charities: s 162(2). As to the Minister see PARA 586.
11 As to the meaning of 'gross income' see PARA 218 note 2.
12 In the case of a charity which is constituted as a CIO, the requirement imposed by the Charities Act 2011 s 163(1) applies whatever the charity's gross income and s 163(2) (see text and notes 13–15) does not apply: s 163(3). As to CIOs see PARAS 226–239.
13 Charities Act 2011 s 163(1). This threshold applies for any financial year ending on or after 1 April 2009: Charities Acts 1992 and 1993 (Substitution of Sums) Order 2009, SI 2009/508, art 16. For earlier financial years, the threshold was £10,000: Charities Act 1993 s 45(3) (repealed) (as originally amended by the Deregulation and Contracting Out Act 1994 s 29). The Minister may by order amend the Charities Act 2011 s 163(1) or (2) by substituting a different sum for the sum for the time being specified there: s 174(1), (2). At the date at which this volume states the law, no such order had been made.

If any requirement imposed by s 163(1) or (2) (see the text and notes 14–16) (taken with s 164, s 166(5) and s 168(7) (see the text and notes 17–29, and PARAS 372 text and note 10, 382 text and note 27), as applicable, is not complied with, each person who immediately before the date for compliance specified in the provision in question was a charity trustee of the charity is guilty of an offence and liable on summary conviction to a fine not exceeding level 4 on the standard scale and, for continued contravention, a daily default fine not exceeding 10 per cent of level 4 on the standard scale for so long as the person in question remains a charity trustee of the charity: s 173(1), (2), (4). However, it is a defence for a person charged with such an offence to prove that he took all reasonable steps for securing that the requirement in question would be complied with in time: s 173(3).

However, proceedings may only be instituted by or with the consent of the Director of Public Prosecutions: s 345(1), (2)(d). As to offences by bodies corporate see s 346; and PARA 588. As to the Director of Public Prosecutions see **CRIMINAL PROCEDURE** vol 27 (2010) PARAS 23, 33 et seq.

Any copy of an annual report transmitted to the Commission under the Charities Act 2011 s 162, together with the documents attached to it, must be kept by the Commission for such period as it thinks fit: s 165(1). As to the meaning of 'document' see PARA 263 note 2.

As to the standard scale see **SENTENCING AND DISPOSITION OF OFFENDERS** vol 92 (2010) PARA 142.
14 Charities Act 2011 s 163(2)(a).

15 Charities Act 2011 s 163(2)(b).
16 Charities Act 2011 s 163(2). Persistent default is an offence: see note 13.
17 Ie under the Charities Act 2011 s 132(1): see PARA 342.
18 Ie under the Charities Act 2011 s 133: see PARA 342.
19 Charities Act 2011 s 164(1).
20 Ie under the Charities Act 2011 s 144, s 145, s 146, s 149 or s 150.
21 Charities Act 2011 s 164(2)(a).
22 Ie under the Charities Act 2011 s 145, s 149 or s 150.
23 Charities Act 2011 s 164(2)(b).
24 As to the meaning of 'charitable company' see PARA 241 note 1.
25 Ie the Companies Act 2006 Pt 15: see **COMPANIES**.
26 Charities Act 2011 s 164(3).
27 Ie the Companies Act 2006 Pt 16: see **COMPANIES**.
28 Ie under the Charities Act 2011 s 144, s 145 or s 146: see PARA 356.
29 Charities Act 2011 s 164(4).
30 See PARA 372 et seq.
31 Ie under the Charities Act 2011 s 17(5); see PARA 4.
32 See *CC15b: Charity reporting and accounting: the essentials* (Charity Commission, January 2013) (available, at the date at which this volume states the law, on the government website). As to the Charity Commission's publications see PARA 547.

372. Annual reports: group accounts. Where group accounts are prepared[1] for a financial year of a parent charity[2], then the following additional[3] provisions apply[4]. The annual report prepared[5] by the charity trustees[6] of the parent charity in respect of that year must include such a report by the trustees on the activities of the charity's subsidiary undertakings[7] during that year and such other information relating to any of those undertakings as may be prescribed by regulations made by the Minister[8].

Any copy of any annual report transmitted to the Commission under these provisions must have attached to it both copy of the report made by the auditor on those accounts or, where those accounts have been examined[9], a copy of the report made by the person carrying out the examination[10].

1 Ie under the Charities Act 2011 s 138(2): see PARA 343.
2 As to the meaning of 'financial year' see PARA 218 note 3. As to the meaning of 'parent charity' see PARA 343 note 2.
3 Ie in addition to the Charities Act 2011 s 162–165 (see PARA 371): s 166(6).
4 See the Charities Act 2011 s 166(1). The Charities Act 2011 s 163 (see PARA 371) applies in relation to the annual report referred to in s 166(2) as if any reference to the charity's gross income in the financial year in question were a reference to the aggregate gross income of the group in that year: s 166(4).
5 Ie under the Charities Act 2011 s 162: see PARA 371.
6 As to the meaning of 'charity trustees' see PARA 255.
7 As to the meaning of 'subsidiary undertaking' see PARA 343 text and note 3.
8 Charities Act 2011 s 166(2). Such regulations may make provision in particular: (1) for any such report as is mentioned in s 166(2)(a) to be prepared in accordance with such principles as are specified or referred to in the regulations; (2) enabling the Charity Commission to dispense with any requirement prescribed by virtue of s 166(2)(b) in the case of a particular subsidiary undertaking or a particular class of subsidiary undertaking: s 166(3). As to such regulations see the Charities (Accounts and Reports) Regulations 2008, SI 2008/629.
9 Ie under the Charities Act 2011 s 152: see PARA 360.
10 Charities Act 2011 s 166(5).

373. Contents of annual reports: non-parent charities. The following statutory requirements[1] apply to annual reports prepared[2] by the charity trustees[3] of a non-parent charity[4] in respect of a financial year[5]: (1) which begins on or after 1 April 2008[6]; or (2) which began before that date and in respect of which the charity trustees determine that these requirements are to apply[7].

The report on the activities of a charity during the year which is required to be contained in the annual report must specify the financial year to which it relates and must[8]:

(1) in the case of a charity which is not an auditable charity[9], be a brief summary setting out the main activities undertaken by the charity to further its charitable purposes for the public benefit and the main achievements of the charity during the year[10];

(2) in the case of a charity which is an auditable charity, be a review of the significant activities undertaken by the charity during the relevant financial year to further its charitable purposes for the public benefit or to generate resources to be used to further its purposes, including: (a) details of the aims and objectives which the charity trustees have set for the charity in that year, details of the strategies adopted and of significant activities undertaken, in order to achieve those aims and objectives; (b) details of the achievements of the charity during the year, measured by reference to the aims and objectives which have been set; (c) details of any significant contribution of volunteers to these activities; (d) details of the principal sources of income of the charity; and (e) a statement as to whether the charity trustees have given consideration to the major risks to which the charity is exposed and satisfied themselves that systems or procedures are established in order to manage those risks[11];

(3) in either case, where any fund of the charity was in deficit at the beginning of the relevant financial and the charity is one in respect of which a statement of accounts has been prepared[12] for that financial year, contain particulars of the steps taken by the charity trustees to eliminate that deficit[13];

(4) in either case, contain a statement by the charity trustees as to whether they have complied with the statutory duty[14] to have due regard to guidance published by the Charity Commission relating to the operation of the public benefit requirement[15]; and

(5) in either case, be dated and be signed by one or more of the charity trustees, each of whom has been authorised to do so[16].

1 The statutory requirements as to annual reports for non-parent charities are contained in the Charities (Accounts and Reports) Regulations 2008, SI 2008/629, reg 40. See also PARA 377.

2 Ie in accordance with the Charities Act 2011 s 162(1): see PARA 371.

3 As to the meaning of 'charity trustees' see PARA 255.

4 'Non-parent' charity means a charity which is not an investment fund and is either not a parent charity or is a parent charity but the charity trustees are not required to prepare group accounts in respect of the financial year to which the annual report relates: Charities (Accounts and Reports) Regulations 2008, SI 2008/629, reg 37(2)(a). As to the meaning of 'investment fund' see PARA 348 note 2. As to the meaning of 'parent charity' see PARA 343 text and note 2 (definition applied by virtue of the Charities (Accounts and Reports) Regulations 2008, SI 2008/629, reg 2(1)).

5 As to the meaning of 'financial year' see PARAS 218 note 3, 344 note 4. As to the information to be contained in a report relating to a non-parent charity see PARA 377.

6 Charities (Accounts and Reports) Regulations 2008, SI 2008/629, reg 4(4)(a).

7 Ie the charity trustees may make and make an accounts determination and a report determination: Charities (Accounts and Reports) Regulations 2008, SI 2008/629, reg 4(4)(b), (6)(d). As to accounts determinations see PARA 342 note 6. A report determination for this purpose means a determination that reg 40, rather than reg 11, is to apply to the annual report prepared in respect of the financial year in question: reg 4(6)(c)(i).

The charity trustees of a charity may not make an accounts determination or a report determination in respect of financial year beginning before 1 April 2008 if the charity is a special case charity, or if, before that date, they have either approved the accounts of the charity prepared in respect of that financial year or authorised the signature of an annual report prepared in respect of that financial year in accordance with the Charities (Accounts and Reports) Regulations 2005, SI 2005/572: Charities (Accounts and Reports) Regulations 2008, SI 2008/629, reg 4(7). As to the meaning of 'special case charity' see PARA 347 note 3.

8 Charities (Accounts and Reports) Regulations 2008, SI 2008/629, reg 40(1), (2)(a).

9 'Auditable charity' means a charity the accounts of which for the financial year in question are required to be audited in pursuance of any statutory requirement: Charities (Accounts and Reports) Regulations 2008, SI 2008/629, reg 2(1).

10 Charities (Accounts and Reports) Regulations 2008, SI 2008/629, reg 40(1), (2)(b)(i). The Charity Commission has published guidance on how to report on this aspect of a charity's activities: see *PB3: Public benefit: reporting* (Charity Commission, September 2013) (available, at the date at which this volume states the law, on the government website). As to the Charity Commission see PARAS 543–578. As to the Charity Commission's publications see PARA 547.

11 Charities (Accounts and Reports) Regulations 2008, SI 2008/629, reg 40(1), (2)(b)(ii). See also the guidance mentioned in note 10.

12 Ie under the Charities Act 2011 s 132(1): see PARA 342.

13 Charities (Accounts and Reports) Regulations 2008, SI 2008/629, reg 40(1), (2)(c)(i).

14 Ie under the Charities Act 2011 s 17: see PARA 4.

15 Charities (Accounts and Reports) Regulations 2008, SI 2008/629, reg 40(1), (2)(c)(ii). See also the guidance mentioned in note 10.

16 Charities (Accounts and Reports) Regulations 2008, SI 2008/629, reg 40(1), (2)(c)(iii). See also the guidance mentioned in note 10.

374. Contents of annual reports: qualifying parent charities. The following statutory requirements[1] apply to annual reports prepared[2] by the charity trustees[3] of a qualifying parent charity[4]. The report on the activities of such a parent charity and its subsidiary undertakings[5], during the year which is required to be contained in the annual report in respect of each financial year must specify the financial year to which it relates and must[6]:

(1) be a review of the significant activities undertaken by the charity during the relevant financial year to further its charitable purposes for the public benefit or to generate resources to be used to further its purposes including details of: (a) the aims and objectives which the charity trustees have set for the parent charity and its subsidiary undertakings in that year; (b) the strategies adopted and the significant activities undertaken, in order to achieve those aims and objectives; (c) the achievements of the parent charity and its subsidiary undertakings during the year, measured by reference to the aims and objectives which have been set; (d) any significant contribution of volunteers to these activities; and (e) the principal sources of income of the parent charity and of its subsidiary undertakings[7];

(2) contain a statement as to whether the charity trustees have given consideration to the major risks to which the parent charity and its subsidiary undertakings are exposed, and satisfied themselves that systems or procedures are established in order to manage those risks[8];

(3) where any fund of the parent charity was in deficit at the beginning of the financial year in question, contain particulars of the steps taken by the charity trustees to eliminate that deficit[9];

(4) where the total of capital and reserves in any of the parent charity's subsidiary undertakings was materially in deficit at the beginning of the financial year, contain particulars of the steps taken by the relevant undertaking or undertakings to eliminate that deficit[10];

(5) contain a statement by the charity trustees as to whether they have

complied with the statutory duty[11] to have due regard to guidance published by the Charity Commission relating to the operation of the public benefit requirement[12]; and

(6) be dated and be signed by one or more of the charity trustees, each of whom has been authorised to do so[13].

1 The statutory requirements as to annual reports for qualifying parent charities are contained in the Charities (Accounts and Reports) Regulations 2008, SI 2008/629, reg 41. See also PARA 378.
2 Ie in accordance with the Charities Act 2011 s 162(1): see PARA 371.
3 As to the meaning of 'charity trustees' see PARA 255.
4 Charities (Accounts and Reports) Regulations 2008, SI 2008/629, reg 41(1). 'Qualifying parent charity' means a charity which is not an investment fund and the charity trustees of which are required to prepare group accounts in respect of the financial year to which the annual report relates: reg 37(d). As to the meaning of 'investment fund' see PARA 348 note 2. As to group accounts see PARA 343.
5 As to the meaning of 'subsidiary undertaking' see PARA 343 text and note 3 (definition applied by virtue of the Charities (Accounts and Reports) Regulations 2008, SI 2008/629, reg 2(1)). However, for these purposes, 'subsidiary undertaking' does not include a subsidiary undertaking which is excluded from the group accounts in accordance with reg 19: reg 41(7).
6 Charities (Accounts and Reports) Regulations 2008, SI 2008/629, reg 41(2)(a).
7 Charities (Accounts and Reports) Regulations 2008, SI 2008/629, reg 41(2)(b).
8 Charities (Accounts and Reports) Regulations 2008, SI 2008/629, reg 41(2)(c).
9 Charities (Accounts and Reports) Regulations 2008, SI 2008/629, reg 41(2)(d).
10 Charities (Accounts and Reports) Regulations 2008, SI 2008/629, reg 41(2)(e).
11 Ie the duty in the Charities Act 2011 s 17 (see PARA 4).
12 Charities (Accounts and Reports) Regulations 2008, SI 2008/629, reg 41(2)(f).
13 Charities (Accounts and Reports) Regulations 2008, SI 2008/629, reg 41(2)(g).

375. Contents of annual reports: non-parent investment funds. The following statutory requirements[1] apply to annual reports prepared[2] by the charity trustees[3] of a non-parent investment fund[4]. The report on the activities of the investment fund during the year which is required to be contained in the annual report must specify the financial year to which it relates and must[5]:

(1) be a review of the significant activities of the investment fund during that year, including details of the aims and objectives which have been set for the investment fund during the year, the policies adopted for achieving those aims and objectives and the achievements of the investment fund, measured by reference to the aims and objectives which have been set[6];

(2) provide any other significant information which the charity trustees consider would assist charities participating in the investment fund to make an informed judgement on the suitability to the charity of the investment fund as an investment for the charity[7];

(3) specify any material events affecting the investment fund which have occurred since the end of the year[8];

(4) contain a statement as to the steps (if any) taken to consider whether any person to whom functions in respect of the management of the investment fund have been delegated has complied with the terms of the delegation[9]; and

(5) be signed, (a) if the scheme or schemes regulating the investment fund allocates responsibility for preparing the report to a particular person, by that person, (b) in any other case by at least one of the charity trustees of the investment fund, each of whom has been authorised to do so[10].

1 The statutory requirements as to annual reports for non-parent investment funds are contained in the Charities (Accounts and Reports) Regulations 2008, SI 2008/629, reg 38 and are set out in the following text and PARA 379.
2 Ie in accordance with the Charities Act 2011 s 162(1): see PARA 371.
3 As to the meaning of 'charity trustees' see PARA 255.
4 Charities (Accounts and Reports) Regulations 2008, SI 2008/629, reg 38(1). 'Non-parent investment fund'' means an investment fund which is not a parent charity, or is a parent charity but the charity trustees are not required to prepare group accounts in respect of the financial year to which the annual report relates: reg 37(2)(b). As to the meaning of 'investment fund' see PARA 348 note 2. As to group accounts see PARA 343.
5 Charities (Accounts and Reports) Regulations 2008, SI 2008/629, reg 38(2)(a).
6 Charities (Accounts and Reports) Regulations 2008, SI 2008/629, reg 38(2)(b).
7 Charities (Accounts and Reports) Regulations 2008, SI 2008/629, reg 38(2)(c).
8 Charities (Accounts and Reports) Regulations 2008, SI 2008/629, reg 38(2)(d).
9 Charities (Accounts and Reports) Regulations 2008, SI 2008/629, reg 38(2)(e).
10 Charities (Accounts and Reports) Regulations 2008, SI 2008/629, reg 38(2)(f).

376. Contents of annual reports: parent investment funds. The following statutory requirements[1] apply to annual reports prepared[2] by the charity trustees[3] of a parent investment fund[4]. The report on the activities of such an investment fund and of its subsidiary undertakings[5] during the year which is required to be contained in the annual report must specify the financial year to which it relates and must[6]:

(1) be a review of the significant activities of the investment fund and of its subsidiary undertakings during that year, including details of: (a) the aims and objectives which have been set for the investment fund and its subsidiary undertakings during the year and identifying, in the case of subsidiary undertakings, how these aims and objectives support the investment activities of the investment fund; (b) the policies adopted for achieving those aims and objectives; and (c) the achievements of the investment fund and of its subsidiary undertakings, measured by reference to the aims and objectives which have been set[7];

(2) where the total of capital and reserves in any of the investment fund's subsidiary undertakings was materially in deficit at the beginning of the financial year, contain particulars of the steps taken by the relevant undertaking or undertakings to eliminate that deficit[8];

(3) provide any other significant information which the charity trustees consider would assist charities participating in the investment fund to make an informed judgement on the suitability to the charity of the investment fund as an investment for the charity[9];

(4) specify any material events affecting the investment fund which have occurred since the end of the relevant financial year[10];

(5) contain a statement as to the steps (if any) taken to consider whether any person to whom functions in respect of the management of the investment fund has been delegated has complied with the terms of the delegation[11]; and

(6) be signed, (a) if the scheme or schemes regulating the investment fund allocates responsibility for preparing the report to a particular person, by that person, or (b) in any other case, by at least one of the charity trustees of the investment fund, each of whom has been authorised to do so[12].

1 The statutory requirements as to annual reports for parent investment funds are contained in the Charities (Accounts and Reports) Regulations 2008, SI 2008/629, reg 39 and are set out in the following text and PARA 380.

2 Ie in accordance with the Charities Act 2011 s 162(1): see PARA 371.
3 As to the meaning of 'charity trustees' see PARA 255.
4 Charities (Accounts and Reports) Regulations 2008, SI 2008/629, reg 39(1). 'Parent investment fund' means an investment fund which is a parent charity and the charity trustees of which are required to prepare group accounts in respect of the financial year to which the annual report relates: Charities (Accounts and Reports) Regulations 2008, SI 2008/629, reg 37(2)(c). As to the meaning of 'investment fund' see PARA 348 note 2. As to group accounts see PARA 343.
5 As to the meaning of 'subsidiary undertaking' see PARA 343 text and note 3. However, for these purposes, 'subsidiary undertaking' does not include a subsidiary undertaking which is excluded from the group accounts in accordance with Charities (Accounts and Reports) Regulations 2008, SI 2008/629, reg 19 (see PARA 343): reg 39(4).
6 Charities (Accounts and Reports) Regulations 2008, SI 2008/629, reg 39(1), (2)(a).
7 Charities (Accounts and Reports) Regulations 2008, SI 2008/629, reg 39(2)(b).
8 Charities (Accounts and Reports) Regulations 2008, SI 2008/629, reg 39(2)(c).
9 Charities (Accounts and Reports) Regulations 2008, SI 2008/629, reg 39(2)(d).
10 Charities (Accounts and Reports) Regulations 2008, SI 2008/629, reg 39(2)(e).
11 Charities (Accounts and Reports) Regulations 2008, SI 2008/629, reg 39(2)(f).
12 Charities (Accounts and Reports) Regulations 2008, SI 2008/629, reg 39(2)(g).

377. Information required in annual reports: non-parent charities. The following information relating to a non-parent charity[1] and to its trustees and officers is required to be contained in the annual report[2]:

(1) the name of the charity as it appears in the register of charities and any other name by which it makes itself known[3];
(2) the number assigned to it in the register and, in the case of a charitable company, the number with which it is registered as a company[4];
(3) the principal address of the charity and, in the case of a charitable company, the address of its registered office[5];
(4) the name of any person who is a charity trustee of the charity on the date when the authority to sign and date the annual report[6] is given, and, where any charity trustee on that date is a body corporate, the name of any person who is a director[7] of the body corporate on that date[8];
(5) the name of any other person who has, at any time during the relevant financial year[9], been a charity trustee of the charity[10];
(6) the name of any person who is a trustee for the charity on the date referred to in head (4) above[11];
(7) the name of any other person who has, at any time during the relevant financial year in question, been a trustee for the charity[12];
(8) particulars, including the date if known, of any deed or other document[13] containing provisions which regulate the purposes and administration of the charity[14];
(9) the name of any person or body of persons entitled by the trusts of the charity to appoint one or more new charity trustees, and a description of the method provided by those trusts for such appointment[15];
(10) a description of the policies and procedures (if any) which have been adopted by the charity trustees for the induction and training of charity trustees and where no such policies have been adopted a statement to that effect[16];
(11) a description of the organisational structure of the charity[17];
(12) a summary description of the purposes of the charity[18];
(13) a description of the policies (if any) which have been adopted by the charity trustees for the selection of individuals and institutions who are to receive grants or other forms of financial support out of the assets of the charity[19];

(14) a statement regarding the performance during the financial year of the investments belonging to the charity (if any)[20];

(15) where material investments are owned by a charity, a description of the policies (if any) which have been adopted by the charity trustees for the selection, retention and realisation of investments for the charity including the extent (if any) to which social, environmental or ethical considerations are taken into account[21];

(16) a description of the policies (if any) which have been adopted by the charity trustees for the purpose of determining the level of reserves which it is appropriate for the charity to maintain in order to meet effectively the needs designated by its trusts, together with details of the amount and purpose of any material commitments and planned expenditure not provided for in the balance sheet which have been deducted from the assets in the unrestricted fund[22] of the charity in calculating the amount of reserves, and where no such policies have been adopted, a statement to that effect[23];

(17) a description of the aims and objectives which the charity trustees have set for the charity in the future and of the activities contemplated in furtherance of those aims and objectives[24];

(18) a description of any assets held by the charity or by any charity trustee of, or trustee for, the charity, on behalf of another charity, and particulars of any special arrangements made with respect to the safe custody of such assets and their segregation from assets of the charity not so held and a description of the objects of the charity on whose behalf the assets are held[25].

1 As to the meaning of 'non-parent charity' see PARA 373 note 4.

2 Charities (Accounts and Reports) Regulations 2008, SI 2008/629, reg 40(3). This provision is expressed to be subject to reg 40(4)–(7): see reg 40(3). As to annual reports see PARAS 371–376. These provisions apply to financial years beginning on or after 1 April 2008 or where the charity trustees have so determined: see PARA 373. As to the meaning of 'charity trustees' see PARA 255.

Where it is satisfied that, in the case of a particular charity or class of charities, or in the case of a particular financial year of a charity or class of charities, the disclosure of the name of any person whose name is required by any of reg 40(3)(d), (e), (f), (g) and (i) (see the text and notes 8–16) to be contained in the annual report of a charity could lead to that person being placed in any personal danger, the Charity Commission may dispense with the requirement in any of those provisions so far as it applies to the name of such person: reg 40(4)(a). The Commission may also, where it is satisfied that, in the case of a particular charity or class of charities, or in the case of a particular financial year of a charity or class of charities, the disclosure of the principal address of the charity in accordance with reg 40(3)(c) (see the text and note 5) could lead to any such person being placed in any personal danger, dispense with that requirement: reg 40(4)(b). As to the Charity Commission see PARAS 543–578.

3 Charities (Accounts and Reports) Regulations 2008, SI 2008/629, reg 40(3)(a). As to the register of charities see PARA 307 et seq. In the case of a report prepared under the Charities Act 2011 s 168(3) (see PARA 381) (excepted charities which are not registered), this requirement is modified so that the information required to be contained in the annual report is the name of the charity: see the Charities (Accounts and Reports) Regulations 2008, SI 2008/629, reg 40(6)(a). Note that reg 40(6)(a) purports to amend reg 40(4)(a). However it is submitted this is in error and should instead refer to reg 40(3)(a).

4 Charities (Accounts and Reports) Regulations 2008, SI 2008/629, reg 40(3)(b). As to the meaning of 'charitable company' see PARA 241 note 1. In the case of a report prepared under the Charities Act 2011 s 168(3) (see PARA 381) (excepted charities which are not registered), this requirement is modified so that the information required to be contained in the annual report is, in the case of a charitable company, the number with which it is registered as a company:

Charities (Accounts and Reports) Regulations 2008, SI 2008/629, reg 40(6)(b). Note that reg 40(6)(b) purports to amend reg 40(4)(b). However it is submitted this is in error and should instead refer to reg 40(3)(b).

5 Charities (Accounts and Reports) Regulations 2008, SI 2008/629, reg 40(3)(c).

6 Ie the authority referred to in the Charities (Accounts and Reports) Regulations 2008, SI 2008/629, reg 40(1), (2)(c)(iii): see PARA 373 head (5).

7 'Director' in relation to a body corporate whose affairs are managed by its members, means a member of the body corporate, and in any other case, includes any person occupying the position of a director by whatever name called: Charities (Accounts and Reports) Regulations 2008, SI 2008/629, reg 2(1).

8 Charities (Accounts and Reports) Regulations 2008, SI 2008/629, reg 40(3)(d). In the case of a charity having more than 50 charity trustees on the date referred to in the text, reg 40(3)(d) has effect so that the information required to be contained in the annual report is the names of not less than 50 of the charity trustees of the charity, including any charity trustee who is also an officer of the charity: reg 40(5)(a).

9 As to the meaning of 'financial year' see PARAS 218 note 3, 344 note 4.

10 Charities (Accounts and Reports) Regulations 2008, SI 2008/629, reg 40(3)(e). In the case of a charity having more than 50 charity trustees on the date referred to in head (4) in the text, reg 40(3)(e) is modified so that the information required to be contained in the annual report excludes the name of any charity trustee whose name has been excluded from the report in pursuance of reg 40(3)(d) (see note 8): reg 40(5)(b).

11 Charities (Accounts and Reports) Regulations 2008, SI 2008/629, reg 40(3)(f).

12 Charities (Accounts and Reports) Regulations 2008, SI 2008/629, reg 40(3)(g).

13 As to the meaning of 'document' see PARA 263 note 2.

14 Charities (Accounts and Reports) Regulations 2008, SI 2008/629, reg 40(3)(h).

15 Charities (Accounts and Reports) Regulations 2008, SI 2008/629, reg 40(3)(i).

16 Charities (Accounts and Reports) Regulations 2008, SI 2008/629, reg 40(3)(j). This information is not a requirement for a charity which is not an auditable charity: see reg 40(7). As to the meaning of 'auditable charity' see PARA 373 note 9.

17 Charities (Accounts and Reports) Regulations 2008, SI 2008/629, reg 40(3)(k). This information is not a requirement for a charity which is not an auditable charity: reg 40(7).

18 Charities (Accounts and Reports) Regulations 2008, SI 2008/629, reg 40(3)(l).

19 Charities (Accounts and Reports) Regulations 2008, SI 2008/629, reg 40(3)(m). This information is not a requirement for a charity which is not an auditable charity: reg 40(7).

20 Charities (Accounts and Reports) Regulations 2008, SI 2008/629, reg 40(3)(n). This information is not a requirement for a charity which is not an auditable charity: reg 40(7).

21 Charities (Accounts and Reports) Regulations 2008, SI 2008/629, reg 40(3)(o). This information is not a requirement for a charity which is not an auditable charity: reg 40(7).

22 As to the meaning of 'unrestricted fund' see PARA 346 note 14.

23 Charities (Accounts and Reports) Regulations 2008, SI 2008/629, reg 40(3)(p).

24 Charities (Accounts and Reports) Regulations 2008, SI 2008/629, reg 40(3)(q). This information is not a requirement for a charity which is not an auditable charity: reg 40(7).

25 Charities (Accounts and Reports) Regulations 2008, SI 2008/629, reg 40(3)(r).

378. Information required in annual reports: qualifying parent charities. The following information relating to a qualifying parent charity[1], to its trustees and officers, and to its subsidiary undertakings[2], is required to be contained in the annual report[3]:

(1) the name of the parent charity as it appears in the register of charities and any other name by which it makes itself known[4];

(2) the number assigned to the parent charity in the register and, in the case of a charitable company, the number with which it is registered as a company[5];

(3) the principal address of the parent charity and, in the case of a charitable company, the address of its registered office[6];

(4) the name of any person who is a charity trustee[7] of the parent charity on the date when the authority to sign and date the annual report[8] is given,

and, where any charity trustee on that date is a body corporate, the name of any person who is a director of the body corporate on that date[9];

(5) the name of any other person who has, at any time during the financial year in question, been a charity trustee of the parent charity[10];

(6) the name of any person who is a trustee for the parent charity on the date referred to in head (4)[11];

(7) the name of any other person who has, at any time during the financial year in question, been a trustee for the parent charity[12];

(8) particulars, including the date if known, of any deed or other document containing provisions which regulate the purposes and administration of the parent charity[13];

(9) the name of any person or body of persons entitled by the trusts of the parent charity to appoint one or more new charity trustees, and a description of the method provided by those trusts for such appointment[14];

(10) a description of the policies and procedures (if any) which have been adopted by the charity trustees of the parent charity for the induction and training of charity trustees, and where no such policies have been adopted a statement to this effect[15];

(11) a description of the organisational structure of the parent charity and of its subsidiary undertakings[16];

(12) a summary description of the purposes of the parent charity[17];

(13) a description of the policies (if any) which have been adopted by the charity trustees of the parent charity for the selection of individuals and institutions who are to receive grants, or other forms of financial support, out of the assets of the charity[18];

(14) a statement regarding the performance during the financial year of: (a) any investments belonging to the parent charity; and (b) any investments belonging to the parent charity's subsidiary undertakings, where those investments are material to the group account[19];

(15) where investments are owned by a qualifying parent charity or any of its subsidiary undertakings, and those investments are material to the group accounts, a description of the policies (if any) which have been adopted by the charity trustees, or as the case may be the subsidiary undertaking, for the selection, retention and realisation of investments, including the extent (if any) to which social, environmental or ethical considerations are taken into account[20];

(16) where the charity trustees have adopted polices for the purpose of determining the level of reserves which it is appropriate to maintain in order to meet effectively the needs designated by its trusts: (a) a description of those policies including in particular whether account has been taken of any reserves held by its subsidiary undertakings in determining the appropriate level of reserves; and (b) details of the amount and purpose of any material commitments and planned expenditure not provided for in the balance sheet which have been deducted from the assets in the unrestricted fund of the charity in calculating the amount of reserves[21];

(17) if the charity trustees have not adopted policies falling within head (16) a statement that no such policies have been adopted[22];

(18) a description of the aims and objectives which the charity trustees have

set for the parent charity in the future, and of the activities contemplated in furtherance of those aims and objectives[23]; and

(19) a description of any assets held by the parent charity or by any charity trustee of, or trustee for, the charity, on behalf of another charity, and particulars of any special arrangements made with respect to the safe custody of such assets and their segregation from assets of the charity not so held and a description of the objects of the charity on whose behalf the assets are held[24].

1 As to the meaning of 'qualifying parent charity' see PARA 374 note 4.

2 As to the meaning of 'subsidiary undertaking' see PARA 343 and note 3 (definition applied by virtue of the Charities (Accounts and Reports) Regulations 2008, SI 2008/629, reg 2(1)). However, for these purposes, 'subsidiary undertaking' does not include a subsidiary undertaking which is excluded from the group accounts in accordance with reg 19 (see PARA 343): reg 41(7).

3 Charities (Accounts and Reports) Regulations 2008, SI 2008/629, reg 41(1). This provision is expressed to be subject to reg 41(4)–(6): see reg 41(3).

Where it is satisfied that, in the case of a particular charity or class of charities, or in the case of a particular financial year of a charity or class of charities, the disclosure of the name of any person whose name is required by any of reg 41(3)(d), (e), (f), (g) and (i) (see heads (4)–(7), (9) in the text) to be contained in the annual report of a charity could lead to that person being placed in any personal danger, the Charity Commission may dispense with the requirement in any of those provisions so far as it applies to the name of that person: reg 41(4)(a). The Commission may also, where it is satisfied that, in the case of a particular charity or class of charities, or in the case of a particular financial year of a charity or class of charities, the disclosure of the principal address of the charity in accordance with reg 41(3)(c) (see head (3) in the text) could lead to any such person being placed in any personal danger, dispense with that requirement: reg 41(4)(b). As to the Charity Commission see PARAS 543–578.

4 Charities (Accounts and Reports) Regulations 2008, SI 2008/629, reg 41(3)(a). As to the register of charities see PARA 307 et seq. In the case of a report prepared under the Charities Act 2011 s 168(3) (see PARA 381) (excepted charities which are not registered), this requirement is modified so that the information required to be contained in the annual report is the name of the charity: see the Charities (Accounts and Reports) Regulations 2008, SI 2008/629, reg 41(6)(a).

5 Charities (Accounts and Reports) Regulations 2008, SI 2008/629, reg 41(3)(b). As to the meaning of 'charitable company' see PARA 241 note 1. In the case of a report prepared under the Charities Act 2011 s 168(3) (see PARA 381) (excepted charities which are not registered), this requirement is modified so that the information required to be contained in the annual report is, in the case of a charitable company, the number with which it is registered as a company: Charities (Accounts and Reports) Regulations 2008, SI 2008/629, reg 41(6)(b).

6 Charities (Accounts and Reports) Regulations 2008, SI 2008/629, reg 41(3)(c).

7 As to the meaning of 'charity trustees' see PARA 255.

8 Ie the authority referred to in the Charities (Accounts and Reports) Regulations 2008, SI 2008/629, reg 41(2)(g): see PARA 374 head (6).

9 Charities (Accounts and Reports) Regulations 2008, SI 2008/629, reg 41(3)(d). In the case of a charity having more than 50 charity trustees on the date referred to in the text, reg 41(3)(d) has effect so that the information required to be contained in the annual report is the names of not less than 50 of the charity trustees of the charity, including any charity trustee who is also an officer of the charity: see reg 41(5)(a).

10 Charities (Accounts and Reports) Regulations 2008, SI 2008/629, reg 41(3)(e). In the case of a charity having more than 50 charity trustees on the date referred to in head (4) in the text, reg 41(3)(e) is modified so that the information required to be contained in the annual report excludes the name of any charity trustee whose name has been excluded from the report in pursuance of reg 41(3)(d) (see note 9): see reg 41(5)(b).

11 Charities (Accounts and Reports) Regulations 2008, SI 2008/629, reg 41(3)(f).

12 Charities (Accounts and Reports) Regulations 2008, SI 2008/629, reg 41(3)(g).

13 Charities (Accounts and Reports) Regulations 2008, SI 2008/629, reg 41(3)(h).

14 Charities (Accounts and Reports) Regulations 2008, SI 2008/629, reg 41(3)(i).

15 Charities (Accounts and Reports) Regulations 2008, SI 2008/629, reg 41(3)(j).

16 Charities (Accounts and Reports) Regulations 2008, SI 2008/629, reg 41(3)(k).

17 Charities (Accounts and Reports) Regulations 2008, SI 2008/629, reg 41(3)(l).

18 Charities (Accounts and Reports) Regulations 2008, SI 2008/629, reg 41(3)(m).

19 Charities (Accounts and Reports) Regulations 2008, SI 2008/629, reg 41(3)(n).

20 Charities (Accounts and Reports) Regulations 2008, SI 2008/629, reg 41(3)(o).
21 Charities (Accounts and Reports) Regulations 2008, SI 2008/629, reg 41(3)(p).
22 Charities (Accounts and Reports) Regulations 2008, SI 2008/629, reg 41(3)(q).
23 Charities (Accounts and Reports) Regulations 2008, SI 2008/629, reg 41(3)(r).
24 Charities (Accounts and Reports) Regulations 2008, SI 2008/629, reg 41(3)(s).

379. Information required in annual reports: non-parent investment funds. The following information relating to a non-parent investment fund[1] and to its trustees and officers is required to be contained in the annual report[2]:

(1) the name of the investment fund as it appears in the register of charities and any other name by which it makes itself known[3];
(2) the number assigned to the investment fund in the register[4];
(3) the principal address of the investment fund[5];
(4) particulars, including the date, of any scheme or schemes containing provisions which regulate the purposes and administration of the investment fund[6];
(5) the name of any person or body of persons entitled under any such scheme or schemes to appoint any charity trustee of the investment fund, and a description of the method provided by any such scheme or schemes for such appointment[7];
(6) a description of the objects of the investment fund[8];
(7) a description of the organisational structure of the investment fund[9];
(8) the name of any charity trustee of the investment fund, on the date of the signature of the report if the scheme or schemes regulating the investment fund allocates responsibility for preparing the report to a particular person[10], otherwise on the date when the authority to sign and date the annual report[11] is given, and, where any such person is a body corporate, the name of any person who is a director of the body corporate on that date[12];
(9) the professional qualifications of any individual person referred to in head (5) or (8)[13];
(10) the name of any other person who has, at any time during the financial year in question, been a charity trustee of the investment fund[14];
(11) the name of any person who is, in relation to the investment fund, a trustee for the charity on the date referred to in head (8)[15];
(12) the name of any other person who has, at any time during the financial year in question, been, in relation to the investment fund, a trustee for the charity[16];
(13) a description of any functions relating to the management of the investment fund which have been delegated (including the maintenance of the register of charities participating in the investment fund), and of the procedures adopted to ensure that those functions are discharged consistently with the scheme or schemes by which the investment fund is regulated, and with the investment policies adopted for the investment fund[17];
(14) the name and address of any person to whom any such functions in respect of the management of the investment fund have been delegated or who have been instructed to provide advice on investment matters[18]; and
(15) a statement as to which, if any, of the persons whose names are given in accordance with the provisions of head (8), (10), (11), (12) or (14), are authorised persons[19].

1 As to the meaning of 'non-parent investment fund' see PARA 375 note 4.
2 Charities (Accounts and Reports) Regulations 2008, SI 2008/629, reg 38(1), (3).
3 Charities (Accounts and Reports) Regulations 2008, SI 2008/629, reg 38(3)(a). As to the register of charities see PARA 307 et seq.
4 Charities (Accounts and Reports) Regulations 2008, SI 2008/629, reg 38(3)(b).
5 Charities (Accounts and Reports) Regulations 2008, SI 2008/629, reg 38(3)(c). As to the meaning of 'charity trustees' see PARA 255.
6 Charities (Accounts and Reports) Regulations 2008, SI 2008/629, reg 38(3)(d).
7 Charities (Accounts and Reports) Regulations 2008, SI 2008/629, reg 38(3)(e).
8 Charities (Accounts and Reports) Regulations 2008, SI 2008/629, reg 38(3)(f).
9 Charities (Accounts and Reports) Regulations 2008, SI 2008/629, reg 38(3)(g).
10 Ie under the Charities (Accounts and Reports) Regulations 2008, SI 2008/629, reg 38(2)(f)(i): see PARA 375 head (5).
11 Ie under the Charities (Accounts and Reports) Regulations 2008, SI 2008/629, reg 38(2)(f)(ii): see PARA 375 head (5).
12 Charities (Accounts and Reports) Regulations 2008, SI 2008/629, reg 38(3)(h).
13 Charities (Accounts and Reports) Regulations 2008, SI 2008/629, reg 38(3)(i).
14 Charities (Accounts and Reports) Regulations 2008, SI 2008/629, reg 38(3)(j).
15 Charities (Accounts and Reports) Regulations 2008, SI 2008/629, reg 38(3)(k).
16 Charities (Accounts and Reports) Regulations 2008, SI 2008/629, reg 38(3)(l).
17 Charities (Accounts and Reports) Regulations 2008, SI 2008/629, reg 38(3)(m).
18 Charities (Accounts and Reports) Regulations 2008, SI 2008/629, reg 38(3)(n).
19 Charities (Accounts and Reports) Regulations 2008, SI 2008/629, reg 38(3)(o). As to the meaning of 'authorised person' see the Financial Services and Markets Act 2000 s 31; and FINANCIAL SERVICES AND INSTITUTIONS vol 48 (2008) PARA 314 (definition applied by the Charities (Accounts and Reports) Regulations 2008, SI 2008/629, reg 2(1)).

380. Information required in annual reports: parent investment funds. The following information relating to a parent investment fund[1], to its trustees and officers, and to its subsidiary undertakings[2], is required to be contained in the annual report[3]:

(1) the name of the investment fund as it appears in the register of charities and any other name by which it makes itself known[4];
(2) the number assigned to the investment fund in the register[5];
(3) the principal address of the investment fund[6];
(4) particulars, including the date, of any scheme or schemes containing provisions which regulate the purposes and administration of the investment fund[7];
(5) the name of any person or body of persons entitled under any such scheme or schemes to appoint any charity trustee of the investment fund, and a description of the method provided by any such scheme or schemes for such appointment[8];
(6) a description of the objects of the investment fund[9];
(7) a description of the organisational structure of the investment fund, and of its subsidiary undertakings[10];
(8) the name of any charity trustee of the investment fund, on the date of the signature of the report if the scheme or schemes regulating the investment fund allocates responsibility for preparing the report to a particular person[11] otherwise on the date when the authority to sign and date the annual report[12] is given, and, where any such person is a body corporate, the name of any person who is a director of the body corporate on that date[13];
(9) the professional qualifications of any individual person referred to in head (5) or head (8)[14];
(10) the name of any other person who has, at any time during the financial year in question, been a charity trustee of the investment fund[15];

(11) the name of any person who is, in relation to the investment fund, a trustee for the charity on the date referred to in head (8)[16];

(12) the name of any other person who has, at any time during the financial year in question, been, in relation to the investment fund, a trustee for the charity[17];

(13) a description of any functions relating to the management of the investment fund which have been delegated (including the maintenance of the register of charities participating in the investment fund), and of the procedures adopted to ensure that those functions are discharged consistently with the scheme or schemes by which the investment fund is regulated, and with the investment policies adopted for the investment fund[18];

(14) the name and address of any person to whom any such functions in respect of the management of the investment fund have been delegated or who have been instructed to provide advice on investment matters[19]; and

(15) a statement as to which, if any, of the persons whose names are given in accordance with the provisions of head (8), (10), (11), (12) or (14), are authorised persons[20].

1 As to the meaning of 'non-parent investment fund' see PARA 375 note 4.
2 As to the meaning of 'subsidiary undertaking' see PARA 343 text and note 3 (definition applied by virtue of the Charities (Accounts and Reports) Regulations 2008, SI 2008/629, reg 2(1)). However, for these purposes, 'subsidiary undertaking' does not include a subsidiary undertaking which is excluded from the group accounts in accordance with reg 19 (see PARA 343): reg 39(4).
3 Charities (Accounts and Reports) Regulations 2008, SI 2008/629, reg 39(1), (3).
4 Charities (Accounts and Reports) Regulations 2008, SI 2008/629, reg 39(3)(a).
5 Charities (Accounts and Reports) Regulations 2008, SI 2008/629, reg 39(3)(b).
6 Charities (Accounts and Reports) Regulations 2008, SI 2008/629, reg 39(3)(c).
7 Charities (Accounts and Reports) Regulations 2008, SI 2008/629, reg 39(3)(d).
8 Charities (Accounts and Reports) Regulations 2008, SI 2008/629, reg 39(3)(e).
9 Charities (Accounts and Reports) Regulations 2008, SI 2008/629, reg 39(3)(f).
10 Charities (Accounts and Reports) Regulations 2008, SI 2008/629, reg 39(3)(g).
11 Ie under the Charities (Accounts and Reports) Regulations 2008, SI 2008/629, reg 39(2)(g)(i): see PARA 376 head (6).
12 Ie under the Charities (Accounts and Reports) Regulations 2008, SI 2008/629, reg 39(2)(g)(ii): see PARA 376 head (6).
13 Charities (Accounts and Reports) Regulations 2008, SI 2008/629, reg 39(3)(h).
14 Charities (Accounts and Reports) Regulations 2008, SI 2008/629, reg 39(3)(i).
15 Charities (Accounts and Reports) Regulations 2008, SI 2008/629, reg 39(3)(j).
16 Charities (Accounts and Reports) Regulations 2008, SI 2008/629, reg 39(3)(k).
17 Charities (Accounts and Reports) Regulations 2008, SI 2008/629, reg 39(3)(l).
18 Charities (Accounts and Reports) Regulations 2008, SI 2008/629, reg 39(3)(m).
19 Charities (Accounts and Reports) Regulations 2008, SI 2008/629, reg 39(3)(n).
20 Charities (Accounts and Reports) Regulations 2008, SI 2008/629, reg 39(3)(o). As to the meaning of 'authorised person' see the Financial Services and Markets Act 2000 s 31; and FINANCIAL SERVICES AND INSTITUTIONS vol 48 (2008) PARA 314 (definition applied by the Charities (Accounts and Reports) Regulations 2008, SI 2008/629, reg 2(1)).

381. Special provision as respects accounts and annual reports of exempt and other excepted charities. None of the provisions in the Charities Act 2011 relating to accounts, audits and annual reports[1] applies to an exempt charity[2]. The charity trustees[3], however, must keep proper books of account with respect to the affairs of the charity and, if not required by or under the authority of any other Act to prepare periodical statements of account, must prepare consecutive statements of account consisting on each occasion of an income and expenditure account relating to a period of not more than 15 months and a balance sheet relating to the end of that period[4]. The books of accounts and statements of account relating to an exempt charity must be preserved for a period of six years at least unless the charity ceases to exist and the Charity Commission[5] consents in writing to their being destroyed or otherwise disposed of[6].

However, the statutory provisions relating to the duty of auditors, independent examiners and examiners to report matters to the Charity Commission[7] will also apply to a person appointed to audit, or report on, the accounts of an exempt charity[8] which is not a company[9], but any reference to the Commission or to any of its functions is to be read as a reference to the charity's principal regulator or to any of that person's functions in relation to the charity as such[10].

The provisions of the Charities Act 2011 relating to annual reports and annual audits or examination of charity accounts[11] do not apply to any charity whose gross income does not exceed £5,000[12] and which is not registered[13], unless that charity is an English NHS charity or a Welsh NHS charity[14], in which case the authority under which the Minister may make supplementary provisions for annual audits by regulations applies[15].

A charity whose gross income exceeds £5,000[16] is nevertheless absolved from the obligation to prepare annual reports[17] if it is excepted by the statutory provisions which state which charities are not required to be registered[18] and is not registered[19]. However, in this case, if requested to do so by the Charity Commission, the charity trustees must prepare an annual report in respect of such financial year[20] as is specified in the Commission's request[21]. Any report so prepared must contain such a report by the charity trustees on the activities of the charity during the year in question, and such other information relating to the charity or to its trustees or officers, as may be prescribed by regulations[22] made in relation to annual reports[23]. Where a charity is required to prepare such an annual report in respect of a financial year and: (1) the charity is a parent charity[24] at the end of the year; and (2) group accounts are prepared for that year under the statutory provisions[25], then the copy of the annual report transmitted to the Commission must also have attached to it both a copy of the group accounts and either a copy of the report made by the auditor on those accounts or, where those accounts have been examined[26], a copy of the report made by the person carrying out the examination[27].

An appeal against a decision of the Commission to request charity trustees to prepare an annual report for a charity[28] lies to the Tribunal at the instance of the Attorney General[29], the charity trustees of the charity and, if a body corporate, the charity[30]. The Tribunal has the power to quash the decision and, if appropriate, remit the matter to the Commission[31].

1 Ie the Charities Act 2011 ss 130–134, 137–142, 144–155, 162–166: see PARA 341 et seq.
2 Charities Act 2011 ss 136(1), 143, 160, 167. As to exempt charities see PARAS 318–320. As to the meaning of 'charity' see PARA 1.
3 As to the meaning of 'charity trustees' see PARA 255.
4 Charities Act 2011 s 136(2).
5 As to the Charity Commission see PARAS 543–578.
6 Charities Act 2011 s 136(3).
7 Ie the Charities Act 2011 ss 156(2)–(6), 157: see PARA 367.
8 Including where that charity has a gross income which does not exceed £5,000 and is not registered: see the Charities Act 2011 s 161(4); and note 10.
9 See the Charities Act 2011 s 160(2). Any reference to a person acting in the capacity mentioned in s 156(1) is to be read as a reference to his acting as a person appointed: s 162(2)(a).

Transitional modifications to ss 160, 161 are made by Sch 9 para 22, in relation to exempt charities other than those for whom the equivalent previous statutory provisions had not been brought into force. As to the phasing in of increased regulation for exempt charities see PARA 319.

10 See Charities Act 2011 s 162(2)(b) (see note 9). Sections 156, 157 apply in accordance with s 160(2) to a charity mentioned in s 161(1) (see notes 11–15) which is also an exempt charity: s 161(4) (and see note 9).
11 Ie the Charities Act 2011 ss 144–146: see PARA 356 et seq.
12 Ie any charity excepted from the requirement of registration by the Charities Act 2011 s 30(2)(d) (whether or not it is also excepted from registration by s 30(2)(b) or (c)).
13 Charities Act 2011 s 161(4). See further PARA 309.
14 As to the meaning of 'English NHS charity' see PARA 357 note 2. As to the meaning of 'Welsh NHS charity' see PARA 358 note 2.
15 See Charities Act 2011 s 161(3), applying ss 154–157 (see PARAS 361, 367). As to the Minister see PARA 586.
16 Ie it does not fall within the Charities Act 2011 s 30(2)(d): see PARA 308.
17 Ie those contained in the Charities Act 2011 ss 162–165: see PARA 371.
18 Ie under the Charities Act 2011 s 30(2)(b) or (c): see PARA 308.
19 See the Charities Act 2011 s 168(2).
20 As to the meaning of 'financial year' see PARAS 218 note 3, 344 note 4.
21 Charities Act 2011 s 168(3). In relation to any report required to be prepared under s 168(3), the provisions of ss 163(1), 164, 165(1) apply as if it were an annual report required to be prepared under s 162(1) (PARA 371): see s 168(5).
22 Ie by regulations under the Charities Act 2011 s 162(1) (see PARA 371): see PARA 377.
23 Charities Act 2011 s 168(4).
24 As to the meaning of 'parent charity' see PARA 343 note 2.
25 Ie under the Charities Act 2011 s 138(2): see PARA 343.
26 Ie under the Charities Act 2011 s 152: see PARA 360.
27 Charities Act 2011 s 168(7). This is in addition to the requirement under s 168(4) (see text ant note 23): s 168(8).
28 Ie under the Charities Act 2011 s 168(3).
29 As to the Tribunal see PARA 579 et seq. As to the Attorney General see PARAS 589, 596, 605 et seq; and CONSTITUTIONAL AND ADMINISTRATIVE LAW vol 20 (2014) PARA 273 et seq.
30 See the Charities Act 2011 s 319(2), Sch 6 Table Cols 1, 2.
31 See the Charities Act 2011 Sch 6 Table Col 3.

382. Public inspection of annual reports and other documents. Any copy of an annual report, or accompanying document, kept by the Charity Commission[1] must be open to public inspection at all reasonable times during the period for which it is so kept, or if the Commission so determines, during such lesser period as it may specify[2]. On request the Commission must furnish any person with copies of, or extracts from, any document in its possession which is for the time being open to public inspection[3].

Where any person requests the charity trustees[4] of a charity[5] in writing to provide him with a copy of the charity's most recent accounts[6], or its most recent annual report if such a report has been prepared[7], and pays them such reasonable fee, if any, as they may require in respect of the costs of complying with the request, those trustees must comply with the request within the period of two months beginning with the date on which it is made[8].

1 Ie in pursuance of the Charities Act 2011 s 165(1): see PARA 371. As to the Charity Commission see PARAS 543–578.
2 Charities Act 2011 s 170.
3 Charities Act 2011 s 18.
4 As to the meaning of 'charity trustees' see PARA 255.
5 As to the meaning of 'charity' see PARA 1.
6 The reference to a charity's most recent accounts means:
   (1) in the case of a charity other than one falling within head (2) or (3) below, a reference to the statement of accounts or account and statement prepared in pursuance of the

Charities Act 2011 s 132(1) or s 133 (see PARA 342) in respect of the last financial year of the charity in respect of which a statement of accounts or account and statement has or have been so prepared (s 172(2)(a));

(2) in the case of a charitable company, a reference to the most recent annual accounts of the company prepared under the Companies Act 2006 Pt 16 (see COMPANIES) in relation to which any of the following conditions is satisfied: (a) they have been audited; (b) they have been examined by an independent examiner under the Charities Act 2011 s 145(1)(a) (see PARA 356); or (c) they relate to a year in respect of which the company is exempt from audit under the Companies Act 2006 Pt 16 and neither the Charities Act 2011 s 144(2) nor s 145(1) applied to them (s 172(2)(b); and

(3) in the case of an exempt charity, a reference to the accounts of the charity most recently audited in pursuance of any statutory or other requirement or, if its accounts are not required to be audited, the accounts most recently prepared in respect of the charity (s 172(2)(c)).

As to the meaning of 'financial year' see PARAS 218 note 3, 344 note 4. As to the meaning of 'charitable company' see PARA 241 note 1.

In relation to a charity whose charity trustees have prepared any group accounts (ie under s 138(2): see PARA 343) the reference to its most recent accounts includes the group accounts most recently prepared by them: s 172(3).

7 Ie in pursuance of the Charities Act 2011 s 162(1) or 168(3): s 171(1). The reference to a charity's most recent annual report is a reference to the annual report so prepared in respect of the last financial year of the charity in respect of which an annual report has been so prepared: s 171(3).

8 Charities Act 2011 ss 171(1), 172(1), (3). If any requirement imposed by s 171(1) or s 172(1), (3) is not complied with, each person who immediately before the date for compliance specified in the section in question was a charity trustee of the charity is guilty of an offence and liable on summary conviction to a fine not exceeding level 4 on the standard scale and, for continued contravention, a daily default fine not exceeding 10 per cent of level 4 on the standard scale for so long as the person in question remains a charity trustee of the charity: s 173(1), (2)(c), (d), (4). However, it is a defence for a person charged with such an offence to prove that he took all reasonable steps for securing that the requirement in question would be complied with in time: s 173(3).

However, proceedings may only be instituted by or with the consent of the Director of Public Prosecutions: Charities Act 2011 s 345(1), (2)(d). As to offences by bodies corporate see s 346; and PARA 588. As to the Director of Public Prosecutions see CRIMINAL PROCEDURE vol 27 (2010) PARAS 23, 33 et seq.

As to the standard scale see SENTENCING AND DISPOSITION OF OFFENDERS vol 92 (2010) PARA 142.

383. Annual returns by registered charities. Every registered charity[1] must prepare in respect of each of its financial years[2] an annual return in such form, and containing such information, as may be prescribed by regulations[3] made by the Charity Commission[4]. However, this does not apply in relation to any financial year of a charity in which the gross income does not exceed £10,000[5], unless the charity is constituted as a charitable incorporated organisation (CIO)[6].

Any such return under these provisions must be transmitted to the Commission by the date by which the charity trustees[7] are required[8] to transmit to it the annual report required to be prepared in respect of the financial year in question[9].

The Commission may dispense with these requirements[10] in the case of a particular charity or a particular class of charities, or in the case of a particular financial year of a charity or of any class of charities[11]. An appeal against a decision of the Commission not to so dispense with these requirements lies to the Tribunal at the instance of the Attorney General[12] and the charity trustees of any charity affected by the decision[13]. The Tribunal has power to quash the decision and, if appropriate, remit the matter to the Commission[14].

1 Ie registered under the Charities Act 2011 s 30 (see PARAS 307–310): s 29(3). As to the meaning of 'charity' see PARA 1.

2 As to the meaning of 'financial year' see PARAS 218 note 3, 344 note 4.
3 Such regulations are made and published annually by the Charity Commission. See eg the Charities (Annual Return) Regulations 2013 (Charity Commission, December 2013) (available, at the date at which this volume states the law, on the government website). As to the Charity Commission see PARAS 543–578. As to the Charity Commission's publications see PARA 547.
4 Charities Act 2011 s 169(1).
5 The Minister may by order amend the Charities Act 2011 s 169(2) by substituting a different sum for the sum for the time being specified there: s 174(1), (2). At the date at which this volume states the law no such order had been made. As to the making of orders generally see s 347; and PARA 590. As to the Minister see PARA 586.
6 Charities Act 2011 s 169(2). As to CIOs see PARAS 226–239.
7 As to the meaning of 'charity trustees' see PARA 255.
8 Ie by virtue of the Charities Act 2011 s 163(1): see PARA 371.
9 Charities Act 2011 s 169(3). If any such requirement is not complied with, each person who immediately before the date for compliance specified in the section in question was a charity trustee of the charity is guilty of an offence and liable on summary conviction to a fine not exceeding level 4 on the standard scale and, for continued contravention, a daily default fine not exceeding 10 per cent of level 4 on the standard scale for so long as the person in question remains a charity trustee of the charity: s 173(1), (2)(b). However, it is a defence for a person charged with such an offence to prove that he took all reasonable steps for securing that the requirement in question would be complied with in time: 173(3).

However, proceedings may only be instituted by or with the consent of the Director of Public Prosecutions: Charities Act 2011 s 345(1), (2)(d). As to offences by bodies corporate see s 346; and PARA 588. As to the Director of Public Prosecutions see **CRIMINAL PROCEDURE** vol 27 (2010) PARAS 23, 33 et seq.

As to the standard scale see **SENTENCING AND DISPOSITION OF OFFENDERS** vol 92 (2010) PARA 142.
10 Ie the requirements of the Charities Act 2011 s 169(1): see the text and notes 1–6.
11 Charities Act 2011 s 169(4).
12 As to the Tribunal see PARA 579 et seq. As to the Attorney General see PARAS 589, 596, 605 et seq; and **CONSTITUTIONAL AND ADMINISTRATIVE LAW** vol 20 (2014) PARA 273 et seq.
13 See the Charities Act 2011 s 319(2), Sch 6 Table Cols 1, 2.
14 See the Charities Act 2011 Sch 6 Table Col 3.

(2) POWERS OF CHARITY TRUSTEES

(i) Exercise of Powers generally

384. Exercise of discretionary powers. Trustees invested with discretionary powers must exercise them honestly and with a fair consideration of the subject[1]. They need not give reasons for their actions[2]. Where they state reasons which do not justify their conclusions[3], or where they have acted corruptly or improperly[4], the court will interfere, though there is some doubt as to whether it is necessary that there be dishonesty for the court to interfere[5]. The court is generally reluctant to interfere with the discretion of trustees by means of schemes[6], although in order to retain some control over the trustees it may refuse to dismiss an action seeking the interference of the court[7], or may refuse to order payment out to trustees of a fund in court without an affidavit by them stating how they propose to apply the money[8].

1 *Re Beloved Wilkes' Charity* (1851) 20 LJCh 588 at 597 per Lord Truro LC. The exercise by trustees of discretionary powers was discussed in *McPhail v Doulton* [1971] AC 424 at 449, [1970] 2 All ER 228 at 240, HL, per Lord Wilberforce. Where there is a duty combined with a power, the court can compel trustees to act in a proper manner: *Marwaha v Singh* [2013] PTSR D14, [2013] All ER (D) 229 (Jun); appealed as to costs [2013] EWCA Civ 1878, [2014] PTSR 1166.
2 *Re Beloved Wilkes' Charity* (1851) 20 LJCh 588.
3 *Re Beloved Wilkes' Charity* (1851) 20 LJCh 588. See, however, *A-G v Mosely* (1848) 17 LJCh 446, where it was said that a discretionary consent might be withheld for an insufficient reason or none.

4 *A-G v Glegg* (1738) Amb 584; *A-G v Governors of Harrow School* (1754) 2 Ves Sen 551; *Waldo v Caley* (1809) 16 Ves 206 at 212 per Lord Eldon LC; *Ex p Berkhampstead Free School* (1813) 2 Ves & B 134 at 138 per Lord Eldon LC; *Re Bedford Charity* (1833) 5 Sim 578; *A-G v Boucherett* (1858) 25 Beav 116. See also *A-G v Governors etc of Sherborne Grammar School* (1854) 18 Beav 256 (discretion of visitor).

5 See *Marwaha v Singh* [2013] EWCA Civ 1878 at [30] et seq, [2014] PTSR 1166, where in a hearing as to costs the Court of Appeal stated that the judge in the court below had interpreted the court's power too narrowly: see [2013] PTSR D14, [2013] All ER (D) 229 (Jun).

6 *Powerscourt v Powerscourt* (1824) 1 Mol 616 (trust of a temporary nature); *A-G v Gaskell* (1831) 9 LJOS Ch 188; *Re Lea, Lea v Cooke* (1887) 34 ChD 528 (where no permanent charity was intended). In *Re Hurley, Nichols v Pargiter* (1900) 17 TLR 115 a scheme was ordered by the court, although the trustees were given a discretionary power. In *Marwaha v Singh* [2013] EWCA Civ 1878, [2014] PTSR 1166, the Court of Appeal observed that the court might have directed an amendment to a charity's constitution by a scheme, though the judge had incorrectly (see note 5) decided it could not override trustees' discretion in the absence of dishonesty.

7 *A-G v Governors of Harrow School* (1754) 2 Ves Sen 551.

8 *Re Devlin's Estate, Hagan v Duff* (1889) 23 LR Ir 516.

385. Who may exercise discretionary powers. Where a power to prescribe the mode of applying a charitable gift is contained in the trust instrument, it is a question of construction to determine who is capable of exercising the power[1]. Powers given to trustees, and even to a testator's 'said trustees' (being named earlier in the will) are prima facie regarded as annexed to the office and therefore exercisable by the trustees for the time being[2].

A power given to executors only is exercisable by continuing[3] or surviving[4] executors, but not by one who renounces[5], or by persons subsequently appointed trustees[6]. The question whether it is exercisable by a substituted personal representative appointed by the court under the Administration of Justice Act 1985 has not yet come before the court[7].

A power given to a person who is not a trustee of the property cannot be exercised by any other person[8]; if the named person does not or cannot exercise the power, the court must exercise the discretion[9].

The permissible manner of exercise of a power and its scope also depend upon the construction of the trust instrument[10].

1 *Crawford v Forshaw* [1891] 2 Ch 261 at 267–268, CA, per Bowen LJ; and see the non-charity cases of *Re Smith, Eastick v Smith* [1904] 1 Ch 139; *Re Hayes' Will Trusts, Pattinson v Hayes* [1971] 2 All ER 341, [1971] 1 WLR 758.

2 *Re Smith, Eastick v Smith* [1904] 1 Ch 139. See also *Re Taylor's Charity, ex p Blackburne* (1820) 1 Jac & W 297 (where the selection of objects was left with the persons nominated by the testator as trustees, although new trustees were appointed); *Re Hampton, Public Trustee v Hampton* (1918) 88 LJCh 103. See also the Trustee Act 1925 ss 18, 36(7), 43; the Law of Property Act 1925 s 156; and TRUSTS AND POWERS.

3 *Crawford v Forshaw* [1891] 2 Ch 261, CA.

4 *A-G v Glegg* (1738) Amb 584.

5 *A-G v Fletcher* (1835) 5 LJCh 75; cf the Administration of Estates Act 1925 s 8; and see WILLS AND INTESTACY vol 103 (2010) PARA 629.

6 *Hibbard v Lamb* (1756) Amb 309.

7 See the Administration of Justice Act 1985 s 50; and WILLS AND INTESTACY vol 103 (2010) PARA 1165.

8 *Re M'Auliffe's Goods* [1895] P 290; cf *Re Lalor's Goods* (1901) 85 LT 643.

9 *Moggridge v Thackwell* (1792) 1 Ves 464 at 475 per Lord Thurlow LC; on rehearing (1803) 7 Ves 36 at 86 per Lord Eldon LC; affd (1807) 13 Ves 416, HL; cf *Doyley v A-G* (1735) 4 Vin Abr 485 pl 16 (a trustee who refused to act). See also PARA 124.

10 See PARA 124; and TRUSTS AND POWERS vol 98 (2013) PARA 411 et seq.

386. Powers of majority of trustees or quorum. Apart from powers exercisable under statutory provisions by a majority of trustees, the general rule is that a majority of the trustees of a trust of a public or charitable nature acting within the limits of the instrument of foundation[1] bind the minority[2].

Schemes for the administration of a charity may contain a provision that a certain number of trustees constitute a quorum[3].

1 *Ward v Hipwell* (1862) 3 Giff 547.
2 *Re Whiteley, Bishop of London v Whiteley* [1910] 1 Ch 600; *Doe d Read v Godwin* (1822) 1 Dow & Ry KB 259 (conveyance by majority); but see *Re Ebsworth and Tidy's Contract* (1889) 42 ChD 23, CA (where it was held that without statutory authority a majority of trustees could not pass the legal estate if vested in all); *Re Congregational Church, Smethwick* [1866] WN 196; *A-G v Shearman* (1839) 2 Beav 104 (lease); *Doe d Dupleix v Roe* (1794) 1 Anst 86 (action of ejectment); *Withnell v Gartham* (1795) 6 Term Rep 388; *Wilkinson v Malin* (1832) 2 Cr & J 636; *A-G v Scott* (1750) 1 Ves Sen 413 at 416 per Lord Hardwicke LC; *A-G v Cuming* (1843) 2 Y & C Ch Cas 139 (election of minister of Established Church by advowson trustees); *Davis v Jenkins* (1814) 3 Ves & B 151 at 159 per Lord Eldon LC; *Perry v Shipway* (1859) 4 De G & J 353; *A-G v Lawson* (1866) 36 LJCh 130 (appointment and dismissal of minister of dissenting chapel).
3 Cf *Re Beverley Grammar School* (1839) 9 LJCh 91. Cf PARA 290.

(ii) Authorisation of Dealings by the Charity Commission

387. General power. If it appears to the Charity Commission[1] that an action which is proposed or contemplated in the administration of a charity[2] is expedient in the interests of the charity, the Commission may by order[3] sanction that action, whether or not it would otherwise be within the powers exercisable by the charity trustees[4] in the administration of the charity[5]. Anything done under the authority of such an order is deemed to be properly done in the exercise of those powers[6].

Such an order may be made to authorise a particular transaction, compromise[7] or the like, or a particular application of property, or so as to confer a more general authority[8], and in particular may authorise[9] a charity to use common premises or employ a common staff or otherwise combine for any administrative purpose with another charity[10].

An application for the review of a decision of the Commission not to make such an order lies to the Tribunal at the instance of the Attorney General[11], the charity trustees of the charity and, if a body corporate, the charity itself[12]. The Tribunal has the power to quash the decision and, if appropriate, remit the matter the Commission[13].

1 As to the Charity Commission see PARAS 543–578.
2 As to the meaning of 'charity' see PARA 1.
3 It has been held that the order should be made formally under seal: see *BIU Estates Ltd v Chichester Diocesan Fund and Board of Finance Inc* (1963) 186 Estates Gazette 261 (decided under earlier legislation).
4 As to the meaning of 'charity trustees' see PARA 255.
5 Charities Act 2011 s 105(1). This is subject to the remaining provisions of s 105 (see the text to note 10; and PARA 388 et seq): see s 26(1). See eg *Trustees of the Presbyterian Church in Ireland v A-G for Northern Ireland* [2011] NICh 4 (23 March 2011, unreported), where the power under Northern Ireland legislation in the same terms was exercised in relation to disbursements made to a mutual society by the Presbyterian Church, as being of considerable benefit to Church members and in both reputational and financial sense to the Church itself. See also *R (on the application of O'Callaghan) v Charity Commission for England and Wales* [2007] EWHC 2491 (Admin), [2007] All ER (D) 77 (Oct), where judicial review was successfully sought of an order of the Commission's, the order having been made without the consultation promised at inquiry.
6 Charities Act 2011 s 105(2).
7 See eg *Report of the Charity Commissioners for England and Wales for 1978* (HC Paper (1979–80) no 94) paras 146–149; and *Report of the Charity Commissioners for England and Wales for 1982* (HC Paper (1982–83) no 370) paras 90–96.

8 Eg a general authority to invest in land: see *Report of the Charity Commissioners for England and Wales for 1988* (HC Paper (1988–89) no 319) paras 73–75.
9 Ie without prejudice to the generality of the Charities Act 2011 s 105(1).
10 Charities Act 2011 s 105(3).
11 A decision to offer such orders, rather than to refuse them, is not reviewable under this provision: *Morris v Charity Commission for England and Wales* (2010) First-tier Tribunal, General Regulatory Chamber (Charity), 26 March. As to the Tribunal see PARA 579 et seq. As to the Attorney General see PARAS 589, 596, 605 et seq; and **CONSTITUTIONAL AND ADMINISTRATIVE LAW** vol 20 (2014) PARA 273 et seq. As to reviewable decisions see PARA 580.
12 See the Charities Act 2011 s 319(2), Sch 6 Table Cols 1, 2.
13 See the Charities Act 2011 Sch 6 Table Col 3.

388. Directions as to expenditure. An order of the Charity Commission[1] authorising action in the administration of a charity[2] may give directions as to the manner in which any expenditure is to be borne and as to other matters connected with or arising out of the action thereby authorised[3]. Where anything is done under the authority of such an order, the directions are binding on the charity trustees[4] for the time being as if contained in the trusts[5] of the charity[6]. Any such directions may, on the application of the charity, be modified or superseded by a further order[7]. In particular, such directions include directions for meeting any expenditure out of a specified fund, for charging any expenditure to capital or to income, for requiring expenditure charged to capital to be recouped out of income within a specified period, for restricting the costs to be incurred at the expense of the charity, or for the investment of moneys arising from any transaction[8].

1 As to the Charity Commission see PARAS 543–578.
2 Ie under the Charities Act 2011 s 105(1): see PARA 387. As to the meaning of 'charity' see PARA 1.
3 Charities Act 2011 s 105(4).
4 As to the meaning of 'charity trustees' see PARA 255.
5 As to the meaning of 'trusts' see PARA 218 note 5.
6 Charities Act 2011 s 105(5)(a).
7 Charities Act 2011 s 105(5)(b).
8 Charities Act 2011 s 105(6).

389. Transactions affected by disabling Acts or requiring a court order. An order of the Charity Commission[1] authorising action in the administration of a charity[2] may also authorise any act notwithstanding that it is prohibited by the Ecclesiastical Leases Act 1836[3], and notwithstanding that the trusts[4] of the charity provide for the act to be done by or under the authority of the court[5].

1 As to the Charity Commission see PARAS 543–578.
2 As to the meaning of 'charity' see PARA 1.
3 Charities Act 2011 s 105(7)(a). This power does not extend to acts prohibited by any other Act: see s 105(8)(b), and PARA 391. As to the Ecclesiastical Leases Acts see **ECCLESIASTICAL LAW**.
4 As to the meaning of 'trusts' see PARA 218 note 5.
5 Charities Act 2011 s 105(7)(b). As to the meaning of 'court' see PARA 177 note 12.

390. Transactions affected by a company director's breach of duty. In the case of a charitable company[1], an order of the Charity Commission[2] authorising action in the administration of a charity[3] may also authorise any act notwithstanding that it involves the breach of a duty imposed on a director of the company by the Companies Act 2006[4].

1 As to the meaning of 'charitable company' see PARA 241 note 1.
2 As to the Charity Commission see PARAS 543–578.

3 As to the meaning of 'charity' see PARA 1.
4 Ie under the Companies Act 2006 Pt 10 Ch 2: Charities Act 2011 s 105(9).

391. Acts which may not be authorised. No order of the Charity Commission[1] authorising action in the administration of a charity[2] may authorise the doing of any act expressly prohibited by an Act of Parliament other than the Ecclesiastical Leases Act 1836[3] or by the trusts of the charity[4], or extend or alter the purposes of the charity[5]; nor may it confer any authority in relation to a building which has been consecrated and the use or disposal of which is regulated, and can be further regulated, by a scheme made or having effect under the Mission and Pastoral Measure 2011[6]. The power of the Commission to authorise dealings with trust property[7] is not, however, affected by the Redundant Churches and Other Religious Buildings Act 1969[8].

1 As to the Charity Commission see PARAS 543–578.
2 As to the meaning of 'charity' see PARA 1.
3 See PARA 389.
4 See however PARA 390. As to the meaning of 'trusts' see PARA 218 note 5.
5 See the Charities Act 2011 s 105(8).
6 Charities Act 2011 s 105(10). The reference to a building is taken to include part of a building and any land which under such a scheme is to be used or disposed of with a building to which the scheme applies: s 105(11). As to schemes under the Mission and Pastoral Measure 2011 see ECCLESIASTICAL LAW vol 34 (2011) PARA 641.
7 Ie under the Charities Act 2011 s 105: see PARA 387 et seq.
8 See the Redundant Churches and Other Religious Buildings Act 1969 s 7(2) (substituted by the Charities Act 2011 Sch 7 para 18); and ECCLESIASTICAL LAW vol 34 (2011) PARA 907.

392. Charge for agricultural improvements. The powers conferred by the Agricultural Holdings Act 1986 on landlords as regards charging land with the amount paid or expended as compensation for improvements[1] are not exercisable by trustees for charitable purposes except with the approval in writing of the Charity Commission[2].

1 See the Agricultural Holdings Act 1986 s 86(1)–(3); and AGRICULTURAL LAND vol 1 (2008) PARAS 477, 484.
2 Agricultural Holdings Act 1986 s 86(4) (amended by the Charities Act 2006 Sch 8 para 79). As to the Charity Commission see PARAS 543–578.

(iii) Advice by the Charity Commission

393. Power to give advice. On the written application of any charity trustee[1] or trustee for a charity, the Charity Commission[2] may give him its opinion or advice on any matter relating to the performance of any of his duties as such a trustee in relation to the charity concerned, or otherwise relating to the proper administration of the charity[3]. The accuracy of the Commission's opinion or advice may be challenged under the procedure set up under the Charities Act 2011[4], but a common law action in negligence cannot be brought on the ground that the opinion or advice is not only wrong but was given negligently[5].

1 As to the meaning of 'charity trustees' see PARA 255.
2 As to the Charity Commission see PARAS 543–578.
3 Charities Act 2011 s 110(1).
4 See the Charities Act 2011 s 115; and PARA 592 et seq.
5 *Mills v Winchester Diocesan Board of Finance* [1989] Ch 428, [1989] 2 All ER 317.

394. Consequences of acting on advice. If the Charity Commission[1] gives its opinion or advice with respect to a charity on the application of a charity trustee[2] or trustee for a charity[3], then a charity trustee or trustee for the charity acting in accordance with that opinion or advice, whether made to him or another trustee, is deemed to have acted in accordance with his trust, as regards his responsibility for so acting[4], unless, when he does so act, either he knows or has reasonable cause to suspect that the opinion or advice was given in ignorance of material facts, or the decision of the court[5] or the Tribunal[6] has been obtained on the matter or proceedings are pending to obtain one[7].

1 As to the Charity Commission see PARAS 543–578.
2 Ie under the Charities Act 2011 s 110(1): see PARA 393. As to the meaning of 'charity trustees' see PARA 255.
3 As to the meaning of 'charity' see PARA 1.
4 Charities Act 2011 s 110(2).
5 As to the meaning of 'court' see PARA 177 note 12.
6 As to the Tribunal see PARA 579 et seq.
7 Charities Act 2011 s 110(3).

(iv) Execution of Documents

395. Power to delegate. Subject to the trusts[1] of the charity, charity trustees[2] may confer on any two or more of their body a general authority or authority limited in such manner as the trustees think fit, to execute in the names and on behalf of the trustees assurances or other deeds or instruments for giving effect to transactions to which the trustees are a party[3].

1 As to the meaning of 'trusts' see PARA 218 note 5.
2 As to the meaning of 'charity trustees' see PARA 255.
3 Charities Act 2011 s 333(1). Any deed or instrument executed in pursuance of an authority so given is of the same effect as if executed by the whole body: s 333(2). This power is in addition to and not in derogation of any other powers (eg the general power to act by a majority (see PARA 386)): s 333(6). As to the powers of trustees generally, including the power to execute documents, see **TRUSTS AND POWERS** vol 98 (2013) PARA 411 et seq; and as to their power to delegate see further **TRUSTS AND POWERS** vol 98 (2013) PARA 425 et seq.

396. Manner of delegating authority. An authority to execute any deed or instrument[1] is sufficient if given in writing or by resolution of a meeting of the trustees, notwithstanding the want of any formality which would otherwise be required[2]. It may be given so that the powers conferred are exercisable by any of the trustees or may be restricted to named persons or in any other way[3].

1 Ie under the Charities Act 2011 s 333(1): see PARA 395.
2 Charities Act 2011 s 333(3)(a).
3 Charities Act 2011 s 333(3)(b).

397. Effect of authority. An authority to execute instruments on behalf of charity trustees[1] has effect, subject to any restriction expressed in it and until it is revoked, as a continuing authority given by the charity trustees from time to time of the charity[2] and exercisable by such trustees, notwithstanding any change in the charity trustees[3]. A deed or instrument executed in pursuance of such an authority has the same effect as if executed by all the trustees[4]. Such an authority also includes an implied authority to execute deeds and instruments in the name and on behalf of the official custodian for charities[5], in cases where the charity trustees could do so[6].

Where a deed or instrument purports to be executed in pursuance of such an authority, then in favour of a person who, then or afterwards, in good faith acquires for money or money's worth an interest in or charge on property or the benefit of a covenant or agreement expressed to be entered into by the charity trustees, it is presumed conclusively to have been duly executed under proper authority[7].

1 Ie under the Charities Act 2011 s 333: see PARAS 395–396. As to the meaning of 'charity trustees' see PARA 255.
2 As to the meaning of 'charity' see PARA 1.
3 Charities Act 2011 s 333(3)(c).
4 Charities Act 2011 s 333(2).
5 As to the official custodian for charities see PARA 300 et seq.
6 Charities Act 2011 s 333(4). As to where the charity trustees can execute deeds and instruments on behalf of the official custodian for charities see PARA 304.
7 Charities Act 2011 s 333(5).

(v) Preservation of Charity Documents

398. Enrolment and deposit of documents. The Charity Commission[1] may provide books in which any deed, will and other document[2] relating to a charity[3] may be enrolled[4]. It may also accept for safe keeping any document of or relating to a charity, and the charity trustees[5] or other persons having the custody of such documents, including documents relating to a charity which has ceased to exist, may, with the consent of the Commission, deposit them with it for safe keeping, except in the case of documents required by some enactment other than the Charities Act 2011 to be kept elsewhere[6]. Regulations made by the Minister[7] may make provision for such documents so deposited with the Commission as may be prescribed by the regulations to be destroyed or otherwise disposed of after such period or in such circumstances as may be so prescribed[8].

1 As to the Charity Commission see PARAS 543–578.
2 As to the meaning of 'document' see PARA 263 note 2.
3 As to the meaning of 'charity' see PARA 1.
4 Charities Act 2011 s 340(1).
5 As to the meaning of 'charity trustees' see PARA 255.
6 Charities Act 2011 s 340(2).
7 As to the Minister see PARA 586.
8 Charities Act 2011 s 340(3). At the date at which this volume states the law, no such regulations had been made. This power applies also to any document transmitted to the Commission under s 52, and kept by it under s 52(3) (see PARA 562) as if the document had been deposited with it for safe keeping under s 340: s 340(4). As to evidence of such documents see PARA 399.
The Charities Act 2011 s 340(3), (4) applies to documents enrolled by, deposited or transmitted to the Charity Commissioners under corresponding previous enactments: see s 340(5).

399. Evidence of documents. Evidence of the contents of a document[1] enrolled by or deposited with the Charity Commission[2] may be given by means of a copy certified by any member of its staff generally or specially authorised by it to act for this purpose[3]. A document purporting to be such a copy must be received in evidence without proof of the official position, authority or handwriting of the person certifying it, or of the original document being enrolled or deposited[4].

1 As to the meaning of 'document' see PARA 263 note 2.
2 Ie under the Charities Act 2011 s 340: see PARA 398. As to the Charity Commission see PARAS 543–578.
3 Charities Act 2011 s 341(1), (2).
4 Charities Act 2011 s 341(3). This also applies to any document transmitted to the Commission under s 52, and kept by it under s 52(3) (see PARA 562) as if the document had been deposited with it for safe keeping under s 340: s 341(4).

The Charities Act 2011 s 341(2), (3) applies to documents enrolled by, deposited or transmitted to the Charity Commissioners under corresponding previous enactments: see s 341(5).

(vi) Notices

400. Service of notices. All notices required or authorised by the trusts[1] of a charity[2] to be given to a charity trustee[3], member or subscriber may be sent by post, addressed to any address given as his in the list of charity trustees, members or subscribers for the time being in use at the principal office of the charity[4]. If the charity trustee, member or subscriber has no address in the United Kingdom on that list, no notice of an election or meeting need be given even though required by the trusts of the charity[5]. Where any required notice is given by post, it is deemed to have been given at the time when the letter containing it would be delivered in the ordinary course of post[6].

1 As to the meaning of 'trusts' see PARA 218 note 5.
2 As to the meaning of 'charity' see PARA 1.
3 As to the meaning of 'charity trustees' see PARA 255.
4 Charities Act 2011 s 332(1).
5 See the Charities Act 2011 s 332(2), (4).
6 Charities Act 2011 s 332(2), (3).

(3) MANAGEMENT OF TRUST PROPERTY

(i) Disposal of Property

401. Restrictions on dispositions of charity land. The Charities Act 1992 made new provisions with respect to restrictions on the disposition of land held in trust for a charity and on the charging of charity property, which are consolidated in the Charities Act 2011[1]. The basic rule that no land held by or in trust for a charity may be conveyed, transferred, leased or otherwise disposed of without an order of the court or of the Charity Commission[2] is subject to important exceptions[3], as a result of which many transactions can take place without an order being obtained. The basic rule does not apply to a disposition of such land if the disposition is made to a person who is not a connected person, or a trustee for, or nominee of, a connected person[4]. 'Connected person', in relation to a charity, means a person who, at the time of the disposition in question or at the time of any contract for the disposition in question[5], falls into any of the following categories[6]: (1) a charity trustee or trustee for a charity[7]; (2) a person who is the donor of any land to the charity[8]; (3) a child[9], parent, grandchild, grandparent, brother or sister of any such trustee or donor[10]; (4) an officer, agent or employee of the charity[11]; (5) the spouse[12] or civil partner[13] of any person falling within any of heads (1) to (4) above[14]; (6) a person carrying on business in partnership with any person falling within any of heads (1) to (5) above[15], except in certain limited circumstances[16]; (7) an institution which is controlled[17] by any person falling within any of heads (1) to (6) above, or by two or more such persons taken together[18]; or (8) a body corporate in which any connected person falling within any of heads (1) to (7) above has a substantial interest, or two or more such persons, taken together, have a substantial interest[19].

Where the disposition is made to a person other than a connected person or a trustee for, or nominee of a connected person, an order is not required where, before entering into the agreement for the sale, or as the case may be, for the lease or other disposition of the land[20], the charity trustees comply with the following requirements[21], namely, that they: (a) obtain and consider a written report on the proposed disposition from a qualified surveyor[22] instructed by the trustees and acting exclusively for the charity[23]; (b) advertise the proposed disposition for such period and in such manner as the surveyor has advised in his report[24]; and (c) decide that they are satisfied, having considered the surveyor's report, that the terms on which the disposition is proposed to be made are the best that can reasonably be obtained for the charity[25].

The requirements are modified where the proposed disposition is the granting of a lease for a term ending not more than seven years after it is granted, other than one granted wholly or partly in consideration of a fine[26]. In this case the above requirements[27] do not apply, but the charity trustees must, before entering into the agreement for the lease, obtain and consider the advice on the proposed disposition of a person who is reasonably believed by the trustees to have the requisite ability and practical experience to provide them with competent advice thereon[28]. The charity trustees must also decide that they are satisfied, having considered that person's advice, that the terms on which the disposition is proposed to be made are the best that can reasonably be obtained for the charity[29].

Where any land is held by or in trust for a charity and the trusts[30] on which it is held stipulate that it is to be used for the purposes, or for any particular purposes, of the charity, the land must not be conveyed, transferred, leased or otherwise disposed of unless the charity trustees have before the relevant time[31] previously given public notice of the proposed disposition, inviting representations to be made to them[32], and taken into consideration any representations duly made to them about the proposed disposition[33]. This requirement does not, however, apply if the disposition is to be effected with a view to acquiring by way of replacement other property to be held on the same trusts[34]. Nor does it apply if the disposition is the granting of a lease for a term ending not more than two years after it is granted, other than one granted wholly or partly in consideration of a fine[35]. Moreover, the Charity Commission may direct that this requirement is not to apply to dispositions of land held by or in trust for a charity or class of charities[36], or that it is not to apply to a particular disposition of land held by or in trust for a charity[37]. Such a direction may be given if, on an application made to it in writing by or on behalf of the charity or charities in question, the Commission is satisfied that it would be in the interests of the charity or charities for it to do so[38].

All these restrictions on disposition apply notwithstanding anything in the trusts of a charity[39]. They do not apply, however, to: (i) any disposition for which general or special authority is expressly given[40] by any statutory provision contained in or having effect under an Act of Parliament or by any scheme legally established[41]; or (ii) any disposition for which the authorisation or consent of the Secretary of State is required under the Universities and College Estates Act 1925[42]; or (iii) to any disposition of land held by or in trust for a charity which is made to another charity otherwise than for the best price that can reasonably be obtained, and is authorised to be so made by the trusts of the first mentioned charity[43]; or (iv) to the granting, by or on behalf of a charity and in accordance with its trusts, of a lease to any beneficiary under those trusts, where the lease is granted otherwise than for the best rent that can reasonably be obtained and is intended to enable the demised premises to be occupied for the purposes, or any particular purposes, of the charity[44].

None of the above provisions applies to any disposition of land held by or in trust for an exempt charity[45], to any disposition of land by way of mortgage or other security, or to any disposition of an advowson[46].

An application for the review of a decision of the Commission not to make such an order under the above provisions in relation to land held on or in trust for a charity lies to the Tribunal at the instance of the Attorney General[47], the charity trustees of the charity, the charity itself (if a body corporate), and any other person who is or may be affected by the decision[48]. The Tribunal has the power to quash the decision and, if appropriate, remit the matter to the Commission[49].

1 Charities Act 1992 ss 32–36 (repealed): see now the Charities Act 2011 ss 117–129. Any provision establishing or regulating a particular charity and contained in, or having effect under, any Act of Parliament, or contained in the trusts of a charity, has ceased to have effect if and to the extent that it provides for dispositions of, or other dealings with, land in England and Wales held by or in trust for the charity to require the consent of the Charity Commissioners (now the Charity Commission), whether signified by order or otherwise: Charities Act 1992 s 36(1), (3) (repealed, but the effect of the repeal does not revive so much as of any document as ceased to have effect by virtue of that provisions: Charities Act 2006 Sch 10 para 29(1), (2)(c)). Similarly, any provision of an order or scheme under the Education Acts 1944 (repealed: see now the Education Act 1996) or Education Act 1973 (see EDUCATION vol 36 (2011) PARA 1247) relating to a charity has ceased to have effect if and to the extent that it requires in relation to any sale, lease or other disposition of land in England or Wales held by or in trust for the charity, approval by the Commissioners (now the Commission) or the Secretary of State of the amount payable in respect of the sale, lease or disposition: Charities Act 1992 s 36(2), (3) (repealed, but the effect of the repeal does not revive so much as of any document as ceased to have effect by virtue of that provision: Charities Act 2006 Sch 10 para 29(1), (2)(c)). As to the Secretary of State see PARA 585.

2 Charities Act 2011 s 117(1). For these purposes, 'land' means land in England and Wales: s 129(1). As to the meaning of 'court' see PARA 177 note 12.

3 Ie the exceptions contained in the Charities Act 2011 ss 117(2)–(4), 119–121, 127.

4 Charities Act 2011 s 117(2)(a).

5 This is subject to an exception in the case of a disposition for which the contract was entered into before 28 February 2007: see the Charities Act 2006 (Commencement No 1, Transitional Provisions and Savings) Order 2007, SI 2007/309, art 6(2). The continuity of the law is unaffected by the consolidation of legislation in the Charities Act 2011, but this provision may now be of limited application.

6 Charities Act 2011 s 118(1).

7 Charities Act 2011 s 118(2)(a). As to the meaning of 'charity trustees' see PARA 255. As to the meaning of 'charity' see PARA 1.

8 Charities Act 2011 s 118(2)(b). This applies whether the gift was made on or after the establishment of the charity: s 118(2)(b).

9 'Child' includes a stepchild and an illegitimate child: Charities Act 2011 s 350(1).

10 Charities Act 2011 s 118(2)(c).

11 Charities Act 2011 s 118(2)(d).

12 A person living with another as that person's husband or wife is treated as that person's spouse: Charities Act 2011 s 350(2)(a). As to the effect of the Marriage (Same Sex Couples) Act 2013 see s 1(1), 11(1); and MATRIMONIAL AND CIVIL PARTNERSHIP LAW vol 72 (2009) PARA 1 et seq.

13 Where two persons of the same sex are not civil partners but live together as if they were, each of them is treated as the civil partner of the other: Charities Act 2011 s 350(2)(b).

14 Charities Act 2011 s 118(2)(e).

15 Charities Act 2011 s 118(2)(f).

16 See note 5.

17 A person controls an institution if he is able to secure that the affairs of the institution are conducted in accordance with his wishes: Charities Act 2011 s 351.

18 Charities Act 2011 s 118(2)(g).

19 Charities Act 2011 s 118(2)(h). A connected person has a substantial interest in a body corporate if the person or institution in question: (1) is interested in shares comprised in the

equity share capital of that body of a nominal value of more than one-fifth of that share capital; or (2) is entitled to exercise, or control the exercise of, more than one-fifth of the voting power at any general meeting of that body: s 352(1). The rules relating to the interpretation of 'connected person' set out in the Companies Act 2006 Sch 1 apply for the purposes of the Charities Act 2011 s 352 as they apply for the purposes of the Companies Act 2006 s 254, and the terms 'equity share capital' and 'share' have the same meaning as in that Act: Charities Act 2011 s 352(2), (3). See **COMPANIES**.

20 This applies except where the proposed disposition is the granting of a lease for not more than seven years under the Charities Act 2011 s 120(1), (2): see s 119(2).

21 Charities Act 2011 ss 117(2), 119(1).

22 A person is a qualified surveyor if (1) he is a fellow or professional associate of the Royal Institution of Chartered Surveyors or satisfies such other requirement or requirements as may be prescribed by regulations made by the Minister; and (2) he is reasonably believed by the charity trustees to have ability in, and experience of, the valuation of land of the particular kind, and in the particular area, in question: Charities Act 2011 s 119(3)(a), (b). Any report must contain such information, and deal with such matters, as may be prescribed by regulations: s 119(4). At the date at which this volume states the law no such regulations had been made under s 36(4) but the Charities (Qualified Surveyors' Reports) Regulations 1992, SI 1992/2980, have effect as if made under it. See further PARA 402.

23 Charities Act 2011 s 119(1)(a).

24 Charities Act 2011 s 119(1)(b). This provision applies unless the surveyor has advised in his report that it would not be in the best interests of the charity to advertise the proposed disposition: s 119(1)(b).

25 Charities Act 2011 s 119(1)(c).

26 Charities Act 2011 ss 117(2), 120(1).

27 Ie those under the Charities Act 2011 s 119(1), (2): see the text and notes 23–25.

28 Charities Act 2011 s 120(2)(a).

29 Charities Act 2011 s 120(2)(b).

30 As to the meaning of 'trusts' see PARA 218 note 5.

31 Where the charity trustees enter into an agreement for the sale or, as the case may be, for the lease or other disposition then the 'relevant time' means the time when they enter into that agreement; in any other case 'relevant time' means the time of the disposition: see the Charities Act 2011 s 121(4).

A limited exception applies in relation to a disposition for which the agreement was entered into before 27 February: see note 5.

32 The notice must specify a time within which representations must be made, being not less than one month from the date of the notice: Charities Act 2011 s 121(2)(a).

33 Charities Act 2011 s 121(1), (2). This is subject to s 121(5), (6): see s 121(3).

34 Charities Act 2011 s 121(5)(a).

35 Charities Act 2011 s 121(5)(b).

36 Whether generally or only in the case of a specified class of dispositions or land, or otherwise as may be provided in the direction: Charities Act 2011 s 121(6)(a).

37 Charities Act 2011 s 121(6)(a), (b).

38 Charities Act 2011 s 121(7).

39 Charities Act 2011 s 117(3).

40 Without the authority being made subject to the sanction of an order of the court: Charities Act 2011 s 117(3)(a).

41 Charities Act 2011 s 117(3)(a). See also *Sales of land: Powers of sale and leasing conferred by scheme and the effect of sections 36(1) of the Charities Act 1992 and 36(9)(a) of the Charities Act 1993 (1994)* Decisions of the Charity Commissioners (1997) vol 5 p 21. As to decisions of the Charity Commission see PARA 547.

42 Charities Act 2011 s 117(3)(b).

43 Charities Act 2011 s 117(3)(c).

44 Charities Act 2011 s 117(3)(d).

45 As to exempt charities see PARAS 318–320.

46 Charities Act 2011 s 117(4). As to advowsons see **ECCLESIASTICAL LAW** vol 34 (2011) PARA 550.

47 A decision to offer such orders, rather than to refuse them, is not reviewable under this provision: *Morris v Charity Commission for England and Wales* (2010) First-tier Tribunal, General Regulatory Chamber (Charity), 26 March. As to the Tribunal see PARA 579 et seq. As to the Attorney General see PARAS 589, 596, 605 et seq; and **CONSTITUTIONAL AND ADMINISTRATIVE LAW** vol 20 (2014) PARA 273 et seq. As to reviewable decisions see PARA 580.

48 Charities Act 2011 s 319(2), Sch 6 Table Cols 1, 2. As to the meaning of 'person who is or may be affected' within the meaning of Sch 6 see PARA 317 note 8.
49 Charities Act 2011 Sch 6 Table Col 3.

402. Information to be contained in, and matters to be dealt with by, qualified surveyors' reports. A surveyor's report prepared for the purposes of enabling the disposal of land held by or in trust for a charity[1] (otherwise than with an order of the court or of the Charity Commission[2]) must contain such information and deal with such matters as are prescribed[3] together with such other information and such other matters as the surveyor[4] believes should be drawn to the attention of the charity trustees[5]. The report must contain a description of the relevant land[6] and its location, which includes the measurements of the relevant land, its current use, the number of buildings, if any, included in the relevant land, the measurements of any such buildings, and the number of rooms in any such buildings and the measurements of those rooms[7]. Where any such information required may be clearly given by means of a plan, it may be so given and any such plan need not be drawn to scale[8].

Further information required includes whether the relevant land, or any part of it, is leased by or from the charity trustees and, if it is, details of[9]:

(1) the length of the lease and the period of it which is outstanding[10];
(2) the rent payable under the lease[11];
(3) any service charge which is so payable[12];
(4) the provisions in the lease for any review of the rent payable under it or any service charge so payable[13];
(5) the liability under the lease for repairs and dilapidations[14]; and
(6) any other provision in the lease which, in the opinion of the surveyor, affects the value of the relevant land[15].

The report must further provide information on whether the relevant land is subject to the burden of, or enjoys the benefit of, any easement or restrictive covenant[16] or is subject to any annual or other periodic sum charged on, or issuing out of, the land except rent reserved by a lease or tenancy[17]. It must deal with whether any buildings included in the relevant land are in good repair and, if not, the surveyor's advice: (a) as to whether or not it would be in the best interests of the charity for repairs to be carried out prior to the proposed disposition; (b) as to what those repairs, if any, should be; and (c) as to the estimated cost of any repairs he advises[18]. The report must also include where, in the opinion of the surveyor, it would be in the best interests of the charity to alter any buildings included in the relevant land prior to disposition, because, for example, adaptations to the buildings for their current use are not such as to command the best market price on the proposed disposition, that opinion and an estimate of the outlay required for any alterations which he suggests[19].

The report must further contain advice as to the manner of disposing of the relevant land so that the terms on which it is disposed of are the best that can reasonably be obtained for the charity, including[20]:

(i) where appropriate, a recommendation that the land should be divided for the purposes of the disposition[21];
(ii) unless the surveyor's advice is that it would not be in the best interests of the charity to advertise the proposed disposition, the period for which and the manner in which the proposed disposition should be advertised[22];
(iii) where the surveyor's advice is that it would not be in the best interests of the charity to advertise the proposed disposition, his reasons for that

advice, for example, that the proposed disposition is the renewal of a lease to someone who enjoys statutory protection or that he believes someone with a special interest in acquiring the relevant land will pay considerably more than the market price for it[23]; and

(iv) any view the surveyor may have on the desirability or otherwise of delaying the proposed disposition and, if he believes such delay is desirable, what the period of that delay should be[24].

Where the surveyor feels able to give such advice and where such advice is relevant, the report must contain advice as to the chargeability or otherwise of value added tax on the proposed disposition and the effect of such advice on the valuations given under heads (A) to (E) below[25]. Where either the surveyor does not feel able to give such advice or such advice is not in his opinion relevant, a statement to that effect must be included in the report[26].

The report must also include the surveyor's opinion as to:

(A) the current value of the relevant land having regard to its current state of repair and current circumstances, such as the presence of a tenant who enjoys statutory protection, or, where the proposed disposition is a lease, the rent which could be obtained under it having regard to such matters[27];

(B) what the value of the relevant land or what the rent under the proposed disposition would be where he has given advice[28] if that advice is followed, or where he has expressed an opinion[29] if that opinion is acted upon, or if both that advice is followed and that opinion is acted upon[30];

(C) where he has made a recommendation under head (i) above, the increase in the value of the relevant land or rent in respect of it if the recommendation were followed[31];

(D) where his advice is that it would not be in the best interests of the charity to advertise the proposed disposition because he believes a higher price can be obtained by not doing so, the amount by which that price exceeds the price that could be obtained if the proposed disposition were advertised[32]; and

(E) where he has advised a delay in the proposed disposition under head (iv) above, the amount by which he believes the price which could be obtained consequent on such a delay exceeds the price that could be obtained without it[33].

Where the surveyor is of the opinion that the proposed disposition is not in the best interests of the charity because it is not a disposition that makes the best use of the relevant land, the report must include that opinion and the reasons for it, together with his advice as to the type of disposition which would constitute the best use of the land, including such advice as may be relevant as to the prospects of buying out any sitting tenant or of succeeding in an application for change of use of the land[34] under the laws relating to town and country planning[35].

1 Ie a report for the purposes of the Charities Act 2011 s 119 (see PARA 401) or where the Charities Act 2011 s 120(2) (see PARA 401) applies: Charities (Qualified Surveyors' Reports) Regulations 1992, SI 1992/2980, reg 2. Those regulations have effect under the Charities Act 2011 s 119(3), (4); see Sch 8 Pt I, and the Interpretation Act 1978 s 17(2)(b). As to the meaning of 'charity' see PARA 1.

2 As to the Charity Commission see PARAS 538–572.

3 Ie prescribed by the Charities (Qualified Surveyors' Reports) Regulations 1992, SI 1992/2980, Schedule: see the text and notes 7–35.

4 'Surveyor' means the qualified surveyor from whom such a report is being obtained: Charities (Qualified Surveyors' Reports) Regulations 1992, SI 1992/2980, reg 1(2).
5 Charities (Qualified Surveyors' Reports) Regulations 1992, SI 1992/2980, reg 2. As to the meaning of 'charity trustees' see PARA 255.
6 'Relevant land' means the land in respect of which a report is being obtained for the purposes of the Charities Act 2011 s 119 (see PARA 401): Charities (Qualified Surveyors' Reports) Regulations 1992, SI 1992/2980, reg 1(2); and see note 4.
7 Charities (Qualified Surveyors' Reports) Regulations 1992, SI 1992/2980, Schedule para 1(1).
8 Charities (Qualified Surveyors' Reports) Regulations 1992, SI 1992/2980, Schedule para 1(2).
9 Charities (Qualified Surveyors' Reports) Regulations 1992, SI 1992/2980, Schedule para 2.
10 Charities (Qualified Surveyors' Reports) Regulations 1992, SI 1992/2980, Schedule para 2(a).
11 Charities (Qualified Surveyors' Reports) Regulations 1992, SI 1992/2980, Schedule para 2(b).
12 Charities (Qualified Surveyors' Reports) Regulations 1992, SI 1992/2980, Schedule para 2(c).
13 Charities (Qualified Surveyors' Reports) Regulations 1992, SI 1992/2980, Schedule para 2(d).
14 Charities (Qualified Surveyors' Reports) Regulations 1992, SI 1992/2980, Schedule para 2(e).
15 Charities (Qualified Surveyors' Reports) Regulations 1992, SI 1992/2980, Schedule para 2(f).
16 As to easements and restrictive covenants see **REAL PROPERTY AND REGISTRATION** vol 87 (2012) PARA 1076.
17 Charities (Qualified Surveyors' Reports) Regulations 1992, SI 1992/2980, Schedule para 3.
18 Charities (Qualified Surveyors' Reports) Regulations 1992, SI 1992/2980, Schedule para 4.
19 Charities (Qualified Surveyors' Reports) Regulations 1992, SI 1992/2980, Schedule para 5.
20 Charities (Qualified Surveyors' Reports) Regulations 1992, SI 1992/2980, Schedule para 6.
21 Charities (Qualified Surveyors' Reports) Regulations 1992, SI 1992/2980, Schedule para 6(a).
22 Charities (Qualified Surveyors' Reports) Regulations 1992, SI 1992/2980, Schedule para 6(b).
23 Charities (Qualified Surveyors' Reports) Regulations 1992, SI 1992/2980, Schedule para 6(c).
24 Charities (Qualified Surveyors' Reports) Regulations 1992, SI 1992/2980, Schedule para 6(d).
25 Charities (Qualified Surveyors' Reports) Regulations 1992, SI 1992/2980, Schedule para 7(1).
26 Charities (Qualified Surveyors' Reports) Regulations 1992, SI 1992/2980, Schedule para 7(2).
27 Charities (Qualified Surveyors' Reports) Regulations 1992, SI 1992/2980, Schedule para 8(a).
28 Ie under the Charities (Qualified Surveyors' Reports) Regulations 1992, SI 1992/2980, Schedule para 4: see the text to note 18.
29 Ie under the Charities (Qualified Surveyors' Reports) Regulations 1992, SI 1992/2980, Schedule para 5: see the text to note 19.
30 Charities (Qualified Surveyors' Reports) Regulations 1992, SI 1992/2980, Schedule para 8(b).
31 Charities (Qualified Surveyors' Reports) Regulations 1992, SI 1992/2980, Schedule para 8(c).
32 Charities (Qualified Surveyors' Reports) Regulations 1992, SI 1992/2980, Schedule para 8(d).
33 Charities (Qualified Surveyors' Reports) Regulations 1992, SI 1992/2980, Schedule para 8(e).
34 As to a material change of use of the land see **PLANNING** vol 81 (2010) PARA 297.
35 Charities (Qualified Surveyors' Reports) Regulations 1992, SI 1992/2980, Schedule para 9. See generally **PLANNING**.

403. Supplementary provisions relating to dispositions of charity land. Any contract for the sale, or for a lease or other disposition, of land[1] which is held by or in trust for a charity[2], and any conveyance, transfer, lease or other instrument effecting a disposition of such land[3], must state: (1) that the land is held by or in trust for a charity[4]; (2) whether the charity is an exempt charity[5] and whether the disposition is one excepted[6] from the statutory restrictions[7]; and (3) if it is not an exempt charity and the disposition is not one so excepted, that the land is land to which the statutory restrictions[8] apply[9].

Where any land held by or in trust for a charity is conveyed, transferred, leased or otherwise disposed of[10], the charity trustees must certify in the instrument by which the disposition is effected[11]: (a) in a case where an order of the court or of the Charity Commission is required[12], that the disposition has been sanctioned by an order of the court or of the Commission, as the case may be[13]; or (b) in a case where such an order is not required[14], that the charity trustees have power under the trusts of the charity to effect the disposition, and that they have complied with the statutory provisions so far as applicable to it[15]. In the case of a duly certified disposition it is conclusively presumed, in favour of a person who (whether under the disposition or afterwards) acquires an interest in the land for money or money's worth that the facts were as stated in the certificate[16].

Where a disposition is not duly certified[17], and any land held by or in trust for a charity is conveyed, transferred, leased or otherwise disposed of by a disposition to which these provisions apply[18], the disposition will nevertheless be valid in favour of a person who (whether under the disposition or afterwards) in good faith acquires an interest in the land for money or money's worth[19]. This is so whether or not the disposition has been sanctioned by an order of the court or of the Commission, or whether or not the charity trustees have power under the trusts of the charity to effect the disposition and have complied with the statutory provisions so far applicable to it[20].

Any contract for the sale, or for a lease or other disposition, of land which will, as a result of the disposition, be held by or in trust for a charity, and any conveyance, transfer, lease or other instrument effecting a disposition of such land[21] must state: (i) that the land will, as a result of the disposition, be held by or in trust for a charity[22]; (ii) whether the charity is an exempt charity[23]; and (iii) if it is not an exempt charity, that the statutory restrictions on disposition[24] will apply to the land[25].

There are additional provisions in relation to the Land Registration Act 2002. Where the disposition to be effected by any such conveyance, transfer, lease or other instrument effecting a disposition of such land will be a registrable disposition[26] or a disposition which triggers the requirement of registration[27], the statement which is to be contained in the instrument must be in such form as may be prescribed by land registration rules[28]. Where the registrar approves an application for registration of a disposition of registered land, or a person's title under a disposition of unregistered land, and the instrument effecting the disposition contains a statement complying with provisions above[29], he must enter in the register a restriction reflecting the limitation under the Charities Act 2011 on subsequent disposal[30]. Where any such restriction is entered in the register in respect of any land, and the charity by or in trust for which the land is held becomes an exempt charity, the charity trustees must apply to the registrar for the removal of the entry[31]. On receiving any application duly made, the registrar must remove the entry[32]. Conversely, where any registered land is held by or in trust for an exempt charity and the charity ceases to be an exempt charity, or where any registered land becomes, as a result of a declaration of trust by the registered proprietor, land held in trust for a charity (other than an exempt charity), the charity trustees must apply to the registrar for the entry of a restriction in the prescribed form and, on receiving an application duly made, the registrar must enter it accordingly[33].

Where there is a conveyance of land[34] held on charitable trusts, if neither of the mandatory provisions for inclusion in contracts and dispositive instruments[35] or mortgages[36] applies the conveyance must state the land is held on such trusts and if neither of these provisions has been complied with in relation to the conveyance and a purchaser has notice that the land is held on such trusts, he must see that any consents or orders necessary to authorise the transaction have been obtained[37].

1 For these purposes, references to a disposition of land do not include references to a disposition of land by way of mortgage or other security, any disposition of an advowson, or any release of a rentcharge falling within the Charities Act 2011 s 127(1) (see PARA 406): s 122(9). As to the meaning of 'land' see PARA 401 note 2. As to advowsons see ECCLESIASTICAL LAW vol 34 (2011) PARA 550.

2 As to the meaning of 'charity' see PARA 1.
3 Charities Act 2011 s 122(1)(a), (b).
4 Charities Act 2011 s 122(2)(a).
5 As to exempt charities see PARA 318.
6 Ie excepted by the Charities Act 2011 s 117(3)(a), (b), (c) or (d): see PARA 401 text and notes 40–46.
7 Charities Act 2011 s 122(2)(b).
8 Ie the restrictions imposed by ss 117–121.
9 Charities Act 2011 s 122(2)(c). As to the form of statement required see the Land Registration Rules 2003, SI 2003/1417, r 180(1); and **REAL PROPERTY AND REGISTRATION** vol 87 (2012) PARA 405.
10 Ie by a disposition falling within the Charities Act 2011 s 117(1) or (2): see PARA 401.
11 Charities Act 2011 s 121(3). As to the meaning of 'charity trustees' see PARA 255.
12 Ie where the case falls within the Charities Act 2011 s 117(1): see PARA 401. As to the Charity Commission see PARAS 543–578. As to the meaning of 'court' see PARA 177 note 12.
13 Charities Act 2011 s 122(3)(a).
14 Ie where the case falls within the Charities Act 2011 s 117(2): see PARA 401.
15 Charities Act 2011 s 122(3)(b).
16 See the Charities Act 2011 s 122(4).
17 Ie under the Charities Act 2011 s 122(3): see the text and notes 10–15.
18 Ie under the Charities Act 2011 s 117(1), (2): see PARA 401.
19 Charities Act 2011 s 122(5), (6). This does not make a disposition valid unless it is a disposition to which s 117(1) or (2) (see PARA 401) applies: see *Bayoumi v Women's Total Abstinence Educational Union Ltd* [2003] EWCA Civ 1548, [2004] Ch 46, [2004] 3 All ER 110, decided under the previous equivalent provisions.
20 Charities Act 2011 s 122(6)(a), (b).
21 See the Charities Act 2011 s 122(7)(a), (b).
22 Charities Act 2011 s 122(8)(a).
23 Charities Act 2011 s 122(8)(b).
24 Ie the restrictions imposed by the Charities Act 2011 ss 117–121: see PARA 401. Those provisions, subject to s 117(3), apply to the land: s 122(8).
25 Charities Act 2011 s 122(8)(c). As to the form of statement required see the Land Registration Rules 2003, SI 2003/1417, r 179; and **REAL PROPERTY AND REGISTRATION** vol 87 (2012) PARA 405.
26 As to registrable dispositions see **REAL PROPERTY AND REGISTRATION** vol 87 (2012) PARA 427 et seq.
27 As to dispositions triggering the requirement of registration see **REAL PROPERTY AND REGISTRATION** vol 87 (2012) PARA 540.
28 Charities Act 2011 s 123(1). This is to be construed as one with the Land Registration Act 2006: Charities Act 2011 s 129(3); and see **REAL PROPERTY AND REGISTRATION**.
29 Ie the Charities Act 2011 s 122(8), 123(1): see the text and notes 21–28.
30 Charities Act 2011 s 123(2); and see note 28.
31 Charities Act 2011 s 123(3).
32 Charities Act 2011 s 123(4); and see note 28.
33 Charities Act 2011 s 123(5), (6); and see note 28.
34 This applies to land other than land to which the Universities and College Estates Act 1925 applies (see **EDUCATION** vol 36 (2011) PARA 1575): Trusts of Land and Appointment of Trustees Act 1996 s 2, Sch 1 para 4(1).
35 Ie the Charities Act 2011 s 122(2): see the text and notes 1–9.
36 Ie the Charities Act 2011 s 125(1): see PARA 405.
37 Trusts of Land and Appointment of Trustees Act 1996 Sch 1 para 4(1), (2) (amended by the Charities Act 2011 Sch 7 para 70); and see **SETTLEMENTS** vol 91 (2012) PARA 578. Where any trustees or the majority of any set of trustees have power to transfer or create any legal estate in the land, the estate must be transferred or created by them in the names and on behalf of the persons in whom it is vested: Trusts of Land and Appointment of Trustees Act 1996 Sch 1 para 4(3).

404. Restrictions on mortgaging charity land. The basic rule is that no mortgage[1] of land[2] held by or in trust for a charity[3] is to be granted without an order of the court[4] or of the Charity Commission[5]. However, this does not apply[6] to a mortgage of any such land if the charity trustees have, before executing the mortgage, obtained and considered proper advice, given to them in writing, on the following relevant matters or matter, as the case may be[7]:

(1) in the case of a mortgage to secure the repayment of a proposed loan or grant, the relevant matters are (a) whether the loan or grant is necessary in order for the charity trustees to be able to pursue the particular course of action in connection with which they are seeking the loan or grant; (b) whether the terms of the loan or grant are reasonable having regard to the status of the charity as the prospective recipient of the loan or grant; and (c) the ability of the charity to repay on those terms the sum proposed to be paid by way of loan or grant[8];

(2) in the case of a mortgage to secure the discharge of any other proposed obligation, the relevant matter is whether it is reasonable for the charity trustees to undertake to discharge the obligation, having regard to the charity's purposes[9].

Head (1), or as the case may be, head (2) applies in relation to such a mortgage as is mentioned therein whether the mortgage would only have effect to secure the repayment of the proposed loan or grant or the discharge of the proposed obligation, or would also have effect to secure the repayment of sums paid by way of loan or grant, or the discharge of other obligations undertaken, after the date of its execution[10].

Where the charity trustees of a charity have executed a mortgage of land held by or in trust for a charity having obtained and considered the proper advice[11] and the mortgage has effect to secure the repayment of sums paid by way of loan or grant, or the discharge of other obligations undertaken, after the date of its execution[12], then the charity trustees must not after that date enter into any transaction involving the payment of any such sums, or the undertaking of any such obligations, unless they have, before entering into the transaction, obtained and considered proper advice, given to them in writing, on the matters or matter mentioned in head (1) or (2) above, as the case may be[13].

For these purposes, proper advice is the advice of a person who is reasonably believed by the charity trustees to be qualified by his ability in and practical experience of financial matters, and who has no financial interest in relation to the loan, grant or other transaction in connection with which his advice is given[14]. Such advice may constitute proper advice notwithstanding that the person giving it does so in the course of his employment as an officer or employee of the charity or of the charity trustees[15].

These provisions apply notwithstanding anything in the trusts[16] of a charity, but they do not apply to a mortgage (i) for which general or special authority is expressly given (without the authority being made subject to the sanction of an order of the court) by any statutory provision contained in or having effect under an Act of Parliament or by any scheme legally established[17]; or (ii) for which general or special authority is given for which the authorisation or consent of the Secretary of State is required[18].

An application for the review of a decision of the Commission not to make an order in relation to a mortgage of land held by or in trust for a charity[19] lies to the Tribunal at the instance of the Attorney General[20], the charity trustees of the charity and the charity itself (if a body corporate) and any other person who is or may be affected by the decision[21]. The Tribunal has the power to quash the decision and, if appropriate, remit the matter to the Commission[22].

1 'Mortgage' includes a charge: Charities Act 2011 s 129(2). As to mortgages generally see MORTGAGE.

2 As to the meaning of 'land' see PARA 401 note 2.
3 As to the meaning of 'charity' see PARA 1.
4 As to the meaning of 'court' see PARA 177 note 12.
5 Charities Act 2011 s 124(1). For an example of a security that would contravene this provision see *White v Williams* [2011] EWHC 494 (Ch), [2011] PTSR 1151, [2011] All ER (D) 122 (Mar).
Nothing in the Charities Act 2011 s 124 applies to an exempt charity: s 124(10). As to exempt charities see PARA 318. See also s 117, which removes certain requirements under statutory provisions for consent to dealings with charity land; and PARA 401 note 1. As to the Charity Commission see PARAS 543–578.
6 Charities Act 2011 s 124(1).
7 Charities Act 2011 s 124(2).
8 Charities Act 2011 s 124(3).
9 Charities Act 2011 s 124(4).
10 Charities Act 2011 s 124(5).
11 Ie under the Charities Act 2011 s 124(2).
12 Charities Act 2011 s 124(6).
13 Charities Act 2011 s 124(7).
14 Charities Act 2011 s 124(8).
15 Charities Act 2011 s 124(8).
16 As to the meaning of 'trusts' see PARA 218 note 5.
17 Charities Act 2011 ss 117(3)(a), 124(9)(a).
18 Charities Act 2011 ss 117(3)(b), 124(9)(b).
19 Ie under the Charities Act 2011 s 124.
20 As to the Tribunal see PARA 579 et seq. As to the Attorney General see PARAS 589, 596, 605 et seq; and CONSTITUTIONAL AND ADMINISTRATIVE LAW vol 20 (2014) PARA 273 et seq.
21 Charities Act 2011 s 319(2), Sch 6 Table Cols 1, 2. As to the meaning of 'person who is or may be affected' within the meaning of Sch 6 see PARA 317 note 8.
22 Charities Act 2011 Sch 6 Table Col 3.

405. Supplementary provisions relating to mortgaging of charity land. Any mortgage[1] of land[2] held by or in trust for a charity[3] must state[4]: (1) that the land is held by or in trust for a charity[5]; (2) whether the charity is an exempt charity[6] and whether the mortgage is one for which general or special authority is expressly given[7] (without the authority being made subject to the sanction of an order of the court) by any statutory provision contained in or having effect under an Act of Parliament or by any scheme legally established[8]; and (3) if it is not an exempt charity and it does not fall within head (2) above, that the mortgage is one to which the statutory restrictions[9] apply[10].

Where any such mortgage will be one falling within the statutory provisions relating to the requirements of compulsory registration[11] the statement required[12] must be in such form as may be prescribed by land registration rules and, if the charity is not an exempt charity, the mortgage must also contain a statement, in such form as may be prescribed by land registration rules, that the restrictions on disposition[13] apply to the land[14]. Where the registrar approves an application for registration of a person's title to land in connection with such a mortgage, the mortgage contains statements complying with the above provisions[15] and the charity is not an exempt charity, the registrar must enter in the register a restriction reflecting the limitation on subsequent disposal[16].

Where the restrictions on mortgaging[17] apply to any mortgage of land held by or in trust for a charity, the charity trustees[18] must certify in the mortgage: (a) in the case where an order of the court[19] or the Charity Commission[20] is required[21], that the mortgage has been sanctioned by an order of the court or of the Commission[22]; or (b) in a case where such an order is not required[23], that the charity trustees have power under the trusts of the charity to grant the mortgage, and that they have obtained and considered proper advice[24]. In the case of a duly certified mortgage it is conclusively presumed, in favour of a person who (whether under the mortgage or afterwards) acquires an interest in the land in question for money or money's worth, that the facts were as stated in the certificate[25]. Where a disposition is not duly certified, and the restrictions on mortgaging[26] apply to any mortgage of land held by or in trust for a charity it will nevertheless be valid in favour of a person who (whether under the mortgage or afterwards) in good faith acquires an interest in the land for money or money's worth[27]. This is so whether or not the mortgage has been sanctioned by an order of the court or of the Commission, or whether or not the charity trustees have power under the trusts of the charity to grant the mortgage and have obtained and considered proper advice[28].

Where the statutory provisions apply concerning obtaining and considering proper advice before entering into certain transactions[29], the charity trustees must certify in relation to any such transaction that they have obtained and considered such advice as is mentioned in those provisions[30].

1 As to the meaning of 'mortgage' see PARA 404 note 1. As to mortgages generally see **MORTGAGE**.
2 As to the meaning of 'land' see PARA 401 note 2.
3 As to the meaning of 'charity' see PARA 1.
4 Charities Act 2011 s 125(1). Where the mortgage will be a registered disposition the statement must be in such form as may be prescribed by land registration rules: s 126(1). As to the meanings of 'prescribed' and 'registered disposition' see **REAL PROPERTY AND REGISTRATION** vol 87 (2012) PARA 405. The Charities Act 2011 s 126 is to be construed as one with the Land Registration Act 2002: Charities Act 2011 s 129(3); and see **REAL PROPERTY AND REGISTRATION**.

As to a conveyance of land held on charitable trusts see the Trusts of Land and Appointment of Trustees Act 1996 s 2, Sch 1 para 4; and PARA 403.
5 Charities Act 2011 s 125(1)(a).
6 As to exempt charities see PARA 318.
7 Ie a mortgage falling within the Charities Act 2011 s 124(9): see PARA 404.
8 Charities Act 2011 s 125(1)(b).
9 Ie those imposed by the Charities Act 2011 s 124: see PARA 404.
10 Charities Act 2011 s 125(1)(c).
11 Ie the Land Registration Act 2002 s 4(1)(g): see **REAL PROPERTY AND REGISTRATION** vol 87 (2012) PARA 718.
12 Ie under the Charities Act 2011 s 125(1): see the text and notes 4–10.
13 Ie imposed under the Charities Act 2011 ss 117–121: see PARA 401. Those provisions, subject to s 117(3), apply to the land: s 126(2)(b).
14 Charities Act 2011 s 126(2). See also note 4; and **REAL PROPERTY AND REGISTRATION**.
15 Ie the Charities Act 2011 ss 125(1), 126(2): see the text and notes 2–14.
16 Charities Act 2011 s 126(3). Section s 123(3), (4) apply in relation to any restriction entered under s 126(3) as in relation to any restriction entered under s 123(2) (see PARA 403): s 126(4).
17 Ie the Charities Act 2011 s 124(1), (2): see PARA 404.
18 As to the meaning of 'charity trustees' see PARA 255.
19 As to the meaning of 'court' see PARA 177 note 12.
20 As to the Charity Commission see PARAS 543–578.
21 Ie where the Charities Act 2011 s 124(1) applies: see PARA 404.
22 Charities Act 2011 s 125(2)(a).
23 Ie where the Charities Act 2011 s 124(2) applies: see PARA 404.
24 Charities Act 2011 s 125(2)(b). The reference to proper advice is a reference to the advice mentioned in s 124(2) (see PARA 404 text to notes 6–7): see s 125(2).
25 Charities Act 2011 s 125(3).
26 Ie under the Charities Act 2011 s 124(1), (2): see PARA 404.
27 Charities Act 2011 s 125(4), (5).
28 Charities Act 2011 s 125(5)(a), (b).
29 Ie under the Charities Act 2011 s 124(7): see PARA 404.
30 See the Charities Act 2011 s 125(6). Where this has been complied with in relation to any transaction, then, in favour of a person who (whether under the mortgage or afterwards) has acquired or acquires an interest in the land for money or money's worth, it is conclusively presumed that the facts were as stated in the certificate: s 125(7).

406. Release of charity rentcharges. The restrictions on the disposition of charity land[1] do not apply to the release by a charity of a rentcharge which it is entitled to receive if the release is given in consideration of the payment of an amount which is not less than ten times the annual amount of the rentcharge[2], nor do they apply where a rentcharge which a charity is entitled to receive is redeemed under the provisions of the Rentcharges Act 1977[3]. Where a charity which is entitled to receive a rentcharge releases it in consideration of the payment of an amount not exceeding £1,000[4], any costs incurred by the charity in connection with proving its title are recoverable by the charity from the person or persons in whose favour the rentcharge is being released, but this provision does not apply where a rentcharge which a charity is entitled to receive is redeemed under the provisions of the Rentcharges Act 1977[5].

1 Ie those contained in the Charities Act 2011 s 117(1): see PARA 401. As to the meaning of 'charity' see PARA 1.
2 Charities Act 2011 s 127(1).
3 Ie the Rentcharges Act 1977 ss 8–10: see **REAL PROPERTY AND REGISTRATION** vol 87 (2012) PARAS 1169–171.
4 The specified sum may be altered by the Minister by order: Charities Act 2011 s 128. At the date at which this volume states the law, no such order had been made. As to the making of orders generally see s 347; and PARA 590. As to the Minister see PARA 586.
5 Charities Act 2011 s 127(2), (3). The provisions of the Rentcharges Act 1977 referred to in the text are ss 8–10 (see **REAL PROPERTY AND REGISTRATION** vol 87 (2012) PARAS 1169–1171).

407. Powers to deal with charity land in relation to the Chequers Estate Act 1917 and the Chevening Estate Act 1959. In relation to the deed of settlement set out in the Chequers Estate Act 1917[1] or the trust instrument set out in the Chevening Estate Act 1959[2], all land vested or to be vested in trustees on or for charitable, ecclesiastical or public trusts or purposes is deemed to be settled land[3], and in relation to that land the trustees have all the powers conferred by the Settled Land Act 1925 on a tenant for life and on the trustees of a settlement[4]. Where the land is vested in persons having no powers of management, the Settled Land Act powers are exercisable by the managing trustees or committee of management, and the persons in whom the land is vested are not liable for giving effect to directions given by the managing trustees or committee[5]. The Settled Land Act powers are exercisable subject to obtaining any consents or orders which would, apart from that Act, have been required for the exercise of an express power under the trust instrument[6]. These provisions of the Settled Land Act do not affect the jurisdiction of the court, the Charity Commission, or any other competent authority in regard to the administration of charitable and other trusts[7].

Any conveyance of land held on charitable, ecclesiastical or public trusts must state that the land is held on such trusts[8].

1 Ie in the Chequers Estate Act 1917 s 1, Schedule.
2 Ie in the Chevening Estate Act 1959 s 1, Schedule.
3 Ie for the purposes of the Settled Land Act 1925 s 29 (repealed) (see note 4); see *Re Booth and Southend-on-Sea Estate Co's Contract* [1927] 1 Ch 579.
4 See the Settled Land Act 1925 s 29(1). Section 29 is repealed, except in relation to the deed of settlement set out in the Chequers Estate Act 1917 s 1, Schedule or the trust instrument set out in the Chevening Estate Act 1959 s 1, Schedule: Trusts of Land and Appointment of Trustees Act 1996 s 25(3). As to the powers under the Settled Land Act 1925 see PARAS 410–413. Section 29 does not apply to consecrated land and buildings vested in an incumbent during his incumbency: *Re St Swithin's, Norwich* [1960] P 77, [1959] 3 All ER 301, Consistory Ct; and see **ECCLESIASTICAL LAW** vol 34 (2011) PARA 840.

5 See the Settled Land Act 1925 s 29(2) (amended by the Charities Act 1960 s 48(2), Sch 7 Pt I (repealed)). Where trustees, or a majority of them, have power to transfer or create any legal estate, it must be transferred or created by them in the names of the persons in whom the legal estate is vested: Settled Land Act 1925 s 29(5) (amended by the Charities Act 1960 s 48(2), Sch 7 Pt I (repealed)).

6 See the Settled Land Act 1925 s 29(2). Thus, an order of the court or of the Charity Commission is sometimes required before the Settled Land Act powers may be exercised: see the Charities Act 2011 s 117; and PARA 401. Where a disposition or dealing is to be effected for less than full consideration in money, or where any interest in land is to be acquired, the same consent or order, if any, is required as if the intended transaction were a sale: Settled Land Act 1925 s 29(2) proviso. As to the Charity Commission see PARAS 543–578.

7 See the Settled Land Act 1925 s 29(3) (amended by the Charities Act 1960 Sch 7 Pt I).

8 Settled Land Act 1925 s 29(1).

408. Express powers. Where a trust deed gives to the trustees powers of disposal wider than those under the Settled Land Act 1925, they are not cut down by that Act, nor need they be exercised in accordance with the provisions of that Act as if they were additional powers comprised in a settlement[1]. Nothing in that Act converts revenue into capital money[2]. The statutory restrictions on dispositions of charity land apply notwithstanding anything in the trusts of the charity[3].

Regulations made by the founders of old charities that rents should not be increased have been held ineffective in changed circumstances[4], but regulations fixing the maximum duration of leases were generally upheld[5].

1 *Re Booth and Southend-on-Sea Estate Co's Contract* [1927] 1 Ch 579 (power for a sole trustee to give a good receipt for purchase money).

2 *Re Booth and Southend-on-Sea Estate Co's Contract* [1927] 1 Ch 579 at 588 per Astbury J.

3 See the Charities Act 2011 s 117(3); and PARA 401.

4 *Watson v Hinsworth Hospital* (1707) 2 Vern 596; *A-G v Catherine Hall, Cambridge* (1820) Jac 381.

5 *A-G v Griffith* (1807) 13 Ves 565; *Watson v Master, etc of Hemsworth Hospital* (1807) 14 Ves 324.

409. Powers at common law. Before the disposition of charity land was regulated by statute[1] it was held that charitable corporations and trustees had power to sell, lease or mortgage charity land, but that the transaction was liable to be set aside unless it was shown to be beneficial to the charity, the onus to establish that being on the purchaser[2]. It may be that transactions relating to property which could be dealt with as income were not vulnerable in this way[3].

It is not clear whether the statutory powers supersede the powers which existed at common law, but it is not safe for a purchaser to rely on the common law powers as authorising a transaction. In the absence of statutory power, special authority may be granted by the Charity Commission[4].

1 Ie before the Charitable Trusts Amendment Act 1855 (repealed).

2 See eg *A-G v Warren* (1818) 2 Swan 291; *President etc of St Mary Magdalen College, Oxford v A-G* (1857) 6 HL Cas 189; *A-G v South Sea Co* (1841) 4 Beav 453; *A-G v Brettingham* (1840) 3 Beav 91; *Re Clergy Orphan Corpn* [1894] 3 Ch 145, CA.

3 See *Re Clergy Orphan Corpn* [1894] 3 Ch 145 at 154, CA, obiter per Davey J.

4 Ie under the Charities Act 2011 s 105: see PARA 387. As to the Charity Commission see PARAS 543–578.

410. Statutory powers: sale and exchange. The powers under the Settled Land Act 1925 enjoyed by charity trustees include power to sell the land, any part of it or any easement, right or privilege of any kind over or in relation to the land[1], and to make exchanges for other land or rights over or in relation to land, with or without the payment of money for equality of exchange[2]. Sales must be made for the best consideration in money that can reasonably be obtained[3], which may be in the form of a perpetual or terminable rent[4]. Exchanges must be made for the best consideration in land or in land and money that can reasonably be obtained[5].

1 See the Settled Land Act 1925 s 38(i); and SETTLEMENTS vol 91 (2012) PARA 728.
2 See the Settled Land Act 1925 s 38(iii); and SETTLEMENTS vol 91 (2012) PARA 735.
3 See the Settled Land Act 1925 s 39(1); and SETTLEMENTS vol 91 (2012) PARA 729. However, see also s 39(5) (fully paid shares as consideration on sale to company); and SETTLEMENTS vol 91 (2012) PARA 731.
4 See the Settled Land Act 1925 s 39(2)–(4); and SETTLEMENTS vol 91 (2012) PARAS 729–730.
5 See the Settled Land Act 1925 s 40(1); and SETTLEMENTS vol 91 (2012) PARA 736.

411. Statutory powers: leases. The powers of trustees under the Settled Land Act 1925 include power to grant leases of the land, any part of it or right over or in relation to it, for any purpose for a term not exceeding 999 years in the case of a building or forestry lease, or 100 years in the case of a mining lease, or 50 years in the case of any other lease[1]. The lease must be made by deed, except in the case of a term of not more than three years, and must take effect in possession within one year or in reversion after a current term with seven years or less outstanding[2]. The best rent reasonably obtainable must be reserved, having regard to any fine taken[3] and to the circumstances generally[4], and there must be a covenant by the lessee to pay the rent and a condition of re-entry on non-payment[5]. A counterpart must be executed by the lessee and delivered to the trustees[6].

1 See the Settled Land Act 1925 s 41; and SETTLEMENTS vol 91 (2012) PARA 738. As to mining leases generally see MINES, MINERALS AND QUARRIES vol 76 (2013) PARA 321 et seq.
2 See the Settled Land Act 1925 s 42(1)(i), (5)(ii); and SETTLEMENTS vol 91 (2012) PARA 740.
3 Any fine taken on a lease under the statutory powers is capital money: Settled Land Act 1925 s 42(4).
4 See the Settled Land Act 1925 s 42(1)(ii); and SETTLEMENTS vol 91 (2012) PARA 740.
5 See the Settled Land Act 1925 s 42(1)(iii); and SETTLEMENTS vol 91 (2012) PARA 740. In the case of a short lease in writing, there must be an agreement rather than a covenant: s 42(5)(ii).
6 See the Settled Land Act 1925 s 42(2); and SETTLEMENTS vol 91 (2012) PARA 740.

412. Statutory powers: mortgages. The Settled Land Act 1925 only permits the legal estate in the land to be mortgaged for specified purposes, all of which relate to the well-being of the land, either by authorised improvements or by discharging incumbrances or other liabilities[1].

1 See the Settled Land Act 1925 s 71; and SETTLEMENTS vol 91 (2012) PARAS 750–751.

413. Statutory powers: options. The powers of trustees under the Settled Land Act 1925 include power to grant options over the land, any part of it or any right over or in relation to it, at a price which must be fixed at the time of granting the option[1] and must be the best reasonably obtainable in all the circumstances[2], to be exercisable within an agreed number of years not exceeding ten[3].

1 See the Settled Land Act 1925 s 51(1). See also SETTLEMENTS vol 91 (2012) PARA 772.
2 See the Settled Land Act 1925 s 51(3).
3 See the Settled Land Act 1925 s 51(2).

414. Miscellaneous statutory powers. Trustees holding land for charitable purposes may grant up to one acre of land for the purposes of the School Sites

Act 1841[1]. They may also, with the consent of the Charity Commission[2], or on compliance with certain provisions of the Charities Act 2011[3], grant up to one acre of land as a site for a literary or scientific institution[4].

Where charity trustees, as landlords, are liable to pay compensation for improvements to their tenants, they are expressly empowered to grant a lease which relieves them from that liability[5].

1 See the School Sites Act 1841 ss 2, 6; and EDUCATION vol 36 (2011) PARA 1541.
2 As to the Charity Commission see PARAS 543–578.
3 Ie the applicable provisions of the Charities Act 2011 ss 117(2), 119–121 (see PARA 401 et seq).
4 See the Literary and Scientific Institutions Act 1854 ss 1, 6 (amended by the Charities Act 2011 Sch 7 para 4); and NATIONAL CULTURAL HERITAGE vol 77 (2010) PARA 948.
5 See the Landlord and Tenant Act 1927 s 14. For the circumstances in which such liability exists and the leases which may be granted see generally Pt I (ss 1–17); and LANDLORD AND TENANT vol 63 (2012) PARA 904 et seq.

415. Disposal by local authorities. A principal council[1], parish and community councils[2], and the parish trustees of a parish acting with the consent of the parish meeting[3], may generally dispose of land held by them, including land held for charitable purposes, in any manner they wish[4]. However, this does not authorise local authorities to dispose of land in breach of any trust, covenant or agreement binding on them[5]. Nor does it affect the operation of the provisions of the Charities Act 2011 relating to dispositions of charitable land, and in particular it does not give any special authority to dispose of charitable land, where such special authority is required by that Act[6].

Capital money received by a parish or community council, or the parish trustees of a parish acting with the consent of the parish meeting in respect of a disposal of land held for charitable purposes must be applied in accordance with any directions given under the Charities Act 2011[7].

1 As to the meaning of 'principal council' see the Local Government Act 1972 s 270(1); and LOCAL GOVERNMENT vol 69 (2009) PARA 23.
2 As to parish and community councils see LOCAL GOVERNMENT vol 69 (2009) PARA 33.
3 As to parish trustees and parish meeting see LOCAL GOVERNMENT vol 69 (2009) PARAS 34, 635 et seq.
4 See the Local Government Act 1972 ss 123(1), 127(1); and LOCAL GOVERNMENT vol 69 (2009) PARAS 515, 520. Both of those provisions are expressed to be subject to the provisions of the Playing Fields (Community Involvement in Disposal Decisions) (Wales) Measure 2010.

Unless the disposal is by way of short tenancy, consent is required if the disposal is for a consideration less than the best that could reasonably be expected: see the Local Government Act 1972 ss 123(2), 127(2); and LOCAL GOVERNMENT vol 69 (2009) PARAS 515, 520.
5 See the Local Government Act 1972 s 131(1)(a); and LOCAL GOVERNMENT vol 69 (2009) PARA 515.
6 See the Local Government Act 1972 s 131(3) (amended in this regard by the Charities Act 2011 Sch 7 para 27). The provisions referred to are the Charities Act 2011 ss 117–121, and in particular s 117(3)(a): see PARA 401; and LOCAL GOVERNMENT vol 69 (2009) PARA 515. As to the Charity Commission see PARAS 543–578.
7 See the Local Government Act 1972 s 127(1), (4) (amended in this regard by the Charities Act 2011 Sch 7 para 26); and LOCAL GOVERNMENT vol 69 (2009) PARA 520.

416. Compulsory purchase and tenant's right of first refusal. Charity land is subject to compulsory purchase under statutory procedure[1], and charity trustees have express power to sell by agreement land which is subject to a compulsory purchase order[2]. If the purchase money on a compulsory purchase is paid into court[3], the acquiring authority is liable for the cost of investing the funds in court and may be ordered to pay the cost of reinvestment in land[4]. If the purchase is made by agreement, the acquiring authority may also have to bear the cost of reinvesting in land.

The collective right of first refusal given to qualifying tenants of flats to buy their landlord's interest if he proposes to dispose of it[5] does not apply to a disposal by way of gift to a charity, nor when the flats are the functional property of a charity which is being disposed of to another charity for functional purposes, nor where the landlord is a housing trust, a non-profit private registered provider of social housing, a registered social landlord, or a fully mutual housing association which is neither a private registered provider of social housing nor a registered social landlord[6]. It does apply where flats held as investment property are to be disposed of[7].

1 For the procedure see the Compulsory Purchase Act 1965, which largely superseded the Lands Clauses Consolidation Act 1845; and COMPULSORY ACQUISITION OF LAND. Under the latter Act it was held that unless the statutory procedure was followed strictly owners of land under a disability, such as charity trustees, could not be forced to sell to the acquiring authority: *Wycombe Rly Co v Donnington Hospital* (1866) 1 Ch App 268; *Bridgend Gas and Water Co v Dunraven* (1885) 31 ChD 219.

2 See the Compulsory Purchase Act 1965 ss 2, 3, Sch 1 para 2(2); and COMPULSORY ACQUISITION OF LAND vol 18 (2009) PARA 553. This power is probably superfluous in view of the other statutory powers of sale (see PARA 410).

3 Ie under the Compulsory Purchase Act 1965 ss 2, 3, Sch 1 para 6(2): see COMPULSORY ACQUISITION OF LAND vol 18 (2009) PARA 674.

4 See the Compulsory Purchase Act 1965 s 26(2); and COMPULSORY ACQUISITION OF LAND vol 18 (2009) PARA 666.

5 Ie under the Landlord and Tenant Act 1987: see generally LANDLORD AND TENANT vol 64 (2012) PARA 1852 et seq.

6 See the Landlord and Tenant Act 1987 ss 1(4), 4(1), (2)(f), 58(1)(f), (g), (ga), (gb) (s 58(1)(g)–(gb) substituted by SI 2010/866); and LANDLORD AND TENANT vol 64 (2012) PARA 1852 et seq.

7 Such a sale would not need the consent of the Charity Commission under the Charities Act 2011 s 117 because it would be a transaction for which general or special authority had been given by Act of Parliament: see s 117(3)(a); PARA 401; and *Report of the Charity Commissioners for England and Wales for 1987* (HC Paper (1987–88) no 427) App C(c). As to the Charity Commission see PARAS 543–578.

417. Pre-merger vesting declarations. Provision is made in relation to pre-merger vesting declarations[1]. A declaration which is made by deed by the charity trustees of the transferor[2] for the purposes of creating a declaration under these provisions[3], is made in connection with a relevant charity merger[4], and is to the effect that[5] all of the transferor's property is to vest in the transferee[6] on such date as is specified in the declaration (the 'specified date')[7], operates on the specified date to vest the legal title to all of the transferor's property in the transferee, without the need for any further document transferring it[8].

However this does not apply to:

(1) any land held by the transferor as security for money subject to the trusts of the transferor (other than land held on trust for securing debentures or debenture stock)[9];

(2) any land held by the transferor under a lease or agreement which contains any covenant (however described) against assignment of the transferor's interest without the consent of some other person, unless that consent has been obtained before the specified date[10]; or

(3) any shares, stock, annuity or other property which is only transferable in books kept by a company or other body or in a manner directed by or under any enactment[11].

In the case of a relevant charity merger where the transferee is a charitable incorporated organisation (CIO)[12], the above provisions apply, with modifications so as to include specified trust property[13]. In such a case, the transferee holds specified trust property on the same trusts, so far as is reasonably practicable, on which the property was held immediately before the merger[14]. Where specified trust property vests in the transferee, unless the Charity Commission directs otherwise, the specified trust property and the transferee are to be treated as a single charity for the purposes of provisions relating to the registration of charities and to accounts and reports[15].

1 See the Charities Act 2011 s 310; and the text and notes 2–11.
2 As to the meaning of 'transferor' see the Charities Act 2011 s 306; and PARA 322 (definition applied by s 312(1)(a)). Any reference to all of the transferor's property, where the transferor is a charity within s 306(2), is a reference to all of the transferor's unrestricted property (within the meaning of s 306(2)(a)): s 312(1)(b).
3 Ie for the purposes of the Charities Act 2011 s 310.
4 As to the meaning of 'relevant charity merger' see PARA 322.
5 This is subject to the Charities Act 2011 s 310(3), (4).
6 For these purposes any reference to the transferee, in relation to a relevant charity merger, is a reference to the transferee (within the meaning of the Charities Act 2011 s 306: see PARA 322), if it is a company or other body corporate, and otherwise, to the charity trustees of the transferee (within the meaning of s 306): s 312(2).
7 Charities Act 2011 s 310(1).
8 Charities Act 2011 s 310(2). This is subject to s 310(3), (4). In its application to registered land s 310(2) has effect subject to the Land Registration Act 2002 s 27 (dispositions required to be registered: see **REAL PROPERTY AND REGISTRATION** vol 87 (2012) PARA 427): Charities Act 2011 s 310(4). As to the meaning of 'registered land' see the Land Registration Act 2002; and **REAL PROPERTY AND REGISTRATION** vol 87 (2012) PARA 459.
9 Charities Act 2011 s 310(3)(a).
10 Charities Act 2011 s 310(3)(b).
11 Charities Act 2011 s 310(3)(c).
12 As to CIOs see PARA 226 et seq.
13 'Specified trust property' is any permanent endowment or other property held on special trust which is specified in the declaration: Charities Act 2011 s 310(1)(c) (modified in relation to CIOs by SI 2012/3012). As to the meaning of 'special trust' see PARA 218 note 2.
14 Charities Act 2011 s 310(2) (modified in relation to CIOs by SI 2012/3012).
15 Charities Act 2011 s 310(5) (added in relation to CIOs by SI 2012/3012). The provisions referred to are the Charities Act 2011 Pt 4 (ss 29–45) and Pt 8 (ss 130–176). As to the Charity Commission see PARAS 543–578.

(ii) Investment

418. Powers of investment. The powers and duties of charity trustees in regard to the investment of funds belonging to the charity are, like those of private trustees in relation to private trusts, governed by any special provisions of the trust instrument extending or limiting their statutory powers. The investment clause contained in the trust instrument may, for example, be so drawn as not to permit investment in some securities authorised by law for the investment of trust funds[1]. On the other hand, if the trust instrument directs and requires trustees to make some specified investment, they are under a duty to do so even it is one of which they disapprove[2]. Subject to any express directions contained in that instrument[3], and to any conditions prescribed by it, the trustees may invest[4] the money in any manner authorised by it, provided that in making the selection they use proper care and caution, and avoid investments which are accompanied by risk[5].

Charity trustees should not allow their own personal opinions or moral judgements to affect their investment decisions[6]. If they consider that the charitable purposes for which the funds are held require that certain types of investment should be avoided or that an ethical investment policy is in the interests of the charity they may adopt such a policy but only in so far as this is compatible with obtaining the best possible financial return on capital[7].

1 See eg *Re Warren, Public Trustee v Fletcher* [1939] Ch 684, [1939] 2 All ER 599; *Re Rider's Will Trusts, Nelson v Rider* [1958] 3 All ER 135, [1958] 1 WLR 974.

2 *Beauclerk v Ashburnham* (1845) 8 Beav 322; *Cadogan v Earl of Essex* (1854) 2 Drew 227; *Re Hurst, Addison v Topp* (1890) 63 LT 665 (all private trust cases).

As to the powers of investment under the Trustee Investments Act 1961 (repealed, except in so far as it is applied by another enactment) see PARA 423; and **TRUSTS AND POWERS** vol 98 (2013) PARA 458 et seq. As to the statutory powers of investment under the Trustee Act 2000 see PARAS 420–422; and **TRUSTS AND POWERS** vol 98 (2013) PARA 453 et seq. As to total return investment see PARA 419.

3 *Beauclerk v Ashburnham* (1845) 8 Beav 322; *Cadogan v Earl of Essex* (1854) 2 Drew 227.

4 To 'invest' prima facie means to apply money in the purchase of some property from which interest or profit is expected and which property is purchased in order to be held for the sake of the income it will yield: *Re Wragg, Wragg v Palmer* [1919] 2 Ch 58 at 65 per Lawrence J; *Moss's Trustees v King* 1952 SC 523 at 527 per Lord President Cooper. The purchase of freehold land for some purpose other than the receipt of income is not an investment: *Re Power, Public Trustee v Hastings* [1947] Ch 572, [1947] 2 All ER 282. As to the mode of investment see **TRUSTS AND POWERS** vol 98 (2013) PARA 448.

5 *Re Whiteley, Whiteley v Learoyd* (1886) 33 ChD 347 at 353, CA, per Cotton LJ; affd sub nom *Learoyd v Whiteley* (1887) 12 App Cas 727 at 733, HL, per Lord Watson. As to consent and discretion in relation to investment see **TRUSTS AND POWERS** vol 98 (2013) PARA 472.

6 *Cowan v Scargill* [1985] Ch 270 at 287–288, [1984] 2 All ER 750 per Megarry V-C.

7 *Harries v Church Comrs for England* [1993] 2 All ER 300, [1992] 1 WLR 1241.

419. Total return investment by charities. The Charities Act 2011 makes provision by which funds held on permanent endowment under the trusts of a charity may be freed from the restrictions applicable to them regarding the balance between capital and income, and thereby enable them to spend capital which they would otherwise be prevented from spending. This is known as the total return approach[1].

Under certain circumstances[2], the charity trustees[3] may resolve that the available endowment fund[4] of the charity[5], or a portion of it[6] (1) should be invested without the need to maintain a balance between capital and income returns[7]; and (2) accordingly, should be freed from the restrictions with respect to expenditure of capital that apply to it[8].

The circumstances are that the trustees must be satisfied that it is in the interests of the charity that regulations made by the Charity Commission[9] should apply in place of the restrictions mentioned in head (2) above[10]. Accordingly, while such a resolution has effect, the regulations apply in replace of the restrictions[11].

In pursuance of the provisions described above, the Commission may by regulations make provision about:

(a) resolutions[12],

(b) investment of relevant funds[13] as mentioned in head (1) above, and expenditure from such a fund[14], and

(c) the steps that must be taken by charity trustees in respect of a fund, or portion of a fund, in the event of a resolution ceasing to have effect[15].

1 See the Charities Act 2011 ss 104A, 104B (added by the Trusts (Capital and Income) Act 2013 s 4). The term 'total return' is not used in the primary legislation, other than in the marginal notes to both the amending and the amended provisions; however, this is the term generally used to describe the investment allowed by these provisions, and is used throughout the regulations made by the Charity Commission referred to in text and note 9.

'Total return' in those regulations means the whole of the investment return received by a charity from a relevant fund, regardless of when it has arisen; 'total return approach to investment' means an approach to investment which gives trustees flexibility in the way they allocate the total return arising from the trust for investment between the trust for application and the trust for investment: see the Charities (Total Return) Regulations 2013 reg 2; and note 9.

2 See text and notes 9, 10.

3 As to the meaning of 'charity trustees' see PARA 255.

4 'Available endowment fund', in relation to a charity, means the whole of the charity's permanent endowment if it is all subject to the same trusts; or any part of its permanent endowment which is subject to any particular trusts that are different from those to which any other part is subject: Charities Act 2011 s 104A(5) (as added: see note 1).

A charity is deemed for the purposes of the Charities Act 2011 to have a permanent endowment unless all property held for the purposes of the charity may be expended for those purposes without distinction between capital and income: s 353(3). As to the meaning of 'permanent endowment' see PARA 217 note 1.

5 As to the meaning of 'charity' see PARA 1.

6 Charities Act 2011 s 104A(1), (2) (as added: see note 1).

7 Charities Act 2011 s 104A(2)(a) (as added: see note 1).

8 Charities Act 2011 s 104A(2)(b) (as added: see note 1).

9 As to the Charity Commission's power to make such regulations see the Charities Act 2011 s 104B (as added: see note 1). As to the Charity Commission see PARAS 543–578. Any such regulations must be published by the Commission in such manner as it thinks fit: s 104B(5) (as added: see note 1).

Regulations of the Charity Commission are not made by statutory instrument, but are published by the Commission. For the regulations published in pursuance of this provision see the Charities (Total Return) Regulations 2013 (available, at the date at which this volume states the law, on the government website), which came into effect on 1 January 2014.

10 Charities Act 2011 s 104A(3) (as added: see note 1).

11 Charities Act 2011 s 104A(4) (as added: see note 1).

12 Charities Act 2011 s 104B(1)(a) (as added: see note 1). Such regulations under this head may, in particular: (1) specify steps that must be taken by charity trustees before passing a resolution; (2) make provision about the variation and revocation of such a resolution; (3) require charity trustees to notify the Commission of the passing, variation or revocation of such a resolution; and (4) specify circumstances in which such a resolution is to cease to have effect: s 104B(2) (as so added).

13 'Relevant fund' means a fund, or portion of a fund, in respect of which a resolution under the Charities Act 2011 s 104A(2) has effect, and includes the returns from the investment of the fund or portion: s 104B(6) (as added: see note 1).

14 Charities Act 2011 s 104B(1)(b) (as added: see note 1). Regulations under this head may, in particular (1) make provision requiring a relevant fund to be invested, and the returns from that investment to be allocated, in such a way as to maintain (so far as practicable) the long-term capital value of the fund, (2) make provision about the taking of advice by charity trustees in connection with the investment of, and expenditure from, a relevant fund, (3) confer on the charity trustees of a relevant fund a power (subject to such restrictions as may be specified in the regulations) to accumulate income, (4) make provision about expenditure from a relevant fund (including by imposing limits on expenditure and specifying circumstances in which expenditure requires the Commission's consent), and (5) require charity trustees to report to the Commission on the investment of, and expenditure from, a relevant fund: s 104B(3) (as so added).

A power to accumulate income conferred by regulations under s 104B(1)(b) or (c) (see text and note 15) is not subject to the Perpetuities and Accumulations Act 2009 s 14(3) (certain powers to accumulate income to cease to have effect after 21 years: see PARA 145): Charities Act 2011 s 104B(4) (as so added).

15 Charities Act 2011 s 104B(1)(b) (as added: see note 1). See also s 104B(4); and note 14.

420. Statutory general power of investment. The powers to make specified authorised investments given to trustees under the Trustee Investment Act 1961 have been largely repealed[1]. Under the Trustee Act 2000, a trustee may make any kind of investment that he could make if he were absolutely entitled to the assets of the trust[2]. This statutory power is called the 'general power of investment'[3]. The general power of investment does not permit a trustee to make investments in land other than in loans secured on land[4]. A person invests in a loan secured on land if he has rights under any contract under which one person provides another with credit[5] and the obligation of the borrower to repay is secured on land[6]. An investment for these purposes does not include an asset from which no profit or income is expected[7].

1 See PARA 423. As to the powers of investment under the Trustee Investments Act 1961 see PARA 423 et seq; and **TRUSTS AND POWERS** vol 98 (2013) PARA 458 et seq. As to total return investment schemes see PARA 419.
2 See the Trustee Act 2000 s 3(1); and **TRUSTS AND POWERS** vol 98 (2013) PARA 453. As to statutory powers of investment under the Trustee Act 2000 see further **TRUSTS AND POWERS** vol 98 (2013) PARA 453 et seq. Part II (ss 3–7), Pt III (ss 8–10) and Pt IV (ss 11–27) do not apply to (1) trustees of authorised unit trusts (s 37(1)); (2) trustees managing a fund under a common investment scheme made, or having effect as if made, under the Charities Act 2011 s 96 (see PARA 426), other than such a fund the trusts of which provide that property is not to be transferred to the fund except by or on behalf of a charity the trustees of which are the trustees appointed to manage the fund (Trustee Act 2000 s 38(a)); or (3) trustees managing a fund under a common deposit scheme made, or having effect as if made, under the Charities Act 2011 s 100 (see PARA 427) (Trustee Act 2000 s 38(b)): see **TRUSTS AND POWERS** vol 98 (2013) PARA 453.
3 See the Trustee Act 2000 s 3(2); and **TRUSTS AND POWERS** vol 98 (2013) PARA 453.
4 See the Trustee Act 2000 s 3(3); and **TRUSTS AND POWERS** vol 98 (2013) PARA 453. As to the power to acquire freehold and leasehold land see s 8; and **TRUSTS AND POWERS** vol 98 (2013) PARA 475.
5 'Credit' includes any cash loan or other financial accommodation: Trustee Act 2000 s 3(5). 'Cash' includes money in any form: s 3(6).
6 See the Trustee Act 2000 s 3(4); and **TRUSTS AND POWERS** vol 98 (2013) PARA 453.
7 See the cases cited in PARA 418 note 4.

421. Application of the general power of investment. The general power of investment is in addition to powers conferred on trustees otherwise than by the Trustee Act 2000, but is subject to any restriction or exclusion imposed by the trust instrument or by any enactment or any provision of subordinate legislation[1].

The provisions relating to the general power of investment introduced by the Trustee Act 2000[2] apply in relation to trusts whether created before or after its commencement on 1 February 2001[3]. However, no provision relating to the powers of a trustee contained in an instrument made before 3 August 1961[4] is to be treated as restricting or excluding[5] the general power of investment[6]. A provision contained in a trust instrument made before 1 February 2001 which has effect under the Trustee Investment Act 1961[7] as a power to invest under that Act or confers power to invest under that Act is to be treated as conferring the general power of investment on a trustee[8].

Common investment funds for charities and common deposit funds[9] for charities fall outside the provisions dealing with the statutory general power of investment[10].

1 See the Trustee Act 2000 s 6(1); and **TRUSTS AND POWERS** vol 98 (2013) PARA 453. For these purposes, an enactment or a provision of subordinate legislation is not to be regarded as being, or as being part of, a trust instrument: s 6(2).
2 Ie by the Trustee Act 2000 Pt II (ss 3–7): see **TRUSTS AND POWERS** vol 98 (2013) PARA 453 et seq.
3 See the Trustee Act 2000 s 7(1); Trustee Act 2000 (Commencement) Order 2001, SI 2001/49, art 2; and **TRUSTS AND POWERS** vol 98 (2013) PARA 453.
4 Ie the date of the commencement of the Trustee Investment Act 1961.
5 Ie under the Trustee Act 2000 s 6(1)(b): see **TRUSTS AND POWERS** vol 98 (2013) PARA 453.
6 See the Trustee Act 2000 s 7(2); and **TRUSTS AND POWERS** vol 98 (2013) PARA 453.
7 Ie under the Trustee Investments Act 1961 s 3(2): see PARA 423; and **TRUSTS AND POWERS** vol 98 (2013) PARA 453.

8 See the Trustee Act 2000 s 7(3); and TRUSTS AND POWERS vol 98 (2013) PARA 453.
9 Ie under the Charities Act 2011 ss 96, 100: see PARAS 426–427.
10 See the Trustee Act 2000 s 38; PARA 420 note 2; and TRUSTS AND POWERS vol 98 (2013) PARA 453.

422. Exercising skill and care in investment. When exercising the general power of investment or any other power of investment, however conferred, and when carrying out duties relating to the exercise of a power of investment or to the review of investments[1], trustees are under a duty to exercise such skill and care as is reasonable in the circumstances[2].

Further, in exercising any power of investment, a trustee must have regard to the standard investment criteria[3]. The standard investment criteria, in relation to a trust, are:

(1) the suitability to the trust of investments of the same kind as any particular investment proposed to be made or retained and of that particular investment as an investment of that kind[4]; and
(2) the need for diversification of investments of the trust, in so far as is appropriate to the circumstances of the trust[5].

Before exercising any power of investment, the trustee must, unless the exception applies[6], seek proper advice[7] about the way in which, having regard to the standard investment criteria, the powers ought to be exercised[8].

A trustee must from time to time review the investments of the trust and consider whether, having regard to the standard investment criteria, they ought to be varied[9]. When reviewing the investments of the trust, a trustee must, unless the exception applies[10], obtain and consider proper advice about whether, having regard to the standard investment criteria, the investments ought to be varied[11].

1 Ie under the Trustee Act 2000 ss 4, 5: see TRUSTS AND POWERS vol 98 (2013) PARAS 454–455.
2 See the Trustee Act 2000 ss 1, 2, Sch 1; and TRUSTS AND POWERS vol 98 (2013) PARAS 389–390.
3 See the Trustee Act 2000 s 4(1); and TRUSTS AND POWERS vol 98 (2013) PARA 454.
4 See the Trustee Act 2000 s 4(3)(a); and TRUSTS AND POWERS vol 98 (2013) PARA 454.
5 See the Trustee Act 2000 s 4(3)(b); and TRUSTS AND POWERS vol 98 (2013) PARA 454.
6 The exception is that a trustee need not obtain such advice if he reasonably concludes that in all the circumstances it is unnecessary or inappropriate to do so: Trustee Act 2000 s 5(3).
7 As to proper advice for the purposes of the Trustee Act 2000 s 5 see s 5(4); and TRUSTS AND POWERS vol 98 (2013) PARA 455.
8 See the Trustee Act 2000 s 5(1); and TRUSTS AND POWERS vol 98 (2013) PARA 455.
9 See the Trustee Act 2000 s 4(2); and TRUSTS AND POWERS vol 98 (2013) PARA 454.
10 See note 6.
11 See the Trustee Act 2000 s 5(2); and TRUSTS AND POWERS vol 98 (2013) PARA 455.

423. General investment powers under the Trustee Investment Act 1961. The powers to make specified authorised investments given to trustees under the Trustee Investment Act 1961 have been largely repealed and replaced by the broad general power of investment under the Trustee Act 2000[1], but certain provisions still have effect either in so far as they are applied by or under any other enactment or in so far as they relate to a trustee having a power of investment conferred on him under an enactment passed before 3 August 1961[2] and which has not been amended[3] by the Trustee Act 2000[4].

Trustees of charitable trusts have the same powers of investment as private trustees. Except in so far as they may be limited by any statutory provision, whenever made, or by express provision in any other instrument made after 3 August 1961[5], their powers and duties are laid down and regulated by the Trustee Investment Act 1961, but those statutory powers are in addition to any other power of investment given to the trustees[6].

Where property is held by trustees as an investment, the trustees should normally seek to obtain therefrom the maximum return, whether by way of income or capital growth, which is consistent with commercial prudence. In most case the best interests of the charity require that the trustees' choice of investments should be made solely on the basis of well-established investment criteria, including the need for diversification[7]. Exceptionally, if trustees are satisfied that investing in a company engaged in a particular type of business would conflict with the very objects their charity is seeking to achieve, they should not so invest[8]. Another exceptional case might be where trustees' holdings of particular investments might hamper a charity's work either by making potential recipients of aid unwilling to be helped because of the source of the charity's money, or by alienating some of those who support the charity financially. If the trust deed so provides, trustees would be entitled, or even required, to take into account non-financial criteria[9].

1 The Trustee Investments Act 1961 was generally repealed by the Trustee Act 2000 s 40(1), (3), Sch 2 Pt I para 1, Sch 4 Pt I. As to powers of investment under the Trustee Investments Act 1961 see further **TRUSTS AND POWERS** vol 98 (2013) PARA 458 et seq. As to the statutory powers of investment under the Trustee Act 2000 see PARAS 420–422; and **TRUSTS AND POWERS** vol 98 (2013) PARA 453 et seq.

2 Ie the date on which the Trustee Investment Act 1961 was passed.

3 Ie by the Trustee Act 2000 Sch 2.

4 See the Trustee Act 2000 Sch 2 Pt I para 1(1), (2). The Trustee Investments Act 1961 ss 1, 2, 5, 6, 12, 13 and 15 cease to have effect, except in so far as they are applied by or under any other enactment: Trustee Act 2000 Sch 2 Pt I para 1(1). The Trustee Investments Act 1961 s 3 and Schs 2, 3 cease to have effect, except in so far as they relate to a trustee having a power of investment conferred on him under an enactment which was passed before the passing of the Trustee Investment Act 1961, and which is not amended by the Trustee Act 2000 Sch 2: Sch 2 Pt I para 1(2). As to the Trustee Investments Act 1961 see **TRUSTS AND POWERS** vol 98 (2013) PARA 458 et seq.

5 See the Trustee Investments Act 1961 s 1; and **TRUSTS AND POWERS** vol 98 (2013) PARA 459 et seq.

6 See the Trustee Investments Act 1961 s 3; and **TRUSTS AND POWERS** vol 98 (2013) PARA 459 et seq. Guidance was given by the Charity Commissioners (now the Charity Commission) in the *Report of the Charity Commissioners for England and Wales for 1978* (HC Paper (1979–80) no 94) App G, and the *Report of the Charity Commissioners for England and Wales for 1985* (HC Paper (1985–86) no 391) paras 65–70.

The court has jurisdiction to widen the powers of investment of charitable trustees either by way of an administrative scheme (*Re Royal Society's Charitable Trusts* [1956] Ch 87, [1955] 3 All ER 14; *Re Royal Naval and Royal Marine Children's Homes, Portsmouth, Lloyds Bank Ltd v A-G* [1959] 2 All ER 716n, [1959] 1 WLR 755) or under the Trustee Act 1925 (see the Trustee Act 1925 s 57; *Re Shipwrecked Fishermen and Mariners' Royal Benevolent Society* [1959] Ch 220, [1958] 3 All ER 465; *Mason v Farbrother* [1983] 2 All ER 1078; and **TRUSTS AND POWERS** vol 98 (2013) PARA 646). Initially, the view of the courts was that the powers of investment given by the Trustee Investments Act 1961 should be taken to be prima facie sufficient, though there was power to act if a very special case was made out: *Re London University's Charitable Trusts* [1964] Ch 282, [1963] 3 All ER 859 (applying non-charity trust cases such as *Re Kolb's Will Trusts, Lloyds Bank Ltd v Ullman* [1962] Ch 531, [1961] 3 All ER 811; compromised on appeal 106 Sol Jo 669, CA); *Re Cooper's Settlement, Cooper v Cooper* [1962] Ch 826, [1961] 3 All ER 636. Subsequently it has been held that this principle is no longer applicable: *Trustees of the British Museum v A-G* [1984] 1 All ER 337, [1984] 1 WLR 418. Before the Charities Act 1960 the jurisdiction was sometimes used to permit the funds of several charitable trusts to be consolidated and managed together: *Re Royal Society's Charitable Trusts* [1956] Ch 87, [1955] 3 All ER 14.

7 Expert advice should be taken where appropriate. Due regard should be taken of the need to balance income against capital growth and the need to balance risk against return: *Harries v Church Comrs for England* [1993] 2 All ER 300, [1992] 1 WLR 1241. Note also the observations of Lord Templeman in *Hazell v Hammersmith and Fulham London Borough Council* [1992] 2 AC 1, [1991] 1 All ER 545, HL.

8 Eg cancer research charities investing in tobacco shares. It is very unlikely that this would disable the trustees from choosing a properly diversified portfolio.

9 *Harries v Church Comrs for England* [1993] 2 All ER 300, [1992] 1 WLR 1241. See also *Cowan v Scargill* [1985] Ch 270, [1984] 2 All ER 750 (a non-charity case).

424. Deposits in trustee savings banks. Under the Trustee Savings Bank Act 1981[1] the treasurer of any charitable or provident institution or society, or charitable donation or bequest for the maintenance, education, or benefit of the poor, could, subject to the statutory provisions restricting the amount of deposits, invest the trust funds in the funds of a trustee savings bank. The receipt of the treasurer, trustee, or other officer of the charitable or provident institution or society apparently authorised to require payment discharged the savings bank[2]. These provisions were repealed by the Trustee Savings Bank Act 1985[3], which reorganised trustee savings banks into companies incorporated under the Companies Acts, with savings in relation to funds already invested in the funds of a trustee savings bank and in relation to receipts[4].

1 Trustee Savings Banks Act 1981 s 29(1), consolidating earlier legislation (now repealed: see the text and notes 3–4).

2 Trustee Savings Bank Act 1981 s 29(2) (repealed).

3 See the Trustee Savings Banks Act 1985 s 7(3), Sch 4.

4 See the Trustee Savings Banks Act 1985 ss 4(3), (5), 7(3), Sch 4; Trustee Savings Banks Act 1985 (Appointed Day) (No 4) Order 1986, SI 1986/1223, arts 2(a), 8, 9, 12, Sch 1. See further FINANCIAL SERVICES AND INSTITUTIONS vol 49 (2008) PARA 809.

425. Investment in land. The Trustee Investments Act 1961 did not itself permit investment in land[1]. In the absence of an express power, the purchase of land may be authorised out of capital money arising on the sale of settled land[2], or it may be specially authorised by the Charity Commission[3].

However, under the Trustee Act 2000, trustees may acquire freehold or leasehold land as an investment, for occupation by a beneficiary or for any other reason[4].

1 It did permit investment in certain mortgages: see the Trustee Investments Act 1961 s 1, Sch 1 Pt II para 13; and TRUSTS AND POWERS vol 98 (2013) PARA 464. Section 1 was repealed, with savings, by the Trustee Act 2000: see PARA 423. As to the Trustee Investments Act 1961 see PARA 423; and TRUSTS AND POWERS vol 98 (2013) PARA 458 et seq.

2 See the Settled Land Act 1925 s 73(1)(x); and SETTLEMENTS vol 91 (2012) PARA 709.

3 Ie under the Charities Act 2011 s 105: see PARA 391. See the *Report of the Charity Commissioners for England and Wales for 1988* (HC Paper (1988–89) no 319) paras 73–75. As to the Charity Commission see PARAS 538–572.

4 See the Trustee Act 2000 ss 8–10; and TRUSTS AND POWERS vol 98 (2013) PARA 475.

426. Schemes to establish common investment funds. Under the Charities Act 2011, the court[1] and the Charity Commission[2] may by order[3] make and bring into effect schemes ('common investment schemes') to establish common investment funds providing[4]: (1) for property transferred to the fund by or on behalf of a charity[5] participating in the scheme to be invested under the control of the trustees managing the fund[6]; and (2) for the participating charities to be entitled, subject to the provisions of the scheme, to the capital and income of the fund in shares determined by reference to the amount or value of the property transferred to it by or on behalf of each of them and to the value of the fund at the time of the transfer[7].

Common investment schemes may be made on the application of any two or more charities[8]. Every charity has power to participate in common investment schemes as part of its investment powers, unless that power is excluded specifically by the trusts[9] of the charity[10]. Unless the scheme provides otherwise, the rights of a participating charity may not be assigned or charged[11].

Common investment schemes may be made in terms admitting any charity to participate, or may restrict the right to participate in any manner[12].

A common investment fund is deemed for all purposes to be a charity; and, until a day to be appointed, if the scheme only admits exempt charities[13] the fund is treated as an exempt charity[14].

A common investment scheme may make provision for, and for all matters connected with, the establishment, investment, management and winding up of the common investment fund, and may in particular include provision[15]:

(a) for remunerating persons appointed trustees to hold or manage the fund or any part of it, with or without provision authorising a person to receive the remuneration notwithstanding that he is also a charity trustee[16] of or trustee for a participating charity[17];
(b) for restricting the size of the fund, and for regulating as to time, amount or otherwise the right to transfer property to or withdraw it from the fund, and for enabling sums to be advanced out of the fund by way of loan to a participating charity pending the withdrawal of property from the fund by the charity[18];
(c) for enabling income to be withheld from distribution with a view to avoiding fluctuations in the amounts distributed, and generally for regulating distributions of income[19];
(d) for enabling money to be borrowed temporarily for the purpose of meeting payments to be made out of the funds[20];
(e) for enabling questions arising under the scheme as to the right of a charity to participate, or as to the rights of participating charities, or as to any other matter, to be conclusively determined by the decision of the trustees managing the fund or in any other manner[21];
(f) for regulating the accounts and information to be supplied to participating charities[22].

An application for the review of a decision of the Commission not to make a common investment scheme lies to the Tribunal at the instance of the Attorney General[23], the charity trustees of a charity which applied to the Commission for the scheme, the charity itself (if a body corporate) and any other person who is or may be affected by the decision[24]. The Tribunal has the power to quash the decision and, if appropriate, remit the matter to the Commission[25].

The Charity Commission has made regulations governing the content of annual reports of common investment funds[26].

1 As to the meaning of 'court' see PARA 177 note 12.
2 As to the Charity Commission see PARAS 543–578.
3 By order of the Commissioners dated 4 December 1962 a scheme was made establishing the Charities Official Investment Fund. The original scheme is printed in full in the *Report of the Charity Commissioners for England and Wales for 1962* (HC Paper (1963–64) no 17) pp 34–49, App B, and in Tudor on Charities (6th Edn, 1967) pp 721–735. It has been amended subsequently. As to the unification of trusts by specified universities and colleges under the Universities and Colleges (Trusts) Act 1943 see EDUCATION vol 36 (2011) PARA 827; and *Re Freeston's Charity, Sylvester v Master and Fellows of University College, Oxford* [1979] 1 All ER 51, [1978] 1 WLR 741, CA.
4 Charities Act 2011 s 96(1), (2).
5 As to the meaning of 'charity' see PARA 1.
6 Charities Act 2011 s 96(1)(a). As to the disapplication of the Trustee Act 2000 in relation to common investment schemes see PARA 420 note 2.
7 Charities Act 2011 s 96(1)(b).

8 Charities Act 2011 s 96(3). This means on the application of the trustees of two or more charitable trusts; the trustees may be the same: *Re London University's Charitable Trusts* [1964] Ch 282, [1963] 3 All ER 859 (decided under previous legislation).
9 As to the meaning of 'trusts' see PARA 218 note 5.
10 Charities Act 2011 s 99(2).
11 Charities Act 2011 s 99(1)(a). Trustees and persons concerned in the management of the fund are not required or entitled to take account of any trust or equity affecting participating charities or its property or rights: s 99(1)(b).
12 Charities Act 2011 s 97(1). A common investment scheme may also provide for Scottish recognised bodies or Northern Ireland charities to be admitted to participate in the scheme, in addition to the participating charities, to such extent as the trustees appointed to manage the fund may determine: see ss 97(2)–(4), 104.
13 As to exempt charities see PARAS 318–320.
14 Charities Act 2011 s 99(3). Until a day to be appointed, the classification of such funds under the Charities Act 2011 s 99(3) as exempt charities if they admit only charities which are themselves exempt, remains effective: see the Charities Act 2011 Sch 9 para 2. At the date at which this volume states the law, no such day had been appointed. See further *CC23: Exempt charities* (Charity Commission, September 2013) Annex 1 (available, at the date at which this volume states the law, on the government website). As to the Charity Commission's publications see PARA 547.

The Charities Act 2011 s 99(3) applies not only to the common investment funds established under the powers of s 96 but also to similar funds established under statutory powers for the exclusive benefit of charities by or under any enactment relating to any particular charities or class of charities: s 99(4).
15 Charities Act 2011 s 98(1). A common investment scheme, in addition to the provision for property to be transferred to the fund on the basis that the charity is entitled to a share in the capital and income of the fund, may include provision for enabling sums to be deposited by or on behalf of a charity on the basis that (subject to the provisions of the scheme) the charity is entitled to repayment of the sums deposited and to interest thereon at a rate determined by or under the scheme: s 98(2). Where a scheme makes any such provision it must also provide for excluding from the amount of capital and income to be shared between charities participating otherwise than by way of deposit such amounts (not exceeding the amounts properly attributable to the making of deposits) as are from time to time reasonably required in respect of the liabilities of the fund for the repayment of deposits and for the interest on deposits, including amounts required by way of reserve: s 98(3).
16 As to the meaning of 'charity trustees' see PARA 255.
17 Charities Act 2011 s 98(1)(a).
18 Charities Act 2011 s 98(1)(b).
19 Charities Act 2011 s 98(1)(c).
20 Charities Act 2011 s 98(1)(d).
21 Charities Act 2011 s 98(1)(e).
22 Charities Act 2011 s 98(1)(f).
23 As to the Tribunal see PARA 579 et seq. As to the Attorney General see PARAS 589, 596, 605 et seq; and **CONSTITUTIONAL AND ADMINISTRATIVE LAW** vol 20 (2014) PARA 273 et seq.
24 Charities Act 2011 s 319(2), Sch 6 Table Cols 1, 2. As to the meaning of 'person who is or may be affected' within the meaning of Sch 6 see PARA 317 note 8.
25 Charities Act 2011 Sch 6 Table Col 3.
26 See the Charities (Annual Returns) (Common Investment Funds) Regulations 2008. Regulations of the Charity Commission are not made by statutory instrument, but are published by the Commission and are available, at the date at which this volume states the law, on the government website.

427. Schemes to establish common deposit funds. The court[1] or the Charity Commission[2] may by order make and bring into effect schemes ('common deposit schemes') for the establishment of common deposit funds under trusts which provide[3]: (1) for sums to be deposited by or on behalf of a charity[4] participating in the scheme and invested under the control of trustees appointed to manage the fund[5]; and (2) for any such charity to be entitled to repayment of any sums so deposited and to interest thereon at a rate determined under the scheme[6].

Common deposit schemes may be made on the application of any two or more charities[7]. Every charity has power to participate in common deposit schemes as part of its investment powers, unless that power is excluded specifically by the trusts[8] of the charity[9]. Unless the scheme provides otherwise, the rights of a participating charity may not be assigned or charged[10].

Common deposit schemes may be made in terms admitting any charity to participate, or may restrict the right to participate in any manner[11]. A common deposit fund is deemed for all purposes to be a charity; and, until a day to be appointed, if the scheme only admits exempt charities[12] the fund is treated as an exempt charity[13].

A common deposit scheme may make provision for, and for all matters connected with, the establishment, investment, management and winding up of the common deposit fund, and may in particular include provision[14]:

(a) for remunerating persons appointed trustees to hold or manage the fund or any part of it, with or without provision authorising a person to receive the remuneration notwithstanding that he is also a charity trustee[15] of or trustee for a participating charity[16];

(b) for regulating as to time, amount or otherwise the right to repayment of sums deposited in the fund[17];

(c) for authorising a part of the income for any year to be credited to a reserve account maintained for the purpose of counteracting any losses accruing to the fund, and generally for regulating the manner in which the rate of interest on deposits is to be determined from time to time[18];

(d) for enabling money to be borrowed temporarily for the purpose of meeting payments to be made out of the funds[19];

(e) for enabling questions arising under the scheme as to the right of a charity to participate, or as to the rights of participating charities, or as to any other matter, to be conclusively determined by the decision of the trustees managing the fund or in any other manner[20];

(f) for regulating the accounts and information to be supplied to participating charities[21].

An application for the review of a decision of the Commission not to make a common deposit scheme lies to the Tribunal at the instance of the Attorney General[22], the charity trustees of a charity which applied to the Commission for the scheme, the charity itself (if a body corporate) and any other person who is or may be affected by the decision[23]. The Tribunal has the power to quash the decision and, if appropriate, remit the matter to the Commission[24].

1 As to the meaning of 'court' see PARA 177 note 12.
2 As to the Charity Commission see PARAS 543–578.
3 Charities Act 2011 s 100(1), (2).
4 As to the meaning of 'charity' see PARA 1.
5 Charities Act 2011 s 100(1)(a). As to the disapplication of the Trustee Act 2000 in relation to common deposit schemes see PARA 420 note 2.
6 Charities Act 2011 s 100(1)(b).
7 Charities Act 2011 s 100(3).
8 As to the meaning of 'trusts' see PARA 218 note 5.
9 Charities Act 2011 s 103(2).
10 Charities Act 2011 s 103(1)(a). Trustees and persons concerned in the management of the fund are not required or entitled to take account of any trust or equity affecting participating charities or its property or rights: s 103(1)(b).
11 Charities Act 2011 s 101(1). They may also provide for Scottish recognised bodies or Northern Ireland charities to be admitted to participate in the scheme, in addition to the participating charities, to such extent as the trustees appointed to manage the fund may determine: see ss 101, (3), (4), 104.

12 As to exempt charities see PARA 318.
13 Charities Act 2011 s 103(3). Until a day to be appointed, the classification of such funds as exempt charities if they admit only charities which are themselves exempt, remains effective: see the Charities Act 2011 Sch 9 para 2. At the date at which this volume states the law, no such day had been appointed. See further *CC23: Exempt charities* (Charity Commission, September 2013) Annex 1 (available, at the date at which this volume states the law, on the government website). As to the Charity Commission's publications see PARA 547.

This applies not only to the common deposit funds, but also to similar funds established under statutory powers for the exclusive benefit of charities by or under any enactment relating to any particular charities or class of charities: Charities Act 2011 s 103(4).
14 Charities Act 2011 s 102.
15 As to the meaning of 'charity trustees' see PARA 1 note 10.
16 Charities Act 2011 s 102(a).
17 Charities Act 2011 s 102(b).
18 Charities Act 2011 s 102(c).
19 Charities Act 2011 s 102(d).
20 Charities Act 2011 s 102(e).
21 Charities Act 2011 s 102(f).
22 As to the Tribunal see PARA 579 et seq. As to the Attorney General see PARAS 589, 596, 605 et seq; and **CONSTITUTIONAL AND ADMINISTRATIVE LAW** vol 20 (2014) PARA 273 et seq.
23 Charities Act 2011 s 319(2), Sch 6 Table Cols 1, 2. As to the meaning of 'person who is or may be affected' within the meaning of Sch 6 see PARA 317 note 8.
24 Charities Act 2011 Sch 6 Table Col 3.

(iii) Ex Gratia Payments

428. Circumstances in which payments may be made. Notwithstanding the rule that trust property may only be applied in accordance with the terms of the trust[1], there are cases in which trustees of property for charitable purposes may be authorised to make payments out of the trust property to persons with a moral but no legal claim to the property[2].

Just as trustees have power to compromise claims[3] and the court, acting on the advice of the Attorney General, may relieve charity trustees from the obligation to make good in full breaches of trust for which they are answerable[4], so, where by mistake or owing to some legal technicality a charity has received more than was apparently intended[5], the charity or the trustees may apply for authority to pay out some part of the fund to the persons who have a moral claim to it[6]. The charity or the trustees will not necessarily be authorised to pay out as much as they wish[7].

1 See PARA 333.
2 *Re Snowden, Shackleton v Eddy, Re Henderson, Henderson v A-G* [1970] Ch 700, [1969] 3 All ER 208; but not where doing so would contravene an Act of Parliament: *A-G v Trustees of the British Museum (Commission for Looted Art in Europe intervening)* [2005] EWHC 1089, [2005] Ch 397, [2005] 3 WLR 396. See also *Trustees of the Presbyterian Church in Ireland v A-G for Northern Ireland* [2011] NICh 4 (23 March 2011, unreported) (Presbyterian Church given authority to make disbursement to a mutual society in administration on the basis that it owed a moral obligation to investors suffering hardship, whose membership of the mutual society depended on being a member of the Church).

See further *CC7: Ex gratia payments by charities* (Charity Commission, May 2014) (available, at the date at which this volume states the law, on the government website). As to the Charity Commission's publications see PARA 547.
3 See the Trustee Act 1925 s 15(f); and **TRUSTS AND POWERS** vol 98 (2013) PARA 518. For further protection, they may apply to the court to sanction the compromise. The court will take into account the moral merits of the claim in question: see *Re Snowden, Shackleton v Eddy, Re Henderson, Henderson v A-G* [1970] Ch 700 at 709, [1969] 3 All ER 208 at 213 per Cross J.
4 See *A-G v Brettingham* (1840) 3 Beav 91 at 95 per Lord Langdale MR; *A-G v Exeter Corpn* (1827) 2 Russ 362; *A-G v Pretyman* (1841) 4 Beav 462; *Re Snowden, Shackleton v Eddy, Re Henderson, Henderson v A-G* [1970] Ch 700 at 710, [1969] 3 All ER 208 at 213 per Cross J.

As to the Attorney General see PARAS 589, 596, 605 et seq; and **CONSTITUTIONAL AND ADMINISTRATIVE LAW** vol 20 (2014) PARA 273 et seq.

5 There might be other circumstances, as where a testator had broken a solemn but unenforceable promise to give the property to an individual: see eg *National Provincial Bank Ltd v Moore* (1967) 111 Sol Jo 357. As to this type of case see *Re Snowden, Shackleton v Eddy, Re Henderson, Henderson v A-G* [1970] Ch 700 at 710, [1969] 3 All ER 208 at 214 per Cross J.

6 *Re Snowden, Shackleton v Eddy, Re Henderson, Henderson v A-G* [1970] Ch 700, [1969] 3 All ER 208. The trustees cannot be compelled to apply.

7 See the order made in *Re Snowden, Shackleton v Eddy, Re Henderson, Henderson v A-G* [1970] Ch 700, [1969] 3 All ER 208.

429. Procedure prior to the Charities Act 1992. The procedure prior to the Charities Act 1992 was that if the property was that of a specific charity, application would be made in the first instance to the Charity Commissioners (now the Charity Commission)[1]; if it was held on trust for charitable purposes generally the application would first be made to the Treasury Solicitor[2]. After an investigation into the facts a report might be made to the Attorney General, who might decide himself or might apply ex parte to the court for guidance[3]. This procedure has not been abolished, but it is thought that application will now normally be made under the statutory provisions introduced by the Charities Act 1992 and re-enacted in the Charities Act 2011[4].

1 As to the Charity Commissioners see PARA 543.

2 As to the Treasury Solicitor see **CONSTITUTIONAL AND ADMINISTRATIVE LAW** vol 20 (2014) PARA 281.

3 This procedure was indicated as appropriate in *Re Snowden, Shackleton v Eddy, Re Henderson, Henderson v A-G* [1970] Ch 700 at 711, [1969] 3 All ER 208 at 214 per Cross J. It has been followed since, though it may be modified in the light of experience. Reference may be made to the annual reports of the Charity Commissioners (eg *Report of the Charity Commissioners for England and Wales for 1970* (HC Paper (1970–71) no 409) p 30 and the *Report of the Charity Commissioners for England and Wales for 1976* (HC Paper (1976–77) no 389) paras 113–116 which contain an example of an ex gratia payment authorised by the Attorney General on a proposal by the Commissioners) for guidance on this matter. As to the Attorney General see PARAS 589, 596, 605 et seq; and **CONSTITUTIONAL AND ADMINISTRATIVE LAW** vol 20 (2014) PARA 273 et seq.

4 See the Charities Act 2011 s 106 (see PARA 430), which re-enacts the Charities Act 1960 s 23A (added by the Charities Act 1992 s 17; but now repealed).

430. Power of Charity Commission to authorise ex gratia payments. The Charity Commission[1] may by order[2] exercise the same power as is exercisable by the Attorney General to authorise charity trustees[3] to (1) make any application of property of the charity, or (2) waive to any extent, on behalf of the charity, its entitlement to receive any property[4]. This may be done where the charity trustees otherwise have no power to do so, but in all the circumstances regard themselves as under a moral obligation to do so[5].

The power is exercisable under the supervision of, and in accordance with any directions given by, the Attorney General[6], which may, in particular, require the Commission, in such circumstances as are specified in the directions, to refrain from exercising the power, or to consult the Attorney General before exercising it[7]. Where an application is made to the Commission for it to exercise that power in a case where it is not precluded from doing so by any such directions, but it considers that it would nevertheless be desirable for the application to be entertained by the Attorney General rather than by them, the Commission must refer the application to the Attorney General[8]. Where, in the case of any such application, the Commission determines the application by refusing to authorise charity trustees to take any action under these provisions[9], that refusal does not preclude the Attorney General, on an application subsequently made to him by the trustees, from authorising the trustees to take that action[10].

1 As to the Charity Commission see PARAS 543–578.
2 As to the making or orders generally see the Charities Act 2011 s 347; and PARA 590.
3 As to the meaning of 'charity trustees' see PARA 255. As to the Attorney General see PARAS 589, 596, 605 et seq; and CONSTITUTIONAL AND ADMINISTRATIVE LAW vol 20 (2014) PARA 273 et seq.
4 Charities Act 2011 s 106(1), (2). See further *CC7: Ex gratia payments by charities* (Charity Commission, May 2014) (available, at the date at which this volume states the law, on the government website). As to the Charity Commission's publications see PARA 547.
5 Charities Act 2011 s 106(1)(a), (b).
6 Charities Act 2011 s 106(3).
7 Charities Act 2011 s 106(4).
8 Charities Act 2011 s 106(5).
9 Ie under the Charities Act 2011 s 106(2): see the text and note 4.
10 Charities Act 2011 s 106(6).

(iv) Rating

A. MANDATORY RELIEF FOR CHARITIES

(A) Right to Relief

431. Scope of relief in general. Before new valuation lists came into force in 1956 there was a divergence between the law and practice with regard to the rating of charities. At law, it had long been established that charitable organisations were rateable in respect of the hereditaments they occupied[1], but in practice rating authorities frequently undervalued the hereditaments of charitable and kindred bodies, and by this means those bodies paid only reduced or nominal rates. When rating authorities[2] ceased to be responsible for preparing and amending valuation lists[3] this divergence of law and practice was ended, and in the valuation lists which came into force in 1956 the valuation officers of the Inland Revenue Commissioners[4] assessed such hereditaments at their full value[5].

The Local Government Finance Act 1988, which repealed the General Rate Act 1967, abolished domestic rates and replaced them with a system of community charges[6]. So far as non-domestic rates were concerned a new form of rating was set up, though it is broadly similar to the system it replaced.

Under the Local Government Finance Act 1988, ratepayers that are charities[7] or trustees for a charity qualify for a reduction by 80 per cent of the amount the ratepayer would otherwise have to pay[8] for any occupied hereditament[9] where (1) the ratepayer is a charity or trustees for a charity; and (2) the hereditament is wholly or mainly used for charitable purposes[10] (whether of that charity or of that and other charities)[11]. Previously a similar relief applied to any unoccupied hereditament where (a) the ratepayer is a charity or trustees for a charity; and (b) it appears that when next in use the hereditament will be wholly or mainly used for charitable purposes (whether of that charity or of that and other charities)[12]; however, such unoccupied hereditaments are now zero-rated and thus no rates are payable[13]. Certain hereditaments, namely places of religious worship and property used for the disabled, are wholly exempt from non-domestic rating[14].

1 *Mersey Docks v Cameron, Jones v Mersey Docks* (1865) 11 HL Cas 443; *London Corpn v Stratton* (1875) LR 7 HL 477.
2 Rating authorities have been replaced by billing authorities. As to billing authorities see LOCAL GOVERNMENT FINANCE vol 70 (2012) PARA 54. As to the meaning of 'hereditament' see LOCAL GOVERNMENT FINANCE vol 70 (2012) PARA 82 et seq.

3 Ie by virtue of the Local Government Act 1948 s 33 (repealed). As to valuation lists see LOCAL GOVERNMENT FINANCE vol 70 (2012) PARA 168 et seq.
4 The Inland Revenue Commissioners have been replaced by the Commissioners for Revenue and Customs: see INCOME TAXATION vol 58 (2014) PARA 33. As to the functions of the valuation officers of the Commissioners for Revenue and Customs see LOCAL GOVERNMENT FINANCE vol 70 (2012) PARA 55.
5 As to the history of the rating legislation see LOCAL GOVERNMENT FINANCE vol 70 (2012) PARA 51.
6 Domestic rates were abolished by the Local Government Finance Act 1988 and replaced by the community charge, itself replaced by the council tax in 1993: see the Local Government Finance Act 1992; and LOCAL GOVERNMENT FINANCE vol 70 (2012) PARAS 1, 51. As to the exemption from council tax of a dwelling owned by a body established for charitable purposes only, which is unoccupied and has been so for a period of less than six months, and was last occupied in furtherance of the objects of the charity see the Local Government Finance Act 1992 s 4; the Council Tax (Exempt Dwellings) Order 1992, SI 1992/558, art 3 Class B; *Ealing London Borough Council v Notting Hill Housing Trust* [2015] EWHC 161 (Admin); and LOCAL GOVERNMENT FINANCE vol 70 (2012) PARA 306.
7 As to the meaning of 'charity' for these purposes see PARA 433 note 2.
8 See the Local Government Finance Act 1988 s 43(5), (6)(a); and PARA 433.
9 As to the meaning of 'hereditament' see LOCAL GOVERNMENT FINANCE vol 70 (2012) PARA 82 et seq. As to rateable occupation see LOCAL GOVERNMENT FINANCE vol 70 (2012) PARA 61 et seq. As to occupation by a charity see PARA 434.
10 As to the meaning of 'wholly or mainly used for charitable purposes' see PARA 435.
11 See the Local Government Finance Act 1988 s 43(5), (6)(a); and PARA 433.
12 See the Local Government Finance Act 1988 s 45(5), (6) (repealed).
13 See the Local Government Finance Act 1988 s 45A; and PARA 436.
14 See the Local Government Finance Act 1988 s 51, Sch 5 paras 11, 16; and LOCAL GOVERNMENT FINANCE vol 70 (2012) PARAS 90–91, 101.

432. Establishment of right to relief. Under the General Rate Act 1967 (now repealed)[1], the right to charity rating relief could be established by resisting proceedings in the magistrates' court brought by the rating authority[2] for non-payment of rates[3] or by proceedings in the High Court for a declaration[4]. It would seem that both procedures are still available under the Local Government Finance Act 1988[5].

1 As to the history of the rating legislation see LOCAL GOVERNMENT FINANCE vol 70 (2012) PARA 51.
2 See eg *Meriden RDC v White* [1972] RA 530, DC; *Ealing London Borough Council v Ladyeholme Co Ltd* [1974] RA 399; *Royal Society for the Protection of Birds v Hornsea UDC* [1975] RA 26, DC.
3 Then by means of an application for a distress warrant, now by means of an application for a liability order (as to which see LOCAL GOVERNMENT FINANCE vol 70 (2012) PARA 246 et seq).
4 This was done in eg *Over Seventies Housing Association v Westminster City Council* [1974] RA 247; *Oxfam v Birmingham City District Council* [1976] AC 126, [1975] 2 All ER 289, HL; *Forces Help Society and Lord Roberts Workshops v Canterbury City Council* [1979] RA 68. As to declaratory orders see JUDICIAL REVIEW vol 61 (2010) PARA 716 et seq.
5 A judicial review of a magistrates' court decision, in making a liability order in respect of non-domestic rates that were unpaid on the basis of a claim for charitable relief, was made in *R (on the application of Tower of Refuge Ministry) v Highbury Corner Magistrates' Court* [2004] EWHC 2372 (Admin), [2004] RVR 269, [2004] All ER (D) 414 (Jul) (authority had been entitled to withdraw mandatory relief in the light of the use of a false charity number and lack of evidence that the claimant was a charitable organisation).

(B) Occupied Hereditaments

433. Calculating the amount payable for hereditaments in the local rating list occupied by charities. Where on the day concerned the ratepayer[1] is a charity[2] or trustees for a charity and the occupied hereditament is wholly or mainly used for charitable purposes[3] (whether of that charity or of that and other charities)[4], the chargeable amount[5] for a chargeable day[6] is calculated by multiplying the rateable value[7] by the non-domestic rating multiplier[8] for the financial year, and dividing the product by five times the number of days in the financial year[9]. The result is a reduction by 80 per cent of the amount the ratepayer would have had to pay were he not entitled to the reduction[10].

1 Ie the person subject to the non-domestic rate of a hereditament in a local rating list: see the Local Government Finance Act 1988 s 43(1). As to the meaning of 'hereditament' see LOCAL GOVERNMENT FINANCE vol 70 (2012) PARA 82 et seq. As to the liability to the non-domestic rate for occupied hereditaments in the local non-domestic rating lists see LOCAL GOVERNMENT FINANCE vol 70 (2012) PARA 109. As to rating lists see LOCAL GOVERNMENT FINANCE vol 70 (2012) PARA 168 et seq.

2 For these purposes, 'charity' means an institution or other organisation established for charitable purposes only or any persons administering a trust established for charitable purposes only: Local Government Finance Act 1988 s 67(10). For the general definition of a charity see PARA 1. Registration under the charities legislation is conclusive that the organisation is a charity for the purposes of the relief from rates: see eg *Wynn v Skegness UDC* [1966] 3 All ER 336, [1967] 1 WLR 52, ChD; *Finch v Poplar Borough Council* (1967) 66 LGR 324, [1968] RA 208, ChD; *Meriden RDC v White* [1972] RA 530, 17 RRC 187. See also LOCAL GOVERNMENT FINANCE vol 70 (2012) PARA 122.

The cases cited in this paragraph which were decided prior to the coming into force of the Local Government Finance Act 1988 must now be considered in relation to the non-domestic rating provisions in Pt III (ss 41–67) (see LOCAL GOVERNMENT FINANCE vol 70 (2012) PARA 50 et seq). As to the history of the rating legislation see LOCAL GOVERNMENT FINANCE vol 70 (2012) PARA 51.

3 Local Government Finance Act 1988 s 43(5), (6)(a) (substituted by the Local Government Act 2003 s 64(1)). As to the meaning of 'wholly or mainly used for charitable purposes' see PARA 435. As to occupation by a charity see PARA 434.

4 See the Local Government Finance Act 1988 ss 43(6)(a), 67(7) (amended by the Rating (Empty Properties) Act 2007 Sch 1 para 5).

5 The chargeable amount for occupied property is calculated by the formula in the Local Government Finance Act 1988 s 43(5).

6 A 'chargeable day' is one which falls within the financial year and for which the ratepayer's name is shown in the list: Local Government Finance Act 1988 s 54(3). A 'financial year' is a period of 12 months beginning with 1 April: s 145(3).

7 The 'rateable value' is the value entered in the local non-domestic rating list under s 42(4): s 44(2) (amended by the Local Government and Housing Act 1989 Sch 5 paras 1, 21, 79(3), Sch 12 Pt II).

8 Local Government Finance Act 1988 s 44(4). Where the billing authority is a special authority, this figure is the authority's non-domestic rating multiplier for the financial year: s 44(5) (amended by the Local Government Finance Act 1992 Sch 13 para 61). The multiplier is a uniform amount applying to every billing authority area and is fixed annually by the Secretary of State using the method set out in the Local Government Finance Act 1988 s 56(2), Sch 7: see LOCAL GOVERNMENT FINANCE vol 70 (2012) PARA 136. As to billing authorities see LOCAL GOVERNMENT FINANCE vol 70 (2012) PARA 54; and as to special authorities see LOCAL GOVERNMENT FINANCE vol 70 (2012) PARA 109.

9 Local Government Finance Act 1988 s 44(6). The formula is set out in s 43(5). See further LOCAL GOVERNMENT FINANCE vol 70 (2012) PARA 122.

10 As to the scope of relief in general see PARA 431.

434. Occupation by a charity. Charities registered under the Charities Act 2011[1] are conclusively presumed to be charities for the purposes of the rating legislation[2]. However, a body whose application to be registered as a charity has been rejected by the Charity Commission[3] may still contend that it is a charity for the purposes of the rating legislation[4]. For rating purposes a charity occupies a house in which one of its officers or servants resides if it is essential to the performance of his duties that he should reside in it or in one close by and it is the mutual understanding that he should do so; or, even though it is not essential that he reside in the house or in one close by, if he can by doing so better perform his duties to a material degree and there is an express term in the contract that he should reside there[5]. Charities which provided flats for the dependants of deceased officers of the armed services, and for ex-servicemen, have been held to be in occupation of the flats[6].

1 As to the registration of charities under the Charities Act 2011 see PARA 307 et seq.

2 See eg *Wynn v Skegness UDC* [1966] 3 All ER 336, [1967] 1 WLR 52, ChD; *Finch v Poplar Borough Council* (1967) 66 LGR 324, [1968] RA 208, ChD; *Meriden RDC v White* [1972] RA 530, 17 RRC 187. See also LOCAL GOVERNMENT FINANCE vol 70 (2012) PARA 123.

The cases cited in this paragraph which were decided prior to the coming into force of the Local Government Finance Act 1988 must now be considered in relation to the non-domestic rating provisions in Pt III (ss 41–67) (see LOCAL GOVERNMENT FINANCE vol 70 (2012) PARA 52 et seq). As to the history of the rating legislation see LOCAL GOVERNMENT FINANCE vol 70 (2012) PARA 51.

3 As to the Charity Commission see PARAS 543–578.

4 See *Over Seventies Housing Association v Westminster City Council* [1974] RA 247. See also LOCAL GOVERNMENT FINANCE vol 70 (2012) PARA 123.

5 *Glasgow Corpn v Johnstone* [1965] AC 609, [1965] 1 All ER 730, HL (house occupied by church officer); *Northern Ireland Comr of Valuation v Fermanagh Protestant Board of Education* [1969] 3 All ER 352, [1969] 1 WLR 1708, HL (teachers' houses); *Valuation Comr v Redemptorist Order Trustees* [1972] RA 145, NI CA (monastery where members of religious order lived and from where they carried out its charitable purposes); *Royal Society for the Protection of Birds v Hornsea UDC* [1975] RA 26, DC (house for warden at bird reserve); *Welsh National Water Development Authority (formerly Taf Fechan Water Board) v Mid-Glamorgan County Council (formerly Glamorgan County Council)* [1975] RA 106, CA (caretaker living on school premises). See also LOCAL GOVERNMENT FINANCE vol 70 (2012) PARA 123.

6 *Soldiers', Sailors' and Airmen's Families Association v Merton Corpn* [1966] 3 All ER 780, [1967] 1 WLR 127, CA; *Forces Help Society and Lord Roberts Workshops v Canterbury City Council* [1979] RA 68; and see *Ealing London Borough Council v Ladyeholme Co Ltd* [1974] RA 399. See also LOCAL GOVERNMENT FINANCE vol 70 (2012) PARA 123.

435. Wholly or mainly used for charitable purposes. In deciding whether a hereditament[1] is wholly or mainly[2] used for charitable purposes, the use made of the hereditament by the occupier must be considered[3]. The use must be for purposes which directly facilitate the carrying out of the main charitable purposes of the charity[4], and use for the purpose of raising money to further the charitable objects does not qualify for relief[5]. However, a hereditament is to be treated as wholly or mainly used for charitable purposes at any time if at the time it is wholly or mainly used for the sale of goods donated to a charity and the proceeds of sale of the goods, after any deduction of expenses, are applied for the purposes of a charity[6].

In determining whether premises are wholly or mainly used for charitable purposes the court should look at the whole of the evidence before it and decide the question on a broad basis, referring to the purpose of the use, rather than the amount or extent of the actual use made of the premises[7].

1 As to the meaning of 'hereditament' see LOCAL GOVERNMENT FINANCE vol 70 (2012) PARA 82 et seq.

2 It has been said in another context that 'mainly' probably means 'more than half ': *Fawcett Properties Ltd v Buckingham County Council* [1961] AC 636 at 669, [1960] 3 All ER 503 at 512, HL, per Lord Morton of Henryton.

3 See *Glasgow Corpn v Johnstone* [1965] AC 609, [1965] 1 All ER 730, HL, where the residence of a church officer was held to be occupied by the church authority and used for charitable purposes, because his residence there was of material assistance to the church authority in carrying out its main charitable activities. See further LOCAL GOVERNMENT FINANCE vol 70 (2012) PARA 124.

The cases cited in this paragraph which were decided prior to the coming into force of the Local Government Finance Act 1988 must now be considered in relation to the non-domestic rating provisions in Pt III (ss 41–67) (see LOCAL GOVERNMENT FINANCE vol 70 (2012) PARA 52 et seq). As to the history of the rating legislation see LOCAL GOVERNMENT FINANCE vol 70 (2012) PARA 51.

4 *Glasgow Corpn v Johnstone* [1965] AC 609, [1965] 1 All ER 730, HL; *Oxfam v Birmingham City District Council* [1976] AC 126, [1975] 2 All ER 289, HL. See also *Polish Historical Institution Ltd v Hove Corpn* (1963) 61 LGR 438, DC; *Aldous v Southwark Corpn* [1968] 3 All ER 498, 15 RRC 269, CA. In *Wynn v Skegness UDC* [1966] 3 All ER 336, [1967] 1 WLR 52, trustees of a holiday centre for miners in need of a change of air admitted to it persons other than beneficiaries if there was surplus accommodation at charges sufficient to cover their cost; the admission of such persons, not to raise money, but to assist in keeping the centre functioning, was held to facilitate wholly and directly the carrying out of the trustees' main purpose. See also *Meriden RDC v White* [1972] RA 530, DC (colliery sports and social club); *Royal British Legion Attendants Co (Belfast) Ltd v Valuation Comr* [1979] NI 138, NI Lands Tribunal (employment of ex-servicemen as car park attendants); *MacConnell v Northern Ireland Valuation Comr* [1989] RA 221, NI Lands Tribunal (garage used for servicing charity's buses not exempt because hereditament not used wholly or mainly for charitable purposes); *Re Hatschek's Patents, ex p Zerenner* [1909] 2 Ch 68; *Miller v Ottilie (Owners)* [1944] KB 188, [1944] 1 All ER 277, CA; *Franklin v Gramophone Co Ltd* [1948] 1 KB 542 at 555, [1948] 1 All ER 353 at 358, CA, per Somervell LJ; *Berthelemy v Neale* [1952] 1 All ER 437, CA. As to the meaning of 'charity' for rating purposes see PARA 433 note 2.

5 *Oxfam v Birmingham City District Council* [1976] AC 126, [1975] 2 All ER 289, HL, where shops occupied by a charity and used to sell goods, most of which were donated, in order to raise funds for spending on charitable purposes were held not to be mainly used for charitable purposes. It does not appear to provide relief to trading shops run by charities, i e shops wholly or mainly used to sell goods bought under normal trading conditions, or to ' fifty-fifty' shops in which goods are deposited for sale and the net proceeds of sale are divided between the donor and the charity. Nor did it cover the facts of *Royal Society for the Protection of Birds v Brighton Borough Council* [1982] RA 33.

The actual decision in *Oxfam v Birmingham City District Council* above, but not its reasoning, was reversed by what is now the Local Government Finance Act 1988 s 64(10) (which has its origins in the Rating (Charity Shops) Act 1976 s 1(1) (repealed)) (see the text to note 6). However, the selling in a shop of goods manufactured by blind persons in order to facilitate the provision of employment for the blind has been held to be a use for charitable purposes: *Belfast Association for Employment of Industrious Blind v Northern Ireland Valuation Comr* [1968] NI 21; and see *Royal Society for the Protection of Birds v Brighton Borough Council* above.

6 Local Government Finance Act 1988 s 64(10). This has the effect of reversing the decision in *Oxfam v Birmingham City District Council* [1976] AC 126, [1975] 2 All ER 289, HL (see note 5). However, the reasoning of the decision in *Oxfam v Birmingham City District Council* above is unaffected.

7 *Sheffield City Council v Kenya Aid Programme, R (Kenya Aid Programme) v Sheffield Magistrates' Court* [2013] EWHC 54 (Admin), [2014] QB 62, [2013] All ER (D) 230 (Jan) (efficiency of the furniture storage use at the premises and the necessity for the charity to occupy two premises were irrelevant); applied in *Public Safety Charitable Trust v Milton Keynes Council* [2013] EWHC 1237 (Admin), [2013] 2 EGLR 133, [2013] All ER (D) 268 (May).

(C) Unoccupied Hereditaments

436. Liability for unoccupied hereditaments where the ratepayer is a charity. Where a ratepayer[1] is a charity[2] or trustees for a charity and it appears that when next in use the hereditament[3] will be wholly or mainly used for charitable purposes[4], whether of that charity or of that and other charities[5], the chargeable amount for a chargeable day[6] is zero[7].

1 Ie the person subject to the non-domestic rate: see the Local Government Finance Act 1988 s 45(1); and LOCAL GOVERNMENT FINANCE vol 70 (2012) PARA 111.

2 As to the meaning of 'charity' for rating purposes see PARA 433 note 2.

3 As to the meaning of 'hereditament' see LOCAL GOVERNMENT FINANCE vol 70 (2012) PARA 82 et seq.

4 As to the meaning of 'wholly or mainly used for charitable purposes' see PARA 435.

5 Ie used for the charitable objects of the owning charity, accompanied or not by other charitable purposes; a requirement for it to appear additionally that, when the property is next used, the

currently-owning charity will occupy and use the property cannot be read into the Local Government Finance Act 1988 s 45A(2)(b): *Preston City Council v Oyston Angel Charity* [2012] EWHC 2005 (Admin), [2012] RA 357, [2012] All ER (D) 279 (Jul).

6 As to the meaning of 'chargeable day' see PARA 433 note 6.

7 See the Local Government Finance Act 1988 s 45A(1), (2) (added by the Rating (Empty Properties) Act 2007 s 1(2)); and LOCAL GOVERNMENT FINANCE vol 70 (2012) PARA 127.

B. DISCRETIONARY RELIEF FOR CHARITIES

437. Scope of discretion. Where an unoccupied hereditament is not zero-rated[1] and a billing authority decides that the following provisions apply in respect of a period including a day which is a chargeable day[2], then the chargeable amount for the day is not to be determined by the general rules[3] but is determined by, or found in accordance with rules determined by, the billing authority concerned[4].

The chargeable amount so determined must be less than would otherwise be the case, and may be zero[5].

A general requirement that the authority may not make such a decision unless satisfied that it would be reasonable for it to do so, having regard to the interests of persons liable to pay council tax set by it, does not apply[6]:

(1) if the ratepayer[7] is a charity[8], or trustees for a charity, and the hereditament[9] is wholly or mainly used for charitable purposes (whether of that charity or of that charity and other charities)[10];

(2) if the hereditament is not an excepted hereditament[11], and all or part of it is occupied[12] for the purposes of[13] one or more institutions or other organisations[14] none of which is established or conducted for profit[15] and each of whose main objects[16] are charitable or are otherwise philanthropic or religious[17] or concerned with[18] education[19], social welfare[20], science, literature or the fine arts[21].

1 Ie the provisions of the Local Government Finance Act 1988 s 45A (see PARA 436) do not apply: see s 47(10) (added by the Rating (Empty Properties) Act 2007 Sch 1 para 2); and LOCAL GOVERNMENT FINANCE vol 70 (2012) PARA 129.

2 See the Local Government Finance Act 1988 s 47(3) (amended by the Local Government Finance Act 1992 Sch 13 para 65, and the Localism Act 2011 Sch 25 Pt 10). As to the meaning of 'chargeable day' see PARA 433 note 6.

3 Ie the Local Government Finance Act 1988 ss 43(4)–(6B), 44, 45(4)–(4B), 46, regulations under s 57A or s 58 or any provision of or made under Sch 7A (as the case may be) do not apply as regards the day.

4 See the Local Government Finance Act 1988 s 47(1)(a), (b); and LOCAL GOVERNMENT FINANCE vol 70 (2012) PARA 129.

5 Local Government Finance Act 1988 s 47(4).

6 Local Government Finance Act 1988 s 47(5A) (s 47(5A), (5B) added by the Localism Act 2011 s 69).

The widening by the Localism Act 2011 of the billing authority's discretion to give relief nonetheless replicates the categories and purposes formerly contained in the repealed provisions of the Local Government Finance Act 1988 s 47(2); the cases cited in notes 11–21 may therefore continue to be read as interpretative of the provisions.

A Mayoral development corporation may be given functions under s 47: see s 48A (added by the Localism Act 2011 Sch 22 para 24); and LONDON GOVERNMENT vol 71 (2013) PARA 323.

7 Ie the person subject to the non-domestic rate: see the Local Government Finance Act 1988 s 45(1); and LOCAL GOVERNMENT FINANCE vol 70 (2012) PARA 111.

8 As to the meaning of 'charity' for rating purposes see PARA 433 note 2.

9 As to the meaning of 'hereditament' see LOCAL GOVERNMENT FINANCE vol 70 (2012) PARA 82 et seq.

10 See the Local Government Finance Act 1988 ss 43(6), 47(5A); PARAS 431, 433; and LOCAL GOVERNMENT FINANCE vol 70 (2012) PARA 129. As to the meaning of 'wholly or mainly used for charitable purposes' see PARA 435.

11 See the Local Government Finance Act 1988 s 47(8A), (9); and LOCAL GOVERNMENT FINANCE vol 70 (2012) PARA 129.

12 As to occupation see LOCAL GOVERNMENT FINANCE vol 70 (2012) PARA 61 et seq. If a hereditament is wholly unoccupied but it appears that it or any part of it when next occupied will be occupied for particular purposes, the hereditament or part concerned, as the case may be, is to be treated as occupied for these purposes: see Local Government Finance Act 1988 s 48(5).

13 The phrase 'occupied for the purposes of' is not to be read as 'occupied exclusively for the purposes of': *Royal London Mutual Insurance Society Ltd v Hendon Corpn* (1958) 3 RRC 76, 56 LGR 285, 122 JP 310, 171 Estates Gazette 605.

The cases cited in this paragraph which were decided prior to the coming into force of the Local Government Finance Act 1988 must now be considered in relation to the non-domestic rating provisions in Pt III (ss 41–67) (see LOCAL GOVERNMENT FINANCE vol 70 (2012) PARA 52 et seq). As to the history of the rating legislation see LOCAL GOVERNMENT FINANCE vol 70 (2012) PARA 51.

14 On similar wording in the Rating and Valuation (Miscellaneous Provisions) Act 1955 s 8 (repealed), it was held to be not always right to take the occupier and treat him as the organisation: *Skegness UDC v Derbyshire Miners' Welfare Committee* [1959] AC 807 at 827, [1959] 2 All ER 258 at 265, HL, per Lord Denning; *Isaacs v Market Bosworth RDC* [1960] 1 All ER 433, [1960] 1 WLR 277 (trustees of trade union memorial home; organisation for whose purposes hereditament occupied was the trade union; hereditament not entitled to relief); cf *National Children's Home and Orphanage Registered Trustees v Penarth UDC* (1960) 53 R & IT 166 (trustees of approved school not occupying for purposes of Home Secretary; school entitled to relief); *Trustees of the Benevolent and Orphan Fund, National and Local Government Officers' Association v Bournemouth Corpn* (1957) 1 RRC 363 (quarter sessions).

15 The same words in the Rating and Valuation (Miscellaneous Provisions) Act 1955 s 8 (repealed) were held to mean not established or conducted for the purpose of making profit; accordingly a direction to the trustees of a charity to make investments in order to produce revenue and increase capital does not make the organisation one which is established or conducted for profit: *Guinness Trust (London Fund) Founded 1890, Registered 1902 v West Ham Corpn* [1959] 1 All ER 482, [1959] 1 WLR 233, CA. The financial gains made by a friendly society from investments do not make the society one which is established or conducted for profit: *Trustees of National Deposit Friendly Society v Skegness UDC* [1959] AC 293, [1958] 2 All ER 601, HL. A zoo held to be an educational charity is not conducted for profit merely because it makes a financial surplus on its operations: *North of England Zoological Society v Chester RDC* [1959] 3 All ER 116, [1959] 1 WLR 773, CA. See also *Working Men's Club and Institute Union Ltd v Swansea Corpn* [1959] 3 All ER 769, [1959] 1 WLR 1197, CA, where a society registered under what is now the Co-operative and Community Benefit Societies Act 2014 was held not to be established or conducted for profit. See also *Ladbroke Park Golf Club Ltd v Stratford-on-Avon RDC* (1957) 1 RRC 202; *Reinshaw Park Golf Club v Chesterfield RDC* (1957) 1 RRC 281; *Mid-Kent Golf Club Ltd v Gravesend Borough Council* (1957) 50 R & IT 613, where golf clubs were held, at quarter sessions, not to be established or conducted for profit merely because of incidental financial gains.

16 On the same words in the Rating and Valuation (Miscellaneous Provisions) Act 1955 (repealed), it was held that the main objects must be sought in the written constitution, if there is one: *Berry v St Marylebone Borough Council* [1958] Ch 406, [1957] 3 All ER 677, CA; *General Nursing Council for England and Wales v St Marylebone Borough Council* [1959] AC 540 at 559, [1959] 1 All ER 325 at 332, HL, per Lord Keith of Avonholm; *Victory (Ex-Services) Association Ltd v Paddington Borough Council* [1960] 1 All ER 498, [1960] 1 WLR 106, DC; *Royal College of Nursing v St Marylebone Corpn* [1959] 3 All ER 663, [1959] 1 WLR 1077, CA. The activities of the organisation may be relevant in determining which of the objects are the main objects (*Berry v St Marylebone Borough Council; Working Men's Club and Institute Union Ltd v Swansea Corpn* [1959] 3 All ER 769, [1959] 1 WLR 1197, CA; *Trustees of National Deposit Friendly Society v Skegness UDC* [1959] AC 293 at 320, [1958] 2 All ER 601 at 612, HL, per Lord Denning); or where there is ambiguity in the objects (*North of England Zoological Society v Chester RDC* [1959] 3 All ER 116, [1959] 1 WLR 773, CA; *Nottingham Mechanics Institution v City of Nottingham* (1958) 3 RRC 359; *English-Speaking Union v Westminster City Council* (1959) 4 RRC 97, DC).

17 The objects of theosophy were held not to be 'concerned with the advancement of religion' within the meaning of the Rating and Valuation (Miscellaneous Provisions) Act 1955 s 8 (repealed) (*Berry v St Marylebone Borough Council* [1958] Ch 406, [1957] 3 All ER 677, CA); and so were the objects of freemasonry (*United Grand Lodge of Ancient Free and Accepted Masons of England v Holborn Borough Council* [1957] 3 All ER 281, [1957] 1 WLR 1080, CA). See also *Trustees of National Deposit Friendly Society v Skegness UDC* [1959] AC

293 at 322, [1958] 2 All ER 601 at 614, HL, per Lord Denning. As to the advancement of religion within the meaning of the Charities Act 2011 see PARA 27 et seq.

18 On the words in the Rating and Valuation (Miscellaneous Provisions) Act 1955 s 8 (repealed) 'concerned with the advancement of religion, education or social welfare', it was held that the organisation must be substantially altruistic or benevolent in its purposes, although not necessarily in the limited sense applied to charities: *Trustees of National Deposit Friendly Society v Skegness UDC* [1959] AC 293, [1958] 2 All ER 601, HL; *Independent Order of Odd Fellows, Manchester Unity Friendly Society v Manchester Corpn* [1958] 3 All ER 378, [1958] 1 WLR 1171, CA; *Working Men's Club and Institute Union Ltd v Swansea Corpn* [1959] 3 All ER 769, [1959] 1 WLR 1197, CA. The crucial test was the purpose to which the money was devoted, not the motives of its donors: *Skegness UDC v Derbyshire Miners' Welfare Committee* [1959] AC 807 at 824, [1959] 2 All ER 258 at 263, HL, per Viscount Simonds; explained in *Waterson v Hendon Borough Council* [1959] 2 All ER 760, [1959] 1 WLR 985. The size of the class of persons to be benefited was irrelevant: *Skegness UDC v Derbyshire Miners' Welfare Committee* above.

19 The main objects of the Chartered Insurance Institute are not the advancement of education but the benefit of the profession of insurance generally: *Chartered Insurance Institute v London Corpn* [1957] 2 All ER 638, [1957] 1 WLR 867, DC. The main objects of the English-Speaking Union are not concerned with the advancement of education (*English-Speaking Union v Westminster City Council* (1959) 4 RRC 97); nor are those of the Theosophical Society (*Berry v St Marylebone Borough Council* [1958] Ch 406, [1957] 3 All ER 677, CA). See *Trustees of National Deposit Friendly Society v Skegness UDC* [1959] AC 293 at 322, [1958] 2 All ER 601 at 613, HL, per Lord Denning. At quarter sessions, the Oxford Union Society (*Oxford Union Society v City of Oxford* (1957) 2 RRC 54) and two dramatic societies (*Newport Playgoers' Society v Newport County Borough Council* (1957) 1 RRC 279; *Trustees of Stoke-on-Trent Repertory Players v Stoke-on-Trent Corpn* (1957) 1 RRC 353) have been held to be concerned with the advancement of education. As to the advancement of education within the meaning of the Charities Act 2011 see PARA 20 et seq.

20 It has been said that 'social welfare' is not the same as 'social well-being', but savours more of those needs of the community which, as a matter of social ethics, ought to be met in the attainment of some acceptable standard: *Trustees of National Deposit Friendly Society v Skegness UDC* [1959] AC 293 at 314, [1958] 2 All ER 601 at 609, HL, per Lord MacDermott. The needs which are met need not be financial: *Victory (Ex-Services) Association Ltd v Paddington Borough Council* [1960] 1 All ER 498, [1960] 1 WLR 106, DC, where it was held that to promote comradeship between and improve the conditions and welfare of all ranks past and present advanced social welfare. Public benefit alone is not the test of social welfare (*General Nursing Council for England and Wales v St Marylebone Borough Council* [1959] AC 540, [1959] 1 All ER 325, HL); and 'social welfare' is a narrower phrase than 'social improvement' (*Nottingham Mechanics Institution v City of Nottingham* (1958) 3 RRC 359). An organisation which provides benefits only for its members is not concerned with the advancement of social welfare: *Working Men's Club and Institute Union Ltd v Swansea Corpn* [1959] 3 All ER 769, [1959] 1 WLR 1197, CA; *Waterson v Hendon Borough Council* [1959] 2 All ER 760, [1959] 1 WLR 985. A holiday camp run by a miners' welfare committee has been held to be concerned with the advancement of 'social welfare': *Skegness UDC v Derbyshire Miners' Welfare Committee* [1959] AC 807, [1959] 2 All ER 258, HL. See also *Independent Order of Odd Fellows, Manchester Unity Friendly Society v Manchester Corpn* [1958] 3 All ER 378, [1958] 1 WLR 1171, CA; *Berry v St Marylebone Borough Council* [1958] Ch 406, [1957] 3 All ER 677, CA; and, at quarter sessions, *Trustees of West Ham Boys' and Amateur Boxing Club v West Ham County Borough Council* (1957) 2 RRC 44; *Trustees of Fegg Hayes Welfare Club and Institute v Stoke-on-Trent Corpn* (1957) 1 RRC 353; *Trustees of Wearmouth Colliery Welfare Fund v Sunderland County Borough Council* (1956) 1 RRC 272; *Wearmouth Colliery Cricket Club v Sunderland County Borough Council* (1956) 1 RRC 277.

21 See the Local Government Finance Act 1988 s 47(5A), (5B) (as added: see note 6). Societies which were instituted for the purpose of science, literature or the fine arts exclusively were at one stage exempted from rates, provided that certain other conditions were fulfilled, by the Scientific Societies Act 1843 s 1 (repealed). Many decisions were made as to societies which were to be treated as exempt, and as to others which were so instituted but were not exempt because a condition of exemption was not satisfied; some societies were held not to be exclusively instituted for the requisite purposes but might now qualify for discretionary relief on the ground that their main objects are concerned with science, literature or the fine arts. 'Science' has been held to include applied science: *R v Royal Medical and Chirurgical Society of London* (1857) 21 JP 789 at 791. The fine arts must be distinguished from the arts: *R v Institution of Civil Engineers* (1879) 5 QBD 48 at 52, DC. Music is one of the fine arts (*Royal*

College of Music v Westminster Vestry [1898] 1 QB 809, CA), and drama and acting may be (*Nonentities Society v Linley (Valuation Officer) and Kidderminster Borough Council* (1954) 47 R & IT 426, CA), but folk dancing is not (*O'Sullivan (Valuation Officer) v English Folk Dance and Song Society* [1955] 2 All ER 845, [1955] 1 WLR 907, CA). As to the advancement of arts, culture, heritage or science within the meaning of the Charities Act 2011 see PARA 36 et seq.

(v) Taxes

438. Eligibility for tax relief. Charities and charitable trusts may be eligible for reliefs and exemption in respect of various direct and indirect taxes, which are dealt with in detail elsewhere in this work[1].

As well as any specific conditions for such eligibility, a body must satisfy Her Majesty's Revenue and Customs that it is a charity; and while this is connected to the meaning of 'charity' in the Charities Act 2011, it is not identical[2].

For the purposes of the enactments relating to (1) income tax[3]; (2) capital gains tax[4]; (3) corporation tax[5]; (4) value added tax[6]; (5) inheritance tax[7]; (6) stamp duty[8]; (7) stamp duty land tax[9]; and (8) stamp duty reserve tax[10], a charity is a body of persons or trust that[11]:

(a) is established for charitable purposes only[12];
(b) meets the jurisdiction condition[13];
(c) meets the registration condition[14]; and
(d) meets the management condition[15].

A body or trust meets the jurisdiction condition if it falls to be subject to the control of a relevant UK court[16] in the exercise of its jurisdiction with respect to charities, or any other court in the exercise of a corresponding jurisdiction under the law of a relevant territory[17].

A body or trust meets the registration condition if (i) in the case of a charity within the meaning of the Charities Act 2011, it has complied with any requirement to be registered in the register of charities under that Act[18], and (ii) in the case of any other body of persons or trust, it has complied with any corresponding requirement under the law of a territory outside England and Wales[19].

A body or trust meets the management condition if its managers[20] are fit and proper persons to be managers of the body or trust[21].

The Charity Commission takes the view that sensible and prudent tax planning, including taking advantage of specific tax reliefs for charities, is consistent with the fiduciary duties of charity trustees, but regards tax fraud, evasion and avoidance as being matters of regulatory concern[22].

1 See notes 3–10.

2 As to the meaning of 'charity' under the Charities Act 2011 see PARA 1.

3 See the Income Tax Act 2007 Pt 10 (ss 518–564); and INCOME TAXATION vol 58A (2014) PARA 1633 et seq.

As to the gift aid regime, whereunder charities may claim tax relief on donations, see INCOME TAXATION vol 58A (2014) PARA 1633. As to the eligibility for charities to receive top-up payments in respect of small donations, similar to gift aid but without a gift aid declaration having been made, see the Small Charitable Donations Act 2012 s 1; and INCOME TAXATION vol 58A (2014) PARA 1659.

4 See the Taxation of Chargeable Gains Act 1992 s 256(1); and CAPITAL GAINS TAXATION vol 6 (2011) PARA 878.

5 See the Corporation Tax Act 2010 Pt 11 (ss 466–517); and INCOME TAXATION vol 58A (2014) PARA 1633 et seq.

6 See the Value Added Tax Act 1994 s 4(1); and VALUE ADDED TAX vol 99 (2012) PARA 36.

7 See the Inheritance Tax Act 1984 s 23(1), (6); and INHERITANCE TAXATION vol 59A (2014) PARA 134.

8 See STAMP TAXES vol 96 (2012) PARA 363.

9 See STAMP TAXES vol 96 (2012) PARA 470.
10 See STAMP TAXES vol 96 (2012) PARA 410.
11 Finance Act 2011 Sch 6 paras 1, 7.
12 Finance Act 2011 Sch 6 para 1(1)(a) (amended by the Charities Act 2011 Sch 7 para 143). See text and notes 16, 17. The meaning of 'charitable purpose' in the Charities Act 2011 s 2 (see PARA 2) is applied for this purpose: Finance Act 2011 Sch 6 para 1(4) (as so amended).
13 Finance Act 2011 Sch 6 para 1(1)(b). See text and notes 16, 17.
14 Finance Act 2011 Sch 6 para 1(1)(c). See text and notes 18, 19.
15 Finance Act 2011 Sch 6 para 1(1)(d). See text and notes 20, 21.
16 'Relevant UK court' means the High Court, the Court of Session or the High Court in Northern Ireland: Finance Act 2011 Sch 6 para 2(2).
17 Finance Act 2011 Sch 6 para 2(1). As to the meaning of 'relevant territory' see Sch 6 para 2(3); regulations made under that provision; and INCOME TAXATION vol 58A (2014) PARA 1622.
18 Ie under the Charities Act 2011 s 29: see PARA 307 et seq.
19 Finance Act 2011 Sch 6 para 3(1)–(3) (amended by the Charities Act 2011 Sch 7 para 143).
20 'Managers' means the persons having the general control and management of the administration of the body or trust: Finance Act 2011 Sch 6 para 4(2).
21 Finance Act 2011 Sch 6 para 4(1). This condition can be treated as met if HMRC are satisfied that the charitable purposes have not been prejudiced by it not being strictly complied with: see Sch 6 para 5.
22 See *Charity tax reliefs: guidance on Charity Commission policy* (Charity Commission, January 2015) (available, at the date at which this volume states the law, on the government website). As to the Charity Commission's publications see PARA 547.

(4) RECOVERY OF TRUST PROPERTY

(i) Recovery in general

439. Payment of legacies to charity. Trustees of charities or charitable institutions who are entitled absolutely to legacies may demand immediate payment, notwithstanding any direction for accumulation[1]. In the case of a charitable bequest which remained unapplied and accumulated for 30 years, the accumulations were held to pass with the original bequest[2]. It is a different matter where there is an indefinite gift of income. It is a well-established proposition that such a gift to an individual carries the right to corpus, but that principle does not apply to a bequest to a charity, as a charity continues in perpetuity and effect can be given to a perpetual trust of income for its purposes[3].

Interest is allowed on a charitable legacy as from the end of a year after the testator's death[4].

1 *Harbin v Masterman* [1894] 2 Ch 184, CA (affd sub nom *Wharton v Masterman* [1895] AC 186, HL, overruling a previous doubt upon this point expressed in *Harbin v Masterman* (1871) LR 12 Eq 559); *Re Knapp, Spreckley v A-G* [1929] 1 Ch 341, where a direction to accumulate was held not to be binding, but to be a directory provision which the trustees ought prima facie to bear in mind and carry out.
2 *Forbes v Forbes* (1854) 18 Beav 552.
3 *Re Levy, Barclays Bank Ltd v Board of Guardians and Trustees for the Relief of the Jewish Poor* [1960] Ch 346, [1960] 1 All ER 42, CA; *Re Beesty's Will Trusts, Farrar v Royal Alfred Merchant Seamen's Society* [1966] Ch 223, [1964] 3 All ER 82. See PARAS 88, 131, 141.
4 *Fisher v Brierley (No 3)* (1861) 30 Beav 268.

440. Remedies for recovery of trust property. In addition to their right of action against the trustees for breach of trust[1], beneficiaries who have suffered from an improper alienation of the trust estate may in many instances follow the trust estate into the hands of the alienee[2], or attach the property into which the trust estate has been improperly converted[3]. They are entitled to take whichever remedy appears more beneficial[4]. To this extent, they have an equitable right to recover money paid to charitable institutions by executors under a mistake[5], and that money may be traced, provided that it can be identified or disentangled where it has been mixed with other assets of the recipient institution[6].

Unless the purchaser is protected by reason of the statutes of limitation[7] or on the ground that he is a purchaser for value without notice, a conveyance to him of charity property which constitutes a breach of trust may be set aside[8]. The same rule applies in the case of a lease in breach of trust[9]. In the absence of collusion or fraud, the court, on setting aside a sale[10] or a lease[11], may direct that an allowance should be made in respect of buildings or other permanent improvements erected or made on the land.

1 See PARAS 450–457; and **TRUSTS AND POWERS** vol 98 (2013) PARA 665 et seq.
2 *A-G v Kell* (1840) 2 Beav 575; *A-G v Compton* (1842) 1 Y & C Ch Cas 417.
3 *A-G v Newcastle Corpn* (1842) 5 Beav 307; affd sub nom *Newcastle-upon-Tyne Corpn v A-G* (1845) 12 Cl & Fin 402, HL.
4 *A-G v Newcastle Corpn* (1842) 5 Beav 307 at 314 per Lord Langdale MR.
5 *Ministry of Health v Simpson* [1951] AC 251, [1950] 2 All ER 1137, HL. See further **WILLS AND INTESTACY** vol 103 (2010) PARAS 1094–1105.
6 *Re Diplock, Diplock v Wintle* [1948] Ch 465, [1948] 2 All ER 318, CA; affd, without reference to tracing of money, sub nom *Ministry of Health v Simpson* [1951] AC 251, [1950] 2 All ER 1137, HL. See further **EQUITABLE JURISDICTION** vol 47 (2014) PARA 238 et seq.
7 For the statutory provisions governing the limitation of actions see generally the Limitation Act 1980; and **LIMITATION PERIODS**.
8 *A-G v Christ's Hospital* (1834) 3 My & K 344; *A-G v Brettingham* (1840) 3 Beav 91; *A-G v Kerr* (1840) 2 Beav 420; *A-G v Bishop of Manchester* (1867) LR 3 Eq 436. See also **TRUSTS AND POWERS**.
9 *Re Lawford Charity, ex p Skinner* (1817) 2 Mer 453 at 457 per Lord Eldon LC.
10 *A-G v Magdalen College, Oxford* (1854) 18 Beav 223.
11 *A-G v Kerr* (1840) 2 Beav 420.

441. Purchaser with notice of trust. A purchaser for value with notice that the property purchased is subject to charitable trusts takes subject to those trusts[1], and apart from the Statutes of Limitation[2], no length of possession will protect him[3]. Notice given at any time prior to the execution of the conveyance binds the purchaser[4].

A person acquiring a charity estate for no valuable consideration is not entitled to protection, whether he had notice of the trusts or not[5].

Where a person who purchased land with notice of an equitable right sells to another for value without notice, the latter is protected, even where the right is vested in a charity[6].

After getting notice of the trust a purchaser for value without notice of a trust cannot subsequently protect himself by taking a conveyance of the legal estate from the trustee, for by taking such a conveyance he becomes a trustee himself[7].

1 *Harding v Edge* (1682) 2 Cas in Ch 94; *A-G v Christ's Hospital* (1834) 3 My & K 344; *A-G v Flint* (1844) 4 Hare 147; *A-G v Hall* (1853) 16 Beav 388 at 392 per Romilly MR.
2 See *Incorporated Society in Dublin v Richards* (1841) 1 Dr & War 258; *A-G v Payne* (1859) 27 Beav 168; *A-G v Davey* (1859) 4 De G & J 136; and PARAS 447–448. As to the Limitation Act 1980 (which consolidated previous legislation relating to limitation of actions) generally see **LIMITATION PERIODS**.
3 *A-G v Christ's Hospital* (1834) 3 My & K 344; and see *Churcher v Martin* (1889) 42 ChD 312.
4 *Woodford Inhabitants v Parkhurst* (1639) Duke 70; and see *Roots v Williamson* (1888) 38 ChD 485 at 497–498 per Stirling J.
5 *Mansell v Mansell* (1732) 2 P Wms 678 at 681 per Lord King LC.
6 *Re Alms Corn Charity, Charity Comrs v Bode* [1901] 2 Ch 750, where, however, the early cases to the contrary, namely *East-Greensted's Case* (1633) Duke 64, and *Sutton Colefield Case* (1635) Duke 68, were not quoted. See also *Charitable Donations and Bequests Comrs v*

Wybrants (1845) 2 Jo & Lat 182 at 194 per Lord Sugden LC; *A-G v Lord Gower* (1736) 2 Eq Cas Abr 195; Dart's Vendor and Purchaser (8th Edn, 1929) p 712; and EQUITABLE JURISDICTION vol 47 (2014) PARA 238.

7 *Mumford v Stohwasser* (1874) LR 18 Eq 556 at 563 per Jessel MR, approving *Saunders v Dehew* (1692) 2 Vern 271.

442. Boundaries of charity land. A tenant of charity land is under an obligation to the charity to keep that land distinct from his own property during the tenancy[1]. If the charity land has become intermixed with other land, the boundaries of the charity land must be ascertained by inquiry at chambers[2], and if they cannot be pointed out, then the value of the land formerly belonging to the charity must be ascertained[3].

1 *A-G v Fullerton* (1813) 2 Ves & B 263; *Spike v Harding* (1878) 7 ChD 871, where it was said that the obligation rests on the tenant not merely at the end of the term when he comes to deliver up the property, but during the subsistence of the term also.

2 *Spike v Harding* (1878) 7 ChD 871. Formerly the procedure used was to issue a commission to inquire: see *A-G v Fullerton* (1813) 2 Ves & B 263 at 266 per Lord Eldon LC; *Reresby v Farrer* (1700) 2 Vern 414; *A-G v Bowyer* (1800) 5 Ves 300; *Solicitor-General v Bath Corpn* (1849) 18 LJCh 275; *A-G v Stephens* (1855) 6 De GM & G 111. In *Spike v Harding* above this practice was said to have fallen into disuse in 1852.

3 *A-G v Fullerton* (1813) 2 Ves & B 263.

(ii) Rentcharges

443. Purchase of land subject to charitable rentcharge. A purchaser for value of land subject to a legal or equitable rentcharge in favour of a charity will take subject to that rentcharge unless (1) the rentcharge is registrable as a land charge and is void against him for want of registration[1]; or (2) the sale is made in exercise of powers under the Settled Land Act 1925, and the rentcharge is capable of being overreached on such a sale[2]; or (3) in the case of an equitable rentcharge, the purchaser had no notice of it[3].

1 See the Land Charges Act 1972 ss 2, 4; the Law of Property Act 1969 s 24; the Law of Property Act 1925 s 2(1)(i); and REAL PROPERTY AND REGISTRATION vol 87 (2012) PARAS 708, 714 et seq. As to rentcharges generally see REAL PROPERTY AND REGISTRATION vol 87 (2012) PARA 1104.

2 See the Settled Land Act 1925 s 72; the Law of Property Act 1925 s 2(1)(i); and SETTLEMENTS vol 91 (2012) PARA 775; REAL PROPERTY AND REGISTRATION vol 87 (2012) PARA 261.

3 *Re Alms Corn Charity, Charity Comrs v Bode* [1901] 2 Ch 750 at 760 per Stirling LJ. In the case of a legal rentcharge not within head (1) or (2) in the text, a purchaser for value takes subject to the charge whether or not he has notice: *East-Greensted's Case* (1633) Duke 64; *Peacock v Thewer* (1638) Duke 82; *Wharton v Charles* (1673) Cas *temp* Finch 81; Sugden's Law of Vendors and Purchasers (14th Edn, 1862) p 722. See *Ind Coope & Co v Emmerson* (1887) 12 App Cas 300 at 306–307, HL, per Earl of Selborne; and cf *A-G v Wilkins* (1853) 17 Beav 285, discussed in Sugden's Law of Vendors and Purchasers (14th Edn, 1862) p 794 et seq.

444. Remedies: in general. Rentcharges created for charitable purposes and rentcharges created out of land belonging to charity are both subject to the same incidents and recoverable by the same remedies as other rentcharges[1].

Actions to recover or compel payment of rentcharges which appear to belong to charities may be brought by the Attorney General[2], or by the Charity Commission[3]. Charity trustees may also institute such proceedings[4]; and the county court has jurisdiction[5].

If in any such proceedings it is shown that the rentcharge or other payment has at any time been paid for 12 consecutive years to or for the benefit of the charity, that is prima facie evidence of perpetual liability to the payment, and no proof of its origin is necessary[6].

The repeal[7] of the provisions in the Charities Act 1960[8] relating to the redemption of rentcharges does not affect any notice to treat given prior to 1 January 1993[9].

1 See REAL PROPERTY AND REGISTRATION vol 87 (2012) PARA 1149.
2 See *A-G v Bolton* (1796) 3 Anst 820; *A-G v Jackson* (1805) 11 Ves 365; *A-G v Gascoigne* (1833) 2 My & K 647; *A-G v Naylor* (1863) 1 Hem & M 809. As to the Attorney General see PARAS 589, 596, 605 et seq; and CONSTITUTIONAL AND ADMINISTRATIVE LAW vol 20 (2014) PARA 273 et seq.
3 Under the Charities Act 2011 s 114: see PARA 558. As to the Charity Commission see PARAS 543–572.
4 Such proceedings do not require the consent of the Commission under the Charities Act 2011 s 115 (see PARA 594), nor did they under the old law (see *Bassano v Bradley* [1896] 1 QB 645, DC).
5 See *Bassano v Bradley* [1896] 1 QB 645, DC; the County Courts Act 1984 s 21(2); and COURTS AND TRIBUNALS vol 24 (2010) PARA 772.
6 See the Charities Act 2011 s 344(1), (2).
7 Ie by the Charities Act 1992 ss 37(5), 78(2), Sch 7 (repealed).
8 Ie the Charities Act 1960 s 27(2)–(8).
9 See the Charities Act 1992 (Commencement No 1 and Transitional Provisions) Order 1992, SI 1992/1900, art 4(3).

445. Uncertainty as to land charged. Where there is a confusion of boundaries, or it is not known out of what land the rentcharge issues[1], or the legal title is not clear or is defective[2], a legal rentcharge may be enforced in equity in favour of a charity where the right could not be enforced at law[3].

1 *A-G v Wilkins* (1853) 22 LJCh 830 at 832 per Romilly MR. See also REAL PROPERTY AND REGISTRATION vol 87 (2012) PARA 1104 et seq.
2 *Re Herbage Rents, Greenwich, Charity Comrs v Green* [1896] 2 Ch 811 at 825 per Stirling J; *Foley's Charity Trustees v Dudley Corpn* [1910] 1 KB 317, CA.
3 The law here enunciated is in accordance with the well-established principle that equity will aid defective assurances in favour of charity: see Shelford's Law of Mortmain (1836) 514.

446. Time for recovery. A defence founded on the Limitation Act 1980[1] may be a complete bar to an action to recover a charitable rentcharge[2], but time does not run where, by reason of the circumstances, no beneficiary is in a position to make a claim[3].

1 The Limitation Act 1980 consolidated previous legislation relating to the limitation of actions. See generally LIMITATION PERIODS.
2 *A-G v Wilkins* (1853) 17 Beav 285 at 293 per Romilly MR; *A-G v Stephens* (1855) 6 De GM & G 111 at 146 per Lord Cranworth LC; *President etc of St Mary Magdalen College, Oxford v A-G* (1857) 6 HL Cas 189.
3 *A-G v Persse* (1842) 2 Dr & War 67, where a rentcharge was given as a salary for a schoolmaster to be appointed by a certain person; no appointment was made for 27 years, but nevertheless the rentcharge was not barred. See also *Incorporated Society in Dublin v Richards* (1841) 1 Dr & War 258 at 288 per Lord Sugden LC.

(iii) Limitation of Actions

447. Limitation periods. In proceedings against trustees[1], whether express or constructive, the general rule is that, except in cases of fraud, retention of the trust property, or conversion by the trustee to his own use[2], the right of a beneficiary to recover trust property, whether real or personal, or to sue in respect of any breach of trust, is barred after the expiration of six years[3]. Time runs from the date on which the right of action accrued[4] or the date of the breach of trust[5]. It is very doubtful, however, whether these provisions have any application to a charitable trust because in most, if not all, charitable trusts there are no individual beneficiaries[6]. Certainly it has no application to an action by the Attorney General to enforce public charitable trusts[7].

Claims by charities to land or rent are barred after the expiration of 12 years[8], and claims by charities to an interest in the estate of a deceased person are also barred after the expiration of 12 years, and claims to arrears of interest of a legacy after the expiration of six years[9].

1 'Trustee' has the same meaning as in the Trustee Act 1925 (see TRUSTS AND POWERS vol 98 (2013) PARA 1): Limitation Act 1980 s 38(1).
2 See the Limitation Act 1980 s 21(1); and LIMITATION PERIODS vol 68 (2008) PARA 1140 et seq. See also s 21(2); and LIMITATION PERIODS vol 68 (2008) PARA 1140.
3 See the Limitation Act 1980 s 21(3); and LIMITATION PERIODS vol 68 (2008) PARA 1143.
4 See the Limitation Act 1980 s 21(3); and LIMITATION PERIODS vol 68 (2008) PARA 1144. As to what is the date of accrual of the right of action to recover land see s 15(6), (7), Sch 1; and LIMITATION PERIODS vol 68 (2008) PARA 1034 et seq.
5 *Thorne v Heard and Marsh* [1895] AC 495, HL.
6 *A-G v Cocke* [1988] Ch 414, [1988] 2 All ER 391, citing *Thomson v Trustees of the Honourable Society of the Inner Temple* (30 May 1967, unreported).
7 *A-G v Cocke* [1988] Ch 414 at 421, [1988] 2 All ER 391 at 395 per Harman J where it was also held that an action for an account was not 'an action ... to recover trust property or in respect of any breach of trust' within the wording of the Limitation Act 1980 s 21(3). As to the Attorney General see PARAS 589, 596, 605 et seq; and CONSTITUTIONAL AND ADMINISTRATIVE LAW vol 20 (2014) PARA 273 et seq.
8 See the Limitation Act 1980 s 15; and LIMITATION PERIODS vol 68 (2008) PARA 1159 et seq.
9 See the Limitation Act 1980 s 22; and LIMITATION PERIODS vol 68 (2008) PARA 1161. Cf *Cadbury v Smith* (1869) LR 9 Eq 37.

448. Possession of land under void lease or conveyance. Charity trustees may acquire a valid title to land by possession under a void lease[1]. If no rent is paid, no tenancy is created, and the period of limitation runs from the date on which possession is acquired[2]. The payment of rent, however small, establishes the relation of landlord and tenant; and where there is a tenancy at will the period of limitation runs from the actual termination of the tenancy[3], but where there is a tenancy from year to year or other period without a lease in writing, it runs from the end of the first year or other period[4] or from the last payment of rent[5].

1 *President and Governors of Magdalen Hospital v Knotts* (1879) 4 App Cas 324, HL (disabling Acts); *Bunting v Sargent* (1879) 13 ChD 330; *Webster v Southey* (1887) 36 ChD 9 at 19 per Kay J (mortmain); cf *Bishop of Bangor v Parry* [1891] 2 QB 277 (lack of consent of Charity Commissioners). It was held in *Churcher v Martin* (1889) 42 ChD 312 that under the Statutes of Limitation charity trustees might also acquire a valid title to land of which they had enjoyed possession under a conveyance rendered void for not complying with the Mortmain and Charitable Uses Act 1888 (repealed: see PARA 83).
2 *President and Governors of Magdalen Hospital v Knotts* (1879) 4 App Cas 324 at 334, HL, per Earl Cairns LC.
3 See LIMITATION PERIODS vol 68 (2008) PARA 1068. The Limitation Act 1939 s 9, which provided that a tenancy of will was deemed to be determined at the expiration of one year from its commencement, unless determined earlier, has been repealed: see LIMITATION PERIODS vol 68 (2008) PARA 1068.
4 See the Limitation Act 1980 s 15(6), Sch 1 para 5(1); and LIMITATION PERIODS vol 68 (2008) PARAS 1058, 1159.
5 See the Limitation Act 1980 Sch 1 para 5(2); and LIMITATION PERIODS vol 68 (2008) PARAS 1058, 1159. See also *Bunting v Sargent* (1879) 13 ChD 330; *Webster v Southey* (1887) 36 ChD 9; *President and Governors of Magdalen Hospital v Knotts* (1879) 4 App Cas 324 at 335, HL, per Lord Selborne.

449. Claims adverse to charity barred. The right to claim the benefit of a gift over of land from one charity to another, or of a reverter to the grantor, may be barred by effluxion of time[1]. The charity trustees remain in possession under the original trusts, and not for their own benefit[2].

Time does not run in favour of a person who has obtained possession of charity land by fraud so long as the fraud is concealed, but it begins to run from the date of discovery or the date when with reasonable diligence it could have been discovered[3].

1 See *Re Orchard Street Schools Trustees* [1878] WN 211; *Christ's Hospital v Grainger* (1849) 1 Mac & G 460; *Re Ingleton Charity, Croft v A-G* [1956] Ch 585, [1956] 2 All ER 881.
2 *Re Ingleton Charity, Croft v A-G* [1956] Ch 585, [1956] 2 All ER 881.
3 See the Limitation Act 1980 s 32; and LIMITATION PERIODS vol 68 (2008) PARA 1220 et seq. See also *Hovenden v Lord Annesley* (1806) 2 Sch & Lef 607 at 634 per Lord Redesdale LC; *Charitable Donations and Bequests Comrs v Wybrants* (1845) 2 Jo & Lat 182.

(5) LIABILITY OF TRUSTEES

450. Misapplication of trust property. In the absence of evidence to the contrary, it is presumed that trustees have faithfully discharged their duty[1].

Charity trustees, whether a corporate body or individuals, using trust money for their own purposes[2], for purposes not in accordance with the trusts[3], occasioning the destruction of the trust property[4], improperly alienating it[5], or negligently allowing others to misappropriate it[6], are strictly liable to make good any deficiency or loss[7]. A threatened application of charity property for non-charitable purposes will be restrained by injunction[8].

Parish officials are not liable for breaches of trust committed by their predecessors in office[9].

Although the court has been severe with trustees who wilfully, corruptly or negligently misapply the trust property, it has acted leniently where the administration of the funds has been honest but mistaken[10], as, for example, where a wrong construction has been put on an ambiguous instrument of trust[11]. Where a corporation is trustee, the court has tended to leniency more than in the case of individual trustees[12].

In certain circumstances the Charity Commission and the court have statutory powers to relieve a trustee from liability for breach of trust or duty[13].

1 *A-G v Earl of Stamford* (1843) 1 Ph 737 at 747 per Lord Cottenham LC. As to the liabilities of trustees generally see TRUSTS AND POWERS vol 98 (2013) PARA 665 et seq.
2 *Kennington Hastings Case* (1612) Duke 71 (retainer by trustee of increase of rent on reletting of charity lands); *A-G v Bedford Corpn* (1754) 2 Ves Sen 505 (retainer by schoolmaster of charity school of usher's salary); *A-G v Bolton* (1796) 3 Anst 820 (retainer by vicar of charity annuity payable to preacher); *A-G v Dixie, ex p Bosworth School* (1805) 13 Ves 519.
3 *A-G v Brewers' Co* (1816) 1 Mer 495; *A-G v Cambridge Corpn* (1836) 5 LJCh 357.
4 *Ex p Greenhouse* (1815) 1 Madd 92 at 109 per Plumer V-C (chapel pulled down by trustees).
5 *A-G v East Retford Corpn* (1838) 3 My & Cr 484; *A-G v Wisbeach Corpn* (1842) 11 LJCh 412 (innocent but improper sale of charity lands in redemption of land tax on other lands belonging to the trustees); and see *A-G v Newark-upon-Trent Corpn* (1842) 1 Hare 395.
6 *A-G v Leicester Corpn* (1844) 7 Beav 176.
7 Charity trustees may obtain complete protection by seeking the advice of the Charity Commission under the Charities Act 2011 s 110 (see PARAS 393–394), or their authorisation for transactions under s 105 (see PARAS 387–391). They may also pay trust money into court under the Trustee Act 1925 s 63 (see PARA 611). As to funding of indemnity insurance by charities for trustees, see the Charities Act 2011 s 189; and PARA 452.
8 *Baldry v Feintuck* [1972] 2 All ER 81, [1972] 1 WLR 552.
9 *Ex p Fowlser* (1819) 1 Jac & W 70; *French v Dear* (1800) 5 Ves 547.
10 *A-G v Exeter Corpn* (1826) 2 Russ 45 at 54 per Lord Eldon LC ('to act on any other principles would be to deter all prudent persons from becoming trustees of charities); *A-G v Dean and Canons of Christ Church* (1826) 2 Russ 321; *A-G v Pretyman* (1841) 4 Beav 462 at 464;

Andrews v M'Guffog (1886) 11 App Cas 313 at 324, HL, per Lord Watson. See also *A-G v Bowyer* (1798) 3 Ves 714 at 729 per Lord Thurlow LC.

11 *A-G v Master, Wardens etc of the Wax Chandlers' Co* (1873) LR 6 HL 1. See, however, *Ministry of Health v Simpson* [1951] AC 251, [1950] 2 All ER 1137, HL; affg *Re Diplock, Diplock v Wintle* [1948] Ch 465, [1948] 2 All ER 318, CA.

12 *A-G v Baliol College, Oxford* (1744) 9 Mod Rep 407 at 409–410 per Lord Hardwicke LC; *A-G v East Retford Corpn* (1833) 2 My & K 35 at 37–38 per Leach MR; *A-G v Newbury Corpn* (1834) 3 My & K 647 at 651 per Lord Brougham LC; *A-G v Caius College* (1837) 2 Keen 150 at 169 per Lord Langdale MR; *Edinburgh Corpn v Lord Advocate* (1879) 4 App Cas 823, HL.

13 See PARA 451.

451. Power to relieve trustee etc from liability for breach of trust or duty. The Charities Act 2011 makes provision for the Charity Commission[1] to make orders relieving a person wholly or partly from liability for breach of trust or breach of duty[2]. The provision applies to a person who is or has been: (1) a charity trustee or trustee for a charity[3]; (2) a person appointed to audit a charity's accounts[4] (whether appointed under an enactment or otherwise)[5]; or (3) an independent examiner, reporting accountant or other person appointed to examine or report on a charity's accounts (whether appointed under an enactment or otherwise)[6]. If the Commission considers that a person is or may be personally liable for a breach of trust or breach of duty committed in his capacity as such a person, but that he has acted honestly and reasonably and ought fairly to be excused for the breach of trust or duty, it may make an order relieving him wholly or partly from any such liability[7]. Such an order may grant the relief on such terms as the Commission thinks fit[8].

The Act also extends the court's power under the Companies Act 2006 to grant relief to a person employed as an auditor by a company[9] to: (a) a person falling within head (2) or (3) above, where the provisions of the Companies Act 2006 would not apply to him in that capacity[10]; and (b) a charity trustee of a CIO[11].

If it appears to the court that a trustee is or may be personally liable for any breach of trust but has acted honestly and reasonably and ought fairly to be excused for the breach and for omitting to obtain the court's directions in the matter in which he committed the breach, the court may relieve him wholly or partly from that personal liability[12]. In such a case the onus is upon the trustee to prove that he acted both honestly and reasonably[13]: this is a question of fact depending on the circumstances of each case[14].

1 As to the Charity Commission see PARAS 543–578.

2 See the Charities Act 2011 s 191. The Charities Act 2011 ss 191, 192 have effect in relation to acts or omissions whether before 27 February 2007: see Sch 8 Pt 1. The Charities Act 2011 s 191 does not affect the operation of the Trustee Act 1925 s 61 (power of court to grant relief to trustees: see note 12), the Companies Act 2006 s 1157 (power of court to grant relief to officers or auditors of companies: see **COMPANIES**) or the Charities Act 2011 s 192 (which extends the Companies Act 2006 s 1157 to auditors etc of charities which are not companies): Charities Act 2011 s 191(6).

3 Charities Act 2011 s 191(1)(a). As to the meaning of 'charity trustee' see PARA 255.

4 For the purposes of the Charities Act 2011 ss 191, 192 this is to be read as including a reference to the Auditor General for Wales acting as auditor under Pt 8 (see PARA 358) and any reference to a charity's accounts is to be read as including any group accounts prepared by the charity trustees of a charity: s 191(5). See also note 2.

5 Charities Act 2011 s 191(1)(b).

6 Charities Act 2011 s 191(1)(c).

7 Charities Act 2011 s 191(2). This does not however apply to any personal contractual liability of a charity trustee or trustee for a charity: s 191(4).

8 Charities Act 2011 s 191(3).

9 Charities Act 2011 s 192(1). See also note 2.

10 Charities Act 2011 s 192(2)(a).
11 Charities Act 2011 s 192(2)(b). As to CIOs see PARA 226 et seq.
12 See the Trustee Act 1925 s 61; and **TRUSTS AND POWERS** vol 98 (2013) PARA 707. As to the court's jurisdiction under this provision see *Re Allsop, Whittaker v Bamford* [1914] 1 Ch 1, CA (decided under earlier legislation); *Re Pauling's Settlement Trusts, Younghusband v Coutts & Co* [1964] Ch 303, [1963] 3 All ER 1, CA. As to when relief will be granted see **TRUSTS AND POWERS** vol 98 (2013) PARA 707.
13 *National Trustees Co of Australasia v General Finance Co of Australasia* [1905] AC 373, PC; *Re Stuart, Smith v Stuart* [1897] 2 Ch 583.
14 *Re Turner, Barker v Ivimey* [1897] 1 Ch 536.

452. Trustees' indemnity insurance. The charity trustees of a charity[1] may arrange for the purchase, out of the funds of the charity, of insurance designed to indemnify the charity trustees or any trustees for the charity against any personal liability in respect of any breach of trust or breach of duty committed by them in their capacity as charity trustees or trustees for the charity, or any negligence, default, breach of duty or breach of trust committed by them in their capacity as directors or officers of the charity (if it is a body corporate) or of any body corporate carrying on any activities on behalf of the charity[2]. The terms of such insurance must, however, be so framed as to exclude the provision of any indemnity for a person in respect of: (1) any liability incurred by him to pay a fine imposed in criminal proceedings, or a sum payable to a regulatory authority by way of a penalty in respect of non-compliance with any requirement of a regulatory nature (however arising)[3]; (2) any liability incurred by him in defending any criminal proceedings in which he is convicted[4] of an offence arising out of any fraud or dishonesty, or wilful or reckless misconduct, by him[5]; or (3) any liability incurred by him to the charity that arises out of any conduct which he knew (or must reasonably be assumed to have known) was not in the interests of the charity or in the case of which he did not care whether it was in the best interests of the charity or not[6].

The charity trustees of a charity may not purchase insurance under this provision unless they decide that they are satisfied that it is in the best interests of the charity for them to do so[7]. The statutory duty of care[8] applies to a charity trustee when making such a decision[9]. These provisions do not authorise the purchase of any insurance whose purchase is expressly prohibited by the trusts of the charity, but have effect despite any provision prohibiting the charity trustees or trustees for the charity receiving any personal benefit out of the funds of the charity[10].

1 As to the meaning of 'charity trustees' see PARA 255. As the meaning of 'charity' see PARA 1.
2 Charities Act 2011 s 189(1).
3 Charities Act 2011 s 189(2)(a).
4 For these purposes the reference to any such conviction is a reference to one that has become final; a conviction becomes final, if not appealed against, at the end of the period for bringing an appeal, or if appealed against, at the time when the appeal (or any further appeal) is disposed of; and an appeal is disposed of if it is determined and the period for bringing any further appeal has ended or if it is abandoned or otherwise ceases to have effect: Charities Act 2011 s 189(3). The Minister may by order make such amendments of s 189(2), (3) as he considers appropriate: s 190. At the date at which this volume states the law, no such orders had been made.
5 Charities Act 2011 s 189(2)(b).
6 Charities Act 2011 s 189(2)(c).
7 Charities Act 2011 s 189(4).
8 Ie the duty of care in the Trustee Act 2000 s 1(1) (see PARA 334).
9 Charities Act 2011 s 189(5).
10 Charities Act 2011 s 189(6).

453. Accounts against defaulting trustees. The general rule is that, in the absence of special circumstances[1], accounts are to be taken against the trustees from the date at which the misapplication commenced[2]. Each case is, however, decided on its merits at the court's discretion, and therefore the dates to which accounts against charity trustees are carried back differ widely[3]. The court may decline to direct an account where the litigation would be expensive and the benefit to the charity problematical or trifling[4].

Where the misapplication has been innocent, accounts are usually directed from the commencement of the action[5]; but they may also be ordered from the date at which notice was given to the trustees questioning the propriety of the application[6], from the date of the decree declaring the application improper[7], or from the date of the last appointment of a new trustee[8]. An account is not, it seems, directed against innocent trustees where their co-trustees are entirely responsible for the breach of trust[9].

In dealing with charitable corporations which have acted mistakenly but honestly the court likewise has a considerable measure of discretion[10].

1 Eg innocent misapplication: see the text and notes 5–9.

2 *A-G v Cashel Corpn* (1842) 3 Dr & War 294; *A-G v Davey* (1854) 19 Beav 521 at 527 per Romilly MR, where accounts were ordered from the dates when improper leases were granted. See also *A-G v Newbury Corpn* (1834) 3 My & K 647 at 653 per Lord Brougham LC, where the question of directing an account from the date of the foundation of the charity was discussed.

3 *A-G v Davey* (1854) 19 Beav 521 at 527 per Romilly MR. In *A-G v Pretyman* (1841) 4 Beav 462 at 467 per Lord Langdale MR, the question was referred by the court to the consideration of the Attorney General. As to the Attorney General's power to sanction compromises in such cases see *A-G v Exeter Corpn* (1822) Jac 443 at 448 per Plumer MR; *A-G v Exeter Corpn* (1827) 2 Russ 362; *A-G v Brettingham* (1840) 3 Beav 91; and cf *A-G v Carlisle Corpn* (1831) 4 Sim 275. As to the Attorney General see PARAS 589, 596, 605 et seq; and CONSTITUTIONAL AND ADMINISTRATIVE LAW vol 20 (2014) PARA 273 et seq.

4 *A-G v Dixie, ex p Bosworth School* (1805) 13 Ves 519; *A-G v Cullum* (1836) 1 Keen 104; *A-G v Shearman* (1839) 2 Beav 104.

5 *A-G v Joliffe* (1822) 1 LJOS Ch 43; *A-G v Winchester Corpn* (1824) 3 LJOS Ch 64; *A-G v Stationers' Co* (1831) 9 LJOS Ch 229; *A-G v Caius College* (1837) 2 Keen 150 at 166 per Lord Langdale MR; *A-G v Harper, A-G v Nash* (1838) 8 LJCh 12; *A-G v Drapers' Co, Kendrick's Charity* (1841) 4 Beav 67; *A-G v Drapers' Co, Kendrick's Charity* (1847) 10 Beav 558; *A-G v Christ's Hospital* (1841) 4 Beav 73; *A-G v Hall* (1853) 16 Beav 388 at 395 per Romilly MR; *A-G v Davey* (1854) 19 Beav 521; *A-G v Master, Wardens etc of the Wax Chandlers' Co* (1873) LR 6 HL 1 at 15 per Lord Chelmsford.

6 *A-G v Berwick-upon-Tweed Corpn* (1829) Taml 239; *A-G v East Retford Corpn* (1833) 2 My & K 35 at 37 per Leach MR; *A-G v Cambridge Corpn* (1836) 5 LJCh 357.

7 *A-G v Tufnell* (1849) 12 Beav 35.

8 *A-G v Newbury Corpn* (1834) 3 My & K 647.

9 *A-G v Joliffe* (1822) 1 LJOS Ch 43; *A-G v Holland* (1837) 2 Y & C Ex 683, where co-trustees of a charity under a will were directed to act annually in rotation.

10 *Re Freeston's Charity, Sylvester v Master and Fellows of University College, Oxford* [1978] 1 All ER 481, [1978] 1 WLR 120; affd [1979] 1 All ER 51, [1978] 1 WLR 741, CA.

454. Liability for interest or profits. It has been held that, where a charity trustee uses the trust funds for trading purposes, he is accountable to the charity for any profit made, or for interest at the rate of 5 per cent if the latter is the larger amount[1]; but in general a defaulting trustee is charged with interest at 4 per cent[2]. However, these rates have been thought to be unrealistic in modern conditions[3], and in some relatively recent non-charity cases it has been held that the proper rate of interest is 1 per cent above bank rate[4], while in others it has been said that it should be that allowed from time to time on the court's short term investment account[5]. Whether the interest is simple or compound is in the discretion of the court[6].

1 *A-G v Solly* (1829) 2 Sim 518, where a charity trustee who used the trust property for trading purposes was charged 5 per cent, but not compound interest; *A-G v Cambridge Corpn* (1836) 5 LJCh 357; *Re Davis, Davis v Davis* [1902] 2 Ch 314, applied in the non-charity case of *Gordon v Gonda* [1955] 2 All ER 762, [1955] 1 WLR 885, CA.

2 *Jones v Foxall* (1852) 15 Beav 388 at 392 per Romilly MR; *A-G v Alford* (1855) 4 De GM & G 843 at 851 per Lord Cranworth LC; *Re Emmet's Estate, Emmet v Emmet* (1881) 17 ChD 142. In *A-G v Cambridge Corpn* (1836) 5 LJCh 357, the interest was 5 per cent. As to trustees' liability to pay interest see TRUSTS AND POWERS vol 98 (2013) PARAS 690–692.

3 See *Bartlett v Barclays Bank Trust Co Ltd (No 2)* [1980] Ch 515 at 547, [1980] 2 All ER 92 at 98 per Brightman LJ.

4 See *Belmont Finance Corpn Ltd v Williams Furniture Ltd (No 2)* [1980] 1 All ER 393, CA; *O'Sullivan v Management Agency and Music Ltd* [1985] QB 428, [1985] 3 All ER 351, CA.

5 See *Bartlett v Barclays Bank Trust Co Ltd (No 2)* [1980] Ch 515, [1980] 2 All ER 92. As to the management and investment of funds in court see the Administration of Justice Act 1982 Pt VI (ss 38–48).

6 See the cases cited in notes 1–5; *Incorporated Society in Dublin v Richards* (1841) 1 Dr & War 258 (where a trustee who set up a title adverse to the charity was charged compound interest); *A-G v Alford* (1855) 4 De GM & G 843 at 851 per Lord Cranworth LC. In other cases relating to private trusts (*Heighington v Grant* (1840) 5 My & Cr 258; *Jones v Foxall* (1852) 15 Beav 388) compound interest has been charged where trust funds had been employed in trade. See also the non-charity cases of *Burdick v Garrick* (1870) 5 Ch App 233; *Re Davis, Davis v Davis* [1902] 2 Ch 314; and TRUSTS AND POWERS vol 98 (2013) PARA 692.

455. Liability of trustee's agent. Where a trustee administers a charity by means of a mere agent, the latter is usually accountable in case of default only to his principal and not to the charity, as the ordinary law of agency is applicable to charity cases[1]; but if the agent, knowing that a breach of trust is being committed, interferes and assists in the breach, or if a stranger intermeddles with the affairs and administration of a charity, each makes himself a quasi-trustee and as such personally answerable[2].

1 *A-G v Earl of Chesterfield* (1854) 18 Beav 596. Note that in that case it was not alleged that the agent himself was in any sense a trustee. As to the relationship between principal and agent see further AGENCY vol 1 (2008) PARA 71 et seq.

2 *A-G v Earl of Chesterfield* (1854) 18 Beav 596 at 599 per Romilly MR. See also *A-G v Leicester Corpn* (1844) 7 Beav 176 (where a town clerk who retained trust funds with the consent of a municipal corporation, the actual trustee of the charity, was held jointly liable with the corporation for the breach of trust); *A-G v Wilson* (1840) Cr & Ph 1 (where a corporation was trustee of a charity and the members of the governing body were held liable for injury to the charity occasioned by their default); *Charitable Corpn v Sutton* (1742) 2 Atk 400 at 405 per Lord Hardwicke LC. See also TRUSTS AND POWERS vol 98 (2013) PARAS 125, 669.

456. Remedy against trustee corporation. When a corporation is declared liable to make good a loss caused by a breach of trust, the court does not charge the loss upon the general property of the corporation. The remedy is enforceable by process of sequestration[1].

1 *A-G v East Retford Corpn* (1838) 3 My & Cr 484.

457. Liability of trust property. Charity property cannot be taken to indemnify a person injured by a breach of trust committed by the trustees of the charity[1].

1 *Heriot's Hospital (Feoffees) v Ross* (1846) 12 Cl & Fin 507, HL (a Scottish case).

(6) EDUCATIONAL CHARITIES

(i) Educational Charities generally

458. Endowments for maintenance of voluntary schools. Where the trust deed[1] of a voluntary school requires that the income of any endowment is to be applied towards the maintenance of a school which a local authority is required to maintain as a voluntary school, any such income must not be paid to the local authority but must be applied by the governors of the school towards the discharge of their obligations, if any[2], with respect to the maintenance of the school, or in such other manner, if any, as may be determined by a scheme[3] for the administration of the endowment[4].

1 'Trust deed' means, in relation to any voluntary school, any instrument, other than an instrument of government, regulating the constitution of the school's governing body or the maintenance, management or conduct of the school: Education Act 1996 s 579(1) (definition added by the School Standards and Framework Act 1998 s 140(1), Sch 30 para 183(a)(iv); and applied by s 142(8)). As to voluntary schools see EDUCATION vol 35 (2011) PARA 108.

2 In the case of a controlled school, the governors have no obligations with respect to the maintenance of the school. The governors of aided and special agreement schools are responsible for the expenses referred to in the School Standards and Framework Act 1998 s 22, Sch 3 para 3: see EDUCATION vol 35 (2011) PARA 284. As to controlled schools and aided and special agreement schools see EDUCATION vol 35 (2011) PARA 106.

3 Ie a scheme made by the Charity Commission. As to the Charity Commission see PARAS 538–572.

4 See the School Standards and Framework Act 1998 Sch 3 para 11 (amended by SI 2010/1158); and EDUCATION vol 35 (2011) PARA 281.

459. Power of local authorities to accept gifts for educational purposes. A local authority is empowered to accept, hold and administer any property on trust for purposes connected with education[1]. Any intention on the part of the authority that a school should be vested in the authority as trustees is treated[2] as an intention to establish a new community school[3], community special school[4] or maintained nursery school[5], and the relevant procedure applies[6]. Any school which is so vested in a local education authority as trustees, is a community school, a community special school or a maintained nursery school[7].

1 See the Education Act 1996 s 529(1); and EDUCATION vol 36 (2011) PARA 1625. As to the application of an endowment of an existing school transferred to the local education authority see *Re Poplar and Blackwall Free School* (1878) 8 ChD 543.

2 Ie in England treated for the purposes of the Education and Inspections Act 2006 ss 7, 10, 11, and in Wales treated for the purposes of the School Standards and Framework Act 1998 ss 28, 31: see EDUCATION vol 35 (2011) PARA 123.

3 As to community schools see EDUCATION vol 35 (2011) PARA 107.

4 As to community special schools see EDUCATION vol 36 (2011) PARA 1227 et seq.

5 As to maintained nursery schools see EDUCATION vol 35 (2011) PARA 177.

6 See the Education Act 1996 s 529(1A), (2); and EDUCATION vol 36 (2011) PARA 1625.

7 See the Education Act 1996 s 529(3); and EDUCATION vol 36 (2011) PARA 1625.

460. Extent of local authority's powers relating to charitable purposes. It is the duty of the local authority to contribute towards the spiritual, moral, mental and physical development of the community by securing that efficient primary education and secondary education are available to meet the needs of the population of its area, so far as its powers extend[1]. This duty does not extend to matters in respect of which the Chief Executive of Skills Funding[2], the Welsh Ministers[3], or the higher education funding councils[4] have a duty[5]. A local education authority has no locus standi to institute legal proceedings for the construction of a will purporting to create a charitable trust[6]. However, a local authority may help with education matters by establishing a trust fund to provide free or assisted places at independent schools[7].

1 See the Education Act 1996 s 13(1); and EDUCATION vol 35 (2011) PARA 26.
2 See EDUCATION vol 36 (2011) PARA 1279.
3 Ie under the Learning and Skills Act 2000 Pt 2 (ss 31–41).
4 Ie established under the Further and Higher Education Act 1992 s 62: see EDUCATION vol 36 (2011) PARA 887.
5 See the Education Act 1996 s 13(2); and EDUCATION vol 35 (2011) PARA 26.
6 *Re Belling, Enfield London Borough Council v Public Trustee* [1967] Ch 425, [1967] 1 All ER 105.
7 *Manchester City Council v Greater Manchester Metropolitan County Council* (1980) 78 LGR 560, HL. This was decided on the basis that the authority so enabled was not a local education authority; since the abolition of separate local education authorities (see EDUCATION vol 35 (2011) PARA 25), it is conceived that this applies more generally. As to independent schools see EDUCATION vol 35 (2011) PARA 440 et seq.

(ii) Trusts

461. Powers as to educational trusts. The Secretary of State or, in relation to Wales, the Welsh Ministers may by order make modifications of any trust deed[1] or other instrument relating to[2]: (1) a school which is or is to become a foundation, voluntary or foundation special school[3]; or (2) property held on trust for the purposes of such a school[4]. Such an order may be made so as to have permanent effect or to have effect for such period as is specified in the order[5]. However, before making such an order the Secretary of State or, in relation to Wales, the Welsh Ministers, must consult: (a) the governing body of the school in question; (b) any trustees holding property on trust for the purposes of the school; (c) in the case of a Church of England, Church in Wales or Roman Catholic Church school, the appropriate diocesan authority[6]; and (d) such other persons as he considers appropriate[7].

The Secretary of State or, in relation to Wales, the Welsh Ministers may by order make such modifications of any trust deed or other instrument relating to or regulating any institution that provides or is concerned in the provision of educational services, or is concerned in educational research, as, after consultation with the persons responsible for the management of the institution, appear to him to be requisite to enable them to fulfil any condition or meet any requirement imposed by regulations[8]. Any modification made by such an order may be made to have permanent effect or to have effect for such period as may be specified in the order[9].

1 As to the meaning of 'trust deed' see PARA 458 note 1.
2 See the School Standards and Framework Act 1998 s 82(1); and EDUCATION vol 35 (2011) PARA 117.
3 See the School Standards and Framework Act 1998 s 82(1)(a); and EDUCATION vol 35 (2011) PARA 117. As to foundation, voluntary and foundation special schools see EDUCATION vol 35 (2011) PARA 108.
4 See the School Standards and Framework Act 1998 s 82(1)(b); and EDUCATION vol 35 (2011) PARA 117.
5 See the School Standards and Framework Act 1998 s 82(3); and EDUCATION vol 35 (2011) PARA 117.
6 As to the appropriate diocesan authority for a Church of England, Church in Wales or Roman Catholic Church school see EDUCATION vol 35 (2011) PARA 117.
7 See the School Standards and Framework Act 1998 s 82(2); and EDUCATION vol 35 (2011) PARA 117. Where any scheme for the regulation of endowed charities includes any provision for the benefit of children who are or have been scholars in a county or voluntary school, an army

school is deemed to be a county or voluntary school within the meaning of those provisions: see the Army Schools Act 1891 s 1(1); and EDUCATION vol 35 (2011) PARA 117. An army school is a school established for the purpose of affording education to children of non-commissioned officers and men of Her Majesty's regular land forces and conducted under the authority of a Secretary of State: see the Army Schools Act 1891 s 1(2); and EDUCATION vol 35 (2011) PARA 117. As to voluntary schools see EDUCATION vol 35 (2011) PARA 108.

8 Education Act 1996 s 489(3). As to the regulations made under s 485 (grants in aid of educational services or research) see EDUCATION vol 35 (2011) PARA 81.

9 Education Act 1996 s 489(4).

462. Powers as to trusts for religious education. Where in relation to any time before the appointed day[1], the premises of a voluntary or grant-maintained school[2] ceased to be used for such a school[3], or in relation to any time on or after the appointed day[4]: (1) the premises of a foundation or voluntary school[5] have ceased to be used for such a school[6]; or (2) in the opinion of the Secretary of State or, in relation to Wales, the Welsh Ministers[7] it is likely such premises will cease to be so used[8], he or they may by order[9] made by statutory instrument make new provision as to the use of any endowment[10] if it is shown[11] either[12]: (a) that the endowment is or has been held wholly or partly for or in connection with the provision at the school of religious education in accordance with the tenets of a particular religion or religious denomination[13]; or (b) that the endowment is or has been used wholly or partly for or in connection with the provision at the school of such religious education and that the following requirements are fulfilled[14], namely (i) that the school was or has been maintained as a voluntary or grant-maintained school[15] or as a foundation or voluntary school[16] since 1 April 1945[17]; and (ii) that religious education in accordance with the tenets of the religion or denomination concerned is, and from that date has been, provided at the school or, where the premises have ceased to be used for the purposes of the school, was provided at the school from that date until immediately before the premises ceased to be so used[18].

Such an order by the Secretary of State or, in relation to Wales, the Welsh Ministers may require or authorise the disposal by sale or otherwise of any land or other property forming part of an endowment affected by the order, including the premises of the school and any teacher's dwelling-house, and may also consolidate any endowments to be dealt with by the scheme[19]. Subject to this and to any statutory provisions affecting the endowments, the order must establish and give effect, with a view to enabling the denomination concerned to participate more effectively in the administration of the statutory system of public education, to a scheme or schemes[20] for the endowments dealt with by the order to be used[21] for appropriate educational purposes[22]. The order may include any necessary or expedient incidental or supplementary provisions[23].

1 The appointed day is 1 September 1999: School Standards and Framework Act 1998 s 20(7); School Standards and Framework Act 1998 (Appointed Day) Order 1998, SI 1998/2083, art 2.

2 As to voluntary schools and grant-maintained schools see EDUCATION vol 35 (2011) PARA 108.

3 Education Act 1996 s 554(1)(a) (s 554(1) substituted by the School Standards and Framework Act 1998 Sch 30 para 168(2)).

4 Education Act 1996 s 554(1)(b) (as substituted: see note 3).

5 Ie within the meaning of the School Standards and Framework Act 1998: see EDUCATION vol 35 (2011) PARA 108. As to foundation schools see EDUCATION vol 35 (2011) PARA 108.

6 Education Act 1996 s 554(1)(b)(i) (as substituted: see note 3).

7 As to the Secretary of State and the Welsh Ministers see PARA 585.

8 Education Act 1996 s 554(1)(b)(ii) (as substituted: see note 3).

9 The order may be made only on the application of the persons appearing to the Secretary of State or, in relation to Wales, the Welsh Ministers to be the appropriate authority of the denomination concerned: Education Act 1996 s 555(1). The Secretary of State or, in relation to

Wales, the Welsh Ministers must, not less than one month before making the order give notice of the proposed order and of the right of persons interested to make representations on it: s 555(2). The order must take into account any representations that may be made to the Secretary of State or, in relation to Wales, the Welsh Ministers by any person interested in it before the order is made: s 555(4). The notice must be given: (1) by giving to any persons appearing to the Secretary of State or, in relation to Wales, the Welsh Ministers to be trustees of an endowment affected by the proposed order a notice of the proposal to make it, together with a draft or summary of the provisions proposed to be included; and (2) by publishing, in such manner as the Secretary of State, or in relation to Wales, the Welsh Ministers think sufficient for informing any other persons interested, a notice of the proposal to make the order and of the place where any person interested may, during a period of not less than a month, inspect such a draft or summary, and by keeping a draft or summary available for inspection in accordance with the notice: s 555(3).

10 'Endowment' includes property not subject to any restriction on the expenditure of capital: Education Act 1996 s 554(5). As to the extension to army schools of certain provisions relating to endowments see EDUCATION vol 35 (2011) PARA 117.

11 'Shown' means shown to the satisfaction of the Secretary of State: Education Act 1996 s 554(5).

12 Education Act 1996 s 554(2), which is expressed to be subject to s 555 (see note 9), and s 556(1), (2) (see the text and notes 19–22).

13 Education Act 1996 s 554(2)(a).

14 Education Act 1996 s 554(2)(b), which is expressed to be subject to s 554(4) (see the text and note 18).

15 Ie within the meaning of the Education Act 1996: see EDUCATION vol 35 (2011) PARA 106.

16 Ie within the meaning of the School Standards and Framework Act 1998: see EDUCATION vol 35 (2011) PARA 108.

17 Education Act 1996 s 554(3)(a) (substituted by the School Standards and Framework Act 1998 Sch 30 para 168(3)(a)). The text refers to the date on which the Education Act 1944 Pt II (ss 6–69) (now repealed) came into force.

18 Education Act 1996 s 554(3)(b). 'Used' in this context means used in pursuance of ss 377, 378, 380, 381 (all repealed) (or any corresponding earlier enactment), or the School Standards and Framework Act 1998 Sch 19 para 3 or 4 (see EDUCATION vol 36 (2011) PARAS 1118–1119): Education Act 1996 s 554(3)(b) (amended by the School Standards and Framework Act 1998 Sch 30 para 168(3)(b)). Where religious education in accordance with such tenets is shown to have been given to any pupils at: (1) a controlled school (within the meaning of the Education Act 1996); (2) a grant-maintained school (within the meaning of the Education Act 1996) which was a controlled school immediately before it became a grant-maintained school; or (3) a foundation or voluntary controlled school with a religious character (within the meaning of the School Standards and Framework Act 1998 Pt II (ss 22–83)), the religious education is taken to have been given to them at the request of their parents, unless the contrary is shown: Education Act 1996 s 554(4)(b) (substituted by the School Standards and Framework Act 1998 Sch 30 para 168(4)). As to controlled schools see EDUCATION vol 35 (2011) PARA 106.

As to the adoption of uniform statutory trusts as the trusts on which endowments regulated by an order under the Education Act 1996 s 554 are to be held see s 557, Sch 36; and EDUCATION vol 36 (2011) PARA 1629.

19 Education Act 1996 s 556(1).

20 Such a scheme may provide for the retention of the capital of any endowment and the application of the accruing income, or may authorise the application or expenditure of capital to such extent and on such conditions as may be determined under the scheme: see Education Act 1996 s 556(4).

21 Ie either in connection with schools which are foundation schools or voluntary schools or partly in connection with such schools (or either description of such schools) and partly in other ways related to the locality served by the school at the premises referred to in the Education Act 1996 s 554(1) (see the text and notes 1–8): s 556(2) (amended by the School Standards and Framework Act 1998 Sch 30 para 169(a), (b)).

22 Education Act 1996 s 556(2). 'Use for appropriate educational purposes' means use for educational purposes in connection with the provision of religious education in accordance with the tenets of the religion or denomination concerned (including use for any purpose specified in Sch 36 (uniform statutory trusts for educational endowments): see EDUCATION vol 35 (2011) PARA 129): s 556(3).

23 See the Education Act 1996 s 556(6). Thus it may provide for the appointment and powers of trustees and for vesting property in trustees: see s 556(6).

463. Sex discrimination: application by trustees to remove or modify restriction. Where a trust deed or other instrument concerns property applicable for or in connection with the provision of education in certain establishments[1] and in any way restricts the benefits available under the instrument to persons of one sex[2], the trustees or the responsible body[3] may apply to a Minister of the Crown for the removal or modification of the restriction[4]. If, on such an application, the Minister is satisfied that the removal or modification of the restriction would conduce to the advancement of education without sex discrimination, he may by order make such modifications of the instrument as appear expedient for removing or modifying the restriction[5]. If the trust was created by gift or bequest, no such order may be made until 25 years after the date on which the gift or bequest took effect, unless the donor or his personal representatives, or the personal representatives of the testator, have consented in writing to the making of the application for the order[6].

The Minister must require the applicant to publish a notice containing particulars of the proposed order and stating that representations may be made to him within a period specified in the notice[7]. That period must be not less than one month from the date of the notice[8]. The applicant must publish the notice in such manner as may be specified by the Minister, and the cost of any publication of the notice may be defrayed out of the property of the trust[9]. Before making the order the Minister must take into account any representations duly made in accordance with the notice[10].

1 Equality Act 2010 Sch 14 para 1(1)(a). The establishments mentioned in the text are those to which the Equality Act 2010 s 85 or s 91 applies: see further DISCRIMINATION vol 33 (2013) PARAS 166 et seq, 175 et seq.
2 Equality Act 2010 Sch 14 para 1(1)(b).
3 The 'responsible body' in respect of the establishments specified in note 1 is the body specified in the Equality Act 2010 s 85 or s 91 respectively.
4 See the Equality Act 2010 Sch 14 para 1(2).
5 See the Equality Act 2010 Sch 14 para 1(2), (3).
6 See the Equality Act 2010 Sch 14 para 1(4), (5).
7 Equality Act 2010 Sch 14 para 1(6).
8 Equality Act 2010 Sch 14 para 1(7).
9 Equality Act 2010 Sch 14 para 1(8), (9).
10 Equality Act 2010 Sch 14 para 1(10).

9. CONTROL OF CHARITABLE FUND RAISING

(1) STATUTORY CONTROLS

464. Statutory control of charitable fund raising. Fund raising for charities is subject to various statutory controls. The House to House Collections Act 1939, which provides for the regulation of house to house collection for charitable purposes, is prospectively repealed[1]. The regime introduced by the Charities Act 1992 deals with control of fund raising for charitable institutions[2]. The 1992 Act also provided for public charitable collections[3], being charitable appeals made in any public place or by means of visits from house to house[4], but the relevant provisions were never brought into force and have since been repealed[5]. The Charities Act 2006 provides a new regime for public charitable collections[6], but the relevant provisions are, except for limited purposes[7], not yet in force[8].

The Charity Commission[9] has published guidance on the legal and practical aspects of fundraising by charities and how it is regulated[10].

1 The House to House Collections Act 1939 is repealed by the Charities Act 1992 s 78(2), Sch 7 as from a day to be appointed under s 79(2). At the date at which this volume states the law no such day had been appointed, and the likelihood of that repeal being brought into force is unclear. As to the House to House Collections Act 1939 see PARAS 465–475. Certain functions under the House to House Collections Act 1939 are 'relevant functions' for the purposes of the Regulatory Enforcement and Sanctions Act 2008 s 4, Sch 3: see LOCAL GOVERNMENT vol 69 (2009) PARA 733.

2 See the Charities Act 1992 Pt II (ss 58–64A); and PARAS 477–494.

3 See the Charities Act 1992 Pt III (ss 65–74) (repealed).

4 See the Charities Act 1992 s 65(1)(a) (repealed).

5 Charities Act 2006 s 75(2), Sch 9 para 1.

6 See the Charities Act 2006 Pt 3 Ch 1 (ss 45–66); and PARAS 495–511.

7 See PARA 495 notes 2, 10.

8 The Charities Act 2006 Pt 3 Ch 1 is to be brought into force by order made by the Minister under s 79(2) as from a day to be appointed. At the date at which this volume states the law only certain provisions were in force, and the likelihood of the regime under the Act being given full statutory force is unclear. As to the Minister see PARA 586.

9 As to the Charity Commission see PARAS 543–578.

10 See *CC20: Charities and fundraising* (Charity Commission, May 2011) (available, at the date at which this volume states the law, on the government website). As to the Charity Commission's publications see PARA 547.

(2) HOUSE TO HOUSE COLLECTIONS, WAR CHARITIES AND CHARITIES FOR THE DISABLED

465. Promoter must be licensed. It is generally necessary to have a licence[1] to promote[2] a house to house collection for any charitable purpose[3]. If a person promotes a collection for a charitable purpose, and a collection for that purpose is made in any locality pursuant to his promotion, then, unless there is in force, throughout the period during which the collection is made in that locality, a licence authorising him, or authorising another under whose authority he acts, to promote a collection in that locality for that purpose, he is guilty of an offence[4]. A collector who acts in any locality for the purposes of a collection for a charitable purpose without there being in force, at all times when he so acts, a licence authorising a promoter under whose authority he acts, or authorising the collector himself, to promote a collection in that locality for that purpose is guilty of an offence[5].

1 'Licence' means a licence under the House to House Collections Act 1939: s 11(1) (prospectively repealed: see PARA 464).

2 'Promoter' means, in relation to a collection, a person who causes others to act, whether for remuneration or otherwise, as collectors for the purposes of the collection; and 'promote' and 'promotion' have corresponding meanings: House to House Collections Act 1939 s 11(1) (prospectively repealed: see PARA 464). 'Collection' means an appeal to the public, made by means of visits from house to house, to give, whether for consideration or not, money or other property; and 'collector' means, in relation to a collection, a person who makes the appeal in the course of such visits as aforesaid: s 11(1) (prospectively repealed: see PARA 464). See also *Carasu Ltd v Smith* [1968] 2 QB 383, [1968] 2 All ER 529, DC ('collection' included a case where a person is induced to purchase an article on the representation that part of the proceeds will go to charity); followed in *Cooper v Coles* [1987] QB 230, [1987] 1 All ER 91, DC, where the view of Forbes J in *Murphy v Duke* [1985] QB 905, [1985] 2 All ER 274 that the earlier decision was made per incuriam was said to be wrong.

'House' includes place of business: House to House Collections Act 1939 s 11(1) (prospectively repealed: see PARA 464). A public house has been held to be a place of business within the House to House Collections Act 1939: see *Report of the Charity Commissioners for England and Wales for 1986* (HC Paper (1986–87) no 306) para 66.

3 See the House to House Collections Act 1939 s 1(1) (prospectively repealed: see PARA 464). 'Charitable purpose' means any charitable, benevolent or philanthropic purpose, whether or not charitable within the meaning of any rule of law: s 11(1) (prospectively repealed: see PARA 464). A collection is deemed to be made for a particular purpose where the appeal is made in association with a representation that the money or other property appealed for, or part of it, will be applied for that purpose: s 11(2) (prospectively repealed: see PARA 464). The Act did not apply to house to house collections made by a registered pool promoter who held a licence under the Pool Competitions Act 1971 permitting house to house collection of entry money etc: s 3(5). However, the Pool Competitions Act 1971 expired on 26 July 1987 (the date to which it was continued in force by the Pool Competitions Act 1971 (Continuance) Order 1986, SI 1986/1234 (spent)). At the date at which this volume states the law no subsequent order has been made continuing it in force.

4 House to House Collections Act 1939 s 1(2) (prospectively repealed: see PARA 464). See also *Carasu Ltd v Smith* [1968] 2 QB 383, [1968] 2 All ER 529, DC. Any promoter guilty of such an offence is liable on summary conviction to a penalty not exceeding six months' imprisonment or a fine not exceeding level 3 on the standard scale or both such imprisonment and such fine: House to House Collections Act 1939 s 8(1) (amended by virtue of the Criminal Justice Act 1982 ss 38, 46). The House to House Collections Act 1939 is prospectively repealed: see PARA 464. As to the standard scale see **SENTENCING AND DISPOSITION OF OFFENDERS** vol 92 (2010) PARA 142.

5 House to House Collections Act 1939 s 1(3) (prospectively repealed: see PARA 464). See also *Carasu Ltd v Smith* [1968] 2 QB 383, [1968] 2 All ER 529, DC. Any collector guilty of such an offence is liable, on summary conviction, to a fine not exceeding level 2 on the standard scale or to imprisonment for a term currently not exceeding three months and, from a day to be appointed, not exceeding three months, or to both such imprisonment and such fine: House to House Collections Act 1939 s 8(2) (amended by virtue of the Criminal Justice Act 1982 ss 35, 46). The House to House Collections Act 1939 is prospectively repealed: see PARA 464. As from a day to be appointed the maximum term of imprisonment is 51 weeks: see the House to House Collections Act 1939 s 8(2) (prospectively amended by the Criminal Justice Act 2003 Sch 26 para 10). At the date at which this volume states the law, no such day had been appointed. It must be proved that the person charged went from house to house or was about to do so when found collecting in one house: *Hankinson v Dowland* [1974] 3 All ER 655, [1974] 1 WLR 1327.

466. Local exemption certificate. If the chief officer of police for the police area[1] comprising a locality in which a collection[2] for a charitable purpose[3] is being or is proposed to be made is satisfied that the purpose is local in character and that the collection is likely to be completed within a short period of time, he may grant to the person appearing to be principally concerned in the promotion[4] a certificate in the prescribed[5] form exempting the grantee, or any person authorised by him to act as promoter[6] or collector[7] in relation to that collection, from the provisions of the House to House Collections Act 1939 (other than those relating to the unauthorised use of badges[8] and the requirement of collectors' names[9]), within the locality and for the period specified in the certificate[10], and from the provisions of regulations made under the Act within the same locality and period[11].

1 As to chief officers of police see POLICE AND INVESTIGATORY POWERS vol 84 (2013) PARA 112 et seq. As to police areas see POLICE AND INVESTIGATORY POWERS vol 84 (2013) PARAS 52–54. The functions conferred on a chief officer of police by the House to House Collections Act 1939 or any regulations made under it may be delegated by him to any officer not below the rank of inspector: s 7(2) (prospectively repealed: see PARA 464). The functions which may be so delegated do not include any functions conferred on the Metropolitan Police Commissioner by virtue of his being a licensing authority within the meaning of s 2 (see PARA 468): s 9(2) (amended by the Local Government Act 1972 Sch 29 para 23(5)). The House to House Collections Act 1939 is prospectively repealed: see PARA 464. As to the Metropolitan Police Commissioner see POLICE AND INVESTIGATORY POWERS vol 84 (2013) PARA 117 et seq.
2 As to the meaning of 'collection' see PARA 465 note 2.
3 As to the meaning of 'charitable purposes' see PARA 465 note 3.
4 As to the meaning of 'promotion' see PARA 465 note 2.
5 'Prescribed' means prescribed by regulations made under the House to House Collections Act 1939: s 11(1) (prospectively repealed: see PARA 464). For the form of the certificate see the House to House Collections Regulations 1947, SR & O 1947/2662, reg 3(1), Sch 1.
6 As to the meaning of 'promoter' see PARA 465 note 2.
7 As to the meaning of 'collector' see PARA 465 note 2.
8 Ie the House to House Collections Act 1939 ss 5, 8(4): see PARA 470.
9 Ie the House to House Collections Act 1939 ss 6, 8(5): see PARA 471.
10 House to House Collections Act 1939 s 1(4) (prospectively repealed: see PARA 464).
11 See the House to House Collections Regulations 1947, SR & O 1947/2662, reg 3(2).

467. Exemption of collections over wide areas. Where the Minister[1] is satisfied that a person pursues a charitable purpose[2] throughout the whole or a substantial part of England and is desirous of promoting collections[3] for that purpose, he may by order[4], direct that that person is exempt from the necessity of having a licence[5] as respects all collections for that purpose in the localities prescribed in the order[6]. Whilst the order is in force as respects collections in any locality, the House to House Collections Act 1939 has effect in relation to the person exempted, to a promoter[7] of a collection in that locality for that purpose acting under the authority of the person exempted, and to a person who so acts as a collector[8] for the purposes of any such collection, as if a licence authorising the exempted person to promote[9] a collection in that locality for that purpose were in force[10].

1 As to the Minister see PARA 586.
2 As to the meaning of 'charitable purposes' see PARA 465 note 3.
3 As to the meaning of 'collection' see PARA 465 note 2.
4 At the date at which this volume states the law no such orders had been made. Any order made under the House to House Collections Act 1939 s 3 (prospectively repealed) may be revoked or varied by a subsequent order made by the Minister: s 3(2) (amended by SI 2006/2951; and prospectively repealed (see PARA 464)).
5 As to the meaning of 'licence' see PARA 461 note 1.
6 House to House Collections Act 1939 s 3(1) (amended by SI 2006/2951; and prospectively repealed (see PARA 464)). An application for an order must be made not later than the first day of the month preceding that in which it is proposed to commence the collection, but the licensing authority or, as the case may be, the Minister may grant an application made out of time if satisfied that there are special reasons for doing so: House to House Collections Regulations 1947, SR & O 1947/2662, reg 4(2) (modified by SI 1974/595 reg 4; and amended by virtue of SI 2006/2951).
7 As to the meaning of 'promoter' see PARA 465 note 2.
8 As to the meaning of 'collector' see PARA 465 note 2.
9 As to the meaning of 'promote' see PARA 465 note 2.
10 House to House Collections Act 1939 s 3(1) (as amended (see note 6); and prospectively repealed: see PARA 464).

468. Grant or refusal of licences. If a person promoting or proposing to promote[1] a collection[2] in any locality for a charitable purpose[3] makes to the licensing authority[4] for the area comprising that locality an application in the prescribed manner[5] specifying the purpose of the collection and the locality, whether being the whole of the area of the authority or a part of it, within which the collection is to be made, and furnishes it with the prescribed information[6], the authority must, subject to the provisions following, grant him a licence[7] to promote a collection within that locality for that purpose[8]. The licence is generally granted for such period, not being longer than 12 months, as is specified in the application, and remains in force for that period unless revoked[9], provided that, if it appears to a licensing authority to be expedient to provide for the simultaneous expiration of licences to be granted by it in respect of collections which in its opinion are likely to be proposed to be made annually or continuously over a long period, it may, on the grant of such a licence, grant it for a period shorter or longer than that specified in the application, or for a period longer than 12 months (but not exceeding 18 months), as may be requisite for that purpose[10].

The licensing authority may refuse or revoke the grant of a licence if it appears to it that[11]:

(1) the total amount likely to be applied for charitable purposes as a result of the collection, including any amount already so applied, is inadequate in proportion to the value of the proceeds[12] likely to be or already received[13];

(2) remuneration which is excessive in relation to that total amount is likely to be, or has been, retained out of the proceeds of the collection by any person[14];

(3) the grant of a licence would be likely to facilitate the commission of an offence of begging[15], or that such an offence has been committed in connection with the collection[16];

(4) the applicant or licensee is not a fit and proper person to hold a licence by reason of conviction in the United Kingdom of certain offences[17], or conviction in any part of the Queen's dominions of any offence conviction for which necessarily involved a finding that he acted fraudulently or dishonestly, or of an offence of a kind the commission of which would be likely to be facilitated by the grant of a licence[18];

(5) the applicant or licensee has failed, in promoting a licensed collection, to exercise due diligence to secure that persons authorised by him to act as collectors[19] were fit and proper persons, to secure the compliance of persons so authorised with regulations under the House to House Collections Act 1939, or to prevent prescribed badges or certificates of authority[20] being obtained by unauthorised persons[21]; or

(6) the applicant or licensee has refused or neglected to furnish the authority with such information as it has reasonably required for informing itself as to matters specified in heads (1) to (5) above[22].

If the authority refuses or revokes a licence, it must forthwith give written notice to the applicant or licensee stating the ground or grounds on which the licence has been refused or revoked and informing him of the right of appeal, and he may, within 14 days of the notice, appeal to the Minister, whose decision is final[23]. If the appeal is allowed, the authority must forthwith issue a licence or cancel the revocation, as the case may be[24].

1 As to the meaning of 'promote' see PARA 465 note 2.

2 As to the meaning of 'collection' see PARA 465 note 2.
3 As to the meaning of 'charitable purposes' see PARA 465 note 3.
4 The 'licensing authority' means: (1) in relation to the City of London, the Common Council of the City of London; (2) in relation to the metropolitan police district the Metropolitan Police Commissioner; and (3) in relation to a district exclusive of any part of it within the metropolitan police district, the district council: House to House Collections Act 1939 s 2(1A) (added by the Local Government Act 1972 Sch 29 para 23(2)). The House to House Collections Act 1939 is prospectively repealed: see PARA 464. As to the delegation of functions of the Metropolitan Police Commissioner see PARA 466 note 1. As to the Common Council of the City of London see **LONDON GOVERNMENT** vol 71 (2013) PARA 34. As to the metropolitan police district see **POLICE AND INVESTIGATORY POWERS** vol 84 (2013) PARA 53. As to the Metropolitan Police Commissioner see **POLICE AND INVESTIGATORY POWERS** vol 84 (2013) PARA 117 et seq. As to district councils see **LOCAL GOVERNMENT** vol 69 (2009) PARA 24.
5 Ie prescribed by regulations made under the House to House Collections Act 1939. An application for a licence must be in the form specified in the House to House Collections Regulations 1947, SR & O 1947/2662, reg 4(1), Sch 2, and must give the particulars there specified; it must be made not later than the first day of the month preceding that in which it is proposed to commence the collection, but the licensing authority or, as the case may be, the Minister may grant an application made out of time if satisfied there are special reasons for doing so: reg 4(2) (modified by SI 1974/595, reg 4; and amended by virtue of SI 2006/2951). As to the Minister see PARA 586.
6 See note 5.
7 As to the meaning of 'licence' see PARA 465 note 1.
8 House to House Collections Act 1939 s 2(1) (amended by the Local Government Act 1972 Sch 29 para 23(1), Sch 30). The House to House Collections Act 1939 is prospectively repealed: see PARA 464.
9 House to House Collections Act 1939 s 2(2) (prospectively repealed: see PARA 464).
10 House to House Collections Act 1939 s 2(2) proviso (amended by the Local Government Act 1972 Sch 29 para 23(3)). The House to House Collections Act 1939 is prospectively repealed: see PARA 464.
11 House to House Collections Act 1939 s 2(3) (amended by the Local Government Act 1972 Sch 29 para 23(3)). The House to House Collections Act 1939 is prospectively repealed: see PARA 464.
12 'Proceeds' means, in relation to a collection, all money and other property given, whether for consideration or not, in response to the appeal: House to House Collections Act 1939 s 11(1) (prospectively repealed: see PARA 464).
13 House to House Collections Act 1939 s 2(3)(a) (prospectively repealed: see PARA 464).
14 House to House Collections Act 1939 s 2(3)(b) (prospectively repealed: see PARA 464).
15 Ie an offence under the Vagrancy Act 1824 s 3: see **CRIMINAL LAW** vol 26 (2010) PARA 772.
16 House to House Collections Act 1939 s 2(3)(c) (prospectively repealed: see PARA 464).
17 The offences are: (1) offences under the Offences Against the Person Act 1861 s 47 (assault occasioning bodily harm); (2) robbery, burglary and blackmail; (3) offences under the Police, Factories, etc (Miscellaneous Provisions) Act 1916 s 5 (regulation of street collections): House to House Collections Act 1939 s 2(3)(d), Schedule (amended by the Theft Act 1968 s 33(2), Sch 2 Pt III). The House to House Collections Act 1939 is prospectively repealed: see PARA 464. See further **CRIMINAL LAW** vol 25 (2010) PARA 159.
18 House to House Collections Act 1939 s 2(3)(d) (prospectively repealed: see PARA 464).
19 As to the meaning of 'collector' see PARA 465 note 2.
20 As to badges and certificates of authority see PARA 470.
21 House to House Collections Act 1939 s 2(3)(e) (prospectively repealed: see PARA 464).
22 House to House Collections Act 1939 s 2(3)(f) (prospectively repealed: see PARA 464).
23 House to House Collections Act 1939 s 2(4), (5) (s 2(4) amended by the Local Government Act 1972 Sch 29 para 23(3); and SI 2006/2951). The House to House Collections Act 1939 is prospectively repealed: see PARA 464.
24 House to House Collections Act 1939 s 2(6) (amended by the Local Government Act 1972 Sch 29 para 23(3); and SI 2006/2951). The House to House Collections Act 1939 is prospectively repealed: see PARA 464.

469. Conduct of collections; offences against regulations. The Minister[1] may make regulations[2] for prescribing anything which by the House to House Collections Act 1939 is required to be prescribed[3], and for regulating the manner in which collections[4], in respect of which licences[5] have been granted or orders have been made[6], may be carried out and the conduct of promoters[7] and collectors[8] in relation to such collections[9].

Such regulations may make provision for all or any of the following matters:

(1) for requiring and regulating the use by collectors, of prescribed badges and prescribed certificates of authority[10], and the issue, custody, production and return thereof, and, in particular, for requiring collectors on demand by a police constable or by any occupant of a house visited to produce their certificates of authority[11];

(2) in the case of collections in respect of which licences have been granted, for requiring that the prescribed certificates of authority of the collectors must be authenticated in a manner approved by the chief officer of police[12] for the area in respect of which the licence was granted, and that their prescribed badges must have inserted therein or annexed thereto in a manner and form so approved a general indication of the purpose of the collection[13];

(3) for prohibiting persons below a prescribed age from acting, and others from causing them to act, as collectors[14];

(4) for preventing annoyance to the occupants of houses visited by collectors[15];

(5) for requiring the prescribed information with respect to the expenses, proceeds[16] and application of the proceeds of collections to be furnished, in the case of collections in respect of which licences have been granted, by the person to whom the licence was granted to the authority by whom it was granted, and, in the case of collections in respect of which an order has been made, by the person thereby exempted[17] to the Minister, and for requiring the information furnished to be vouched and authenticated in such manner as may be prescribed[18].

Any person who contravenes or fails to comply with the provisions of a regulation made under the House to House Collections Act 1939 is guilty of an offence[19].

Street collections for charities, as distinct from house to house collections, are governed by other statutory provisions and regulations[20].

1 As to the Minister see PARA 586.
2 See the House to House Collections Regulations 1947, SR & O 1947/2662 (amended by SI 1963/684; SI 1974/595).
3 Ie required to be prescribed by regulations made under the House to House Collections Act 1939.
4 As to the meaning of 'collection' see PARA 465 note 2.
5 As to the meaning of 'licence' see PARA 465 note 1.
6 Ie under the House to House Collections Act 1939 s 3: see PARA 467.
7 As to the meaning of 'promoter' see PARA 465 note 2.
8 As to the meaning of 'collector' see PARA 465 note 2.
9 House to House Collections Act 1939 s 4(1) (prospectively repealed: see PARA 464). Any regulations so made must be laid before Parliament as soon as may be after they are made, and if either House of Parliament, within the period of 40 days beginning with the date on which the regulations are laid before it, resolves that the regulations be annulled, the regulations thereupon become void, without prejudice, however, to anything previously done thereunder or to the making of new regulations: s 4(4) (prospectively repealed: see PARA 464). In reckoning any such period of 40 days, no account is to be taken of any time during which Parliament is dissolved or prorogued or during which both Houses are adjourned for more than four days: s 4(4) (prospectively repealed: see PARA 464).
10 As to badges and certificates of authority see PARA 470.
11 House to House Collections Act 1939 s 4(2)(a) (prospectively repealed: see PARA 464). See PARA 470.

12 As to chief officers of police see POLICE AND INVESTIGATORY POWERS vol 84 (2013) PARA 113 et seq.
13 House to House Collections Act 1939 s 4(2)(b) (prospectively repealed: see PARA 464). See PARA 470.
14 House to House Collections Act 1939 s 4(2)(c) (prospectively repealed: see PARA 464). See PARA 471.
15 House to House Collections Act 1939 s 4(2)(d) (prospectively repealed: see PARA 464). See PARA 471.
16 As to the meaning of 'proceeds' see PARA 468 note 12.
17 Ie exempted from the provisions of the House to House Collections Act 1939 s 1(2): see PARA 465.
18 House to House Collections Act 1939 s 4(2)(e) (amended by SI 2006/2951; and prospectively repealed (see PARA 464)). See PARA 472.
19 House to House Collections Act 1939 s 4(3) (prospectively repealed: see PARA 464). Any person guilty of such an offence is liable, on summary conviction, to a fine not exceeding level 1 on the standard scale: s 8(3) (amended by virtue of the Criminal Justice Act 1982 ss 38, 46). The House to House Collections Act 1939 is prospectively repealed: see PARA 464. As to the standard scale see SENTENCING AND DISPOSITION OF OFFENDERS vol 92 (2010) PARA 143.
20 See the Police, Factories, etc (Miscellaneous Provisions) Act 1916 s 5 (see POLICE AND INVESTIGATORY POWERS vol 84 (2013) PARA 106); the Local Government (Miscellaneous Provisions) Act 1982 s 3, Sch 4; the London Local Authorities Act 1990 Pt III (ss 21–41); and regulations made thereunder. It was held in *Meaden v Wood* [1985] Crim LR 678, DC, that the Home Secretary had acted within his powers under the Police, Factories, etc (Miscellaneous Provisions) Act 1916 s 5 in setting up the system contained in the Street Collections (Metropolitan Police District) Regulations 1979, SI 1979/1230 (see POLICE AND INVESTIGATORY POWERS vol 84 (2013) PARA 106), by which the Metropolitan Police Commissioner was empowered to regulate persons wishing to make street collections. As to the Metropolitan Police Commissioner see POLICE AND INVESTIGATORY POWERS vol 84 (2013) PARA 118 et seq.

470. Badges and certificates of authority. A promoter[1] of a house to house collection[2] must provide a collector[3] with a prescribed certificate of authority[4] and a prescribed badge[5] and, if money is to be collected, a collecting box or receipt book[6]. He must also exercise all due diligence to secure that all certificates of authority and prescribed badges obtained for the purposes of a collection are destroyed when no longer required[7].

A person who, in connection with any appeal[8] made by him to the public in association with a representation that the appeal is for a charitable purpose[9], displays or uses: (1) a prescribed badge or prescribed certificate of authority not being a badge or certificate for the time being held by him[10] for the purposes of the appeal; or (2) any badge or device, or any certificate or other document so nearly resembling a prescribed badge or, as the case may be, a prescribed certificate of authority as to be calculated to deceive[11], is guilty of an offence[12].

1 As to the meaning of 'promoter' see PARA 465 note 2.
2 As to the meaning of 'collection' see PARA 465 note 2.
3 As to the meaning of 'collector' see PARA 465 note 2.
4 'Prescribed certificate of authority' means a certificate in the form set out in the House to House Collections Regulations 1947, SR & O 1947/2662, regs 2(1), 6, Sch 3: see reg 2(1). The House to House Collections Regulations 1947, SR & O 1947/2662, are made under the House to House Collections Act 1939 which is prospectively repealed: see PARA 464.
5 'Prescribed badge' means a badge in the form set out in the House to House Collections Regulations 1947, SR & O 1947/2662, Sch 4: see reg 2(1).
6 See the House to House Collections Regulations 1947, SR & O 1947/2662, reg 6(1). 'Collecting box' means a box or other receptacle for monetary contributions, securely closed and sealed in such a way that it cannot be opened without breaking the seal: reg 2(1). 'Receipt book' means a book of detachable forms of receipt consecutively numbered with counterfoils or duplicates correspondingly numbered: reg 2(1).
7 See the House to House Collections Regulations 1947, SR & O 1947/2662, reg 17.
8 An appeal is not limited to an appeal by way of house to house collections: *R v Davison* [1972] 3 All ER 1121, [1972] 1 WLR 1540, CA.

9 As to the meaning of 'charitable purposes' see PARA 465 note 3.
10 Ie pursuant to the House to House Collections Regulations 1947, SR & O 1947/2662.
11 'Calculated to deceive' means likely to deceive: *R v Davison* [1972] 3 All ER 1121, [1972] 1 WLR 1540, CA. See also that case for the proper direction to be given to the jury.
12 House to House Collections Act 1939 s 5 (prospectively repealed: see PARA 464). Any person guilty of such an offence is liable, on summary conviction, to imprisonment for a term not exceeding six months or to a fine not exceeding level 3 on the standard scale, or to both such imprisonment and such fine: s 8(4) (amended by virtue of the Criminal Justice Act 1982 ss 38, 46). The House to House Collections Act 1939 is prospectively repealed: see PARA 464. As to the standard scale see **SENTENCING AND DISPOSITION OF OFFENDERS** vol 92 (2010) PARA 143.
There is no power to grant exemptions from s 5 under s 1(4): see PARA 466.

471. Collectors. Promoters[1] must exercise due diligence to ensure that collectors[2] are fit and proper persons to act as such and to secure their compliance with the provisions of the regulations governing house to house collections[3]. No collector may importune any person to his annoyance, or remain in or at the door of any house if requested by the occupant to leave[4]. No person under the age of 16 years may act or be authorised to act as a collector of money[5].

Collectors must sign the prescribed certificate of authority[6] and prescribed badge[7], produce the certificate on demand, wear the badge during collecting, and return both to the promoter when the collection is completed or on demand of the promoter[8]. A police constable may require any person whom he believes to be acting as a collector for the purpose of a collection[9] for a charitable purpose[10] to declare to him immediately his name and address and to sign his name[11]. If any person fails to comply with such a requirement he is guilty of an offence[12].

A collector collecting money by a means of a collecting box[13] may receive it only by permitting the person from whom it is received to place it in the box, and when he is collecting money by other means he must give a signed receipt[14]. Collectors are trustees of the funds they collect[15]. Collecting boxes, with seals unbroken, and receipt books[16], together with the total sum of money which is entered in them, must be returned to the promoter when the collecting box is full or the receipt book is exhausted, upon the demand of the promoter, when the collector does not desire to act as a collector or upon completion of the collection[17].

1 As to the meaning of 'promoter' see PARA 465 note 2.
2 As to the meaning of 'collector' see PARA 465 note 2.
3 See the House to House Collections Regulations 1947, SR & O 1947/2662, reg 5. The House to House Collections Regulations 1947, SR & O 1947/2662, which govern house to house collections, are made under the House to House Collections Act 1939 which is prospectively repealed: see PARA 464.
4 See the House to House Collections Regulations 1947, SR & O 1947/2662, reg 9.
5 House to House Collections Regulations 1947, SR & O 1947/2662, reg 8 (substituted by SI 1963/684).
6 As to the meaning of 'prescribed certificate of authority' see PARA 470 note 4.
7 As to the meaning of 'prescribed badge' see PARA 470 note 5.
8 See the House to House Collections Regulations 1947, SR & O 1947/2662, reg 7. As to badges and certificates see PARA 470.
9 As to the meaning of 'collection' see PARA 465 note 2.
10 As to the meaning of 'charitable purposes' see PARA 465 note 3.
11 House to House Collections Act 1939 s 6 (prospectively repealed: see PARA 464).
12 House to House Collections Act 1939 s 6 (prospectively repealed: see PARA 464). Any person guilty of such an offence is liable, on summary conviction, to a fine not exceeding level 1 on the standard scale: s 8(5) (amended by virtue of the Criminal Justice Act 1982 ss 38, 46). The House to House Collections Act 1939 is prospectively repealed see PARA 464. As to the standard scale see **SENTENCING AND DISPOSITION OF OFFENDERS** vol 92 (2010) PARA 143.
There is no power to grant exemptions from s 6 under s 1(4): see PARA 466.

13 As to the meaning of 'collecting box' see PARA 470 note 6.
14 See the House to House Collections Regulations 1947, SR & O 1947/2662, reg 10. Where a promoter has been granted an order of exemption (see PARA 467) he may, with the Minister's permission, arrange an envelope collection: see reg 13 (amended by virtue of SI 2006/2951). As to the Minister see PARA 586.
15 *Jones v A-G* (1976) Times, 10 November.
16 As to the meaning of 'receipt book' see PARA 470 note 6.
17 See House to House Collections Regulations 1947, SR & O 1947/2662, reg 11. Collecting boxes must be opened in the presence of the promoter and another responsible person, or by an official of a bank: reg 12(1), (2). Receipt books and sums received with them must be examined by the promoter and another responsible person: reg 12(4). In each case the amount collected must be listed with the distinguishing number of the box or book: reg 12(3), (4).

472. Accounts. An account of the collections[1] for which a licence[2] has been granted must be furnished by the chief promoter[3] to the authority[4] granting the licence within one month of the expiry of the licence[5], and where an order of exemption[6] has been made an account must be made annually to the Minister[7]. The time for furnishing the account may in either case be extended[8]. In appropriate cases the account for the house to house collections may be combined with that required[9] for street collections[10]. The account must be in the prescribed form, duly certified and vouched[11].

1 As to the meaning of 'collection' see PARA 465 note 2.
2 As to the meaning of 'licence' see PARA 465 note 1.
3 'Chief promoter', in relation to a collection, means a person to whom a licence has been granted authorising him to promote that collection or in respect of whom an order has been made directing that he is exempt from the provisions of the House to House Collections Act 1939 s 1(2) (see PARA 465) as respects that collection: House to House Collections Regulations 1947, SR & O 1947/2662, reg 2(1). As to the meaning of 'promoter' see PARA 465 note 2. The House to House Collections Regulations 1947, SR & O 1947/2662, are made under the House to House Collections Act 1939 which is prospectively repealed: see PARA 464.
4 As to licensing authorities see PARA 468 note 4.
5 As to the duration of a licence see PARA 468.
6 Ie under the House to House Collections Act 1939 s 3: see PARA 467.
7 See the House to House Collections Regulations 1947, SR & O 1947/2662, reg 14(1), (2) (amended by SI 1974/595; and amended by virtue of SI 2006/2951). As to the Minister see PARA 586.
8 See the House to House Collections Regulations 1947, SR & O 1947/2662, reg 14(3) (amended by SI 1974/595).
9 Ie under the Police, Factories, etc (Miscellaneous Provisions) Act 1916 or regulations made thereunder: see PARA 469 note 20.
10 See the House to House Collections Regulations 1947, SR & O 1947/2662, reg 14(4) (amended by SI 1974/595).
11 See the House to House Collections Regulations 1947, SR & O 1947/2662, regs 15, 16, Schs 5–7.

473. False statements. A person who, in furnishing any information for the purposes of the House to House Collections Act 1939, knowingly or recklessly makes a statement false in a material particular is guilty of an offence[1].

1 House to House Collections Act 1939 s 8(6) (prospectively repealed: see PARA 464). Any person guilty of such an offence is liable, on summary conviction, to imprisonment for a term not exceeding six months or to a fine not exceeding level 3 on the standard scale, or to both such imprisonment and such fine: s 8(6) (amended by virtue of the Criminal Justice Act 1982 ss 38, 46). The House to House Collections Act 1939 is prospectively repealed: see PARA 464. As to the standard scale see **SENTENCING AND DISPOSITION OF OFFENDERS** vol 92 (2010) PARA 143.

474. Offences by corporations. Where an offence under the House to House Collections Act 1939 committed by a corporation is proved to have been committed with the consent and connivance of, or to be attributable to any culpable neglect of duty on the part of, any director, manager, secretary or other officer of the corporation, he, as well as the corporation, is deemed to be guilty of an offence and is liable to be proceeded against and punished accordingly[1].

1 House to House Collections Act 1939 s 8(7) (prospectively repealed: see PARA 464).

475. War charities and charities for the disabled. The War Charities Act 1940, which had been extended to cover the disabled[1], was repealed by the Charities Act 1992[2], which contains new and different provisions designed to deal with the same problems and is considered elsewhere in this title[3].

1 Ie by the National Assistance Act 1948 s 41 (repealed).
2 Ie by the Charities Act 1992 s 78(2), Sch 7.
3 As to the control of charitable fund raising under the Charities Act 1992 Pt II (ss 58–64A) see PARAS 477–494. As to public charitable collections under the Charities Act 2006 Pt 3 Ch 1 (ss 45–66) see PARAS 495–511. Pt 3 Ch 1 is in force only for limited purposes. At the date this volume states the law no day had been appointed bringing Pt 3 Ch 1 into force for any remaining purposes.
As to the statutory regulation of street collections and street trading see the Police, Factories, etc (Miscellaneous Provisions) Act 1916 s 5 (see **POLICE AND INVESTIGATORY POWERS** vol 84 (2013) PARA 106); the Local Government (Miscellaneous Provisions) Act 1982 s 3, Sch 4; and the London Local Authorities Act 1990 Pt III (ss 21–41).

(3) TRADING REPRESENTATIONS

476. Trading representations. The Consumer Protection from Unfair Trading Regulations 2008[1] prohibits unfair commercial practices[2] and the promotion of unfair commercial practices by persons responsible for codes of conduct for traders[3], and provides for a range of connected offences[4]. 'Commercial practice' means any act, omission, course of conduct, representation or commercial communication (including advertising and marketing) by a trader[5], which is directly connected with the promotion, sale or supply of a product to or from consumers, whether occurring before, during or after a commercial transaction, if any, in relation to a product[6]. A commercial practice is unfair if: (1) it contravenes the requirements of professional diligence and it materially distorts or is likely to materially distort the economic behaviour of the average consumer with regard to the product[7]; or (2) it is a misleading action[8], a misleading omission[9], aggressive[10], or a specified unfair commercial practice[11]. A charity is not exempt from these provisions.

1 Ie the Consumer Protection from Unfair Trading Regulations 2008, SI 2008/1277, which implements European Parliament and Council Directive (EC) 2005/29 (OJ L149, 11.6.2005, p 22) concerning unfair business-to-consumer commercial practices. See **CONSUMER PROTECTION** vol 21 (2011) PARA 501 et seq.
2 Consumer Protection from Unfair Trading Regulations 2008, SI 2008/1277, reg 3(1).
3 See the Consumer Protection from Unfair Trading Regulations 2008, SI 2008/1277, reg 4.
4 See the Consumer Protection from Unfair Trading Regulations 2008, SI 2008/1277, regs 8–12. A person guilty of an offence under these provisions is liable: (1) on summary conviction, to a fine not exceeding the statutory maximum; or (2) on conviction on indictment, to a fine or imprisonment for a term not exceeding two years or both: reg 13. As to the statutory maximum see **SENTENCING AND DISPOSITION OF OFFENDERS** vol 92 (2010) PARA 141. There are defences of due diligence and of the innocent publication of an advertisement: see regs 17, 18.
5 'Trader' means a person acting for purposes relating to his business, whether personally or through another acting in his name, and anyone acting in the name of or on behalf of a trader: see the Consumer Protection from Unfair Trading Regulations 2008, SI 2008/1277, reg 2(1) (definition substituted by SI 2014/870).
6 Consumer Protection from Unfair Trading Regulations 2008, SI 2008/1277, reg 2(1).
7 Consumer Protection from Unfair Trading Regulations 2008, SI 2008/1277, reg 3(2), (3).

8 See the Consumer Protection from Unfair Trading Regulations 2008, SI 2008/1277, regs 3(2), (4), 5.
9 See the Consumer Protection from Unfair Trading Regulations 2008, SI 2008/1277, regs 3(2), (4), 6 (amended by SI 2014/870).
10 See the Consumer Protection from Unfair Trading Regulations 2008, SI 2008/1277, regs 3(2), (4), 7.
11 See the Consumer Protection from Unfair Trading Regulations 2008, SI 2008/1277, regs 3(2), (4), Sch 1 (amended by SI 2013/3134, SI 2014/870).

(4) CONTROLS UNDER THE CHARITIES ACT 1992

477. Charitable institutions; professional fund raisers; commercial participators. The provisions of the Charities Act 1992 which deal with the control of fund raising extend beyond charities within the meaning of the Charities Act 2011[1]. They apply to any 'charitable institution', which is defined as a charity or an institution[2], other than a charity, which is established for charitable, benevolent or philanthropic purposes[3]. The main controls are on professional fund raisers and commercial participators.

A professional fund raiser is: (1) any person, apart from a charitable institution or a company[4] connected with such an institution[5], who carries on a fund raising business[6]; or (2) any other person who for reward solicits[7] money or other property for the benefit of a charitable institution, if he does so otherwise than in the course of any fund raising venture undertaken by a person falling within head (1) above[8]. There are important exceptions to this definition. Head (2) above does not apply to any of the following:

(a) any charitable institution or any company connected with any such institution[9];
(b) any officer or employee of any such institution or company, or any trustee of any such institution, acting (in each case) in his capacity as such[10];
(c) any person acting as a collector[11] in respect of a public charitable collection[12];
(d) any person who in the course of a relevant programme, that is to say a radio or television programme in the course of which a fund-raising venture is undertaken by a charitable institution, or a company connected with such an institution, makes any solicitation at the instance of that institution or company[13]; or
(e) any commercial participator[14].

Nor does head (2) apply to a person if he does not receive: (i) more than £10 per day, or £1,000 per year, by way of remuneration in connection with soliciting money or other property for the benefit of the charitable institution[15]; or (ii) more than £1,000 by way of remuneration in connection with any fund-raising venture in the course of which he solicits money or other property for the benefit of that institution[16].

'Commercial participator', in relation to any charitable institution, means any person (apart from a company connected with the institution) who carries on for gain a business other than a fund raising business, but in the course of that business, engages in any promotional venture[17] in the course of which it is represented that charitable contributions[18] are to be given to or applied for the benefit of the institution[19].

1 See the Charities Act 1992 s 58(1) (see notes 2–8); and PARA 1. As to fund raising for charitable purposes otherwise than by professional fund raisers or commercial participators see the Charities Act 1992 s 64(2)(e); the Charitable Institutions (Fund Raising) Regulations 1994, SI 1994/3024, regs 7, 8; and PARAS 488, 490.
2 'Institution' includes any trust or undertaking: Charities Act 1992 s 58(1). 'Charitable purposes', where the term occurs in the context of a reference to charitable, benevolent or philanthropic purposes, is a reference to charitable purposes as defined by the Charities Act 2011 s 2(1): Charities Act 1992 s 58(4) (amended by the Charities Act 2011 Sch 7 para 65).
3 Charities Act 1992 s 58(1).
4 As to the meaning of 'company' see PARA 246; definition applied by the Charities Act 1992 s 58(1) (definition amended by the Charities Act 2011 Sch 7 para 65).
5 A company is connected with a charitable institution if the institution, or the institution and one or more other charitable institutions taken together, is or are entitled (whether directly or through one or more nominees) to exercise, or control the exercise of, the whole of the voting power at any general meeting of the company: Charities Act 1992 s 58(5).
6 Charities Act 1992 s 58(1) (definition amended by the Deregulation and Contracting Out Act 1994 s 25). The definition of 'professional fund raiser' applies to any person apart from a person excluded by virtue of the Charities Act 1992 s 58(2), (3): see the text and notes 9–16. 'Fund raising business' means any business carried on for gain and wholly or primarily engaged in soliciting or otherwise procuring money or other property for charitable, benevolent or philanthropic purposes: s 58(1).
7 'Represent' and 'solicit' mean respectively represent and solicit in any manner whatever, whether expressly or impliedly and whether done by speaking directly to the person or persons to whom the representation or solicitation is addressed (whether when in his or their presence or not), or by means of a statement published in any newspaper, film or radio or television programme, or otherwise and references to a representation or solicitation must be construed accordingly: Charities Act 1992 s 58(6)(a). Any reference to soliciting or otherwise procuring money or other property is a reference to soliciting or otherwise procuring money or other property whether any consideration is, or is to be, given in return for the money or other property or not: s 58(6)(b). Where any solicitation of money or other property for the benefit of a charitable institution is made in accordance with arrangements between any person and that institution, and under those arrangements that person will be responsible for receiving on behalf of the institution money or other property given in response to the solicitation, then that person is to be regarded as soliciting money or other property for the benefit of the institution: s 58(7). Where any fund raising venture is undertaken by a professional fund raiser in the course of a radio or television programme, any solicitation which is made by a person in the course of the programme at the instance of the fund raiser is to be regarded as made by the fund raiser and not by that person, whether or not the solicitation is made by that person for any reward: s 58(8). 'Radio or television programme' includes any item included in a programme service within the meaning of the Broadcasting Act 1990 s 201 (see **TELECOMMUNICATIONS** vol 97 (2010) PARA 16): Charities Act 1992 s 58(1).
8 Charities Act 1992 s 58(1). The definition of 'professional fund raiser' applies to any person apart from a person excluded by virtue of s 58(2), (3): see the text and notes 9–16.
9 Charities Act 1992 s 58(2)(a).
10 Charities Act 1992 s 58(2)(b).
11 As to the meaning of 'collector' see PARA 495 note 15; definition applied by the Charities Act 1992 s 58(2) (amended by the Charities Act 2006 Sch 8 paras 89, 90(1), (3)).
12 Charities Act 1992 s 58(2)(c). This provision applies to any person acting as a collector in respect of a public charitable collection apart from a person who is a promoter of such a collection by virtue of the Charities Act 2006 s 47(1) (not yet in force save for the purposes listed in PARA 495 note 10): see the Charities Act 1992 s 58(2)(c) (amended by the Charities Act 2006 Sch 8 paras 89, 90(1), (3)(a)). As to the meaning of 'public charitable collection' see PARA 495; definition applied by the Charities Act 1992 s 58(2) (amended by the Charities Act 2006 Sch 8 paras 89, 90(1), (3)).
13 Charities Act 1992 s 58(2)(d).
14 Charities Act 1992 s 58(2)(e).
15 Charities Act 1992 s 58(3)(a) (amended by SI 2009/508). The Minister may by order amend the Charities Act 1992 s 58(3) by substituting a different sum for any sum for the time being specified there: s 58(10) (amended by SI 2006/2951). As to the making of orders generally see the Charities Act 1992 s 77; and PARA 590. As to the Minister see PARA 586.
16 Charities Act 1992 s 58(3)(b) (amended by SI 2009/508). See note 15.
17 'Promotional venture' means any advertising or sales campaign or any other venture undertaken for promotional purposes: Charities Act 1992 s 58(1).

18 'Charitable contributions', in relation to any representation made by any commercial participator or other person, means:

(1) the whole or part of the consideration given for goods or services sold or supplied by him, or of any proceeds (other than such consideration) of a promotional venture undertaken by him; or

(2) sums given by him by way of donation in connection with the sale or supply of any such goods or services (whether the amount of such sums is determined by reference to the value of any such goods or services or otherwise) (Charities Act 1992 s 58(1)).

'Services' includes facilities, and in particular access to any premises or event, membership of any organisation, the provision of advertising space, and the provision of any financial facilities, and references to the supply of services are to be construed accordingly: s 58(9).

19 Charities Act 1992 s 58(1) (definition amended by the Deregulation and Contracting Out Act 1994 s 25).

478. Prescribed agreement with charitable institution. It is unlawful for a professional fund raiser[1] to solicit[2] money or other property for the benefit of a charitable institution[3], or for a commercial participator[4] to represent[5] that charitable contributions[6] are to be given to or applied for the benefit of a charitable institution unless, in either case, he does so in accordance with an agreement with the institution satisfying the prescribed requirements[7]. Where on the application of a charitable institution the court[8] is satisfied that any person has contravened or is contravening these provisions in relation to the institution, and that, unless restrained, any such contravention is likely to continue or be repeated, the court may grant an injunction restraining the contravention, but no other remedy is available[9].

Where (1) a charitable institution makes any agreement with a professional fund raiser or a commercial participator by virtue of which the professional fund raiser is authorised to solicit money or other property for the benefit of the institution or the commercial participator is authorised to represent that charitable contributions are to be given to or applied for the benefit of the institution, as the case may be[10]; but (2) the agreement does not satisfy the prescribed requirements in any respect[11], the agreement is not enforceable against the institution except to such extent, if any, as may be provided by an order of the court[12]. A professional fund raiser or commercial participator who is a party to any such agreement is not entitled to receive any amount by way of remuneration or expenses in respect of anything done by him in pursuance of the agreement unless[13]: (a) he is so entitled under any provision of the agreement[14]; and (b) either the agreement satisfies the prescribed requirements or any such provision has effect[15] by virtue of an order of the court[16].

1 As to the meaning of 'professional fund raiser' see PARA 477.

2 As to the meaning of 'solicit' see PARA 477 note 7.

3 As to the meaning of 'charitable institution' see PARA 477.

4 As to the meaning of 'commercial participator' see PARA 477.

5 As to the meaning of 'represent' see PARA 477 note 7.

6 As to the meaning of 'charitable contributions' see PARA 477 note 18. As to references to soliciting money or other property for the benefit of the institution see PARA 477 note 7. As to the meaning of 'institution' see PARA 477 note 2.

7 Charities Act 1992 s 59(1), (2). 'Prescribed requirements' means such requirements as are prescribed by regulations made by virtue of s 64(2)(a) (see the Charitable Institutions (Fund Raising) Regulations 1994, SI 1994/3024; and PARA 486 et seq): Charities Act 1992 s 59(6).

8 'Court' means the High Court or the county court: Charities Act 1992 s 58(1) (definition amended by the Crime and Courts Act 2013 Sch 9 para 52).

9 Charities Act 1992 s 59(3).

10 Charities Act 1992 s 59(4)(a).

11 Charities Act 1992 s 59(4)(b).

12 Charities Act 1992 s 59(4).

13 Charities Act 1992 s 59(5).
14 Charities Act 1992 s 59(5)(a).
15 Ie under the Charities Act 1992 s 59(4): see the text and notes 10–12.
16 Charities Act 1992 s 59(5)(b).

479. Requirement to indicate institutions benefiting and arrangements for remuneration: professional fund raisers and commercial participators. Where a professional fund raiser[1] solicits[2] money or other property for the benefit of one or more particular charitable institutions[3], the solicitation must be accompanied by a statement clearly indicating: (1) the name or names of the institution or institutions concerned; (2) if more than one, the proportions in which they are respectively to benefit; and (3) the method by which the fund raiser's remuneration in connection with the appeal[4] is to be determined and the notifiable amount of that remuneration[5]. Where a professional fund raiser solicits money or other property for charitable, benevolent or philanthropic purposes[6] of any description, rather than for the benefit of one or more particular charitable institutions, the solicitation must be accompanied by a statement clearly indicating[7]: (a) the fact that he is soliciting money or other property for those purposes and not for the benefit of any particular charitable institution or institutions[8]; (b) the method by which it is to be determined how the proceeds of the appeal are to be distributed between different charitable institutions[9]; and (c) the method by which his remuneration in connection with the appeal is to be determined and the notifiable amount of that remuneration[10].

Where any representation[11] is made by a commercial participator[12] to the effect that charitable contributions[13] are to be given to or applied for the benefit of one or more particular charitable institutions, the representation must be accompanied by a statement clearly indicating[14]: (i) the name or names of the institution or institutions concerned[15]; (ii) if there is more than one institution concerned, the proportions in which they are respectively to benefit[16]; and (iii) the notifiable amount of whichever of the following sums is applicable in the circumstances: (A) the sum representing so much of the consideration given for goods or services[17] sold or supplied by him as is to be given to or applied for the benefit of the institution or institutions concerned; (B) the sum representing so much of any other proceeds of a promotional venture[18] undertaken by him as is to be so given or applied; or (C) the sum of the donations by him in connection with the sale or supply of any such goods or services which are to be so given or supplied[19].

If any such solicitation or representation as is referred to above is made in the course of a radio or television programme[20], and in association with an announcement to the effect that payment may be made by means of a credit or debit card[21], the statement required must include full details of the right to have refunded[22] any payment of £100 or more which is so made[23].

If any such solicitation or representation as is referred to above is made orally, but is not made by speaking directly to the particular person or persons to whom it is addressed and in his or their presence, or in the course of any radio or television programme, the professional fund raiser or commercial participator concerned must within seven days of any payment of £100 or more being made to him in response to the solicitation or representation, give the person making the payment[24] a written statement of the matters which are required to be contained in the statements[25], and full details of the right to cancel an agreement made in response to his solicitation or representation[26] and the right to a refund[27] of the payment made in response[28].

Where any requirement of the above mentioned provisions[29] is not complied with in relation to any solicitation or representation, the professional fund raiser or commercial participator concerned is guilty of an offence[30]. It is a defence for such a person to prove that he took all reasonable precautions and exercised all due diligence to avoid the commission of the offence[31].

1 As to the meaning of 'professional fund raiser' see PARA 477.
2 As to the meaning of 'solicit' see PARA 477 note 7.
3 As to the meaning of 'charitable institution' see PARA 477. As to references to soliciting money or other property for the benefit of an institution: see PARA 477 note 7.
4 In relation to any solicitation by a professional fund raiser, 'appeal' means the campaign or other fund raising venture in the course of which the solicitation is made: Charities Act 1992 s 60(10).
5 Charities Act 1992 s 60(1) (amended by the Charities Act 2006 s 67(1), (2)). A reference to the 'notifiable amount' of any remuneration or other sum is a reference to the actual amount of the remuneration or sum, if that is known at the time when the statement is made, and otherwise to the estimated amount of the remuneration or sum, calculated as accurately as is reasonably possible in the circumstances: Charities Act 1992 s 60(3A) (added by the Charities Act 2006 s 67(1), (5)).

   Regulations may specify the manner in which money or other property acquired by professional fund raisers or commercial participators for the benefit of, or otherwise falling to be given to or applied by such persons for the benefit of, charitable institutions is to be transmitted to such institutions: see the Charities Act 1992 s 64(2)(c); and PARA 486. Regulations may also provide for s 60 to apply, with any specified modifications, in relation to solicitations or representations made in the course of radio or television programmes by charitable institutions or by companies connected with such institutions: see s 64(2)(d); and PARA 486.
6 As to the meaning of 'charitable purposes' see PARA 477 note 2.
7 Charities Act 1992 s 60(2).
8 Charities Act 1992 s 60(2)(a).
9 Charities Act 1992 s 60(2)(b).
10 Charities Act 1992 s 60(2)(c) (substituted by the Charities Act 2006 s 67(1), (3)). As to the meaning of 'notifiable amount' see note 5.
11 As to the meaning of 'representation' see PARA 477 note 7.
12 As to the meaning of 'commercial participator' see PARA 477.
13 As to the meaning of 'charitable contributions' see PARA 477 note 18.
14 Charities Act 1992 s 60(3).
15 Charities Act 1992 s 60(3)(a).
16 Charities Act 1992 s 60(3)(b).
17 As to the meaning of 'services' see PARA 477 note 18.
18 As to the meaning of 'promotional venture' see PARA 477 note 17.
19 Charities Act 1992 s 60(3)(c) (substituted by the Charities Act 2006 s 67(1), (4)).
20 As to the meaning of 'radio or television programme' see PARA 477 note 7.
21 'Credit card' means a card which is a credit-token within the meaning of the Consumer Credit Act 1974 (see **CONSUMER CREDIT** vol 21 (2011) PARA 59): Charities Act 1992 s 58(1). 'Debit card' means a card the use of which by its holder to make a payment results in a current account of his at a bank, or at any other institution providing banking services, being debited with the payment: s 58(1).
22 Ie under the Charities Act 1992 s 61(1): see PARA 482. The Minister may by order amend s 61(1) by substituting a different sum for the sum for the time being specified there and make such consequential amendments in s 60 as he considers appropriate: see s 61(8) (amended by SI 2006/2951); and PARA 482. As to the Minister see PARA 586. As to the making of orders generally see the Charities Act 1992 s 77; and PARA 590.
23 Charities Act 1992 s 60(4) (amended by SI 2009/508). Regulations may provide for the Charities Act 1992 s 60(4) to apply, with any specified modifications, in relation to solicitations or representations made in the course of radio or television programmes by charitable institutions or by companies connected with such institutions: see s 64(2)(d); and PARA 486.
24 The reference to the making of a payment is a reference to the making of a payment of whatever nature and by whatever means, including a payment made by means of a credit card or a debit card, and for these purposes: (1) where the person making any such payment makes it in person, it is regarded as made at the time when it is so made; (2) where the person making any such payment sends it by post, it is regarded as made at the time when it is posted; and (3) where the

person making any such payment makes it by giving, by telephone or by means of any other electronic communications apparatus, authority for an account to be debited with the payment, it is regarded as made at the time when any such authority is given: Charities Act 1992 s 60(6) (amended by the Communications Act 2003 Sch 17 para 118).

25 Ie those required by the Charities Act 1992 s 60(1), (2) or (3): see the text and notes 1–19.

26 Ie under the Charities Act 1992 s 61(2): see PARA 482.

27 Ie under the Charities Act 1992 s 61(2), (3): see PARA 482.

28 Charities Act 1992 s 60(5) (amended by SI 2009/508).

29 Ie those contained in the Charities Act 1992 s 60(1)–(5): see the text and notes 1–28.

30 Charities Act 1992 s 60(7). A person guilty of such an offence is liable on summary conviction to a fine not exceeding level 5 on the standard scale: s 60(7). As to the standard scale see SENTENCING AND DISPOSITION OF OFFENDERS vol 92 (2010) PARA 143. Where the commission by any person of an offence under s 60(7) is due to the act or default of some other person, that other person is also guilty of the offence and may be charged and convicted whether or not proceedings are taken against the first named person: s 60(9). As to offences by a body corporate see s 75; and PARA 588.

31 Charities Act 1992 s 60(8).

480. Requirement to indicate institutions benefiting and arrangements for remuneration: officers, employees and trustees of charitable institutions or connected companies. The Charities Act 1992 provides disclosure requirements for a person who: (1) is an officer or employee of a charitable institution[1] or a company connected with any such institution, or a trustee of any such institution; (2) is acting as a collector in that capacity; and (3) receives remuneration either in his capacity as officer, employee or trustee or for acting as a collector[2]. Where such a person solicits[3] money or other property for the benefit of one or more particular charitable institutions, the solicitation must be accompanied by a statement clearly indicating: (a) the name or names of the institution or institutions for whose benefit the solicitation is being made; (b) if there is more than one such institution, the proportions in which the institutions are respectively to benefit; (c) the fact that he is an officer, employee or trustee of the institution or company; and (d) the fact that he is receiving remuneration as an officer, employee or trustee or, as the case may be, for acting as a collector[4]. Where such a person solicits money or other property for charitable, benevolent or philanthropic purposes[5] of any description, rather than for the benefit of one or more particular charitable institutions, the solicitation must be accompanied by a statement clearly indicating: (i) the fact that he is soliciting money or other property for those purposes and not for the benefit of any particular charitable institution or institutions; (ii) the method by which it is to be determined how the proceeds of the appeal[6] are to be distributed between different charitable institutions; (iii) the fact that he is an officer, employee or trustee of the institution or company mentioned; and (iv) the fact that he is receiving remuneration as an officer, employee or trustee or, as the case may be, for acting as a collector[7].

Where any of the above requirements is not complied with in relation to any solicitation, the collector concerned is guilty of an offence[8]. It is a defence for such a person to prove that he took all reasonable precautions and exercised all due diligence to avoid the commission of the offence[9].

1 As to the meaning of 'charitable institution' see PARA 477.

2 Charities Act 1992 s 60A(6) (ss 60A, 60B added by the Charities Act 2006 s 68). However, a person does not fall within these provisions if he is under the earnings limit: Charities Act 1992 ss 60A(7), 60B(4) (as so added).

A person is under the earnings limit if the remuneration received by him is not more than £10 per day or £1,000 per year or, if a lump sum, is not more than £1,000: s 60B(5) (as so added; and amended by SI 2009/508). The Minister may by order amend the Charities Act 1992 s 60B(5) by substituting a different sum for any specified sum for the time being specified there: s 60B(6) (as so added). As to the making of orders generally see s 77; and PARA 590. As to the Minister see PARA 586.

'Collector' has the meaning given by the Charities Act 2006 s 47(1) (not yet in force, save for the purposes listed in PARA 495 note 1: see PARA 495 note 15): Charities Act 1992 s 60A(10) (as so added).

3 As to the meaning of 'solicit' see PARA 477 note 7.
4 Charities Act 1992 s 60A(4) (as added: see note 2).
5 As to the meaning of 'charitable purposes' see PARA 477 note 2.
6 'Appeal', in relation to any solicitation by a collector, means the campaign or other fund raising venture in the course of which the solicitation is made: Charities Act 1992 s 60A(10) (as added: see note 2).
7 Charities Act 1992 s 60A(5) (as added: see note 2).
8 Charities Act 1992 s 60A(8) (as added: see note 2). A person guilty of such an offence is liable on summary conviction to a fine not exceeding level 5 on the standard scale: s 60A(8) (as so added). As to the standard scale see **SENTENCING AND DISPOSITION OF OFFENDERS** vol 92 (2010) PARA 143. Where the commission by any person of such an offence is due to the act or default of some other person, that other person is guilty of the offence and may be charged with and convicted of the offence whether or not proceedings are taken against the first-mentioned person: ss 60(9), 60A(9) (as so added). As to offences by a body corporate see s 75; and PARA 588.
9 Charities Act 1992 ss 60(8), 60A(9) (as added: see note 2).

481. Requirement to indicate institutions benefiting and arrangements for remuneration: other persons. From a day to be appointed[1], the Charities Act 1992 provides for the following disclosure requirements for persons other than professional fund raisers[2] and the officers, employees and trustees of charitable institutions or connected companies[3]. Where a person acting for reward as a collector in respect of a public charitable collection[4] solicits[5] money or other property for the benefit of one or more particular charitable institutions[6], the solicitation must meet the same requirements as if the soliciting were carried on by a professional fund raiser[7]. However, these provisions will not apply to a person if, in relation to his acting for reward as a collector in respect of the collection, he is a promoter[8] or falls under the statutory earnings limit[9].

Where any of the above requirements is not complied with in relation to any solicitation, the collector concerned is guilty of an offence[10]. It is a defence for such a person to prove that he took all reasonable precautions and exercised all due diligence to avoid the commission of the offence[11].

1 The Charities Act 1992 s 60A is added by the Charities Act 2006 s 68 as from a day to be appointed under s 79(2). At the date at which this volume states the Charities Act 1992 s 60A was in force only in relation to s 60A(4)–(7), (8)(b), (10) and no such day had been appointed in relation to s 60A(1)–(3), (8)(a).
2 As to the meaning of 'professional fund raiser' see PARA 477. As to the requirements for professional fund raisers see PARA 479.
3 As to the requirements for such officers, employees and trustees see PARA 480.
4 'Public charitable collection' has the meaning given by the Charities Act 2006 s 45 (see PARA 495): Charities Act 1992 s 60A(10) (as added: see note 1). 'Collector' has the meaning given by the Charities Act 2006 s 47(1) (not yet in force, save for the purposes listed in PARA 495 note 1: see PARA 495 note 14): Charities Act 1992 s 60A(10) (as so added).
5 As to the meaning of 'solicit' see PARA 477 note 7. As to the meaning of 'solicitation' see PARA 477 note 7.
6 As to the meaning of 'charitable institution' see PARA 477. As to references to soliciting money or other property for the benefit of an institution: see PARA 477 note 7.
7 Charities Act 1992 s 60A(1) (as prospectively added: see note 1).
8 Charities Act 1992 s 60A(2)(a), (3)(a) (as prospectively added: see note 1). 'Promoter' has the same meaning as in relation to public charitable collections: see PARA 496 note 3.
9 Charities Act 1992 s 60A(2)(b) (as prospectively added: see note 1). As to the statutory earnings limit see s 60B(1); and PARA 480 note 2.

10 Charities Act 1992 s 60A(8)(a) (as prospectively added: see note 1). A person guilty of such an offence is liable on summary conviction to a fine not exceeding level 5 on the standard scale: s 60A(8) (as so added). As to the standard scale see **SENTENCING AND DISPOSITION OF OFFENDERS** vol 92 (2010) PARA 143. Where the commission by any person of an offence under s 60A(8)(a) is due to the act or default of some other person, that other person is also guilty of the offence and may be charged with and convicted of the offence whether or not proceedings are taken against the first-mentioned person: ss 60(9), 60A(9) (as added: see note 1). As to offences by a body corporate see s 75; and PARA 588.

11 Charities Act 1992 ss 60(8), 60A(9) (as added: see note 1).

482. Cancellation of payments and agreements made in response to appeals. Where: (1) a person (the 'donor') in response to solicitation[1] by a professional fund raiser[2] or a representation[3] by a commercial participator[4] which is made in the course of a radio or television programme[5], makes any payment[6] of £100[7] or more to the relevant fund raiser[8] by means of a credit card or a debit card[9]; but (2) before the end of a period of seven days beginning with the date of the solicitation or representation, the donor serves on the relevant fund raiser a notice in writing which, however expressed, indicates the donor's intention to cancel the payment[10], the donor is entitled[11] to have the payment refunded to him forthwith by the relevant fund raiser[12].

Certain agreements entered into by a donor in response to any solicitation or representation made orally but not made by speaking directly to the particular person or persons to whom it is addressed and in his or their presence, or in the course of any radio or television programme[13] may be cancelled[14]. This can be done in the case of an agreement with the relevant fund raiser under which the donor is, or may be, liable to make any payment or payments[15] to the relevant fund raiser, and the amount or the aggregate amount which the donor is, or may be, liable to pay to him under the agreement is £100 or more[16]. If, before the end of the period of seven days beginning with the date when he is given the required written statement[17], the donor serves on the relevant fund raiser a notice in writing which, however expressed, indicates the donor's intention to cancel the agreement[18], the notice operates, as from the time when it is served, to cancel the agreement and any liability of any person other than the donor in connection with the making of any such payment or payments[19]. The donor is further entitled[20] to have any payment of £100 or more[21] made by him under the agreement refunded to him forthwith by the relevant fund raiser[22]. Where no such agreement has been entered into but, in response to such solicitation or representation as is referred to above[23], the donor has made any payment of £100[24] or more to the relevant fund raiser, the donor may before the end of the period of seven days beginning with the date when the donor is given any such written statement as is required[25] serve on the relevant fund raiser a notice in writing indicating his intention to cancel the payment[26]. However the notice is expressed, it entitles the donor to have the payment refunded to him forthwith by the relevant fund raiser[27].

Further, none of the above provisions[28] has effect in relation to any payment made or to be made in respect of services[29] which have been supplied at the time when the relevant notice is served[30]. In any of the cases mentioned above the right of any person to have a payment refunded to him[31]: (a) is a right to have refunded to him the amount of the payment less any administrative expenses reasonably incurred by the relevant fund raiser in connection with the making of the refund or, as the case may require[32], in dealing with the notice of cancellation served upon him[33]; and (b) is, in the case of a payment for goods already received, conditional upon the restitution being made of the goods in question[34].

1 As to the meaning of 'solicitation' see PARA 477 note 7.
2 Ie under the Charities Act 1992 s 60(1), (2) (see PARA 479). As to the meaning of 'professional fund raiser' see PARA 477.
3 As to the meaning of 'representation' see PARA 477 note 7.
4 Ie under the Charities Act 1992 s 60(3) (see PARA 479). As to the meaning of 'commercial participator' see PARA 477.
5 As to the meaning of 'radio or television programme' see PARA 477 note 7.
6 For these purposes, any reference to the making of a payment is a reference to the making of a payment of whatever nature and, in the case of the Charities Act 1992 s 61(2) or (3) (see the text and notes 7–21), a payment made by whatever means, including a payment made by means of a credit card or a debit card: s 61(6). As to when a payment is to be regarded as having been made see s 60(6) (see PARA 479 note 24); applied by s 61(6). As to the meanings of 'credit card' and 'debit card' PARA 479 note 21.
7 The Minister may by order amend any provision of the Charities Act 1992 s 61 by substituting a different sum for the sum for the time being specified there and make such consequential amendments in s 60 (see PARA 479) as he considers appropriate: s 61(8) (amended by SI 2006/2951). As to the making of orders generally see the Charities Act 1992 s 77; and PARA 590. As to the Minister see PARA 586.
8 'Relevant fund raiser', in relation to any solicitation or representation, means the professional fund raiser or commercial participator by whom it is made: Charities Act 1992 s 61(7).
9 Charities Act 1992 s 61(1)(a) (amended by SI 2009/508).
10 Charities Act 1992 s 61(1)(b).
11 Ie subject to the Charities Act 1992 s 61(4) (see the text and notes 31–33).
12 Charities Act 1992 s 61(1). Regulations may provide for s 61 to apply, with any specified modifications, in relation to solicitations or representations made in the course of radio or television programmes by charitable institutions or by companies connected with such institutions: see s 64(2)(d); and PARA 486.
13 Ie one falling within the Charities Act 1992 s 60(5) (see PARA 479 text and notes 25–28). As to the meaning of 'radio or television programme' see PARA 477 note 7.
14 See the Charities Act 1992 s 61(2).
15 See note 6.
16 See the Charities Act 1992 s 61(2)(a) (amended by SI 2009/508). See also note 7.
17 Ie the statement required under the Charities Act 1992 s 60(5)(a) (see PARA 479).
18 Charities Act 1992 s 61(2)(b).
19 See the Charities Act 1992 s 61(2).
20 Ie subject to the Charities Act 1992 s 61(4) (see the text and notes 31–33).
21 See note 7.
22 Charities Act 1992 s 61(2) (amended by SI 2009/508).
23 Ie one falling within the Charities Act 1992 s 60(5) (see PARA 479 text and notes 25–28).
24 See note 7.
25 Ie the statement required under the Charities Act 1992 s 60(5)(a) (see PARA 479).
26 Charities Act 1992 s 61(3) (amended by SI 2009/508).
27 Charities Act 1992 s 61(3) (as amended: see note 26).
28 Ie under the Charities Act 1992 s 61(1)–(3) (see the text and notes 1–27).
29 As to the meaning of 'services' see PARA 477 note 18.
30 Charities Act 1992 s 61(5).
31 See note 28.
32 Ie under the Charities Act 1992 s 61(2) (see the text and notes 13–14).
33 Charities Act 1992 s 61(4)(a).
34 Charities Act 1992 s 61(4)(b).

483. Right of charitable institutions to prevent unauthorised fund raising. Where on the application of any charitable institution[1]:

(1) the court[2] is satisfied that any person has done or is doing either of the following, namely: (a) soliciting money or other property for the benefit of the institution[3]; or (b) representing that charitable contributions[4] are to be given to or applied for the benefit of the institution, and that, unless restrained, he is likely to do further acts of that nature[5]; and

(2) the court is also satisfied as to one or more of the following: (a) that the person in question is using methods of fund raising to which the

institution objects; (b) that that person is not a fit and proper person to raise funds for the institution; and (c) where the conduct complained of is the making of such representations as are mentioned in head (1)(b) above, that the institution does not wish to be associated with the particular promotional or other fund raising venture in which that person is engaged[6],

then the court may grant an injunction restraining the doing of any such acts[7]. However, the power to grant an injunction is not exercisable on the application of a charitable institution unless the institution has, not less than 28 days before making the application, served on the person in question a notice in writing[8]:

(i) requesting him to cease forthwith soliciting money or other property for the benefit of the institution or representing that charitable contributions are to be given to or applied for the benefit of the institution, as the case may be[9]; and

(ii) stating that, if he does not comply with the notice, the institution will make an application under these provisions for an injunction[10].

Where (A) a charitable institution has served on any person such a notice and that person has complied with the notice[11]; but (B) that person has subsequently begun to carry on activities which are the same, or substantially the same, as those in respect of which the relevant notice was served[12], the institution is not, in connection with an application made by it under these provisions in respect of the activities carried on by that person, required to serve a further notice on him, if the application is made not more than 12 months after the date of service of the relevant notice[13].

1 As to the meaning of 'charitable institution' see PARA 477.
2 As to the meaning of 'court' see PARA 478 note 8.
3 As to references to soliciting money or other property for the benefit of an institution see PARA 477 note 7. As to the meaning of 'solicit' see PARA 477 note 7.
4 As to the meaning of 'charitable contributions' see PARA 477 note 18. As to the meaning of 'represent' see PARA 477 note 7.
5 Charities Act 1992 s 62(1)(a).
6 Charities Act 1992 s 62(1)(b), (2). As to the meaning of 'promotional venture' see PARA 477 note 17.
7 Charities Act 1992 s 62(1). Section 62 does not have the effect of authorising a charitable institution to make an application in respect of anything done by a professional fund raiser or commercial participator in relation to the institution: s 62(5). As to the meanings of 'professional fund raiser' and 'commercial participator' see PARA 477. As to injunctions see **CIVIL PROCEDURE** vol 11 (2009) PARA 335 et seq.
8 Charities Act 1992 s 62(3). The notice served must specify the circumstances which gave rise to the serving of the notice and the grounds on which an application for an injunction is to be made: see the Charitable Institutions (Fund Raising) Regulations 1994, SI 1994/3024, reg 4.
9 Charities Act 1992 s 62(3)(a).
10 Charities Act 1992 s 62(3)(b).
11 Charities Act 1992 s 62(4)(a).
12 Charities Act 1992 s 62(4)(b).
13 Charities Act 1992 s 62(4).

484. False statements relating to institutions which are not registered charities. Where a person solicits money or other property for the benefit of an institution[1] in association with a representation[2] that the institution is a registered charity[3] and the institution is not such a charity, he is guilty of an offence[4]. However, in any proceedings for such an offence, it is a defence for the accused to prove that he believed, on reasonable grounds, that the institution was a registered charity[5].

1 As to references to soliciting money or other property for the benefit of an institution see PARA 477 note 7. As to the meaning of 'solicit' see PARA 477 note 7. As to the meaning of 'institution' see PARA 477 note 2.
2 As to the meaning of 'representation' see PARA 477 note 7.
3 For these purposes, 'registered charity' means a charity which is for the time being registered in the register of charities kept under the Charities Act 2011 s 29 (see PARA 307): Charities Act 1992 s 63(2) (amended by the Deregulation and Contracting Out Act 1994 s 26(3); and the Charities Act 2011 Sch 7 para 66).
4 Charities Act 1992 s 63(1). A person guilty of such an offence is liable on summary conviction to a fine not exceeding level 5 on the standard scale: s 63(1). As to the standard scale see **SENTENCING AND DISPOSITION OF OFFENDERS** vol 92 (2010) PARA 143.
5 Charities Act 1992 s 63(1A) (added by the Deregulation and Contracting Out Act 1994 s 26(2)).

485. Service of notices and other documents. Any notice or other document required or authorised to be given or served in connection with the control of fund raising for charitable institutions[1] may be served or given to a person (other than a body corporate) by delivering it to that person, by leaving it at his last known address in the United Kingdom[2], or by sending it by post to him at that address[3]. In the case of a body corporate, such notice or document may be served or given by delivering it or sending it by post to the registered or principal office of the body in the United Kingdom, or, if it has no such office in the United Kingdom, to any place in the United Kingdom where it carries on business or conducts its activities, as the case may be[4]. Any such document may also be served on or given to a person (including a body corporate) by sending it by post to that person at an address notified by that person for these purposes to the person or persons by whom it is required or authorised to be served or given[5].

1 Ie under the Charities Act 1992 Pt II (ss 58–64A) (see PARAS 477–494).
2 As to the meaning of 'United Kingdom' see PARA 189 note 17.
3 Charities Act 1992 s 76(1)(b), (2).
4 Charities Act 1992 s 76(3).
5 Charities Act 1992 s 76(4).

486. Minister's power to make regulations in relation to the provisions of the Charities Act 1992. The Minister[1] may make such regulations[2] as appear to him to be necessary or desirable for any purposes connected with the provisions of the Charities Act 1992[3] relating to the control of charitable fund raising[4].

Any such regulations may[5]:

(1) prescribe the form and content of agreements made in relation to raising funds for charitable institutions[6], and notices served[7] in relation to injunctions granted by the court preventing unauthorised fund raising[8];
(2) require professional fund raisers[9] or commercial participators[10] who are parties to such agreements with charitable institutions[11] to make available to the institutions books, documents or other records (however kept) which relate to the institutions[12];
(3) specify the manner in which money or other property acquired by professional fund raisers or commercial participators for the benefit of, or otherwise falling to be given to or applied by such persons for the benefit of, charitable institutions is to be transmitted to such institutions[13];
(4) provide for: (a) the provisions relating to the requirement to indicate institutions benefiting and arrangements for remuneration[14]; and (b) the provisions relating to the cancellation of payments and agreements made in response to appeals[15], which have effect in relation to solicitations or representations made in the course of radio or television

programmes[16] to have effect, subject to any modifications specified in the regulations, in relation to solicitations or representations made in the course of such programmes by charitable institutions, or by companies connected with such institutions[17], and, in that connection, provide for any other provisions of Part II of the Charities Act 1992 to have effect for the purposes of the regulations subject to any modifications so specified[18];

(5) make other provision regulating the raising of funds for charitable, benevolent or philanthropic purposes[19], whether by professional fund raisers or commercial participators or otherwise[20].

Regulations under these provisions may provide that any failure to comply with a specified provision of the regulations is an offence[21].

1 As to the Minister see PARA 586.

2 In the exercise of this power, the Charitable Institutions (Fund Raising) Regulations 1994, SI 1994/3024, have been made. As to the making of regulations generally see the Charities Act 1992 s 77; and PARA 590.

3 Ie the Charities Act 1992 Pt II (ss 58–64A): see PARAS 477–494.

4 Charities Act 1992 s 64(1) (amended by SI 2006/2951).

5 Charities Act 1992 s 64(2). This provision is expressed to be without prejudice to s 64(1) (see the text and notes 1–4): s 64(2).

6 Ie agreements under the Charities Act 1992 s 59: see PARA 478.

7 Ie under the Charities Act 1992 s 62(3): see PARA 483.

8 Charities Act 1992 s 64(2)(a). As to regulations in relation to agreements between charitable institutions and professional fund raisers see the Charitable Institutions (Fund Raising) Regulations 1994, SI 1994/3024, reg 2; and PARA 488. As to regulations in relation to agreements between charitable institutions and commercial participators see reg 3; and PARA 489. As to regulations in relation to notices prior to injunction to prevent unauthorised fund raising see reg 4; and PARA 490.

9 As to the meaning of 'professional fund raiser' see PARA 477.

10 As to the meaning of 'commercial participator' see PARA 477.

11 As to the meaning of 'charitable institution' see PARA 477.

12 Charities Act 1992 s 64(2)(b). As to regulations in relation to the availability of books, documents or other records see the Charitable Institutions (Fund Raising) Regulations 1994, SI 1994/3024, reg 5; and PARA 493.

13 Charities Act 1992 s 64(2)(c). For these purposes, the reference to such money or other property mentioned in s 64(2)(c) includes a reference to money or other property which, in the case of a professional fund raiser or commercial participator: (1) has been acquired by him otherwise than in accordance with an agreement with a charitable institution; but (2) by reason of any solicitation or representation in consequence of which it has been acquired, is held by him on trust for such an institution: s 64(3). As to the meanings of 'solicitations' and 'representations' see PARA 477 note 7.

As to regulations in relation to the transmission of money and other property to charitable institutions see the Charitable Institutions (Fund Raising) Regulations 1994, SI 1994/3024, reg 6; and PARA 491.

14 Ie the Charities Act 1992 s 60: see PARA 479.

15 Ie the Charities Act 1992 s 61: see PARA 482.

16 As to the meaning of 'radio or television programmes' see PARA 477 note 7.

17 As to references to a company connected with charitable institutions see PARA 477 note 5. As to the meaning of 'company' see PARA 246; definition applied by the Charities Act 1992 s 58(1).

18 Charities Act 1992 s 64(2)(d).

19 As to the meaning of 'charitable purposes' see PARA 477 note 2.

20 Charities Act 1992 s 64(2)(e). As to regulations in relation to fund raising for charitable, benevolent or philanthropic purposes otherwise than by professional fund raisers or commercial participators see the Charitable Institutions (Fund Raising) Regulations 1994, SI 1994/3024, reg 7; and PARA 492.

21 Charities Act 1992 s 64(4). Such regulations may also provide that any such offence is punishable on summary conviction by a fine not exceeding level 2 on the standard scale: s 64(4). As to the standard scale see **SENTENCING AND DISPOSITION OF OFFENDERS** vol 92 (2010) PARA 143.

As to regulations in relation to offences and penalties for failure to comply with specified provisions see the Charitable Institutions (Fund Raising) Regulations 1994, SI 1994/3024, reg 8; and PARA 494.

487. Minister's reserve power to make regulations about fund raising generally. The Minister[1] may make such regulations as appear to him to be necessary or desirable for or in connection with regulating charity fund raising[2]. 'Charity fund raising' means activities which are carried on by charitable institutions[3], persons managing charitable institutions, or persons or companies connected with such institutions[4], and which involve soliciting or otherwise procuring funds[5] for the benefit of such institutions or companies connected with them, or for general charitable, benevolent or philanthropic purposes[6]. However, 'activities' does not include primary purpose trading[7].

Such regulations may, in particular, impose a good practice requirement on the persons managing charitable institutions in circumstances where those institutions, the persons managing them, or persons or companies connected with such institutions, are engaged in charity fund raising[8]. A 'good practice requirement' is a requirement to take all reasonable steps to ensure that the fund raising is carried out in such a way that: (1) it does not unreasonably intrude on the privacy of those from whom funds are being solicited or procured; (2) it does not involve the making of unreasonably persistent approaches to persons to donate funds; (3) it does not result in undue pressure being placed on persons to donate funds; and (4) it does not involve the making of any false or misleading representation about any of the following matters: (a) the extent or urgency of any need for funds on the part of any charitable institution or company connected with such an institution; (b) any use to which funds donated in response to the fund raising are to be put by such an institution or company; (c) the activities, achievements or finances of such an institution or company[9].

Such regulations may provide that a person who persistently fails, without reasonable excuse, to comply with any specified requirement of the regulations is guilty of an offence[10].

1 As to the Minister see PARA 586.
2 Charities Act 1992 s 64A(1) (s 64A added by the Charities Act 2006 s 69).
3 As to the meaning of 'charitable institution' see PARA 477.
4 The persons 'managing' a charitable institution are the charity trustees or other persons having the general control and management of the administration of the institution: Charities Act 1992 s 64A(7)(c) (as added: see note 2). As to the meaning of 'charity trustees' see PARA 1 note 10. A person is 'connected' with a charitable institution if he is an employee or agent of the institution, the persons managing it, or a company connected with it, or he is a volunteer acting on behalf of the institution or such a company: s 64A(7)(d) (as so added).
5 'Funds' means money or other property: Charities Act 1992 s 64A(7)(a) (as added: see note 2).
6 Charities Act 1992 s 64A(2) (as added: see note 2). 'General charitable, benevolent or philanthropic purposes' means charitable, benevolent or philanthropic purposes other than those associated with one or more particular institutions: s 64A(7)(b) (as so added).
7 Charities Act 1992 s 64A(2) (as added: see note 2). For these purposes, 'primary purpose trading' in relation to a charitable institution, means any trade carried on by the institution or a company connected with it where the trade is carried on in the course of the actual carrying out of a primary purpose of the institution or the work in connection with the trade is mainly carried out by beneficiaries of the institution: s 64A(8) (as so added).
8 Charities Act 1992 s 64A(3) (as added: see note 2).
9 Charities Act 1992 s 64A(4), (5) (as added: see note 2).
10 Charities Act 1992 s 64A(6) (as added: see note 2). Such regulations may also provide that any such offence is punishable on summary conviction by a fine not exceeding level 2 on the standard scale: s 64A(6) (as so added). As to the standard scale see SENTENCING AND DISPOSITION OF OFFENDERS vol 92 (2010) PARA 143.

488. Agreements between charitable institutions and professional fund raisers. An agreement between a professional fund raiser and a charitable institution enabling the fund raiser to solicit money or other property for the benefit of the charitable institution[1] must fulfil the following requirements as to form and content[2]. Such an agreement must be in writing and be signed by or on behalf of the charitable institution and the professional fund raiser[3]. It must specify:

(1) the name and address of each of the parties to the agreement[4];
(2) the date on which the agreement was signed by or on behalf of each of those parties[5];
(3) the period for which the agreement is to subsist[6];
(4) any terms relating to the termination of the agreement prior to the date on which that period expires[7]; and
(5) any terms relating to the variation of the agreement during that period[8].

The agreement must also contain: (a) a statement of its principal objectives and the methods to be used in pursuit of those objectives[9]; (b) if there is more than one charitable institution party to the agreement, provision as to the manner in which the proportion in which the institutions are respectively to benefit under the agreement is to be determined[10]; and (c) provision as to the amount by way of remuneration or expenses which the professional fund raiser is entitled to receive in respect of things done by him in pursuance of the agreement and the manner in which that amount is to be determined[11].

1 Ie under the Charities Act 1992 s 59(1): see PARA 478. For these purposes any reference, in relation to an agreement made for the purposes of s 59 (see PARA 478), to a charitable institution, commercial participator or professional fund raiser, is, unless the contrary intention appears, to be construed as a reference to any charitable institution, commercial participator or professional fund raiser, respectively, which is or who is a party to the agreement: Charitable Institutions (Fund Raising) Regulations 1994, SI 1994/3024, reg 1(3). As to the meanings of 'professional fund raiser', 'charitable institution' and 'commercial participator' see PARA 477.
2 Charitable Institutions (Fund Raising) Regulations 1994, SI 1994/3024, reg 2(1).
3 Charitable Institutions (Fund Raising) Regulations 1994, SI 1994/3024, reg 2(2).
4 Charitable Institutions (Fund Raising) Regulations 1994, SI 1994/3024, reg 2(3)(a).
5 Charitable Institutions (Fund Raising) Regulations 1994, SI 1994/3024, reg 2(3)(b).
6 Charitable Institutions (Fund Raising) Regulations 1994, SI 1994/3024, reg 2(3)(c).
7 Charitable Institutions (Fund Raising) Regulations 1994, SI 1994/3024, reg 2(3)(d).
8 Charitable Institutions (Fund Raising) Regulations 1994, SI 1994/3024, reg 2(3)(e).
9 Charitable Institutions (Fund Raising) Regulations 1994, SI 1994/3024, reg 2(4)(a).
10 Charitable Institutions (Fund Raising) Regulations 1994, SI 1994/3024, reg 2(4)(b).
11 Charitable Institutions (Fund Raising) Regulations 1994, SI 1994/3024, reg 2(4)(c).

489. Agreements between charitable institutions and commercial participators. An agreement between a commercial participator[1] and a charitable institution[2] enabling the commercial participator to represent that charitable contributions are to be given to or applied for the benefit of the charitable institution[3] must fulfil the following requirements as to form and content[4]. Such an agreement must be in writing and be signed by or on behalf of the charitable institution and the commercial participator[5]. It must specify:

(1) the name and address of each of the parties to the agreement[6];
(2) the date on which the agreement was signed by or on behalf of each of those parties[7];
(3) the period for which the agreement is to subsist[8];
(4) any terms relating to the termination of the agreement prior to the date on which that period expires[9]; and

(5) any terms relating to the variation of the agreement during that period[10].

The agreement must also contain a statement of its principal objectives and the methods to be used in pursuit of those objectives[11]. Additionally it must contain provision as to the manner in which are to be determined:

(a) if there is more than one charitable institution party to the agreement, the proportion in which the institutions which are so party are respectively to benefit under the agreement[12]; and

(b) the proportion of the consideration given for goods or services sold or supplied by the commercial participator, or of any other proceeds of a promotional venture undertaken by him, which is to be given to or applied for the benefit of the charitable institution[13]; or

(c) the sums by way of donations by the commercial participator in connection with the sale or supply of any goods or services sold or supplied by him which are to be so given or applied[14],

as the case may require[15]. The agreement must also contain provision as to any amount by way of remuneration or expenses which the commercial participator is to be entitled to receive in respect of things done by him in pursuance of the agreement and the manner in which any such amount is to be determined[16].

1 As to the meaning of 'commercial participator' see PARA 477. A reference to a commercial participator is to be construed as a reference to any commercial participator who is a party to the agreement: see the Charitable Institutions (Fund Raising) Regulations 1994, SI 1994/3024, reg 1(3); and PARA 488 note 1.

2 As to the meaning of 'charitable institution' see PARA 477. A reference to a charitable institution is to be construed as a reference to any charitable institution who is a party to the agreement: see the Charitable Institutions (Fund Raising) Regulations 1994, SI 1994/3024, reg 1(3); and PARA 488 note 1.

3 Ie under the Charities Act 1992 s 59(2): see PARA 478.

4 Charitable Institutions (Fund Raising) Regulations 1994, SI 1994/3024, reg 3(1).

5 Charitable Institutions (Fund Raising) Regulations 1994, SI 1994/3024, reg 3(2).

6 Charitable Institutions (Fund Raising) Regulations 1994, SI 1994/3024, reg 3(3)(a).

7 Charitable Institutions (Fund Raising) Regulations 1994, SI 1994/3024, reg 3(3)(b).

8 Charitable Institutions (Fund Raising) Regulations 1994, SI 1994/3024, reg 3(3)(c).

9 Charitable Institutions (Fund Raising) Regulations 1994, SI 1994/3024, reg 3(3)(d).

10 Charitable Institutions (Fund Raising) Regulations 1994, SI 1994/3024, reg 3(3)(e).

11 Charitable Institutions (Fund Raising) Regulations 1994, SI 1994/3024, reg 3(4)(a). The statement of methods must include, in relation to each method specified, a description of the type of charitable contributions which are to be given to, or applied for the benefit of, the charitable institution and of the circumstances in which they are to be so given or applied: reg 3(5). As to the meaning of 'charitable contributions' see PARA 477 note 18.

12 Charitable Institutions (Fund Raising) Regulations 1994, SI 1994/3024, reg 3(4)(b)(i).

13 Charitable Institutions (Fund Raising) Regulations 1994, SI 1994/3024, reg 3(4)(b)(ii).

14 Charitable Institutions (Fund Raising) Regulations 1994, SI 1994/3024, reg 3(4)(b)(iii). As to the supply of services see PARA 477 note 18.

15 Charitable Institutions (Fund Raising) Regulations 1994, SI 1994/3024, reg 3(4)(b).

16 Charitable Institutions (Fund Raising) Regulations 1994, SI 1994/3024, reg 3(4)(c).

490. Notice prior to injunction to prevent unauthorised fund raising. A notice served by a charitable institution[1] to prevent unauthorised fund raising[2] must[3] specify the circumstances which gave rise to the serving of the notice and the grounds on which an application to prevent unauthorised fundraising[4] is to be made[5].

1 As to the meaning of 'charitable institution' see PARA 477.

2 Ie under the Charities Act 1992 s 62(3): see PARA 483.

3 Ie in addition to satisfying the requirements of Charities Act 1992 s 62(3): see PARA 483.

4 Ie under Charities Act 1992 s 62: see PARA 483.
5 Charitable Institutions (Fund Raising) Regulations 1994, SI 1994/3024, reg 4.

491. Transmission of money and other property to charitable institutions. Any money or other property[1] acquired by a professional fund raiser[2] or commercial participator[3] for the benefit of, or otherwise falling to be given to or applied by such a person for the benefit of, a charitable institution[4] must, notwithstanding any inconsistent term in the agreement[5] with the charitable institution, be transmitted to that institution in accordance with the following provisions[6].

A professional fund raiser or commercial participator holding any such money or property must, unless he has a reasonable excuse[7]:

(1) in the case of any money, and any negotiable instrument which is payable to or to the account of the charitable institution, as soon as is reasonably practicable after its receipt and in any event not later than the expiration of 28 days after that receipt or such other period as may be agreed with the institution[8]: (a) pay it to the person or persons having the general control and management of the administration of the institution[9]; or (b) pay it into an account held by an authorised deposit taker[10] in the name of or on behalf of the institution which is under the control of the person, or any of the persons, specified in head (a) above[11]; and

(2) in the case of any other property, deal with it in accordance with any instructions given for that purpose, either generally or in a particular case, by the charitable institution provided that[12]: (a) any property in the possession of the professional fund raiser or commercial participator either pending the obtaining of such instructions as are referred to above or in accordance with such instructions must be securely held by him[13]; (b) the proceeds of the sale or other disposal of any property are, from the time of their receipt by the professional fund raiser or commercial participator, subject to the requirements of head (1) above[14].

Failure to comply with these provisions is an offence punishable on summary conviction by a fine[15].

1 Including such money or other property referred to in the Charities Act 1992 s 64(3): see PARA 486.
2 As to the meaning of 'professional fund raiser' see PARA 477. A reference to a professional fund raiser is to be construed as a reference to any professional fund raiser who is a party to the agreement: see the Charitable Institutions (Fund Raising) Regulations 1994, SI 1994/3024, reg 1(3); and PARA 488 note 1.
3 As to the meaning of 'commercial participator' see PARA 477. A reference to a commercial participator is to be construed as a reference to any commercial participator who is a party to the agreement: see the Charitable Institutions (Fund Raising) Regulations 1994, SI 1994/3024, reg 1(3); and PARA 488 note 1.
4 As to the meaning of 'charitable institution' see PARA 477. A reference to a charitable institution is to be construed as a reference to any charitable institution which is a party to the agreement: see the Charitable Institutions (Fund Raising) Regulations 1994, SI 1994/3024, reg 1(3); and PARA 488 note 1.
5 Ie an agreement made for the purposes of the Charities Act 1992 s 59: see PARA 478.
6 Charitable Institutions (Fund Raising) Regulations 1994, SI 1994/3024, reg 6(1).
7 Charitable Institutions (Fund Raising) Regulations 1994, SI 1994/3024, reg 6(2).
8 Charitable Institutions (Fund Raising) Regulations 1994, SI 1994/3024, reg 6(2)(a).
9 Charitable Institutions (Fund Raising) Regulations 1994, SI 1994/3024, reg 6(2)(a)(i).
10 'Authorised deposit taker' means the Bank of England, a person who has permission under the Financial Services and Markets Act 2000 Pt 4 (ss 40–55) to accept deposits, or an EEA firm of

the kind mentioned in Sch 3 para 5(b) which has permission under Sch 3 para 15 (as a result of qualifying for authorisation under Sch 3 para 12(1) to accept deposits (see FINANCIAL SERVICES AND INSTITUTIONS vol 48 (2008) PARA 318)): Charitable Institutions (Fund Raising) Regulations 1994, SI 1994/3024, reg 1(2) (definition substituted by SI 2001/3649). This definition must be read with the Financial Services and Markets Act 2000 s 22, any relevant order under that provision, and Sch 3: Charitable Institutions (Fund Raising) Regulations 1994, SI 1994/3024, reg 1(2A) (added by SI 2001/3649). See FINANCIAL SERVICES AND INSTITUTIONS vol 48 (2008) PARA 84.

11 Charitable Institutions (Fund Raising) Regulations 1994, SI 1994/3024, reg 6(2)(a)(ii) (amended by SI 2001/3649). The Financial Services and Markets Act 2000 (Consequential Amendments and Repeals) Order 2001, SI 2001/3649, art 480(4) refers to the Charitable Institutions (Fund Raising) Regulations 1994, SI 1994/3024, reg 6(2)(a)(iii); however, no such provision exists and accordingly that must be taken to refer to reg 6(2)(a)(ii).

12 Charitable Institutions (Fund Raising) Regulations 1994, SI 1994/3024, reg 6(2)(b).

13 Charitable Institutions (Fund Raising) Regulations 1994, SI 1994/3024, reg 6(2)(b)(i).

14 Charitable Institutions (Fund Raising) Regulations 1994, SI 1994/3024, reg 6(2)(b)(ii).

15 Charitable Institutions (Fund Raising) Regulations 1994, SI 1994/3024, reg 8(1), (2)(b). The fine must not exceed level 2 on the standard scale: reg 8(1). As to the standard scale see SENTENCING AND DISPOSITION OF OFFENDERS vol 92 (2010) PARA 143.

492. Fund raising for charitable etc purposes otherwise than by professional fund raisers or commercial participators. The following requirements apply to any person who carries on for gain a business other than a fund raising business[1] but, in the course of that business, engages in any promotional venture in the course of which it is represented that charitable contributions[2] are to be applied for charitable, benevolent or philanthropic purposes[3] of any description, rather than for the benefit of one or more particular charitable institutions[4].

Where such a person makes a representation to the effect that charitable contributions are to be applied for such charitable, benevolent or philanthropic purposes he must, unless he has a reasonable excuse, ensure that the representation is accompanied by a statement clearly indicating[5]:

(1) the fact that the charitable contributions referred to in the representation are to be applied for those purposes and not for the benefit of any particular charitable institution or institutions[6];

(2) the notifiable amount[7] of whichever of the following sums is applicable in the circumstances: (a) the sum representing so much of the consideration given for goods or services sold or supplied by him as is to be applied for those purposes; (b) the sum representing so much of any other proceeds of a promotional venture undertaken by him as is to be so applied; or (c) the sum of the donations by him in connection with the sale or supply of any such goods or services which are to be so applied[8]; and

(3) the method by which it is to be determined how the charitable contributions referred to in the representation are to be distributed between different charitable institutions[9].

Failure to comply with these provisions is an offence punishable on summary conviction by a fine[10].

1 As to the meaning of 'fund raising business' see PARA 477 note 6.

2 As to the meaning of 'charitable contributions' see PARA 477 note 18.

3 As to references to charitable, benevolent or philanthropic purposes see PARA 477 note 2.

4 Charitable Institutions (Fund Raising) Regulations 1994, SI 1994/3024, reg 7(1). As to the meaning of 'charitable institution' see PARA 477.

5 Charitable Institutions (Fund Raising) Regulations 1994, SI 1994/3024, reg 7(2).

6 Charitable Institutions (Fund Raising) Regulations 1994, SI 1994/3024, reg 7(2)(a).

7 'Notifiable amount' in relation to any sum is a reference: (1) to the actual amount of the sum, if that is known at the time when the statement is made; and (2) otherwise to the estimated

amount of the sum, calculated as accurately as is reasonably possible in the circumstances: Charitable Institutions (Fund Raising) Regulations 1994, SI 1994/3024, reg 7(3) (added by SI 2009/1060).

8 Charitable Institutions (Fund Raising) Regulations 1994, SI 1994/3024, reg 7(2)(b) (substituted by SI 2009/1060).

9 Charitable Institutions (Fund Raising) Regulations 1994, SI 1994/3024, reg 7(2)(c).

10 Charitable Institutions (Fund Raising) Regulations 1994, SI 1994/3024, reg 8(1), (2)(c). The fine must not exceed level 2 on the standard scale: reg 8(1). As to the standard scale see **SENTENCING AND DISPOSITION OF OFFENDERS** vol 92 (2010) PARA 143.

493. Availability of books, documents or other records. A professional fund raiser[1] or commercial participator[2] who is a party to an agreement[3] with a charitable institution[4] must, on request and at all reasonable times, make available[5] to any charitable institution which is a party to that agreement any books, documents or other records, however kept, which relate to that institution and are kept for the purposes of the agreement[6]. Failure to comply with these provisions is an offence punishable on summary conviction by a fine[7].

1 As to the meaning of professional fund raiser see PARA 477. A reference to a professional fund raiser is to be construed as a reference to any professional fund raiser who is a party to the agreement: see the Charitable Institutions (Fund Raising) Regulations 1994, SI 1994/3024, reg 1(3); and PARA 488 note 1.

2 As to the meaning of 'commercial participator' see PARA 477. A reference to a commercial participator is to be construed as a reference to any commercial participator who is a party to the agreement: see the Charitable Institutions (Fund Raising) Regulations 1994, SI 1994/3024, reg 1(3); and PARA 488 note 1.

3 Ie an agreement made for the purposes of the Charities Act 1992 s 59: see PARA 478.

4 As to the meaning of 'charitable institution' see PARA 477. A reference to a charitable institution is to be construed as a reference to any charitable institution which is a party to the agreement: see the Charitable Institutions (Fund Raising) Regulations 1994, SI 1994/3024, reg 1(3); and PARA 488 note 1.

5 In the case of any record which is kept otherwise than in legible form, the reference in the text to making that record available is to be construed as a reference to making it available in legible form: Charitable Institutions (Fund Raising) Regulations 1994, SI 1994/3024, reg 5(2).

6 Charitable Institutions (Fund Raising) Regulations 1994, SI 1994/3024, reg 5(1).

7 Charitable Institutions (Fund Raising) Regulations 1994, SI 1994/3024, reg 8(1), (2)(a). The fine must not exceed level 2 on the standard scale: reg 8(1). As to the standard scale see **SENTENCING AND DISPOSITION OF OFFENDERS** vol 92 (2010) PARA 143.

494. Offences and penalties. Failure to comply with any of the provisions relating to: (1) the availability of books, documents or other records[1]; (2) a professional fund raiser[2] or commercial participator[3] holding money or property[4]; and (3) the statement accompanying a representation to the effect that charitable contributions[5] are to be applied for charitable, benevolent or philanthropic purposes[6] of any description[7], is an offence punishable on summary conviction by a fine[8].

1 Ie under the Charitable Institutions (Fund Raising) Regulations 1994, SI 1994/3024, reg 5(1): see PARA 493.

2 As to the meaning of 'professional fund raiser' see PARA 477.

3 As to the meaning of 'commercial participator' see PARA 477.

4 Ie under Charitable Institutions (Fund Raising) Regulations 1994, SI 1994/3024, reg 6(2): see PARA 491.

5 As to the meaning of 'charitable contributions' see PARA 477 note 18.

6 As to references to charitable, benevolent or philanthropic purposes see PARA 477 note 2.

7 Ie under the Charitable Institutions (Fund Raising) Regulations 1994, SI 1994/3024, reg 7(2): see PARA 492.

8 Charitable Institutions (Fund Raising) Regulations 1994, SI 1994/3024, reg 8(1), (2). The fine must not exceed level 2 on the standard scale: reg 8(1). As to the standard scale see **SENTENCING AND DISPOSITION OF OFFENDERS** vol 92 (2010) PARA 143.

(5) CONTROLS UNDER THE CHARITIES ACT 2006

495. Public charitable collections. The following provisions have effect as from a day to be appointed. The Charities Act 2006 provides for the regulation of public charitable collections[1]. A 'public charitable collection' is defined as a charitable appeal which is made in any public place[2] ('collection in a public place'[3]) or by means of visits to houses[4] or business premises[5] ('door to door collection'[6]), or both[7].

A 'charitable appeal' means an appeal to members of the public which is: (1) an appeal to them to give money or other property[8], or the making of an offer to sell goods or to supply services, or the exposing of goods for sale, to them[9], or both; and (2) made in association with a representation that the whole or any part of its proceeds[10] is to be applied for charitable, benevolent or philanthropic purposes[11]. However, a charitable appeal is not a public charitable collection if the appeal: (a) is made in the course of a public meeting[12]; (b) is made on land within a churchyard or burial ground contiguous or adjacent to a place of public worship or on other land occupied for the purposes of a place of public worship and contiguous or adjacent to it, where the land is enclosed or substantially enclosed (whether by any wall or building or otherwise)[13]; (c) is made on land to which members of the public have access only by virtue of the express or implied permission of the occupier of the land, or by virtue of any enactment, and the occupier is the promoter of the collection[14]; or (d) is an appeal to members of the public to give money or other property by placing it in an unattended receptacle[15].

1 Charities Act 2006 s 45(1) (not yet in force).

The provisions of the Charities Act 2006 governing public charitable collections (see Pt 3 Ch 1 (ss 45–66)) are to be brought into force by order made by the Minister under s 79(2) as from a day to be appointed. At the date at which this volume states the law the only provisions brought into force are ss 45(2)–(6), 46, 47(1), for the purposes of the definition of 'professional fund raiser' in the Charities Act 1992 Pt 2 (ss 58–64A) (see PARA 477): see the Charities Act 2006 (Commencement No 2, Transitional Provisions and Savings) Order 2007, SI 2007/3286, art 3, Sch 2.

The likelihood of the regime under these provisions of the Charities Act 2006 being given full statutory force is unclear.

2 'Public place' means any highway and any other place to which, at any time when the appeal is made, members of the public have or are permitted to have access and which either is not within a building, or if within a building, is a public area within any station, airport or shopping precinct or any other similar public area: Charities Act 2006 s 45(5) (not in force: see note 1). However, it does not include: (1) any place to which members of the public are permitted to have access only if any payment or ticket required as a condition of access has been made or purchased; or (2) any place to which members of the public are permitted to have access only by virtue of permission given for the purposes of the appeal in question: s 45(6) (not in force: see note 1).

3 Charities Act 2006 s 45(2)(c) (not in force: see note 1).

4 'House' includes any part of a building constituting a separate dwelling: Charities Act 2006 s 45(5) (not in force: see note 1).

5 'Business premises' means any premises used for business or other commercial purposes: Charities Act 2006 s 45(5) (not in force: see note 1).

6 Charities Act 2006 s 45(2)(d) (not in force: see note 1).

7 Charities Act 2006 s 45(2)(a) (not in force: see note 1).

8 The reference to the giving of money is to doing so by whatever means and it does not matter whether the giving of money or other property is for consideration or otherwise: Charities Act 2006 s 45(3) (not in force: see note 1).

9 Charities Act 2006 s 45(4) (not in force: see note 1).

10 'Proceeds', in relation to a public charitable collection, means all money or other property given, whether for consideration or otherwise, in response to the charitable appeal in question: Charities Act 2006 s 47(1) (not in force: see note 1).

11 Charities Act 2006 s 45(2)(b) (not in force: see note 1). 'Charitable, benevolent or philanthropic institution' means a charity or an institution (other than a charity) which is established for charitable, benevolent, or philanthropic purposes: s 47(1) (not in force: see note 1).
12 Charities Act 2006 s 46(1)(a) (not in force: see note 1).
13 Charities Act 2006 s 46(1)(b) (not in force: see note 1).
14 Charities Act 2006 s 46(1)(c) (not in force: see note 1). 'Occupier', in relation to unoccupied land, means the person entitled to occupy it: s 46(2) (not in force: see note 1).
15 Charities Act 2006 s 46(1)(d) (not in force: see note 1). A receptacle is unattended if it is not in the possession or custody of a person acting as a collector: s 46(3) (not in force: see note 1). 'Collector', in relation to a public charitable collection, means any person by whom the appeal in question is made, whether made by him alone or with others and whether made by him for remuneration or otherwise: s 47(1) (not in force: see note 1).

496. Restrictions on conducting collections in a public place. The following provisions have effect as from a day to be appointed. Collection in a public place[1] which is not an exempt collection[2] must not be conducted unless the promoters[3] of the collection hold a public collections certificate[4] in respect of the collection and the collection is conducted in accordance with a permit issued by the local authority[5] in whose area it is conducted[6].

Where a collection in a public place is conducted in contravention of these provisions and the circumstances of the case do not fall within the statutory provisions for offences relating to local short-term collections[7], every promoter of the collection is guilty of an offence[8].

1 Charities Act 2006 s 45(1) (not in force: see PARA 495 note 1). As to the Minister see PARA 586. As to the meaning of 'collection in a public place' see PARA 495.
2 Ie by virtue of the Charities Act 2006 s 50 (see PARA 498): s 48(2) (not in force: see PARA 495 note 1).
3 'Promoter', in relation to a public charitable collection, means a person who (whether alone or with others and whether for remuneration or otherwise) organises or controls the conduct of the charitable appeal in question, or, where there is no such person, any person who acts as a collector in respect of the collection; and associated expressions are to be construed accordingly: Charities Act 2006 s 47(1) (not in force: see PARA 495 note 1). As to the meaning of 'collector' see PARA 495 note 15.
4 'Public collections certificate' means a certificate issued by the Charity Commission under the Charities Act 2006 s 52 (see PARA 500): s 47(1) (not in force: see PARA 495 note 1). As to the Charity Commission see PARAS 543–578.
5 Ie a permit issued under the Charities Act 2006 s 59 (see PARAS 504–507). 'Local authority' means a unitary authority, the council of a district so far as it is not a unitary authority, the council of a London borough or of a Welsh county or county borough, the Common Council of the City of London or the Council of the Isles of Scilly: s 47(1) (not in force: see PARA 495 note 1). 'Unitary authority' means the council of a county, so far as it is the council for an area for which there are no district councils, and the council of any district comprised in an area for which there is no county council: s 47(2) (not in force: see PARA 495 note 1). The functions exercisable under the provisions relating to public charitable collections (ie under Pt 3 Ch 1 (ss 45–66)) by a local authority are to be exercisable as respects the Inner Temple, by its Sub-Treasurer, and as respects the Middle Temple, by its Under Treasurer, and references in Pt 3 Ch 1 to a local authority or to the area of a local authority are to be construed accordingly: s 47(3) (not in force: see PARA 495 note 1). As to the London borough councils and the Common Council of the City of London see **LONDON GOVERNMENT** vol 71 (2013) PARAS 20 et seq, 34 et seq. As to local government areas and authorities in England and Wales generally see **LOCAL GOVERNMENT** vol 69 (2009) PARA 22 et seq.
6 Charities Act 2006 s 48(1) (not in force: see PARA 495 note 1). As to such permits see PARAS 504–507.
7 Ie under the Charities Act 2006 s 50(6) (see PARA 498). As to local short-term collections see PARA 498.
8 Charities Act 2006 s 48(3) (not in force: see PARA 495 note 1). A person guilty of such an offence is liable on summary conviction to a fine not exceeding level 5 on the standard scale: s 48(3) (not in force: see PARA 495 note 1). As to the standard scale see **SENTENCING AND DISPOSITION OF OFFENDERS** vol 92 (2010) PARA 143.

497. Restrictions on conducting door to door collections. The following provisions have effect as from a day to be appointed. A door to door collection[1] which is not an exempt collection[2] must not be conducted unless the promoters[3] of the collection hold a public collections certificate[4] in respect of the collection and have, within the prescribed[5] period falling before the day, or the first of the days, on which the collection takes place, notified the local authority[6] in whose area the collection is to be conducted of certain matters and provided that authority with a copy of the public collections certificate[7]. The matters to be notified to the local authority are: (1) the purpose for which the proceeds[8] of the appeal are to be applied; (2) the prescribed particulars of when the collection is to be conducted; (3) the locality within which the collection is to be conducted; and (4) such other matters as may be prescribed[9].

Where a door to door collection is conducted in contravention of these provisions and the circumstances of the case do not fall within the statutory provisions for offences relating to local short-term collections[10], every promoter of the collection is guilty of an offence[11].

1 As to the meaning of 'door to door collection' see PARA 495.
2 Ie by virtue of the Charities Act 2006 s 50 (see PARA 498): s 49(2) (not in force: see PARA 495 note 1).
3 As to the meaning of 'promoter' see PARA 496 note 3.
4 As to the meaning of 'public collections certificate' see PARA 496 note 4. As to public collections certificates see PARAS 499–503.
5 'Prescribed' means prescribed by regulations under the Charities Act 2006 s 63 (see PARA 509): s 47(1) (not in force: see PARA 495 note 1). At the date at which this volume states the law no such regulations had been made.
6 As to the meaning of 'local authority' see PARA 496 note 5.
7 Charities Act 2006 s 49(1) (not in force: see PARA 495 note 1).
8 As to the meaning of 'proceeds' see PARA 495 note 10.
9 Charities Act 2006 s 49(3) (not in force: see PARA 495 note 1). See note 5.
10 Ie under the Charities Act 2006 s 50(6) (see PARA 498). As to local short-term collections see PARA 498.
11 Charities Act 2006 s 49(4) (not in force: see PARA 495 note 1). A person guilty of such an offence is liable on summary conviction to a fine not exceeding level 5 on the standard scale (s 49(4) (not in force: see PARA 495 note 1)), unless the appeal is for goods only, in which case such a promoter is liable on summary conviction to a fine not exceeding level 3 on the standard scale (s 49(5) (not in force: see PARA 495 note 1)). 'Goods' includes all personal chattels other than things in action and money: s 49(6) (not in force: see PARA 495 note 1). As to the standard scale see **SENTENCING AND DISPOSITION OF OFFENDERS** vol 92 (2010) PARA 143.

498. Exemptions for local, short term collections. The following provisions have effect as from a day to be appointed. A public charitable collection[1] is an exempt collection if it is a local, short term collection and the promoters[2] notify the local authority[3] in whose area it is to be conducted of certain matters within the prescribed[4] period falling before the day (or the first of the days) on which the collection takes place, unless, within the prescribed period beginning with the date when they are so notified, the local authority serves a statutory notice[5] on the promoters[6]. A public charitable collection is a local, short term collection if the appeal is local in character and the duration of the appeal does not exceed the prescribed period of time[7]. The matters to be notified to the local authority are the purpose for which the proceeds[8] of the appeal are to be applied, the date or dates on which the collection is to be conducted, the place at which, or the locality within which, the collection is to be conducted and such other matters as may be prescribed in regulations[9].

Where it appears to the local authority that the collection is not a local, short term collection, or that the promoters or any of them have or has on any occasion breached any relevant regulations[10] or been convicted of a relevant offence[11], it must serve on the promoters written notice of its decision to that effect and the reasons for its decision[12]. The notice must also state that there is a right of appeal[13] and the time within which such an appeal must be brought[14].

Where a collection in a public place[15] or a door to door collection[16] is conducted otherwise than in accordance with the relevant statutory provisions[17] and the collection is a local, short term collection but the promoters do not notify the local authority[18], every promoter of the collection is guilty of an offence[19].

1 As to the meaning of 'public charitable collection' see PARA 495.
2 As to the meaning of 'promoter' see PARA 496 note 3.
3 As to the meaning of 'local authority' see PARA 496 note 5.
4 Ie such period as is prescribed by regulations under the Charities Act 2006 s 63: see PARA 509.
5 Ie under the Charities Act 2006 s 50(4): see the text to notes 10–12. As to the service of notices see PARA 511.
6 Charities Act 2006 s 50(1) (not in force: see PARA 495 note 1).
7 Charities Act 2006 s 50(2) (not in force: see PARA 495 note 1).
8 As to the meaning of 'proceeds' see PARA 495 note 10.
9 Charities Act 2006 s 50(3) (not in force: see PARA 495 note 1).
10 Ie regulations prescribed under the Charities Act 2006 s 63: see PARA 509.
11 Ie an offence under the Charities Act 2006 s 53(2)(a)(i)–(v): see PARA 500.
12 Charities Act 2006 s 50(4) (not in force: see PARA 495 note 1).
13 Ie the right conferred by the Charities Act 2006 s 62(1): see PARA 508.
14 Charities Act 2006 s 50(5) (not in force: see PARA 495 note 1).
15 As to the meaning of 'collection in a public place' see PARA 495.
16 As to the meaning of 'door to door collection' see PARA 495.
17 Ie under the Charities Act 2006 s 48(1) (see PARA 496) or s 49(1) (see PARA 497), as the case may be.
18 Ie under the Charities Act 2006 s 50(1)(b) (see the text to notes 2–6).
19 Charities Act 2006 s 50(6) (not in force: see PARA 495 note 1). A person guilty of such an offence is liable on summary conviction to a fine not exceeding level 3 on the standard scale: s 50(6) (not yet in force). As to the standard scale see **SENTENCING AND DISPOSITION OF OFFENDERS** vol 92 (2010) PARA 143.

499. Applications for public collections certificates. The following provisions have effect as from a day to be appointed. A person or persons proposing to promote public charitable collections[1] other than exempt collections[2] may apply to the Charity Commission[3] for a public collections certificate in respect of those collections[4]. An application must be made within the specified[5] period falling before the first of the collections is to commence, or before such later date as the Commission may allow in the case of that application[6]. The application must be made in such form as may be specified[7], specify the period for which the certificate is sought (which must be no more than five years), and contain such other information as may be specified in regulations[8]. An application may be made for a public collections certificate in respect of a single collection[9].

1 As to the meaning of 'public charitable collection' see PARA 495.
2 'Exempt collection' means a public charitable collection which is an exempt collection by virtue of the Charities Act 2006 s 50 (see PARA 498): s 51(7) (not in force: see PARA 495 note 1).
3 As to the Charity Commission see PARAS 543–578.
4 Charities Act 2006 s 51(1) (not in force: see PARA 495 note 1).
5 'Specified' means specified in regulations made by the Commission after consulting such persons or bodies of persons as it considers appropriate: Charities Act 2006 s 51(5) (not in force: see PARA 495 note 1). Such regulations must be published in such manner as the Commission considers appropriate, may make different provision for different cases or descriptions of case, and may make such incidental, supplementary, consequential or transitional provision as the Commission considers appropriate: s 51(6) (not in force: see PARA 495 note 1).
6 Charities Act 2006 s 51(2) (not in force: see PARA 495 note 1).

7 See note 5.
8 Charities Act 2006 s 51(3) (not in force: see PARA 495 note 1).
9 Charities Act 2006 s 51(4) (not in force: see PARA 495 note 1). The references to public charitable collections in Pt 3 Ch 1 (ss 45–66) in the context of such certificates are to be read accordingly: s 51(4) (not in force).

500. Determination of applications and issue of public collections certificates. The following provisions have effect as from a day to be appointed. On receiving an application for a public collections certificate[1] the Charity Commission[2] may make such inquiries[3] as it thinks fit[4] and must, after making any such inquiries, determine the application by either issuing a public collections certificate in respect of the collections, or refusing the application on one or more of the statutory grounds[5].

A public collections certificate must specify such matters as may be prescribed, and is in force for the period specified in the application[6] or such shorter period as the Commission thinks fit[7]. The Commission may, at the time of issuing a public collections certificate, attach to it such conditions as it thinks fit[8].

Where the Commission refuses to issue a certificate, or attaches any condition to it, it must serve on the applicant written notice of its decision and the reasons for its decision[9]. That notice must also state that there is a right of appeal[10] and the time within which such an appeal must be brought[11].

The Commission may refuse an application for a public collections certificate on the following grounds[12]:

(1) that the applicant has been convicted of a relevant offence[13];
(2) where the applicant is a person other than a charitable, benevolent or philanthropic institution[14] for whose benefit the collections are proposed to be conducted, that the Commission is not satisfied that the applicant is authorised (whether by any such institution or by any person acting on behalf of any such institution) to promote the collections[15];
(3) that it appears to the Commission that the applicant, in promoting any other collection authorised under the Charities Act 2006[16] or the Civic Government (Scotland) Act 1982[17], failed to exercise the required due diligence[18];
(4) that the Commission is not satisfied that the applicant will exercise the required due diligence in promoting the proposed collections[19];
(5) that it appears to the Commission that the amount likely to be applied for charitable, benevolent or philanthropic purposes in consequence of the proposed collections would be inadequate, having regard to the likely amount of the proceeds[20] of the collections[21];
(6) that it appears to the Commission that the applicant or any other person would be likely to receive an amount by way of remuneration in connection with the collections that would be excessive, having regard to all the circumstances[22];
(7) that the applicant has failed to provide information required for the purposes of the application for the certificate or a previous application, or in response to a request for information[23];
(8) that it appears to the Commission that information so provided to it by the applicant is false or misleading in a material particular[24];
(9) that it appears to the Commission that the applicant, or any person authorised by him, has breached any conditions attached to a previous public collections certificate, or has persistently breached any conditions attached to a permit[25];

(10) that it appears to the Commission that the applicant or any person authorised by him has on any occasion breached any provision of relevant regulations[26].

The Commission may request any applicant for a public collections certificate, or any person to whom such a certificate has been issued, to provide it with any information in his possession, or document in his custody or under his control, which is relevant to the exercise of any of its functions under the Charities Act 2006[27] in relation to public charitable collections[28].

1 Ie an application made in accordance with the Charities Act 2006 s 51: see PARA 499.
2 As to the Charity Commission see PARAS 543–578.
3 Ie whether under the Charities Act 2006 s 54 (see the text and note 28) or otherwise.
4 Charities Act 2006 s 52(1) (not in force: see PARA 495 note 1).
5 Charities Act 2006 s 52(2) (not in force: see PARA 495 note 1). As to the statutory grounds see s 53(1); and the text and notes 13–26.
6 Ie in accordance with the Charities Act 2006 s 51(3)(b): see PARA 499. However, this is specifically stated to be subject to the statutory provisions for the withdrawal and variation of certificates under s 56 (see PARA 502): s 52(3)(b) (not in force: see PARA 495 note 1).
7 Charities Act 2006 s 52(3) (not in force: see PARA 495 note 1).
8 Charities Act 2006 s 52(4) (not in force: see PARA 495 note 1). Such conditions attached may include conditions prescribed for the purposes of s 52(4): s 52(5) (not in force: see PARA 495 note 1). The Commission must secure that the terms of any conditions attached under s 52(4) are consistent with the provisions of any regulations under s 63 (see PARA 509), whether or not prescribing conditions for the purposes of s 52(4): s 52(6) (not in force: see PARA 495 note 1).
9 Charities Act 2006 s 52(7) (not in force: see PARA 495 note 1). As to the service of notices see PARA 511.
10 Ie the right conferred by Charities Act 2006 s 57(1): see PARA 502.
11 Charities Act 2006 s 52(8) (not in force: see PARA 495 note 1).
12 Where an application for a certificate is made by more than one person, any reference to the applicant in the Charities Act 2006 s 53(1) or (2) (see the text and notes 13–26) is to be construed as a reference to any of the applicants: s 53(3) (not in force: see PARA 495 note 1).
13 Charities Act 2006 s 53(1)(a) (not in force: see PARA 495 note 1). A 'relevant offence' is an offence: (1) under the Police, Factories, etc (Miscellaneous Provisions) Act 1916 s 5 (see **POLICE AND INVESTIGATORY POWERS** vol 84 (2013) PARA 105); (2) under the House to House Collections Act 1939 (see PARAS 465–474); (3) under the Civic Government (Scotland) Act 1982 s 119; (4) under the Charities Act 2006 Pt 3 Ch 1 (ss 45–66) (see PARAS 495–511); (5) involving dishonesty; or (6) of a kind the commission of which would, in the opinion of the Commission, be likely to be facilitated by the issuing to the applicant of a public collections certificate: s 53(2)(a), (8) (not in force: see PARA 495 note 1).
14 'Charitable, benevolent or philanthropic institution' means a charity or an institution (other than a charity) which is established for charitable, benevolent, or philanthropic purposes: Charities Act 2006 s 47(1) (not in force: see PARA 495 note 1). As to the meaning of 'charitable, benevolent, or philanthropic purposes' see PARA 495 note 11.
15 Charities Act 2006 s 53(1)(b) (not in force: see PARA 495 note 1).
16 A reference to a collection authorised under the Charities Act 2006 Pt 3 Ch 1 is a reference to a public charitable collection that is conducted in accordance with s 48 (see PARA 496) or s 49 (see PARA 497), or is an exempt collection by virtue of s 50 (see PARA 498): s 53(7) (not in force: see PARA 495 note 1).
17 Ie under the Civic Government (Scotland) Act 1982 s 119.
18 Charities Act 2006 s 53(1)(c) (not in force: see PARA 495 note 1). The 'required due diligence' is due diligence: (1) to secure that persons authorised by the applicant to act as collectors for the purposes of the collection were (or will be) fit and proper persons; (2) to secure that such persons complied (or will comply) with the provisions of regulations under s 63(1)(b) (see PARA 509) or, as the case may be, the Civic Government (Scotland) Act 1982 s 119; or (3) to prevent badges or certificates of authority being obtained by persons other than those the applicant had so authorised: Charities Act 2006 s 53(2)(b) (not in force: see PARA 495 note 1). Subject to s 53(5), (6), the reference to badges or certificates of authority is a reference to badges or certificates of authority in a form prescribed by regulations under s 63(1)(b) (see PARA 509) or, as the case may be, the Civic Government (Scotland) Act 1982 s 119: Charities Act 2006 s 53(4) (not in force: see PARA 495 note 1).

The due diligence requirement applies to the conduct of the applicant (or any of the applicants) in relation to any public charitable collection authorised under the Police, Factories, etc (Miscellaneous Provisions) Act 1916 s 5 (see **POLICE AND INVESTIGATORY POWERS** vol 84 (2013) PARA 105) or under the House to House Collections Act 1939 (see PARAS 465–474) as it applies to his conduct in relation to a collection authorised under the Charities Act 2006 Pt 3 Ch 1 (see note 16) but subject to modifications set out in s 53(6): s 53(5) (not in force: see PARA 495 note 1).

19 Charities Act 2006 s 53(1)(d) (not in force: see PARA 495 note 1). As to the required due diligence see note 18.

20 As to the meaning of 'proceeds' see PARA 495 note 10.

21 Charities Act 2006 s 53(1)(e) (not in force: see PARA 495 note 1).

22 Charities Act 2006 s 53(1)(f) (not in force: see PARA 495 note 1).

23 Charities Act 2006 s 53(1)(g) (not in force: see PARA 495 note 1). A request for information is made under s 54(1) (see the text and notes 28).

24 Charities Act 2006 s 53(1)(h) (not in force: see PARA 495 note 1).

25 Charities Act 2006 s 53(1)(i) (not in force: see PARA 495 note 1). A permit is issued under s 59 (see PARAS 504–507).

26 Charities Act 2006 s 53(1)(j) (not in force: see PARA 495 note 1). Regulations are made under s 63(1)(b) (see PARA 509).

27 Ie under the Charities Act 2006 Pt 3 Ch 1 (ss 45–66) (see PARA 495 et seq).

28 Charities Act 2006 s 54(1) (not in force: see PARA 495 note 1). This provision does not affect the power conferred on the Commission by the Charities Act 2011 s 52 (see PARA 562): Charities Act 2006 s 54(2) (not in force: see PARA 495 note 1) (amended by the Charities Act 2011 Sch 7 para 118).

501. Transfer of public collections certificate between trustees of unincorporated charity. The following provisions have effect as from a day to be appointed. A public collections certificate[1] is not transferable[2] except that one or more individuals to whom a public collections certificate has been issued (the 'holders') may apply to the Charity Commission[3] for a direction that the certificate be transferred to one or more other individuals (the 'recipients')[4]. Such an application must be in such form as may be specified[5], and contain such information as may be specified[6]. The Commission may direct that the certificate be transferred if it is satisfied that each of the holders is or was a trustee of a charity which is not a body corporate, each of the recipients is a trustee of that charity and consents to the transfer, and the charity trustees[7] consent to the transfer[8].

Where the Commission refuses to direct that a certificate be transferred, it must serve on the holders written notice of its decision and the reasons for its decision[9]. The notice must also state that there is a right of appeal[10] and the time within which such an appeal must be brought[11].

1 As to the meaning of 'public collections certificate' see PARA 496 note 4. As to public collections certificates generally see PARA 499.

2 Charities Act 2006 s 55(7) (not in force: see PARA 495 note 1).

3 As to the Charity Commission see PARAS 543–578.

4 Charities Act 2006 s 55(1) (not in force: see PARA 495 note 1).

5 'Specified' means specified in regulations made by the Commission after consulting such persons or bodies of persons as it considers appropriate and such regulations must be published in such manner as the Commission considers appropriate, may make different provision for different cases or descriptions of case, and may make such incidental, supplementary, consequential or transitional provision as the Commission considers appropriate: Charities Act 2006 s 51(5), (6); applied by s 55(6) (not in force: see PARA 495 note 1).

6 Charities Act 2006 s 55(2) (not in force: see PARA 495 note 1).

7 As to the meaning of 'charity trustees' see PARA 1 note 10.

8 Charities Act 2006 s 55(3) (not in force: see PARA 495 note 1).

9 Charities Act 2006 s 55(4) (not in force: see PARA 495 note 1). As to the service of notices see PARA 511.

10 Ie under the Charities Act 2006 57(2): see PARA 503.

11 Charities Act 2006 s 55(5) (not in force: see PARA 495 note 1).

502. Withdrawal, suspension and variation of public collections certificates. The following provisions have effect as from a day to be appointed. In certain circumstances[1], the Charity Commission[2] may withdraw a public collections certificate[3], suspend such a certificate, attach any condition, or further condition, to such a certificate, or vary any existing condition of such a certificate[4]. The circumstances are:

(1) where the Commission has reason to believe there has been a change in the circumstances which prevailed at the time when it issued the certificate[5] and is of the opinion that, if the application for the certificate had been made in the new circumstances, it would not have issued the certificate or would have issued it subject to different or additional conditions[6];

(2) where the holder of a certificate has unreasonably refused to provide any information or document in response to a request under the Commission's statutory power to request information in relation to a public collections certificate[7], or the Commission has reason to believe that information provided to it by the holder of a certificate (or, where there is more than one holder, by any of them) for the purposes of the application for the certificate, or in response to such a request, was false or misleading in a material particular[8];

(3) where the Commission has reason to believe that there has been or is likely to be a breach of any condition of a certificate, or that a breach of such a condition is continuing[9].

Any such condition imposed at any time by the Commission, whether by attaching a new condition to the certificate or by varying an existing condition, must be one that it would be appropriate for the Commission to attach to the certificate[10] if the holder was applying for it in the circumstances prevailing at that time[11].

Where the Commission withdraws or suspends a certificate, attaches a condition to a certificate, or varies an existing condition of a certificate, it must serve on the holder written notice of its decision and the reasons for its decision[12]. That notice must also state the right of appeal[13] and the time within which such an appeal must be brought[14]. However, if the Commission considers that the interests of the public require a decision by it to withdraw or vary a certificate to have immediate effect, and includes a statement to that effect and the reasons for it in the notice so served[15] the decision takes effect when that notice is served on the holder[16]. In any other case the certificate continues to have effect as if it had not been withdrawn or suspended or (as the case may be) as if the condition had not been attached or varied until the time for bringing an appeal has expired, or if such an appeal is duly brought, until the determination or abandonment of the appeal[17].

A certificate suspended under the above provisions, subject to any appeal and any withdrawal of the certificate, remains suspended until such time as the Commission may by notice direct that the certificate is again in force, or the end of the period of six months beginning with the date on which the suspension takes effect, whichever is the sooner[18].

1 See heads (1)–(3) in the text.

2 As to the Charity Commission see PARAS 543–578.

3 As to the meaning of 'public collections certificate' see PARA 496 note 4. As to public collections certificates generally see PARA 499.

4 Charities Act 2006 s 56(1) (not in force: see PARA 495 note 1). The exercise by the Commission of the power to suspend, attach conditions or vary existing conditions on one occasion does not prevent it from exercising any of the powers conferred by s 56(1) on a subsequent occasion: s 56(6) (not in force: see PARA 495 note 1).
5 Or, where the Commission has previously exercised its power under the Charities Act 2006 s 56(1) in relation to the certificate in question, at the time when it last exercised any of those powers: s 56(6) (not in force: see PARA 495 note 1).
6 Charities Act 2006 s 56(2) (not in force: see PARA 495 note 1).
7 Ie under the Charities Act 2006 s 54(1): see PARA 500 note 28.
8 Charities Act 2006 s 56(3) (not in force: see PARA 495 note 1).
9 Charities Act 2006 s 56(4) (not in force: see PARA 495 note 1).
10 Ie under the Charities Act 2006 s 52(4): see PARA 500.
11 Charities Act 2006 s 56(5) (not in force: see PARA 495 note 1).
12 Charities Act 2006 s 56(7) (not in force: see PARA 495 note 1). As to the service of notices see PARA 511.
13 Ie under the Charities Act 2006 s 57(2): see PARA 503.
14 Charities Act 2006 s 56(8) (not in force: see PARA 495 note 1).
15 Ie under the Charities Act 2006 s 56(7): see the text to note 12.
16 Charities Act 2006 s 56(9) (not in force: see PARA 495 note 1).
17 Charities Act 2006 s 56(10) (not in force: see PARA 495 note 1).
18 Charities Act 2006 s 56(11) (not in force: see PARA 495 note 1).

503. Appeals against decisions of the Charity Commission relating to public collections certificates. The following provisions have effect as from a day to be appointed. A person who has duly applied to the Charity Commission[1] for a public collections certificate[2] may appeal to the Tribunal[3] against a decision of the Commission[4] to refuse to issue the certificate, or to attach any condition to it[5]. A person to whom a public collections certificate has been issued may appeal to the Tribunal against a decision of the Commission not to direct that the certificate be transferred between trustees[6]. Such a person may also appeal to the Tribunal against a decision of the Commission[7] to withdraw or suspend the certificate, to attach a condition to the certificate, or to vary an existing condition of the certificate[8].

The Attorney General[9] may appeal to the Tribunal against a decision of the Commission: (1) to issue, or to refuse to issue, a certificate; (2) to attach, or not to attach, any condition to a certificate[10]; (3) to direct, or not to direct, that a certificate be transferred between trustees[11]; (4) to withdraw or suspend, or not to withdraw or suspend, a certificate; or (5) to vary, or not to vary, an existing condition of a certificate[12].

In determining such an appeal, the Tribunal must consider afresh the decision appealed against, and may take into account evidence which was not available to the Commission[13]. The Tribunal may dismiss the appeal, quash the decision, or substitute for the decision another decision of a kind that the Commission could have made[14]. In any case, the Tribunal may give such directions as it thinks fit, having regard to the provisions of the Charities Act 2006 relating to public charitable collections[15] and associated regulations[16]. If the Tribunal quashes the decision, it may remit the matter to the Commission, either generally or for determination in accordance with a finding made or direction given by the Tribunal[17].

1 As to the Charity Commission see PARAS 543–578.
2 As to the meaning of 'public collections certificate' see PARA 496 note 4. As to public collections certificates generally see PARA 499.
3 'Tribunal', in relation to any appeal under the Charities Act 2006 s 57, means: (1) the Upper Tribunal, in any case where it is determined by or under Tribunal Procedure Rules that the Upper Tribunal is to hear the appeal; or (2) the First-tier Tribunal, in any other case: s 57(8) (not in force: see PARA 495 note 1) (added by SI 2009/1834). See **COURTS AND TRIBUNALS**.

4 Ie under the Charities Act 2006 s 52: see PARA 500.
5 Charities Act 2006 s 57(1) (not in force (see PARA 495 note 1); amended by SI 2009/1834).
6 Charities Act 2006 s 57(2) (not in force: see PARA 495 note 1). A certificate is transferred under s 55 (see PARA 501).
7 Ie under the Charities Act 2006 s 56: see PARA 502.
8 Charities Act 2006 s 57(3) (not in force: see PARA 495 note 1).
9 As to the Attorney General see PARAS 589, 596, 605 et seq; and **CONSTITUTIONAL AND ADMINISTRATIVE LAW** vol 20 (2014) PARA 273 et seq.
10 Ie under the Charities Act 2006 s 52 (see PARA 500) or s 56 (see PARA 502).
11 Ie under the Charities Act 2006 s 55 (see PARA 501).
12 Charities Act 2006 s 57(4) (not in force: see PARA 495 note 1).
13 Charities Act 2006 s 57(5) (not in force: see PARA 495 note 1).
14 Charities Act 2006 s 57(6) (not in force: see PARA 495 note 1).
15 Ie under the Charities Act 2006 Pt 3 Ch 1 (ss 45–66) (see PARA 495 et seq).
16 Charities Act 2006 s 57(6) (not in force: see PARA 495 note 1). The regulations are those made under s 63 (see PARA 509).
17 Charities Act 2006 s 57(7) (not in force: see PARA 495 note 1).

504. Applications for permits to conduct collections in public places. The following provisions have effect as from a day to be appointed. A person or persons proposing to promote a collection in a public place[1] other than an exempt collection[2] in the area of a local authority[3] may apply to the authority for a permit to conduct that collection[4]. The application must be made within the prescribed[5] period falling before the day, or the first of the days, on which the collection is to take place[6], save that where an application has been made for a public collections certificate[7] in respect of the collection and either the certificate application has not been determined by the end of this period, or the certificate application has been determined by the issue of such a certificate but at a time when there is insufficient time remaining for the permit application to be made by the end of that period, the permit application must be made as early as practicable before the day, or the first of the days, on which the collection is to take place[8].

The application must: (1) specify the date or dates in respect of which it is desired that the permit, if issued, should have effect, which in the case of two or more dates must not span a period of more than 12 months; (2) be accompanied by a copy of the public collections certificate in force in respect of the proposed collection[9]; and (3) contain such information as may be prescribed[10].

1 As to the meaning of 'collection in a public place' see PARA 495.
2 As to exempt collections see the Charities Act 2006 s 50 (see PARA 498); definition applied by s 58(5) (not in force: see PARA 495 note 1).
3 As to the meaning of 'local authority' see PARA 496 note 5.
4 Charities Act 2006 s 58(1) (not in force: see PARA 495 note 1).
5 As to the meaning of 'prescribed' see PARA 497 note 5. See also PARA 509.
6 Charities Act 2006 s 58(2) (not in force: see PARA 495 note 1).
7 Ie under the Charities Act 2006 s 51: see PARA 499. As to the meaning of 'public collections certificate' see PARA 496 note 4.
8 Charities Act 2006 s 58(4) (not in force: see PARA 495 note 1).
9 Ie under the Charities Act 2006 s 52: see PARA 500.
10 Charities Act 2006 s 58(3) (not in force: see PARA 495 note 1).

505. Determination of applications and issue of permits. The following provisions have effect as from a day to be appointed. On receiving an application for a permit[1] in respect of a collection in a public place[2], a local authority[3] must determine the application within the prescribed period[4] by either issuing a permit in respect of the collection or refusing the application on the statutory ground[5].

Where a local authority issues such a permit, it has effect in respect of the date or dates specified[6] in the application[7]. At the time of issuing a permit under these provisions, a local authority may attach to it such of the following conditions as it thinks fit, having regard to the local circumstances of the collection[8]: (1) conditions specifying the day of the week, date, time or frequency of the collection[9]; (2) conditions specifying the locality or localities within their area in which the collection may be conducted[10]; (3) conditions regulating the manner in which the collection is to be conducted[11]; (4) such other conditions as may be prescribed for this purpose[12]. A local authority must secure that the terms of any conditions so attached are consistent with the provisions of any relevant regulations[13].

Where a local authority refuses to issue a permit, or attach any condition to it, the authority must serve on the applicant written notice of its decision and the reasons for its decision[14]. The notice must also state that there is a right of appeal[15] and the time within which such an appeal must be brought[16].

1 Ie in accordance with the Charities Act 2006 s 58: see PARA 504.
2 As to the meaning of 'collection in a public place' see PARA 495.
3 As to the meaning of 'local authority' see PARA 496 note 5.
4 Ie such period as is prescribed by regulations under the Charities Act 2006 s 63: see PARA 509.
5 Charities Act 2006 s 59(1) (not in force: see PARA 495 note 1). As to the statutory ground for refusal see s 60(1); and PARA 506.
6 Ie in accordance with the Charities Act 2006 s 58(3)(a) (see PARA 504 head (1)).
7 Charities Act 2006 s 59(2) (not in force: see PARA 495 note 1). However, this is subject to any subsequent withdrawal or modification under s 61 (see PARA 507): s 59(2) (not in force).
8 Charities Act 2006 s 59(3) (not in force: see PARA 495 note 1).
9 Charities Act 2006 s 59(3)(a) (not in force: see PARA 495 note 1).
10 Charities Act 2006 s 59(3)(b) (not in force: see PARA 495 note 1).
11 Charities Act 2006 s 59(3)(c) (not in force: see PARA 495 note 1).
12 Charities Act 2006 s 59(3)(d) (not in force: see PARA 495 note 1).
13 Charities Act 2006 s 59(4) (not in force: see PARA 495 note 1). Relevant regulations are those made under s 63 (see PARA 509), whether or not prescribing conditions for the purposes of s 59(3) (see the text to notes 8–12): s 59(4) (not in force).
14 Charities Act 2006 s 59(5) (not in force: see PARA 495 note 1). As to the service of notices see PARA 511.
15 Ie conferred by the Charities Act 2006 s 62(2): see PARA 508.
16 Charities Act 2006 s 59(6) (not in force: see PARA 495 note 1).

506. Refusal of permits. The following provisions have effect as from a day to be appointed. The only ground on which a local authority[1] may refuse an application for a permit[2] to conduct a collection in a public place[3] is that it appears to it that the collection would cause undue inconvenience to members of the public by reason of: (1) the day or the week or the date on or in which; (2) the time at which; (3) the frequency with which; or (4) the locality or localities in which, it is proposed to be conducted[4].

In making this decision, a local authority may have regard to the fact, where it is the case, that the collection is proposed to be conducted wholly or partly in a locality in which another collection in a public place is already authorised to be conducted under the Charities Act 2006 Pt 3 Ch 1[5] and on a day on which that other collection is already so authorised, or on the day falling immediately before, or immediately after, any such day[6]. However, a local authority must not have regard to these matters if it appears to it that the proposed collection would be conducted only in one location, which is on land to which members of the public would have access only by virtue of the express or implied permission of the occupier[7] of the land or by virtue of any enactment, and that the occupier of the land consents to that collection being conducted there[8].

1 As to the meaning of 'local authority' see PARA 496 note 5.
2 As to such permits see PARA 504.
3 As to the meaning of 'collection in a public place' see PARA 495.
4 Charities Act 2006 s 60(1) (not in force: see PARA 495 note 1).
5 A reference to a collection in a public place authorised under the Charities Act 2006 Pt 3 Ch 1 (ss 45–66) is a reference to a collection in a public place that is conducted in accordance with s 48 (see PARA 496), or is an exempt collection by virtue of s 50 (see PARA 498): s 60(4) (not in force: see PARA 495 note 1).
6 Charities Act 2006 s 60(2) (not in force: see PARA 495 note 1).
7 'Occupier' in relation to unoccupied land means the person entitled to occupy it: Charities Act 2006 s 60(3) (not in force: see PARA 495 note 1).
8 Charities Act 2006 s 60(3) (not in force: see PARA 495 note 1).

507. Withdrawal and modification of permits. The following provisions have effect as from a day to be appointed. In certain circumstances[1], a local authority[2] which has issued a permit[3] may withdraw the permit, attach any condition, or further condition, to the permit, or vary any existing condition of the permit[4]. The circumstances are:

(1) where the local authority has reason to believe that there has been a change in the circumstances which prevailed at the time when it issued the permit and is of the opinion that, if the application for the permit had been made in the new circumstances, it would not have issued the permit or would have issued it subject to different or additional conditions[5];

(2) where the local authority has reason to believe that any information provided to it by the holder of a permit (or, where there is more than one holder, by any of them) for the purposes of the application for the permit was false or misleading in a material particular[6];

(3) where the local authority has reason to believe that there has been or is likely to be a breach of any condition of a permit issued by it, or that a breach of such a condition is continuing[7].

Any such condition imposed at any time by a local authority, whether by attaching a new condition to the permit or by varying an existing condition, must be one that it would be appropriate for the authority to attach to the permit[8] if the holder was applying for it in the circumstances prevailing at that time[9].

Where a local authority withdraws a permit, attaches a condition to a permit, or varies an existing condition of a permit, it must serve on the holder written notice of its decision and the reasons for its decision[10]. The notice must also state that there is a right of appeal[11] and the time within which such an appeal must be brought[12]. Where a local authority withdraws a permit it must send a copy of its decision and the reasons for it to the Charity Commission[13]. Where a local authority withdraws a permit, attaches any condition to a permit, or varies an existing condition of a permit, the permit continues to have effect as if it had not been withdrawn or, as the case may be, as if the condition had not been attached or varied until the time for bringing an appeal has expired or, if such an appeal is duly brought, until the determination or abandonment of the appeal[14].

1 See heads (1)–(3) in the text.
2 As to the meaning of 'local authority' see PARA 496 note 5.
3 Ie under the Charities Act 2006 s 59: see PARA 505. As to such permits see PARA 504.
4 Charities Act 2006 s 61(1) (not in force: see PARA 495 note 1). The exercise by a local authority of the power to attach conditions or vary existing conditions on one occasion does not prevent it from exercising any of the powers conferred by s 61(1) on a subsequent occasion: s 61(6) (not in force: see PARA 495 note 1).

5 Charities Act 2006 s 61(2) (not in force: see PARA 495 note 1).
6 Charities Act 2006 s 61(3) (not in force: see PARA 495 note 1).
7 Charities Act 2006 s 61(4) (not in force: see PARA 495 note 1).
8 Ie under the Charities Act 2006 s 59(3): see PARA 505.
9 Charities Act 2006 s 61(5) (not in force: see PARA 495 note 1).
10 Charities Act 2006 s 61(7) (not in force: see PARA 495 note 1). As to the service of notices see PARA 511.
11 Ie under the Charities Act 2006 s 62(3): see PARA 508.
12 Charities Act 2006 s 61(8) (not in force: see PARA 495 note 1).
13 Charities Act 2006 s 61(9) (not in force: see PARA 495 note 1). As to the Charity Commission see PARAS 543–578.
14 Charities Act 2006 s 61(10) (not in force: see PARA 495 note 1).

508. Appeals against decisions of local authority. The following provisions have effect as from a day to be appointed. A person who, in relation to a public charitable collection[1], has duly notified a local authority[2] of the matters necessary for an exempt collection[3] may appeal to a magistrates' court against a decision of the local authority[4] that the collection is not a local, short-term collection[5], or that the promoters[6] or any of them has breached any relevant regulations[7] or been convicted of a relevant offence[8].

A person who has duly applied to a local authority for a permit to conduct a collection in a public place in the authority's area may appeal to a magistrates' court against a decision of the authority[9] to refuse to issue a permit, or to attach any condition to it[10].

A person to whom a permit has been issued may appeal to a magistrates' court against a decision of the local authority[11] to withdraw the permit, to attach a condition to the permit, or to vary an existing condition of the permit[12].

Such an appeal must be by way of complaint for an order and the Magistrates' Courts Act 1980 applies to the proceedings[13]. Any such appeal must be brought within 14 days of the date of service on the person in question of the relevant notice[14] and for these purposes an appeal is taken to be brought when the complaint is made[15]. An appeal against the decision of a magistrates' court on such an appeal may be brought to the Crown Court[16].

On an appeal to a magistrates' court or the Crown Court, the court may confirm, vary or reverse the local authority's decision and generally give such directions as it thinks fit, having regard to the relevant provisions of the Charities Act 2006[17] and associated regulations[18]. If the appeal relates to exemption collection status[19], such directions may include a direction that the collection may be conducted on the date or dates notified by the promoters[20] or on such other date or dates as may be specified in the direction, and if so conducted the collection is to be regarded as one that is an exempt collection[21].

It is the duty of the local authority to comply with any such directions given by the court, but the authority need not comply with any directions given by a magistrates' court until the time for bringing an appeal to the Crown Court has expired or, if such an appeal is duly brought, until the determination or abandonment of the appeal[22].

1 As to the meaning of 'public charitable collection' see PARA 495.
2 As to the meaning of 'local authority' see PARA 496 note 5.
3 Ie under the Charities Act 2006 s 50(3): see PARA 498.
4 Ie under the Charities Act 2006 s 50(4): see PARA 498.
5 As to local, short-term collections see PARA 498.
6 As to the meaning of 'promoter' see PARA 496 note 3.
7 Ie under the Charities Act 2006 s 63: see PARA 509.
8 Charities Act 2006 s 62(1) (not in force: see PARA 495 note 1). A relevant offence is an offence under s 53(2)(a)(i)–(v): see PARA 500.

9 Ie under the Charities Act 2006 s 59: see PARA 505.
10 Charities Act 2006 s 62(2) (not in force: see PARA 495 note 1).
11 Ie under the Charities Act 2006 s 61: see PARA 507.
12 Charities Act 2006 s 62(3) (not in force: see PARA 495 note 1).
13 Charities Act 2006 s 62(4) (not in force: see PARA 495 note 1). See **MAGISTRATES** vol 71 (2013) PARA 527.
14 Ie under the Charities Act 2006 s 50(4) (see PARA 498), s 59(5) (see PARA 505) or s 61(7) (see PARA 507) as the case may be. As to the service of notices see PARA 511.
15 Charities Act 2006 s 62(5) (not in force: see PARA 495 note 1).
16 Charities Act 2006 s 62(6) (not in force: see PARA 495 note 1). As to appeals from magistrates' courts generally see **MAGISTRATES** vol 71 (2013) PARA 697 et seq.
17 Ie the provisions of the Charities Act 2006 Pt 3 Ch 1 (ss 45–66): see PARA 495 et seq.
18 Charities Act 2006 s 62(7) (not in force: see PARA 495 note 1). As to regulations see s 63; and PARA 509.
19 Ie under the Charities Act 2006 s 50(4): see PARA 498.
20 Ie in accordance with the Charities Act 2006 s 50(3)(b): see PARA 498.
21 Charities Act 2006 s 62(8) (not in force: see PARA 495 note 1). As to exempt collections see s 50; and PARA 498.
22 Charities Act 2006 s 62(9) (not in force: see PARA 495 note 1).

509. Regulations. The following provisions have effect as from a day to be appointed. The Minister[1] may make regulations[2]:

(1) prescribing the matters which a local authority[3] is to take into account in determining whether a collection is local in character for the purposes of determining whether a collection is local, short-term collection[4];

(2) for the purpose of regulating the conduct of public charitable collections[5];

(3) prescribing anything falling to be prescribed by virtue of any provision of the Charities Act 2006 relating to public charitable collections[6].

The matters which may be prescribed by regulations under head (1) above include the extent of the area within which the appeal is to be conducted, whether the appeal forms part of a series of appeals, the number of collectors[7] making the appeal and whether they are acting for remuneration or otherwise, the financial resources (of any description) of any charitable, benevolent or philanthropic institution[8] for whose benefit the appeal is to be conducted, and where the promoters live or have any place of business[9].

Regulations under head (2) above may make provision:

(a) about the keeping and publication of accounts[10];

(b) for the prevention of annoyance to members of the public[11];

(c) with respect to the use by collectors of badges and certificates of authority, or badges incorporating such certificates, including, in particular, provision prescribing the form of such badges and certificates, requiring a collector, on request, to permit his badge, or any certificate of authority held by him of the purposes of the collection, to be inspected by a constable or a duly authorised officer of a local authority, or by an occupier of any premises visited by him in the course of the collection[12];

(d) for prohibiting persons under a prescribed age from acting as collectors, and prohibiting others from causing them so to act[13].

Such regulations may provide that any failure to comply with a specified provision of the regulations is to be an offence punishable on summary conviction by a fine[14].

Before making regulations under these provisions, the Minister must consult such persons or bodies of persons as he considers appropriate[15].

1 As to the Minister see PARA 586.
2 Charities Act 2006 s 63(1) (not in force: see PARA 495 note 1).
3 As to the meaning of 'local authority' see PARA 496 note 5.
4 Charities Act 2006 s 63(1)(a) (not in force: see PARA 495 note 1). As to local, short-term collections see PARA 498.
5 Charities Act 2006 s 63(1)(b) (not in force: see PARA 495 note 1). As to the meaning of 'public charitable collection' see PARA 495.
6 Charities Act 2006 s 63(1)(c) (not in force: see PARA 495 note 1). The relevant provisions of the Charities Act 2006 are in Pt 3 Ch 1 (ss 45–66): see PARA 495 et seq.
7 As to the meaning of 'collector' see PARA 495 note 15.
8 As to the meaning of 'charitable, benevolent or philanthropic institution' see PARA 500 note 14.
9 Charities Act 2006 s 63(2) (not in force: see PARA 495 note 1). However, this does not prejudice the generality of head (1) in the text: s 63(4) (not in force: see PARA 495 note 1).
10 Charities Act 2006 s 63(3)(a) (not in force: see PARA 495 note 1). However, this does not prejudice the generality of head (2) in the text: s 63(4) (not in force: see PARA 495 note 1).
11 Charities Act 2006 s 63(3)(b) (not in force: see PARA 495 note 1). See note 10.
12 Charities Act 2006 s 63(3)(c) (not in force: see PARA 495 note 1). See note 10.
13 Charities Act 2006 s 63(3)(d) (not in force: see PARA 495 note 1). See note 10.
14 Charities Act 2006 s 63(5) (not in force: see PARA 495 note 1). The fine must not exceed level 2 on the standard scale: s 63(5) (not in force). As to the standard scale see **SENTENCING AND DISPOSITION OF OFFENDERS** vol 92 (2010) PARA 143.
15 Charities Act 2006 s 63(6) (not in force: see PARA 495 note 1).

510. Offences. The following provisions have effect as from a day to be appointed. A person commits an offence if, in connection with any charitable appeal[1], he displays or uses a prescribed badge[2] or prescribed certificate of authority[3] which is not for the time being held by him for the purposes of the appeal pursuant to regulations[4], or any badge or article, or any certificate or other document, so nearly resembling a prescribed badge or, as the case may be, a prescribed certificate of authority as to be likely to deceive a member of the public[5].

A person commits an offence if he knowingly or recklessly furnishes any information which is false or misleading in a material particular, for the purposes of: (1) an application for a public collections certificate[6]; (2) an application for a permit to conduct a collection in a public place[7]; (3) conducting a door to door collection[8]; or (4) obtaining an exemption[9] for a local, short-term collection[10].

Where any offence under the provisions for public charitable collections in the Charities Act 2006[11] or any regulations made thereunder is committed by a body corporate, and is proved to have been committed with the consent or connivance of, or to be attributable to any neglect on the part of, any director[12], manager, secretary or other similar officer of the body corporate, or any person who was purporting to act in any such capacity, he as well as the body corporate is guilty of that offence and is liable to be proceeded against and punished accordingly[13].

1 As to the meaning of 'charitable appeal' see PARA 495.
2 'Prescribed badge' means a badge in such form as may be prescribed by regulations under the Charities Act 2006 s 63 (see PARA 509): ss 47(1), 64(4) (not in force: see PARA 495 note 1).
3 'Prescribed certificate of authority' means a certificate of authority in such form as may be prescribed by regulations under the Charities Act 2006 s 63 (see PARA 509): ss 47(1), 64(4) (not in force: see PARA 495 note 1).
4 Ie regulations under the Charities Act 2006 s 63: see PARA 509.
5 Charities Act 2006 s 64(1) (not in force: see PARA 495 note 1). A person guilty of such an offence is liable on summary conviction to a fine not exceeding level 5 on the standard scale: s 64(3) (not in force: see PARA 495 note 1). As to the standard scale see **SENTENCING AND DISPOSITION OF OFFENDERS** vol 92 (2010) PARA 143.
6 Ie under the Charities Act 2006 s 51: see PARA 499.
7 Ie under the Charities Act 2006 s 58: see PARA 504.
8 Ie under the Charities Act 2006 s 49: see PARA 497.

9 Ie under the Charities Act 2006 s 50: see PARA 498.
10 Charities Act 2006 s 64(2) (not in force: see PARA 495 note 1). A person guilty of such an offence is liable on summary conviction to a fine not exceeding level 5 on the standard scale: s 64(3) (not in force: see PARA 495 note 1).
11 Ie the Charities Act 2006 Pt 3 Ch 1 (ss 45–66): see PARA 495 et seq.
12 'Director', in relation to a body corporate whose affairs are managed by its members, means a member of the body corporate: Charities Act 2006 s 65(2) (not in force: see PARA 495 note 1).
13 Charities Act 2006 s 65(1) (not in force: see PARA 495 note 1).

511. Service of documents. The following provisions have effect as from a day to be appointed. Any notice required to be served under the provisions of the Charities Act 2006 relating to public charitable collections[1] may be served on a person, other than a body corporate, by delivering it to that person, by leaving it at his last known address in the United Kingdom[2], or by sending it by post to him at that address[3]. Such a notice may be served on a body corporate by delivering it or sending it by post to the registered or principal office of the body in the United Kingdom or, if it has no such office in the United Kingdom, to any place in the United Kingdom where it carries on business or conducts its activities, as the case may be[4]. Such a notice may also be served on a person, including a body corporate, by sending it by post to that person at an address notified by that person for these purposes to the person or persons by whom it is required to be served[5].

1 Ie under the Charities Act 2006 Pt 3 Ch 1 (ss 45–66): see PARA 495 et seq.
2 As to the meaning of 'United Kingdom' see PARA 189 note 17.
3 Charities Act 2006 s 66(1), (2) (not in force: see PARA 495 note 1).
4 Charities Act 2006 s 66(3) (not in force: see PARA 495 note 1).
5 Charities Act 2006 s 66(4) (not in force: see PARA 495 note 1).

10. JURISDICTION OVER CHARITIES

(1) THE CROWN

512. The Crown as protector of charitable trusts. The Crown as parens patriae is the constitutional protector of all property subject to charitable trusts, such trusts being essentially matters of public concern[1]. The Attorney General, who represents the Crown for all forensic purposes, is accordingly the proper person to take proceedings on behalf of and to protect charities[2].

The Crown also, acting through such persons as the Crown may nominate[3], exercises a visitatorial jurisdiction over certain charitable corporations[4].

1 *A-G v Brown* (1818) 1 Swan 265 at 291 per Lord Eldon LC; *A-G v Compton* (1842) 1 Y & C Ch Cas 417 at 427 per Knight Bruce V-C. As to the Crown as parens patriae see CONSTITUTIONAL AND ADMINISTRATIVE LAW vol 20 (2014) PARA 137.

2 *Eyre v Countess of Shaftsbury* (1724) 2 P Wms 103 at 118 per Lord Macclesfield; *Wellbeloved v Jones* (1822) 1 Sim & St 40 at 43 per Leach V-C; *A-G v Magdalen College, Oxford* (1854) 18 Beav 223 at 241 per Romilly MR; *A-G v Dean and Canons of Windsor* (1860) 8 HL Cas 369; *Wallis v Solicitor General for New Zealand* [1903] AC 173 at 182, PC; *Strickland v Weldon* (1885) 28 ChD 426; *Re Belling, Enfield London Borough Council v Public Trustee* [1967] Ch 425, [1967] 1 All ER 105; and see PARA 598 et seq. As to the Attorney General see PARAS 589, 596, 605 et seq; and CONSTITUTIONAL AND ADMINISTRATIVE LAW vol 20 (2014) PARA 273 et seq.

3 In *R v HM the Queen in Council, ex p Vijayatunga* [1990] 2 QB 444, sub nom *R v University of London Visitor, ex p Vijayatunga* [1989] 2 All ER 843, CA, the Crown had nominated a committee of the Privy Council. See further PARA 520 note 1 per Samuel Romilly.

4 See PARAS 517, 527–528.

513. Gift of charity generally, without trust. When no trust is created and property is given to charity generally, that is to say, where no trustees are nominated and the charitable objects are not defined, the duty of disposing of the property devolves on the Crown, as constitutional trustee[1]. Thus, in the case of an assurance, devise or bequest to charity[2], or to the poor[3], simpliciter, or where the testator intended but failed to name the objects of his bounty[4], the disposition of the property is made by the Crown in its character of *parens patriae*, not by means of a scheme settled by the court. So also, a legacy in exoneration of the National Debt[5], or to 'my country England'[6], or a legacy to an institution dissolved after the testator's death but before payment[7], or to a non-existent institution[8], is disposable by the Crown. The result is the same as when a charitable purpose is carried out by the court, though the procedure differs[9].

The power of the Crown to dispose of charitable gifts under the royal sign manual has been delegated to the Attorney General[10].

1 *Moggridge v Thackwell* (1803) 7 Ves 36 at 83 per Lord Eldon LC; *Cary v Abbot* (1802) 7 Ves 490; *Morice v Bishop of Durham* (1805) 10 Ves 522 at 541 per Lord Eldon LC; *Paice v Archbishop of Canterbury* (1807) 14 Ves 364; *Ommanney v Butcher* (1823) Turn & R 260 at 271 per Plumer MR; *Re Davis, Hannen v Hillyer* [1902] 1 Ch 876 at 888 per Buckley J; *Re Pyne, Lilley v A-G* [1903] 1 Ch 83; *Re Bennett, Sucker v A-G* [1960] Ch 18, [1959] 3 All ER 295. Formerly (ie before the series of relieving Acts: see PARA 63), the Crown was also called upon to exercise its prerogative in the case of gifts to superstitious uses which were also charitable: see Boyle on Charities (1837) pp 242–280; *A-G v Bowyer* (1798) 3 Ves 714 at 729 per Lord Thurlow LC.

2 *Clifford v Francis* (1679) Freem Ch 330; *A-G v Syderfen* (1683) 1 Vern 224; *Jones' Case* (1690) cited in [1893] 2 Ch 49n, HL; *A-G v Herrick* (1772) Amb 712; *A-G v Bowyer* (1798) 3 Ves 714 at 729 per Lord Thurlow LC; *Legge v Asgill* (1818) Turn & R 265n; *Kane v Cosgrave* (1873) IR 10 Eq 211.

3 *A-G v Peacock* (1676) Cas *temp* Finch 245; *Ware v A-G* (1824) 3 Hare 194n.
4 *A-G v Syderfen* (1683) 1 Vern 224; *Moggridge v Thackwell* (1803) 7 Ves 36 at 75 per Lord Eldon LC. Cf the cases relating to the jurisdiction of the court: see PARAS 534–535.
5 *Newland v A-G* (1809) 3 Mer 684.
6 *Re Smith, Public Trustee v Smith* [1932] 1 Ch 153, CA.
7 *Re Slevin, Slevin v Hepburn* [1891] 2 Ch 236, CA. See further PARAS 158, 159.
8 *Re Bennett, Sucker v A-G* [1960] Ch 18, [1959] 3 All ER 295.
9 *A-G v Peacock* (1676) Cas *temp* Finch 245; *Moggridge v Thackwell* (1803) 7 Ves 36 at 87 per Lord Eldon LC; Boyle on Charities (1837) pp 239–240.
10 *Report of the Charity Commissioners for England and Wales for 1989* (HC Paper (1989–90) no 343) para 38. See also *De Costa v De Paz* (1754) 2 Swan 487n; *A-G v Herrick* (1772) Amb 712; *Kane v Cosgrave* (1873) IR 10 Eq 211; and see PARA 608. As to the royal sign manual see CONSTITUTIONAL AND ADMINISTRATIVE LAW vol 20 (2014) PARA 582. As to the Attorney General see PARAS 589, 596, 605 et seq; and CONSTITUTIONAL AND ADMINISTRATIVE LAW vol 20 (2014) PARA 273 et seq.

(2) THE VISITOR

(i) Nature of Visitatorial Power

514. Settlement of disputes and correction of abuses. A visitatorial power attaches as a necessary incident to all eleemosynary corporations[1], and may be exercisable in respect of all corporations[2]. It enables the person exercising it, who is called the visitor, to settle disputes between the members of the corporation, to inspect and regulate their actions and behaviour, and generally to correct all abuses and irregularities in the administration of the charity[3].

The tribunal of the visitor is *forum domesticum*, in other words, the court of the founder[4], its jurisdiction being derived from the founder's right to determine concerning his own creation[5].

A visitor's decision on matters within his jurisdiction is exclusive[6] and final, and not subject to review by the High Court[7]. Even the visitor himself cannot relieve against his own sentence[8]; but an action for damages will lie against him for exceeding his jurisdiction[9].

The extent of the power varies according to the terms of the foundation. If the power given to the visitor is unlimited and universal he has, in respect of the foundation and property moving from the founder, no rule but his sound discretion. If there are particular statutes they are the rule by which he is bound, and if he acts contrary to or exceeds them, he acts without jurisdiction, and consequently his act is a nullity[10].

1 *Appleford's Case* (1672) 1 Mod Rep 82 at 85 per Hale CJ; *Philips v Bury* (1694) Skin 447 at 483–484, HL. As to the meaning of 'eleemosynary corporation' see PARA 225.
2 See Tudor on Charities (7th Edn, 1984) p 312; cf Tudor on Charities (8th Edn, 1995) p 369.
3 1 Bl Com 467; *Philips v Bury* (1694) Skin 447 at 484, HL. As to the visitor's power to settle questions see PARA 525.
4 *Green v Rutherforth* (1750) 1 Ves Sen 462 at 472 per Lord Hardwicke LC; *St John's College, Cambridge v Todington* (1757) 1 Burr 158 at 200 per Lord Mansfield; *Spencer v All Souls College* (1762) Wilm 163; *Philips v Bury* (1694) Skin 447, HL.
5 *Green v Rutherforth* (1750) 1 Ves Sen 462 at 472 per Lord Hardwicke LC; *R v Lord President of the Privy Council* [1993] AC 682, sub nom *Page v Hull University Visitor* [1993] 1 All ER 97, HL. Cf the maxim *cuius est dare, eius est disponere*: he who gives something may also direct how it is to be used.
6 *Thomas v University of Bradford* [1987] AC 795, [1987] 1 All ER 834, HL; *Philips v Bury* (1694) Skin 447, HL; *A-G v Talbot* (1748) 3 Atk 662; *St John's College, Cambridge v Todington* (1757) 1 Burr 158; *R v Dean and Chapter of Chester* (1850) 15 QB 513; *R v Hertford College* (1878) 3 QBD 693, CA; *Thomson v University of London* (1864) 10 Jur NS 669; *Patel v University of Bradford Senate* [1978] 3 All ER 841, [1978] 1 WLR 1488 (affd

[1979] 2 All ER 582, [1979] 1 WLR 1006, CA); *Re Wislang's Application* [1984] NI 63; *Hines v Birkbeck College* [1986] Ch 524, [1985] 3 All ER 156 (appeal dismissed [1987] Ch 457n, [1987] 3 All ER 1040n, CA). See also *Herring v Templeman* [1973] 2 All ER 581; affd on grounds not material to the present point [1973] 3 All ER 569, CA. As to the limits on jurisdiction see PARA 523.

7 See PARAS 529–530.

8 *Philips v Bury* (1694) as reported in Show Parl Cas 35 at 52.

9 *Green v Rutherforth* (1750) 1 Ves Sen 462 at 470 per Lord Hardwicke LC.

10 Shelford's Law of Mortmain 360; *Philips v Bury* (1694) as reported in 1 Ld Raym 5, HL. As to the extensive and arbitrary nature of the visitatorial power see also *A-G v Archbishop of York* (1831) 2 Russ & M 461 at 468 per Lord Brougham. As to the court's control over the visitor see PARAS 529–533.

515. Visitors to the Inns of Court. In general visitatorial powers only exist in relation to corporations. An Inn of Court is not a corporation: it does not have statutes, nor does it have a founder who nominated a visitor to hear and determine internal disputes. The Inns of Court are not eleemosynary corporations[1]: they are voluntary societies, some of whose activities, such as education, are charitable, but some of which are not, including call to the Bar and disciplining of barristers[2]. Nevertheless it is well established that there is an appeal from decisions of the benchers of the Inns of Court and the disciplinary tribunals of the Inns of Court to the judges as visitors, exercising a normal visitatorial jurisdiction[3]. Thus they may hear appeals against decisions on property matters such as the letting of chambers within the Inn and dues payable to the Inn by members; they may also hear appeals against disciplinary decisions, such as disbarment for professional misconduct[4]. The limited judicial review jurisdiction available in respect of visitors generally[5] is equally applicable to visitors to the Inns of Court[6].

1 As to the meaning of 'eleemosynary corporation' see PARA 225.

2 See **LEGAL PROFESSIONS** vol 66 (2015) PARA 910 et seq.

3 *R v Visitors to the Inns of Court, ex p Calder, ex p Persaud* [1994] QB 1, [1993] 2 All ER 876, CA; *R v Gray's Inn* (1780) 1 Doug KB 353; *Manisty v Kenealy* (1876) 24 WR 918; *Lincoln v Daniels* [1962] 1 QB 237, [1961] 3 All ER 740, CA; *Re S (A Barrister)* [1981] QB 683, [1981] 2 All ER 952. See generally **LEGAL PROFESSIONS**.

4 *R v Visitors to the Inns of Court, ex p Calder, ex p Persaud* [1994] QB 1, [1993] 2 All ER 876, CA.

5 See PARA 529 et seq.

6 *R v Visitors to the Inns of Court, ex p Calder, ex p Persaud* [1994] QB 1, [1993] 2 All ER 876, CA. The visitors sit as an appeal tribunal. In *R v Visitors to the Inns of Court, ex p Calder, ex p Persaud* the visitors apparently thought that they were sitting as a reviewing tribunal; this was a serious misapprehension of their function. On judicial review the Court of Appeal allowed the appeal on this ground and quashed the decision of the visitors.

516. Quasi-visitatorial powers. The Charity Commission[1] may reserve to itself a quasi-visitatorial power to determine disputes in schemes settled by it under the Charities Act 2011[2]. However, true visitatorial powers can only exist in relation to corporations[3].

1 As to the Charity Commission see PARAS 543–578.

2 See *Re Hodgson's School* (1878) 3 App Cas 857, PC; *R v Wilson* [1888] WN 12. It is not, apparently, the modern practice to seek to oust the court's jurisdiction completely in this way. As to schemes under the Charities Act 2011 see PARA 189 et seq.

3 Formerly there was a statutory exception to this principle under the Grammar Schools Act 1840 s 15, but this was repealed by the Charities Act 1960 (itself now repealed).

(ii) Constitution of Visitor

517. The visitor. Where no visitor has been appointed by the founder, the rule is that the Monarch and her successors are visitors of all lay charitable corporations founded by the Crown alone[1], or by the Crown jointly with a private person, and of all royal foundations endowed by a private person[2]. Where a university is incorporated by royal charter which provides for the appointment of a visitor by the Crown, but no such appointment has been made, the Crown is the visitor[3].

Where a private person alone was founder, the law before 1926 was that he and his heirs were visitors[4], unless the heirs' jurisdiction was expressly excluded[5]. If the heirs of the founder failed[6], were not discoverable[7], or were lunatic[8], and there was no appointment by the founder, the visitatorial power devolved upon the Crown. Descent to the heir has been abolished, but the effect of this upon visitatorial rights does not appear clear[9].

The visitor of an ecclesiastical charitable corporation is the Ordinary[10].

1 *A-G v Dedham School* (1857) 23 Beav 350 at 356 per Romilly MR; *Eden v Foster* (1726) 2 P Wms 325; and see *Re Christ Church* (1866) 1 Ch App 526. See also PARA 518.
2 Shelford's Law of Mortmain (1836) 332, 339–340.
3 *Patel v University of Bradford Senate* [1978] 3 All ER 841, [1978] 1 WLR 1488 (affd [1979] 2 All ER 582, [1979] 1 WLR 1066, CA); *Thomas v University of Bradford* [1987] AC 795 at 811, [1987] 1 All ER 834 at 839, HL, per Lord Griffiths. It is thought to have been wrongly conceded in *R v Aston University Senate, ex p Roffey* [1969] 2 QB 538, sub nom *R v Senate of University of Aston, ex p Roffey* [1969] 2 All ER 964, DC, that the university had no visitor. It should be noted that those new universities which have acquired that title under the Further and Higher Education Act 1992 s 77 (see EDUCATION vol 36 (2011) PARA 812) were not created by royal charter and there is no provision for them to have a visitor.
4 *Eden v Foster* (1726) 2 P Wms 325; *Philips v Bury* (1694) Skin 447 at 483, HL.
5 *St John's College, Cambridge v Todington* (1757) 1 Burr 158 at 200 per Lord Mansfield.
6 *Anon* (1698) 12 Mod Rep 232; *R v Master and Fellows of St Catherine's Hall* (1791) 4 Term Rep 233; *Ex p Wrangham* (1795) 2 Ves 609; *A-G v Earl of Clarendon* (1810) 17 Ves 491 at 498 per Grant MR; *A-G v Ewelme Hospital* (1853) 17 Beav 366 at 381 per Romilly MR.
7 *A-G v Black* (1805) 11 Ves 191.
8 *A-G v Dixie, ex p Bosworth School* (1805) 13 Ves 519 at 533 per Lord Eldon LC.
9 It may be presumed, however, that if there is any residual inherited visitatorial jurisdiction, references to 'lunatic' and 'lunacy' may be regarded as obsolete, and would now refer to lacking necessary mental capacity.
10 *Philips v Bury* (1694) Skin 447, HL; *A-G v Archbishop of York* (1831) 2 Russ & M 461 at 466 per Lord Brougham LC. See also the Cathedrals Measure 1963 s 6 (repealed, with savings in relation to cathedrals existing on 30 June 1999); and ECCLESIASTICAL LAW vol 34 (2011) PARA 350. As to the Ordinary see ECCLESIASTICAL LAW vol 34 (2011) PARA 177. Some of the colleges of Oxford are visitable by the Bishop of Lincoln, in whose diocese Oxford originally was included; the colleges were formerly deemed ecclesiastical foundations, hence the bishop's jurisdiction: see 1 Bl Com 470.

518. Visitatorial jurisdiction of the Crown. The visitatorial jurisdiction of the Crown is exercised upon application by petition[1]. Like a private visitor, the Crown is not bound by any particular forms of procedure[2]. Unless the petitioner can prove that the Crown is in fact visitor, the Crown has no authority to hear the petition[3]. Previously the jurisdiction was exercised by the Lord Chancellor[4], or such other person as he might advise Her Majesty to nominate, on behalf of the Crown[5]. However, since the abolition of the Lord Chancellor's judicial functions by the Constitutional Reform Act 2005[6], a representative will be appointed on a case-by-case basis on the advice of the Secretary of State for Justice[7]. Where the Lord Chancellor previously acted as visitor in his own right, this function is now vested in the Crown or other another suitable office[8].

1 *Ex p Wrangham* (1795) 2 Ves 609; *A-G v Black* (1805) 11 Ves 191; *Re Catharine Hall, ex p Inge* (1831) 2 Russ & M 590; *Re Queen's College, Cambridge* (1828) 5 Russ 64; *Re University College, Oxford* (1848) 2 Ph 521; *Re Christ Church* (1866) 1 Ch App 526.

2 *Queen's College, Cambridge, Case* (1821) Jac 1 at 19 per Lord Eldon LC.

3 *Re Garstang Church Town School, ex p Pedder* (1829) 7 LJOS Ch 169 at 172 per Lord Lyndhurst LC. As to the costs of petitions to the Lord Chancellor see *Ex p Dann* (1804) 9 Ves 547; *Re Masters, Governors and Trustees of Bedford Charity* (1819) 2 Swan 470 at 532 per Lord Eldon LC.

4 Co Litt 96a; Shelford's Law of Mortmain (1836) 333; *R v Master and Fellows of St Catherine's Hall* (1791) 4 Term Rep 233 at 244 per Lord Kenyon CJ; *A-G v Dixie, ex p Bosworth School* (1805) 13 Ves 519; *A-G v Earl of Clarendon* (1810) 17 Ves 491 at 498 per Grant MR; *Re Christ Church* (1866) 1 Ch App 526. See PARAS 510, 513. As to costs in hearings before the Lord Chancellor as visitor see *Queen's College, Cambridge, Case* (1821) Jac 1 at 47 per Lord Eldon LC; *A-G v Master and Fellows of Catherine Hall, Cambridge* (1820) Jac 381 at 401–402 per Lord Eldon LC.

5 *Thomas v University of Bradford* [1987] AC 795 at 811, [1987] 1 All ER 834 at 839, HL, per Lord Griffiths. In *R v HM The Queen in Council, ex p Vijayatunga* [1990] 2 QB 444, sub nom *R v University of London Visitor, ex p Vijayatunga* [1989] 2 All ER 843, CA, the Crown nominated a committee of the Judicial Committee of the Privy Council, in *R v Lord President of the Privy Council, ex p Page* [1993] AC 682, sub nom *Page v Hull University Visitor* [1993] 1 All ER 97, HL, the Lord President of the Privy Council, and in *Thomas v University of Bradford (No 2)* [1992] 1 All ER 964, Lord Browne-Wilkinson, a Lord of Appeal in Ordinary. As to the Judicial Committee of the Privy Council see CONSTITUTIONAL AND ADMINISTRATIVE LAW vol 20 (2014) PARA 147; COURTS AND TRIBUNALS vol 24 (2010) PARA 673. As to Lords of Appeal in Ordinary see COURTS AND TRIBUNALS vol 24 (2010) PARA 673.

6 See the Constitutional Reform Act 2005 Pt II (ss 2–22); and CONSTITUTIONAL AND ADMINISTRATIVE LAW vol 20 (2014) PARAS 128, 131, 259 et seq.

7 See 658 HL Official Report (5th series), 2 March 2004, col WS51–WS52.

8 See the Lord Chancellor (Transfer of Functions and Supplementary Provisions) Order 2007, SI 2007/661.

519. Appointment of general and special visitors by founder. The founder may delegate the visitatorial power wholly or partially to any other person and his heirs[1], thereby appointing them general or special visitors.

A person appointed in general terms is a general visitor, having the same jurisdiction as the founder[2] unless his powers are expressly restricted[3]. Special visitors are those who are appointed for particular purposes, and their jurisdiction is limited accordingly[4]. A general visitor may also have jurisdiction as a special visitor and may proceed in either character in appropriate circumstances[5]. In addition to a general visitor there may also be a special visitor for a particular purpose, in which case that purpose will be excluded from the powers of the general visitor[6]. The visitatorial power may be divided among a number of special visitors, each appointed for special purposes[7]. In the absence of clear words to the contrary which remove his jurisdiction, it is normally inherent in the visitor that he has all the general powers of visitation and determination of disputes arising under the foundation's statutes. The mere fact that, in certain respects, his powers may be limited in the manner in which they can be exercised does not cut down his status from that of a general visitor to that of a special visitor[8].

1 *Eden v Foster* (1726) 2 P Wms 325; *A-G v Lock* (1744) 3 Atk 164; *A-G v Talbot* (1748) 1 Ves Sen 78; *St John's College, Cambridge v Todington* (1757) 1 Burr 158. But see PARA 517 text and notes 4–10. Before the abolition of descent to the heir, the power of appointing and removing visitors might be vested in the heirs of a named person: *A-G v Middleton* (1751) 2 Ves Sen 327. See also *A-G v Talbot*; *St John's College, Cambridge v Todington*.

2 *A-G v Talbot* (1748) 1 Ves Sen 78; *St John's College, Cambridge v Todington* (1757) 1 Burr 158.

3 *R v Bishop of Worcester* (1815) 4 M & S 415 at 420 per Lord Ellenborough CJ.

4 *St John's College, Cambridge v Todington* (1757) 1 Burr 158 at 200 per Lord Mansfield. See also Shelford's Law of Mortmain (1836) 343 et seq; *Bishop of Ely v Bentley* (1732) 2 Bro Parl Cas 220, HL; *R v Bishop of Ely* (1788) 2 Term Rep 290 at 336 per Ashurst J; *R v Bishop of Worcester* (1815) 4 M & S 415 at 420 per Lord Ellenborough CJ.

5 *Bishop of Ely v Bentley* (1732) 2 Bro Parl Cas 220, HL.

6 *St John's College, Cambridge v Todington* (1757) 1 Burr 158.

7 *A-G v Middleton* (1751) 2 Ves Sen 327 at 329 per Lord Hardwicke LC.

8 *Oakes v Sidney Sussex College, Cambridge* [1988] 1 All ER 1004, [1988] 1 WLR 431.

520. Appointment of visitor expressly and by implication. No technical words are necessary for the appointment of a visitor; it is sufficient if the intention to appoint is manifested[1]. The question is invariably one of construction[2].

Moreover, a visitor may be appointed by implication[3], but the fact that the person has the power of construing statutes does not of itself constitute him a visitor if other visitatorial functions are exercisable by other persons[4]. The express exclusion of the jurisdiction of the founder's heirs implies an intention to appoint another as visitor[5].

By being appointed governors of an institution persons do not ipso facto become visitors[6], unless an appointment as visitors is implied or expressed[7]; but the appointment as governors may constitute them visitors as well, if they are not concerned in the management of the charity property, and if there is a manifested intention that they should visit[8]. However, the receipt and application of the charity revenues excludes governors from exercising visitatorial jurisdiction[9], although the bare possession of the legal estate does not do so[10].

If the charity property is not vested in the persons who are to partake, but in trustees for their benefit, there can be no visitor by implication, but the trustees have the powers of a visitor[11].

A beneficial interest in a charity prevents a person from becoming visitor of that charity[12].

1 *A-G v Talbot* (1748) 1 Ves Sen 78; *A-G v Middleton* (1751) 2 Ves Sen 327; *St John's College, Cambridge v Todington* (1757) 1 Burr 158.

2 *St John's College, Cambridge v Todington* (1757) 1 Burr 158; *Bishop of Ely v Bentley* (1732) 2 Bro Parl Cas 220 at 232, HL (where the words 'visitator Episcopus Eliensis sit', no Christian name being mentioned, were held to confer the visitatorial power on the Bishop of Ely and his successors); and see *Ex p Kirkby Ravensworth Hospital* (1808) 15 Ves 305 at 315 per Lord Eldon LC.

3 Eg by conferring powers of correction, removal or of construing statutes upon a person: *A-G v Lock* (1744) 3 Atk 164; *A-G v Talbot* (1748) 1 Ves Sen 78; *St John's College, Cambridge v Todington* (1757) 1 Burr 158.

4 *Ex p Kirkby Ravensworth Hospital* (1808) 15 Ves 305.

5 *St John's College, Cambridge v Todington* (1757) 1 Burr 158. See also PARAS 517–519.

6 *Eden v Foster* (1726) 2 P Wms 325; *A-G v Governors of Harrow School* (1754) 2 Ves Sen 551.

7 *Sutton's Hospital Case* (1612) 10 Co Rep 1a at 23a, 31a, Ex Ch; *A-G v Lock* (1744) 3 Atk 164.

8 *Eden v Foster* (1726) 2 P Wms 325.

9 *Eden v Foster* (1726) 2 P Wms 325. In these circumstances they are simply trustees: *A-G v Lubbock* (1837) Coop Pr Cas 15.

10 *A-G v Middleton* (1751) 2 Ves Sen 327 at 329 per Lord Hardwicke LC.

11 *Green v Rutherforth* (1750) 1 Ves Sen 462 at 472 per Lord Hardwicke LC.

12 *R v Bishop of Chester* (1728) 2 Stra 797; *R v Dean and Chapter of Rochester* (1851) 17 QB 1. This is on the principle that a man cannot visit himself.

521. Suspension of visitatorial powers. If the visitatorial power is at any time suspended, the jurisdiction vests in the court[1]. Such powers may cease and revive in appropriate circumstances[2].

1 *R v Bishop of Chester* (1728) 2 Stra 797 (where the visitor was appointed warden of the college and therefore could not visit himself); and see *R v Bishop of Ely* (1788) 2 Term Rep 290; *Green v Rutherforth* (1750) 1 Ves Sen 462 at 471 per Lord Hardwicke LC.
2 *R v Bishop of Chester* (1728) 2 Stra 797; Shelford's Law of Mortmain (1836) 368.

522. Substitution of bishops by Charity Commission. The Charity Commission's powers[1] to substitute the bishop of one diocese for the bishop of another as trustee of charitable trusts[2] do not extend to or affect trusts of a visitatorial nature exercised in or over the colleges, halls or schools of the universities of Oxford or Cambridge, or the schools of Eton, Winchester or Westminster[3].

1 As to the Charity Commission see PARAS 543–578.
2 Ie under the Bishops Trust Substitution Act 1858: see PARA 270.
3 See the Bishops Trust Substitution Act 1858 s 4.

(iii) Visitor's Powers and Duties

523. Limits of jurisdiction. The general jurisdiction[1] of a visitor is limited by the statutes regulating the charity[2], although under express powers he may be authorised to dispense with or alter those statutes[3]. The powers of a special visitor are confined within the limits imposed by the founder[4].

Where a dispute between a university and a member of its academic staff over his contract of employment concerns questions of the domestic laws of the university, the visitor has exclusive jurisdiction[5]. However, the exclusivity of the jurisdiction of the visitor may be modified by statute[6]. In particular, the jurisdiction of the visitor in relation to universities has been considerably eroded by first the Education Reform Act 1988[7] and then the Higher Education Act 2004[8].

The Higher Education Act 2004 provides that the visitor of a qualifying institution[9] has no jurisdiction in respect of: (1) any dispute relating to a member of the academic staff which concerns his appointment or employment or the termination of his appointment or employment[10]; (2) any other dispute between a member of staff and the qualifying institution in respect of which proceedings could be brought before any court or tribunal[11]; (3) any dispute as to the application of the statutes or other internal laws of the institution in relation to a matter falling within head (1) or head (2)[12]; (4) any complaint made in respect of an application for admission to the qualifying institution as a student[13]; or (5) any complaint made by a person as a student or former student at the qualifying institution, or as a student or former student at another institution[14] undertaking a course of study, or programme of research, leading to the grant of one of the qualifying institution's awards[15].

1 See PARA 514. As to the procedure of visitors see PARA 528.
2 *Green v Rutherforth* (1750) 1 Ves Sen 462 at 472 per Lord Hardwicke LC; *Philips v Bury* (1694) Skin 447 at 490, HL.
3 *St John's College, Cambridge v Todington* (1757) 1 Burr 158 at 201 per Lord Mansfield ('It must be collected from the whole purview of the statutes considered together what power the founder meant to give the visitor').
4 *Philips v Bury* (1694) Skin 447 at 478, HL.
5 See *Thomas v University of Bradford* [1987] AC 795, [1987] 1 All ER 834, HL; *R v Lord President of the Privy Council, ex p Page* [1993] AC 682, sub nom *Page v Hull University Visitor* [1993] 1 All ER 97, HL; and the cases cited in PARA 514 note 6.
6 See *Thomas v University of Bradford* [1987] AC 795, [1987] 1 All ER 834, HL, where Lord Griffiths said at 824, 849, that, if in proceedings under the Employment Protection (Consolidation) Act 1978 (now repealed) a question arises concerning the interpretation or

application of the internal laws of a university, the proceedings will not be adjourned and the question will have to be resolved for the purpose of the case by the tribunal hearing the application.

7 The Education Reform Act 1988 provides for University Commissioners, with powers relating to dismissal and disciplinary procedures for academic staff (see ss 202–205); however, the Commissioners' powers and duties were of limited duration (see Sch 11 para 3), and although continued for some time by ministerial order, it seems that the provisions and powers have now lapsed. See further **EDUCATION** vol 36 (2011) PARA 821.

8 See the text and notes 9–15.

9 Ie any of the following institutions in England or Wales: (1) a university (whether or not receiving financial support under the Further and Higher Education Act 1992 s 65) whose entitlement to grant awards is conferred or confirmed by an Act of Parliament, a royal charter, or an order under the Education Reform Act 1988 s 76; (2) a constituent college, school or hall or other institution of a university falling within head (1); (3) an institution conducted by a higher education corporation; (4) a designated institution, as defined by s 72(3): Higher Education Act 2004 ss 11, 46(2).

10 See the Higher Education Act 2004 s 46(1)(a); and **EDUCATION** vol 36 (2011) PARA 820. This supersedes a similar provision in the Education Reform Act 1988 s 206, which is now repealed: see the Higher Education Act 2004 s 46(4). See also *Hines v Birkbeck College (No 2)* [1992] Ch 33, [1991] 4 All ER 450, CA, where it was held, in relation to the earlier provision, that the reference to the visitor may be made either by the member of the academic staff or by the university.

11 See the Higher Education Act 2004 s 46(1)(b); and **EDUCATION** vol 36 (2011) PARA 820. In determining whether a dispute falls within s 46(1)(b) it is to be assumed that the visitor does not have jurisdiction to determine the dispute: s 46(3).

12 See the Higher Education Act 2004 s 46(1)(c); and **EDUCATION** vol 36 (2011) PARA 820.

13 See the Higher Education Act 2004 s 20(1), (2); and **EDUCATION** vol 36 (2011) PARA 1242.

14 Ie whether or not a qualifying institution.

15 See the Higher Education Act 2004 s 20(1), (3); and **EDUCATION** vol 36 (2011) PARA 1242.

524. Time of visitations. As a rule the statutes of a charitable corporation provide for general visitations being made at fixed intervals of time, or upon the special request of the corporators. If made otherwise the proceedings are void[1]. General visitations have been said to be at least obsolescent[2]. A visitor may at all times hear complaints and appeals of individual members of the corporation and decree an appropriate remedy[3] which may be the award of damages[4].

1 *Philips v Bury* (1694) Skin 447 at 478, HL.

2 *Patel v University of Bradford Senate* [1978] 3 All ER 841 at 846, [1978] 1 WLR 1488 at 1493 per Megarry V-C; affd [1979] 2 All ER 582, [1979] 1 WLR 1066, CA.

3 *Philips v Bury* (1694) Skin 447 at 478, HL; *A-G v Price* (1744) 3 Atk 108.

4 *Thomas v University of Bradford* [1987] AC 795 at 823–824, [1987] 1 All ER 834 at 848–849, HL, per Lord Griffiths, disapproving dictum of Lord Hailsham of St Marylebone LC in *Casson v University of Aston in Birmingham* [1983] 1 All ER 88 at 91, Visitor.

525. Power to settle questions. The jurisdiction of the visitor is sometimes referred to as a domestic jurisdiction. It includes not only the interpretation and enforcement of the internal laws of the foundation but also those internal powers and discretions that derive from the internal laws, such as the discretion necessarily bestowed on those in authority in the exercise of their disciplinary functions over members of the foundation[1]. It extends beyond members of the foundation to other persons claiming to enforce rights which they enjoy under its internal laws[2]. The visitor's duties include the settling of questions arising as to the interpretation of the statutes relating to the foundation[3], and the internal management of a charitable corporation, such as abuses in the internal regulation[4], the increase of a professor's stipend out of unappropriated revenue[5], the refusal of the chairman of a university convocation to summon a meeting to consider certain matters[6], the conduct of examinations by a university[7], or the election of fellows of a college[8]; the residence of the master of a hospital in the master's house[9] or the performance of Divine Service by him[10], or his election[11]; or the election or removal of members of a corporation such as governors[12] or schoolmasters[13]. A visitor has power also to determine whether a person is entitled to become a member of the corporation[14], and whether a person has been properly removed from membership[15].

A member of a corporation refusing to recognise the authority of the visitor may be removed, whether or not the statutes expressly authorise this[16].

1 'A visitor is ... a Judge, not for the single purpose of interpreting laws, but also for the application of laws, that are perfectly clear: requiring no interpretation; and, farther, for the interpretations of questions of fact, involving no interpretation of laws': *Ex p Kirkby Ravensworth Hospital* (1808) 15 Ves 305 at 311 per Sir Samuel Romilly, cited as authoritative by Lord Griffiths in *Thomas v University of Bradford* [1987] AC 795 at 815, [1987] 1 All ER 834 at 846, HL.

2 *Oakes v Sidney Sussex College, Cambridge* [1988] 1 All ER 1004, [1988] 1 WLR 431.

3 *A-G v Stephens* (1737) 1 Atk 358 at 360 per Lord Hardwicke LC; *Ex p Berkhampstead Free School* (1813) 2 Ves & B 134; *A-G v Smythies* (1836) 2 My & Cr 135 (where the question was whether a fellow of a college might let his rooms).

4 *A-G v Dulwich College* (1841) 4 Beav 255; *A-G v Magdalen College, Oxford* (1847) 10 Beav 402. See *Thomas v University of Bradford* [1987] AC 795, [1987] 1 All ER 834, HL (the question whether the university council had correctly followed its disciplinary procedures in dismissing a lecturer was a matter exclusively within the jurisdiction of the visitor), approving *Hines v Birkbeck College* [1986] Ch 524, [1985] 3 All ER 156 (appeal dismissed [1987] Ch 457n [1987] 3 All ER 1040n, CA); *Casson v University of Aston in Birmingham* [1983] 1 All ER 88, Visitor (visitor's jurisdiction to hear petition alleging breach of contract by corporation).

5 *Re Christ Church* (1866) 1 Ch App 526.

6 *R v Dunsheath, ex p Meredith* [1951] 1 KB 127, [1950] 2 All ER 741.

7 *Thomson v London University* (1864) 10 Jur NS 669; *Thorn v University of London* [1966] 2 QB 237, [1966] 2 All ER 338, CA; cf *Herring v Templeman* [1973] 2 All ER 581 (affd on other grounds [1973] 3 All ER 569, CA) (dismissal of student at teacher-training college). See also *R v HM The Queen in Council, ex p Vijayatunga* [1990] 2 QB 444, sub nom *R v University of London Visitor, ex p Vijayatunga* [1989] 2 All ER 843, CA (claim that examiners not qualified to assess thesis: visitor properly refused to intervene).

8 *A-G v Talbot* (1748) 3 Atk 662 at 675 per Lord Hardwicke LC; *Ex p Wrangham* (1795) 2 Ves 609; *Re Catharine Hall, ex p Inge* (1831) 2 Russ & M 590.

9 *Re St Mary Magdalen Hospital, Colchester* (1843) 12 LJCh 375; *Ex p Berkhampstead Free School* (1813) 2 Ves & B 134; *A-G v Smythies* (1836) 2 My & Cr 135 at 142 per Lord Cottenham LC.

10 *A-G v Crook* (1836) 1 Keen 121.

11 *A-G v Archbishop of York* (1831) 2 Russ & M 461 at 468 per Lord Brougham LC.

12 *A-G v Dixie, ex p Bosworth School* (1805) 13 Ves 519; *A-G v Earl of Clarendon* (1810) 17 Ves 491 at 498 per Grant MR.

13 *Whiston v Dean and Chapter of Rochester* (1849) 7 Hare 532.

14 Eg in cases of claims of rejected candidates for fellowships and scholarships: *R v Warden of All Souls College, Oxford* (1681) T Jo 174; *St John's College, Cambridge v Todington* (1757) 1 Burr 158; *R v Master and Fellows of St Catharine's Hall* (1791) 4 Term Rep 233; *Ex p Wrangham* (1795) 2 Ves 609; *R v Hertford College* (1878) 3 QBD 693, CA.

15 *Re Wislang's Application* [1984] NI 63; *Thomas v University of Bradford* [1987] AC 795, [1987] 1 All ER 834, HL. It 'extends to all questions of disputed membership': *Patel v University of Bradford Senate* [1979] 2 All ER 582 at 584, [1979] 1 WLR 1066 at 1069, CA, per Orr LJ.

16 *Philips v Bury* (1694) Skin 447 at 477–478, HL.

526. Restrictions on visitor's power. A visitor is not entitled to interfere with the proceedings of corporators in matters over which they have discretion[1], unless their discretion has been exercised improperly[2]; nor may he insist upon a corporation performing some act which according to the statutes regulating the corporation may be performed by another if the corporation fails to do it[3], or interfere with the internal management of the charitable corporation unless the trusts of the foundation are disregarded[4], or appoint a master of a free school on the ground that the appointments previously made by the proper electors were invalid[5].

As the visitor's jurisdiction extends only over the members of the corporation[6], he has no power to compel specific performance of an agreement between the corporators and other parties[7], or to reverse a decision of a corporation concerning strangers to the foundation[8].

Except under an express power, a visitor cannot be judge in his own cause[9], nor can he alter the general constitution of the trust[10].

1 *Ex p Wrangham* (1795) 2 Ves 609 at 625 per Lord Thurlow LC (election of fellows).
2 *Re Catharine Hall, ex p Inge* (1831) 2 Russ & M 590 at 601 per Lord Brougham LC; *R v Hertford College* (1878) 3 QBD 693 at 701, CA, per Lord Coleridge CJ.
3 *Ex p Wrangham* (1795) 2 Ves 609 at 621 per Lord Thurlow LC, where the statutes provided that if a college failed to elect fellows, the right should be exercised by the master.
4 *A-G v Earl of Clarendon* (1810) 17 Ves 491 at 507 per Grant MR.
5 *A-G v Black* (1805) 11 Ves 191.
6 See *Herring v Templeman* [1973] 3 All ER 569, CA, in relation to a student at a teacher-training college. See also *Casson v University of Aston in Birmingham* [1983] 1 All ER 88, Visitor (no jurisdiction to hear petition alleging breach of pre-admission contract by corporation); *Oakes v Sidney Sussex College, Cambridge* [1988] 1 All ER 1004, [1988] 1 WLR 431 (visitor's jurisdiction dependent on whether claim arose under domestic law of college, not on nature of claimant's college membership).
7 *R v Windham* (1776) 1 Cowp 377.
8 *Ex p Davison* (1772) cited in 1 Cowp 319 (expulsion of commoners by a college). See also *R v Grundon* (1775) 1 Cowp 315.
9 This is upon the principle that the same person cannot be visitor and visited: *R v Bishop of Ely* (1788) 2 Term Rep 290; *A-G v Middleton* (1751) 2 Ves Sen 327 at 329 per Lord Hardwicke LC; and see *R v Hertford College* (1878) 3 QBD 693 at 703, CA, per Lord Coleridge CJ. See also *Re P (A Barrister)* [2005] 1 WLR 3019 (lay member of the Visitors to the Inns of Courts should not have acted in that capacity when she was also a member of the Professional Conduct and Complaints Committee).
10 *Ex p Bolton School* (1789) 2 Bro CC 662.

527. Accession to the foundation. In the case of an accession of a new to an old foundation the visitor of the old foundation has no jurisdiction over the new foundation unless the visitatorial power is especially given to him by the subsequent founder, or his appointment as visitor is to be implied[1].

Where new property is annexed to an old foundation without a special trust being declared or a new visitor being appointed, the necessary implication is that the new property is intended to be subject to the existing visitatorial jurisdiction[2]. However, the visitor of the old foundation has no jurisdiction over an annexed estate concerning which a special trust has been declared[3]. If the Queen is visitor of an old foundation, which accepts an accession, it seems that she becomes visitor of the new foundation, even if the founder declares there shall be no visitor[4].

A lay corporation composed of an indefinite number of members may incorporate additional members, who will thereupon become subject to the jurisdiction of the visitor[5].

1 *Green v Rutherforth* (1750) 1 Ves Sen 462 at 472 per Lord Hardwicke LC.
2 *Green v Rutherforth* (1750) 1 Ves Sen 462 at 473 per Lord Hardwicke LC; *A-G v Talbot* (1748) 3 Atk 662 (accession of fellowship to college foundation); *A-G v Flood* (1816) Hayes & Jo App xxi at p xxv. See also *Re Catharine Hall, ex p Inge* (1831) 2 Russ & M 590 at 596 per Lord Brougham LC.
3 *Green v Rutherforth* (1750) 1 Ves Sen 462 at 468–469, 473 per Lord Hardwicke LC.

4 *A-G v Catherine Hall, Cambridge* (1820) Jac 381 at 400 per Lord Eldon LC. It was doubted whether a college of which the King was visitor could accept an accession without his consent.

5 *A-G v Talbot* (1748) 3 Atk 662 at 675 per Lord Hardwicke LC.

528. Procedure and duties of visitor. Whether a visitor is exercising his jurisdiction upon a general visitation or upon a special appeal[1], he need not proceed according to the rules of common law[2] so long as he pays regard to the positive forms prescribed by the statutes regulating the foundation[3], and subject to this condition, and provided he acts judicially, the actual manner of hearing is within his discretion[4]. He must hear all appeals not of a frivolous nature[5].

A visitor should cite the interested parties to appear before him[6], and no proceedings ought to be taken against an absent party until he has been cited[7]. The visitor may decide questions upon written or oral evidence[8], on oath or otherwise[9]; but he cannot give his decision without hearing the parties concerned or, at least, affording them an opportunity of being heard[10].

The visitor must make the relevant decision, but there is nothing to prevent him appointing a competent person to advise him, and that person may conduct any hearing and obtain all necessary information[11]. Provided that he acts fairly, and the visitor makes the final decision, there is no delegation which could be regarded as unlawful[12]. The 'competent person' should normally be a lawyer of standing and most of the more modern cases show that a judge or a Queen's Counsel has been appointed[13].

Like a private visitor, the Crown is not bound by any particular forms of procedure[14].

1 As to the jurisdiction of general or special visitors see PARA 519.

2 *R v Bishop of Ely* (1788) 2 Term Rep 290 at 338 per Buller J. See, however, the text and note 10.

3 Com Dig Visitor, C.

4 *A-G v Governors of Atherstone Free School* (1834) 3 My & K 544 at 550 per Lord Brougham LC; *R v HM The Queen in Council, ex p Vijayatunga* [1990] 2 QB 444, sub nom *R v University of London Visitor, ex p Vijayatunga* [1989] 2 All ER 843, CA (in some cases he should exercise a merely supervisory jurisdiction, and in others an appellate jurisdiction). In *Thomas v University of Bradford (No 2)* [1992] 1 All ER 964, the jurisdiction was said to be similar to that which the High Court exercises by way of judicial review. See also *Re Dean of York* (1841) 2 QB 1.

5 Shelford's Law of Mortmain (1836) 379.

6 *R v Cambridge University* (1723) 8 Mod Rep 148 at 163 per Pratt CJ. See also *Watson and Freemantle v Warden etc of All Souls College, Oxford* (1864) 11 LT 166.

7 Com Dig Visitor, C.

8 *R v Bishop of Ely* (1794) 5 Term Rep 475.

9 Shelford's Law of Mortmain (1836) 379. However, see *Green v Rutherforth* (1750) 1 Ves Sen 462 at 473 per Lord Hardwicke LC.

10 *R v Bishop of Ely* (1788) 2 Term Rep 290 at 336 per Ashurst J; *R v Cambridge University* (1723) 8 Mod Rep 148; see also *R v Gaskin* (1799) 8 Term Rep 209; *Doe d Earl of Thanet v Gartham* (1823) 8 Moore CP 368 at 371 per Park J.

11 *R (on the application of Varma) v HRH The Duke of Kent* [2004] EWHC 1705 (Admin) at [16], [2004] ELR 616 per Collins J.

12 *R (on the application of Varma) v HRH The Duke of Kent* [2004] EWHC 1705 (Admin) at [16], [2004] ELR 616 per Collins J.

13 *R (on the application of Varma) v HRH The Duke of Kent* [2004] EWHC 1705 (Admin) at [16], [2004] ELR 616 per Collins J.

14 *Queen's College, Cambridge, Case* (1821) Jac 1 at 19 per Lord Eldon LC. And see further PARA 518.

(iv) Court's Control over Visitors

529. Discretionary powers of visitors. The court's jurisdiction does not extend to matters within the properly exercised discretion of the visitor[1], or the trustee[2], governors[3] or other authority[4], but the court controls the visitor's discretionary powers if exercised corruptly or dishonestly[5].

1 *A-G v Harrow School Governors* (1754) 2 Ves Sen 551; *A-G v Dulwich College* (1841) 4 Beav 255; *A-G v Magdalen College, Oxford* (1847) 10 Beav 402; *Thomson v London University* (1864) 33 LJCh 625 at 634; *Thorne v University of London* [1966] 2 QB 237, [1966] 2 All ER 338, CA; *Herring v Templeman* [1973] 2 All ER 581; affd on other grounds [1973] 3 All ER 569, CA. As to what matters are within the visitor's discretion see PARA 514 et seq.

2 *A-G v Harrow School Governors* (1754) 2 Ves Sen 551.

3 *Eden v Foster* (1726) 2 P Wms 325. Cf *R v Governors of Christ's Hospital, ex p Dunn* [1917] 1 KB 19, a case where the matter was not within the governors' discretion.

4 *A-G v Bedford Corpn* (1754) 2 Ves Sen 505; *Costabadie v Costabadie* (1847) 6 Hare 410; *Hayman v Governors of Rugby School* (1874) LR 18 Eq 28.

5 *Ex p Kirkby Ravensworth Hospital* (1808) 15 Ves 305 at 314 per Lord Eldon LC; and see *A-G v Harrow School Governors* (1754) 2 Ves Sen 551.

530. Visitors acting in excess of authority. The court will grant a prohibiting order[1] if a visitor exceeds the limits of his visitatorial authority[2], or proceeds contrary to his citation, or inflicts different penalties from those which the statutes prescribe[3]; or where a person purports to act as visitor when he has no jurisdiction[4]. Mere irregularity in the proceedings or informality in the acts of a visitor will not render him liable to a prohibiting order[5]. Where he has no jurisdiction, appearance or answer does not give him jurisdiction. If there is a want of jurisdiction it may be called in question at any time, even after sentence[6]. An order may also be granted to quash a decision of the visitor which amounts to an abuse of his powers, or if he has acted in breach of the rules of natural justice[7]. Judicial review does not, however, lie to impeach the decisions of a visitor taken within his jurisdiction (in the narrow sense[8]) on questions of either law or fact[9]. This is because the applicable law is not the common law of England but a peculiar or domestic law of which the visitor is the sole judge[10].

1 A prohibiting order (previously referred to simply as a prohibition) must be made by an application for judicial review: see the Senior Courts Act 1981 s 31(1); and JUDICIAL REVIEW vol 61 (2010) PARA 691.

2 *Bishop of Chichester v Harvard and Webber* (1787) 1 Term Rep 650.

3 *Bishop of Ely v Bentley* (1732) 2 Bro Parl Cas 220, HL.

4 *R v Bishop of Chester* (1748) 1 Wm Bl 22 at 25; *Whiston v Dean and Chapter of Rochester* (1849) 7 Hare 532 at 558 per Shadwell V-C.

5 *Bishop of Ely v Bentley* (1732) 2 Bro Parl Cas 220, HL.

6 *Green v Rutherforth* (1750) 1 Ves Sen 462 at 471 per Lord Hardwicke LC.

7 *R v Lord President of the Privy Council, ex p Page* [1993] AC 682, sub nom *Page v Hull University Visitor* [1993] 1 All ER 97, HL; *Thomas v University of Bradford* [1987] AC 795 at 825, [1987] 1 All ER 834 at 850, HL, per Lord Griffiths; *R v Committee of the Lords of the Judicial Committee of the Privy Council acting for the Visitor of the University of London, ex p Vijayatunga* [1988] QB 322, sub nom *R v University of London Visitor, ex p Vijayatunga* [1987] 3 All ER 204; affd sub nom *R v HM The Queen in Council, ex p Vijayatunga* [1990] 2 QB 444, sub nom *R v University of London Visitor, ex p Vijayatunga* [1989] 2 All ER 843, CA. As to quashing orders see JUDICIAL REVIEW vol 61 (2010) PARA 693 et seq; CIVIL PROCEDURE.

8 Ie where he has power under the regulating documents to enter into the adjudication of the dispute.

9 Apart from the anomalous and unique case of the visitor, any error of law made by an administrative tribunal or inferior court may be a ground for quashing the decision on judicial review: *Anisminic Ltd v Foreign Compensation Commission* [1969] 2 AC 147, [1969] 1 All ER 208, HL; *O'Reilly v Mackman* [1983] 2 AC 237, [1982] 3 All ER 1124, HL; *R v Lord President*

of the Privy Council, ex p Page [1993] AC 682, sub nom *Page v Hull University Visitor* [1993] 1 All ER 97, HL. As to judicial review see JUDICIAL REVIEW.

10 *R v Lord President of the Privy Council, ex p Page* [1993] AC 682, sub nom *Page v Hull University Visitor* [1993] 1 All ER 97, HL; *Appleford's Case* (1672) 1 Mod Rep 82; *R v Bishop of Chester* (1747) 1 WM Bl 22; *R v Bishop of Ely* (1794) 5 Term Rep 475; *Ex p Buller* (1855) 1 Jur NS 709. See also *A-G v Lock* (1744) 3 Atk 164 at 165 per Lord Hardwicke LC; *A-G v Talbot* (1748) 3 Atk 662 at 674 per Lord Hardwicke LC; *A-G v Catherine Hall, Cambridge* (1820) Jac 381 at 392 per Lord Eldon LC; *A-G v Dedham School* (1857) 23 Beav 350.

531. Where Charity Commission is visitor. Where visitatorial jurisdiction is reserved by a scheme to the Charity Commission[1], the court will not interfere in matters coming within that jurisdiction which have already been determined conclusively within the meaning of the scheme, before any application is made to the court[2].

1 See the Charity Commissioners' (now the Charity Commission) powers under the Endowed Schools Act 1869 s 23 (repealed), and the decision thereunder in *Re Hodgson's School* (1878) 3 App Cas 857, PC. As to the Charity Commissioners, and the transfer of their functions and liabilities to the Charity Commission, see PARA 543. As to the Charity Commission see PARAS 543–578.

2 *R v Wilson* [1888] WN 12, DC (where the court refused to consider a question regarding the validity of the election of a governor which had already been determined conclusively by the Commissioners under the scheme). Judicial review proceedings can only be brought against a decision of the Commission where it can be shown that, in making the decision, it had acted outside its jurisdiction; no such proceedings can be brought in the case of an error of law: *R v Charity Comrs for England and Wales, ex p Baldwin* (2000) 33 HLR 538. See also PARA 516.

532. Mandatory order to put visitatorial power in motion. The object and effect of a mandatory order is no more than to put the visitatorial power in motion, whereupon the visitor is at liberty to pursue his own course without review by the court[1].

The court may make a mandatory order to compel a visitor to exercise his visitatorial power where he has not acted, declines to act, or acts improperly[2]; or to compel him to receive and hear an appeal, although the court cannot force him to decide on the merits if he considers the appeal is brought too late[3]; so, too, the court may make a mandatory order against the head of a college and the fellows where the laws of the land have been disobeyed by the fellows, even though there is a visitor[4].

A mandatory order will lie against the governors of a charity to compel them to appoint a person duly recommended to an office where, by the constitution of the charity, the governors are bound to act on the recommendation[5].

The court refuses, however, to make such an order where it is doubtful whether the visitatorial power is in the persons required to exercise it[6], or to compel an inferior officer of a college to execute the visitor's sentence in accordance with the statutes[7], or to restore a fellow or member of a college[8], or a chaplain[9] or a sister of a hospital[10].

1 *A-G v Archbishop of York* (1831) 2 Russ & M 461 at 468 per Lord Brougham LC. A mandatory order was formerly known as an order of mandamus: see JUDICIAL REVIEW vol 61 (2010) PARA 703 et seq. An application for a mandatory order must be made by an application for judicial review: see the Senior Courts Act 1981 s 31(1); and JUDICIAL REVIEW vol 61 (2010) PARA 691.

2 *R v Bishop of Ely* (1788) 2 Term Rep 290; *R v Cambridge University* (1723) 8 Mod Rep 148; *R v Bishop of Worcester* (1815) 4 M & S 415; *Whiston v Dean and Chapter of Rochester* (1849) 7 Hare 532 at 558 per Shadwell V-C. See also *Gunston v Dare* (1738) West *temp* Hard 573 at 576 per Lord Hardwicke LC.

3 *R v Bishop of Ely* (1794) 5 Term Rep 475. See also *R v Bishop of Lincoln* (1785) 2 Term Rep 338n; *Ferguson v Kinnoul* (1842) 4 State Tr NS 785 at 820, HL, per Lord Brougham.

4 *R v St John's College, Cambridge* (1693) 4 Mod Rep 233; but see *R v Gower* (1694) 3 Salk 230.
5 *R v Governors of Christ's Hospital, ex p Dunn* [1917] 1 KB 19.
6 *R v Bishop of Ely* (1750) 1 Wm Bl 52; *Brideoak's Case* (1714) cited in 1 Wm Bl 58.
7 *A-G v Aspinall* (1837) 2 My & Cr 613 at 627 per Lord Cottenham LC; *Stevens v Chown* [1901] 1 Ch 894 at 905 per Farwell J; *A-G v De Winton* [1906] 2 Ch 106 at 115 per Farwell J.
8 *Dr Widdrington's Case* (1662) 1 Lev 23; *Appleford's Case* (1672) 1 Mod Rep 82; *Parkinson's Case* (1689) 3 Mod Rep 265; *R v Warden of All Souls College, Oxford* (1681) T Jo 174; *A-G v Governors of Atherstone Free School* (1834) 3 My & K 544 at 550 per Lord Brougham LC; *R v Hertford College* (1878) 3 QBD 693, CA.
9 *Prohurst's Case* (1691) Carth 168.
10 *R v Wheeler* (1674) 3 Keb 360.

533. Remedies against visitor. The remedy, if any, of a person deprived or removed by a visitor has been said[1] to lie in an action of ejectment, long since replaced by an action to recover possession of land[2], or, if the visitor has acted contrary to or exceeded his jurisdiction, in a claim against him on that ground[3]. The appropriate modern procedure is by way of an application for judicial review[4].

1 In *R v Bishop of Chester* (1748) 1 Wils 206 at 209 per Lee CJ.
2 See *Gledhill v Hunter* (1880) 14 ChD 492.
3 See *Green v Rutherforth* (1750) 1 Ves Sen 462 at 472 per Lord Hardwicke LC.
4 See PARAS 530, 532. As to judicial review see JUDICIAL REVIEW.

(3) THE COURTS

534. Jurisdiction to enforce trusts. As a general rule the High Court has jurisdiction to enforce the observance or redress breaches of all trusts, charitable as well as private[1]. The court cannot exercise its charitable jurisdiction if no trust is ascertained[2]. The jurisdiction in the case of charities is more extensive than in the case of private trusts[3]; where the trust is charitable, the court has jurisdiction not only to enforce it and to redress all breaches[4], but also, in certain circumstances, to make schemes for the administration of the charity[5] and to alter or modify the trust to a greater or less degree by virtue of the cy-près doctrine[6].

The court equally enforces the execution of trusts where corporations eleemosynary[7], ecclesiastical[8], or civil[9] are trustees for charitable or public purposes.

1 *Dick v Audsley* [1908] AC 347 at 351, HL, per Lord Loreburn LC. This jurisdiction, formerly exercised by the Court of Chancery, is now vested in the High Court of Justice and exercised by the Chancery Division: see the Senior Courts Act 1981 ss 5(4), (5), 19, 61(1), 64, 65, Sch 1. The jurisdiction has been exercised by the court from the earliest times: see *Wakeryng v Bayle* (circa 1422–70) 1 Calendar of Proceedings in Chancery lvii; *Lyon v Hewe* (circa 1465–83) 2 Calendar of Proceedings in Chancery xliv; *Payne's Case* (temp Eliz) Duke ed Bridgman, 154. For an account of the early history of charitable trusts and uses, see Gareth Jones *History of the Law of Charity*.
2 *Ommanney v Butcher* (1823) Turn & R 260 at 270 per Plumer MR; *A-G v St John's Hospital, Bedford* (1865) 2 De GJ & Sm 621 at 635 per Turner LJ; but see also *Re Bennett, Sucker v A-G* [1960] Ch 18 at 26, [1959] 3 All ER 295 at 296 per Vaisey J. In this context the word 'trust' may have to be understood in a sense wider than usual, as companies and other corporate bodies are clearly subject to the court's charity jurisdiction where they are established for charitable purposes, although they may not necessarily be trustees of their property in a conventional sense. See also *Construction Industry Training Board v A-G* [1973] Ch 173, [1972] 2 All ER 1339, CA; and PARA 254.
3 *A-G v Governors etc of Sherborne Grammar School* (1854) 18 Beav 256 at 280 per Romilly MR; *Clephane v Edinburgh Corpn* (1869) LR 1 Sc & Div 417 at 421, HL, per Lord Westbury; *Andrews v M'Guffog* (1886) 11 App Cas 313 at 316, HL, per Lord Watson.

The courts are, perhaps, even more reluctant to sanction the remuneration of trustees in the case of a charity than in the case of a private trust: see *Report of the Charity Commissioners for England and Wales for 1990* (HC Paper (1990–91) no 362) App D (c); and TRUSTS AND POWERS vol 98 (2013) PARA 370 et seq. See also *Report of the Charity Commissioners for England and Wales for 1981* (HC Paper (1981–82) no 363) para 64; and *Report of the Charity Commissioners for England and Wales for 1988* (HC Paper (1988–89) no 319) para 38. As to the Charity Commission's publications see PARA 547.

4 *A-G v Governors etc of Sherborne Grammar School* (1854) 18 Beav 256. See also *Incorporated Society in Dublin v Richards* (1841) 1 Con & Law 58; *A-G v Dublin Corpn* (1827) 1 Bli NS 312 at 347, HL per Lord Redesdale; *A-G v St John's Hospital, Bedford* (1865) 2 De GJ & Sm 621.

5 See *Re Royal Society's Charitable Trusts* [1956] Ch 87, [1955] 3 All ER 14. As to schemes see PARA 179 et seq.

6 As to the doctrine of cy-près see PARA 209 et seq.

7 As to the court's jurisdiction over corporations see PARA 254; and *A-G v Magdalen College, Oxford* (1847) 10 Beav 402 at 409 per Lord Langdale MR (where a college was trustee of a grammar school); *Whiston v Dean and Chapter of Rochester* (1849) 7 Hare 532 at 560 per Shadwell V-C (dean and chapter trustees); *Daugars v Rivaz* (1860) 28 Beav 233. The duty of appointing and removing schoolmasters may be (*Willis v Childe* (1851) 13 Beav 117), but is not necessarily, in the nature of a trust (*A-G v Magdalen College, Oxford* at 409 per Lord Langdale MR; *Whiston v Dean and Chapter of Rochester*). If it is a trust, an improper removal is restrained by injunction. If it is not a trust but only a duty imposed on trustees, any breach must be redressed by the visitor and not by the court: *A-G v Magdalen College, Oxford*. As to the meaning of 'eleemosynary corporation' see PARA 225.

8 *A-G v St John's Hospital, Bedford* (1865) 2 De GJ & Sm 621 at 635 per Turner LJ. See also *A-G v Brereton* (1752) 2 Ves Sen 425.

9 *Coventry Corpn v A-G* (1720) 7 Bro Parl Cas 235, HL; *A-G v Shrewsbury Town* (1726) Bunb 215; *A-G v Governors of Foundling Hospital* (1793) 2 Ves 42 at 46 per Lord Commissioner Eyre; *Viscount Gort v A-G* (1817) 6 Dow 136, HL; *A-G v Brewers' Co* (1816) 1 Mer 495; *A-G v Stafford Corpn* (1826) 1 Russ 547; *A-G v Exeter Corpn* (1827) 2 Russ 362; *A-G v Dublin Corpn* (1827) 1 Bli NS 312, HL; *A-G v Carlisle Corpn* (1828) 2 Sim 437 at 449 per Shadwell V-C; *A-G v Liverpool Corpn* (1835) 1 My & Cr 171 at 201 per Pepys MR; and see *A-G v Plymouth Corpn* (1845) 9 Beav 67.

535. Extent of jurisdiction. After some conflict of judicial opinion among ancient authorities[1] the rule became established that, when there is a gift to charity and the donor either created or intended to create a trust, whether the objects are specified or indefinite, the court has jurisdiction to enforce the execution of the trust, and, if necessary, to apply the gift to charitable purposes by means of a scheme[2].

1 *A-G v Berryman* (1755) Dick 168; *A-G v Herrick* (1772) Amb 712; *A-G v Marchioness of Londonderry* (1825) 3 Hare 195n; *A-G v Fletcher* (1835) 5 LJCh 75; *Felan v Russell* (1842) 4 I Eq R 701 (in the last-mentioned cases, though a trust was created, the disposition of the property was held to devolve on the Crown and not on the court).

2 *Cook v Duckenfield* (1743) 2 Atk 562 at 567, 569 per Lord Hardwicke LC; *Moggridge v Thackwell* (1803) 7 Ves 36 (affd (1807) 13 Ves 416, HL); *Mills v Farmer* (1815) 1 Mer 55; *Paice v Archbishop of Canterbury* (1807) 14 Ves 364; *Ommanney v Butcher* (1823) Turn & R 260 at 271 per Plumer MR; *Hayter v Trego* (1830) 5 Russ 113; *A-G v Ironmongers' Co* (1834) 2 My & K 576; *Reeve v A-G* (1843) 3 Hare 191 at 197 per Wigram V-C; *Re Davis, Hannen v Hillyer* [1902] 1 Ch 876 at 888 per Buckley J; *Re Pyne, Lilley v A-G* [1903] 1 Ch 83; *Re Bennett, Sucker v A-G* [1960] Ch 18, [1959] 3 All ER 295. As to the exercise of the court's jurisdiction to make schemes see PARA 200 et seq.

536. Limits of jurisdiction. It is not within the court's jurisdiction to determine whether ecclesiastical duties enjoined under a charitable foundation are properly performed[1]. The court cannot give a charity a larger interest in property than that intended by the testator[2], and it is extremely reluctant to prevent a gift over of property from one charity to another in circumstances expressly contemplated by the donor[3].

The court will not adjudicate upon the truth of religious rites, but can address questions of religious belief and practice in order to settle questions arising from the charity's trusts or from the contractual rights of members[4].

1 *A-G v Smithies* (1836) 1 Keen 289; cf *A-G v Dean and Chapter of Ripon Cathedral* [1945] Ch 239, [1945] 1 All ER 479.

2 *Re Randell, Randell v Dixon* (1888) 38 ChD 213 at 216 per North J; *Re Blunt's Trusts, Wigan v Clinch* [1904] 2 Ch 767.

3 In *Re Hanbey's Will Trusts, Cutlers' Co v President and Governors of Christ's Hospital, London* [1956] Ch 264, [1955] 3 All ER 874, Danckwerts J held that there was jurisdiction to make such a scheme, but did not exercise it. See also *Christ's Hospital v Grainger* (1849) 1 Mac & G 460 at 465 per Lord Cottenham LC; *Re Tyler, Tyler v Tyler* [1891] 3 Ch 252, CA. Quaere whether the court has jurisdiction even to defeat a resulting trust in this way: see PARA 183 note 7.

4 See *Shergill v Khaira* [2014] UKSC 33, [2014] 3 All ER 243; and PARA 27 text and note 7.

537. No charitable gift. The court cannot exercise its charitable jurisdiction where the gift is not charitable in the legal sense, as in the case of a private charity[1], or where a gift fails entirely owing to the charitable intention not taking effect[2], or where the gift was never subject to a charitable trust[3], as in the case of a gift to charity subject to the fulfilment of a condition which was never satisfied[4], or in the case of voluntary subscriptions or funds impressed with no charitable trust[5].

1 *Ommanney v Butcher* (1823) Turn & R 260 at 273 per Plumer MR. As to private charities see PARA 59.

2 *A-G v Boultbee* (1794) 2 Ves 380 at 387 per Arden MR (charitable object to build a church in parish of A, which the parish did not permit); *Biscoe v Jackson* (1887) 35 ChD 460 at 463, CA, per Kay J; *Re Wilson, Twentyman v Simpson* [1913] 1 Ch 314.

3 *De Themmines v De Bonneval* (1828) 5 Russ 288.

4 *Chamberlayne v Brockett* (1872) 8 Ch App 206 at 211 per Lord Selborne LC. See also *Re Gyde, Ward v Little* (1898) 79 LT 261, CA; *Re University of London Medical Sciences Institute Fund, Fowler v A-G* [1909] 2 Ch 1, CA.

5 *Anon* (1745) 3 Atk 277; *Leslie v Birnie* (1826) 2 Russ 114 at 119 per Lord Eldon LC.

538. Charity founded by royal charter. On the principle that the authority of the Crown is higher than that of the court[1], the court has generally no jurisdiction to refound or re-establish charities founded by royal charter[2], but it does have jurisdiction to regulate or control the charity by way of scheme[3], especially on financial grounds and in altered circumstances[4], and to see that the provisions of the charter are observed[5] where improper conduct is alleged[6].

The court has power under the Charities Act 2011 to make schemes in relation to chartered charities, including cy-près schemes[7], which necessitate altering the charter, but the schemes are not to come into operation until the charter has been amended[8], which may be done by Order in Council[9].

1 *A-G v Smart* (1748) 1 Ves Sen 72; *A-G v Middleton* (1751) 2 Ves Sen 327; *A-G v Bedford Corpn* (1754) 2 Ves Sen 505; *A-G v Governors of Foundling Hospital* (1793) 2 Ves 42 at 47 per Lord Commissioner Eyre; *A-G v Earl of Clarendon* (1810) 17 Ves 491; *A-G v Dedham School* (1857) 23 Beav 350 at 356 per Romilly MR; *A-G v Governors of Christ's Hospital* [1896] 1 Ch 879 at 888 per Chitty J. See also *Re Chertsey Market, ex p Walthew* (1819) 6 Price 261; *Re Browne's Hospital v Stamford* (1889) 60 LT 288.

2 Ie except where the charter is subsequent to the original foundation: *A-G v Dedham School* (1857) 23 Beav 350 at 356 per Romilly MR. See also *A-G v St Olave's Grammar School, Southwark* (1837) Coop Pr Cas 267.

3 *Re Whitworth Art Gallery Trusts, Manchester Whitworth Institute v Victoria University of Manchester* [1958] Ch 461, [1958] 1 All ER 176; *A-G v Hicks* (1810) 3 Bro CC 166n; *Re Yarm*

Free Grammar School (1853) 10 Hare App I, V; *Re Berkhampsted Grammar School* [1908] 2 Ch 25; *Manchester School Case* (1867) 2 Ch App 497; and see *Berkhampstead School Case* (1865) LR 1 Eq 102.

4 *Re Whitworth Art Gallery Trusts, Manchester Whitworth Institute v Victoria University of Manchester* [1958] Ch 461, [1958] 1 All ER 176; *Clephane v Edinburgh Corpn* (1869) LR 1 Sc & Div 417, HL.

5 *Green v Rutherforth* (1750) 1 Ves Sen 462 at 468 per Lord Hardwicke LC; *A-G v Governors of Foundling Hospital* (1793) 2 Ves 42; *A-G v Earl of Mansfield* (1827) 2 Russ 501; *A-G v Smythies* (1833) 2 Russ & M 717 at 749 per Lord Brougham LC; *A-G v Wyggeston Hospital* (1849) 12 Beav 113 at 123 per Lord Langdale MR; and see *A-G v St John's Hospital, Bedford* (1865) 2 De GJ & Sm 621.

6 *A-G v Bedford Corpn* (1754) 2 Ves Sen 505.

7 As to cy-près schemes see PARA 209 et seq.

8 See the Charities Act 2011 s 68(1), (2); and PARA 184.

9 See the Charities Act 2011 s 68(3), (4); and PARA 184.

539. Charity regulated by statute. If there were an institution established and regulated in every respect by statute, the court would have no jurisdiction to interfere in its administration, notwithstanding that its purposes were charitable[1], unless the statute gave the court such jurisdiction[2]. However, the court may make a scheme in respect of matters not provided for by the statute[3] or in aid of and supplemental to the provisions of the statute[4], and may enforce the observance of those provisions[5].

Certain statutes are declared not to exclude or restrict the court's jurisdiction with respect to charities, so that the court can make schemes superseding the statutory provisions[6].

The Charity Commission, but not the court, may make schemes (which are put into effect by statutory instrument) amending statutory provisions[7].

1 Cf *Re Shrewsbury Grammar School* (1849) 1 Mac & G 324. See also *London Parochial Charities Trustees v A-G* [1955] 1 All ER 1, [1955] 1 WLR 42; *Construction Industry Training Board v A-G* [1973] Ch 173, [1972] 2 All ER 1339, CA.

2 *Re Shrewsbury Grammar School* (1849) 1 Mac & G 324 at 331 per Lord Cottenham LC; *Ex p Bolton* (1789) 2 Bro CC 662; *Re Bedford Charity* (1833) 5 Sim 578. In *London Parochial Charities Trustees v A-G* [1955] 1 All ER 1, [1955] 1 WLR 42, the regulating scheme, which had statutory force, gave the Charity Commissioners (now the Charity Commission) power to make modifying schemes. Such provisions are not uncommon. As to the Charity Commissioners, and the transfer of their functions and liabilities to the Charity Commission, see PARA 543. As to the Charity Commission see PARAS 543–578.

3 *Re Shrewsbury Grammar School* (1849) 1 Mac & G 324.

4 *Re Shipwrecked Fishermen and Mariners' Royal Benevolent Society* [1959] Ch 220, [1958] 3 All ER 465.

5 *A-G v Wyggeston Hospital* (1849) 12 Beav 113. For the distinction between charities established by gifts, but with no regulations as to their exercise, in which cases the court has a general jurisdiction, and charities established and regulated by charter or Act of Parliament, in which cases the court only has jurisdiction in case of abuse: see Chitty's Prerogatives of the Crown (1820) 161; 3 Bl Com (14th Edn) 426–427.

6 See the Charities Act 2011 s 68(5), (6), Sch 5; and PARA 185.

7 See the Charities Act 2011 ss 73–75; and PARAS 193–194.

540. When the court will interfere. The court does not interfere with the execution of a charitable trust unless it appears that its interference will benefit the charity[1]. However, the court has a general controlling power over all charitable institutions[2]. Thus it can always enforce the performance of trusts and redress breaches of trust, whether the trustee is an individual or an eleemosynary corporation[3], and whether or not the corporation is subject to the control of a visitor[4]. On this ground it exercises jurisdiction with respect to the dealings and conduct of governors who receive and apply the revenues of charity property or manage charity estates[5].

Accordingly, the court may set aside a lease of charity property to one of the governors, though there is no suggestion that the transaction was fraudulent[6], and interfere when a school chapel is turned into a chapel of ease[7], and where the master of a school is collusively appointed and takes his salary without fulfilling the duties of his post[8]. On rare occasions it may be appropriate to appoint a receiver or receiver and manager of a charity[9].

1 *A-G v Bosanquet* (1841) 11 LJCh 43.

2 See *A-G v Governors of Foundling Hospital* (1793) 2 Ves 42 at 49.

3 *Green v Rutherforth* (1750) 1 Ves Sen 462 at 475 per Lord Hardwicke LC; *Re Chertsey Market, ex p Walthew* (1819) 6 Price 261; *A-G v Earl of Clarendon* (1810) 17 Ves 491; *A-G v Earl of Mansfield* (1827) 2 Russ 501; *A-G v Lubbock* (1837) Coop Pr Cas 15; *A-G v Dedham School* (1857) 23 Beav 350; *A-G v St Cross Hospital* (1853) 17 Beav 435; *Willis v Childe* (1851) 13 Beav 117; and see also *A-G v Bedford Corpn* (1754) 2 Ves Sen 505. As to the meaning of 'eleemosynary corporation' see PARA 225.

4 *Daugars v Rivaz* (1860) 28 Beav 233; see also the cases cited in note 3. As to the control of charitable trusts by their visitors see PARA 513 et seq.

5 *Eden v Foster* (1726) 2 P Wms 325; *A-G v Lock* (1744) 3 Atk 164 at 165 per Lord Hardwicke LC; *A-G v Governors of Foundling Hospital* (1793) 2 Ves 42; *A-G v Middleton* (1751) 2 Ves Sen 327; *Ex p Kirkby Ravensworth Hospital* (1808) 15 Ves 305 at 314 per Lord Eldon LC; and note *Hynshaw v Morpeth Corpn* (1629) Duke 69; and *Sutton Colefield Case* (1635) Duke 68.

6 *A-G v Earl of Clarendon* (1810) 17 Ves 491.

7 *A-G v Earl of Mansfield* (1827) 2 Russ 501.

8 *A-G v Bedford Corpn* (1754) 2 Ves Sen 505.

9 *A-G v Schonfeld* [1980] 3 All ER 1, [1980] 1 WLR 1182. As to the statutory power of the Charity Commission to appoint a receiver and manager see PARA 568. As to the Charity Commission see PARAS 543–578. As to receivers generally see **RECEIVERS**.

541. Jurisdiction not excluded by special remedies. The fact that special remedies are given by a statute to another authority or under a special procedure for the infringement of a right does not exclude the ordinary jurisdiction of the court, unless that jurisdiction is expressly excluded by the statute[1].

1 *R v Bishop of Ely* (1738) Andr 176; *Dr Walker's Case* (1736) Lee *temp* Hard 212 at 218 per Lord Hardwicke LC. See also PARA 247 note 2.

542. County court jurisdiction. The county court has jurisdiction in proceedings for the execution of a charitable trust, or for a declaration that a charitable trust subsists, where the fund subject to the trust does not exceed the county court limit[1]. It is doubtful whether it will ever be called upon to exercise this jurisdiction.

1 See the County Courts Act 1984 s 23(b); and **COURTS AND TRIBUNALS** vol 24 (2010) PARA 776. 'County court limit' for the purposes of s 23 is £350,000: see s 147(1) (definition amended by SI 1991/724); the County Court Jurisdiction Order 2014, SI 2014/503, art 3, Table; and the Interpretation Act 1978 s 17(2)(b). Subject to the financial limit, the county court is included within the definition of 'court' in the Charities Act 2011 s 353(1): see PARA 177 note 12. It also has jurisdiction under the Open Spaces Act 1906 s 4 to sanction the transfer of an open space within its district by charity trustees to the local authority: see **OPEN SPACES AND COUNTRYSIDE** vol 78 (2010) PARA 574.

(4) THE CHARITY COMMISSION

(i) Constitution and Functions of the Charity Commission

543. The Charity Commission. The Charity Commission for England and Wales is a statutory body regulated by the Charities Act 2011 with functions under that and other Acts[1]. The functions of the Charity Commission are performed on behalf of the Crown[2] and, in the exercise of its functions, the Commission is not subject to the direction or control of any Minister of the Crown or other government department[3].

The Commission has a number of statutory objectives[4], functions[5] and duties[6]. The Commission has the power to do anything which is calculated to facilitate, or is conducive or incidental to, the performance of any of its functions or general duties[7].

However, the Commission must not exercise functions corresponding to those of a charity trustee in relation to a charity or otherwise be directly involved in the administration of a charity[8].

1 See the Charities Act 2011 s 13. Prior to 27 February 2007, all regulatory powers and duties were vested in the statutory offices of the Charity Commissioners for England and Wales, but on that day the office of Charity Commissioner was abolished by the Charities Act 2006 and the functions, property, rights and liabilities of the Charity Commissioners transferred to a new body corporate, the Charity Commission for England and Wales, which is now established under the Charities Act 2011 s 13(1).

In Welsh, the Commission is known as 'Comisiwn Elusennau Cymru a Lloegr': s 13(2).

As to the continuity of the law in relation to functions of, and acts done by, the Commissioners and their transfer to the Commission, see the Charities Act 2011 Sch 7 para 2, Sch 8 Pt 1.

The Charity Commission is a designated regulator for the purposes of the Regulatory Enforcement and Sanctions Act 2008: see Sch 5; and CONSTITUTIONAL AND ADMINISTRATIVE LAW vol 20 (2014) PARA 331.

2 Charities Act 2011 s 13(3).

3 Charities Act 2011 s 13(4). However, s 13(4) does not affect any provision made by or under any enactment or any administrative control exercised over the Commission's expenditure by the Treasury: s 13(5). As to the Treasury see CONSTITUTIONAL AND ADMINISTRATIVE LAW vol 20 (2014) PARA 262 et seq.

4 See the Charities Act 2011 s 14; and PARA 544.

5 See the Charities Act 2011 s 15; and PARA 545.

6 See the Charities Act 2011 s 16; and PARA 546.

7 Charities Act 2011 s 20(1).

8 Charities Act 2011 s 20(2). However, this does not affect the power of the Commission to give directions as to action to be taken or as to application of charity property under ss 84–85: s 20(3). As to the power to give such directions see PARAS 567, 571.

544. Statutory objectives. The Charity Commission has the following statutory objectives[1]:

(1) the public confidence objective, which is to increase public trust and confidence in charities[2];

(2) the public benefit objective, which is to promote awareness and understanding of the operation of the public benefit requirement[3];

(3) the compliance objective, which is to promote compliance by charity trustees[4] with their legal obligations in exercising control and management of the administration of their charities[5];

(4) the charitable resources objective, which is to promote the effective use of charitable resources[6]; and

(5) the accountability objective, which is to enhance the accountability of charities to donors, beneficiaries and the general public[7].

1 Charities Act 2011 s 14.
2 Charities Act 2011 s 14 para 1. As to the meaning of 'charity' see PARA 1.
3 Charities Act 2011 s 14 para 2. As to the meaning of 'public benefit requirement' see PARA 4.
4 As to the meaning of 'charity trustees' see PARA 1 note 10.
5 Charities Act 2011 s 14 para 3.
It is the role of the Commission to promote compliance by charity trustees with their legal obligations in exercising control and management over the administration of charities and their accountability to donors, beneficiaries and the general public. One aspect of those overarching objectives is to ensure that charity trustees act in accordance with the standards of ordinary prudent men of business and independently of any conflicted party: see *Mountstar (PTC) Ltd v Charity Commission for England and Wales* (2013) First-tier Tribunal, General Regulatory Chamber (Charity), 17 October.
6 Charities Act 2011 s 14 para 4.
7 Charities Act 2011 s 14 para 5. See also note 5.

545. General statutory functions. The Charity Commission has the following statutory general functions[1]:

(1) determining whether institutions are or are not charities[2];
(2) encouraging and facilitating the better administration of charities[3];
(3) identifying and investigating apparent misconduct or mismanagement in the administration of charities and taking remedial or protective action in connection with misconduct or mismanagement therein[4];
(4) obtaining, evaluating and disseminating information in connection with the performance of any of the Commission's functions or meeting any of its objectives[5], including, among other things, the maintenance of an accurate and up-to-date register of charities[6]; and
(5) giving information or advice, or making proposals, to any Minister of the Crown on matters relating to any of the Commission's functions or meeting any of its objectives[7], including among other things, complying, so far as is reasonably practicable, with any request made by a Minister of the Crown for information or advice on any matter relating to any of its functions[8].

As from a day to be appointed[9], the Commission will also have the statutory general function of determining whether public collections certificates should be issued, and remain in force, in respect of public charitable collections[10].

1 Charities Act 2011 s 15(1).
2 Charities Act 2011 s 15(1) para 1.
3 Charities Act 2011 s 15(1) para 2. The Commission may, in connection with this function, give such advice or guidance with respect to the administration of charities as it considers appropriate: s 15(2). Any advice or guidance so given may relate to charities generally, any class of charities, or any particular charity, and may take such form, and be given in such manner, as the Commission considers appropriate: s 15(3).
4 Charities Act 2011 s 15(1) para 3.
5 Charities Act 2011 s 15(1) para 5.
6 Charities Act 2011 s 15(4). As to the register of charities see ss 29, 34; and PARAS 307–320.
7 Charities Act 2011 s 15(1) para 6.
8 Charities Act 2011 s 15(5).
9 The Charities Act 2011 s 15(1) para 4, (6) depend upon the commencement of provisions of the Charities Act 2006, which at the date at which this volume states the law had not been brought into force: see PARA 495.
10 Charities Act 2011 s 15(1) para 4. 'Public charitable collection' and 'public collections certificate' have the same meanings as in the Charities Act 2006 Pt 3 Ch 1 (see PARA 495): Charities Act 2011 s 15(5). As to public charitable collections see PARA 495 et seq. As to public collections certificates see PARA 496.

546. General duties. The Charity Commission has a number of statutory general duties[1]. So far as is reasonably practicable, it must, in performing its functions, act in a way which is (1) compatible with its objectives, and which it considers most appropriate for the purpose of meeting those objectives[2]; and (2) compatible with the encouragement of all forms of charitable giving, and voluntary participation in charity work[3]. In performing its functions, the Commission must have regard to: (a) the need to use its resources in the most efficient, effective and economic way[4]; (b) so far as relevant, the principles of best regulatory practice, including the principles under which regulatory activities should be proportionate, accountable, consistent, transparent and targeted only at cases in which action is needed[5]; and (c) in appropriate cases, have regard to the desirability of facilitating innovation by or on behalf of charities[6]. In managing its affairs the Commission must have regard to such generally accepted principles of good corporate governance as it is reasonable to regard as applicable to it[7].

1 See the Charities Act 2011 s 16.
2 Charities Act 2011 s 16 para 1.
3 Charities Act 2011 s 16 para 2.
4 Charities Act 2011 s 16 para 3.
5 Charities Act 2011 s 16 para 4.
6 Charities Act 2011 s 16 para 5.
7 Charities Act 2011 s 16 para 6.

547. **Publications issued by the Charity Commission.** The Charity Commission produces publications which provide information on a wide range of issues affecting charities, including the Commission's role, the duties of charity trustees and charity law. These publications are available from the Commission[1]. They include information and guidance in relation to, for example, charity trustees[2], charity accounts[3], registration[4], investment[5] and fund raising[6]. The publications are generally for guidance only, although trustees have a duty to have regard to the public benefit guidance[7]. The Commission also publishes the technical publication the *Statement of Recommended Practice for Accounting and Reporting by Charities* (the 'SORP')[8] and various associated documents which set out the recommended best practice and guidance for charities in relation to the preparation of financial reports and accounts.

The Charity Commission is under a duty to make a report to Parliament on its operations during each year; such reports are House of Commons Parliamentary Papers[9].

The Stationery Office used to publish the decisions of the Charity Commissioners[10], which include decisions on points of law and individual cases, and guidance on matters of practice or policy in areas where there is no leaflet available on the subject; decisions made after August 2001 are now published by the Commission on its website[11].

1 For a list of the range of publications available from the Charity Commission see the government website.
2 As to trustees see PARA 331 et seq.
3 As to the duties of charity trustees in relation to accounts see PARA 356 et seq.
4 As to the registration of charities see PARA 307 et seq.
5 As to the duties of charity trustees in relation to investment see PARA 418 et seq.
6 As to the control of charitable fund raising see PARA 464 et seq.
7 See the Charities Act 2011 s 17(5); and PARA 4.
8 As to the SORP see PARA 345 note 12.
9 The reports are published as House of Commons Parliamentary Papers, before 2007 under the titles *Report of the Charity Commissioners for England and Wales* for the appropriate year, and from 2007 onwards under the titles *Report of the Charity Commission for England and Wales* for the appropriate year. See PARA 551. These reports are also available via the website: see note 1.

10 As to the Charity Commissioners, and the transfer of their functions and liabilities to the Charity Commission, see PARA 543.

11 See note 1.

548. Constitution. The Charity Commission consists of a chairman and at least four, but not more than eight, other members[1]. The members must be appointed by the Minister[2], who must exercise his power of appointment so as to secure that: (1) the knowledge and experience of the members of the Commission (taken together) includes knowledge and experience of the law relating to charities, charity accounts and the financing of charities and the operation and regulation of charities of different sizes and descriptions[3]; (2) at least two of the members must have a seven year general qualification[4]; and (3) at least one member, excluding the chairman, must know about conditions in Wales and have been appointed following the necessary consultation requirements[5]. The members of the Commission must hold and vacate office as such in accordance with the terms of their respective appointments[6], and an appointment of a person to hold office as a member of the Commission must be for a term not exceeding three years[7]. No person may hold office as a member of the Commission for more than ten years in total[8]. The Commission must pay to its members such remuneration, and such other allowances, as may be determined by the Minister[9].

The Commission must appoint a chief executive and may appoint such other staff as it may determine[10]. It may establish committees and any of its committees may establish sub-committees[11]. The members of a committee may include persons who are not members of the Commission, and the members of a sub-committee may include persons who are not members of the committee or of the Commission[12].

The Commission may regulate its own procedure, including quorum[13]. The validity of anything done by the Commission is not affected by a vacancy among its members or by a defect in the appointment of a member[14]. Anything authorised or required to be done by the Commission may be done by (a) any member or member of staff of the Commission who is authorised by it for that purpose, whether generally or specially[15]; or (b) any committee of the Commission which has been so authorised[16].

1 Charities Act 2011 Sch 1 para 1(1). Provision was made by the Charities Act 2006 Sch 2 (repealed) for the continuation in office of persons on the abolition of the Charity Commissioners and their replacement with the Charity Commission (see PARA 543). The provisions of the Charities Act 2011 relating to terms of appointment to the Commission, length of term of office and resignation or removal from office (ie Sch 1 paras 2, 3 (see notes 6–7)) do not apply in relation to a person while he holds office as a member of the Commission by virtue of these provisions: Charities Act 2006 Sch 2 para 2(6); Charities Act 2011 Sch 8 Pt 1.

2 Charities Act 2011 Sch 1 para 1(1)(a), (2).

3 Charities Act 2011 Sch 1 para 1(2)(a), (3).

4 Charities Act 2011 Sch 1 para 1(2)(b). The seven year general qualification is a qualification within the meaning of the Courts and Legal Services Act 1990 s 71 (see **LEGAL PROFESSIONS** vol 65 (2015) PARA 540).

5 Charities Act 2011 Sch 1 para 1(2)(c), (4).

6 Charities Act 2011 Sch 1 para 2.

7 Charities Act 2011 Sch 1 para 3(1). A person holding office as a member of the Commission may resign that office by giving notice in writing to the Minister, and may be removed from office by the Minister on the ground of incapacity or misbehaviour: Sch 1 para 3(2). However, before removing a member of the Commission the Minister must consult the Commission and, if the member was appointed following consultation with the Welsh Ministers, those Ministers: Sch 1 para 3(3). As to the Minister see PARA 586. As to the Welsh Ministers see PARA 585.

8 Charities Act 2011 Sch 1 para 3(4). Time spent holding office as a Charity Commissioner for England and Wales is counted as time spent holding office as a member of the Commission: Sch 1 para 3(5) (see note 1). As to the Charity Commissioners, and the transfer of their functions and liabilities to the Charity Commission, see PARA 543.

9 Charities Act 2011 Sch 1 para 4(1). In addition, if required to do so by the Minister, the Commission must pay such pension, allowances or gratuities as may be determined by the Minister to or in respect of a person who is or has been a member of the Commission, or make such payments as may be so determined towards provision for the payment of a pension, allowances or gratuities to or in respect of such a person: Sch 1 para 4(2). If the Minister determines that there are special circumstances which make it right for a person ceasing to hold office as a member of the Commission to receive compensation, the Commission must pay to him a sum by way of compensation of such amount as may be determined by the Minister: Sch 1 para 4(3), (4).

10 Charities Act 2011 Sch 1 para 5(1). The terms and conditions of service of persons so appointed are to be such as the Commission may determine with the approval of the Minister for the Civil Service: Sch 1 para 5(2).

11 Charities Act 2011 Sch 1 para 6(1).

12 Charities Act 2011 Sch 1 para 6(2).

13 Charities Act 2011 Sch 1 para 7(1).

14 Charities Act 2011 Sch 1 para 7(2).

15 Charities Act 2011 Sch 1 para 8(a).

16 Charities Act 2011 Sch 1 para 8(b).

549. Documents. Prima facie evidence of any proclamation, order, or regulation, including any document[1], issued by or under the authority of the Charity Commission may be given in all courts of justice, and in all legal proceedings whatsoever[2].

A document is executed by the Commission by the fixing of its common seal to the document[3], but the fixing of that seal to a document must be authenticated by the signature of any member of the Commission, or any member of its staff, who is authorised for the purpose by the Commission[4]. A document which is expressed (in whatever form of words) to be so executed and is so signed has the same effect as if so executed[5]. A document executed by the Commission which makes it clear on its face that it is intended to be a deed has effect, upon delivery, as a deed; and it is to be presumed (unless a contrary intention is proved) to be delivered upon its being executed[6]. In favour of a purchaser[7], a document is to be deemed to have been duly executed by the Commission if it purports to be signed on its behalf by any member of the Commission or any member of its staff, and, where it makes it clear on its face that it is intended to be a deed, it is to be deemed to have been delivered upon its being executed[8].

As a general rule, the Commission no longer provides paper copies of schemes and orders; they are now usually sent out by email.

1 See the Documentary Evidence Act 1868 s 2, Schedule; Charities Act 2011 Sch 1 para 9(c); and **CIVIL PROCEDURE** vol 11 (2009) PARAS 889, 892.

2 See the Documentary Evidence Act 1868 s 2, Schedule; Charities Act 2011 Sch 1 para 9(a), (b); and **CIVIL PROCEDURE** vol 11 (2009) PARAS 889, 892.

3 Charities Act 2011 Sch 1 para 10(1).

4 Charities Act 2011 Sch 1 para 10(2). 'Authorised' means authorised whether generally or specially: Sch 1 para 10(6).

5 Charities Act 2011 Sch 1 para 10(3).

6 Charities Act 2011 Sch 1 para 10(4).

7 'Purchaser' means a purchaser in good faith for valuable consideration and includes a lessee, mortgagee or other person who for valuable consideration acquired an interest in property: Charities Act 2011 Sch 1 para 10(6).

8 Charities Act 2011 Sch 1 para 10(5).

550. Jurisdiction. Any institution which is a charity within the statutory definition[1] is subject to the jurisdiction of the Charity Commission, but many of the specific powers given to the Commission are not exercisable in relation to exempt charities[2]. It may direct that institutions[3] established for special charitable purposes[4] of or in connection with a charity be treated for all or any of the purposes of the Charities Act 2011 as part of that charity or as forming a distinct charity[5]. They may also direct that for all or any of the purposes of the Charities Act 2011 two or more charities having the same charity trustees[6] are to be treated as a single charity[7].

An appeal against a decision of the Commission not to give such a direction in relation to an institution or charity lies to the Tribunal at the instance of the Attorney General[8] and the trustees of the institution or charity concerned[9]. The Tribunal has the power to quash the decision and, if appropriate, remit the matter to the Commission[10].

1 See the Charities Act 2011 ss 1, 10; and PARAS 1, 196. As to territorial limitations on the operation of the Charities Act 2011 (which does not generally extend to Scotland or Northern Ireland) see s 356(1)–(4); and cf *Re Duncan, Re Taylor's Trusts* (1867) 2 Ch App 356; *Construction Industry Training Board v A-G* [1973] Ch 173, [1972] 2 All ER 1339, CA.

2 See eg the Charities Act 2011 s 30(2)(a) (see PARA 318), s 46(1), (2) (see PARA 559), s 52 and Sch 9 para 13 (see PARA 562), s 115 and Sch 9 para 21 (see PARA 594), s 124(10) (see PARA 404). As to exempt charities see PARAS 318–320. However, note that with the increased regulation of exempt charities a number of these powers are being phased in so far as regards specified exempt charities: see PARA 319.

3 As to the meaning of 'institution' see PARA 1.

4 As to the meaning of 'charitable purposes' see PARA 2.

5 Charities Act 2011 s 12(1).

6 As to the meaning of 'charity trustees' see PARA 255.

7 Charities Act 2011 s 12(2).

8 As to the Tribunal see PARA 579 et seq. As to the Attorney General see PARAS 589, 596, 605 et seq; and CONSTITUTIONAL AND ADMINISTRATIVE LAW vol 20 (2014) PARA 273 et seq.

9 Charities Act 2011 s 319(2), Sch 6 Table Cols 1, 2.

10 Charities Act 2011 Sch 6 Table Col 3.

551. Duty to report. The Charity Commission[1] is required, as soon as practicable after the end of each financial year[2], to publish a report, on the following matters during that year[3]: (1) the discharge of its functions[4]; (2) the extent to which, in its opinion, its objectives have been met[5]; (3) the performance of its general duties[6]; and (4) the management of its affairs[7].

The Charity Commission is subject to investigation by the Parliamentary Commissioner for Administration[8].

1 As to the Charity Commission see PARAS 543–578.

2 'Financial year' means the 12 months ending with 31 March in any year: Charities Act 2011 Sch 1 para 11(3).

3 Charities Act 2011 Sch 1 para 11(1). The reports are published as House of Commons Parliamentary Papers, under the titles *Report of the Charity Commission for England and Wales* for the appropriate year. See further, as to publications of the Charity Commission, PARA 547.

4 Charities Act 2011 Sch 1 para 11(1)(a).

5 Charities Act 2011 Sch 1 para 11(1)(b). As to the Commission's general objectives see s 14; and PARA 544.

6 Charities Act 2011 Sch 1 para 11(1)(c). As to the Commission's general duties see s 16; and PARA 546.

7 Charities Act 2011 Sch 1 para 11(1)(d).

8 See the Parliamentary Commissioner Act 1967 s 4(1), Sch 2; and CONSTITUTIONAL AND ADMINISTRATIVE LAW vol 20 (2014) PARA 634.

552. Annual public meeting. The Charity Commission[1] is required to hold an annual public meeting for the purpose of enabling its annual report[2] to be considered[3]. The meeting must be held within the period of three months beginning with the day on which the report is published[4]. The Commission must organise the annual meeting so as to allow a general discussion of the contents of the report which is being considered and a reasonable opportunity for those attending the meeting to put questions to the Commission about matters to which the report relates[5]. Subject to these restrictions, the annual meeting is to be organised and conducted in such a way as the Commission considers appropriate[6].

The Commission must take such steps as are reasonable in the circumstances to ensure that notice of the annual meeting is given to every registered charity and publish notice of the annual meeting in the way appearing to it to be best calculated to bring it to the attention of members of the public[7], each such notice giving details of the time and place at which the meeting is to be held, setting out the proposed agenda for the meeting, indicating the proposed duration of the meeting and giving details of the Commission's arrangements for enabling persons to attend[8]. If the Commission proposes to alter any of the arrangements which have been included in such notices it must give reasonable notice of the alteration and publish the notice in the way appearing to it to be best calculated to bring it to the attention of registered charities and members of the public[9].

1 As to the Charity Commission see PARAS 543–578.
2 Ie the report that must be made under the Charities Act 2011 Sch 1 para 11: see PARA 551.
3 Charities Act 2011 Sch 1 para 12(1).
4 Charities Act 2011 Sch 1 para 12(2).
5 Charities Act 2011 Sch 1 para 12(3).
6 Charities Act 2011 Sch 1 para 12(4).
7 Charities Act 2011 Sch 1 para 12(5).
8 Charities Act 2011 Sch 1 para 12(6).
9 Charities Act 2011 Sch 1 para 12(7).

553. Specific functions under the Charities Act 2011. The Charity Commission[1] has a number of specific functions and powers under the Charities Act 2011, which are dealt with elsewhere in this title:

(1) the duty to maintain the central register of charities[2] and duties in relation to registration[3];
(2) the power to exchange information with regard to institutions treated as charitable[4];
(3) the jurisdiction to make schemes, to appoint and remove trustees and officers and to make vesting orders in relation to charities[5];
(4) the power to make common investment schemes or common deposit funds[6];
(5) the power to authorise beneficial transactions[7];
(6) the power to authorise ex gratia payments etc[8];
(7) the power to give directions about dormant bank accounts[9];
(8) the power to give advice to charity trustees[10];
(9) the power to determine membership of a charity[11];
(10) the power to provide for the enrolment and preservation of documents belonging to charities[12];
(11) the power to order the taxation of a solicitor's bill of costs for work done for a charity[13];
(12) powers to take legal proceedings and compromise claims[14];

(13) the requirement of its consent to the taking of charity proceedings[15];
(14) the requirement of its consent to the expenditure of charity money on promoting legislation in Parliament[16];
(15) the requirement of its consent to certain dispositions of charity property[17];
(16) the power to relieve trustees and others from liability for breach of trust of duty[18];
(17) the power to amend certificates of incorporation[19];
(18) the power to dissolve defunct incorporated bodies[20];
(19) the requirement of its consent for certain matters relating to charitable companies[21];
(20) the duty to establish and maintain a register of charity mergers and associated duties[22];
(21) as from a day to be appointed, the duties and powers relating to the registration and constitution of charitable incorporated organisations (CIOs)[23].

It also has various powers to act for the protection of charities by inquiry, audit, calling for documents, entering premises and seizing documents, and by giving specific directions and making orders in consequence of their investigations[24].

1 As to the Charity Commission see PARAS 543–578.
2 As to the meaning of 'charities' see PARA 1.
3 See the Charities Act 2011 ss 29–34, 38; and PARAS 307–308.
4 See the Charities Act 2011 ss 54–59; and PARA 321.
5 See the Charities Act 2011 ss 69–72; and PARAS 189, 191–192, 298.
6 See the Charities Act 2011 ss 96–102; and PARAS 426–427.
7 See the Charities Act 2011 s 105; and PARAS 387–390.
8 See the Charities Act 2011 s 106; and PARA 430.
9 See the Charities Act 2011 s 107–109; and PARA 575.
10 See the Charities Act 2011 ss 15, 110; and PARAS 393–394, 545.
11 See the Charities Act 2011 s 111; and PARA 576.
12 See the Charities Act 2011 ss 340–341; and PARAS 398–399.
13 See the Charities Act 2011 s 112; and PARA 648.
14 See the Charities Act 2011 s 114; and PARA 558.
15 See the Charities Act 2011 s 115; and PARA 594.
16 See the Charities Act 2011 s 74(1); and PARA 331 text and note 19.
17 See the Charities Act 2011 s 117; and PARA 401.
18 See the Charities Act 2011 s 191; and PARA 451.
19 See the Charities Act 2011 s 262; and PARA 263.
20 See the Charities Act 2011 s 263; and PARA 265.
21 See the Charities Act 2011 ss 201, 202; and PARA 243.
22 See the Charities Act 2011 ss 305–309; and PARA 322.
23 See the Charities Act 2011 Pt 11 Ch 1: see PARA 226 et seq.
24 See the Charities Act 2011 ss 46–53, 76–85, 48, 49, 147; and PARAS 558–574. As to the exclusion of actions in negligence see *Mills v Winchester Diocesan Board of Finance* [1989] Ch 428, [1989] 2 All ER 317; and PARA 393.

554. Ancillary provisions as to Charity Commission orders. The Charities Act 2011 contains various ancillary provisions in relation to any order made under that Act by the Charity Commission[1]. Thus, an order made by the Commission may include such incidental or supplementary provisions as it thinks expedient for carrying into effect the objects of the order, and where the Commission exercises any jurisdiction to make such an order on an application or reference to them, it may insert any such provisions in the order notwithstanding that the application or reference does not propose their insertion[2]. Where the Commission makes an order under the Charities Act 2011, then it may itself give such public notice as it thinks fit of the making or contents of the order, or may require it to be given by any person on whose application the order is made or by any charity[3] affected by the order[4].

Except for the purposes of discharging the order[5], or for the purposes of an appeal under the Charities Act 2011, an order made by the Commission under the Charities Act 2011 is deemed to have been duly and formally made and is not to be called in question on the ground only of irregularity or informality, and, subject to any further order, has effect according to its tenor[6].

Any order made by the Commission under any provision of the Charities Act 2011 may be varied or revoked by a subsequent order so made[7].

Any direction[8] given by the Commission[9] under any provision contained in the Charities Act 2011 must be given in writing, and may be varied or revoked by a further direction given under that provision[10].

At any time within 12 months of making an order under the Charities Act 2011, the Commission, if it is satisfied that the order was made by mistake or on misrepresentation or otherwise than in conformity with Charities Act 2011, may with or without any application or reference to it discharge the order in whole or in part, and subject or not to any savings or other transitional provisions[11].

1 The provisions of the Charities Act 2011 s 337 (see the text and notes 2–7) also apply to orders under:
   (1) the Places of Worship Registration Act 1855 s 9(1)(b) (see s 9(2) (substituted by the Charities Act 2011 Sch 7 para 5));
   (2) the Open Spaces Act 1906 s 4 (see s 4(4) (substituted by the Charities Act 2011 Sch 7 para 8); and OPEN SPACES AND COUNTRYSIDE vol 78 (2010) PARA 574); and
   (3) the New Parishes Measure 1943 s 14(1)(b) (see s 14(4) (substituted by the Charities Act 2011 Sch 7 para 9); and ECCLESIASTICAL LAW vol 34 (2011) PARA 828).

2 Charities Act 2011 s 337(1), (2). The provisions of s 337 apply in relation to charitable incorporated organisations (CIOs): see the Charitable Incorporated Organisations (General) Regulations 2012, SI 2012/3012, reg 26(5); and PARA 239. As to CIOs see PARA 226 et seq.

3 As to the meaning of 'charity' see PARA 1.

4 Charities Act 2011 s 337(3).

5 Ie under the Charities Act 2011 s 337(4): see the text and note 11.

6 Charities Act 2011 s 337(5).

7 Charities Act 2011 s 337(6).

8 Except a direction contained in an order made by the Commission under the Charities Act 2011 s 335(1) (see PARA 556): s 338(4).

9 For these purposes, the reference to the Commission includes, in relation to a direction under the Charities Act 2011 s 47(2) (see PARA 559), a reference to a person conducting an inquiry under that provision: s 338(3).

10 Charities Act 2011 s 338(1). Section 336 (see PARA 556) (enforcement of orders of the Commission) and s 337(1)–(3), (5) (see the text and notes 2–6) apply to any such directions as they apply to an order of the Commission: s 338(2).

11 Charities Act 2011 s 337(4). This does not apply to an order under s 263 (see PARA 265): see s 337(4)(a).

555. Service of orders and directions. Any order or direction made or given by the Charity Commission[1] under the Charities Act 2011 may be served on a person (other than a body corporate) either by delivering it to that person, or by leaving it at his last known address in the United Kingdom[2], or by sending it by post to him at that address[3]. In the case of a body corporate it may be served by delivering it or sending it by post either to the registered or principal office of the body in the United Kingdom, or, if it has no such office in the United Kingdom, to any place in the United Kingdom where it carries on business or conducts its activities[4]. Any such order or direction may also be served on a person, including a body corporate, by sending it by post to that person at an address notified by that person to the Commission for that purpose[5].

1 For these purposes, the reference to the Commission includes, in relation to a direction under the Charities Act 2011 s 47(2) (see PARA 559), a reference to a person conducting an inquiry under s 46: s 339(5).
2 As to the meaning of 'United Kingdom' see PARA 189 note 17.
3 Charities Act 2011 s 339(1), (2). There are corresponding provisions in relation to any order or direction made or given by the Commission under the Charities Act 1992 Pt II (ss 58–64) or any notice required to be served under Pt 3 (ss 65–74) (not yet in force): see s 76(1)–(4); and PARA 485.
4 Charities Act 2011 s 339(3).
5 Charities Act 2011 s 339(4).

556. Enforcement of Charity Commission orders. A person guilty of disobedience to orders of the Charity Commission:

(1) calling for information or documents[1]; or
(2) in connection with the dissolution of an incorporated body[2]; or
(3) relating to a person acting as a charity trustee or trustee for a charity while disqualified[3]; or
(4) for the protection of certain Scottish charities[4]; or
(5) requiring a transfer of property or payment to be called for or made[5]; or
(6) requiring a default to be made good[6]; or
(7) to take action which the Commission considers to be expedient in the interests of the charity following an inquiry[7]; or
(8) directing the application of property[8]; or
(9) requiring a disqualified trustee to reimburse a charity[9],

may be dealt with on the application of the Commission to the High Court as for disobedience to an order of the High Court[10].

If a person fails to comply with any requirement imposed by or under the Charities Act 2011, the Commission may by order give him such directions as it considers appropriate for securing that the default is made good[11], and disobedience to such an order likewise renders him liable to be dealt with as for disobedience to an order of the High Court[12]. These provisions[13] do not apply, however, to any such requirement imposed by or under the Charities Act 2011 if: (a) the requirement is one imposed by an order of the Commission falling within any of the above provisions[14], or is imposed by a direction of the Commission to which those provisions apply[15]; or (b) a person who fails to comply with, or is persistently in default in relation to, the requirement is liable to any criminal penalty[16].

1 Ie under the Charities Act 2011 s 52(1) (see PARA 562) or regulations under s 155 (see PARA 361).
2 Ie under the Charities Act 2011 s 263: see PARA 265.
3 Ie under the Charities Act 2011 s 184: see PARA 277. As to the meaning of 'charity trustees' see PARA 255. As to the meaning of 'charity' see PARA 1.
4 Ie under the Charities Act 2011 s 87.
5 Ie under the Charities Act 2011 ss 69, 76, 79–81: see PARAS 292, 572–573.
6 See, eg, the Charities Act 2011 s 147(5); and PARA 566.
7 Ie under the Charities Act 2011 s 84: see PARA 567.
8 Ie under the Charities Act 2011 s 85: see PARA 571.
9 Ie under the Charities Act 2011 s 186: see PARA 337.
10 Charities Act 2011 s 336(1), (2). The application is made to a single judge of the Chancery Division: see CPR 81.15(3). As to the enforcement of High Court orders see generally CIVIL PROCEDURE vol 12 (2009) PARA 1223 et seq.

The provisions of the Charities Act 2011 s 336 apply in relation to charitable incorporated organisations (CIOs): see the Charitable Incorporated Organisations (General) Regulations 2012, SI 2012/3012, reg 26(5); and PARA 239. As to CIOs see PARA 226 et seq.

11 Charities Act 2011 s 335(1). As to the application of s 335 to CIOs see the Charitable Incorporated Organisations (General) Regulations 2012, SI 2012/3012, reg 26(6).

12 See the Charities Act 2011 s 336; and text and note 6.

13 Ie the Charities Act 2011 s 335(1): see the text and note 11.

14 Ie the Charities Act 2011 s 336: see the text and notes 1–10.

15 Ie under the Charities Act 2011 s 338(2): see PARA 554.

16 Charities Act 2011 s 335(2).

557. Fees and other amounts payable to Charity Commission. The Minister[1] may by regulations[2] require the payment to the Charity Commission of such fees as may be prescribed by the regulations in respect of the discharge by the Commission of such functions under the enactments relating to charities as may be so prescribed, and the inspection of the register of charities[3] or of other material kept by it under those enactments, or the furnishing of copies of or extracts from documents[4] so kept[5]. Such regulations may confer, or provide for the conferring of, exemptions from liability to pay a prescribed fee, or provide for the remission or refunding of a prescribed fee in prescribed circumstances[6]. The Commission may also impose charges of such amounts as it considers reasonable in respect of the supply of any publications produced by it[7].

1 As to the Minister see PARA 586.

2 Such regulations must be made by statutory instrument: see the Charities Act 2011 s 347(1). At the date at which this volume states the law no such regulations had been made under s 19 but, by virtue of the Interpretation Act 1978 s 17(2)(b), the Charity Commissioners' Fees (Copies and Extracts) Regulations 1992, SI 1992/2986, have effect as if made under it.

3 As to the register of charities see PARA 307.

4 As to the meaning of 'document' see PARA 263 note 2.

5 Charities Act 2011 s 19(1).

6 Charities Act 2011 s 19(2).

7 Charities Act 2011 s 19(3). As to publications issued by the Charity Commission see PARA 547.

(ii) Power to Act for Protection of Charities

558. Power of Charity Commission to bring proceedings with respect to charities. Except that it can present a petition for the winding up of a charitable company only in limited circumstances[1], the Charity Commission may exercise the same powers with respect to the taking of legal proceedings with reference to charities[2] or the property or affairs of charities, or the compromise of claims with a view to avoiding or ending such proceedings, as are exercisable by the Attorney General acting ex officio[3]. The practice and procedure to be followed in relation to any such proceedings are in all respects, and in particular as regards costs, the same as if they were proceedings taken by the Attorney General acting ex officio[4]. No rule of law or practice is to be taken to require the Attorney General to be a party to any such proceedings[5]. Although these powers are exercisable by the Commission of its own motion, they are exercisable only with the agreement of the Attorney General on each occasion[6].

1 Ie under the Charities Act 2011 s 113(2)–(4): see PARA 253.

2 As to the meaning of 'charity' see PARA 1.

3 Charities Act 2011 s 114(1), (2). As to the Attorney General see PARAS 589, 596, 605 et seq; and CONSTITUTIONAL AND ADMINISTRATIVE LAW vol 20 (2014) PARA 273 et seq.

4 Charities Act 2011 s 114(3).

5 Charities Act 2011 s 114(4).

6 Charities Act 2011 s 114(5).

559. Power to institute inquiries. The Charity Commission may from time to time institute inquiries with regard to charities[1] or a particular charity or class of charities, either generally or for particular purposes[2]. No such inquiry may extend to any exempt charity[3] except where it has been requested by its principal regulator[4].

For the purposes of any such inquiry the Commission, or a person appointed by it to conduct the inquiry, may direct any person[5]:

(1) to provide accounts and statements in writing with respect to any matter in question at the inquiry, being a matter on which he has or can reasonably obtain information, or to return answers in writing to any questions or inquiries addressed to him on any such matter, and to verify any such accounts, statements or answers by statutory declaration[6];

(2) to provide copies of documents[7] in his custody or under his control which relate to any matter in question at the inquiry, and to verify the same by statutory declaration[8]; and

(3) also to attend and give evidence or produce any such documents[9].

Where an inquiry has been held under these provisions, the Commission may either cause the report of the person conducting the inquiry or such other statement of the results of the inquiry as it thinks fit to be printed and published, or publish any such report or statement in some other way which is calculated in its opinion to bring it to the attention of persons who might wish to make representations about the action to be taken[10].

An application for the review of a decision of the Commission to institute an inquiry under these provisions with regard to a particular institution lies to the Tribunal at the instance of the Attorney General[11], the persons who have control or management of the institution and, if a body corporate, the institution itself[12]. The Tribunal has the power to direct the Commission to end the inquiry[13].

An application for the review of a decision of the Commission to institute an inquiry under these provisions with regard to a class of institutions lies to the Tribunal at the instance of the Attorney General, the persons who have control or management of any institution which is a member of the class of institutions and, if a body corporate, any such institution[14]. The Tribunal has the power to do either or both of the following: (a) direct the Commission that the inquiry should not consider a particular institution; (b) direct the Commission to end the inquiry[15].

1 As to the meaning of 'charity' see PARA 1.

2 Charities Act 2011 s 46(1). As to determining the matters in respect of which the power conferred by s 46 may be exercised see s 109(6), (7); and PARA 575.

The Commission may either conduct such an inquiry itself or appoint a person to conduct it and make a report to the Commission: s 46(3). This power and the related powers under s 147 (see PARA 566) and s 76 (see PARA 567) have been used in a few cases: see *Report of the Charity Commissioners for England and Wales for 1964* (HC Paper (1965–66) no 8) paras 53–61; *Report of the Charity Commissioners for England and Wales for 1970* (HC Paper (1970–71) no 409) paras 50–52; *Report of the Charity Commissioners for England and Wales for 1971* (HC Paper (1971–72) no 269) paras 90–96; *Report of the Charity Commissioners for England and Wales for 1972* (HC Paper (1972–73) no 259) para 80; *Report of the Charity Commissioners for England and Wales for 1979* (HC Paper (1979–80) no 608) paras 24–36; and *Report of the Charity Commissioners for England and Wales for 1980* (HC Paper (1980–81) no 332) para 31.

For a consideration of the threshold that must be met for the Commission to open an inquiry under this power, and the approach of the Tribunal if it reviews such a decision, see *Regentford v Charity Commission for England and Wales* [2014] UKUT 0364 (TCC).

For the purposes of any such inquiry evidence may be taken on oath, and the person conducting the inquiry may for that purpose administer oaths, or may instead of administering an oath require the person examined to make and subscribe a declaration of the truth of the matters about which he is examined: Charities Act 2011 s 47(3). See generally CIVIL PROCEDURE vol 11 (2009) PARA 749 et seq.

3 As to exempt charities see PARA 318 et seq.
4 Charities Act 2011 s 46(2). As to the phasing in of increased regulation of exempt charities (prior to which the reference to an exception in the case of a request by the principal regulator is omitted), see Sch 9 para 11; and PARA 319.
5 Charities Act 2011 s 47(1), (2). As to directions of the Commission generally see s 338; and PARA 554. As to the service of directions see s 339; and PARA 555.
6 Charities Act 2011 s 47(2)(a).
7 As to the meaning of 'document' see PARA 263 note 2.
8 Charities Act 2011 s 47(2)(b).
9 Charities Act 2011 s 47(2)(c). A person may not be required in obedience to a direction under s 47(2)(c) to go more than ten miles from his place of residence unless the expenses of his attendance are paid to him: see s 47(5); and PARA 560.
10 Charities Act 2011 s 50(1), (2).
11 As to the Tribunal see PARA 579 et seq. As to the Attorney General see PARAS 589, 596, 605 et seq; and CONSTITUTIONAL AND ADMINISTRATIVE LAW vol 20 (2014) PARA 273 et seq.
12 Charities Act 2011 s 319(2), Sch 6 Table Cols 1, 2.
13 Charities Act 2011 Sch 6 Table Col 3.
14 Charities Act 2011 s 319(2), Sch 6 Table Cols 1, 2.
15 Charities Act 2011 Sch 6 Table Col 3.

560. Expenses in relation to inquiries. The Charity Commission may pay to any person the necessary expenses of his attendance to give evidence or produce documents for the purpose of an inquiry[1]. No person may be required, in obedience to a direction to attend and give evidence or produce documents[2], to travel more than ten miles from his residence unless those expenses are paid or tendered to him[3].

A county or district council, a county borough council or London borough council, or the Common Council of the City of London[4] may contribute to the expenses of the Commission in connection with inquiries into local charities[5] in the council's area[6].

1 Charities Act 2011 s 47(4).
2 Ie in obedience to a direction under the Charities Act 2011 s 47(2)(c): see PARA 559.
3 Charities Act 2011 s 47(5).
4 As to the London borough councils and the Common Council of the City of London see LONDON GOVERNMENT vol 71 (2013) PARAS 20 et seq, 34 et seq. As to local government areas and authorities in England and Wales generally see LOCAL GOVERNMENT vol 69 (2009) PARA 22 et seq.
5 As to the meaning of 'local charity' see PARA 189 note 10.
6 Charities Act 2011 s 51(1), (2).

561. Offences in connection with inquiries. Persons wilfully giving false evidence on oath before an inquiry[1] are guilty of perjury[2].

Any person who knowingly or recklessly provides the Charity Commission[3] with information which is false or misleading in a material particular is guilty of an offence[4] if the information was provided in purported compliance with a requirement imposed by or under the Charities Act 2011, or in other circumstances in which the person providing the information intended, or could reasonably be expected to have known, that it would be used by the Commission for the purpose of discharging its functions under that Act[5]. Any person who wilfully alters, suppresses, conceals or destroys any document which he is or is liable to be required, by or under the Charities Act 2011, to produce to the Commission is likewise guilty of an offence[6]. No proceedings may be instituted for either of the above offences except by or with the consent of the Director of Public Prosecutions[7].

Persons who disobey orders calling for information or documents[8] may be dealt with as for disobedience to an order of the High Court[9].

1 As to inquiries see PARA 559.
2 See the Perjury Act 1911 s 1; and **CIVIL PROCEDURE** vol 11 (2009) PARA 1021; **CRIMINAL LAW** vol 26 (2010) PARA 688 et seq.
3 For these purposes, references to the Commission include references to a person conducting an inquiry under the Charities Act 2011 s 46 (see PARA 559): s 60(4).
4 Any person guilty of an offence under the Charities Act 2011 s 60 is liable on summary conviction to a fine not exceeding the statutory maximum, and on conviction on indictment to a term of imprisonment not exceeding two years or to a fine, or both: s 60(3). As to the statutory maximum see **SENTENCING AND DISPOSITION OF OFFENDERS** vol 92 (2010) PARA 140. As to offences by bodies corporate see s 346; and PARA 588.
5 Charities Act 2011 s 60(1).
6 Charities Act 2011 s 60(2). The offender is liable to the punishment set out in note 4.
7 Charities Act 2011 s 345(1), (2)(b). As to the Director of Public Prosecutions see **CRIMINAL PROCEDURE** vol 27 (2010) PARAS 23, 33 et seq.
8 Ie under the Charities Act 2011 s 52(1): see PARA 562.
9 See the Charities Act 2011 s 336; and PARA 556.

562. Power to call for documents. The Charity Commission may by order[1]:

(1) require any person to furnish it with any information in his possession which relates to any charity[2] and is relevant to the discharge of the Commission's functions or of the functions of the official custodian for charities[3];

(2) require any person who has in his custody or under his control any document[4] which relates to any charity and is relevant to the discharge of the Commission's functions or of the functions of the official custodian for charities: (a) to furnish it with a copy of, or extract from, the document; or (b) unless the document forms port of the records or other documents of a court or of a public or local authority, to transmit the document itself to the Commission for its inspection[5].

The Commission may without payment keep any such copies or extracts[6]. Where an original document transmitted to it for inspection relates only to one or more charities and is not held by a person entitled as trustee or otherwise to the custody of it, the Commission may keep it or deliver it to charity trustees[7] or other persons who are so entitled[8].

An appeal against a decision of the Commission requiring a person to supply information or a document under these provisions lies to the Tribunal at the instance of the Attorney General[9] and any person who is required to supply the information or document[10]. The Tribunal has the power to do any of the following: (i) quash the order; (ii) substitute for all or part of the order any other order which could have been made by the Commission[11].

1 Charities Act 2011 s 52(1). A person guilty of disobedience to an order of the Charity Commission under s 52(1) may on the application of the Commission to the High Court be dealt with as for disobedience to an order of the High Court: see s 336(2)(a); and PARA 556.

In relation to exempt charities for whom the increased regulation provisions have not been brought into force, no person properly having the custody of documents relating only to an exempt charity may be required to transmit to the Commission any of those documents or to furnish any copy of, or extracts from, any of them: s 52(1A) (added by Sch 9 para 13). As to exempt charities see PARA 318 et seq; as to the phasing in of increased regulation of exempt charities see PARA 319.

2 As to the meaning of 'charity' see PARA 1.
3 Charities Act 2011 s 52(1)(a). As to the official custodian for charities see PARA 300 et seq.
4 As to the meaning of 'document' see PARA 263 note 2.

5 Charities Act 2011 s 52(1)(b). As to the power to inspect records see PARA 564. As to determining the matters in respect of which the power conferred by the Charities Act 2011 s 52 may be exercised see s 109(6); and PARA 575.
6 Charities Act 2011 s 52(2).
7 As to the meaning of 'charity trustees' see PARA 255.
8 Charities Act 2011 s 52(3).
9 As to the Tribunal see PARA 579 et seq. As to the Attorney General see PARAS 589, 596, 605 et seq; and **CONSTITUTIONAL AND ADMINISTRATIVE LAW** vol 20 (2014) PARA 273 et seq.
10 Charities Act 2011 s 319(2), Sch 6 Table Cols 1, 2. As to ambit of the Tribunal's scope in relation to orders under s 52 see PARA 579 note 6.
11 Charities Act 2011 Sch 6 Table Col 3.

563. Disclosure of information in relation to inquiries. Information held by the Charity Commission as a result of an inquiry[1] falls generally within the exemption from disclosure contained in the Freedom of Information Act 2000[2] relating to court records[3]. Disclosure may nonetheless be required under the common law or other statutory provisions[4], on evaluation of the balance between the competing reasons for and against disclosure[5].

1 Ie an inquiry under what is now the Charities Act 2011 s 46: see PARA 560.
2 Ie the exemption relation to court records, documents and similar materials contained in the Freedom of Information Act 2000 s 32: see **CONSTITUTIONAL AND ADMINISTRATIVE LAW** vol 20 (2014) PARA 446.
3 See *Kennedy v Charity Commission* [2014] UKSC 20 at [101], [2014] 2 All ER 847, [2014] IP & T 733. In so far as this decision rested on charities legislation it was decided under the provisions of the Charities Act 1993.
4 Eg the Commission's general objective under the Charities Act 2011 s 14 to increase public trust and confidence in charities: see PARA 544. Such powers are expressly preserved by the Freedom of Information Act 2000 s 78: see **CONSTITUTIONAL AND ADMINISTRATIVE LAW** vol 20 (2014) PARA 425.
5 See *Kennedy v Charity Commission* [2014] UKSC 20 at [101], [2014] 2 All ER 847, [2014] IP & T 733.

564. Power to inspect records. Any member of staff of the Charity Commission (including the official custodian for charities even if he is not a member of staff of the Commission[1]), if so authorised by it, is entitled without payment to inspect and take copies of or extracts from the records or other documents[2] of any court, public registry or office of records, for any purpose connected with the discharge of the functions of the Commission or of the official custodian for charities[3]. These rights, in relation to information recorded otherwise than in legible form, include the right to require the information to be made available in legible form for inspection or for a copy or extract to be made of or from it[4].

1 Charities Act 2011 s 53(2). As to the official custodian for charities see PARA 300 et seq.
2 As to the meaning of 'document' see PARA 263 note 2.
3 Charities Act 2011 s 53(1).
4 Charities Act 2011 s 53(3).

565. Power to enter premises and seize documents etc. A justice of the peace may issue a warrant if satisfied, on information given on oath by a member of the Charity Commission's staff, that there are reasonable grounds for believing that each of the following conditions is satisfied[1]:

(1) that an inquiry has been instituted[2] by the Commission[3];
(2) that there is on the premises to be specified in the warrant any document or information relevant to that inquiry which the Commission could require[4] to be produced or furnished[5]; and

(3) that, if the Commission were to make an order requiring the document or information to be so produced or furnished, the order would not be complied with or the document or information would be removed, tampered with, concealed or destroyed[6].

Such a warrant authorises the member of the Commission's staff who is named in it to do the following:

(a) to enter and search the premises specified in it[7];

(b) to take such other persons with him as the Commission considers are needed to assist him in doing anything that he is authorised to do under the warrant[8];

(c) to take possession of any documents which appear to fall within head (2) above, or to take any other steps which appear to be necessary for preserving, or preventing interference with, any such documents[9];

(d) to take possession of any computer disk or other electronic storage device which appears to contain information falling within head (2) above, or information contained in a document so falling, or to take any other steps which appear to be necessary for preserving, or preventing interference with, any such information[10];

(e) to take copies of, or extracts from, any documents or information falling within head (c) or head (d) above[11];

(f) to require any person on the premises to provide an explanation of any such document or information or to state where any such documents or information may be found[12];

(g) to require any such person to give him such assistance as he may reasonably require for the taking of copies or extracts as mentioned in head (e) above[13].

Entry and search under such a warrant must be at a reasonable hour and within one month of the date of its issue[14]. The member of the Commission's staff who is authorised under such a warrant must, if required to do so, produce the warrant and documentary evidence that he is a member of the Commission's staff for inspection by the occupier of the premises or anyone acting on his behalf[15].

The member of the Commission's staff who is authorised under such a warrant must make a written record of the date and time of his entry on the premises, the number of persons (if any) who accompanied him onto the premises, and the names of any such persons, the period for which he (and any such persons) remained on the premises, what he (and any such persons) did while on the premises, and any document or device of which he took possession while there[16]. If required to do so, he must give a copy of the record to the occupier of the premises or someone acting on his behalf[17]. Unless it is not reasonably practicable to do so, the member of the Commission's staff who is authorised under such a warrant must comply with these requirements before leaving the premises[18].

Where possession of any document or device is taken under these provisions, the document may be retained for so long as the Commission considers that it is necessary to retain it (rather than a copy of it) for the purposes of the relevant inquiry, or the device may be retained for so long as the Commission considers that it is necessary to retain it for the purposes of that inquiry, as the case may be[19]. Once it appears to the Commission that the retention of any document or device has ceased to be so necessary, it must arrange for the document or device to be returned as soon as is reasonably practicable to the person from whose possession it was taken, or to any of the charity trustees of the charity to which it belonged or related[20].

A person who intentionally obstructs the exercise of any rights conferred by a warrant under this section is guilty of an offence[21].

1 Charities Act 2011 s 48(1).
2 Ie under the Charities Act 2011 s 46: see PARA 559.
3 Charities Act 2011 s 48(2)(a).
4 Ie under the Charities Act 2011 s 52(1): see PARA 562.
5 Charities Act 2011 s 48(2)(b).
6 Charities Act 2011 s 48(2)(c).
7 Charities Act 2011 s 48(3)(a).
8 Charities Act 2011 s 48(3)(b).
9 Charities Act 2011 s 48(3)(c).
10 Charities Act 2011 s 48(3)(d).
11 Charities Act 2011 s 48(3)(e).
12 Charities Act 2011 s 48(3)(f).
13 Charities Act 2011 s 48(3)(g).
14 Charities Act 2011 s 49(1).
15 Charities Act 2011 s 49(2).
16 Charities Act 2011 s 49(3).
17 Charities Act 2011 s 49(4).
18 Charities Act 2011 s 49(5).
19 Charities Act 2011 s 49(6).
20 Charities Act 2011 s 49(7).
21 Charities Act 2011 s 49(8). Such a person is liable on summary conviction to imprisonment for a term not exceeding 51 weeks, a fine not exceeding level 5 on the standard scale, or both: see s 49(9). As to the standard scale see **SENTENCING AND DISPOSITION OF OFFENDERS** vol 92 (2010) PARA 142.

566. Investigation and audit of charity accounts. In the case of a charitable company[1] the Charity Commission may by order require that the condition and relevant accounts[2] of the charity for such period as the Commission thinks fit be investigated and audited by an auditor appointed by it[3]. The Commission must pay the expenses of the audit, including the remuneration of the auditor[4].

The auditor has a right of access to all books, accounts and documents[5] relating to the charity which are in the possession or control of the charity trustees[6] or to which they have access[7]. The auditor is entitled to require from any past or present charity trustee, and from any past or present officer or employee of the charity, such information and explanation as he thinks necessary for the performance of his duties[8]. If a person fails to afford to the auditor any such facilities, the Commission may by order give to that person or to charity trustees for the time being directions as it thinks appropriate for securing that the default is made good[9].

At the conclusion or during the progress of the audit, the auditor must make such reports to the Commission about the audit or the charity's accounts or affairs as he thinks the case requires, and must send a copy of any such report to the charity trustees[10].

An application for a review of an order of the Commission requiring such an audit[11] lies to the Tribunal at the instance of the Attorney General[12], the directors of the company, the company itself and any other person who is or may be affected by the order[13]. The Tribunal has the power to do any of the following: (1) quash the order and, if appropriate, remit the matter to the Commission; (2) substitute for the order any other order which could have been made by the Commission; (3) add to the order anything which could have been contained in an order made by the Commission[14].

An appeal against an order giving directions for securing a default in respect of the provision of information and explanation to an auditor[15], or not to make such an order, lies to the Tribunal at the instance of the Attorney General, the charity trustees, the company itself, the auditor (in the case of decision not to make an order), and any other person who is or may be affected by the order or decision[16]. The Tribunal has the power to do any of the following: (a) quash the order or decision; (b) substitute for the order any other order which could have been made by the Commission; (c) make any order which the Commission could have made[17].

1 As to the meaning of 'charitable company' see PARA 231.
2 Ie the accounts required to be audited under the Companies Act 2006 Pt 16 (see **COMPANIES**): see the Charities Act 2011 s 147(1).
3 Charities Act 2011 s 147(2). The auditor must be a person eligible for appointment as a statutory auditor under the Companies Act 2006 Pt 42 (see **COMPANIES**): Charities Act 2011 s 147(2)(a), (b). As to the use made of this power see PARA 559 note 2.
4 Charities Act 2011 s 147(4).
5 As to the meaning of 'document' see PARA 263 note 2.
6 As to the meaning of 'charity trustees' see PARA 255.
7 Charities Act 2011 s 147(3)(a).
8 Charities Act 2011 s 147(3)(b).
9 Charities Act 2011 s 147(5). As to the enforcement of such an order see PARA 559.
10 Charities Act 2011 s 147(3)(c).
11 Ie under the Charities Act 2011 s 147(2): see text and note 3.
12 As to the Tribunal see PARA 579 et seq. As to the Attorney General see PARAS 589, 596, 605 et seq; and **CONSTITUTIONAL AND ADMINISTRATIVE LAW** vol 20 (2014) PARA 273 et seq.
13 Charities Act 2011 s 319(2), Sch 6 Table Cols 1, 2. As to the meaning of 'person who is or may be affected' within the meaning of Sch 6 see PARA 317 note 8.
14 Charities Act 2011 Sch 6 Table Col 3.
15 Ie under the Charities Act 2011 s 147(5): see text and note 9.
16 Charities Act 2011 s 319(2), Sch 6 Table Cols 1, 2. See note 13.
17 Charities Act 2011 Sch 6 Table Col 3.

567. Power to protect charities from mismanagement. Where, at any time after it has instituted an inquiry[1], the Charity Commission is satisfied[2] that there is or has been any misconduct or mismanagement[3] in the administration of the charity[4] or that it is necessary or desirable to act for the purpose of protecting the property of the charity or securing a proper application for the purposes of the charity of that property or of property coming to the charity[5]; it may of its own motion do one or more of the following things, namely[6]:

(1) by order suspend any trustee, charity trustee, officer, agent or employee of the charity from the exercise of his office or employment pending consideration being given to his removal, whether under these provisions or otherwise[7];
(2) by order appoint such number of additional charity trustees as it considers necessary for the proper administration of the charity[8];
(3) by order vest any property held by or in trust for the charity in the official custodian for charities, or require the persons in whom any such property is vested to transfer it to him, or appoint any person to transfer any such property to him[9];
(4) order any person who holds any property on behalf of the charity, or of any trustee for it, not to part with the property without the approval of the Commission[10];

(5) order any debtor of the charity not to make any payment in or towards the discharge of his liability to the charity without the approval of the Commission[11];

(6) by order restrict, notwithstanding anything in the trusts of the charity, the transactions which may be entered into, or the nature or amount of the payments which may be made, in the administration of the charity without the approval of the Commission[12];

(7) by order appoint an interim manager who must act as receiver and manager in respect of the property and affairs of the charity[13];

(8) by order direct the charity trustees, any trustee of the charity, any officer or employee of the charity or, if a body corporate, the charity itself to take any action specified in the order which the Commission considers to be expedient in the interests of the charity[14].

The Commission must, at such intervals as it thinks fit, review any order made by it under these provisions, other than one appointing additional charity trustees[15] or one directing action it considers expedient[16], and if it appears to them that it would be appropriate to discharge the order in whole or in part, they must so discharge it, whether subject to any savings or other transitional provisions or not[17].

Further, if both heads (1) and (2) above are satisfied, the Commission may of its own motion do either or both of the following things[18]:

(a) by order remove any trustee, charity trustee, officer, agent or employee of the charity who has been responsible for or privy to the misconduct or mismanagement or has by his conduct contributed to it or facilitated it[19];

(b) by order establish a scheme for the administration of the charity[20].

For these purposes, misconduct or mismanagement extends, notwithstanding anything in the trusts[21] of the charity, to the employment for the remuneration or reward of persons acting in the affairs of the charity, or for other administrative purposes, of sums which are excessive in relation to the property which is likely to be applied or applicable for the purposes of the charity[22].

Where the Commission makes such an order removing a person from his office or employment under the above provisions, and that person is a member of the charity[23], then the Commission may also make an order terminating his membership of the charity and prohibiting him from resuming it without the Commission's consent[24].

An appeal against an of the order of the Commission under heads (1) to (7) or (a) to (b) above lies to the Tribunal at the instance of the Attorney General[25], the charity trustees of the charity, the charity itself (if a body corporate), any person suspended by the order, and any other person who is or may be affected by the order[26]. The Tribunal has the power to do any of the following: (i) quash the order in whole or in part and, if appropriate, remit the matter to the Commission; (ii) substitute for all or part of the order any other order which could have been made by the Commission; (iii) add to the order anything which could have been made by the Commission[27].

An appeal against an order of the Commission under head (8) above lies to the Tribunal at the instance of the Attorney General and any person who is directed by the order to take the specified action[28]. The Tribunal has the power to quash the order and, if appropriate, remit the matter to the Commission[29].

An appeal against a decision of the Commission to discharge, or not to discharge an order[30] following a review lies to the Tribunal at the instance of the

Attorney General, the charity trustees of the charity to which the order relates, the charity itself (if a body corporate), any person suspended by it and any other person who is or may be affected by the order[31]. The Tribunal has the power to do any of the following: (A) quash the decision and, if appropriate, remit the matter to the Commission; (B) make the discharge of the order subject to savings or transitional provisions; (C) remove any such savings or transitional provisions; (D) discharge the order in whole or in part, whether subject to any savings or other transitional provisions or not[32].

1 Ie under the Charities Act 2011 s 46: see PARAS 559–560.
2 Charities Act 2011 s 76(1).
3 As to the meaning of 'misconduct or mismanagement' see the text to notes 20–21.
4 Charities Act 2011 s 76(1)(a). As to the meaning of 'charity' see PARA 1.
Sections 76–82 do not apply to exempt charities for whom the increased regulation provisions have not been brought into force: s 82A (added by Sch 9 para 18). See also s 81(3). As to exempt charities see PARA 318 et seq; as to the phasing in of increased regulation of exempt charities see PARA 319.
5 Charities Act 2011 s 76(1)(b).
6 Charities Act 2011 s 76(3). A person guilty of disobedience to an order of the Commission under the Charities Act 2011 s 84 requiring a transfer of property or payment to be called for or made, may on the application of the Commission to the High Court be dealt with as for disobedience to an order of the High Court: see s 336; and PARA 556.
The power of the Commission under s 76 to remove or appoint charity trustees of its own motion includes power to make any such order with respect to the vesting in or transfer to the charity trustees of any property as the Commission could make on the removal or appointment of a charity trustee by it under s 69: s 81(1). As to the meaning of 'charity trustees' see PARA 255.
7 Charities Act 2011 s 76(3)(a). See *Jones v A-G* [1974] Ch 148, [1973] 3 All ER 518, CA; further proceedings (1976) Times, 10 November. The power of the Commission to make an order under the Charities Act 2011 s 76(3)(a) is not exercisable so as to suspend any person from the exercise of his office or employment for a period of more than 12 months: s 76(4). However, without prejudice to the generality of the Charities Act 2011 s 337(1), (2) (see PARA 554), any such order made in the case of any person may make provision as respects the period of his suspension for matters arising out of it, and in particular for enabling any person to execute any instrument in his name or otherwise act for him and, in the case of a charity trustee, for adjusting any rules governing the proceedings of the charity trustees to take account of the reduction in the number capable of acting: s 76(5).
Where the Commission makes such an order suspending a person his office or employment under the above provisions, and that person is a member of the charity, then the Commission may also make an order suspending his membership of the charity for the period for which he is suspended from his office or employment: s 83(1), (2).
An appeal against such an order which suspends a person's membership of a charity lies to the Tribunal at the instance of the Attorney General, the person whose membership is affected and any other person who is or may be affected by the order: Charities Act 2011 s 319(2), Sch 6 Table Cols 1, 2. The Tribunal has the power to quash the order and, if appropriate, remit the matter to the Commission: Sch 6 Table Col 3.
8 Charities Act 2011 s 76(3)(b).
9 Charities Act 2011 s 76(3)(c). As to the official custodian for charities see PARA 300 et seq.
10 Charities Act 2011 s 76(3)(d). Contravention of an order under s 76(3)(d), (e) or (f) (see the text and notes 11–12) is an offence punishable on summary conviction with a fine not exceeding level 5 on the standard scale: s 77(1), (2). As to the standard scale see **SENTENCING AND DISPOSITION OF OFFENDERS** vol 92 (2010) PARA 142. However, proceedings for such an offence may only be instituted by or with the consent of the Director of Public Prosecutions: s 345(1), (2)(c). As to the Director of Public Prosecutions see **CRIMINAL PROCEDURE** vol 27 (2010) PARAS 23, 33 et seq. Section 77(1), (2) is not to be taken to preclude the bringing of proceedings for breach of trust against any charity trustee or trustee for a charity in respect of any such contravention of an order under s 76(3)(d) or (f), whether the proceedings in respect of the contravention are brought against him under s 77 or not: s 77(3). As to offences by bodies corporate see PARA 588.
11 Charities Act 2011 s 76(3)(e). Contravention of such an order is an offence: see note 10.
12 Charities Act 2011 s 76(3)(f). Contravention of such an order is an offence: see note 10.

13 Charities Act 2011 s 76(3)(g). The appointment must be made in accordance with the Charities Act 2011 s 78 (see PARA 568): see s 76(3)(g).
14 See the Charities Act 2011 s 84(1), (2). Such an order may require action to be taken whether or not it would otherwise be within the powers exercisable by the person or persons concerned, or by the charity, in relation to the administration of the charity or to its property, but may not require any action to be taken which is prohibited by any Act of Parliament or expressly prohibited by the trusts of the charity or is inconsistent with its purposes: s 84(3). Anything done by a person or body under the authority of an order under s 84 is deemed to be properly done in the exercise of these powers but this does not affect any contractual or other rights arising in connection with anything which has been done under the authority of such an order: s 84(4), (5).
15 Ie under the Charities Act 2011 s 76(3)(b): see the text and note 8.
16 Ie under the Charities Act 2011 s 84(1), (2): see the text and note 15.
17 Charities Act 2011 s 76(6).
18 Charities Act 2011 s 79(1), (2).
19 Charities Act 2011 s 79(2)(a). See *Scargill v Charity Comrs* (4 September 1998, unreported), Ch D, noted in (1998) 12 TLI 254.
20 Charities Act 2011 s 79(2)(b).
21 As to the meaning of 'trusts' see PARA 218 note 5.
22 Charities Act 2011 s 76(2).
23 Charities Act 2011 s 83(3).
24 Charities Act 2011 s 83(4). If an application for the Commission's consent under s 83(4)(b) is made five years or more after the order was made, the Commission must grant the application unless satisfied that, by reason of any special circumstances, it should be refused: s 83(5).
25 As to the Tribunal see PARA 579 et seq. As to the Attorney General see PARAS 589, 596, 605 et seq; and **CONSTITUTIONAL AND ADMINISTRATIVE LAW** vol 20 (2014) PARA 273 et seq.
26 Charities Act 2011 s 319(2), Sch 6 Table Cols 1, 2. As to the meaning of 'person who is or may be affected' within the meaning of Sch 6 see PARA 317 note 8.
27 Charities Act 2011 Sch 6 Table Col 3.
28 Charities Act 2011 s 319(2), Sch 6 Table Cols 1, 2. See note 26.
29 Charities Act 2011 s 319(2), Sch 6 Table Col 3.
30 Ie under the Charities Act 2011 s 76(6): see text and note 17.
31 Charities Act 2011 s 319(2), Sch 6 Table Cols 1, 2.
32 Charities Act 2011 s 319(2), Sch 6 Table Col 3. See note 26.

568. Power to appoint interim manager for a charity. The Charity Commission may appoint[1] to be interim manager in respect of the property and affairs of a charity[2] such person, other than a member of its staff, as it thinks fit[3]. The order appointing him may make provision with respect to the functions to be discharged by the interim manager appointed by the order, and those functions are to be discharged by him under the supervision of the Commission[4]. In connection with the discharge of those functions any such order may provide for the interim manager appointed by the order to have such powers and duties of the charity trustees[5] of the charity concerned, whether arising under the Charities Act 2011 or otherwise, as are specified in the order, and for such powers or duties to be performed by the interim manager to the exclusion of the charity trustees[6]. The Commission has the same power to advise an interim manager as it has to advise charity trustees[7], and it may apply to the High Court for directions in relation to any particular matter arising in connection with the functions of the interim manager[8]. The High Court may on such an application give such directions, or make such orders declaring the rights of any persons, whether before the court or not, as it thinks just, and the costs of any such application must be paid by the charity concerned[9].

Regulations made by the Minister[10] may make provision with respect to the appointment and removal of persons appointed in accordance with these provisions, the remuneration of such persons out of the income of the charities concerned and the making of reports to the Commission by such persons[11]. Such regulations may, in particular, authorise the Commission to require security for the due discharge of his functions to be given by a person so appointed, to determine the amount of such a person's remuneration and to disallow any amount of remuneration in such circumstances as are prescribed by the regulations[12].

1 Ie under the Charities Act 2011 s 76(3)(g): see PARA 567.
2 As to the meaning of 'charity' see PARA 1.
3 Charities Act 2011 s 78(1).
4 Charities Act 2011 s 78(2), (3). Section 78(2) does not affect the generality of s 337(1), (2) (inclusion of incidental or supplemental provisions in the Commission's orders) (see PARA 554): see s 78(2).
5 As to the meaning of 'charity trustees' see PARA 255.
6 Charities Act 2011 s 78(4).
7 Ie under the Charities Act 2011 s 110: see PARAS 393–394.
8 Charities Act 2011 s 78(5).
9 Charities Act 2011 s 78(6), (7).
10 As to the Minister see PARA 586.
11 Charities Act 2011 s 78(8). By virtue of the Interpretation Act 1978 s 17(2)(b), the Charities (Receiver and Manager) Regulations 1992, SI 1992/2355, have effect as if made under the Charities Act 2011 s 78: see PARAS 569–570. As to the making of regulations generally see the Charities Act 2011 s 347; and as to the power to make regulations amending charity legislation in light of changes in company law see PARA 590.
12 Charities Act 2011 s 78(9); and see PARAS 569–570.

569. Appointment, remuneration and removal of the interim manager. The Charity Commission[1] is authorised to require the person appointed by order to be receiver and manager in respect of the property and affairs of the charity (the 'appointed person')[2] to give security to it for the due discharge of his functions within such time and in such form as it may specify[3]. It is also authorised to determine the amount of an appointed person's remuneration[4], which is payable out of the income of the relevant charity[5].

Where it appears to the Commission that an appointed person has failed: (1) to give security within such time or in such form as it has specified[6]; or (2) satisfactorily to discharge any function imposed on him by or by virtue of the relevant order[7] or in relation to the report made by him to the Commission[8], and it wishes to consider exercising its powers to disallow any amount of remuneration[9] or remove the appointed person[10], it must give him, whether in person or by post, a written notice complying with the following requirements[11]. Such a notice must inform him of:

(a) any such failure in respect of which the notice is issued[12];
(b) the Commission's power to authorise the disallowance of any amount of remuneration if satisfied as to any such failure[13];
(c) its power to remove him if satisfied as to any such failure[14]; and
(d) his right to make representations to it in respect of any such alleged failure within such reasonable time as is specified in the notice[15].

The Commission is authorised to disallow any amount of remuneration of an appointed person where, on the expiry of the time specified in the notice[16] for making representations and after consideration of such representations, if any, as are duly made in response to such a notice, it is satisfied that he has failed to give security or satisfactorily discharge any of his functions in such manner as is set out in the notice[17]. In addition, on the expiry of the time specified in the notice and after consideration of such representations, if any, as are duly made in response to such a notice, the Commission may remove an appointed person where it is satisfied that he has failed in such manner as is specified in the notice, whether or not it also exercises its power to disallow any amount of remuneration[18].

1 The Charities (Receiver and Manager) Regulations 1992, SI 1992/2355, make the provisions detailed in this paragraph with reference to the Charity Commissioners; this takes effect as a reference to the Charity Commission: see PARA 543. As to the Charity Commissioners, and the transfer of their functions and liabilities to the Charity Commission, see PARA 543.
2 Ie the interim manager appointed by order under the Charities Act 2011 s 76(3)(g) (see PARA 567) to be receiver and manager in respect of the property and affairs of a charity: Charities (Receiver and Manager) Regulations 1992, SI 1992/2355, reg 1(2); Interpretation Act 1978 s 17(2)(b).
3 Charities (Receiver and Manager) Regulations 1992, SI 1992/2355, reg 2.
4 Charities (Receiver and Manager) Regulations 1992, SI 1992/2355, reg 3(1).
5 Charities (Receiver and Manager) Regulations 1992, SI 1992/2355, reg 3(2). 'Relevant charity' means the charity in respect of which that person was appointed: reg 1(2).
6 Charities (Receiver and Manager) Regulations 1992, SI 1992/2355, reg 4(1)(a).
7 'Relevant order' means the order by which that person was appointed: Charities (Receiver and Manager) Regulations 1992, SI 1992/2355, reg 1(2).
8 Ie a report made under the Charities (Receiver and Manager) Regulations 1992, SI 1992/2355, reg 5: see PARA 570.
9 Charities (Receiver and Manager) Regulations 1992, SI 1992/2355, reg 4(1)(b). The text refers to the Commission's powers under reg 3(3): see the text and note 17.
10 Ie its powers under the Charities (Receiver and Manager) Regulations 1992, SI 1992/2355, reg 4(3): see the text to note 18.
11 Charities (Receiver and Manager) Regulations 1992, SI 1992/2355, reg 4(1).
12 Charities (Receiver and Manager) Regulations 1992, SI 1992/2355, reg 4(2)(a).
13 Charities (Receiver and Manager) Regulations 1992, SI 1992/2355, reg 4(2)(b). The text refers to the Commission's power under reg 3(3): see the text and note 17.
14 Charities (Receiver and Manager) Regulations 1992, SI 1992/2355, reg 4(2)(c). The text refers to the Commission's power under reg 4(3): see the text to note 18.
15 Charities (Receiver and Manager) Regulations 1992, SI 1992/2355, reg 4(2)(d).
16 Ie the notice referred to in the Charities (Receiver and Manager) Regulations 1992, SI 1992/2355, reg 4(2): see the text and notes 12–15.
17 Charities (Receiver and Manager) Regulations 1992, SI 1992/2355, reg 3(3). The text refers to the appointed person having failed in such manner as is set out in reg 4(1)(a) or (b): see the text to notes 6, 9.
18 Charities (Receiver and Manager) Regulations 1992, SI 1992/2355, reg 4(3).

570. Reports by the appointed interim manager. Reports which are to be made to the Charity Commission[1] by the person appointed to be interim manager[2], in addition to the matters which are required to be included set out below, may also include particulars of any matter which, in the opinion of the appointed person, should be brought to the Charity Commission's attention[3]. An appointed person must make a report to the Charity Commission not later than three months after the date of his appointment setting out[4]:

(1) an estimate by him of the total value of the property of the relevant charity[5] on, or shortly after, the date of his appointment[6];
(2) such information about the property and affairs of the relevant charity immediately prior to his appointment as he believes should be included in the report, notwithstanding that it may also be eventually included in another report[7];
(3) his strategy for discharging the functions conferred on him by or by virtue of the relevant order[8].

For as long as an appointed person holds office as such, he must make a report to the Charity Commission not later than one month after each anniversary of his appointment setting out[9]:

(a) an estimate by him of the total value of the property of the relevant charity on that anniversary of his appointment in respect of which the report is required to be made[10];

(b) a summary of the discharge by him of the functions conferred on him by or by virtue of the relevant order during the 12 months ending with that anniversary[11]; and

(c) where there are changes to his strategy as last set out in a report[12] those changes[13].

An appointed person must make a report to the Charity Commission not later than three months after the date when he ceased to hold office as such setting out[14]: (i) an estimate by him of the total value of the property of the relevant charity on that date[15]; and (ii) a summary of the discharge by him of the functions conferred on him by or by virtue of the relevant order during the period ending with that date and beginning with either the date of his appointment, or if that date is more than 12 months before the date when he ceased to hold office as an appointed person, the day immediately after the last anniversary of his appointment[16].

1 See PARA 569 note 1. As to the Charity Commissioners, and the transfer of their functions and liabilities to the Charity Commission, see PARA 543.
2 See PARA 569 note 2.
3 Charities (Receiver and Manager) Regulations 1992, SI 1992/2355, reg 5(1).
4 Charities (Receiver and Manager) Regulations 1992, SI 1992/2355, reg 5(2).
5 As to the meaning of 'relevant charity' see PARA 569 note 5.
6 Charities (Receiver and Manager) Regulations 1992, SI 1992/2355, reg 5(2)(a).
7 Charities (Receiver and Manager) Regulations 1992, SI 1992/2355, reg 5(2)(b). The text refers to a report which may be made under the Charities Act 2011 s 50 (see PARAS 559–560): Charities (Receiver and Manager) Regulations 1992, SI 1992/2355, reg 5(2)(b); Interpretation Act 1978 s 17(2)(b).
8 Charities (Receiver and Manager) Regulations 1992, SI 1992/2355, reg 5(2)(c). As to the meaning of 'relevant order' see PARA 569 note 7.
9 Charities (Receiver and Manager) Regulations 1992, SI 1992/2355, reg 5(3).
10 Charities (Receiver and Manager) Regulations 1992, SI 1992/2355, reg 5(3)(a).
11 Charities (Receiver and Manager) Regulations 1992, SI 1992/2355, reg 5(3)(b).
12 Ie changes to his strategy as last set out in a report in accordance with the Charities (Receiver and Manager) Regulations 1992, SI 1992/2355, reg 5(2)(c) (see head (3) in the text) or reg 5(3)(c) (see head (c) in the text): see reg 5(3)(c).
13 Charities (Receiver and Manager) Regulations 1992, SI 1992/2355, reg 5(3)(c).
14 Charities (Receiver and Manager) Regulations 1992, SI 1992/2355, reg 5(4), which is expressed to be subject to reg 5(5): see note 16.
15 Charities (Receiver and Manager) Regulations 1992, SI 1992/2355, reg 5(4)(a). See note 16.
16 Charities (Receiver and Manager) Regulations 1992, SI 1992/2355, reg 5(4)(b). Regulation 5(4) does not apply where an appointed person ceased to hold office one month or less after an anniversary of his appointment and a report had been made to the Charity Commission in accordance with heads (a)–(c) in the text in respect of that anniversary: reg 5(5).

571. Power to direct application of trust property. Where the Charity Commission is satisfied that a person, or persons, in possession or control of any property held by or on trust for a charity is, or are, unwilling to apply it properly for the purposes of the charity and that it is necessary or desirable for the purpose of securing a proper application of that property for the purposes of the charity[1], it may by order direct the person or persons concerned to apply the property in such manner as is specified in the order[2]. Such an order may require action to be taken whether or not it would otherwise be within the powers exercisable by the person or persons concerned in relation to the property[3], but may not require any action to be taken which is prohibited by any Act of Parliament or expressly prohibited by the trusts of the charity[4].

An appeal against such an order lies to the Tribunal at the instance of the Attorney General[5] and any person who is directed by the order to apply the property in the specified manner[6]. The Tribunal has the power to quash the order and, if appropriate, remit the matter to the Commission[7].

1 Charities Act 2011 s 85(1).
2 Charities Act 2011 s 85(2).
3 Anything done by a person under the authority of such an order must be deemed to be properly done in the exercise of these powers: Charities Act 2011 s 85(4). This does not affect any contractual or other rights arising in connection with anything which has been done under the authority of such an order: s 85(5).
4 Charities Act 2011 s 85(3).
5 As to the Tribunal see PARA 579 et seq. As to the Attorney General see PARAS 589, 596, 605 et seq; and **CONSTITUTIONAL AND ADMINISTRATIVE LAW** vol 20 (2014) PARA 273 et seq.
6 Charities Act 2011 s 319(2), Sch 6 Table Cols 1, 2.
7 Charities Act 2011 Sch 6 Table Col 3.

572. Power to remove and appoint charity trustees. The Charity Commission has power to remove a charity trustee[1] by order made of its own motion[2]:

(1) where, within the last five years, the trustee[3]:
  (a) having previously been adjudged bankrupt or had his estate sequestrated, has been discharged[4]; or
  (b) having previously made a composition or arrangement with, or granted a trust deed for, his creditors, has been discharged in respect of it[5];
  (c) having previously been the subject of a debt relief order, has been discharged from all the disqualifying debts under the debt relief order[6];
(2) where the trustee is a corporation in liquidation[7];
(3) where the trustee is incapable of acting by reason of mental disorder within the meaning of the Mental Health Act 1983[8];
(4) where the trustee has not acted and will not declare his willingness or unwillingness to act[9]; or
(5) where the trustee is outside England and Wales or cannot be found or does not act, and his absence or failure to act impedes the proper administration of the charity[10].

The Commission may by order made of its own motion appoint a person to be a charity trustee of a charity[11]:

(i) in place of a charity trustee removed by the Commission under these provisions or otherwise[12];
(ii) where there are no charity trustees, or where by reason of vacancies in their number or the absence or incapacity of any of their number the charity cannot apply for the appointment[13];
(iii) where there is a single charity trustee, not being a corporation aggregate, and the Commission is of opinion that it is necessary for the proper administration of the charity to increase the number[14]; or
(iv) where the Commission is of the opinion that it is necessary for the proper administration of the charity to have an additional trustee because one of the existing charity trustees who ought nevertheless to remain a charity trustee is outside England and Wales or cannot be found, or does not act[15].

An order for the appointment or removal of a charity trustee or trustee for a charity, or for the vesting or transfer of property under these powers, has the same effect as a similar order[16] made on the application of the charity or of other persons[17].

An appeal against an order of the Commission removing a charity trustee[18] lies to the Tribunal at the instance of the Attorney General[19], the charity trustee, the remaining charity trustees of the charity of which he was a charity trustee, the charity itself (if a body corporate) and any other person who is or may be affected by the order[20]. An appeal against an order of the Commission appointing a charity trustee[21] lies to the Tribunal at the instance of the Attorney General, the other charity trustees of the charity, the charity itself (if a body corporate) and any other person who is or may be affected by the order[22].

In either case, the Tribunal has the power to do any of the following: (A) quash the order in whole or in part and, if appropriate, remit the matter to the Commission; (B) substitute for all or part of the order any other order which could have been made by the Commission; (C) add to the order anything which could have been contained in an order made by the Commission[23].

1 As to the meaning of 'charity trustees' see PARA 255.
The Charities Act 2011 ss 76–82 do not apply to exempt charities for whom the increased regulation provisions have not been brought into force: see ss 80(4), 82A (added by Sch 9 para 18). As to exempt charities see PARA 318 et seq; as to the phasing in of increased regulation of exempt charities see PARA 319.
2 Charities Act 2011 s 80(1). The powers of the Commission under s 80 to remove or appoint charity trustees of its own motion includes power to make any such order with respect to the vesting in or transfer to the charity trustees of any property as the Commission could make on the removal or appointment of a charity trustee by it under s 69 (see PARAS 189, 191–192, 298): s 81(1). The vesting or transfer of any property in accordance with such an order does not operate as a breach of any covenant or condition against alienation or give rise to a forfeiture: see PARA 189 note 6.
3 Charities Act 2011 s 80(1)(a).
4 Charities Act 2011 s 80(1)(a)(i), (3). See generally **BANKRUPTCY AND INDIVIDUAL INSOLVENCY.**
5 Charities Act 2011 s 80(1)(a)(ii). See generally **BANKRUPTCY AND INDIVIDUAL INSOLVENCY.**
6 Charities Act 2011 s 80(1)(a)(iii) (added by SI 2012/2404). See **BANKRUPTCY AND INDIVIDUAL INSOLVENCY** vol 5 (2013) PARA 91.
7 Charities Act 2011 s 80(1)(b). See **COMPANIES.**
8 Charities Act 2011 s 80(1)(c). As to mental disorders within the meaning of the Mental Health Act 1983 see **MENTAL HEALTH AND CAPACITY** vol 75 (2013) PARA 761.
9 Charities Act 2011 s 80(1)(d).
10 Charities Act 2011 s 80(1)(e).
11 Charities Act 2011 s 80(2).
12 Charities Act 2011 s 80(2)(a).
13 Charities Act 2011 s 80(2)(b).
14 Charities Act 2011 s 80(2)(c).
15 Charities Act 2011 s 80(2)(d).
16 Ie under the Charities Act 2011 s 69: see PARAS 189, 191–192, 298.
17 Charities Act 2011 s 81(2). See also note 2.
18 Ie under the Charities Act 2011 s 80(1): see notes 3–10.
19 As to the Tribunal see PARA 579 et seq. As to the Attorney General see PARAS 589, 596, 605 et seq; and **CONSTITUTIONAL AND ADMINISTRATIVE LAW** vol 20 (2014) PARA 273 et seq.
20 Charities Act 2011 s 319(2), Sch 6 Table Cols 1, 2. As to the meaning of 'person who is or may be affected' within the meaning of Sch 6 see PARA 317 note 8.
21 Ie under the Charities Act 2011 s 80(2): see notes 11–15.
22 Charities Act 2011 s 319(2), Sch 6 Table Cols 1, 2. See note 20.
23 Charities Act 2011 Sch 6 Table Col 3.

573. Notice of orders. Before exercising any of the powers relating to the protection of charities[1], other than the emergency powers[2], the Charity

Commission must give notice[3] to each of the charity trustees[4] of its intention to do so[5]. It must also normally give public notice of its intention to make orders appointing, discharging or removing a charity trustee or trustee for a charity[6].

Before making an order removing a charity trustee or trustee for a charity or officer, employee or agent of a charity, without his consent, the Commission must give him not less than one month's notice of its proposal inviting representations to be made to it within a time specified in the notice, save where he cannot be found or has no known address in the United Kingdom[7].

1 Ie the jurisdiction under the Charities Act 2011 ss 79, 80: see PARAS 567, 572.
2 Ie under the Charities Act 2011 s 76(1): see PARA 567.
3 Notice may be given by post and, if so, may be addressed to the recipient's last known address in the United Kingdom: Charities Act 2011 s 82(2). As to the meaning of 'United Kingdom' see PARA 189 note 17.
4 However, notice need not be given to any that cannot be found or has no known address in the United Kingdom: Charities Act 2011 s 82(1). As to the meaning of 'charity trustees' see PARA 255.
5 Charities Act 2011 s 82(1).
6 See the Charities Act 2011 s 89(1), (2); and PARA 292.
7 Charities Act 2011 s 89(5). As to the contents of the notice see s 89(7); and PARA 292.

The Commission must take into account any representations made to it within the period specified in the notice, and may (without further notice) proceed with the proposals either without modifications or with such modifications as it thinks desirable: see s 89(6); and PARA 292.

Notice (other than public notice) may be given by post and, if given by post, be addressed to the recipient's last known address in the United Kingdom: see s 89(8); and PARA 292.

574. Copy of orders and Commission's reasons to be sent to charity. Where the Commission makes an order for the protection of charities[1], it must send a copy of the order and a statement of its reasons for making it to the charity concerned, if a body corporate, or else to each of the charity trustees[2]. These documents must be sent to the charity or charity trustees as soon as practicable after the making of the order[3]. However, the Commission need not send the documents or, as the case may be, the statement of reasons at this time if it considers that to do so would prejudice any inquiry or investigation or would not be in the interests of the charity, in which case once the Commission considers that this is no longer the case, it must send the documents or, as the case may be, the statement to the charity or charity trustees as soon as practicable[4].

1 Ie under the Charities Act 2011 ss 76, 79, 80, 81, 83, 84 or 85: see PARA 567 et seq.
2 Charities Act 2011 s 86(1), (2), (3). Nothing in s 86 requires any document to be sent to a person who cannot be found or who has no known address in the United Kingdom: s 86(6). Any documents required to be sent to a person under s 86 may be sent to, or otherwise served on, that person in the same way as an order made by the Commission under the Charities Act 2011 could be served on him in accordance with s 339 (see PARA 555): s 86(7).
3 Charities Act 2011 s 86(4).
4 Charities Act 2011 s 86(5).

(iii) Miscellaneous Statutory Powers of the Charity Commission

575. Dormant bank accounts of charities. Where the Charity Commission[1]: (1) is informed by a relevant institution[2] that it holds one or more accounts in the name or on behalf of a particular charity (the 'relevant charity')[3], and that the account or, if it holds two or more accounts, each of the accounts is dormant[4]; and (2) the Commission is unable, after making reasonable inquiries, to locate that charity or any of its trustees[5], it may give a direction[6] which:

(a) requires the institution concerned to transfer the amount[7], or, as the case may be, the aggregate amount, standing to the credit of the relevant charity in the account or accounts in question to such other charity as is specified[8] in the direction[9]; or
(b) requires the institution concerned to transfer such part of that amount or aggregate amount as is specified to each of two or more other specified charities[10].

In such a direction the Commission may specify such other charity or charities as it considers appropriate, having regard, in a case where the purposes of the relevant charity are known to it, to those purposes and to the purposes of the other charity or charities[11]. Any amount received by a charity under these provisions is received on the terms that it will be held and applied by the charity for the purposes of the charity, but will, as property of the charity, nevertheless be subject to any restrictions on expenditure to which it was subject as property of the relevant charity[12].

Where the Commission has been informed by any relevant institution under head (1) above, and before any transfer is made by the institution in pursuance of a direction, the institution has, by reason of any circumstances, cause to believe that the account, or, as the case may be, any of the accounts is or are no longer dormant, it must forthwith notify those circumstances in writing to the Commission[13]. If it appears to the Commission that the account or accounts in question is or are no longer dormant, it must revoke the direction which has previously been given by it to the institution with respect to the relevant charity[14]. No obligation as to secrecy or other restriction precludes a relevant institution from disclosing any information to the Commission for the purpose of enabling it to discharge the above functions[15].

An appeal against such a direction of the Commission lies to the Tribunal at the instance of the Attorney General[16], the charity trustees of the charity, the charity itself (if a body corporate) and any other person who is or may be affected by the order[17]. The Tribunal has the power to do any of the following: (i) quash the direction and, if appropriate, remit the matter to the Commission; (ii) substitute for all or part of the direction any other direction which could have been made by the Commission; (iii) add to the direction anything which could have been contained in a direction given by the Commission[18].

1 Charities Act 2011 s 107(1).

2 Charities Act 2011 s 107(1)(a). A 'relevant institution' means: (1) the Bank of England; (2) a person who has permission under the Financial Services and Markets Act 2000 Pt 4A to accept deposits; (3) an EEA firm of the kind mentioned in Sch 3 para 5 which has permission under Sch 3 para 15 (as a result of qualifying for authorisation under Sch 3 para 12(1)) to accept deposits; or (4) such other person who may lawfully accept deposits in the United Kingdom as may be prescribed by the Minister: Charities Act 2011 s 109(3) (amended by the Financial Services Act 2012 Sch 18 para 136). Heads (2)–(4) must be read with the Financial Services and Markets Act 2000 s 22, any relevant order under s 22 and Sch 2: Charities Act 2011 s 109(4). See also FINANCIAL SERVICES AND INSTITUTIONS vol 49 (2008) PARA 791. As to the Minister see PARA 586.

3 Charities Act 2011 s 107(1)(a)(i). As to the meaning of 'charity' see PARA 1.

In relation to exempt charities for whom the increased regulation provisions have not been brought into force, s 107(1) does not apply to any account held in the name of or on behalf of an exempt charity: s 107(6) (added by Sch 9 para 20). As to exempt charities see PARA 318 et seq; as to the phasing in of increased regulation of exempt charities see PARA 319.

4 Charities Act 2011 s 107(1)(a)(ii). An account is dormant if no transaction other than: (1) a transaction consisting in a payment into the account; or (2) a transaction which the institution holding the account has itself caused to be effected, has been effected in relation to the account within the period of five years immediately preceding the date when the Commission was so informed under s 107(1)(a): s 109(2).

5 Charities Act 2011 s 107(1)(b).
6 Charities Act 2011 s 107(1). For the purpose of determining the matters in respect of which any of the powers conferred by the Charities Act 2011 ss 46–53 (see PARA 559 et seq) may be exercised, it is to be assumed that the Commission has no functions under s 107 or s 108 in relation to accounts to which this provision applies, with the result that, for example, a relevant institution is not, in connection with the functions of the Commission under ss 107, 108, required under s 47(2)(a) to furnish any statements, or answer any questions or inquiries, with respect to any such accounts held by the institution: s 109(6). This applies to accounts which are dormant accounts by virtue of s 109(2) (see note 4) but would not be dormant accounts if s 109(2)(a) (see note 4 head (1)) were omitted: s 109(7).
7 Reference to the transfer of any amount to a charity are references to its transfer to the charity trustees, or to any trustee for the charity, as the charity trustees may determine, and any reference to any amount received by the charity is to be construed accordingly: Charities Act 2011 s 109(5). As to the meaning of 'charity trustees' see PARA 255.
8 Ie in accordance with the Charities Act 2011 s 107(3): see the text and note 11.
9 Charities Act 2011 s 107(2)(a).
10 Charities Act 2011 s 107(2)(b).
11 Charities Act 2011 s 107(3)(a). The Commission, however, must not specify any charity unless it has received from the charity trustees written confirmation that those trustees are willing to accept the amount proposed to be transferred to the charity: s 107(3)(b).
12 Charities Act 2011 s 107(4). The receipt of any charity trustees or trustees for a charity in respect of any amount received from a relevant institution under these provisions is a complete discharge of the institution in respect of that amount: s 107(5).
13 Charities Act 2011 s 108(1), (2).
14 Charities Act 2011 s 108(3).
15 Charities Act 2011 s 109(1).
16 As to the Tribunal see PARA 579 et seq. As to the Attorney General see PARAS 589, 596, 605 et seq; and CONSTITUTIONAL AND ADMINISTRATIVE LAW vol 20 (2014) PARA 273 et seq.
17 Charities Act 2011 s 319(2), Sch 6 Table Cols 1, 2. As to the meaning of 'person who is or may be affected' within the meaning of Sch 6 see PARA 317 note 8.
18 Charities Act 2011 Sch 6 Table Col 3.

576. Power to determine membership of charity. The Charity Commission may on the application of a charity, or at any time after the institution of an inquiry, determine who are the members of the charity[1]. This power may also be exercised by a person appointed by the Commission for the purpose[2] and the Commission may, if it thinks fit, so appoint the person appointed to conduct the inquiry[3].

1 Charities Act 2011 s 111(1).
2 Charities Act 2011 s 111(2).
3 Charities Act 2011 s 111(3).

577. Miscellaneous powers. Apart from its powers under the Charities Act 2011, the Charity Commission has specific powers and functions under a variety of other Acts: the Bishops Trusts Substitution Act 1858[1], the Voluntary Hospitals (Paying Patients) Act 1936[2], the Reserve Forces Act 1980[3], the Mission and Pastoral Measure 2011[4] and the Redundant Churches and Other Religious Buildings Act 1969[5].

The Commission also has the power, on application by any person interested, to make such provision for the apportionment and management of endowments held partly for ecclesiastical purposes and partly for other purposes as seems to it necessary or expedient for giving effect to the Local Government Act 1894[6].

The Commission's office is a place of deposit for those of its records selected for permanent preservation[7].

1 See PARA 270.
2 See PARA 578.
3 See PARA 198.

4 See PARA 196.

5 See PARA 197.

6 See the Local Government Act 1894 s 75(2); PARA 267 note 4; and LOCAL GOVERNMENT vol 69 (2009) PARA 537.

7 Ie by virtue of an appointment by the Lord Chancellor under the Public Records Act 1958 s 4(1) (see CONSTITUTIONAL AND ADMINISTRATIVE LAW vol 20 (2014) PARA 346): see the *Report of the Charity Commissioners for England and Wales for 1961* (HC Paper (1962–63) no 30) para 43; and the Charities Act 2011 Sch 7 para 2(1).

578. Paying patients in voluntary hospitals. On the application of the committee of management of a voluntary hospital[1], the Charity Commission may, by order, authorise the provision of specified facilities for the accommodation and treatment of patients able and willing to pay for it by the committee for specified periods[2]. The committee may charge for accommodation and maintenance, including medical and surgical attendance and treatment given by the resident staff, in accordance with the scale specified in the Commission's order[3], which may include any consequential or incidental provisions appearing to the Commission to be necessary or desirable[4]. The order may authorise the committee to defray out of any fund applicable to the general purposes of the hospital the difference between the full expense of accommodation and maintenance and the sum charged to a paying patient[5], but except to this extent no order may be construed as authorising any application of funds[6].

On the application of the committee, the Commission may from time to time vary an order, and may of its own motion vary or revoke an order if it considers that there has been a material change in the circumstances and it first gives the committee and others concerned an opportunity of making representations[7].

Generally the Commission must not make an order authorising any use or application of property or funds which, apart from the order, would involve a breach of any trusts upon which the property or funds are held, or a contravention of any prohibition or restriction expressly relating to the hospital[8]. But it may make such an order:

(1) in the case of an application to use land, if it is satisfied that, if the order were not made, the land would not come into use for the purposes for which the trusts were created or the prohibition or restriction was imposed until after the expiration of a substantial period from the date of the application[9];

(2) in the case of an application to use existing buildings or part of such buildings, if satisfied either[10]:

   (a) that such use for the purposes for which the trusts were created or the prohibition or restriction was imposed is impracticable, or is likely soon so to become, because the committee of management have not at their disposal, and will be unable to obtain, sufficient funds to enable the buildings or part to be, or to continue to be, so used[11]; or

   (b) that use for those purposes is impracticable, or is likely soon so to become, because of a shortage of demand for accommodation on the part of the persons for whose benefit the trusts were created or the prohibition or restriction was imposed[12]; or

   (c) that the committee has, or is likely soon to have, at its disposal premises which could be put to the use to which the application relates without breach of any trust upon which those premises are held or contravention of any such prohibition or restriction, and that the buildings or part will be used by way of exchange for those premises[13];

(3) in any case, if satisfied that the authorisation will not diminish or restrict the accommodation for such persons for whose benefit the trusts were created or the prohibition or restriction imposed which is provided in the hospital at the date of the application and which the committee would be able to continue to provide if the order were not made[14].

1 'Committee of management' includes any body or persons having the management or control of a voluntary hospital: Voluntary Hospitals (Paying Patients) Act 1936 s 1. 'Voluntary hospital' means an institution, not being an institution carried on for profit or which is maintained wholly or mainly at the expense of the rates or which is vested in an NHS trust or an NHS foundation trust or which is vested in the Secretary of State, which provides medical or surgical treatment for in-patients: s 1 (definition amended by the National Health Service Act 1946 s 76, Sch 10 Pt I (repealed with savings by the National Health Service Act 1977 s 129, Sch 14 paras 1–3, 13, Sch 16); the National Health Service and Community Care Act 1990 s 66(1), Sch 9 para 2; SI 2000/90; the Health and Social Care (Community Health and Standards) Act 2003 Sch 4 para 2; and the Health and Social Care Act 2012 Sch 5 para 1(a)).

The functions of the Secretary of State under the Voluntary Hospitals (Paying Patients) Act 1936 are exercised, in relation to England, by the Secretary of State for Health, and in relation to Wales, by the Secretary of State for Wales: see the Secretary of State for Social Services Order 1968, SI 1968/1699; Transfer of Functions (Wales) Order 1969, SI 1969/388; Transfer of Functions (Health and Social Security) Order 1988, SI 1988/1843.

'NHS trust' means a National Health Service trust established under the National Health Service Act 2006 or the National Health Service (Wales) Act 2006 (see HEALTH SERVICES vol 54 (2008) PARA 83): Voluntary Hospitals (Paying Patients) Act 1936 s 1 (definition added by the National Health Service and Community Care Act 1990 s 66(1), Sch 9 para 2(b); and amended by the National Health Service (Consequential Provisions) Act 2006 Sch 1 para 2(a)). As from a day to be appointed, the reference to the National Health Service Act 2006 is repealed by the Health and Social Care Act 2012 Sch 14 Pt 2 para 41. At the date at which this volume states the law, no such day had been appointed.

2 See the Voluntary Hospitals (Paying Patients) Act 1936 s 2(1) (s 2 amended by the Charities Act 2006 Sch 8 para 23). As to the power of the Charity Commission to make rules for these purposes see the Voluntary Hospitals (Paying Patients) Act 1936 s 5 (s 5 amended by the Charities Act 2006 Sch 8 para 26). As to the rules relating to applications see the Rules made by the Charity Commissioners under section 5(1) of the Voluntary Hospitals (Paying Patients) Act 1936, SR & O 1936/1025. The Commission may require a sum to cover their costs and expenses to be provided out of hospital funds: see the Voluntary Hospitals (Paying Patients) Act 1936 s 5(3) (as so amended). The powers conferred on the Charity Commission by the Voluntary Hospitals (Paying Patients) Act 1936 are in addition to and not in derogation of any other powers exercisable by it: s 6(2) (s 6 amended by the Charities Act 2006 Sch 8 para 27).

3 See the Voluntary Hospitals (Paying Patients) Act 1936 s 2(2). Except where satisfied that it would be inappropriate to do so, the Commission must include, in the scale of charges, charges fixed with a view to meeting the needs of patients who, although able to make some payment, are unable to pay sufficient to meet the full expense to the hospital of their accommodation and maintenance: see s 3(1) (amended by the Charities Act 2006 Sch 8 para 24). The Commission must make it a condition that, in the use of a specified number of authorised beds, priority is to be given to such patients: see the Voluntary Hospitals (Paying Patients) Act 1936 s 3(1).

4 See the Voluntary Hospitals (Paying Patients) Act 1936 s 2(3) (as amended: see note 2).

5 See the Voluntary Hospitals (Paying Patients) Act 1936 s 3(2).

6 See the Voluntary Hospitals (Paying Patients) Act 1936 s 6(3).

7 See the Voluntary Hospitals (Paying Patients) Act 1936 s 2(4) (as amended: see note 2).

8 See the Voluntary Hospitals (Paying Patients) Act 1936 s 4 (amended by the Charities Act 2006 Sch 8 para 25).

9 See the Voluntary Hospitals (Paying Patients) Act 1936 s 4(a).

10 See the Voluntary Hospitals (Paying Patients) Act 1936 s 4(b) (as amended: see note 8).

11 See the Voluntary Hospitals (Paying Patients) Act 1936 s 4(b)(i).

12 See the Voluntary Hospitals (Paying Patients) Act 1936 s 4(b)(ii).

13 See the Voluntary Hospitals (Paying Patients) Act 1936 s 4(b)(iii).

14 See the Voluntary Hospitals (Paying Patients) Act 1936 s 4(c) (as amended: see note 8).

(5) APPEALS TO THE TRIBUNAL

579. Appeals to the Tribunal. The Tribunal[1] has jurisdiction to hear and determine appeals against many of the decisions, directions or orders of the Charity Commission[2], which are dealt with as appropriate elsewhere in this title.

An appeal may be brought by the Attorney General or any person specified for each appeal in the Charities Act 2011[3], and the Commission is the respondent to such an appeal[4]. However, where an order, decision or direction gives effect to a decision of the Tribunal deciding a question referred to the Tribunal by the Commission or the Attorney General, no appeal may be made in respect of that order by a person who was at any stage party to the proceedings in which the question was referred[5].

In determining an appeal the Tribunal must consider afresh the decision, direction or order appealed against[6]. The Tribunal may take into account evidence which was not available to the Commission[7].

The Tribunal may dismiss the appeal or, if it allows the appeal, exercise any of the powers as specified for each of the decisions, directions and orders[8]. Where this includes the power to remit a matter to the Commission, the power is to remit the matter generally or for determination in accordance with a finding made or direction given by the Tribunal[9].

The Tribunal's jurisdiction is restricted to the matters laid down by the statute; it does not have a general supervisory jurisdiction allowing it to provide public law remedies[10].

1 Until 1 September 2009 this Tribunal was the Charity Tribunal. However the Charity Tribunal was abolished and its functions transferred to the First-tier Tribunal and the Upper Tribunal: see the Transfer of Functions of the Charity Tribunal Order 2009, SI 2009/1834, art 2. As to the Tribunal see COURTS AND TRIBUNALS vol 24 (2010) PARA 874 et seq. The following offices held before 1 September 2009 are also transferred: (1) the office of the President of the Charity Tribunal appointed under the Charities Act 1993 Sch 1B para 1(2)(a) now holds the office of deputy judge of the Upper Tribunal and transferred-in judge of the First-tier Tribunal; (2) a legal member of the Charity Tribunal appointed under Sch 1B para 1(2)(b) now holds the office of transferred-in judge of the First-tier Tribunal; and (3) an ordinary member of the Charity Tribunal appointed under Sch 1B para 1(2)(c) now holds the office of transferred-in other member of the First-tier Tribunal: see the Transfer of Functions of the Charity Tribunal Order 2009, SI 2009/1834, art 3. Appeals, applications and matters referred to the Tribunal under the Charities Act 2011 Pt 17 Chs 2, 3 (ss 319–331) must be heard and determined by the Tribunal in accordance with the relevant provisions, taken with rules made under s 316(2) (see PARA 582) and Tribunal Procedure Rules: Charities Act 2011 s 315(3).

2 Charities Act 2011 s 315(2), Sch 6 Table Col 1. Provisions relating to appeal do not apply in the case of a reviewable matter: see s 319(1). As to reviewable matters see PARA 580. The Minister may by order amend or otherwise modify an entry in the Table, add an entry to the Table or remove an entry from the Table: s 324(1). Such an order may make such amendments, repeals or other modifications of ss 319–323, or of an enactment which applies Ch 2 and Sch 6, as the Minister considers appropriate in consequence of any change in the Table made by the order: s 324(2). The Charitable Incorporated Organisations (Consequential Amendments) Order 2012, SI 2012/3014, art 8 is made under this provision.

A letter highly directive in tone and containing an action plan which the Charity Commission expected the charity to take was not a decision, direction or order so as to make it an appealable matter under these provisions: *Eyob Ghebre-Sellassie (African AIDS Action) v Charity Commission for England and Wales* (2010) First-tier Tribunal, General Regulatory Chamber (Charity), 9 February.

As to the Charity Commission see PARAS 543–578. As to the Minister see PARA 586. These provisions apply, with the necessary modifications, in relation to the Charities Act 2006 s 57 (see PARA 503) as if that section were contained within the Charities Act 2011 Pt 17 Ch 2 (ss 319–324) and the reference in s 324(2) included a reference to any other provision relating to appeals to the Tribunal which in contained in Pt 3 Chapter 1 of the Charities Act 2006: Charities Act 2011 s 324(3).

3 Charities Act 2011 s 319(2), Sch 6 Table Col 2. As to the Attorney General see PARAS 589, 596, 605 et seq; and CONSTITUTIONAL AND ADMINISTRATIVE LAW vol 20 (2014) PARA 273 et seq.
4 Charities Act 2011 s 319(3).
5 Charities Act 2011 s 330(1), (2): see PARA 579.
6 Charities Act 2011 s 319(4)(a). This does not apply in relation to an appeal relating to an order under s 52 (call for documents: see PARA 562): s 320(1). In such an appeal, the Tribunal must consider whether the information or document in question:
   (1) relates to a charity; or
   (2) is relevant to the discharge of the functions of the Commission or the official custodian,
and it may allow the appeal only if either head (1) or head (2) is satisfied: s 320(2), (3). As to the official custodian see PARA 300 et seq.
7 Charities Act 2011 s 319(4)(b).
8 Charities Act 2011 Sch 6 Col 3.
9 Charities Act 2011 s 323.
10 Thus, where the Charities Act 2011 made the refusal of an order a reviewable decision, a decision to offer such orders, rather than to refuse them, was not reviewable under this provision: *Holland v Charity Commission for England and Wales* (2011) First-tier Tribunal, General Regulatory Chamber (Charity), 6 January, para 3.6, 3.7. As to the Tribunal see PARA 579 et seq. As to reviewable decisions see PARA 580.

580. Applications for review by the Tribunal. An application may be made to the Tribunal[1] for the review of a reviewable matter[2]. The following decisions and orders of the Charity Commission[3] are 'reviewable matters'[4], and are dealt with elsewhere in this title:

(1) a decision[5] to institute an inquiry with regard to a particular institution or class of institutions[6];
(2) a decision[7] not to make a common investment scheme[8];
(3) a decision[9] not to make a common deposit scheme[10];
(4) a decision[11] not to make an order authorising dealings with charity property etc in relation to a charity[12];
(5) a decision[13] not to make an order for the conveyance, transfer, lease or other disposal of land held by or in trust for a charity[14];
(6) a decision[15] not to make an order in relation to a mortgage of land held by or in trust for a charity[16];
(7) an order[17] for the investigation and audit of the accounts of a company which is a charity[18].

An application for the review of a reviewable matter may be made by the Attorney General or any person specified for each reviewable matter in the Charities Act 2011[19], and the Commission is the respondent to such an application[20]. However, where an order or decision gives effect to a decision of the Tribunal deciding a question referred to the Tribunal by the Commission or the Attorney General, no application for review may be made in respect of that order by a person who was at any stage party to the proceedings in which the question was referred[21].

In determining the application the Tribunal must apply the principles which would be applied by the High Court on an application for judicial review[22]. It may dismiss the application or, if it allows the application, exercise any of the powers as specified for each of the directions and the order above[23]. Where this includes the power to remit a matter to the Commission, the power is to remit the matter generally or for determination in accordance with a finding made or direction given by the Tribunal[24].

1 As to the Tribunal see PARA 579 note 1.
2 Charities Act 2011 s 321(1). Where the Charities Act 2011 made the refusal of an order a reviewable decision, a decision to offer such orders, rather than to refuse them, was not

reviewable under this provision: *Holland v Charity Commission for England and Wales* (2011) First-tier Tribunal, General Regulatory Chamber (Charity), 6 January, para 3.6, 3.7.

3 As to the Charity Commission see PARAS 543–578.

4 Charities Act 2011 s 322(1). As to the Minister's power to make amendments or other modifications to this provision see PARA 579 note 2. As to the Minister see PARA 586.

5 Ie under the Charities Act 2011 s 46: see PARA 559.

6 Charities Act 2011 s 322(2)(a), (b).

7 Ie under the Charities Act 2011 s 96: see PARA 426.

8 Charities Act 2011 s 322(2)(c).

9 Ie under the Charities Act 2011 s 100: see PARA 427.

10 See the Charities Act 2011 s 322(2)(d).

11 Ie under the Charities Act 2011 s 105: see PARAS 387–391.

12 See the Charities Act 2011 322(2)(e).

13 Ie under the Charities Act 2011 s 117: see PARA 401.

14 See the Charities Act 2011 s 322(2)(f).

15 Ie under the Charities Act 2011 s 124: see PARA 404.

16 See the Charities Act 2011 s 322(2)(f).

17 Ie under the Charities Act 2011 s 147(2): see PARA 566.

18 Charities Act 2011 s 322(3).

19 Charities Act 2011 s 321(2). As to the Attorney General see PARAS 589, 596, 605 et seq; and **CONSTITUTIONAL AND ADMINISTRATIVE LAW** vol 20 (2014) PARA 273 et seq.

20 Charities Act 2011 s 321(3).

21 Charities Act 2011 s 330(1), (2); see PARA 579.

22 Charities Act 2011 s 321(4). However, it appears that Tribunal is not required in every case to test, in a formulaic manner, the Commission's decision against the 'classic' grounds for judicial review: *Regentford v Charity Commission for England and Wales* [2014] UKUT 0364 (TCC) at para [37]. As to judicial review see **JUDICIAL REVIEW**.

23 Charities Act 2011 s 321(5).

24 Charities Act 2011 s 323.

581. References to the Tribunal. A question which has arisen in connection with the exercise by the Charity Commission[1] of any of its functions, and involves either the operation of charity law[2] in any respect or its application to a particular state of affairs, may be referred to the Tribunal[3] by the Commission if the Commission considers it desirable to do so[4]. However, such a reference may only be made with the consent of the Attorney General[5]. The Commission must be a party to proceedings before the Tribunal on the reference[6] and the Attorney General is entitled to be a party to such proceedings[7]. In addition, the following are entitled to be parties to such proceedings with the Tribunal's permission: (1) the charity trustees of any charity which is likely to be affected by the Tribunal's decision on the reference; (2) any such charity which is a body corporate; and (3) any other person who is likely to be so affected[8].

A question which involves either the operation of charity law in any respect, or the application of charity law to a particular state of affairs, may be referred to the Tribunal by the Attorney General if he considers it desirable to do so[9]. The Attorney General must be a party to proceedings before the Tribunal on the reference[10] and the Commission is entitled to be a party to such proceedings[11]. In addition, the following are entitled to be parties to such proceedings with the Tribunal's permission: (a) the charity trustees of any charity which is likely to be affected by the Tribunal's decision on the reference; (b) any such charity which is a body corporate; and (c) any other person who is likely to be so affected[12].

Where a question which involves the application of charity law to a particular state of affairs has been referred to the Tribunal under either of the provisions above, the Commission must not take any steps in reliance on any view as to the application of charity law to that state of affairs until proceedings on the reference, including any proceedings on appeal, have been concluded, and any period during which an appeal, or further appeal, may ordinarily be made has ended[13]. However, this restriction does not apply in relation to any steps taken by the Commission with the agreement of: (i) the persons who are parties to the proceedings on the reference at the time when those steps are taken; and (ii) if not within head (i), the charity trustees of any charity which is likely to be directly affected by the taking of those steps and is not a party to the proceedings at that time[14].

Where proceedings, including any proceedings on appeal, have been concluded, any period during which an appeal, or further appeal, may ordinarily be made has ended, and the question has been decided in proceedings on the reference, the Commission must give effect to that decision when dealing with the particular state of affairs to which the reference related[15]. No appeal[16] or application for review[17] in respect of an order, decision or direction by which the Commission so gives effect to the decision may be made to the Tribunal by a person who was at any stage a party to proceedings in which the question was referred[18].

1 As to the Charity Commission see PARAS 543–578.

2 For these purposes 'charity law' means any enactment contained in, or made under, the Charities Act 2011 or the Charities Act 2006, any other enactment specified in regulations made by the Minister and any rule of law which relates to charities: Charities Act 2011 s 331(1). 'Enactment' means an enactment comprised in subordinate legislation within in the meaning of the Interpretation Act 1978 and includes an enactment whenever passed and made: Charities Act 2011 s 331(1). The exclusions from the definition of charity in s 10(2) (see PARA 196) do not have effect for these purposes: s 331(2).

3 As to the Tribunal see PARAS 579–582.

4 Charities Act 2011 ss 315(2)(b), 325(1).

5 Charities Act 2011 s 325(2). As to the Attorney General see PARAS 589, 596, 605 et seq; and CONSTITUTIONAL AND ADMINISTRATIVE LAW vol 20 (2014) PARA 273 et seq.

6 Charities Act 2011 s 325(3).

7 Charities Act 2011 s 325(4)(a).

8 Charities Act 2011 s 325(4)(b).

9 Charities Act 2011 s 326(1).

10 Charities Act 2011 s 326(2).

11 Charities Act 2011 s 326(3)(a).

12 Charities Act 2011 s 326(3)(b).

13 Charities Act 2011 s 327(1), (2). If this prevents the Commission from taking any steps which it would otherwise be permitted or required to take, and the steps in question may be taken only during a period specified in an enactment (the 'specified period'), then the running of the specified period is suspended for the period which begins with the date on which the question is referred to the Tribunal, and ends with the date on which (1) proceedings, including any proceedings on appeal, have been concluded; and (2) any period during which an appeal, or further appeal, may ordinarily be made has ended: s 328(1), (2). Nothing in s 328 or s 271 or s 278 (see PARA 218) prevents the specified period being suspended concurrently by virtue of those provisions: s 328(3).

14 Charities Act 2011 s 329(1). The Commission may take those steps despite the suspension in accordance with s 328(2) of any period during which it would otherwise be permitted or required to take them: s 329(2).

15 Charities Act 2011 s 327(3). This does not require the Commission to give effect to a decision as to the application of charity law to a particular state of affairs to the extent that the decision is inconsistent with any steps already taken by the Commission in relation to that state of affairs in accordance with s 329: s 329(3).

16 As to appeals to the Tribunal see PARA 579.

17 As to applications for review by Tribunal see PARA 580.

18 Charities Act 2011 s 330(1), (2). Any enactment, including one contained in the Charities Act 2011, which provides for an appeal or application to be made to the Tribunal has effect subject to this provision: s 330(3).

582. Practice and procedure. The following applies in relation to appeals, applications or references to the Tribunal in relation to decisions, directions or orders[1] of the Charity Commission[2].

The Lord Chancellor[3] may make rules: (1) specifying steps which must be taken before appeals, applications or references are made to the Tribunal (and the period within which any steps much be taken); (2) requiring the Commission to inform persons of their right to appeal or apply to the Tribunal following a final decision, direction or order of the Commission[4].

Tribunal rules may make any other provision regulating the exercise of rights to appeal or to apply to the Tribunal and matters relating to the making of references to it[5].

Rules made under the above provisions may confer a discretion on the Tribunal or any other person[6].

1 Ie appeals, applications or references to the Tribunal which are mentioned in the Charities Act 2011 s 315(2) (see PARA 579 et seq). As to the Tribunal see PARA 579 note 1.
2 Charities Act 2011 s 316(1), (5), (6).
3 As to the Lord Chancellor see CONSTITUTIONAL AND ADMINISTRATIVE LAW vol 20 (2014) PARA 255 et seq.
4 Charities Act 2011 s 316(2). Such rules must be made by statutory instrument: see s 316(5)(a). At the date at which this volume states the law no such rules were in force explicitly under this power, but the Tribunal Procedure (First-tier Tribunal) (General Regulatory Chamber) Rules 2009, SI 2009/1976, extend to charities cases: see r 1(2). See further COURTS AND TRIBUNALS vol 24 (2010) PARAS 918, 919.
5 Charities Act 2011 s 316(3). See also note 4.
6 Charities Act 2011 s 316(4). See also note 4.

583. Appeals from the Tribunal. In the case of an appeal[1] against a decision of the Tribunal[2] which determines a question referred to it by the Charity Commission or the Attorney General[3], the tribunal or court hearing the appeal must consider afresh the question referred to the Tribunal, and may take into account evidence which was not available to the Tribunal[4].

1 Ie an appeal under the Tribunals, Courts and Enforcement Act 2007 s 11 or s 13 (see COURTS AND TRIBUNALS vol 24 (2010) PARAS 928, 929.
2 As to the Tribunal see PARA 579 note 1.
3 As to the Charity Commission see PARAS 543–578. As to the Attorney General see PARAS 589, 596, 605 et seq; and CONSTITUTIONAL AND ADMINISTRATIVE LAW vol 20 (2014) PARA 273 et seq. For the purposes of the Tribunals, Courts and Enforcement Act 2007 s 11(2) and s 13(2) the Commission and the Attorney General are to be treated as parties to cases before the Tribunal in respect of any such appeal, application or reference as is mentioned in the Charities Act 2011 s 315(2) (see PARA 579 et seq): s 317(1).
4 Charities Act 2011 s 317(2).

584. Intervention by the Attorney General. In the case of any proceedings before the Tribunal[1], or on an appeal from the Tribunal, to which the Attorney General is not a party[2], the appropriate body[3], may at any stage of the proceedings direct that all the necessary papers in the proceedings be sent to the Attorney General[4]. Such a direction may be made by the appropriate body of its own motion or on the application of any party to the proceedings[5].

The Attorney General may intervene in the proceedings in such manner as he thinks necessary or expedient, and argue before the appropriate body any question in relation to the proceedings which the appropriate body considers it necessary to have fully argued[6], whether or not a direction is given[7] as above[8].

1 As to the Tribunal see PARA 579 note 1.
2 Charities Act 2011 s 318(1). As to the Attorney General see PARAS 589, 596, 605 et seq; and CONSTITUTIONAL AND ADMINISTRATIVE LAW vol 20 (2014) PARA 273 et seq.

3 For these purposes 'appropriate body' means the Tribunal or, in the case of an appeal from the Tribunal, the tribunal or court hearing the appeal: Charities Act 2011 s 318(6).
4 Charities Act 2011 s 318(2).
5 Charities Act 2011 s 318(3).
6 Charities Act 2011 s 318(4).
7 Ie under the Charities Act 2011 s 318(2).
8 Charities Act 2011 s 318(5).

(6) THE SECRETARY OF STATE AND THE WELSH MINISTERS

585. The role of the Secretary of State and the Welsh Ministers. In law 'Secretary of State' means one of Her Majesty's Principal Secretaries of State[1]. Accordingly, many modern statutes refer simply to the 'Secretary of State' without reference to a particular department or ministry[2]. Previously, the Secretary of State had numerous functions under the Charities Acts but these are now vested in the Minister[3].

At one time, the Secretary of State for Education and Science[4] had functions concurrent with the Charity Commissioners[5], as did the Secretary of State for Wales in relation to primary and secondary education in Wales[6]. By the Education Act 1973[7] these functions were terminated, and first the Charity Commissioners, and then subsequently the Charity Commission[8], became responsible for educational trusts, having jurisdiction over them in exactly the same way as they have jurisdiction over other charitable trusts. However, certain functions formerly exercised by the Secretary of State for Children, Schools and Families in relation to the modification of trusts deeds relating to certain schools[9] or relating to the provision of educational services or educational research[10], are now exercised by the Secretary of State for Education[11]. He also has powers in relation to religious educational trusts[12].

The Secretary of State has power as a 'relevant Minister'[13] under the Charities Act 2006 to give financial assistance to any charitable, benevolent or philanthropic institution[14] in respect of any of the institution's activities which directly or indirectly benefit the whole or any part of England, whether or not they also benefit any other area[15]. Such financial assistance may be given in any form, in particular by way of grants, loans, guarantees or incurring expenditure for the benefit of the person assisted[16], and on such terms and conditions as he considers appropriate[17]. Those terms and conditions may, in particular, include provision as to:

(1) the purposes for which the assistance may be used[18];
(2) circumstances in which the assistance is to be repaid, or otherwise made good, to him, and the manner in which that is to be done[19];
(3) the making of reports to him regarding the uses to which the assistance has been put[20];
(4) the keeping, and making available for inspection, of accounts and other records[21];
(5) the carrying out of examinations by the Comptroller and Auditor General[22] into the economy, efficiency and effectiveness with which the assistance has been used[23];
(6) the giving by the institution of financial assistance in any form to other persons on such terms and conditions as the institution or he considers appropriate[24].

A person receiving assistance under these provisions must comply with the terms and conditions on which it is given, and compliance may be enforced by the relevant Minister[25]. The relevant Minister may make arrangements for such financial assistance and any of his associated functions to be exercised by some other person[26]. Such arrangements may make provision for the functions concerned to be so exercised either wholly or to such extent as may be specified in the arrangements, and either generally or in such cases or circumstances as may be so specified, but do not prevent the functions concerned from being exercised by a relevant Minister[27]. As soon as possible after 31 March in each year, a relevant Minister must make a report on any exercise by him of any powers under this section during the period of 12 months ending on that day[28].

In Wales certain functions relating to discrimination[29], education[30] and places of worship[31] have been transferred to the Welsh Ministers.

1 See the Interpretation Act 1978 s 5, Sch 1.
2 As to the office of Secretary of State see CONSTITUTIONAL AND ADMINISTRATIVE LAW vol 20 (2014) PARA 153 et seq.
3 As to the transfer of functions see PARA 586.
4 References to the Secretary of State were substituted for the original references to the Minister of Education by the Secretary of State for Education and Science Order 1964, SI 1964/490, art 2(1) (lapsed).
5 See the Charities Act 1960 s 2(1) (repealed).
6 See the Transfer of Functions (Wales) Order 1970, SI 1970/1536, art 2(2) (lapsed).
7 Education Act 1973 s 1(1)(a), Sch 1 para 1, Sch 2 Pt III. The functions were transferred as from 1 February 1974: see s 1(5); Education Act 1973 (Commencement) Order 1973, SI 1973/1661.
8 As to the Charity Commissioners, and the transfer of their functions and liabilities to the Charity Commission, see PARA 543.
9 See the School Standards and Framework Act 1998 s 82; and EDUCATION vol 35 (2011) PARA 117.
10 See the Education Act 1996 s 489(3), (4); and EDUCATION vol 35 (2011) PARA 82.
11 The office of Secretary of State for Children, Schools and Families was superseded by that of Secretary of State for Education: see the Secretary of State for Education Order 2010, SI 2010/1836; and EDUCATION vol 35 (2011) PARA 60.
12 See the Education Act 1996 ss 554–556; and EDUCATION vol 36 (2011) PARA 1628.
13 'Relevant Minister' means the Secretary of State or the Minister of the Cabinet Office: Charities Act 2006 s 70(11) (amended by SI 2007/2914, and SI 2010/1839). As to the Minister see PARA 586.

Similar powers to give financial assistance exist in respect of Wales (see text and notes 12–21) in relation to any charitable, benevolent or philanthropic institution in respect of any of the institution's activities which directly or indirectly benefit the whole or any part of Wales, whether or not they also benefit any other area: see the Charities Act 2006 s 71.
14 'Charitable, benevolent or philanthropic institution' means a charity or an institution other than a charity which is established for charitable, benevolent or philanthropic purposes: Charities Act 2006 s 70(10).
15 Charities Act 2006 s 70(1).
16 Charities Act 2006 s 70(2).
17 Charities Act 2006 s 70(3).
18 Charities Act 2006 s 70(4)(a).
19 Charities Act 2006 s 70(4)(b).
20 Charities Act 2006 s 70(4)(c).
21 Charities Act 2006 s 70(4)(d).
22 In relation to Wales the power under the Charities Act 2006 s 71 (see note 13), applies to the Auditor General for Wales instead of the Comptroller and Auditor General: see s 71(4)(e).
23 Charities Act 2006 s 70(4)(e).
24 Charities Act 2006 s 70(4)(f).
25 Charities Act 2006 s 70(5).
26 Charities Act 2006 s 70(6).
27 Charities Act 2006 s 70(7).

28 Charities Act 2006 s 70(8). In relation to s 71 a report must be published after 31 March each years on the exercise of powers under s 71 during the period of 12 months ending on that day: s 71(8).
29 See PARAS 9, 463.
30 See PARAS 70, 461, 462.
31 See PARA 197.

(7) THE MINISTER FOR THE CABINET OFFICE

586. The role of the Minister for the Cabinet Office. All references to the 'Minister' in the Charities Acts 1992, 2006 and 2011 are to the Minister for the Cabinet Office[1]. The functions previously held by the Secretary of State[2] under the House to House Collections Act 1939[3] and the Charities Act 1992 and 1993 were transferred to the Minister on 13 December 2006 by the Transfer of Functions (Third Sector, Communities and Equality) Order 2006[4].

The Charities Act 2006 made provision for the Minister to appoint a person to review generally the operation of the Act[5]. Provisions of the Act which are repealed and replaced by the Charities Act 2011 are within the scope of this review[6].

1 Charities Act 1992 s 58(1) (definition added by the Charities Act 2006 Sch 8 para 90(1), (2)); Charities Act 2006 s 78(6); Charities Act 2011 s 353(1).
2 As to the Secretary of State see PARA 585.
3 Ie functions of the Secretary of State under the House to House Collections Act 1939 ss 2–4. Functions are also transferred in relation to the House to House Collections Regulations 1947, SR & O 1947/2662, which is made under the House to House Collections Act 1939 s 4. See generally PARA 465 et seq.
4 Ie the Transfer of Functions (Third Sector, Communities and Equality) Order 2006, SI 2006/2951.
5 See the Charities Act 2006 s 73(1)–(5) (s 73(5) amended by the Charities Act 2011 Sch 8 Pt 1).
6 See the Charities Act 2006 s 73(6) (added by the Charities Act 2011 Sch 7 para 120).

(8) THE DIRECTOR OF PUBLIC PROSECUTIONS

587. Consent of Director of Public Prosecutions to instigation of certain proceedings. Proceedings for certain specified offences relating to charities may only be instigated by or with the consent of the Director of Public Prosecutions[1]. The offences in question relate to omission of a registered charity's status on official publications[2]; supplying false or misleading information[3]; failure to comply with orders made by the Charity Commission[4]; failure to comply with requirements as to annual reports and annual returns[5]; and acting as a trustee while disqualified[6].

1 Charities Act 2011 s 345(1). As to the Director of Public Prosecutions see CRIMINAL PROCEDURE vol 27 (2010) PARAS 23, 33 et seq.
2 Ie under the Charities Act 2011 s 41: see PARA 311.
3 Ie under the Charities Act 2011 s 60: see PARA 561.
4 Ie under the Charities Act 2011 s 77(1): see PARA 567. As to the Charity Commission see PARAS 543–578.
5 Ie under the Charities Act 2011 s 173: see PARAS 371, 382–383.
6 Charities Act 2011 s 345(2). The reference to the offence of acting as a trustee while disqualified is a reference to an offence under s 183(1) (see PARA 277).

588. Offences by bodies corporate. Where any offence under the Charities Act 2011, or any offence under the Charities Act 1992 or any regulations made under it, is committed by a body corporate and is proved to have been committed with the consent or connivance of, or to be attributable to any neglect on the part of, any director[1], manager, secretary or other similar officer of the body corporate, or any person who was purporting to act in any such capacity, he as well as the body corporate is guilty of that offence and is liable to be proceeded against and punished accordingly[2].

1 In relation to a body corporate the affairs of which are managed by its members, 'director' means a member of the body corporate: Charities Act 1992 s 75; Charities Act 2011 s 346(2).
2 Charities Act 1992 s 75 (amended by the Charities Act 1993 Sch 7); Charities Act 2011 s 346(1). In relation to the Charities Act 2011, s 346 is not limited to cases where the Director of Public Prosecutions is necessarily involved under s 345: see PARA 587.

(9) THE ATTORNEY GENERAL

589. The role of the Attorney General. The Attorney General[1] represents the beneficial interest, or 'objects', of the charity[2]. His duty is to protect the interests of charity generally, and in so doing he contributes to a framework of supervision and control over charities in which the Charity Commission plays a significant, statutory role[3]. However, his role is particularly important in relation to exempt charities, which until such time as the increased regulation introduced by the Charities Act 2006 is fully in force[4] are largely outside the Charity Commission's jurisdiction[5].

The Attorney General is generally a necessary party to all claims relating to charities[6], and he may appear either in person or by counsel[7]. Where the Attorney General is a proper party, the Solicitor General[8] is the proper person to take his place if the Attorney General's office is vacant or if he is ill or concerned in the action in another capacity[9].

1 As to the Attorney General see also PARAS 596, 605 et seq; and **CONSTITUTIONAL AND ADMINISTRATIVE LAW** vol 20 (2014) PARA 273 et seq.
2 See *A-G v Brodie* (1846) 6 Moo PCC 12; *A-G v Bishop of Worcester* (1851) 9 Hare 328 at 361 per Turner V-C; *Ware v Cumberlege* (1855) 20 Beav 503; *Re Sekeford's Charity* (1861) 5 LT 488. See also *Brooks v Richardson* [1986] 1 All ER 952, [1986] 1 WLR 385.
3 As to the Charity Commission see PARAS 543–578.
4 As to the increased regulation introduced by the Charities Act 2006 and maintained by the Charities Act 2011 see PARA 319.
5 As to exempt charities see PARAS 318–320.
6 As to the role of the Attorney General in charity proceedings see further PARAS 596, 604 et seq. As to the costs of the Attorney General see PARAS 623–626. As to when the Attorney General is not a necessary party see PARA 609.
7 See PARA 615.
8 As to the Solicitor General see **CONSTITUTIONAL AND ADMINISTRATIVE LAW** vol 20 (2014) PARA 273 et seq.
9 See *R v Wilkes* (1770) 4 Burr 2527 at 2554, HL, per Lord Mansfield; *Ludlow Corpn v Greenhouse* (1827) 1 Bli NS 17 at 51, HL, per Lord Redesdale; *A-G v Bristol Corpn* (1820) 2 Jac & W 294; *A-G v Ironmongers' Co* (1834) 2 My & K 576; *A-G v Dean and Canons of Windsor* (1860) 8 HL Cas 369; *Brookes v Richardson* [1986] 1 All ER 952, [1986] 1 WLR 385; and PARAS 594, 604.

(10) REGULATIONS AND ORDERS AMENDING CHARITY LEGISLATION

590. Amendment of charity legislation to reflect changes to company law. The Minister may make such amendments to the Charities Act 2006[1] or the Charities Act 2011[2] as he considers appropriate: (1) in consequence of, or in connection with, any changes made or to be made by any enactment to the provisions of company law[3] relating to the accounts[4] of charitable companies[5] or to the auditing of, or preparation of reports in respect of, such accounts[6]; (2) for the purposes of, or in connection with, applying the statutory provisions for group accounts[7] to charitable companies that are not required to produce group accounts under company law[8].

1 For these purposes this includes repeals and modifications: Charities Act 2006 s 77(2). As to the Minister see PARA 586.
2 Ie, in so far as the Charities Act 2011 repeals and re-enacts provisions of the Charities Act 2006, the Minister may amend the equivalent provisions of the Charities Act 2011: Sch 8 para 3.
3 'Company law' means the enactments relating to companies: Charities Act 2006 s 77(2).
4 For these purpose 'accounts' includes group accounts: Charities Act 2006 s 77(2).
5 'Charitable companies' means companies which are charities: Charities Act 2006 s 77(2).
6 Charities Act 2006 s 77(1)(a).
7 Ie the Charities Act 2011 ss 137–175: see PARAS 343, 359–361.
8 Charities Act 2006 s 77(1)(b).

11. COURT PROCEEDINGS

(1) PROCEEDINGS INVOLVING CHARITIES

591. Litigation involving charities. A charity or a charity trustee may be involved in various different kinds of civil proceedings[1]. These include ordinary litigation involving charities relating to disputes about contracts[2], allegations of tortious conduct[3], property disputes[4], interpretation of wills[5] and other documents referring to charities or charitable purposes, applications under the Inheritance (Provision for Family and Dependants) Act 1975[6], appeals from certain decisions of the Charity Commission[7], applications for judicial review by or against the charity[8], and 'charity proceedings'[9]. The following paragraphs are concerned exclusively with 'charity proceedings'.

1 Even when proceedings are not charity proceedings per se, a party's charitable status may have bearing: see eg *Hackney Empire Ltd v Aviva Insurance UK Ltd* [2013] EWHC 2212 (TCC), 149 ConLR 213, [2013] All ER (D) 97 (Aug), where the claimant's charitable status had a bearing on the degree of latitude the court allowed in regard to late commencement of proceedings and on the determination of interest.
2 See generally CONTRACT vol 22 (2012) PARA 201 et seq.
3 See generally TORT vol 97 (2010) PARA 401 et seq.
4 See eg LANDLORD AND TENANT; REAL PROPERTY AND REGISTRATION.
5 As to wills generally see WILLS AND INTESTACY.
6 See WILLS AND INTESTACY vol 103 (2010) PARA 565 et seq.
7 As to the Charity Commission see PARAS 543–578.
8 As to judicial review see JUDICIAL REVIEW vol 61 (2010) PARA 601 et seq; CIVIL PROCEDURE vol 12 (2009) PARA 1530.
9 See PARA 592 et seq.

(2) RESTRICTIONS ON CHARITY PROCEEDINGS

592. Meaning of 'charity proceedings'. The Charities Act 2011 imposes restrictions on the taking of charity proceedings[1]. 'Charity proceedings' means proceedings in any court in England or Wales brought under the court's jurisdiction with respect to charities[2] or under the court's jurisdiction with respect to trusts in relation to the administration of a trust for charitable purposes[3]. The definition does not include proceedings to determine whether a valid charitable trust has been created[4]. The statutory provisions with regard to the taking of charity proceedings[5] are concerned with jurisdiction over the domestic aspects of an institution, not with issues lying between the institution and outsiders[6]. Charity proceedings relate to the constitution and administration of a charity, which are internal matters, as opposed to disputes over contract, tort or property rights between a charity and a third party[7], but they may involve as parties persons who are not trustees who have an interest in ensuring that the charity is properly administered[8].

1 See the Charities Act 2011 s 115; the text and notes 2–3; and PARAS 593–594. The Charities Act 1960 s 28(9) (repealed) provided that the Charities Procedure Act 1812 and also the provisions of any local or private Act regulating the persons by whom or the manner or form in which charity proceedings may be brought should cease to have effect. The repeal did not, however, affect any proceedings begun before 1 January 1961 (ie the commencement of the Charities Act 1960): s 48(5) (repealed). The Charities Procedure Act 1812 (repealed), otherwise known as Romilly's Act, provided a summary procedure on petition for determining simple questions arising in the administration of a charitable trust.
2 This phrase has been considered in *Construction Industry Training Board v A-G* [1973] Ch 173, [1972] 2 All ER 1339, CA (affg [1971] 3 All ER 449, [1971] 1 WLR 1303) (decided under

previous legislation): see PARA 632. In the Charities Act 2011 s 115, 'charity' does not include an institution established under the laws of another legal system: *Gaudiya Mission v Brahmachary* [1998] Ch 341, [1997] 4 All ER 957, CA. As to the meaning of 'charity' in the Charities Act 2011 see PARA 1. As to the meaning of 'court' see PARA 177 note 12.

3 Charities Act 2011 s 115(8). See also *Brooks v Richardson* [1986] 1 All ER 952, [1986] 1 WLR 385; *Scott v National Trust for Places of Historic Interest or Natural Beauty* [1998] 2 All ER 705, sub nom *Ex p Scott* [1998] 1 WLR 226. See also CPR 64.5(2)(a), (b) which defines charity proceedings as having the same meaning as in the Charities Act 1993 s 33(8) (repealed) (now the Charities Act 2011 s 115(8)). As to the CPR see PARA 595.

4 See *Re Belling, Enfield London Borough Council v Public Trustee* [1967] Ch 425, [1967] 1 All ER 105; *Hauxwell v Barton-upon-Humber UDC* [1974] Ch 432, [1973] 2 All ER 1022; *Mills v Winchester Diocesan Board of Finance* [1989] Ch 428, [1989] 2 All ER 317 (all decided under previous legislation).

5 Ie the Charities Act 2011 s 115: see the text and note 3; and PARAS 593–594.

6 *Construction Industry Training Board v A-G* [1973] Ch 173, [1972] 2 All ER 1339, CA (decided under previous legislation). The Charitable Trusts Act 1853 s 17 proviso (repealed by the Charities Act 1960) contained a similar restriction, in different terms, as to which see *Re Shum's Trusts* (1904) 91 LT 192; *Bassano v Bradley* [1896] 1 QB 645, DC; *Holme v Guy* (1877) 5 ChD 901, CA; *Rendall v Blair* (1890) 45 ChD 139, CA; *Re St Giles' and St George's, Bloomsbury, Volunteer Corps* (1858) 25 Beav 313; *Re Poplar and Blackwall Free School* (1878) 8 ChD 543; *Re Lister's Hospital* (1855) 6 De GM & G 184; *Falconer v Stearn* [1932] 1 Ch 509; *Braund v Earl of Devon* (1868) 3 Ch App 800; *Rooke v Dawson* [1895] 1 Ch 480. See also *Cifci v Erbil* [2012] EWHC 3170 (Ch), [2012] All ER (D) 142 (Nov).

7 See *Rendall v Blair* (1890) 45 ChD 139, CA. For a modern example of charity proceedings of this type, in which the court gave a detailed judgment on the constitution and internal proceedings of a charity, see *Cifci v Erbil* [2012] EWHC 3170 (Ch), [2012] All ER (D) 142 (Nov).

8 See eg *Gunning v Buckfast Abbey Trustees Registered* (1994) Times, 9 June. See also *Scott v National Trust for Places of Historic Interest or Natural Beauty* [1998] 2 All ER 705, sub nom *Ex p Scott* [1998] 1 WLR 226, which indicated a wider meaning for charity proceedings, to include an application for judicial review of the decision of a charity's governing body where the charity is a public body susceptible to judicial review; and *R (on the application of Heather) v Leonard Cheshire Foundation* [2001] EWHC Admin 429 at [97], [2001] All ER (D) 156 (Jun) per Stanley Burton J ('judicial review proceedings against a charity exercising public functions are charity proceedings'). Cf *R (on the application of Brent London Borough Council) v Fed 2000* [2005] EWHC 2771 (Admin), [2005] All ER (D) 264 (Oct), where proceedings for judicial review were held not to be charity proceedings where there was no challenge to the due administration of the charity. Bringing charity proceedings in the Chancery Division is the procedure which must be followed in all but the most exceptional cases: *Scott v National Trust for Places of Historic Interest or Natural Beauty* [1998] 2 All ER 705 at 716 per Robert Walker J.

593. Claimants in charity proceedings. Charity proceedings[1] may be taken with reference to a charity[2] by the charity, or by any of the charity trustees[3], or by any person interested in the charity[4], or, if it is a local charity[5], by any two or more inhabitants of the area of the charity, but not by any other person[6]. This, however, does not prevent the taking of proceedings by the Charity Commission[7] or by the Attorney General[8], with or without a relator[9].

1 As to the meaning of 'charity proceedings' see PARA 592.

2 As to the meaning of 'charity' see PARA 1.

3 As to the meaning of 'charity trustees' see PARA 255.

4 See *Re Hampton Fuel Allotment Charity* [1989] Ch 484, sub nom *Richmond upon Thames London Borough Council v Rogers* [1988] 2 All ER 761, CA (to qualify as a claimant in his own right a person needs to have an interest materially greater than or different from that possessed by ordinary members of the public); applied in *Rosenzweig v NMC Recordings Ltd* [2013] EWHC 3792 (Ch), [2014] PTSR 261, [2014] 1 P & CR D46, [2013] All ER (D) 74 (Dec) (composer whose work had been rejected was a person interested in a charity concerned with the promotion of new music). A contract with the trustees relating to property of the charity does not suffice: *Haslemere Estates Ltd v Baker* [1982] 3 All ER 525, [1982] 1 WLR 1109. Nor are the executors of the will of the founder of a charity persons interested in the charity:

Bradshaw v University College of Wales, Aberystwyth [1987] 3 All ER 200, [1988] 1 WLR 190. See also *Scott v National Trust for Places of Historic Interest or Natural Beauty* [1998] 2 All ER 705, sub nom *Ex p Scott* [1998] 1 WLR 226.

See also *Gunning v Buckfast Abbey Trustees* (1994) Times, 9 June, where charity proceedings were properly brought by parents of children attending an independent school run by a charity, and although the parents had a contractual relationship with the school, they were not suing on their contracts but seeking the proper administration of the charity. They were persons interested in the charity because they had a moral and legal duty regarding the education of their children and thus had a concern that the charity should fulfil its functions properly which was greater than the concern of an ordinary member of the public.

5 As to the meaning of 'local charity' see PARA 189 note 10.

6 Charities Act 2011 s 115(1).

7 Ie under the Charities Act 2011 s 114: see PARA 558. As to the Charity Commission see PARAS 543–578.

8 As to the Attorney General see PARAS 589, 596, 605 et seq; and **CONSTITUTIONAL AND ADMINISTRATIVE LAW** vol 20 (2014) PARA 273 et seq.

9 Charities Act 2011 s 115(6). As to relators see further PARA 613 et seq. Relator proceedings are now rare in practice.

594. Authority or permission to bring charity proceedings. Apart from proceedings by the Attorney General, those taken by the Charity Commission under the powers conferred by the Charities Act 2011[1], and (as applicable) proceedings relating to an exempt charity[2], no charity proceedings[3] relating to a charity[4] may be entertained or proceeded with in any court unless the Charity Commission has by order authorised the taking of the proceedings[5]. The Commission must not, without special reasons, authorise the taking of proceedings where in its opinion the case can be dealt with by it under the other powers[6] conferred by the Charities Act 2011[7].

If an order of the Commission has been applied for and refused, the proceedings may nevertheless be entertained or proceeded with if, after the refusal, permission to take the proceedings is obtained from one of the judges of the High Court attached to the Chancery Division[8].

These provisions do not make necessary an order for the taking of proceedings[9] in a pending cause or matter, or for the bringing of any appeal[10].

Under previous legislation[11] it was held that where proceedings were commenced without the authority which ought to have been obtained, the proper course was to stay the proceedings to see if authority could be obtained[12].

1 Ie under the Charities Act 2011 s 114: see PARA 558. As to the Charity Commission see PARAS 543–578. As to the Attorney General see PARAS 589, 596, 605 et seq; and **CONSTITUTIONAL AND ADMINISTRATIVE LAW** vol 20 (2014) PARA 273 et seq.

2 Exempt charities are excluded from these provisions except where the increased regulation of exempt charities has effect in relation to the charity or class of charity in question: Charities Act 2011 s 115(2), (7)(a) (amended by Sch 9 para 21). As to exempt charities see PARAS 318–321. As to the increased regulation of exempt charities see PARA 319.

3 As to the meaning of 'charity proceedings' see PARA 592.

4 As to the meaning of 'charity' see PARA 1.

5 Charities Act 2011 s 115(2), (6) (and see note 2). See also PARA 592. It appears that the Charity Commission has power to give such authorisation retrospectively: *Park v Cho* [2014] EWHC 55 (Ch), [2014] PTSR 769, [2014] All ER (D) 151 (Jan), in which the Charity Commission was said to have proceeded on a false premise in stating that it did not have that power.

6 Ie powers other than those conferred by the Charities Act 2011 s 114: see PARA 558.

7 Charities Act 2011 s 115(3).

8 See the Charities Act 2011 s 115(5). In such proceedings the court is exercising an original jurisdiction and not acting as an appellate court against the decision of the Charity Commissioners; nonetheless, the Commission's refusal of permission is part of the evidence: *Garcha v Charity Commission for England and Wales* [2014] EWHC 2754 (Ch), [2014] PTSR D28, (2014) Times, 1 September.

The application is made without notice at first and must be made within 21 days of the refusal of the order. As to the application for permission to take charity proceedings see CPR 64.6; and PARA 621. Leave was not granted in a case concerning Dulwich College Picture Gallery: see the *Report of the Charity Commissioners for England and Wales for 1979* (HC Paper (1979–80) no 608) paras 56–58.

The intended proceedings must disclose a legally sustainable case: *Rai v Charity Commission for England and Wales* [2012] EWHC 1111 (Ch), [2012] PTSR D33, [2012] All ER (D) 22 (May); *Rosenzweig v NMC Recordings Ltd* [2013] EWHC 3792 (Ch), [2014] PTSR 261, [2014] 1 P & CR D46, [2013] All ER (D) 74 (Dec), where the court would not allow the taking of proceedings which had no legally sustainable case, were imperfectly pleaded and would have destroyed the charity; *Garcha v Charity Commission for England and Wales* (the court may take the wider view in reaching its decision, not solely the precise proceedings which it is being invited to authorise).

The claim must be advanced in good faith, though that is not of itself a sufficient reason to grant permission: *Rai v Charity Commission for England and Wales*; *Garcha v Charity Commission for England and Wales*.

9 The 'taking of proceedings' includes both initiating or commencing proceedings from their inception and the taking of steps within any existing proceedings: *Park v Cho* [2014] EWHC 55 (Ch), [2014] PTSR 769, [2014] All ER (D) 151 (Jan).

10 Charities Act 2011 s 115(4). An equivalent provision under previous legislation (ie the Charitable Trusts Act 1853 s 17 (repealed)) was held to mean pending at the date of the commencement of the proceedings in question: *Re Lister's Hospital* (1855) 6 De GM & G 184. The question is to be determined on the facts of each case: *Ford's Charity* (1855) 3 Drew 324; *Re Jarvis' Charity* (1859) 1 Drew & Sm 97.

11 See note 10.

12 *Rendall v Blair* (1890) 45 ChD 139, CA.

595. Procedure. Charity proceedings[1] and any appeal to the High Court, case stated or question referred for the opinion of that court under the Charities Act 2011 are assigned to the Chancery Division[2], and must be begun by a claim form[3], except for applications for permission to appeal[4] and applications for committal[5].

1 As to the meaning of 'charity proceedings' see PARA 592.

2 CPR 64.1(3).

3 See CPR 7.2; and CIVIL PROCEDURE vol 11 (2009) PARA 116 et seq. Unless there is a serious dispute of fact requiring particulars of claim, it is usual to commence charity proceedings by the alternative procedure under CPR Pt 8 (see CIVIL PROCEDURE vol 11 (2009) PARA 127 et seq) supported by witness statement. Application for permission to take charity proceedings must be brought under CPR Pt 8: see CPR 64.6(2); and PARA 621.

4 In the case of appeals, the appeal must be brought by an appeal notice: see CPR 52.3(2)(b); *Practice Direction—Estates, Trusts and Charities* PD64A para 10; and PARA 621.

5 See CPR 81.15.

(3) CLAIMS AND OTHER PROCEEDINGS

(i) Claims and Proceedings in general

596. Parties. In the case of proceedings involving charities the general rules as to who are the proper parties[1] are subject to two qualifications. In the first place, as already stated, only specified persons may take charity proceedings[2]; in the second place, the Attorney General is generally a necessary party[3].

He may either act alone ex officio as the officer of the Crown and, as such, the protector of charities, or at the request of a private individual, called a relator, who thinks that the charity is being or has been abused[4].

With the sanction of the Attorney General an ordinary action may be turned into a relator action, by amendment of the particulars of claim[5]. Otherwise claims of this kind, if instituted by parties other than the Attorney General or the

Solicitor General[6], are dismissed[7], unless the Attorney General applies to be substituted[8] as claimant and the court gives permission for the substitution[9].

1 See generally CIVIL PROCEDURE vol 11 (2009) PARA 207 et seq. In a claim for the court to determine any question arising in the administration of a deceased person's estate or the execution of a trust, for an order for the administration of a deceased person's estate or for the execution of a trust: (1) all the trustees must be parties; (2) if the claim is made by trustees then any of them who do not consent to being a claimant must be a defendant; and (3) the claimant may make parties to the claim any persons with an interest in or claim against the estate, or an interest under the trust, who it is appropriate to make parties having regard to the nature of the order sought: CPR 64.2, 64.4(1). This does not apply to the power of the High Court to authorise action to be taken in reliance on counsel's opinion as to the construction of a will or trust under the Administration of Justice Act 1985 s 48 (see TRUSTS AND POWERS vol 98 (2013) PARA 48): CPR 64.4(1). Cf *Re HMF* [1976] Ch 33, [1975] 2 All ER 795.

2 See the Charities Act 2011 s 115(1); and PARA 593. As to the meaning of 'charity proceedings' see PARA 592.

3 Where the Attorney General is a proper party, the Solicitor General is the proper person to take his place if the Attorney General's office is vacant or if he is ill or concerned in the action in another capacity: *R v Wilkes* (1770) 4 Burr 2527 at 2554, HL, per Lord Mansfield; *Ludlow Corpn v Greenhouse* (1827) 1 Bli NS 17 at 51, HL, per Lord Redesdale; *A-G v Bristol Corpn* (1820) 2 Jac & W 294; *A-G v Ironmongers' Co* (1834) 2 My & K 576; *A-G v Dean and Canons of Windsor* (1860) 8 HL Cas 369; *Brookes v Richardson* [1986] 1 All ER 952, [1986] 1 WLR 385; and see PARAS 599, 606. As to when the Attorney General is not a necessary party see PARA 609. As to the Attorney General see also PARAS 589, 605 et seq; and CONSTITUTIONAL AND ADMINISTRATIVE LAW vol 20 (2014) PARA 273 et seq. As to the Solicitor General see CONSTITUTIONAL AND ADMINISTRATIVE LAW vol 20 (2014) PARA 273 et seq.

Before the creation of the High Court of Chancery, proceedings by the Attorney General ex officio or at the relation of plaintiffs were taken by information, it being a public privilege that the Crown should be entitled to intervene by its officer for the purpose of asserting a public right: *A-G v Compton* (1842) 1 Y & C Ch Cas 417 at 427 per Knight Bruce V-C. After 1873 these proceedings became actions commenced by writ: cf *A-G v Shrewsbury Bridge Co* (1880) 42 LT 79. These actions were not affected by the abolition of Latin and English informations by the Crown Proceedings Act 1947 s 13, Sch 1; but, except so far as they are excepted by s 23(3)(a) as being relator proceedings, they appear to be civil proceedings by the Crown within s 23(1)(b): see CROWN AND CROWN PROCEEDINGS vol 29 (2014) PARAS 90, 99. See further PARAS 599, 606.

4 *A-G v Logan* [1891] 2 QB 100 at 103, DC, per Wills J; and see *A-G v Cockermouth Local Board* (1874) LR 18 Eq 172 at 176 per Jessel MR. Except for the purposes of costs there is no practical difference between proceedings ex officio and on relation. As to relators see further PARA 613 et seq. Relator proceedings are now rare in practice.

5 *Caldwell v Pagham Harbour Reclamation Co* (1876) 2 ChD 221 (reclamation of land covered by sea); *Wallasey Local Board v Gracey* (1887) 36 ChD 593 at 599 per Stirling J (public nuisance). For earlier practice see *President etc of St Mary Magdalen College, Oxford v Sibthorp* (1826) 1 Russ 154; *A-G v Newcombe* (1807) 14 Ves 1 at 6 per Lord Eldon LC; *A-G v Vivian* (1826) 1 Russ 226; *A-G v East India Co* (1840) 11 Sim 380; *A-G v Cuming* (1843) 2 Y & C Ch Cas 139 at 149 per Knight Bruce V-C. If the claim is or becomes one within the statutory definition of 'charity proceedings' (see PARA 592), it should be begun by a claim form (see CPR 7.2; and PARA 595), but the court could, no doubt, permit it to proceed with particulars of claim (cf CPR 8.1(3); and see CIVIL PROCEDURE vol 11 (2009) PARA 127 et seq). The claim should normally be a CPR Part 8 claim.

6 See note 3.

7 *A-G v Hewitt* (1804) 9 Ves 232; *A-G v Green* (1820) 1 Jac & W 303 at 305 per Lord Eldon LC; *Strickland v Weldon* (1885) 28 ChD 426; *A-G v Wyggeston Hospital* (1853) 16 Beav 313, where a petition presented in the name, but without the authority, of the Attorney General was dismissed.

8 Ie under CPR 19.2: see CIVIL PROCEDURE vol 11 (2009) PARA 213.

9 Cf *Hauxwell v Barton-upon-Humber UDC* [1974] Ch 432, [1973] 2 All ER 1022.

597. Control of proceedings by the court. The court has a duty to actively manage cases[1] and its general powers of management are set out in the Civil Procedure Rules[2].

1 See CPR 1.4; and CIVIL PROCEDURE vol 11 (2009) PARAS 35, 246.
2 See CPR Pt 3; and CIVIL PROCEDURE vol 11 (2009) PARA 247 et seq. Formerly, it was the case that the Attorney General had entire control of the proceedings, whether they were ex officio or at the request of a relator: *Andrew v Master and Wardens of the Merchant Taylors' Co* (1800) 7 Ves 223, HL; *A-G v Hewitt* (1804) 9 Ves 232; *Ludlow Corpn v Greenhouse* (1827) 1 Bli NS 17 at 65, HL, per Lord Redesdale; *A-G v Ironmongers' Co* (1840) 2 Beav 313 at 328–329 per Lord Langdale MR; *A-G v Haberdashers' Co* (1852) 15 Beav 397. See also the non-charity case of *LCC v A-G* [1902] AC 165, HL. As to relators see further PARA 613 et seq. Relator proceedings are now rare in practice.
The Attorney General had control even where he did not act personally: *A-G v Hewitt* (1804) 9 Ves 232. No amendment could be made (*A-G v Fellows* (1820) 1 Jac & W 254), or notice of motion given (*A-G v Wright* (1841) 3 Beav 447), without his consent. He could also, at any time, stay the proceedings: *A-G v Ironmongers' Co* (1840) 2 Beav 313 at 329 per Lord Langdale MR; *A-G v Newark-upon-Trent Corpn* (1842) 1 Hare 395. A reference to arbitration could only be made with his sanction: *A-G v Hewitt* (1804) 9 Ves 232; *A-G v Fea* (1819) 4 Madd 274; and see *Prior v Hembrow* (1841) 8 M & W 873. His consent was also necessary before an award could be acted upon: *A-G v Hewitt* (1804) 9 Ves 232; and see *A-G v Clements* (1823) Turn & R 58 at 61 per Lord Eldon LC.
As to the Attorney General see PARAS 589, 596, 605 et seq; and CONSTITUTIONAL AND ADMINISTRATIVE LAW vol 20 (2014) PARA 273 et seq.

598. Duty of the Attorney General and of the court. It has been held that it is not the duty of the Attorney General[1] in all charity cases to contend for his strict legal rights when the result of enforcing them would be oppressive to individuals. If, however, he insists on his strict rights, the court will enforce them[2].

The court formerly exercised a quasi-custodial jurisdiction over a charity when proceedings were brought for its regulation or administration[3].

1 As to the Attorney General see PARAS 589, 596, 605 et seq; and CONSTITUTIONAL AND ADMINISTRATIVE LAW vol 20 (2014) PARA 273 et seq.
2 *A-G v Brettingham* (1840) 3 Beav 91 at 95 per Lord Langdale MR. See also *Re Snowden, Shackleton v Eddy, Re Henderson, Henderson v A-G* [1970] Ch 700, [1969] 3 All ER 208; and PARA 429.
3 See *A-G v Governors of Harrow School* (1754) 2 Ves Sen 551 at 552 per Lord Hardwicke LC: 'though I will make no decree at present, yet I will not dismiss the information, but still keep a hand over them'. The principal example of this attitude was that the wrong prayer was never fatal in a charity case where it appeared that some relief might be given; cf *A-G v Coopers' Co* (1812) 19 Ves 187 at 194 per Lord Eldon LC: 'the court is not only to attend to an actual complaint but to see whether there is any cause for complaint'. Actions were generally not dismissed for want of form, though care was taken not to injure the defendant. These principles may be regarded as obsolete for general relief may now be given (see the Senior Courts Act 1981 s 49; and EQUITABLE JURISDICTION vol 47 (2014) PARAS 98–99), and amendment to statements of case is more freely available (see CPR Pt 17; and CIVIL PROCEDURE vol 11 (2009) PARA 607 et seq).
In addition, the Charity Commission has powers of supervision, guidance and inquiry in relation to charities: see PARA 543 et seq. As to the Charity Commission see PARAS 543–578.

599. Information to Attorney General with a view to proceedings by him. Where it appears to the Charity Commission[1] that it is desirable for legal proceedings to be taken with reference to any charity[2] or its property or affairs, and for the proceedings to be taken by the Attorney General, it must so inform him and send him such statements and particulars as it thinks necessary to explain the matter[3].

1 As to the Charity Commission see PARAS 543–578.
2 As to the meaning of 'charity' see PARA 1. Exempt charities are excluded from these provisions except where the increased regulation of exempt charities has effect in relation to the charity or class of charity in question: Charities Act 2011 s 115(2), (7)(a) (amended by Sch 9 para 21). As to exempt charities see PARAS 318–321. As to the increased regulation of exempt charities see PARA 319.

3 Charities Act 2011 s 115(7). This may arise out of an application for the Commission's authority under s 115 to take charity proceedings or otherwise: s 115(7). As to the meaning of 'charity proceedings' see PARA 592. The Charity Commission may, by its own motion, also bring legal proceedings with reference to charities or the property or affairs of charities, with the agreement of the Attorney General: see s 114(5); and PARA 558. As to the Attorney General see PARAS 589, 596, 605 et seq; and **CONSTITUTIONAL AND ADMINISTRATIVE LAW** vol 20 (2014) PARA 273 et seq.

600. Proceedings by trustees. If the Attorney General declines to interfere in a dispute over the administration of a trust, and the trustees of the charity differ amongst themselves as to the proper mode of administration, a certain number may bring the matter before the court by a claim on behalf of themselves and others, making some of the dissentients and the Attorney General defendants[1].

1 *Lang v Purves* (1862) 8 Jur NS 523 at 525, PC. Such proceedings would require the consent of the Charity Commission or the permission of the court: see PARA 594. As to representative actions, i e one or more of numerous parties suing or defending on behalf of all, see CPR 19.6; *A-G v Fowler* (1808) 15 Ves 85 at 87; *Milligan v Mitchell* (1837) 3 My & Cr 72; and **CIVIL PROCEDURE** vol 11 (2009) PARA 229.

It is now relatively uncommon for the Attorney General to commence charity proceedings. It is more usual for one or more of the trustees to do so, making any dissentient trustees, as well as the Attorney General, defendants: see *Varsani v Jesani* [1999] Ch 219, [1998] 3 All ER 273, CA.

As to the Attorney General see PARAS 589, 596, 605 et seq; and **CONSTITUTIONAL AND ADMINISTRATIVE LAW** vol 20 (2014) PARA 273 et seq.

601. Evidence. In any proceedings, the printed copies of the reports of the Charity Commissioners[1] for inquiring concerning charities between 1818 and 1837[2] and the printed copies of the reports which were made for various counties and county boroughs to the Charity Commissioners by their assistant Commissioners and presented to the House of Commons as returns to orders of various dates between 8 December 1890 and 9 September 1909, are admissible as evidence of the documents[3] and facts stated in them[4].

Evidence of any order, certificate or other document issued by the Charity Commission[5] or the Charity Commissioners[6] may be given by means of a copy which it retained, or which is taken from a copy so retained and evidence of an entry in any register kept by it may be given by means of a certified copy of the entry[7]. In each case, the copy must be certified to be a true copy by any member of the staff of the Commission generally or specially authorised by the Commission to act for that purpose[8].

The official seal of the official custodian for charities is judicially noticed[9].

In any legal proceedings instituted[10] by the Charity Commission, or instituted by the Attorney General in respect of a charity[11], a copy of the report of the person conducting an inquiry[12] is admissible, if certified by the Commission to be a true copy, as evidence of any fact stated in the report, and as evidence of the opinion of that person as to any matter referred to in it[13].

1 As to the Charity Commissioners see PARA 543.
2 Ie who were appointed under the Act 58 Geo 3 c 91 (the Inquiry Concerning Charities Act 1838) (repealed).
3 As to the meaning of 'document' see PARA 263 note 2.
4 Charities Act 2011 s 344(3).
5 As to the Charity Commission see PARAS 543–578.
6 Charities Act 2011 s 343(4).
7 Charities Act 2011 s 343(1), (2).
8 Charities Act 2011 s 343(1), (2). A document purporting to be such a copy must be received in evidence without proof of the official position, authority or handwriting of the person certifying it: s 343(3).

9 See the Charities Act 2011 Sch 2 para 1; and PARA 300. As to the official custodian see PARA 300 et seq.
10 Ie under the Charities Act 2011 Pt 6 (ss 61–116).
11 As to the meaning of 'charity' see PARA 1. As to the Attorney General see PARAS 589, 596, 605 et seq; and **CONSTITUTIONAL AND ADMINISTRATIVE LAW** vol 20 (2014) PARA 273 et seq.
12 Ie under the Charities Act 2011 s 46: see PARAS 559–560.
13 Charities Act 2011 s 342(1), (2). A document purporting to be a certificate issued for these purposes must be received in evidence and is deemed to be such a certificate, unless the contrary is proved: s 342(3).

602. Court's discretion. Modern practice of the courts has been to consider what is in the interests of the charity in determining the issues arising in the case, and if it considers that the proceedings themselves are against its interests it will make this very clear, and either encourage the parties to settle or refuse relief on grounds of expense[1]. By its wide discretion over costs the court can discourage parties taking useless proceedings even if the proceedings are sanctioned by the Attorney General[2].

The court has disapproved of charity proceedings being promoted by public meetings and supported by public subscriptions[3].

Actual or contemplated breaches of trust may be restrained by injunction[4]. When necessary a claim for an injunction may be brought by a trustee against his co-trustees[5].

1 See eg *Governing Body of the Henrietta Barnett School v Hampstead Garden Suburb Institute* (1995) 93 LGR 470, sub nom *Re Hampstead Garden Suburb Institute* (1995) Times, 13 April; *Varsani v Jesani* [1999] Ch 219, [1998] 3 All ER 273, CA. However, there are many cases in which the sole question for the court is whether proposed proceedings are in the interests of the charity: see eg *Weth v A-G* (3 December 1997, unreported); affd [2001] EWCA Civ 263, [2001] All ER (D) 314 (Feb) (proposed appeal against appointment of receiver and manager for charity held not in the interests of the charity because of charity's limited financial resources).
2 *A-G (ex rel Everett and Bottomley) v Merchant Tailors' Co* (1834) 5 LJCh 62; but see *A-G v Cullum* (1836) 1 Keen 104; and PARA 453. As to the Attorney General see PARAS 589, 596, 605 et seq; and **CONSTITUTIONAL AND ADMINISTRATIVE LAW** vol 20 (2014) PARA 273 et seq.

Instead of acting according to the strict rules of law, the court had discretion to refer matters arising out of proceedings to the Attorney General, and to act on his certificate or report: *A-G v Exeter Corpn* (1827) 2 Russ 362 (where the court referred the matter to the Attorney General to certify whether a charity might accept from its debtor a smaller sum than was actually due); *A-G v Green* (1820) 1 Jac & W 303; *A-G v Carlisle Corpn* (1831) 4 Sim 275; *A-G v Pretyman* (1841) 4 Beav 462 at 467 per Lord Langdale MR; *A-G v Tufnell* (1849) 12 Beav 35 at 41 per Lord Langdale MR; and see *A-G v Brettingham* (1840) 3 Beav 91 (where, in a hard case, the decision was postponed in order that the Attorney General might come to some arrangement). However, questions arising on the construction of wills and other documents were not referred to the Attorney General: *A-G v Fea* (1819) 4 Madd 274.
3 *A-G v Bishop of Worcester* (1851) 21 LJCh 25 at 46 per Turner V-C.
4 *Rigall v Foster* (1853) 18 Jur 39 (to restrain improper mortgage by charity trustees); *A-G v Welsh* (1844) 4 Hare 572 (to prevent user of chapel for unauthorised form of worship); *A-G v Murdoch* (1849) 7 Hare 445 (affd (1852) 1 De GM & G 86); *Cooper v Gordon* (1869) LR 8 Eq 249 (to restrain ministers from officiating); *Milligan v Mitchell* (1833) 1 My & K 446 (to prevent election of unlicensed minister). As to injunctions generally see **CIVIL PROCEDURE** vol 11 (2009) PARA 335 et seq.
5 *Re Chertsey Market, ex p Walthew* (1819) 6 Price 261 at 279; *Perry v Shipway* (1859) 4 De G & J 353 (where an improper retainer of a chapel by the minority of the trustees was prevented by the majority).

603. Compromise. Questions relating to charities may be compromised and the terms of the compromise confirmed by the court[1].

Trustees for charities have power to compromise claims under the Trustee Act 1925[2]. In addition, a compromise may be approved by the Charity Commission[3] under the Charities Act 2011[4].

Where the Attorney General is a party to any legal proceedings affecting a charity, no compromise can be enforced without his sanction[5]. Where, in proceedings in which a charity is cited but does not appear, the Attorney General assents to a compromise on behalf of the absent charity, that charity is bound by the compromise[6].

1 This may happen, for example, in cases where it is doubtful whether a bequest or devise to charity is valid, and a compromise is arrived at by a division of the property between the charity and other claimants, such as the persons entitled on intestacy, and residuary legatees: *A-G v Landerfield* (1743) 9 Mod Rep 286; *Re Simpson's Will* (circa 1786) cited in 5 Ves 304; *A-G v Bishop of Oxford* (1786) cited in 4 Ves 431; *Andrew v Master and Wardens of the Merchant Taylors' Co* (1800) 7 Ves 223; *Andrew v Trinity Hall, Cambridge* (1804) 9 Ves 525 at 532–533 per Grant MR. See also *A-G v Trevelyan* (1847) 16 LJCh 521 and *Re Freeston's Charity, Sylvester v Master and Fellows of University College, Oxford* [1978] 1 All ER 481 at 490, [1978] 1 WLR 120 at 130 per Fox J; affd [1979] 1 All ER 51, [1978] 1 WLR 741, CA, without discussing this point.

2 See the Trustee Act 1925 s 15; and TRUSTS AND POWERS vol 98 (2013) PARA 518.

3 As to the Charity Commission see PARAS 543–578.

4 See the Charities Act 2011 s 105(3); and PARA 387.

5 *Andrew v Master and Wardens of the Merchant Taylors' Co* (1800) 7 Ves 223; *Andrew v Trinity Hall, Cambridge* (1804) 9 Ves 525 at 532–533 per Grant MR; *A-G v Exeter Corpn* (1827) 2 Russ 362; *A-G v Fishmongers' Co* (1837) Coop Pr Cas 85; *A-G v Ludlow Corpn* (1842) 6 Jur 1003; *A-G v Trevelyan* (1847) 16 LJCh 521; *A-G v Boucherett* (1858) 25 Beav 116. As to the Attorney General see PARAS 589, 596, 605 et seq; and CONSTITUTIONAL AND ADMINISTRATIVE LAW vol 20 (2014) PARA 273 et seq.

6 *Re King, Jackson v A-G* [1917] 2 Ch 420.

604. Service on Treasury Solicitor. In all charity proceedings, any document required or authorised to be served on the Charity Commission[1] or the Attorney General[2] must also be served on the Treasury Solicitor[3].

1 As to the Charity Commission see PARAS 543–578.

2 As to the Attorney General see PARAS 589, 596, 605 et seq; and CONSTITUTIONAL AND ADMINISTRATIVE LAW vol 20 (2014) PARA 273 et seq.

3 CPR *Practice Direction—Estates, Trusts and Charities* PD 64A para 8. This must be in accordance with *Practice Direction—Crown Proceedings* PD 66 para 2.1. As to the Treasury Solicitor see CONSTITUTIONAL AND ADMINISTRATIVE LAW vol 20 (2014) PARA 281. *Practice Direction—Estates, Trusts and Charities* PD 64A para 8 refers to the Charity Commissioners; this has effect as if it were a reference to the Charity Commission: see PARA 543.

(ii) The Attorney General as a Party

605. Attorney General a necessary party. The Attorney General[1] is a necessary party to all charity proceedings[2], other than any commenced by the Charity Commission[3], and must be joined as a defendant if he is not a claimant[4].

Thus where proceedings[5] are necessary to test the validity of an alleged charitable gift[6], even where the class to benefit is a foreign community[7], or to determine whether a claim to the benefit of a charity is properly founded[8], or to enforce the execution of a charitable purpose, or to remedy abuse or misapplication of charitable funds, or to administer a charity[9], the Attorney General is generally[10] a necessary party[11], and is normally the proper claimant[12]. He represents the beneficial interest, in other words the objects, of the charity[13]. Even if all the subscribers to a charitable fund are made claimants, a claim for the regulation of the charity is defective unless the Attorney General is also a party[14].

1 The Solicitor General may in some circumstances discharge the Attorney General's functions: see PARA 596 note 3. As to the Attorney General see also PARAS 589, 596; and CONSTITUTIONAL AND ADMINISTRATIVE LAW vol 20 (2014) PARA 273 et seq.

2 As to the meaning of 'charity proceedings' see PARA 592. The Attorney General's right to file an information (which was the procedure prior to the creation of the High Court of Chancery: see PARA 596 note 3), and consequently his right to take proceedings today, was founded on the Crown's prerogative as parens patriae (see CONSTITUTIONAL AND ADMINISTRATIVE LAW vol 20 (2014) PARA 137) to inform the court of and demand a remedy for an injustice perpetrated against a subject of the Crown (eg a charity) who was incompetent to enforce a claim in person: see Shelford's Law of Mortmain (1836) 399; *A-G v Brown* (1818) 1 Swan 265 at 291; *Wellbeloved v Jones* (1822) 1 Sim & St 40; *A-G v Compton* (1842) 1 Y & C Ch Cas 417 at 427 per Knight Bruce V-C; *A-G v Magdalen College, Oxford* (1854) 23 LJCh 844 at 852 per Romilly MR. See also *Re Weir Hospital* [1910] 2 Ch 124 at 130, CA; *Re Belling, Enfield London Borough Council v Public Trustee* [1967] Ch 425, [1967] 1 All ER 105; *Hauxwell v Barton-upon-Humber UDC* [1974] Ch 432, [1973] 2 All ER 1022. Moreover, the Attorney General is the protector of the interests of all charities beneficially entitled under charitable gifts, and all beneficiaries are bound if he is made a party: *Re Sekeford's Charity* (1861) 5 LT 488; *Ware v Cumberlege* (1855) 20 Beav 503.

3 *Practice Direction—Estates, Trusts and Charities* PD 64A para 7 refers to the Charity Commissioners rather than the Charity Commission; however, this has effect as if it were a reference to the Charity Commission for England and Wales: see PARA 543. As to the Charity Commissioners, and the transfer of their functions and liabilities to the Charity Commission, see PARA 543. As to the Charity Commission see PARAS 543–578.

4 *Practice Direction—Estates, Trusts and Charities* PD 64A para 7.

5 See PARA 596 note 3.

6 See eg *Kirkbank v Hudson* (1819) 7 Price 212.

7 See *Re Love, Naper v Barlow* [1932] WN 17 (gift for benefit of parishes in Republic of Ireland: Attorney General of the Republic held not to be a proper party and struck out; Attorney General directed to be added).

8 *Re Magdalen Land Charity, Hastings* (1852) 9 Hare 624, where the proceeds of the charity had for many years been applied for other purposes.

9 See PARA 606.

10 *Wellbeloved v Jones* (1822) 1 Sim & St 40; *Ware v Cumberlege* (1855) 20 Beav 503; *Boughey v Minor* [1893] P 181 (compromise). The cases distinguish between gifts for charity generally, which cannot be represented by anyone other than the Attorney General, and cases where there are specified individual charities, when the Attorney General's presence is not universally necessary. However, if there is a gift to charity trustees and the question is whether the trust is validly established, the persons named as trustees are the proper parties, and it may not be necessary for the Attorney General to be a party: *Practice Note* [1945] WN 38. See also *Re HMF* [1976] Ch 33, [1975] 2 All ER 795.

11 *Wellbeloved v Jones* (1822) 1 Sim & St 40; *Christ's Hospital Governors v A-G* (1846) 5 Hare 257 (Attorney General as defendant); *Philipps v A-G* [1932] WN 100 (dormant fund, raised by subscription; cy-près application; Attorney General as defendant).

12 *Strickland v Weldon* (1885) 28 ChD 426 at 430 per Pearson J; *Re Belling, Enfield London Borough Council v Public Trustee* [1967] Ch 425, [1967] 1 All ER 105; *Hauxwell v Barton-upon-Humber UDC* [1974] Ch 432, [1973] 2 All ER 1022; but see *Baldry v Feintuck* [1972] 2 All ER 81, [1972] 1 WLR 552, where the Attorney General was not a party. When appearing on behalf of a charity, the Attorney General is not like an ordinary claimant endeavouring to obtain redress for a private wrong. It is one of his duties to protect the defendant against any hardship which he might suffer at the hands of the relators, eg if they mislead him or withhold documents or other necessary information: *A-G v Clapham* (1853) 10 Hare App II, lxviii at lxx per Wood V-C. Although the Attorney General is a proper claimant, he is most often involved as the defendant: see PARA 608. As to relators see further PARA 613 et seq. Relator proceedings are now rare in practice.

In High Court proceedings for the construction of wills or other documents or by personal representatives for directions, the Attorney General, if a party where a charity is concerned, is usually made a defendant: see eg *Re Lawton, Gartside v A-G* [1936] 3 All ER 378 (question whether bequest should lapse or be applied cy-près).

13 *A-G v Brodie* (1846) 6 Moo PCC 12; *A-G v Bishop of Worcester* (1851) 9 Hare 328 at 361 per Turner V-C; *Ware v Cumberlege* (1855) 20 Beav 503; *Re Sekeford's Charity* (1861) 5 LT 488. See also *Brooks v Richardson* [1986] 1 All ER 952, [1986] 1 WLR 385.

14 *Stickland v Weldon* (1885) 28 ChD 426. See also *Minn v Stant* (1851) 15 Beav 49, where, for a special transaction, it was held that the subscribers were necessary parties; but see *Baldry v Feintuck* [1972] 2 All ER 81, [1972] 1 WLR 552.

606. Administration proceedings. In administration proceedings where a question arises as to the application of a gift for charitable purposes, the Attorney General is a necessary party to represent the interests of charity in general[1]. Where there are gifts to specified individual charities and the establishment of a scheme or rules is required for the regulation of the internal conduct of the charity, the presence of the Attorney General is necessary[2]. Similarly, he is generally a necessary party when the question is whether a particular bequest is charitable[3], or is applicable cy-près[4], or where there is a gift to an established charitable institution to be held upon trusts differing from those upon which the general funds of the institution are held[5].

The Attorney General is not a necessary party in administration proceedings where the legacy is to an established charitable institution as part of its general funds[6], or to named trustees and the question is the validity of the trusts of which they are trustees[7], or to an action for account in respect of a legacy given to a charity[8], or where annual sums are given to specified trustees to be distributed in charity[9], or where a capital sum is given for immediate distribution[10]. Where the question is whether a charity is entitled to a particular legacy or not, the Attorney General may be made a party as being in the nature of a trustee for the charity, but his presence is not necessary, and the court prefers that the charity should itself appear rather than that the Attorney General should represent it[11].

1 *Ware v Cumberlege* (1855) 20 Beav 503 at 511 per Romilly MR. See also *A-G v Bowyer* (1798) 3 Ves 714 at 726 per Lord Hardwicke LC; *Boughey v Minor* [1893] P 181; *Re Pyne, Lilley v A-G* [1903] 1 Ch 83; and *Practice Note* [1945] WN 38. As to the Attorney General see PARAS 589, 596, 605 et seq; and CONSTITUTIONAL AND ADMINISTRATIVE LAW vol 20 (2014) PARA 273 et seq.

2 *Ware v Cumberlege* (1855) 20 Beav 503. See also *Practice Direction—Estates, Trusts and Charities* PD 64A para 7; and PARA 605.

3 *Cook v Duckenfield* (1743) 2 Atk 562 at 564 per Lord Hardwicke LC; and see PARA 605.

4 *Re Taylor, Martin v Freeman* (1888) 58 LT 538. A legacy may be ordered to be paid to a legatee on his undertaking to the Attorney General to apply the sum for charitable purposes: see *Re Reddish, Penton v Waters* [1934] WN 198. As to the doctrine of cy-près see PARA 209 et seq.

5 *Wellbeloved v Jones* (1822) 1 Sim & St 40; *Sons of the Clergy Corpn v Mose* (1839) 9 Sim 610; and see *A-G v Warren* (1818) 2 Swan 291.

6 *Wellbeloved v Jones* (1822) 1 Sim & St 40; *Re M'Auliffe's Goods* [1895] P 290.

7 See *Practice Note* [1945] WN 38: in such cases the position is that there is no universal rule that the Attorney General must be a party.

8 *Chitty v Parker* (1792) 4 Bro CC 38.

9 *Waldo v Caley* (1809) 16 Ves 206; *M'Coll v Atherton* (1848) 12 Jur 1042. See also *Horde v Earl of Suffolk* (1833) 2 My & K 59 (where the Attorney General was a party but appeared to claim the legacy on behalf of the Crown, alleging failure of the charitable bequest and of the next of kin).

10 *Re Barnett* (1860) 29 LJCh 871. But see *Re Lea, Lea v Cooke* (1887) 34 ChD 528 (where the Attorney General was a party, the question being whether a charitable legacy should be paid over without a scheme).

11 *Ware v Cumberlege* (1855) 20 Beav 503.

607. Claims by Crown. The Attorney General represents the Crown where the Crown is claiming beneficially[1]. Therefore, when the Crown's private rights conflict with its rights as protector of charities, one of the law officers appears on behalf of the Crown's private interests and the other represents the charitable interest[2].

The Attorney General had to be a party to legal proceedings where the question concerned the Crown's right to appoint under the sign manual, even before the right was delegated to him[3].

1 *A-G v Magdalen College, Oxford* (1854) 18 Beav 223 at 241 per Romilly MR. As to the Attorney General see PARAS 589, 596, 605 et seq; and CONSTITUTIONAL AND ADMINISTRATIVE LAW vol 20 (2014) PARA 273 et seq.

2 *A-G v Bristol Corpn* (1820) 2 Jac & W 294 at 312 per Lord Eldon LC; *A-G v Ironmongers' Co* (1834) 2 My & K 576 at 578; *A-G v Dean and Canons of Windsor* (1860) 8 HL Cas 369.

3 *De Themmines v De Bonneval* (1828) 5 Russ 288. See PARA 513.

608. Attorney General as defendant. The Attorney General may be made a defendant in a claim by charity trustees for an account of the charity property and a personal discharge[1]; or for the purpose of protecting the interests of a charity[2], as, for example, where a claim is brought by executors to determine the validity of a doubtful charitable bequest[3]; or to decide whether a testator's general charitable intention should be carried into effect by a court scheme or under the royal sign manual[4].

1 *Clum Hospital Warden and Brethren v Lord Powys* (1842) 6 Jur 252; *Christ's Hospital Governors v A-G* (1846) 5 Hare 257. In such claims the trustees must render such accounts as the Attorney General demands, and, if he desires it, the court may direct a scheme. As to proceedings by trustees see PARA 600. As to the direction of schemes see PARA 179 et seq. As to the Attorney General see PARAS 589, 596, 605 et seq; and CONSTITUTIONAL AND ADMINISTRATIVE LAW vol 20 (2014) PARA 273 et seq.

2 *Ludlow Corpn v Greenhouse* (1827) 1 Bli NS 17 at 66, HL, per Lord Redesdale.

3 See *Re Waring, Hayward v A-G* [1907] 1 Ch 166; *Re Pardoe, McLaughlin v A-G* [1906] 2 Ch 184; *Re Mann, Hardy v A-G* [1903] 1 Ch 232.

4 *Re Pyne, Lilley v A-G* [1903] 1 Ch 83; *Re Bennett, Sucker v A-G* [1960] Ch 18, [1959] 3 All ER 295.

609. When Attorney General is not a necessary party. The Attorney General is not a necessary party where the proceedings concern a private charity[1], or where the trust is not charitable[2], or where, whether the trust is charitable or not, the parties taking the proceedings do so under express statutory powers[3], or where third persons are taking proceedings against charity trustees for specific performance of an agreement[4].

1 *Anon* (1745) 3 Atk 277 (society for providing for necessities of its members and their widows, being in the nature of a private charity, the Attorney General on behalf of the Crown is not concerned to see to its proper application). A private charity (see PARA 59) in this sense is one for the benefit of private individuals, and not of the public or a section of the public (see PARA 6). Quaere whether this would now be followed. If it is right, it is on the basis that the institution is not charitable at all in the legal sense. As to the Attorney General see PARAS 589, 596, 605 et seq; and CONSTITUTIONAL AND ADMINISTRATIVE LAW vol 20 (2014) PARA 273 et seq.

2 *A-G v Hewer* (1700) 2 Vern 387 (school not a charity school); *A-G v Whorwood* (1750) 1 Ves Sen 534 at 536 per Lord Hardwicke LC (where it was held, in the case of a devise to a college, that there were no grounds for an information (see PARA 596 note 3) by the Attorney General); *A-G v Brereton* (1752) 2 Ves Sen 425 at 426 per Lord Hardwicke LC; *A-G v Newcombe* (1807) 14 Ves 1 at 7 per Lord Eldon LC; *Prestney v Colchester Corpn and A-G* (1882) 21 ChD 111.

The cases deciding that advowsons held on trust for parishioners were not charity property and that therefore an information by the Attorney General was not maintainable with regard to such trusts (see *A-G v Parker* (1747) 1 Ves Sen 43; *A-G v Forster* (1804) 10 Ves 335; *A-G v Newcombe*; *A-G v Webster* (1875) LR 20 Eq 483 at 491 per Jessel MR) cannot be supported on that point since the cases of *Re St Stephen, Coleman Street, Re St Mary the Virgin, Aldermanbury* (1888) 39 ChD 492 and *Hunter v A-G* [1899] AC 309 at 315, HL, per Earl of Halsbury LC, which decided that such trusts are charitable. See PARA 31. As to advowsons see ECCLESIASTICAL LAW vol 34 (2011) PARA 550.

3 *Prestney v Colchester Corpn and A-G* (1882) 21 ChD 111 at 119–120 per Hall V-C (action by some freemen of a borough, on behalf of all, to establish a right for the benefit of all the freemen, suing under powers conferred by the Municipal Corporations Act 1835 s 2 (repealed)); cf *A-G v Meyrick* [1893] AC 1, HL (where the Act did not contain similar provisions and the Attorney General was a party).

4 *A-G v Warren* (1818) 2 Swan 291 at 311 per Plumer MR; *Neville Estates Ltd v Madden* [1962] Ch 832, [1961] 3 All ER 769. See also *Rendall v Blair* (1890) 45 ChD 139, CA.

610. Parties bound by proceedings. All beneficiaries are bound by the result of proceedings to which the Attorney General is a party[1], but the Attorney General is not bound by any proceedings taken by beneficiaries to which he is not made a party[2].

1 *Vince v Walsh* (1854) 3 WR 7. As to the Attorney General see PARAS 589, 596, 605 et seq; and CONSTITUTIONAL AND ADMINISTRATIVE LAW vol 20 (2014) PARA 273 et seq.
2 *A-G v Leage* (1881) Tudor on Charities (4th Edn, 1906) 1041 at p 1044 per Kay J, discussing *Saunders v Howes* (1857) cited in Tudor on Charities (4th Edn, 1906) p 1043.

611. Payment into court by trustees. If a trustee pays money or securities into court[1], unless the court orders otherwise, he must immediately serve notice of the payment into court on every person interested in or entitled to the money or securities[2]. This includes the Attorney General who has an interest in the funds as representing the public[3]. The payment into court discharges the trustees, and all future applications in regard to the fund so paid in must be made by the Attorney General only[4].

1 See the Trustee Act 1925 s 63; and TRUSTS AND POWERS vol 98 (2013) PARA 357 et seq.
2 *Practice Direction—Miscellaneous Provisions about Payments into Court* PD 37 para 6.3; and CIVIL PROCEDURE vol 11 (2009) PARA 742.
3 *Re Poplar and Blackwall Free School* (1878) 8 ChD 543 at 546 per Jessel MR. As to the Attorney General see PARAS 589, 596, 605 et seq; and CONSTITUTIONAL AND ADMINISTRATIVE LAW vol 20 (2014) PARA 273 et seq.
4 *Re Poplar and Blackwall Free School* (1878) 8 ChD 543.

612. Appeal by Attorney General. With the permission of the Court of Appeal, the Attorney General may appeal against a decision in proceedings to which he was not a party in the court of first instance[1]. However, after a decree which he did not oppose in proceedings to which he was a party he should not reopen the discussion by an appeal, although the court will not dismiss the appeal on that ground alone[2].

1 *Re Faraker, Faraker v Durell* [1912] 2 Ch 488, CA. As to the Attorney General see PARAS 589, 596, 605 et seq; and CONSTITUTIONAL AND ADMINISTRATIVE LAW vol 20 (2014) PARA 273 et seq.
2 *Christ's Hospital v Grainger* (1849) 19 LJCh 33 at 36 per Lord Cottenham LC.

(iii) The Relator

613. Introduction of relator. The introduction of a relator in claims relating to charities is not essential[1]. The Attorney General may, if he pleases, take proceedings without a relator[2], or may require one to be introduced even in cases certified by the Charity Commission[3], the object being to have before the court a person who may be made liable for any costs which may be awarded against the Crown[4]. In connection with the award of costs, the Crown is not deemed to be a party to proceedings by reason only that the proceedings are brought by the Attorney General on the relation of some other person[5].

Relator proceedings are now rare in practice.

1 *Mucklow v A-G* (1816) 4 Dow 1 at 15 per Lord Redesdale; *Re Masters, Governors and Trustees of the Bedford Charity* (1819) 2 Swan 470 at 520 per Lord Eldon LC; *A-G v Dublin Corpn* (1827) 1 Bli NS 312 at 351, HL, per Lord Redesdale.

2 *A-G v Logan* [1891] 2 QB 100 at 107, DC, per Williams J; *A-G v Lewis* (1845) 8 Beav 179. As to the Attorney General see PARAS 589, 596, 605 et seq; and CONSTITUTIONAL AND ADMINISTRATIVE LAW vol 20 (2014) PARA 273 et seq.
3 *A-G v Boucherett* (1858) 25 Beav 116. As to the Charity Commission see PARAS 543–578.
4 Shelford's Law of Mortmain (1836) 424, 425; *A-G v Brown* (1818) 1 Swan 265 at 305 per Lord Eldon LC; *Re Masters, Governors and Trustees of the Bedford Charity* (1819) 2 Swan 470; *A-G v Dublin Corpn* (1827) 1 Bli NS 312 at 351–352, HL, per Lord Redesdale; *A-G v Boucherett* (1858) 25 Beav 116 at 120 per Romilly MR; *A-G v Logan* [1891] 2 QB 100 at 106 per Vaughan Williams J: the practice of making the relator directly responsible for the costs of the action had its origin not in the protection of the defendant but of the Crown. However, see *Ludlow Corpn v Greenhouse* (1827) 1 Bli NS 17 at 48, HL, where Lord Redesdale suggests that a relator was joined in the interests of the defendant. See PARA 623.
5 See the Administration of Justice (Miscellaneous Provisions) Act 1933 s 7(2); and CIVIL PROCEDURE vol 11 (2009) PARA 409. This provision is not affected by the Crown Proceedings Act 1947: see s 23(3)(a); and CROWN AND CROWN PROCEEDINGS vol 29 (2014) PARA 99. See further PARA 623.

614. Who may be relators. The following persons and bodies have been held to have capacity to act as relators[1]: any private individual who thinks that a charity has been abused[2], several individuals[3], the trustees of the charities concerned or any of them[4], corporations[5], companies[6], district councils[7], local education authorities[8], and ratepayers[9]. A relator need not have any interest in the charity, its administration, or the subject of the suit[10], but he must not be a person in indigent circumstances[11].

The restrictions on the bringing of charity proceedings[12] do not apply to the taking of such proceedings by the Attorney General with a relator[13].

1 Relator proceedings are now rare in practice.
2 Shelford's Law of Mortmain (1836) 424.
3 *A-G v Earl of Clarendon* (1810) 17 Ves 491 (several inhabitants).
4 *A-G v Griffith* (1807) 13 Ves 565 at 571, citing *A-G v Talbot* (circa 1800, unreported).
5 *A-G v Logan* [1891] 2 QB 100 at 104 per Wills J; *A-G v Ashborne Recreation Ground Co* [1903] 1 Ch 101. As to corporations generally see CORPORATIONS.
6 *A-G v Merthyr Tydfil Union* [1900] 1 Ch 516, CA. As to companies generally see COMPANIES.
7 *A-G v Wimbledon House Estate Co Ltd* [1904] 2 Ch 34. As to local government areas and authorities in England and Wales see LOCAL GOVERNMENT vol 69 (2009) PARA 22 et seq.
8 *A-G v Price* (1908) 72 JP 208. As to the abolition of local education authorities and the transfer of their functions to local authorities see EDUCATION vol 35 (2011) PARA 25. It is to be presumed that this transfer of functions does not have any effect on the principle here set out.
9 *LCC v A-G* [1902] AC 165, HL. Domestic rates were replaced first by the community charge, and subsequently by the council tax: see LOCAL GOVERNMENT FINANCE vol 70 (2012) PARA 298. The reference in the text to ratepayers can be taken to refer to council tax payers in this context.
10 *A-G v Bucknall* (1742) 2 Atk 328; *A-G v Green* (1789) 2 Bro CC 492 at 497; *A-G v Vivian* (1826) 1 Russ 226 at 236 per Lord Gifford MR. See also *Southmolton Corpn v A-G* (1854) 5 HL Cas 1 at 27 per Lord Cranworth LC (where the court appeared to look with disfavour upon a relator who was a complete stranger to the charity). A paragraph in the statement of claim indicating the relator's interest has been held not irrelevant: *A-G v Rickards* (1843) 6 Beav 444; affd (1844) 1 Ph 383; on appeal, sub nom *Rickards v A-G* (1845) 12 Cl & Fin 30, HL.
11 *Fellows v Barrett* (1836) 1 Keen 119 at 120 per Lord Langdale MR. This is because he is liable for costs: see PARA 627. A solicitor's certificate of the relator's fitness to act and ability to pay costs is necessary.
12 See PARA 592 et seq.
13 See the Charities Act 2011 s 115(6); and PARA 593. The Attorney General may take such proceedings without a relator: s 115(6). As to the Attorney General see PARAS 589, 596, 605 et seq; and CONSTITUTIONAL AND ADMINISTRATIVE LAW vol 20 (2014) PARA 273 et seq.

615. Relator and Attorney General. The introduction of a relator's name does not make him a claimant[1], except where he is personally interested in the relief sought[2], and then he may be a co-claimant in his personal capacity. The Crown, acting through the Attorney General, is the real claimant[3].

A relator's claim is the claim of the Attorney General, and therefore the relator cannot appear separately[4], or take an opposite view[5] from the Attorney General; nor, when a relator is claimant, can he be heard in person on behalf of the Attorney General[6].

Before the claim form is issued the Attorney General's fiat must be obtained, and for this purpose counsel must certify that the proceedings are proper to be begun by the Attorney General[7].

The Attorney General may appear either in person or by counsel[8], or he may authorise the relator to conduct the case and instruct counsel on his behalf. The Attorney General cannot then appear independently[9] except by the court's special permission[10].

1 *A-G v Logan* [1891] 2 QB 100 at 106 per Williams J. Relator proceedings are now rare in practice.
2 *A-G v Heelis* (1824) 2 Sim & St 67; *A-G v Vivian* (1826) 1 Russ 226 at 236 per Lord Gifford MR; *Lang v Purves* (1862) 15 Moo PCC 389. Under the old practice, where the relator joined as plaintiff, the proceeding was called 'a bill and information'.
3 *A-G v Logan* [1891] 2 QB 100. Under the Rules of the Supreme Court, it was the practice that before a person's name was used as a relator he was required to give a written authorisation, which had to be filed: see RSC Ord 15 r 11 (revoked). As to the Attorney General see PARAS 589, 596, 605 et seq; and CONSTITUTIONAL AND ADMINISTRATIVE LAW vol 20 (2014) PARA 273 et seq.
4 *A-G v Ironmongers' Co* (1840) 2 Beav 313 at 328 per Lord Langdale MR.
5 *A-G v Governors etc of Sherborne Grammar School* (1854) 18 Beav 256. However, in *Shore v Wilson* (1842) 9 Cl & Fin 355 at 475, HL, the Attorney General appeared for the defendants in an action by the Attorney with a relator.
6 *A-G v Barker* (1838) 4 My & Cr 262.
7 As to costs see PARA 626. Cf *Gouriet v Union of Post Office Workers* [1978] AC 435, [1977] 3 All ER 70, HL.
8 *A-G v Green* (1820) 1 Jac & W 303 at 305 per Lord Eldon LC; *Ludlow Corpn v Greenhouse* (1827) 1 Bli NS 17 at 65, HL, per Lord Redesdale.
9 *A-G v Governors etc of Sherborne Grammar School* (1854) 18 Beav 256 at 264 per Romilly MR. See also *A-G v Dove* (1823) Turn & R 328; *A-G v Barker* (1838) 4 My & Cr 262; *A-G v Ironmongers' Co* (1840) 2 Beav 313.
10 *A-G v Dove* (1823) Turn & R 328; *A-G v Earl of Stamford* (1843) 10 LJCh 58 at 66 per Lord Cottenham LC. See also *Re Hanson's Trust* (1852) 9 Hare, App I, liv; Seton's Judgments and Orders (7th Edn, 1912) 1246. See also PARA 625.

616. Death of relator. Where there are several relators the death of one does not affect the proceedings, but if all die, or if the sole relator dies[1] or becomes mentally disordered[2], the court will stay the proceedings until a new relator is appointed, in order that some person may be made answerable for costs[3]. The Attorney General's consent is required before an order appointing a new relator can be obtained[4], or the Attorney General must make the application himself[5].

1 *A-G v Powel* (1763) 1 Dick 355; *A-G v Haberdashers' Co* (1852) 15 Beav 397 at 404 per Romilly MR. Relator proceedings are now rare in practice.
2 *A-G v Tyler* (1764) 2 Eden 230.
3 *A-G v Smart* (1748) 1 Ves Sen 72.
4 *Anon* (1726) Cas *temp* King 69. As to the Attorney General see PARAS 589, 596, 605 et seq; and CONSTITUTIONAL AND ADMINISTRATIVE LAW vol 20 (2014) PARA 273 et seq.
5 *A-G v Plumptree* (1820) 5 Madd 452.

(iv) Other Persons as Parties

617. Persons interested and strangers. Apart from the statutory restriction on the persons who may take proceedings in relation to the administration of a charity[1], all persons interested[2] in the subject of the claim ought, generally speaking, to be parties, if they are within the jurisdiction of the court[3].

In a claim to establish a charity rentcharge it is not necessary for all the persons whose estates may be liable to be joined as parties; the court will decide whether the rentcharge in question is charged on the estate of the person actually before the court[4].

It depends upon the circumstances in each case whether persons who have a contingent interest in a charitable fund should be made parties to any proceedings concerning it[5].

Where the Attorney General appears on behalf of a charity the court may allow the trustees to argue in support of the Attorney General[6], and it will hear the trustees when, in good faith, they differ from the relators[7].

Strangers to a charitable trust who are not joined as relators[8] are not proper parties to any legal proceedings relating to it[9]; as for example the original subscribers to a charitable fund[10], or an agent employed by charity trustees to manage the affairs of the charity[11].

Persons showing an apparent right of intervention in legal proceedings to which they are not parties may be allowed by the court to attend[12]. Again, if any necessary parties are omitted or unnecessary parties are added, the court upon application will usually allow the proper alterations to be made[13].

1 See the Charities Act 2011 s 115(1); and PARA 593.

2 This does not include persons who merely conceive themselves to be interested in establishing the validity of the trust: *Practice Note* [1945] WN 38; cf *Re Belling, Enfield London Borough Council v Public Trustee* [1967] Ch 425, [1967] 1 All ER 105.

3 Persons who have been held to be interested parties include: purchasers, where land subject to a charge in favour of charity was alleged to have been improperly sold (*Southmolton Corpn v A-G* (1854) 5 HL Cas 1); executors, where a legacy charged on land was given to a charity and an action to ascertain the profits of the lands was instituted (*A-G v Twisden* (1678) Cas *temp* Finch 336); one tenant in common of lands, where a charity was claiming against the other tenant in common (*A-G v Flint* (1844) 4 Hare 147); the heir-at-law, where the proceedings were to decide whether surplus funds belonged to him or to a charity (*A-G v Haberdashers' Co* (1792) 4 Bro CC 103 at 106; *Ludlow Corpn v Greenhouse* (1827) 1 Bli NS 17 at 55, HL, per Lord Redesdale), or whether there was a resulting trust for his benefit (*A-G v Green* (1789) 2 Bro CC 492), or where he was by implication visitor of a charity and an action was instituted for the execution of the trusts (*A-G v Gaunt* (1790) 3 Swan 148n); a schoolmaster, where the action was to have surplus charity funds applied for his benefit (*A-G v Smart* (1748) 1 Ves Sen 72); lessees, underlessees and assignees of charity lands in an action to set aside the lease (*A-G v Backhouse* (1810) 17 Ves 283 at 285; *Ludlow Corpn v Greenhouse* at 73 per Lord Redesdale; *A-G v Greenhill* (1863) 33 Beav 193. See also *A-G v Pretyman* (1845) 8 Beav 316, where a lessee, though not made a party, was given leave to attend). Where certain parishioners, on behalf of themselves and others, claiming to be interested in certain charities, applied to the court to be served with notice of all proceedings in the matter and for liberty to attend an inquiry, their application was refused on the ground that the public was already represented by the Attorney General: *Ironmongers' Co v Roberts* (1909) Times, 24 June. As to the Attorney General see PARAS 589, 596, 605 et seq; and **CONSTITUTIONAL AND ADMINISTRATIVE LAW** vol 20 (2014) PARA 273 et seq.

4 *A-G v Jackson* (1805) 11 Ves 365 at 367, 372 per Lord Eldon LC; *A-G v Naylor* (1863) 1 Hem & M 809. It is otherwise where the rentcharge is not charitable: *A-G v Jackson* at 367 per Lord Eldon LC.

5 *A-G v St John's College* (1835) 7 Sim 241 (where the information was held defective for want of parties because the person who was entitled to appoint the master of a charity school if he was not appointed by other persons within a limited period was not joined as party); *A-G v Goddard* (1823) Turn & R 348 (where trustees of a charity who had a contingent interest in a legacy given to another charity were held not to be necessary parties to a suit establishing the second charity).

6 *Solicitor-General v Bath Corpn* (1849) 18 LJCh 275 at 276 per Wigram V-C; *Whicker v Hume* (1851) 14 Beav 509 at 528 per Romilly MR; affd (1858) 7 HL Cas 124.

7 *Solicitor-General v Bath Corpn* (1849) 18 LJCh 275 at 277 per Wigram V-C. As to relators see further PARA 613 et seq. Relator proceedings are now rare in practice.
8 See PARAS 613–616.
9 *Lang v Purves* (1862) 15 Moo PCC 389.
10 *A-G v Gardner* (1848) 2 De G & Sm 102; *A-G v Munro* (1848) 2 De G & Sm 122 at 161–162 per Shadwell V-C. However, see *Minn v Stant* (1851) 15 Beav 49, where the original subscribers were in special circumstances held still to have an interest, and were joined as parties.
11 *A-G v Earl of Chesterfield* (1854) 18 Beav 596. As regards actions by some agents against others see also *Strickland v Weldon* (1885) 28 ChD 426.
12 *A-G v Shore* (1836) 1 My & Cr 394; *A-G v Pretyman* (1845) 8 Beav 316; *Re Shrewsbury Grammar School* (1849) 1 Mac & G 324; and see PARA 620. See also *Royal Society for the Prevention of Cruelty to Animals v A-G* (2001) Times, 13 February.
13 See CPR 19.2; and CIVIL PROCEDURE vol 11 (2009) PARA 213. See also *Re Church Patronage Trust, Laurie v A-G* [1904] 1 Ch 41; affd on another point [1904] 2 Ch 643. CA.

618. Proceedings against trustees. Where proceedings are taken against charity trustees, all must be joined, and not only the acting trustees[1]; but in a claim to remedy a breach of trust it is not necessary to make every person participating in the breach party to the suit[2].

New trustees appointed during the course of proceedings who ought to be, but are not, parties to proceedings for the administration of a charity are not so bound by a decree made in such proceedings as to be absolutely precluded from making a case by way of defence to the suit[3].

1 *Re Chertsey Market, ex p Walthew* (1819) 6 Price 261.
2 *A-G v Leicester Corpn* (1844) 7 Beav 176. See the following cases of *McCheane v Gyles (No 2)* [1902] 1 Ch 911, where a claim was brought by a beneficiary against one of two trustees liable for breach of trust, and *Ideal Films Ltd v Richards* [1927] 1 KB 374, CA, neither of which involved charities. See also CPR 19.6 (see CIVIL PROCEDURE vol 11 (2009) PARA 229), which provides that where more than one person has the same interest in a claim, the claim may be begun or the court may order that the claim be continued, by or against one or more of the persons who have the same interest as representatives of any other persons who have that interest.
3 *A-G v Foster* (1842) 2 Hare 81. See also PARA 619 text and note 18.

(4) PROCEDURE RELATING TO SCHEMES

619. Drafting and settling schemes. In many non-contentious cases schemes are settled by the Charity Commission[1], either on an application to them for the purpose[2] or on a reference by the court[3]. Otherwise, where the court directs a scheme to be settled, the matter may be referred to a master and settled in private before the judge[4]; the scheme settled by the judge is scheduled to the order approving it. In simple cases, where a slight modification of a trust is required[5] or where the fund is small[6], a reference to the master may be dispensed with and the scheme set out in the order[7]. Sometimes a reference to the master is directed to apportion a fund without settling a scheme[8].

When a scheme is directed to be settled, the draft may be prepared by the Attorney General[9], or by other applicants, who would usually be the trustees of the charity[10]. If the draft is not prepared by the Attorney General it must be submitted to the Treasury Solicitor[11] for the Attorney General's approval. The draft scheme is brought before the judge in private for approval[12]. If there are any points objected to, the summons may be adjourned into court[13].

The Attorney General, whose presence at the settlement of a scheme is generally[14], but not invariably[15], required, should be served with a summons to attend[16], and he may then raise any objections[17].

On an application for an order approving a scheme for the administration of a charity estate, a newly appointed trustee who has not been served with the proceedings may oppose the application on grounds not appearing upon the report or brought before the master[18].

1 As to the Charity Commission see PARAS 543–578.
2 Ie under the Charities Act 2011 s 69(1), (2): see PARA 189.
3 Ie under the Charities Act 2011 s 69(3): see PARA 191.
4 *Wellbeloved v Jones* (1822) 1 Sim & St 40; and see *AG v Doyley* (1735) 7 Ves 58n; *Baylis v A-G* (1741) 2 Atk 239 at 240n per Lord Hardwicke LC; *Paice v Archbishop of Canterbury* (1807) 14 Ves 364 at 372 per Lord Eldon LC; *Waldo v Caley* (1809) 16 Ves 206 at 211 per Grant MR; *Re Hanson's Trust* (1852) 9 Hare, App I, liv. In practice, it is only in some cases that the court directs the scheme be settled by the master: where the scheme is either very short or particularly contentious the judge may make the scheme.
5 *Re Richardson's Will* (1887) 58 LT 45.
6 *Re Lousada, Bacon v Bacon* (1887) 82 LT Jo 358.
7 *A-G v Brandreth* (1842) 1 Y & C Ch Cas 200; *Clum Hospital Warden and Brethren v Lord Powys* (1842) 6 Jur 252; *Re Delmar Charitable Trust* [1897] 2 Ch 163 at 168 per Stirling J. See also *Gillan v Gillan* (1878) 1 LR Ir 114; *A-G v Earl of Mansfield, ex p Wardens and Governors of Highgate Free Grammar School* (1845) 14 Sim 601.
8 *White v White* (1778) 1 Bro CC 12 at 15 per Lord Thurlow LC; *Re Hyde's Trusts* (1873) 22 WR 69.
9 *Smith v Kerr (No 2)* (1905) 74 LJCh 763 at 767 per Farwell J. As to the Attorney General see PARAS 589, 596, 605 et seq; and CONSTITUTIONAL AND ADMINISTRATIVE LAW vol 20 (2014) PARA 273 et seq.
10 *A-G v Stepney* (1804) 10 Ves 22 at 29 per Lord Eldon LC; *Jemmit v Verril* (1826) Amb 585n; and cf *Re Lea, Lea v Cooke* (1887) 34 ChD 528 at 533 per North J.
11 As to the Treasury Solicitor see CONSTITUTIONAL AND ADMINISTRATIVE LAW vol 20 (2014) PARA 281.
12 *Re Wyersdale School* (1853) 10 Hare, App II, lxxiv.
13 *Re Wyersdale School* (1853) 10 Hare, App II, lxxiv.
14 *Re Hanson's Trust* (1852) 9 Hare, App I, liv; *A-G v Goldsmiths' Co* (1833) Coop Pr Cas 292 at 312 per Leach MR; *A-G v Earl of Stamford* (1843) 1 Ph 737 at 739; *A-G v St Cross Hospital* (1854) 18 Beav 475; *Re Clergy Society* (1856) 2 K & J 615; *Re Taylor, Martin v Freeman* (1888) 58 LT 538.
15 Eg where the fund is small: *A-G v Haberdashers' Co* (1835) 2 My & K 817 (fund of £1,100).
16 *Re Hanson's Trust* (1852) 9 Hare, App I, liv.
17 *Re Lea, Lea v Cooke* (1887) 34 ChD 528.
18 *Re Loppington Parish* (1850) 8 Hare 198.

620. Attendance on settlement of scheme. As the Attorney General attends the settlement of a scheme to protect the interests of all concerned in the charity, the court may refuse to allow the attendance of interested persons, even at their own expense[1]. As a rule strangers to the suit are not allowed to intervene or to attend the settlement of a scheme[2], unless their intervention or attendance will clearly be beneficial to the charity[3], or it is necessary, for the purpose of deciding a particular point, that someone should be allowed to intervene for the purpose of arguing a particular contention[4]. Permission to attend may be given to persons who are not parties, on the understanding that only one set of costs will be allowed[5], or that they do so at their own expense[6]. However, the Attorney General is always ready to listen to any suggestion made by persons who have any real interest in the matter[7].

1 *A-G v St Cross Hospital* (1854) 18 Beav 475; *A-G v Wimborne School* (1847) 10 Beav 209 (Ecclesiastical Commissioners refused leave to attend); *Re Shrewsbury Grammar School* (1849) 1 Mac & G 324 at 334–335 per Lord Cottenham LC; *Re Sekeford's Charity* (1861) 5 LT 488. As to the Attorney General see PARAS 589, 596, 605 et seq; and CONSTITUTIONAL AND ADMINISTRATIVE LAW vol 20 (2014) PARA 273 et seq.
2 *A-G v Attwood* (1852) 1 WR 64 at 91; *Smith v Kerr (No 2)* (1905) 74 LJCh 763 at 767 per Farwell J. See also the cases cited in note 1.

3 *Smith v Kerr (No 2)* (1905) 74 LJCh 763 at 767 per Farwell J.
4 *Re Hyde Park Place Charity* [1911] 1 Ch 678, CA.
5 *A-G v Shore* (1836) 1 My & Cr 394.
6 *Re Shrewsbury Grammar School* (1849) 1 Mac & G 324 at 335 per Lord Cottenham LC.
7 *Smith v Kerr (No 2)* (1905) 74 LJCh 763. See also *Royal Society for the Prevention of Cruelty to Animals v A-G* (2001) Times, 13 February.

(5) PROCEDURE ON APPLICATIONS AND APPEALS

621. Applications. Where it is necessary to obtain the authority or certificate of the Charity Commission[1] to take charity proceedings[2], and the authority or certificate or permission is refused[3], the leave of one of the judges of the High Court attached to the Chancery Division may instead be obtained[4].

Application for permission to take charity proceedings[5] must be made within 21 days after the refusal by the Commission of an order authorising proceedings[6]. The application must be made by issuing a Part 8 claim form, which must contain the following information[7]:

(1) the name, address and description of the applicant;
(2) details of the proceedings which he wishes to take;
(3) the date of the Commission's refusal to grant an order authorising the taking of proceedings;
(4) the grounds on which the applicant alleges that it is a proper case for taking proceedings; and
(5) if the application is made with the consent of any other party to the proposed proceedings, that fact[8].

If the Commission has given reasons for refusing to grant an order, a copy of its reasons must be filed with the claim form[9]. The Commission must be made defendant to the claim, but the claim form need not be served on it or on any other person[10]. If the judge on considering the application so directs, the Commission must file a written statement of its reasons for its decision[11], and the court will serve on the applicant a copy of any statement so filed[12]. The judge may either give permission without a hearing or fix a hearing[13].

Application for permission to appeal a decision of the Tribunal must be made according to the standard rules for appeals[14].

1 As to the Charity Commission see PARAS 543–578.
2 As to what are charity proceedings, and when the Charity Commission's authority or the permission of a judge is required, see PARAS 592, 594.
3 The authority or certificate must first have been applied for and refused: see the Charities Act 2011 s 115(5); *Khaira v Grewal* [2005] EWHC 1413 (Ch), [2005] All ER (D) 336 (Feb); and PARA 594.
4 See the Charities Act 2011 s 115(5); and PARA 594.
5 Ie under the Charities Act 2011 s 115(5): see PARA 594.
6 CPR 64.6(1). CPR 64.6(1) refers to the Charity Commissioners rather than the Charity Commission; however, this has effect as if it were a reference to the Charity Commission for England and Wales: see PARA 543. As to the Charity Commissioners, and the transfer of their functions and liabilities to the Charity Commission, see PARA 543. As to the Charity Commission see PARAS 543–578.
7 CPR 64.6(2). As to claims under CPR Pt 8 see CIVIL PROCEDURE vol 11 (2009) PARA 127 et seq.
8 *Practice Direction—Estates, Trusts and Charities* PD 64A para 9.1.
9 *Practice Direction—Estates, Trusts and Charities* PD 64A para 9.2.
10 CPR 64.6(3).
11 CPR 64.6(4).
12 CPR 64.6(5).
13 CPR 64.6(6).
14 Ie CPR Pt 52: see CIVIL PROCEDURE vol 12 (2009) PARA 1660 et seq.

(6) COSTS

(i) General Discretion as to Costs

622. Discretion as to costs. The court has a very wide discretionary jurisdiction to determine allocation of costs[1].

The fact that a party is a charitable body, acting not out of private self-interest but seeking to improve the services available to its clients, is not of itself a basis for an award of costs[2].

In any civil proceedings to which the Crown is a party the costs of the proceedings are in the discretion of the court. The court must exercise this discretion in the same manner and on the same principles as in cases between subjects, and may order the payment of costs by or to the Crown accordingly[3].

1 See *Aiden Shipping Co Ltd v Interbulk Ltd, The Vimeira* [1986] AC 965, [1986] 2 All ER 409, HL; and CIVIL PROCEDURE vol 12 (2009) PARA 1732 et seq. The principles set out and the cases cited in the following paragraphs are indicative of how the court has awarded costs in charity proceedings, but should be read in light of the principle enunciated in this paragraph.
For a modern example of an order in charity proceedings see *Marwaha v Singh* [2013] EWCA Civ 1878, [2014] PTSR 1166.

2 *British Pregnancy Advisory Service v Secretary of State for Health* [2011] EWHC 637 (Admin), [2011] All ER (D) 214 (Mar).

3 See the Administration of Justice (Miscellaneous Provisions) Act 1933 s 7(1); and CROWN AND CROWN PROCEEDINGS vol 29 (2014) PARA 112.

(ii) The Attorney General

623. Discretion as to costs. Where the Attorney General as such is required to be made a party to proceedings, the court must have regard to the nature of the proceedings[1] and the character and circumstances in which the Attorney General appears and, in the exercise of its discretion, may order any other party to pay the Attorney General's costs whatever the result of the proceedings may be[2]; but the Crown is not deemed to be a party by reason only that the proceedings are by the Attorney General on the relation of some other person[3].

The Attorney General, it was formerly said, never pays costs when he sues as an officer of the Crown in the performance of a public duty, for example on behalf of a charity, even when he loses his case[4]. It is not clear whether this rule has survived the statutory provisions described above[5].

Where the Attorney General brings a claim for an injunction on behalf of the Crown as parens patriae he will not normally be required to give the usual cross-undertaking[6]. However, if the Crown is asserting proprietary rights and seeking to recover property alleged to belong to or to be owed to the charity, the court may think it right to give the defendant the benefit of a cross-undertaking if possible[7].

1 See, however, PARA 622 text and note 2. As to the Attorney General see PARAS 589, 596, 605 et seq; and CONSTITUTIONAL AND ADMINISTRATIVE LAW vol 20 (2014) PARA 273 et seq.

2 See the Administration of Justice (Miscellaneous Provisions) Act 1933 s 7(1) proviso (a); and CROWN AND CROWN PROCEEDINGS vol 29 (2014) PARA 112. See eg *Marwaha v Singh* [2013] EWCA Civ 1878, [2014] PTSR 1166.

3 See the Administration of Justice (Miscellaneous Provisions) Act 1933 s 7(2); and CROWN AND CROWN PROCEEDINGS vol 29 (2014) PARA 112. It seems that the Act does not affect the practice as to costs in charity proceedings: cf *A-G v Dean and Canons of Windsor* (1860) 8 HL Cas 369 at 459.

4 Shelford's Law of Mortmain (1836) 474; *A-G v Earl of Ashburnham* (1823) 1 Sim & St 394 at 397 per Leach V-C; *A-G v Dublin Corpn* (1827) 1 Bli NS 312 at 351–352, HL, per

Lord Redesdale; *Ludlow Corpn v Greenhouse* (1827) 1 Bli NS 17 at 48, HL, per Lord Redesdale; *A-G v Chester Corpn* (1851) 14 Beav 338; *Re Macduff, Macduff v Macduff* [1896] 2 Ch 451 at 475, CA, per Rigby LJ. As to the general principle said to apply in courts of common law that 'the Crown neither receives nor pays costs' see also *A-G v London Corpn* (1850) 2 Mac & G 247 at 271 per Lord Cottenham LC; *R v Archbishop of Canterbury* [1902] 2 KB 503 at 572 per Wright J; *Thomas v Pritchard* [1903] 1 KB 209 at 215 per Lord Alverstone CJ; *Sanderson v Blyth Theatre Co* [1903] 2 KB 533 at 542, CA, per Stirling LJ; *Re Cardwell, A-G v Day* [1912] 1 Ch 779. As to the payment of costs by the Crown generally see CONSTITUTIONAL AND ADMINISTRATIVE LAW vol 20 (2014) PARA 201; CROWN AND CROWN PROCEEDINGS vol 29 (2014) PARA 112.

5 Ie the Administration of Justice (Miscellaneous Provisions) Act 1933 s 7(1): see the text and notes 1–2; and CROWN AND CROWN PROCEEDINGS vol 29 (2014) PARA 112. See Tudor on Charities (9th Edn, 2003) pp 402–403.

6 *A-G v Wright* [1987] 3 All ER 579, [1988] 1 WLR 164; *F Hoffmann-La Roche & Co A-G v Secretary of State for Trade and Industry* [1975] AC 295, [1974] 2 All ER 1128, HL. See CIVIL PROCEDURE vol 11 (2009) PARAS 419–423.

7 There may be a difficulty about requiring an undertaking from the Attorney General since he does not have any right ex officio to resort to the charity funds for reimbursement. In *A-G v Wright* [1987] 3 All ER 579, [1988] 1 WLR 164, where the matter arose, a receiver of the charity had been appointed who would have such a right and the injunction was granted to the Attorney General conditional on the giving of a cross-undertaking by the receiver limited, however, to what he could recover by way of indemnity from the charity.

624. When Attorney General receives costs. As a rule in charity cases the Attorney General is entitled to receive costs which would have been awarded to him as a private litigant; but he is not entitled to receive costs in proceedings brought by him where, if he had brought them as a private individual, he could have been called upon to pay them[1].

Where the court sanctions an application to Parliament to effect certain changes in the constitution of a charity, the Attorney General's costs are allowed out of the charity estate, even if the application fails[2]. Costs may also be given to him in interim applications made independently of the relator[3].

If a defendant who has been ordered to pay the Attorney General's costs becomes insolvent, the costs may be ordered to be paid out of the charity estate[4].

In administration actions where the Attorney General is joined as the guardian of a charitable, or supposed charitable, legacy, he is usually given his costs on the standard basis[5] out of the estate[6], even if the proceedings are unsuccessful so far as the charity is concerned[7].

When the Attorney General takes proceedings as a result of information given to him by the Charity Commission[8], he is entitled to be put in the same position as any other claimant with regard to costs, and to have his costs out of the fund[9].

1 *A-G v London Corpn* (1850) 2 Mac & G 247 at 269 per Lord Cottenham LC; but see *Re Cardwell, A-G v Day* [1912] 1 Ch 779. The court has a very wide discretion to determine allocation of costs: see PARA 622. As to the Attorney General see PARAS 589, 596, 605 et seq; and CONSTITUTIONAL AND ADMINISTRATIVE LAW vol 20 (2014) PARA 273 et seq.

2 *Re Bedford Charity* (1857) 26 LJCh 613.

3 *A-G v Earl of Ashburnham* (1823) 1 Sim & St 394. As to relators see further PARA 613 et seq. Relator proceedings are now rare in practice.

4 *A-G v Lewis* (1845) 8 Beav 179.

5 Previously the common fund basis. As to the basis of assessment now see CPR 44.3; and CIVIL PROCEDURE vol 12 (2009) PARA 1729 et seq.

6 See eg *Mills v Farmer* (1815) 19 Ves 483 at 490 per Lord Eldon LC; and *Re Preston's Estate, Raby v Port of Hull Society's Sailors' Orphans' Homes* [1951] Ch 878 at 881, [1951] 2 All ER 421 at 423 per Vaisey J; *Re Amory, Westminster Bank Ltd v British Sailors' Society Inc at Home and Abroad* [1951] 2 All ER 947n. See also *Hunter v A-G* [1899] AC 309 at 325, HL, per Earl of Halsbury LC, where the Attorney General attempted unsuccessfully to support a judgment of the Court of Appeal in his favour, and the court intimated that, if the estate had not been large,

costs would not necessarily have been given to the Attorney General. See also *Construction Industry Training Board v A-G* [1973] Ch 173, [1972] 2 All ER 1339, CA (appeal by Attorney General dismissed with costs).

7 *Moggridge v Thackwell* (1803) 7 Ves 36 at 88 per Lord Eldon LC; *A-G v Earl of Ashburnham* (1823) 1 Sim & St 394 at 396 per Leach V-C.

8 Ie under the Charities Act 2011 s 115(7); see PARA 599. As to the Charity Commission see PARAS 543–578.

9 Cf *Re Cardwell, A-G v Day* [1912] 1 Ch 779.

625. Costs allowed. Where the Attorney General takes proceedings at the instance of relators[1], he is not allowed the costs of attending separately by his own solicitor[2]; but if there is a suspicion of collusion between the relators and the defendant, for example where the same solicitor appears for both, application ought to be made for permission of the court for the Attorney General to appear separately[3].

Even when the Attorney General does not appear personally at the hearing of proceedings instituted by him, the costs of his brief should be allowed upon detailed assessment, on the ground that the Attorney General's duty is distinct from the mere duty and responsibility of counsel attending at the hearing to argue the cause[4].

Costs of particular proceedings taken and abandoned by the Attorney General in the course of an ex officio claim may be excepted from the general costs of the claim[5].

It has been held that costs of persons who, on public grounds, give advice to the Attorney General to secure the appointment of fit persons as charity trustees, are not allowed out of the charity funds[6].

1 This does not of itself make the Crown a party to the proceedings so as to give the court discretion to order costs as between subjects: see the Administration of Justice (Miscellaneous Provisions) Act 1933 s 7(2); and **CROWN AND CROWN PROCEEDINGS** vol 29 (2014) PARA 112. As to relators see further PARA 544 et seq. Relator proceedings are now rare in practice. As to the Attorney General see PARAS 589, 596, 605 et seq; and **CONSTITUTIONAL AND ADMINISTRATIVE LAW** vol 20 (2014) PARA 273 et seq.

2 *A-G v Dove* (1823) Turn & R 328.

3 *A-G v Wyggeston Hospital* (1855) Seton's Judgments and Orders (6th Edn, 1901) 1290; *A-G v Dove* (1823) Turn & R 328. The court has a very wide discretion to determine allocation of costs: see PARA 622.

4 *A-G v Drapers' Co* (1841) 4 Beav 305; and see *Cockburn v Raphael* (1843) 12 LJCh 263.

5 *A-G v Ward* (1848) 11 Beav 203 at 208 per Lord Langdale MR.

6 *Re Gloucester Charities* (1853) 10 Hare, App I, iii, where prior to the appointment by the court of new trustees of a charity under the Municipal Corporations Act 1835 s 71 (repealed: see now the Municipal Corporations Act 1882 s 133; and PARA 256), a public notice was issued inviting parties to lay before the Attorney General any objections or suggestions with reference to the proposed appointments.

626. Costs of application for fiat. The costs of obtaining the Attorney General's fiat before taking proceedings requiring it, such as a relator action[1], and the costs of proceedings before the Attorney General with reference to the withdrawal of his fiat pending an appeal, may be made costs in the claim[2].

Where an application is made to the Attorney General without the direction or sanction of the court, the court has no jurisdiction to order payment of the costs occasioned by it[3].

1 See PARA 615. As to relators see further PARA 613 et seq. Relator proceedings are now rare in practice.

2 *A-G v Halifax Corpn* (1871) LR 12 Eq 262. The court has a very wide discretion to determine allocation of costs: see PARA 622. As to the Attorney General see PARAS 589, 596, 605 et seq; and **CONSTITUTIONAL AND ADMINISTRATIVE LAW** vol 20 (2014) PARA 273 et seq.

3 *A-G v Harper* (1838) 8 LJCh 12, where certain persons, who were purchasers in good faith of an improvident lease of charity lands, presented a memorial to the Attorney General praying that the matter might be referred to the master to approve a proper lease.

(iii) The Relator

627. Relator's liability for costs. As the relator is answerable for costs, he should be a person of substance[1]. He may be directed to give security for costs[2], but this is not done where he sues as claimant as well as relator[3].

When proceedings are unnecessary[4], or are instituted from improper motives, such as private revenge[5], or where wrong parties are joined[6], the court may order the relator to pay costs, or such part as is occasioned by his misconduct.

1 *A-G v Knight* (1837) 3 My & Cr 154. As to relators see further PARA 613 et seq. Relator proceedings are now rare in practice. The court has a very wide discretion to determine allocation of costs: see PARA 622.
2 *A-G v Rochester Corpn* (1680) Shelford's Law of Mortmain (1836) 425.
3 *A-G v Knight* (1837) 3 My & Cr 154.
4 *A-G v Glegg* (1738) Amb 584 (where the relators were charged with costs on the dismissal of an information which sought specific performance of an agreement between three executors, trustees of a charity, giving each a right to nominate to a third part of the charity funds absolutely); *A-G v Parker* (1747) 3 Atk 576; *A-G v Smart* (1748) 1 Ves Sen 72 (information in contradiction to the charity rights as established by its charter); *A-G v Hartley* (1820) 2 Jac & W 353 at 370 per Lord Eldon LC (where an information was filed involving most expensive inquiries, containing gross imputations on the conduct of individuals and allegations not proved, upon which no relief was or could be given); *A-G v Earl of Mansfield* (1827) 2 Russ 501 at 538 per Lord Eldon LC (information containing unfounded charges against officers of a charity). See also *Southmolton Corpn v A-G* (1854) 5 HL Cas 1 at 39 per Lord St Leonards.
5 *A-G v Middleton* (1751) 2 Ves Sen 327 at 330 per Lord Hardwicke LC; *A-G v Bosanquet* (1841) 11 LJCh 43.
6 *A-G v Berry* (1847) 11 Jur 114.

628. When costs denied to relator. Where a relator totally fails in substantiating the case, no costs can be given to him; the utmost he can then claim is to be discharged without costs[1]. This rule is applied where a relator acts in good faith but in error with a view to protecting a charity[2], or with similar motives seeks to divert charitable funds to purposes not contemplated by the trust[3]. Even if his application is partially successful, the relator may not obtain his costs where the proceedings have been conducted with unnecessary expense[4].

1 *A-G v Oglander* (1790) 1 Ves 246. As to relators see further PARA 613 et seq. Relator proceedings are now rare in practice. The court has a very wide discretion to determine allocation of costs: see PARA 622.
2 *A-G v Bolton* (1796) 3 Anst 820; and see *A-G v Bosanquet* (1841) 11 LJCh 43.
3 *A-G v Braithwaite* (1885) 2 TLR 56, CA.
4 *A-G v Cullum* (1836) 1 Keen 104, where no costs up to the hearing were given to the relators.

629. Costs given to relator. Where there is nothing to impeach the propriety of the proceedings and no special circumstances to justify a special order, the relator in charity proceedings which terminate successfully is entitled to his costs on the standard basis[1], and to be paid out of the charity estate the difference between the amount of those costs and the amount recovered from the defendant[2]. In special circumstances a relator may also be given his charges and expenses[3]. Again, even though costs may be refused him, he may be allowed money actually expended by him although without the sanction of the master, if in the result the expenditure has been of use to the charity[4].

A relator who, with the Attorney General's consent, proceeds by action when the relief desired might otherwise have been obtained, may be allowed his costs[5]. So also may costs be given to a relator who is changed before the hearing of the proceedings[6], or to a relator who acts in error but with the intention in good faith of benefiting the charity[7].

1 See PARA 624 note 5.
2 *A-G v Berwick-upon-Tweed Corpn* (1829) Taml 239; *A-G v Kerr* (1841) 4 Beav 297. As to relators see further PARA 613 et seq. Relator proceedings are now rare in practice. The court has a very wide discretion to determine allocation of costs: see PARA 622.
3 *A-G v Kerr* (1841) 4 Beav 297 at 303 per Lord Langdale MR; *A-G v Taylor* (1802) cited in 7 Ves 424; *A-G v Skinners' Co* (1821) Jac 629 at 630 per Lord Eldon LC; *A-G v Winchester Corpn* (1824) 3 LJOS Ch 64.
4 *A-G v Ironmongers' Co* (1847) 10 Beav 194.
5 *A-G v Biddulph* (1853) 22 LTOS 114. He may not be allowed costs where the Attorney General's sanction is not first obtained: *A-G v Holland* (1837) 2 Y & C Ex 683. As to the Attorney General see PARAS 589, 596, 605 et seq; and CONSTITUTIONAL AND ADMINISTRATIVE LAW vol 20 (2014) PARA 273 et seq.
6 *A-G v Tyler* (1838) Coop Pr Cas 358.
7 *A-G v Bosanquet* (1841) 11 LJCh 43.

630. When further parties allowed to intervene. Where, owing to their peculiar character and position, relators are incapable of adequately representing and protecting the interests of all the objects of a charity, persons who are not parties to the proceedings may be allowed to intervene in the proceedings, on the understanding, however, that only one bill of costs will be allowed against the charity estate[1].

1 *A-G v Shore* (1836) 1 My & Cr 394. See also *Royal Society for the Prevention of Cruelty to Animals v A-G* (2001) Times, 13 February. As to relators see further PARA 613 et seq. Relator proceedings are now rare in practice. The court has a very wide discretion to determine allocation of costs: see PARA 622.

(iv) Charity Trustees

631. Charity trustees' right to costs. The rules with respect to the costs of trustees of charities are for the most part the same as those with respect to the costs of trustees for other purposes[1].

Thus, in general, charity trustees who have not been guilty of misconduct expect to be paid out of the trust funds all costs, charges and expenses properly incurred by them in the execution of or in connection with the trust[2]. In particular, under the Civil Procedure Rules, in every detailed assessment of a trustee's costs where he is or has been a party to any proceedings in that capacity and he is entitled to be paid his costs out of the proceedings of any fund which he holds in that capacity, costs are to be assessed on the indemnity basis[3]. If parties to proceedings who are ordered to pay the trustees' costs are unable to do so, the trustees may recoup themselves out of the charity funds or estate[4].

1 Shelford's Law of Mortmain (1836) 467; *Man v Ballet* (1682) 1 Vern 43 at 44 per Lord Nottingham LC; and see *A-G v Drummond* (1842) 3 Dr & War 162 at 163–164, where Sugden LC pointed out how in some ways charity trustees are more favoured than ordinary trustees. As to the costs of trustees generally see TRUSTS AND POWERS vol 98 (2013) PARAS 346–353. The court has a very wide discretion to determine allocation of costs: see PARA 622.
2 *A-G v Norwich Corpn* (1837) 2 My & Cr 406 at 424 per Lord Cottenham LC.
3 See CPR 46.3; and CIVIL PROCEDURE vol 12 (2009) PARA 1807.
4 *A-G v Lewis* (1845) 8 Beav 179.

632. Charity trustees' liability for costs. Where a succession of charity trustees has for a long period acted wrongly but innocently in the administration of the trust, the court may refuse to visit the error of their predecessors upon the present trustees by depriving the latter of their costs[1], but the court's discretion is guided by the circumstances of each case[2]. So, too, if trustees take steps promptly to remedy an innocent and accidental breach of trust, they will not be made to pay the costs[3].

Charity trustees ought not to be visited with costs because of the misapprehension of the Charity Commission as to the construction of a public statute[4].

In relation to an exempt charity[5], the court may give charity trustees the costs of a successful application to Parliament for an Act to regulate the charity, even though the application is made without the previous sanction of the court[6]; or of an unsuccessful application to which the court's consent has previously been given[7].

Where the court orders charity trustees to pay costs personally, they may not pay them out of the charity fund. If they do so they will be directed to refund the amount so misapplied[8].

1 *A-G v Drummond* (1842) 3 Dr & War 162 at 163 per Lord Sugden LC, where the trustees had in error allowed Unitarians to participate in a trust property confined to another body; *A-G v Caius College* (1837) 2 Keen 150, where, notwithstanding certain misapplications, the trustees and their predecessors had accumulated a large amount for the benefit of the foundation.

2 *Shore v Wilson* (1842) 9 Cl & Fin 355, HL, where the trustees in similar circumstances were not allowed their costs. The Charity Commission has power to advise charity trustees: see the Charities Act 2011 s 110; and PARAS 393–394. As to the Charity Commission see PARAS 543–578. The court has a very wide discretion to determine allocation of costs: see PARA 622.

3 *A-G v Drapers' Co, Kendrick's Charity* (1841) 4 Beav 67.

4 *Moore v Clench* (1875) 1 ChD 447 at 450–451 per Jessel MR.

5 As to exempt charities see PARAS 318–321.

6 *A-G v Vigor, Downing College Case* (1805) cited in 2 Russ at 519 per Lord Eldon LC. Costs will not be given where the application is unsuccessful: *A-G v Earl of Mansfield* (1827) 2 Russ 501 at 519 per Lord Eldon LC. See also *Solicitor General for Ireland v Dublin Corpn* (1877) 1 LR Ir 166.

7 *Re Bedford Charity* (1857) 26 LJCh 613. The Charity Commission may give permission to trustees to promote a private Bill: see the Charities Act 2011 s 74(1), (2); and PARA 331.

8 See *A-G v Daugars* (1864) 33 Beav 621 at 624 per Romilly MR; and *A-G v Mercers' Co, Re St Paul's School* (1870) 18 WR 448. See PARA 450.

633. Charity benefited by breach of trust. Where a breach of trust has been committed, the trustees may be refused the costs of an inquiry into the matter, even where the breach has benefited the charity, although the fact that the property has been improved may properly be taken into account in disposing of the costs[1].

1 *Solicitor-General v Bath Corpn* (1849) 18 LJCh 275 at 277 per Wigram V-C, distinguishing *A-G v Caius College* (1837) 2 Keen 150, where, in somewhat similar circumstances, costs were given to trustees who had innocently misapplied trust property to the advantage of the charity; *A-G v Armitstead* (1854) 19 Beav 584, where trustees greatly exceeded the estimate authorised by the court for erecting a building. Cf *Bartlett v Barclays Bank Trust Co Ltd (No 2)* [1980] Ch 515, [1980] 2 All ER 92, where gains made in breach of trust were set off against losses made in breach of trust: see **TRUSTS AND POWERS** vol 98 (2013) PARA 665 et seq.

The court has a very wide discretion to determine allocation of costs: see PARA 622.

634. Severance of defence in claim for breach of trust. Where, in a claim against charity trustees charged with breaches of trust, one of the trustees severs his defence and adopts the view taken by the claimant, he may be allowed to recover his costs on the standard basis out of the charity property, the costs to be recovered from the other trustees[1].

1 *A-G v Mercers' Co, Re St Paul's School* (1870) 18 WR 448. In this case costs were awarded against the other trustees on a party and party basis. This basis was abolished when RSC Ord 62 was reformed and recast by the RSC (Amendment) 1986, SI 1986/632. As to the standard basis of assessment see now CPR 44.3; and CIVIL PROCEDURE vol 12 (2009) PARA 1729 et seq.
The court has a very wide discretion to determine allocation of costs: see PARA 622.

635. Proceedings occasioned by trustees' misconduct. If proceedings are rendered necessary by any particular instance of misconduct on the part of trustees, whether they be private individuals or a corporation[1], or by their general dereliction of duty, even where they have not acted corruptly[2], they must expect to pay the costs occasioned by their improper behaviour[3]. Thus they may be fixed with the costs of proceedings where they have claimed unsuccessfully to be entitled beneficially to property belonging to a charity[4], or have committed a breach of trust and acted in a spirit of animosity[5], or have wilfully suppressed evidence thereby obstructing the course of justice[6], or have negligently professed ignorance of matters which they might have ascertained from an examination of their documents[7]; or where they adopt a wrong mode of procedure[8]; or where, pending proceedings instituted for the purpose of having new trustees appointed, they appoint new trustees themselves and this appointment is subsequently set aside[9].

So, too, on being removed from the trusts on account of their misconduct, charity trustees may be ordered to pay the cost of vesting the trust property in the new trustees[10]. Again, where trustees of a religious congregation who refuse to retire on account of holding opinions incompatible with the terms of the trust are removed by the court, they may be made to pay the costs of appointing new trustees[11].

When proceedings are necessary to force charity trustees to comply with orders of the Charity Commission[12], the trustees must expect to pay the costs of the proceedings[13].

1 Eg an appointment of officials contrary to the terms of the trust: *Salop Town v A-G* (1726) 2 Bro Parl Cas 402, HL; *A-G v Lord Carrington* (1850) 4 De G & Sm 140.

2 *East v Ryal* (1725) 2 P Wms 284; *A-G v Stafford Corpn* (1740) Barn Ch 33.

3 *Haberdashers' Co v A-G* (1702) 2 Bro Parl Cas 370, HL (negligent trustees ordered to pay costs of original suit and part of those of the appeal); *A-G v Wilson* (1840) Cr & Ph 1; *A-G v Mercers' Co* (1833) 2 My & K 654 (where a corporation, trustee of a charity, which had failed to apply properly a number of charitable legacies, was ordered to pay the costs of an information filed against it, but not of the subsequent reference to the master to settle a scheme). The court has a very wide discretion to determine allocation of costs: see PARA 622.

4 *A-G v Drapers' Co, Kendrick's Charity* (1841) 4 Beav 67; *A-G v Christ's Hospital* (1841) 4 Beav 73 (where trustees, who had for a long period administered charitable funds erroneously, on being called upon to administer them duly, unsuccessfully insisted on their own rights adversely to the charity); *A-G v Webster* (1875) LR 20 Eq 483 at 492 per Jessel MR (where the trustees disregarded the opinion of their own counsel that the property was charitable, but the Attorney General, by whom this was an ex officio information, did not press the costs against the trustees personally); *Re St Stephen, Coleman Street, Re St Mary the Virgin, Aldermanbury* (1888) 39 ChD 492 (a test case instituted by trustees claiming that certain property was not charitable). See also *A-G v Brewer's Co* (1717) 1 P Wms 376; *A-G v Gibbs* (1847) 1 De G & Sm 156 (affd 2 Ph 327); *A-G v Mercers' Co, Re St Paul's School* (1870) 18 WR 448.

5 *A-G v Stroud* (1868) 19 LT 545.

6 *Hertford Corpn v Hertford Poor* (1713) 2 Bro Parl Cas 377, HL.

7 *A-G v East Retford Corpn* (1833) 2 My & K 35; revsd without affecting this point (1838) 3 My & Cr 484. In *Solicitor-General v Bath Corpn* (1849) 18 LJCh 275 at 277 per Wigram V-C, it

was suggested that the court might be compelled to fix charity trustees with constructive notice of a document which they had innocently failed to disclose.

8 *Ludlow Corpn v Greenhouse* (1827) 1 Bli NS 17 at 93, HL.
9 *A-G v Clack* (1839) 1 Beav 467.
10 *Coventry Corpn v A-G* (1720) 7 Bro Parl Cas 235 at 237–238, HL; *Ex p Greenhouse* (1815) 1 Madd 92 at 109 per Plumer V-C.
11 *A-G v Murdoch* (1856) 2 K & J 571. They will not be made to pay costs where they retire voluntarily, though whether they will receive them is a question for the court's discretion, and may depend upon the circumstances of their retirement: *A-G v Murdoch* at 573 per Wood V-C.
12 As to the enforcement of orders of the Commission see PARA 556. As to the Charity Commission see PARAS 543–578.
13 Cf *Re St Brides', Fleet Street, Church or Parish Estate* (1877) 35 ChD 147n (affd [1877] WN 149, CA); *Re Gilchrist Educational Trust* [1895] 1 Ch 367.

636. Mistaken application for scheme. Where, having paid a fund into court and thereby discharged themselves from the office of trustees, charity trustees prepared an application to the court for a scheme to administer the charity, to which the Attorney General refused his fiat, the trustees were not allowed the costs of the abortive application, although they might have been given their costs in connection with an application by the Attorney General for the same purpose[1].

1 *Re Poplar and Blackwall Free School* (1878) 8 ChD 543. The court has a very wide discretion to determine allocation of costs: see PARA 622. As to the Attorney General see PARAS 589, 596, 605 et seq; and CONSTITUTIONAL AND ADMINISTRATIVE LAW vol 20 (2014) PARA 273 et seq.

637. Proceedings to obtain accounts. As it is the duty of charity trustees to render accounts without application to those to whom they are accountable, they are liable to the costs of proceedings to compel an account, even if in the result the charity proves to be indebted to the trustees. However, if the accounts show that the trustees are not debtors to the trust, no subsequent costs on either side are likely to be given[1]. So, too, trustees refusing to render accounts to the Charity Commission[2] may be ordered to pay the costs of an order for committal[3].

1 *A-G v Gibbs* (1847) 2 Ph 327. The court has a very wide discretion to determine allocation of costs: see PARA 622.
2 As to the Charity Commission see PARAS 543–578.
3 *Re Gilchrist Educational Trust* [1895] 1 Ch 367.

638. Trustees allowed costs. Trustees who are made claimants in proceedings without their consent are allowed their costs of having their names struck out[1].

Where unjustifiable proceedings are taken against trustees of a charity, the claimant may be ordered to pay the trustees' costs on the standard basis, so that the charity fund may be preserved intact[2].

When the official custodian for charities[3] has been made a party to legal proceedings the claimants have been ordered to pay his costs[4].

1 *A-G v Maryatt* (1838) 2 Jur 1060. The court has a very wide discretion to determine allocation of costs: see PARA 622.
2 *Edenborough v Archbishop of Canterbury* (1826) 2 Russ 93 at 112 per Lord Eldon LC; *A-G v Cuming* (1843) 2 Y & C Ch Cas 139 at 155 per Knight Bruce V-C; *Andrews v Barnes* (1888) 39 ChD 133, CA. See *A-G v Holland* (1837) 2 Y & C Ex 683, where an information, which contained false charges against the existing trustees of culpable mismanagement, was in part dismissed with costs, though the earlier part of the information was successful. See PARA 624 note 5.
3 As to the official custodian for charities see PARA 300 et seq.
4 *Re Church Patronage Trust, Laurie v A-G* [1904] 1 Ch 41 at 51 per Buckley J, where the plaintiffs failed in their summons and were ordered to pay the costs of the Official Trustee of Charity Lands (now replaced by the official custodian for charities).

639. Costs where property is forfeited. Where, owing to a breach of a condition by charity trustees, part of the charity property is held to be forfeited, the trustees are not entitled to their costs of an unsuccessful appeal against the decision, the only fund out of which those costs would be payable being no longer in their possession[1].

1 *A-G v Grainger* (1859) 7 WR 684. The court has a very wide discretion to determine allocation of costs: see PARA 622.

(v) Costs in relation to Charitable Gifts by Will

640. Costs of construction claim. As a rule the costs of a claim for construction occasioned by obscurity in a will, for example to determine whether a particular charitable bequest is valid[1], are payable out of the testator's residuary personal estate[2]; but there is no absolute right to costs out of the estate, and the causing of unnecessary expense is discouraged by withholding costs[3]. Costs of an administration action are included in the words 'testamentary expenses', a direction as to which is often included in a will[4].

If a dispute arises between persons claiming a charitable legacy and persons claiming the residue as to whether the legacy is or is not payable, the costs of the litigation are payable out of the estate[5]. An executor cannot relieve the residue of its proper burden by paying a disputed charitable legacy into court[6].

1 *Kirkbank v Hudson* (1819) 7 Price 212 at 222 per Lord Richards CB; *A-G v Hinxman* (1820) 2 Jac & W 270 at 278 per Plumer MR; *Giblett v Hobson* (1833) 5 Sim 651 at 662 per Shadwell V-C (affd (1834) 3 My & K 517); *Daly v A-G* (1860) 11 I Ch R 41.
2 *Philpott v President and Governors of St George's Hospital, A-G v Philpott* (1857) 6 HL Cas 338 at 374 per Lord Wensleydale; *Wilson v Squire* (1842) 13 Sim 212; *Daly v A-G* (1860) 11 I Ch R 41 at 49; and see WILLS AND INTESTACY vol 103 (2010) PARA 1198 et seq.
3 See *Re Amory, Westminster Bank Ltd v British Sailors' Society Inc at Home and Abroad* [1951] 2 All ER 947n (costs withheld); *Re Daysh, Dale v Duke of Richmond and Gordon* [1951] 1 TLR 257 per Wynn-Parry J, where the costs were allowed in the particular circumstances of the case. Costs may also be disallowed where they are incurred in preferring hopeless claims: see PARA 642 note 1. The court has a very wide discretion to determine allocation of costs: see PARA 622.
4 *Penny v Penny* (1879) 11 ChD 440.
5 *A-G v Lawes* (1849) 8 Hare 32 at 43 per Knight Bruce V-C.
6 *Re Birkett* (1878) 9 ChD 576 at 581 per Jessel MR.

641. Dispute as to legacy severed from estate. If executors admit a legacy to be payable and sever it from the estate, and a dispute afterwards arises between the persons to whom or to some of whom the legacy belongs, and the court has to decide to whom it belongs, the legacy bears the cost[1]. Thus, where executors have appropriated a charitable legacy and divided the residue, the costs of proceedings to secure the legacy must be paid out of it[2]. The mere fact that executors have set apart a sum to meet the legacy, if payable, does not constitute a severance[3].

An admission by an executor of assets for the payment of a charitable legacy extends to an admission of assets for the payment of costs to secure payment of the legacy, if the court thinks fit to direct them[4].

1 *A-G v Lawes* (1849) 8 Hare 32 at 43 per Knight Bruce V-C; *Re Lycett, Riley v King's College Hospital* (1897) 13 TLR 373 (ambiguous bequest to charitable institution wrongly described). The court has a very wide discretion to determine allocation of costs: see PARA 622.
2 *Governesses' Benevolent Institution v Rusbridger* (1854) 18 Beav 467.
3 *A-G v Lawes* (1849) 8 Hare 32.
4 *Philanthropic Society v Hobson* (1833) 2 My & K 357.

642. Charities claiming bequest. Where a testator occasions difficulty to his executors in administering his estate by misdescribing a charitable institution which he intends should receive a legacy, and more than one institution claims the legacy, the costs even of the unsuccessful claimants, on the standard basis, notwithstanding the opposition of the residuary legatees, are often directed to be paid out of the estate; but where in the court's opinion a claim is hopeless and not made in good faith, the unsuccessful claimant may be ordered to pay his own costs, and in some cases may be ordered to pay the costs of other parties[1].

1 *Re Clarke, Clarke v St Mary's Convalescent Home* (1907) 97 LT 707; and cf *Re Lycett, Riley v King's College Hospital* (1897) 13 TLR 373, where the costs were made payable out the legacy, presumably on the ground that it had been severed from the estate. Farwell J stated that a society which appeared in court to support a claim which was not admitted must not expect as of right to be paid its costs out of the estate, and might in certain events have to pay costs: *Re Millington* (1932) Times, 14 January referred to in *Re Preston's Estate, Raby v Port of Hull Society's Sailors' Orphans' Homes* [1951] Ch 878, [1951] 2 All ER 421 (costs of claimants not allowed after a point in the proceedings where it had become clear that the claims were hopeless); *Re Vernon's Will Trusts, Lloyds Bank Ltd v Group 20 Hospital Management Committee (Coventry)* [1972] Ch 300n, [1971] 3 All ER 1061n (where (although this does not appear from the report) the second defendant was not allowed its costs out of the estate). See also PARA 651.

The court has a very wide discretion to determine allocation of costs: see PARA 622.

In practice, proceedings can often be avoided by an approach to the Treasury Solicitor to discover what view would be taken by the Attorney General were the matter to come before the court, and, if a firm view is given, to act on that basis. This is an inexpensive way of dealing with the misdescription of charities in a will and apparent cases of initial failure where a cy-près scheme may be made by the Charity Commission if all concerned agree. As to the cy-près doctrine see PARA 209 et seq. As to the Treasury Solicitor see **CONSTITUTIONAL AND ADMINISTRATIVE LAW** vol 20 (2014) PARA 281. As to the Attorney General see PARAS 589, 596, 605 et seq; and **CONSTITUTIONAL AND ADMINISTRATIVE LAW** vol 20 (2014) PARA 273 et seq.

643. Costs in administration claim. Where the next of kin[1] are made parties to a claim for administration relating to a charity and raise no improper point, they are as a rule, though not as of right[2], allowed their costs on the standard basis, even where their claim does not succeed[3], and they may be allowed charges and expenses as well[4].

The rule that the costs of an administration action were payable out of residue generally, and not primarily out of a lapsed share, applied when that share was given to a charity and lapsed[5], but the rule seems to have been superseded[6].

1 Most of the cases referred to in notes 2–5 are cases in which it was the heir at law who was made a party. The principle must apply in just the same way to persons entitled under the Administration of Estates Act 1925 s 46: see **WILLS AND INTESTACY** vol 102 (2010) PARA 529 et seq. If the heir at law brought an unnecessary suit, the costs were directed to be paid out of the real estate: *Leacroft v Maynard* (1791) 1 Ves 279.

2 *Whicker v Hume* (1851) 14 Beav 509 at 528 per Romilly MR (where the heir was only given party and party costs); *Aria v Emanuel* (1861) 9 WR 366; *Wilkinson v Barber* (1872) LR 14 Eq 96 at 99 (next of kin).

3 *A-G v Haberdashers' Co* (1793) 4 Bro CC 178; *Currie v Pye* (1811) 17 Ves 462; *A-G v Kerr* (1841) 4 Beav 297 at 299; *James v James* (1849) 11 Beav 397 (heir at law cases); *Gaffney v Hevey* (1837) 1 Dr & Wal 12 at 25; *Carter v Green* (1857) 3 K & J 591 at 608; *Lewis v Allenby* (1870) LR 10 Eq 668 (next of kin cases).

4 *A-G v Haberdashers' Co* (1793) 4 Bro CC 178; *A-G v Kerr* (1841) 4 Beav 297. The court has a very wide discretion to determine allocation of costs: see PARA 622.

5 *Blann v Bell* (1877) 7 ChD 382; contra, *Taylor v Mogg* (1858) 27 LJCh 816; and see *Linley v Taylor* (1859) 1 Giff 67.

6 See the Administration of Estates Act 1925 s 34(3), Sch 1 Pt II para 1, whereby, as regards solvent estates, property of the deceased undisposed of by will becomes primarily liable, subject

to the retention of a fund to meet pecuniary legacies, for testamentary and administration expenses; but this is subject to any contrary provision in the will. See also WILLS AND INTESTACY vol 103 (2010) PARA 998.

(vi) Payment and Apportionment of Costs Payable out of Charity Funds

644. Costs charged on estates or income. A charge[1] of the whole or part of the charity estates may be ordered for the payment of costs. Sometimes the payment of costs may be directed out of the income of a charity fund[2].

It has been held that, where proceedings are taken in respect of one only of several gifts belonging to a charity, the costs should in the first instance fall on the property which is the subject of the proceedings; but a different provision may be made if justice to the relator or the interests of the charity require it[3].

1 *A-G v Atherstone School Governors* (1833) Shelford's Law of Mortmain 477; *A-G v Bishop of St David's* (1849) Seton's Judgments and Orders (7th Edn, 1912) 1269; *Re Lambeth Charities* (1850) Seton's Judgments and Orders (7th Edn, 1912) 1247; *A-G v Archbishop of York* (1853) 17 Beav 495; *A-G v Murdoch* (1856) 2 K & J 571. The court might possibly order a sale of part of the charity estates for the same purpose under its general power to authorise a sale of charity lands: *A-G v Newark-upon-Trent Corpn* (1842) 1 Hare 395; *A-G v Nethercoat* (1840) cited in 1 Hare 400. As to mortgages generally see MORTGAGE.

2 *A-G v Smythies* (1853) 16 Beav 385, where the costs of an application by a new master of a hospital for payment of the income of a fund in court was held payable out of the income. It was held that where a charitable corporation is ordered to pay costs, and it is entitled to a fund representing the proceeds of sale of part of its property, the party to whom the costs are payable may charge them upon that fund: *A-G v Thetford Corpn* (1860) 8 WR 467.

The court has a very wide discretion to determine allocation of costs: see PARA 622.

3 *A-G v Kerr* (1841) 4 Beav 297 at 303 per Lord Langdale. As to relators see further PARA 613 et seq. Relator proceedings are now rare in practice.

645. Apportionment of costs. The costs of settling one scheme for a number of charities are apportioned rateably, though primarily they may be made payable out of a fund not belonging to all the charities[1]. Where a charity includes two classes of estates, both of which are the subject of proceedings, the costs of establishing a scheme for the regulation of one estate only are borne by that estate[2]. Similarly, where several distinct charities are vested in the same set of trustees, the costs of proceedings relating to one charity alone must be borne entirely by that charity[3].

1 *Re Stafford Charities* (1858) 26 Beav 567. For a form of order apportioning costs see *Re Saffron Walden Charity* (1857) Seton's Judgments and Orders (7th Edn, 1912) 1250. The court has a very wide discretion to determine allocation of costs: see PARA 622.

2 *A-G v Skinners' Co* (1827) 2 Russ 407 at 446 per Lord Eldon LC.

3 *A-G v Grainger* (1859) 7 WR 684.

(vii) Costs where Charity Land is Compulsorily Acquired

646. Costs on compulsory acquisition. Where land belonging to a charity is compulsorily acquired under the provisions of the Compulsory Purchase Act 1965[1], and the compensation is paid into court under those provisions[2], the High Court may order[3] the acquiring authority to pay the costs, including all reasonable charges and expenses, of or incurred in consequence of the purchase of the land[4], of the investment of the compensation in court or of its reinvestment in the purchase of other land[5], and of all proceedings relating to orders for those matters except such as are occasioned by litigation between adverse claimants[6].

Where the legal estate in the land is vested in the official custodian for charities[7], and the compensation has been fixed, the official custodian is under no obligation to receive the compensation so as to relieve the acquiring authority from the cost of payment into court and investment[8].

1 As to sales under compulsory purchase powers see PARA 416; and **COMPULSORY ACQUISITION OF LAND.**

2 See the Compulsory Purchase Act 1965 s 2, Sch 1 para 6(2); and **COMPULSORY ACQUISITION OF LAND** vol 18 (2009) PARA 555.

3 The power does not apply where payment into court was necessitated by wilful refusal to accept the money or convey the property, or wilful neglect to make a good title: see Compulsory Purchase Act 1965 s 26(1); and **COMPULSORY ACQUISITION OF LAND** vol 18 (2009) PARA 666.

4 See the Compulsory Purchase Act 1965 s 26(2)(a), (3); and **COMPULSORY ACQUISITION OF LAND** vol 18 (2009) PARA 666.

5 See the Compulsory Purchase Act 1965 s 26(2)(b), (3); and **COMPULSORY ACQUISITION OF LAND** vol 18 (2009) PARA 666. As to when the costs of more than one application for reinvestment in land are allowed see s 26(4); and **COMPULSORY ACQUISITION OF LAND** vol 18 (2009) PARA 666.

6 See the Compulsory Purchase Act 1965 s 26(3)(d); and **COMPULSORY ACQUISITION OF LAND** vol 18 (2009) PARA 666. The court has a very wide discretion to determine allocation of costs: see PARA 622.

7 As to the official custodian for charities see PARA 300 et seq.

8 Cf *Re Leeds Grammar School* [1901] 1 Ch 228.

647. Costs of payment out of compensation or dividends on it. An application by charity trustees for the transfer to the account of the official custodian for charities[1] of a fund paid into court and invested in government securities is regarded as an application for the payment of money out of court, and the acquiring authority is liable for the costs of the application[2]. After the fund has been paid or transferred to the official custodian, the costs of the subsequent reinvestment are not payable by the acquiring authority[3].

The acquiring authority is not liable for costs where the dividends arising from a fund in court have been ordered to be paid to existing trustees of a charity and a fresh application to the court is rendered necessary owing to the appointment of new trustees[4].

Where, after land belonging to a charity has been compulsorily acquired[5] and the usual order for investment of the compensation and payment of the dividend to the then trustees of the charity has been made, the constitution of the charity is altered by a scheme, the acquiring authority may be directed to pay the cost of an application for payment out of part of the fund to cover the expenses of the new scheme[6]. Again, where in such a case an application is made to sanction a scheme applying the compensation cy-près and for payment out to trustees to carry out the scheme, the costs, so far as they are increased by the necessity for a scheme, may be excepted from the costs payable by the acquiring authority[7].

1 As to the official custodian for charities see PARA 300 et seq.

2 *Re Bristol Free Grammar School Estates* (1878) 47 LJCh 317; *Re Bishop Monk's Horfield Trust* (1881) 43 LT 793; *Re Rector and Churchwardens of St Alban's, Wood Street* (1891) 66 LT 51. See *Re London, Brighton and South Coast Rly Co* (1854) 18 Beav 608. The court has a very wide discretion to determine allocation of costs: see PARA 622.

3 *Re Bishop Monk's Horfield Trust* (1881) 43 LT 793.

4 *Re Andenshaw School* (1863) 1 New Rep 255. It is otherwise where the charity has been reconstituted under a scheme: *Re Shakespeare Walk School* (1879) 12 ChD 178; cf *Re St Paul's Schools, Finsbury* (1883) 52 LJCh 454.

5 As to the compulsory acquisition of land see PARA 646; and **COMPULSORY ACQUISITION OF LAND.**

6 *Re Shakespeare Walk School* (1879) 12 ChD 178; *Re Wood Green Gospel Hall Charity, ex p Middlesex County Council* [1909] 1 Ch 263. As to the direction of schemes see PARA 179 et seq.
7 *Re St Paul's Schools, Finsbury* (1883) 52 LJCh 454.

(viii) Miscellaneous Provisions as to Costs

648. Assessment on order of Charity Commission. The Charity Commission[1] may order that a solicitor's bill of costs for business done for a charity[2], or for charity trustees[3] or trustees for a charity, be assessed, together with the costs of the assessment, by a costs officer in such division of the High Court as may be specified in the order, or by the costs officer of any other court having jurisdiction to order the assessment of the bill[4]. On any such order the assessment must proceed, and the costs officer has the same powers and duties, and the costs of the assessment must be borne, as if the order had been made, on the application of the person chargeable with the bill, by the court in which the costs are assessed[5]. If the bill has already been paid, an order may not be made under this provision unless the Commission thinks it contains exorbitant charges[6]. No such order may be made where the solicitor's costs are not subject to an assessment on an order of the High Court by reason either of an agreement as to his remuneration or of the lapse of time since payment of the bill[7].

An appeal against an order of the Commission for the assessment of a solicitor's bill lies to the Tribunal at the instance of the Attorney General[8], the solicitor, any person for whom the work was done by the solicitor, and any other person who is or may be affected by the order[9]. The Tribunal has the power to do any of the following: (1) quash the order; (2) substitute for the order any other order which could have been made by the Commission; (3) add anything to the order which could have been contained in an order made by the Commission[10].

1 As to the Charity Commission see PARAS 543–578.
2 As to the meaning of 'charity' see PARA 1.
3 As to the meaning of 'charity trustees' see PARA 255.
4 Charities Act 2011 s 112(1). In practice, the Charity Commission does not exercise its power to order assessment of a solicitor's bill of costs. The Law Society has a procedure in non-contentious business whereby on the application of a party it can issue a remuneration certificate.
5 Charities Act 2011 s 112(2).
6 Charities Act 2011 s 112(3).
7 Charities Act 2011 s 112(4). As to the relevance of lapse of time see in particular the Solicitors Act 1974 s 70; and LEGAL PROFESSIONS vol 66 (2015) PARA 743.
8 As to the Tribunal see PARA 579 et seq. As to the Attorney General see PARAS 589, 596, 605 et seq; and CONSTITUTIONAL AND ADMINISTRATIVE LAW vol 20 (2014) PARA 273 et seq.
9 Charities Act 2011 Sch 6 Table Cols 1, 2. As to the meaning of 'person who is or may be affected' within the meaning of Sch 6 see PARA 317 note 8.
10 Charities Act 2011 Sch 6 Table Col 3.

649. Costs on the standard basis. In matters of equitable jurisdiction the court has power to order an unsuccessful litigant to pay the costs of the claim on the standard basis[1]. In many cases costs have been allowed out of a charity fund to all parties[2], or to some of them[3].

1 *Andrews v Barnes* (1888) 39 ChD 133, CA. The court has a very wide discretion to determine allocation of costs: see PARA 622.
2 *A-G v Carte* (1746) 1 Dick 113; *Moggridge v Thackwell* (1803) 7 Ves 36 at 69, 88 per Lord Eldon LC; *Bishop of Hereford v Adams* (1802) 7 Ves 324 at 332 per Lord Eldon LC; *Mills v Farmer* (1815) 1 Mer 55; *Gaffney v Hevey* (1837) 1 Dr & Wal 12 at 25; *Wickham v Marquis*

of Bath (1865) LR 1 Eq 17 at 25 per Romilly MR; *Re Cardwell, A-G v Day* [1912] 1 Ch 779 at 784 per Warrington J (where the costs of all parties were directed to be paid out of three charitable funds in proportion to their respective values).

3 *A-G v Stewart* (1872) LR 14 Eq 17.

650. Interest on costs. Although interest is recoverable[1] on costs which one party is ordered to pay to another, it is not recoverable on costs directed to be raised out of a charity estate[2], unless the court in the exercise of its discretion as to costs so directs[3].

1 See the Judgments Act 1838 ss 17, 18; the Administration of Justice Act 1970 s 44; and CIVIL PROCEDURE vol 12 (2009) PARA 1149. See the non-charity case *Taylor v Roe* [1894] 1 Ch 413. As to interests on judgment debts expressed in currencies other than sterling, see the Administration of Justice Act 1970 s 44A; and CIVIL PROCEDURE vol 12 (2009) PARA 1149.

2 *A-G v Nethercote* (1841) 11 Sim 529.

3 *A-G v Bishop of St David's* (1849) Seton's Judgments and Orders (7th Edn, 1912) 1269 (and see Seton's Judgments and Orders (6th Edn, 1901) 1290 for the form of order), where 4 per cent interest was given. This rate might now be 8 per cent, which is the rate applicable under the Judgments Act 1838 s 17: see CIVIL PROCEDURE vol 12 (2009) PARA 1149.

The court has a very wide discretion to determine allocation of costs: see PARA 622.

651. When costs allowed out of charity funds. The costs of making an unsuccessful application to the court in a charity matter may be given out of the charity funds, if there are substantial grounds for the application, although it may be induced by private interest[1], or even if the grounds of the application are based in good faith on a misconception of law[2]. The costs of vexatious proceedings[3], or of proceedings taken under an inappropriate procedure[4], are not allowed out of the charity funds. In some cases unsuccessful applications in charity matters are dismissed without costs[5].

Where an unnecessary party, by setting up a claim, renders service of process upon him necessary, costs will not be paid to him out of the charity funds[6]. Where a person who is not personally interested in a charity attends proceedings before a master, he will not be given his costs out of the charity funds[7] unless he can show that the charity is likely to derive benefit from his attendance[8].

Even though it is the court's duty in charity cases to grant the proper relief, whether it has been asked or not[9], the question of costs may depend upon the form of the application[10].

1 *Re Storie's University Gift* (1860) 2 De GF & J 529.

2 *Re Betton's Charity* [1908] 1 Ch 205 at 212 per Swinfen Eady J. The court has a very wide discretion to determine allocation of costs: see PARA 622.

3 *Re Chertsey Market, ex p Walthew* (1819) 6 Price 261, where there was great delay in bringing forward charges of breach of trust against the representatives of deceased trustees, and the proceedings were accordingly held vexatious.

4 *Re Phillipott's Charity* (1837) 8 Sim 381. The summary procedure on petition provided by the Charities Procedure Act 1812 (Romilly's Act; repealed by the Charities Act 1960 ss 28(9), 48(2), Sch 7) was held to be appropriate only for simple cases: *Ludlow Corpn v Greenhouse* (1827) 1 Bli NS 17, HL.

5 *A-G v Stewart* (1872) LR 14 Eq 17 at 25 per Malins V-C.

6 *Re Shrewsbury School* (1849) 1 Mac & G 85.

7 *Re Shrewsbury Grammar School* (1849) 1 Mac & G 324 at 334 per Lord Cottenham LC.

8 *Re Shrewsbury Grammar School* (1849) 1 Mac & G 324 at 335 per Lord Cottenham LC.

9 As to this principle, which is in practice now obsolete, see PARA 598 note 3.

10 *A-G v Hartley* (1820) 2 Jac & W 353 at 369 per Lord Eldon LC. See also PARA 598.

652. Co-defendant liable for trustee defendants' costs. Where the Attorney General takes proceedings on behalf of a charity and there are two sets of defendants, namely the trustees of the charity and another party who, in the event, is adjudged liable to pay the costs, the court may direct the defendant so liable to pay the costs of the trustees directly instead of ordering the trustees' costs to be paid out of the charity funds and afterwards to be repaid by that defendant[1].

1 *A-G v Chester Corpn* (1851) 14 Beav 338 at 341. See also *A-G v Mercers' Co, Re St Paul's School* (1870) 18 WR 448 at 450 per James V-C, and the non-charity cases of *Rudow v Great Britain Mutual Life Assurance Society* (1881) 17 ChD 600 at 608, CA, per Jessel MR, and *Sanderson v Blyth Theatre Co* [1903] 2 KB 533, CA. As to the Attorney General see PARAS 589, 596, 605 et seq; and CONSTITUTIONAL AND ADMINISTRATIVE LAW vol 20 (2014) PARA 273 et seq.

The court has a very wide discretion to determine allocation of costs: see PARA 622.

653. Costs of proceedings to set aside lease. As a rule the costs of proceedings to set aside an improvident lease of charity lands are paid by the lessee[1]; but the costs of setting aside a lease at an undervalue made in pursuance of a direction in a will which the court holds to be void as a perpetuity may be directed to be paid by the lessor[2].

1 *A-G v Lord Hotham* (1823) Turn & R 209 at 220–222 per Plumer MR. The court has a very wide discretion to determine allocation of costs: see PARA 622.

2 *A-G v Greenhill* (1863) 33 Beav 193, where the costs were awarded on what is now the standard basis.

654. Costs of appeals. There must be a substantial ground for an appeal by defendants in a charity suit to exempt them from payment of costs if the appeal is unsuccessful[1]. As a rule, in the case of appeals, costs of all parties should not be given out of the charity funds, as such a practice tends to encourage groundless appeals[2].

1 *A-G v Rochester Corpn* (1854) 5 De GM & G 797. The court has a very wide discretion to determine allocation of costs: see PARA 622.

2 *Bruce v Deer Presbytery* (1867) LR 1 Sc & Div 96 at 98, HL, per Lord Cranworth.

INDEX

Charities

References are to paragraph numbers; superior figures refer to notes

Words and Phrases

Words in parentheses indicate the context in which the word or phrase is used